CHILDREN LAW

AN INTERDISCIPLINARY HANDBOOK

CHILDREN LAW
AN INTERDISCIPLINARY HANDBOOK

Charles Prest

Solicitor

Stephen Wildblood QC

Albion Chambers, Bristol

Family Law

2005

Published by
Jordan Publishing Limited
21 St Thomas Street
Bristol BS1 6JS

British Library Cataloguing-in-Publication Data
A catalogue record for this book is available from the British Library.

ISBN 0 85308 9442

Typeset by Jordan Publishing Ltd
Printed in Great Britain by MPG Books Limited, Bodmin, Cornwall

FOREWORD

It is now well recognised that family justice, and in particular justice for children, can only be achieved through the collaboration of people of different professional backgrounds. Such thinking may have become mainstream, but there is still a long way to go to realise the full potential of interdisciplinary working. To do this it is vital for the separate professions to communicate and to learn from one another. The professions must also be able critically to re-examine their own practices in light of what they have learnt. This is very much the thinking that has led to the creation of the Family Justice Council, with its local councils that are soon to follow, and similar thinking lies behind this book.

The book guides, informs and stimulates both lawyers and readers from other professions. It guides by its Overviews, which can be read individually or as a whole. It informs by providing a wealth of primary materials, the most important of which are amplified by concise and practical notes. And it stimulates with its selection of quotations and comments, and its eye to the future. Strikingly, it dares to start its approach to the subject of children law in England and Wales from outside the jurisdiction, a reflection of the fact that the subject is, in all sorts of ways, increasingly international as well as increasingly interdisciplinary.

I am extremely pleased that CAFCASS officers will each be provided with a copy of this book. They are in a unique position within the family justice system. It is not that they must all become lawyers, but their work is particularly defined by law and they need to have a sound understanding of the legal framework within which they operate as well as knowing where to turn for advice. This book gives them that framework and much useful detail besides, and is a foundation that can be built upon in any particular case by the advice of lawyers with whom they work, whether in private practice locally or from CAFCASS Legal.

I commend this book not only to CAFCASS officers but to lawyers and all other professionals working in the family justice system. It will refresh, encourage and challenge, and it reminds us of the common enterprise in which we are involved despite the different parts we each have to play.

THE RT HON DAME ELIZABETH BUTLER-SLOSS GBE
President of the Family Division

ACKNOWLEDGEMENTS

Many people have kindly provided us with help and encouragement in writing this Handbook. In particular we would like to thank Richard Barr, Alison Bone, Harriet Bretherton, Rachelle Correia, Mark Everall QC, Fiona Ford, Paul Gardner, Dr Danya Glaser, Mike Hinchliffe, Joan Hunt, Graham Lambert, Charlotte McCafferty, Mick McNeill, the Hon Mr Justice Munby, Janet Sivills, Dr Claire Sturge, Gill Timmis, Jonathan Tross, and the Rt Hon Lord Justice Wall.

The authors and publishers would like to thank the following for granting permission to reproduce extracts from their copyright material in this work:

Bennion on Statutory Interpretation, 4th edn – Publisher: Reed Elsevier (UK) Limited

Christine Olsen's screenplay, *Rabbit Proof Fence* – Publisher: Currency Press Ltd, Sydney, Australia

Homer, *The Odyssey* (Oxford World's Classics), ed Walter Shewring (1980) – Publisher: Oxford University Press

Leo Tolstoy, *Anna Karenina* (Oxford World's Classics), ed Louise and Aylmer Maude (1979) – Publisher: Oxford University Press

Bren Neale and Amanda Wade, *Parent Problems!* – Publisher: Young Voice

Isaac Asimov, *The Caves of Steel* – Publisher: HarperCollins Publishers Ltd

Jacqueline Wilson, *The Story of Tracy Beaker* – Publisher: Corgi Yearling

Physical Signs of Sexual Abuse in Children, 2nd edition. Publisher: Royal College of Physicians

Judith Timms and June Thoburn, *Your Shout* – Publisher: NSPCC

Agatha Christie, *The Mousetrap* – Publisher: HarperCollins Publishers Ltd

Gill Timmis 'Explaining the Welfare Checklist for Children and Young People', first published in (2001) *Seen and Heard* (NAGALRO), Vol 11

We, of course, remain responsible for any errors. We would welcome corrections, comments and suggestions for improvement, which should be sent to us c/o Family Law, 21 St Thomas Street, Bristol BS1 6JS.

CHARLES PREST
London

STEPHEN WILDBLOOD QC
Bristol

CONTENTS

TABLE OF CASES

References are to page numbers. References in bold indicate cases or practice directions set out in full or in part in Part 5 or Part 6.

PART 1

INTRODUCTION

'Over the course of the last decade the crucial importance of interdisciplinary collaboration in the family justice system has been more plainly recognised. Disciplines are not ranged hierarchically. Hopefully self-importance does not figure in the culture. The inter-dependence of the disciplines should preclude that.'

Lord Justice Thorpe in *Re M (Disclosure: Children and Family Reporter)*
[2002] 2 FLR 893

'... the challenge is to provide busy staff in each of the agencies with something of real practical help and of manageable length. The test is simply one of ensuring the material actually helps staff do their job.'

Lord Laming, Report of the Victoria Climbié Inquiry
(The Stationery Office, 2003), para 1.61

'We all make mistakes, in the law as elsewhere; and we can all learn and improve. The only failing is to pretend it is not so.'

Bennion on Statutory Interpretation, 4th edn (LexisNexis, 2002), pp 4–5[1]

'Lawyers, I suppose, were children once.'

Charles Lamb

---

[1]   Reproduced by permission of Reed Elsevier (UK) Limited, trading as LexisNexis UK.

1.1 INTRODUCTION AND HOW TO USE THIS HANDBOOK

Structure

There are three elements to this Handbook. The first is an **Overview** of children law. This is split into eleven parts, each of which is a short overview of key features in a particular area.[1] The aim is not to try to say everything that can be said about children law but instead to pick out the main features of the subject and to present it as a whole within its wider international, constitutional and interdisciplinary context.

We hope, by placing each part of the Overview immediately in front of the primary material to which it relates, that as well as drawing readers to the primary sources, this will make the subject easier to digest and will give a greater sense of progress than if the Overview had been placed at the beginning of the Handbook in its entirety. At the end of some parts of the Overview we have suggested a few key texts to look up and read. It is entirely a matter for individual readers whether to do this, but the purpose is to help make clear the main points and, for readers who are not lawyers, to give a lead into the primary sources.

The second element of the Handbook operates as a **Reference Book**, like a dictionary. It is not intended to be like the *Oxford English Dictionary* but more like the *Concise Oxford Dictionary*, which is quite sufficient for most people most of the time. The Reference Book contains primary sources of children law – treaties, statutes, statutory instruments, case law and guidance. Where those primary sources are particularly important we have annotated them. Some pages in the Reference Book are likely to be referred to on many occasions. Others will never need to be referred to at all by some readers, but they are there in case of need, and even having them in the Handbook is itself important to an overall impression of the subject.

The third element is an assortment of information which we have entitled a **Jackdaw's Collection**, and which appears as Part 7 of the Handbook. We believe this information will help an understanding of children law, set it in its proper context or may otherwise be useful in practice.

---

[1] The eleven parts of the Overview are: (1) international, human rights and European Union law, (2) the European Convention on Human Rights 1950, (3) the United Nations Convention on the Rights of the Child 1989, (4) statutes, (5) adoption legislation, (6) the Children Act 1989, (7) the Human Rights Act 1998, (8) statutory instruments, (9) the Family Proceedings Rules 1991, (10) case-law, and (11) Practice Directions, Practice Notes, circulars and other guidance.

Audiences

This Handbook is intended for two audiences. It is intended for professionals who are not lawyers but who nevertheless have to deal with the family justice system as part of their professional work with children. This includes social workers in both the public and voluntary sectors, CAFCASS officers, paediatricians, psychiatrists, health visitors and other medical professionals, psychologists, police officers, lay magistrates, and others such as teachers who may have a particular interest in aspects of children law. It is our attempt, as lawyers, to welcome you to our world and to introduce you to it, a world in which you are entitled to be treated with courtesy[2] and respect.

For such readers we hope that the overviews will provide an overall understanding, answers to some specific questions and, if you want to do so, sufficient confidence and knowledge to begin to explore further, to look things up and to participate in discussions with lawyers. We have tried to assume little or no knowledge but an interest in the subject. It aims to be enough to stretch but not to overwhelm.

This Handbook is also intended for lawyers. The invitation to lawyers is to use the overviews to look at our own world afresh. The pressures of practice can easily prevent professionals from standing back, looking at their subject as a whole and seeing it in its wider context.[3] Besides, answers to difficult issues are often found in getting the basics right. Even if the Overview only serves to stimulate disagreement with the way in which we have described the shape and direction of the subject then that in itself will be healthy.

The Reference Book is likely to be particularly important to lawyers and to other professionals, notably CAFCASS officers, whose work constantly brings them into contact with the family courts. Our aim has been to provide enough to refresh the memory of professional lawyers appearing in a court of first instance rather than to write a book for use when preparing a skeleton argument for the Court of Appeal. Other professionals may want, at least from time to time, to know something more about the primary materials that make up the subject, and this Handbook is intended to contain all they are ever likely to need for that purpose. As for the 'Jackdaw's Collection', different items are likely to interest and be of use to different readers.

Whether from the legal or other professions, readers will almost certainly agree that whilst good law and proper process are good ends in themselves, they are never the principal end for children law, which must always be better outcomes for children, families and for society in general. There is always something much bigger at stake, and this will not be achieved without an interdisciplinary understanding between all concerned. We hope that, in a

---

2   Note the stem of the word!

3   For example, what proportion of practising children lawyers have in fact read the United Nations Convention on the Rights of the Child, given that it is not directly enforceable in the domestic courts?

modest way, this Handbook will contribute to that understanding and, in turn, to that greater end.

One complex jurisdiction among several

Once upon a time, not very long ago, if it was thought necessary to say anything at all about the jurisdiction,[4] a book like this would simply have said that the jurisdiction comprised England and Wales. The jurisdiction with which this Handbook is concerned is indeed England and Wales, but today something more needs to be said.

The Irish Sea and Hadrian's Wall[5] still separate this jurisdiction from those in Northern Ireland and Scotland, each of which is distinct from the other, but Offa's Dyke has also once again become an important landmark. The Welsh Language Act 1993 established the principle that, in the conduct of public business and the administration of justice in Wales, there should be equality between Welsh and English. Next came the Government of Wales Act 1998 which gave the newly created National Assembly for Wales the power and responsibility to pass secondary legislation and to issue guidance in areas including health, education and social services. This was followed by the Children's Commissioner for Wales Act 2001.[6]

Even more importantly, the English Channel is now far from being an absolute divide. The UK's consent to the Treaty of Rome 1957 and the European Convention on Human Rights 1950, enacted through the European Communities Act 1972 and the Human Rights Act 1998 respectively, created a fundamental change. As Lord Denning put it (in relation to what in this Handbook is called the law of the European Union, but which is just as apt to describe the effect of the law of the European Convention on Human Rights):

> 'All this shows that the flowing tide of Community Law is coming in fast. It has not stopped at high-water mark. It has broken the dykes and the banks. It has submerged the surrounding land. So much so that we have to learn to become amphibious if we wish to keep our heads above water.'[7]

---

4   In this context, 'the jurisdiction' means the geographical territory to which a law applies. In other contexts, 'the jurisdiction' means the range of powers of a particular court. So, for example, the jurisdiction to which the Human Rights Act 1998 applies is the United Kingdom, but only certain judges have the jurisdiction to make a declaration of incompatibility under s 4.

5   It is a small irony of history that whilst Hadrian's Wall marked the north-western extent of the Roman Empire it was Scotland – not England and Wales – that ended up with a legal system significantly influenced by Roman law.

6   The next step, set out in the Children Act 2004, is for CAFCASS Cymru to be transferred from CAFCASS (and beyond CAFCASS, the DfES) to the National Assembly for Wales. This is due to happen on 1 April 2005.

7   *Shields v E Coomes (Holdings) Limited* [1978] 1 WLR 1408 at 1416.

It is partly for this reason that this Handbook begins not with the statutes of the Parliament of the United Kingdom but with international, human rights and European Union law. Whilst the sovereignty of Parliament[8] has been carefully preserved, it is nevertheless at least arguable that the current day-to-day reality in court is the supremacy of European law[9] over domestic law. Add to that the influence of treaties of the wider international community[10] and the way in which children law increasingly has to deal with issues arising from families whose members are from different nations[11] and we have felt able to suggest that this is now at least a proper starting point from which to view the subject.

Content and scope

In writing and assembling this Handbook we have had to make a number of decisions about its content and scope.

- We have had to make decisions about what is and is not 'children law'. We have essentially followed the common practice in this jurisdiction of confining it to those aspects of the law affecting children that fall to be dealt with by the Family Division of the High Court.[12] This restricted definition is not, however, the only one that could be used. All sorts of other laws affect children. For example, some other jurisdictions, including some in the United States of America, routinely treat the criminal law affecting children as coming within their definition of family law, and indeed this is an approach that fits well with the provisions of Article 40 of the United Nations Convention of the Rights of the Child.

- In order to make room for the inclusion of other materials, and to try to help readers distinguish the wood from the trees, we have edited the primary materials. We have even removed a large portion of the Children Act 1989 and most of its Schedules and hope the book is more helpful for it. As a general rule we have sought to include what we think readers may most need to know in the form most likely to help find it and understand it.

---

[8] See further the Overview of Statute Law at **3.1** below.

[9] By which we mean both the European Convention on Human Rights 1950 and the law of the European Union.

[10] Notably, but by no means exclusively, the United Nations Convention on the Rights of the Child 1989.

[11] Internationalism, the advances in medical science and rapid social change are three of the main forces to which children law has to respond.

[12] See Supreme Court Act 1981, Sch 1. The main exception to this is the notes about judicial review contained at **7.14**, and see also the comments about Part III of the Children Act 1989 in the Overview of that Act at **3.6**.

- With apologies to magistrates, judges who sit in family proceedings courts,[13] justices' clerks and legal advisers, for similar reasons, and in order to emphasise the essential sameness of the rules, we have omitted rules that apply in the family proceedings court in favour of those that apply in the county court and High Court.[14]

- We have made two decisions arising from the enactment but, to date, limited implementation of the Adoption and Children Act 2002. First, we have included both the 'current' law and the 'future' law. Indeed one of the purposes of the book is to help readers with the transition from one adoption regime to the other.[15] Secondly, we have incorporated directly into the text of the Children Act 1989 (and other legislation) amendments made by the Adoption and Children Act 2002 where they are already in force.[16] Where they have yet to come into force they have been left within the text of Part 2 of the Adoption and Children Act 2002 but are cross-referred to from the relevant section of the Children Act 1989 (or other legislation) to be amended.

- In several instances we have produced a very personal selection, for example, the eight cases we have chosen to include in Part 5, Case-law.

- We have allowed ourselves some freedom of expression[17] – more in some places and less in others – in the hope of stimulating interest and provoking thought and discussion.

- In dealing with gender in the text, we have taken our lead from s 6 of the Interpretation Act 1978 – 'unless the contrary intention appears, words importing the masculine gender include the feminine and vice versa'.

We have tried to set out the law as at 1 January 2005, although there are a number of exceptions to this. Most obviously, and as already mentioned, we have included the Adoption and Children Act 2002, although the main provisions are not due to come into force until September 2005. Note also that some of the international instruments are not in force (at least in respect of the United Kingdom). Further details about these are given in the Overview of International, Human Rights and European Union Law at **2.1**. We have included them in the belief that one cannot properly understand the present without being aware of these wider developments.

---

[13] As magistrates' courts are known when dealing with children and family law cases.

[14] This also anticipates the day when there will be only one set of rules: see further at **4.20** below.

[15] See further the Overview of adoption legislation at **3.3** below.

[16] Including, most recently, the amended definition of 'harm' in Children Act 1989, s 31(9).

[17] As to which, see Article 10 of the European Convention on Human Rights.

How to use this Handbook

In the end, all that matters is whether or not you find this Handbook useful as you go about your own professional work. So it is very much a matter for you how you use it. Our own suggestion, which is reflected in the way we have structured the book, is:

- to spend five or ten minutes reading the Contents pages and briefly leafing through the Handbook;
- to read the overview sections. These are intended to be read as a whole, even though they are distributed throughout the Handbook. Some readers, perhaps particularly lawyers, may want to read them in one go and can probably do so in an afternoon or an evening. Others may prefer to read one element at a time or in sessions of 30–40 minutes. This is probably the better way to read these sections for those who are not lawyers;
- next, read any parts of the Jackdaw's Collection (Part 7) you identify as being likely to be particularly helpful or relevant to your work;
- if you want to pursue any part of the subject in greater depth, the time will have come for you to explore more closely the Reference Book of primary materials; and
- thereafter use the Handbook to refer to as and when occasion arises in your work.

The Handbook is for you to use as you think best, but we would be delighted to think of it as being covered with post-its, flags, fluorescent highlighting and your own notes.

The Overview begins at **2.1** International, Human Rights and European Union Law.

1.2 REFERENCES TO LAW REPORTS AND THE USE OF ABBREVIATIONS

References to law reports

Understanding references to law reports is probably best done by working through an example: *Re O (Care Proceedings: Evidence)* [2003] EWHC 2011 (Fam), [2004] 1 FLR 161. To see what this all means we will look at it in three parts.

The first element is *Re O (Care Proceedings: Evidence)*. It is a reference to the judgment in a case called 'Re O' (most children law cases are known by only the initial letter of the child's surname in order to protect the child's identity) and tells us a little about the key legal issue in the judgment (it is something to do with evidence in care proceedings).

The second element is [2003] EWHC 2011 (Fam). Since 14 January 2002 a form of 'neutral citation' has been in operation throughout the higher courts (High Court and above) which has created a structured approach to the way in which judgments are identified.[1] The main reason for this has been to facilitate the publication of judgments on the worldwide web. '[2003]' refers to the year in which the judgment was given. 'EWHC (Fam)' is shorthand for 'England and Wales, High Court, Family Division'.[2] 2011 means that it was the 2011th judgment recorded under the system that year.

The third element is '[2004] 1 FLR 161'. This means the judgment was reported in 2004, in the first volume of the *Family Law Reports* at page 161. Finally, the second and third elements may each be followed by 'at [38]' or some other number. This simply means 'at paragraph 38' of that particular judgment.[3]

---

[1] *Practice Direction* [2001] 1 WLR 194, [2001] 1 All ER 193 and *Practice Direction* [2002] 1 WLR 346, [2002] 1 All ER 351.

[2] Judgments of all the higher courts are readily identified by this shorthand. 'UKHL' refers to 'United Kingdom, House of Lords' (its jurisdiction not being confined to England and Wales). 'EWCA' refers to 'England and Wales, Court of Appeal' and is followed by (Crim) or (Civ) depending on whether the judgment is that of the Criminal or Civil Division of the Court of Appeal. 'EWHC', as we have seen, refers to 'England and Wales, High Court' and can be followed by a variety of abbreviations of which (Fam) – Family Division – and (Admin) – Administrative Court – are the ones most likely to matter to readers of this Handbook.

[3] Older reports do not have numbered paragraphs, and the convention then was to refer to the page followed by a letter of the alphabet which indicated whereabouts on the particular

How would you find a copy of the full judgment if you wanted it? The answer is by looking it up, either in the law report using its reference (still the preferred way for most lawyers who have ready access to them), or on the internet using the neutral citation (but remember that judgments before 2002 will not have a neutral citation). As yet there is no website that we know of that routinely records all decisions of the higher courts,[4] but there is useful access to many important judgments through, for example, www.courtservice.gov.uk and www.bailii.org.

Decisions of the European Court of Human Rights are identified by a reference comprising the year and the application number. Judgments can be accessed through www.echr.coe.int.

Abbreviations used in this Handbook and/or commonly used elsewhere

AA 1976	Adoption Act 1976
AC	Appeal Cases
ACA 2002	Adoption and Children Act 2002
All ER/AER	*All England Reports*
CA	Court of Appeal
CA 1989	Children Act 1989
CAFCASS	Children and Family Court Advisory and Support Service
CC	county court
CFR	children and family reporter
CO	care order
CPR 1998	Civil Procedure Rules 1998
DCA	Department for Constitutional Affairs
DfES	Department for Education and Skills
ECHR	European Convention on Human Rights 1950
ECJ	European Court of Justice

---

page the relevant comment was to be found, the law reports having identifying letters running down their margin.

4   This will surely happen one day, but perhaps even more urgent is the need for a website that sets out all legislation in its current form (the HMSO website, www.hmso.gov.uk, which is nevertheless useful, only gives legislation in the form in which it was originally passed). It would be very helpful if, for example, the Department for Constitutional Affairs were to do this, perhaps as part of its response to the general principles underlying the Freedom of Information Act 2000 and given its new focus on 'consumers'.

ECR	*European Court Reports*
ECtHR	European Court of Human Rights
EHRR	*European Human Rights Reports*
EPO	emergency protection order
Fam Law	*Family Law*
FCR	*Family Court Reports*
FLR	*Family Law Reports*
FPC	Family Proceedings Court
FPC(CA)R 1991	Family Proceedings Courts (Children Act 1989) Rules 1991
FPR 1991	Family Proceedings Rules 1991
HC	High Court
HL	House of Lords
HRA 1998	Human Rights Act 1998
ICO	interim care order
INLR	*Immigration and Nationality Law Reports*
ISO	interim supervision order
r	rule
s	section
SO	supervision order
UNCRC	United Nations Convention on the Rights of the Child 1989
WLR	*Weekly Law Reports*

1.3   A WINDOW INTO THE HISTORY OF CHILDREN LAW[1]

The following is an extract from the leading judgment of Lord Fraser of Tullybelton in the House of Lords' decision in October 1985 in *Gillick v West Norfolk and Wisbech Area Health Authority*.[2] The issue was whether guidelines issued by the DHSS, which left it to the clinical judgement of a doctor whether to give advice on contraception to a child under 16 years of age without informing the child's parents, were lawful. We have included it because of the light it sheds on the law relating children over more than one hundred years preceding the decision and because the decision itself marked a watershed in that law.[3]

> 'From the parents' right and duty of custody flows their right and duty of control of the child, but the fact that custody is its origin throws but little light on the question of the legal extent of control at any particular age. Counsel for Mrs Gillick placed some reliance on the Children Act 1975. Section 85(1) provides that in that Act the expression "the parental rights and duties" means "all the rights and duties which by law the mother and father have in relation to a legitimate child and his property", but the subsection does not define the extent of the right and duties which by law the mother and father have. Section 86 of the Act provides:
>
> > "In this Act, unless, the context otherwise requires, 'legal custody' means, as respects a child, so much of the parental rights and duties as relate to the person of the child (including the place and manner in which his time is spent)."
>
> In the Court of Appeal, Parker LJ attached much importance to that section especially to the words in brackets. He considered that the right relating to the place and manner in which the child's time is spent included the right, as he put it, "completely to control the child", subject of course always to the intervention of the court. The Lord Justice went on thus at [1985] FLR 736, 745E:
>
> > "Indeed there must, it seems to me, be such a right from birth to a fixed age unless whenever, short of majority, a question arises it must be determined, in relation to a particular child and a particular matter, whether he or she is of sufficient understanding to make a responsible and reasonable decision. This alternative appears to me singularly unattractive and impracticable, particularly in the context of medical treatment."

---

[1]   For readers wanting a window into the philosophy of children law – of what it can and cannot do – see the dissenting opinion in *Nuutinen v Finland* (2002) 34 EHRR 407.

[2]   [1986] 1 AC 112, [1986] 1 FLR 224. It is perhaps the only children law case that is known among the general public.

[3]   It is also worth considering the way and extent to which children law has developed in the two decades since the decision in *Gillick*. Even a quick look at the Contents of this Handbook will reveal something of how much has happened in that time.

My Lords, I have, with the utmost respect, reached a different conclusion from that of the Lord Justice. It is, in my view, contrary to the ordinary experience of mankind, at least in Western Europe in the present century, to say that a child or a young person remains in fact under the complete control of his parents until he attains the definite age of majority, now 18 in the United Kingdom, and that on attaining that age he suddenly acquires independence. In practice most wise parents relax their control gradually as the child develops and encourage him or her to become increasingly independent. Moreover, the degree of parental control actually exercised over a particular child does in practice vary considerably according to his understanding and intelligence and it would, in my opinion, be unrealistic for the courts not to recognize these facts. Social customs change, and the law ought to, and does in fact, have regard to such changes when they are of major importance. An example of such recognition is to be found in the view recently expressed in your Lordships' House by my noble and learned friend Lord Brandon of Oakbrook, with which the other noble and learned Lords who were present agreed, in *Regina v D* [1984] FLR 847, 858C. Dealing with the question of whether the consent of a child to being taken away by a stranger would be a good defence to a charge of kidnapping, my noble and learned friend said:

> "In the case of a very young child, it would not have the understanding or the intelligence to give its consent, so that absence of consent would be a necessary inference from its age. In the case of an older child, however, it must, I think be a question of fact for a jury whether the child concerned has sufficient understanding and intelligence to give its consent; if, but only if, the jury considers that a child has these qualities, it must then go on to consider whether it has been proved that the child did not give its consent. While the matter will always be for the jury alone to decide, I should not expect a jury to find at all frequently that a child under 14 had sufficient understanding and intelligence to give its consent."

That expression of opinion seems to me entirely contradictory of the view expressed by Cockburn CJ in *R v Howes* (1860) 1 E&E 332, 336–337:

> "We repudiate utterly, as most dangerous, the notion that any intellectual precocity in an individual female child can hasten the period which appears to have been fixed by statute for the arrival at the age of discretion; for that very precocity, if uncontrolled, might very probably lead to her irreparable injury. The legislature has given us a guide, which we may safely follow, in pointing out 16 as the age up to which the father's right to custody of his female child is to continue; and short of which such a child has no discretion to consent to leaving him."

The question for decision in that case was different from that in the present, but the view that the child's intellectual ability is irrelevant cannot, in my opinion, now be accepted. It is a question of fact for the judge (or jury) to decide whether a particular child can give effective consent to contraceptive treatment.

In times gone by the father had almost absolute authority over his children until they attained majority. A rather remarkable example of such authority being upheld by the court was the case of *Re Agar-Ellis* (1883) 24 ChD 317 which was much relied on by the Court of Appeal. The father in that case restricted the communication which his daughter aged 17 was allowed to have with her mother, against whose moral character nothing was alleged, to an extent that would be universally condemned today as quite unreasonable. The case has been much criticised in recent years and, in my opinion, with good reason. In *Hewer v Bryant* [1970] 1 QB 357, 369 Lord Denning MR said:

> "I would get rid of the rule in *Re Agar-Ellis* and of the suggested exceptions to it. That case was decided in the year 1883. It reflects the attitude of a Victorian parent towards his children. He expected unquestioning obedience to his commands. If a son disobeyed, his father would cut him off with a shilling. If a daughter had an illegitimate child, he would turn her out of the house. His power only ceased when the child became 21. I decline to accept a view so much out of date. The common law can, and should, keep pace with the times. It should declare, in conformity with the recent Report of the Committee on the Age of Majority [Cmnd 3342, 1967], that the legal right of a parent to the custody of a child ends at the 18th birthday; and even up till then, it is a dwindling right which the courts will hesitate to enforce against the wishes of the child, and the more so the older he is. It starts with a right of control and ends with little more than advice."

I respectfully agree with every word of that and especially with the description of the father's authority as a dwindling right. In *J v C* [1970] AC 668, Lord Guest and Lord MacDermott referred to the decision in *Agar-Ellis* as an example of the almost absolute power asserted by the father over his children before the Judicature Act 1873 and plainly thought such an assertion was out of place at the present time: see Lord MacDermott at pp 703–704. In *Regina v D* [1984] FLR 847, Lord Brandon of Oakbrook cited *Agar-Ellis* as an example of the older view of a father's authority which his Lordship and the other members of the House rejected. In my opinion, the view of absolute paternal authority continuing until a child attains majority which was applied in *Agar-Ellis* is so out of line with present-day views that it should no longer be treated as having any authority. I regard it as an historical curiosity. As Fox LJ pointed out in the Court of Appeal, [1985] FLR 736, 762F, the *Agar-Ellis* cases, (1878) 10 ChD 49; 24 ChD 317, seemed to have been regarded as somewhat extreme even in their own day, as they were quickly followed by the Guardianship of Infants Act 1886 (49 & 50 Vict c 27) which, by s 5, provided that the court may:

> "... upon the application of the mother of any infant (whether over 16 or not) make such order as it may think fit regarding the custody of such infant and the right of access thereto of either parent, *having regard to the welfare of the infant*, and to the conduct of the parents ..." (Emphasis added.)

Once the rule of the parents' absolute authority over minor children is abandoned, the solution to the problem in this appeal can no longer be found by referring to rigid parental rights at any particular age. The solution depends upon a judgment of what is best for the welfare of the particular child. Nobody doubts, certainly I do not doubt, that in the overwhelming majority of cases the best judges of a child's welfare are his or her parents. Nor do I doubt that any important medical treatment of a child under 16 would normally only be carried out with the parents' approval. That is why it would and should be "most unusual" for a doctor to advise a child without the knowledge and consent of the parents on contraceptive matters. But, as I have already pointed out, Mrs Gillick has to go further if she is to obtain the first declaration that she seeks. She has to justify the absolute right of veto in a parent. But there may be circumstances in which a doctor is a better judge of the medical advice and treatment which will conduce to a girl's welfare than her parents. It is notorious that children of both sexes are often reluctant to confide in their parents about sexual matters, and the DHSS guidance under consideration shows that to abandon the principle of confidentiality for contraceptive advice to girls under 16 might cause some of them not to seek professional advice at all, with the consequence of exposing them to "the immediate risks of pregnancy and of sexually-transmitted diseases". No doubt the risk could be avoided if the patient were to abstain from sexual intercourse, and one of the doctor's responsibilities will be to decide whether a particular patient can reasonably be expected to act upon advice to abstain. We were told that in a significant number of cases such abstinence could not reasonably be expected. An example is the case of *Re P (A Minor)* [[1986] 1 FLR 272]; (1981) 80 LGR 301, in which Butler-Sloss J ordered that a girl aged 15 who had been pregnant for the second time and who was in the care of a local authority should be fitted with a contraceptive appliance because, as the judge is reported to have said at p 312:

> "I assume that it is impossible for this local authority to monitor her sexual activities, and, therefore, contraception appears to be the only alternative."

There may well be other cases where the doctor feels that because the girl is under the influence of her sexual partner or for some other reason there is no realistic prospect of her abstaining from intercourse. If that is right it points strongly to the desirability of the doctor being entitled in some cases, in the girl's best interest, to give her contraceptive advice and treatment if necessary without the consent or even the knowledge of her parents. The only practicable course is, in my opinion, to entrust the doctor with a discretion to act in accordance with his view of what is best in the interests of the girl who is his patient. He should, of course, always seek to persuade her to tell her parents that she is seeking contraceptive advice, and the nature of the advice that she receives. At least he should seek to persuade her to agree to the doctor's informing the parents. But there may well be cases, and I think there will be some cases, where the girl refuses either to tell the parents herself or to permit the doctor to do so and in such cases, the doctor will, in my opinion, be justified in proceeding without the parents' consent or even knowledge provided he is satisfied on the following matters:

(1)   that the girl (although under 16 years of age) will understand his advice;
(2)   that he cannot persuade her to inform her parents or to allow him to inform the parents that she is seeking contraceptive advice;
(3)   that she is very likely to begin or to continue having sexual intercourse with or without contraceptive treatment;
(4)   that unless she receives contraceptive advice or treatment her physical or mental health or both are likely to suffer;
(5)   that her best interest requires him to give her contraceptive advice, treatment or both without the parental consent.

That result ought not to be regarded as a licence for doctors to disregard the wishes of parents on this matter whenever they find it convenient to do so. Any doctor who behaves in such a way would, in my opinion, be failing to discharge his professional responsibilities, and I would expect him to be disciplined by his own professional body accordingly. The medical profession have in modern times come to be entrusted with very wide discretionary powers going beyond the strict limits of clinical judgment and, in my opinion, there is nothing strange about entrusting them with this further responsibility which they alone are in a position to discharge satisfactorily.'

PART 2

INTERNATIONAL, HUMAN RIGHTS AND EUROPEAN UNION LAW

'To look into some aspects of the future, we do not need projections by supercomputers. Much of the next millennium can be seen in how we care for our children today. Tomorrow's world may be influenced by science and technology, but more than anything it is already taking shape in the bodies and minds of our children.'

Kofi Annan, United Nations' Secretary-General

'1979 was the International Year of the Child. It marked the 20th anniversary of the United Nations Declaration of the Rights of the Child. To celebrate, the Great Children's Party was held here in Hyde Park. 180,000 children came to the party from all over the United Kingdom. By coming and joining in the fun they showed how important the United Nations Declaration is for children everywhere. The Queen came and so did the Duke of Edinburgh, Princess Anne and many other famous people. This drinking fountain was put here so that people will remember the party and why it was held. It was unveiled by the Prime Minister Mrs Margaret Thatcher on 4 December 1981.'

Inscription on a drinking fountain in Hyde Park,
close to the site of the Reformer's Tree[1]

'Whoever we are, wherever we live, these rights belong to all children under the sun and the moon and the stars, whether we live in cities or towns or villages, or in mountains or valleys or deserts or forests or jungles. Anywhere and everywhere in the big, wide world, these are the rights of every child.'

Extract from 'For every child', explaining the UN Convention on the Rights of the Child to children, published in association with Unicef

'We walked for nine weeks, a long way all the way home. Then we went straight away and hid in the desert. Got married. I had two baby girls. Then they took me and my kids back to that Moore River place. And I walked all the way back to Jigalong again, carrying Annabella, the little one. When she was three that Mr Neville took her away. I have never seen her again. Gracie is dead now. She never made it back to Jigalong. Daisy and me, we're here, living in our own country, Jigalong. We're never going back to that place.'

Molly Craig in the closing scene of *Rabbit Proof Fence*[2]

---

[1] The inscription is faded in places and the drinking fountain does not work.

[2] Taken from *Rabbit Proof Fence* (screenplay) by Christine Olsen, first published in 2002 by Currency Press Pty Ltd, Sydney Australia.

2.1 OVERVIEW OF INTERNATIONAL, HUMAN RIGHTS AND EUROPEAN UNION LAW

This overview begins by considering international law in general and its application to, and influence upon, children law in England and Wales. It then turns to consider human rights and European Union law as special categories of international law, and concludes with a note about international courts.

Sources of international law

The International Court of Justice, which exists to determine disputes between States and not disputes about children, may seem a strange place to begin an overview of children law in England and Wales. But international law is of ever-increasing importance to domestic children law, and it is the Statute of the International Court of Justice 1945 that most authoritatively[1] sets out the various *sources of international law* when it says:

> 'the Court ... shall apply:
>
> (a) international conventions, whether general or particular, establishing rules expressly recognised by the contesting states;
> (b) international custom, as evidence of a general practice accepted as law;
> (c) the general principles of law recognised by civilised nations;
> (d) subject to the provisions of Article 59, judicial decisions and the teachings of the most highly qualified publicists of the various nations, as subsidiary means for the determination of rules of law.' [2]

Of these sources, international conventions ('treaties') are the most important for children law in England and Wales, and it is to these that we must first turn.

Treaties

Key points about *treaties* are:

- 'treaties' is the general term most commonly used to describe written and binding legal agreements entered into between States. Individual treaties are known by a variety of names including 'treaty', 'convention', 'charter', 'statute' and 'declaration';
- States that do not consent[3] to a particular treaty are not bound by its terms;

---

[1] Although technically limited to the sources of international law that the International Court must apply, in practice the statement is treated as authoritative, as all Member States of the United Nations are necessarily parties to the Statute of the International Court of Justice 1945.

[2] Article 38(1).

[3] 'Consent' is also a general term. There are various ways in which treaties become effective, the process for each particular treaty being set out within its text. A common process is for consent to be a two-

- the power to enter into a treaty varies between States and depends upon each State's own constitution. For the United Kingdom the power to enter into a treaty is a matter of royal prerogative;

- whilst treaty-making power is the prerogative of the Crown in the United Kingdom, it is also a basic tenet of our constitution that legislation is a matter for Parliament, and that before a treaty can become part of the law of England and Wales there must be an Act of Parliament;

- the constitutional position is summarised by the comments of two Law Lords:

  > 'Treaties, as it is sometimes expressed, are not self-executing. Quite simply, a treaty is not part of English law unless and until it has been incorporated into the law by legislation';[4]

  > 'Except to the extent that a treaty becomes incorporated into the laws of the United Kingdom by statute, the courts of the United Kingdom have no power to enforce treaty rights and obligations at the behest of a sovereign government or at the behest of a private individual.'[5]

Does international law matter?

Given this constitutional position in relation to treaties, *does international law really matter?* The answer is that it does and for all sorts of reasons. These include:

- customary international law (as opposed to treaties) may be directly enforceable in the courts of the United Kingdom irrespective of whether or not it has been incorporated into domestic law by legislation;[6]

- in some circumstances, the fact that the United Kingdom has given its consent to a treaty may give rise to a legitimate expectation that the executive will act in conformity with the treaty;[7]

- there is a presumption that domestic legislation is to be construed so as to avoid a conflict with international law, although if the meaning of a statute is clear the courts must apply it irrespective of any conflict with international law;[8]

- international law influences thinking and discussion within the legal community of England and Wales. This does not itself achieve change, but change will not happen without such thinking and discussion;

---

stage process – signature and later ratification – and even then, if the treaty is a multilateral one, it will probably not come into effect until a certain time has elapsed after a certain number of States have consented to it.

[4]   Lord Oliver in *Maclaine Watson v Department of Trade and Industry* [1989] 3 All ER 523 at 544.

[5]   Lord Templeman in the same case at 526.

[6]   See eg Lord Lloyd in *Ex parte Pinochet (No 1)* [2000] 1 AC 61 at 98, and Lord Millett in *Ex parte Pinochet (No 3)* [2000] 1 AC 147 at 276.

[7]   Lord Woolf in *Ex parte Ahmed and Patel* [1998] INLR 570 at 584.

[8]   *Ex parte Brind* [1991] 1 AC 696 at 748; *IRC v Collco Dealings Ltd* [1962] AC 1. As to statutory construction more generally, see **3.1** below.

- international law provides a focus for public and political pressure concerning domestic legislation;
- the United Nations Convention on the Rights of the Child has important indirect effects;[9]
- of the utmost importance, the European Convention on Human Rights has direct effect for those States that have consented to it through the European Court of Human Rights;[10]
- of increasing importance, certain laws made by the European Union have direct effect in Member States (see further below).

Particular treaties included in this Handbook

Before turning in more detail to two particularly important categories of international law – human rights and European Union law – a brief overview of the treaties contained in this Handbook is necessary. They can be divided into three categories:

- treaties to which the United Kingdom has consented and to which direct effect has been given by legislation in Parliament: these include: (1) the Hague Convention on the Civil Aspects of International Child Abduction 1980; and (2) the European Convention on the Recognition and Enforcement of Decisions concerning the Custody of Children 1985;[11] (3) the Hague Convention on Protection of Children and Co-operation in respect of Intercountry Adoption 1993;[12] and, most importantly, (4) the European Convention on Human Rights 1950;[13]
- treaties to which the United Kingdom has consented but to which direct effect has not been given by legislation in Parliament: these include the United Nations Convention on the Rights of the Child;[14]
- treaties to which the United Kingdom has not consented: these include the European Convention on the Exercise of Children's Rights 1996.[15]

Of the primary documents included in this Handbook, this leaves the two instruments of the European Union – (1) Brussels II[16] and (2) the Charter of Fundamental Rights of the European Union[17] – which we will consider below

---

[9] See **2.9**.

[10] See **2.4**.

[11] See **2.8** and **2.6** respectively. Both enacted by the Child Abduction and Custody Act 1985.

[12] See **2.7**. Enacted by the Adoption (Intercountry Aspects) Act 1999.

[13] See **2.4**. This already had direct effect in the sense that, even before the Human Rights Act 1998, individuals could bring claims against the State in the European Court of Human Rights. However, it was the Human Rights Act 1998 that gave the Convention direct effect in courts in the United Kingdom.

[14] See **2.9**.

[15] See **2.5**.

[16] See **2.3**.

[17] See **2.2**. Note that this is explicitly referred to at para 33 of the recitals to Brussels II.

under the heading 'European Union law' after we have first looked at human rights law as a special category of international law.

Human rights law

Although it can be seen as the head of the family of human rights treaties, the United Nations Universal Declaration of Human Rights 1948 has not been included in this Handbook.[18] It has no direct means of enforcement and its provisions are mostly general to all people rather than specific to children. The striking exception to this is Article 25(2) which states:

> 'Motherhood and childhood are entitled to special care and assistance. All children, whether born in or out of wedlock, shall enjoy the same social protection.'[19]

The most important international human rights treaties for the purposes of children law in England and Wales are the European Convention on Human Rights 1950 and the United Nations Convention on the Rights of the Child 1989. Both are of such importance that each has its own overview in this Handbook.[20]

There are a growing number of other human rights treaties relevant to children law. We have chosen to include the European Convention on the Exercise of Children's Rights 1996, which is in force among certain States,[21] but not including the United Kingdom which is still to decide whether to consent to it, partly to draw attention to it and partly because it may nevertheless contribute to shaping future developments within England and Wales.[22]

European Union law[23]

Whether in fact the law of the European Union is a special category of international law or whether it is something altogether different ('supranational law') is an issue that lies well beyond a Handbook such as this. However, as with so much other international law, European Union law is founded upon treaties made between States, most notably the Treaty of

---

[18] It is, however, readily available on the internet, eg at www.un.org/overview/rights or at www.unicef.org/crc.

[19] This provision may have some relevance, surely, to the equal parenting debate albeit that much has changed in many societies since 1948.

[20] See **2.4** and **2.9** respectively.

[21] Currently the Czech Republic, Germany, Greece, Italy, Latvia, Poland, Slovenia, Turkey and the former Yugoslav Republic of Macedonia.

[22] For example, if the European Court of Human Rights were to rely on it in decisions it makes. Another example is the European Convention on Contact concerning Children 2002, which the Government is considering whether or not the United Kingdom should consent to. It has currently been consented to by Austria, Belgium, Bulgaria, Croatia, Cyprus, the Czech Republic, Italy, Malta, Moldova, Portugal, San Marino and the Ukraine.

[23] This is more usually called 'European law', but we have chosen to call it 'European Union law' to try to avoid confusion with the European Convention on Human Rights 1950 – the two are quite separate.

Rome[24] and the Treaty of Maastricht.[25] Within the United Kingdom these treaties have been given effect by the European Communities Act 1972[26] and the European Communities (Amendment) Act 1993.[27]

What is beyond dispute is that the combined effect of the treaties and Acts of Parliament is striking. For example, at an early stage, the European Court of Justice said that:

> 'by creating a community of unlimited duration, having its own institutions, its own personality, its own legal capacity and capacity of representation on the international plane and, more particularly, real powers stemming from a limitation of sovereignty or a transfer of powers from the states to the Community, Member States have limited their sovereign rights, albeit within limited fields, and have created a body of law which binds both their nationals and themselves'[28]

whilst s 2(1) of the European Communities Act 1972 states:

> 'All such rights, powers, liabilities, obligations and restrictions from time to time created or arising by or under the Treaties,[29] and all such remedies and procedures from time to time provided for by or under the Treaties, as in accordance with the Treaties are without further enactment to be given legal effect or used in the United Kingdom, shall be recognised and available in law, and be enforced, allowed and followed accordingly ...'

The bottom line is that the European Union creates rights and obligations[30] that have direct effect in each Member State[31] without the need for any further national implementing legislation. Individuals are bound by such regulations and can rely on them in domestic courts.

---

[24] Signed on 25 March 1957 and coming into effect between Member States on 1 January 1958, by which the European Economic Community was established, fundamentally concerned with 'a harmonious development of economic activities'.

[25] Signed on 7 February 1992 and coming into effect on 1 November 1993, and since modified by the Treaty of Amsterdam (signed on 2 October 1997) and the Treaty of Nice (signed on 26 February 2001). The 'current version' is known as the European Union Treaty. As a result of the Treaty of Maastricht, the European Economic Community became the European Union, marking a 'new stage in the process of creating an ever closer union among the peoples of Europe', founded on three 'pillars': (1) the European Communities (ie trade and economic development, the original concern of the Treaty of Rome); (2) a common foreign and security policy; and (3) justice and home affairs. It is the last of these that is particularly significant for readers of this Handbook.

[26] Followed by the Single European Act 1987.

[27] Followed by the European Union (Accession) Act 2003.

[28] *Costa v ENEL* [1964] ECR 585 at 593.

[29] 'The Treaties' is defined in the European Communities Act 1972, s 1(2).

[30] Council Regulations are 'directly applicable in all Member States' (Article 249(2)). By contrast, Directives may have direct effect, particularly if the time limit for their implementation has passed, but there will be some latitude given to Member States as to the exact way in which they are implemented. In practice Directives have not (yet) been relevant to children law.

[31] Except Denmark, which has chosen to opt out.

Until relatively recently, however important this may have been in other areas of law,[32] there was little impact on family law in general or children law in particular. This has begun to change. The Council Regulation 2201/2003 concerning the Jurisdiction and the Recognition and Enforcement of Judgments in Matrimonial Matters and the Matters of Parental Responsibility (Brussels II)[33] entered into force on 1 August 2004 and comes into effect from 1 March 2005. It determines between Member States which court has jurisdiction in cases involving children. The general rule is that it is the court of the State in which the child is habitually resident,[34] to which there are a number of exceptions.[35] It also addresses the issue of child abduction within the European Union[36] and the recognition and enforcement of orders.

And this is perhaps just a foretaste of what is to come. The direct impact of European Union law on the domestic law relating to children must be expected to grow. For example, the European Union is considering legislating about mediation in civil and commercial law, and this would be likely to apply to alternative dispute resolution work in children law cases. Again, Article 24[37] of the Charter of Fundamental Rights of the European Union is incorporated into the new constitution of the European Union. It is headed 'The rights of the child', and if the new constitution is adopted by the European Union and consented to by the United Kingdom it will effectively become part of our children law.

A note about international courts

There are a plethora of international courts that we hear about through the media, three of which have been mentioned in this overview. It is important to keep them distinct. In summary:

- the International Court of Justice is the court of the United Nations and deals with disputes between States. It has been referred to here only because of its helpful definition of the sources of international law;
- the European Court of Justice[38] is the court of the European Union. It resolves disputes arising under the European Union treaty and, in limited circumstances, can resolve disputes as to the proper interpretation of regulations on applications brought by individuals;

---

[32] Especially in areas of law relating to economic activities, reflecting the original purpose of what has now become the European Union.

[33] It is also known as Brussels II bis or Brussels IIA. It replaces the current Brussels II, Council Regulation 1347/2000.

[34] Article 8.

[35] Articles 9–15.

[36] Articles 10–11 and 40–42, supplementing the Hague Abduction Convention 1980.

[37] Which is derived from Articles 2(1), 3(1) and 9(3) of the United Nations Convention on the Rights of the Child, and is set out at **2.2** below.

[38] Strictly speaking the European Court of Justice now comprises: (1) the Court of Justice; (2) the Court of First Instance; and (3) judicial panels attached to the Court of First Instance.

- the European Court of Human Rights[39] deals with claims by individuals against States under the terms of the European Convention on Human Rights 1950. Its jurisdiction is quite separate from that of the European Court of Justice.[40]

> The Overview continues at **2.4** European Convention on Human Rights 1950.

---

[39] The European Court of Human Rights is considered in a little more detail in **2.4** below.

[40] Although the rights guaranteed by the European Convention on Human Rights are part of the 'general principles' of the law of the European Union: European Union Treaty, Article 6(2).

2.2 CHARTER OF FUNDAMENTAL RIGHTS OF THE EUROPEAN UNION
(Art 24)

ARTICLE 24

The rights of the child

1 Children shall have the right to such protection and care as is necessary for their well-being. They may express their views freely. Such views shall be taken into consideration on matters which concern them in accordance with their age and maturity.

2 In all actions relating to children, whether taken by public authorities or private institutions, the child's best interests must be a primary consideration.

3 Every child shall have the right to maintain on a regular basis a personal relationship and direct contact with both his or her parents, unless that is contrary to his or her interests.

2.3 COUNCIL REGULATION (EC) NO 2201/2003 (BRUSSELS II)[1]

of 27 November 2003

concerning jurisdiction and the recognition and enforcement of judgments in matrimonial matters and the matters of parental responsibility, repealing Regulation (EC) No 1347/2000

THE COUNCIL OF THE EUROPEAN UNION

Having regard to the Treaty establishing the European Community, and in particular Article 61(c) and Article 67(1) thereof,

Having regard to the proposal from the Commission,[2]

Having regard to the opinion of the European Parliament,[3]

Having regard to the opinion of the European Economic and Social Committee,[4]

Whereas:

(1) The European Community has set the objective of creating an area of freedom, security and justice, in which the free movement of persons is ensured. To this end, the Community is to adopt, among others, measures in the field of judicial cooperation in civil matters that are necessary for the proper functioning of the internal market.

(2) The Tampere European Council endorsed the principle of mutual recognition of judicial decisions as the cornerstone for the creation of a genuine judicial area, and identified visiting rights as a priority.

(3) Council Regulation (EC) No 1347/2000[5] sets out rules on jurisdiction, recognition and enforcement of judgments in matrimonial matters and matters of parental responsibility for the children of both spouses rendered on the occasion of the matrimonial proceedings. The content of this Regulation was substantially taken over from the Convention of 28 May 1998 on the same subject matter.[6]

(4) On 3 July 2000 France presented an initiative for a Council Regulation on the mutual enforcement of judgments on rights of access to children.[7]

---

[1]   Note that a helpful practice guide to Brussels II is being produced and should be available through the Official Solicitor (contact details at **7.21**) who is the Central Authority for such matters in England and Wales.

[2]   OJ C 203 E, 27 August 2002, p 155.

[3]   Opinion delivered on 20 September 2002 (not yet published in the *Official Journal*).

[4]   OJ C 61, 14 March 2003, p 76.

[5]   OJ L 160, 30 June 2000, p 19.

[6]   At the time of the adoption of Regulation (EC) No 1347/2000 the Council took note of the explanatory report concerning that Convention prepared by Professor Alegria Borras (OJ C 221, 16 July 1998, p 27).

[7]   OJ C 234, 15 August 2000, p 7.

(5) In order to ensure equality for all children, this Regulation covers all decisions on parental responsibility, including measures for the protection of the child, independently of any link with a matrimonial proceeding.

(6) Since the application of the rules on parental responsibility often arises in the context of matrimonial proceedings, it is more appropriate to have a single instrument for matters of divorce and parental responsibility.

(7) The scope of this Regulation covers civil matters, whatever the nature of the court or tribunal.

(8) As regards judgments on divorce, legal separation or marriage annulment, this Regulation should apply only to the dissolution of matrimonial ties and should not deal with issues such as the grounds for divorce, property consequences of the marriage or any other ancillary measures.

(9) As regards the property of the child, this Regulation should apply only to measures for the protection of the child, ie (i) the designation and functions of a person or body having charge of the child's property, representing or assisting the child, and (ii) the administration, conservation or disposal of the child's property. In this context, this Regulation should, for instance, apply in cases where the parents are in dispute as regards the administration of the child's property. Measures relating to the child's property which do not concern the protection of the child should continue to be governed by Council Regulation (EC) No 44/2001 of 22 December 2000 on jurisdiction and the recognition and enforcement of judgments in civil and commercial matters.[8]

(10) This Regulation is not intended to apply to matters relating to social security, public measures of a general nature in matters of education or health or to decisions on the right of asylum and on immigration. In addition it does not apply to the establishment of parenthood, since this is a different matter from the attribution of parental responsibility, nor to other questions linked to the status of persons. Moreover, it does not apply to measures taken as a result of criminal offences committed by children

(11) Maintenance obligations are excluded from the scope of this Regulation as these are already covered by Council Regulation No 44/2001. The courts having jurisdiction under this Regulation will generally have jurisdiction to rule on maintenance obligations by application of Article 5(2) of Council Regulation No 44/2001.

(12) The grounds of jurisdiction in matters of parental responsibility established in the present Regulation are shaped in the light of the best interests of the child, in particular on the criterion of proximity. This means that jurisdiction should lie in the first place with the Member State of the child's habitual residence, except for certain cases of a change in the child's residence or pursuant to an agreement between the holders of parental responsibility.

(13) In the interest of the child, this Regulation allows, by way of exception and under certain conditions, that the court having jurisdiction may transfer a case to a court of another Member State if this court is better placed to hear the case. However, in this case the second court should not be allowed to transfer the case to a third court.

---

[8]   OJ L 12, 16 January 2001, p 1. Regulation as last amended by Commission Regulation (EC) No 1496/2002 (OJ L 225, 22 August 2002, p 13).

(14) This Regulation should have effect without prejudice to the application of public international law concerning diplomatic immunities. Where jurisdiction under this Regulation cannot be exercised by reason of the existence of diplomatic immunity in accordance with international law, jurisdiction should be exercised in accordance with national law in a Member State in which the person concerned does not enjoy such immunity.

(15) Council Regulation (EC) No 1348/2000 of 29 May 2000 on the service in the Member States of judicial and extrajudicial documents in civil or commercial matters[9] should apply to the service of documents in proceedings instituted pursuant to this Regulation.

(16) This Regulation should not prevent the courts of a Member State from taking provisional, including protective measures, in urgent cases, with regard to persons or property situated in that State.

(17) In cases of wrongful removal or retention of a child, the return of the child should be obtained without delay, and to this end the Hague Convention of 25 October 1980 would continue to apply as complemented by the provisions of this Regulation, in particular Article 11. The courts of the Member State to or in which the child has been wrongfully removed or retained should be able to oppose his or her return in specific, duly justified cases. However, such a decision could be replaced by a subsequent decision by the court of the Member State of habitual residence of the child prior to the wrongful removal or retention. Should that judgment entail the return of the child, the return should take place without any special procedure being required for recognition and enforcement of that judgment in the Member State to or in which the child has been removed or retained.

(18) Where a court has decided not to return a child on the basis of Article 13 of the 1980 Hague Convention, it should inform the court having jurisdiction or central authority in the Member State where the child was habitually resident prior to the wrongful removal or retention. Unless the court in the latter Member State has been seised, this court or the central authority should notify the parties. This obligation should not prevent the central authority from also notifying the relevant public authorities in accordance with national law.

(19) The hearing of the child plays an important role in the application of this Regulation, although this instrument is not intended to modify national procedures applicable.

(20) The hearing of a child in another Member State may take place under the arrangements laid down in Council Regulation (EC) No 1206/2001 of 28 May 2001 on cooperation between the courts of the Member States in the taking of evidence in civil or commercial matters.[10]

(21) The recognition and enforcement of judgments given in a Member State should be based on the principle of mutual trust and the grounds for non-recognition should be kept to the minimum required.

(22) Authentic instruments and agreements between parties that are enforceable in one Member State should be treated as equivalent to 'judgments' for the purpose of the application of the rules on recognition and enforcement.

---

[9]   OJ L 160, 30 June 2000, p 37.

[10]   OJ L 174, 27 June 2001, p 1.

(23) The Tampere European Council considered in its conclusions (point 34) that judgments in the field of family litigation should be 'automatically recognised throughout the Union without any intermediate proceedings or grounds for refusal of enforcement'. This is why judgments on rights of access and judgments on return that have been certified in the Member State of origin in accordance with the provisions of this Regulation should be recognised and enforceable in all other Member States without any further procedure being required. Arrangements for the enforcement of such judgments continue to be governed by national law.

(24) The certificate issued to facilitate enforcement of the judgment should not be subject to appeal. It should be rectified only where there is a material error, ie where it does not correctly reflect the judgment.

(25) Central authorities should cooperate both in general matter and in specific cases, including for purposes of promoting the amicable resolution of family disputes, in matters of parental responsibility. To this end central authorities shall participate in the European Judicial Network in civil and commercial matters created by Council Decision 2001/470/EC of 28 May 2001 establishing a European Judicial Network in civil and commercial matters.[11]

(26) The Commission should make publicly available and update the lists of courts and redress procedures communicated by the Member States.

(27) The measures necessary for the implementation of this Regulation should be adopted in accordance with Council Decision 1999/468/EC of 28 June 1999 laying down the procedures for the exercise of implementing powers conferred on the Commission.[12]

(28) This Regulation replaces Regulation (EC) No 1347/2000 which is consequently repealed.

(29) For the proper functioning of this Regulation, the Commission should review its application and propose such amendments as may appear necessary.

(30) The United Kingdom and Ireland, in accordance with Article 3 of the Protocol on the position of the United Kingdom and Ireland annexed to the Treaty on European Union and the Treaty establishing the European Community, have given notice of their wish to take part in the adoption and application of this Regulation.

(31) Denmark, in accordance with Articles 1 and 2 of the Protocol on the position of Denmark annexed to the Treaty on European Union and the Treaty establishing the European Community, is not participating in the adoption of this Regulation and is therefore not bound by it nor subject to its application.

(32) Since the objectives of this Regulation cannot be sufficiently achieved by the Member States and can therefore be better achieved at Community level, the Community may adopt measures, in accordance with the principle of subsidiarity as set out in Article 5 of the Treaty. In accordance with the principle of proportionality, as set out in that Article, this Regulation does not go beyond what is necessary in order to achieve those objectives.

(33) This Regulation recognises the fundamental rights and observes the principles of the Charter of Fundamental Rights of the European Union. In particular, it seeks to

---

[11]   OJ L 174, 27 June 2001, p 25.

[12]   OJ L 184, 17 July 1999, p 23.

ensure respect for the fundamental rights of the child as set out in Article 24 of the Charter of Fundamental Rights of the European Union,

HAS ADOPTED THE PRESENT REGULATION:

CHAPTER I

SCOPE AND DEFINITIONS

ARTICLE 1

Scope

1 This Regulation shall apply, whatever the nature of the court or tribunal, in civil matters relating to:

    (a) divorce, legal separation or marriage annulment;

    (b) the attribution, exercise, delegation, restriction or termination of parental responsibility.

2 The matters referred to in paragraph 1(b) may, in particular, deal with:

    (a) rights of custody and rights of access;

    (b) guardianship, curatorship and similar institutions;

    (c) the designation and functions of any person or body having charge of the child's person or property, representing or assisting the child;

    (d) the placement of the child in a foster family or in institutional care;

    (e) measures for the protection of the child relating to the administration, conservation or disposal of the child's property.

3 This Regulation shall not apply to:

    (a) the establishment or contesting of a parent-child relationship;

    (b) decisions on adoption, measures preparatory to adoption, or the annulment or revocation of adoption;

    (c) the name and forenames of the child;

    (d) emancipation;

    (e) maintenance obligations;

    (f) trusts or succession;

    (g) measures taken as a result of criminal offences committed by children.

ARTICLE 2

Definitions

For the purposes of this Regulation:

1 the term 'court' shall cover all the authorities in the Member States with jurisdiction in the matters falling within the scope of this Regulation pursuant to Article 1;

2 the term 'judge' shall mean the judge or an official having powers equivalent to those of a judge in the matters falling within the scope of the Regulation;

3 the term 'Member State' shall mean all Member States with the exception of Denmark;

4 the term 'judgment' shall mean a divorce, legal separation or marriage annulment, as well as a judgment relating to parental responsibility, pronounced by a court of a Member State, whatever the judgment may be called, including a decree, order or decision;

5 the term 'Member State of origin' shall mean the Member State where the judgment to be enforced was issued;

6 the term 'Member State of enforcement' shall mean the Member State where enforcement of the judgment is sought;

7 the term 'parental responsibility' shall mean all rights and duties relating to the person or the property of a child which are given to a natural or legal person by judgment, by operation of law or by an agreement having legal effect. The term shall include rights of custody and rights of access;

8 the term 'holder of parental responsibility' shall mean any person having parental responsibility over a child;

9 the term 'rights of custody' shall include rights and duties relating to the care of the person of a child, and in particular the right to determine the child's place of residence;

10 the term 'rights of access' shall include in particular the right to take a child to a place other than his or her habitual residence for a limited period of time;

11 the term 'wrongful removal or retention' shall mean a child's removal or retention where:

(a)   it is in breach of rights of custody acquired by judgment or by operation of law or by an agreement having legal effect under the law of the Member State where the child was habitually resident immediately before the removal or retention; and

(b)   provided that, at the time of removal or retention, the rights of custody were actually exercised, either jointly or alone, or would have been so exercised but for the removal or retention. Custody shall be considered to be exercised jointly when, pursuant to a judgment or by operation of law, one holder of parental responsibility cannot decide on the child's place of residence without the consent of another holder of parental responsibility.

CHAPTER II

JURISDICTION

Section 1

Divorce, legal separation and marriage annulment

ARTICLE 3

General jurisdiction

1 In matters relating to divorce, legal separation or marriage annulment, jurisdiction shall lie with the courts of the Member State

(a) in whose territory:
   – the spouses are habitually resident, or
   – the spouses were last habitually resident, insofar as one of them still resides there, or
   – the respondent is habitually resident, or
   – in the event of a joint application, either of the spouses is habitually resident, or
   – the applicant is habitually resident if he or she resided there for at least a year immediately before the application was made, or
   – the applicant is habitually resident if he or she resided there for at least six months immediately before the application was made and is either a national of the Member State in question or, in the case of the United Kingdom and Ireland, has his or her 'domicile' there;
(b) of the nationality of both spouses or, in the case of the United Kingdom and Ireland, of the 'domicile' of both spouses.

2 For the purpose of this Regulation, 'domicile' shall have the same meaning as it has under the legal systems of the United Kingdom and Ireland.

ARTICLE 4

Counterclaim

The court in which proceedings are pending on the basis of Article 3 shall also have jurisdiction to examine a counterclaim, insofar as the latter comes within the scope of this Regulation.

ARTICLE 5

Conversion of legal separation into divorce

Without prejudice to Article 3, a court of a Member State that has given a judgment on a legal separation shall also have jurisdiction for converting that judgment into a divorce, if the law of that Member State so provides.

ARTICLE 6

Exclusive nature of jurisdiction under Articles 3, 4 and 5

A spouse who:

(a)   is habitually resident in the territory of a Member State; or

(b)   is a national of a Member State, or, in the case of the United Kingdom and Ireland, has his or her 'domicile' in the territory of one of the latter Member States,

may be sued in another Member State only in accordance with Articles 3, 4 and 5.

ARTICLE 7

Residual jurisdiction

1 Where no court of a Member State has jurisdiction pursuant to Articles 3, 4 and 5, jurisdiction shall be determined, in each Member State, by the laws of that State.

2 As against a respondent who is not habitually resident and is not either a national of a Member State or, in the case of the United Kingdom and Ireland, does not have his 'domicile' within the territory of one of the latter Member States, any national of a Member State who is habitually resident within the territory of another Member State may, like the nationals of that State, avail himself of the rules of jurisdiction applicable in that State.

Section 2

Parental responsibility

ARTICLE 8

General jurisdiction

1 The courts of a Member State shall have jurisdiction in matters of parental responsibility over a child who is habitually resident in that Member State at the time the court is seised.

2 Paragraph 1 shall be subject to the provisions of Articles 9, 10 and 12.

ARTICLE 9

Continuing jurisdiction of the child's former habitual residence

1 Where a child moves lawfully from one Member State to another and acquires a new habitual residence there, the courts of the Member State of the child's former habitual residence shall, by way of exception to Article 8, retain jurisdiction during a three-month period following the move for the purpose of modifying a judgment on access rights issued in that Member State before the child moved, where the holder of

access rights pursuant to the judgment on access rights continues to have his or her habitual residence in the Member State of the child's former habitual residence.

2 Paragraph 1 shall not apply if the holder of access rights referred to in paragraph 1 has accepted the jurisdiction of the courts of the Member State of the child's new habitual residence by participating in proceedings before those courts without contesting their jurisdiction.

ARTICLE 10

Jurisdiction in cases of child abduction

In case of wrongful removal or retention of the child, the courts of the Member State where the child was habitually resident immediately before the wrongful removal or retention shall retain their jurisdiction until the child has acquired a habitual residence in another Member State and:

(a) each person, institution or other body having rights of custody has acquiesced in the removal or retention; or

(b) the child has resided in that other Member State for a period of at least one year after the person, institution or other body having rights of custody has had or should have had knowledge of the whereabouts of the child and the child is settled in his or her new environment and at least one of the following conditions is met:

    (i) within one year after the holder of rights of custody has had or should have had knowledge of the whereabouts of the child, no request for return has been lodged before the competent authorities of the Member State where the child has been removed or is being retained;

    (ii) a request for return lodged by the holder of rights of custody has been withdrawn and no new request has been lodged within the time limit set in paragraph (i);

    (iii) a case before the court in the Member State where the child was habitually resident immediately before the wrongful removal or retention has been closed pursuant to Article 11(7);

    (iv) a judgment on custody that does not entail the return of the child has been issued by the courts of the Member State where the child was habitually resident immediately before the wrongful removal or retention.

ARTICLE 11

Return of the child

1 Where a person, institution or other body having rights of custody applies to the competent authorities in a Member State to deliver a judgment on the basis of the Hague Convention of 25 October 1980 on the Civil Aspects of International Child Abduction (hereinafter 'the 1980 Hague Convention'), in order to obtain the return of a child that has been wrongfully removed or retained in a Member State other than the Member State where the child was habitually resident immediately before the wrongful removal or retention, paragraphs 2 to 8 shall apply.

2 When applying Articles 12 and 13 of the 1980 Hague Convention, it shall be ensured that the child is given the opportunity to be heard during the proceedings unless this appears inappropriate having regard to his or her age or degree of maturity.

3 A court to which an application for return of a child is made as mentioned in paragraph 1 shall act expeditiously in proceedings on the application, using the most expeditious procedures available in national law.

Without prejudice to the first subparagraph, the court shall, except where exceptional circumstances make this impossible, issue its judgment no later than six weeks after the application is lodged.

4. A court cannot refuse to return a child on the basis of Article 13b of the 1980 Hague Convention if it is established that adequate arrangements have been made to secure the protection of the child after his or her return.

5 A court cannot refuse to return a child unless the person who requested the return of the child has been given an opportunity to be heard.

6 If a court has issued an order on non-return pursuant to Article 13 of the 1980 Hague Convention, the court must immediately either directly or through its central authority, transmit a copy of the court order on non-return and of the relevant documents, in particular a transcript of the hearings before the court, to the court with jurisdiction or central authority in the Member State where the child was habitually resident immediately before the wrongful removal or retention, as determined by national law. The court shall receive all the mentioned documents within one month of the date of the non-return order.

7 Unless the courts in the Member State where the child was habitually resident immediately before the wrongful removal or retention have already been seised by one of the parties, the court or central authority that receives the information mentioned in paragraph 6 must notify it to the parties and invite them to make submissions to the court, in accordance with national law, within three months of the date of notification so that the court can examine the question of custody of the child.

Without prejudice to the rules on jurisdiction contained in this Regulation, the court shall close the case if no submissions have been received by the court within the time limit.

8 Notwithstanding a judgment of non-return pursuant to Article 13 of the 1980 Hague Convention, any subsequent judgment which requires the return of the child issued by a court having jurisdiction under this Regulation shall be enforceable in accordance with Section 4 of Chapter III below in order to secure the return of the child.

ARTICLE 12

Prorogation of jurisdiction

1 The courts of a Member State exercising jurisdiction by virtue of Article 3 on an application for divorce, legal separation or marriage annulment shall have jurisdiction in any matter relating to parental responsibility connected with that application where:

    (a)   at least one of the spouses has parental responsibility in relation to the child; and

(b)   the jurisdiction of the courts has been accepted expressly or otherwise in an unequivocal manner by the spouses and by the holders of parental responsibility, at the time the court is seised, and is in the superior interests of the child.

2 The jurisdiction conferred in paragraph 1 shall cease as soon as:

(a)   the judgment allowing or refusing the application for divorce, legal separation or marriage annulment has become final;

(b)   in those cases where proceedings in relation to parental responsibility are still pending on the date referred to in (a), a judgment in these proceedings has become final;

(c)   the proceedings referred to in (a) and (b) have come to an end for another reason.

3 The courts of a Member State shall also have jurisdiction in relation to parental responsibility in proceedings other than those referred to in paragraph 1 where:

(a)   the child has a substantial connection with that Member State, in particular by virtue of the fact that one of the holders of parental responsibility is habitually resident in that Member State or that the child is a national of that Member State; and

(b)   the jurisdiction of the courts has been accepted expressly or otherwise in an unequivocal manner by all the parties to the proceedings at the time the court is seised and is in the best interests of the child.

4 Where the child has his or her habitual residence in the territory of a third State which is not a contracting party to the Hague Convention of 19 October 1996 on jurisdiction, applicable law, recognition, enforcement and cooperation in respect of parental responsibility and measures for the protection of children, jurisdiction under this Article shall be deemed to be in the child's interest, in particular if it is found impossible to hold proceedings in the third State in question.

ARTICLE 13

Jurisdiction based on the child's presence

1 Where a child's habitual residence cannot be established and jurisdiction cannot be determined on the basis of Article 12, the courts of the Member State where the child is present shall have jurisdiction.

2 Paragraph 1 shall also apply to refugee children or children internationally displaced because of disturbances occurring in their country.

ARTICLE 14

Residual jurisdiction

Where no court of a Member State has jurisdiction pursuant to Articles 8 to 13, jurisdiction shall be determined, in each Member State, by the laws of that State

ARTICLE 15

Transfer to a court better placed to hear the case

1 By way of exception, the courts of a Member State having jurisdiction as to the substance of the matter may, if they consider that a court of another Member State, with which the child has a particular connection, would be better placed to hear the case, or a specific part thereof, and where this is in the best interests of the child:

(a)   stay the case or the part thereof in question and invite the parties to introduce a request before the court of that other Member State in accordance with paragraph 4; or

(b)   request a court of another Member State to assume jurisdiction in accordance with paragraph 5.

2 Paragraph 1 shall apply:

(a)   upon application from a party; or

(b)   of the court's own motion; or

(c)   upon application from a court of another Member State with which the child has a particular connection, in accordance with paragraph 3.

A transfer made of the court's own motion or by application of a court of another Member State must be accepted by at least one of the parties.

3 The child shall be considered to have a particular connection to a Member State as mentioned in paragraph 1, if that Member State:

(a)   has become the habitual residence of the child after the court referred to in paragraph 1 was seised; or

(b)   is the former habitual residence of the child; or

(c)   is the place of the child's nationality; or

(d)   is the habitual residence of a holder of parental responsibility; or

(e)   is the place where property of the child is located and the case concerns measures for the protection of the child relating to the administration, conservation or disposal of this property.

4 The court of the Member State having jurisdiction as to the substance of the matter shall set a time limit by which the courts of that other Member State shall be seised in accordance with paragraph 1.

If the courts are not seised by that time, the court which has been seised shall continue to exercise jurisdiction in accordance with Articles 8 to 14.

5 The courts of that other Member State may, where due to the specific circumstances of the case, this is in the best interests of the child, accept jurisdiction within six weeks of their seisure in accordance with paragraph 1(a) or 1(b). In this case, the court first seised shall decline jurisdiction. Otherwise, the court first seised shall continue to exercise jurisdiction in accordance with Articles 8 to 14.

6 The courts shall cooperate for the purposes of this Article, either directly or through the central authorities designated pursuant to Article 53.

Section 3

Common provisions

ARTICLE 16

Seising of a Court

1 A court shall be deemed to be seised:

(a) at the time when the document instituting the proceedings or an equivalent document is lodged with the court, provided that the applicant has not subsequently failed to take the steps he was required to take to have service effected on the respondent; or

(b) if the document has to be served before being lodged with the court, at the time when it is received by the authority responsible for service, provided that the applicant has not subsequently failed to take the steps he was required to take to have the document lodged with the court.

ARTICLE 17

Examination as to jurisdiction

Where a court of a Member State is seised of a case over which it has no jurisdiction under this Regulation and over which a court of another Member State has jurisdiction by virtue of this Regulation, it shall declare of its own motion that it has no jurisdiction.

ARTICLE 18

Examination as to admissibility

1 Where a respondent habitually resident in a State other than the Member State where the action was brought does not enter an appearance, the court with jurisdiction shall stay the proceedings so long as it is not shown that the respondent has been able to receive the document instituting the proceedings or an equivalent document in sufficient time to enable him to arrange for his defence, or that all necessary steps have been taken to this end.

2 Article 19 of Regulation (EC) No 1348/2000 shall apply instead of the provisions of paragraph 1 of this Article if the document instituting the proceedings or an equivalent document had to be transmitted from one Member State to another pursuant to that Regulation.

3 Where the provisions of Regulation (EC) No 1348/2000 are not applicable, Article 15 of the Hague Convention of 15 November 1965 on the service abroad of judicial and extrajudicial documents in civil or commercial matters shall apply if the document instituting the proceedings or an equivalent document had to be transmitted abroad pursuant to that Convention.

ARTICLE 19

Lis pendens and dependent actions

1 Where proceedings relating to divorce, legal separation or marriage annulment between the same parties are brought before courts of different Member States, the court second seised shall of its own motion stay its proceedings until such time as the jurisdiction of the court first seised is established.

2 Where proceedings relating to parental responsibility relating to the same child and involving the same cause of action are brought before courts of different Member States, the court second seised shall of its own motion stay its proceedings until such time as the jurisdiction of the court first seised is established.

3 Where the jurisdiction of the court first seised is established, the court second seised shall decline jurisdiction in favour of that court.

In that case, the party who brought the relevant action before the court second seised may bring that action before the court first seised.

ARTICLE 20

Provisional, including protective, measures

1 In urgent cases, the provisions of this Regulation shall not prevent the courts of a Member State from taking such provisional, including protective, measures in respect of persons or assets in that State as may be available under the law of that Member State, even if, under this Regulation, the court of another Member State has jurisdiction as to the substance of the matter.

2 The measures referred to in paragraph 1 shall cease to apply when the court of the Member State having jurisdiction under this Regulation as to the substance of the matter has taken the measures it considers appropriate.

CHAPTER III

RECOGNITION AND ENFORCEMENT

Section 1

Recognition

ARTICLE 21

Recognition of a judgment

1 A judgment given in a Member State shall be recognised in the other Member States without any special procedure being required.

2 In particular, and without prejudice to paragraph 3, no special procedure shall be required for updating the civil-status records of a Member State on the basis of a judgment relating to divorce, legal separation or marriage annulment given in another

Member State, and against which no further appeal lies under the law of that Member State.

3 Without prejudice to Section 4 of this Chapter, any interested party may, in accordance with the procedures provided for in Section 2 of this Chapter, apply for a decision that the judgment be or not be recognised

The local jurisdiction of the court appearing in the list notified by each Member State to the Commission pursuant to Article 68 shall be determined by the internal law of the Member State in which proceedings for recognition or non-recognition are brought.

4 Where the recognition of a judgment is raised as an incidental question in a court of a Member State, that court may determine that issue.

****

ARTICLE 23

Grounds of non-recognition for judgments relating to parental responsibility

A judgment relating to parental responsibility shall not be recognised:

- (a) if such recognition is manifestly contrary to the public policy of the Member State in which recognition is sought taking into account the best interests of the child;
- (b) if it was given, except in case of urgency, without the child having been given an opportunity to be heard, in violation of fundamental principles of procedure of the Member State in which recognition is sought;
- (c) where it was given in default of appearance if the person in default was not served with the document which instituted the proceedings or with an equivalent document in sufficient time and in such a way as to enable that person to arrange for his or her defence unless it is determined that such person has accepted the judgment unequivocally;
- (d) on the request of any person claiming that the judgment infringes his or her parental responsibility, if it was given without such person having been given an opportunity to be heard;
- (e) if it is irreconcilable with a later judgment relating to parental responsibility given in the Member State in which recognition is sought;
- (f) if it is irreconcilable with a later judgment relating to parental responsibility given in another Member State or in the non-Member State of the habitual residence of the child provided that the later judgment fulfils the conditions necessary for its recognition in the Member State in which recognition is sought, or
- (g) if the procedure laid down in Article 56 has not been complied with.

ARTICLE 24

Prohibition of review of jurisdiction of the court of origin

The jurisdiction of the court of the Member State of origin may not be reviewed. The test of public policy referred to in Articles 22(a) and 23(a) may not be applied to the rules relating to jurisdiction set out in Articles 3 to 14.

ARTICLE 25

Differences in applicable law

The recognition of a judgment may not be refused because the law of the Member State in which such recognition is sought would not allow divorce, legal separation or marriage annulment on the same facts.

ARTICLE 26

Non-review as to substance

Under no circumstances may a judgment be reviewed as to its substance.

ARTICLE 27

Stay of proceedings

1 A court of a Member State in which recognition is sought of a judgment given in another Member State may stay the proceedings if an ordinary appeal against the judgment has been lodged.

2 A court of a Member State in which recognition is sought of a judgment given in Ireland or the United Kingdom may stay the proceedings if enforcement is suspended in the Member State of origin by reason of an appeal.

Section 2

Application for a declaration of enforceability

ARTICLE 28

Enforceable judgments

1 A judgment on the exercise of parental responsibility in respect of a child given in a Member State which is enforceable in that Member State and has been served shall be enforced in another Member State when, on the application of any interested party, it has been declared enforceable there.

2 However, in the United Kingdom, such a judgment shall be enforced in England and Wales, in Scotland or in Northern Ireland only when, on the application of any

interested party, it has been registered for enforcement in that part of the United Kingdom.

ARTICLE 29

Jurisdiction of local courts

1 An application for a declaration of enforceability shall be submitted to the court appearing in the list notified by each Member State to the Commission pursuant to Article 68.

2 The local jurisdiction shall be determined by reference to the place of habitual residence of the person against whom enforcement is sought or by reference to the habitual residence of any child to whom the application relates.

Where neither of the places referred to in the first subparagraph can be found in the Member State of enforcement, the local jurisdiction shall be determined by reference to the place of enforcement.

ARTICLE 30

Procedure

1 The procedure for making the application shall be governed by the law of the Member State of enforcement.

2 The applicant must give an address for service within the area of jurisdiction of the court applied to. However, if the law of the Member State of enforcement does not provide for the furnishing of such an address, the applicant shall appoint a representative ad litem.

3 The documents referred to in Articles 37 and 39 shall be attached to the application.

ARTICLE 31

Decision of the court

1 The court applied to shall give its decision without delay. Neither the person against whom enforcement is sought, nor the child shall, at this stage of the proceedings, be entitled to make any submissions on the application.

2 The application may be refused only for one of the reasons specified in Articles 22, 23 and 24.

3 Under no circumstances may a judgment be reviewed as to its substance.

ARTICLE 32

Notice of the decision

The appropriate officer of the court shall without delay bring to the notice of the applicant the decision given on the application in accordance with the procedure laid down by the law of the Member State of enforcement.

ARTICLE 33

Appeal against the decision

1 The decision on the application for a declaration of enforceability may be appealed against by either party.

2 The appeal shall be lodged with the court appearing in the list notified by each Member State to the Commission pursuant to Article 68.

3 The appeal shall be dealt with in accordance with the rules governing procedure in contradictory matters.

4 If the appeal is brought by the applicant for a declaration of enforceability, the party against whom enforcement is sought shall be summoned to appear before the appellate court. If such person fails to appear, the provisions of Article 18 shall apply.

5 An appeal against a declaration of enforceability must be lodged within one month of service thereof. If the party against whom enforcement is sought is habitually resident in a Member State other than that in which the declaration of enforceability was given, the time for appealing shall be two months and shall run from the date of service, either on him or at his residence. No extension of time may be granted on account of distance.

ARTICLE 34

Courts of appeal and means of contest

The judgment given on appeal may be contested only by the proceedings referred to in the list notified by each Member State to the Commission pursuant to Article 68.

ARTICLE 35

Stay of proceedings

1 The court with which the appeal is lodged under Articles 33 or 34 may, on the application of the party against whom enforcement is sought, stay the proceedings if an ordinary appeal has been lodged in the Member State of origin, or if the time for such appeal has not yet expired. In the latter case, the court may specify the time within which an appeal is to be lodged.

2 Where the judgment was given in Ireland or the United Kingdom, any form of appeal available in the Member State of origin shall be treated as an ordinary appeal for the purposes of paragraph 1.

ARTICLE 36

Partial enforcement

1 Where a judgment has been given in respect of several matters and enforcement cannot be authorised for all of them, the court shall authorise enforcement for one or more of them.

2 An applicant may request partial enforcement of a judgment.

Section 3

Provisions common to Sections 1 and 2

ARTICLE 37

Documents

1 A party seeking or contesting recognition or applying for a declaration of enforceability shall produce:

(a) a copy of the judgment which satisfies the conditions necessary to establish its authenticity; and

(b) the certificate referred to in Article 39.

2 In addition, in the case of a judgment given in default, the party seeking recognition or applying for a declaration of enforceability shall produce:

(a) the original or certified true copy of the document which establishes that the defaulting party was served with the document instituting the proceedings or with an equivalent document; or

(b) any document indicating that the defendant has accepted the judgment unequivocally.

ARTICLE 38

Absence of documents

1 If the documents specified in Article 37(1)(b) or (2) are not produced, the court may specify a time for their production, accept equivalent documents or, if it considers that it has sufficient information before it, dispense with their production.

2 If the court so requires, a translation of such documents shall be furnished. The translation shall be certified by a person qualified to do so in one of the Member States.

ARTICLE 39

Certificate concerning judgments in matrimonial matters and certificate concerning judgments on parental responsibility

The competent court or authority of a Member State of origin shall, at the request of any interested party, issue a certificate using the standard form set out in Annex I (judgments in matrimonial matters) or in Annex II (judgments on parental responsibility).

Section 4

Enforceability of certain judgments concerning rights of access and of certain judgments which require the return of the child

ARTICLE 40

Scope

1 This Section shall apply to:

    (a)   rights of access; and

    (b)   the return of a child entailed by a judgment given pursuant to Article 11(8).

2 The provisions of this Section shall not prevent a holder of parental responsibility from seeking recognition and enforcement of a judgment in accordance with the provisions in Sections 1 and 2 of this Chapter.

ARTICLE 41

Rights of access

1 The rights of access referred to in Article 40(1)(a) granted in an enforceable judgment given in a Member State shall be recognised and enforceable in another Member State without the need for a declaration of enforceability and without any possibility of opposing its recognition if the judgment has been certified in the Member State of origin in accordance with paragraph 2.

Even if national law does not provide for enforceability by operation of law of a judgment granting access rights, the court of origin may declare that the judgment shall be enforceable, notwithstanding any appeal.

2 The judge of origin shall issue the certificate referred to in paragraph 1 using the standard form in Annex III (certificate concerning rights of access) only if:

    (a)   where the judgment was given in default, the person defaulting was served with the document which instituted the proceedings or with an equivalent document in sufficient time and in such a way as to enable that person to arrange for his or her defense, or, the person has been served with the document but not in compliance with these conditions, it is nevertheless established that he or she accepted the decision unequivocally;

    (b)   all parties concerned were given an opportunity to be heard; and

(c)   the child was given an opportunity to be heard, unless a hearing was considered inappropriate having regard to his or her age or degree of maturity.

The certificate shall be completed in the language of the judgment.

3 Where the rights of access involve a cross-border situation at the time of the delivery of the judgment, the certificate shall be issued ex officio when the judgment becomes enforceable, even if only provisionally. If the situation subsequently acquires a cross-border character, the certificate shall be issued at the request of one of the parties.

ARTICLE 42

Return of the child

1 The return of a child referred to in Article 40(1)(b) entailed by an enforceable judgment given in a Member State shall be recognised and enforceable in another Member State without the need for a declaration of enforceability and without any possibility of opposing its recognition if the judgment has been certified in the Member State of origin in accordance with paragraph 2.

Even if national law does not provide for enforceability by operation of law, notwithstanding any appeal, of a judgment requiring the return of the child mentioned in Article 11(b)(8), the court of origin may declare the judgment enforceable.

2 The judge of origin who delivered the judgment referred to in Article 40(1)(b) shall issue the certificate referred to in paragraph 1 only if:

(a)   the child was given an opportunity to be heard, unless a hearing was considered inappropriate having regard to his or her age or degree of maturity;
(b)   the parties were given an opportunity to be heard; and
(c)   the court has taken into account in issuing its judgment the reasons for and evidence underlying the order issued pursuant to Article 13 of the 1980 Hague Convention.

In the event that the court or any other authority takes measures to ensure the protection of the child after its return to the State of habitual residence, the certificate shall contain details of such measures.

The judge of origin shall of his or her own motion issue that certificate using the standard form in Annex IV (certificate concerning return of the child(ren)).

The certificate shall be completed in the language of the judgment.

ARTICLE 43

Rectification of the certificate

1 The law of the Member State of origin shall be applicable to any rectification of the certificate.

2 No appeal shall lie against the issuing of a certificate pursuant to Articles 41(1) or 42(1).

ARTICLE 44

Effects of the certificate

The certificate shall take effect only within the limits of the enforceability of the judgment.

ARTICLE 45

Documents

1 A party seeking enforcement of a judgment shall produce:

(a)   a copy of the judgment which satisfies the conditions necessary to establish its authenticity; and

(b)   the certificate referred to in Article 41(1) or Article 42(1).

2 For the purposes of this Article,

–   the certificate referred to in Article 41(1) shall be accompanied by a translation of point 12 relating to the arrangements for exercising right of access,

–   the certificate referred to in Article 42(1) shall be accompanied by a translation of its point 14 relating to the arrangements for implementing the measures taken to ensure the child's return.

The translation shall be into the official language or one of the official languages of the Member State of enforcement or any other language that the Member State of enforcement expressly accepts. The translation shall be certified by a person qualified to do so in one of the Member States.

Section 5

Authentic instruments and agreements

ARTICLE 46

Documents which have been formally drawn up or registered as authentic instruments and are enforceable in one Member State and also agreements between the parties that are enforceable in the Member State in which they were concluded shall be recognised and declared enforceable under the same conditions as judgments.

Section 6
Other provisions

ARTICLE 47

Enforcement procedure

1 The enforcement procedure is governed by the law of the Member State of enforcement.

2 Any judgment delivered by a court of another Member State and declared to be enforceable in accordance with Section 2 or certified in accordance with Article 41(1) or Article 42(1) shall be enforced in the Member State of enforcement in the same conditions as if it had been delivered in that Member State.

In particular, a judgment which has been certified according to Article 41(1) or Article 42(1) cannot be enforced if it is irreconcilable with a subsequent enforceable judgment.

ARTICLE 48

Practical arrangements for the exercise of rights of access

1 The courts of the Member State of enforcement may make practical arrangements for organising the exercise of rights of access, if the necessary arrangements have not or have not sufficiently been made in the judgment delivered by the courts of the Member State having jurisdiction as to the substance of the matter and provided the essential elements of this judgment are respected

2 The practical arrangements made pursuant to paragraph 1 shall cease to apply pursuant to a later judgment by the courts of the Member State having jurisdiction as to the substance of the matter.

ARTICLE 49

Costs

The provisions of this Chapter, with the exception of Section 4, shall also apply to the determination of the amount of costs and expenses of proceedings under this Regulation and to the enforcement of any order concerning such costs and expenses.

ARTICLE 50

Legal aid

An applicant who, in the Member State of origin, has benefited from complete or partial legal aid or exemption from costs or expenses shall be entitled, in the procedures provided for in Articles 21, 28, 41, 42 and 48 to benefit from the most favourable legal aid or the most extensive exemption from costs and expenses provided for by the law of the Member State of enforcement.

ARTICLE 51

Security, bond or deposit

No security, bond or deposit, however described, shall be required of a party who in one Member State applies for enforcement of a judgment given in another Member State on the following grounds

(a)   that he or she is not habitually resident in the Member State in which enforcement is sought; or

(b)   that he or she is either a foreign national or, where enforcement is sought in either the United Kingdom or Ireland, does not have his or her 'domicile' in either of those Member States.

ARTICLE 52

Legalisation or other similar formality

No legalisation or other similar formality shall be required in respect of the documents referred to in Articles 37, 38 and 45 or in respect of a document appointing a representative ad litem.

CHAPTER IV

COOPERATION BETWEEN CENTRAL AUTHORITIES IN MATTERS OF PARENTAL RESPONSIBILITY

ARTICLE 53

Designation

Each Member State shall designate one or more central authorities to assist with the application of this Regulation and shall specify the geographical or functional jurisdiction of each. Where a Member State has designated more than one central authority, communications shall normally be sent direct to the relevant central authority with jurisdiction. Where a communication is sent to a central authority without jurisdiction, the latter shall be responsible for forwarding it to the central authority with jurisdiction and informing the sender accordingly.

ARTICLE 54

General functions

The central authorities shall communicate information on national laws and procedures and take measures to improve the application of this Regulation and strengthening their cooperation. For this purpose the European Judicial Network in civil and commercial matters created by Decision No 2001/470/EC shall be used.

ARTICLE 55

Cooperation on cases specific to parental responsibility

The central authorities shall, upon request from a central authority of another Member State or from a holder of parental responsibility, cooperate on specific cases to achieve the purposes of this Regulation. To this end, they shall, acting directly or through public authorities or other bodies, take all appropriate steps in accordance with the law of that Member State in matters of personal data protection to

(a) collect and exchange information:
   (i) on the situation of the child;
   (ii) on any procedures under way; or
   (iii) on decisions taken concerning the child;
(b) provide information and assistance to holders of parental responsibility seeking the recognition and enforcement of decisions on their territory, in particular concerning rights of access and the return of the child;
(c) facilitate communications between courts, in particular for the application of Article 11(6) and (7) and Article 15;
(d) provide such information and assistance as is needed by courts to apply Article 56; and
(e) facilitate agreement between holders of parental responsibility through mediation or other means, and facilitate cross-border cooperation to this end.

ARTICLE 56

Placement of a child in another Member State

1 Where a court having jurisdiction under Articles 8 to 15 contemplates the placement of a child in institutional care or with a foster family and where such placement is to take place in another Member State, it shall first consult the central authority or other authority having jurisdiction in the latter State where public authority intervention in that Member State is required for domestic cases of child placement.

2 The judgment on placement referred to in paragraph 1 may be made in the requesting State only if the competent authority of the requested State has consented to the placement.

3 The procedures for consultation or consent referred to in paragraphs 1 and 2 shall be governed by the national law of the requested State

4 Where the authority having jurisdiction under Articles 8 to 15 decides to place the child in a foster family, and where such placement is to take place in another Member State and where no public authority intervention is required in the latter Member State for domestic cases of child placement, it shall so inform the central authority or other authority having jurisdiction in the latter State.

ARTICLE 57

Working method

1 Any holder of parental responsibility may submit, to the central authority of the Member State of his or her habitual residence or to the central authority of the Member State where the child is habitually resident or present, a request for assistance as mentioned in Article 55. In general, the request shall include all available information of relevance to its enforcement. Where the request for assistance concerns the recognition or enforcement of a judgment on parental responsibility that falls within the scope of this Regulation, the holder of parental responsibility shall attach the relevant certificates provided for in Articles 39, 41(1) or 42(1).

2 Member States shall communicate to the Commission the official language or languages of the Community institutions other than their own in which communications to the central authorities can be accepted.

3 The assistance provided by the central authorities pursuant to Article 55 shall be free of charge.

4 Each central authority shall bear its own costs.

ARTICLE 58

Meetings

1 In order to facilitate the application of this Regulation, central authorities shall meet regularly.

2 These meetings shall be convened in compliance with Decision No 2001/470/EC establishing a European Judicial Network in civil and commercial matters.

CHAPTER V

RELATIONS WITH OTHER INSTRUMENTS

ARTICLE 59

Relation with other instruments

1 Subject to the provisions of Articles 60, 63, 64 and paragraph 2 of this Article, this Regulation shall, for the Member States, supersede conventions existing at the time of entry into force of this Regulation which have been concluded between two or more Member States and relate to matters governed by this Regulation

2 (a)   Finland and Sweden shall have the option of declaring that the Convention of 6 February 1931 between Denmark, Finland, Iceland, Norway and Sweden comprising international private law provisions on marriage, adoption and guardianship, together with the Final Protocol thereto, will apply, in whole or in part, in their mutual relations, in place of the rules of this Regulation. Such declarations shall be annexed to this Regulation and

published in the Official Journal of the European Union. They may be withdrawn, in whole or in part, at any moment by the said Member States.

(b)   The principle of non-discrimination on the grounds of nationality between citizens of the Union shall be respected.

(c)   The rules of jurisdiction in any future agreement to be concluded between the Member States referred to in subparagraph (a) which relate to matters governed by this Regulation shall be in line with those laid down in this Regulation.

(d)   Judgments handed down in any of the Nordic States which have made the declaration provided for in subparagraph (a) under a forum of jurisdiction corresponding to one of those laid down in Chapter II of this Regulation, shall be recognised and enforced in the other Member States under the rules laid down in Chapter III of this Regulation.

3 Member States shall send to the Commission:

(a)   a copy of the agreements and uniform laws implementing these agreements referred to in paragraph 2(a) and (c);

(b)   any denunciations of, or amendments to, those agreements or uniform laws.

ARTICLE 60

Relations with certain multilateral conventions

In relations between Member States, this Regulation shall take precedence over the following Conventions in so far as they concern matters governed by this Regulation:

(a)   the Hague Convention of 5 October 1961 concerning the Powers of Authorities and the Law Applicable in respect of the Protection of Minors;

(b)   the Luxembourg Convention of 8 September 1967 on the Recognition of Decisions Relating to the Validity of Marriages;

(c)   the Hague Convention of 1 June 1970 on the Recognition of Divorces and Legal Separations;

(d)   the European Convention of 20 May 1980 on Recognition and Enforcement of Decisions concerning Custody of Children and on Restoration of Custody of Children; and

(e)   the Hague Convention of 25 October 1980 on the Civil Aspects of International Child Abduction.

ARTICLE 61

Relation with the Hague Convention of 19 October 1996 on Jurisdiction, Applicable law, Recognition, Enforcement and Cooperation in Respect of Parental Responsibility and Measures for the Protection of Children

As concerns the relation with the Hague Convention of 19 October 1996 on Jurisdiction, Applicable law, Recognition, Enforcement and Cooperation in Respect of Parental Responsibility and Measures for the Protection of Children, this Regulation shall apply:

(a)   where the child concerned has his or her habitual residence on the territory of a Member State;

(b)   as concerns the recognition and enforcement of a judgment given in a court of a Member State on the territory of another Member State, even if the child concerned has his or her habitual residence on the territory of a third State which is a contracting Party to the said Convention.

ARTICLE 62

Scope of effects

1 The agreements and conventions referred to in Articles 59(1), 60 and 61 shall continue to have effect in relation to matters not governed by this Regulation.

2 The conventions mentioned in Article 60, in particular the 1980 Hague Convention, continue to produce effects between the Member States which are party thereto, in compliance with Article 60.

****

CHAPTER VI

TRANSITIONAL PROVISIONS

ARTICLE 64

1 The provisions of this Regulation shall apply only to legal proceedings instituted, to documents formally drawn up or registered as authentic instruments and to agreements concluded between the parties after its date of application in accordance with Article 72.

2 Judgments given after the date of application of this Regulation in proceedings instituted before that date but after the date of entry into force of Regulation (EC) No 1347/2000 shall be recognised and enforced in accordance with the provisions of Chapter III of this Regulation if jurisdiction was founded on rules which accorded with those provided for either in Chapter II or in Regulation (EC) No 1347/2000 or in a convention concluded between the Member State of origin and the Member State addressed which was in force when the proceedings were instituted.

3 Judgments given before the date of application of this Regulation in proceedings instituted after the entry into force of Regulation (EC) No 1347/2000 shall be recognised and enforced in accordance with the provisions of Chapter III of this Regulation provided they relate to divorce, legal separation or marriage annulment or parental responsibility for the children of both spouses on the occasion of these matrimonial proceedings.

4 Judgments given before the date of application of this Regulation but after the date of entry into force of Regulation (EC) No 1347/2000 in proceedings instituted before the date of entry into force of Regulation (EC) No 1347/2000 shall be recognised and enforced in accordance with the provisions of Chapter III of this Regulation provided they relate to divorce, legal separation or marriage annulment or parental

responsibility for the children of both spouses on the occasion of these matrimonial proceedings and that jurisdiction was founded on rules which accorded with those provided for either in Chapter II of this Regulation or in Regulation (EC) No 1347/2000 or in a convention concluded between the Member State of origin and the Member State addressed which was in force when the proceedings were instituted.

CHAPTER VII
FINAL PROVISIONS

ARTICLE 65

Review

No later than 1 January 2012, and every five years thereafter, the Commission shall present to the European Parliament, to the Council and to the European Economic and Social Committee a report on the application of this Regulation on the basis of information supplied by the Member States. The report shall be accompanied if need be by proposals for adaptations.

ARTICLE 66

Member States with two or more legal systems

With regard to a Member State in which two or more systems of law or sets of rules concerning matters governed by this Regulation apply in different territorial units:

  (a)   any reference to habitual residence in that Member State shall refer to habitual residence in a territorial unit;

  (b)   any reference to nationality, or in the case of the United Kingdom 'domicile', shall refer to the territorial unit designated by the law of that State;

  (c)   any reference to the authority of a Member State shall refer to the authority of a territorial unit within that State which is concerned;

  (d)   any reference to the rules of the requested Member State shall refer to the rules of the territorial unit in which jurisdiction, recognition or enforcement is invoked.

ARTICLE 67

Information on central authorities and languages accepted

The Member States shall communicate to the Commission within three months following the entry into force of this Regulation:

  (a)   the names, addresses and means of communication for the central authorities designated pursuant to Article 53;

  (b)   the languages accepted for communications to central authorities pursuant to Article 57(2); and

(c)   the languages accepted for the certificate concerning rights of access pursuant to Article 45(2).

The Member States shall communicate to the Commission any changes to this information.

The Commission shall make this information publicly available.

ARTICLE 68

Information relating to courts and redress procedures

The Member States shall notify to the Commission the lists of courts and redress procedures referred to in Articles 21, 29, 33 and 34 and any amendments thereto.

The Commission shall update this information and make it publicly available through the publication in the Official Journal of the European Union and any other appropriate means.

****

ARTICLE 71

Repeal of Regulation (EC) No 1347/2000

1 Regulation (EC) No 1347/2000 shall be repealed as from the date of application of this Regulation.

2 Any reference to Regulation (EC) No 1347/2000 shall be construed as a reference to this Regulation according to the comparative table in Annex V.

ARTICLE 72

Entry into force

This Regulation shall enter into force on 1 August 2004.

The Regulation shall apply from 1 March 2005, with the exception of Articles 67, 68, 69 and 70, which shall apply from 1 August 2004.

This Regulation shall be binding in its entirety and directly applicable in the Member States in accordance with the Treaty establishing the European Community.

Done at Brussels, 27 November 2003.

For the Council
The President
R. Castelli

2.4 EUROPEAN CONVENTION ON HUMAN RIGHTS 1950

OVERVIEW

A general introduction[1]

The Convention for the Protection of Human Rights and Fundamental Freedoms – to give the ECHR its full title – was opened for signature in 1950 and came into force in 1958.[2] It was born in the aftermath of the Second World War and had as one of its underlying concerns the protection of the individual from the government of her State. It was the first convention to establish a procedure that enabled an individual to bring proceedings against the State in an international court.[3] Whilst children are generally not singled out for special protection, the ECHR applies to them every bit as much as it does to their parents or any other adults.

As well as being governed by the principles set out in the Vienna Convention on the Law of Treaties, there are a number of well-established principles governing the interpretation and application of the ECHR. These include:

- the ECHR is *a 'living' (or 'dynamic' or 'evolutive') document.* So, for example, when determining whether an interference with someone's Article 8 rights is 'necessary in a democratic society ... for the protection of the rights and freedoms of others', this must be considered in a contemporary context and might lead to a different conclusion from one reached some years earlier. Society changes, and the application of the ECHR evolves with it;
- the ECHR is to be *interpreted purposively (also known as 'the principle of effective protection').* In other words, the European Court of Human Rights ('ECtHR') will seek to give effect to the underlying purpose of the ECHR and to make its provisions real and practical;
- *the principle of proportionality.* The means employed by the State must be proportionate to the intended end, and a fair balance may have to be

---

[1] This is the most detailed of the overviews in this Handbook. Readers – particularly those who are not lawyers – may find it helpful also to refer to the summaries at **7.1** and **7.2**.

[2] This is why it is sometimes referred to as the ECHR 1950 and sometimes as the ECHR 1958.

[3] 'The European Court of Human Rights was set up in Strasbourg by the Council of Europe Member States in 1959 to deal with alleged violations of the 1950 European Convention on Human Rights. Since 1 November 1998 it has sat as a full-time Court composed of an equal number of judges to that of the States party to the Convention. The Court examines the admissibility and merits of applications submitted to it. It sits in Chambers of 7 judges or, in exceptional cases, as a Grand Chamber of 17 judges. The Committee of Ministers of the Council of Europe supervises the execution of the Court's judgments' – quotation taken from the European Court of Human Rights website: www.echr.coe.int/.

struck between the rights of an individual and the rights or interests of others or what it is feasible for a State to achieve;

- *the margin of appreciation.* The ECtHR recognises that some degree of latitude may properly be given to individual States in dealing with particular issues. This margin of appreciation is likely to be narrow on issues where a common practice is apparent between States, but broader where a common practice is not widespread;

- *positive obligations and horizontality.* Derived from the principle of a purposive approach to ensure effective protection, the ECtHR has determined that not only can the ECHR require a State to refrain from taking certain action (a negative obligation) it can also require a State to take action (a positive obligation). The next step was to derive from this that not only were the ECHR obligations 'vertical' (ie applying between the State and the individual) they might also be 'horizontal' (ie a positive obligation upon the State to protect an individual's rights against infringement by other individuals).[4] So, for example, one can ask whether, and if so to what extent, because of the Article 2 right to life, a State must take steps to protect someone from the risk of being killed by his or her partner.[5]

Which provisions of the ECHR matter most in children law?

Among the provisions of the ECHR, and the various Protocols that have supplemented it from time to time, two stand out head and shoulders above the others for those involved in children law proceedings. These are Article 6 (the right to a fair trial) and Article 8 (the right to respect for private and family life).

It is important to understand that Articles 6 and 8 are very different from each other. Article 6 is an absolute right. No interference with it can be lawful. But Article 8 is a qualified right. The State, acting through public authorities, can lawfully interfere with the right provided it:

> 'is in accordance with the law and is necessary in a democratic society in the interests of national security, public safety or the economic well-being of the country, for the prevention of disorder or crime, for the protection of health or morals, or for the protection of rights and freedoms of others.'[6]

We will now look at Articles 6 and 8 in more detail. In the case of Article 8 this means looking first at three main rights within Article 8(1)[7] and then at the circumstances in which an interference with those rights can be justified in accordance with Article 8(2), including the place of the best interests of the child.

---

[4] Eg *Hokkanen v Finland* (1994) 19 EHRR 139, [1996] 1 FLR 289.

[5] Cf *Osman v United Kingdom* (2000) 29 EHRR 245.

[6] Article 8(2) of the ECHR.

[7] (1) Procedural rights inherent within the right to respect for family life; (2) substantive rights within the right to respect for family life; and (3) the right to respect for private life.

Article 6: the right to a fair trial

Elements of the Article 6 right include:

- the right to a tribunal[8] that is independent, impartial and established by law;[9]
- the right to a public hearing unless one of the exceptions set out within Article 6 applies. Although family law in England and Wales has become used to its proceedings being conducted in private, the extent to which 'the interests of juveniles or protection of the private life of the parties' requires this is certainly an area of potential contention;
- the right to be present and to participate effectively. In children law this lends support to the practice of litigants in person being allowed a so-called 'McKenzie friend' to assist them;
- 'equality of arms' (see below);
- the right to a reasoned and enforceable judgment. This particularly takes those involved in children law to the difficult issue of enforcing orders for contact;[10]
- the right to a determination of the issue within a reasonable time.[11]

Here is a selection of comments made by the ECtHR in cases in which Article 6 issues have been raised:

> 'The court has ... to ascertain whether the proceedings considered as a whole, including the way in which the evidence was taken, were fair'[12]

> 'The reasonableness of the length of proceedings is to be considered in the light of the criteria laid down in the Court's case law, in particular the complexity of the case, the conduct of the applicant and that of the relevant authorities. On the latter point the importance of what is at stake for the applicant in the litigation has to be taken into account. It is thus essential that custody cases be dealt with speedily. A delay at some stage may be tolerated if the overall duration of the proceedings cannot be deemed excessive.'[13]

> '... as regards litigation involving opposing private interests, "equality of arms" implies that each party must be afforded a reasonable opportunity to present his

---

[8]   See further the consideration of 'tribunal' in *McMichael v United Kingdom* (1995) 20 EHRR 205 at [78]–[82], and in particular, the comment: 'The court accepts that in this sensitive domain of family law there may be good reasons for opting for an adjudicatory body that does not have the composition or procedures of a court of law of the classic kind.'

[9]   Cf the concept of 'natural justice' referred to in the notes about judicial review at **7.14** below.

[10] Eg *Hornsby v Greece* (1997) 24 EHRR 250 at [40]. This is also very much a current issue for the ECtHR in relation to Article 8, as we will see below.

[11] Also something that is very much a current issue for the ECtHR in relation to Article 8, again as we will see below.

[12] *Mantovanelli v France* (1997) 24 EHRR 370 at [34].

[13] *Nuutinen v Finland* (2002) 34 EHRR 358 at [110] (a private law case) following the wording used in *Olsson v Sweden (No 2)* (1992) 17 EHRR 134 at [99] (a public law case).

case – including his evidence – under conditions that do not place him at a substantial disadvantage vis-à-vis his opponent'[14]

'The right to an adversarial trial means the opportunity for the parties to have knowledge of and comment on the observations filed or evidence adduced by the other party.'[15]

This last quotation serves as a reminder that, however non-adversarial family proceedings should be in the manner in which they are conducted, they remain adversarial in the technical sense described.

Two common fallacies about Article 8

Before going any further we need to go to the wording of Article 8(1) and expose two fallacies that are contained within the popular description of Article 8 as being 'the right to family life'. First, the right is not confined to protecting family life. It expressly extends to four concepts – private life, family life, one's home and one's correspondence – which, although they may sometimes overlap, are each distinct from one another. 'Family life' may be the concept most often referred to, but each of the others is important, particularly 'private life'.

Secondly, it is not a right to these four things, but a right to respect for them that is protected by Article 8. As the ECtHR said in *Botta v Italy*:

'… the concept of respect is not precisely defined. In order to determine whether such obligations exist, regard must be had to the fair balance that has to be struck between the general interest and the interests of the individual, while the State has, in any event, a margin of appreciation.'[16]

The meaning of 'family life'

The first question that arises is 'what is family life?'. In the seminal case of *Marckx v Belgium* the ECtHR stated:

'Article 8 makes no distinction between the "legitimate" and the "illegitimate" family. Such a distinction would not be consonant with the word "everyone", and this is confirmed by article 14 with its prohibition, in the enjoyment of the rights and freedoms enshrined in the Convention, of discrimination grounded on "birth". In addition, the Court notes that the Committee of Ministers of the Council of Europe regards the single woman and her child as one form of family no less than others.'[17]

Although *Marckx v Belgium* establishes that the existence of family life does not depend on legal status it still doesn't precisely answer the question 'what is family life?'. Some examples follow:

---

[14] *Dombo Beheer BV v The Netherlands* (1994) 18 EHRR 213 at [33].

[15] *Ruiz-Mateos v Spain* (1993) 16 EHRR 505 at para 63, cited in *McMichael v United Kingdom* (1995) 20 EHRR 205 at [80].

[16] (1998) 26 EHRR 241.

[17] (1979)] 2 EHRR 330 at [31].

- family life may exist even though a couple do not live together;[18]
- family life may exist between a 'father' who has undergone gender reassignment from female to male and a child who had been born to the 'father's' female partner following IVF treatment;[19] but
- family life may not exist where one of two women in a long-term lesbian relationship has a child by artificial insemination.[20]

In the end, whether or not there is 'family life' is a question of fact to be determined in each individual case. Principles, such as that in *Marckx v Belgium*, are well established and must be applied but they cannot by themselves give the answer in any particular case. That is why in each of the three examples we have just given we have spoken of 'may'. And it is important to remember that the ECHR is a living document and what was true ten years ago may not be true now. In its time, *Marckx v Belgium* was ground-breaking; today, that same thinking has become a cornerstone of our understanding of Article 8. If the third of the three cases in the examples given above were to be determined today it is possible that the ECtHR might now conclude that family life existed.

The ECtHR has recently stated:

'The existence or non-existence of "family life" for the purposes of Art 8 is essentially a question of fact depending upon the real existence in practice of close personal ties (see *K and T v Finland* (2000) 31 EHRR 484, [2000] 2 FLR 79). Where it concerns a potential relationship which could develop between a child born out of wedlock and its natural father, relevant factors include the nature of the relationship between the natural parents and the demonstrable interest in and commitment by the father to the child both before and after its birth (see *Nylund v Finland* (Application No 27110/95)).'[21]

Article 8(1): procedural rights inherent within the right to respect for private and family life

It is well established that procedural requirements are inherent within Article 8 in order to ensure respect for family life, and it is therefore quite common for (strictly different) procedural arguments to be raised under each of Articles 6 and 8 from the (same) set of facts. The key advantage of the procedural right inherent within Article 8 is that it applies to administrative procedures as well as to judicial proceedings.[22] Comments from the ECtHR include:

---

18   *Kroon v Netherlands* (1994) 19 EHRR 263 at [30].

19   *X, Y and Z v United Kingdom* (1997) 24 EHRR 143.

20   *Kerkhoven v Netherlands*, Application 15666/89.

21   *Lebbink v The Netherlands* [2004] 2 FLR 463. This passage was cited by both Dyson LJ and Munby J in *Singh v Entry Clearance Officer, New Delhi* [2004] EWCA Civ 1075, [2005] 1 FLR 308.

22   '... administrative decision-makers should be under no illusions. Article 8 imposes procedural safeguards that impose on administrative decision makers whose decisions impinge on private or family life burdens significantly greater than I suspect many of them really appreciate. And the burden of parents – and particularly children – are properly represented when decisions fundamental to the children's welfare are being taken': Munby J in 'Making Sure the Child is Heard', a lecture for the

'The Court would point to the difference in the nature of the interests protected by Articles 6(1) and 8. Thus, Article 6(1) affords a procedural safeguard, namely the "right to a court" in the determination of one's "civil rights and obligations", whereas not only does the procedural requirement inherent in Article 8 cover administrative procedures as well as judicial proceedings, but it is ancillary to the wider purpose of ensuring proper respect for, inter alia, family life. The difference between the purpose pursued by the respective safeguards afforded by Articles 6(1) and 8 may, in the light of the particular circumstances, justify the examination of the same set of facts under both Articles.'[23]

'Whilst Article 8 contains no explicit procedural requirements, the decision-making process leading to measures of interference must be fair and such as to afford due respect to the interests safeguarded by Article 8.'[24]

'The positive obligation on the Contracting State to protect the interests of the family requires that this material be made available to the parent concerned, even in the absence of any request by the parent. If there were doubts as to whether this posed a risk to the welfare of the child, the matter should have been submitted to the court by the local authority at the earliest stage in the proceedings possible for it to resolve the issues involved.'[25]

'... What therefore has to be determined is whether, having regard to the particular circumstances of the case and notably the serious nature of the decisions to be taken, the parents have been involved in the decision-making process, seen as a whole, to a degree sufficient to provide them with the requisite protection of their interests. If they have not, there will have been a failure to respect their family life and the interference resulting from the decision will not be capable of being regarded as "necessary" within the meaning of Article 8.'[26]

The *'sufficient involvement'*[27] of those concerned has become a key concept in children law proceedings, not only in the ECtHR but also in the domestic courts.

Article 8(1): substantive rights within the right to respect for family life

Once it has been established that 'family life' exists, the next question in relation to the right to respect for family life is *'has there been an interference in that family life by the State?'*. This is where the concept of the State's positive obligations inherent within Article 8 is so powerful. It is well settled that the State has all sorts of obligations that might not appear obvious from a quick

---

National Youth Advocacy Service given at the Law Society, London, in February 2004 and published at [2004] Fam Law 427 at 430.

23 *McMichael v United Kingdom* (1995) 20 EHRR 205 at [91].

24 The same case at [87].

25 *TP and KM v United Kingdom* (2001) 2 FLR 549 at [82].

26 *W v United Kingdom* (1988) 10 EHRR 29 at [64].

27 'Sufficient involvement' embraces having the information and opportunity necessary to put one's case (see, in particular, *Kosmopoulou v Greece* [2004] 1 FLR 800 at [48]–[50]) and, crucially, requires that the reasons for the decision and the evidence on which it is based must themselves be relevant and sufficient to found the decision, and in this regard the importance of the decision itself is also highly relevant (see, eg *Elsholz v Germany* [2000] 2 FLR 486 at [52], *Sahin v Germany* [2003] 2 FLR 671 at [77]).

reading of Article 8. Here are some examples of interferences by the State in family members' rights to respect for family life:

- any decision to take a child into care. This is perhaps the most obvious such interference, carried out by the State through the local authority social services department. It is such a serious interference in family life that it must be supported by 'sufficiently sound and weighty considerations in the interests of the child',[28] all the more so where it is proposed to remove a child from his parents shortly after his birth, when there must be 'extraordinarily compelling reasons' before doing so;[29]

- not only the decision to take a child into care but also the refusal to terminate care, for similar reasons; again, the terms of the care plan and its actual implementation must comply with the requirements of Article 8;[30]

- the failure, whether in public or private law,[31] to meet the State's positive obligation to reunite those between whom family life exists. We will look at this in more detail below;

- the failure to take realistic measures (including, potentially, 'coercive' measures) effectively to enforce such reunification. This is particularly important in relation to the enforcement of contact orders in private law cases;[32]

- delay in determining an application, whether in public or private law, where it materially affects the outcome;[33]

- the failure to involve the mother and father in the process of adoption.[34]

There is a particularly strong positive obligation on the State inherent within Article 8 to take all the necessary steps that can reasonably be expected in the circumstances of the particular case to effect *reunification of those between whom family life exists.* This obligation applies to both public and private law cases[35] and embraces both the return of a child to live within her family (eg return from foster care) and achieving contact between family members.[36]

---

[28] Eg *Olsson v Sweden (No 1)* (1988) 11 EHRR 259 at [72]–[74], and *Johansen v Norway* (1996) 23 EHRR 33 at [64].

[29] Eg *P, C and S v United Kingdom* [2002] 2 FLR 631 at [116], reproduced at **5.6** below.

[30] Eg *Olsson v Sweden (No 1)* (1988) 11 EHRR 259 at [75]–[77] and [78]–[83].

[31] 'Public' and 'private' law are explained at **3.6** below.

[32] Eg *Hansen v Turkey* [2004] 1 FLR 142 at [103]–[108].

[33] Eg *H v United Kingdom* (1987) 10 EHRR 95 at [89]–[90]; *W v United Kingdom* (1987) 10 EHRR 29 at [65]; *Sylvester v Austria* [2003] 2 FLR 210 at [69].

[34] *X v United Kingdom,* Application No 7626/76 (mother); *Keegan v Ireland* (1994)] 18 EHRR 342 (father).

[35] See *Olsson v Sweden (No 2)* (1992) 17 EHRR 134 at [90] (public law) and *Hokkanen v Finland* [1996] 1 FLR 289 at [55] and [58] (private law). It is important to remember that Article 8 is essentially blind to any such distinction: the right to respect for private and family life exists irrespective of the kind of case it is, although the application of that right may vary – the interference with the right is normally greater in public law situations and will therefore require more to justify it under Article 8(2).

[36] The same principle is also why, as a matter of law, local authorities should look to place children within their wider family whenever possible.

A classic statement of this in relation to public law cases is contained in the decision of the ECtHR in *Johansen v Norway* when it said:

> 'taking a child into care should normally be regarded as a temporary measure to be discontinued as soon as circumstances permit and ... any measures of implementation of temporary care should be consistent with the ultimate aim of reuniting the natural parent and child. In this regard, a fair balance has to be struck between the interests of the child in remaining in public care and those of the parent in being reunited with the child. In carrying out this balancing exercise, the Court will attach particular importance to the best interests of the child, which, depending on their nature and seriousness, may override those of the parent. In particular ... the parent cannot be entitled under Article 8 of the Convention to have such measures taken as would harm the child's health and development.' [37]

To illustrate the application of the principle of reunification in private law cases see, for example, *Kosmopoulou v Greece*, a case concerning the domestic courts' failure to enforce contact between a mother and her daughter:

> 'As to the state's obligation to take positive measures, the court has repeatedly held that Article 8 includes a right for parents to have measures taken with a view to their being reunited with their children and an obligation for the national authorities to take such measures. This applies not only to cases dealing with the compulsory taking of children into public care and the implementation of care measures but also to cases where contact and residence disputes concerning children arise between parents and/or other members of the children's family.' [38]

This obligation is not, however, absolute. For example, in *Sylvester v Austria*, the ECtHR said:

> 'the national authorities' obligation to take such measures is not absolute, since the reunion of a parent with a child who has lived for some time with the other parent may not be able to take place immediately and may require preparatory measures to be taken. Any obligation to apply coercion in this area must be limited since the interests as well as the rights and freedoms of all concerned must be taken into account and more particularly the best interests of the child and his or her rights under the Convention. Where contacts with the parent might appear to threaten those interests or interfere with those rights, it is for the national authority to strike a fair balance between them.' [39]

Article 8(1): the right to respect for private life

Just because it is perhaps not as important as the right to respect for family life does not mean that the right to respect for private life is unimportant. Far from it. It is ripe for further development.

Private life is a broad concept:

---

[37]　(1996) 23 EHRR 33 at [78].

[38]　[2004] 1 FLR 800 at [44].

[39]　[2003] 2 FLR 210 at [58]. See also *Hansen v Turkey* [2004] 1 FLR 142 at [98].

'Private life, in the Court's view, includes a person's physical and psychological integrity; the guarantee afforded by article 8 of the Convention is primarily intended to ensure the development, without outside interference, of the personality of each individual in his relations with other human beings.'[40]

Elements include the right to live privately (away from unwanted attention), to physical and moral integrity,[41] and to self-fulfilment (to develop one's own personality, to make the relationships one chooses). It is particularly relevant in children law to any issue of self-determination by children as they grow up.[42]

As with the right to respect for family life, once an interference with the right to respect for private life has been established, that interference will be unlawful unless justified in accordance with Article 8(2), and it is to this we must now turn.

Article 8(2): justifying an interference in an Article 8(1) right

It has already been noted that Article 8 (unlike Article 6) is a qualified right, ie a right that is not absolute but which can lawfully be interfered with in certain circumstances. Assuming an interference with an Article 8(1) right has been established for which the State is responsible (whether as a result of its positive or its negative obligations),[43] the next step is to turn to Article 8(2) to determine whether that interference was lawful or not. There are three elements all of which must be made out before the interference will have been lawful:

(1) the interference must be *'in accordance with the law'*. This means not only that it must have a basis in the relevant domestic law but also that that law 'must be adequately accessible' and 'formulated with sufficient precision';[44]

(2) the interference must be *in pursuit of a legitimate aim*, ie one or more of the six (or nine, depending on how you count them) aims set out in Article 8(2); and

---

[40] *Botta v Italy* (1998) 26 EHRR 241 at [32].

[41] Eg *X and Y v The Netherlands* (1985) 8 EHRR 235, in which the ECtHR held there to have been a breach of Article 8 because the Netherlands Criminal Code provided no practical or effective protection for a mentally handicapped 16-year-old girl who had been sexually assaulted (an example of a positive and horizontal obligation). See also in relation to consent to medical treatment *Glass v United Kingdom* [2004] 1 FLR 1019.

[42] Had Mrs Gillick brought her case today it is surely inconceivable that it could have been determined without reference to her daughters' right to respect for private life under Article 8. See '1.3 A window into the history of children law' at the start of this Handbook.

[43] Ie there has been 'a prima facie breach' of Article 8 or, as it is more commonly expressed, Article 8 'is engaged'.

[44] *Sunday Times v United Kingdom* (1979) 2 EHRR 245 at [49] and *Olsson v Sweden (No 1)* (1988) 11 EHRR 259 at [61]. This has the potential to deliver a knock-out blow to a State against which an application has been brought, although the ECtHR recognises that 'it is primarily for the national authorities, notably the courts, to interpret and apply national law': *Yousef v The Netherlands* [2003] 1 FLR 210 at [57].

(3) the interference must be *'necessary in a democratic society'*. This is often the main area of argument in a case about Article 8. Hallmarks of a democratic society are 'tolerance', 'pluralism' and 'broadmindedness'; the word 'necessary' implies a pressing social need; and the interference must be proportionate to the legitimate aim, which means that the reasons advanced to support it must be relevant and sufficient having regard to the nature and extent of the actual interference.[45] As well as proportionality, it is particularly in this area where the margin of appreciation may be brought to bear, and on this, inevitably, there is room for disagreement.[46]

Article 8(2): the best interests of the child

Exactly where do the child's best interests and rights[47] fit within all this? The answer is broadly, but not precisely, clear. At its lowest, the interests and rights of the child must be balanced against those of others involved. In fact, the ECtHR routinely states (something like) that they are 'particularly' to be taken in to account,[48] 'of particular importance ... which, depending on their nature and seriousness, may override those of the parent',[49] or that they are 'of crucial importance'.[50] However, in *Yousef v The Netherlands* the ECtHR went an important step further and said:

> 'The court reiterates that in judicial considerations where the rights under Article 8 of parents and those of a child are at stake, the child's rights must be the paramount consideration. If any balancing of interests is necessary, the interests of the child must prevail.'[51]

Other provisions of the ECHR that may be relevant to matters relating to children law

In passing, attention should be drawn to:

*   Article 3 (prohibition of torture and of inhuman or degrading treatment or punishment);[52]

---

[45] *Dudgeon v United Kingdom* (1981) 4 EHRR 149 at [50]–[54], in which the ECtHR held that the interference was disproportionate and therefore unlawful even though the United Kingdom had acted carefully and in good faith.

[46] See, for example, the very different conclusions of the Chamber of the ECtHR at [2002] 1 FLR 119 and those of the Grand Chamber at [2003] 2 FLR 671 in the cases of *Sahin v Germany* and *Sommerfeld v Germany*.

[47] The ECtHR speaks in terms of (best) interest(s) and rights and not, as in the domestic legislation, in terms of welfare.

[48] *Hansen v Turkey* [2004] 2 FLR 142 at [98].

[49] *Elsholz v Germany* [2000] 2 FLR 486 at [50].

[50] *Hoppe v Germany* [2003] 1 FLR 384 at [48].

[51] [2003] 1 FLR 210 at [73]. Although the ECtHR has not consistently stated this in subsequent decisions, it has recently done so in *Maire v Portugal* [2004] 2 FLR 653 at [77].

[52] See, for example, *A v United Kingdom (Human Rights: Punishment of Child)* [1998] 2 FLR 959: by allowing parents and others in loco parentis the defence of 'reasonable chastisement' in criminal proceedings the State had failed in its positive obligation under Article 3.

- Article 5 (right to liberty and security);
- Article 9 (freedom of thought, conscience and religion) and Article 10 (freedom of expression);
- Article 14 (prohibition of discrimination). It is important to note that this is not a free-standing provision but must be taken in conjunction with another Article;[53]
- Article 2 of Protocol 1 (the right to education).

Consequences of a decision in the ECtHR

Where the ECtHR decides against a State it often creates great pressure for that State to amend its domestic law to prevent the same contravention being repeated in the future. For the individual who has successfully brought the case, as well as establishing their rights in the matter in question, the ECtHR can, and frequently does, award damages[54] (now calculated, of course, in euros, including when the award is against a State, like the United Kingdom, that is not part of the monetary union).

The extracts from the primary materials we recommend you read now are Articles 6 and 8 of the ECHR.

The Overview continues at **2.9** United Nations Convention on the Rights of the Child 1989.

---

[53] Eg a decision essentially based upon the fact the mother is raising the children as Jehovah's Witnesses, or because the father is a homosexual and living with another man, may involve breaches of Article 14 in conjunction with Article 8: *Hoffman v Austria* (1993)] 17 EHRR 293 at [36]. See also the extract from *Marckx v Belgium* quoted earlier in this section of the overview.

[54] Article 41: 'If the court finds that there has been a violation of the Convention or the Protocols thereto, and if the internal law of the High Contracting party concerned allows only partial reparation to be made, the court shall, if necessary, afford just satisfaction to the injured party'.

European Convention on Human Rights 1950

(As set out in the Schedule to the Human Rights Act 1998)

Rights and Freedoms

Article 2 – Right to life

1 Everyone's right to life shall be protected by law. No one shall be deprived of his life intentionally save in the execution of a sentence of a court following his conviction of a crime for which this penalty is provided by law.

2 Deprivation of life shall not be regarded as inflicted in contravention of this Article when it results from the use of force which is no more than absolutely necessary:

  (a) in defence of any person from unlawful violence;
  (b) in order to effect a lawful arrest or to prevent the escape of a person lawfully detained;
  (c) in action lawfully taken for the purpose of quelling a riot or insurrection.

Article 2

In *Pretty v UK* [2002] 2 FLR 45 at [5] it was said that 'the thrust of this is to reflect the sanctity which, particularly in Western eyes, attaches to life'. The Article protects the right to life and prevents the deliberate taking of life save in very narrowly defined circumstances. An Article with that effect cannot be interpreted as conferring a right to die or to enlist the aid of another in bringing about one's own death. It has been considered by the European Court of Human Rights (ECtHR) in relation to:

(1) a refusal of the DPP to give immunity from prosecution in the event that a husband assisted the suicide of his wife (who suffered from motor neurone disease). Held: no breach by reason of the DPP's refusal (*Pretty v UK*);
(2) allegations that police failed to protect the Osman family from interference by their daughter's teacher leading to killing of Mr Osman and the death of the deputy headmaster's son. Held: no breach of Article 2 by the police (*Osman v UK* [1998] 5 BHRC 293, [1999] 1 FLR 193, ECHR);
(3) the suicide of a young prisoner whose mother complained of a failure by the prison authorities to protect his life. The complaint under Article 2 was rejected (*Keenan v UK* (2001) 10 BHRC 319).

In *Re A (Children) (Conjoined Twins: Surgical Separation)* [2001] Fam 147, [2000] 4 All ER 961, [2001] 2 WLR 480, CA, Robert Walker LJ said: 'The Convention is to be construed as an autonomous text, without regard to any special rules of English law, and the word "intentionally" in art 2(1) must be given its natural and ordinary meaning. In my judgment the word, construed in that way, applies only to cases where the purpose of the prohibited action is to cause death. It does not import any prohibition of the proposed operation other than those which are to be found in the common law of England.'

In *R v Her Majesty's Coroner for the Western District of Somerset (Respondent) and Another (Appellant) ex parte Middleton (FC) (Respondent)* [2004] UKHL 10, on appeal from [2002] EWCA Civ 390, Lord Bingham said:

'The European Court of Human Rights has repeatedly interpreted Article 2 of the European Convention as imposing on member states substantive obligations not to take life without justification and also to establish a framework of laws, precautions, procedures and means of enforcement which will, to the greatest extent reasonably practicable, protect life. See, for example, *LCB v United Kingdom* (1998) 27 EHRR 212, para 36; *Osman v United Kingdom* (1998) 29 EHRR 245; *Powell v United Kingdom* (App No 45305/99) (unreported) 4 May 2000, 16–17; *Keenan v United Kingdom* (2001) 33 EHRR 913, paras 88–90; *Edwards v United Kingdom* (2002) 35 EHRR 487, para 54; *Calvelli and Ciglio v Italy* (App No 32967/96) (unreported) 17 January 2002; *Öneryildiz v Turkey* (App No 48939/99) (unreported) 18 June 2002.

3. The European Court has also interpreted Article 2 as imposing on member states a procedural obligation to initiate an effective public investigation by an independent official body into any death occurring in circumstances in which it appears that one or other of the foregoing substantive obligations has been, or may have been, violated and it appears that agents of the state are, or may be, in some way implicated. See, for example, *Taylor v United Kingdom* (1994) 79-A DR 127, 137; *McCann v United Kingdom* (1995) 21 EHRR 97, para 161; *Powell v United Kingdom*, supra p 17; *Salman v Turkey* (2000) 34 EHRR 425, para 104; *Sieminska v Poland* (App No 37602/97) (unreported) 29 March 2001; *Jordan v United Kingdom* (2001) 37 EHRR 52, para 105; *Edwards v United Kingdom*, supra, para 69; *Öneryildiz v Turkey*, supra, paras 90–91; *Mastromatteo v Italy* (App No 37703/97) (unreported) 24 October 2002.

4. The scope of the state's substantive obligations has been the subject of previous decisions such as *Osman* and *Keenan* but is not in issue in this appeal. Nor does any issue arise about participation in the official investigation by the family or next of kin of the deceased, as recently considered by the House in *R (Amin) v Secretary of State for the Home Department* [2003] UKHL 51, [2003] 3 WLR 1169.' (The House then went on to consider the role of inquests in satisfying the State's procedural obligations under Article 2.)

Article 3 – Prohibition of torture

No one shall be subjected to torture or to inhuman or degrading treatment or punishment.

Article 3

In *DP and Another v United Kingdom* (App No 38719/97) [2003] 1 FLR 50, ECHR, it was said:

'Article 3 enshrines one of the most fundamental values of democratic society. It prohibits in absolute terms torture or inhuman or degrading treatment or punishment. The obligation on high contracting parties under art 1 of the Convention to secure to everyone within their jurisdiction the rights and freedoms defined in the Convention, taken together with art 3, requires states to take measures designed to ensure that individuals within their jurisdiction are not subjected to torture or inhuman or degrading treatment, including such ill-treatment administered by private individuals (see *A v UK* [1998] 3 FCR 597 at 602 (para 22)). These measures should provide effective protection, in particular, of children and other vulnerable persons and include reasonable steps to prevent ill-treatment of which the authorities had or ought to have had knowledge (mutatis mutandis, *Osman v UK* (1998) 5 BHRC 293 at 321 (para 116)). Thus a failure, over four and a half years, to protect children from serious neglect and abuse of which the local authority were aware disclosed a breach of art 3 of the Convention in the case of *Z v UK* [2001] 2 FCR 246 at 265 (paras 74–75).'

Article 4 – Prohibition of slavery and forced labour

1 No one shall be held in slavery or servitude.

2 No one shall be required to perform forced or compulsory labour.

3 For the purpose of this Article the term 'forced or compulsory labour' shall not include:

(a) any work required to be done in the ordinary course of detention imposed according to the provisions of Article 5 of this Convention or during conditional release from such detention;

(b) any service of a military character or, in case of conscientious objectors in countries where they are recognised, service exacted instead of compulsory military service;

(c) any service exacted in case of an emergency or calamity threatening the life or well-being of the community;

(d) any work or service which forms part of normal civic obligations.

Article 5 – Right to liberty and security

1 Everyone has the right to liberty and security of person. No one shall be deprived of his liberty save in the following cases and in accordance with a procedure prescribed by law –

(a) the lawful detention of a person after conviction by a competent court;

(b) the lawful arrest or detention of a person for non-compliance with the lawful order of a court or in order to secure the fulfilment of any obligation prescribed by law;

(c) the lawful arrest or detention of a person effected for the purpose of bringing him before the competent legal authority on reasonable suspicion of having committed an offence or when it is reasonably considered necessary to prevent his committing an offence or fleeing after having done so;

(d) the detention of a minor by lawful order for the purpose of educational supervision or his lawful detention for the purpose of bringing him before the competent legal authority;

(e) the lawful detention of persons for the prevention of the spreading of infectious diseases, of persons of unsound mind, alcoholics or drug addicts or vagrants;

(f) the lawful arrest or detention of a person to prevent his effecting an unauthorised entry into the country or of a person against whom action is being taken with a view to deportation or extradition.

2 Everyone who is arrested shall be informed promptly, in a language which he understands, of the reasons for his arrest and of any charge against him.

3 Everyone arrested or detained in accordance with the provisions of paragraph 1(c) of this Article shall be brought promptly before a judge or other officer authorised by law to exercise judicial power and shall be entitled to trial within a reasonable time or to release pending trial. Release may be conditioned by guarantees to appear for trial.

4 Everyone who is deprived of his liberty by arrest or detention shall be entitled to take proceedings by which the lawfulness of his detention shall be decided speedily by a court and his release ordered if the detention is not lawful.

5 Everyone who has been the victim of arrest or detention in contravention of the provisions of this Article shall have an enforceable right to compensation.

Article 5

In *Nowicka v Poland* [2003] 1 FLR 417, ECtHR, it was said that: 'Article 5(1) requires in the first place that the detention be "lawful", which includes the condition of compliance with a procedure prescribed by law. The convention here essentially refers back to national law and states the obligation to conform to the substantive and procedural rules thereof, but it requires in addition that any deprivation of liberty should be consistent with the purpose of

Article 5, namely to protect individuals from arbitrariness. A period of detention will in principle be lawful if it is carried out pursuant to a court order (see *Benham v UK* (1996) 22 EHRR 293, at paras 40 and 42). [59] Furthermore, the list of exceptions to the right to liberty secured in art 5(1) is an exhaustive one and only a narrow interpretation of those exceptions is consistent with the aim of that provision, namely to ensure that no one is arbitrarily deprived of his liberty (see, inter alia, *Giulia Manzoni v Italy* [1997] ECHR 19218/91, at para 25). [60] Moreover, detention is authorised under sub-para (b) of art 5(1) only to "secure the fulfilment" of the obligation prescribed by law. It follows that, at the very least, there must be an unfulfilled obligation incumbent on the person concerned and the arrest and detention must be for the purpose of securing its fulfilment and not punitive in character. As soon as the relevant obligation has been fulfilled, the basis for detention under art 5(1)(b) ceases to exist. [61] Finally, a balance must be drawn between the importance in a democratic society of securing the immediate fulfilment of the obligation in question, and the importance of the right to liberty. The duration of detention is also a relevant factor in drawing such a balance (see *McVeigh v UK* (1981) 25 DR 15 at 37–38 and 42; *Johansen v Norway* (1985) 44 DR 155).'

It has also been held that parents may restrict the movement of their children (*Nielsen v Denmark* (1988) 11 EHRR 175).

The UK law relating to the making of secure accommodation orders is not in breach of Article 5(1) since such orders fall within the exemption in Article 5(1)(d) (*Re K (Secure Accommodation Order: Right to Liberty)* [2001] Fam 377, [2001] 2 All ER 719, [2001] 1 FLR 526, CA).

Article 6 – Right to a fair trial

1 In the determination of his civil rights and obligations or of any criminal charge against him, everyone is entitled to a fair and public hearing within a reasonable time by an independent and impartial tribunal established by law. Judgment shall be pronounced publicly but the press and public may be excluded from all or part of the trial in the interest of morals, public order or national security in a democratic society, where the interests of juveniles or the protection of the private life of the parties so require, or to the extent strictly necessary in the opinion of the court in special circumstances where publicity would prejudice the interests of justice.

2 Everyone charged with a criminal offence shall be presumed innocent until proved guilty according to law.

3 Everyone charged with a criminal offence has the following minimum rights –

    (a)   to be informed promptly, in a language which he understands and in detail, of the nature and cause of the accusation against him;

    (b)   to have adequate time and facilities for the preparation of his defence;

    (c)   to defend himself in person or through legal assistance of his own choosing or, if he has not sufficient means to pay for legal assistance, to be given it free when the interests of justice so require;

    (d)   to examine or have examined witnesses against him and to obtain the attendance and examination of witnesses on his behalf under the same conditions as witnesses against him;

    (e)   to have the free assistance of an interpreter if he cannot understand or speak the language used in court.

Article 6

In *P, C and S v United Kingdom* [2002] 2 FLR 631, (2002) 35 EHRR 31, ECtHR, the court expressed some general principles about Article 6 at paras [90]–[91] (see **5.6** where this case is set out).

The Convention rights are engaged where a party is within the jurisdiction of England and Wales. The fact that a mother's Convention rights might not be respected in a foreign court (eg Saudi Arabia) did not make it a breach of the Convention for the UK court to return the children to that country (*Re J (Child Returned Abroad: Human Rights)* [2004] EWCA Civ 417, [2004] 2 FLR 85, CA).

The Article has been considered in the following cases (amongst others):

Case	Topic	Summary
Fayed v UK (1994) 18 EHRR 393	Article 6 and creation of new domestic civil right.	The Convention enforcement bodies may not create by way of interpretation of Article 6(1) a substantive civil right which has no legal basis in the State concerned.
Re P (A Child) (Residence Order: Child's Welfare) [2000] Fam 15, [1999] 3 All ER 734, [1999] 3 WLR 1164, [1999] 2 FLR 573, CA	CA 1989, s 91(14).	Section 91(14) of the CA 1989 is ECHR-compliant.
Re F (Care: Termination of Contact) [2000] 2 FCR 481	CA 1989, s 34.	Section 34 of the CA 1989 is ECHR-compliant.
L v UK [2000] 2 FLR 322, ECtHR	Disclosure of experts' reports.	The compulsory disclosure of experts' reports in proceedings under the CA 1989 does not offend Article 6.
Re B (Disclosure to Other Parties) [2001] 2 FLR 1017, FD	Non-disclosure of information to other parties.	Unlike Article 8, Article 6 is not qualified by words of limitation. Non-disclosure to other parties should only be allowed where the case for it is compelling and it is strictly necessary
Re H; Re G (Adoption: Consultation of Unmarried Fathers) [2001] 1 FLR 646, FD	Father unaware of child's birth.	'If the father is a father who is found to have a family life with his child then one would expect Art 6(1) prima facie to apply. This raises the difficult question of the impact of the rights of other parties under Art 8, and the welfare principles, on the right to a fair trial. There must, however, in principle, be some qualification of the right of a party to be heard in proceedings. This would be likely to arise under two separate categories, namely, a policy decision of the court, in the exercise of its right to run its own proceedings within the requirements that there should be a fair trial, and, secondly, the practicalities of service on a potential litigant or his attendance at the hearing. There will be cases where notice to a father would create a significant physical risk to the mother, to children in the family, or to other people concerned in the case, (see for instance *Re X (Care: Notice of Proceedings)* [1996] 1 FLR 186). That might result in the court balancing the fairness to the father of notice, against the real risks of the consequences of such notice. The practicalities of finding the father have also to be taken into account. There will be cases where the adoption agency, despite taking reasonable steps to ascertain the father's whereabouts, have been unable to locate him, and it will be necessary to dispense with service.'
P, C and S v United Kingdom [2002] 2 FLR 631, ECtHR	Legal representation.	Mother should have had legal representation where the local authority sought a care order and adoption.

Case	Topic	Summary
Clibbery v Allan [2002] EWCA Civ 45, [2002] Fam 261, [2002] 1 FLR 565	Hearings in private.	There is nothing in Article 6 that requires all cases to be heard in open court (see also *P v BW (Children Cases: Hearings in Public)* [2004] EWCA Civ 845, also *B v United Kingdom* (2002) 34 EHRR 19, [2001] 2 FLR 261, ECtHR).
Re M (Disclosure: Children and Family Reporter) [2002] EWCA Civ 1199, [2002] 2 FLR 893, CA.	CAFCASS officers.	CAFCASS officers may be cross-examined.
Re H (A Child) (Interim Care Order) [2002] EWCA Civ 1932, [2003] 1 FCR 350.	Premature decision.	The rights of parents under Articles 6 and 8 of the ECHR will require a judge to abstain from a premature determination of the case unless the welfare of the child demands it. Immediate separation will only be contemplated if the child's safety so demands.
Re L (Care: Assessment: Fair Trial) [2002] EWHC 1379 (Fam), [2002] 2 FLR 730, FD.	Care proceedings.	The rights under Article 6 are not limited to the purely judicial part of the proceedings. Article 8 does not water down Article 6.
Re S (Minors) (Care Order: Implementation of Care Plan); Re W (Minors) (Care Order: Adequacy of Care Plan) [2002] UKHL 10, [2002] 2 All ER 192, HL.	Extent of Article 6.	'[74] In taking this step the jurisprudence of the European Court of Human Rights has drawn back from holding that Art 6(1) requires that all administrative decisions should be susceptible of, in effect, substantive appeal to a court, with the court substituting its views for the decision made by the administrator. Article 6(1) is not so crude or, I might add, so unrealistic. Article 6(1) is more discerning in its requirements. The extent of judicial control required depends on the subject matter of the decision and the extent to which this lends itself to judicial decision. This area of the law has recently been discussed by Lord Hoffmann in *R (On the Application of Alconbury Developments Ltd) v Secretary of State for the Environment, Transport and the Regions* [2001] UKHL 23, [2001] 2 All ER 929, [2001] 2 WLR 1389, at [77]–[122].'
P v BW (Children Cases: Hearings in Public) [2004] EWCA Civ 845 (and see also *B v United Kingdom* (2002) 34 EHRR 19, [2001] 2 FLR 261, ECtHR).	CA 1989, s 97.	Section 97 of the CA 1989 is ECHR-compliant.
Evans v Amicus Healthcare Ltd and Others, Hadley v Midland Fertility Services Ltd and Others [2003] EWHC 2161 (Fam), [2004] 1 FLR 67, FD.	Human Fertilisation and Embryology Act 1990.	The Act does not breach the ECHR.

Case	Topic	Summary
D v East Berkshire Community Health NHS Trust K and Another v Dewsbury Healthcare NHS Trust and Another RK and Another v Oldham NHS Trust and Another [2003] EWCA Civ 1151, [2003] 4 All ER 796, CA.	Duty of care of local authority where child abuse occurs.	'The procedure that has given rise to these appeals involves determining, by way of preliminary issues, whether the test of what is "fair just and reasonable", applied with that respect for case precedent which our law requires, precludes the existence of a duty of care, even if all the facts alleged by the claimants are established. Those preliminary issues have reached the Court of Appeal and may well reach the House of Lords. No violation of art 6 is involved in this procedure, as the Strasbourg Court expressly recognised in *Z v UK* and *TP and KM v UK*.'
Re K (Children) (Committal Proceedings) [2003] 2 FCR 336, CA.	Committal.	Committal proceedings invoke the protection of Article 6. The mother had the right not to be committed for not complying with contact orders without legal representation (an unreasonable litigant may lose that right).
Newham London Borough Council v Kibata [2003] EWCA Civ 1785, [2003] 3 FCR 724, CA.	Notice to quit.	Service by local authority on a husband of notice to quit after the wife's departure was not in breach of Article 6.
Re V (Care Proceedings: Human Rights Claims) [2004] EWCA Civ 54, [2004] 1 FLR 944, CA.	CA 1989 and ECHR-compatibility.	The CA 1989 generally and Part IV in particular are ECHR-compliant.
R (On the Application of M) v Inner London Crown Court [2003] EWHC 301 (Admin), [2003] 1 FLR 994 DC.	Parenting orders under s 8 of the Crime and Disorder Act 1998.	Such orders do not create a breach of Article 6.

Article 7 – No punishment without law

1 No one shall be held guilty of any criminal offence on account of any act or omission which did not constitute a criminal offence under national or international law at the time when it was committed. Nor shall a heavier penalty be imposed than the one that was applicable at the time the criminal offence was committed.

2 This Article shall not prejudice the trial and punishment of any person for any act or omission which, at the time when it was committed, was criminal according to the general principles of law recognised by civilised nations.

Article 8 – Right to respect for private and family life

1 Everyone has the right to respect for his private and family life, his home and his correspondence.

2 There shall be no interference by a public authority with the exercise of this right except such as is in accordance with the law and is necessary in a democratic society in the interests of national security, public safety or the economic well-being of the

country, for the prevention of disorder or crime, for the protection of health or morals, or for the protection of the rights and freedoms of others.

Article 8

Generally (ECtHR decisions)—In the case of *P, C and S v United Kingdom* [2002] 2 FLR 631, [2002] 3 FCR 1, ECtHR, the court gave a full explanation of Article 8 at [113]–[120] (see **5.6** where this case is set out).

Generally (domestic authority)—Article 8 provides parents involved in care proceedings with procedural rights as well as substantive rights – those rights are not confined to the trial of the application but extend to all stages of the decision-making process (*Re G (Care: Challenge to Local Authority's Decision)* [2003] EWHC 551 (Fam), [2003] 2 FLR 42, FD).

In *B County Council v L* [2002] EWHC 2327 (Fam), Charles J said:

'In *Re W & B (Re W Care Plan)* [2001] 2 FLR 582 at paras 52–58, Hale LJ gives an overview of Article 8 which demonstrates the overlap between the purposes that underlie Article 8 and the Children Act and makes the point that sometimes not to interfere where interference is called for may also violate a child's Convention rights and fail to satisfy the positive obligation to secure a new family for a child who has been deprived of life with his family of birth. I have also considered *Re C & B (Care Order: Future Harm)* [2001] 1 FLR 611 and in particular paras 33 and 34 of the judgment of Hale LJ therein where she says this:

"**[33]** I would have reached that conclusion without reference to the European Convention for the Protection of Human Rights and Fundamental Freedoms 1950, but I do note that under Art 8 of the Convention both the children and the parents have the right to respect for their family and private life. If the state is to interfere with that there are three requirements: first, that it be in accordance with the law; secondly, that it be for a legitimate aim (in this case the protection of the welfare and interests of the children); and thirdly, that it be 'necessary in a democratic society'.

[34] There is a long line of European Court of Human Rights jurisprudence on that third requirement, which emphasises that the intervention has to be proportionate to the legitimate aim. Intervention in the family may be appropriate, but the aim should be to reunite the family when the circumstances enable that, and the effort should be devoted towards that end. Cutting off all contact and the relationship between the child or children and their family is only justified by the overriding necessity of the interests of the child."

In my judgment that guidance from Hale LJ is not undermined in any way by the decision of the House of Lords in *Re S, Re W*. Indeed it seems to me that the speeches therein confirm this general guidance as to the approach to be adopted albeit that the House of Lords allowed the appeal from the decision of the Court of Appeal reported as *Re W & B (Re W Care Plan)*.'

Child's welfare—There is nothing in s 1 of the Children Act 1989 which is incompatible with Article 8 of the ECHR (*Dawson v Wearmouth* [1999] 2 AC 329, [1999] 2 All ER 353, [1999] 1 FLR 1167, HL).

In the case of *Re L (A Child) (Contact: Domestic Violence)* [2000] 4 All ER 609, [2001] 2 WLR 339, [2000] 2 FCR 404, 424–425, [2000] 2 FLR 334, CA, the President said: 'In *Hendriks v Netherlands* (1982) 5 EHRR 223 the court held that where there was a serious conflict between the interests of a child and one of its parents which could only be resolved to the disadvantage of one of them, the interests of the child had to prevail under art 8(2). The principle of the crucial importance of the best interests of the child has been upheld in all subsequent decisions of the European Court of Human Rights. The observation by the court in *Johansen v Norway* (1996) 23 EHRR 33 is particularly apposite to this appeal. The court said: "In particular the parent cannot be entitled under Article 8 of the Convention to have such measures taken as would harm the child's health and development".'

Private life—In *X (A Woman Formerly Known as Mary Bell) and Another v O'Brien and Others* [2003] EWHC 1101, [2003] 2 FCR 686, QBD, the President said:

'[20] In numerous decisions on Art 8, the European Court of Human Rights at Strasbourg has set out the general principles and enlarged the meaning of "private life". It covers the physical and psychological integrity of a person (see *X v Netherlands* (1985) 8 EHRR 235 at para 22). It protects a right to personal development and to establish and develop relationships with other human beings and the outside world (see *Botta v Italy* (1998) 4 BHRC 81 and *Bensaid v UK* (2001) 11 BHRC 297). [21] In *Botta v Italy* (1998) 4 BHRC 81 at 88 the European Court of Human Rights said: "[32] Private life, in the court's view, includes a person's physical and psychological integrity; the guarantee afforded by Art 8 of the Convention is primarily intended to ensure the development, without outside interference, of the personality of each individual in his relations with other human beings ...". [22] In *Bensaid v UK* (2001) 11 BHRC 297 at 309–310 the court said: "[46] Not every act or measure which adversely affects moral or physical integrity will interfere with the right to respect to private life guaranteed by art 8. However, the court's case law does not exclude that treatment which does not reach the severity of art 3 treatment may nonetheless breach Art 8 in its private life aspect where there are sufficiently adverse effects on physical and moral integrity ... [47] Private life is a broad term not susceptible to exhaustive definition. The court has already held that elements such as gender identification, name and sexual orientation and sexual life are important elements of the personal sphere protected by Art 8 ... Mental health must also be regarded as a crucial part of private life associated with the aspect of moral integrity. Article 8 protects a right to identity and personal development, and the right to establish and develop relationships with other human beings and the outside world ... The preservation of mental stability is in that context an indispensable precondition to effective enjoyment of the right to respect for private life." [23] One important factor in X's case, to which I refer below in more detail, is the potential effect of publicity upon her mental health. [24] Article 8 has to be balanced against the rights to be found in Art 10.'

In *Palau-Martinez v France* [2004] 2 FLR 810, ECtHR, it was held that the French court had acted in breach of the mother's Article 8 rights by granting residence to the father because of the mother's religious convictions as a Jehovah's witness (there being no direct concrete evidence that residence with the mother would be contrary to the children's welfare).

Family life—This has an extensive meaning and is not limited to legitimate families, see *Lebbink v The Netherlands* [2004] 2 FLR 463, ECtHR. In *Marckx v Belgium* (1979) 2 EHRR 330 the court said; 'Article 8 makes no distinction between the "legitimate" and the "illegitimate" family. Such a distinction would not be consonant with the word "everyone", and this is confirmed by Art 14 with its prohibition, in the enjoyment of the rights and freedoms enshrined in the Convention, of discrimination grounded on "birth". In addition, the ECtHR notes that the Committee of Ministers of the Council of Europe regards the single woman and her child as one form of family no less than others'.

Relations between grandparents and grandchildren (as well as those between other family members) fall within the ambit of family life and therefore attract the protection of Article 8 of that Convention (*Scozzari and Giunta v Italy* (2002) 35 EHRR 12).

In *Kroon v Netherlands* (1994) 19 EHRR 263, ECtHR, the Court said:

'In any case the court recalls that the notion of "family life" in Article 8 is not confined solely to marriage-based relationships and may encompass other de facto "family ties" where parties are living together outside marriage (see as the most recent authority, the *Keegan v Ireland* judgment of 26 May 1994, Series A no 290, pp 17–18, § 44 and reported at [1994] 18 EHRR 342, [1994] 3 FCR 165). Although, as a rule, living together may be a requirement for such a relationship, exceptionally other factors may also serve to demonstrate that a relationship has sufficient constancy to create de facto "family ties"; such is the case here, as since 1987 four children have been born to Mrs Kroon and Mr Zerrouk. A child born of such a relationship is ipso jure part of that "family unit" from the moment of its birth and by the very fact of it (see the *Keegan* judgment, ibid).'

In *X, Y and Z v United Kingdom* [1997] 2 FLR 892, 24 EHRR 143, it was held that family life existed between a transsexual, his partner and his partner's child. In *Boyle v UK* [1994] 2 FCR 822, 19 EHRR 179, the Commission had decided that a claim by an uncle that family life existed between himself and his nephew but the case was settled before the full court could rule upon the application. In *Lebbink v The Netherlands* [2004] 2 FLR 463, ECtHR, (unmarried father of child) it was held that the question of whether there has been 'family life' is one of fact – mere biological kinship, without any further legal or factual elements indicating the existence of a close personal relationship, could not be regarded as sufficient to attract the protection of Article 8.

The ECtHR said at [36]:

'The existence or non-existence of "family life" for the purpose of Article 8 is essentially a question of fact depending upon the real existence in practice of close personal ties (see *K and T v Finland* [2000] 31 EHRR 484, [2000] 2 FLR 79). Where it concerns a potential relationship which could develop between a child born out of wedlock and its natural father, relevant factors include the nature of the relationship between the natural parents and the demonstrable interest in and commitment by the father to the child both before and after its birth (see *Nylund v Finland* (Application No 27110/95) (unreported)).'

Restoration/maintenance of family life —The State must take measures to restore the family where children are removed into public care, although this is not an absolute duty (*Hansen v Turkey* [2003] 1 FLR 142 at [98]). This applies not only in relation to cases where children are taken into public care (*Gorgulu v Germany* [2004] 1 FLR 894, ECtHR) but also in 'private law' disputes (*Kosmopoulou v Greece* [2004] 1 FLR 800, ECtHR, and *Maire v Portugal* [2004] 2 FLR 653). In *Hokkanen v Finland* [1995] 19 EHRR 139, [1996] 1 FLR 289, ECtHR, the court said: 'In previous cases dealing with issues relating to the compulsory taking of children into public care and the implementation of care measures, the court has consistently held that Article 8 includes a right for the parent to have measures taken with a view to his or her being reunited with the child and an obligation for the national authorities to take such action (see, for instance, the *Eriksson v Sweden* judgment of 22 June 1989, Series A no 156, p 26, § 71; the *Margareta and Roger Andersson v Sweden* judgment of 25 February 1992, Series A no 226-A, p 30, § 91; and the *Olsson v Sweden (No 2)* judgment of 27 November 1992, Series A no 250, pp 35–36, § 90). In the opinion of the court, this principle must be taken as also applying to cases such as the present where the origin of the provisional transfer of care is a private agreement'. Where parents have learning difficulties, the investigation of rehabilitation should be intensive (*Kutzner v Germany* (2002) 35 EHRR 25, ECtHR). The summary removal of children from their parents requires extraordinarily compelling reasons (*Haase v Germany* [2004] 2 FLR 39, ECtHR).

There must be extraordinarily compelling reasons to justify the removal of a new born baby from its mother's care (*P, C and S v United Kingdom* [2002] 2 FLR 631, ECtHR, and *Haase v Germany* [2004] 2 FLR 39, ECtHR).

Contact—In *S and G v Italy* [2000] 2 FLR 771, ECtHR, it was held: '**[181]** Article 8 demands that decisions of courts aimed in principle at facilitating visits between parents and their children so that they can re-establish relations with a view to reunification of the family be implemented in an effective and coherent manner. No logical purpose would be served in deciding that visits may take place if the manner in which the decision is implemented means that de facto the child is irreversibly separated from its natural parent. Accordingly, the relevant authorities, in this case the Youth Court, have a duty to exercise constant vigilance, particularly as regards action taken by social services, to ensure the latter's conduct does not defeat the authorities' decisions. ... **[221]** ... The court noted, firstly, that it was common ground that issues relating to the relations between the second applicant and her grandchildren were covered by Art 8 of the Convention. It also pointed out in that connection that "family life", within the meaning of Art 8 includes at least the ties between near relatives, for instance those between grandparents and grandchildren, since such relatives may play a considerable part in family life ... "Respect" for a family life so understood implies an obligation for the State to act in a manner calculated to allow these ties to develop normally (see *Marckx v Belgium* (1979) 2 EHRR 330, 348, para 45).' See also the cases in the paragraph above ('Article 8: Restoration/maintenance of family life').

Where a child is abducted, effective measures should be implemented to secure the return of the child (*Maire v Portugal* [2004] 2 FLR 653, ECtHR).

Article 9 – Freedom of thought, conscience and religion

1 Everyone has the right to freedom of thought, conscience and religion; this right includes freedom to change his religion or belief and freedom, either alone or in community with others and in public or private, to manifest his religion or belief, in worship, teaching, practice and observance.

2 Freedom to manifest one's religion or beliefs shall be subject only to such limitations as are prescribed by law and are necessary in a democratic society in the interests of public safety, for the protection of public order, health or morals, or for the protection of the rights and freedoms of others.

Article 9

There may have to be a balance struck between a parent's wish to practice his/her religion and the welfare of a child concerned. In the case of *Re J (Specific Issue Order: Child's Religious Upbringing and Circumcision)* [2000] 1 FLR 571, CA, the President said: 'The judge correctly held that the father's right to manifest his religion had to be balanced against the welfare of the child and the rights of the mother' (see also *Hoffman v Austria* (1993) 17 EHRR 293).

Article 10 – Freedom of expression

1 Everyone has the right to freedom of expression. This right shall include freedom to hold opinions and to receive and impart information and ideas without interference by public authority and regardless of frontiers. This Article shall not prevent States from requiring the licensing of broadcasting, television or cinema enterprises.

2 The exercise of these freedoms, since it carries with it duties and responsibilities, may be subject to such formalities, conditions, restrictions or penalties as are prescribed by law and are necessary in a democratic society, in the interests of national security, territorial integrity or public safety, for the prevention of disorder or crime, for the protection of health or morals, for the protection of the reputation or rights of others, for preventing the disclosure of information received in confidence, or for maintaining the authority and impartiality of the judiciary.

Article 10

In *B v United Kingdom* (2002) 34 EHRR 19, [2001] 2 FLR 261, the ECtHR rejected the father's argument that the UK courts were in breach of Article 6 in holding that the whole of the evidence, submissions and judgment relating to the residence of a child should be in open court; the court found that it was not necessary to consider Article 10. Munby J in *Kelly v BBC* [2001] 1 All ER 323 at 337 said: 'if those who seek to bring themselves within para (2) of Art 10 are to establish "convincingly" that they are – and that is what they have to establish – they cannot do so by mere assertion, however eminent the person making the assertion, nor by simply inviting the court to make assumptions; what is required is proper evidence'. In *Venables and Another v News Group Newspapers Ltd and Others* [2001] Fam 430, [2001] 1 All ER 908, [2001] 2 WLR 1038, [2001] 1 FLR 791, the President gives an extensive examination of the principles that arise under this Article.

Article 11 – Freedom of assembly and association

1 Everyone has the right to freedom of peaceful assembly and to freedom of association with others, including the right to form and to join trade unions for the protection of his interests.

2 No restrictions shall be placed on the exercise of these rights other than such as are prescribed by law and are necessary in a democratic society in the interests of national security or public safety, for the prevention of disorder or crime, for the protection of health or morals or for the protection of the rights and freedoms of others. This Article shall not prevent the imposition of lawful restrictions on the exercise of these rights by members of the armed forces, of the police or of the administration of the State.

Article 12 – Right to marry

Men and women of marriageable age have the right to marry and to found a family, according to the national laws governing the exercise of this right.

Article 14 – Prohibition of discrimination

The enjoyment of the rights and freedoms set forth in this Convention shall be secured without discrimination on any ground such as sex, race, colour, language, religion, political or other opinion, national or social origin, association with a national minority, property, birth or other status.

Article 14

Although Article 14 does not create new rights, it is not necessary for there to be a breach of other Articles before it becomes relevant. Thus it has been said:

(1) 'Article 14 protects individuals placed in similar situations from discrimination in their enjoyment of their rights under the Convention and its Protocols. However, a difference in the treatment of one of those individuals will only be discriminatory if it "has no objective and reasonable justification," that is if it does not pursue a "legitimate aim" and if there is no "reasonable relationship of proportionality between the means employed and the aim sought to be realised".' (*Darby v Sweden* (1990) 13 EHRR 774, ECtHR, at para 31);

(2) 'The European Court of Human Rights has repeatedly held that Art 14 is not autonomous but has effect only in relation to Convention rights. As it was put in *Van Raalte v Netherlands* (1997) 24 EHRR 503 at 516–517: "As the court has consistently held, Article 14 of the Convention complements the other substantive provisions of the Convention and the Protocols. It has no independent existence since it has effect solely in relation to 'the enjoyment of the rights and freedoms' safeguarded by those provisions. Although the application of Article 14 does not presuppose a breach of those provisions – and to this extent it is autonomous – there can be no room for its application unless the facts at issue fall within the ambit of one or more of the latter".' (*Pretty v UK* [2002] 2 FLR 45, ECtHR) (and see also *Botta v Italy* (1998) 4 BHRC 81 at 90 (para 39));

(3) 'An uninformed reading of the bare words of that provision might suggest that a complainant had to establish an actual breach of another Article of the Convention before he could rely on Article 14. Jurisprudence has however established that that is not so. As it is put in Grosz, Beatson & Duffy *Human Rights* (2000), § C14-10: "It would appear, however, that even the most tenuous link with another provision in the Convention will suffice for Article 14 to enter into play." A recent illustration is to be found in *Petrovic v Austria* (2001) 33 EHRR 14, a complaint about the refusal of the Austrian authorities to grant to men a parental leave allowance that was available to mothers. The Court held, at §26, that Article 8 itself was not infringed since it did not impose any positive obligation on the state to provide the financial assistance in question. Nonetheless, at §§27–29: "this allowance paid by the State is intended to promote family life and necessarily affects the way in which the latter is organised as, in conjunction with parental leave, it enables one of the parents to stay at home to look after the children. The Court has said on many occasions that Article 14 comes into

play whenever 'the subject-matter of the disadvantage constitutes one of modalities of the exercise of a right guaranteed', or the measures complained of are 'linked to the exercise of a right guaranteed'. By granting parental leave allowance States are able to demonstrate their respect for family life within the meaning of Article 8 of the Convention; the allowance therefore comes within the scope of that provision. It follows that Article 14 – taken together with Article 8 – is applicable." We therefore have to apply that wide view of the ambit of Article 14 in relation to the two other provisions of the Convention that are relied on in conjunction with Article 14': Buxton LJ in *Ghaidan v Mendoza* [2002] EWCA Civ 1533, [2003] Ch 380, [2003] 2 WLR 478, CA;

(4) 'It is important to bear in mind that there does not have to be a breach of one of the substantive Articles of the Convention before Article 14 comes into play. The usual test, as was indicated by Brooke LJ in *Michalak*, is whether the facts "fall within the ambit of one or more of the substantive Convention provisions" (para 20). That phrase "fall within the ambit" is one regularly found in judgments of the Strasbourg Court on this issue: see, for example, *Rasmussen v Denmark* (1985) 7 EHRR 371, para 29; *Van der Mussele v Belgium* (1983) 6 EHRR 163, para 43. One can readily understand why such an approach is adopted, since there would be little force in Article 14 if an infringement of another Article had first to be established. There would always be a breach, irrespective of Article 14': Keene LJ in *Ghaidan v Mendoza* [2002] EWCA Civ 1533, [2003] Ch 380, [2003] 2 WLR 478, CA.

When the case of *Ghaidan v Mendoza* came before the House of Lords (and was dismissed – [2004] UKHL 30, [2004] 3 WLR 113), Lord Nicholls said at [9] and [10]:

'[9] It goes without saying that Article 14 is an important Article of the Convention. Discrimination is an insidious practice. Discriminatory law undermines the rule of law because it is the antithesis of fairness. It brings the law into disrepute. It breeds resentment. It fosters an inequality of outlook which is demeaning alike to those unfairly benefited and those unfairly prejudiced. Of course all law, civil and criminal, has to draw distinctions. One type of conduct, or one factual situation, attracts one legal consequence, another type of conduct or situation attracts a different legal consequence. To be acceptable these distinctions should have a rational and fair basis. Like cases should be treated alike, unlike cases should not be treated alike. The circumstances which justify two cases being regarded as unlike, and therefore requiring or susceptible of different treatment, are infinite. In many circumstances opinions can differ on whether a suggested ground of distinction justifies a difference in legal treatment. But there are certain grounds of factual difference which by common accord are not acceptable, without more, as a basis for different legal treatment. Differences of race or sex or religion are obvious examples. Sexual orientation is another. This has been clearly recognised by the European Court of Human Rights: see, for instance, *Fretté v France* [2003] 2 FLR 9, 23, at para 32. Unless some good reason can be shown, differences such as these do not justify differences in treatment. Unless good reason exists, differences in legal treatment based on grounds such as these are properly stigmatised as discriminatory.

[10] Unlike Article 1 of the 12th Protocol, Article 14 of the Convention does not confer a free-standing right of non-discrimination. It does not confer a right of non-discrimination in respect of all laws. Article 14 is more limited in its scope. It precludes discrimination in the "enjoyment of the rights and freedoms set forth in this Convention". The court at Strasbourg has said this means that, for Article 14 to be applicable, the facts at issue must "fall within the ambit2 of one or more of the Convention rights. Article 14 comes into play whenever the subject matter of the disadvantage "constitutes one of the modalities" of the exercise of a right guaranteed or whenever the measures complained of are "linked" to the exercise of a right guaranteed: *Petrovic v Austria* (2001) 33 EHRR 14 at paras 22, 28.'

Article 16 – Restrictions on political activity of aliens

Nothing in Articles 10, 11 and 14 shall be regarded as preventing the High Contracting Parties from imposing restrictions on the political activity of aliens.

Article 17 – Prohibition of abuse of rights

Nothing in this Convention may be interpreted as implying for any State, group or person any right to engage in any activity or perform any act aimed at the destruction of any of the rights and freedoms set forth herein or at their limitation to a greater extent than is provided for in the Convention.

Article 18 – Limitation on use of restrictions on rights

The restrictions permitted under this Convention to the said rights and freedoms shall not be applied for any purpose other than those for which they have been prescribed.

****

2.5 EUROPEAN CONVENTION ON THE EXERCISE OF CHILDREN'S RIGHTS 1996

Strasbourg, 25 January 1996

Preamble

The member States of the Council of Europe and the other States signatory hereto,

Considering that the aim of the Council of Europe is to achieve greater unity between its members;

Having regard to the United Nations Convention on the rights of the child and in particular Article 4 which requires States Parties to undertake all appropriate legislative, administrative and other measures for the implementation of the rights recognised in the said Convention;

Noting the contents of Recommendation 1121 (1990) of the Parliamentary Assembly on the rights of the child;

Convinced that the rights and best interests of children should be promoted and to that end children should have the opportunity to exercise their rights, in particular in family proceedings affecting them;

Recognising that children should be provided with relevant information to enable such rights and best interests to be promoted and that due weight should be given to the views of children;

Recognising the importance of the parental role in protecting and promoting the rights and best interests of children and considering that, where necessary, States should also engage in such protection and promotion;

Considering, however, that in the event of conflict it is desirable for families to try to reach agreement before bringing the matter before a judicial authority,

Have agreed as follows:

CHAPTER I

SCOPE AND OBJECT OF THE CONVENTION AND DEFINITIONS

ARTICLE 1

Scope and object of the Convention

1 This Convention shall apply to children who have not reached the age of 18 years.

2 The object of the present Convention is, in the best interests of children, to promote their rights, to grant them procedural rights and to facilitate the exercise of these rights by ensuring that children are, themselves or through other persons or

bodies, informed and allowed to participate in proceedings affecting them before a judicial authority.

3 For the purposes of this Convention proceedings before a judicial authority affecting children are family proceedings, in particular those involving the exercise of parental responsibilities such as residence and access to children.

4 Every State shall, at the time of signature or when depositing its instrument of ratification, acceptance, approval or accession, by a declaration addressed to the Secretary General of the Council of Europe, specify at least three categories of family cases before a judicial authority to which this Convention is to apply.

5 Any Party may, by further declaration, specify additional categories of family cases to which this Convention is to apply or provide information concerning the application of Article 5, paragraph 2 of Article 9, paragraph 2 of Article 10 and Article 11.

6 Nothing in this Convention shall prevent Parties from applying rules more favourable to the promotion and the exercise of children's rights.

ARTICLE 2

Definitions

For the purposes of this Convention:

(a) the term 'judicial authority' means a court or an administrative authority having equivalent powers;

(b) the term 'holders of parental responsibilities' means parents and other persons or bodies entitled to exercise some or all parental responsibilities;

(c) the term 'representative' means a person, such as a lawyer, or a body appointed to act before a judicial authority on behalf of a child;

(d) the term 'relevant information' means information which is appropriate to the age and understanding of the child, and which will be given to enable the child to exercise his or her rights fully unless the provision of such information were contrary to the welfare of the child.

CHAPTER II

PROCEDURAL MEASURES TO PROMOTE THE EXERCISE OF CHILDREN'S RIGHTS

A Procedural rights of a child

ARTICLE 3

Right to be informed and to express his or her views in proceedings

A child considered by internal law as having sufficient understanding, in the case of proceedings before a judicial authority affecting him or her, shall be granted, and shall be entitled to request, the following rights:

(a)   to receive all relevant information;
(b)   to be consulted and express his or her views;
(c)   to be informed of the possible consequences of compliance with these
        views and the possible consequences of any decision.

ARTICLE 4

Right to apply for the appointment of a special representative

1 Subject to Article 9, the child shall have the right to apply, in person or through
other persons or bodies, for a special representative in proceedings before a judicial
authority affecting the child where internal law precludes the holders of parental
responsibilities from representing the child as a result of a conflict of interest with the
latter.

2 States are free to limit the right in paragraph 1 to children who are considered by
internal law to have sufficient understanding.

ARTICLE 5

Other possible procedural rights

Parties shall consider granting children additional procedural rights in relation to
proceedings before a judicial authority affecting them, in particular:

(a)   the right to apply to be assisted by an appropriate person of their choice in
        order to help them express their views;
(b)   the right to apply themselves, or through other persons or bodies, for the
        appointment of a separate representative, in appropriate cases a lawyer;
(c)   the right to appoint their own representative;
(d)   the right to exercise some or all of the rights of parties to such
        proceedings.

B Role of judicial authorities

ARTICLE 6

Decision-making process

In proceedings affecting a child, the judicial authority, before taking a decision, shall:

(a)   consider whether it has sufficient information at its disposal in order to
        take a decision in the best interests of the child and, where necessary, it
        shall obtain further information, in particular from the holders of parental
        responsibilities;
(b)   in a case where the child is considered by internal law as having sufficient
        understanding:
        –   ensure that the child has received all relevant information;

> – consult the child in person in appropriate cases, if necessary privately, itself or through other persons or bodies, in a manner appropriate to his or her understanding, unless this would be manifestly contrary to the best interests of the child;
> – allow the child to express his or her views;

(c) give due weight to the views expressed by the child.

ARTICLE 7

Duty to act speedily

In proceedings affecting a child the judicial authority shall act speedily to avoid any unnecessary delay and procedures shall be available to ensure that its decisions are rapidly enforced. In urgent cases the judicial authority shall have the power, where appropriate, to take decisions which are immediately enforceable.

ARTICLE 8

Acting on own motion

In proceedings affecting a child the judicial authority shall have the power to act on its own motion in cases determined by internal law where the welfare of a child is in serious danger.

ARTICLE 9

Appointment of a representative

1 In proceedings affecting a child where, by internal law, the holders of parental responsibilities are precluded from representing the child as a result of a conflict of interest between them and the child, the judicial authority shall have the power to appoint a special representative for the child in those proceedings.

2 Parties shall consider providing that, in proceedings affecting a child, the judicial authority shall have the power to appoint a separate representative, in appropriate cases a lawyer, to represent the child.

C Role of representatives

ARTICLE 10

1 In the case of proceedings before a judicial authority affecting a child the representative shall, unless this would be manifestly contrary to the best interests of the child:

(a) provide all relevant information to the child, if the child is considered by internal law as having sufficient understanding;

(b) provide explanations to the child if the child is considered by internal law as having sufficient understanding, concerning the possible consequences of compliance with his or her views and the possible consequences of any action by the representative;

(c) determine the views of the child and present these views to the judicial authority.

2 Parties shall consider extending the provisions of paragraph 1 to the holders of parental responsibilities.

D Extension of certain provisions

ARTICLE 11

Parties shall consider extending the provisions of Articles 3, 4 and 9 to proceedings affecting children before other bodies and to matters affecting children which are not the subject of proceedings.

E National bodies

ARTICLE 12

1 Parties shall encourage, through bodies which perform, *inter alia*, the functions set out in paragraph 2, the promotion and the exercise of children's rights.

2 The functions are as follows:

(a) to make proposals to strengthen the law relating to the exercise of children's rights;

(b) to give opinions concerning draft legislation relating to the exercise of children's rights;

(c) to provide general information concerning the exercise of children's rights to the media, the public and persons and bodies dealing with questions relating to children;

(d) to seek the views of children and provide them with relevant information.

F Other matters

ARTICLE 13

Mediation or other processes to resolve disputes

In order to prevent or resolve disputes or to avoid proceedings before a judicial authority affecting children, Parties shall encourage the provision of mediation or other processes to resolve disputes and the use of such processes to reach agreement in appropriate cases to be determined by Parties.

ARTICLE 14

Legal aid and advice

Where internal law provides for legal aid or advice for the representation of children in proceedings before a judicial authority affecting them, such provisions shall apply in relation to the matters covered by Articles 4 and 9.

ARTICLE 15

Relations with other international instruments

This Convention shall not restrict the application of any other international instrument which deals with specific issues arising in the context of the protection of children and families, and to which a Party to this Convention is, or becomes, a Party.

2.6 EUROPEAN CONVENTION ON THE RECOGNITION AND ENFORCEMENT OF DECISIONS CONCERNING CUSTODY OF CHILDREN 1980

(As set out in Schedule 2 of the Child Abduction and Custody Act 1985)

ARTICLE 1

For the purposes of this Convention:

(a) child means a person of any nationality, so long as he is under 16 years of age and has not the right to decide on his own place of residence under the law of his habitual residence, the law of his nationality or the internal law of the State addressed;

(b) authority means a judicial or administrative authority;

(c) decision relating to custody means a decision of an authority in so far as it relates to the care of the person of the child, including the right to decide on the place of his residence, or to the right of access to him;

(d) improper removal means the removal of a child across an international frontier in breach of a decision relating to his custody which has been given in a Contracting State and which is enforceable in such a State; improper removal also includes:

   (i) the failure to return a child across an international frontier at the end of a period of the exercise of the right of access to this child or at the end of any other temporary stay in a territory other than that where the custody is exercised;

   (ii) a removal which is subsequently declared unlawful within the meaning of Art 12.

PART I

CENTRAL AUTHORITIES

ARTICLE 2

1 Each Contracting State shall appoint a central authority to carry out the functions provided for by this Convention.

2 Federal States and States with more than one legal system shall be free to appoint more than one central authority and shall determine the extent of their competence.

3 The Secretary General of the Council of Europe shall be notified of any appointment under this Article.

ARTICLE 3

1 The central authorities of the Contracting States shall co-operate with each other and promote co-operation between the competent authorities in their respective countries. They shall act with all necessary despatch.

2 With a view to facilitating the operation of this Convention, the central authorities of the Contracting States:

(a) shall secure the transmission of requests for information coming from competent authorities and relating to legal or factual matters concerning pending proceedings;

(b) shall provide each other on request with information about their law relating to the custody of children and any changes in that law;

(c) shall keep each other informed of any difficulties likely to arise in applying the Convention and, as far as possible, eliminate obstacles to its application.

ARTICLE 4

1 Any person who has obtained in a Contracting State a decision relating to the custody of a child and who wishes to have that decision recognised or enforced in another Contracting State may submit an application for this purpose to the central authority in any Contracting State.

2 The application shall be accompanied by the documents mentioned in Art 13.

3 The central authority receiving the application, if it is not the central authority in the State addressed, shall send the documents directly and without delay to that central authority.

4 The central authority receiving the application may refuse to intervene where it is manifestly clear that the conditions laid down by this Convention are not satisfied.

5 The central authority receiving the application shall keep the applicant informed without delay of the progress of his application.

Article 4

Registration is effected in accordance with s 16, and rr 6.1–6.16 of the FPR 1991.

Although Brussels II (Council Regulation (EC) No 2201/2003 of 27 November 2003 on Jurisdiction and the Recognition and Enforcement of Judgments in Matrimonial Matters and in Matters of Parental Responsibility) (reproduced at **2.3**) takes precedence over the European Convention on the Recognition and Enforcement of Decisions Concerning Custody of Children, it does not take precedence over the Hague Convention on the Civil Aspects of International Child Abduction. See, in particular, paras 17 and 18 of the Recitals to, and Article 11 of, Brussels II and, under the 'old' Brussels II, *Re G (Foreign Contact Order: Enforcement)* [2003] EWCA Civ 1607, [2004] 1 FLR 378, CA. The provisions of the 'old' Brussels II did not cease to apply when the divorce was made final (although in *Re G* the exclusive jurisdiction of the French Court was terminated by the French order giving permission for the children to be permanently removed from France).

ARTICLE 5

1 The central authority in the State addressed shall take or cause to be taken without delay all steps which it considers to be appropriate, if necessary by instituting proceedings before its competent authorities, in order:

(a) to discover the whereabouts of the child;
(b) to avoid, in particular by any necessary provisional measures, prejudice to the interests of the child or of the applicant;
(c) to secure the recognition or enforcement of the decision;
(d) to secure the delivery of the child to the applicant where enforcement is granted;
(e) to inform the requesting authority of the measures taken and their results.

2 Where the central authority in the State addressed has reason to believe that the child is in the territory of another Contracting State it shall send the documents directly and without delay to the central authority of that State.

3 With the exception of the cost of repatriation, each Contracting State undertakes not to claim any payment from an applicant in respect of any measures taken under para 1 of this Article by the central authority of that State on the applicant's behalf, including the costs of proceedings and, where applicable, the costs incurred by the assistance of a lawyer.

4 If recognition or enforcement is refused, and if the central authority of the State addressed considers that it should comply with a request by the applicant to bring in that State proceedings concerning the substance of the case, that authority shall use its best endeavours to secure the representation of the applicant in the proceedings under conditions no less favourable than those available to a person who is resident in and a national of that State and for this purpose it may, in particular, institute proceedings before its competent authorities.

ARTICLE 6

1 Subject to any special agreements made between the central authorities concerned and to the provisions of para 3 of this Article:

(a) communications to the central authority of the State addressed shall be made in the official language or in one of the official languages of that State or be accompanied by a translation into that language;
(b) the central authority of the State addressed shall nevertheless accept communications made in English or in French or accompanied by a translation into one of these languages.

2 Communications coming from the central authority of the State addressed, including the results of enquiries carried out, may be made in the official language or one of the official languages of that State or in English or French.

3 A Contracting State may exclude wholly or partly the provisions of para 1(b) of this Article. When a Contracting State has made this reservation any other Contracting State may also apply the reservation in respect of that State.

PART II

RECOGNITION AND ENFORCEMENT OF DECISIONS AND RESTORATION OF CUSTODY OF CHILDREN

ARTICLE 7

A decision relating to custody given in a Contracting State shall be recognised and, where it is enforceable in the State of origin, made enforceable in every other Contracting State.

ARTICLE 8

1 In the case of an improper removal, the central authority of the State addressed shall cause steps to be taken forthwith to restore the custody of the child where:

(a)   at the time of the institution of the proceedings in the State where the decision was given or at the time of the improper removal, if earlier, the child and his parents had as their sole nationality the nationality of that State and the child had his habitual residence in the territory of that State, and

(b)   a request for the restoration was made to a central authority within a period of six months from the date of the improper removal.

2 If, in accordance with the law of the State addressed, the requirements of para 1 of this Article cannot be complied with without recourse to a judicial authority, none of the grounds of refusal specified in this Convention shall apply to the judicial proceedings.

3 Where there is an agreement officially confirmed by a competent authority between the person having the custody of the child and another person to allow the other person a right of access, and the child, having been taken abroad, has not been restored at the end of the agreed period to the person having the custody, custody of the child shall be restored in accordance with paras 1(b) and 2 of this Article. The same shall apply in the case of a decision of the competent authority granting such a right to a person who has not the custody of the child.

ARTICLE 9

1 In cases of improper removal, other than those dealt with in Art 8, in which an application has been made to a central authority within a period of six months from the date of the removal, recognition and enforcement may be refused only if:

(a)   in the case of a decision given in the absence of the defendant or his legal representative, the defendant was not duly served with the document which instituted the proceedings or an equivalent document in sufficient time to enable him to arrange his defence; but such a failure to effect service cannot constitute a ground for refusing recognition or enforcement where service was not effected because the defendant had concealed his whereabouts from the person who instituted the proceedings in the State of origin;

(b) in the case of a decision given in the absence of the defendant or his legal representative, the competence of the authority giving the decision was not founded:
    (i) on the habitual residence of the defendant, or
    (ii) on the last common habitual residence of the child's parents, at least one parent being still habitually resident there, or
    (iii) on the habitual residence of the child;

(c) the decision is incompatible with a decision relating to custody which became enforceable in the State addressed before the removal of the child, unless the child has had his habitual residence in the territory of the requesting State for one year before his removal.

2 Where no application has been made to a central authority, the provisions of para 1 of this Article shall apply equally, if recognition and enforcement are requested within six months from the date of the improper removal.

3 In no circumstances may the foreign decision be reviewed as to its substance.

ARTICLE 10

1 In cases other than those covered by Arts 8 and 9, recognition and enforcement may be refused not only on the grounds provided for in Art 9 but also on any of the following grounds:

(a) if it is found that the effects of the decision are manifestly incompatible with the fundamental principles of the law relating to the family and children in the State addressed;

(b) if it is found that by reason of a change in the circumstances including the passage of time but not including a mere change in the residence of the child after an improper removal, the effects of the original decision are manifestly no longer in accordance with the welfare of the child;

(c) if at the time when the proceedings were instituted in the State of origin:
    (i) the child was a national of the State addressed or was habitually resident there and no such connection existed with the State of origin;
    (ii) the child was a national both of the State of origin and of the State addressed and was habitually resident in the State addressed;

(d) if the decision is incompatible with a decision given in the State addressed or enforceable in that State after being given in a third State, pursuant to proceedings begun before the submission of the request for recognition or enforcement, and if the refusal is in accordance with the welfare of the child.

2 In the same cases, proceedings for recognition or enforcement may be adjourned on any of the following grounds:

(a) if an ordinary form of review of the original decision has been commenced;

(b) if proceedings relating to the custody of the child, commenced before the proceedings in the State of origin were instituted, are pending in the State addressed;

(c) if another decision concerning the custody of the child is the subject of proceedings for enforcement or of any other proceedings concerning the recognition of the decision.

Article 10

The question of contact following divorce between the parents of a child is covered by Brussels II, which takes precedence over the European Convention.

Manifestly incompatible—This must be construed stringently (*Re G (Foreign Contact Order: Enforcement)* [2003] EWCA Civ 1607, [2004] 1 FLR 378, CA, at [24]).

Change in circumstances—In *Re A (Foreign Access Order: Enforcement)* [1996] 1 FLR 561, CA, Leggatt LJ said: 'The judge therefore had to ask herself whether the Art 10(1)(b) ground was made out by the mother. That depended on (1) whether there had been a change of circumstances, including the passage of time as a possible change of circumstances; and (2) whether by reason of any such change, the effects of the original decision were manifestly no longer in accordance with the welfare of the children. This was a "yes" or "no" decision. Unless there had been a change of circumstances, there could be no refusal of recognition and then only if such a change had rendered the custody order manifestly no longer in accordance with the welfare of the children.'

Incompatible with a decision, etc—This condition was considered in the case of *Re M (Child Abduction) (European Convention)* [1994] 1 FLR 551, FD (Rattee J).

ARTICLE 11

1 Decisions on rights of access and provisions of decisions relating to custody which deal with the right of access shall be recognised and enforced subject to the same conditions as other decisions relating to custody.

2 However, the competent authority of the State addressed may fix the conditions for the implementation and exercise of the right of access taking into account, in particular, undertakings given by the parties on this matter.

3 Where no decision on the right of access has been taken or where recognition or enforcement of the decision relating to custody is refused, the central authority of the State addressed may apply to its competent authorities for a decision on the right of access, if the person claiming a right of access so requests.

Article 11

Article 11(2) should be liberally construed to enable courts to attach conditions with the intention of ensuring that orders were complied with (*Re G (Foreign Contact Order: Enforcement)* [2003] EWCA Civ 1607, [2004] 1 FLR 378, CA).

ARTICLE 12

Where, at the time of the removal of a child across an international frontier, there is no enforceable decision given in a Contracting State relating to his custody, the provisions of this Convention shall apply to any subsequent decision, relating to the custody of that child and declaring the removal to be unlawful, given in a Contracting State at the request of any interested person.

PART III

PROCEDURE

ARTICLE 13

1 A request for recognition or enforcement in another Contracting State of a decision relating to custody shall be accompanied by:

(a) a document authorising the central authority of the State addressed to act on behalf of the applicant or to designate another representative for that purpose;

(b) a copy of the decision which satisfies the necessary conditions of authenticity;

(c) in the case of a decision given in the absence of the defendant or his legal representative, a document which establishes that the defendant was duly served with the document which instituted the proceedings or an equivalent document;

(d) if applicable, any document which establishes that, in accordance with the law of the State of origin, the decision is enforceable;

(e) if possible, a statement indicating the whereabouts or likely whereabouts of the child in the State addressed;

(f) proposals as to how the custody of the child should be restored.

2 The documents mentioned above shall, where necessary, be accompanied by a translation according to the provisions laid down in Art 6.

ARTICLE 14

Each Contracting State shall apply a simple and expeditious procedure for recognition and enforcement of decisions relating to the custody of a child. To that end it shall ensure that a request for enforcement may be lodged by simple application.

ARTICLE 15

1 Before reaching a decision under para 1(b) of Art 10, the authority concerned in the State addressed:

(a) shall ascertain the child's views unless this is impracticable having regard in particular to his age and understanding; and

(b) may request that any appropriate enquiries be carried out.

2 The cost of enquiries in any Contracting State shall be met by the authorities of the State where they are carried out.

3 Request for enquiries and the results of enquiries may be sent to the authority concerned through the central authorities.

ARTICLE 16

For the purposes of this Convention, no legalisation or any like formality may be required.

****

2.7 HAGUE CONVENTION ON PROTECTION OF CHILDREN AND CO-OPERATION IN RESPECT OF INTERCOUNTRY ADOPTION 1993

(As set out in the Adoption (Intercountry Aspects) Act 2002, Sch 1)

Preamble

The States signatory to the present Convention.

Recognising that the child, for the full and harmonious development of his or her personality, should grow up in a family environment, in an atmosphere of happiness, love and understanding,

Recalling that each State should take, as a matter of priority, appropriate measures to enable the child to remain in the care of his or her family of origin,

Recognising that intercountry adoption may offer the advantage of a permanent family to a child for whom a suitable family cannot be found in his or her State of origin,

Convinced of the necessity to take measures to ensure that intercountry adoptions are made in the best interests of the child and with respect for his or her fundamental rights, and to prevent the abduction, the sale of, or traffic in children,

Desiring to establish common provisions to this effect, taking into account the principles set forth in international instruments, in particular the United Nations Convention on the Rights of the Child, of 20 November 1989, and the United Nations Declaration on Social and Legal Principles relating to the Protection and Welfare of Children, with Special Reference to Foster Placement and Adoption Nationally and Internationally (General Assembly Resolution 41/85, of 3 December 1986),

Have agreed upon the following provisions –

CHAPTER I

SCOPE OF THE CONVENTION

ARTICLE 1

The objects of the present Convention are –

(a) to establish safeguards to ensure that intercountry adoptions take place in the best interests of the child and with respect for his or her fundamental rights as recognised in international law;

(b) to establish a system of co-operation amongst Contracting States to ensure that those safeguards are respected and thereby prevent the abduction, the sale of, or traffic in children;

(c)   to secure the recognition in Contracting States of adoptions made in accordance with the Convention.

ARTICLE 2

1 The Convention shall apply where a child habitually resident in one Contracting State ('the State of origin') has been, is being, or is to be moved to another Contracting State ('the receiving State') either after his or her adoption in the State of origin by spouses or a person habitually resident in the receiving State, or for the purposes of such an adoption in the receiving State or in the State of origin.

2 The Convention covers only adoptions which create a permanent parent-child relationship.

ARTICLE 3

The Convention ceases to apply if the agreements mentioned in Article 17, sub-paragraph (c), have not been given before the child attains the age of eighteen years.

CHAPTER II

REQUIREMENTS FOR INTERCOUNTRY ADOPTIONS

ARTICLE 4

An adoption within the scope of the Convention shall take place only if the competent authorities of the State of origin –

- (a)   have established that the child is adoptable;
- (b)   have determined, after possibilities for placement of the child within the State of origin have been given due consideration, that an intercountry adoption is in the child's best interests;
- (c)   have ensured that –
  - (i)   the persons, institutions and authorities whose consent is necessary for adoption, have been counselled as may be necessary and duly informed of the effects of their consent, in particular whether or not an adoption will result in the termination of the legal relationship between the child and his or her family of origin,
  - (ii)   such persons, institutions and authorities have given their consent freely, in the required legal form, and expressed or evidenced in writing,
  - (iii) the consents have not been induced by payment or compensation of any kind and have not been withdrawn, and
  - (iv)   the consent of the mother, where required, has been given only after the birth of the child; and
- (d)   have ensured, having regard to the age and degree of maturity of the child, that –
  - (i)   he or she has been counselled and duly informed of the effects of the adoption and of his or her consent to the adoption, where such consent is required,
  - (ii)   consideration has been given to the child's wishes and opinions,

(iii) the child's consent to the adoption, where such consent is required, has been given freely, in the required legal form, and expressed or evidenced in writing, and

(iv) such consent has not been induced by payment or compensation of any kind.

ARTICLE 5

An adoption within the scope of the Convention shall take place only if the competent authorities of the receiving State –

(a) have determined that the prospective adoptive parents are eligible and suited to adopt;

(b) have ensured that the prospective adoptive parents have been counselled as may be necessary; and

(c) have determined that the child is or will be authorised to enter and reside permanently in that State.

CHAPTER III

CENTRAL AUTHORITIES AND ACCREDITED BODIES

ARTICLE 6

1 A Contracting State shall designate a Central Authority to discharge the duties which are imposed by the Convention upon such authorities.

2 Federal States, States with more than one system of law or States having autonomous territorial units shall be free to appoint more than one Central Authority and to specify the territorial or personal extent of their functions. Where a State has appointed more than one Central Authority, it shall designate the Central Authority to which any communication may be addressed for transmission to the appropriate Central Authority within that State.

ARTICLE 7

1 Central Authorities shall co-operate with each other and promote co-operation amongst the competent authorities in their States to protect children and to achieve the other objects of the Convention.

2 They shall take directly all appropriate measures to –

(a) provide information as to the laws of their States concerning adoption and other general information, such as statistics and standard forms;

(b) keep one another informed about the operation of the Convention and, as far as possible, eliminate any obstacles to its application.

ARTICLE 8

Central Authorities shall take, directly or through public authorities, all appropriate measures to prevent improper financial or other gain in connection with an adoption and to deter all practices contrary to the objects of the Convention.

ARTICLE 9

Central Authorities shall take, directly or through public authorities or other bodies duly accredited in their State, all appropriate measures, in particular to –

    (a)   collect, preserve and exchange information about the situation of the child and the prospective adoptive parents, so far as is necessary to complete the adoption;

    (b)   facilitate, follow and expedite proceedings with a view to obtaining the adoption;

    (c)   promote the development of adoption counselling and post-adoption services in their States;

    (d)   provide each other with general evaluation reports about experience with intercountry adoption;

    (e)   reply, in so far as is permitted by the law of their State, to justified requests from other Central Authorities or public authorities for information about a particular adoption situation.

ARTICLE 10

Accreditation shall only be granted to and maintained by bodies demonstrating their competence to carry out properly the tasks with which they may be entrusted.

ARTICLE 11

An accredited body shall –

    (a)   pursue only non-profit objectives according to such conditions and within such limits as may be established by the competent authorities of the State of accreditation;

    (b)   be directed and staffed by persons qualified by their ethical standards and by training or experience to work in the field of intercountry adoption; and

    (c)   be subject to supervision by competent authorities of that State as to its composition, operation and financial situation.

ARTICLE 12

A body accredited in one Contracting State may act in another Contracting State only if the competent authorities of both States have authorised it to do so.

ARTICLE 13

The designation of the Central Authorities and, where appropriate, the extent of their functions, as well as the names and addresses of the accredited bodies shall be communicated by each Contracting State to the Permanent Bureau of the Hague Conference on Private International Law.

CHAPTER IV

PROCEDURAL REQUIREMENTS IN INTERCOUNTRY ADOPTION

ARTICLE 14

Persons habitually resident in a Contracting State, who wish to adopt a child habitually resident in another Contracting State, shall apply to the Central Authority in the State of their habitual residence.

ARTICLE 15

1 If the Central Authority of the receiving State is satisfied that the applicants are eligible and suited to adopt, it shall prepare a report including information about their identity, eligibility and suitability to adopt, background, family and medical history, social environment, reasons for adoption, ability to undertake an intercountry adoption, as well as the characteristics of the children for whom they would be qualified to care.

2 It shall transmit the report to the Central Authority of the State of origin.

ARTICLE 16

1 If the Central Authority of the State of origin is satisfied that the child is adoptable, it shall –

(a) prepare a report including information about his or her identity, adoptability, background, social environment, family history, medical history including that of the child's family, and any special needs of the child;

(b) give due consideration to the child's upbringing and to his or her ethnic, religious and cultural background;

(c) ensure that consents have been obtained in accordance with Article 4; and

(d) determine, on the basis in particular of the reports relating to the child and the prospective adoptive parents, whether the envisaged placement is in the best interests of the child.

2 It shall transmit to the Central Authority of the receiving State its report on the child, proof that the necessary consents have been obtained and the reasons for its determination on the placement, taking care not to reveal the identity of the mother and the father if, in the State of origin, these identities may not be disclosed.

ARTICLE 17

Any decision in the State of origin that a child should be entrusted to prospective adoptive parents may only be made if –

(a) the Central Authority of that State has ensured that the prospective adoptive parents agree;

(b) the Central Authority of the receiving State has approved such decision, where such approval is required by the law of that State or by the Central Authority of the State of origin;

(c)   the Central Authorities of both States have agreed that the adoption may proceed; and

(d)   it has been determined, in accordance with Article 5, that the prospective adoptive parents are eligible and suited to adopt and that the child is or will be authorised to enter and reside permanently in the receiving State.

ARTICLE 18

The Central Authorities of both States shall take all necessary steps to obtain permission for the child to leave the State of origin and to enter and reside permanently in the receiving State.

ARTICLE 19

1 The transfer of the child to the receiving State may only be carried out if the requirements of Article 17 have been satisfied.

2 The Central Authorities of both States shall ensure that this transfer takes place in secure and appropriate circumstances and, if possible, in the company of the adoptive or prospective adoptive parents.

3 If the transfer of the child does not take place, the reports referred to in Articles 15 and 16 are to be sent back to the authorities who forwarded them.

ARTICLE 20

The Central Authorities shall keep each other informed about the adoption process and the measures taken to complete it, as well as about the progress of the placement if a probationary period is required.

ARTICLE 21

1 Where the adoption is to take place after the transfer of the child to the receiving State and it appears to the Central Authority of that State that the continued placement of the child with the prospective adoptive parents is not in the child's best interests, such Central Authority shall take the measures necessary to protect the child, in particular –

(a)   to cause the child to be withdrawn from the prospective adoptive parents and to arrange temporary care;

(b)   in consultation with the Central Authority of the State of origin, to arrange without delay a new placement of the child with a view to adoption or, if this is not appropriate, to arrange alternative long-term care; an adoption shall not take place until the Central Authority of the State of origin has been duly informed concerning the new prospective adoptive parents;

(c)   as a last resort, to arrange the return of the child, if his or her interests so require.

2 Having regard in particular to the age and degree of maturity of the child, he or she shall be consulted and, where appropriate, his or her consent obtained in relation to measures to be taken under this Article.

ARTICLE 22

1 The functions of a Central Authority under this Chapter may be performed by public authorities or by bodies accredited under Chapter III, to the extent permitted by the law of its State.

2 Any Contracting State may declare to the depositary of the Convention that the functions of the Central Authority under Articles 15 to 21 may be performed in that State, to the extent permitted by the law and subject to the supervision of the competent authorities of that State, also by bodies or persons who –

(a) meet the requirements of integrity, professional competence, experience and accountability of that State; and

(b) are qualified by their ethical standards and by training or experience to work in the field of intercountry adoption.

3 A Contracting State which makes the declaration provided for in paragraph 2 shall keep the Permanent Bureau of the Hague Conference on Private International Law informed of the names and addresses of these bodies and persons.

4 Any Contracting State may declare to the depositary of the Convention that adoptions of children habitually resident in its territory may only take place if the functions of the Central Authorities are performed in accordance with paragraph 1.

5 Notwithstanding any declaration made under paragraph 2, the reports provided for in Articles 15 and 16 shall, in every case, be prepared under the responsibility of the Central Authority or other authorities or bodies in accordance with paragraph 1.

CHAPTER V
RECOGNITION AND EFFECTS OF THE ADOPTION

ARTICLE 23

1 An adoption certified by the competent authority of the State of the adoption as having been made in accordance with the Convention shall be recognised by operation of law in the other Contracting States. The certificate shall specify when and by whom the agreements under Article 17, sub-paragraph (c), were given.

2 Each Contracting State shall, at the time of signature, ratification, acceptance, approval or accession, notify the depositary of the Convention of the identity and the functions of the authority or the authorities which, in that State, are competent to make the certification. It shall also notify the depositary of any modification in the designation of these authorities.

ARTICLE 24

The recognition of an adoption may be refused in a contracting State only if the adoption is manifestly contrary to its public policy, taking into account the best interests of the child.

ARTICLE 25

Any Contracting State may declare to the depositary of the convention that it will not be bound under this Convention to recognise adoptions made in accordance with an agreement concluded by application of Article 39, paragraph 2.

ARTICLE 26

1 The recognition of an adoption includes recognition of –

(a) the legal parent-child relationship between the child and his or her adoptive parents;

(b) parental responsibility of the adoptive parents for the child;

(c) the termination of a pre-existing legal relationship between the child and his or her mother and father, if the adoption has this effect in the Contracting State where it was made.

2 In the case of an adoption having the effect of terminating a pre-existing legal parent-child relationship, the child shall enjoy in the receiving State, and in any other Contracting State where the adoption is recognised, rights equivalent to those resulting from adoptions having this effect in each such State.

3 The preceding paragraphs shall not prejudice the application of any provision more favourable for the child, in force in the Contracting State which recognises the adoption.

ARTICLE 27

1 Where an adoption granted in the State of origin does not have the effect of terminating a pre-existing legal parent-child relationship, it may, in the receiving State which recognises the adoption under the Convention, be converted into an adoption having such an effect –

(a) if the law of the receiving State so permits; and

(b) if the consents referred to in Article 4, sub-paragraphs (c) and (d), have been or are given for the purpose of such an adoption.

2 Article 23 applies to the decision converting the adoption.

CHAPTER VI

GENERAL PROVISIONS

ARTICLE 28

The Convention does not affect any law of a State of origin which requires that the adoption of a child habitually resident within that State take place in that State or which prohibits the child's placement in, or transfer to, the receiving State prior to adoption.

ARTICLE 29

There shall be no contact between the prospective adoptive parents and the child's parents or any other person who has care of the child until the requirements of Article 4, sub-paragraphs (a) to (c), and Article 5, sub-paragraph (a), have been met, unless the adoption takes place within a family or unless the contact is in compliance with the conditions established by the competent authority of the State of origin.

ARTICLE 30

1 The competent authorities of a Contracting State shall ensure that information held by them concerning the child's origin, in particular information concerning the identity of his or her parents, as well as the medical history, is preserved.

2 They shall ensure that the child or his or her representative has access to such information, under appropriate guidance, in so far as is permitted by the law of that State.

ARTICLE 31

Without prejudice to Article 30, personal data gathered or transmitted under the Convention, especially data referred to in Articles 15 and 16, shall be used only for the purposes for which they were gathered or transmitted.

ARTICLE 32

1 No one shall derive improper financial or other gain from an activity related to an intercountry adoption.

2 Only costs and expenses, including reasonable professional fees of persons involved in the adoption, may be charged or paid.

3 The directors, administrators and employees of bodies involved in an adoption shall not receive remuneration which is unreasonably high in relation to services rendered.

ARTICLE 33

A competent authority which finds that any provision of the Convention has not been respected or that there is a serious risk that it may not be respected, shall immediately inform the Central Authority of its State. This Central Authority shall be responsible for ensuring that appropriate measures are taken.

ARTICLE 34

If the competent authority of the State of destination of a document so requests, a translation certified as being in conformity with the original must be furnished. Unless otherwise provided, the costs of such translation are to be borne by the prospective adoptive parents.

ARTICLE 35

The competent authorities of the contracting States shall act expeditiously in the process of adoption.

ARTICLE 36

In relation to a State which has two or more systems of law with regard to adoption applicable in different territorial units –

(a) any reference to habitual residence in that State shall be construed as referring to habitual residence in a territorial unit of that State;

(b) any reference to the law of that State shall be construed as referring to the law in force in the relevant territorial unit;

(c) any reference to the competent authorities or to the public authorities of that State shall be construed as referring to those authorised to act in the relevant territorial unit;

(d) any reference to the accredited bodies of that State shall be construed as referring to bodies accredited in the relevant territorial unit.

ARTICLE 37

In relation to a State which with regard to adoption has two or more systems of law applicable to different categories of persons, any reference to the law of that State shall be construed as referring to the legal system specified by the law of that State.

ARTICLE 38

A State within which different territorial units have their own rules of law in respect of adoption shall not be bound to apply the Convention where a State with a unified system of law would not be bound to do so.

ARTICLE 39

1 The Convention does not affect any international instrument to which Contracting States are Parties and which contains provisions on matters governed by the Convention, unless a contrary declaration is made by the States parties to such instrument.

2 Any Contracting State may enter into agreements with one or more other Contracting States, with a view to improving the application of the Convention in their mutual relations. These agreements may derogate only from the provisions of Articles 14 to 16 and 18 to 21. The States which have concluded such an agreement shall transmit a copy to the depositary of the Convention.

ARTICLE 40

No reservation to the Convention shall be permitted.

ARTICLE 41

The Convention shall apply in every case where an application pursuant to Article 14 has been received after the Convention has entered into force in the receiving State and the State of origin.

ARTICLE 42

The Secretary General of the Hague Conference on Private International Law shall at regular intervals convene a Special Commission in order to review the practical operation of the Convention.

****

2.8 HAGUE CONVENTION ON THE CIVIL ASPECTS OF INTERNATIONAL CHILD ABDUCTION 1980

(As set out in Schedule 1 to the Child Abduction and Custody Act 1985)

CHAPTER I
SCOPE OF THE CONVENTION

ARTICLE 1

The objects of the present Convention are:

(a) to secure the prompt return of children wrongfully removed to or retained in any Contracting State; and

(b) to ensure that rights of custody and of access under the law of one Contracting State are effectively respected in the other Contracting States.

ARTICLE 2

Contracting States shall take all appropriate measures to secure within their territories the implementation of the objects of the Convention. For this purpose they shall use the most expeditious procedures available.

ARTICLE 3

The removal or the retention of a child is to be considered wrongful where:

(a) it is in breach of rights of custody attributed to a person, an institution or any other body, either jointly or alone, under the law of the State in which the child was habitually resident immediately before the removal or retention; and

(b) at the time of removal or retention those rights were actually exercised, either jointly or alone, or would have been so exercised but for the removal or retention.

The rights of custody mentioned in sub-para (a) above, may arise in particular by operation of law or by reason of a judicial or administrative decision, or by reason of an agreement having legal effect under the law of that State.

Article 3

Purpose of the Convention—Lord Browne-Wilkinson in *Re H (Minors) (Abduction: Acquiescence)* [1998] AC 72 at 81 said: 'The recitals and Article 1 of the Convention set out its underlying purpose. Although they are not specifically incorporated into the law of the United Kingdom, they are plainly relevant to the construction of an international treaty. The object of the Convention is to protect children from the harmful effects of their wrongful removal from the country of their habitual residence to another country or their wrongful retention in some country other than that of their habitual residence. This is to be achieved by establishing a procedure to ensure the prompt return of the child to the State of his habitual residence.'

Although Brussels II (Council Regulation (EC) No 2201/2003 of 27 November 2003 on Jurisdiction and the Recognition and Enforcement of Judgments in Matrimonial Matters and in Matters of Parental Responsibility) (reproduced at **2.3**) takes precedence over the European Convention on the Recognition and Enforcement of Decisions Concerning Custody of Children, it does not take precedence over the Hague Convention on the Civil Aspects of International Child Abduction. See, in particular, paras 17 and 18 of the Recitals to, and Article 11 of, Brussels II and, under the 'old' Brussels II, *Re G (Foreign Contact Order: Enforcement)* [2003] EWCA Civ 1607, [2004] 1 FLR 378, CA, and *Re L (Child's Objections to Return)* [2002] EWHC Civ 1864, [2002] 2 FLR 1042.

Rights of custody—See the definition of this at Article 5(a) below and the House of Lords' decision in *Re H (A Child) (Abduction: Rights of Custody)* [2000] 2 All ER 1, [2000] 2 WLR 337, [2000] 1 FLR 374, HL (a court may have rights of custody which would generally be invoked when an application is served, rather than when a later interim order is made, cf *B v UK* [2000] 1 FLR 1, ECtHR, and *Re B (Abduction) (Rights of Custody)* [1997] 2 FLR 594, CA). In *C v C (Minor: Abduction: Rights of Custody Abroad)* [1989] 2 All ER 465, following *B v B (Abduction: Custody Rights)* [1993] Fam 32, Lord Donaldson of Lymington MR said (at 473): 'This is "the right to determine the child's place of residence". This right may be in the court, the mother, the father, some caretaking institution, such as a local authority, or it may, as in this case, be a divided right—insofar as the child is to reside in Australia, the right being that of the mother; but, insofar as any question arises as to the child residing outside of Australia, it being a joint right subject always, of course, to the overriding rights of the court' – see also the Canadian case of *Thomson v Thomson* [1994] 3 SCR 551, *Re S (Abduction: Children: Separate Representation)* [1997] 1 FLR 486, the Irish case of *HI v MG* [1999] 2 IRLM 1 and *Re A (Abduction: Rights of Custody: Imprisonment)* [2004] 1 FLR 1, FD (child wrongfully removed from Australia in breach of unmarried father's custody rights).

The relevant rights of custody are those 'under the law of the State in which the child was habitually resident immediately before the removal or retention'; in the case of *Re JB (Child Abduction) (Rights of Custody: Spain)* [2003] EWHC 2130 (Fam), [2004] 1 FLR 796, the unmarried Spanish father's rights in relation to the child were governed by the personal law of the child under Spanish law; since the child's personal law was that of the UK (being a British National) the father failed to show that the removal was wrongful (see also *Re C (A Child) (Unmarried Father: Custody Rights)* [2002] EWHC 2219, [2003] 1 WLR 493, [2003] 1 FLR 252).

In the case of *Re V-B (Abduction: Custody Rights)* [1999] 2 FLR 192, CA, it was held that the application of the respondent for guardianship did not confer rights of custody on the Irish court since a right merely to be consulted on residence, or any other issue, without an associated right to object did not amount to a right relating to the care of the person of the child; while consultation was of considerable importance, it had little legal effect and did not amount to a veto (*Re V-B* was referred to by Lord Mackay in his speech in *Re H* without disapproval and also by Thorpe LJ in the Court of Appeal judgment in *Re H* [2000] 1 FCR 225 at 238, in which he said: 'an application that in its substance seeks only the determination, definition or quantification of contact cannot vest rights of custody in the court (see *Re V-B*)'.

Wrongful removal—For the meaning of this see *Re H (Minors) (Abduction: Custody Rights)* [1991] 2 AC 476, [1991] 3 WLR 68, [1991] 3 All ER 230, [1991] 2 FLR 262, HL (per Lord Brandon: 'it appears to me that, once it is accepted that retention is not a continuing state of affairs but an event occurring on a specific occasion, it necessarily follows that removal or retention are mutually exclusive concepts. For the purposes of the Convention, removal occurs when a child, which has previously been in the State of its habitual residence, is taken away across the frontier of that State; whereas retention occurs where a child, which has previously been for a limited period of time outside the State of its habitual residence, is not returned to that State on the expiry of such limited period. That being so, it seems to me that removal and retention are basically different concepts, so that it is impossible either for them to overlap each other or for either to follow upon the other').

Wrongful retention—Removal and retention can both occur in relation to the same child, albeit on different dates. An initial lawful removal of a child may become a wrongful retention if the child is retained beyond an agreed period (per Lord Slynn in *Re S (Custody: Habitual Residence)* [1998] AC 750, [1998] 1 FLR 122, HL: 'Thus a parent or parents having rights of custody may agree that a child shall go on 1 January to stay with a friend abroad for a period of six months. The friend takes the child abroad. That is clearly not a wrongful removal. The friend keeps the child abroad until 30 June: that is clearly not a wrongful retention. On 1 July the friend keeps the child and refuses to return him. The parent's consent has gone and the retention becomes wrongful. The time runs from that date. The flaw in the appellants' argument is that it looks only at the date of retention whereas what has to be considered is the date of wrongful retention (see *Re H and Anor (Minors) (Abduction: Custody Rights), Re S and Anor (Minors) (Abduction: Custody Rights)* [1991] 3 All ER 230 at 239, [1991] 2 AC 476 at 499)').

Habitual residence—In *Re J (A Minor) (Abduction: Custody Rights)* [1990] 2 AC 562, [1990] 3 WLR 492, [1990] 2 All ER 961, [1990] 2 FLR 442, HL, Lord Brandon gave this guidance as to the meaning of habitual residence: 'The first point is that the expression "habitually resident", as used in Article 3 of the Convention, is nowhere defined. It follows, I think, that the expression is not to be treated as a term of art with some special meaning, but is rather to be understood according to the ordinary and natural meaning of the two words which it contains. The second point is that the question whether a person is or is not habitually resident in a specified country is a question of fact to be decided by reference to all the circumstances of any particular case. The third point is that there is a significant difference between a person ceasing to be habitually resident in country A, and his subsequently becoming habitually resident in country B. A person may cease to be habitually resident in country A in a single day if he or she leaves it with a settled intention not to return to it but to take up long-term residence in country B instead. Such a person cannot, however, become habitually resident in country B in a single day. An appreciable period of time and a settled intention will be necessary to enable him or her to become so. During that appreciable period of time the person will have ceased to be habitually resident in country A but not yet have become habitually resident country B. The fourth point is that, where a child of J's age is in the sole lawful custody of the mother, his situation with regard to habitual residence will necessarily be the same as hers.' This passage was further considered by the House of Lords in *Nessa v Chief Adjudication Officer* [1999] 1 WLR 1937, [1999] 4 All ER 677, [1999] 2 FLR 1116, and in *Re S (Custody: Habitual Residence)* [1998] AC 750, [1998] 1 FLR 122, HL.

In *Re N (Abduction: Habitual Residence)* [2000] 2 FLR 899 (applied by Charles J in *B v H (Habitual Residence: Wardship)* [2002] 1 FLR 388, FD), Black J said: '"Habitual residence" is not defined by the Hague Convention or by the statute: the words are to be understood according to their ordinary and natural meaning. It refers to a person's abode in a particular place or country which he has adopted voluntarily and for settled purposes as part of the regular order of his life for the time being whether of short or long duration. The question of whether a person is or is not habitually resident in a specified country is a question of fact to be decided by reference to all the circumstances of any particular case. Habitual residence can be lost in a single day if a person leaves a country with the settled intention not to return but to take up long-term residence elsewhere. There is no fixed period of residence required in the new country before habitual residence there can be established. What must be shown is residence for a period which shows that the residence has become habitual and will or is likely to continue to be habitual. A short period of residence may suffice in some cases and there may be special cases where someone is resuming residence in a country where they were formerly habitually resident rather than coming for the first time'.

The phrase 'for a settled purpose' does not invoke a test 'that one does not lose one's habitual residence in a particular country absent a settled intention not to return there'. The test is whether the residence in a particular country was for a settled purpose, albeit for a period of short duration (*Re R (Abduction: Habitual Residence)* [2003] EWHC 1968 (Fam), [2004] 1 FLR 216, FD, and *Al Habtoor v Fotheringham* [2001] EWCA Civ 186, [2001] 1 FLR 951, CA).

ARTICLE 4

The Convention shall apply to any child who was habitually resident in a Contracting State immediately before any breach of custody or access rights. The Convention shall cease to apply when the child attains the age of 16 years.

Article 4

Where a child has attained the age of 16 at the time of the court hearing the Convention will no longer apply, even if the child was under the age of 16 when the application was made; an application for the return of a child of 16 or over will have to be considered under the inherent jurisdiction of the High Court (*Re H (Abduction: Child of Sixteen)* [2000] 2 FLR 51, FD).

ARTICLE 5

For the purposes of this Convention:

(a) 'rights of custody' shall include rights relating to the care of the person of the child and, in particular, the right to determine the child's place of residence;

(b) 'rights of access' shall include the right to take a child for a limited period of time to a place other than the child's habitual residence.

CHAPTER II

CENTRAL AUTHORITIES

ARTICLE 6

A Contracting State shall designate a Central Authority to discharge the duties which are imposed by the Convention upon such authorities.

Federal States, States with more than one system of law or States having autonomous territorial organisations shall be free to appoint more than one Central Authority and to specify the territorial extent of their powers. Where a State has appointed more than one Central Authority, it shall designate the Central Authority to which applications may be addressed for transmission to the appropriate Central Authority within that State.

ARTICLE 7

Central Authorities shall co-operate with each other and promote co-operation amongst the competent authorities in their respective State to secure the prompt return of children and to achieve the other objects of this Convention.

In particular, either directly or through any intermediary, they shall take all appropriate measures:

(a)   to discover the whereabouts of a child who has been wrongfully removed or retained;

(b)   to prevent further harm to the child or prejudice to interested parties by taking or causing to be taken provisional measures;

(c)   to secure the voluntary return of the child or to bring about an amicable resolution of the issues;

(d)   to exchange, where desirable, information relating to the social background of the child;

(e)   to provide information of a general character as to the law of their State in connection with the application of the Convention;

(f)   to initiate or facilitate the institution of judicial or administrative proceedings with a view to obtaining the return of the child and, in a proper case, to make arrangements for organising or securing the effective exercise of rights of access;

(g)   where the circumstances so require, to provide or facilitate the provision of legal aid and advice, including the participation of legal counsel and advisers;

(h)   to provide such administrative arrangements as may be necessary and appropriate to secure the safe return of the child;

(i)   to keep each other informed with respect to the operation of this Convention and, as far as possible, to eliminate any obstacles to its application.

Article 7

See s 24A of the Child Abduction and Custody Act 1985 for the power of the court to order any person to provide information of a child's whereabouts, and s 6 for the provision of reports relating to the child.

The Convention draws a distinction between rights of custody and rights of access – see *S v H (Abduction: Access Rights)* [1998] Fam 49, FD. However, the access/contact order of a foreign court should be given the greatest possible weight consistent with the overriding consideration that the welfare of the child is paramount (*Re G (A Minor) (Enforcement of Access Abroad)* [1993] Fam 216, [1993] 2 WLR 824, [1993] 3 All ER 657, CA).

A failure by a State to effect the return under the Convention of a child wrongfully removed or retained may be a breach of Article 8 of ECHR (*Ignaccolo-Zenide v Romania* (2001) 31 EHRR 7 and *Sylvester v Austria* [2003] 2 FLR 210, ECtHR). For an example of a case being adjourned in order to facilitate co-operation between the Californian courts and the UK courts, see *Re M and J (Abduction: International Judicial Collaboration)* [2000] 1 FLR 803, although the court will avoid excessive 'dotting of I's and crossing of T's' (*Re M (Abduction: Intolerable Situation)* [2000] 1 FLR 930, FD).

CHAPTER III

RETURN OF CHILDREN

ARTICLE 8

Any person, institution or other body claiming that a child has been removed or retained in breach of custody rights may apply either to the Central Authority of the child's habitual residence or to the Central Authority of any other Contracting State for assistance in securing the return of the child.

The application shall contain:

(a)   information concerning the identity of the applicant, of the child and of the person alleged to have removed or retained the child;

(b)   where available, the date of birth of the child;

(c)   the grounds on which the applicant's claim for return of the child is based;

(d)   all available information relating to the whereabouts of the child and the identity of the person with whom the child is presumed to be.

The application may be accompanied or supplemented by:

(e)   an authenticated copy of any relevant decision or agreement;

(f)   a certificate or an affidavit emanating from a Central Authority, or other competent authority of the State of the child's habitual residence, or from a qualified person, concerning the relevant law of that State;

(g)   any other relevant document.

Article 8

The procedure in the UK is governed by FPR 1991, rr 6.1–6.14.

ARTICLE 9

If the Central Authority which receives an application referred to in Art 8 has reason to believe that the child is in another Contracting State, it shall directly and without delay transmit the application to the Central Authority of that Contracting State and inform the requesting Central Authority, or the applicant, as the case may be.

ARTICLE 10

The Central Authority of the State where the child is shall take or cause to be taken all appropriate measures in order to obtain the voluntary return of the child.

ARTICLE 11

The judicial or administrative authorities of Contracting States shall act expeditiously in proceedings for the return of children.

If the judicial or administrative authority concerned has not reached a decision within six weeks from the date of commencement of the proceedings, the applicant or the Central Authority of the requested State, on its own initiative or if asked by the Central Authority of the requesting State, shall have the right to request a statement of the reasons for the delay. If a reply is received by the Central Authority of the requested State, that Authority shall transmit the reply to the Central Authority of the requesting State, or to the applicant, as the case may be.

ARTICLE 12

Where a child has been wrongfully removed or retained in terms of Art 3 and, at the date of the commencement of the proceedings before the judicial or administrative authority of the Contracting State where the child is, a period of less than one year has elapsed from the date of the wrongful removal or retention, the authority concerned shall order the return of the child forthwith.

The judicial or administrative authority, even where the proceedings have been commenced after the expiration of the period of one year referred to in the preceding paragraph, shall also order the return of the child, unless it is demonstrated that the child is now settled in its new environment.

Where the judicial or administrative authority in the requested State has reason to believe that the child has been taken to another State, it may stay the proceedings or dismiss the application for the return of the child.

Article 12

In relation to when the period of one year starts where wrongful retention is alleged see the passage from *Re S (Custody: Habitual Residence)* [1998] AC 750, [1998] 1 FLR 122, HL, set out above under Article 3 (under the heading 'wrongful retention'). In the case of *Cannon v Cannon* [2004] EWCA Civ 1330, [2005] 1 FLR 169, CA, Thorpe LJ said at para 61: 'I would unhesitatingly uphold the well-recognised construction of the concept of settlement in Article 12(2): it is not enough to regard only the physical characteristics of settlement. Equal regard must be paid to the emotional and psychological elements. In cases of concealment and subterfuge the burden of demonstrating the necessary elements of emotional and psychological settlement is much increased. The judges in the Family Division should not apply a rigid rule of disregard but they should look critically at any alleged settlement that is built on concealment and deceit especially if the defendant is a fugitive from criminal justice. ... Even if settlement is established on the facts the court retains a residual discretion to order a return under the Convention. The discretion is specifically conferred by Article 18'.

Settlement has to be considered as at the date of commencement of the proceedings, and it is to be given its ordinary meaning with two constituents, physical and emotional (*Re H (Abduction: Child of Sixteen)* [2000] 2 FLR 51, FD). In *Re L (Abduction: Pending Criminal Proceedings)* [1999] 1 FLR 433, FD, Wilson J said: 'In *Re S (A Minor) (Abduction)* [1991] FCR 656 at 676 Purchas LJ described what was required as a long-term settled position; and in *Re N (Minors) (Abduction)* [1991] 1 FLR 413 ... Bracewell J observed that the position had to be as permanent as anything in life could be said to be permanent. Whether a Danish mother who has been present with the children in England for a year only because it has been a good hiding-place and who faces likely extradition proceedings could demonstrate the children's settlement in England within the meaning of those authorities is doubtful'.

ARTICLE 13

Notwithstanding the provisions of the preceding Article, the judicial or administrative authority of the requested State is not bound to order the return of the child if the person, institution or other body which opposes its return establishes that:

(a) the person, institution or other body having the care of the person of the child was not actually exercising the custody rights at the time of removal or retention, or had consented to or subsequently acquiesced in the removal or retention; or

(b) there is a grave risk that his or her return would expose the child to physical or psychological harm or otherwise place the child in an intolerable situation.

The judicial or administrative authority may also refuse to order the return of the child if it finds that the child objects to being returned and has attained an age and degree of maturity at which it is appropriate to take account of its views.

In considering the circumstances referred to in this Article, the judicial and administrative authorities shall take into account the information relating to the social background of the child provided by the Central Authority or other competent authority of the child's habitual residence.

Article 13

Acquiescence—The leading case on this is *Re H (Minors) (Abduction: Acquiescence)* [1998] AC 72, [1997] 2 All ER 225, [1997] 1 FLR 872, HL (Question of fact. Subjective intention of the wronged parent, save that where the words or actions of the wronged parent clearly and unequivocally show and have led the other parent to believe that the wronged parent is not asserting or going to assert his right to the summary return of the child and are inconsistent with such return, justice requires that the wronged parent be held to have acquiesced. Judges should be slow to infer an intention to acquiesce from attempts by the wronged parent to effect a reconciliation or to reach an agreed voluntary return of the abducted child).

In *Re S (A Minor) (Abduction: Acquiescence)* [1998] 2 FLR 115, CA, at 122, Butler-Sloss LJ said: 'In earlier decisions of this court the lack of knowledge and misleading legal advice have been considered relevant factors to which the court should have regard, see *Re A (Minors) (Abduction: Custody Rights)* [1992] Fam 106 and *Re S (Minors) (Abduction: Acquiescence)* [1994] 1 FLR 819 ... In *Re AZ (A Minor) (Abduction: Acquiescence)* [1993] 1FLR 682 this court held that it is not necessary, in order for a defence under art 13 to succeed, to show that the applicant had specific knowledge of the Hague Convention. Knowledge of the facts and that the act of removal or retention is wrongful will normally usually be necessary. But to expect the applicant necessarily to have knowledge of the rights which can be enforced under the Convention is to set too high a standard. The degree of knowledge as a relevant factor will, of course, depend on the facts of each case' (see also *Re D (Abduction: Acquiescence)* [1998] 2 FLR 335, CA)). In *Re P (Abduction: Consent)* [2004] EWCA 971, [2004] 2 FLR 1057, CA, it was held that the judge had been wrong to hear the contested evidence from two handwriting experts to decide whether the mother had forged a document by which the father had purportedly consented to the removal of the child from New York; consent does not fall to be considered for the purpose of establishing the wrongfulness of a removal or a breach of custody rights, but only for purposes of invoking the court's discretion under Article 13.

Grave risk of physical/psychological harm, etc—In *Re H (Abduction: Grave Risk)* [2003] EWCA Civ 355, [2003] 2 FLR 71, CA, the President said:

'**[30]** The threshold to be crossed when an Art 13(b) defence is raised is a high one and difficult to surmount. Hence the courts in this country have always adopted a strict view of Art 13(b). The risk must be grave and the harm must be serious. The courts are also anxious that the wrongdoer should not benefit from the wrong: that is, that the person removing the children should not be able to rely on the consequences of that removal to create a risk of harm or an intolerable situation on return. This is summed up, after a review of the authorities, in the words of Ward LJ in *Re C (Abduction) (Grave Risk of Psychological Harm)* [1999] 2 FCR 507 at 517, cited by the judge in the present case: "There is, therefore, an established line of authority that the court should require clear and compelling evidence of the grave risk of harm or other intolerability which must be measured as substantial, not trivial, and of a severity which is much more than is inherent in the inevitable disruption, uncertainty and anxiety which follows an unwelcome return to the jurisdiction of the court of habitual residence".

[31] There are two parts to Art 13(b). Even if the threshold is crossed there still remains a discretion in the court whether to return the child.'

Domestic violence will not, of itself, fulfil that threshold (*Re W (Abduction: Domestic Violence)* [2004] EWHC 1247, [2004] 2 FLR 499, FD).

Child objects—The principles are set out in the cases of *S v S (Child Abduction)* [1993] Fam 242, [1993] 2 WLR 775, [1993] 2 All ER 683, [1992] 2 FLR 492, CA; *Re T (Abduction: Child's Objections to Return)* [2000] 2 FLR 192, CA; and *Re J (Children) (Abduction: Child's Objections to Return)* [2004] EWCA Civ 428, [2004] 2 FLR 64, CA. In *Re T*, Ward LJ summarised the principles thus:

'(1) The part of Art 13 which relates to the child's objections to being returned is completely separate from para (b) and there is no reason to interpret this part of the article as importing a requirement to establish a grave risk that the return of the child would expose her to harm, or otherwise place her in an intolerable situation.

(2) The questions whether: (i) a child objects to being returned; and (ii) has attained an age and a degree of maturity at which it is appropriate to take account of its views, are questions of fact which are peculiarly within the province of the trial judge.

(3) It will usually be necessary for the judge to find out why the child objects to being returned. If the only reason is because it wants to remain with the abducting parent, who is asserting that he or she is unwilling to return, then this will be a highly relevant factor when the judge comes to consider the exercise of discretion.

(4) Article 13 does not seek to lay down any age below which a child is to be considered as not having attained sufficient maturity for its views to be taken into account. (As a matter of fact, the child in S, whose objections prevailed, was only nine years old.)

(5) If the court should come to the conclusion that the child's views have been influenced by some other person, for example the abducting parent, or that the objection to return is because of a wish to remain with the abducting parent, then it is probable that little or no weight will be given to those views.

(6) On the other hand, where the court finds that the child has valid reasons for her objection to being returned, then it may refuse to order the return.

(7) Nevertheless it is only in exceptional cases under the Hague Convention that the court should refuse to order the immediate return of a child who has been wrongfully removed.

(8) As to the difficult problem of deciding whether a child is mature enough, Waite LJ helpfully said in *Re S (Minors) (Abduction: Acquiescence)* [1994] 2 FCR 945 at 954: "When Article 13 speaks of an age and maturity level at which it is appropriate to take account of a child's views, the inquiry which it envisages is not restricted to a generalized appraisal of the child's capacity to form and express views which bear the hallmark of maturity. It is permissible (and indeed will often be necessary) for the court to make specific inquiry as to whether the child has reached a stage of development at which, when asked the question 'Do you object to a return to your home country?' he or she can be relied on to give an answer which does not depend upon instinct alone, but is influenced by the discernment which a mature child brings to the question's implications for his or her own best interests in the long and the short-term."

(9) Thus it seems to me that the matters to establish are as follows.

(10) Whether the child objects to being returned to the country of habitual residence, bearing in mind that there may be cases where this is so inevitably and inextricably linked with an objection to living with the other parent that the two factors cannot be separated. Hence there is a need to ascertain why the child objects;

(11) The age and degree of maturity of the child. Is the child more mature or less mature than or as mature as her chronological age? By way of example only, I note that in *Re R (Minors: Child Abduction)* (unreported) 14 October 1994 Ewbank J's decision that boys aged seven and a half and six were mature enough was upheld by Balcombe LJ and Sir Ralph Gibson, Millett LJ dissenting (see [1995] 1 FLR 717). I would not wish to venture any definition of maturity. Clearly the child has to know what has happened to her and to understand that there is a range of choice. A child may be mature enough for it to be appropriate for her views to be taken into account even though she may not have gained that level of maturity that she is fully emancipated from parental dependence and can claim autonomy of decision-making. The child's 'right' – and I use the word loosely – is, consistently with art 12 of the United Nations Convention on The Rights of a Child 1989 (New York, 20 November 1989; TS 44 (1998); Cm 1976), to have the opportunity to express her views and to be heard, not a right to self-determination. Article 12, which is often judged to be one of the most important in that convention, assures to children capable of forming their own views – 'the right to express those views freely in all matters affecting (them), the views of the child being given due weight in accordance with the age and maturity of the child.'

(12)The sentiments in both conventions are the same and they give strong support to the idea that the purpose of the exception to the general rule of immediate return is to defer to the wishes of the child *for Convention purposes*, even if the child's wishes may not prevail if welfare were the paramount consideration. Thus once the child is judged to be of an age and maturity for it to be appropriate for the court to take account of her views then the art 13 defence is established and the court moves to the separate exercise of discretion as it is required to be conducted under the Hague Convention. Each case will, of course, depend upon its own facts.

(13)So a discrete finding as to age and maturity is necessary in order to judge the next question which is whether it is appropriate to take account of child's views. That requires an ascertainment of the strength and validity of those views which will call for an examination of the following matters, among others.

(i) What is the child's own perspective of what is in her interests, short, medium and long term? Self-perception is important because it is *her* views which have to be judged appropriate.

(ii) To what extent, if at all, are the reasons for objection rooted in reality or might reasonably appear to the child to be so grounded?

(iii) To what extent have those views been shaped or even coloured by undue influence and pressure, directly or indirectly exerted by the abducting parent?

(iv) To what extent will the objections be mollified on return and, where it is the case, on removal from any pernicious influence from the abducting parent?'

In the case of *Re J (Abduction: Child's Objections to Return)* [2004] EWCA Civ 428, [2004] 2 FLR 64, it was held that the court should make discrete findings about the child's age and maturity in order to decide whether it is appropriate to take account of a child's views. The court should also consider the extent, if any, to which the child's views may have been influenced by the abducting parent. It is very unusual for a child to have separate representation in an application under the Convention.

ARTICLE 14

In ascertaining whether there has been a wrongful removal or retention within the meaning of Art 3, the judicial or administrative authorities of the requested State may take notice directly of the law of, and of judicial or administrative decisions, formally recognised or not in the State of the habitual residence of the child, without recourse to the specific procedures for the proof of that law or for the recognition of foreign decisions which would otherwise be applicable.

ARTICLE 15

The judicial or administrative authorities of a Contracting State may, prior to the making of an order for the return of the child, request that the applicant obtain from the authorities of the State of the habitual residence of the child a decision or other determination that the removal or retention was wrongful within the meaning of Art 3 of the Convention, where such a decision or determination may be obtained in that State. The Central Authorities of the Contracting States shall so far as practicable assist applicants to obtain such a decision or determination.

ARTICLE 16

After receiving notice of a wrongful removal or retention of a child in the sense of Art 3, the judicial or administrative authorities of the Contracting State to which the child has been removed or in which it has been retained shall not decide on the merits of rights of custody until it has been determined that the child is not to be returned under this Convention or unless an application under this Convention is not lodged within a reasonable time following receipt of the notice.

ARTICLE 17

The sole fact that a decision relating to custody has been given in or is entitled to recognition in the requested State shall not be a ground for refusing to return a child under this Convention, but the judicial or administrative authorities of the requested State may take account of the reasons for that decision in applying this Convention.

ARTICLE 18

The provisions of this Chapter do not limit the power of a judicial or administrative authority to order the return of the child at any time.

ARTICLE 19

A decision under this Convention concerning the return of the child shall not be taken to be a determination on the merits of any custody issue.

ARTICLE 20

The return of the child under the provisions of Art 12 may be refused if this would not be permitted by the fundamental principles of the requested State relating to the protection of human rights and fundamental freedoms.

CHAPTER IV

RIGHTS OF ACCESS

ARTICLE 21

An application to make arrangements for organizing or securing the effective exercise of rights of access may be presented to the Central Authorities of the Contracting States in the same way as an application for the return of a child.

The Central Authorities are bound by the obligations of co-operation which are set forth in Art 7 to promote the peaceful enjoyment of access rights and the fulfilment of any conditions to which the exercise of those rights may be subject. The Central Authorities shall take steps to remove, as far as possible, all obstacles to the exercise of such rights.

The Central Authorities, either directly or through intermediaries, may initiate or assist in the institution of proceedings with a view to organizing or protecting these rights and securing respect for the conditions to which the exercise of these rights may be subject.

Article 21

See *Re G (A Minor) (Hague Convention: Access)* [1993] Fam 216, [1993] 3 All ER 65, [1993] 1 FLR 669, CA (the existence of an order of the court where the child was then habitually residing is, however, of crucial importance and is a factor to be given the greatest possible weight consistent with the overriding consideration that the welfare of the child is paramount, agreeing with Eastham J, in *Re C (Minors) (Enforcing Foreign Access Order)* [1993] 1 FCR 770).

****

2.9 UNITED NATIONS CONVENTION ON THE RIGHTS OF THE CHILD 1989

OVERVIEW

Article 42 of the United Nations Convention of the Rights of the Child 1989 (UNCRC) requires that:

> 'States Parties undertake to make the principles and provisions of the Convention widely known, by appropriate and active means to adults and children alike'

and only the convention of alphabetical ordering of materials prevents it from being the first primary text in this Handbook. In the early twenty-first century, this text of the whole international community demands consideration in any review of children law.

A little history

The origins of the UNCRC are in the Declaration of the Rights of the Child adopted by the League of Nations in 1924. That first Declaration of the Rights of the Child was in significant part inspired by the concerns of two non-governmental organisations, the Save the Children Fund and the International Council of Women.[1] At its heart was the phrase '... recognising that mankind owes to the child the best it has to give ...'. It was followed by a second Declaration of the Rights of the Child, adopted by the United Nations in 1959 that introduced 'the best interests of the child' as a touchstone.

In the 65 years between the first Declaration of the Rights of the Child and the UNCRC two important shifts are broadly clear. First, obligations moved from being the responsibility of adult citizens to being the responsibility of the States themselves. Secondly, children moved from being essentially objects of international law requiring legal protection to being also its subjects, entitled to enjoy their own rights.

The UNCRC was drafted, adopted and entered into force in what was, for the international community, double-quick time. Certain things were lost as a result including provisions about medical treatment, but these losses were small when compared with the sense of urgency and widespread support the UNCRC engendered. It is, apparently, the most widely accepted human rights instrument there has ever been with, at the time of writing, only Somalia, Timor-Leste and the United States of America not having consented to it.

---

[1] It is also worth noting that the path through the United Nations to the UNCRC later included notable contributions from countries such as Poland and Afghanistan.

A summary of the principles within the UNCRC

There is general agreement about the principles that run through the UNCRC, although there is some variation in the way in which these are described.[2] Our version is that there are four key principles:

- the right of children to participate in decisions affecting them (see Article 12);
- the right of children to protection and to prevention from harm (see, for example, Articles 2, 3, 8, 11, 16, 19, 22 and 32–38);
- the right of children to provision for basic needs (see, for example, Articles 17, 24, 26–28 and 31);
- the right of children to priority, ie that a key test in determining an issue should be the best interests of the child (see, generally, Article 3 but also, for example, Articles 9 and 21).[3]

The enforceability of the UNCRC

Unlike with the European Convention on Human Rights, there is no international court to which an individual can bring a claim against a State for breaching his rights under the UNCRC. However, the UNCRC can be and is sometimes directly referred to in arguments and judgments in cases within the domestic courts, but because it has not been incorporated into domestic law by primary legislation, it can only be of persuasive effect. It is not binding law in such circumstances. And, if some part of the UNCRC is incorporated into the reasoning of the European Court of Human Rights on a particular issue, then by virtue of s 2 of the Human Rights Act 1998[4] the domestic courts will have to take it into account. This is not the same as saying the domestic courts must apply it, but it is much closer to it.[5]

The pressure upon States to comply with the UNCRC is increased by the work of the Committee on the Rights of the Child and, in particular, the five-yearly review it conducts in relation to each State.

---

[2] The UNCRC is sometimes described to children (and adults) as 'the friendly crocodile' which is derived from the initials CRC.

[3] But here lies a tension: to what extent are the best interests of the child to be determined by reference to the child's welfare or the child's rights, such as the child's right to participate? And note that Article 3 speaks of the best interests of the child being 'a' primary consideration, not 'the' primary consideration.

[4] See the overview of the Human Rights Act 1998 at **3.16**.

[5] One measure of the extent to which the UNCRC is used by the domestic courts and the European Court of Human Rights is to look at the annual index of the *Family Law Reports*. For recent examples, see, eg, *R(G) v Barnet London Borough Council, R(W) v Lambeth London Borough Council and R(A) v Lambeth London Borough Council* [2003] UKHL 57, [2004] 1 FLR 454 at [68] and *Sahin v Germany* [2003] 2 FLR 671 at [39]–[41] and [64].

An example of the relevance of the UNCRC

An important debate has been opened up in England and Wales about a whole range of private law issues from parental responsibility (who should have it, how it should be acquired, what it means and how it should be exercised) to contact for non-resident parents (whether there should be a general principle in favour of contact incorporated into the Children Act 1989, when shared residence is appropriate, whether the norms for contact orders that currently exist are appropriate in today's society, how and when contact should be enforced).

One factor which it is relevant to consider as part of that debate is to look to what the United Kingdom has agreed in its international obligations, including Article 9 of the UNCRC, as well as the way in which other States have developed their domestic law, mindful themselves of similar international obligations they too have entered into.[6]

> The extracts from the primary materials we recommend you read now are Articles 3, 9 and 12 of the UNCRC.
>
> The Overview continues at **3.1** Overview of Statute Law.

6　For example, the German Civil Code, amended by the Law on Family Matters 1997 (Reform zum Kindschaftsrecht), which came into force on 1 July 1998. The following summary is taken from the judgment of the European Court of Human Rights in *Sahin v Germany* [2003] 2 FLR 671 at [32]: 'the parents of a minor child born out of wedlock jointly exercise custody if they make a declaration to that effect (declaration on joint custody) or if they marry ... a child is entitled to have access to both parents; each parent is obliged to have contact with, and entitled to have access to, the child ... parents must not do anything that would harm the child's relationship with the other parent or seriously interfere with the child's upbringing ... family courts can determine the scope of the right of access and prescribe more specific rules for its exercise, also with regard to third parties; and they may order the parties to fulfil their obligations towards the child. The family courts can, however, restrict or suspend that right if such a measure is necessary for the child's welfare. A decision restricting or suspending that right for a lengthy period or permanently may only be taken if the child's well-being would otherwise be endangered. The family courts may order that the right of access be exercised in the presence of a third party, such as a youth office authority or an association'.

United Nations Convention on the Rights of the Child 1989

The Convention on the Rights of the Child was adopted and opened for signature, ratification and accession by General Assembly resolution 44/25 of 20 November 1989. It entered into force 2 September 1990, in accordance with Article 49.

Preamble

The States Parties to the present Convention,

Considering that, in accordance with the principles proclaimed in the Charter of the United Nations, recognition of the inherent dignity and of the equal and inalienable rights of all members of the human family is the foundation of freedom, justice and peace in the world,

Bearing in mind that the peoples of the United Nations have, in the Charter, reaffirmed their faith in fundamental human rights and in the dignity and worth of the human person and have determined to promote social progress and better standards of life in larger freedom,

Recognising that the United Nations has, in the Universal Declaration of Human Rights and in the International Covenants on Human Rights, proclaimed and agreed that everyone is entitled to all the rights and freedoms set forth therein, without distinction of any kind, such as race, colour, sex, language, religion, political or other opinion, national or social origin, property, birth or other status,

Recalling that, in the Universal Declaration of Human Rights, the United Nations has proclaimed that childhood is entitled to special care and assistance,

Convinced that the family, as the fundamental group of society and the natural environment for the growth and well-being of all its members and particularly children, should be afforded the necessary protection and assistance so that it can fully assume its responsibilities within the community,

Recognising that the child, for the full and harmonious development of his or her personality, should grow up in a family environment, in an atmosphere of happiness, love and understanding,

Considering that the child should be fully prepared to live an individual life in society and brought up in the spirit of the ideals proclaimed in the Charter of the United Nations and in particular in the spirit of peace, dignity, tolerance, freedom, equality and solidarity,

Bearing in mind that the need to extend particular care to the child has been stated in the Geneva Declaration of the Rights of the Child of 1924 and in the Declaration of the Rights of the Child adopted by the General Assembly on 20 November 1959 and recognized in the Universal Declaration of Human Rights, in the International Covenant on Civil and Political Rights (in particular in Articles 23 and 24), in the International Covenant on Economic, Social and Cultural Rights (in particular in Article 10) and in the statutes and relevant instruments of specialised agencies and international organisations concerned with the welfare of children,

Bearing in mind that, as indicated in the Declaration of the Rights of the Child, 'the child, by reason of his physical and mental immaturity, needs special safeguards and care, including appropriate legal protection, before as well as after birth',

Recalling the provisions of the Declaration on Social and Legal Principles relating to the Protection and Welfare of Children, with Special Reference to Foster Placement and Adoption Nationally and Internationally; the United Nations Standard Minimum Rules for the Administration of Juvenile Justice (The Beijing Rules); and the Declaration on the Protection of Women and Children in Emergency and Armed Conflict,

Recognising that, in all countries in the world, there are children living in exceptionally difficult conditions and that such children need special consideration,

Taking due account of the importance of the traditions and cultural values of each people for the protection and harmonious development of the child,

Recognising the importance of international co-operation for improving the living conditions of children in every country, in particular in the developing countries,

Have agreed as follows:

PART I

ARTICLE 1

For the purposes of the present Convention, a child means every human being below the age of eighteen years unless under the law applicable to the child, majority is attained earlier.

ARTICLE 2

1 States Parties shall respect and ensure the rights set forth in the present Convention to each child within their jurisdiction without discrimination of any kind, irrespective of the child's or his or her parent's or legal guardian's race, colour, sex, language, religion, political or other opinion, national, ethnic or social origin, property, disability, birth or other status.

2 States Parties shall take all appropriate measures to ensure that the child is protected against all forms of discrimination or punishment on the basis of the status, activities, expressed opinions, or beliefs of the child's parents, legal guardians, or family members.

ARTICLE 3

1 In all actions concerning children, whether undertaken by public or private social welfare institutions, courts of law, administrative authorities or legislative bodies, the best interests of the child shall be a primary consideration.

2 States Parties undertake to ensure the child such protection and care as is necessary for his or her well-being, taking into account the rights and duties of his or her

parents, legal guardians, or other individuals legally responsible for him or her, and, to this end, shall take all appropriate legislative and administrative measures.

3 States Parties shall ensure that the institutions, services and facilities responsible for the care or protection of children shall conform with the standards established by competent authorities, particularly in the areas of safety, health, in the number and suitability of their staff, as well as competent supervision.

ARTICLE 4

States Parties shall undertake all appropriate legislative, administrative and other measures for the implementation of the rights recognised in the present Convention. With regard to economic, social and cultural rights, States Parties shall undertake such measures to the maximum extent of their available resources and, where needed, within the framework of international co-operation.

ARTICLE 5

States Parties shall respect the responsibilities, rights and duties of parents or, where applicable, the members of the extended family or community as provided for by local custom, legal guardians or other persons legally responsible for the child, to provide, in a manner consistent with the evolving capacities of the child, appropriate direction and guidance in the exercise by the child of the rights recognised in the present Convention.

ARTICLE 6

1 States Parties recognize that every child has the inherent right to life.

2 States Parties shall ensure to the maximum extent possible the survival and development of the child.

ARTICLE 7

1 The child shall be registered immediately after birth and shall have the right from birth to a name, the right to acquire a nationality and. as far as possible, the right to know and be cared for by his or her parents.

2 States Parties shall ensure the implementation of these rights in accordance with their national law and their obligations under the relevant international instruments in this field, in particular where the child would otherwise be stateless.

ARTICLE 8

1 States Parties undertake to respect the right of the child to preserve his or her identity, including nationality, name and family relations as recognised by law without unlawful interference.

2 Where a child is illegally deprived of some or all of the elements of his or her identity, States Parties shall provide appropriate assistance and protection, with a view to re-establishing speedily his or her identity.

ARTICLE 9

1 States Parties shall ensure that a child shall not be separated from his or her parents against their will, except when competent authorities subject to judicial review determine, in accordance with applicable law and procedures, that such separation is necessary for the best interests of the child. Such determination may be necessary in a particular case such as one involving abuse or neglect of the child by the parents, or one where the parents are living separately and a decision must be made as to the child's place of residence.

2 In any proceedings pursuant to paragraph 1 of the present article, all interested parties shall be given an opportunity to participate in the proceedings and make their views known.

3 States Parties shall respect the right of the child who is separated from one or both parents to maintain personal relations and direct contact with both parents on a regular basis, except if it is contrary to the child's best interests.

4 Where such separation results from any action initiated by a State Party, such as the detention, imprisonment, exile, deportation or death (including death arising from any cause while the person is in the custody of the State) of one or both parents or of the child, that State Party shall, upon request, provide the parents, the child or, if appropriate, another member of the family with the essential information concerning the whereabouts of the absent member(s) of the family unless the provision of the information would be detrimental to the well-being of the child. States Parties shall further ensure that the submission of such a request shall of itself entail no adverse consequences for the person(s) concerned.

ARTICLE 10

1 In accordance with the obligation of States Parties under Article 9, paragraph 1, applications by a child or his or her parents to enter or leave a State Party for the purpose of family reunification shall be dealt with by States Parties in a positive, humane and expeditious manner. States Parties shall further ensure that the submission of such a request shall entail no adverse consequences for the applicants and for the members of their family.

2 A child whose parents reside in different States shall have the right to maintain on a regular basis, save in exceptional circumstances personal relations and direct contacts with both parents. Towards that end and in accordance with the obligation of States Parties under Article 9, paragraph 1, States Parties shall respect the right of the child and his or her parents to leave any country, including their own and to enter their own country. The right to leave any country shall be subject only to such restrictions as are prescribed by law and which are necessary to protect the national security, public order (ordre public), public health or morals or the rights and freedoms of others and are consistent with the other rights recognised in the present Convention.

ARTICLE 11

1 States Parties shall take measures to combat the illicit transfer and non-return of children abroad.

2 To this end, States Parties shall promote the conclusion of bilateral or multilateral agreements or accession to existing agreements.

ARTICLE 12

1 States Parties shall assure to the child who is capable of forming his or her own views the right to express those views freely in all matters affecting the child, the views of the child being given due weight in accordance with the age and maturity of the child.

2 For this purpose, the child shall in particular be provided the opportunity to be heard in any judicial and administrative proceedings affecting the child, either directly, or through a representative or an appropriate body, in a manner consistent with the procedural rules of national law.

ARTICLE 13

1 The child shall have the right to freedom of expression; this right shall include freedom to seek, receive and impart information and ideas of all kinds, regardless of frontiers, either orally, in writing or in print, in the form of art, or through any other media of the child's choice.

2 The exercise of this right may be subject to certain restrictions, but these shall only be such as are provided by law and are necessary:

    (a)   For respect of the rights or reputations of others; or
    (b)   For the protection of national security or of public order (ordre public), or of public health or morals.

ARTICLE 14

1 States Parties shall respect the right of the child to freedom of thought, conscience and religion.

2 States Parties shall respect the rights and duties of the parents and, when applicable, legal guardians, to provide direction to the child in the exercise of his or her right in a manner consistent with the evolving capacities of the child.

3 Freedom to manifest one's religion or beliefs may be subject only to such limitations as are prescribed by law and are necessary to protect public safety, order, health or morals, or the fundamental rights and freedoms of others.

ARTICLE 15

1 States Parties recognise the rights of the child to freedom of association and to freedom of peaceful assembly.

2 No restrictions may be placed on the exercise of these rights other than those imposed in conformity with the law and which are necessary in a democratic society in the interests of national security or public safety, public order (ordre public), the protection of public health or morals or the protection of the rights and freedoms of others.

ARTICLE 16

1 No child shall be subjected to arbitrary or unlawful interference with his or her privacy, family, home or correspondence, nor to unlawful attacks on his or her honour and reputation.

2 The child has the right to the protection of the law against such interference or attacks.

ARTICLE 17

States Parties recognize the important function performed by the mass media and shall ensure that the child has access to information and material from a diversity of national and international sources, especially those aimed at the promotion of his or her social, spiritual and moral well-being and physical and mental health. To this end, States Parties shall:

- (a) Encourage the mass media to disseminate information and material of social and cultural benefit to the child and in accordance with the spirit of Article 29;
- (b) Encourage international co-operation in the production, exchange and dissemination of such information and material from a diversity of cultural, national and international sources;
- (c) Encourage the production and dissemination of children's books;
- (d) Encourage the mass media to have particular regard to the linguistic needs of the child who belongs to a minority group or who is indigenous;
- (e) Encourage the development of appropriate guidelines for the protection of the child from information and material injurious to his or her well-being, bearing in mind the provisions of Articles 13 and 18.

ARTICLE 18

1 States Parties shall use their best efforts to ensure recognition of the principle that both parents have common responsibilities for the upbringing and development of the child. Parents or, as the case may be, legal guardians, have the primary responsibility for the upbringing and development of the child. The best interests of the child will be their basic concern.

2 For the purpose of guaranteeing and promoting the rights set forth in the present Convention, States Parties shall render appropriate assistance to parents and legal guardians in the performance of their child-rearing responsibilities and shall ensure the development of institutions, facilities and services for the care of children.

3 States Parties shall take all appropriate measures to ensure that children of working parents have the right to benefit from child-care services and facilities for which they are eligible.

ARTICLE 19

1 States Parties shall take all appropriate legislative, administrative, social and educational measures to protect the child from all forms of physical or mental violence, injury or abuse, neglect or negligent treatment, maltreatment or exploitation, including sexual abuse, while in the care of parent(s), legal guardian(s) or any other person who has the care of the child.

2 Such protective measures should, as appropriate, include effective procedures for the establishment of social programmes to provide necessary support for the child and for those who have the care of the child, as well as for other forms of prevention and for identification, reporting, referral, investigation, treatment and follow-up of instances of child maltreatment described heretofore, and, as appropriate, for judicial involvement.

ARTICLE 20

1 A child temporarily or permanently deprived of his or her family environment, or in whose own best interests cannot be allowed to remain in that environment, shall be entitled to special protection and assistance provided by the State.

2 States Parties shall in accordance with their national laws ensure alternative care for such a child.

3 Such care could include, inter alia, foster placement, kafalah of Islamic law, adoption or if necessary placement in suitable institutions for the care of children. When considering solutions, due regard shall be paid to the desirability of continuity in a child's upbringing and to the child's ethnic, religious, cultural and linguistic background.

ARTICLE 21

States Parties that recognize and/or permit the system of adoption shall ensure that the best interests of the child shall be the paramount consideration and they shall:

(a) Ensure that the adoption of a child is authorised only by competent authorities who determine, in accordance with applicable law and procedures and on the basis of all pertinent and reliable information, that the adoption is permissible in view of the child's status concerning parents, relatives and legal guardians and that, if required, the persons concerned have given their informed consent to the adoption on the basis of such counselling as may be necessary;

(b) Recognise that inter-country adoption may be considered as an alternative means of child's care, if the child cannot be placed in a foster or an adoptive family or cannot in any suitable manner be cared for in the child's country of origin;

(c) Ensure that the child concerned by inter-country adoption enjoys safeguards and standards equivalent to those existing in the case of national adoption;

(d) Take all appropriate measures to ensure that, in inter-country adoption, the placement does not result in improper financial gain for those involved in it;

(e)   Promote, where appropriate, the objectives of the present article by concluding bilateral or multilateral arrangements or agreements and endeavour, within this framework, to ensure that the placement of the child in another country is carried out by competent authorities or organs.

ARTICLE 22

1 States Parties shall take appropriate measures to ensure that a child who is seeking refugee status or who is considered a refugee in accordance with applicable international or domestic law and procedures shall, whether unaccompanied or accompanied by his or her parents or by any other person, receive appropriate protection and humanitarian assistance in the enjoyment of applicable rights set forth in the present Convention and in other international human rights or humanitarian instruments to which the said States are Parties.

2 For this purpose, States Parties shall provide, as they consider appropriate, co-operation in any efforts by the United Nations and other competent intergovernmental organizations or non-governmental organisations co-operating with the United Nations to protect and assist such a child and to trace the parents or other members of the family of any refugee child in order to obtain information necessary for reunification with his or her family. In cases where no parents or other members of the family can be found, the child shall be accorded the same protection as any other child permanently or temporarily deprived of his or her family environment for any reason, as set forth in the present Convention.

ARTICLE 23

1 States Parties recognise that a mentally or physically disabled child should enjoy a full and decent life, in conditions which ensure dignity, promote self-reliance and facilitate the child's active participation in the community.

2 States Parties recognise the right of the disabled child to special care and shall encourage and ensure the extension, subject to available resources, to the eligible child and those responsible for his or her care, of assistance for which application is made and which is appropriate to the child's condition and to the circumstances of the parents or others caring for the child.

3 Recognising the special needs of a disabled child, assistance extended in accordance with paragraph 2 of the present article shall be provided free of charge, whenever possible, taking into account the financial resources of the parents or others caring for the child and shall be designed to ensure that the disabled child has effective access to and receives education, training, health care services, rehabilitation services, preparation for employment and recreation opportunities in a manner conducive to the child's achieving the fullest possible social integration and individual development, including his or her cultural and spiritual development

4 States Parties shall promote, in the spirit of international cooperation, the exchange of appropriate information in the field of preventive health care and of medical, psychological and functional treatment of disabled children, including dissemination of and access to information concerning methods of rehabilitation, education and vocational services, with the aim of enabling States Parties to improve their capabilities and skills and to widen their experience in these areas. In this regard, particular account shall be taken of the needs of developing countries.

ARTICLE 24

1 States Parties recognise the right of the child to the enjoyment of the highest attainable standard of health and to facilities for the treatment of illness and rehabilitation of health. States Parties shall strive to ensure that no child is deprived of his or her right of access to such health care services.

2 States Parties shall pursue full implementation of this right and, in particular, shall take appropriate measures:

(a) To diminish infant and child mortality;

(b) To ensure the provision of necessary medical assistance and health care to all children with emphasis on the development of primary health care;

(c) To combat disease and malnutrition, including within the framework of primary health care, through, inter alia, the application of readily available technology and through the provision of adequate nutritious foods and clean drinking-water, taking into consideration the dangers and risks of environmental pollution;

(d) To ensure appropriate pre-natal and post-natal health care for mothers;

(e) To ensure that all segments of society, in particular parents and children, are informed, have access to education and are supported in the use of basic knowledge of child health and nutrition, the advantages of breastfeeding, hygiene and environmental sanitation and the prevention of accidents;

(f) To develop preventive health care, guidance for parents and family planning education and services.

3 States Parties shall take all effective and appropriate measures with a view to abolishing traditional practices prejudicial to the health of children.

4 States Parties undertake to promote and encourage international co-operation with a view to achieving progressively the full realisation of the right recognised in the present article. In this regard, particular account shall be taken of the needs of developing countries.

ARTICLE 25

States Parties recognize the right of a child who has been placed by the competent authorities for the purposes of care, protection or treatment of his or her physical or mental health, to a periodic review of the treatment provided to the child and all other circumstances relevant to his or her placement.

ARTICLE 26

1 States Parties shall recognise for every child the right to benefit from social security, including social insurance and shall take the necessary measures to achieve the full realization of this right in accordance with their national law.

2 The benefits should, where appropriate, be granted, taking into account the resources and the circumstances of the child and persons having responsibility for the maintenance of the child, as well as any other consideration relevant to an application for benefits made by or on behalf of the child.

ARTICLE 27

1 States Parties recognise the right of every child to a standard of living adequate for the child's physical, mental, spiritual, moral and social development.

2 The parent(s) or others responsible for the child have the primary responsibility to secure, within their abilities and financial capacities, the conditions of living necessary for the child's development.

3 States Parties, in accordance with national conditions and within their means, shall take appropriate measures to assist parents and others responsible for the child to implement this right and shall in case of need provide material assistance and support programmes, particularly with regard to nutrition, clothing and housing.

4 States Parties shall take all appropriate measures to secure the recovery of maintenance for the child from the parents or other persons having financial responsibility for the child, both within the State Party and from abroad. In particular, where the person having financial responsibility for the child lives in a State different from that of the child, States Parties shall promote the accession to international agreements or the conclusion of such agreements, as well as the making of other appropriate arrangements.

ARTICLE 28

1 States Parties recognise the right of the child to education and with a view to achieving this right progressively and on the basis of equal opportunity, they shall, in particular:

(a)   Make primary education compulsory and available free to all;

(b)   Encourage the development of different forms of secondary education, including general and vocational education, make them available and accessible to every child and take appropriate measures such as the introduction of free education and offering financial assistance in case of need;

(c)   Make higher education accessible to all on the basis of capacity by every appropriate means;

(d)   Make educational and vocational information and guidance available and accessible to all children;

(e)   Take measures to encourage regular attendance at schools and the reduction of drop-out rates.

2 States Parties shall take all appropriate measures to ensure that school discipline is administered in a manner consistent with the child's human dignity and in conformity with the present Convention.

3 States Parties shall promote and encourage international cooperation in matters relating to education, in particular with a view to contributing to the elimination of ignorance and illiteracy throughout the world and facilitating access to scientific and technical knowledge and modern teaching methods. In this regard, particular account shall be taken of the needs of developing countries.

ARTICLE 29

1 States Parties agree that the education of the child shall be directed to:

(a)   The development of the child's personality, talents and mental and physical abilities to their fullest potential;

(b)   The development of respect for human rights and fundamental freedoms, and for the principles enshrined in the Charter of the United Nations;

(c)   The development of respect for the child's parents, his or her own cultural identity, language and values, for the national values of the country in which the child is living, the country from which he or she may originate, and for civilizations different from his or her own;

(d)   The preparation of the child for responsible life in a free society, in the spirit of understanding, peace, tolerance, equality of sexes, and friendship among all peoples, ethnic, national and religious groups and persons of indigenous origin;

(e)   The development of respect for the natural environment.

2 No part of the present article or Article 28 shall be construed so as to interfere with the liberty of individuals and bodies to establish and direct educational institutions, subject always to the observance of the principle set forth in paragraph 1 of the present article and to the requirements that the education given in such institutions shall conform to such minimum standards as may be laid down by the State.

ARTICLE 30

In those States in which ethnic, religious or linguistic minorities or persons of indigenous origin exist, a child belonging to such a minority or who is indigenous shall not be denied the right, in community with other members of his or her group, to enjoy his or her own culture, to profess and practise his or her own religion, or to use his or her own language.

ARTICLE 31

1 States Parties recognize the right of the child to rest and leisure, to engage in play and recreational activities appropriate to the age of the child and to participate freely in cultural life and the arts.

2 States Parties shall respect and promote the right of the child to participate fully in cultural and artistic life and shall encourage the provision of appropriate and equal opportunities for cultural, artistic, recreational and leisure activity.

ARTICLE 32

1 States Parties recognize the right of the child to be protected from economic exploitation and from performing any work that is likely to be hazardous or to interfere with the child's education, or to be harmful to the child's health or physical, mental, spiritual, moral or social development.

2 States Parties shall take legislative, administrative, social and educational measures to ensure the implementation of the present article. To this end and having regard to the relevant provisions of other international instruments, States Parties shall in particular:

(a)   Provide for a minimum age or minimum ages for admission to employment;

(b) Provide for appropriate regulation of the hours and conditions of employment;

(c) Provide for appropriate penalties or other sanctions to ensure the effective enforcement of the present article.

ARTICLE 33

States Parties shall take all appropriate measures, including legislative, administrative, social and educational measures, to protect children from the illicit use of narcotic drugs and psychotropic substances as defined in the relevant international treaties and to prevent the use of children in the illicit production and trafficking of such substances.

ARTICLE 34

States Parties undertake to protect the child from all forms of sexual exploitation and sexual abuse. For these purposes, States Parties shall in particular take all appropriate national, bilateral and multilateral measures to prevent:

(a) The inducement or coercion of a child to engage in any unlawful sexual activity;

(b) The exploitative use of children in prostitution or other unlawful sexual practices;

(c) The exploitative use of children in pornographic performances and materials.

ARTICLE 35

States Parties shall take all appropriate national, bilateral and multilateral measures to prevent the abduction of, the sale of or traffic in children for any purpose or in any form.

ARTICLE 36

States Parties shall protect the child against all other forms of exploitation prejudicial to any aspects of the child's welfare.

ARTICLE 37

States Parties shall ensure that:

(a) No child shall be subjected to torture or other cruel, inhuman or degrading treatment or punishment. Neither capital punishment nor life imprisonment without possibility of release shall be imposed for offences committed by persons below 18 years of age;

(b) No child shall be deprived of his or her liberty unlawfully or arbitrarily. The arrest, detention or imprisonment of a child shall be in conformity with the law and shall be used only as a measure of last resort and for the shortest appropriate period of time;

(c) Every child deprived of liberty shall be treated with humanity and respect for the inherent dignity of the human person and in a manner which takes into account the needs of persons of his or her age. In particular, every child deprived of liberty shall be separated from adults unless it is considered in the child's best interest not to do so and shall have the right to maintain contact with his or her family through correspondence and visits, save in exceptional circumstances;

(d) Every child deprived of his or her liberty shall have the right to prompt access to legal and other appropriate assistance, as well as the right to challenge the legality of the deprivation of his or her liberty before a court or other competent, independent and impartial authority and to a prompt decision on any such action.

ARTICLE 38

1 States Parties undertake to respect and to ensure respect for rules of international humanitarian law applicable to them in armed conflicts which are relevant to the child.

2 States Parties shall take all feasible measures to ensure that persons who have not attained the age of fifteen years do not take a direct part in hostilities.

3 States Parties shall refrain from recruiting any person who has not attained the age of fifteen years into their armed forces. In recruiting among those persons who have attained the age of fifteen years but who have not attained the age of eighteen years, States Parties shall endeavour to give priority to those who are oldest.

4 In accordance with their obligations under international humanitarian law to protect the civilian population in armed conflicts, States Parties shall take all feasible measures to ensure protection and care of children who are affected by an armed conflict.

ARTICLE 39

States Parties shall take all appropriate measures to promote physical and psychological recovery and social reintegration of a child victim of: any form of neglect, exploitation, or abuse; torture or any other form of cruel, inhuman or degrading treatment or punishment; or armed conflicts. Such recovery and reintegration shall take place in an environment which fosters the health, self-respect and dignity of the child.

ARTICLE 40

1 States Parties recognize the right of every child alleged as, accused of, or recognized as having infringed the penal law to be treated in a manner consistent with the promotion of the child's sense of dignity and worth, which reinforces the child's respect for the human rights and fundamental freedoms of others and which takes into account the child's age and the desirability of promoting the child's reintegration and the child's assuming a constructive role in society.

2 To this end and having regard to the relevant provisions of international instruments, States Parties shall, in particular, ensure that:

(a)   No child shall be alleged as, be accused of, or recognized as having infringed the penal law by reason of acts or omissions that were not prohibited by national or international law at the time they were committed;

(b)   Every child alleged as or accused of having infringed the penal law has at least the following guarantees:

   (i)   To be presumed innocent until proven guilty according to law;

   (ii)   To be informed promptly and directly of the charges against him or her, and, if appropriate, through his or her parents or legal guardians and to have legal or other appropriate assistance in the preparation and presentation of his or her defence;

   (iii) To have the matter determined without delay by a competent, independent and impartial authority or judicial body in a fair hearing according to law, in the presence of legal or other appropriate assistance and, unless it is considered not to be in the best interest of the child, in particular, taking into account his or her age or situation, his or her parents or legal guardians;

   (iv)   Not to be compelled to give testimony or to confess guilt; to examine or have examined adverse witnesses and to obtain the participation and examination of witnesses on his or her behalf under conditions of equality;

   (v)   If considered to have infringed the penal law, to have this decision and any measures imposed in consequence thereof reviewed by a higher competent, independent and impartial authority or judicial body according to law;

   (vi)   To have the free assistance of an interpreter if the child cannot understand or speak the language used;

   (vii) To have his or her privacy fully respected at all stages of the proceedings.

3 States Parties shall seek to promote the establishment of laws, procedures, authorities and institutions specifically applicable to children alleged as, accused of, or recognised as having infringed the penal law, and, in particular:

(a)   The establishment of a minimum age below which children shall be presumed not to have the capacity to infringe the penal law;

(b)   Whenever appropriate and desirable, measures for dealing with such children without resorting to judicial proceedings, providing that human rights and legal safeguards are fully respected.

4 A variety of dispositions, such as care, guidance and supervision orders; counselling; probation; foster care; education and vocational training programmes and other alternatives to institutional care shall be available to ensure that children are dealt with in a manner appropriate to their well-being and proportionate both to their circumstances and the offence.

ARTICLE 41

Nothing in the present Convention shall affect any provisions which are more conducive to the realisation of the rights of the child and which may be contained in:

(a)   The law of a State party; or

(b)   International law in force for that State.

PART II

ARTICLE 42

States Parties undertake to make the principles and provisions of the Convention widely known, by appropriate and active means, to adults and children alike.

ARTICLE 43

1 For the purpose of examining the progress made by States Parties in achieving the realization of the obligations undertaken in the present Convention, there shall be established a Committee on the Rights of the Child, which shall carry out the functions hereinafter provided.

2 The Committee shall consist of ten experts of high moral standing and recognized competence in the field covered by this Convention. The members of the Committee shall be elected by States Parties from among their nationals and shall serve in their personal capacity, consideration being given to equitable geographical distribution, as well as to the principal legal systems.

3–12 *Not reproduced*

ARTICLE 44

1 States Parties undertake to submit to the Committee, through the Secretary-General of the United Nations, reports on the measures they have adopted which give effect to the rights recognised herein and on the progress made on the enjoyment of those rights:

    (a)   Within two years of the entry into force of the Convention for the State Party concerned;

    (b)   Thereafter every five years.

2 Reports made under the present article shall indicate factors and difficulties, if any, affecting the degree of fulfilment of the obligations under the present Convention. Reports shall also contain sufficient information to provide the Committee with a comprehensive understanding of the implementation of the Convention in the country concerned.

3 A State Party which has submitted a comprehensive initial report to the Committee need not, in its subsequent reports submitted in accordance with paragraph 1(b) of the present article, repeat basic information previously provided.

4 The Committee may request from States Parties further information relevant to the implementation of the Convention.

5 The Committee shall submit to the General Assembly, through the Economic and Social Council, every two years, reports on its activities.

6 States Parties shall make their reports widely available to the public in their own countries.

****

PART 3

STATUTES

'[The Cyclops] have no assemblies to debate in, they have no ancestral ordinances; they live in arching caves on the tops of high hills, and the head of each family heeds no other, but makes his own ordinances for wife and children.'

Homer, *The Odyssey*, Book 9[1]

'There is but one law for all, namely, that law which governs all law, the law of our Creator, the law of humanity, justice, equity – the law of nature and of nations.'

Edmund Burke, Impeachment of Warren Hastings, 28 May 1794

'My family just is. It's different from other people's families, but I don't mind because who says what a family should be like?'

Hope, aged 14, in Bren Neale and Amanda Wade,
Parent Problems! (Young Voice)[2]

'... I assure you that the essence of the robot mind lies in a completely literal interpretation of the universe. It recognises no spirit in the First Law, only the letter ...'

Isaac Asimov, *The Caves of Steel* (Harper Collins Publishers Ltd), Chapter 8[3]

' 'Tis often seen adoption strives with nature'

William Shakespeare, *All's Well that Ends Well*, Act 1, Scene 3

---

[1] By permission of Oxford University Press. Book 9, p 101 (40 words) from *The Odyssey* (OWC), edited by Shewring, Walter (1980). Free permission.

[2] By permission of Young Voice.

[3] By permission of HarperCollins Publishers Ltd. (c) 1954 Asimov. Copyright in the customised version vests in Jordans. Asimov is consciously alluding to 2 Corinthians 3:6. Law, justice and mercy are important themes throughout the book, but particularly in this chapter, which includes the robot Daneel's definition of justice, 'Justice, Elijah, is that which exists when all the laws are enforced'. Daneel would not, therefore, regard what happens in cases in which contact orders are unenforced as amounting to justice.

3.1 OVERVIEW OF STATUTE LAW

Statutes and the sovereignty of Parliament

'Statutes' refers to Acts of Parliament,[1] which are described as primary legislation, distinguishing them from 'statutory instruments',[2] which are described as secondary legislation.

The *sovereignty of Parliament* is one of the most important principles of our constitution. It has been expressed in a variety of ways. In practice it means that:

- Parliament can make the laws it chooses;
- those laws cannot be challenged as being unconstitutional;[3]
- judges are bound to apply the laws made by Parliament.[4]

It is because of the sovereignty of Parliament that most books of this sort would begin with 'statutes' rather than 'international law'. But, for all that the principle of the sovereignty of Parliament has been carefully preserved,[5] the political and legal reality is rather different today. [6]

So what is the bottom-line? As a matter of strict law, the United Kingdom, as a sovereign State, is entitled to make its own law in accordance with its own constitution, in which Parliament is sovereign. But because: (1) the United Kingdom, as a sovereign State, has consented to treaties that provide extra-national remedies,[7] including, in the case of the European Convention on Human Rights, by individuals against the State; and (2) our sovereign Parliament has legislated for the direct application of European Union law and the European Convention on Human Rights, the reality is the supremacy of

---

[1] 'Parliament' in this context means the House of Commons, the House of Lords and the Queen, whose Royal Assent is required to complete the process of enactment.

[2] As to 'Statutory Instruments', see further below at **4.1**.

[3] Being made by Parliament, which is sovereign, they are by definition, constitutional. Contrast, for example, with the position in the United States of America where legislation can be challenged under the Bill of Rights.

[4] '... it cannot be emphasised too strongly that the British Constitution, though largely unwritten, is firmly based on the separation of powers; Parliament makes the laws, the judiciary interpret them ...': Lord Diplock in *Duport Steels Ltd v Sirs* [1980] 1 All ER 529 at 541.

[5] Because the derogations have themselves been made by Parliament which, being sovereign, has power to take back what it has previously given ('Parliament giveth, and Parliament taketh away').

[6] See, for example, the judgment of Lord Denning MR in *Blackburn v Attorney-General* [1971] 1 WLR 1037.

[7] The right to litigate on matters of European Union law before the European Court of Justice, and on matters of the European Convention on Human Rights before the European Court of Human Rights.

European law[8] over domestic law. Put simply, the Children Act 1989 is judged against the European Convention on Human Rights, but the European Convention on Human Rights is not judged against the Children Act 1989.

Finding your way around Acts of Parliament

This is not always easy but there are some general tips worth knowing. To begin with, try to understand the general structure of an Act by looking at the 'Arrangement of Sections' immediately preceding the Act itself. This is, in effect, a list of contents. Here you will be able to pick out the main divisions of the Act (called 'Parts'[9]) and its basic elements ('sections'). It is always easier and often essential to an understanding of a section to understand its context.

Important general principles are often found at the beginning of an Act, or Part of an Act, or a section; and the definitions of key words and phrases are usually to be found in an 'Interpretation' section at or near the end of the Act.

Statutory interpretation

Imagine all the different areas of law (contract law, criminal law, constitutional law, and so on) as countries set out on a map or globe. Family law, of which children law as we treat it in this Handbook is a part, has some distinctive features, so it might be an island country, and since it forms one of the three Divisions of the High Court it might approximate to a continent.[10] Linking the lands are the seas and oceans. These might be the legal skills and knowledge that apply across the different areas of law – skills like drafting and advocacy, and knowledge such as jurisprudence, professional ethics and rules of evidence and procedure. If so, then among these, *statutory interpretation* is an ocean.[11] Yet despite this the subject is little taught to lawyers. It is, of course, impossible to rectify this in a Handbook but it is possible to point the way.

Bennion, in his book on *Statutory Interpretation*,[12] puts it like this:

- the interpreter's duty is to arrive at the legal meaning of the enactment, which is not necessarily the same as its grammatical meaning. This must be done in accordance with the rules, principles, presumptions and canons which govern statutory interpretation;

- if, on an informed interpretation, there is no real doubt that a particular meaning of an enactment is to be applied, that is to be taken as its legal meaning;

---

[8] By which we mean both the law of the European Union and the law of the European Convention on Human Rights, as explained in 'Introduction and How to Use this Handbook' at **1.1**.

[9] Themselves sometimes subdivided into 'chapters'.

[10] Australia, perhaps, rather than Antarctica!

[11] Indeed, it is perhaps the Pacific Ocean, for it is commonly said that the majority of cases that reach the Court of Appeal or the House of Lords are determined as a matter of statutory interpretation.

[12] Bennion *Statutory Interpretation* (Butterworths Lexis Nexis, 4th edn, 2002).

- the basic rule of statutory interpretation is that it is taken to be the legislator's intention that the enactment shall be construed in accordance with the general guides to legislative intention laid down by law; and that where these conflict the problem is to be resolved by weighing and balancing interpretative factors concerned;

- the interpretative criteria may be divided into: (1) binding rules, eg that the court must strive to implement rather than defeat the object of the legislation in question, and the rules of interpretation set out in the Interpretation Act 1978; (2) principles derived from general legal policy eg law should not in general operate retrospectively; (3) presumptions derived from the nature of legislation, eg the literal meaning is the most likely to convey the legislative intention; and (4) linguistic canons of construction, eg that an Act is to be construed as a whole.

More specifically, s 3 of the Human Rights Act 1998 establishes a rule of construction – that legislation must be read and given effect in a way which is compatible with rights under the European Convention on Human Rights.[13]

The Overview continues at **3.3** Overview of Adoption Legislation.

---

[13] See further at **3.15**.

3.2 ADMINISTRATION OF JUSTICE ACT 1960
(s 12)

12 Publication of information relating to proceedings in private

(1) The publication of information relating to proceedings before any court sitting in private shall not of itself be contempt of court except in the following cases, that is to say –

    (a) where the proceedings –
        (i) relate to the exercise of the inherent jurisdiction of the High Court with respect to minors;
        (ii) are brought under the Children Act 1989; or
        (iii) otherwise relate wholly or mainly to the maintenance or upbringing of a minor;
  (b)–(e) ...

(2) Without prejudice to the foregoing subsection, the publication of the text or a summary of the whole or part of an order made by a court sitting in private shall not of itself be contempt of court except where the court (having power to do so) expressly prohibits the publication.

(3) In this section references to a court include references to a judge and to a tribunal and to any person exercising the functions of a court, a judge or a tribunal; and references to a court sitting in private include references to a court sitting in camera or in chambers.

(4) Nothing in this section shall be construed as implying that any publication is punishable as contempt of court which would not be so punishable apart from this section.

Section 12

Prospective amendments—Section prospectively amended by Adoption and Children Act 2002, s 101(2) (see **3.3B**), and by Children Act 2004, s 62(2) (see **3.7**).

Other statutory provisions—This section has to be read in conjunction with s 97 of the Children Act 1989 and r 4.23 of the FPR 1991 (and see the case-law referred to under those sections, in particular: *Re EC (Disclosure of Material)* [1997] Fam 76, [1997] 2 WLR 322, [1996] 2 FLR 725, CA; *A Chief Constable v A County Council and Others* [2002] EWHC 2198 (Fam), [2003] 2 FCR 384, FD; *Re R (Children: Disclosure)* [2003] EWCA Civ 13, [2003] 1 FCR 192, CA; *Pelling v Bruce-Williams (Secretary of State for Constitutional Affairs Intervening)* [2004] EWCA Civ 845, [2004] 2 FLR 823, CA; and *B v United Kingdom* (2002) 34 EHRR 19, [2001] 2 FLR 261, ECtHR).

Disclosure by social worker and court and family reporter—In *Re G (Social Worker: Disclosure)* [1996] 1 FLR 276 it was said that a social worker did not need permission of the court to inform the police that oral admissions had been made, since r 4.23 only required that leave should be sought in respect of documents filed with and held by the court (see also *Re W (Minors) (Social Worker: Disclosure)* [1998] 2 FLR 135, CA). A court and family reporter does not require permission from a court to disclose to social services information obtained whilst preparing a court report in private law proceedings that raised concern about a child's welfare (*Re M (Disclosure: Children and Family Reporter)* [2002] EWCA Civ 1199, [2002] 2 FLR 593, CA).

Teenage mothers wishing to publish—For the human rights considerations that may arise where teenage minors have children and one of them wishes to publish an account in the media, see *Re Roddy (A Child) (Identification: Restriction on Publication)* [2003] EWHC 2927 (Fam), [2004] 2 FLR 949, FD.

Website disclosure—In the case of *Re G (Contempt: Committal)* [2003] EWCA Civ 489, [2003] 2 FLR 58, CA, the father had published information about the child on a website and identified volunteers at a contact centre. The President said as follows:

'**[27]** Without breach of a court order, the contempt had to lie in a breach of s 12(1) of the Administration of Justice Act 1960 or of r 4.23 of the Family Proceedings Rules 1991, SI 1991/1247, in relation to the disclosure without leave of documents. The judge's decision did not rest on the disclosure of documents. Section 12(1) of the 1960 Act makes the publication of "information relating to proceedings before any court sitting in private ... where the proceedings ... are brought under the Children Act 1989" contempt of court. What is protected from publication are details of the actual proceedings of the court (*Re F (A Minor) (Publication of Information)* [1977] 1 All ER 114 at 130, [1977] Fam 58 at 99). In the absence of an order, as under s 39(1) of the Children and Young Persons Act 1933, it is not a breach of s 12 to publish the name and address of, or to indicate the identity of, the child nor to publish the fact that proceedings are taking place (*Re W and Others (Wards) (Publication of Information)* [1989] 1 FLR 246). It is a breach to publish details of the actual proceedings. These include the evidence given before the court, the proofs of witnesses, the contents of experts' reports and the Official Solicitor's report and the submissions of the advocates (*Re F* [1977] 1 All ER 114 at 135, [1977] Fam 58 at 105).

[28] Thus, in the absence of an order forbidding it, identifying volunteers at the contact centre was neither a contempt nor an offence. Identifying the child was probably not a contempt in itself. It might have been a criminal offence under s 97 of the 1989 Act, but the judge was not exercising that jurisdiction and the father may have had a defence under s 97(3). Some of the other material which he published may well have been a technical contempt under s 12(1) of the 1960 Act as being details of the actual proceedings of the court. But the father was seeking advice and the publication was on a website for that purpose with restricted access. The technical contempt was not as wide as the judge considered. This all contributes to the view of this court that, on the hypothetical facts we are considering, a suspended committal order would have been disproportionate and a wrong exercise of the court's discretion.

...

[30] A judge sitting in the county court has power under s 118 of the County Courts Act 1984 to commit for contempt where the contempt occurs in the face of the court; and power under Ord 29 of the County Court Rules (which applies generally to family proceedings) to make a committal order for a party's breach of a judgment or order of a county court or for breach of an undertaking given to the court (*Bush v Green* [1985] 3 All ER 721, [1985] 1 WLR 1143). The present case was neither of these. The court in *Bush v Green* considered the powers conferred by s 38 of the 1984 Act, which has since been amended. The section now provides that "in any proceedings in a county court the court may make any order which could be made by the High Court if the proceedings were in the High Court". The former version of s 38 was different but said much the same thing. The facts of *Bush v Green* were in substance close to those in the present case. What was decisive to the decision that the county court did not have jurisdiction in that case, notwithstanding the powers in Ord 29 of the County Court Rules 1981, was RSC Ord 52, r 1(2)(1)(iii) as it then was. This provided that "where contempt of court ... is committed in connection with ... proceedings in an inferior court ... an order for committal may only be made by a Divisional Court of the Queen's Bench Division". That rule in substance remains today in RSC Ord 52, r 1(2) in Sch 1 to the CPR. It is subject to r 1(4) which provides that in certain circumstances the power may be exercised by a single judge of the Queen's Bench Division.

[31] In *Re M (Contempt of Court: Committal of Court's Own Motion)* [1999] Fam 263, [1999] 2 WLR 810, this court decided that a judge in a county court has power to initiate committal proceedings for contempt of court by virtue of RSC Ord 52, rr 1 and 5 as applied by s 38 of the 1984 Act. The question in that case was whether the judge could initiate the proceedings on his own initiative, not whether there was jurisdiction in the first place. Ward LJ examined the authorities in detail. His conclusion is in para [32] of his judgment where he said that counsel did not seriously challenge the jurisdiction of the judge to proceed on his own initiative. The alleged contempt was breach of a contact order endorsed with a penal notice. So apart from the "own initiative" point, the judge did have jurisdiction in accordance with *Bush v Green*. It thus appears that, on the authority of *Bush v Green* and by virtue of RSC Ord 52, r 1(2), contempt of court "in connection with" proceedings in the county court, which is not contempt in the face of the court nor disobedience of an order of a county court, is only punishable by an order of committal made in the Queen's Bench Division. We have not overlooked para 1.1 of the *Practice Direction (Family Proceedings: Committal)* {2001} 1 WLR 1253 which provides for family proceedings that, where the alleged contempt is in connection with existing proceedings (other than contempt in the face of the court), or with an order made or an undertaking given in existing proceedings, the committal application shall be made in those proceedings. But we fear that this is inconsistent with RSC Ord 52, r 1(2) and that a practice direction cannot override a rule.'

3.3 OVERVIEW OF ADOPTION LEGISLATION

Introduction

This overview of adoption legislation is written at a time of transition. At the moment the main primary legislation in force is the Adoption Act 1976 (AA 1976).[1] At the same time, Parliament has enacted the Adoption and Children Act 2002 (ACA 2002), the main provisions of which are due, on current information, to come into force in September 2005.

Adoption is sometimes thought of as coming within the public law side of a private law/public law dichotomy.[2] It should not be. Indeed if anything it should probably be treated as a part of private law since, most fundamentally of all, as we will shortly see, adoption is a legal rearrangement of the relationships and responsibilities of private individuals. However, adoption is sufficiently striking in its own right and sufficiently distinguishable from both private and public law cases as they are usually thought of, that we prefer to treat it as its own category. This creates a threefold basic structure of children law: private law/public law/adoption.

Adoption has been used in different ways at different times. At the moment, there are three main, common, but very different, kinds of case:

- in the first, the adopters are one of the child's natural parents (usually the mother) and a step-parent (usually, therefore, the step-father). Typically the parties are asking that the law should reflect what for them has probably been the reality for some time, that they are 'a family';
- in the second, the adopters are unrelated to the child. They are a new, substitute family, typically identified by a local authority following care proceedings. The child may not have lived for very long with the prospective adopters.[3] Here the law is being used to help create a new family unit that is to some extent inchoate;
- the third kind of case again involves adopters who are unrelated to the child and who are asking the law to create a new family unit, but this time the distinguishing feature is that the child has previously been living overseas – adoption with a foreign element. This often involves couples who are otherwise childless.

---

[1] The main secondary legislation is the Adoption Rules 1984 for cases proceeding in the county court and High Court, and the Magistrates' Courts (Adoption) Rules 1984 for cases proceeding in the family proceedings court.

[2] Private law and public law are explained at the start of **3.4**.

[3] The basic rule under the current law is that the child must have had his home with at least one of the adopters at all times during the 13 weeks preceding the adoption order: AA 1976, s 13(1). Various different periods of time are prescribed by ACA 2002, s 42.

Adoption Act 1976

Consequences of adoption

The legal consequences of an adoption order are that it gives parental responsibility for a child to the adopter(s) and it extinguishes the parental responsibility that any person has for the child immediately before the making of the adoption order.[4] Further, an adopted child is treated in law as being the child of the adopter(s) and no longer the child of the natural parents.[5]

So, as a matter of law, a child's parents can be changed. As a matter of genetics, however, they cannot and this leads to all sorts of important questions about the child's future well-being (adoption registers, post-adoption contact, inherited medical conditions and consanguinity in future relationships are examples) some of which grow in accordance with the amount of time the child has lived with his natural family as the effects of nurture are added to those of nature.

Two routes to adoption; two ways of dealing with parental agreement; and a two-stage test for dispensing with agreement

Within current adoption law it is important to know that:

- there are two different routes to an adoption order: it is sometimes achieved in two stages (*'freeing for adoption'* followed by 'adoption') and sometimes all in one (simply 'adoption'). Where it is done in two stages, the order freeing a child for adoption acts as a halfway house, extinguishing the parental responsibility of anyone who held it previously and vesting it in the adoption agency that brought the application;[6]

- whether following the one-stage or the two-stage process, at some point before an adoption order can be made the *agreement*[7] of those who have parental responsibility for the child must be dealt with. There are two ways in which this can be done: either agreement to the making of an adoption order is given[8] or it must be dispensed with by the court on the basis of one or more grounds.[9] Those grounds are set out in AA 1976, s 16(2):

---

[4]   AA 1976, s 12.

[5]   AA 1976, s 39.

[6]   The practical effect of this is that the adoption agency has been able to reassure possible adopters that there is little prospect of the interests of the natural family intervening in any future adoption.

[7]   Often called 'consent', but 'agreement' is the word used in the AA 1976.

[8]   AA 1976, s 16(1)(b)(i), which requires that 'he freely, and with full understanding of what is involved, agrees unconditionally to the making of an adoption order ...'. Such agreement must be formally evidenced in accordance with the AA 1976, s 61. A CAFCASS officer to whom such agreement is given is called a reporting officer. The statutory provisions concerning the various roles of CAFCASS officers are set out below at **7.13**.

[9]   AA 1976, s 16(1)(b)(ii). A CAFCASS officer acting in these circumstances is called a children's guardian.

'the parent or guardian:

(a)   cannot be found or is incapable of giving his consent;

(b)   is withholding his consent unreasonably;[10]

(c)   has persistently failed without reasonable cause to discharge his parental responsibility for the child;

(d)   has abandoned or neglected the child;

(e)   has persistently ill-treated the child;

(f)   has seriously ill-treated the child[11] ...';

- there is a twofold test for courts to apply before dispensing with agreement: first, whether adoption is in the best interests of the child (as to the welfare of the child, see immediately below); and secondly, whether parental agreement is given or one (or more) of the statutory grounds for dispensing with such agreement is proved.[12] The parental interests are therefore protected by the second question.

The welfare of the child

This brings us to the welfare of the child. AA 1976, s 6 states:

'In reaching any decision relating to the adoption of a child a court or adoption agency shall have regard to all the circumstances, first consideration being given to the need to safeguard and promote the welfare of the child throughout his childhood; and shall so far as practicable ascertain the wishes and feelings of the child regarding the decision and give due consideration to them, having regard to his age and understanding.'

So the welfare of the child is firmly in the picture, but it does not dominate the scene in quite the same way that it does under Children Act 1989, s 1. There is a difference between it being the 'first' consideration and being the 'paramount' consideration.

Adoption with a foreign element

The current law[13]

On 1 June 2003 the United Kingdom ratified the Hague Convention on Protection of Children and Co-operation in respect of Inter-Country Adoption 1993. There are now three different types of intercountry adoption to distinguish between:

---

[10]   This is much the most commonly used ground and has developed its own important body of case-law stemming from the decision of the House of Lords in *Re W (An Infant)* [1971] AC 682, [1971] 2 All ER 49.

[11]   This ground does not apply unless the rehabilitation of the child within the household of the parent or guardian is unlikely: AA 1976, s 16(5).

[12]   The two questions must be considered in this order: *Re D (A Minor) (Adoption: Freeing Order)* [1991] 1 FLR 48.

[13]   Note also the Adoption (Intercountry Aspects) Act 1999 (see **3.3C**), and the main secondary legislation relating to adoptions with a foreign element: the Adoption (Designation of Overseas Adoptions) Order 1973, the Adoption of Children from Overseas Regulations 2001, the Adoption (Bringing Children into the United Kingdom) Regulations 2003, the Intercountry Adoption (Hague Convention) Regulations 2003 and the Registration of Foreign Adoptions Regulations 2003.

- Convention adoptions: under the Hague Convention, central authorities make agreements to entrust children to applicants so that orders made in the country of origin can be recognised automatically in England and Wales;

- overseas adoptions (formerly known as 'the designated list'): adoption orders from these countries are also recognised automatically in England and Wales. The difference from Convention adoptions is that it is still necessary to apply for entry clearance and the child will not acquire British citizenship automatically;

- the common law: adoption orders from other countries are not recognised in England and Wales. So it is still necessary for an adoption order to be made in a court here if the adoptive parent–child relationship is to be recognised.

Adoption and Children Act 2002

Repeal of the Adoption Act 1976

When the ACA 2002 is fully in force, the whole of the AA 1976, with the exception of Part IV and Sch 2, para 6,[14] will be repealed.

Basic structure of the Adoption and Children Act 2002

The ACA 2002 is in three Parts: 'Adoption' (ss 1–110), 'Amendments of the Children Act 1989' (ss 111–122) and 'Miscellaneous and final provisions' (ss 123–150). It also has six Schedules.

Adoption and Children Act 2002, Part 1: Adoption

Our concern here is to highlight the principal ways in which the new law on adoption will be the same as or different from the current law. These include:

- first and foremost, the new adoption law will operate within general principles that are virtually (but not entirely) the same as those that govern much of the Children Act 1989. Section 1 of the ACA 2002 provides that:

    '... whenever a court or adoption agency is coming to a decision relating to the adoption of a child'[15] 'the paramount consideration ... must be the child's welfare, throughout his life',[16]

    and they must 'at all times bear in mind that, in general, any delay in coming to a decision is likely to prejudice the child's welfare.[17] Like the Children Act 1989, the ACA 2002 provides a list of matters to which the

---

14   These deal with the status of adopted children, in particular in relation to their property and other such rights.

15   ACA 2002, s 1(1).

16   ACA 2002, s 1(2). The phrase 'throughout his life' is an important difference from the wording in s 1 of the Children Act 1989.

17   ACA 2002, s 1(3).

court or adoption agency must have regard.[18] This will no doubt also be called 'the welfare checklist', although in neither Act is this phrase actually used. Similarly, the ACA 2002 contains a menu principle and a no-order principle[19] both of which are explained in the Overview of the Children Act 1989;[20]

- an adoption order will still have the effect of terminating the legal relationship between the natural parent(s) and child,[21] and creating such a relationship with the adopter(s),[22] but the basic inflexibility that has often surrounded this will be modified. Most importantly of all:

  'before making an adoption order, the court must consider whether there should be arrangements for allowing any person contact with the child; and for that purpose the court must consider any existing or proposed arrangements and obtain any views of the parties to the proceedings.'[23]

  This is certainly not to say that 'open'[24] adoption will become the norm but it does open the way to it becoming a norm. Although this has been entirely possible under the current legislation,[25] it has nevertheless been a way the courts have often been reluctant to take because of a philosophy that adoption would and should normally mean a complete break between the child and the family of his birth. At best, this has been uncomfortable territory under the current law, and while the difficulties will not disappear the new law does adjust the context within which those difficulties must be considered;

- the opportunity has also been taken to remove what was an uncomfortable legal construct. Under the AA 1976, a step-parent adoption results, in law, in the mother[26] losing her responsibilities as a natural parent and re-acquiring them as an adoptive parent. This consequence of adoption, which is so difficult to explain to any parent, will be removed;[27]

- some flexibility in adoption law had already been achieved by the Children Act 1989 including the AA 1976 within its definition of 'family proceedings'. This means that on an application for an adoption order the court is not restricted to making orders under the AA 1976 but can,

---

[18] ACA 2002, s 1(4), which is not identical to the welfare checklist in s 1(3) of the Children Act 1989, and note also the additional requirement under s 1(5) that 'in placing the child for adoption, the adoption agency must give due consideration to the child's religious persuasion, racial origin and cultural and linguistic background'.

[19] Both in ACA 2002, s 1(6).

[20] See **3.6**.

[21] ACA 2002, s 46(2).

[22] ACA 2002, s 46(1).

[23] ACA 2002, s 46(6).

[24] Ie adoption in which there is continuing face-to-face contact between the child and her birth family.

[25] See the decision of the House of Lords in *Re C (A Minor) (Adoption Order: Conditions)* [1988] 2 FLR 159.

[26] As it usually is, but it applies equally to a natural father applying to adopt his child.

[27] ACA 2002, s 46(2)(a).

instead or in combination, make orders under the Children Act 1989.[28] Even more flexible solutions are provided by the ACA 2002, including the acquisition of parental responsibility by step-parents,[29] relaxing the restrictions upon local authority foster-parents[30] and, in particular, by creating a new order altogether, a *special guardianship order*.[31] Such an order falls significantly short of adoption as it does not extinguish the parental responsibility of the natural parent(s), but provides significantly more certainty and authority than does a residence order as:

> 'a special guardian is entitled to exercise parental responsibility to the exclusion of any other person with parental responsibility for the child (apart from another special guardian)';[32]

- freeing for adoption will be abolished altogether;[33]

- *placement for adoption* will become a key new concept – indeed we suggest that understanding and applying the new law about placement for adoption will be one of the greater challenges for the various professionals when the new adoption law comes into effect.[34] The basic provisions about placement are set out in ss 18–35 of the ACA 2002. Placement for adoption will either be by consent[35] or by court order.[36] Before it can make a placement order the court must consider two things. First, unless the child has no parent or guardian or is already the subject of a care order, the court must be satisfied that the threshold criteria in s 31(2) of the Children Act 1989 are met; and secondly, either the necessary parental consent has been given (and not withdrawn) or it should be dispensed with.[37] The natural parent(s) continue to have parental responsibility for the child while she is placed for adoption, as do the prospective adopter(s) and the adoption agency, but it is the

---

[28] The 'menu principle' of the Children Act 1989, s 10(1)(b) referred to in the Overview of the Children Act 1989 (at **3.6** below). See the decision of the Court of Appeal in *Re M (Adoption or Residence Order)* [1998] 1 FLR 570.

[29] ACA 2002, s 112.

[30] ACA 2002, s 113 and Sch 3, para 56(c).

[31] ACA 2002, s 115, which will create new ss 14A–14G of the Children Act 1989, when brought into force (provisionally in September 2005).

[32] Children Act 1989, s 14C(1)(b), when brought into force.

[33] Freeing for adoption was always thought by some to be an unsatisfactory halfway house and was rarely, if ever, used in some parts of England and Wales. Growing concerns about the human rights of the natural family (including the human rights of the child herself), about whether in fact it operated in the long-term interests of the child (if adoptive parents need the shutting out of the natural family, are they in fact the right people to adopt the child?), together with examples of children left in the legal limbo of having been freed for adoption but not having been adopted, have all played their part in its demise.

[34] It is worth noting that underlying the provisions about placement for adoption is a concern that it currently often takes too long for children in care to reach permanent homes within new families, which is why ACA 2002, s 22 states that local authorities 'must' in certain circumstances apply for a placement order.

[35] ACA 2002, ss 19 and 20.

[36] ACA 2002, ss 21–24.

[37] ACA 2002, s 21(2) and (3).

adoption agency that may determine the extent to which others exercise the responsibility they have.[38] There are also important provisions about contact;[39]

- parental consent must still either be given or dispensed with. Where consent is given, it can still be given in advance but if an application for an adoption order has been made the advance consent cannot be withdrawn and leave to oppose the adoption order can only be given if the court is satisfied there has been a change in circumstances. Where consent has to be dispensed with there will effectively only be three grounds on which this can be done:[40] that the parent or guardian cannot be found, that he or she is incapable of giving consent, or that the welfare of the child requires the consent to be dispensed with;[41]
- unmarried couples, including same-sex couples, will be able to make joint applications to adopt.[42]

Adoption and Children Act 2002, Part 2: Amendments to the Children Act 1989

The occasion of major reform to adoption legislation was also an opportunity to effect a series of other changes to children law. As well as the acquisition of parental responsibility by a step-parent, reducing restrictions on foster-parents and the creation of the wholly new order of special guardianship that have just been referred to, these include:

- extending parental responsibility to the unmarried father when he is registered as the child's father;[43]
- strengthening provisions about the review of cases of looked after children and the provision of advocacy services for them;[44]
- extending the definition of 'harm' in s 31(9) of the Children Act 1989 by adding the words 'including, for example, impairment suffered from seeing or hearing the ill-treatment of another';[45]
- introducing statutory provisions about care plans;[46] and

---

[38] Rather like the position under Children Act 1989, s 33(3) when a care order has been made.

[39] ACA 2002, ss 26–27.

[40] Contrast with the six grounds of the AA 1976, s 16 referred to above.

[41] See generally ACA 2002, ss 20, 47 and 52. In determining whether the welfare of the child requires consent to be dispensed with the court will, of course, have to apply the provisions of ACA 2002, s 1.

[42] ACA 2002, ss 49, 50 and 144(4). Contrast with the AA 1976 which confines applications by a couple to married couples (s 14).

[43] ACA 2002, s 111, and note that this has been in force since 1 December 2003. It does not apply retrospectively to unmarried fathers who were registered before this date.

[44] ACA 2002, ss 118 and 119, in force from 21 May 2004 and 1 April 2004, respectively. These are in part a response to the decision of the House of Lords in *Re S; Re W (Minors)* [2002] 1 FLR 815.

[45] ACA 2002, s 120, which came into effect on 31 January 2005. This is an important element in restructuring the statutory approach to domestic violence.

[46] ACA 2002, s 121.

- extending the categories of specified proceedings set out in s 41 of the Children Act 1989.[47]

Adoption and Children Act 2002, Part 3: Miscellaneous and final provisions, and the Schedules

Part 3 deals with the sort of things that are commonly dealt with at the end of any such legislation including amendments, transitional provisions and repeals,[48] the powers to make subordinate legislation[49] and general interpretation.[50] Among the miscellaneous provisions are restrictions on advertising relating to adoption[51] and provision for the creation of a national Adoption and Children Act Register containing prescribed information about children who are suitable for adoption and prospective adopter(s) who are suitable to adopt a child.[52] There are also provisions about the registration of adoptions and the disclosure of birth records.[53]

Adoptions with a foreign element after the implementation of the Adoption and Children Act 2002

When the ACA 2002 is fully in force it will replace most of the Adoption (Intercountry Aspects) Act 1999.[54] The provisions of the 1999 Act which enabled the UK to ratify the Hague Convention will remain in effect, as will the three-fold categorisation of intercountry adoptions outlined above. It is expected that the number of Hague Adoption Convention ratifications will grow, and the countries on 'the designated list'[55] will be reviewed. The common law will therefore apply to fewer adoptions with a foreign element.

The Overview continues at **3.6** Children Act 1989.

---

[47] ACA 2002, s 122.

[48] ACA 2002, s 139 and Schs 3, 4 and 5 respectively. Note that Sch 3, para 118, which came into effect in November 2003, has repealed the former s 12(5)(b) of the Criminal Justice and Court Services Act 2000 which Wall J had used to enable the court to direct that there should be a continuing role for a children's guardian during the lifetime of a supervision order: *Re MH; Re SB and MB* [2001] 2 FLR 1334.

[49] ACA 2002, ss 140–142.

[50] ACA 2002, ss 144 and 147, and Sch 6.

[51] ACA 2002, ss 123 and 124.

[52] ACA 2002, ss 125–131.

[53] ACA 2002, Schs 1 and 2, respectively.

[54] The position is not easy to piece together, but see: (1) ss 83–91; (2) Sch 3, paras 95–101; and (3) Sch 5, of the ACA 2002.

[55] Now 'overseas adoptions'.

3.3A ADOPTION ACT 1976
(ss 6, 7, 11–36, 38–41, 61, 65, 72)

General note on provisional repeal—The whole Act, except Part 4 and para 6 of Sch 2, is repealed by Adoption and Children Act 2002, s 139(3), Sch 5, which is currently expected to come into force in September 2005.

PART I
THE ADOPTION SERVICE

****

6 Duty to promote welfare of child

In reaching any decision relating to the adoption of a child a court or adoption agency shall have regard to all the circumstances, first consideration being given to the need to safeguard and promote the welfare of the child throughout his childhood; and shall so far as practicable ascertain the wishes and feelings of the child regarding the decision and give due consideration to them, having regard to his age and understanding.

> **Section 6**—This section does not provide that the child's welfare is the *paramount* consideration in adoption proceedings and thus it is dissimilar to s 1 of the Children Act 1989 (*Re D (An Infant) (Adoption: Parent's Consent)* [1977] AC 602 at 641, [1977] 1 All ER 145). In contested adoption proceedings the court should consider whether the application fulfils the requirements of this section before considering whether to dispense with the parents' consent under s 16.
>
> In *Soderback v Sweden* [1999] 1 FLR 250, ECtHR, the mother and her new husband applied for adoption. The order was made in the face of opposition from the natural father. The father alleged breach of Article 8 of the ECHR (respect for family life). The court held that the adoption order amounted to an interference with respect for the father's family life. However, due to the infrequent and limited contact between the father and the child, and the strong family ties between the new husband and the child, the decision was in accordance with the law, fulfilled the requirements of Article 8(2) and fell within the state's margin of appreciation.

7 Religious upbringing of adopted child

An adoption agency shall in placing a child for adoption have regard (so far as is practicable) to any wishes of a child's parents and guardians as to the religious upbringing of the child.

Supplemental

****

11 Restriction on arranging adoptions and placing of children

(1) A person other than an adoption agency shall not make arrangements for the adoption of a child, or place a child for adoption, unless –

    (a) the proposed adopter is a relative of the child, or

    (b) he is acting in pursuance of an order of the High Court.

(2) An adoption society which is –

    (a) approved as respects Scotland under section 3 of the Adoption (Scotland) Act 1978; or

    (b) registered as respects Northern Ireland under Article 4 of the Adoption (Northern Ireland) Order 1987,

but which is not an appropriate voluntary organisation, shall not act as an adoption society in England and Wales except to the extent that the society considers it necessary to do so in the interests of a person mentioned in section 1 of the Act of 1978 or Article 3 of the Order of 1987.

(3) A person who –

    (a) takes part in the management or control of a body of persons which exists wholly or partly for the purpose of making arrangements for the adoption of children and which is not an adoption agency; or

    (b) contravenes subsection (1) or

    (c) receives a child placed with him in contravention of subsection (1),

shall be guilty of an offence and liable on summary conviction to imprisonment for a term not exceeding 3 months or to a fine not exceeding level 5 on the standard scale or to both.

(4) In any proceedings for an offence under paragraph (a) of subsection (3), proof of things done or of words written, spoken or published (whether or not in the presence of any party to the proceedings) by any person taking part in the management or control of a body of persons, or in making arrangements for the adoption of children on behalf of the body, shall be admissible as evidence of the purpose for which that body exists.

(5) *(repealed)*

PART II

ADOPTION ORDERS

The making of adoption orders

12 Adoption orders

(1) An adoption order is an order giving parental responsibility for a child to the adopters, made on their application by an authorised court.

(2) The order does not affect parental responsibility so far as it relates to any period before the making of the order.

(3) The making of an adoption order operates to extinguish –

(a) the parental responsibility which any person has for the child immediately before the making of the order;

(aa) any order under the Children Act 1989; and

(b) any duty arising by virtue of an agreement or the order of a court to make payments, so far as the payments are in respect of the child's maintenance or upbringing for any period after the making of the order.

(4) Subsection (3)(b) does not apply to a duty arising by virtue of an agreement –

(a) which constitutes a trust, or

(b) which expressly provides that the duty is not to be extinguished by the making of an adoption order.

(5) An adoption order may not be made in relation to a child who is or has been married.

(6) An adoption order may contain such terms and conditions as the court thinks fit.

(7) An adoption order may be made notwithstanding that the child is already an adopted child.

13 Child to live with adopters before order is made

(1) Where –

(a) (subject to subsection (1A)) the applicant, or one of the applicants, is a parent, step-parent or relative of the child, or

(b) the child was placed with the applicants by an adoption agency or in pursuance of an order of the High Court,

an adoption order shall not be made unless the child is at least 19 weeks old and at all times during the preceding 13 weeks had his home with the applicants or one of them.

(1A) Where an adoption is proposed to be effected by a Convention adoption order, the order shall not be made unless at all times during the preceding six months the child had his home with the applicants or one of them.

(2) Where subsection (1) or (1A) does not apply, an adoption order shall not be made unless the child is at least 12 months old and at all times during the preceding 12 months had his home with the applicants or one of them.

(3) An adoption order shall not be made unless the court is satisfied that sufficient opportunities to see the child with the applicant or, in the case of an application by a married couple, both applicants together in the home environment have been afforded –

(a) where the child was placed with the applicant by an adoption agency, to that agency, or

(b) in any other case, to the local authority within whose area the home is.

14 Adoption by married couple

(1) An adoption order shall not be made on the application of more than one person except in the circumstances specified in subsections (1A) and (1B).

(1A) An adoption order may be made on the application of a married couple where both the husband and the wife have attained the age of 21 years.

(1B) An adoption order may be made on the application of a married couple where –

> (a) the husband or the wife –
>> (i) is the father or mother of the child; and
>> (ii) has attained the age of 18 years;
>> and
> (b) his or her spouse has attained the age of 21 years.

(2) An adoption order shall not be made on the application of a married couple unless –

> (a) at least one of them is domiciled in a part of the United Kingdom, or in the Channel Islands or the Isle of Man, or
> (b) the application is for a Convention adoption order and the requirements of regulations under section 17 are complied with.

(3) *(repealed)*

15 Adoption by one person

(1) An adoption order may be made on the application of one person where he has attained the age of 21 years and –

> (a) is not married, or
> (b) is married and the court is satisfied that –
>> (i) his spouse cannot be found, or
>> (ii) the spouses have separated and are living apart, and the separation is likely to be permanent, or
>> (iii) his spouse is by reason of ill-health, whether physical or mental, incapable of making an application for an adoption order.

(2) An adoption order shall not be made on the application of one person unless –

> (a) he is domiciled in a part of the United Kingdom, or in the Channel Islands or the Isle of Man, or
> (b) the application is for a Convention adoption order and the requirements of regulations under section 17 are complied with.

(3) An adoption order shall not be made on the application of the mother or father of the child alone unless the court is satisfied that –

> (a) the other natural parent is dead or cannot be found or, by virtue of section 28 of the Human Fertilisation and Embryology Act 1990, there is no other parent, or
> (b) there is some other reason justifying the exclusion of the other natural parent,

and where such an order is made the reason justifying the exclusion of the other natural parent shall be recorded by the court.

(4) *(repealed)*

16 Parental agreement

(1) An adoption order shall not be made unless –

(a) the child is free for adoption by virtue of an order made –
    (i) in England and Wales, under section 18;
    (ii) in Scotland, under section 18 of the Adoption (Scotland) Act 1978; or
    (iii) in Northern Ireland, under Article 17(1) or 18(1) of the Adoption (Northern Ireland) Order 1987; or

(b) in the case of each parent or guardian of the child the court is satisfied that –
    (i) he freely, and with full understanding of what is involved, agrees unconditionally to the making of an adoption order (whether or not he knows the identity of the applicants), or
    (ii) his agreement to the making of the adoption order should be dispensed with on a ground specified in subsection (2).

(2) The grounds mentioned in subsection (1)(b)(ii) are that the parent or guardian –

    (a) cannot be found or is incapable of giving agreement;
    (b) is withholding his agreement unreasonably;
    (c) has persistently failed without reasonable cause to discharge his parental responsibility for the child;
    (d) has abandoned or neglected the child;
    (e) has persistently ill-treated the child;
    (f) has seriously ill-treated the child (subject to subsection (5)).

(3) *(repealed)*

(4) Agreement is ineffective for the purposes of subsection (1)(b)(i) if given by the mother less than six weeks after the child's birth.

(5) Subsection (2)(f) does not apply unless (because of the ill-treatment or for other reasons) the rehabilitation of the child within the household of the parent or guardian is unlikely.

Section 16

Agreement—Although agreement to adoption should be in writing (Form 7 and r 20 of the Adoption Rules 1984 provide for a standard form), those rules are directory rather than mandatory (*Re T (A Minor) (Adoption: Validity of Order)* [1986] Fam 160, sub nom *Re T (A Minor) (Adoption: Parental Consent)* [1986] 1 All ER 817, CA). Agreement is ineffective for the purposes of AA 1976, s 16(1)(b)(i) if given by the mother less than six weeks after the child's birth (AA 1976, s 16(4)). A parent may withdraw consent to adoption prior to the making of an adoption order, although the withdrawal of consent may be a factor that the court takes into account when deciding whether to hold that a parent is withholding agreement to adoption unreasonably (*Re H (Infants) (Adoption: Parental Consent)* [1977] 2 All ER 339, CA).

Cannot be found—All reasonable steps to find a parent must be taken before the court will conclude that the parent cannot be found (*Re S (Adoption)* [1999] 2 FLR 374, Ct Sess: adoption order made on basis that mother could not be found. After referring to English authority on the point, the court held that 'cannot be found' meant that all reasonable steps had been taken to find the mother; if one reasonable step was omitted it could not be said that the person could not be found).

Incapable of giving agreement—It has been held that a parent living in a totalitarian regime might be held to be incapable of giving agreement (*Re R (Adoption)* [1966] 3 All ER 613).

Withholding agreement unreasonably—In *Re W (An Infant)* [1971] 2 All ER 49 the House of Lords stressed that the test is 'reasonableness and not anything else'. There is a band of reasonable decisions that a reasonable hypothetical parent might make which the court should not invade. The parent's decisions must be judged as at the time of the hearing. Welfare of a child is decisive only to the extent that the reasonable, hypothetical parent would regard it as such on the facts of the individual case.

The *Re W* test has been examined in more recent authority. In *Re F (Children) (Adoption: Freeing Order)* [2000] 2 FLR 505, CA, the court approved the following passage from the joint judgment of Steyn and Hoffmann LJJ in *Re C (A Minor) (Adoption: Parental Agreement)* [1993] 2 FLR 260, [1994] 2 FCR 485. Steyn and Hoffmann LJJ, having commented on the difficulties created by lawyers in their conceptualisation of hypothetical reasonable parents, went on to say (at [1994] 2 FCR 498):

> 'The characteristics of the notional reasonable parent have been expounded on many occasions: see for example Lord Wilberforce in *Re D (Adoption: Parent's Consent)* [1977] AC 602 at 625 ("endowed with a mind and temperament capable of making reasonable decisions"). The views of such a parent will not necessarily coincide with the judge's views as to what the child's welfare requires. As Lord Hailsham of St. Marylebone, LC said in *Re W (An Infant)* [1971] AC 682, 700: "Two reasonable parents can perfectly reasonably come to opposite conclusions on the same set of facts without forfeiting their title to be regarded as reasonable." Furthermore, although the reasonable parent will give great weight to the welfare of the child, there are other interests of herself and her family which she may legitimately take into account. All this is well-settled by authority. Nevertheless, for those who feel some embarrassment at having to consult the views of so improbable a legal fiction, we venture to observe that precisely the same question may be raised in a demythologized form by the Judge asking himself whether, having regard to the evidence and applying the current values of our society, the advantages of adoption for the welfare of the child appear sufficiently strong to justify overriding the views and interests of the objecting parent or parents. The reasonable parent is only a piece of machinery invented to provide the answer to this question. If authority is required for this statement of the obvious, it can be found in the analysis of a similar question by Lord Radcliffe in *Davis Contractors Limited v Fareham UDC* [1956] AC 696, 728–729.'

That approach is again advanced as the correct test in *Re B-M (A Child) (Adoption: Parental Agreement)* [2001] 1 FCR 1, CA.

In *Re D (Grant of Care Order: Refusal of Freeing Order)* [2001] 1 FCR 501, CA, the judge disagreed with the guardian. It was held that when a judge is considering the test of the reasonable hypothetical parent, the judge should not give prominence to a theoretical possibility (mother give up heroin, father establish himself independently) unless it was realistic. There was no expert evidence on behalf of the parents but the judge preferred their evidence over that of the local authority and the guardian. When departing from the views of a CAFCASS officer it is essential that a judge should explain his reasons for doing so.

Where there are two opposing reasonable views and a parent adopts one of these views, it cannot be said that the parent was withholding agreement unreasonably (*Re B (Adoption Order)* [2001] EWCA Civ 347, [2001] 2 FLR 26, CA, and *Re F (Adoption: Welfare of Child: Financial Considerations)* [2003] EWHC 3448 (Fam), [2004] 2 FLR 440, FD). In the latter case, the guardian, the child psychologist and the independent social worker opposed the proposed adoption; the judge held that the mother could not be held to be withholding her agreement unreasonably in agreeing with them.

Other grounds for dispensing with agreement

– **Section 16(2)(c):** 'Persistently failed without reasonable cause to discharge his parental responsibility for the child' means that the failure must be culpable to a high degree (*Re D (Minors) (Adoption by Parent)* [1973] 3 All ER 1001).

– **Section 16(2)(d):** 'Abandoned or neglected the child'. It has been held that this involves abandonment or neglect that would meet the meaning of those words under criminal law (*Re P (Infants)* [1962] 3 All ER 789).

– **Section 16(2)(e):** 'Persistently ill-treated the child' – see *Re A (A Minor) (Adoption: Dispensing with Agreement)* [1981] 2 FLR 173 (must be a persistent course of conduct towards the child which would render the parent criminally liable).

– **Section 16(2)(f):** 'Seriously ill-treated the child' implies treatment that would amount to criminal behaviour (*Re PB (A Minor) (Application to Free for Adoption)* [1985] FLR 394,

CA). Under s 16(5), s 16(2)(f) does not apply unless (because of the ill-treatment or for other reasons) the rehabilitation of the child within the household of the parent or guardian is unlikely.

17 Convention adoption orders

An adoption order shall be made as a Convention adoption order if –

    (a) the application is for a Convention adoption order; and

    (b) such requirements as may be prescribed by regulations made by the Secretary of State are complied with.

Freeing for adoption

18 Freeing child for adoption

(1) Where, on an application by an adoption agency, an authorised court is satisfied in the case of each parent or guardian of the child that –

    (a) he freely, and with full understanding of what is involved, agrees generally and unconditionally to the making of an adoption order, or

    (b) his agreement to the making of an adoption order should be dispensed with on a ground specified in section 16(2),

the court shall make an order declaring the child free for adoption.

(2) No application shall be made under subsection (1) unless –

    (a) it is made with the consent of a parent or guardian of a child, or

    (b) the adoption agency is applying for dispensation under subsection (1)(b) of the agreement of each parent or guardian of the child, and the child is in the care of the adoption agency.

(2A) For the purposes of subsection (2) a child is in the care of an adoption agency if the adoption agency is a local authority and he is in their care.

(3) No agreement required under subsection (1)(a) shall be dispensed with under subsection (1)(b) unless the child is already placed for adoption or the court is satisfied that it is likely that the child will be placed for adoption.

(4) An agreement by the mother of the child is ineffective for the purposes of this section if given less than 6 weeks after the child's birth.

(5) On the making of an order under this section, parental responsibility for the child is given to the adoption agency, and subsections (2) to (4) of section 12 apply as if the order were an adoption order and the agency were the adopters.

(6) Before making an order under this section, the court shall satisfy itself, in relation to each parent or guardian of the child who can be found, that he has been given an opportunity of making, if he so wishes, a declaration that he prefers not to be involved in future questions concerning the adoption of the child; and any such declaration shall be recorded by the court.

(7) Before making an order under this section in the case of a child whose father does not have parental responsibility for him, the court shall satisfy itself in relation to any person claiming to be the father that –

    (a) he has no intention of applying for –

(i)   an order under section 4(1) of the Children Act 1989, or

(ii) a residence order under section 10 of that Act, or

(b) if he did make any such application, it would be likely to be refused.

(8) Subsections (5) and (7) of section 12 apply in relation to the making of an order under this section as they apply in relation to the making of an order under that section.

> **Section 18**—Although it has been said that an application to free for adoption is inappropriate where potential adopters have been identified (see *Re H (A Minor) (Freeing Order)* [1993] 2 FLR 325, CA), in *Re S* (unreported) 3 April 2000, CA, the court approved the making of a freeing application even though adopters had been identified. Thorpe LJ said:
>
> > 'That leaves Miss Small's reliance upon the decision of this Court in *Re H (A Minor) (Freeing Order)* (CA) [1993] 2 FLR 325. Again, the leading judgment was given by Butler-Sloss LJ. She, on the facts of that case, held that the freeing procedure was misconceived when it was a clear case for going direct to the adoption application, bearing in mind the length of time the child had been with the foster family. But Miss Archer points out that there are a number of very valid factual distinctions between the case that this Court then considered and the case which is before us today. In the case of *Re H* the foster parents had not even been assessed, so there was absolutely no assurance that they would be the carers ultimately involved in the management of future contact.'

19 Progress reports to former parents

(1) This section and section 20 apply to any person ('the former parent'), who was required to be given an opportunity of making a declaration under section 18(6) but did not do so.

(2) Within the 14 days following the date 12 months after the making of the order under section 18 the adoption agency to which parental responsibility was given on the making of the order, unless it has previously by notice to the former parent informed him that an adoption order has been made in respect of the child, shall by notice to the former parent inform him –

(a) whether an adoption order has been made in respect of the child, and (if not)

(b) whether the child has his home with a person with whom he has been placed for adoption.

(3) If at the time when the former parent is given notice under subsection (2) an adoption order has not been made in respect of the child, it is thereafter the duty of the adoption agency to give notice to the former parent of the making of an adoption order (if and when made), and meanwhile to give the former parent notice whenever the child is placed for adoption or ceases to have his home with a person with whom he has been placed for adoption.

(4) If at any time the former parent by notice makes a declaration to the adoption agency that he prefers not to be involved in future questions concerning the adoption of the child –

(a) the agency shall secure that the declaration is recorded by the court which made the order under section 18, and

(b) the agency is released from the duty of complying further with subsection (3) as respects that former parent.

20 Revocation of s 18 order

(1) The former parent, at any time more than 12 months after the making of the order under section 18 when –

    (a) no adoption order has been made in respect of the child, and
    (b) the child does not have his home with a person with whom he has been placed for adoption,

may apply to the court which made the order for a further order revoking it on the ground that he wishes to resume parental responsibility.

(2) While the application is pending the adoption agency having parental responsibility shall not place the child for adoption without the leave of the court.

(3) The revocation of an order under section 18 ('a section 18 order') operates –

    (a) to extinguish the parental responsibility given to the adoption agency under the section 18 order;
    (b) to give parental responsibility for the child to –
        (i) the child's mother; and
        (ii) where the child's father and mother were married to each other at the time of his birth, the father; and
    (c) to revive –
        (i) any parental responsibility agreement,
        (ii) any order under section 4(1) of the Children Act 1989, and
        (iii) any appointment of a guardian in respect of the child (whether made by a court or otherwise),
    extinguished by the making of the section 18 order.

(3A) Subject to subsection (3)(c), the revocation does not –

    (a) operate to revive –
        (i) any order under the Children Act 1989, or
        (ii) any duty referred to in section 12(3)(b),
    extinguished by the making of the section 18 order; or
    (b) affect any person's parental responsibility so far as it relates to the period between the making of the section 18 order and the date of revocation of that order.

(4) Subject to subsection (5), if the application is dismissed on the ground that to allow it would contravene the principle embodied in section 6 –

    (a) the former parent who made the application shall not be entitled to make any further application under subsection (1) in respect of the child, and
    (b) the adoption agency is released from the duty of complying further with section 19(3) as respects that parent.

(5) Subsection (4)(a) shall not apply where the court which dismissed the application gives leave to the former parent to make a further application under subsection (1), but such leave shall not be given unless it appears to the court that because of a change in circumstances or for any other reason it is proper to allow the application to be made.

Section 20—In *Re C (Adoption: Freeing Order)* [1999] Fam 240, [1999] 1 WLR 1079, [1999] 1 FLR 348, the child had been freed for adoption. The mother made a declaration under s 18(6) stating that she did not wish to be involved in future questions about the child. The child was not adopted and the mother wished to have some involvement with her life. The child was in 'pre-adoptive limbo' – the local authority's care order had ended, the mother had no legal rights and parental responsibility was vested in the adoption agency (even though adoption was no longer viable). All parties agreed that it was appropriate for the freeing order to be revoked and for the child to become subject to a care order. The mother was not in a position to apply for the revocation of the freeing order nor was the adoption agency (AA 1976, ss 19(1) and 20). It was held that the court could revoke the freeing order under its inherent jurisdiction (see also *Re J (Freeing for Adoption)* [2000] 2 FLR 58, FD).

21 Variation of s 18 order so as to substitute one adoption agency for another

(1) On an application to which this section applies, an authorised court may vary an order under section 18 so as to give parental responsibility for the child to another adoption agency ('the substitute agency') in place of the agency for the time being having parental responsibility for the child under the order ('the existing agency').

(2) This section applies to any application made jointly by –

    (a) the existing agency; and
    (b) the would-be substitute agency.

(3) Where an order under section 18 is varied under this section, section 19 shall apply as if the substitute agency had been given responsibility for the child on the making of the order.

Supplemental

22 Notification to local authority of adoption application

(1) An adoption order shall not be made in respect of a child who was not placed with the applicant by an adoption agency unless the applicant has, at least 3 months before the date of the order, given notice to the local authority within whose area he has his home of his intention to apply for the adoption order.

(1A) An application for such an adoption order shall not be made unless the person wishing to make the application has, within the period of two years preceding the making of the application, given notice as mentioned in subsection (1).

(1B) In subsections (1) and (1A) the references to the area in which the applicant or person has his home are references to the area in which he has his home at the time of giving the notice.

(2) On receipt of such a notice the local authority shall investigate the matter and submit to the court a report of their investigation.

(3) Under subsection (2), the local authority shall in particular investigate, –

    (a) so far as is practicable, the suitability of the applicant, and any other matters relevant to the operation of section 6 in relation to the application; and
    (b) whether the child was placed with the applicant in contravention of section 11.

(4) A local authority which receive notice under subsection (1) in respect of a child whom the authority know to be looked after by another local authority shall, not more than 7 days after the receipt of the notice, inform that other local authority in writing, that they have received the notice.

23 Reports where child placed by agency

Where an application for an adoption order relates to a child placed by an adoption agency, the agency shall submit to the court a report on the suitability of the applicants and any other matters relevant to the operation of section 6, and shall assist the court in any manner the court may direct.

24 Restrictions on making adoption orders

(1) The court shall not proceed to hear an application for an adoption order in relation to a child where a previous application for a British adoption order made in relation to the child by the same persons was refused by any court unless –

(a) in refusing the previous application the court directed that this subsection should not apply or
(b) it appears to the court that because of a change in circumstances or for any other reason it is proper to proceed with the application.

(2) The court shall not make an adoption order in relation to a child unless it is satisfied that the applicants have not, as respects the child, contravened section 57.

25 Interim orders

(1) Where on an application for an adoption order the requirements of sections 16(1) and 22(1) are complied with, the court may postpone the determination of the application and make an order giving parental responsibility for the child to the applicants for a probationary period not exceeding 2 years upon such terms for the maintenance of the child and otherwise as the court thinks fit.

(2) Where the probationary period specified in an order under subsection (1) is less than 2 years, the court may by a further order extend the period to a duration not exceeding 2 years in all.

26 *(repealed)*

PART III
CARE AND PROTECTION OF CHILDREN AWAITING ADOPTION

27 Restrictions on removal where adoption agreed or application made under s 18

(1) While an application for an adoption is pending in a case where a parent or guardian of the child has agreed to the making of the adoption order, (whether or not he knows the identity of the applicant), the parent or guardian is not entitled, against the will of the person with whom the child has his home, to remove the child from the home of that person except with the leave of the court.

(2) While an application is pending for an order freeing a child for adoption and –

    (a) the child is in the care of the adoption agency making the application, and

    (b) the application was not made with the consent of each parent or guardian of the child,

no parent or guardian of the child is entitled, against the will of the person with whom the child has his home, to remove the child from the home of that person except with the leave of the court.

(2A) For the purposes of subsection (2) a child is in the care of an adoption agency if the adoption agency is a local authority and he is in their care.

(3) Any person who contravenes subsection (1) or (2) shall be guilty of an offence and liable on summary conviction to imprisonment for a term not exceeding 3 months or a fine not exceeding level 5 on the standard scale or both.

(4), (5) (*repealed*)

28 Restrictions on removal where applicant has provided home for 5 years

(1) While an application for an adoption order in respect of a child made by the person with whom the child has had his home for the 5 years preceding the application is pending, no person is entitled, against the will of the applicant, to remove the child from the applicant's home except with the leave of the court or under authority conferred by any enactment or on the arrest of the child.

(2) Where a person ('the prospective adopter') gives notice to the local authority within whose area he has his home that he intends to apply for an adoption order in respect of a child who for the preceding 5 years has had his home with the prospective adopter, no person is entitled, against the will of the prospective adopter, to remove the child from the prospective adopter's home, except with the leave of a court or under authority conferred by any enactment or on the arrest of the child, before –

    (a) the prospective adopter applies for the adoption order, or

    (b) the period of 3 months from the receipt of the notice by the local authority expires,

whichever occurs first.

(2A) The reference in subsections (1) and (2) to any enactment does not include a reference to section 20(8) of the Children Act 1989.

(3) In any case where subsection (1) or (2) applies and –

    (a) the child was being looked after by a local authority before he began to have his home with the applicant or, as the case may be, the prospective adopter, and

    (b) the child is still being looked after by a local authority,

the authority which are looking after the child shall not remove him from the home of the applicant or the prospective adopter except in accordance with section 30 or 31 or with the leave of a court.

(4) In subsections (2) and (3) 'a court' means a court with jurisdiction to make adoption orders.

(5) A local authority which receive such notice as is mentioned in subsection (2) in respect of a child whom the authority know to be looked after by another local authority shall, not more than 7 days after the receipt of the notice, inform that other authority, in writing, that they have received the notice.

(6) Subsection (2) does not apply to any further notice served by the prospective adopter on any local authority in respect of the same child during the period referred to in paragraph (b) of that subsection or within 28 days after its expiry.

(7) Any person who contravenes subsection (1) or (2) shall be guilty of an offence and liable on summary conviction to imprisonment for a term not exceeding 3 months or a fine not exceeding level 5 on the standard scale or both.

(8), (9) (*repealed*)

(10) The Secretary of State may by order amend subsection (1) or (2) to substitute a different period for the period of 5 years mentioned in that subsection (or the period which, by a previous order under this subsection, was substituted for that period).

29 Return of child taken away in breach of s 27 or 28

(1) An authorised court may, on the application of a person from whose home a child has been removed in breach of –

  (a) section 27 or 28,
  (b) section 27 or 28 of the Adoption (Scotland) Act 1978, or
  (c) Article 28 or 29 of the Adoption (Northern Ireland) Order 1987,

order the person who has so removed the child to return the child to the applicant.

(2) An authorised court may, on the application of a person who has reasonable grounds for believing that another person is intending to remove a child from his home in breach of –

  (a) section 27 or 28,
  (b) section 27 or 28 of the Adoption (Scotland) Act 1978, or
  (c) Article 28 or 29 of the Adoption (Northern Ireland) Order 1987,

by order direct that other person not to remove the child from the applicant's home in breach of any of those provisions.

(3) If, in the case of an order made by the High Court under subsection (1), the High Court or, in the case of an order made by a county court under subsection (1), a county court is satisfied that the child has not been returned to the applicant, the court may make an order authorising an officer of the court to search such premises as may be specified in the order for the child and, if the officer finds the child, to return the child to the applicant.

(4) If a justice of the peace is satisfied by information on oath that there are reasonable grounds for believing that a child to whom an order under subsection (1) relates is in premises specified in the information, he may issue a search warrant authorising a constable to search the premises for the child; and if a constable acting in pursuance of a warrant under this section finds the child, he shall return the child to the person on whose application the order under subsection (1) was made.

(5) An order under subsection (3) may be enforced in like manner as a warrant for committal.

30 Return of children placed for adoption by adoption agencies

(1) Subject to subsection (2), at any time after a child has been placed with any person in pursuance of arrangements made by an adoption agency for the adoption of the child by that person, and before an adoption order has been made on the application of that person in respect of the child, –

    (a) that person may give notice to the agency of his intention not to give the child a home; or

    (b) the agency may cause notice to be given to that person of their intention not to allow the child to remain in his home.

(2) No notice under paragraph (b) of subsection (1) shall be given in respect of a child in relation to whom an application has been made for an adoption order except with the leave of the court to which the application has been made.

(3) Where a notice is given to an adoption agency by any person or by an adoption agency to any person under subsection (1), or where an application for an adoption order made by any person in respect of a child placed with him by an adoption agency is refused by the court or withdrawn, that person shall, within 7 days after the date on which notice was given or the application refused or withdrawn, as the case may be, cause the child to be returned to the agency, who shall receive the child.

(4) Where the period specified in an interim order made under section 25 (whether as originally made or as extended under subsection (2) of that section) expires without an adoption order having been made in respect of the child, subsection (3) shall apply as if the application for an adoption order upon which the interim order was made, had been refused at the expiration of that period.

(5) It shall be sufficient compliance with the requirements of subsection (3) if the child is delivered to, and is received by, a suitable person nominated for the purpose by the adoption agency.

(6) Where an application for an adoption order is refused the court may, if it thinks fit at any time before the expiry of the period of 7 days mentioned in subsection (3), order that period to be extended to a duration, not exceeding 6 weeks, specified in the order.

(7) Any person who contravenes the provisions of this section shall be guilty of an offence and liable on summary conviction to imprisonment for a term not exceeding 3 months or to a fine not exceeding level 5 on the standard scale or to both; and the court by which the offender is convicted may order the child in respect of whom the offence is committed to be returned to his parent or guardian or to the adoption agency which made the arrangements referred to in subsection (1).

31 Application of s 30 where child not placed for adoption

(1) Where a person gives notice in pursuance of section 22(1) to the local authority within whose area he has his home of his intention to apply for an adoption order in respect of a child –

    (a) who is (when the notice is given) being looked after by a local authority; but

    (b) who was placed with that person otherwise than in pursuance of such arrangements as are mentioned in section 30(1),

that section shall apply as if the child had been placed in pursuance of such arrangements except that where the application is refused by the court or withdrawn the child need not be returned to the local authority in whose care he is unless that authority so require.

(2) Where notice of intention is given as aforesaid in respect of any child who is (when the notice is given) being looked after by a local authority then, until the application for an adoption order has been made and disposed of, any right of the local authority to require the child to be returned to them otherwise than in pursuance of section 30 shall be suspended.

(3) While the child has his home with the person by whom the notice is given no contribution shall be payable (whether under a contribution order or otherwise) in respect of the child by any person liable under Part III of Schedule 2 to the Children Act 1989 to make contributions in respect of him (but without prejudice to the recovery of any sum due at the time the notice is given), unless 12 weeks have elapsed since the giving of the notice without the application being made or the application has been refused by the court or withdrawn.

(4) Nothing in this section affects the right of any person who has parental responsibility for a child to remove him under section 20(8) of the Children Act 1989.

Protected children

32 Meaning of 'protected child'

(1) Where a person gives notice in pursuance of section 22(1) to the local authority within whose area he lives of his intention to apply for an adoption order in respect of a child, the child is for the purposes of this Part a protected child while he has his home with that person.

(2) A child shall be deemed to be a protected child for the purposes of this Part if he is a protected child within the meaning of –

    (a) section 32 of the Adoption (Scotland) Act 1978; or
    (b) Article 33 of the Adoption (Northern Ireland) Order 1987.

(3) A child is not a protected child by reason of any such notice as is mentioned in subsection (1) while –

    (a) he is in the care of any person –
        (i) in any children's home in respect of which a person is registered under Part II of the Care Standards Act 2000;
        (ii) in any school in which he is receiving full-time education;
        (iii) in any health service hospital; or
    (b) he is –
        (i) suffering from mental disorder within the meaning of the Mental Health Act 1983; and
        (ii) resident in a residential care home, within the meaning of Part I of Schedule 4 to the Health and Social Services and Social Security Adjudications Act 1983; or
    (c) he is liable to be detained or subject to guardianship under the Mental Health Act 1983; or

(d) he is in the care of any person in any home or institution not specified in this subsection but provided, equipped and maintained by the Secretary of State.

(3A) In subsection (3) 'children's home', 'school' and 'health service hospital' have the same meaning as in the Children Act 1989.

(4) A protected child ceases to be a protected child –

(a) on the grant or refusal of the application for an adoption order;

(b) on the notification to the local authority for the area where the child has his home that the application for an adoption order has been withdrawn;

(c) in a case where no application is made for an adoption order, on the expiry of the period of two years from the giving of the notice;

(d) on the making of a residence order, a care order or a supervision order under the Children Act 1989 in respect of the child;

(e) on the appointment of a guardian for him under that Act;

(f) on his attaining the age of 18 years; or

(g) on his marriage,

whichever first occurs.

(5) In subsection (4)(d) the references to a care order and a supervision order do not include references to an interim care order or interim supervision order.

33 Duty of local authorities to secure well-being of protected children

(1) It shall be the duty of every local authority to secure that protected children within their area are visited from time to time by officers of the authority, who shall satisfy themselves as to the well-being of the children and give such advice as to their care and maintenance as may appear to be needed.

(2) Any officer of a local authority authorised to visit protected children may, after producing, if asked to do so, some duly authenticated document showing that he is so authorised, inspect any premises in the area of the authority in which such children are to be or are being kept.

34 *(repealed)*

35 Notices and information to be given to local authorities

(1) Where a person with whom a protected child has his home changes his permanent address he shall, not less than 2 weeks before the change, or, if the change is made in an emergency, not later than one week after the change, give notice specifying the new address to the local authority in whose area his permanent address is before the change, and if the new address is in the area of another local authority, the authority to whom the notice is given shall inform that other local authority and give them such of the following particulars as are known to them, that is to say –

(a) the name, sex and date and place of birth of the child;

(b) the name and address of every person who is a parent or guardian or acts as a guardian of the child or from whom the child was received.

(2) If a protected child dies, the person with whom he had his home at his death shall within 48 hours give notice of the child's death to the local authority.

36 Offences relating to protected children

(1) A person shall be guilty of an offence if –

(a) being required, under section 35 to give any notice or information, he fails to give the notice within the time specified in that provision or fails to give the information within a reasonable time, or knowingly makes or causes or procures another person to make any false or misleading statement in the notice of information;

(b) he refuses to allow the visiting of a protected child by a duly authorised officer of a local authority or the inspection, under the power conferred by section 33(2) of any premises;

(c) (*repealed*)

(2) A person guilty of an offence under this section shall be liable on summary conviction to imprisonment for a term not exceeding 3 months or a fine not exceeding level 5 on the standard scale or both.

****

PART IV

STATUS OF ADOPTED CHILDREN

38 Meaning of 'adoption' in Part IV

(1) In this Part 'adoption' means adoption –

(a) by an adoption order;

(b) by an order made under the Children Act 1975, the Adoption Act 1958, the Adoption Act 1950 or any enactment repealed by the Adoption Act 1950;

(c) by an order made in Scotland, Northern Ireland, the Isle of Man or in any of the Channel Islands;

(cc) which is a Convention adoption;

(d) which is an overseas adoption; or

(e) which is an adoption recognised by the law of England and Wales and effected under the law of any other country,

and cognate expressions shall be construed accordingly.

(2) The definition of adoption includes, where the context admits, an adoption effected before the passing of the Children Act 1975, and the date of an adoption effected by an order is the date of the making of the order.

Section 38

Prospective amendments—Section prospectively amended by Adoption and Children Act 2002, Sch 3, para 19 (see **3.3B** below).

39 Status conferred by adoption

(1) An adopted child shall be treated in law –

(a) where the adopters are a married couple, as if he had been born as a child of the marriage (whether or not he was in fact born after the marriage was solemnised);

(b) in any other case, as if he had been born to the adopter in wedlock (but not as a child of any actual marriage of the adopter).

(2) An adopted child shall, subject to subsections (3) and (3A), be treated in law as if he were not the child of any person other than the adopters or adopter.

(3) In the case of a child adopted by one of its natural parents as sole adoptive parent, subsection (2) has no effect as respects entitlement to property depending on relationship to that parent, or as respects anything else depending on that relationship.

(3A) Where, in the case of a Convention adoption, the High Court is satisfied, on an application under this subsection –

(a) that under the law of the country in which the adoption was effected the adoption is not a full adoption;

(b) that the consents referred to in Article 4(c) and (d) of the Convention have not been given for a full adoption, or that the United Kingdom is not the receiving State (within the meaning of Article 2 of the Convention); and

(c) that it would be more favourable to the adopted child for a direction to be given under this subsection,

the Court may direct that subsection (2) shall not apply, or shall not apply to such extent as may be specified in the direction.

In this subsection 'full adoption' means an adoption by virtue of which the adopted child falls to be treated in law as if he were not the child of any person other than the adopters or adopter.

(3B) The following provisions of the Family Law Act 1986 –

(a) section 59 (provisions relating to the Attorney General); and

(b) section 60 (supplementary provision as to declarations),

shall apply in relation to, and to an application for, a direction under subsection (3A) as they apply in relation to, and to an application for, a declaration under Part III of that Act.

(4) It is hereby declared that this section prevents an adopted child from being illegitimate.

(5) This section has effect –

(a) in the case of an adoption before 1 January 1976, from that date, and

(b) in the case of any other adoption, from the date of the adoption.

(6) Subject to the provisions of this Part, this section –

(a) applies for the construction of enactments or instruments passed or made before the adoption or later, and so applies subject to any contrary indication; and

(b) has effect as respects things done, or events occurring, after the adoption, or after 31 December 1975, whichever is the later.

40 *(repealed)*

41 Adoptive relatives

A relationship existing by virtue of section 39 may be referred to as an adoptive relationship, and –

(a) a male adopter may be referred to as the adoptive father;

(b) a female adopter may be referred to as the adoptive mother;

(c) any other relative of any degree under an adoptive relationship may be referred to as an adoptive relative of that degree,

but this section does not prevent the term 'parent', or any other term not qualified by the word 'adoptive' being treated as including an adoptive relative.

****

PART VI

MISCELLANEOUS AND SUPPLEMENTAL

****

61 Evidence of agreement and consent

(1) Any agreement or consent which is required by this Act to be given to the making of an order or application for an order may be given in writing, and, if the document signifying the agreement or consent is witnessed in accordance with rules, it shall be admissible in evidence without further proof of the signature of the person by whom it was executed.

(2) A document signifying such agreement or consent which purports to be witnessed in accordance with rules shall be presumed to be so witnessed, and to have been executed and witnessed on the date and at the place specified in the document, unless the contrary is proved.

****

65 Duties of officers of the Service

(1) For the purpose of any application for an adoption order or an order freeing a child for adoption or an order under section 20 or 55 rules shall provide for the appointment, in such cases as are prescribed of an officer of the service –

(a) to act on behalf of the child upon the hearing of the application, with the duty of safeguarding the interests of the child in the prescribed manner;

(b) for the purpose of witnessing agreements to adoption and performing such other duties as the rules may prescribe.

(2) A person who is employed –

(a) in the case of an application for an adoption order, by the adoption agency
     by whom the child was placed; or

(b) in the case of an application for an order freeing a child for adoption, by the
     adoption agency by whom the application was made; or

(c) in the case of an application under section 20, by the adoption agency with
     the parental rights and duties relating to the child,

shall not be appointed to act under subsection (1) for the purposes of the application
but, subject to that, the same person may if the court thinks fit act under both
paragraphs (a) and (b) of subsection (1).

(3) Rules of court may make provision as to the assistance which an officer of the
Service may be required by the court to give it.

(4) In this section 'officer of the Service' has the same meaning as in the Criminal
Justice and Court Services Act 2000.

****

72 Interpretation

(1) In this Act, unless the context otherwise requires –

'adoption agency' in sections 11, 13, 18 to 23 and 27 to 31 includes an adoption
     agency within the meaning of –
     (a) section 1 of the Adoption (Scotland) Act 1978; and
     (b) Article 3 of the Adoption (Northern Ireland) Order 1987;
'adoption order' –
     (a) means an order under section 12(1); and
     (b) in sections 12(3) and (4), 18 to 20, 27, 28, and 30 to 32 and in the
          definition of 'British adoption order' in this subsection includes an
          order under section 12 of the Adoption (Scotland) Act 1978 and Article
          12 of the Adoption (Northern Ireland) Order 1987 (Adoption orders in
          Scotland and Northern Ireland respectively); and
     (c) in sections 27, 28 and 30 to 32 includes an order under section 55,
          section 49 of the Adoption (Scotland) Act 1978 and Article 57 of the
          Adoption (Northern Ireland) Order 1987 (orders in relation to children
          being adopted abroad);
'adoption society' means a body of persons whose functions consist of or
     include the making of arrangements for the adoption of children;
'appropriate voluntary organisation' has the meaning assigned by section 1(5);
'authorised court' shall be construed in accordance with section 62;
'body of persons' means any body of persons, whether incorporated or
     unincorporated;
'British adoption order' means –
     (a) an adoption order as defined in this subsection, and
     (b) an order under any provision for the adoption of a child effected under
          the law of any British territory outside the United Kingdom;
'British territory' means, for the purposes of any provision of this Act, any of the
     following countries, that is to say, Great Britain, Northern Ireland, the
     Channel Islands, the Isle of Man and a colony, being a country designated
     for the purposes of that provision by order of the Secretary of State or, if no
     country is so designated, any of those countries;

'child', except where used to express a relationship, means a person who has not attained the age of 18 years;

'the Convention' means the Convention on Protection of Children and Co-operation in respect of Intercountry Adoption, concluded at the Hague on 29 May 1993;

'Convention adoption' means an adoption effected under the law of a Convention country outside the British Islands, and certified in pursuance of Article 23(1) of the Convention;

'Convention adoption order' means an adoption order made in accordance with section 17;

'Convention country' means any country or territory in which the Convention is in force.

'existing' in relation to an enactment or other instrument, means one passed or made at any time before 1 January 1976;

'guardian' has the same meaning as in the Children Act 1989;

'internal law' has the meaning assigned by section 71;

'local authority' means the council of a county (other than a metropolitan county), a metropolitan district, a London borough or the Common Council of the City of London but, in relation to Wales, means the council of a county or county borough;

'notice' means a notice in writing;

'order freeing a child for adoption' means an order under section 18 and in sections 27(2) and 59 includes an order under –

    (a)   section 18 of the Adoption (Scotland) Act 1978; and

    (b)   Article 17 or 18 of the Adoption (Northern Ireland) Act 1987;

'overseas adoption' has the meaning assigned by subsection (2);

'parent' means, in relation to a child, any parent who has parental responsibility for the child under the Children Act 1989;

'parental responsibility' and 'parental responsibility agreement' have the same meaning as in the Children Act 1989;

'prescribed' means prescribed by rules;

'relative' in relation to a child means grandparent, brother, sister, uncle or aunt, whether of the full blood or half-blood or by affinity and includes, where the child is illegitimate, the father of the child and any person who would be a relative within the meaning of this definition if the child were the legitimate child of his mother and father;

'rules' means rules made under section 66(1) or made by virtue of section 66(2) under section 144 of the Magistrates' Courts Act 1980;

'United Kingdom national' means, for the purposes for any provision of this Act, a citizen of the United Kingdom and colonies satisfying such conditions, if any, as the Secretary of State may by order specify for the purposes of that provision;

'upbringing' has the same meaning as in the Children Act 1989;

'voluntary organisation' means a body other than a public or local authority the activities of which are not carried on for profit.

(1A) In this Act, in determining with what person, or where, a child has his home, any absence of the child at a hospital or boarding school and any other temporary absence shall be disregarded.

(1B) In this Act, references to a child who is in the care of or looked after by a local authority have the same meaning as in the Children Act 1989.

(2) In this Act 'overseas adoption' means an adoption of such a description as the Secretary of State may by order specify, being a description of adoptions of children appearing to him to be effected under the law of any country outside the British Islands; and an order under this subsection may contain provision as to the manner in which evidence of an overseas adoption may be given.

(3) For the purposes of this Act a person shall be deemed to make arrangements for the adoption of a child if he enters into or makes any agreement for, or for facilitating, the adoption of the child by any other person, whether the adoption is effected, or is intended to be effected, in Great Britain or elsewhere, or if he initiates or takes part in any negotiations of which the purpose or effect is the conclusion of any agreement or the making of any arrangement therefor, and if he causes another person to do so.

(3A) In this Act, in relation to the proposed adoption of a child resident outside the British Islands, references to arrangements for the adoption of a child include references to arrangements for an assessment for the purpose of indicating whether a person is suitable to adopt a child or not.

(3B) *(repealed)*

(4) Except so far as the context otherwise requires, any reference in this Act to an enactment shall be construed as a reference to that enactment as amended by or under any other enactment, including this Act.

(5) In this Act, except where otherwise indicated –

  (a) a reference to a numbered Part, section or Schedule is a reference to the Part or section of, or the Schedule to, this Act so numbered, and
  (b) a reference in a section to a numbered subsection is a reference to the subsection of that section so numbered, and
  (c) a reference in a section, subsection or Schedule to a numbered paragraph is a reference to the paragraph of that section, subsection or schedule so numbered.

****

3.3B ADOPTION AND CHILDREN ACT 2002
(ss 1–68, 74, 77–104, 109–131, 135–150, Schs 1–3, 6)

Note on commencement—The following provisions are fully in force as at 1 February 2005: ss 2, 4(6), (7), 9–11, 16, 27(3), 45, 53(1)–(3), 54, 63–65, 87(1)(b), (4), 98, 108, 111, 116, 118–120, 122(1)(b), (2), 135–136, 140–146, 148–150, Sch 3, paras 6, 7, 53, 105–106, 118, Sch 4, paras 3–5, 10, 13, 14, Sch 6.

PART 1

ADOPTION

Chapter 1
Introductory

1 Considerations applying to the exercise of powers

(1) This section applies whenever a court or adoption agency is coming to a decision relating to the adoption of a child.

(2) The paramount consideration of the court or adoption agency must be the child's welfare, throughout his life.

(3) The court or adoption agency must at all times bear in mind that, in general, any delay in coming to the decision is likely to prejudice the child's welfare.

(4) The court or adoption agency must have regard to the following matters (among others) –

    (a) the child's ascertainable wishes and feelings regarding the decision (considered in the light of the child's age and understanding),
    (b) the child's particular needs,
    (c) the likely effect on the child (throughout his life) of having ceased to be a member of the original family and become an adopted person,
    (d) the child's age, sex, background and any of the child's characteristics which the court or agency considers relevant,
    (e) any harm (within the meaning of the Children Act 1989) which the child has suffered or is at risk of suffering,
    (f) the relationship which the child has with relatives, and with any other person in relation to whom the court or agency considers the relationship to be relevant, including –
        (i) the likelihood of any such relationship continuing and the value to the child of its doing so,
        (ii) the ability and willingness of any of the child's relatives, or of any such person, to provide the child with a secure environment in which the child can develop, and otherwise to meet the child's needs,

(iii) the wishes and feelings of any of the child's relatives, or of any such person, regarding the child.

(5) In placing the child for adoption, the adoption agency must give due consideration to the child's religious persuasion, racial origin and cultural and linguistic background.

(6) The court or adoption agency must always consider the whole range of powers available to it in the child's case (whether under this Act or the Children Act 1989); and the court must not make any order under this Act unless it considers that making the order would be better for the child than not doing so.

(7) In this section, 'coming to a decision relating to the adoption of a child', in relation to a court, includes –

(a) coming to a decision in any proceedings where the orders that might be made by the court include an adoption order (or the revocation of such an order), a placement order (or the revocation of such an order) or an order under section 26 (or the revocation or variation of such an order),

(b) coming to a decision about granting leave in respect of any action (other than the initiation of proceedings in any court) which may be taken by an adoption agency or individual under this Act,

but does not include coming to a decision about granting leave in any other circumstances.

(8) For the purposes of this section –

(a) references to relationships are not confined to legal relationships,

(b) references to a relative, in relation to a child, include the child's mother and father.

Chapter 2
The Adoption Service

2 Basic definitions

(1) The services maintained by local authorities under section 3(1) may be collectively referred to as 'the Adoption Service', and a local authority or registered adoption society may be referred to as an adoption agency.

(2) In this Act, 'registered adoption society' means a voluntary organisation which is an adoption society registered under Part 2 of the Care Standards Act 2000; but in relation to the provision of any facility of the Adoption Service, references to a registered adoption society or to an adoption agency do not include an adoption society which is not registered in respect of that facility.

(3) A registered adoption society is to be treated as registered in respect of any facility of the Adoption Service unless it is a condition of its registration that it does not provide that facility.

(4) No application for registration under Part 2 of the Care Standards Act 2000 may be made in respect of an adoption society which is an unincorporated body.

(5) In this Act –

'the 1989 Act' means the Children Act 1989,

'adoption society' means a body whose functions consist of or include making arrangements for the adoption of children,

'voluntary organisation' means a body other than a public or local authority the activities of which are not carried on for profit.

(6) In this Act, 'adoption support services' means –

    (a)   counselling, advice and information, and

    (b)   any other services prescribed by regulations,

in relation to adoption.

(7) The power to make regulations under subsection (6)(b) is to be exercised so as to secure that local authorities provide financial support.

(8) In this Chapter, references to adoption are to the adoption of persons, wherever they may be habitually resident, effected under the law of any country or territory, whether within or outside the British Islands.

3 Maintenance of Adoption Service

(1) Each local authority must continue to maintain within their area a service designed to meet the needs, in relation to adoption, of –

    (a)   children who may be adopted, their parents and guardians,

    (b)   persons wishing to adopt a child, and

    (c)   adopted persons, their parents, natural parents and former guardians;

and for that purpose must provide the requisite facilities.

(2) Those facilities must include making, and participating in, arrangements –

    (a)   for the adoption of children, and

    (b)   for the provision of adoption support services.

(3) As part of the service, the arrangements made for the purposes of subsection (2)(b) –

    (a)   must extend to the provision of adoption support services to persons who are within a description prescribed by regulations,

    (b)   may extend to the provision of those services to other persons.

(4) A local authority may provide any of the requisite facilities by securing their provision by –

    (a)   registered adoption societies, or

    (b)   other persons who are within a description prescribed by regulations of persons who may provide the facilities in question.

(5) The facilities of the service must be provided in conjunction with the local authority's other social services and with registered adoption societies in their area, so that help may be given in a co-ordinated manner without duplication, omission or avoidable delay.

(6) The social services referred to in subsection (5) are the functions of a local authority which are social services functions within the meaning of the Local Authority Social Services Act 1970 (which include, in particular, those functions in so far as they relate to children).

4 Assessments etc for adoption support services

(1) A local authority must at the request of –

    (a) any of the persons mentioned in paragraphs (a) to (c) of section 3(1), or

    (b) any other person who falls within a description prescribed by regulations (subject to subsection (7)(a)),

carry out an assessment of that person's needs for adoption support services.

(2) A local authority may, at the request of any person, carry out an assessment of that person's needs for adoption support services.

(3) A local authority may request the help of the persons mentioned in paragraph (a) or (b) of section 3(4) in carrying out an assessment.

(4) Where, as a result of an assessment, a local authority decide that a person has needs for adoption support services, they must then decide whether to provide any such services to that person.

(5) If –

    (a) a local authority decide to provide any adoption support services to a person, and

    (b) the circumstances fall within a description prescribed by regulations,

the local authority must prepare a plan in accordance with which adoption support services are to be provided to the person and keep the plan under review.

(6) Regulations may make provision about assessments, preparing and reviewing plans, the provision of adoption support services in accordance with plans and reviewing the provision of adoption support services.

(7) The regulations may in particular make provision –

    (a) as to the circumstances in which a person mentioned in paragraph (b) of subsection (1) is to have a right to request an assessment of his needs in accordance with that subsection,

    (b) about the type of assessment which, or the way in which an assessment, is to be carried out,

    (c) about the way in which a plan is to be prepared,

    (d) about the way in which, and time at which, a plan or the provision of adoption support services is to be reviewed,

    (e) about the considerations to which a local authority are to have regard in carrying out an assessment or review or preparing a plan,

    (f) as to the circumstances in which a local authority may provide adoption support services subject to conditions,

    (g) as to the consequences of conditions imposed by virtue of paragraph (f) not being met (including the recovery of any financial support provided by a local authority),

    (h) as to the circumstances in which this section may apply to a local authority in respect of persons who are outside that local authority's area,

    (i) as to the circumstances in which a local authority may recover from another local authority the expenses of providing adoption support services to any person.

(8) A local authority may carry out an assessment of the needs of any person under this section at the same time as an assessment of his needs is made under any other enactment.

(9) If at any time during the assessment of the needs of any person under this section, it appears to a local authority that –

(a) there may be a need for the provision of services to that person by a Primary Care Trust (in Wales, a Health Authority or Local Health Board), or

(b) there may be a need for the provision to him of any services which fall within the functions of a local education authority (within the meaning of the Education Act 1996),

the local authority must notify that Primary Care Trust, Health Authority, Local Health Board or local education authority.

(10) Where it appears to a local authority that another local authority could, by taking any specified action, help in the exercise of any of their functions under this section, they may request the help of that other local authority, specifying the action in question.

(11) A local authority whose help is so requested must comply with the request if it is consistent with the exercise of their functions.

5 Local authority plans for adoption services

(1) Each local authority must prepare a plan for the provision of the services maintained under section 3(1) and secure that it is published.

(2) The plan must contain information of a description prescribed by regulations (subject to subsection (4)(b)).

(3) The regulations may make provision requiring local authorities –

(a) to review any plan,

(b) in the circumstances prescribed by the regulations, to modify that plan and secure its publication or to prepare a plan in substitution for that plan and secure its publication.

(4) The appropriate Minister may direct –

(a) that a plan is to be included in another document specified in the direction,

(b) that the requirements specified in the direction as to the description of information to be contained in a plan are to have effect in place of the provision made by regulations under subsection (2).

(5) Directions may be given by the appropriate Minister for the purpose of making provision in connection with any duty imposed by virtue of this section including, in particular, provision as to –

(a) the form and manner in which, and the time at which, any plan is to be published,

(b) the description of persons who are to be consulted in the preparation of any plan,

(c) the time at which any plan is to be reviewed.

(6) Subsections (2) to (5) apply in relation to a modified or substituted plan (or further modified or substituted plan) as they apply in relation to a plan prepared under subsection (1).

(7) Directions given under this section may relate –

(a) to a particular local authority,
(b) to any class or description of local authorities, or
(c) except in the case of a direction given under subsection (4)(b), to local authorities generally,

and accordingly different provision may be made in relation to different local authorities or classes or descriptions of local authorities.

6 Arrangements on cancellation of registration

Where, by virtue of the cancellation of its registration under Part 2 of the Care Standards Act 2000, a body has ceased to be a registered adoption society, the appropriate Minister may direct the body to make such arrangements as to the transfer of its functions relating to children and other transitional matters as seem to him expedient.

7 Inactive or defunct adoption societies etc

(1) This section applies where it appears to the appropriate Minister that –

(a) a body which is or has been a registered adoption society is inactive or defunct, or
(b) a body which has ceased to be a registered adoption society by virtue of the cancellation of its registration under Part 2 of the Care Standards Act 2000 has not made such arrangements for the transfer of its functions relating to children as are specified in a direction given by him.

(2) The appropriate Minister may, in relation to such functions of the society as relate to children, direct what appears to him to be the appropriate local authority to take any such action as might have been taken by the society or by the society jointly with the authority.

(3) A local authority are entitled to take any action which –

(a) apart from this subsection the authority would not be entitled to take, or would not be entitled to take without joining the society in the action, but
(b) they are directed to take under subsection (2).

(4) The appropriate Minister may charge the society for expenses necessarily incurred by him or on his behalf in securing the transfer of its functions relating to children.

(5) Before giving a direction under subsection (2) the appropriate Minister must, if practicable, consult both the society and the authority.

8 Adoption support agencies

(1) In this Act, 'adoption support agency' means an undertaking the purpose of which, or one of the purposes of which, is the provision of adoption support services; but an undertaking is not an adoption support agency –

(a) merely because it provides information in connection with adoption other than for the purpose mentioned in section 98(1), or

(b) if it is excepted by virtue of subsection (2).

'Undertaking' has the same meaning as in the Care Standards Act 2000.

(2) The following are excepted –

(a) a registered adoption society, whether or not the society is registered in respect of the provision of adoption support services,

(b) a local authority,

(c) a local education authority (within the meaning of the Education Act 1996),

(d) a Special Health Authority, Primary Care Trust (in Wales, a Health Authority or Local Health Board) or NHS trust,

(e) the Registrar General,

(f) any person, or description of persons, excepted by regulations.

(3) In section 4 of the Care Standards Act 2000 (basic definitions) –

(a) after subsection (7) there is inserted –

'(7A) 'Adoption support agency' has the meaning given by section 8 of the Adoption and Children Act 2002.',

(b) in subsection (9)(a) (construction of references to descriptions of agencies), for 'or a voluntary adoption agency' there is substituted 'a voluntary adoption agency or an adoption support agency'.

Regulations

9 General power to regulate adoption etc agencies

(1) Regulations may make provision for any purpose relating to –

(a) the exercise by local authorities or voluntary adoption agencies of their functions in relation to adoption, or

(b) the exercise by adoption support agencies of their functions in relation to adoption.

(2) The extent of the power to make regulations under this section is not limited by sections 10 to 12, 45, 54, 56 to 65 and 98 or by any other powers exercisable in respect of local authorities, voluntary adoption agencies or adoption support agencies.

(3) Regulations may provide that a person who contravenes or fails to comply with any provision of regulations under this section is to be guilty of an offence and liable on summary conviction to a fine not exceeding level 5 on the standard scale.

(4) In this section and section 10, 'voluntary adoption agency' means a voluntary organisation which is an adoption society.

10 Management etc of agencies

(1) In relation to local authorities, voluntary adoption agencies and adoption support agencies, regulations under section 9 may make provision as to –

(a) the persons who are fit to work for them for the purposes of the functions mentioned in section 9(1),

(b) the fitness of premises,

   (c) the management and control of their operations,

   (d) the number of persons, or persons of any particular type, working for the purposes of those functions,

   (e) the management and training of persons working for the purposes of those functions,

   (f) the keeping of information.

(2) Regulations made by virtue of subsection (1)(a) may, in particular, make provision for prohibiting persons from working in prescribed positions unless they are registered in, or in a particular part of, one of the registers maintained under section 56(1) of the Care Standards Act 2000 (registration of social care workers).

(3) In relation to voluntary adoption agencies and adoption support agencies, regulations under section 9 may –

   (a) make provision as to the persons who are fit to manage an agency, including provision prohibiting persons from doing so unless they are registered in, or in a particular part of, one of the registers referred to in subsection (2),

   (b) impose requirements as to the financial position of an agency,

   (c) make provision requiring the appointment of a manager,

   (d) in the case of a voluntary adoption agency, make provision for securing the welfare of children placed by the agency, including provision as to the promotion and protection of their health,

   (e) in the case of an adoption support agency, make provision as to the persons who are fit to carry on the agency.

(4) Regulations under section 9 may make provision as to the conduct of voluntary adoption agencies and adoption support agencies, and may in particular make provision –

   (a) as to the facilities and services to be provided by an agency,

   (b) as to the keeping of accounts,

   (c) as to the notification to the registration authority of events occurring in premises used for the purposes of an agency,

   (d) as to the giving of notice to the registration authority of periods during which the manager of an agency proposes to be absent, and specifying the information to be given in such a notice,

   (e) as to the making of adequate arrangements for the running of an agency during a period when its manager is absent,

   (f) as to the giving of notice to the registration authority of any intended change in the identity of the manager,

   (g) as to the giving of notice to the registration authority of changes in the ownership of an agency or the identity of its officers,

   (h) requiring the payment of a prescribed fee to the registration authority in respect of any notification required to be made by virtue of paragraph (g),

   (i) requiring arrangements to be made for dealing with complaints made by or on behalf of those seeking, or receiving, any of the services provided by an agency and requiring the agency or manager to take steps for publicising the arrangements.

11 Fees

(1) Regulations under section 9 may prescribe –

(a) the fees which may be charged by adoption agencies in respect of the provision of services to persons providing facilities as part of the Adoption Service (including the Adoption Services in Scotland and Northern Ireland),

(b) the fees which may be paid by adoption agencies to persons providing or assisting in providing such facilities.

(2) Regulations under section 9 may prescribe the fees which may be charged by local authorities in respect of the provision of prescribed facilities of the Adoption Service where the following conditions are met.

(3) The conditions are that the facilities are provided in connection with –

(a) the adoption of a child brought into the United Kingdom for the purpose of adoption, or

(b) a Convention adoption, an overseas adoption or an adoption effected under the law of a country or territory outside the British Islands.

(4) Regulations under section 9 may prescribe the fees which may be charged by adoption agencies in respect of the provision of counselling, where the counselling is provided in connection with the disclosure of information in relation to a person's adoption.

12 Independent review of determinations

(1) Regulations under section 9 may establish a procedure under which any person in respect of whom a qualifying determination has been made by an adoption agency may apply to a panel constituted by the appropriate Minister for a review of that determination.

(2) The regulations must make provision as to the description of determinations which are qualifying determinations for the purposes of subsection (1).

(3) The regulations may include provision as to –

(a) the duties and powers of a panel (including the power to recover the costs of a review from the adoption agency by which the determination reviewed was made),

(b) the administration and procedures of a panel,

(c) the appointment of members of a panel (including the number, or any limit on the number, of members who may be appointed and any conditions for appointment),

(d) the payment of expenses of members of a panel,

(e) the duties of adoption agencies in connection with reviews conducted under the regulations,

(f) the monitoring of any such reviews.

(4) The appropriate Minister may make an arrangement with an organisation under which functions in relation to the panel are performed by the organisation on his behalf.

(5) If the appropriate Minister makes such an arrangement with an organisation, the organisation is to perform its functions under the arrangement in accordance with any general or special directions given by the appropriate Minister.

(6) The arrangement may include provision for payments to be made to the organisation by the appropriate Minister.

(7) Where the appropriate Minister is the Assembly, subsections (4) and (6) also apply as if references to an organisation included references to the Secretary of State.

(8) In this section, 'organisation' includes a public body and a private or voluntary organisation.

Supplemental

13 Information concerning adoption

(1) Each adoption agency must give to the appropriate Minister any statistical or other general information he requires about –

    (a) its performance of all or any of its functions relating to adoption,
    (b) the children and other persons in relation to whom it has exercised those functions.

(2) The following persons –

    (a) the justices' chief executive for each magistrates' court,
    (b) the relevant officer of each county court,
    (c) the relevant officer of the High Court,

must give to the appropriate Minister any statistical or other general information he requires about the proceedings under this Act of the court in question.

(3) In subsection (2), 'relevant officer', in relation to a county court or the High Court, means the officer of that court who is designated to act for the purposes of that subsection by a direction given by the Lord Chancellor.

(4) The information required to be given to the appropriate Minister under this section must be given at the times, and in the form, directed by him.

(5) The appropriate Minister may publish from time to time abstracts of the information given to him under this section.

14 Default power of appropriate Minister

(1) If the appropriate Minister is satisfied that any local authority have failed, without reasonable excuse, to comply with any of the duties imposed on them by virtue of this Act or of section 1 or 2(4) of the Adoption (Intercountry Aspects) Act 1999 , he may make an order declaring that authority to be in default in respect of that duty.

(2) An order under subsection (1) must give the appropriate Minister's reasons for making it.

(3) An order under subsection (1) may contain such directions as appear to the appropriate Minister to be necessary for the purpose of ensuring that, within the period specified in the order, the duty is complied with.

(4) Any such directions are enforceable, on the appropriate Minister's application, by a mandatory order.

15 Inspection of premises etc

(1) The appropriate Minister may arrange for any premises in which –

(a) a child is living with a person with whom the child has been placed by an adoption agency, or

(b) a child in respect of whom a notice of intention to adopt has been given under section 44 is, or will be, living,

to be inspected from time to time.

(2) The appropriate Minister may require an adoption agency –

(a) to give him any information, or

(b) to allow him to inspect any records (in whatever form they are held),

relating to the discharge of any of its functions in relation to adoption which the appropriate Minister specifies.

(3) An inspection under this section must be conducted by a person authorised by the appropriate Minister.

(4) An officer of a local authority may only be so authorised with the consent of the authority.

(5) A person inspecting any premises under subsection (1) may –

(a) visit the child there,

(b) make any examination into the state of the premises and the treatment of the child there which he thinks fit.

(6) A person authorised to inspect any records under this section may at any reasonable time have access to, and inspect and check the operation of, any computer (and associated apparatus) which is being or has been used in connection with the records in question.

(7) A person authorised to inspect any premises or records under this section may –

(a) enter the premises for that purpose at any reasonable time,

(b) require any person to give him any reasonable assistance he may require.

(8) A person exercising a power under this section must, if required to do so, produce a duly authenticated document showing his authority.

(9) Any person who intentionally obstructs another in the exercise of a power under this section is guilty of an offence and liable on summary conviction to a fine not exceeding level 3 on the standard scale.

16 Distribution of functions in relation to registered adoption societies

After section 36 of the Care Standards Act 2000 there is inserted –

'36A Voluntary adoption agencies: distribution of functions

(1) This section applies to functions relating to voluntary adoption agencies conferred on the registration authority by or under this Part or under Chapter 2 of Part 1 of the Adoption and Children Act 2002.

(2) Subject to the following provisions, functions to which this section applies are exercisable –

(a) where the principal office of an agency is in England, by the Commission,

(b)   where the principal office of an agency is in Wales, by the Assembly.

(3) So far as those functions relate to the imposition, variation or removal of conditions of registration, they may only be exercised after consultation with the Assembly or (as the case may be) the Commission.

(4) But –

(a)   where such a function as is mentioned in subsection (3) is exercisable by the Commission in relation to an agency which has a branch in Wales, it is exercisable only with the agreement of the Assembly,

(b)   where such a function as is mentioned in subsection (3) is exercisable by the Assembly in relation to an agency which has a branch in England, it is exercisable only with the agreement of the Commission.

(5) The functions conferred on the registration authority by sections 31 and 32 of this Act in respect of any premises of a voluntary adoption agency are exercisable –

(a)   where the premises are in England, by the Commission

(b)   where the premises are in Wales, by the Assembly.

(6) In spite of subsections (2) to (5), regulations may provide for any function to which this section applies to be exercisable by the Commission instead of the Assembly, or by the Assembly instead of the Commission, or by one concurrently with the other, or by both jointly or by either with the agreement of or after consultation with the other.

(7) In this section, "regulations" means regulations relating to England and Wales.'

17 Inquiries

(1) The appropriate Minister may cause an inquiry to be held into any matter connected with the functions of an adoption agency.

(2) Before an inquiry is begun, the appropriate Minister may direct that it is to be held in private.

(3) Where no direction has been given, the person holding the inquiry may if he thinks fit hold it, or any part of it, in private.

(4) Subsections (2) to (5) of section 250 of the Local Government Act 1972 (powers in relation to local inquiries) apply in relation to an inquiry under this section as they apply in relation to a local inquiry under that section.

Chapter 3
Placement for Adoption and Adoption Orders

Placement of children by adoption agency for adoption

18 Placement for adoption by agencies

(1) An adoption agency may –

(a) place a child for adoption with prospective adopters, or

(b) where it has placed a child with any persons (whether under this Part or not), leave the child with them as prospective adopters,

but, except in the case of a child who is less than six weeks old, may only do so under section 19 or a placement order.

(2) An adoption agency may only place a child for adoption with prospective adopters if the agency is satisfied that the child ought to be placed for adoption.

(3) A child who is placed or authorised to be placed for adoption with prospective adopters by a local authority is looked after by the authority.

(4) If an application for an adoption order has been made by any persons in respect of a child and has not been disposed of –

(a) an adoption agency which placed the child with those persons may leave the child with them until the application is disposed of, but

(b) apart from that, the child may not be placed for adoption with any prospective adopters.

'Adoption order' includes a Scottish or Northern Irish adoption order.

(5) References in this Act (apart from this section) to an adoption agency placing a child for adoption –

(a) are to its placing a child for adoption with prospective adopters, and

(b) include, where it has placed a child with any persons (whether under this Act or not), leaving the child with them as prospective adopters;

and references in this Act (apart from this section) to a child who is placed for adoption by an adoption agency are to be interpreted accordingly.

(6) References in this Chapter to an adoption agency being, or not being, authorised to place a child for adoption are to the agency being or (as the case may be) not being authorised to do so under section 19 or a placement order.

(7) This section is subject to sections 30 to 35 (removal of children placed by adoption agencies).

19 Placing children with parental consent

(1) Where an adoption agency is satisfied that each parent or guardian of a child has consented to the child –

(a) being placed for adoption with prospective adopters identified in the consent, or

(b) being placed for adoption with any prospective adopters who may be chosen by the agency,

and has not withdrawn the consent, the agency is authorised to place the child for adoption accordingly.

(2) Consent to a child being placed for adoption with prospective adopters identified in the consent may be combined with consent to the child subsequently being placed for adoption with any prospective adopters who may be chosen by the agency in circumstances where the child is removed from or returned by the identified prospective adopters.

(3) Subsection (1) does not apply where –

(a) an application has been made on which a care order might be made and the application has not been disposed of, or

(b) a care order or placement order has been made after the consent was given.

(4) References in this Act to a child placed for adoption under this section include a child who was placed under this section with prospective adopters and continues to be placed with them, whether or not consent to the placement has been withdrawn.

(5) This section is subject to section 52 (parental etc consent).

20 Advance consent to adoption

(1) A parent or guardian of a child who consents to the child being placed for adoption by an adoption agency under section 19 may, at the same or any subsequent time, consent to the making of a future adoption order.

(2) Consent under this section –

(a) where the parent or guardian has consented to the child being placed for adoption with prospective adopters identified in the consent, may be consent to adoption by them, or

(b) may be consent to adoption by any prospective adopters who may be chosen by the agency.

(3) A person may withdraw any consent given under this section.

(4) A person who gives consent under this section may, at the same or any subsequent time, by notice given to the adoption agency –

(a) state that he does not wish to be informed of any application for an adoption order, or

(b) withdraw such a statement.

(5) A notice under subsection (4) has effect from the time when it is received by the adoption agency but has no effect if the person concerned has withdrawn his consent.

(6) This section is subject to section 52 (parental etc consent).

21 Placement orders

(1) A placement order is an order made by the court authorising a local authority to place a child for adoption with any prospective adopters who may be chosen by the authority.

(2) The court may not make a placement order in respect of a child unless –

(a) the child is subject to a care order,

(b) the court is satisfied that the conditions in section 31(2) of the 1989 Act (conditions for making a care order) are met, or

(c) the child has no parent or guardian.

(3) The court may only make a placement order if, in the case of each parent or guardian of the child, the court is satisfied –

(a) that the parent or guardian has consented to the child being placed for adoption with any prospective adopters who may be chosen by the local authority and has not withdrawn the consent, or

(b) that the parent's or guardian's consent should be dispensed with.

This subsection is subject to section 52 (parental etc consent).

(4) A placement order continues in force until –

    (a) it is revoked under section 24,

    (b) an adoption order is made in respect of the child, or

    (c) the child marries or attains the age of 18 years.

'Adoption order' includes a Scottish or Northern Irish adoption order.

22 Applications for placement orders

(1) A local authority must apply to the court for a placement order in respect of a child if –

    (a) the child is placed for adoption by them or is being provided with accommodation by them,

    (b) no adoption agency is authorised to place the child for adoption,

    (c) the child has no parent or guardian or the authority consider that the conditions in section 31(2) of the 1989 Act are met, and

    (d) the authority are satisfied that the child ought to be placed for adoption.

(2) If –

    (a) an application has been made (and has not been disposed of) on which a care order might be made in respect of a child, or

    (b) a child is subject to a care order and the appropriate local authority are not authorised to place the child for adoption,

the appropriate local authority must apply to the court for a placement order if they are satisfied that the child ought to be placed for adoption.

(3) If –

    (a) a child is subject to a care order, and

    (b) the appropriate local authority are authorised to place the child for adoption under section 19,

the authority may apply to the court for a placement order.

(4) If a local authority –

    (a) are under a duty to apply to the court for a placement order in respect of a child, or

    (b) have applied for a placement order in respect of a child and the application has not been disposed of,

the child is looked after by the authority.

(5) Subsections (1) to (3) do not apply in respect of a child –

    (a) if any persons have given notice of intention to adopt, unless the period of four months beginning with the giving of the notice has expired without them applying for an adoption order or their application for such an order has been withdrawn or refused, or

    (b) if an application for an adoption order has been made and has not been disposed of.

'Adoption order' includes a Scottish or Northern Irish adoption order.

(6) Where –

(a) an application for a placement order in respect of a child has been made and has not been disposed of, and
(b) no interim care order is in force,

the court may give any directions it considers appropriate for the medical or psychiatric examination or other assessment of the child; but a child who is of sufficient understanding to make an informed decision may refuse to submit to the examination or other assessment.

(7) The appropriate local authority –

(a) in relation to a care order, is the local authority in whose care the child is placed by the order, and
(b) in relation to an application on which a care order might be made, is the local authority which makes the application.

23 Varying placement orders

(1) The court may vary a placement order so as to substitute another local authority for the local authority authorised by the order to place the child for adoption.

(2) The variation may only be made on the joint application of both authorities.

24 Revoking placement orders

(1) The court may revoke a placement order on the application of any person.

(2) But an application may not be made by a person other than the child or the local authority authorised by the order to place the child for adoption unless –

(a) the court has given leave to apply, and
(b) the child is not placed for adoption by the authority.

(3) The court cannot give leave under subsection (2)(a) unless satisfied that there has been a change in circumstances since the order was made.

(4) If the court determines, on an application for an adoption order, not to make the order, it may revoke any placement order in respect of the child.

(5) Where –

(a) an application for the revocation of a placement order has been made and has not been disposed of, and
(b) the child is not placed for adoption by the authority,

the child may not without the court's leave be placed for adoption under the order.

25 Parental responsibility

(1) This section applies while –

(a) a child is placed for adoption under section 19 or an adoption agency is authorised to place a child for adoption under that section, or
(b) a placement order is in force in respect of a child.

(2) Parental responsibility for the child is given to the agency concerned.

(3) While the child is placed with prospective adopters, parental responsibility is given to them.

(4) The agency may determine that the parental responsibility of any parent or guardian, or of prospective adopters, is to be restricted to the extent specified in the determination.

26 Contact

(1) On an adoption agency being authorised to place a child for adoption, or placing a child for adoption who is less than six weeks old, any provision for contact under the 1989 Act ceases to have effect.

(2) While an adoption agency is so authorised or a child is placed for adoption –

    (a) no application may be made for any provision for contact under that Act, but

    (b) the court may make an order under this section requiring the person with whom the child lives, or is to live, to allow the child to visit or stay with the person named in the order, or for the person named in the order and the child otherwise to have contact with each other.

(3) An application for an order under this section may be made by –

    (a) the child or the agency,

    (b) any parent, guardian or relative,

    (c) any person in whose favour there was provision for contact under the 1989 Act which ceased to have effect by virtue of subsection (1),

    (d) if a residence order was in force immediately before the adoption agency was authorised to place the child for adoption or (as the case may be) placed the child for adoption at a time when he was less than six weeks old, the person in whose favour the order was made,

    (e) if a person had care of the child immediately before that time by virtue of an order made in the exercise of the High Court's inherent jurisdiction with respect to children, that person,

    (f) any person who has obtained the court's leave to make the application.

(4) When making a placement order, the court may on its own initiative make an order under this section.

(5) This section does not prevent an application for a contact order under section 8 of the 1989 Act being made where the application is to be heard together with an application for an adoption order in respect of the child.

(6) In this section, 'provision for contact under the 1989 Act' means a contact order under section 8 of that Act or an order under section 34 of that Act (parental contact with children in care).

27 Contact: supplementary

(1) An order under section 26 –

    (a) has effect while the adoption agency is authorised to place the child for adoption or the child is placed for adoption, but

    (b) may be varied or revoked by the court on an application by the child, the agency or a person named in the order.

(2) The agency may refuse to allow the contact that would otherwise be required by virtue of an order under that section if –

    (a) it is satisfied that it is necessary to do so in order to safeguard or promote the child's welfare, and

    (b) the refusal is decided upon as a matter of urgency and does not last for more than seven days.

(3) Regulations may make provision as to –

    (a) the steps to be taken by an agency which has exercised its power under subsection (2),

    (b) the circumstances in which, and conditions subject to which, the terms of any order under section 26 may be departed from by agreement between the agency and any person for whose contact with the child the order provides,

    (c) notification by an agency of any variation or suspension of arrangements made (otherwise than under an order under that section) with a view to allowing any person contact with the child.

(4) Before making a placement order the court must –

    (a) consider the arrangements which the adoption agency has made, or proposes to make, for allowing any person contact with the child, and

    (b) invite the parties to the proceedings to comment on those arrangements.

(5) An order under section 26 may provide for contact on any conditions the court considers appropriate.

28 Further consequences of placement

(1) Where a child is placed for adoption under section 19 or an adoption agency is authorised to place a child for adoption under that section –

    (a) a parent or guardian of the child may not apply for a residence order unless an application for an adoption order has been made and the parent or guardian has obtained the court's leave under subsection (3) or (5) of section 47,

    (b) if an application has been made for an adoption order, a guardian of the child may not apply for a special guardianship order unless he has obtained the court's leave under subsection (3) or (5) of that section.

(2) Where –

    (a) a child is placed for adoption under section 19 or an adoption agency is authorised to place a child for adoption under that section, or

    (b) a placement order is in force in respect of a child,

then (whether or not the child is in England and Wales) a person may not do either of the following things, unless the court gives leave or each parent or guardian of the child gives written consent.

(3) Those things are –

    (a) causing the child to be known by a new surname, or

    (b) removing the child from the United Kingdom.

(4) Subsection (3) does not prevent the removal of a child from the United Kingdom for a period of less than one month by a person who provides the child's home.

29 Further consequences of placement orders

(1) Where a placement order is made in respect of a child and either –

(a) the child is subject to a care order, or

(b) the court at the same time makes a care order in respect of the child,

the care order does not have effect at any time when the placement order is in force.

(2) On the making of a placement order in respect of a child, any order mentioned in section 8(1) of the 1989 Act, and any supervision order in respect of the child, ceases to have effect.

(3) Where a placement order is in force –

(a) no prohibited steps order, residence order or specific issue order, and

(b) no supervision order or child assessment order,

may be made in respect of the child.

(4) Subsection (3)(a) does not apply in respect of a residence order if –

(a) an application for an adoption order has been made in respect of the child, and

(b) the residence order is applied for by a parent or guardian who has obtained the court's leave under subsection (3) or (5) of section 47 or by any other person who has obtained the court's leave under this subsection.

(5) Where a placement order is in force, no special guardianship order may be made in respect of the child unless –

(a) an application has been made for an adoption order, and

(b) the person applying for the special guardianship order has obtained the court's leave under this subsection or, if he is a guardian of the child, has obtained the court's leave under section 47(5).

(6) Section 14A(7) of the 1989 Act applies in respect of an application for a special guardianship order for which leave has been given as mentioned in subsection (5)(b) with the omission of the words 'the beginning of the period of three months ending with'.

(7) Where a placement order is in force –

(a) section 14C(1)(b) of the 1989 Act (special guardianship: parental responsibility) has effect subject to any determination under section 25(4) of this Act,

(b) section 14C(3) and (4) of the 1989 Act (special guardianship: removal of child from UK etc) does not apply.

Removal of children who are or may be placed by adoption agencies

30 General prohibitions on removal

(1) Where –

(a) a child is placed for adoption by an adoption agency under section 19, or

(b) a child is placed for adoption by an adoption agency and either the child is less than six weeks old or the agency has at no time been authorised to place the child for adoption, a person (other than the agency) must not remove the child from the prospective adopters.

(2) Where –

    (a)   a child who is not for the time being placed for adoption is being provided with accommodation by a local authority, and

    (b)   the authority have applied to the court for a placement order and the application has not been disposed of,

only a person who has the court's leave (or the authority) may remove the child from the accommodation.

(3) Where subsection (2) does not apply, but –

    (a)   a child who is not for the time being placed for adoption is being provided with accommodation by an adoption agency, and

    (b)   the agency is authorised to place the child for adoption under section 19 or would be so authorised if any consent to placement under that section had not been withdrawn,

a person (other than the agency) must not remove the child from the accommodation.

(4) This section is subject to sections 31 to 33 but those sections do not apply if the child is subject to a care order.

(5) This group of sections (that is, this section and those sections) apply whether or not the child in question is in England and Wales.

(6) This group of sections does not affect the exercise by any local authority or other person of any power conferred by any enactment, other than section 20(8) of the 1989 Act (removal of children from local authority accommodation).

(7) This group of sections does not prevent the removal of a child who is arrested.

(8) A person who removes a child in contravention of this section is guilty of an offence and liable on summary conviction to imprisonment for a term not exceeding three months, or a fine not exceeding level 5 on the standard scale, or both.

31 Recovery by parent etc where child not placed or is a baby

(1) Subsection (2) applies where –

    (a)   a child who is not for the time being placed for adoption is being provided with accommodation by an adoption agency, and

    (b)   the agency would be authorised to place the child for adoption under section 19 if consent to placement under that section had not been withdrawn.

(2) If any parent or guardian of the child informs the agency that he wishes the child to be returned to him, the agency must return the child to him within the period of seven days beginning with the request unless an application is, or has been, made for a placement order and the application has not been disposed of.

(3) Subsection (4) applies where –

    (a)   a child is placed for adoption by an adoption agency and either the child is less than six weeks old or the agency has at no time been authorised to place the child for adoption, and

    (b) any parent or guardian of the child informs the agency that he wishes the child to be returned to him,

unless an application is, or has been, made for a placement order and the application has not been disposed of.

(4) The agency must give notice of the parent's or guardian's wish to the prospective adopters who must return the child to the agency within the period of seven days beginning with the day on which the notice is given.

(5) A prospective adopter who fails to comply with subsection (4) is guilty of an offence and liable on summary conviction to imprisonment for a term not exceeding three months, or a fine not exceeding level 5 on the standard scale, or both.

(6) As soon as a child is returned to an adoption agency under subsection (4), the agency must return the child to the parent or guardian in question.

32 Recovery by parent etc where child placed and consent withdrawn

(1) This section applies where –

    (a) a child is placed for adoption by an adoption agency under section 19, and
    (b) consent to placement under that section has been withdrawn,

unless an application is, or has been, made for a placement order and the application has not been disposed of.

(2) If a parent or guardian of the child informs the agency that he wishes the child to be returned to him –

    (a) the agency must give notice of the parent's or guardian's wish to the prospective adopters, and
    (b) the prospective adopters must return the child to the agency within the period of 14 days beginning with the day on which the notice is given.

(3) A prospective adopter who fails to comply with subsection (2)(b) is guilty of an offence and liable on summary conviction to imprisonment for a term not exceeding three months, or a fine not exceeding level 5 on the standard scale, or both.

(4) As soon as a child is returned to an adoption agency under this section, the agency must return the child to the parent or guardian in question.

(5) Where a notice under subsection (2) is given, but –

    (a) before the notice was given, an application for an adoption order (including a Scottish or Northern Irish adoption order), special guardianship order or residence order, or for leave to apply for a special guardianship order or residence order, was made in respect of the child, and
    (b) the application (and, in a case where leave is given on an application to apply for a special guardianship order or residence order, the application for the order) has not been disposed of,

the prospective adopters are not required by virtue of the notice to return the child to the agency unless the court so orders.

33 Recovery by parent etc where child placed and placement order refused

(1) This section applies where –

    (a) a child is placed for adoption by a local authority under section 19,

    (b) the authority have applied for a placement order and the application has been refused, and

    (c) any parent or guardian of the child informs the authority that he wishes the child to be returned to him.

(2) The prospective adopters must return the child to the authority on a date determined by the court.

(3) A prospective adopter who fails to comply with subsection (2) is guilty of an offence and liable on summary conviction to imprisonment for a term not exceeding three months, or a fine not exceeding level 5 on the standard scale, or both.

(4) As soon as a child is returned to the authority, they must return the child to the parent or guardian in question.

34 Placement orders: prohibition on removal

(1) Where a placement order in respect of a child –

    (a) is in force, or

    (b) has been revoked, but the child has not been returned by the prospective adopters or remains in any accommodation provided by the local authority,

a person (other than the local authority) may not remove the child from the prospective adopters or from accommodation provided by the authority.

(2) A person who removes a child in contravention of subsection (1) is guilty of an offence.

(3) Where a court revoking a placement order in respect of a child determines that the child is not to remain with any former prospective adopters with whom the child is placed, they must return the child to the local authority within the period determined by the court for the purpose; and a person who fails to do so is guilty of an offence.

(4) Where a court revoking a placement order in respect of a child determines that the child is to be returned to a parent or guardian, the local authority must return the child to the parent or guardian as soon as the child is returned to the authority or, where the child is in accommodation provided by the authority, at once.

(5) A person guilty of an offence under this section is liable on summary conviction to imprisonment for a term not exceeding three months, or a fine not exceeding level 5 on the standard scale, or both.

(6) This section does not affect the exercise by any local authority or other person of a power conferred by any enactment, other than section 20(8) of the 1989 Act.

(7) This section does not prevent the removal of a child who is arrested.

(8) This section applies whether or not the child in question is in England and Wales.

35 Return of child in other cases

(1) Where a child is placed for adoption by an adoption agency and the prospective adopters give notice to the agency of their wish to return the child, the agency must –

    (a) receive the child from the prospective adopters before the end of the period of seven days beginning with the giving of the notice, and

    (b) give notice to any parent or guardian of the child of the prospective adopters' wish to return the child.

(2) Where a child is placed for adoption by an adoption agency, and the agency –

    (a) is of the opinion that the child should not remain with the prospective adopters, and

    (b) gives notice to them of its opinion,

the prospective adopters must, not later than the end of the period of seven days beginning with the giving of the notice, return the child to the agency.

(3) If the agency gives notice under subsection (2)(b), it must give notice to any parent or guardian of the child of the obligation to return the child to the agency.

(4) A prospective adopter who fails to comply with subsection (2) is guilty of an offence and liable on summary conviction to imprisonment for a term not exceeding three months, or a fine not exceeding level 5 on the standard scale, or both.

(5) Where –

    (a) an adoption agency gives notice under subsection (2) in respect of a child,

    (b) before the notice was given, an application for an adoption order (including a Scottish or Northern Irish adoption order), special guardianship order or residence order, or for leave to apply for a special guardianship order or residence order, was made in respect of the child, and

    (c) the application (and, in a case where leave is given on an application to apply for a special guardianship order or residence order, the application for the order) has not been disposed of,

prospective adopters are not required by virtue of the notice to return the child to the agency unless the court so orders.

(6) This section applies whether or not the child in question is in England and Wales.

Removal of children in non-agency cases

36 Restrictions on removal

(1) At any time when a child's home is with any persons ('the people concerned') with whom the child is not placed by an adoption agency, but the people concerned –

    (a) have applied for an adoption order in respect of the child and the application has not been disposed of,

    (b) have given notice of intention to adopt, or

    (c) have applied for leave to apply for an adoption order under section 42(6) and the application has not been disposed of,

a person may remove the child only in accordance with the provisions of this group of sections (that is, this section and sections 37 to 40).

The reference to a child placed by an adoption agency includes a child placed by a Scottish or Northern Irish adoption agency.

(2) For the purposes of this group of sections, a notice of intention to adopt is to be disregarded if –

> (a) the period of four months beginning with the giving of the notice has expired without the people concerned applying for an adoption order, or
>
> (b) the notice is a second or subsequent notice of intention to adopt and was given during the period of five months beginning with the giving of the preceding notice.

(3) For the purposes of this group of sections, if the people concerned apply for leave to apply for an adoption order under section 42(6) and the leave is granted, the application for leave is not to be treated as disposed of until the period of three days beginning with the granting of the leave has expired.

(4) This section does not prevent the removal of a child who is arrested.

(5) Where a parent or guardian may remove a child from the people concerned in accordance with the provisions of this group of sections, the people concerned must at the request of the parent or guardian return the child to the parent or guardian at once.

(6) A person who –

> (a) fails to comply with subsection (5), or
>
> (b) removes a child in contravention of this section,

is guilty of an offence and liable on summary conviction to imprisonment for a term not exceeding three months, or a fine not exceeding level 5 on the standard scale, or both.

(7) This group of sections applies whether or not the child in question is in England and Wales.

37 Applicants for adoption

If section 36(1)(a) applies, the following persons may remove the child –

> (a) a person who has the court's leave,
>
> (b) a local authority or other person in the exercise of a power conferred by any enactment, other than section 20(8) of the 1989 Act.

38 Local authority foster parents

(1) This section applies if the child's home is with local authority foster parents.

(2) If –

> (a) the child has had his home with the foster parents at all times during the period of five years ending with the removal and the foster parents have given notice of intention to adopt, or
>
> (b) an application has been made for leave under section 42(6) and has not been disposed of,

the following persons may remove the child.

(3) They are –

(a) a person who has the court's leave,

(b) a local authority or other person in the exercise of a power conferred by any enactment, other than section 20(8) of the 1989 Act.

(4) If subsection (2) does not apply but –

(a) the child has had his home with the foster parents at all times during the period of one year ending with the removal, and

(b) the foster parents have given notice of intention to adopt,

the following persons may remove the child.

(5) They are –

(a) a person with parental responsibility for the child who is exercising the power in section 20(8) of the 1989 Act,

(b) a person who has the court's leave,

(c) a local authority or other person in the exercise of a power conferred by any enactment, other than section 20(8) of the 1989 Act.

39 Partners of parents

(1) This section applies if a child's home is with a partner of a parent and the partner has given notice of intention to adopt.

(2) If the child's home has been with the partner for not less than three years (whether continuous or not) during the period of five years ending with the removal, the following persons may remove the child –

(a) a person who has the court's leave,

(b) a local authority or other person in the exercise of a power conferred by any enactment, other than section 20(8) of the 1989 Act.

(3) If subsection (2) does not apply, the following persons may remove the child –

(a) a parent or guardian,

(b) a person who has the court's leave,

(c) a local authority or other person in the exercise of a power conferred by any enactment, other than section 20(8) of the 1989 Act.

40 Other non-agency cases

(1) In any case where sections 37 to 39 do not apply but –

(a) the people concerned have given notice of intention to adopt, or

(b) the people concerned have applied for leave under section 42(6) and the application has not been disposed of,

the following persons may remove the child.

(2) They are –

(a) a person who has the court's leave,

(b) a local authority or other person in the exercise of a power conferred by any enactment, other than section 20(8) of the 1989 Act.

Breach of restrictions on removal

41 Recovery orders

(1) This section applies where it appears to the court –

   (a) that a child has been removed in contravention of any of the preceding provisions of this Chapter or that there are reasonable grounds for believing that a person intends to remove a child in contravention of those provisions, or

   (b) that a person has failed to comply with section 31(4), 32(2), 33(2), 34(3) or 35(2).

(2) The court may, on the application of any person, by an order –

   (a) direct any person who is in a position to do so to produce the child on request to any person mentioned in subsection (4),

   (b) authorise the removal of the child by any person mentioned in that subsection,

   (c) require any person who has information as to the child's whereabouts to disclose that information on request to any constable or officer of the court,

   (d) authorise a constable to enter any premises specified in the order and search for the child, using reasonable force if necessary.

(3) Premises may only be specified under subsection (2)(d) if it appears to the court that there are reasonable grounds for believing the child to be on them.

(4) The persons referred to in subsection (2) are –

   (a) any person named by the court,

   (b) any constable,

   (c) any person who, after the order is made under that subsection, is authorised to exercise any power under the order by an adoption agency which is authorised to place the child for adoption.

(5) A person who intentionally obstructs a person exercising a power of removal conferred by the order is guilty of an offence and liable on summary conviction to a fine not exceeding level 3 on the standard scale.

(6) A person must comply with a request to disclose information as required by the order even if the information sought might constitute evidence that he had committed an offence.

(7) But in criminal proceedings in which the person is charged with an offence (other than one mentioned in subsection (8)) –

   (a) no evidence relating to the information provided may be adduced, and

   (b) no question relating to the information may be asked,

by or on behalf of the prosecution, unless evidence relating to it is adduced, or a question relating to it is asked, in the proceedings by or on behalf of the person.

(8) The offences excluded from subsection (7) are –

   (a) an offence under section 2 or 5 of the Perjury Act 1911 (false statements made on oath otherwise than in judicial proceedings or made otherwise than on oath),

(b) an offence under section 44(1) or (2) of the Criminal Law (Consolidation) (Scotland) Act 1995 (false statements made on oath or otherwise than on oath).

(9) An order under this section has effect in relation to Scotland as if it were an order made by the Court of Session which that court had jurisdiction to make.

Preliminaries to adoption

42 Child to live with adopters before application

(1) An application for an adoption order may not be made unless –

    (a) if subsection (2) applies, the condition in that subsection is met,

    (b) if that subsection does not apply, the condition in whichever is applicable of subsections (3) to (5) applies.

(2) If –

    (a) the child was placed for adoption with the applicant or applicants by an adoption agency or in pursuance of an order of the High Court, or

    (b) the applicant is a parent of the child,

the condition is that the child must have had his home with the applicant or, in the case of an application by a couple, with one or both of them at all times during the period of ten weeks preceding the application.

(3) If the applicant or one of the applicants is the partner of a parent of the child, the condition is that the child must have had his home with the applicant or, as the case may be, applicants at all times during the period of six months preceding the application.

(4) If the applicants are local authority foster parents, the condition is that the child must have had his home with the applicants at all times during the period of one year preceding the application.

(5) In any other case, the condition is that the child must have had his home with the applicant or, in the case of an application by a couple, with one or both of them for not less than three years (whether continuous or not) during the period of five years preceding the application.

(6) But subsections (4) and (5) do not prevent an application being made if the court gives leave to make it.

(7) An adoption order may not be made unless the court is satisfied that sufficient opportunities to see the child with the applicant or, in the case of an application by a couple, both of them together in the home environment have been given –

    (a) where the child was placed for adoption with the applicant or applicants by an adoption agency, to that agency,

    (b) in any other case, to the local authority within whose area the home is.

(8) In this section and sections 43 and 44(1) –

    (a) references to an adoption agency include a Scottish or Northern Irish adoption agency,

    (b) references to a child placed for adoption by an adoption agency are to be read accordingly.

43 Reports where child placed by agency

Where an application for an adoption order relates to a child placed for adoption by an adoption agency, the agency must –

    (a) submit to the court a report on the suitability of the applicants and on any other matters relevant to the operation of section 1, and

    (b) assist the court in any manner the court directs.

44 Notice of intention to adopt

(1) This section applies where persons (referred to in this section as 'proposed adopters') wish to adopt a child who is not placed for adoption with them by an adoption agency.

(2) An adoption order may not be made in respect of the child unless the proposed adopters have given notice to the appropriate local authority of their intention to apply for the adoption order (referred to in this Act as a 'notice of intention to adopt').

(3) The notice must be given not more than two years, or less than three months, before the date on which the application for the adoption order is made.

(4) Where –

    (a) if a person were seeking to apply for an adoption order, subsection (4) or (5) of section 42 would apply, but

    (b) the condition in the subsection in question is not met,

the person may not give notice of intention to adopt unless he has the court's leave to apply for an adoption order.

(5) On receipt of a notice of intention to adopt, the local authority must arrange for the investigation of the matter and submit to the court a report of the investigation.

(6) In particular, the investigation must, so far as practicable, include the suitability of the proposed adopters and any other matters relevant to the operation of section 1 in relation to the application.

(7) If a local authority receive a notice of intention to adopt in respect of a child whom they know was (immediately before the notice was given) looked after by another local authority, they must, not more than seven days after the receipt of the notice, inform the other local authority in writing that they have received the notice.

(8) Where –

    (a) a local authority have placed a child with any persons otherwise than as prospective adopters, and

    (b) the persons give notice of intention to adopt,

the authority are not to be treated as leaving the child with them as prospective adopters for the purposes of section 18(1)(b).

(9) In this section, references to the appropriate local authority, in relation to any proposed adopters, are –

    (a) in prescribed cases, references to the prescribed local authority,

(b) in any other case, references to the local authority for the area in which, at the time of giving the notice of intention to adopt, they have their home,

and 'prescribed' means prescribed by regulations.

45 Suitability of adopters

(1) Regulations under section 9 may make provision as to the matters to be taken into account by an adoption agency in determining, or making any report in respect of, the suitability of any persons to adopt a child.

(2) In particular, the regulations may make provision for the purpose of securing that, in determining the suitability of a couple to adopt a child, proper regard is had to the need for stability and permanence in their relationship.

The making of adoption orders

46 Adoption orders

(1) An adoption order is an order made by the court on an application under section 50 or 51 giving parental responsibility for a child to the adopters or adopter.

(2) The making of an adoption order operates to extinguish –

(a) the parental responsibility which any person other than the adopters or adopter has for the adopted child immediately before the making of the order,

(b) any order under the 1989 Act or the Children (Northern Ireland) Order 1995 (SI 1995/755 (NI 2)),

(c) any order under the Children (Scotland) Act 1995 other than an excepted order, and

(d) any duty arising by virtue of an agreement or an order of a court to make payments, so far as the payments are in respect of the adopted child's maintenance or upbringing for any period after the making of the adoption order.

'Excepted order' means an order under sections 9, 11(1)(d) or 13 of the Children (Scotland) Act 1995 or an exclusion order within the meaning of section 76(1) of that Act.

(3) An adoption order –

(a) does not affect parental responsibility so far as it relates to any period before the making of the order, and

(b) in the case of an order made on an application under section 51(2) by the partner of a parent of the adopted child, does not affect the parental responsibility of that parent or any duties of that parent within subsection (2)(d).

(4) Subsection (2)(d) does not apply to a duty arising by virtue of an agreement –

(a) which constitutes a trust, or

(b) which expressly provides that the duty is not to be extinguished by the making of an adoption order.

(5) An adoption order may be made even if the child to be adopted is already an adopted child.

(6) Before making an adoption order, the court must consider whether there should be arrangements for allowing any person contact with the child; and for that purpose the court must consider any existing or proposed arrangements and obtain any views of the parties to the proceedings.

47 Conditions for making adoption orders

(1) An adoption order may not be made if the child has a parent or guardian unless one of the following three conditions is met; but this section is subject to section 52 (parental etc consent).

(2) The first condition is that, in the case of each parent or guardian of the child, the court is satisfied –

  (a) that the parent or guardian consents to the making of the adoption order,
  (b) that the parent or guardian has consented under section 20 (and has not withdrawn the consent) and does not oppose the making of the adoption order, or
  (c) that the parent's or guardian's consent should be dispensed with.

(3) A parent or guardian may not oppose the making of an adoption order under subsection (2)(b) without the court's leave.

(4) The second condition is that –

  (a) the child has been placed for adoption by an adoption agency with the prospective adopters in whose favour the order is proposed to be made,
  (b) either –
    (i) the child was placed for adoption with the consent of each parent or guardian and the consent of the mother was given when the child was at least six weeks old, or
    (ii) the child was placed for adoption under a placement order, and
  (c) no parent or guardian opposes the making of the adoption order.

(5) A parent or guardian may not oppose the making of an adoption order under the second condition without the court's leave.

(6) The third condition is that the child is free for adoption by virtue of an order made –

  (a) in Scotland, under section 18 of the Adoption (Scotland) Act 1978, or
  (b) in Northern Ireland, under Article 17(1) or 18(1) of the Adoption (Northern Ireland) Order 1987 (SI 1987/2203 (NI 22)).

(7) The court cannot give leave under subsection (3) or (5) unless satisfied that there has been a change in circumstances since the consent of the parent or guardian was given or, as the case may be, the placement order was made.

(8) An adoption order may not be made in relation to a person who is or has been married.

(9) An adoption order may not be made in relation to a person who has attained the age of 19 years.

48 Restrictions on making adoption orders

(1) The court may not hear an application for an adoption order in relation to a child, where a previous application to which subsection (2) applies made in relation to the child by the same persons was refused by any court, unless it appears to the court that, because of a change in circumstances or for any other reason, it is proper to hear the application.

(2) This subsection applies to any application –

    (a) for an adoption order or a Scottish or Northern Irish adoption order, or

    (b) for an order for adoption made in the Isle of Man or any of the Channel Islands.

49 Applications for adoption

(1) An application for an adoption order may be made by –

    (a) a couple, or

    (b) one person,

but only if it is made under section 50 or 51 and one of the following conditions is met.

(2) The first condition is that at least one of the couple (in the case of an application under section 50) or the applicant (in the case of an application under section 51) is domiciled in a part of the British Islands.

(3) The second condition is that both of the couple (in the case of an application under section 50) or the applicant (in the case of an application under section 51) have been habitually resident in a part of the British Islands for a period of not less than one year ending with the date of the application.

(4) An application for an adoption order may only be made if the person to be adopted has not attained the age of 18 years on the date of the application.

(5) References in this Act to a child, in connection with any proceedings (whether or not concluded) for adoption, (such as 'child to be adopted' or 'adopted child') include a person who has attained the age of 18 years before the proceedings are concluded.

50 Adoption by couple

(1) An adoption order may be made on the application of a couple where both of them have attained the age of 21 years.

(2) An adoption order may be made on the application of a couple where –

    (a) one of the couple is the mother or the father of the person to be adopted and has attained the age of 18 years, and

    (b) the other has attained the age of 21 years.

51 Adoption by one person

(1) An adoption order may be made on the application of one person who has attained the age of 21 years and is not married.

(2) An adoption order may be made on the application of one person who has attained the age of 21 years if the court is satisfied that the person is the partner of a parent of the person to be adopted.

(3) An adoption order may be made on the application of one person who has attained the age of 21 years and is married if the court is satisfied that –

    (a) the person's spouse cannot be found,

    (b) the spouses have separated and are living apart, and the separation is likely to be permanent, or

    (c) the person's spouse is by reason of ill-health, whether physical or mental, incapable of making an application for an adoption order.

(4) An adoption order may not be made on an application under this section by the mother or the father of the person to be adopted unless the court is satisfied that –

    (a) the other natural parent is dead or cannot be found,

    (b) by virtue of section 28 of the Human Fertilisation and Embryology Act 1990, there is no other parent, or

    (c) there is some other reason justifying the child's being adopted by the applicant alone,

and, where the court makes an adoption order on such an application, the court must record that it is satisfied as to the fact mentioned in paragraph (a) or (b) or, in the case of paragraph (c), record the reason.

Placement and adoption: general

52 Parental etc consent

(1) The court cannot dispense with the consent of any parent or guardian of a child to the child being placed for adoption or to the making of an adoption order in respect of the child unless the court is satisfied that –

    (a) the parent or guardian cannot be found or is incapable of giving consent, or

    (b) the welfare of the child requires the consent to be dispensed with.

(2) The following provisions apply to references in this Chapter to any parent or guardian of a child giving or withdrawing –

    (a) consent to the placement of a child for adoption, or

    (b) consent to the making of an adoption order (including a future adoption order).

(3) Any consent given by the mother to the making of an adoption order is ineffective if it is given less than six weeks after the child's birth.

(4) The withdrawal of any consent to the placement of a child for adoption, or of any consent given under section 20, is ineffective if it is given after an application for an adoption order is made.

(5) 'Consent' means consent given unconditionally and with full understanding of what is involved; but a person may consent to adoption without knowing the identity of the persons in whose favour the order will be made.

(6) 'Parent' (except in subsections (9) and (10) below) means a parent having parental responsibility.

(7) Consent under section 19 or 20 must be given in the form prescribed by rules, and the rules may prescribe forms in which a person giving under any other provision of this Part may do so (if he wishes).

(8) Consent given under section 19 or 20 must be withdrawn –

(a) in the form prescribed by rules, or
(b) by notice given to the agency.

(9) Subsection (10) applies if –

(a) an agency has placed a child for adoption under section 19 in pursuance of consent given by a parent of the child, and
(b) at a later time, the other parent of the child acquires parental responsibility for the child.

(10) The other parent is to be treated as having at that time given consent in accordance with this section in the same terms as those in which the first parent gave consent.

53 Modification of 1989 Act in relation to adoption

(1) Where –

(a) a local authority are authorised to place a child for adoption, or
(b) a child who has been placed for adoption by a local authority is less than six weeks old,

regulations may provide for the following provisions of the 1989 Act to apply with modifications, or not to apply, in relation to the child.

(2) The provisions are –

(a) section 22(4)(b), (c) and (d) and (5)(b) (duty to ascertain wishes and feelings of certain persons),
(b) paragraphs 15 and 21 of Schedule 2 (promoting contact with parents and parents' obligation to contribute towards maintenance).

(3) Where a registered adoption society is authorised to place a child for adoption or a child who has been placed for adoption by a registered adoption society is less than six weeks old, regulations may provide –

(a) for section 61 of that Act to have effect in relation to the child whether or not he is accommodated by or on behalf of the society,
(b) for subsections (2)(b) to (d) and (3)(b) of that section (duty to ascertain wishes and feelings of certain persons) to apply with modifications, or not to apply, in relation to the child.

(4) Where a child's home is with persons who have given notice of intention to adopt, no contribution is payable (whether under a contribution order or otherwise) under Part 3 of Schedule 2 to that Act (contributions towards maintenance of children looked after by local authorities) in respect of the period referred to in subsection (5).

(5) That period begins when the notice of intention to adopt is given and ends if –

(a) the period of four months beginning with the giving of the notice expires without the prospective adopters applying for an adoption order, or
(b) an application for such an order is withdrawn or refused.

(6) In this section, 'notice of intention to adopt' includes notice of intention to apply for a Scottish or Northern Irish adoption order.

54 Disclosing information during adoption process

Regulations under section 9 may require adoption agencies in prescribed circumstances to disclose in accordance with the regulations prescribed information to prospective adopters.

55 Revocation of adoptions on legitimation

(1) Where any child adopted by one natural parent as sole adoptive parent subsequently becomes a legitimated person on the marriage of the natural parents, the court by which the adoption order was made may, on the application of any of the parties concerned, revoke the order.

(2) In relation to an adoption order made by a magistrates' court, the reference in subsection (1) to the court by which the order was made includes a court acting for the same petty sessions area.

Disclosure of information in relation to a person's adoption

56 Information to be kept about a person's adoption

(1) In relation to an adopted person, regulations may prescribe –

    (a) the information which an adoption agency must keep in relation to his adoption,

    (b) the form and manner in which it must keep that information.

(2) Below in this group of sections (that is, this section and sections 57 to 65), any information kept by an adoption agency by virtue of subsection (1)(a) is referred to as section 56 information.

(3) Regulations may provide for the transfer in prescribed circumstances of information held, or previously held, by an adoption agency to another adoption agency.

57 Restrictions on disclosure of protected etc information

(1) Any section 56 information kept by an adoption agency which –

    (a) is about an adopted person or any other person, and

    (b) is or includes identifying information about the person in question,

may only be disclosed by the agency to a person (other than the person the information is about) in pursuance of this group of sections.

(2) Any information kept by an adoption agency –

    (a) which the agency has obtained from the Registrar General on an application under section 79(5) and any other information which would enable the adopted person to obtain a certified copy of the record of his birth, or

    (b) which is information about an entry relating to the adopted person in the Adoption Contact Register,

may only be disclosed to a person by the agency in pursuance of this group of sections.

(3) In this group of sections, information the disclosure of which to a person is restricted by virtue of subsection (1) or (2) is referred to (in relation to him) as protected information.

(4) Identifying information about a person means information which, whether taken on its own or together with other information disclosed by an adoption agency, identifies the person or enables the person to be identified.

(5) This section does not prevent the disclosure of protected information in pursuance of a prescribed agreement to which the adoption agency is a party.

(6) Regulations may authorise or require an adoption agency to disclose protected information to a person who is not an adopted person.

58 Disclosure of other information

(1) This section applies to any section 56 information other than protected information.

(2) An adoption agency may for the purposes of its functions disclose to any person in accordance with prescribed arrangements any information to which this section applies.

(3) An adoption agency must, in prescribed circumstances, disclose prescribed information to a prescribed person.

59 Offence

Regulations may provide that a registered adoption society which discloses any information in contravention of section 57 is to be guilty of an offence and liable on summary conviction to a fine not exceeding level 5 on the standard scale.

60 Disclosing information to adopted adult

(1) This section applies to an adopted person who has attained the age of 18 years.

(2) The adopted person has the right, at his request, to receive from the appropriate adoption agency –

   (a) any information which would enable him to obtain a certified copy of the record of his birth, unless the High Court orders otherwise,
   (b) any prescribed information disclosed to the adopters by the agency by virtue of section 54.

(3) The High Court may make an order under subsection (2)(a), on an application by the appropriate adoption agency, if satisfied that the circumstances are exceptional.

(4) The adopted person also has the right, at his request, to receive from the court which made the adoption order a copy of any prescribed document or prescribed order relating to the adoption.

(5) Subsection (4) does not apply to a document or order so far as it contains information which is protected information.

61 Disclosing protected information about adults

(1) This section applies where –

> (a) a person applies to the appropriate adoption agency for protected information to be disclosed to him, and
>
> (b) none of the information is about a person who is a child at the time of the application.

(2) The agency is not required to proceed with the application unless it considers it appropriate to do so.

(3) If the agency does proceed with the application it must take all reasonable steps to obtain the views of any person the information is about as to the disclosure of the information about him.

(4) The agency may then disclose the information if it considers it appropriate to do so.

(5) In deciding whether it is appropriate to proceed with the application or disclose the information, the agency must consider –

> (a) the welfare of the adopted person,
>
> (b) any views obtained under subsection (3),
>
> (c) any prescribed matters,

and all the other circumstances of the case.

(6) This section does not apply to a request for information under section 60(2) or to a request for information which the agency is authorised or required to disclose in pursuance of regulations made by virtue of section 57(6).

62 Disclosing protected information about children

(1) This section applies where –

> (a) a person applies to the appropriate adoption agency for protected information to be disclosed to him, and
>
> (b) any of the information is about a person who is a child at the time of the application.

(2) The agency is not required to proceed with the application unless it considers it appropriate to do so.

(3) If the agency does proceed with the application, then, so far as the information is about a person who is at the time a child, the agency must take all reasonable steps to obtain –

> (a) the views of any parent or guardian of the child, and
>
> (b) the views of the child, if the agency considers it appropriate to do so having regard to his age and understanding and to all the other circumstances of the case,

as to the disclosure of the information.

(4) And, so far as the information is about a person who has at the time attained the age of 18 years, the agency must take all reasonable steps to obtain his views as to the disclosure of the information.

(5) The agency may then disclose the information if it considers it appropriate to do so.

(6) In deciding whether it is appropriate to proceed with the application, or disclose the information, where any of the information is about a person who is at the time a child –

(a) if the child is an adopted child, the child's welfare must be the paramount consideration,
(b) in the case of any other child, the agency must have particular regard to the child's welfare.

(7) And, in deciding whether it is appropriate to proceed with the application or disclose the information, the agency must consider –

(a) the welfare of the adopted person (where subsection (6)(a) does not apply),
(b) any views obtained under subsection (3) or (4),
(c) any prescribed matters,

and all the other circumstances of the case.

(8) This section does not apply to a request for information under section 60(2) or to a request for information which the agency is authorised or required to disclose in pursuance of regulations made by virtue of section 57(6).

63 Counselling

(1) Regulations may require adoption agencies to give information about the availability of counselling to persons –

(a) seeking information from them in pursuance of this group of sections,
(b) considering objecting or consenting to the disclosure of information by the agency in pursuance of this group of sections, or
(c) considering entering with the agency into an agreement prescribed for the purposes of section 57(5).

(2) Regulations may require adoption agencies to make arrangements to secure the provision of counselling for persons seeking information from them in prescribed circumstances in pursuance of this group of sections.

(3) The regulations may authorise adoption agencies –

(a) to disclose information which is required for the purposes of such counselling to the persons providing the counselling,
(b) where the person providing the counselling is outside the United Kingdom, to require a prescribed fee to be paid.

(4) The regulations may require any of the following persons to provide counselling for the purposes of arrangements under subsection (2) –

(a) a local authority, a council constituted under section 2 of the Local Government etc (Scotland) Act 1994 or a Health and Social Services Board established under Article 16 of the Health and Personal Social Services (Northern Ireland) Order 1972 (SI 1972/1265 (NI 14)),
(b) a registered adoption society, an organisation within section 144(3)(b) or an adoption society which is registered under Article 4 of the Adoption (Northern Ireland) Order 1987 (SI 1987/2203 (NI 22)),
(c) an adoption support agency in respect of which a person is registered under Part 2 of the Care Standards Act 2000.

(5) For the purposes of subsection (4), where the functions of a Health and Social Services Board are exercisable by a Health and Social Services Trust, the reference in sub-paragraph (a) to a Board is to be read as a reference to the Health and Social Services Trust.

64 Other provision to be made by regulations

(1) Regulations may make provision for the purposes of this group of sections, including provision as to –

    (a)   the performance by adoption agencies of their functions,

    (b)   the manner in which information may be received, and

    (c)   the matters mentioned below in this section.

(2) Regulations may prescribe –

    (a)   the manner in which agreements made by virtue of section 57(5) are to be recorded,

    (b)   the information to be provided by any person on an application for the disclosure of information under this group of sections.

(3) Regulations may require adoption agencies –

    (a)   to give to prescribed persons prescribed information about the rights or opportunities to obtain information, or to give their views as to its disclosure, given by this group of sections,

    (b)   to seek prescribed information from, or give prescribed information to, the Registrar General in prescribed circumstances.

(4) Regulations may require the Registrar General –

    (a)   to disclose to any person (including an adopted person) at his request any information which the person requires to assist him to make contact with the adoption agency which is the appropriate adoption agency in the case of an adopted person specified in the request (or, as the case may be, in the applicant's case),

    (b)   to disclose to the appropriate adoption agency any information which the agency requires about any entry relating to the adopted person on the Adoption Contact Register.

(5) Regulations may provide for the payment of a prescribed fee in respect of the disclosure in prescribed circumstances of any information in pursuance of sections 60, 61 or 62; but an adopted person may not be required to pay any fee in respect of any information disclosed to him in relation to any person who (but for his adoption) would be related to him by blood (including half-blood) or marriage.

(6) Regulations may provide for the payment of a prescribed fee by an adoption agency obtaining information under subsection (4)(b).

65 Sections 56 to 65: interpretation

(1) In this group of sections –

    'appropriate adoption agency', in relation to an adopted person or to information relating to his adoption, means –

(a) if the person was placed for adoption by an adoption agency, that agency or (if different) the agency which keeps the information in relation to his adoption,

(b) in any other case, the local authority to which notice of intention to adopt was given,

'prescribed' means prescribed by subordinate legislation,

'regulations' means regulations under section 9,

'subordinate legislation' means regulations or, in relation to information to be given by a court, rules.

(2) But –

(a) regulations under section 63(2) imposing any requirement on a council constituted under section 2 of the Local Government etc (Scotland) Act 1994, or an organisation within section 144(3)(b), are to be made by the Scottish Ministers,

(b) regulations under section 63(2) imposing any requirement on a Health and Social Services Board established under Article 16 of the Health and Personal Social Services (Northern Ireland) Order 1972 (SI 1972/1265 (NI 14)), or an adoption society which is registered under Article 4 of the Adoption (Northern Ireland) Order 1987 (SI 1987/2203 (NI 22)), are to be made by the Department of Health, Social Services and Public Safety.

(3) The power of the Scottish Ministers or of the Department of Health, Social Services and Public Safety to make regulations under section 63(2) includes power to make –

(a) any supplementary, incidental or consequential provision,

(b) any transitory, transitional or saving provision,

which the person making the regulations considers necessary or expedient.

(4) Regulations prescribing any fee by virtue of section 64(6) require the approval of the Chancellor of the Exchequer.

(5) Regulations making any provision as to the manner in which any application is to be made for the disclosure of information by the Registrar General require his approval.

Chapter 4
Status of Adopted Children

66 Meaning of adoption in Chapter 4

(1) In this Chapter 'adoption' means –

(a) adoption by an adoption order or a Scottish or Northern Irish adoption order,

(b) adoption by an order made in the Isle of Man or any of the Channel Islands,

(c) an adoption effected under the law of a Convention country outside the British Islands, and certified in pursuance of Article 23(1) of the Convention (referred to in this Act as a 'Convention adoption'),

(d) an overseas adoption, or

(e) an adoption recognised by the law of England and Wales and effected under the law of any other country;

and related expressions are to be interpreted accordingly.

(2) But references in this Chapter to adoption do not include an adoption effected before the day on which this Chapter comes into force (referred to in this Chapter as 'the appointed day').

(3) Any reference in an enactment to an adopted person within the meaning of this Chapter includes a reference to an adopted child within the meaning of Part 4 of the Adoption Act 1976.

67 Status conferred by adoption

(1) An adopted person is to be treated in law as if born as the child of the adopters or adopter.

(2) An adopted person is the legitimate child of the adopters or adopter and, if adopted by –

    (a) a couple, or
    (b) one of a couple under section 51(2),

is to be treated as the child of the relationship of the couple in question.

(3) An adopted person –

    (a) if adopted by one of a couple under section 51(2), is to be treated in law as not being the child of any person other than the adopter and the other one of the couple, and
    (b) in any other case, is to be treated in law, subject to subsection (4), as not being the child of any person other than the adopters or adopter;

but this subsection does not affect any reference in this Act to a person's natural parent or to any other natural relationship.

(4) In the case of a person adopted by one of the person's natural parents as sole adoptive parent, subsection (3)(b) has no effect as respects entitlement to property depending on relationship to that parent, or as respects anything else depending on that relationship.

(5) This section has effect from the date of the adoption.

(6) Subject to the provisions of this Chapter and Schedule 4, this section –

    (a) applies for the interpretation of enactments or instruments passed or made before as well as after the adoption, and so applies subject to any contrary indication, and
    (b) has effect as respects things done, or events occurring, on or after the adoption.

68 Adoptive relatives

(1) A relationship existing by virtue of section 67 may be referred to as an adoptive relationship, and –

    (a) an adopter may be referred to as an adoptive parent or (as the case may be) as an adoptive father or adoptive mother,
    (b) any other relative of any degree under an adoptive relationship may be referred to as an adoptive relative of that degree.

(2) Subsection (1) does not affect the interpretation of any reference, not qualified by the word 'adoptive', to a relationship.

(3) A reference (however expressed) to the adoptive mother and father of a child adopted by –

(a) a couple of the same sex, or

(b) a partner of the child's parent, where the couple are of the same sex,

is to be read as a reference to the child's adoptive parents.

****

74 Miscellaneous enactments

(1) Section 67 does not apply for the purposes of –

(a) the table of kindred and affinity in Schedule 1 to the Marriage Act 1949,

(b) sections 10 and 11 of the Sexual Offences Act 1956 (incest), or

(c) section 54 of the Criminal Law Act 1977 (inciting a girl to commit incest).

(2) Section 67 does not apply for the purposes of any provision of –

(a) the British Nationality Act 1981,

(b) the Immigration Act 1971,

(c) any instrument having effect under an enactment within paragraph (a) or (b), or

(d) any other provision of the law for the time being in force which determines British citizenship, British overseas territories citizenship, the status of a British National (Overseas) or British Overseas citizenship.

****

Chapter 5
The Registers

Adopted Children Register etc

77 Adopted Children Register

(1) The Registrar General must continue to maintain in the General Register Office a register, to be called the Adopted Children Register.

(2) The Adopted Children Register is not to be open to public inspection or search.

(3) No entries may be made in the Adopted Children Register other than entries –

(a) directed to be made in it by adoption orders, or

(b) required to be made under Schedule 1.

(4) A certified copy of an entry in the Adopted Children Register, if purporting to be sealed or stamped with the seal of the General Register Office, is to be received as evidence of the adoption to which it relates without further or other proof.

(5) Where an entry in the Adopted Children Register contains a record –

(a) of the date of birth of the adopted person, or

(b) of the country, or the district and sub-district, of the birth of the adopted person,

a certified copy of the entry is also to be received, without further or other proof, as evidence of that date, or country or district and sub-district, (as the case may be) in all respects as if the copy were a certified copy of an entry in the registers of live-births.

(6) Schedule 1 (registration of adoptions and the amendment of adoption orders) is to have effect.

78 Searches and copies

(1) The Registrar General must continue to maintain at the General Register Office an index of the Adopted Children Register.

(2) Any person may –

(a) search the index,

(b) have a certified copy of any entry in the Adopted Children Register.

(3) But a person is not entitled to have a certified copy of an entry in the Adopted Children Register relating to an adopted person who has not attained the age of 18 years unless the applicant has provided the Registrar General with the prescribed particulars.

'Prescribed' means prescribed by regulations made by the Registrar General with the approval of the Chancellor of the Exchequer.

(4) The terms, conditions and regulations as to payment of fees, and otherwise, applicable under the Births and Deaths Registration Act 1953, and the Registration Service Act 1953, in respect of –

(a) searches in the index kept in the General Register Office of certified copies of entries in the registers of live-births,

(b) the supply from that office of certified copies of entries in those certified copies,

also apply in respect of searches, and supplies of certified copies, under subsection (2).

79 Connections between the register and birth records

(1) The Registrar General must make traceable the connection between any entry in the registers of live-births or other records which has been marked 'Adopted' and any corresponding entry in the Adopted Children Register.

(2) Information kept by the Registrar General for the purposes of subsection (1) is not to be open to public inspection or search.

(3) Any such information, and any other information which would enable an adopted person to obtain a certified copy of the record of his birth, may only be disclosed by the Registrar General in accordance with this section.

(4) In relation to a person adopted before the appointed day the court may, in exceptional circumstances, order the Registrar General to give any information mentioned in subsection (3) to a person.

(5) On an application made in the prescribed manner by the appropriate adoption agency in respect of an adopted person a record of whose birth is kept by the Registrar General, the Registrar General must give the agency any information relating to the adopted person which is mentioned in subsection (3).

'Appropriate adoption agency' has the same meaning as in section 65.

(6) In relation to a person adopted before the appointed day, Schedule 2 applies instead of subsection (5).

(7) On an application made in the prescribed manner by an adopted person a record of whose birth is kept by the Registrar General and who –

(a) is under the age of 18 years, and
(b) intends to be married,

the Registrar General must inform the applicant whether or not it appears from information contained in the registers of live-births or other records that the applicant and the person whom the applicant intends to marry may be within the prohibited degrees of relationship for the purposes of the Marriage Act 1949.

(8) Before the Registrar General gives any information by virtue of this section, any prescribed fee which he has demanded must be paid.

(9) In this section –

'appointed day' means the day appointed for the commencement of sections 56 to 65,
'prescribed' means prescribed by regulations made by the Registrar General with the approval of the Chancellor of the Exchequer.

Adoption Contact Register

80 Adoption Contact Register

(1) The Registrar General must continue to maintain at the General Register Office in accordance with regulations a register in two Parts to be called the Adoption Contact Register.

(2) Part 1 of the register is to contain the prescribed information about adopted persons who have given the prescribed notice expressing their wishes as to making contact with their relatives.

(3) The Registrar General may only make an entry in Part 1 of the register for an adopted person –

(a) a record of whose birth is kept by the Registrar General,
(b) who has attained the age of 18 years, and
(c) who the Registrar General is satisfied has such information as is necessary to enable him to obtain a certified copy of the record of his birth.

(4) Part 2 of the register is to contain the prescribed information about persons who have given the prescribed notice expressing their wishes, as relatives of adopted persons, as to making contact with those persons.

(5) The Registrar General may only make an entry in Part 2 of the register for a person –

(a) who has attained the age of 18 years, and

(b) who the Registrar General is satisfied is a relative of an adopted person and
has such information as is necessary to enable him to obtain a certified copy
of the record of the adopted person's birth.

(6) Regulations may provide for –

(a) the disclosure of information contained in one Part of the register to persons
for whom there is an entry in the other Part,

(b) the payment of prescribed fees in respect of the making or alteration of
entries in the register and the disclosure of information contained in the
register.

81 Adoption Contact Register: supplementary

(1) The Adoption Contact Register is not to be open to public inspection or search.

(2) In section 80, 'relative', in relation to an adopted person, means any person who
(but for his adoption) would be related to him by blood (including half-blood) or
marriage.

(3) The Registrar General must not give any information entered in the register to any
person except in accordance with subsection (6)(a) of that section or regulations made
by virtue of section 64(4)(b).

(4) In section 80, 'regulations' means regulations made by the Registrar General with
the approval of the Chancellor of the Exchequer, and 'prescribed' means prescribed
by such regulations.

General

82 Interpretation

(1) In this Chapter –

'records' includes certified copies kept by the Registrar General of entries in any
register of births,
'registers of live-births' means the registers of live-births made under the Births
and Deaths Registration Act 1953.

(2) Any register, record or index maintained under this Chapter may be maintained in
any form the Registrar General considers appropriate; and references (however
expressed) to entries in such a register, or to their amendment, marking or
cancellation, are to be read accordingly.

Chapter 6
Adoptions with a Foreign Element

Bringing children into and out of the United Kingdom

83 Restriction on bringing children in

(1) This section applies where a person who is habitually resident in the British
Islands (the 'British resident') –

    (a) brings, or causes another to bring, a child who is habitually resident outside the British Islands into the United Kingdom for the purpose of adoption by the British resident, or

    (b) at any time brings, or causes another to bring, into the United Kingdom a child adopted by the British resident under an external adoption effected within the period of six months ending with that time.

The references to adoption, or to a child adopted, by the British resident include a reference to adoption, or to a child adopted, by the British resident and another person.

(2) But this section does not apply if the child is intended to be adopted under a Convention adoption order.

(3) An external adoption means an adoption, other than a Convention adoption, of a child effected under the law of any country or territory outside the British Islands, whether or not the adoption is –

    (a) an adoption within the meaning of Chapter 4, or

    (b) a full adoption (within the meaning of section 88(3)).

(4) Regulations may require a person intending to bring, or to cause another to bring, a child into the United Kingdom in circumstances where this section applies –

    (a) to apply to an adoption agency (including a Scottish or Northern Irish adoption agency) in the prescribed manner for an assessment of his suitability to adopt the child, and

    (b) to give the agency any information it may require for the purpose of the assessment.

(5) Regulations may require prescribed conditions to be met in respect of a child brought into the United Kingdom in circumstances where this section applies.

(6) In relation to a child brought into the United Kingdom for adoption in circumstances where this section applies, regulations may –

    (a) provide for any provision of Chapter 3 to apply with modifications or not to apply,

    (b) if notice of intention to adopt has been given, impose functions in respect of the child on the local authority to which the notice was given.

(7) If a person brings, or causes another to bring, a child into the United Kingdom at any time in circumstances where this section applies, he is guilty of an offence if –

    (a) he has not complied with any requirement imposed by virtue of subsection (4), or

    (b) any condition required to be met by virtue of subsection (5) is not met,

before that time, or before any later time which may be prescribed.

(8) A person guilty of an offence under this section is liable –

    (a) on summary conviction to imprisonment for a term not exceeding six months, or a fine not exceeding the statutory maximum, or both,

    (b) on conviction on indictment, to imprisonment for a term not exceeding twelve months, or a fine, or both.

(9) In this section, 'prescribed' means prescribed by regulations and 'regulations' means regulations made by the Secretary of State, after consultation with the Assembly.

84 Giving parental responsibility prior to adoption abroad

(1) The High Court may, on an application by persons who the court is satisfied intend to adopt a child under the law of a country or territory outside the British Islands, make an order giving parental responsibility for the child to them.

(2) An order under this section may not give parental responsibility to persons who the court is satisfied meet those requirements as to domicile, or habitual residence, in England and Wales which have to be met if an adoption order is to be made in favour of those persons.

(3) An order under this section may not be made unless any requirements prescribed by regulations are satisfied.

(4) An application for an order under this section may not be made unless at all times during the preceding ten weeks the child's home was with the applicant or, in the case of an application by two people, both of them.

(5) Section 46(2) to (4) has effect in relation to an order under this section as it has effect in relation to adoption orders.

(6) Regulations may provide for any provision of this Act which refers to adoption orders to apply, with or without modifications, to orders under this section.

(7) In this section, 'regulations' means regulations made by the Secretary of State, after consultation with the Assembly.

85 Restriction on taking children out

(1) A child who –

    (a) is a Commonwealth citizen, or
    (b) is habitually resident in the United Kingdom,

must not be removed from the United Kingdom to a place outside the British Islands for the purpose of adoption unless the condition in subsection (2) is met.

(2) The condition is that –

    (a) the prospective adopters have parental responsibility for the child by virtue of an order under section 84, or
    (b) the child is removed under the authority of an order under section 49 of the Adoption (Scotland) Act 1978 or Article 57 of the Adoption (Northern Ireland) Order 1987 (SI 1987/2203 (NI 22)).

(3) Removing a child from the United Kingdom includes arranging to do so; and the circumstances in which a person arranges to remove a child from the United Kingdom include those where he –

    (a) enters into an arrangement for the purpose of facilitating such a removal of the child,
    (b) initiates or takes part in any negotiations of which the purpose is the conclusion of an arrangement within paragraph (a), or
    (c) causes another person to take any step mentioned in paragraph (a) or (b).

An arrangement includes an agreement (whether or not enforceable).

(4) A person who removes a child from the United Kingdom in contravention of subsection (1) is guilty of an offence.

(5) A person is not guilty of an offence under subsection (4) of causing a person to take any step mentioned in paragraph (a) or (b) of subsection (3) unless it is proved that he knew or had reason to suspect that the step taken would contravene subsection (1).

But this subsection only applies if sufficient evidence is adduced to raise an issue as to whether the person had the knowledge or reason mentioned.

(6) A person guilty of an offence under this section is liable –

    (a) on summary conviction to imprisonment for a term not exceeding six months, or a fine not exceeding the statutory maximum, or both,

    (b) on conviction on indictment, to imprisonment for a term not exceeding twelve months, or a fine, or both.

(7) In any proceedings under this section –

    (a) a report by a British consular officer or a deposition made before a British consular officer and authenticated under the signature of that officer is admissible, upon proof that the officer or the deponent cannot be found in the United Kingdom, as evidence of the matters stated in it, and

    (b) it is not necessary to prove the signature or official character of the person who appears to have signed any such report or deposition.

86 Power to modify sections 83 and 85

(1) Regulations may provide for section 83 not to apply if –

    (a) the adopters or (as the case may be) prospective adopters are natural parents, natural relatives or guardians of the child in question (or one of them is), or

    (b) the British resident in question is a partner of a parent of the child,

and any prescribed conditions are met.

(2) Regulations may provide for section 85(1) to apply with modifications, or not to apply, if –

    (a) the prospective adopters are parents, relatives or guardians of the child in question (or one of them is), or

    (b) the prospective adopter is a partner of a parent of the child,

and any prescribed conditions are met.

(3) On the occasion of the first exercise of the power to make regulations under this section –

    (a) the statutory instrument containing the regulations is not to be made unless a draft of the instrument has been laid before, and approved by a resolution of, each House of Parliament, and

    (b) accordingly section 140(2) does not apply to the instrument.

(4) In this section, 'prescribed' means prescribed by regulations and 'regulations' means regulations made by the Secretary of State after consultation with the Assembly.

Overseas adoptions

87 Overseas adoptions

(1) In this Act, 'overseas adoption' –

   (a) means an adoption of a description specified in an order made by the
        Secretary of State, being a description of adoptions effected under the law of
        any country or territory outside the British Islands, but
   (b) does not include a Convention adoption.

(2) Regulations may prescribe the requirements that ought to be met by an adoption
of any description effected after the commencement of the regulations for it to be an
overseas adoption for the purposes of this Act.

(3) At any time when such regulations have effect, the Secretary of State must
exercise his powers under this section so as to secure that subsequently effected
adoptions of any description are not overseas adoptions for the purposes of this Act if
he considers that they are not likely within a reasonable time to meet the prescribed
requirements.

(4) In this section references to this Act include the Adoption Act 1976.

(5) An order under this section may contain provision as to the manner in which
evidence of any overseas adoption may be given.

(6) In this section –

   'adoption' means an adoption of a child or of a person who was a child at the
      time the adoption was applied for,
   'regulations' means regulations made by the Secretary of State after consultation
      with the Assembly.

Miscellaneous

88 Modification of section 67 for Hague Convention adoptions

(1) If the High Court is satisfied, on an application under this section, that each of the
following conditions is met in the case of a Convention adoption, it may direct that
section 67(3) does not apply, or does not apply to any extent specified in the direction.

(2) The conditions are –

   (a) that under the law of the country in which the adoption was effected, the
        adoption is not a full adoption,
   (b) that the consents referred to in Article 4(c) and (d) of the Convention have
        not been given for a full adoption or that the United Kingdom is not the
        receiving State (within the meaning of Article 2 of the Convention),
   (c) that it would be more favourable to the adopted child for a direction to be
        given under subsection (1).

(3) A full adoption is an adoption by virtue of which the child is to be treated in law
as not being the child of any person other than the adopters or adopter.

(4) In relation to a direction under this section and an application for it, sections 59
and 60 of the Family Law Act 1986 (declarations under Part 3 of that Act as to marital
status) apply as they apply in relation to a direction under that Part and an application
for such a direction.

89 Annulment etc of overseas or Hague Convention adoptions

(1) The High Court may, on an application under this subsection, by order annul a Convention adoption or Convention adoption order on the ground that the adoption is contrary to public policy.

(2) The High Court may, on an application under this subsection –

(a) by order provide for an overseas adoption or a determination under section 91 to cease to be valid on the ground that the adoption or determination is contrary to public policy or that the authority which purported to authorise the adoption or make the determination was not competent to entertain the case, or

(b) decide the extent, if any, to which a determination under section 91 has been affected by a subsequent determination under that section.

(3) The High Court may, in any proceedings in that court, decide that an overseas adoption or a determination under section 91 is to be treated, for the purposes of those proceedings, as invalid on either of the grounds mentioned in subsection (2)(a).

(4) Subject to the preceding provisions, the validity of a Convention adoption, Convention adoption order or overseas adoption or a determination under section 91 cannot be called in question in proceedings in any court in England and Wales.

90 Section 89: supplementary

(1) Any application for an order under section 89 or a decision under subsection (2)(b) or (3) of that section must be made in the prescribed manner and within any prescribed period.

'Prescribed' means prescribed by rules.

(2) No application may be made under section 89(1) in respect of an adoption unless immediately before the application is made –

(a) the person adopted, or
(b) the adopters or adopter,

habitually reside in England and Wales.

(3) In deciding in pursuance of section 89 whether such an authority as is mentioned in section 91 was competent to entertain a particular case, a court is bound by any finding of fact made by the authority and stated by the authority to be so made for the purpose of determining whether the authority was competent to entertain the case.

91 Overseas determinations and orders

(1) Subsection (2) applies where any authority of a Convention country (other than the United Kingdom) or of the Channel Islands, the Isle of Man or any British overseas territory has power under the law of that country or territory –

(a) to authorise, or review the authorisation of, an adoption order made in that country or territory, or

(b) to give or review a decision revoking or annulling such an order or a Convention adoption.

(2) If the authority makes a determination in the exercise of that power, the determination is to have effect for the purpose of effecting, confirming or terminating the adoption in question or, as the case may be, confirming its termination.

(3) Subsection (2) is subject to section 89 and to any subsequent determination having effect under that subsection.

Chapter 7
Miscellaneous

Restrictions

92 Restriction on arranging adoptions etc

(1) A person who is neither an adoption agency nor acting in pursuance of an order of the High Court must not take any of the steps mentioned in subsection (2).

(2) The steps are –

(a) asking a person other than an adoption agency to provide a child for adoption,

(b) asking a person other than an adoption agency to provide prospective adopters for a child,

(c) offering to find a child for adoption,

(d) offering a child for adoption to a person other than an adoption agency,

(e) handing over a child to any person other than an adoption agency with a view to the child's adoption by that or another person,

(f) receiving a child handed over to him in contravention of paragraph (e),

(g) entering into an agreement with any person for the adoption of a child, or for the purpose of facilitating the adoption of a child, where no adoption agency is acting on behalf of the child in the adoption,

(h) initiating or taking part in negotiations of which the purpose is the conclusion of an agreement within paragraph (g),

(i) causing another person to take any of the steps mentioned in paragraphs (a) to (h).

(3) Subsection (1) does not apply to a person taking any of the steps mentioned in paragraphs (d), (e), (g), (h) and (i) of subsection (2) if the following condition is met.

(4) The condition is that –

(a) the prospective adopters are parents, relatives or guardians of the child (or one of them is), or

(b) the prospective adopter is the partner of a parent of the child.

(5) References to an adoption agency in subsection (2) include a prescribed person outside the United Kingdom exercising functions corresponding to those of an adoption agency, if the functions are being exercised in prescribed circumstances in respect of the child in question.

(6) The Secretary of State may, after consultation with the Assembly, by order make any amendments of subsections (1) to (4), and any consequential amendments of this Act, which he considers necessary or expedient.

(7) In this section –

(a) 'agreement' includes an arrangement (whether or not enforceable),

(b) 'prescribed' means prescribed by regulations made by the Secretary of State after consultation with the Assembly.

93 Offence of breaching restrictions under section 92

(1) If a person contravenes section 92(1), he is guilty of an offence; and, if that person is an adoption society, the person who manages the society is also guilty of the offence.

(2) A person is not guilty of an offence under subsection (1) of taking the step mentioned in paragraph (f) of section 92(2) unless it is proved that he knew or had reason to suspect that the child was handed over to him in contravention of paragraph (e) of that subsection.

(3) A person is not guilty of an offence under subsection (1) of causing a person to take any of the steps mentioned in paragraphs (a) to (h) of section 92(2) unless it is proved that he knew or had reason to suspect that the step taken would contravene the paragraph in question.

(4) But subsections (2) and (3) only apply if sufficient evidence is adduced to raise an issue as to whether the person had the knowledge or reason mentioned.

(5) A person guilty of an offence under this section is liable on summary conviction to imprisonment for a term not exceeding six months, or a fine not exceeding £10,000, or both.

94 Restriction on reports

(1) A person who is not within a prescribed description may not, in any prescribed circumstances, prepare a report for any person about the suitability of a child for adoption or of a person to adopt a child or about the adoption, or placement for adoption, of a child.

'Prescribed' means prescribed by regulations made by the Secretary of State after consultation with the Assembly.

(2) If a person –

(a) contravenes subsection (1), or

(b) causes a person to prepare a report, or submits to any person a report which has been prepared, in contravention of that subsection,

he is guilty of an offence.

(3) If a person who works for an adoption society –

(a) contravenes subsection (1), or

(b) causes a person to prepare a report, or submits to any person a report which has been prepared, in contravention of that subsection,

the person who manages the society is also guilty of the offence.

(4) A person is not guilty of an offence under subsection (2)(b) unless it is proved that he knew or had reason to suspect that the report would be, or had been, prepared in contravention of subsection (1).

But this subsection only applies if sufficient evidence is adduced to raise an issue as to whether the person had the knowledge or reason mentioned.

(5) A person guilty of an offence under this section is liable on summary conviction to imprisonment for a term not exceeding six months, or a fine not exceeding level 5 on the standard scale, or both.

95 Prohibition of certain payments

(1) This section applies to any payment (other than an excepted payment) which is made for or in consideration of –

    (a) the adoption of a child,

    (b) giving any consent required in connection with the adoption of a child,

    (c) removing from the United Kingdom a child who is a Commonwealth citizen, or is habitually resident in the United Kingdom, to a place outside the British Islands for the purpose of adoption,

    (d) a person (who is neither an adoption agency nor acting in pursuance of an order of the High Court) taking any step mentioned in section 92(2),

    (e) preparing, causing to be prepared or submitting a report the preparation of which contravenes section 94(1).

(2) In this section and section 96, removing a child from the United Kingdom has the same meaning as in section 85.

(3) Any person who –

    (a) makes any payment to which this section applies,

    (b) agrees or offers to make any such payment, or

    (c) receives or agrees to receive or attempts to obtain any such payment,

is guilty of an offence.

(4) A person guilty of an offence under this section is liable on summary conviction to imprisonment for a term not exceeding six months, or a fine not exceeding £10,000, or both.

96 Excepted payments

(1) A payment is an excepted payment if it is made by virtue of, or in accordance with provision made by or under, this Act, the Adoption (Scotland) Act 1978 or the Adoption (Northern Ireland) Order 1987 (SI 1987/2203 (NI 22)).

(2) A payment is an excepted payment if it is made to a registered adoption society by –

    (a) a parent or guardian of a child, or

    (b) a person who adopts or proposes to adopt a child,

in respect of expenses reasonably incurred by the society in connection with the adoption or proposed adoption of the child.

(3) A payment is an excepted payment if it is made in respect of any legal or medical expenses incurred or to be incurred by any person in connection with an application to a court which he has made or proposes to make for an adoption order, a placement order, or an order under section 26 or 84.

(4) A payment made as mentioned in section 95(1)(c) is an excepted payment if –

(a) the condition in section 85(2) is met, and

(b) the payment is made in respect of the travel and accommodation expenses reasonably incurred in removing the child from the United Kingdom for the purpose of adoption.

97 Sections 92 to 96: interpretation

In sections 92 to 96 –

(a) 'adoption agency' includes a Scottish or Northern Irish adoption agency,

(b) 'payment' includes reward,

(c) references to adoption are to the adoption of persons, wherever they may be habitually resident, effected under the law of any country or territory, whether within or outside the British Islands.

Information

98 Pre-commencement adoptions: information

(1) Regulations under section 9 may make provision for the purpose of –

(a) assisting persons adopted before the appointed day who have attained the age of 18 to obtain information in relation to their adoption, and

(b) facilitating contact between such persons and their relatives.

(2) For that purpose the regulations may confer functions on –

(a) registered adoption support agencies,

(b) the Registrar General,

(c) adoption agencies.

(3) For that purpose the regulations may –

(a) authorise or require any person mentioned in subsection (2) to disclose information,

(b) authorise or require the disclosure of information contained in records kept under section 8 of the Public Records Act 1958 (court records),

and may impose conditions on the disclosure of information, including conditions restricting its further disclosure.

(4) The regulations may authorise the charging of prescribed fees by any person mentioned in subsection (2) or in respect of the disclosure of information under subsection (3)(b).

(5) An authorisation or requirement to disclose information by virtue of subsection (3)(a) has effect in spite of any restriction on the disclosure of information in Chapter 5.

(6) The making of regulations by virtue of subsections (2) to (4) which relate to the Registrar General requires the approval of the Chancellor of the Exchequer.

(7) In this section –

'appointed day' means the day appointed for the commencement of sections 56 to 65, 'registered adoption support agency' means an adoption support agency in respect of which a person is registered under Part 2 of the Care Standards Act 2000,

'relative', in relation to an adopted person, means any person who (but for his adoption) would be related to him by blood (including half-blood) or marriage.

Proceedings

99 Proceedings for offences

Proceedings for an offence by virtue of section 9 or 59 may not, without the written consent of the Attorney General, be taken by any person other than the National Care Standards Commission or the Assembly.

100 Appeals

In section 94 of the 1989 Act (appeals under that Act), in subsections (1)(a) and (2), after 'this Act' there is inserted 'or the Adoption and Children Act 2002'.

101 Privacy

(1) Proceedings under this Act in the High Court or a County Court may be heard and determined in private.

(2) In section 12 of the Administration of Justice Act 1960 (publication of information relating to proceedings in private), in subsection (1)(a)(ii), after '1989' there is inserted 'or the Adoption and Children Act 2002'.

(3) In section 97 of the 1989 Act (privacy for children involved in certain proceedings), after 'this Act' in subsections (1) and (2) there is inserted 'or the Adoption and Children Act 2002'.

The Children and Family Court Advisory and Support Service

102 Officers of the Service

(1) For the purposes of –

(a) any relevant application,
(b) the signification by any person of any consent to placement or adoption,

rules must provide for the appointment in prescribed cases of an officer of the Children and Family Court Advisory and Support Service ('the Service').

(2) The rules may provide for the appointment of such an officer in other circumstances in which it appears to the Lord Chancellor to be necessary or expedient to do so.

(3) The rules may provide for the officer –

(a) to act on behalf of the child upon the hearing of any relevant application, with the duty of safeguarding the interests of the child in the prescribed manner,
(b) where the court so requests, to prepare a report on matters relating to the welfare of the child in question,

    (c) to witness documents which signify consent to placement or adoption,

    (d) to perform prescribed functions.

(4) A report prepared in pursuance of the rules on matters relating to the welfare of a child must –

    (a) deal with prescribed matters (unless the court orders otherwise), and

    (b) be made in the manner required by the court.

(5) A person who –

    (a) in the case of an application for the making, varying or revocation of a placement order, is employed by the local authority which made the application,

    (b) in the case of an application for an adoption order in respect of a child who was placed for adoption, is employed by the adoption agency which placed him, or

    (c) is within a prescribed description,

is not to be appointed under subsection (1) or (2).

(6) In this section, 'relevant application' means an application for –

    (a) the making, varying or revocation of a placement order,

    (b) the making of an order under section 26, or the varying or revocation of such an order,

    (c) the making of an adoption order, or

    (d) the making of an order under section 84.

(7) Rules may make provision as to the assistance which the court may require an officer of the Service to give to it.

103 Right of officers of the Service to have access to adoption agency records

(1) Where an officer of the Service has been appointed to act under section 102(1), he has the right at all reasonable times to examine and take copies of any records of, or held by, an adoption agency which were compiled in connection with the making, or proposed making, by any person of any application under this Part in respect of the child concerned.

(2) Where an officer of the Service takes a copy of any record which he is entitled to examine under this section, that copy or any part of it is admissible as evidence of any matter referred to in any –

    (a) report which he makes to the court in the proceedings in question, or

    (b) evidence which he gives in those proceedings.

(3) Subsection (2) has effect regardless of any enactment or rule of law which would otherwise prevent the record in question being admissible in evidence.

Evidence

104 Evidence of consent

(1) If a document signifying any consent which is required by this Part to be given is witnessed in accordance with rules, it is to be admissible in evidence without further proof of the signature of the person by whom it was executed.

(2) A document signifying any such consent which purports to be witnessed in accordance with rules is to be presumed to be so witnessed, and to have been executed and witnessed on the date and at the place specified in the document, unless the contrary is proved.

****

General

109 Avoiding delay

(1) In proceedings in which a question may arise as to whether an adoption order or placement order should be made, or any other question with respect to such an order, the court must (in the light of any rules made by virtue of subsection (2)) –

    (a) draw up a timetable with a view to determining such a question without delay, and

    (b) give such directions as it considers appropriate for the purpose of ensuring that the timetable is adhered to.

(2) Rules may –

    (a) prescribe periods within which prescribed steps must be taken in relation to such proceedings, and

    (b) make other provision with respect to such proceedings for the purpose of ensuring that such questions are determined without delay.

110 Service of notices etc

Any notice or information required to be given by virtue of this Act may be given by post.

PART 2

AMENDMENTS OF THE CHILDREN ACT 1989

111 Parental responsibility of unmarried father

(1)–(6) (*not reproduced here*)

(7) Paragraph (a) of section 4(1) of the 1989 Act, as substituted by subsection (2) of this section, does not confer parental responsibility on a man who was registered under an enactment referred to in paragraph (a), (b) or (c) of section 4(1A) of that Act, as inserted by subsection (3) of this section, before the commencement of subsection (3) in relation to that paragraph.

Section 111

See Children Act 1989, ss 2, 4, 104 for effect of amendments (in force from 1 December 2003).

112 Acquisition of parental responsibility by step-parent

After section 4 of the 1989 Act there is inserted –

'4A Acquisition of parental responsibility by step-parent

(1) Where a child's parent ("parent A") who has parental responsibility for the child is married to a person who is not the child's parent ("the step-parent")—

(a) parent A or, if the other parent of the child also has parental responsibility for the child, both parents may by agreement with the step-parent provide for the step-parent to have parental responsibility for the child; or

(b) the court may, on the application of the step-parent, order that the step-parent shall have parental responsibility for the child.

(2) An agreement under subsection (1)(a) is also a "parental responsibility agreement", and section 4(2) applies in relation to such agreements as it applies in relation to parental responsibility agreements under section 4.

(3) A parental responsibility agreement under subsection (1)(a), or an order under subsection (1)(b), may only be brought to an end by an order of the court made on the application –

(a) of any person who has parental responsibility for the child; or
(b) with the leave of the court, of the child himself.

(4) The court may only grant leave under subsection (3)(b) if it is satisfied that the child has sufficient understanding to make the proposed application.'

113 Section 8 orders: local authority foster parents

In section 9 of the 1989 Act (restrictions on making section 8 orders) –

(a) in subsection (3)(c), for 'three years' there is substituted 'one year', and
(b) subsection (4) is omitted.

114 Residence orders: extension to age of 18

(1) In section 12 of the 1989 Act (residence orders and parental responsibility), after subsection (4) there is inserted –

'(5) The power of a court to make a residence order in favour of any person who is not the parent or guardian of the child concerned includes power to direct, at the request of that person, that the order continue in force until the child reaches the age of eighteen (unless the order is brought to an end earlier); and any power to vary a residence order is exercisable accordingly.

(6) Where a residence order includes such a direction, an application to vary or discharge the order may only be made, if apart from this subsection the leave of the court is not required, with such leave'.

(2) In section 9 of that Act (restrictions on making section 8 orders), at the beginning of subsection (6) there is inserted 'Subject to section 12(5)'.

(3) In section 91 of that Act (effect and duration of orders), in subsection (10), after '9(6)' there is inserted 'or 12(5)'.

115 Special guardianship

(1) After section 14 of the 1989 Act there is inserted –

'*Special guardianship*

14A Special guardianship orders

(1) A "special guardianship order" is an order appointing one or more individuals to be a child's "special guardian" (or special guardians).

(2) A special guardian –

 (a) must be aged eighteen or over; and
 (b) must not be a parent of the child in question,

and subsections (3) to (6) are to be read in that light.

(3) The court may make a special guardianship order with respect to any child on the application of an individual who –

 (a) is entitled to make such an application with respect to the child; or
 (b) has obtained the leave of the court to make the application,

or on the joint application of more than one such individual.

(4) Section 9(3) applies in relation to an application for leave to apply for a special guardianship order as it applies in relation to an application for leave to apply for a section 8 order.

(5) The individuals who are entitled to apply for a special guardianship order with respect to a child are –

 (a) any guardian of the child;
 (b) any individual in whose favour a residence order is in force with respect to the child;
 (c) any individual listed in subsection (5)(b) or (c) of section 10 (as read with subsection (10) of that section);
 (d) a local authority foster parent with whom the child has lived for a period of at least one year immediately preceding the application.

(6) The court may also make a special guardianship order with respect to a child in any family proceedings in which a question arises with respect to the welfare of the child if –

 (a) an application for the order has been made by an individual who falls within subsection (3)(a) or (b) (or more than one such individual jointly); or
 (b) the court considers that a special guardianship order should be made even though no such application has been made.

(7) No individual may make an application under subsection (3) or (6)(a) unless, before the beginning of the period of three months ending with the date of

the application, he has given written notice of his intention to make the application –

(a)　if the child in question is being looked after by a local authority, to that local authority, or

(b)　otherwise, to the local authority in whose area the individual is ordinarily resident.

(8) On receipt of such a notice, the local authority must investigate the matter and prepare a report for the court dealing with –

(a)　the suitability of the applicant to be a special guardian;

(b)　such matters (if any) as may be prescribed by the Secretary of State; and

(c)　any other matter which the local authority consider to be relevant.

(9) The court may itself ask a local authority to conduct such an investigation and prepare such a report, and the local authority must do so.

(10) The local authority may make such arrangements as they see fit for any person to act on their behalf in connection with conducting an investigation or preparing a report referred to in subsection (8) or (9).

(11) The court may not make a special guardianship order unless it has received a report dealing with the matters referred to in subsection (8).

(12) Subsections (8) and (9) of section 10 apply in relation to special guardianship orders as they apply in relation to section 8 orders.

(13) This section is subject to section 29(5) and (6) of the Adoption and Children Act 2002.

14B Special guardianship orders: making

(1) Before making a special guardianship order, the court must consider whether, if the order were made –

(a)　a contact order should also be made with respect to the child, and

(b)　any section 8 order in force with respect to the child should be varied or discharged.

(2) On making a special guardianship order, the court may also –

(a)　give leave for the child to be known by a new surname;

(b)　grant the leave required by section 14C(3)(b), either generally or for specified purposes.

14C Special guardianship orders: effect

(1) The effect of a special guardianship order is that while the order remains in force –

(a)　a special guardian appointed by the order has parental responsibility for the child in respect of whom it is made; and

(b)　subject to any other order in force with respect to the child under this Act, a special guardian is entitled to exercise parental responsibility to the exclusion of any other person with parental responsibility for the child (apart from another special guardian).

(2) Subsection (1) does not affect –

(a) the operation of any enactment or rule of law which requires the consent of more than one person with parental responsibility in a matter affecting the child; or

(b) any rights which a parent of the child has in relation to the child's adoption or placement for adoption.

(3) While a special guardianship order is in force with respect to a child, no person may –

(a) cause the child to be known by a new surname; or

(b) remove him from the United Kingdom,

without either the written consent of every person who has parental responsibility for the child or the leave of the court.

(4) Subsection (3)(b) does not prevent the removal of a child, for a period of less than three months, by a special guardian of his.

(5) If the child with respect to whom a special guardianship order is in force dies, his special guardian must take reasonable steps to give notice of that fact to –

(a) each parent of the child with parental responsibility; and

(b) each guardian of the child,

but if the child has more than one special guardian, and one of them has taken such steps in relation to a particular parent or guardian, any other special guardian need not do so as respects that parent or guardian.

(6) This section is subject to section 29(7) of the Adoption and Children Act 2002.

14D Special guardianship orders: variation and discharge

(1) The court may vary or discharge a special guardianship order on the application of –

(a) the special guardian (or any of them, if there are more than one);

(b) any parent or guardian of the child concerned;

(c) any individual in whose favour a residence order is in force with respect to the child;

(d) any individual not falling within any of paragraphs (a) to (c) who has, or immediately before the making of the special guardianship order had, parental responsibility for the child;

(e) the child himself;

(f) a local authority designated in a care order with respect to the child.

(2) In any family proceedings in which a question arises with respect to the welfare of a child with respect to whom a special guardianship order is in force, the court may also vary or discharge the special guardianship order if it considers that the order should be varied or discharged, even though no application has been made under subsection (1).

(3) The following must obtain the leave of the court before making an application under subsection (1) –

(a)   the child;

(b)   any parent or guardian of his;

(c)   any step-parent of his who has acquired, and has not lost, parental responsibility for him by virtue of section 4A;

(d)   any individual falling within subsection (1)(d) who immediately before the making of the special guardianship order had, but no longer has, parental responsibility for him.

(4) Where the person applying for leave to make an application under subsection (1) is the child, the court may only grant leave if it is satisfied that he has sufficient understanding to make the proposed application under subsection (1).

(5) The court may not grant leave to a person falling within subsection (3)(b)(c) or (d) unless it is satisfied that there has been a significant change in circumstances since the making of the special guardianship order.

14E Special guardianship orders: supplementary

(1) In proceedings in which any question of making, varying or discharging a special guardianship order arises, the court shall (in the light of any rules made by virtue of subsection (3)) –

(a)   draw up a timetable with a view to determining the question without delay; and

(b)   give such directions as it considers appropriate for the purpose of ensuring, so far as is reasonably practicable, that the timetable is adhered to.

(2) Subsection (1) applies also in relation to proceedings in which any other question with respect to a special guardianship order arises.

(3) The power to make rules in subsection (2) of section 11 applies for the purposes of this section as it applies for the purposes of that.

(4) A special guardianship order, or an order varying one, may contain provisions which are to have effect for a specified period.

(5) Section 11(7) (apart from paragraph (c)) applies in relation to special guardianship orders and orders varying them as it applies in relation to section 8 orders.

14F Special guardianship support services

(1) Each local authority must make arrangements for the provision within their area of special guardianship support services, which means –

(a)   counselling, advice and information; and

(b)   such other services as are prescribed,

in relation to special guardianship.

(2) The power to make regulations under subsection (1)(b) is to be exercised so as to secure that local authorities provide financial support.

(3) At the request of any of the following persons –

(a)   a child with respect to whom a special guardianship order is in force;

(b) a special guardian;
(c) a parent;
(d) any other person who falls within a prescribed description,

a local authority may carry out an assessment of that person's needs for special guardianship support services (but, if the Secretary of State so provides in regulations, they must do so if he is a person of a prescribed description, or if his case falls within a prescribed description, or if both he and his case fall within prescribed descriptions).

(4) A local authority may, at the request of any other person, carry out an assessment of that person's needs for special guardianship support services.

(5) Where, as a result of an assessment, a local authority decide that a person has needs for special guardianship support services, they must then decide whether to provide any such services to that person.

(6) If –

(a) a local authority decide to provide any special guardianship support services to a person, and
(b) the circumstances fall within a prescribed description,

the local authority must prepare a plan in accordance with which special guardianship support services are to be provided to him, and keep the plan under review.

(7) The Secretary of State may by regulations make provision about assessments, preparing and reviewing plans, the provision of special guardianship support services in accordance with plans and reviewing the provision of special guardianship support services.

(8) The regulations may in particular make provision–

(a) about the type of assessment which is to be carried out, or the way in which an assessment is to be carried out;
(b) about the way in which a plan is to be prepared;
(c) about the way in which, and the time at which, a plan or the provision of special guardianship support services is to be reviewed;
(d) about the considerations to which a local authority are to have regard in carrying out an assessment or review or preparing a plan;
(e) as to the circumstances in which a local authority may provide special guardianship support services subject to conditions (including conditions as to payment for the support or the repayment of financial support);
(f) as to the consequences of conditions imposed by virtue of paragraph (e) not being met (including the recovery of any financial support provided);
(g) as to the circumstances in which this section may apply to a local authority in respect of persons who are outside that local authority's area;
(h) as to the circumstances in which a local authority may recover from another local authority the expenses of providing special guardianship support services to any person.

(9) A local authority may provide special guardianship support services (or any part of them) by securing their provision by –

(a) another local authority; or

(b) a person within a description prescribed in regulations of persons who may provide special guardianship support services,

and may also arrange with any such authority or person for that other authority or that person to carry out the local authority's functions in relation to assessments under this section.

(10) A local authority may carry out an assessment of the needs of any person for the purposes of this section at the same time as an assessment of his needs is made under any other provision of this Act or under any other enactment.(11) Section 27 (co-operation between authorities) applies in relation to the exercise of functions of a local authority under this section as it applies in relation to the exercise of functions of a local authority under Part 3.

14G Special guardianship support services: representations

(1) Every local authority shall establish a procedure for considering representations (including complaints) made to them by any person to whom they may provide special guardianship support services about the discharge of their functions under section 14F in relation to him.

(2) Regulations may be made by the Secretary of State imposing time limits on the making of representations under subsection (1).

(3) In considering representations under subsection (1), a local authority shall comply with regulations (if any) made by the Secretary of State for the purposes of this subsection.'

(2) The 1989 Act is amended as follows.

(3) In section 1 (welfare of the child), in subsection (4)(b), after 'discharge' there is inserted 'a special guardianship order or'.

(4) In section 5 (appointment of guardians) –

    (a) in subsection (1) –
        (i) in paragraph (b), for 'or guardian' there is substituted ', guardian or special guardian', and
        (ii) at the end of paragraph (b) there is inserted:

'; or
    (c) paragraph (b) does not apply, and the child's only or last surviving special guardian dies.',

    (b) in subsection (4), at the end there is inserted '; and a special guardian of a child may appoint another individual to be the child's guardian in the event of his death', and
    (c) in subsection (7), at the end of paragraph (b) there is inserted 'or he was the child's only (or last surviving) special guardian'.

116 (*not reproduced here*)

Section 116

See Children Act 1989, ss 17, 22, 24A for effect of amendments (in force from 7 November 2002).

117 Inquiries by local authorities into representations

(1) In section 24D of the 1989 Act (representations: sections 23A to 24B), after subsection (1) there is inserted –

'(1A) Regulations may be made by the Secretary of State imposing time limits on the making of representations under subsection (1).'

(2) Section 26 of that Act (procedure for considering other representations) is amended as follows.

(3) In subsection (3) (which makes provision as to the persons by whom, and the matters in respect of which, representations may be made), for 'functions under this Part' there is substituted 'qualifying functions'.

(4) After that subsection there is inserted –

'(3A) The following are qualifying functions for the purposes of subsection (3) –

(a) functions under this Part,
(b) such functions under Part 4 or 5 as are specified by the Secretary of State in regulations.

(3B) The duty under subsection (3) extends to representations (including complaints) made to the authority by –
(a)
any person mentioned in section 3(1) of the Adoption and Children Act 2002 (persons for whose needs provision is made by the Adoption Service) and any other person to whom arrangements for the provision of adoption support services (within the meaning of that Act) extend,
(b) such other person as the authority consider has sufficient interest in a child who is or may be adopted to warrant his representations being considered by them,

about the discharge by the authority of such functions under the Adoption and Children Act 2002 as are specified by the Secretary of State in regulations.'

(5) In subsection (4) (procedure to require involvement of independent person), after paragraph (b) there is inserted –

'but this subsection is subject to subsection (5A).'

(6) After that subsection there is inserted –

'(4A) Regulations may be made by the Secretary of State imposing time limits on the making of representations under this section.'

(7) After subsection (5) there is inserted –

'(5A) Regulations under subsection (5) may provide that subsection (4) does not apply in relation to any consideration or discussion which takes place as part of a procedure for which provision is made by the regulations for the purpose of resolving informally the matters raised in the representations.'

118 (*not reproduced here*)

Section 118

See Children Act 1989, s 26 for effect of amendments (in force from 21 May 2004).

119 (*not reproduced here*)

Section 119

See Children Act 1989, s 26A for effect of amendments (in force from 1 April 2004).

120 (*not reproduced here*)

Section 120

See Children Act 1989, s 31 for effect of amendments (in force from 31 January 2005).

121 Care plans

(1) In section 31 of the 1989 Act (care and supervision orders), after subsection (3) there is inserted –

'(3A) No care order may be made with respect to a child until the court has considered a section 31A plan.'

(2) After that section there is inserted –

'31A Care orders: care plans

(1) Where an application is made on which a care order might be made with respect to a child, the appropriate local authority must, within such time as the court may direct, prepare a plan ("a care plan") for the future care of the child.

(2) While the application is pending, the authority must keep any care plan prepared by them under review and, if they are of the opinion some change is required, revise the plan, or make a new plan, accordingly.

(3) A care plan must give any prescribed information and do so in the prescribed manner.

(4) For the purposes of this section, the appropriate local authority, in relation to a child in respect of whom a care order might be made, is the local authority proposed to be designated in the order.

(5) In section 31(3A) and this section, references to a care order do not include an interim care order.

(6) A plan prepared, or treated as prepared, under this section is referred to in this Act as a "section 31A plan".'

(3) If –

  (a) before subsection (2) comes into force, a care order has been made in respect of a child and a plan for the future care of the child has been prepared in connection with the making of the order by the local authority designated in the order, and

  (b) on the day on which that subsection comes into force the order is in force, or would be in force but for section 29(1) of this Act, the plan is to have effect as if made under section 31A of the 1989 Act.

122 Interests of children in proceedings

(1) In section 41 of the 1989 Act (specified proceedings) –

   (a) in subsection (6), after paragraph (h) there is inserted –

   '(hh) on an application for the making or revocation of a placement order (within the meaning of section 21 of the Adoption and Children Act 2002);',

   (b) after that subsection there is inserted –

   '(6A) The proceedings which may be specified under subsection (6)(i) include (for example) proceedings for the making, varying or discharging of a section 8 order.'

(2) In section 93 of the 1989 Act (rules of court), in subsection (2), after paragraph (b) there is inserted –

   '(bb) for children to be separately represented in relevant proceedings,'

PART 3

MISCELLANEOUS AND FINAL PROVISIONS

Chapter 1
Miscellaneous

Advertisements in the United Kingdom

123 Restriction on advertisements etc

(1) A person must not –

   (a) publish or distribute an advertisement or information to which this section applies, or
   (b) cause such an advertisement or information to be published or distributed.

(2) This section applies to an advertisement indicating that –

   (a) the parent or guardian of a child wants the child to be adopted,
   (b) a person wants to adopt a child,
   (c) a person other than an adoption agency is willing to take any step mentioned in paragraphs (a) to (e), (g) and (h) and (so far as relating to those paragraphs) (i) of section 92(2),
   (d) a person other than an adoption agency is willing to receive a child handed over to him with a view to the child's adoption by him or another, or
   (e) a person is willing to remove a child from the United Kingdom for the purposes of adoption.

(3) This section applies to –

   (a) information about how to do anything which, if done, would constitute an offence under section 85 or 93, section 11 or 50 of the Adoption (Scotland)

Act 1978 or Article 11 or 58 of the Adoption (Northern Ireland) Order 1987 (SI 1987/2203 (NI 22)) (whether or not the information includes a warning that doing the thing in question may constitute an offence),

(b)   information about a particular child as a child available for adoption.

(4) For the purposes of this section and section 124 –

   (a)   publishing or distributing an advertisement or information means publishing it or distributing it to the public and includes doing so by electronic means (for example, by means of the internet),

   (b)   the public includes selected members of the public as well as the public generally or any section of the public.

(5) Subsection (1) does not apply to publication or distribution by or on behalf of an adoption agency.

(6) The Secretary of State may by order make any amendments of this section which he considers necessary or expedient in consequence of any developments in technology relating to publishing or distributing advertisements or other information by electronic or electro-magnetic means.

(7) References to an adoption agency in this section include a prescribed person outside the United Kingdom exercising functions corresponding to those of an adoption agency, if the functions are being exercised in prescribed circumstances.

'Prescribed' means prescribed by regulations made by the Secretary of State.

(8) Before exercising the power conferred by subsection (6) or (7), the Secretary of State must consult the Scottish Ministers, the Department of Health, Social Services and Public Safety and the Assembly.

(9) In this section –

   (a)   'adoption agency' includes a Scottish or Northern Irish adoption agency,

   (b)   references to adoption are to the adoption of persons, wherever they may be habitually resident, effected under the law of any country or territory, whether within or outside the British Islands.

124 Offence of breaching restriction under section 123

(1) A person who contravenes section 123(1) is guilty of an offence.

(2) A person is not guilty of an offence under this section unless it is proved that he knew or had reason to suspect that section 123 applied to the advertisement or information.

But this subsection only applies if sufficient evidence is adduced to raise an issue as to whether the person had the knowledge or reason mentioned.

(3) A person guilty of an offence under this section is liable on summary conviction to imprisonment for a term not exceeding three months, or a fine not exceeding level 5 on the standard scale, or both.

Adoption and Children Act Register

125 Adoption and Children Act Register

(1) Her Majesty may by Order in Council make provision for the Secretary of State to establish and maintain a register, to be called the Adoption and Children Act Register, containing –

    (a) prescribed information about children who are suitable for adoption and prospective adopters who are suitable to adopt a child,

    (b) prescribed information about persons included in the register in pursuance of paragraph (a) in respect of things occurring after their inclusion.

(2) For the purpose of giving assistance in finding persons with whom children may be placed for purposes other than adoption, an Order under this section may –

    (a) provide for the register to contain information about such persons and the children who may be placed with them, and

    (b) apply any of the other provisions of this group of sections (that is, this section and sections 126 to 131), with or without modifications.

(3) The register is not to be open to public inspection or search.

(4) An Order under this section may make provision about the retention of information in the register.

(5) Information is to be kept in the register in any form the Secretary of State considers appropriate.

126 Use of an organisation to establish the register

(1) The Secretary of State may make an arrangement with an organisation under which any function of his under an Order under section 125 of establishing and maintaining the register, and disclosing information entered in, or compiled from information entered in, the register to any person is performed wholly or partly by the organisation on his behalf.

(2) The arrangement may include provision for payments to be made to the organisation by the Secretary of State.

(3) If the Secretary of State makes an arrangement under this section with an organisation, the organisation is to perform the functions exercisable by virtue of this section in accordance with any directions given by the Secretary of State and the directions may be of general application (or general application in any part of Great Britain) or be special directions.

(4) An exercise of the Secretary of State's powers under subsection (1) or (3) requires the agreement of the Scottish Ministers (if the register applies to Scotland) and of the Assembly (if the register applies to Wales).

(5) References in this group of sections to the registration organisation are to any organisation for the time being performing functions in respect of the register by virtue of arrangements under this section.

127 Use of an organisation as agency for payments

(1) An Order under section 125 may authorise an organisation with which an arrangement is made under section 126 to act as agent for the payment or receipt of

sums payable by adoption agencies to other adoption agencies and may require adoption agencies to pay or receive such sums through the organisation.

(2) The organisation is to perform the functions exercisable by virtue of this section in accordance with any directions given by the Secretary of State; and the directions may be of general application (or general application in any part of Great Britain) or be special directions.

(3) An exercise of the Secretary of State's power to give directions under subsection (2) requires the agreement of the Scottish Ministers (if any payment agency provision applies to Scotland) and of the Assembly (if any payment agency provision applies to Wales).

128 Supply of information for the register

(1) An Order under section 125 may require adoption agencies to give prescribed information to the Secretary of State or the registration organisation for entry in the register.

(2) Information is to be given to the Secretary of State or the registration organisation when required by the Order and in the prescribed form and manner.

(3) An Order under section 125 may require an agency giving information which is entered on the register to pay a prescribed fee to the Secretary of State or the registration organisation.

(4) But an adoption agency is not to disclose any information to the Secretary of State or the registration organisation –

   (a) about prospective adopters who are suitable to adopt a child, or persons who were included in the register as such prospective adopters, without their consent,
   (b) about children suitable for adoption, or persons who were included in the register as such children, without the consent of the prescribed person.

(5) Consent under subsection (4) is to be given in the prescribed form.

129 Disclosure of information

(1) Information entered in the register, or compiled from information entered in the register, may only be disclosed under subsection (2) or (3).

(2) Prescribed information entered in the register may be disclosed by the Secretary of State or the registration organisation –

   (a) where an adoption agency is acting on behalf of a child who is suitable for adoption, to the agency to assist in finding prospective adopters with whom it would be appropriate for the child to be placed,
   (b) where an adoption agency is acting on behalf of prospective adopters who are suitable to adopt a child, to the agency to assist in finding a child appropriate for adoption by them.

(3) Prescribed information entered in the register, or compiled from information entered in the register, may be disclosed by the Secretary of State or the registration organisation to any prescribed person for use for statistical or research purposes, or for other prescribed purposes.

(4) An Order under section 125 may prescribe the steps to be taken by adoption agencies in respect of information received by them by virtue of subsection (2).

(5) Subsection (1) does not apply –

    (a) to a disclosure of information with the authority of the Secretary of State, or

    (b) to a disclosure by the registration organisation of prescribed information to the Scottish Ministers (if the register applies to Scotland) or the Assembly (if the register applies to Wales).

(6) Information disclosed to any person under subsection (2) or (3) may be given on any prescribed terms or conditions.

(7) An Order under section 125 may, in prescribed circumstances, require a prescribed fee to be paid to the Secretary of State or the registration organisation –

    (a) by a prescribed adoption agency in respect of information disclosed under subsection (2), or

    (b) by a person to whom information is disclosed under subsection (3).

(8) If any information entered in the register is disclosed to a person in contravention of subsection (1), the person disclosing it is guilty of an offence.

(9) A person guilty of an offence under subsection (8) is liable on summary conviction to imprisonment for a term not exceeding three months, or a fine not exceeding level 5 on the standard scale, or both.

130　Territorial application

(1) In this group of sections, 'adoption agency' means –

    (a) a local authority in England,

    (b) a registered adoption society whose principal office is in England.

(2) An Order under section 125 may provide for any requirements imposed on adoption agencies in respect of the register to apply –

    (a) to Scottish local authorities and to voluntary organisations providing a registered adoption service,

    (b) to local authorities in Wales and to registered adoption societies whose principal offices are in Wales,

and, in relation to the register, references to adoption agencies in this group of sections include any authorities or societies mentioned in paragraphs (a) and (b) to which an Order under that section applies those requirements.

(3) For the purposes of this group of sections, references to the register applying to Scotland or Wales are to those requirements applying as mentioned in paragraph (a) or, as the case may be, (b) of subsection (2).

(4) An Order under section 125 may apply any provision made by virtue of section 127 –

    (a) to Scottish local authorities and to voluntary organisations providing a registered adoption service,

    (b) to local authorities in Wales and to registered adoption societies whose principal offices are in Wales.

(5) For the purposes of this group of sections, references to any payment agency provision applying to Scotland or Wales are to provision made by virtue of section 127 applying as mentioned in paragraph (a) or, as the case may be, (b) of subsection (4).

131 Supplementary

(1) In this group of sections –

    (a) 'organisation' includes a public body and a private or voluntary organisation,

    (b) 'prescribed' means prescribed by an Order under section 125,

    (c) 'the register' means the Adoption and Children Act Register,

    (d) 'Scottish local authority' means a local authority within the meaning of the Regulation of Care (Scotland) Act 2001,

    (e) 'voluntary organisation providing a registered adoption service' has the same meaning as in section 144(3).

(2) For the purposes of this group of sections –

    (a) a child is suitable for adoption if an adoption agency is satisfied that the child ought to be placed for adoption,

    (b) prospective adopters are suitable to adopt a child if an adoption agency is satisfied that they are suitable to have a child placed with them for adoption.

(3) Nothing authorised or required to be done by virtue of this group of sections constitutes an offence under section 93, 94 or 95.

(4) No recommendation to make an Order under section 125 is to be made to Her Majesty in Council unless a draft has been laid before and approved by resolution of each House of Parliament.

(5) If any provision made by an Order under section 125 would, if it were included in an Act of the Scottish Parliament, be within the legislative competence of that Parliament, no recommendation to make the Order is to be made to Her Majesty in Council unless a draft has been laid before, and approved by resolution of, the Parliament.

(6) No recommendation to make an Order under section 125 containing any provision in respect of the register is to be made to Her Majesty in Council if the register applies to Wales or the Order would provide for the register to apply to Wales, unless a draft has been laid before, and approved by resolution of, the Assembly.

(7) No recommendation to make an Order under section 125 containing any provision by virtue of section 127 is to be made to Her Majesty in Council if any payment agency provision applies to Wales or the Order would provide for any payment agency provision to apply to Wales, unless a draft has been laid before, and approved by resolution of, the Assembly.

****

135 Adoption and fostering: criminal records

(1) Part 5 of the Police Act 1997 (certificates of criminal records) is amended as follows.

(2) In section 113 (criminal record certificates), in subsection (3A), for 'his suitability' there is substituted 'the suitability of the applicant, or of a person living in the same household as the applicant, to be a foster parent or'.

(3) In section 115 (enhanced criminal record certificates), in subsection (6A), for 'his suitability' there is substituted 'the suitability of the applicant, or of a person living in the same household as the applicant, to be a foster parent or'.

136 Payment of grants in connection with welfare services

(1) Section 93 of the Local Government Act 2000 (payment of grants for welfare services) is amended as follows.

(2) In subsection (1) (payment of grants by the Secretary of State), for the words from 'in providing' to the end there is substituted –

> '(a) in providing, or contributing to the provision of, such welfare services as may be determined by the Secretary of State, or
> (b) in connection with any such welfare services.'

(3) In subsection (2) (payment of grants by the Assembly), for the words from 'in providing' to the end there is substituted –

> '(a) in providing, or contributing to the provision of, such welfare services as may be determined by the Assembly, or
> (b) in connection with any such welfare services.'

(4) After subsection (6) there is inserted –

> '(6A) Before making any determination under subsection (3) or (5) the Secretary of State must obtain the consent of the Treasury.'

137 Extension of the Hague Convention to British overseas territories

(1) Her Majesty may by Order in Council provide for giving effect to the Convention in any British overseas territory.

(2) An Order in Council under subsection (1) in respect of any British overseas territory may, in particular, make any provision corresponding to provision which in relation to any part of Great Britain is made by the Adoption (Intercountry Aspects) Act 1999 or may be made by regulations under section 1 of that Act.

(3) The British Nationality Act 1981 is amended as follows.

(4) In section 1 (acquisition of British citizenship by birth or adoption) –

> (a) in subsection (5), at the end of paragraph (b) there is inserted 'effected under the law of a country or territory outside the United Kingdom',
> (b) at the end of subsection (5A)(b) there is inserted 'or in a designated territory',
> (c) in subsection (8), the words following 'section 50' are omitted.

(5) In section 15 (acquisition of British overseas territories citizenship) –

> (a) after subsection (5) there is inserted –
>
> '(5A) Where –
>
>> (a) a minor who is not a British overseas territories citizen is adopted under a Convention adoption,

(b)   on the date on which the adoption is effected –

    (i)   the adopter or, in the case of a joint adoption, one of the adopters is a British overseas territories citizen, and

    (ii)   the adopter or, in the case of a joint adoption, both of the adopters are habitually resident in a designated territory, and

(c)   the Convention adoption is effected under the law of a country or territory outside the designated territory,

the minor shall be a British overseas territories citizen as from that date.',

(b)   in subsection (6), after 'order' there is inserted 'or a Convention adoption'.

(6) In section 50 (interpretation), in subsection (1) –

(a)   after the definition of 'company' there is inserted –

'"Convention adoption" means an adoption effected under the law of a country or territory in which the Convention is in force, and certified in pursuance of Article 23(1) of the Convention',

(b)   after the definition of 'Crown service under the government of the United Kingdom' there is inserted –

'"designated territory" means a qualifying territory, or the Sovereign Base Areas of Akrotiri and Dhekelia, which is designated by Her Majesty by Order in Council under subsection (14)'.

(7) After subsection (13) of that section there is inserted –

'(14) For the purposes of the definition of "designated territory" in subsection (1), an Order in Council may –

(a)   designate any qualifying territory, or the Sovereign Base Areas of Akrotiri and Dhekelia, if the Convention is in force there, and

(b)   make different designations for the purposes of section 1 and section 15;

and, for the purposes of this subsection and the definition of "Convention adoption" in subsection (1), "the Convention" means the Convention on the Protection of Children and Co-operation in respect of Intercountry Adoption, concluded at the Hague on 29th May 1993.

An Order in Council under this subsection shall be subject to annulment in pursuance of a resolution of either House of Parliament.'

138 Proceedings in Great Britain

Proceedings for an offence by virtue of section 9, 59, 93, 94, 95 or 129 –

(a)   may not be brought more than six years after the commission of the offence but, subject to that,

(b)   may be brought within a period of six months from the date on which evidence sufficient in the opinion of the prosecutor to warrant the proceedings came to his knowledge.

(words apply to Scotland only).

Amendments etc

139 Amendments, transitional and transitory provisions, savings and repeals

(1) Schedule 3 (minor and consequential amendments) is to have effect.

(2) Schedule 4 (transitional and transitory provisions and savings) is to have effect.

(3) The enactments set out in Schedule 5 are repealed to the extent specified.

Chapter 2
Final provisions

140 Orders, rules and regulations

(1) Any power to make subordinate legislation conferred by this Act on the Lord Chancellor, the Secretary of State, the Scottish Ministers, the Assembly or the Registrar General is exercisable by statutory instrument.

(2) A statutory instrument containing subordinate legislation made under any provision of this Act (other than section 14 or 148 or an instrument to which subsection (3) applies) is to be subject to annulment in pursuance of a resolution of either House of Parliament.

(3) A statutory instrument containing subordinate legislation –

    (a) under section 9 which includes provision made by virtue of section 45(2),
    (b) under section 92(6), 94 or 123(6), or
    (c) which adds to, replaces or omits any part of the text of an Act,

is not to be made unless a draft of the instrument has been laid before, and approved by resolution of, each House of Parliament.

(4) Subsections (2) and (3) do not apply to an Order in Council or to subordinate legislation made –

    (a) by the Scottish Ministers, or
    (b) by the Assembly, unless made jointly by the Secretary of State and the Assembly.

(5) A statutory instrument containing regulations under section 63(2) made by the Scottish Ministers is to be subject to annulment in pursuance of a resolution of the Scottish Parliament.

(6) The power of the Department of Health, Social Services and Public Safety to make regulations under section 63(2) is to be exercisable by statutory rule for the purposes of the Statutory Rules (Northern Ireland) Order 1979 (SI 1979/1573 (NI 12)); and any such regulations are to be subject to negative resolution within the meaning of section 41(6) of the Interpretation Act (Northern Ireland) 1954 as if they were statutory instruments within the meaning of that Act.

(7) Subordinate legislation made under this Act may make different provision for different purposes.

(8) A power to make subordinate legislation under this Act (as well as being exercisable in relation to all cases to which it extends) may be exercised in relation to –

(a) those cases subject to specified exceptions, or

(b) a particular case or class of case.

(9) In this section, 'subordinate legislation' does not include a direction.

141 Rules of procedure

(1) The Lord Chancellor may make rules in respect of any matter to be prescribed by rules made by virtue of this Act and dealing generally with all matters of procedure.

(2) Subsection (1) does not apply in relation to proceedings before magistrates' courts, but the power to make rules conferred by section 144 of the Magistrates' Courts Act 1980 includes power to make provision in respect of any of the matters mentioned in that subsection.

(3) In the case of an application for a placement order, for the variation or revocation of such an order, or for an adoption order, the rules must require any person mentioned in subsection (4) to be notified –

(a) of the date and place where the application will be heard, and

(b) of the fact that, unless the person wishes or the court requires, the person need not attend.

(4) The persons referred to in subsection (3) are –

(a) in the case of a placement order, every person who can be found whose consent to the making of the order is required under subsection (3)(a) of section 21 (or would be required but for subsection (3)(b) of that section) or, if no such person can be found, any relative prescribed by rules who can be found,

(b) in the case of a variation or revocation of a placement order, every person who can be found whose consent to the making of the placement order was required under subsection (3)(a) of section 21 (or would have been required but for subsection (3)(b) of that section),

(c) in the case of an adoption order –

   (i) every person who can be found whose consent to the making of the order is required under subsection (2)(a) of section 47 (or would be required but for subsection (2)(c) of that section) or, if no such person can be found, any relative prescribed by rules who can be found,

   (ii) every person who has consented to the making of the order under section 20 (and has not withdrawn the consent) unless he has given a notice under subsection (4)(a) of that section which has effect,

   (iii) every person who, if leave were given under section 47(5), would be entitled to oppose the making of the order.

(5) Rules made in respect of magistrates' courts may provide –

(a) for enabling any fact tending to establish the identity of a child with a child to whom a document relates to be proved by affidavit, and

(b) for excluding or restricting in relation to any facts that may be so proved the power of a justice of the peace to compel the attendance of witnesses.

Section 141

Prospective amendment—Section prospectively amended by Children Act 2004, s 62(7) (see **3.7**).

142 Supplementary and consequential provision

(1) The appropriate Minister may by order make –

    (a) any supplementary, incidental or consequential provision,

    (b) any transitory, transitional or saving provision,

which he considers necessary or expedient for the purposes of, in consequence of or for giving full effect to any provision of this Act.

(2) For the purposes of subsection (1), where any provision of an order extends to England and Wales, and Scotland or Northern Ireland, the appropriate Minister in relation to the order is the Secretary of State.

(3) Before making an order under subsection (1) containing provision which would, if included in an Act of the Scottish Parliament, be within the legislative competence of that Parliament, the appropriate Minister must consult the Scottish Ministers.

(4) Subsection (5) applies to any power of the Lord Chancellor, the Secretary of State or the Assembly to make regulations, rules or an order by virtue of any other provision of this Act or of Her Majesty to make an Order in Council by virtue of section 125.

(5) The power may be exercised so as to make –

    (a) any supplementary, incidental or consequential provision,

    (b) any transitory, transitional or saving provision,

which the person exercising the power considers necessary or expedient.

(6) The provision which may be made under subsection (1) or (5) includes provision modifying Schedule 4 or amending or repealing any enactment or instrument.

In relation to an Order in Council, 'enactment' in this subsection includes an enactment comprised in, or in an instrument made under, an Act of the Scottish Parliament.

(7) The power of the Registrar General to make regulations under Chapter 5 of Part 1 may, with the approval of the Chancellor of the Exchequer, be exercised so as to make –

    (a) any supplementary, incidental or consequential provision,

    (b) any transitory, transitional or saving provision,

which the Registrar General considers necessary or expedient.

143 Offences by bodies corporate and unincorporated bodies

(1) Where an offence under this Act committed by a body corporate is proved to have been committed with the consent or connivance of, or to be attributable to any neglect on the part of, any director, manager, secretary or other similar officer of the body, or a person purporting to act in any such capacity, that person as well as the body is guilty of the offence and liable to be proceeded against and punished accordingly.

(2) Where the affairs of a body corporate are managed by its members, subsection (1) applies in relation to the acts and defaults of a member in connection with his functions of management as it applies to a director of a body corporate.

(3) Proceedings for an offence alleged to have been committed under this Act by an unincorporated body are to be brought in the name of that body (and not in that of any of its members) and, for the purposes of any such proceedings in England and Wales or Northern Ireland, any rules of court relating to the service of documents have effect as if that body were a corporation.

(4) A fine imposed on an unincorporated body on its conviction of an offence under this Act is to be paid out of the funds of that body.

(5) If an unincorporated body is charged with an offence under this Act –

    (a) in England and Wales, section 33 of the Criminal Justice Act 1925 and Schedule 3 to the Magistrates' Courts Act 1980 (procedure on charge of an offence against a corporation),

    (b) in Northern Ireland, section 18 of the Criminal Justice Act (Northern Ireland) 1945 and Schedule 4 to the Magistrates' Courts (Northern Ireland) Order 1981 (SI 1981/1675 (NI 26)) (procedure on charge of an offence against a corporation),

have effect in like manner as in the case of a corporation so charged.

(6) Where an offence under this Act committed by an unincorporated body (other than a partnership) is proved to have been committed with the consent or connivance of, or to be attributable to any neglect on the part of, any officer of the body or any member of its governing body, he as well as the body is guilty of the offence and liable to be proceeded against and punished accordingly.

(7) Where an offence under this Act committed by a partnership is proved to have been committed with the consent or connivance of, or to be attributable to any neglect on the part of, a partner, he as well as the partnership is guilty of the offence and liable to be proceeded against and punished accordingly.

144 General interpretation etc

(1) In this Act –

    'appropriate Minister' means –
        (a) in relation to England, Scotland or Northern Ireland, the Secretary of State,
        (b) in relation to Wales, the Assembly,
    and in relation to England and Wales means the Secretary of State and the Assembly acting jointly,
    'the Assembly' means the National Assembly for Wales,
    'body' includes an unincorporated body,
    'by virtue of' includes 'by' and 'under',
    'child', except where used to express a relationship, means a person who has not attained the age of 18 years,
    'the Convention' means the Convention on Protection of Children and Co-operation in respect of Intercountry Adoption, concluded at the Hague on 29th May 1993,
    'Convention adoption order' means an adoption order which, by virtue of regulations under section 1 of the Adoption (Intercountry Aspects) Act 1999 (regulations giving effect to the Convention), is made as a Convention adoption order,

'Convention country' means a country or territory in which the Convention is in force,

'court' means, subject to any provision made by virtue of Part 1 of Schedule 11 to the 1989 Act, the High Court, a county court or a magistrates' court,

'enactment' includes an enactment comprised in subordinate legislation,

'fee' includes expenses,

'guardian' has the same meaning as in the 1989 Act and includes a special guardian within the meaning of that Act,

'information' means information recorded in any form,

'local authority' means any unitary authority, or any county council so far as they are not a unitary authority,

'Northern Irish adoption agency' means an adoption agency within the meaning of Article 3 of the Adoption (Northern Ireland) Order 1987 (SI 1987/2203 (NI 22)),

'Northern Irish adoption order' means an order made, or having effect as if made, under Article 12 of the Adoption (Northern Ireland) Order 1987,

'notice' means a notice in writing,

'registration authority' (in Part 1) has the same meaning as in the Care Standards Act 2000,

'regulations' means regulations made by the appropriate Minister, unless they are required to be made by the Lord Chancellor, the Secretary of State or the Registrar General,

'relative', in relation to a child, means a grandparent, brother, sister, uncle or aunt, whether of the full blood or half-blood or by marriage,

'rules' means rules made under section 141(1) or made by virtue of section 141(2) under section 144 of the Magistrates' Courts Act 1980,

'Scottish adoption order' means an order made, or having effect as if made, under section 12 of the Adoption (Scotland) Act 1978,

'subordinate legislation' has the same meaning as in the Interpretation Act 1978,

'unitary authority' means –

    (a) the council of any county so far as they are the council for an area for which there are no district councils,

    (b) the council of any district comprised in an area for which there is no county council,

    (c) the council of a county borough,

    (d) the council of a London borough,

    (e) the Common Council of the City of London.

(2) Any power conferred by this Act to prescribe a fee by Order in Council or regulations includes power to prescribe –

    (a) a fee not exceeding a prescribed amount,

    (b) a fee calculated in accordance with the Order or, as the case may be, regulations,

    (c) a fee determined by the person to whom it is payable, being a fee of a reasonable amount.

(3) In this Act, 'Scottish adoption agency' means –

    (a) a local authority, or

    (b) a voluntary organisation providing a registered adoption service;

but in relation to the provision of any particular service, references to a Scottish adoption agency do not include a voluntary organisation unless it is registered in respect of that service or a service which, in Scotland, corresponds to that service.

Expressions used in this subsection have the same meaning as in the Regulation of Care (Scotland) Act 2001 and 'registered' means registered under Part 1 of that Act.

(4) In this Act, a couple means –

    (a) a married couple, or

    (b) two people (whether of different sexes or the same sex) living as partners in an enduring family relationship.

(5) Subsection (4)(b) does not include two people one of whom is the other's parent, grandparent, sister, brother, aunt or uncle.

(6) References to relationships in subsection (5) –

    (a) are to relationships of the full blood or half blood or, in the case of an adopted person, such of those relationships as would exist but for adoption, and

    (b) include the relationship of a child with his adoptive, or former adoptive, parents,

but do not include any other adoptive relationships.

(7) For the purposes of this Act, a person is the partner of a child's parent if the person and the parent are a couple but the person is not the child's parent.

145 Devolution: Wales

(1) The references to the Adoption Act 1976 and to the 1989 Act in Schedule 1 to the National Assembly for Wales (Transfer of Functions) Order 1999 (SI 1999/672) are to be treated as referring to those Acts as amended by virtue of this Act.

(2) This section does not affect the power to make further Orders varying or omitting those references.

(3) In Schedule 1 to that Order, in the entry for the Adoption Act 1976, '9' is omitted.

(4) The functions exercisable by the Assembly under sections 9 and 9A of the Adoption Act 1976 (by virtue of paragraphs 4 and 5 of Schedule 4 to this Act) are to be treated for the purposes of section 44 of the Government of Wales Act 1998 (parliamentary procedures for subordinate legislation) as if made exercisable by the Assembly by an Order in Council under section 22 of that Act.

146 Expenses

There shall be paid out of money provided by Parliament –

    (a) any expenditure incurred by a Minister of the Crown by virtue of this Act,

    (b) any increase attributable to this Act in the sums payable out of money so provided under any other enactment.

147 Glossary

Schedule 6 (glossary) is to have effect.

148 Commencement

(1) This Act (except sections 116 and 136, this Chapter and the provisions mentioned in subsections (5) and (6)) is to come into force on such day as the Secretary of State may by order appoint.

(2) Before making an order under subsection (1) (other than an order bringing paragraph 53 of Schedule 3 into force) the Secretary of State must consult the Assembly.

(3) Before making an order under subsection (1) bringing sections 123 and 124 into force, the Secretary of State must also consult the Scottish Ministers and the Department of Health, Social Services and Public Safety.

(4) Before making an order under subsection (1) bringing sections 125 to 131 into force, the Secretary of State must also consult the Scottish Ministers.

(5) The following are to come into force on such day as the Scottish Ministers may by order appoint –

- (a) section 41(5) to (9), so far as relating to Scotland,
- (b) sections 132 to 134,
- (c) paragraphs 21 to 35 and 82 to 84 of Schedule 3,
- (d) paragraphs 15 and 23 of Schedule 4,
- (e) the entries in Schedule 5, so far as relating to the provisions mentioned in paragraphs (c) and (d),
- (f) section 139, so far as relating to the provisions mentioned in the preceding paragraphs.

(6) Sections 2(6), 3(3) and (4), 4 to 17, 27(3), 53(1) to (3), 54, 56 to 65 and 98, paragraphs 13, 65, 66 and 111 to 113 of Schedule 3 and paragraphs 3 and 5 of Schedule 4 are to come into force on such day as the appropriate Minister may by order appoint.

149 Extent

(1) The amendment or repeal of an enactment has the same extent as the enactment to which it relates.

(2) Subject to that and to the following provisions, this Act except section 137 extends to England and Wales only.

(3) The following extend also to Scotland and Northern Ireland –

- (a) sections 63(2) to (5), 65(2)(a) and (b) and (3), 123 and 124,
- (b) this Chapter, except sections 141 and 145.

(4) The following extend also to Scotland –

- (a) section 41(5) to (9),
- (b) sections 125 to 131,
- (c) section 138,
- (d) section 139, so far as relating to provisions extending to Scotland.

(5) In Schedule 4, paragraph 23 extends only to Scotland.

150 Short title

This Act may be cited as the Adoption and Children Act 2002.

SCHEDULES

Schedule 1

Registration of Adoptions

1 Registration of adoption orders

(1) Every adoption order must contain a direction to the Registrar General to make in the Adopted Children Register an entry in the form prescribed by regulations made by the Registrar General with the approval of the Chancellor of the Exchequer.

(2) Where, on an application to a court for an adoption order in respect of a child, the identity of the child with a child to whom an entry in the registers of live-births or other records relates is proved to the satisfaction of the court, any adoption order made in pursuance of the application must contain a direction to the Registrar General to secure that the entry in the register or, as the case may be, record in question is marked with the word 'Adopted'.

(3) Where an adoption order is made in respect of a child who has previously been the subject of an adoption order made by a court in England or Wales under Part 1 of this Act or any other enactment –

    (a) sub-paragraph (2) does not apply, and

    (b) the order must contain a direction to the Registrar General to mark the previous entry in the Adopted Children Register with the word 'Re-adopted'.

(4) Where an adoption order is made, the prescribed officer of the court which made the order must communicate the order to the Registrar General in the prescribed manner; and the Registrar General must then comply with the directions contained in the order.

'Prescribed' means prescribed by rules.

2 Registration of adoptions in Scotland, Northern Ireland, the Isle of Man and the Channel Islands

(1) Sub-paragraphs (2) and (3) apply where the Registrar General is notified by the authority maintaining a register of adoptions in a part of the British Islands outside England and Wales that an order has been made in that part authorising the adoption of a child.

(2) If an entry in the registers of live-births or other records (and no entry in the Adopted Children Register) relates to the child, the Registrar General must secure that the entry is marked with –

    (a) the word 'Adopted', followed by

    (b) the name, in brackets, of the part in which the order was made.

(3) If an entry in the Adopted Children Register relates to the child, the Registrar General must mark the entry with –

(a)   the word 'Re-adopted', followed by

(b)   the name, in brackets, of the part in which the order was made.

(4) Where, after an entry in either of the registers or other records mentioned in sub-paragraphs (2) and (3) has been so marked, the Registrar General is notified by the authority concerned that –

(a)   the order has been quashed,

(b)   an appeal against the order has been allowed, or

(c)   the order has been revoked,

the Registrar General must secure that the marking is cancelled.

(5) A copy or extract of an entry in any register or other record, being an entry the marking of which is cancelled under sub-paragraph (4), is not to be treated as an accurate copy unless both the marking and the cancellation are omitted from it.

3 Registration of other adoptions

(1) If the Registrar General is satisfied, on an application under this paragraph, that he has sufficient particulars relating to a child adopted under a registrable foreign adoption to enable an entry to be made in the Adopted Children Register for the child he must make the entry accordingly.

(2) If he is also satisfied that an entry in the registers of live-births or other records relates to the child, he must –

(a)   secure that the entry is marked 'Adopted', followed by the name, in brackets, of the country in which the adoption was effected, or

(b)   where appropriate, secure that the overseas registers of births are so marked.

(3) An application under this paragraph must be made, in the prescribed manner, by a prescribed person and the applicant must provide the prescribed documents and other information.

(4) An entry made in the Adopted Children Register by virtue of this paragraph must be made in the prescribed form.

(5) In this Schedule 'registrable foreign adoption' means an adoption which satisfies prescribed requirements and is either –

(a)   adoption under a Convention adoption, or

(b)   adoption under an overseas adoption.

(6) In this paragraph –

(a)   'prescribed' means prescribed by regulations made by the Registrar General with the approval of the Chancellor of the Exchequer,

(b)   'overseas register of births' includes –

  (i)   a register made under regulations made by the Secretary of State under section 41(1)(g), (h) or (i) of the British Nationality Act 1981 ,

  (ii)   a record kept under an Order in Council made under section 1 of the Registration of Births, Deaths and Marriages (Special Provisions) Act 1957 (other than a certified copy kept by the Registrar General).

4 Amendment of orders and rectification of Registers and other records

(1) The court by which an adoption order has been made may, on the application of the adopter or the adopted person, amend the order by the correction of any error in the particulars contained in it.

(2) The court by which an adoption order has been made may, if satisfied on the application of the adopter or the adopted person that within the period of one year beginning with the date of the order any new name –

    (a) has been given to the adopted person (whether in baptism or otherwise), or

    (b) has been taken by the adopted person,

either in place of or in addition to a name specified in the particulars required to be entered in the Adopted Children Register in pursuance of the order, amend the order by substituting or, as the case may be, adding that name in those particulars.

(3) The court by which an adoption order has been made may, if satisfied on the application of any person concerned that a direction for the marking of an entry in the registers of live-births, the Adopted Children Register or other records included in the order in pursuance of paragraph 1(2) or (3) was wrongly so included, revoke that direction.

(4) Where an adoption order is amended or a direction revoked under sub-paragraphs (1) to (3), the prescribed officer of the court must communicate the amendment in the prescribed manner to the Registrar General.

'Prescribed' means prescribed by rules.

(5) The Registrar General must then –

    (a) amend the entry in the Adopted Children Register accordingly, or

    (b) secure that the marking of the entry in the registers of live-births, the Adopted Children Register or other records is cancelled,

as the case may be.

(6) Where an adoption order is quashed or an appeal against an adoption order allowed by any court, the court must give directions to the Registrar General to secure that –

    (a) any entry in the Adopted Children Register, and

    (b) any marking of an entry in that Register, the registers of live-births or other records as the case may be, which was effected in pursuance of the order,

is cancelled.

(7) Where an adoption order has been amended, any certified copy of the relevant entry in the Adopted Children Register which may be issued pursuant to section 78(2)(b) must be a copy of the entry as amended, without the reproduction of –

    (a) any note or marking relating to the amendment, or

    (b) any matter cancelled in pursuance of it.

(8) A copy or extract of an entry in any register or other record, being an entry the marking of which has been cancelled, is not to be treated as an accurate copy unless both the marking and the cancellation are omitted from it.

(9) If the Registrar General is satisfied –

(a) that a registrable foreign adoption has ceased to have effect, whether on annulment or otherwise, or

(b) that any entry or mark was erroneously made in pursuance of paragraph 3 in the Adopted Children Register, the registers of live-births, the overseas registers of births or other records,

he may secure that such alterations are made in those registers or other records as he considers are required in consequence of the adoption ceasing to have effect or to correct the error.

'Overseas register of births' has the same meaning as in paragraph 3.

(10) Where an entry in such a register is amended in pursuance of sub-paragraph (9), any copy or extract of the entry is not to be treated as accurate unless it shows the entry as amended but without indicating that it has been amended.

5 Marking of entries on re-registration of birth on legitimation

(1) Without prejudice to paragraphs 2(4) and 4(5), where, after an entry in the registers of live-births or other records has been marked in accordance with paragraph 1 or 2, the birth is re-registered under section 14 of the Births and Deaths Registration Act 1953 (re-registration of births of legitimated persons), the entry made on the re-registration must be marked in the like manner.

(2) Without prejudice to paragraph 4(9), where an entry in the registers of live-births or other records is marked in pursuance of paragraph 3 and the birth in question is subsequently re-registered under section 14 of that Act, the entry made on re-registration must be marked in the like manner.

6 Cancellations in registers on legitimation

(1) This paragraph applies where an adoption order is revoked under section 55(1).

(2) The prescribed officer of the court must communicate the revocation in the prescribed manner to the Registrar General who must then cancel or secure the cancellation of –

(a) the entry in the Adopted Children Register relating to the adopted person, and

(b) the marking with the word 'Adopted' of any entry relating to the adopted person in the registers of live-births or other records.

'Prescribed' means prescribed by rules.

(3) A copy or extract of an entry in any register or other record, being an entry the marking of which is cancelled under this paragraph, is not to be treated as an accurate copy unless both the marking and the cancellation are omitted from it.

Schedule 2

Disclosure of Birth Records by Registrar General

1

On an application made in the prescribed manner by an adopted person –

(a) a record of whose birth is kept by the Registrar General, and

(b) who has attained the age of 18 years,

the Registrar General must give the applicant any information necessary to enable the applicant to obtain a certified copy of the record of his birth.

'Prescribed' means prescribed by regulations made by the Registrar General with the approval of the Chancellor of the Exchequer.

2

(1) Before giving any information to an applicant under paragraph 1, the Registrar General must inform the applicant that counselling services are available to the applicant –

(a) from a registered adoption society, an organisation within section 144(3)(b) or an adoption society which is registered under Article 4 of the Adoption (Northern Ireland) Order 1987 (SI 1987/2203 (NI 22)),

(b) if the applicant is in England and Wales, at the General Register Office or from any local authority or registered adoption support agency,

(c) if the applicant is in Scotland, from any council constituted under section 2 of the Local Government etc (Scotland) Act 1994 ,

(d) if the applicant is in Northern Ireland, from any Board.

(2) In sub-paragraph (1)(b), 'registered adoption support agency' means an adoption support agency in respect of which a person is registered under Part 2 of the Care Standards Act 2000.

(3) In sub-paragraph (1)(d), 'Board' means a Health and Social Services Board established under Article 16 of the Health and Personal Social Services (Northern Ireland) Order 1972 (SI 1972/1265 (NI 14)); but where the functions of a Board are exercisable by a Health and Social Services Trust, references in that sub-paragraph to a Board are to be read as references to the Health and Social Services Trust.

(4) If the applicant chooses to receive counselling from a person or body within sub-paragraph (1), the Registrar General must send to the person or body the information to which the applicant is entitled under paragraph 1.

3

(1) Where an adopted person who is in England and Wales –

(a) applies for information under paragraph 1 or Article 54 of the Adoption (Northern Ireland) Order 1987, or

(b) is supplied with information under section 45 of the Adoption (Scotland) Act 1978,

the persons and bodies mentioned in sub-paragraph (2) must, if asked by the applicant to do so, provide counselling for the applicant.

(2) Those persons and bodies are –

(a) the Registrar General,

(b) any local authority,

(c) a registered adoption society, an organisation within section 144(3)(b) or an adoption society which is registered under Article 4 of the Adoption (Northern Ireland) Order 1987.

4

(1) Where a person –

    (a) was adopted before 12th November 1975, and

    (b) applies for information under paragraph 1,

the Registrar General must not give the information to the applicant unless the applicant has attended an interview with a counsellor arranged by a person or body from whom counselling services are available as mentioned in paragraph 2.

(2) Where the Registrar General is prevented by sub-paragraph (1) from giving information to a person who is not living in the United Kingdom, the Registrar General may give the information to any body which –

    (a) the Registrar General is satisfied is suitable to provide counselling to that person, and

    (b) has notified the Registrar General that it is prepared to provide such counselling.

****

Schedule 3
Minor and Consequential Amendments

1–11 (*not reproduced here*)

The Local Authority Social Services Act 1970 (c 42)

12 The Local Authority Social Services Act 1970 is amended as follows.

13 In section 7D (default powers of Secretary of State as respects social services functions of local authorities), in subsection (1), after 'the Children Act 1989' there is inserted 'section 1 or 2(4) of the Adoption (Intercountry Aspects) Act 1999 or the Adoption and Children Act 2002'.

14–15 (*not reproduced here*)

The Legitimacy Act 1976 (c 31)

16 The Legitimacy Act 1976 is amended as follows.

17 In section 4 (legitimation of adopted child) –

    (a) in subsection (1), after '1976' there is inserted 'or section 67 of the Adoption and Children Act 2002',

    (b) in subsection (2) –

        (i) in paragraph (a), after '39' there is inserted 'or subsection (3)(b) of the said section 67',

        (ii) in paragraph (b), after '1976' there is inserted 'or section 67, 68 or 69 of the Adoption and Children Act 2002'.

18 In section 6 (dispositions depending on date of birth), at the end of subsection (2) there is inserted 'or section 69(2) of the Adoption and Children Act 2002'.

The Adoption Act 1976 (c 36)

19 In section 38 of the Adoption Act 1976 (meaning of 'adoption' in Part 4), in subsection (2), after '1975' there is inserted 'but does not include an adoption of a kind mentioned in paragraphs (c) to (e) of subsection (1) effected on or after the day which is the appointed day for the purposes of Chapter 4 of Part 1 of the Adoption and Children Act 2002'.

20–35 (*not reproduced here*)

The Magistrates' Courts Act 1980 (c 43)

36 The Magistrates' Courts Act 1980 is amended as follows.

37 In section 65 (meaning of family proceedings), in subsection (1), for paragraph (h) there is substituted –

'(h) the Adoption and Children Act 2002;'.

38 In section 69 (sitting of magistrates' courts for family proceedings), in subsections (2) and (3), for 'the Adoption Act 1976' there is substituted 'the Adoption and Children Act 2002'.

39 In section 71 (newspaper reports of family proceedings) –

  (a) in subsection (1), '(other than proceedings under the Adoption Act 1976)' is omitted,
  (b) in subsection (2)-
      (i) for 'the Adoption Act 1976' there is substituted 'the Adoption and Children Act 2002',
      (ii) the words following '(a) and (b)' are omitted.

40–41 (*not reproduced here*)

The Child Abduction Act 1984 (c 37)

42 (1) Section 1 of the Child Abduction Act 1984 (offence of abduction of child by parent, etc.) is amended as follows.

(2) In subsection (2), after paragraph (c) there is inserted –

'(ca) he is a special guardian of the child; or'.

(3) In subsection (3)(a), after sub-paragraph (iii) there is inserted –

'(iiia) any special guardian of the child;'.

(4) In subsection (4), for paragraphs (a) and (b) there is substituted –

  '(a) he is a person in whose favour there is a residence order in force with respect to the child, and he takes or sends the child out of the United Kingdom for a period of less than one month; or
  (b) he is a special guardian of the child and he takes or sends the child out of the United Kingdom for a period of less than three months.'

(5) In subsection (5A), the 'or' at the end of sub-paragraph (i) of paragraph (a) is omitted, and after that sub-paragraph there is inserted –

'(ia) who is a special guardian of the child; or'.

(6) In subsection (7)(a), after '"guardian of a child,"' there is inserted '"special guardian,"'.

43 (1) The Schedule to that Act (modifications of section 1 for children in certain cases) is amended as follows.

(2) In paragraph 3 (adoption and custodianship), for sub-paragraphs (1) and (2) there is substituted –

> '(1) This paragraph applies where –
>
> > (a) a child is placed for adoption by an adoption agency under section 19 of the Adoption and Children Act 2002, or an adoption agency is authorised to place the child for adoption under that section; or
> > (b) a placement order is in force in respect of the child; or
> > (c) an application for such an order has been made in respect of the child and has not been disposed of; or
> > (d) an application for an adoption order has been made in respect of the child and has not been disposed of; or
> > (e) an order under section 84 of the Adoption and Children Act 2002 (giving parental responsibility prior to adoption abroad) has been made in respect of the child, or an application for such an order in respect of him has been made and has not been disposed of.
>
> (2) Where this paragraph applies, section 1 of this Act shall have effect as if –
>
> > (a) the reference in subsection (1) to the appropriate consent were –
> > > (i) in a case within sub-paragraph (1)(a) above, a reference to the consent of each person who has parental responsibility for the child or to the leave of the High Court;
> > > (ii) in a case within sub-paragraph (1)(b) above, a reference to the leave of the court which made the placement order;
> > > (iii) in a case within sub-paragraph (1)(c) or (d) above, a reference to the leave of the court to which the application was made;
> > > (iv) in a case within sub-paragraph (1)(e) above, a reference to the leave of the court which made the order or, as the case may be, to which the application was made;
> > (b) subsection (3) were omitted;
> > (c) in subsection (4), in paragraph (a), for the words from "in whose favour" to the first mention of "child" there were substituted "who provides the child's home in a case falling within sub-paragraph (1)(a) or (b) of paragraph 3 of the Schedule to this Act"; and
> > (d) subsections (4A), (5), (5A) and (6) were omitted.'

(3) In paragraph 5 (interpretation), in sub-paragraph (a), for the words from 'and "adoption order"' to the end there is substituted ', "adoption order", "placed for adoption by an adoption agency" and "placement order" have the same meaning as in the Adoption and Children Act 2002; and'.

40–41 (*not reproduced here*)

The Family Law Act 1986 (c 55)

46 The Family Law Act 1986 is amended as follows.

47 In section 1 (orders to which Part 1 applies), in subsection (1), after paragraph (a) there is inserted –

'(aa) a special guardianship order made by a court in England and Wales under the Children Act 1989;
(ab) an order made under section 26 of the Adoption and Children Act 2002 (contact), other than an order varying or revoking such an order'.

48 In section 2 (jurisdiction: general), after subsection (2) there is inserted –

'(2A) A court in England and Wales shall not have jurisdiction to make a special guardianship order under the Children Act 1989 unless the condition in section 3 of this Act is satisfied.

(2B) A court in England and Wales shall not have jurisdiction to make an order under section 26 of the Adoption and Children Act 2002 unless the condition in section 3 of this Act is satisfied.'

49 In section 57 (declarations as to adoptions effected overseas) –

(a) for subsection (1)(a) there is substituted –

'(a) a Convention adoption, or an overseas adoption, within the meaning of the Adoption and Children Act 2002, or',

(b) in subsection (2)(a), after '1976' there is inserted 'or section 67 of the Adoption and Children Act 2002'.

The Family Law Reform Act 1987 (c 42)

50 The Family Law Reform Act 1987 is amended as follows.

51 In section 1 (general principle), for paragraph (c) of subsection (3) there is substituted –

'(c) is an adopted person within the meaning of Chapter 4 of Part 1 of the Adoption and Children Act 2002'.

The Children Act 1989 (c 41)

54 The Children Act 1989 is amended as follows.

55 In section 8 (residence, contact and other orders with respect to children), in subsection (4), for paragraph (d) there is substituted –

'(d) the Adoption and Children Act 2002;'.

56 In section 10 (power of court to make section 8 orders) –

(a) in subsection (4)(a), for 'or guardian' there is substituted ', guardian or special guardian',
(b) after subsection (4)(a) there is inserted –

'(aa) any person who by virtue of section 4A has parental responsibility for the child;',

(c) after subsection (5) there is inserted –

'(5A) A local authority foster parent is entitled to apply for a residence order with respect to a child if the child has lived with him for a period of at least one year immediately preceding the application.',

(d)   after subsection (7) there is inserted –

'(7A) If a special guardianship order is in force with respect to a child, an application for a residence order may only be made with respect to him, if apart from this subsection the leave of the court is not required, with such leave.'

57 In section 12 (residence orders and parental responsibility), in subsection (3) –

(a)   paragraph (a) is omitted,
(b)   in paragraph (b), for 'section 55 of the Act of 1976' there is substituted 'section 84 of the Adoption and Children Act 2002'.

58 In section 16 (family assistance orders), in subsection (2)(a), for 'or guardian' there is substituted ', guardian or special guardian'.

59 In section 20 (provision of accommodation for children: general), in subsection (9), the 'or' at the end of paragraph (a) is omitted and after that paragraph there is inserted –

'(aa)   who is a special guardian of the child; or'.

60 In section 24 (persons qualifying for advice and assistance) –

(a)   for subsection (1) there is substituted –

'(1)   In this Part 'a person qualifying for advice and assistance' means a person to whom subsection (1A) or (1B) applies.

(1A)   This subsection applies to a person –

(a)   who has reached the age of sixteen but not the age of twenty-one;
(b)   with respect to whom a special guardianship order is in force (or, if he has reached the age of eighteen, was in force when he reached that age); and
(c)   who was, immediately before the making of that order, looked after by a local authority.

(1B)   This subsection applies to a person to whom subsection (1A) does not apply, and who –

(a)   is under twenty-one; and
(b)   at any time after reaching the age of sixteen but while still a child was, but is no longer, looked after, accommodated or fostered.',

(b)   in subsection (2), for 'subsection (1)(b)' there is substituted 'subsection (1B)(b)',
(c)   in subsection (5), before paragraph (a) there is inserted –

'(za)   in the case of a person to whom subsection (1A) applies, a local authority determined in accordance with regulations made by the Secretary of State;'.

61 In section 24A (advice and assistance for qualifying persons) –

(a)   in subsection (2)(b), after 'a person' there is inserted 'to whom section 24(1A) applies, or to whom section 24(1B) applies and',

(b) in subsection (3)(a), after 'if' there is inserted 'he is a person to whom section 24(1A) applies, or he is a person to whom section 24(1B) applies and'.

62 In section 24B (assistance with employment, education and training), in each of subsections (1) and (3)(b), after 'of' there is inserted 'section 24(1A) or'.

63 In section 33 (effect of care order) –

(a) in subsection (3)(b), for 'a parent or guardian of the child' there is substituted –

'(i) a parent, guardian or special guardian of the child; or
(ii) a person who by virtue of section 4A has parental responsibility for the child,',

(b) in subsection (5), for 'a parent or guardian of the child who has care of him' there is substituted 'a person mentioned in that provision who has care of the child',

(c) in subsection (6)(b) –
(i) sub-paragraph (i) is omitted,
(ii) in sub-paragraph (ii), for 'section 55 of the Act of 1976' there is substituted 'section 84 of the Adoption and Children Act 2002',

(d) in subsection (9), for 'a parent or guardian of the child' there is substituted 'a person mentioned in that provision'.

64 In section 34 (parental contact etc. with children in care) –

(a) in subsection (1)(b), after 'guardian' there is inserted 'or special guardian', and

(b) after subsection (1)(b) there is inserted –

'(ba) any person who by virtue of section 4A has parental responsibility for him;'.

65 In section 80 (inspection of children's homes by persons authorised by Secretary of State), in subsection (1), paragraphs (e) and (f) are omitted.

66 In section 81 (inquiries), in subsection (1), paragraph (b) is omitted.

67 In section 88 (amendments of adoption legislation), subsection (1) is omitted.

68 In section 91 (effect and duration of orders, etc) –

(a) after subsection (5) there is inserted –

'(5A) The making of a special guardianship order with respect to a child who is the subject of –

(a) a care order; or
(b) an order under section 34,

discharges that order.',

(b) in subsection (7), after '4(1)' there is inserted '4A(1)',
(c) in subsection (8)(a), after '4' there is inserted 'or 4A'.

69 In section 102 (power of constable to assist in exercise of certain powers to search for children or inspect premises), in subsection (6), paragraph (c) is omitted.

70 In section 105 (interpretation), in subsection (1) –

(a) in the definition of 'adoption agency', for 'section 1 of the Adoption Act 1976' there is substituted 'section 2 of the Adoption and Children Act 2002',

(b) at the appropriate place there is inserted –

'"section 31A plan" has the meaning given by section 31A(6);',

(c) in the definition of 'parental responsibility agreement', for 'section 4(1)' there is substituted 'sections 4(1) and 4A(2)',

(d) the definition of 'protected child' is omitted,

(e) after the definition of 'special educational needs' there is inserted –

'"special guardian" and "special guardianship order" have the meaning given by section 14A;'.

71 *(not reproduced here)*

72 In Schedule 2, in paragraph 19 (arrangements by local authorities to assist children to live abroad) –

(a) in sub-paragraph (4) (arrangements to assist children to live abroad), after 'guardian,' there is inserted 'special guardian,',

(b) in sub-paragraph (6), for the words from the beginning to 'British subject)' there is substituted 'Section 85 of the Adoption and Children Act 2002 (which imposes restrictions on taking children out of the United Kingdom)',

(c) after sub-paragraph (8) there is inserted –

'(9) This paragraph does not apply to a local authority placing a child for adoption with prospective adopters.'

73–75 *(not reproduced here)*

The Human Fertilisation and Embryology Act 1990 (c 37)

76 The Human Fertilisation and Embryology Act 1990 is amended as follows.

77 In section 27 (meaning of mother), in subsection (2), for 'child of any person other than the adopter or adopters' there is substituted 'woman's child'.

78 In section 28 (meaning of father), in subsection (5)(c), for 'child of any person other than the adopter or adopters' there is substituted 'man's child'.

79 In section 30 (parental orders in favour of gamete donors), in subsection (10) for 'Adoption Act 1976' there is substituted 'Adoption and Children Act 2002'.

The Family Law Act 1996 (c 27)

85 The Family Law Act 1996 is amended as follows.

86 In section 62 (meaning of 'relevant child' etc) –

(a) in subsection (2), in paragraph (b), after 'the Adoption Act 1976' there is inserted ', the Adoption and Children Act 2002',

(b) in subsection (5), for the words from 'has been freed' to '1976' there is substituted 'falls within subsection (7)'.

87 At the end of that section there is inserted –

'(7) A child falls within this subsection if –

(a) an adoption agency, within the meaning of section 2 of the Adoption and Children Act 2002, has power to place him for adoption under section 19 of that Act (placing children with parental consent) or he has become the subject of an order under section 21 of that Act (placement orders), or

(b) he is freed for adoption by virtue of an order made –

   (i) in England and Wales, under section 18 of the Adoption Act 1976,

   (ii) in Scotland, under section 18 of the Adoption (Scotland) Act 1978, or

   (iii) in Northern Ireland, under Article 17(1) or 18(1) of the Adoption (Northern Ireland) Order 1987.'

88 In section 63 (interpretation of Part 4) –

(a) in subsection (1), for the definition of 'adoption order', there is substituted –

'"adoption order" means an adoption order within the meaning of section 72(1) of the Adoption Act 1976 or section 46(1) of the Adoption and Children Act 2002;',

(b) in subsection (2), after paragraph (h) there is inserted –

'(i) the Adoption and Children Act 2002.'

89–94 *(not reproduced here)*

The Adoption (Intercountry Aspects) Act 1999 (c 18)

95 The following provisions of the Adoption (Intercountry Aspects) Act 1999 cease to have effect in relation to England and Wales: sections 3, 6, 8, 9 and 11 to 13.

96 Section 2 of that Act (accredited bodies) is amended as follows.

97 In subsection (2A) –

(a) for the words from the beginning to '2000' there is substituted 'A registered adoption society',

(b) for 'agency' there is substituted 'society'.

98 For subsection (5) there is substituted –

'(5) In this section, "registered adoption society" has the same meaning as in section 2 of the Adoption and Children Act 2002 (basic definitions); and expressions used in this section in its application to England and Wales which are also used in that Act have the same meanings as in that Act.'

99 In subsection (6) –

(a) the words 'in its application to Scotland' are omitted,

(b) after 'expressions' there is inserted 'used in this section in its application to Scotland'.

100 Section 14 (restriction on bringing children into the United Kingdom for adoption) is omitted.

101 In section 16(1) (devolution: Wales), the words ', or section 17 or 56A of the 1976 Act,' are omitted.

****

Schedule 6

Glossary

In this Act, the expressions listed in the left-hand column below have the meaning given by, or are to be interpreted in accordance with, the provisions of this Act or (where stated) of the 1989 Act listed in the right-hand column.

Expression	Provision
the 1989 Act	section 2(5)
Adopted Children Register	section 77
Adoption and Children Act Register	section 125
adoption (in relation to Chapter 4 of Part 1)	section 66
adoption agency	section 2(1)
adoption agency placing a child for adoption	section 18(5)
Adoption Contact Register	section 80
adoption order	section 46(1)
Adoption Service	section 2(1)
adoption society	section 2(5)
adoption support agency	section 8
adoption support services	section 2(6)
appointed day (in relation to Chapter 4 of Part 1)	section 66(2)
appropriate Minister	section 144
Assembly	section 144
body	section 144
by virtue of	section 144
care order	section 105(1) of the 1989 Act
child	sections 49(5) and 144
child assessment order	section 43(2) of the 1989 Act
child in the care of a local authority	section 105(1) of the 1989 Act
child looked after by a local authority	section 22 of the 1989 Act
child placed for adoption by an adoption agency	section 18(5)
child to be adopted, adopted child	section 49(5)

consent (in relation to making adoption orders or placing for adoption)	section 52
the Convention	section 144
Convention adoption	section 66(1)(c)
Convention adoption order	section 144
Convention country	section 144
couple	section 144(4)
court	section 144
disposition (in relation to Chapter 4 of Part 1)	section 73
enactment	section 144
fee	section 144
guardian	section 144
information	section 144
interim care order	section 38 of the 1989 Act
local authority	section 144
local authority foster parent	section 23(3) of the 1989 Act
Northern Irish adoption agency	section 144
Northern Irish adoption order	section 144
notice	section 144
notice of intention to adopt	section 44(2)
overseas adoption	section 87
parental responsibility	section 3 of the 1989 Act
partner, in relation to a parent of a child	section 144(7)
placement order	section 21
placing, or placed, for adoption	sections 18(5) and 19(4)
prohibited steps order	section 8(1) of the 1989 Act
records (in relation to Chapter 5 of Part 1)	section 82
registered adoption society	section 2(2)
registers of live-births (in relation to Chapter 5 of Part 1)	section 82
registration authority (in Part 1)	section 144
regulations	section 144
relative	section 144, read with section 1(8)

residence order	section 8(1) of the 1989 Act
rules	section 144
Scottish adoption agency	section 144(3)
Scottish adoption order	section 144
specific issue order	section 8(1) of the 1989 Act
subordinate legislation	section 144
supervision order	section 31(11) of the 1989 Act
unitary authority	section 144
voluntary organisation	section 2(5)

3.3C ADOPTION (INTERCOUNTRY ASPECTS) ACT 1999
(ss 1, 2, 16, 17)

Implementation of Convention

1 Regulations giving effect to Convention

(1) Subject to the provisions of this Act, regulations made by the Secretary of State may make provision for giving effect to the Convention on Protection of Children and Co-operation in respect of Intercountry Adoption, concluded at the Hague on 29th May 1993 ('the Convention').

(2) The text of the Convention (so far as material) is set out in Schedule 1 to this Act.

(3) Regulations under this section may –

(a) apply, with or without modifications, any provision of the enactments relating to adoption;

(b) provide that any person who contravenes or fails to comply with any provision of the regulations is to be guilty of an offence and liable on summary conviction to imprisonment for a term not exceeding three months, or a fine not exceeding level 5 on the standard scale, or both;

(c) make different provision for different purposes or areas; and

(d) make such incidental, supplementary, consequential or transitional provision as appears to the Secretary of State to be expedient.

(4) Regulations under this section shall be made by statutory instrument which shall be subject to annulment in pursuance of a resolution of either House of Parliament.

(5) Subject to subsection (6), any power to make subordinate legislation under or for the purposes of the enactments relating to adoption includes power to do so with a view to giving effect to the provisions of the Convention.

(6) Subsection (5) does not apply in relation to any power which is exercisable by the National Assembly for Wales.

2 Central Authorities and accredited bodies

(1) The functions under the Convention of the Central Authority are to be discharged –

(a) separately in relation to England and Scotland by the Secretary of State; and

(b) in relation to Wales by the National Assembly for Wales.

(2) A communication may be sent to the Central Authority in relation to any part of Great Britain by sending it (for forwarding if necessary) to the Central Authority in relation to England.

(2A) A voluntary adoption agency in respect of which a person is registered under Part II of the Care Standards Act 2000 is an accredited body for the purposes of the

Convention if, in accordance with the conditions of the registration, the agency may provide facilities in respect of Convention adoptions and adoptions effected by Convention adoption orders.

(3) An approved adoption society is an accredited body for the purposes of the Convention if the approval extends to the provision of facilities in respect of Convention adoptions and adoptions effected by Convention adoption orders.

(4) The functions under Article 9(a) to (c) of the Convention are to be discharged by local authorities and accredited bodies on behalf of the Central Authority.

(5) In this section in its application to England and Wales, 'voluntary adoption agency' has the same meaning as in the Care Standards Act 2000; and expressions which are also used in the Adoption Act 1976 ('the 1976 Act') have the same meanings as in that Act.

(6) *(applies to Scotland only)*

Section 2

Prospective amendment—Section prospectively amended by Adoption and Children Act 2002, s 139(1), Sch 3, paras 95–99 (see **3.3B**).

****

16 Devolution

(1) Any function of the Secretary of State under section 1 or 18(3), or section 17 or 56A of the 1976 Act, is exercisable only after consultation with the National Assembly for Wales.

Section 16

Prospective amendment—Section prospectively amended by Adoption and Children Act 2002, s 139(1), Sch 3, paras 95, 101 (see **3.3B**).

17 Savings for adoptions etc under 1965 Convention

(1) In relation to –

(a) a 1965 Convention adoption order or an application for such an order; or
(b) a 1965 Convention adoption,

the 1976 and 1978 Acts shall have effect without the amendments made by sections 3 to 6 and 8 and Schedule 2 to this Act and the associated repeals made by Schedule 3 to this Act.

(2) In subsection (1) in its application to the 1976 or 1978 Act –

'1965 Convention adoption order' has the meaning which 'Convention adoption order' has in that Act as it has effect without the amendments and repeals mentioned in that subsection;

'1965 Convention adoption' has the meaning which 'regulated adoption' has in that Act as it so has effect.

Schedule 1

Convention on Protection of Children and Co-operation in respect of Intercountry Adoption

(*Not reproduced here*)

Schedule 1

The Hague Convention on Protection of Children and Co-operation in respect of Intercountry Adoption is set out in Part 2 as **2.7**.

3.4 CHILD ABDUCTION ACT 1984

1 Offence of abduction of child by parent, etc

(1) Subject to subsections (5) and (8) below, a person connected with a child under the age of sixteen commits an offence if he takes or sends the child out of the United Kingdom without the appropriate consent.

(2) A person is connected with a child for the purposes of this section if –

    (a) he is a parent of the child; or

    (b) in the case of a child whose parents were not married to each other at the time of his birth, there are reasonable grounds for believing that he is the father of the child; or

    (c) he is a guardian of the child; or

    (d) he is a person in whose favour a residence order is in force with respect to the child; or

    (e) he has custody of the child.

(3) In this section 'the appropriate consent', in relation to a child, means –

    (a) the consent of each of the following –

        (i) the child's mother;

        (ii) the child's father, if he has parental responsibility for him;

        (iii) any guardian of the child;

        (iv) any person in whose favour a residence order is in force with respect to the child;

        (v) any person who has custody of the child; or

    (b) the leave of the court granted under or by virtue of any provision of Part II of the Children Act 1989; or

    (c) if any person has custody of the child, the leave of the court which awarded custody to him.

(4) A person does not commit an offence under this section by taking or sending a child out of the United Kingdom without obtaining the appropriate consent if –

    (a) he is a person in whose favour there is a residence order in force with respect to the child, and

    (b) he takes or sends him out of the United Kingdom for a period of less than one month.

(4A) Subsection (4) above does not apply if the person taking or sending the child out of the United Kingdom does so in breach of an order under Part II of the Children Act 1989.

(5) A person does not commit an offence under this section by doing anything without the consent of another person whose consent is required under the foregoing provisions if –

    (a) he does it in the belief that the other person –

        (i) has consented; or

        (ii) would consent if he was aware of all the relevant circumstances; or

(b) he has taken all reasonable steps to communicate with the other person but has been unable to communicate with him; or

(c) the other person has unreasonably refused to consent.

(5A) Subsection (5)(c) above does not apply if –

(a) the person who refused to consent is a person –
    (i) in whose favour there is a residence order in force with respect to the child;
    (ii) who has custody of the child; or

(b) the person taking or sending the child out of the United Kingdom is, by so acting, in breach of an order made by a court in the United Kingdom.

(6) Where, in proceedings for an offence under this section, there is sufficient evidence to raise an issue as to the application of subsection (5) above, it shall be for the prosecution to prove that that subsection does not apply.

[(7) For the purposes of this section –

(a) 'guardian of a child', 'residence order' and 'parental responsibility' have the same meaning as in the Children Act 1989; and

(b) a person shall be treated as having custody of a child if there is in force an order of a court in the United Kingdom awarding him (whether solely or jointly with another person) custody, legal custody or care and control of the child.

(8) This section shall have effect subject to the provisions of the Schedule to this Act in relation to a child who is in the care of a local authority detained in a place of safety, remanded to a local authority accommodation or the subject of proceedings or an order relating to adoption.

Section 1

Section prospectively amended by Adoption and Children Act 2002, s 139(1), Sch 3, para 42 (see **3.3B**).

2   Offence of abduction of child by other persons

(1) Subject to subsection (3) below, a person, other than one mentioned in subsection (2) below commits an offence if, without lawful authority or reasonable excuse, he takes or detains a child under the age of sixteen –

(a) so as to remove him from the lawful control of any person having lawful control of the child; or

(b) so as to keep him out of the lawful control of any person entitled to lawful control of the child.

(2) The persons are –

(a) where the father and mother of the child in question were married to each other at the time of his birth, the child's father and mother;

(b) where the father and mother of the child in question were not married to each other at the time of his birth, the child's mother; and

(c) any other person mentioned in section 1(2)(c) to (e) above.

(3) In proceedings against any person for an offence under this section, it shall be a defence for that person to prove –

(a) where the father and mother of the child in question were not married to each other at the time of his birth –

    (i)   that he is the child's father; or

    (ii) that, at the time of the alleged offence, he believed, on reasonable grounds, that he was the child's father; or

(b) that, at the time of the alleged offence, he believed that the child had attained the age of sixteen.

3 Construction of references to taking, sending and detaining

For the purposes of this Part of this Act –

(a) a person shall be regarded as taking a child if he causes or induces the child to accompany him or any other person or causes the child to be taken;

(b) a person shall be regarded as sending a child if he causes the child to be sent;

(c) a person shall be regarded as detaining a child if he causes the child to be detained or induces the child to remain with him or any other person; and

(d) references to a child's parents and to a child whose parents were (or were not) married to each other at the time of his birth shall be construed in accordance with section 1 of the Family Law Reform Act 1987 (which extends their meaning).

4 Penalties and prosecutions

(1) A person guilty of an offence under this Part of this Act shall be liable–

(a) on summary conviction, to imprisonment for a term not exceeding six months or to a fine not exceeding the statutory maximum, or to both such imprisonment and fine;

(b) on conviction on indictment, to imprisonment for a term not exceeding seven years.

(2) No prosecution for an offence under section 1 above shall be instituted except by or with the consent of the Director of Public Prosecutions.

5 Restriction on prosecutions for offence of kidnapping

Except by or with the consent of the Director of Public Prosecutions no prosecution shall be instituted for an offence of kidnapping if it was committed –

(a) against a child under the age of sixteen; and

(b) by a person connected with the child, within the meaning of section 1 above.

****

11 Consequential amendments and repeals

(1), (2) (*not reproduced*)

(3) The reference to abduction in section 1(1) of the Internationally Protected Persons Act 1978 – shall be construed as not including an offence under section 1 above or any corresponding provision in force in Northern Ireland or Part II of this Act.

(4), (5) (*not reproduced*)

****

13 Short title, commencement and extent

(1) This Act may be cited as the Child Abduction Act 1984.

(2) This Act shall come into force at the end of the period of three months beginning with the day on which it is passed.

(3) Part I of this Act extends to England and Wales only, Part II extends to Scotland only and in Part III section 11(1) and (5)(a) and section 12 do not extend to Scotland and section 11(1), (2) and (5)(a) and (c) does not extend to Northern Ireland.

SCHEDULE

MODIFICATIONS OF SECTION 1 FOR CHILDREN IN CERTAIN CASES

1 Children in care of local authorities and voluntary organisations

(1) This paragraph applies in the case of a child who is in the care of a local authority within the meaning of the Children Act 1989 in England or Wales.

(2) Where this paragraph applies, section 1 of this Act shall have effect as if–

- (a) the reference in subsection (1) to the appropriate consent were a reference to the consent of the local authority in whose care the child is; and
- (b) subsections (3) to (6) were omitted.

2 Children in places of safety

(1) This paragraph applies in the case of a child who is –

- (a) detained in a place of safety under paragraph 7(4) of Schedule 7 to the Powers of Criminal Courts (Sentencing) Act 2000; or
- (b) remanded to local authority accommodation under section 23 of the Children and Young Persons Act 1969.

(2) Where this paragraph applies, section 1 of this Act shall have effect as if –

- (a) the reference in subsection (1) to the appropriate consent were a reference to the leave of any magistrates' court acting for the area in which the place of safety is; and
- (b) subsections (3) to (6) were omitted.

3 Adoption and custodianship

(1) This paragraph applies in the case of a child –

- (a) who is the subject of an order under section 18 of the Adoption Act 1976 freeing him for adoption: or
- (b) who is the subject of a pending application for such an order; or
- (c) who is the subject of a pending application for an adoption order; or
- (d) who is the subject of an order under section 55 of the Adoption Act 1976 relating to adoption abroad or of a pending application for such an order; or
- (e) ...

(2) Where this paragraph applies, section 1 of this Act shall have effect as if –

   (a) the reference in subsection (1) to the appropriate consent were a reference –

      (i) in a case within sub-paragraph (1)(a) above, to the consent of the adoption agency which made the application for the section 18 order or, if the section 18 order has been varied under section 21 of that Act so as to give parental responsibility to another agency, to the consent of that other agency;

      (ii) in a case within sub-paragraph (1)(b), or (c) above, to the leave of the court to which the application was made; and

      (iii) in a case within sub-paragraph (1)(d) above, to the leave of the court which made the order or, as the case may be, to which the application was made; and

   (b) subsections (3) to (6) were omitted.

(3) Sub-paragraph (2) above shall be construed as if the references to the court included, in any case where the court is a magistrates' court, a reference to any magistrates' court acting for the same area as that court.

4 Cases within paragraphs 1 and 3

In the case of a child falling within both paragraph 1 and paragraph 3 above, the provisions of paragraph 3 shall apply to the exclusion of those in paragraph 1.

5 Interpretation

In this Schedule –

   (a) 'adoption agency' and 'adoption order' have the same meaning as in the Adoption and Children Act 2002; and]

   (b) 'area', in relation to a magistrates' court, means the petty sessions area.

Schedule

Schedule prospectively amended by Adoption and Children Act 2002, s 139(1), Sch 3, para 43 (see **3.3B**).

3.5 CHILD ABDUCTION AND CUSTODY ACT 1985

PART I

INTERNATIONAL CHILD ABDUCTION

1 The Hague Convention

(1) In this Part of this Act 'the Convention' means the Convention on the Civil Aspects of International Child Abduction which was signed at The Hague on 25 October 1980.

(2) Subject to the provisions of this Part of this Act, the provisions of that Convention set out in Schedule 1 to this Act shall have the force of law in the United Kingdom.

2 Contracting States

(1) For the purposes of the Convention as it has effect under this Part of this Act the Contracting States other than the United Kingdom shall be those for the time being specified by an Order in Council under this section.

(2) An Order in Council under this section shall specify the date of the coming into force of the Convention as between the United Kingdom and any State specified in the Order; and except where the Order otherwise provides, the Convention shall apply as between the United Kingdom and that State only in relation to wrongful removals or retentions occurring on or after that date.

(3) Where the Convention applies, or applies only, to a particular territory or particular territories specified in a declaration made by a Contracting State under Article 39 or 40 of the Convention references to that State in subsections (1) and (2) above shall be construed as references to that territory or those territories.

Section 2

Although Brussels II (Council Regulation (EC) No 2201/2003 of 27 November 2003 on Jurisdiction and the Recognition and Enforcement of Judgments in Matrimonial Matters and in Matters of Parental Responsibility) (reproduced at **2.3**) takes precedence over the European Convention on the Recognition and Enforcement of Decisions Concerning Custody of Children, it does not take precedence over the Hague Convention on the Civil Aspects of International Child Abduction. See, in particular, paras 17 and 18 of the recitals to, and Article 11 of, Brussels II and, under the 'old' Brussels II, *Re G (Foreign Contact Order: Enforcement)* [2003] EWCA Civ 1607, [2004] 1 FLR 378, CA. As to the court's jurisdiction under Brussels II, see also *C v FC (Brussels II: Freestanding Applications for Parental Responsibility)* [2004] 1 FLR 317, FD (the 'old' Brussels II did not apply to freestanding applications relating to parental responsibility in a country where there are no divorce proceedings).

The following countries are now signatories to the Hague Convention (see the Child Abduction and Custody (Parties to Conventions) (Amendment) Order 2004, SI 2004/3040); the dates of ratification of the Convention by the party States are given since the Convention is not retrospective (*Re H (Minors) (Abduction: Custody Rights)* [1991] 2 AC 476, [1991] 3 All ER 230, [1991] 2 FLR 262, HL):

State	Date in force		State	Date in force
Argentina	1 June 1991		Greece	1 June 1993
Australia. Australian States and mainland Territories	1 January 1987		Honduras	1 March 1994
Austria	1 October 1988		Hungary	1 September 1986
The Bahamas	1 January 1994		Iceland	1 November 1996
Belarus	1 September 2003		Ireland	1 October 1991
Belgium	1 May 1999		Israel	1 December 1991
Belize	1 October 1989		Italy	1 May 1995
Bosnia and Herzegovina	7 April 1992		Latvia	1 September 2003
Brazil	1 March 2005		Lithuania	1 March 2005
Burkina Faso	1 August 1992		Luxembourg	1 January 1987
Canada:			Macedonia	1 December 1991
Canada – Ontario	1 August 1986		Malta	1 March 2002
Canada – New Brunswick	1 August 1986		Mauritius	1 June 1993
Canada – British Columbia	1 August 1986		Mexico	1 September 1991
Canada – Manitoba	1 August 1986		Monaco	1 February 1993
Canada – Nova Scotia	1 August 1986		Netherlands	1 September 1990
Canada – Newfoundland	1 August 1986		New Zealand	1 August 1991
Canada – Prince Edward Island	1 August 1986		Norway	1 April 1989
Canada – Quebec	1 August 1986		Panama	1 May 1994
Canada – Yukon Territory	1 August 1986		Peru	1 September 2003
Canada – Saskatchewan	1 November 1986		Poland	1 November 1992
Canada – Alberta	1 February 1987		Portugal	1 August 1986

State	Date in force	State	Date in force
Canada – Northwest Territories	1 April 1988	Romania	1 February 1993
Chile	1 May 1994	St Kitts and Nevis	1 August 1994
China – Hong Kong Special Administrative Region	1 September 1997	Serbia and Montenegro	27 April 1992
China – Macau Special Administrative Region	1 March 1999	Slovakia	1 February 2001
Colombia	1 March 1996	Slovenia	1 June 1994
Croatia	1 December 1991	South Africa	1 October 1997
Cyprus	1 February 1995	Spain	1 September 1987
Czech Republic	1 March 1998	Sweden	1 June 1989
Denmark	1 July 1991	Switzerland	1 August 1986
Ecuador	1 April 1992	Turkey	1 August 2001
Estonia	1 September 2003	Turkmenistan	1 March 1998
Fiji	1 September 2003	United States of America	1 July 1988
Finland	1 August 1994	Uruguay	1 September 2003
France	1 August 1986	Uzbekistan	1 September 2003
Georgia	1 October 1997	Venezuela	1 January 1997
Germany	1 December 1990	Zimbabwe	1 July 1995

3 Central Authorities

(1) Subject to subsection (2) below, the functions under the Convention of a Central Authority shall be discharged –

(a) in England and Wales and in Northern Ireland by the Lord Chancellor; and

(b) in Scotland by the Secretary of State.

(2) Any application made under the Convention by or on behalf of a person outside the United Kingdom may be addressed to the Lord Chancellor as the Central Authority in the United Kingdom.

(3) Where any such application relates to a function to be discharged under subsection (1) above by the Secretary of State it shall be transmitted by the Lord Chancellor to the Secretary of State and where such an application is addressed to the

Secretary of State but relates to a function to be discharged under subsection (1) above by the Lord Chancellor the Secretary of State shall transmit it to the Lord Chancellor.

4 Judicial authorities

The courts having jurisdiction to entertain applications under this Convention shall be –

(a) in England and Wales or in Northern Ireland the High Court; and
(b) in Scotland the Court of Session.

Section 4

By art 2(a)(ii) of the High Court (Distribution of Business Order) 1991, SI 1991/1210, all proceedings under this Act are assigned to the Family Division. FPR 1991, rr 6.1–6.15 set out the procedure for such proceedings. The case will usually be heard on affidavit evidence only, in accordance with FPR 1991, r 6.7 (*Re F (A Minor) (Child Abduction)* [1992] 1 FLR 548, CA). The child will seldom be joined as a party under r 6.5 (*Re P (Abduction: Minor's View)* [1998] 2 FLR 825, CA).

5 Interim powers

Where an application has been made to a court in the United Kingdom under the Convention, the court may, at any time before the application is determined, give such interim directions as it thinks fit for the purpose of securing the welfare of the child concerned or of preventing changes in the circumstances relevant to the determination of the application.

Section 5

See FPR 1991, rr 6.1–6.16 for the various directions that may be given. Under r 6.13 'an application for interim directions under section 5 or section 19 of the Act may where the case is one of urgency be made ex parte on affidavit but shall otherwise be made by summons'. Under s 24A of the Act, the court may order any person who may have relevant information to disclose it to the court.

6 Reports

Where the Lord Chancellor or the Secretary of State is requested to provide information relating to a child under Article 7(d) of the Convention he may –

(a) request a local authority or an officer of the Service to make a report to him in writing with respect to any matter which appears to him to be relevant;
(b) request the Department of Health and Social Services for Northern Ireland to arrange for a suitably qualified person to make such a report to him;
(c) request any court to which a written report relating to the child has been made to send him a copy of the report;

and such a request shall be duly complied with.

Section 6

Thus an officer of CAFCASS may be ordered to file a report under s 6(a) on any matter that appears to the judge to be relevant. A similar provision applies in relation to the European Convention under s 21 of the Act.

7 Proof of documents and evidence

(1) For the purposes of Article 14 of the Convention a decision or determination of a judicial or administrative authority outside the United Kingdom may be proved by a duly authenticated copy of the decision or determination; and any document purporting to be such a copy shall be deemed to be a true copy unless the contrary is shown.

(2) For the purposes of subsection (1) above a copy is duly authenticated if it bears the seal, or is signed by a judge or officer, of the authority in question.

(3) For the purposes of Articles 14 and 30 of the Convention any such document as is mentioned in Article 8 of the Convention, or a certified copy of any such document, shall be sufficient evidence of anything stated in it.

8 Declarations by United Kingdom courts

The High Court or Court of Session may, on an application made for the purposes of Article 15 of the Convention by any person appearing to the court to have an interest in the matter, make a declaration or declarator that the removal of any child from, or his retention outside, the United Kingdom was wrongful within the meaning of Article 3 of the Convention.

9 Suspension of court's powers in cases of wrongful removal

The reference in Article 16 of the Convention to deciding on the merits of rights of custody shall be construed as a reference to –

  (a) making, varying or revoking a custody order, or a supervision order under section 31 of the Children Act 1989 or Article 50 of the Children (Northern Ireland) Order 1995;
  (aa) enforcing under section 29 of the Family Law Act 1986 a custody order within the meaning of Chapter V of Part I of that Act;
  (b) registering or enforcing a decision under Part II of this Act;
  (c) *(repealed)*
  (d) making, varying or discharging an order under section 86 of the Children (Scotland) Act 1995;
  (e) *(repealed)*

10 Rules of court

(1) An authority having power to make rules of court may make such provision for giving effect to this Part of this Act as appears to that authority to be necessary or expedient.

(2) Without prejudice to the generality of subsection (1) above, rules of court may make provision –

  (a) with respect to the procedure on applications for the return of a child and with respect to the documents and information to be furnished and the notices to be given in connection with any such application;
  (b) for the transfer of any such application between the appropriate courts in the different parts of the United Kingdom;

(c) for the giving of notices by or to a court for the purposes of the provisions of Article 16 of the Convention and section 9 above and generally as respects proceedings to which those provisions apply;

(d) for enabling a person who wishes to make an application under the Convention in a Contracting State other than the United Kingdom to obtain from any court in the United Kingdom an authenticated copy of any decision of that court relating to the child to whom the application is to relate.

11 Cost of applications

The United Kingdom having made such a reservation as is mentioned in the third paragraph of Article 26 of the Convention, the costs mentioned in that paragraph shall not be borne by any Minister or other authority in the United Kingdom except so far as they fall to be so borne by virtue of –

(a) the provision of any service funded by the Legal Services Commission as part of the Community Legal Service, or

(b) the grant of legal aid or legal advice and assistance under the Legal Aid (Scotland) Act 1967, Part I of the Legal Advice and Assistance Act 1972 or the Legal Aid Advice and Assistance (Northern Ireland) Order 1981.

PART II

RECOGNITION AND ENFORCEMENT OF CUSTODY DECISIONS

12 The European Convention

(1) In this Part of this Act 'the Convention' means the European Convention on Recognition and Enforcement of Decisions concerning Custody of Children and on the Restoration of Custody of Children which was signed in Luxembourg on 20 May 1980.

(2) Subject to the provisions of this Part of this Act, the provisions of that Convention set out in Schedule 2 to this Act (which include Articles 9 and 10 as they have effect in consequence of a reservation made by the United Kingdom under Article 17) shall have the force of law in the United Kingdom.

(3) But those provisions of the Convention are subject to Article 37 of Council Regulation (EC) No 1347/2000 of 29 May 2000 on jurisdiction and the recognition and enforcement of judgments in matrimonial matters and in matters of parental responsibility for children of both spouses (under which the Regulation takes precedence over the Convention), and the provisions of this Part of this Act, and any rules of court made pursuant to section 24 of this Act, shall be construed accordingly.

13 Contracting States

(1) For the purposes of the Convention as it has effect under this Part of this Act the Contracting States other than the United Kingdom shall be those for the time being specified by an Order in Council under this section.

(2) An Order in Council under this section shall specify the date of the coming into force of the Convention as between the United Kingdom and any State specified in the Order.

(3) Where the Convention applies, or applies only, to a particular territory or particular territories specified by a Contracting State under Article 24 or 25 of the Convention references to that State in subsections (1) and (2) above shall be construed as references to that territory or those territories.

Section 13

The procedure under this Convention is set out in FPR 1991, rr 6.1–6.16.

The following are signatories to the Convention (see the Child Abduction and Custody (Parties to Conventions) (Amendment) Order 2004, SI 2003/3040), which will apply where an order has been made in a Contracting State before that State signed the Convention (*Re L (Child Abduction: European Convention)* [1992] 2 FLR 178, FD):

State	Date in force	State	Date in force
Austria	1 August 1986	Liechtenstein	1 August 1997
Belgium	1 August 1986	Lithuania	1 March 2005
Cyprus	1 October 1986	Luxembourg	1 August 1986
Czech Republic	1 July 2000	Malta	1 February 2000
Denmark	1 August 1991	Netherlands	1 September 1990
Finland	1 August 1994	Norway	1 May 1989
France	1 August 1986	Poland	1 March 1996
Germany	1 February 1991	Portugal	1 August 1986
Greece	1 July 1993	Spain	1 August 1986
Iceland	1 November 1996	Sweden	1 July 1989
Ireland	1 October 1991	Switzerland	1 August 1986
Italy	1 June 1995	Turkey	1 June 2000
Latvia	1 August 2002		

14 Central Authorities

(1) Subject to subsection (2) below, the functions under the Convention of a Central Authority shall be discharged –

    (a) in England and Wales and in Northern Ireland by the Lord Chancellor; and

    (b) in Scotland by the Secretary of State.

(2) Any application made under the Convention by or on behalf of a person outside the United Kingdom may be addressed to the Lord Chancellor as the Central Authority in the United Kingdom.

(3) Where any such application relates to a function to be discharged under subsection (1) above by the Secretary of State it shall be transmitted by the Lord Chancellor to the Secretary of State and where such an application is addressed to the Secretary of State but relates to a function to be discharged under subsection (1) above by the Lord Chancellor, the Secretary of State shall transmit it to the Lord Chancellor.

15 Recognition of decisions

(1) Articles 7 and 12 of the Convention shall have effect in accordance with this section.

(2) A decision to which either of those Articles applies which was made in a Contracting State other than the United Kingdom shall be recognised in each part of the United Kingdom as if made by a court having jurisdiction to make it in that part but –

    (a) the appropriate court in any part of the United Kingdom may, on the application of any person appearing to it to have an interest in the matter, declare on any of the grounds specified in Article 9 or 10 of the Convention that the decision is not to be recognised in any part of the United Kingdom; and

    (b) the decision shall be enforceable in any part of the United Kingdom unless registered in the appropriate court under section 16 below.

(3) The references in Article 9(1)(c) of the Convention to the removal of the child are to his improper removal within the meaning of the Convention.

16 Registration of decisions

(1) A person on whom any rights are conferred by a decision relating to custody made by an authority in a Contracting State other than the United Kingdom may make an application for the registration of the decision in an appropriate court in the United Kingdom.

(2) The Central Authority in the United Kingdom shall assist a person in making such an application if a request for such assistance is made by him or on his behalf by the Central Authority of the Contracting State in question.

(3) An application under subsection (1) above or a request under subsection (2) above shall be treated as a request for enforcement for the purposes of Articles 10 and 13 of the Convention.

(4) The High Court or Court of Session shall refuse to register a decision if –

    (a) the court is of the opinion that on any of the grounds specified in Article 9 or 10 of the Convention the decision should not be recognised in any part of the United Kingdom;

    (b) the court is of the opinion that the decision is not enforceable in the Contracting State where it was made and is not a decision to which Article 12 of the Convention applies;

    (c) an application in respect of the child under Part I of this Act is pending.

(5) Where the Lord Chancellor is requested to assist in making an application under this section to the Court of Session he shall transmit the request to the Secretary of

State and the Secretary of State shall transmit to the Lord Chancellor any such request to assist in making an application to the High Court.

(6) In this section 'decision relating to custody' has the same meaning as in the Convention.

17 Variation and revocation of registered decisions

(1) Where a decision which has been registered under section 16 above is varied or revoked by an authority in the Contracting State in which it was made, the person on whose behalf the application for registration of the decision was made shall notify the court in which the decision is registered of the variation or revocation.

(2) Where a court is notified under subsection (1) above of the revocation of a decision, it shall –

    (a) cancel the registration, and
    (b) notify such persons as may be prescribed by rules of court of the cancellation.

(3) Where a court is notified under subsection (1) above of the variation of a decision, it shall –

    (a) notify such persons as may be prescribed by rules of court of the variation; and
    (b) subject to any conditions which may be so prescribed, vary the registration.

(4) The court in which a decision is registered under section 16 above may also, on the application of any person appearing to the court to have an interest in the matter, cancel or vary the registration if it is satisfied that the decision has been revoked or, as the case may be, varied by an authority in the Contracting State in which it was made.

18 Enforcement of decisions

Where a decision relating to custody has been registered under section 16 above, the court in which it is registered shall have the same powers for the purpose of enforcing the decision as if it had been made by that court; and proceedings for or with respect to enforcement may be taken accordingly.

19 Interim powers

Where an application has been made to a court for the registration of a decision under section 16 above or for the enforcement of such a decision, the court may, at any time before the application is determined, give such interim directions as it thinks fit for the purpose of securing the welfare of the child concerned or of preventing changes in the circumstances relevant to the determination of the application or, in the case of an application for registration, to the determination of any subsequent application for the enforcement of the decision.

20 Suspension of court's powers

(1) Where it appears to any court in which such proceedings as are mentioned in subsection (2) below are pending in respect of a child that –

    (a) an application has been made for the registration of a decision in respect of the child under section 16 above (other than a decision mentioned in subsection (3) below) or that such a decision is registered; and

(b)   the decision was made in proceedings commenced before the proceedings which are pending,

the powers of the court with respect to the child in those proceedings shall be restricted as mentioned in subsection (2) below unless, in the case of an application for registration, the application is refused.

(2) Where subsection (1) above applies the court shall not –

    (a)   in the case of custody proceedings, make, vary or revoke any custody order, or a supervision order under section 31 of the Children Act 1989 or Article 50 of the Children (Northern Ireland) Order 1995;

   (aa)   in the case of proceedings under section 29 of the Family Law Act 1986 for the enforcement of a custody order within the meaning of Chapter V or Part I of that Act, enforce that order; or

(b), (c) *(repealed)*

    (d)   in the case of proceedings for, or for the variation or discharge of, a parental responsibilities order under section 86 of the Children (Scotland) Act 1995, make, vary or discharge any such order;

    (e)   *(repealed)*

(2A) Where it appears to the Secretary of State –

    (a)   that an application has been made for the registration of a decision in respect of a child under section 16 above (other than a decision mentioned in subsection (3) below); or

    (b)   that such a decision is registered;

the Secretary of State shall not make, vary or revoke any custody order in respect of the child unless, in the case of an application for registration, the application is refused.

(3) The decision referred to in subsection (1) or (2A) above is a decision which is only a decision relating to custody within the meaning of section 16 of this Act by virtue of being a decision relating to rights of access.

(4) Paragraph (b) of Article 10(2) of the Convention shall be construed as referring to custody proceedings within the meaning of this Act.

(5) This section shall apply to a children's hearing (as defined in section 93(1) of the Children (Scotland) Act 1995) as it does to a court.

21 Reports

Where the Lord Chancellor or the Secretary of State is requested to make enquiries about a child under Article 15(1)(b) of the Convention he may –

    (a)   request a local authority or an officer of the Service to make a report to him in writing with respect to any matter relating to the child concerned which appears to him to be relevant;

    (b)   request the Department of Health and Social Services for Northern Ireland to arrange for a suitably qualified person to make such a report to him;

    (c)   request any court to which a written report relating to the child has been made to send him a copy of the report;

and any such request shall be duly complied with.

22 Proof of documents and evidence

(1) In any proceedings under this Part of this Act a decision of an authority outside the United Kingdom may be proved by a duly authenticated copy of the decision; and any document purporting to be such a copy shall be deemed to be a true copy unless the contrary is shown.

(2) For the purpose of subsection (1) above a copy is duly authenticated if it bears the seal, or is signed by a judge or officer, of the authority in question.

(3) In any proceedings under this Part of this Act any such document as is mentioned in Article 13 of the Convention, or a certified copy of any such document, shall be sufficient evidence of anything stated in it.

23 Decisions of United Kingdom courts

(1) Where a person on whom any rights are conferred by a decision relating to custody made by a court in the United Kingdom makes an application to the Lord Chancellor or the Secretary of State under Article 4 of the Convention with a view to securing its recognition or enforcement in another Contracting State, the Lord Chancellor or the Secretary of State may require the court which made the decision to furnish him with all or any of the documents referred to in Article 13(1)(b), (c) and (d) of the Convention.

(2) Where in any custody proceedings a court in the United Kingdom makes a decision relating to a child who has been removed from the United Kingdom, the court may also, on an application made by any person for the purposes of Article 12 of the Convention, declare the removal to have been unlawful if it is satisfied that the applicant has an interest in the matter and that the child has been taken from or sent or kept out of the United Kingdom without the consent of the person (or, if more than one, all the persons) having the right to determine the child's place of residence under the law of the part of the United Kingdom in which the child was habitually resident.

(3) In this section 'decision relating to custody' has the same meaning as in the Convention.

24 Rules of court

(1) An authority having power to make rules of court may make such provision for giving effect to this Part of this Act as appears to that authority to be necessary or expedient.

(2) Without prejudice to the generality of subsection (1) above, rules of court may make provision –

    (a) with respect to the procedure on application to a court under any provision of this Part of this Act and with respect to the documents and information to be furnished and the notices to be given in connection with any such application;

    (b) for the transfer of any such application between the appropriate courts in the different parts of the United Kingdom;

(c) for the giving of directions requiring the disclosure of information about any child who is the subject of proceedings under this Part of this Act and for safeguarding its welfare.

PART III

SUPPLEMENTARY

24A Power to order disclosure of child's whereabouts

(1) Where –

(a) in proceedings for the return of a child under Part I of this Act; or
(b) on an application for the recognition, registration or enforcement of a decision in respect of a child under Part II of this Act,

there is not available to the court adequate information as to where the child is, the court may order any person who it has reason to believe may have relevant information to disclose it to the court.

(2) A person shall not be excused from complying with an order under subsection (1) above by reason that to do so may incriminate him or his spouse of an offence; but a statement or admission made in compliance with such an order shall not be admissible in evidence against either of them in proceedings for any offence other than perjury.

25 Termination of existing custody orders etc

(1) Where –

(a) an order is made for the return of a child under Part I of this Act; or
(b) a decision with respect to a child (other than a decision mentioned in subsection (2) below) is registered under section 16 of this Act,

any custody order relating to him shall cease to have effect.

(2) The decision referred to in subsection (1)(b) above is a decision which is only a decision relating to custody within the meaning of section 16 of this Act by virtue of being a decision relating to rights of access.

(3)–(7) (*repealed*)

26 Expenses

There shall be paid out of money provided by Parliament –

(a) any expenses incurred by the Lord Chancellor or the Secretary of State by virtue of this Act; and
(b) any increase attributable to this Act in the sums so payable under any other Act.

27 Interpretation

(1) In this Act 'custody order' means (unless contrary intention appears) any such order as is mentioned in Schedule 3 to this Act and 'custody proceedings' means

proceedings in which an order within paragraphs 1, 2, 5, 6, 8 or 9 of that Schedule may be made, varied or revoked.

(2) For the purposes of this Act 'part of the United Kingdom' means England and Wales, Scotland or Northern Ireland and 'the appropriate court', in relation to England and Wales or Northern Ireland means the High Court and, in relation to Scotland, the Court of Session.

(3) In this Act 'local authority' means –

    (a) in relation to England and Wales, the council of a non-metropolitan county, a metropolitan district, a London borough or the Common Council of the City of London; and

    (b) in relation to Scotland, a council constituted under section 2 of the Local Government etc (Scotland) Act 1994.

(4) In this Act a decision relating to rights of access in England and Wales or Scotland or Northern Ireland means a decision as to the contact which a child may, or may not, have with any person.

(5) In this Act 'officer of the Service' has the same meaning as in the Criminal Justice and Court Services Act 2000.

28   Application as respects British Islands and colonies

(1) Her Majesty may by Order in Council direct that any of the provisions of this Act specified in the Order shall extend, subject to such modifications as may be specified in the Order, to –

    (a) the Isle of Man,

    (b) any of the Channel Islands, and

    (c) any colony.

(2) Her Majesty may by Order in Council direct that this Act shall have effect in the United Kingdom as if any reference in this Act, or in any amendment made by this Act, to any order which may be made, or any proceedings which may be brought or any other thing which may be done in, or in any part of, the United Kingdom included a reference to any corresponding order which may be made or, as the case may be, proceedings which may be brought or other thing which may be done in any of the territories mentioned in subsection (1) above.

(3) An Order in Council under this section may make such consequential, incidental and supplementary provision as Her Majesty considers appropriate.

(4) An Order in Council under this section shall be subject to annulment in pursuance of a resolution of either House of Parliament.

29   Short title, commencement and extent

(1) This Act may be cited as the Child Abduction and Custody Act 1985.

(2) This Act shall come into force on such day as may be appointed by an order made by statutory instrument by the Lord Chancellor and the Lord Advocate; and different days may be so appointed for different provisions.

(3) This Act extends to Northern Ireland.

Schedule 1

Convention on the Civil Aspects of International Child Abduction

(*Not reproduced here*)

Schedule 1

The Hague Convention on the Civil Aspects of International Child Abduction is set out in Part 2 as **2.8**.

Schedule 2

European Convention on Recognition and Enforcement of Decisions Concerning Custody of Children

(*Not reproduced here*)

Schedule 2

The European Convention on Recognition and Enforcement of Decisions Concerning Custody of Children is set out in Part 2 as **2.6**.

****

3.6 CHILDREN ACT 1989

OVERVIEW

Whilst the 'European law'[1] may be regarded as the bottom-line in children law in England and Wales,[2] in practice the Children Act 1989 (CA 1989) remains the single document most referred to. It received Royal Assent on 16 November 1989 and came into effect on 14 October 1991.

In trying to get an overview of the CA 1989, it may help to think of it as a three-storey house: Part I ('Introductory') is the foundations on which everything else is built; Part II ('Orders with respect to children in family proceedings') is the ground floor where much of life is lived; Part III ('Local authority support for children and families') is the first floor; Parts IV and V ('Care and supervision' and 'Protection of children') together make up the second floor; Parts VI to XI are the attic, where most people hardly ever go; and Part XII ('Miscellaneous and general') is the roof. The Schedules are rather like fitted furniture.

Before embarking on a tour of the house it is important to understand two terms. '*Private law*' refers to issues that are between individuals – typically between parents but also sometimes involving grandparents, siblings and others. '*Public law*' refers to matters in which the State – typically through a local authority social services department – is a party to the proceedings.[3]

Part I: 'Introductory' (the foundations)

CA 1989, Part I deals with four issues of varying practical importance. First, and of the utmost importance, is s 1. It is the main foundation stone of the CA 1989. It sets out three vital principles the court must generally apply:

- *the paramountcy principle*: that the child's welfare shall be the court's paramount consideration when it determines any question with respect to: (a) the upbringing of the child; or (b) the administration of a child's property or the application of any income arising from it (s 1(1));[4]

---

[1] By which we mean both the law of the European Union and the law of the European Convention on Human Rights, as explained in 'Introduction and How to Use this Handbook' at **1.1**.

[2] Subject to the power of Parliament to repeal the legislation and to the power of the United Kingdom, as a sovereign nation, to withdraw from the treaties.

[3] It has been explained at **3.3** why adoption is best treated as its own, separate category.

[4] The paramountcy principle applies to most applications brought under the CA 1989 as most such matters clearly fall within the definition of being a 'question with respect to the upbringing of a child'. However, there are some exceptions: see further **7.4**.

- *the delay principle*: any delay in determining a question about a child's upbringing is likely to prejudice the welfare of the child (section 1(2));[5] and

- *the no order principle*: the court shall not make an order unless it considers that doing so would be better for the child than making no order at all (s 1(5)).[6]

Where the court is considering whether to make, vary or discharge: (a) a residence, contact, specific issue or prohibited steps order that is opposed by a party; or (b) an order under Part IV[7] of the CA 1989, it 'shall have regard in particular to' seven factors,[8] invariably called *the welfare checklist* although the term is not used by the CA 1989 itself (s 1(3) and (4)). Most applications brought under the CA 1989 therefore become a question of assessing and weighing competing factors from within the welfare checklist. The factors in the welfare checklist, which are not in any order of precedence, are:

(a) the ascertainable wishes and feelings of the child concerned (considered in the light of his age and understanding);
(b) his physical, emotional and educational needs;
(c) the likely effect on him of any change in his circumstances;
(d) his age, sex, background and any characteristics of his which the court considers relevant;
(e) any harm[9] which he has suffered or is at risk of suffering;
(f) how capable each of his parents, and any other person in relation to whom the court considers the question to be relevant, is of meeting his needs;
(g) the range of powers available to the court under this Act in the proceedings in question.

Part I deals with three other matters:

---

[5] The delay principle is a general but not an absolute principle. There are circumstances in which so-called 'planned and purposeful' delay may be in the interests of the child but one must beware lest this too readily becomes an excuse for something else. Delay in determining questions about children's upbringing, both in private law and in public law cases, is a stain on the family justice system – not necessarily the only one but probably the greatest. It has reached the point where (from the lawyer's perspective) this may of itself amount to breaches of the human rights of those involved and (from the policy-maker's perspective) amounts to a failure to achieve the purposes of welfare and social justice. Hence the imperative behind the Protocol for Judicial Case Management in Public Law Children Act Cases – that all such cases should be completed within a maximum of 40 weeks save in exceptional circumstances.

[6] The no order principle is consistent with two of the philosophies underlying the CA 1989, that there should be minimum State intervention in family life (cf Article 8 of the European Convention on Human Rights) and that parents should exercise, and be encouraged to exercise, responsibility for their children. Practice varies as to whether an order is issued saying 'no order is made' or whether no such order is issued. However logical the latter is, it is suggested that the former is much clearer (especially important if the matter comes back to court some time later).

[7] See below in this overview.

[8] Note that the court is not strictly confined to these seven factors.

[9] Defined by CA 1989, s 31(9) – see further below in this overview.

- *parental responsibility*:[10] another key concept introduced by the CA 1989 and defined as 'all the rights, duties, powers, responsibilities and authority which by law a parent of a child has in relation to a child and his property' (s 3(1)).[11] The basic principle is that those with parental responsibility can act independently of each other (s 2(7) and (8)). In practice, unless in an emergency, no big decisions should be taken unilaterally (this would be contrary to the underlying meaning of 'responsibility' itself) and if agreement cannot be reached a court may have to be asked to determine the matter;[12]

- the appointment of guardians (ss 5 and 6);[13]

- *welfare reports*: when a court is considering any question with respect to a child under the CA 1989 it can 'ask': (a) an officer of CAFCASS; or (b) a local authority officer or someone else the authority considers appropriate, to report to the court (s 7).[14]

Part II: 'Orders with respect to children in family and other proceedings' (the ground floor)

CA 1989, Part II deals with private law orders. It is a busy part of the CA 1989, both in the sense that most cases about children are about such orders and in the sense that it contains a lot of detailed rules.[15] An overview is not the place to try to tackle the detail, but Part II is an area that might particularly

---

10 For details of who has parental responsibility, see **7.5**. Note in particular that s 111 of the Adoption and Children Act 2002, which came into effect on 1 December 2003, has amended s 4 of the CA 1989 so that the unmarried father will automatically acquire parental responsibility if registered as the father at birth.

11 Contrast with the much more explicit provisions about parental responsibilities and parental rights in Part I of the Children (Scotland) Act 1995.

12 For a practical example of 'who can take what decisions', see **7.6**.

13 Ie someone who will assume parental responsibility for a child in the event of the death of the appointing person. It is normally done within a will, but it can be done by a separate document or by court order. Note that such a guardian is nothing to do with the roles of a children's guardian (CA 1989, s 41) or of a guardian ad litem (Family Proceedings Rules 1991, r 9.5) which are confined to the participation of a child as a party to family proceedings, nor is it anything to do with special guardianship, a concept that will be inserted into the CA 1989 by Adoption and Children Act 2002, s 115.

14 Where such a report is necessary the court will normally ask CAFCASS to provide it. The obvious occasions on which the court should instead consider asking the local authority to do so are if the local authority social services are known to have had significant dealings with the family already or if the court has concerns that child protection measures may be necessary but those concerns fall short of the court making an order under the CA 1989, s 37 (the principal responsibility for child protection lies with social services, not CAFCASS, and it is the local authority, not CAFCASS, that can issue protective proceedings under the CA 1989, Parts IV and V). Note that if a CAFCASS officer is appointed the role is called 'children and family reporter' and the Family Proceedings Rules 1991, rr 4.11 and 4.11B apply, but if the person appointed is through the local authority they are called a 'welfare officer' and the Family Proceedings Rules 1991, r 4.13 applies. On the relationship between courts and CAFCASS officers, see further *Re M (Disclosure: Children and Family Reporter)* [2002] 2 FLR 893, and **5.8** below where extracts from this judgment are set out.

15 Which means it is not always easy to find what you are looking for, and sometimes some of the rules are overlooked. For example, there are rules about residence orders in all but the last two sections of Part II.

repay returning to (and it is not very long), especially for anyone whose work is mainly in private law matters.

Key features of Part II include:

- definitions of the four key private law orders – a *contact order*, a *prohibited steps order*, a *residence order* and a *specific issue order* (s 8(1));
- the definition of the phrase 'family proceedings' within the CA 1989 (s 8(3)–(4));
- the power of the court in any family proceedings in which a question arises with respect to the welfare of a child to make a s 8 order even though no application has been made for that order (s 10(1)(b)). This power, which is sometimes called *'the menu principle'*, is immensely important. The court can and should itself consider what is the best order (if any) for the child whatever orders are being argued for by the parties;[16]
- provisions about who is entitled to apply for a s 8 order as of right and who has first to obtain the court's permission ('leave') to do so (s 10);
- the responsibility on the court to draw up a timetable with a view to determining any question in relation to a s 8 order without delay, and the power to give such directions as it considers appropriate to achieve this (s 11);
- some important rules about residence orders, including limitations on changing the child's surname or removing her from the United Kingdom (sections 12 to 14);
- *special guardianship orders* (ss 14A to 14G).[17] This will provide an important alternative to be considered in some cases under the menu principle, falling short of adoption but carrying greater authority than a residence order:

  'a special guardian is entitled to exercise parental responsibility to the exclusion of any other person with parental responsibility for the child (apart from another special guardian)';[18]

- provision in relation to financial relief for children (s 15 and Sch 1);[19]
- the power to make *a family assistance order* (s 16). This is an order for up to six months requiring either an officer of CAFCASS or of a local

---

[16] Orders from Part II can be, and often are, used in the course of public law proceedings either instead of any public law order (for example, an application for a care order might result in a residence order to the maternal grandparents and contact orders to the mother and father) or in combination with a public law order (for example, care proceedings resulting in a residence order to the mother and a supervision order to the local authority).

[17] These sections are inserted into the CA 1989 by the Adoption and Children Act 2002, s 115. At the time of writing they are not in force, although it is planned this will happen in September 2005.

[18] CA 1989, s 14C(1)(b) when brought into force.

[19] Financial provision for children is mostly achieved through the Child Support Act 1991 or the Matrimonial Causes Act 1973 but there are circumstances where the CA 1989, s 15 is important, particularly for children whose parents have never been married to each other.

authority 'to advise, assist and (where appropriate) befriend any person named in the order'.[20]

Part III: 'Local authority support for children and families' (the first floor)

There are several features of the CA 1989, Part III as a whole that need to be noticed before attempting any summary of its detailed contents. The first is that it precedes Parts IV and V. It is surely significant that 'Local authority support for children and families' comes before 'Care and supervision' and 'Protection of children'. Not only is it logically prior, but prevention is better than cure as well as usually being cheaper.

The second observation is that Part III must be read in conjunction with Sch 2[21] which shares the same title, 'Local authority support for children and families'. It is also worth being aware that both Part III and Sch 2 have been significantly amended since 1989, notably by the Carers and Disabled Children Act 2000, the Children (Leaving Care) Act 2000 and the Adoption and Children Act 2002.[22]

The third observation is that Part III is difficult for many (perhaps most) people practising within the family justice system. Its architecture[23] is different from that of Parts I, II, IV and V. It is where public law 'in the family lawyer's sense' becomes public law 'in the administrative lawyer's sense'.[24]

Having made these observations we are now in a position to summarise the dense web of powers and duties contained in Part III and Sch 2. They include:

- local authority powers and duties towards all children;[25]
- local authority powers and duties towards children in need. '*Child in need*' is the most important concept within Part III and is defined by s 17(10) as being if:

---

[20] Before a family assistance order can be made for a local authority to provide an officer its consent must be obtained; in the case of CAFCASS no such consent is needed. The circumstances in which, and purposes for which, family assistance orders are made vary throughout England and Wales. It is an issue about which good practice needs to be discussed within the family justice system. It is also an area in which law reform has been recommended: see the report of the Advisory Board on Family Law Children Act Sub-Committee, 'Making Contact Work' (2002), at ch 11.

[21] See CA 1989, ss 17(2) and (4), 23(9) and 29(6). Schedule 2 is itself divided into three Parts: Part I (provision of services for families); Part II (children looked after by local authorities); and Part III (contributions towards maintenance of children looked after by local authorities).

[22] Amendments of this sort to primary legislation are a sure sign that policy from Westminster and Whitehall is continuing to evolve.

[23] Like that of 'the attic' – Parts VI to XI.

[24] The phrases and the distinction are borrowed from Munby J in *Re S (Habeas corpus), S v Haringey London Borough Council* [2003] EWHC 2734, [2004] 1 FLR 590 at [8].

[25] For example, the power to provide day-care for young children (s 18(2)) and the duty to take reasonable steps to reduce the need to bring care or supervision proceedings in relation to children within its area (Sch 2, para 7(a)(i)).

'(a) he is unlikely to achieve or maintain, or to have the opportunity of
      achieving or maintaining, a reasonable standard of health or
      development without the provision for him of services by a local
      authority under this Part;

(b) his health or development is likely to be significantly impaired, or
     further impaired, without the provision for him of such services; or

(c) he is disabled.'[26]

A local authority has both a general duty '(a) to safeguard and promote
the welfare of children within their area who are in need; and (b) so far as
is consistent with that duty, to promote the upbringing of such children
by their families.'[27] It also has specific duties and powers set out in Part I
of Sch 2,[28] as well as other duties set out in Part III of the CA 1989:[29]

• local authority powers and duties to provide accommodation: these are
  extremely important and are particularly set out in the CA 1989, ss 20, 21
  and 23;[30]

• local authority powers and duties towards children looked after by them.
  This introduces the second most important concept within Part III, the
  definition of a *'child who is looked after by a local authority'*. Section 22(1)
  defines this as:

    '... a child who is –

    (a) in their care; or

    (b) provided with accommodation by the local authority in the exercise
         of any functions (in particular those under this Act) which are social
         services functions within the meaning of the Local Authority Social
         Services Act 1970, apart from functions under sections 17, 23B and
         24B.'

  These duties are particularly set out in s 22 (a general duty) and s 23 and
  Part II of Sch 2 (specific duties);[31]

• ongoing local authority powers and duties towards 'relevant children' and
  'persons qualifying for advice and assistance'. These provisions are
  designed to ensure children and young adults are helped in the transition
  to independent adult living: see ss 23A–24C;

• provisions in relation to the review of the cases of 'looked after' children
  in s 26 and for advocacy services in s 26A.

---

[26] Itself defined in CA 1989, s 17(11).

[27] CA 1989, s 17(1). This does not require a local social services authority to meet every need which has
      been identified: see *R(G) v Barnet London Borough Council, R(W) v Lambeth London Borough Council* and
      R(A) v Lambeth London Borough Council [2003] UKHL 57, [2004] 1 FLR 454.

[28] CA 1989, s 17(2): for example, the duty to identify children in need (Sch 2, para 1); the power to assess
      the needs of such a child (Sch 2, para 3); the duty to make provision for children in need living with
      their families (Sch 2, para 8); and the duty to promote contact between a child in need and his family
      who is neither living with his family nor being looked after by the local authority (Sch 2, para 10).

[29] For example, the duty to provide such day care for children in need within their area who are five or
      under and not yet attending school (CA 1989, s 18(1)).

[30] See also Sch 2, paras 5 and 13.

[31] CA 1989, s 23 is a duty to provide accommodation and to maintain. Part II of Sch 2 includes, for
      example, a duty to promote contact between the child and her family (para 15).

Finally, within Part III there is a matter that is familiar to the family lawyer: *secure accommodation*. The consequences of a secure accommodation order are such that it is hardly surprising it should be the subject of its own technical rules.[32] The relevant criteria that have to be established are:

> '(a) that—
>> (i) he has a history of absconding and is likely to abscond from any other description of accommodation; and
>> (ii) if he absconds he is likely to suffer significant harm, or
>
> (b) that if he is kept in any other description of accommodation he is likely to injure himself or other persons.'[33]

Parts IV and V: 'Care and supervision' and 'Protection of children' (the second floor)

Parts IV and V are concerned with public law 'in the family lawyer's sense'. They make provision for the protection of children and for their care and supervision. Underpinning the legislation and subsequent case-law is the principle that there should be the minimum State interference in family life necessary to ensure the safety and wellbeing of the children,[34] and therefore that any such interference should not take place unless a *threshold* has been crossed.

It is crucial to understand three things about the threshold. First, in every case the threshold involves the concept of *significant harm*. 'Significant harm' is not defined within the CA 1989, but 'harm' is:

> '"harm" means ill-treatment or the impairment of health or development including, for example, impairment suffered from seeing or hearing the ill-treatment of another.'[35]

Secondly, and even more importantly, the threshold varies according to the step it is proposed the State – acting through local authority social services[36] – is to take. The more radically the step would intrude upon the child and her family's right to respect for their private and family life, the greater the threshold that has to be crossed. So, for example, the threshold for a care order is higher than the threshold for an interim care order.[37] Thirdly, when

---

[32] For example, the explicit requirements about legal representation (CA 1989, s 25(6)), the fact that the welfare principle does not apply, and the existence of the Children (Secure Accommodation) Regulations 1991 and the Children (Secure Accommodation) (No 2) Regulations 1991.

[33] CA 1989, s 25(1).

[34] A principle derived from Article 8 of the European Convention on Human Rights.

[35] CA 1989, s 31(9). The words 'including ... another' were added when the Adoption and Children Act 2002, s 119 came into force on 31 January 2005, this being a response to concerns about the harm suffered by children who see or hear domestic violence taking place. 'Ill-treatment', 'health' and 'development' are all themselves defined within the same subsection. Note also that s 105 extends this definition of harm throughout the CA 1989 so that, in particular, it also applies to the phrase 'any harm which he has suffered or is at risk of suffering' in the welfare checklist (s 1(3)).

[36] But note also the role of the State acting through the court and of CAFCASS.

[37] The varying thresholds are illustrated at **7.7** below.

the court is asked to make an order under Parts IV or V that requires it to apply a threshold test it must, if it decides the threshold test has been made out, also then go on to apply the welfare principle, the no delay principle and the no order principle set out in s 1 and referred to above.

In our experience, in many contested applications most of the evidence and argument focuses upon the threshold test. It is perhaps not difficult to imagine why this might be so. It is hard enough to admit one's failings in private and to oneself. How much harder it must be for parents to admit, in public and to strangers, that they have caused and/or would be likely to cause significant harm to their children – especially if they are frightened that criminal proceedings may follow. More subtly, the threshold test may lend itself more readily to the methodology of judges and lawyers than does the welfare test.

Should there be a shift of emphasis in many contested cases away from the threshold test and to the welfare test? That is not to say that the threshold test is unimportant. It is vitally important and, of course, the court's findings on the threshold test are highly relevant to the welfare test it must go on to perform. It is to recognise, however, the reality that in most cases the threshold test is made out,[38] that the future is even more important than the past, that it is even harder for the court to predict the future than to analyse the past, and that there are all sorts of potential deficiencies in what any corporate parent (ie the local authority) has to offer. Put baldly, parents often have little prospect of being successful on the threshold argument but almost always have a prospect of being successful on the welfare argument, especially if they can focus on it at an early stage.

It is time to look at the main provisions contained within Parts IV and V that together form a continuum from preliminary assessment and/or immediate protection, through provisions to ensure a child's safety and well-being while thorough assessments and planning are done, to decision-making by a court based on those assessments and planning:[39]

- *the local authority's duty to investigate* (s 47): 'where a local authority…have reasonable cause to suspect that a child who lives, or is found, in their area is suffering or is likely to suffer significant harm, the authority shall make … such enquiries as they consider necessary to enable them to decide whether they should take any action to safeguard or promote the

---

[38] Unfortunately, this information is not disceerible from the annual judicial statistics (www.dca.gov.uk/jsalist.htm)

[39] The balance between various priorities differs depending on where proceedings are within this continuum. In the early stages greater priority will usually be given to the need to provide immediate protection, and the information available may well be incomplete. The emphasis is on the short-term. At the next stage the emphasis is on establishing a holding position and ensuring appropriate investigation is carried out and help made available. At the conclusion of care proceedings the evidence should be complete and long-term plans (albeit sometimes in the alternative) should be clear.

child's welfare.' Note that there is no power under the CA 1989 to compel a local authority to bring proceedings;[40]

- *a child assessment order* (s 43): like the duty to investigate, this is a form of preliminary assessment. It operates on the same essential test of '... reasonable cause to suspect that the child is suffering or is likely to suffer significant harm ...';

- *police protection* (s 46): 'Where a constable has reasonable cause to believe that a child would otherwise be likely to suffer significant harm, he may – (a) remove the child to suitable accommodation and keep him there ...'. The maximum this can last is 72 hours;

- *an emergency protection order* (ss 44–45): 'Where any person ("the applicant") applies to the court for an order to be made under this section with respect to a child, the court may make the order if, but only if, it is satisfied that – (a) there is reasonable cause to believe that the child is likely to suffer significant harm if – (i) he is not removed to accommodation provided by or on behalf of the applicant ...'. The maximum this can last is eight days; it can be renewed once for up to seven days; and there is no appeal against such orders;

- *interim care order or interim supervision order* (s 38): 'A court shall not make an interim care order or interim supervision order ... unless it is satisfied that there are reasonable grounds for believing: [(a) that the child concerned is suffering, or is likely to suffer, significant harm; and (b) that the harm, or likelihood of harm, is attributable to: (i) the care being given to the child, or likely to be given to him if the order were not made, not being what it would be reasonable to expect a parent to give him; or (ii) the child's being beyond parental control].' The maximum[41] this can last is eight weeks from the date of the first order, and four weeks after that period.

- *supervision order* (s 31): 'a court may only make a ... supervision order if it is satisfied: (a) that the child concerned is suffering, or is likely to suffer, significant harm; and (b) that the harm, or likelihood of harm, is attributable to: (i) the care being given to the child, or likely to be given to him if the order were not made, not being what it would be reasonable to expect a parent to give him; or (ii) the child's being beyond parental control.' A supervision order lasts for up to one year and can be extended to a maximum of three years.[42] It does not vest parental responsibility in the local authority. Instead, it is the duty of the supervisor '(a) to advise, assist and befriend the supervised child; (b) to take such steps as are reasonably necessary to give effect to the order; and (c) where (i) the order is not wholly complied with; or (ii) the

---

[40] *Nottinghamshire County Council v P* [1993] 2 FLR 134, although a decision not to do so could, in appropriate circumstances, be challenged by judicial review. As to judicial review, see **7.14** below.

[41] Which is not to say that orders should be made to the maximum length. The principles of minimum interference and no delay may well indicate that shorter lengths should be ordered.

[42] CA 1989, Sch 3, para 6.

supervisor considers the order may no longer be necessary, to consider whether or not to apply to the court for its variation or discharge.'[43] Schedule 3, Parts I and II make further provision with respect to supervision orders and are important.[44]

- *care order* (s 31): 'a court may only make a care order ... if it is satisfied: (a) that the child concerned is suffering, or is likely to suffer, significant harm; and (b) that the harm, or likelihood of harm, is attributable to: (i) the care being given to the child, or likely to be given to him if the order were not made, not being what it would be reasonable to expect a parent to give him; or (ii) the child's being beyond parental control.' A care order lasts until the child is 18, unless brought to an end earlier.[45] Section 33 sets out the effect of a care order. It vests parental responsibility in the local authority. It does not remove it from parents or guardians who otherwise have it, but the extent to which they may meet their parental responsibility for the child may be determined by the local authority, subject to the other provisions of the section.

Pause here for a moment. Go back over the preceding list of bullet points and note which of them are court orders (two are not): then remind yourself that in the case of those that are, not only must the court apply the threshold test referred to, but also it must also apply the welfare test (with reference to the welfare checklist), the no delay principle and the no order principle, and it should apply the menu principle – all before making any order.

Completing these provisions are a variety of others including:

- the responsibility on the court to draw up a timetable with a view to disposing of an application under Part IV without delay, and the power to give such directions as it considers appropriate to achieve this (s 32);[46]
- provisions in relation to contact with children in care (s 34). This is an issue that is immensely important;[47]
- education supervision orders (s 36);
- the power of the court to direct a local authority to undertake an investigation of a child's circumstances 'where, in any family proceedings in which a question arises with respect to the welfare of any child, it appears to the court that it may be appropriate for a care or supervision

---

[43] CA 1989, s 35(1).

[44] There is no power to attach conditions to a supervision order: see *Re V (Care or Supervision Order)* [1996] 1 FLR 776. However, Sch 3 does make provision for directions to be given by the supervisor, requirements that can be imposed with consent, and a regime for the psychiatric and medical examination and treatment of the child.

[45] CA 1989, s 91(12).

[46] Echoing s 11 in relation to private law proceedings, and now supplemented by the Protocol for Judicial Case Management in Public Law Children Act Cases (see below at **6.2**).

[47] It is also an issue in which one can surely expect to see human rights arguments run and indeed which may be a candidate for amending legislation in relation to contact between siblings. One of the most striking results of the 'Your Shout!' survey published by the NSPCC in 2003 was the strength of concern expressed by children in care about the lack of contact they have with their family and friends.

order to be made with respect to him' (s 37). This is an important bridge between private law proceedings and public law responsibilities;[48]

• the power of the court on making an interim care or interim supervision order to include directions with regard to the medical or psychiatric examination or other assessment of the child (s 38(6));[49]

• the power of the court to exclude a relevant person from a dwelling-house when making an interim care order or emergency protection order (ss 38A and 44A).[50] This may enable the child who has suffered or is at risk of suffering abuse to remain living at home rather than being removed into foster care;

• discharge and variation of care and supervision orders (s 39);

• for the representation of a child who is the subject of *specified proceedings*[51] (s 41); and of the rights of a CAFCASS officer to have access to local authority records in such cases (s 42).[52]

Parts VI to XI (the attic)

CA 1989, Part VI is headed 'Community homes', Part VII 'Voluntary homes and voluntary organisations', Part VIII 'Registered children's homes', Part IX 'Private arrangements for fostering children', Part X has been repealed and replaced by Part XA 'Childminding and daycare for children in England and Wales', and Part XI is headed 'Secretary of State's supervisory functions and responsibilities'. We have decided to omit all these parts from this Handbook on the basis that for most interdisciplinary workers within the family justice system it is enough to be aware of their existence.

---

[48] Whilst a court can make an interim care or interim supervision order at the same time as it makes a s 37 direction (see CA 1989, s 38(1)(a)) it cannot thereafter compel a local authority to apply for a care or supervision order: *Nottinghamshire County Council v P* [1993] 2 FLR 134.

[49] See *Re C (Interim Care Order: Residential Assessment)* [1997 AC 489, [1997] 1 FLR 1, and *Re G (Interim Care Order: Residential Assessment)* [2004] EWCA Civ 24, [2004] 1 FLR 876. Note that if the child is of sufficient understanding to make an informed decision he may refuse to submit to the examination or assessment. Similar provisions apply in relation to psychiatric and medical examinations and treatment of children who are the subject of supervision orders (Sch 3, paras 4(4) and 5(5)).

[50] Or to accept an undertaking to similar effect from the relevant person (CA 1989, ss 38B and 44B).

[51] 'Specified proceedings' is defined by s 41(6), a definition that will be extended by the Adoption and Children Act 2002, s 122 once it has been implemented. It is suggested that, under the tandem model it is the role of the solicitor to 'represent' the child, and that of the children's guardian to 'safeguard' her interests (see the wording of CA 1989, s 41, and of FPR, rr 4.10 and 4.11A). Unless the child is able to choose and instruct her own solicitor it is for the children's guardian to do so (FPR 1991, rr 4.11A(1)(a) and 4.12(1)(a)). If there is no children's guardian to do so, it is for the court to appoint the child's solicitor (CA 1989, s 41(3)–(5); Protocol for Judicial Case Management in Public Law Children Act Cases, para 1.4 (see **6.2** below); and the Statement of Good Practice in the Appointment of Solicitors for Children where it falls to the Court to do so in Specified Proceedings (The Law Society, November 2003)), and the solicitor must then represent the child 'in furtherance of the best interests of the child' (FPR 1991, r 4.12(1)(c)).

[52] See *Re J (Care Proceedings: Disclosure)* [2003] EWHC (Fam) 976, [2003] 2 FLR 522. It is suggested that the solicitor for the child has a separate right to obtain relevant information under ordinary rules of disclosure (this right existed anyway and therefore did not need including in the CA 1989, whereas there was no such right otherwise for the children's guardian, hence the need for the CA 1989, s 42).

Part XII: 'Miscellaneous and general' (the roof)

The CA 1989, Part XII contains an assortment of highly important and useful provisions, including:

- about the effect and duration of orders, including the power to order that no further application for an order under the CA 1989 of any specified kind may be made without the leave of the court[53] (s 91 in general, s 91(14) in particular);

- about the attendance of children at hearings and their evidence (ss 95 and 96);[54]

- limiting the general rule that no-one can be required to give evidence that might incriminate him or his spouse of a criminal offence (s 98);[55]

- restricting the use of wardship (s 100);[56]

- the interpretation section, defining the meaning of important words and phrases used within the CA 1989 (s 105).

Schedules (the fitted furniture)

We have decided to include two of the fourteen Schedules to the CA 1989, Sch 2, 'Local authority support for children and families', and Sch 3, 'Supervision orders', both of which have been considered above.

The extracts from the primary materials we recommend you read now are ss 1, 8, 17 and 31 of the CA 1989.[57]

The Overview continues at **3.16** Human Rights Act 1998.

---

53 This has been restrictively interpreted, but might such case-law be distinguished in the case of the older child arguing a right to respect for her private life?

54 See also FPR 1991, r 4.16.

55 The exact meaning of this section, and the extent to which it achieves the right balance between various competing interests (the welfare of the child, of adults who may be charged in criminal proceedings and of the wider public in all such matters), continues to be a matter of debate.

56 Wardship is a part of the inherent jurisdiction, the essential points about which are: (1) it is a jurisdiction of the High Court, not the county court or the family proceedings court; (2) its powers are immensely flexible; and (3) it should not be used when other suitable powers are available.

57 Which are the first sections in each of the first four Parts of the CA 1989. CAFCASS officers should also particularly read ss 7, 41 and 42.

Children Act 1989

PART I

INTRODUCTORY

1 Welfare of the child

(1) When a court determines any question with respect to –

    (a) the upbringing of a child; or

    (b) the administration of a child's property or the application of any income arising from it,

the child's welfare shall be the court's paramount consideration.

(2) In any proceedings in which any question with respect to the upbringing of a child arises, the court shall have regard to the general principle that any delay in determining the question is likely to prejudice the welfare of the child.

(3) In the circumstances mentioned in subsection (4), a court shall have regard in particular to –

    (a) the ascertainable wishes and feelings of the child concerned (considered in the light of his age and understanding);

    (b) his physical, emotional and educational needs;

    (c) the likely effect on him of any change in his circumstances;

    (d) his age, sex, background and any characteristics of his which the court considers relevant;

    (e) any harm which he has suffered or is at risk of suffering;

    (f) how capable each of his parents, and any other person in relation to whom the court considers the question to be relevant, is of meeting his needs;

    (g) the range of powers available to the court under this Act in the proceedings in question.

(4) The circumstances are that –

    (a) the court is considering whether to make, vary or discharge a section 8 order, and the making, variation or discharge of the order is opposed by any party to the proceedings; or

    (b) the court is considering whether to make, vary or discharge an order under Part IV.

(5) Where a court is considering whether or not to make one or more orders under this Act with respect to a child, it shall not make the order or any of the orders unless it considers that doing so would be better for the child than making no order at all.

Section 1

Prospective amendment—Section prospectively amended by Adoption and Children Act 2002, s 115(3) (see **3.3B**).

Generally—Questions with respect to the upbringing of a child will obviously include issues relating to the making of orders under s 8 of the Children Act 1989 (CA 1989) (orders for contact, prohibited steps, residence and specific issues). Further, in proceedings where care/supervision orders are sought and the threshold criteria have been satisfied, the provisions of the CA 1989, s 1 and Article 8 of the European Convention on Human Rights must be considered before the court may make those orders.

Human rights—There is nothing in s 1 of the CA 1989 which is incompatible with Article 8 of the European Convention on Human Rights (*Dawson v Wearmouth* [1999] 2 AC 329, [1999] 2 All ER 353, [1999] 1 FLR 1167). The welfare checklist must be considered and applied in the circumstances specified in s 1(4) – note that by s 1(4)(b) this includes when: 'the court is considering whether to make, vary or discharge [a special guardianship order or] an order under Part IV' (words in square brackets prospectively inserted). In the case of *Re L (A Child) (Contact: Domestic Violence)* [2000] 4 All ER 609, [2001] 2 WLR 339, [2000] 2 FLR 334, CA, the President said (at [2000] 2 FLR 346): 'In *Hendriks v Netherlands* (1982) 5 EHRR 223 the court held that where there was a serious conflict between the interests of a child and one of its parents which could only be resolved to the disadvantage of one of them, the interests of the child had to prevail under Art 8(2). The principle of the crucial importance of the best interests of the child has been upheld in all subsequent decisions of the European Court of Human Rights. The observation by the court in *Johansen v Norway* (1996) 23 EHRR 33 is particularly apposite to this appeal. The court said: "In particular ... the parent cannot be entitled under Article 8 of the Convention to have such measures taken as would harm the child's health and development".'

Infant parent/children's conflicting interests—Where a child ('A') is born to a parent who is himself/herself a child ('B') and care proceedings are taken, the welfare of the child 'A' will be the court's paramount consideration (*Birmingham City Council v H (A Minor)* [1994] 2 AC 212, [1995] 1 All ER 12, [1994] 1 FLR 224, HL, and *F v Leeds City Council* [1994] 2 FLR 60, CA). This may lead to complicated issues where more than one child is concerned in a case (such as in the case of the conjoined twins, *Re A (Children) (Conjoined Twins: Surgical Separation)* [2000] 4 All ER 961, [2001] 1 FLR 1, CA).

Child's welfare not paramount in some proceedings—The child's welfare will be relevant but will not be the court's paramount concern in applications for secure accommodation orders (*Re M (Secure Accommodation Order)* [1995] Fam 108, [1995] 3 All ER 405), orders that blood tests be carried out (*Re H (A Minor) (Blood Tests: Parental Rights)* [1996] 4 All ER 28, [1996] 3 WLR 308), orders under Sch 1 to the Children Act 1989 (application for financial provision relating to a child (*J v C (Child: Financial Provision)* [1999] 1 FLR 152) and orders that a child attend court pursuant to a witness summons (*Re P (Witness Summons)* [1997] 2 FLR 447, CA – see also *Re P (Minor: Compellability as Witness)* reported in (1991) *The Times*, 24 January, and *Re O (Care Proceedings: Evidence)* [2003] EWHC 2011 (Fam), [2004] 1 FLR 161, in which it was said that the general practice is not to hear evidence from children in care proceedings).

Age and understanding—The child's age and understanding must be considered in relation to the individual child concerned. There is no prescribed age at which a child's wishes will be determinative (this reflects the House of Lords decision in *Gillick v West Norfolk and Wisbech Area Health Authority* [1986] AC 112).

Harm—In the case of *Re M and R* [1996] 4 All ER 239 at 247, the Court of Appeal held that, in deciding whether a child is at risk of suffering harm under s 1(2)(e) of the CA 1989, the harm or risk of harm must be proved on the balance of probabilities; if the harm or risk of harm is not proved to that standard there is no basis upon which the court may find that the risk of harm exists. Without deciding the point, Lord Nicholls has said in *Re O and N* that he finds the conclusions of the Court of Appeal in *Re M and R* (and also in *Re P (Sexual Abuse: Standard of Proof)* [1996] 2 FLR 333) attractive (*Re O and N; Re B* [2003] UKHL 18, [2003] 2 All ER 305, [2003] 1 FLR 1169, HL).

Delay—Although delay will normally be inimical to a child's welfare, delay may in certain circumstances be purposive and therefore of benefit to the child: see, eg, *C v Solihull*

Metropolitan Borough Council [1993] 1 FLR 290. This issue frequently arises where an assessment of a child is sought in care proceedings under s 38(6) of the CA 1989 (as to which see, in particular, *Re G (Interim Care Order: Residential Assessment)* [2004] EWCA Civ 24, [2004] 1 FLR 876, CA).

No order—If the court makes no order on an application, it should issue an order stating this: *S v R (Parental Responsibility)* [1993] 1 FCR 331.

McKenzie friend—If a party wishes to be assisted by a McKenzie friend the following principles were identified in *R v Bow County Court, ex parte Pelling* [1999] 4 All ER 751, [1999] 1 WLR 1807, [1999] 2 FLR 1126, CA:

(1) in relation to proceedings in public, a litigant in person should be allowed to have the assistance of a McKenzie friend unless the judge is satisfied that fairness and the interests of justice do not require a litigant in person to have the assistance of a McKenzie friend;

(2) the position is the same where the proceedings are in chambers unless the proceedings are in private;

(3) where the proceedings are in private then the nature of the proceedings which make it appropriate for them to be heard in private may make it undesirable in the interests of justice for a McKenzie friend to assist;

(4) a judge should give reasons for refusing to allow a litigant in person the assistance of a McKenzie friend;

(5) the assistance of a McKenzie friend is available for the benefit of the litigant in person and whether or not a McKenzie friend is paid or unpaid for his services he has no right to provide those services; the court is solely concerned with the interests of the litigant in person.

See also: *Re M (Contact: Family Assistance: McKenzie Friend)* [1999] 1 FLR 75, CA; *Re H (Chambers Proceedings: McKenzie Friend)* [1997] 2 FLR 423, CA; and *Re H (McKenzie Friend: Pre-trial Determination)* [2001] EWCA Civ 1444, [2002] 1 FLR 39, CA.

2 Parental responsibility for children

(1) Where a child's father and mother were married to each other at the time of his birth, they shall each have parental responsibility for the child.

(2) Where a child's father and mother were not married to each other at the time of his birth –

    (a) the mother shall have parental responsibility for the child;

    (b) the father shall have parental responsibility for the child if he has acquired it (and has not ceased to have it) in accordance with the provisions of this Act.

(3) References in this Act to a child whose father and mother were, or (as the case may be) were not, married to each other at the time of his birth must be read with section 1 of the Family Law Reform Act 1987 (which extends their meaning).

(4) The rule of law that a father is the natural guardian of his legitimate child is abolished.

(5) More than one person may have parental responsibility for the same child at the same time.

(6) A person who has parental responsibility for a child at any time shall not cease to have that responsibility solely because some other person subsequently acquires parental responsibility for the child.

(7) Where more than one person has parental responsibility for a child, each of them may act alone and without the other (or others) in meeting that responsibility; but

nothing in this Part shall be taken to affect the operation of any enactment which requires the consent of more than one person in a matter affecting the child.

(8) The fact that a person has parental responsibility for a child shall not entitle him to act in any way which would be incompatible with any order made with respect to the child under this Act.

(9) A person who has parental responsibility for a child may not surrender or transfer any part of that responsibility to another but may arrange for some or all of it to be met by one or more persons acting on his behalf.

(10) The person with whom any such arrangement is made may himself be a person who already has parental responsibility for the child concerned.

(11) The making of any such arrangement shall not affect any liability of the person making it which may arise from any failure to meet any part of his parental responsibility for the child concerned.

Section 2

Generally—Provisions relating to the acquisition of parental responsibility are to be found in ss 4 and 4A of the CA 1989, and were amended to their current form by the Adoption and Children Act 2002 with effect from 1 December 2003 (SI 2003/3079). Parental responsibility will also be conferred by the making of a residence order within the terms of and for the duration stated within s 12 of the CA 1989, or the making of an adoption order.

Parental responsibility and care orders—A care order does not deprive a parent of parental responsibility although it confers a dominant parental responsibility upon the local authority concerned (CA 1989, s 33(3)). Where a care order has been made, an unmarried father may still acquire parental responsibility by agreement with the mother or order of the court (*D v Hereford and Worcester County Council* [1991] Fam 14, and *Re X (Parental Responsibility Agreement: Children in Care)* [2000] 1 FLR 517).

Special guardianship—When the provisions of CA 1989, ss 14A to 14G come into force, a special guardianship order will confer parental responsibility upon the person in whose favour the order is made (CA 1989, s 14C).

3 Meaning of 'parental responsibility'

(1) In this Act 'parental responsibility' means all the rights, duties, powers, responsibilities and authority which by law a parent of a child has in relation to the child and his property.

(2) It also includes the rights, powers and duties which a guardian of the child's estate (appointed, before the commencement of section 5, to act generally) would have had in relation to the child and his property.

(3) The rights referred to in subsection (2) include, in particular, the right of the guardian to receive or recover in his own name, for the benefit of the child, property of whatever description and wherever situated which the child is entitled to receive or recover.

(4) The fact that a person has, or does not have, parental responsibility for a child shall not affect –

    (a) any obligation which he may have in relation to the child (such as a statutory duty to maintain the child); or

    (b) any rights which, in the event of the child's death, he (or any other person) may have in relation to the child's property.

(5) A person who –

    (a) does not have parental responsibility for a particular child; but

    (b) has care of the child,

may (subject to the provisions of this Act) do what is reasonable in all the circumstances of the case for the purpose of safeguarding or promoting the child's welfare.

4 Acquisition of parental responsibility by father

(1) Where a child's father and mother were not married to each other at the time of his birth, the father shall acquire parental responsibility for the child if –

    (a) he becomes registered as the child's father under any of the enactments specified in subsection (1A);[1]

    (b) he and the child's mother make an agreement (a 'parental responsibility agreement') providing for him to have parental responsibility for the child; or

    (c) the court, on his application, orders that he shall have parental responsibility for the child.

(1A) The enactments referred to in subsection (1)(a) are –

    (a) paragraphs (a), (b) and (c) of section 10(1) and of section 10A(1) of the Births and Deaths Registration Act 1953;

    (b) paragraphs (a), (b)(i) and (c) of section 18(1), and sections 18(2)(b) and 20(1)(a) of the Registration of Births, Deaths and Marriages (Scotland) Act 1965; and

    (c) sub-paragraphs (a), (b) and (c) of Article 14(3) of the Births and Deaths Registration (Northern Ireland) Order 1976.

(1B) The Secretary of State may by order amend subsection (1A) so as to add further enactments to the list in that subsection.

(2) No parental responsibility agreement shall have effect for the purposes of this Act unless –

    (a) it is made in the form prescribed by regulations made by the Lord Chancellor; and

    (b) where regulations are made by the Lord Chancellor prescribing the manner in which such agreements must be recorded, it is recorded in the prescribed manner.

(2A) A person who has acquired parental responsibility under subsection (1) shall cease to have that responsibility only if the court so orders.

(3) The court may make an order under subsection (2A) on the application –

    (a) of any person who has parental responsibility for the child; or

    (b) with leave of the court, of the child himself,

subject, in the case of parental responsibility acquired under subsection (1)(c), to section 12(4).

---

[1]   Note that this does not apply to any registration before 1 December 2004: s 111(7) of the Adoption and Children Act 2002.

(4) The court may only grant leave under subsection (3)(b) if it is satisfied that the child has sufficient understanding to make the proposed application.

Section 4

Prescribed form—The prescribed form for a parental responsibility agreement is that which is set out in the Parental Responsibility Agreement (Amendment) Regulations 2001, SI 2001/2262.

Test for parental responsibility order—In deciding whether to make an order that an unmarried father should have parental responsibility, the court should apply s 1 of the CA 1989 (*Re G (A Minor) (Parental Responsibility Order)* [1994] 1 FLR 504, CA). The court will also take into account the degree of commitment shown by the father to the child, the attachment between the father and the child and the reasons for the father making the application (see, eg *Re G* (above) and *Re P (Parental Responsibility)* [1997] 2 FLR 722, CA). The emphasis should be on the status conferred by parental responsibility rather than on the rights conferred by a parental responsibility order (*Re S (Parental Responsibility)* [1995] 2 FLR 648).

In *Re M (Contact: Parental Responsibility)* [2001] 2 FLR 342, the father's application for a parental responsibility order was rejected due to the concern that he would use it to interfere unduly in the mother's care of the child (cf *D v S* [1995] 3 FCR 783, *Re C and V (Contact and Parental Responsibility)* [1998] 1 FLR 392, and see *Re P (Parental Responsibility)* [1998] 2 FLR 96).

Ending parental responsibility—A parental responsibility order or agreement may be ended by the order of the court made on the application of a person with parental responsibility or, with the court's permission, of the child concerned (*Re P (Terminating Parental Responsibility)* [1995] 1 FLR 1048 and *Re G (Child Case: Parental Involvement)* [1996] 1 FLR 857).

Passports and refusal of parent to apply—Where a person with parental responsibility refuses to sign a passport application form on behalf of the child, the guidance contained in *Guidance from the President's Office (UK Passport Applications on behalf of children in the absence of the signature of a person with parental responsibility)* [2004] 1 FLR 746 should be followed.

Brussels II and parental responsibility—It has been held that Brussels II does not apply where no divorce proceedings have been issued and there is a free-standing application for parental responsibility in an EC country (*C v FC (Brussels II: Free-standing Application for Parental Responsibility)* [2004] 1 FLR 317, FD).

4A (*Section prospectively inserted by Adoption and Children Act 2002, s 112(7) – see* **3.3B** *for text*)

5 Appointment of guardians

(1) Where an application with respect to a child is made to the court by any individual, the court may by order appoint that individual to be the child's guardian if –

    (a) the child has no parent with parental responsibility for him; or

    (b) a residence order has been made with respect to the child in favour of a parent or guardian of his who has died while the order was in force.

(2) The power conferred by subsection (1) may also be exercised in any family proceedings if the court considers that the order should be made even though no application has been made for it.

(3) A parent who has parental responsibility for his child may appoint another individual to be the child's guardian in the event of his death.

(4) A guardian of a child may appoint another individual to take his place as the child's guardian in the event of his death.

(5) An appointment under subsection (3) or (4) shall not have effect unless it is made in writing, is dated and is signed by the person making the appointment or –

- (a) in the case of an appointment made by a will which is not signed by the testator, is signed at the direction of the testator in accordance with the requirements of section 9 of the Wills Act 1837; or
- (b) in any other case, is signed at the direction of the person making the appointment, in his presence and in the presence of two witnesses who each attest the signature.

(6) A person appointed as a child's guardian under this section shall have parental responsibility for the child concerned.

(7) Where –

- (a) on the death of any person making an appointment under subsection (3) or (4), the child concerned has no parent with parental responsibility for him; or
- (b) immediately before the death of any person making such an appointment, a residence order in his favour was in force with respect to the child,

the appointment shall take effect on the death of that person.

(8) Where, on the death of any person making an appointment under subsection (3) or (4) –

- (a) the child concerned has a parent with parental responsibility for him; and
- (b) subsection (7)(b) does not apply,

the appointment shall take effect when the child no longer has a parent who has parental responsibility for him.

(9) Subsections (1) and (7) do not apply if the residence order referred to in paragraph (b) of those subsections was also made in favour of a surviving parent of the child.

(10) Nothing in this section shall be taken to prevent an appointment under subsection (3) or (4) being made by two or more persons acting jointly.

(11) Subject to any provision made by rules of court, no court shall exercise the High Court's inherent jurisdiction to appoint a guardian of the estate of any child.

(12) Where the rules of court are made under subsection (11) they may prescribe the circumstances in which, and conditions subject to which, an appointment of such a guardian may be made.

(13) A guardian of a child may only be appointed in accordance with the provisions of this section.

Section 5

Prospective amendment—Section prospectively amended by Adoption and Children Act 2002, s 115(4) (see **3.3B**).

6 Guardians: revocation and disclaimer

(1) An appointment under section 5(3) or (4) revokes an earlier such appointment (including one made in an unrevoked will or codicil) made by the same person in

respect of the same child, unless it is clear (whether as the result of an express provision in the later appointment or by any necessary implication) that the purpose of the later appointment is to appoint an additional guardian.

(2) An appointment under section 5(3) or (4) (including one made in an unrevoked will or codicil) is revoked if the person who made the appointment revokes it by a written and dated instrument which is signed –

    (a) by him; or
    (b) at his direction, in his presence and in the presence of two witnesses who each attest the signature.

(3) An appointment under section 5(3) or (4) (other than one made in a will or codicil) is revoked if, with the intention of revoking the appointment, the person who made it –

    (a) destroys the instrument by which it was made; or
    (b) has some other person destroy that instrument in his presence.

(3A) An appointment under section 5(3) or (4) (including one made in an unrevoked will or codicil) is revoked if the person appointed is the spouse of the person who made the appointment and either –

    (a) a decree of a court of civil jurisdiction in England and Wales dissolves or annuls the marriage, or
    (b) the marriage is dissolved or annulled and the divorce or annulment is entitled to recognition in England and Wales by virtue of Part II of the Family Law Act 1986,

unless a contrary intention appears by the appointment.

(4) For the avoidance of doubt, an appointment under section 5(3) or (4) made in a will or codicil is revoked if the will or codicil is revoked.

(5) A person who is appointed as a guardian under section 5(3) or (4) may disclaim his appointment by an instrument in writing signed by him and made within a reasonable time of his first knowing that the appointment has taken effect.

(6) Where regulations are made by the Lord Chancellor prescribing the manner in which such disclaimers must be recorded, no such disclaimer shall have effect unless it is recorded in the prescribed manner.

(7) Any appointment of a guardian under section 5 may be brought to an end at any time by order of the court –

    (a) on the application of any person who has parental responsibility for the child;
    (b) on the application of the child concerned, with leave of the court; or
    (c) in any family proceedings, if the court considers that it should be brought to an end even though no application has been made.

7 Welfare reports

(1) A court considering any question with respect to a child under this Act may –

    (a) ask an officer of the Service; or
    (b) ask a local authority to arrange for –
        (i) an officer of the authority; or

(ii)   such other person (other than an officer of the Service) as the authority considers appropriate,

to report to the court on such matters relating to the welfare of that child as are required to be dealt with in the report.

(2) The Lord Chancellor may make regulations specifying matters which, unless the court orders otherwise, must be dealt with in any report under this section.

(3) The report may be made in writing, or orally, as the court requires.

(4) Regardless of any enactment or rule of law which would otherwise prevent it from doing so, the court may take account of –

(a)   any statement contained in the report; and

(b)   any evidence given in respect of the matters referred to in the report,

in so far as the statement or evidence is, in the opinion of the court, relevant to the question which it is considering.

(5) It shall be the duty of the authority or officer of the Service to comply with any request for a report under this section.

Section 7

Generally—This is the general provision by which reports may be ordered by the court in proceedings under the CA 1989. This section has to be distinguished from s 37 of the Act (where a local authority may be ordered to file a report where it appears to the court that it may be appropriate for care or supervision orders to be made). Rules that have been made under this section are Family Proceedings Rules 1991 (FPR 1991), rr 4.11 and 4.11B (Family Proceedings Court (Children Act 1989) Rules 1991 (FPC(CA 1989)R 1991), rr 11 and 11B) when the report is to be provided by an officer of CAFCASS (a 'children and family reporter' or 'CFR'), and FPR 1991, r 4.13 and FPC(CA 1989)R 1991, r 13 when the report is provided by or through a local authority. In the absence of a direction for the attendance of the reporter, he/she will not be expected to attend court.

Child party—FPR 1991, r 9.5 and the role of CAFCASS Legal in representing children are considered under s 41 below and are dealt with in *CAFCASS Practice Note* [2004] 1 FLR 1190 dated 6 April 2004 (see **6.19**), which replaces the Practice Note that was reported at [2001] 2 FLR 151 (and see also *Re W (Contact: Joining Child as Party)* [2001] EWCA Civ 1830, [2003] 1 FLR 681, CA). The CAFCASS Practice Note should be read in conjunction with *President's Direction (Representation of Children in Family Proceedings Pursuant to Rule 9.5 of the FPR 1991)* [2004] 1 FLR 1188, dated April 2004 (see **6.18**). It will be rare for a child to be joined as a party ('a step that will be taken only in cases which involve an issue of significant difficulty').

CAFCASS officer as witness—In *Re M (Disclosure: Children and Family Reporter)* [2002] EWCA Civ 1199, [2002] 2 FLR 893, Wall J said at [78]: 'By s 16 of the Criminal Justice and Court Services Act 2000, and in a significant departure from previous practice (see *Cadman v Cadman* (1982) 3 FLR 275 at 277 referred to at [24] in Thorpe LJ's judgment) CFRs may be cross-examined in any proceedings to the same extent as any witness, although they may not be cross-examined merely because they are exercising a right to conduct litigation or a right of audience granted in accordance with s 15. This change derives from the incorporation into English law of Art 6 of the European Convention on Human Rights and Fundamental Freedoms 1950 (as set out in Sch 1 to the Human Rights Act 1998)'. See also Thorpe LJ's judgment at [43] (extracts from this case are set out at **5.8**).

The CFR, generally, does not give evidence on oath (*Re I and H (Contact: Right to Give Evidence)* [1998] 1 FLR 876). However, any party may question him at the hearing (FPR 1991, r 4.11B(3) and FPC(CA 1989)R 1991, r 11B(3)), although the reporter should not be drawn into the adversarial arena by lengthy cross-examination (*Re B (Residence Order: Status Quo)* [1998] 1 FLR 368, CA).

If the judge is to depart from the recommendations of the reporter, he should hear oral evidence from him, test with him concerns that he has about the report and state his reason for departing from the reporter's recommendations in his judgment (*Re W (Residence)* [1999] 2 FLR 390, CA, and *W v W (A Minor: Custody Appeal)* [1988] 2 FLR 505, CA).

Judge and CAFCASS officer—Only in exceptional circumstances should a judge:

(1) have confidential discussions with the CFR (*Re C (A Minor: Irregularity of Practice)* [1991] 2 FLR 438);

(2) receive evidence relating to a party on the basis that it will not be revealed to that (or another) party (*Official Solicitor v K* [1965] AC 201, [1963] 3 WLR 408, HL). Such issues will require consideration to be given to Articles 6 and 8 of the European Convention on Human Rights (*Re B (Disclosure to Other Parties)* [2002] 1 FLR 1017, FD).

Judge's inadequate reasons—Where a judge does express his reasons inadequately, advocates should draw this to the attention of the judge (*Re T (Contact: Alienation: Permission to Appeal)* [2002] EWCA Civ 1736, [2003] 1 FLR 531, CA); where an appeal is based on such inadequacies, the Court of Appeal may adjourn an appeal in order to allow the judge to give additional reasons (*Re B (Appeal: Lack of Reasons)* [2003] EWCA Civ 881, [2003] 2 FLR 1035, CA).

Confidentiality of material received (and social services)—Where, during the course of his enquiries for the preparation of a court report, a CFR obtains material that causes concerns about a child's welfare, he does not need the judge's permission before revealing that material to the social services (*Re M (Disclosure: Children and Family Reporter)* [2002] EWCA Civ 1199, [2002] 2 FLR 893, CA).

PART II

ORDERS WITH RESPECT TO CHILDREN IN FAMILY PROCEEDINGS

General

8 Residence, contact and other orders with respect to children

(1) In this Act –

    'a contact order' means an order requiring the person with whom a child lives, or is to live, to allow the child to visit or stay with the person named in the order, or for that person and the child otherwise to have contact with each other;

    'a prohibited steps order' means an order that no step which could be taken by a parent in meeting his parental responsibility for a child, and which is of a kind specified in the order, shall be taken by any person without the consent of the court;

    'a residence order' means an order settling the arrangements to be made as to the person with whom a child is to live; and

    'a specific issue order' means an order giving directions for the purpose of determining a specific question which has arisen, or which may arise, in connection with any aspect of parental responsibility for a child.

(2) In this Act 'a section 8 order' means any of the orders mentioned in subsection (1) and any order varying or discharging such an order.

(3) For the purposes of this Act 'family proceedings' means any proceedings –

    (a) under the inherent jurisdiction of the High Court in relation to children; and

    (b) under the enactments mentioned in subsection (4),

but does not include proceedings on an application for leave under section 100(3).

(4) The enactments are –

    (a) Parts I, II and IV of this Act;
    (b) the Matrimonial Causes Act 1973;
    (c) *(repealed)*
    (d) the Adoption Act 1976;
    (e) the Domestic Proceedings and Magistrates' Courts Act 1978;
    (f) *(repealed)*
    (g) Part III of the Matrimonial and Family Proceedings Act 1984;
    (h) the Family Law Act 1996.
    (i) sections 11 and 12 of the Crime and Disorder Act 1998.

Section 8

Prospective amendment—Section prospectively amended by ACA 2002, s 139(1), Sch 3, paras 54, 55 (see **3.3B**).

Generally—'Private law' orders are dealt with in Part II of the CA 1989 (ss 8–16). This Part includes provision relating to 'section 8 orders' (defined by CA 1989, s 8(2) as being orders for contact, prohibited steps, residence and specific issues together with orders varying or discharging them), orders for financial relief in relation to children (s 15 and Sch 1) and family assistance orders (s 16). Special guardianship orders will also be covered once ss 14A–14G of the Adoption and Children Act 2002 are brought into force.

Ancillary provisions relating to section 8 orders—The ancillary provisions of the statute relating to s 8 are: s 9 (restrictions on making of s 8 orders); s 10 (power of the court to make s 8 orders); s 11 (general principles and supplementary provisions); s 12 (residence orders and parental responsibility); and s 13 (change of child's surname and removal from jurisdiction).

Section 8 orders generally—Orders may be made in family proceedings in which a question arises with respect to the welfare of the child, either on application or of the court's own motion (CA 1989, s 10(1) and see *Gloucestershire County Council v P* [2000] Fam 1, [1999] 2 FLR 61, CA). Interim orders may be made (s 11(3)), although it has been said that where there are substantial factual issues and the principle of contact is in dispute, it will rarely be right for an interim contact order to be made (*Re M (Interim Contact: Domestic Violence)* [2000] 2 FLR 377, CA).

An applicant for an ex parte order has a heavy duty to ensure that all material facts are before the court (*Re M and N (Minors) (Wardship: Publication of Information)* [1990] Fam 211 at 229, [1990] FCR 395 at 406, and *W v H (Ex Parte Injunctions)* [2001] 1 All ER 300, [2000] 2 FLR 927, FD (in the latter case Munby J emphasised that the order must be properly drawn and the legal representative of the applicant must ensure that this is so – see also *Re S (A Child) (Ex Parte Orders)* [2001] 1 All ER 362, [2001] 1 WLR 211, [2001] 1 FLR 308, FD)).

The general practice is that orders for costs will not be made (*C v FC (Children Proceedings: Costs)* [2004] 1 FLR 362, FD).

Contact orders

Child's welfare—Issues relating to contact must be determined through the application of CA 1989, s 1; the interests of the child concerned are therefore paramount (*Re O (A Minor) (Contact: Imposition of Conditions)* [1995] 2 FLR 124, CA). It will almost always be in the interests of a child to have contact with a non-residential parent (*Re KD (A Minor) (Ward: Termination of Access)* [1988] AC 806, [1998] 1 All ER 577, HL).

Cogent reasons—There must be cogent reasons (which should be identified in any judgment) before an order is made refusing contact between a child and a parent or before rejecting an application for contact to be introduced/reintroduced (*Re H (Minors) (Access)* [1992] 1 FLR 148, CA; *Re K (A Minor) (Access Order: Breach)* [1977] 2 All ER 737, [1977] 1 WLR 533; and *Re S (Contact: Promoting Relationship with Absent Parent)* [2004] EWCA Civ 18, [2004] 1 FLR 1279, CA, in which the Court of Appeal held that it had been premature to abandon any possibility of contact between the father and the child, and the Recorder should have ordered a psychiatric/psychological assessment of the family in order to examine the issue further).

Implacable hostility—Although the implacable hostility of one parent to contact by the other may amount to a cogent reason for refusing contact to the other parent (*Re D (A Minor) (Contact: Mother's Hostility)* [1993] 2 FLR 1, CA), the court will be reluctant to allow that hostility to dominate the issue of contact (*Re J (A Minor) (Contact)* [1994] 1 FLR 729, CA, and *Re P (Contact: Discretion)* [1998] 2 FLR 696, FD). Where a father is denied or inhibited from an ordinary relationship with a child due to the mother's determined efforts to excise him from the child's life, the court should not abandon endeavours to right the wrongs within the family dynamics (*Re B (Section 91(14) Order: Duration)* [2003] EWCA Civ 1966, [2004] 1 FLR 871, CA). The analysis on implacable hostility by Hale J sitting in the Court of Appeal in *Re D (Contact: Reasons for Refusal)* [1997] 2 FLR 48 is particularly helpful:

'It is important to bear in mind that the label "implacable hostility" is sometimes imposed by the law reporters and can be misleading. It is, as Mrs MacGregor points out, an umbrella term that sometimes is applied to cases not only where there is hostility, but no good reason can be discerned either for the hostility or for the opposition to contact, but also to cases where there are such good reasons. In the former sort of case the court will be very slow indeed to reach the conclusion that contact will be harmful to the child. It may eventually have to reach that conclusion but it will want to be satisfied that there is indeed a serious risk of major emotional harm before doing so. It is rather different in the cases where the judge or the court finds that the mother's fears, not only for herself but also for the child, are genuine and rationally held; as indeed the court did in this case.'

In the case of *Re D (Intractable Contact Dispute: Publicity)* [2004] EWHC 727 (Fam), [2004] 1 FLR 1226, FD, Munby J gave detailed consideration to the manner in which courts should deal with cases where a mother deliberately obstructs contact. He made particular reference to *Re M (Intractable Contact Dispute: Interim Care Order)* [2003] EWHC 1024 (Fam), [2003] 2 FLR 636; *Re O (Contact: Withdrawal of Application)* [2003] EWHC 3031 (Fam), [2004] 1 FLR 1258; and *A v A (Shared Residence)* [2004] EWHC 142 (Fam), [2004] 1 FLR 1195. Munby J advanced the following ideas:

- tracking of contact cases – simple cases being fast-tracked, difficult cases being multi-tracked and subject to a clear timetable that must be measured in months, not years;
- there must be judicial continuity (at most two judges);
- hard-headed directions should be given and delay avoided by firm timetabling;
- allegations of fact (eg misconduct by the non-residential parent) should be resolved swiftly;
- (at para [51] of the judgment) 'As Wall J pointed out in *Re M* at para [15], intractable contact disputes are one of the "prime categories" for separate representation of the children. I agree. I also agree that in this situation the court can with great advantage make use of organisations such as the National Youth Advisory Service (NYAS), an organisation whose assistance in *A v A* was justifiably lauded by Wall J (see at paras [24], [131]–[133])';
- experts should not only be regarded as a source of court reports. They may be able to help directly with the restoration of contact;
- other things being equal, swift, efficient, enforcement of existing court orders is surely called for at the first sign of trouble. It may be that committal is the remedy of last resort but, as Wall J recognised in *Re M* at [115], the strategy for a case may properly

involve the use of imprisonment (paras [56] and [57]). A willingness to impose very short sentences – of one, two or three days – may suffice to achieve the necessary deterrent or coercive effect without significantly impairing a mother's ability to look after her children.

In the case of *V v V (Contact: Implacable Hostility)* [2004] EWHC 1215 (Fam), [2004] 2 FLR 851, Bracewell J made a number of suggestions for dealing with cases where contact orders were thwarted (judicial continuity, case management, timetabling and proactive orders); she also made a number of suggestions for legislative change (eg referral to mediation/psychiatric services, making of probation orders and awards of financial compensation to offended parent). A court should not be unduly passive in accepting a therapist's view that family therapy 'would not work'; although the court does not have the power to order a parent to attend family therapy, if the parent refused to participate the court might draw adverse inferences against him or her (*Re S (Unco-operative Mother)* [2004] EWCA Civ 597, [2004] 2 FLR 710, CA).

Parental alienation—Where parental alienation is alleged (ie one parent alienating the other from the child) the existence, cause and effect of that alienation should be investigated by the court (*Re T (Contact: Alienation: Permission to Appeal)* [2003] 1 FLR 531, CA).

Violence—Domestic violence does not necessarily mean that there should be no contact but it is a factor that should be considered where it arises in relation to the welfare of the child (*Re L (A Child: Domestic Violence)* [2000] 4 All ER 609, [2000] 2 WLR 339, [200] 2 FLR 334, CA, and *Re M & B (Children) (Contact: Domestic Violence)* [2001] FCR 116, CA). Where there is a split hearing (allegations of violence/contact), the same court should hear both parts (*M v A (Contact: Domestic Violence)* [2002] 2 FLR 921).

Grandparents—It has been held that there is no presumption in favour of contact by a grandparent (*Re A (Section 8 Order: Grandparent Application)* [1995] 2 FLR 153, CA), although in the case of *Re W (A Child) (Contact: Leave to Apply)* [2000] 1 FCR 185, FD, it was held that the absence of such a presumption may be open to challenge under Article 8 of the European Convention on Human Rights. Relations between grandparents and grandchildren (as well as those between other family members) fall within the ambit of family life and therefore attract the protection of Article 8 of that Convention (*S and G v Italy* (2002) 35 EHRR 12).

Disobedience—Where an order for contact expressed in mandatory terms is disobeyed, an order for committal or a fine may be made, but a committal order will be regarded as a very last resort (*A v N (Committal: Refusal of Contact)* [1997] FLR 533, CA, and *Re H (A Child) (Contact: Mother's Opposition)* [2001] 1 FCR 59, CA). In an appropriate case where a contact order is ignored, the court may need to consider whether a change of residence is in the child's interests (*Re S (Minors: Access)* [1990] 2 FLR 166, CA, and *V v V (Contact: Implacable Hostility)* [2004] EWHC 1215 (Fam), [2004] 2 FLR 851). Alternatively, the court may consider making an order for a report under CA 1989, s 37 so that consideration can then be given to public law proceedings on the grounds of the harm being caused to the children by the contact dispute (*Re M (Intractable Contact Dispute: Interim Care Order)* [2003] 2 FLR 636). The issue of enforcement of contact orders is currently being investigated by the Government, and is one of the issues referred to in the Green Paper 'Parental separation: children's needs and parents' responsibilities' (July 2004).

Human rights—A Member State that is party to the European Convention on Human Rights should ensure that effective measures exist and are taken to enforce contact (*Hokkanen v Finland* [1996] 1 FLR 289; *Glaser v The United Kingdom* [2001] 1 FLR 153; *Hansen v Turkey* [2004] 1 FLR 142, ECtHR; and *Kosmopoulou v Greece* [2004] 1 FLR 800, ECtHR). For the enforcement of foreign contact orders, see *Re G (Foreign Contact Order: Enforcement)* [2003] EWCA Civ 607, [2004] 1 FLR 378, CA, and *Re A (Foreign Contact Order: Jurisdiction)* [2003] EWHC 2911 (Fam), [2004] 1 FLR 641, FD.

Conditions—Conditions may be attached to orders for contact, including a requirement that the residential parent send photographs, medical reports and school reports to the non-residential parent (*Re O (Contact: Imposition of Conditions)* [1995] 2 FLR 124, CA).

Supervision—In the case of *Re B* [2004] EWCA Civ 197, CA, Thorpe LJ said that judges should be alive to the artificiality that results from the maintenance of supervision and should see supervised contact as a stepping stone to something more normal.

Striking out—A contact application should only be struck out in the most exceptional circumstances and an order to that effect should only be made where the contact application has no prospect whatsoever of success (*Re T (A Minor) (Parental Responsibility: Contact)* [1993] 2 FLR 450, CA; *Re B (Minors) (Contact)* [1994] 2 FLR 1, CA; and *Re U (Children) (Contact)* [2004] 1 FCR 768, CA). When experts' reports become available and demonstrate the lack of merit in the application, the legal representatives should refer the matter back to the Legal Services Commission in a case where a party is publicly funded (*Re N (Contested Care Application)* [1994] 2 FLR 992, CA). A contact application may only be withdrawn with leave (*Re O (Contact: Withdrawal of Application)* [2004] 1 FLR 1258, FD).

Prohibited steps orders

Generally—Section 9(5) contains specific restrictions on the power of the court to make prohibited steps orders. It has been said that it is not necessary for the person against whom the order is made to be a parent or party to the proceedings; nor, in an appropriate case, is it necessary for that person to be present in the court (*Re H (Minors) (Prohibited Steps Orders)* [1995] 4 All ER 110, [1995] 1 WLR 667, CA) (although it may be questioned whether such an approach remains 'human rights compliant').

Residence orders

Parental responsibility—If a residence order is granted to a father who does not have parental responsibility (PR), the court must make a PR order under s 12(1) in his favour. Where residence orders are made in favour of others who are not parents of a child, PR is conferred on them (if they do not already have it) within the terms of s 12(2) of the CA 1989. If the residence order is later revoked, PR remains for fathers under s 12(1), but not for others under s 12(2).

Section 13 of the CA 1989 contains restrictions upon the ability of a person with a residence order to change a child's surname or remove the child from the United Kingdom.

General principles

Case	What the case says
Re K (A Minor) (Ward: Care and Control) [1990] 3 All ER 795, [1991] WLR 431, CA	The correct person to bring up a child is a parent, unless the child's welfare positively demands otherwise – see also, eg, *Re M (A Minor) (Custody Appeal)* [1990] 1 FLR 291; *Re W (A Minor) (Residence Order)* [1993] 2 FLR 625, CA; *Re D (Care: Natural Parent: Presumption)* [1999] 1 FLR 134, CA.
Re W (A Minor) (Residence Order) [1992] 2 FLR 332	There is no presumption in favour of either parent; however, it will often be in the interests of a very young child to reside with the mother (and this is a factor that should be taken into account) – see also *Brixey v Lynas* [1996] 2 FLR 499.
C v C (Minors) (Custody) [1988] 2 FLR 291	Siblings should be kept together in the absence of good reason to the contrary – see also *Re B(T) (A Minor) (Residence Order)* [1995] 2 FCR 240, CA.
Re G (Minors) (Ex Parte Residence Orders) [1992] 2 FCR 720, CA	Ex parte residence orders should only be made in cases of real necessity (such as where a child has been snatched).

Shared residence—The term 'shared residence' may have two meanings (and it is necessary to identify the sense in which the phrase is being used):

(1) an arrangement where the child spends an equal amount of time with each parent; and
(2) an arrangement where the child spends an unequal amount of time with each parent but where each parent has a residence order.

There has been an increasing recognition of the benefits to a child in the making of shared residence orders even where the child does not spend an equal amount of time with both parents; such orders do not require exceptional circumstances nor do 'positive benefits' have to be shown to arise from the order (*D v D (Shared Residence Order)* [2001] 1 FLR 495, CA; *Re A (Children) (Shared Residence)* [2002] EWCA Civ 1343, [2003] 3 FCR 656, CA; and *Re F (Shared Residence Order)* [2003] EWCA Civ 592, [2003] 2 FLR 397, CA). Where parents are unable to work in harmony, a shared residence order may bear a positive benefit, since a sole residence order might be misinterpreted as enabling the residential parent to exercise greater control (*A v A (Shared Residence)* [2004] EWHC 142 (Fam), [2004] 1 FLR 1195).

Homosexuality—In *Salgueiro da Silva Mouta v Portugal* (2001) 31 EHRR 1055, ECtHR, it was held that a father's homosexuality should not be a decisive factor in a 'custody' dispute. In *C v C (Custody of Child) (No 2)* [1992] 1 FCR 206, FD, it was held that, the fact that the mother was lesbian was only one of the factors to be taken into account.

Specific issue orders

Generally—Section 9(5) contains specific restrictions on the ability of the court to make specific issue orders. Examples of issues that may fall for determination are those relating to where a child is to be educated (*Re A (Specific Issue Order: Parental Disagreement)* [2001] 1 FLR 121, CA – there are no governing principles that arise in such applications, save that the child's welfare is paramount), whether a child should leave the jurisdiction (see notes on s 13 below), and whether a child should undergo medical treatment (although medical issues will often be dealt with under the inherent jurisdiction of the High Court in relation to children – see, eg, *Re R (A Minor) (Blood Transfusion)* [1993] 2 FLR 757). In *Re C (Welfare of Child: Immunisation)* [2003] EWCA Civ 1148, [2003] 2 FLR 1095, CA, orders were made on the application of fathers for the vaccination of children, notwithstanding the objections of the mothers.

In *Re K (Specific Issue Order)* [1999] 2 FLR 280, FD, a father applied for an order that the child be informed of his identity; it was held that, in the light of the mother's obsessional hatred of the father and the effect that an order would have upon the emotional stability of the mother (and, consequently, upon the child), there were cogent reasons why the child should not be informed of his paternity and, therefore, the father's application rejected. See also: (1) *Re R (Minor: Contact)* [1993] 2 FLR 762, CA – father's application adjourned for the court to receive assistance from Official Solicitor about whether and how a 5-year-old child should be informed of the true identity of her father who she had not seen for 3 years; and (3) *Re AB (Care Proceedings: Service on Husband Ignorant of Child's Existence)* [2003] EWCA Civ 1842, [2004] 1 FLR 541, FD – mother's attempt to prevent the father learning about the birth of the child failed.

9 Restrictions on making section 8 orders

(1) No court shall make any section 8 order, other than a residence order, with respect to a child who is in the care of a local authority.

(2) No application may be made by a local authority for a residence order or contact order and no court shall make such an order in favour of a local authority.

(3) A person who is, or was at any time within the last six months, a local authority foster parent of a child may not apply for leave to apply for a section 8 order with respect to the child unless –

(a) he has the consent of the authority;
(b) he is a relative of the child; or
(c) the child has lived with him for at least three years preceding the application.

(4) The period of three years mentioned in subsection (3)(c) need not be continuous but must have begun not more than five years before the making of the application.

(5) No court shall exercise its powers to make a specific issue order or prohibited steps order –

(a) with a view to achieving a result which could be achieved by making a residence or contact order; or
(b) in any way which is denied to the High Court (by section 100(2)) in the exercise of its inherent jurisdiction with respect to children.

(6) No court shall make any section 8 order which is to have effect for a period which will end after the child has reached the age of sixteen unless it is satisfied that the circumstances of the case are exceptional.

(7) No court shall make any section 8 order, other than one varying or discharging such an order, with respect to a child who has reached the age of sixteen unless it is satisfied that the circumstances of the case are exceptional.

Section 9

Prospective amendment—Section prospectively amended by Adoption and Children Act 2002, ss 113(b), 114, 139(3), Sch 5 (see **3.3B**).

10 Power of court to make section 8 orders

(1) In any family proceedings in which a question arises with respect to the welfare of any child, the court may make a section 8 order with respect to the child if –

(a) an application for the order has been made by a person who –
    (i) is entitled to apply for a section 8 order with respect to the child; or
    (ii) has obtained the leave of the court to make the application; or
(b) the court considers that the order should be made even though no such application has been made.

(2) The court may also make a section 8 order with respect to any child on the application of a person who –

(a) is entitled to apply for a section 8 order with respect to the child; or
(b) has obtained the leave of the court to make the application.

(3) This section is subject to the restrictions imposed by section 9.

(4) The following persons are entitled to apply to the court for any section 8 order with respect to a child –

(a) any parent or guardian of the child;
(b) any person in whose favour a residence order is in force with respect to the child.

(5) The following persons are entitled to apply for a residence or contact order with respect to a child –

   (a) any party to a marriage (whether or not subsisting) in relation to whom the child is a child of the family;

   (b) any person with whom the child has lived for a period of at least three years;

   (c) any person who –

      (i) in any case where a residence order is in force with respect to the child, has the consent of each of the persons in whose favour the order was made;

      (ii) in any case where the child is in the care of a local authority, has the consent of that authority; or

      (iii) in any other case, has the consent of each of those (if any) who have parental responsibility for the child.

(6) A person who would not otherwise be entitled (under the previous provisions of this section) to apply for the variation or discharge of a section 8 order shall be entitled to do so if –

   (a) the order was made on his application; or

   (b) in the case of a contact order, he is named in the order.

(7) Any person who falls within a category of person prescribed by rules of court is entitled to apply for any such section 8 order as may be prescribed in relation to that category of person.

(8) Where the person applying for leave to make an application for a section 8 order is the child concerned, the court may only grant leave if it is satisfied that he has sufficient understanding to make the proposed application for the section 8 order.

(9) Where the person applying for leave to make an application for a section 8 order is not the child concerned, the court shall, in deciding whether or not to grant leave, have particular regard to –

   (a) the nature of the proposed application for the section 8 order;

   (b) the applicant's connection with the child;

   (c) any risk there might be of that proposed application disrupting the child's life to such an extent that he would be harmed by it; and

   (d) where the child is being looked after by a local authority –

      (i) the authority's plans for the child's future; and

      (ii) the wishes and feelings of the child's parents.

(10) The period of three years mentioned in subsection (5)(b) need not be continuous but must not have begun more than five years before, or ended more than three months before, the making of the application.

Section 10

Prospective amendment—Section prospectively amended by Adoption and Children Act 2002, s 139(1), Sch 3, paras 54, 56 (see **3.3B**).

Generally—Where an application for leave is made, the provisions of s 10(8) of the CA 1989 must be considered where the applicant for leave is the child concerned. In any other case, the provisions of s 10(9) must be considered. On an application for leave, the child's welfare, although of obvious importance, is not the court's paramount consideration (*Re C (Residence: Child's Application for Leave)* [1995] 1 FLR 927, FD). In *Re M (Care: Contact: Grandmother's Application for Leave)* [1995] 2 FLR 86, CA, it was said that the applicant for leave should show that he/she has a good arguable case. However, in the case of *Re J (Leave* *to Issue Application for Residence Order)* [2003] 1 FLR 114, it was said that, although the test in *Re M* had served a valuable purpose in its day, the test expounded in that case should not be used as a substitute for s 10(9) on applications for permission to apply under s 8.

There has been a growing appreciation of 'what grandparents have to offer', and judges should be careful not to dismiss applications for grandparents without a full enquiry (*Re J (Leave to Issue Application for Residence Order)* [2003] 1 FLR 114).

Following the grant of leave, there is no presumption that the person granted leave should secure the substantive order sought (*Re A (Section 8 Order: Grandparent: Application)* [1995] 1 FLR 153, CA). Another example is *Re S (Specific Issue Order: Religion: Circumcision)* [2004] EWHC 1282 (Fam), [2005] 1 FLR 236, in which a Muslim mother sought an order that children of 10 and 8 should be brought up in the Muslim faith, and that the 8-year-old boy should be circumcised; the judge rejected the mother's application, favouring the arguments of the Jainist Hindu father that children of a mixed cultural heritage should be allowed to decide for themselves which, if any, religion they wished to follow.

11 General principles and supplementary provisions

(1) In proceedings in which any question of making a section 8 order, or any other question with respect to such an order, arises, the court shall (in the light of any rules made by virtue of subsection (2)) –

    (a) draw up a timetable with a view to determining the question without delay; and

    (b) give such directions as it considers appropriate for the purpose of ensuring, so far as is reasonably practicable, that that timetable is adhered to.

(2) Rules of court may –

    (a) specify periods within which specified steps must be taken in relation to proceedings in which such questions arise; and

    (b) make other provision with respect to such proceedings for the purpose of ensuring, so far as is reasonably practicable, that such questions are determined without delay.

(3) Where a court has power to make a section 8 order, it may do so at any time during the course of the proceedings in question even though it is not in a position to dispose finally of those proceedings.

(4) Where a residence order is made in favour of two or more persons who do not themselves all live together, the order may specify the periods during which the child is to live in the different households concerned.

(5) Where –

    (a) a residence order has been made with respect to a child; and

    (b) as a result of the order the child lives, or is to live, with one of two parents who each have parental responsibility for him,

the residence order shall cease to have effect if the parents live together for a continuous period of more than six months.

(6) A contact order which requires the parent with whom a child lives to allow the child to visit, or otherwise have contact with, his other parent shall cease to have effect if the parents live together for a continuous period of more than six months.

(7) A section 8 order may –

    (a) contain directions about how it is to be carried into effect;

(b) impose conditions which must be complied with by any person –
  (i) in whose favour the order is made;
  (ii) who is a parent of the child concerned;
  (iii) who is not a parent of his but who has parental responsibility for him; or
  (iv) with whom the child is living,
  and to whom the conditions are expressed to apply;
(c) be made to have effect for a specified period, or contain provisions which are to have effect for a specified period;
(d) make such incidental, supplemental or consequential provision as the court thinks fit.

Section 11

It would be rare for the court to restrict the right of a residential parent to move with the child within the United Kingdom; however, in unusual circumstances, such a restriction may be ordered – see *Re H (Children) (Residence Order: Condition)* [2001] EWCA Civ 1338, [2001] 2 FLR 1277; *Re S (A Child) (Residence Order: Condition)* [2001] EWCA Civ 847, [2001] 3 FCR 154; and *B v B (Residence: Condition Limiting Geographic Area)* [2004] 2 FLR 979, FD.

In the case of *Re O (Contact: Imposition of Conditions)* [1995] 2 FLR 124, CA, the Court of Appeal held that it was lawful for the court to impose a condition requiring the residential parent to send photographs, medical reports and school reports to the non-residential parent.

12 Residence orders and parental responsibility

(1) Where the court makes a residence order in favour of the father of a child it shall, if the father would not otherwise have parental responsibility for the child, also make an order under section 4 giving him that responsibility.

(2) Where the court makes a residence order in favour of any person who is not the parent or guardian of the child concerned that person shall have parental responsibility for the child while the residence order remains in force.

(3) Where a person has parental responsibility for a child as a result of subsection (2), he shall not have the right –

(a) to consent, or refuse to consent, to the making of an application with respect to the child under section 18 of the Adoption Act 1976;
(b) to agree, or refuse to agree, to the making of an adoption order, or an order under section 55 of the Act of 1976, with respect to the child; or
(c) to appoint a guardian for the child.

(4) Where subsection (1) requires the court to make an order under section 4 in respect of the father of a child, the court shall not bring that order to an end at any time while the residence order concerned remains in force.

Section 12

Prospective amendment—Section prospectively amended by Adoption and Children Act 2002, ss 114, 139(1), Sch 3, paras 54, 57 (see **3.3B**).

13 Change of child's name or removal from jurisdiction

(1) Where a residence order is in force with respect to a child, no person may –

(a) cause the child to be known by a new surname; or
(b) remove him from the United Kingdom;

without either the written consent of every person who has parental responsibility for the child or the leave of the court.

(2) Subsection (1)(b) does not prevent the removal of a child, for a period of less than one month, by the person in whose favour the residence order is made.

(3) In making a residence order with respect to a child the court may grant the leave required by subsection (1)(b), either generally or for specified purposes.

Section 13

Applications for the change of a child's surname should be determined by applying the provisions of s 1 of the CA 1989. Such applications raise important issues for the child (*Dawson v Wearmouth* [1999] 2 AC 308, [1999] 2 WLR 960, [1999] 2 All ER 353, [1999] 1 FLR 1167, HL). The case of *Re W, Re A, Re B (Change of Name)* [1999] 2 FLR 930, CA, gives the following guidance (which is stated not to be exhaustive):

(1) if parents are married, they both have the power and the duty to register their child's names;
(2) if they are not married the mother has the sole duty and power to do so;
(3) after registration of the child's names, the grant of a residence order obliges any person wishing to change the surname to obtain the leave of the court or the written consent of all those who have parental responsibility;
(4) in the absence of a residence order, the person wishing to change the surname from the registered name ought to obtain the relevant written consent or the leave of the court by making an application for a specific issue order;
(5) on any application, the welfare of the child is paramount and the judge must have regard to the s 1(3) criteria;
(6) among the factors to which the court should have regard is the registered surname of the child and the reasons for the registration, for instance recognition of the biological link with the child's father. Registration is always a relevant and an important consideration but it is not in itself decisive. The weight to be given to it by the court will depend upon the other relevant factors or valid countervailing reasons which may tip the balance the other way;
(7) the relevant considerations should include factors which may arise in the future as well as the present situation;
(8) reasons given for changing or seeking to change a child's name based on the fact that the child's name is or is not the same as the parent making the application do not generally carry much weight;
(9) the reasons for an earlier unilateral decision to change a child's name may be relevant;
(10) any changes of circumstances of the child since the original registration may be relevant;
(11) in the case of a child whose parents were married to each other, the fact of the marriage is important and there would have to be strong reasons to change the name from the father's surname if the child was so registered;
(12) where the child's parents were not married to each other, the mother has control over registration. Consequently, on an application to change the surname of the child, the degree of commitment of the father to the child, the quality of contact, if it occurs, between father and child, and the existence or absence of parental responsibility are all relevant factors to take into account.

In an appropriate case it may be sensible for the child's surname to be a combination of the parents' surnames, eg Smith-Jones (*Re R (Surname: Using Both Parents')* [2001] EWCA Civ 1344, [2002] 2 FLR 1358, CA).

Applications to remove a child from the jurisdiction—In the case of *Payne v Payne* [2001] 1 FLR 1052, the President stated that the following principles should apply (at para [85] of her judgment):

(1) the welfare of the child is always paramount;

(2) there is no presumption created by s 13(1)(b) in favour of the applicant parent;

(3) the reasonable proposals of the parent with a residence order wishing to live abroad carry great weight;

(4) consequently, the proposals have to be scrutinised with care, and the court needs to be satisfied that there is a genuine motivation for the move and not the intention to bring contact between the child and the other parent to an end;

(5) the effect upon the applicant parent and the new family of the child of a refusal of leave is very important;

(6) the effect on the child of the denial of contact with the other parent and in some cases his family is very important;

(7) the opportunity for continuing contact between the child and the parent left behind may be very significant.

The principles to be applied in such cases have not shifted materially from those expressed in the case of *Poel v Poel* [1970] 1 WLR 1469, [1970] 3 All ER 659 (as was stated in the case of *Re B, Re S (Children) (Removal from Jurisdiction)* [2003] EWCA Civ 1149, [2003] 2 FLR 1043, CA). The continuing thread within the case-law can be seen in cases such as *Chamberlain v De La Mare* (1982) 4 FLR 434, *Tyler v Tyler* [1989] 2 FLR 158, and *Re A (Permission to Remove Child from Jurisdiction: Human Rights)* [2000] 2 FLR 225, CA. In the case of *Re Y (Leave to Remove from Jurisdiction)* [2004] 2 FLR 330, FD, the child's home was equally with both parents. The mother sought to emigrate with the child to the United States. Refusing her application, the judge held that the case fell outside the factual ambit of the established authorites due to the equal care of the child. The overbearing consideration was that of the welfare of the child. The child's welfare required that the child should remain in Wales.

14 Enforcement of residence orders

(1) Where –

(a) a residence order is in force with respect to a child in favour of any person; and

(b) any other person (including one in whose favour the order is also in force) is in breach of the arrangements settled by that order,

the person mentioned in paragraph (a) may, as soon as the requirement in subsection (2) is complied with, enforce the order under section 63(3) of the Magistrates' Courts Act 1980 as if it were an order requiring the other person to produce the child to him.

(2) The requirement is that a copy of the residence order has been served on the other person.

(3) Subsection (1) is without prejudice to any other remedy open to the person in whose favour the residence order is in force.

[14A–14G *(Sections prospectively inserted by Adoption and Children Act 2002, s 115(1) – see* **3.3B** *for text)*]

Sections 14A–14G

The Adoption and Children Act 2002 makes provision for the making of special guardianship orders. Special guardianship orders can only be made in favour of those who are aged 18 or over and who are not a parent of the child in question. Section 14A(5) specifies those who are entitled to apply for an order without prior leave. Those who need leave must fulfil the requirements of either s 10(8) or s 10(9) of the CA 1989. The court may also make an order in family proceedings of its own motion (ie even where no application has been made). Joint applications may be made (s 14A(3)).

At least 3 months' notice must be given to a relevant local authority of the intention to apply for such an order (s 14A(7)). Thereafter, the local authority has a duty to investigate the application and prepare a report for the court.

The effect of a special guardianship order is that, while the order remains in force, the special guardian appointed by the order will have parental responsibility for the child and, subject to any other orders in force in respect to the child under the CA 1989, a special guardian is entitled to exercise parental responsibility to the exclusion of any other person with parental responsibility for the child (apart from another special guardian) (s 14C(1)). Special guardianship orders are capable of variation and discharge (s 14D). Conditions may be attached to the order under s 11(7) of the CA 1989 (see s 14E, but note that it is not possible to include a condition under s 11(7)(c) – ie a condition cannot be imposed that the special guardianship order should have effect for a specified period or should contain provisions which are to have effect for a specified period). A local authority must make arrangements for the provision within its area of special guardianship support services (s 14F). Further, the local authority must set up a procedure for considering representations (including complaints) made to them by any person to whom they may provide special guardianship support services (s 14G).

Financial relief

15 Orders for financial relief with respect to children

(1) Schedule 1 (which consists primarily of the re-enactment, with consequential amendments and minor modifications, of provisions of section 6 of the Family Law Reform Act 1969, the Guardianship of Minors Acts 1971 and 1973, the Children Act 1975 and of sections 15 and 16 of the Family Law Reform Act 1987) makes provision in relation to financial relief for children.

(2) The powers of a magistrates' court under section 60 of the Magistrates' Courts Act 1980 to revoke, revive or vary an order for the periodical payment of money and the power of a clerk of a magistrates' court to vary such an order shall not apply in relation to an order made under Schedule 1.

Section 15

Schedule 1 to the CA 1989 (which is implemented by s 15 of the Act) introduces a complete statutory code in relation to orders for financial relief with respect to children. The power to make orders for child periodical payments is heavily confined by the provisions of the Child Support Act 1991.

When making orders in relation to properties under Sch 1 to the CA 1989 the court will usually order that the property should revert to the respondent parent upon the child ceasing to be dependent (*A v A (A Minor: Financial Provision)* [1994] 1 FLR 657, FD, and *T v S (Financial Provision for Children)* [1994] 2 FLR 883, FD). In the case of *Re P (Child: Financial Provision)* [2003] EWCA Civ 837, [2003] 2 FLR 865, the Court of Appeal gave guidance to the correct approach to such applications where the respondent father was 'fabulously wealthy'. In the case of *J v C (Child: Financial Provision)* [1999] 1 FLR 152, FD, it was said that a child should be brought up in the circumstances which bore some sort of relationship with the father's resources and standard of living. Orders have been made for lump sums to be paid outright to mothers for chattels such as furniture and cars, without the chattels reverting to the father upon the child attaining majority (eg *Phillips v Peace* [1996] 2 FLR 230, FD – £90,000 for a house which would revert to the father but £15,000 outright to mother for furniture; *J v C* (above) – £70,000 for a house which would revert to the father and £21,000 outright to mother for furniture, car and house maintenance).

Orders may be made against either or both parents of a child (see Sch 1, para 1). Under Sch 1, para 16 a parent includes any party to a marriage (whether or not subsisting) in relation to whom the child concerned is a child of the family. A cohabitee will not fall within that definition (since there will be no 'marriage') – see *J v J (A Minor) (Property*

Transfer) [1993] 2 FLR 56. A child of the family is defined in s 105 of the CA 1989 as being either a child of both parties or any other child, not being a child who is placed with those parties as foster parents by a local authority or voluntary organisation, who has been treated by both of those parties as a child of the family. Plainly, it is not possible to 'treat' a child as a child of the family prior to its birth (*A v A (Family: Unborn Child)* [1974] Fam 6, [1974] 1 All ER 755, CA). The fact that a father is bankrupt does not preclude the court from making an order under Sch 1 against him (*Re G (Children Act 1989: Schedule 1)* [1996] 2 FLR 171, FD). The court retains the power to make orders for child periodical payments in circumstances that fall outside the Child Support Act 1991 (*B v B (Adult Student: Liability to Support)* [1998] 1 FLR 373, CA – maintenance for student daughter; *C v F (Disabled Child: Maintenance Orders)* [1998] 2 FLR 1 – disabled child).

It has been held that the court does not have jurisdiction under s 15 of and Sch 1 to the CA 1989 to order one parent to pay the other's legal costs by way of 'up front' payment (*W v J (Child: Variation of Financial Provision)* [2003] EWHC 2657 (Fam), [2004] 2 FLR 300, FD).

Family assistance orders

16 Family assistance orders

(1) Where, in any family proceedings, the court has power to make an order under this Part with respect to any child, it may (whether or not it makes such an order) make an order requiring –

    (a) an officer of the Service to be made available; or

    (b) a local authority to make an officer of the authority available,

to advise, assist and (where appropriate) befriend any person named in the order.

(2) The persons who may be named in an order under this section ('a family assistance order') are –

    (a) any parent or guardian of the child;

    (b) any person with whom the child is living or in whose favour a contact order is in force with respect to the child;

    (c) the child himself.

(3) No court may make a family assistance order unless –

    (a) it is satisfied that the circumstances of the case are exceptional; and

    (b) it has obtained the consent of every person to be named in the order other than the child.

(4) A family assistance order may direct –

    (a) the person named in the order; or

    (b) such of the persons named in the order as may be specified in the order,

to take such steps as may be so specified with a view to enabling the officer concerned to be kept informed of the address of any person named in the order and to be allowed to visit any such person.

(5) Unless it specifies a shorter period, a family assistance order shall have effect for a period of six months beginning with the day on which it is made.

(6) Where –

    (a) a family assistance order is in force with respect to a child; and

    (b) a section 8 order is also in force with respect to the child, the officer concerned may refer to the court the question whether the section 8 order should be varied or discharged.

(7) A family assistance order shall not be made so as to require a local authority to make an officer of theirs available unless –

(a) the authority agree; or

(b) the child concerned lives or will live within their area.

(8), (9) (*repealed*)

Section 16

Prospective amendment—Section prospectively amended by Adoption and Children Act 2002, s 139(1), Sch 3, para 58 (see **3.3B**).

Generally—A family assistance order may be used to provide encouragement to a local authority to assist with the supervision of contact in private law proceedings (*Re E (Family Assistance Order)* [1999] 2 FLR 512).

PART III

LOCAL AUTHORITY SUPPORT FOR CHILDREN AND FAMILIES

Provision of services for children and their families

17 Provision of services for children in need, their families and others

(1) It shall be the general duty of every local authority (in addition to the other duties imposed on them by this Part) –

(a) to safeguard and promote the welfare of children within their area who are in need; and

(b) so far as is consistent with that duty, to promote the upbringing of such children by their families,

by providing a range and level of services appropriate to those children's needs.

(2) For the purpose principally of facilitating the discharge of their general duty under this section, every local authority shall have the specific duties and powers set out in Part I of Schedule 2.

(3) Any service provided by an authority in the exercise of functions conferred on them by this section may be provided for the family of a particular child in need or for any member of his family, if it is provided with a view to safeguarding or promoting the child's welfare.

(4) The Secretary of State may by order amend any provision of Part I of Schedule 2 or add any further duty or power to those for the time being mentioned there.

(5) Every local authority –

(a) shall facilitate the provision by others (including in particular voluntary organisations) of services which the authority have power to provide by virtue of this section, or section 18, 20, 23, 23B to 23D, 24A or 24B; and

(b) may make such arrangements as they see fit for any person to act on their behalf in the provision of any such service.

(6) The services provided by a local authority in the exercise of functions conferred on them by this section may include providing accommodation and giving assistance in kind or, in exceptional circumstances, in cash.

(7) Assistance may be unconditional or subject to conditions as to the repayment of the assistance or of its value (in whole or in part).

(8) Before giving any assistance or imposing any conditions, a local authority shall have regard to the means of the child concerned and of each of his parents.

(9) No person shall be liable to make any repayment of assistance or of its value at any time when he is in receipt of income support under Part VII of the Social Security Contributions and Benefits Act 1992, of any element of child tax credit other than the family element, of working tax credit or of an income-based jobseeker's allowance.

(10) For the purposes of this Part a child shall be taken to be in need if –

(a) he is unlikely to achieve or maintain, or to have the opportunity of achieving or maintaining, a reasonable standard of health or development without the provision for him of services by a local authority under this Part;

(b) his health or development is likely to be significantly impaired, or further impaired, without the provision for him of such services; or

(c) he is disabled,

and 'family,' in relation to such a child, includes any person who has parental responsibility for the child and any other person with whom he has been living.

(11) For the purposes of this Part, a child is disabled if he is blind, deaf or dumb or suffers from mental disorder of any kind or is substantially and permanently handicapped by illness, injury or congenital deformity or such other disability as may be prescribed; and in this Part –

'development' means physical, intellectual, emotional, social or behavioural development; and
'health' means physical or mental health.

(12) The Treasury may by regulations prescribe circumstances in which a person is to be treated for the purposes of this Part (or for such of those purposes as are prescribed) as in receipt of any element of child tax credit other than the family element or of working tax credit.

Section 17

The duties of a local authority to provide support for children and families are detailed in Sch 2 of the CA 1989. Guidance upon the exercise of those duties is given in *The Children Act 1989 Guidance and Regulations* (HMSO, 1991), vol 2: *Family Support, Day Care and Educational Provision for Young Children*, and vol 6, *Children with Disabilities*. Social work assessments of children and families should be conducted in accordance with the 'Framework for the assessment of children in need and their families' which was published by the Department of Health in April 2000. Although the local authority has a power to offer a family accommodation under Sch 2 to the Act, there is no specific obligation upon it to do so, since the duties under s 17 are general duties rather than duties owed to individual children (*R (G) v Barnet London Borough Council; R (W) v Lambeth London Borough Council; R (A) v Lambeth London Borough Council* [2003] UKHL 57, [2004] 1 All ER 97, HL). See also the cases listed in the notes on Local Authority Social Services Act 1970, s 7.

17A Direct payments

(1) The Secretary of State may by regulations make provision for and in connection with requiring or authorising the responsible authority in the case of a person of a prescribed description who falls within subsection (2) to make, with that person's consent, such payments to him as they may determine in accordance with the regulations in respect of his securing the provision of the service mentioned in that subsection.

(2) A person falls within this subsection if he is–

- (a) a person with parental responsibility for a disabled child,
- (b) a disabled person with parental responsibility for a child, or
- (c) a disabled child aged 16 or 17,

and a local authority ('the responsible authority') have decided for the purposes of section 17 that the child's needs (or, if he is such a disabled child, his needs) call for the provision by them of a service in exercise of functions conferred on them under that section.

(3) Subsections (3) to (5) and (7) of section 57 of the 2001 Act shall apply, with any necessary modifications, in relation to regulations under this section as they apply in relation to regulations under that section.

(4) Regulations under this section shall provide that, where payments are made under the regulations to a person falling within subsection (5)–

- (a) the payments shall be made at the rate mentioned in subsection (4)(a) of section 57 of the 2001 Act (as applied by subsection (3)); and
- (b) subsection (4)(b) of that section shall not apply.

(5) A person falls within this subsection if he is–

- (a) a person falling within subsection (2)(a) or (b) and the child in question is aged 16 or 17, or
- (b) a person who is in receipt of income support, working families' tax credit or disabled person's tax credit under Part 7 of the Social Security Contributions and Benefits Act 1992 of any element of child tax credit other than the family element, of working tax credit or of an income-based jobseeker's allowance.

(6) In this section–

'the 2001 Act' means the Health and Social Care Act 2001;
'disabled' in relation to an adult has the same meaning as that given by section 17(11) in relation to a child;
'prescribed' means specified in or determined in accordance with regulations under this section (and has the same meaning in the provisions of the 2001 Act mentioned in subsection (3) as they apply by virtue of that subsection).

18 Day care for pre-school and other children

(1) Every local authority shall provide such day care for children in need within their area who are –

- (a) aged five or under; and

(b) not yet attending schools,

as is appropriate.

(2) A local authority may provide day care for children within their area who satisfy the conditions mentioned in subsection (1)(a) and (b) even though they are not in need.

(3) A local authority may provide facilities (including training, advice, guidance and counselling) for those –

(a) caring for children in day care; or

(b) who at any time accompany such children while they are in day care.

(4) In this section 'day care' means any form of care or supervised activity provided for children during the day (whether or not it is provided on a regular basis).

(5) Every local authority shall provide for children in need within their area who are attending any school such care or supervised activities as is appropriate –

(a) outside school hours; or

(b) during school holidays.

(6) A local authority may provide such care or supervised activities for children within their area who are attending any school even though those children are not in need.

(7) In this section 'supervised activity' means an activity supervised by a responsible person.

Section 18

The main provisions relating to day care and child minding are to be found in Part XA (CA 1989, ss 79A–79X). Further guidance is given in *The Children Act 1989 Guidance and Regulations* (HMSO, 1991), vol 2: *Family Support, Day Care and Educational Provision for Young Children.*

19 Review of provision for day care, child minding etc

(1) Every local authority in England and Wales shall review –

(a) the provision which they make under section 18;

(b) the extent to which the services of child minders are available within their area with respect to children under the age of eight; and

(c) the provision for day care within their area made for children under the age of eight by persons other than the authority, required to register under Part XA.

(2) A review under subsection (1) shall be conducted –

(a) together with the appropriate local education authority; and

(b) at least once in every review period.

(3) *(applies to Scotland only)*

(4) In conducting any such review, the two authorities or, in Scotland, the authority shall have regard to the provision made with respect to children under the age of eight in relevant establishments within their area.

(5) In this section –

'relevant establishment' means–

(a) in relation to Scotland, any establishment which is mentioned in paragraphs 3 and 4 of Schedule 9 (establishments exempt from the registration requirements which apply in relation to the provision of day care in Scotland); and

(b) in relation to England and Wales, any establishment which is mentioned in paragraphs 1 and 2 of Schedule 9A (establishments exempt from the registration requirements which apply in relation to the provision of day care in England and Wales);

'review period' means the period of one year beginning with the commencement of this section and each subsequent period of three years beginning with an anniversary of that commencement.

(6) Where a local authority have conducted a review under this section they shall publish the result of the review –

(a) as soon as is reasonably practicable;

(b) in such form as they consider appropriate; and

(c) together with any proposals they may have with respect to the matters reviewed.

(7) The authorities conducting any review under this section shall have regard to –

(a) any representations made to any one of them by any relevant Health Authority, Special Health Authority, Primary Care Trust or health board; and

(b) any other representations which they consider to be relevant.

(8) *(applies to Scotland only)*

Section 19

Italicised subsections repealed except in relation to Wales.

Provision of accommodation for children

20 Provision of accommodation for children: general

(1) Every local authority shall provide accommodation for any child in need within their area who appears to them to require accommodation as a result of –

(a) there being no person who has parental responsibility for him;

(b) his being lost or having been abandoned; or

(c) the person who has been caring for him being prevented (whether or not permanently, and for whatever reason) from providing him with suitable accommodation or care.

(2) Where a local authority provide accommodation under subsection (1) for a child who is ordinarily resident in the area of another local authority, that other local authority may take over the provision of accommodation for the child within –

(a) three months of being notified in writing that the child is being provided with accommodation; or

(b) such other longer period as may be prescribed.

(3) Every local authority shall provide accommodation for any child in need within their area who has reached the age of sixteen and whose welfare the authority consider is likely to be seriously prejudiced if they do not provide him with accommodation.

(4) A local authority may provide accommodation for any child within their area (even though a person who has parental responsibility for him is able to provide him with accommodation) if they consider that to do so would safeguard or promote the child's welfare.

(5) A local authority may provide accommodation for any person who has reached the age of sixteen but is under twenty-one in any community home which takes children who have reached the age of sixteen if they consider that to do so would safeguard or promote his welfare.

(6) Before providing accommodation under this section, a local authority shall, so far as is reasonably practicable and consistent with the child's welfare –

    (a) ascertain the child's wishes regarding the provision of accommodation; and

    (b) give due consideration (having regard to his age and understanding) to such wishes of the child as they have been able to ascertain.

(7) A local authority may not provide accommodation under this section for any child if any person who –

    (a) has parental responsibility for him; and

    (b) is willing and able to –

        (i) provide accommodation for him; or

        (ii) arrange for accommodation to be provided for him,

objects.

(8) Any person who has parental responsibility for a child may at any time remove the child from accommodation provided by or on behalf of the local authority under this section.

(9) Subsections (7) and (8) do not apply while any person –

    (a) in whose favour a residence order is in force with respect to the child; or

    (b) who has care of the child by virtue of an order made in the exercise of the High Court's inherent jurisdiction with respect to children,

agrees to the child being looked after in accommodation provided by or on behalf of the local authority.

(10) Where there is more than one such person as is mentioned in subsection (9), all of them must agree.

(11) Subsections (7) and (8) do not apply where a child who has reached the age of sixteen agrees to being provided with accommodation under this section.

Section 20

Prospective amendment—Section prospectively amended by Adoption and Children Act 2002, s 139(1), Sch 3, paras 54, 59 (see **3.3B**).

21 Provision of accommodation for children in police protection or detention or on remand etc

(1) Every local authority shall make provision for the reception and accommodation of children who are removed or kept away from home under Part V.

(2) Every local authority shall receive, and provide accommodation for, children –

    (a) in police protection whom they are requested to receive under section 46(3)(f);

    (b) whom they are requested to receive under section 38(6) of the Police and Criminal Evidence Act 1984;

    (c) who are –

        (i) on remand under paragraph 7(5) of Schedule 7 to the Powers of Criminal Courts (Sentencing) Act 2000 or section 23(1) of the Children and Young Persons Act 1969; or

        (ii) the subject of a supervision order imposing a local authority residence requirement under paragraph 5 of Schedule 6 to that Act,

    and with respect to whom they are the designated authority.

(3) Where a child has been –

    (a) removed under Part V; or

    (b) detained under section 38 of the Police and Criminal Evidence Act 1984,

and he is not being provided with accommodation by a local authority or in a hospital vested in the Secretary of State or a Primary Care Trust or otherwise made available pursuant to arrangements made by a Health Authority or a Primary Care Trust, any reasonable expenses of accommodating him shall be recoverable from the local authority in whose area he is ordinarily resident.

Duties of local authorities in relation to children looked after by them

22 General duty of local authority in relation to children looked after by them

(1) In this Act, any reference to a child who is looked after by a local authority is a reference to a child who is –

    (a) in their care; or

    (b) provided with accommodation by the authority in the exercise of any functions (in particular those under this Act) which are social services functions within the meaning of the Local Authority Social Services Act 1970, apart from functions under sections 17, 23B and 24B.

(2) In subsection (1) 'accommodation' means accommodation which is provided for a continuous period of more than 24 hours.

(3) It shall be the duty of a local authority looking after any child –

    (a) to safeguard and promote his welfare; and

    (b) to make such use of services available for children cared for by their own parents as appears to the authority reasonable in his case.

(4) Before making any decision with respect to a child whom they are looking after, or proposing to look after, a local authority shall, so far as is reasonably practicable, ascertain the wishes and feelings of –

    (a) the child;

    (b) his parents;

    (c) any person who is not a parent of his but who has parental responsibility for him; and

    (d) any other person whose wishes and feelings the authority consider to be relevant, regarding the matter to be decided.

(5) In making any such decision a local authority shall give due consideration –

    (a) having regard to his age and understanding, to such wishes and feelings of the child as they have been able to ascertain;

    (b) to such wishes and feelings of any person mentioned in subsection (4)(b) to (d) as they have been able to ascertain; and

    (c) to the child's religious persuasion, racial origin and cultural and linguistic background.

(6) If it appears to a local authority that it is necessary, for the purposes of protecting members of the public from serious injury, to exercise their powers with respect to a child whom they are looking after in a manner which may not be consistent with their duties under this section, they may do so.

(7) If the Secretary of State considers it necessary, for the purpose of protecting members of the public from serious injury, to give directions to a local authority with respect to the exercise of their powers with respect to a child whom they are looking after, he may give such directions to the authority.

(8) Where any such directions are given to an authority they shall comply with them even though doing so is inconsistent with their duties under this section.

23 Provision of accommodation and maintenance by local authority for children whom they are looking after

(1) It shall be the duty of any local authority looking after a child –

    (a) when he is in their care, to provide accommodation for him; and

    (b) to maintain him in other respects apart from providing accommodation for him.

(2) A local authority shall provide accommodation and maintenance for any child whom they are looking after by –

    (a) placing him (subject to subsection (5) and any regulations made by the Secretary of State) with –

        (i) a family;

        (ii) a relative of his; or

        (iii) any other suitable person,

    on such terms as to payment by the authority and otherwise as the authority may determine;

    (aa) maintaining him in an appropriate children's home;

  (b)–(e) (*repealed*)

    (f) making such other arrangements as –

        (i) seem appropriate to them; and

        (ii) comply with any regulations made by the Secretary of State.

(2A) Where under subsection (2)(aa) a local authority maintains a child in a home provided, equipped and maintained by the Secretary of State under section 82(5), it shall do so on such terms as the Secretary of State may from time to time determine.

(3) Any person with whom a child has been placed under subsection (2)(a) is referred to in this Act as a local authority foster parent unless he falls within subsection (4).

(4) A person falls within this subsection if he is –

(a) a parent of the child;

(b) a person who is not a parent of the child but who has parental responsibility for him; or

(c) where the child is in care and there was a residence order in force with respect to him immediately before the care order was made, a person in whose favour the residence order was made.

(5) Where a child is in the care of a local authority, the authority may only allow him to live with a person who falls within subsection (4) in accordance with regulations made by the Secretary of State.

(5A) For the purposes of subsection (5) a child shall be regarded as living with a person if he stays with that person for a continuous period of more than 24 hours.

(6) Subject to any regulations made by the Secretary of State for the purposes of this subsection, any local authority looking after a child shall make arrangements to enable him to live with –

(a) a person falling within subsection (4); or

(b) a relative, friend or other person connected with him,

unless that would not be reasonably practicable or consistent with his welfare.

(7) Where a local authority provide accommodation for a child whom they are looking after, they shall, subject to the provisions of this Part and so far as is reasonably practicable and consistent with his welfare, secure that –

(a) the accommodation is near his home; and

(b) where the authority are also providing accommodation for a sibling of his, they are accommodated together.

(8) Where a local authority provide accommodation for a child whom they are looking after and who is disabled, they shall, so far as is reasonably practicable, secure that the accommodation is not unsuitable to his particular needs.

(9) Part II of Schedule 2 shall have effect for the purposes of making further provision as to children looked after by local authorities and in particular as to the regulations that may be made under subsections (2)(a) and (f) and (5).

(10) In this Act –

'appropriate children's home' means a children's home in respect of which a person is registered under Part II of the Care Standards Act 2000; and
'children's home' has the same meaning as in that Act.

Advice and assistance for certain children and young persons

23A The responsible authority and relevant children

(1) The responsible local authority shall have the functions set out in section 23B in respect of a relevant child.

(2) In subsection (1) 'relevant child' means (subject to subsection (3)) a child who –

(a) is not being looked after by any local authority;

(b) was, before last ceasing to be looked after, an eligible child for the purposes of paragraph 19B of Schedule 2; and

(c) is aged sixteen or seventeen.

(3) The Secretary of State may prescribe –

    (a) additional categories of relevant children; and
    (b) categories of children who are not to be relevant children despite falling within subsection (2).

(4) In subsection (1) the 'responsible local authority' is the one which last looked after the child.

(5) If under subsection (3)(a) the Secretary of State prescribes a category of relevant children which includes children who do not fall within subsection (2)(b) (for example, because they were being looked after by a local authority in Scotland), he may in the regulations also provide for which local authority is to be the responsible local authority for those children.

23B Additional functions of the responsible authority in respect of relevant children

(1) It is the duty of each local authority to take reasonable steps to keep in touch with a relevant child for whom they are the responsible authority, whether he is within their area or not.

(2) It is the duty of each local authority to appoint a personal adviser for each relevant child (if they have not already done so under paragraph 19C of Schedule 2).

(3) It is the duty of each local authority, in relation to any relevant child who does not already have a pathway plan prepared for the purposes of paragraph 19B of Schedule 2 –

    (a) to carry out an assessment of his needs with a view to determining what advice, assistance and support it would be appropriate for them to provide him under this Part; and
    (b) to prepare a pathway plan for him.

(4) The local authority may carry out such an assessment at the same time as any assessment of his needs is made under any enactment referred to in sub-paragraphs (a) to (c) of paragraph 3 of Schedule 2, or under any other enactment.

(5) The Secretary of State may by regulations make provision as to assessments for the purposes of subsection (3).

(6) The regulations may in particular make provision about –

    (a) who is to be consulted in relation to an assessment;
    (b) the way in which an assessment is to be carried out, by whom and when;
    (c) the recording of the results of an assessment;
    (d) the considerations to which the local authority are to have regard in carrying out an assessment.

(7) The authority shall keep the pathway plan under regular review.

(8) The responsible local authority shall safeguard and promote the child's welfare and, unless they are satisfied that his welfare does not require it, support him by –

    (a) maintaining him;
    (b) providing him with or maintaining him in suitable accommodation; and
    (c) providing support of such other descriptions as may be prescribed.

(9) Support under subsection (8) may be in cash.

(10) The Secretary of State may by regulations make provision about the meaning of 'suitable accommodation' and in particular about the suitability of landlords or other providers of accommodation.

(11) If the local authority have lost touch with a relevant child, despite taking reasonable steps to keep in touch, they must without delay –

(a) consider how to re-establish contact; and
(b) take reasonable steps to do so,

and while the child is still a relevant child must continue to take such steps until they succeed.

(12) Subsections (7) to (9) of section 17 apply in relation to support given under this section as they apply in relation to assistance given under that section.

(13) Subsections (4) and (5) of section 22 apply in relation to any decision by a local authority for the purposes of this section as they apply in relation to the decisions referred to in that section.

23C Continuing functions in respect of former relevant children

(1) Each local authority shall have the duties provided for in this section towards –

(a) a person who has been a relevant child for the purposes of section 23A (and would be one if he were under eighteen), and in relation to whom they were the last responsible authority; and
(b) a person who was being looked after by them when he attained the age of eighteen, and immediately before ceasing to be looked after was an eligible child,

and in this section such a person is referred to as a 'former relevant child'.

(2) It is the duty of the local authority to take reasonable steps –

(a) to keep in touch with a former relevant child whether he is within their area or not; and
(b) if they lose touch with him, to re-establish contact.

(3) It is the duty of the local authority –

(a) to continue the appointment of a personal adviser for a former relevant child; and
(b) to continue to keep his pathway plan under regular review.

(4) It is the duty of the local authority to give a former relevant child –

(a) assistance of the kind referred to in section 24B(1), to the extent that his welfare requires it;
(b) assistance of the kind referred to in section 24B(2), to the extent that his welfare and his educational or training needs require it;
(c) other assistance, to the extent that his welfare requires it.

(5) The assistance given under subsection (4)(c) may be in kind or, in exceptional circumstances, in cash.

(6) Subject to subsection (7), the duties set out in subsections (2), (3) and (4) subsist until the former relevant child reaches the age of twenty-one.

(7) If the former relevant child's pathway plan sets out a programme of education or training which extends beyond his twenty-first birthday –

    (a) the duty set out in subsection (4)(b) continues to subsist for so long as the former relevant child continues to pursue that programme; and

    (b) the duties set out in subsections (2) and (3) continue to subsist concurrently with that duty.

(8) For the purposes of subsection (7)(a) there shall be disregarded any interruption in a former relevant child's pursuance of a programme of education or training if the local authority are satisfied that he will resume it as soon as is reasonably practicable.

(9) Section 24B(5) applies in relation to a person being given assistance under subsection (4)(b) as it applies in relation to a person to whom section 24B(3) applies.

(10) Subsections (7) to (9) of section 17 apply in relation to assistance given under this section as they apply in relation to assistance given under that section.

Personal advisers and pathway plans

23D Personal advisers

(1) The Secretary of State may by regulations require local authorities to appoint a personal adviser for children or young persons of a prescribed description who have reached the age of sixteen but not the age of twenty-one who are not –

    (a) children who are relevant children for the purposes of section 23A;
    (b) the young persons referred to in section 23C; or
    (c) the children referred to in paragraph 19C of Schedule 2.

(2) Personal advisers appointed under or by virtue of this Part shall (in addition to any other functions) have such functions as the Secretary of State prescribes.

23E Pathway plans

(1) In this Part, a reference to a 'pathway plan' is to a plan setting out –

    (a) in the case of a plan prepared under paragraph 19B of Schedule 2 –
        (i) the advice, assistance and support which the local authority intend to provide a child under this Part, both while they are looking after him and later; and
        (ii) when they might cease to look after him; and
    (b) in the case of a plan prepared under section 23B, the advice, assistance and support which the local authority intend to provide under this Part,

and dealing with such other matters (if any) as may be prescribed.

(2) The Secretary of State may by regulations make provision about pathway plans and their review.

Advice and assistance for certain children and young persons

24 Persons qualifying for advice and assistance

(1) In this Part 'a person qualifying for advice and assistance' means a person who –

- (a) is under twenty-one; and
- (b) at any time after reaching the age of sixteen but while still a child was, but is no longer, looked after, accommodated or fostered.

(2) In subsection (1)(b), 'looked after, accommodated or fostered' means –

- (a) looked after by a local authority;
- (b) accommodated by or on behalf of a voluntary organisation;
- (c) accommodated in a registered children's home;
- (d) accommodated for a consecutive period of at least three months –
    - (i) by any Health Authority, Special Health Authority, Primary Care Trust or local education authority, or
    - (ii) in any residential care home, nursing home or mental nursing home or in any accommodation provided by a National Health Service trust; or
- (e) privately fostered.

(3) Subsection (2)(d) applies even if the period of three months mentioned there began before the child reached the age of sixteen.

(4) In the case of a person qualifying for advice and assistance by virtue of subsection (2)(a), it is the duty of the local authority which last looked after him to take such steps as they think appropriate to contact him at such times as they think appropriate with a view to discharging their functions under sections 24A and 24B.

(5) In each of sections 24A and 24B, the local authority under the duty or having the power mentioned there ('the relevant authority') is –

- (a) in the case of a person qualifying for advice and assistance by virtue of subsection (2)(a), the local authority which last looked after him; or
- (b) in the case of any other person qualifying for advice and assistance, the local authority within whose area the person is (if he has asked for help of a kind which can be given under section 24A or 24B).

Section 24

Prospective amendment—Section prospectively amended by Adoption and Children Act 2002, s 139(1), Sch 3, paras 54, 60 (see **3.3B**).

24A Advice and assistance

(1) The relevant authority shall consider whether the conditions in subsection (2) are satisfied in relation to a person qualifying for advice and assistance.

(2) The conditions are that –

- (a) he needs help of a kind which they can give under this section or section 24B; and
- (b) in the case of a person who was not being looked after by any local authority, they are satisfied that the person by whom he was being looked after does not have the necessary facilities for advising or befriending him.

(3) If the conditions are satisfied –

(a) they shall advise and befriend him if he was being looked after by a local authority or was accommodated by or on behalf of a voluntary organisation; and

(b) in any other case they may do so.

(4) Where as a result of this section a local authority are under a duty, or are empowered, to advise and befriend a person, they may also give him assistance.

(5) The assistance may be in kind and, in exceptional circumstances, assistance may be given –

(a) by providing accommodation, if in the circumstances assistance may not be given in respect of the accommodation under section 24B, or

(b) in cash.

(6) Subsections (7) to (9) of section 17 apply in relation to assistance given under this section or section 24B as they apply in relation to assistance given under that section.

Section 24A

Prospective amendment—Section prospectively amended by Adoption and Children Act 2002, s 139(1), Sch 3, paras 54, 61 (see **3.3B**).

24B Employment, education and training

(1) The relevant local authority may give assistance to any person who qualifies for advice and assistance by virtue of section 24(2)(a) by contributing to expenses incurred by him in living near the place where he is, or will be, employed or seeking employment.

(2) The relevant local authority may give assistance to a person to whom subsection (3) applies by –

(a) contributing to expenses incurred by the person in question in living near the place where he is, or will be, receiving education or training; or

(b) making a grant to enable him to meet expenses connected with his education or training.

(3) This subsection applies to any person who –

(a) is under twenty-four; and

(b) qualifies for advice and assistance by virtue of section 24(2)(a), or would have done so if he were under twenty-one.

(4) Where a local authority are assisting a person under subsection (2) they may disregard any interruption in his attendance on the course if he resumes it as soon as is reasonably practicable.

(5) Where the local authority are satisfied that a person to whom subsection (3) applies who is in full-time further or higher education needs accommodation during a vacation because his term-time accommodation is not available to him then, they shall give him assistance by –

(a) providing him with suitable accommodation during the vacation; or

(b) paying him enough to enable him to secure such accommodation himself.

(6) The Secretary of State may prescribe the meaning of 'full-time', 'further education', 'higher education' and 'vacation' for the purposes of subsection (5).

Section 24B

Prospective amendment—Section prospectively amended by Adoption and Children Act 2002, s 139(1), Sch 3, paras 54, 62 (see **3.3B**).

24C Information

(1) Where it appears to a local authority that a person –

    (a) with whom they are under a duty to keep in touch under section 23B, 23C or 24; or

    (b) whom they have been advising and befriending under section 24A; or

    (c) to whom they have been giving assistance under section 24B,

proposes to live, or is living, in the area of another local authority, they must inform that other authority.

(2) Where a child who is accommodated –

    (a) by a voluntary organisation or in a registered children's home;

    (b) by any Health Authority, Special Health Authority, Primary Care Trust or local education authority; or

    (c) in any residential care home, nursing home or mental nursing home or any accommodation provided by a National Health Service trust,

ceases to be so accommodated, after reaching the age of sixteen, the organisation, authority or (as the case may be) person carrying on the home shall inform the local authority within whose area the child proposes to live.

(3) Subsection (2) only applies, by virtue of paragraph (b) or (c), if the accommodation has been provided for a consecutive period of at least three months.

24D Representations: sections 23A to 24B

(1) Every local authority shall establish a procedure for considering representations (including complaints) made to them by –

    (a) a relevant child for the purposes of section 23A or a young person falling within section 23C;

    (b) a person qualifying for advice and assistance; or

    (c) a person falling within section 24B(2),

about the discharge of their functions under this Part in relation to him.

(2) In considering representations under subsection (1), a local authority shall comply with regulations (if any) made by the Secretary of State for the purposes of this subsection.

Section 24D

Prospective amendment—Section prospectively amended by Adoption and Children Act 2002, s 117(1) (see **3.3B**).

Secure accommodation

25 Use of accommodation for restricting liberty

(1) Subject to the following provisions of this section, a child who is being looked after by a local authority may not be placed, and, if placed, may not be kept, in accommodation provided for the purpose of restricting liberty ('secure accommodation') unless it appears –

(a) that –
   (i) he has a history of absconding and is likely to abscond from any other description of accommodation; and
   (ii) if he absconds, he is likely to suffer significant harm, or
(b) that if he is kept in any other description of accommodation he is likely to injure himself or other persons.

(2) The Secretary of State may by regulations –

(a) specify a maximum period –
   (i) beyond which a child may not be kept in secure accommodation without the authority of the court; and
   (ii) for which the court may authorise a child to be kept in secure accommodation;
(b) empower the court from time to time to authorise a child to be kept in secure accommodation for such further period as the regulations may specify; and
(c) provide that applications to the court under this section shall be made only by local authorities.

(3) It shall be the duty of a court hearing an application under this section to determine whether any relevant criteria for keeping a child in secure accommodation are satisfied in his case.

(4) If a court determines that any such criteria are satisfied, it shall make an order authorising the child to be kept in secure accommodation and specifying the maximum period for which he may be so kept.

(5) On any adjournment of the hearing of an application under this section, a court may make an interim order permitting the child to be kept during the period of the adjournment in secure accommodation.

(6) No court shall exercise the powers conferred by this section in respect of a child who is not legally represented in that court unless, having been informed of his right to apply for representation funded by the Legal Services Commission as part of the Community Legal Service or Criminal Defence Service and having had the opportunity to do so, he refused or failed to apply.

(7) The Secretary of State may by regulations provide that –

(a) this section shall or shall not apply to any description of children specified in the regulations;
(b) this section shall have effect in relation to children of a description specified in the regulations subject to such modifications as may be so specified;
(c) such other provisions as may be so specified shall have effect for the purpose of determining whether a child of a description specified in the regulations may be placed or kept in secure accommodation.

(8) The giving of an authorisation under this section shall not prejudice any power of any court in England and Wales or Scotland to give directions relating to the child to whom the authorisation relates.

(9) This section is subject to section 20(8).

Section 25

It has been held that these provisions do not offend the European Convention on Human Rights (*Re K (Secure Accommodation Order: Right to Liberty)* [2001] 1 FLR 526). Regulations have been made under this section. The Children (Secure Accommodation) Regulations 1991, SI 1991/1505, are the main regulations (and provide, for example, the maximum duration for a secure accommodation order – the period of remand up to 28 days in remand cases, and three months (first application) and six months (further application) in non-remand cases). The other regulations are the Children (Secure Accommodation) (No 2) Regulations 1991, SI 1991/2034. Guidance is given in *The Children Act 1989 Guidance and Regulations* (HMSO, 1991), vols 1 and 4.

Once an application has been made it can only be withdrawn with the court's permission. The child's welfare is relevant but not paramount (*Re M (Secure Accommodation Order)* [1995] Fam 108, [1995] 3 All ER 407, [1995] 1 FLR 418). Hearsay evidence is admissible (*Oxfordshire County Council v R* [1992] Fam 150, [1992] 1 FLR 648). The question of whether an institution is 'secure' is one of fact (*Re C (Detention: Medical Treatment)* [1997] 2 FLR 180). An application may be made in relation to a child remanded or bailed to a local authority by a criminal court (*Re C (Secure Accommodation: Bail)* [1994] 2 FLR 922 – see *Liverpool City Council v B* [1995] 1 WLR 505, [1995] 2 FLR 84 for where a child had been remanded to a magistrates' court). The court may make interim orders where an application is adjourned but the adjournment should not be for longer than would be permitted if a substantive order were made. Where a child is represented by a solicitor or guardian he should only attend court if it is in his interest to do so (*Re W (Secure Accommodation Order: Attendance at Court)* [1994] 2 FLR 1092, FD). Only in very exceptional cases should an application proceed without a child's guardian (*Re AS (Secure Accommodation Order)* [1999] 1 FLR 103). The duties of a local authority during the currency of a secure accommodation order are susceptible to judicial review (*S v Knowsley Borough Council* [2004] EWHC 491 (Fam), [2004] 2 FLR 716).

In an emergency, a child who satisfies the requirements of the section may be detained for up to 72 hours in any 28-day period without the prior authority of the court (see the Children (Secure Accommodation) Regulations 1991, regs 10(3) and 11(1)).

The word 'likely' in s 25(1)(a)(i) and (ii) means a real possibility that cannot sensibly be ignored (*S v Knowsley Borough Council* [2004] EWHC 491 (Fam), [2004] 2 FLR 716).

Supplemental

26 Review of cases and inquiries into representations

(1) The Secretary of State may make regulations requiring the case of each child who is being looked after by a local authority to be reviewed in accordance with the provisions of the regulations.

(2) The regulations may, in particular, make provision –

    (a) as to the manner in which each case is to be reviewed;

    (b) as to the considerations to which the local authority are to have regard in reviewing each case;

    (c) as to the time when each case is first to be reviewed and the frequency of subsequent reviews;

    (d) requiring the authority, before conducting any review, to seek the views of –

        (i) the child;

    (ii) his parents;

    (iii) any person who is not a parent of his but who has parental responsibility for him; and

    (iv) any other person whose views the authority consider to be relevant, including, in particular, the views of those persons in relation to any particular matter which is to be considered in the course of the review;

(e) requiring the authority, in the case of a child who is in their care –

    (i) to keep the section 31A plan for the child under review and, if they are of the opinion that some change is required, to revise the plan, or make a new plan, accordingly;

    (ii) to consider whether an application should be made to discharge the care order;

(f) requiring the authority, in the case of a child in accommodation provided by the authority –

    (i) if there is no plan for the future care of the child, to prepare one;

    (ii) if there is such a plan for the child, to keep it under review and, if they are of the opinion that some change is required, to revise the plan or make a new plan, accordingly;

    (iii) to consider whether the accommodation accords with the requirements of this Part;

(g) requiring the authority to inform the child, so far as is reasonably practicable, of any steps he may take under this Act;

(h) requiring the authority to make arrangements, including arrangements with such other bodies providing services as it considers appropriate, to implement any decision which they propose to make in the course, or as a result, of the review;

(i) requiring the authority to notify details of the result of the review and of any decision taken by them in consequence of the review to –

    (i) the child;

    (ii) his parents;

    (iii) any person who is not a parent of his but who has had parental responsibility for him; and

    (iv) any other person whom they consider ought to be notified;

(j) requiring the authority to monitor the arrangements which they have made with a view to ensuring that they comply with the regulations;

(k) for the authority to appoint a person in respect of each case to carry out in the prescribed manner the functions mentioned in subsection (2A) and any prescribed function.

(2A) The functions referred to in subsection (2)(k) are –

(a) participating in the review of the case in question,

(b) monitoring the performance of the authority's functions in respect of the review,

(c) referring the case to an officer of the Children and Family Court Advisory and Support Service, if the person appointed under subsection (2)(k) considers it appropriate to do so.

(2B) A person appointed under subsection (2)(k) must be a person of a prescribed description.

(2C) In relation to children whose cases are referred to officers under subsection (2A)(c), the Lord Chancellor may by regulations –

    (a) extend any functions of the officers in respect of family proceedings (within the meaning of section 12 of the Criminal Justice and Court Services Act 2000) to other proceedings,

    (b) require any functions of the officers to be performed in the manner prescribed by the regulations.

(3) Every local authority shall establish a procedure for considering any representations (including any complaint) made to them by –

    (a) any child who is being looked after by them or who is not being looked after by them but is in need;

    (b) a parent of his;

    (c) any person who is not a parent of his but who has parental responsibility for him;

    (d) any local authority foster parent;

    (e) such other person as the authority consider has a sufficient interest in the child's welfare to warrant his representations being considered by them,

about the discharge of the authority of any of their functions under this Part in relation to the child.

(4) The procedure shall ensure that at least one person who is not a member or officer of the authority takes part in –

    (a) the consideration; and

    (b) any discussions which are held by the authority about the action (if any) to be taken in relation to the child in the light of the consideration.

(5) In carrying out any consideration of representations under this section a local authority shall comply with any regulations made by the Secretary of State for the purpose of regulating the procedure to be followed.

(6) The Secretary of State may make regulations requiring local authorities to monitor the arrangements that they have made with a view to ensuring that they comply with any regulations made for the purposes of subsection (5).

(7) Where any representation has been considered under the procedure established by a local authority under this section, the authority shall –

    (a) have due regard to the findings of those considering the representation; and

    (b) take such steps as are reasonably practicable to notify (in writing) –

        (i) the person making the representation;

        (ii) the child (if the authority consider that he has sufficient understanding); and

        (iii) such other persons (if any) as appear to the authority to be likely to be affected,

    of the authority's decision in the matter and their reasons for taking that decision and of any action which they have taken, or propose to take.

(8) Every local authority shall give such publicity to their procedure for considering representations under this section as they consider appropriate.

Section 26

Prospective amendment—Section prospectively amended by Adoption and Children Act 2002, s 117 (see **3.3B**).

26A Advocacy services

(1) Every local authority shall make arrangements for the provision of assistance to –

    (a) persons who make or intend to make representations under section 24D; and

    (b) children who make or intend to make representations under section 26.

(2) The assistance provided under the arrangements shall include assistance by way of representation.

(3) The arrangements –

    (a) shall secure that a person may not provide assistance if he is a person who is prevented from doing so by regulations made by the Secretary of State; and

    (b) shall comply with any other provision made by the regulations in relation to the arrangements.

(4) The Secretary of State may make regulations requiring local authorities to monitor the steps that they have taken with a view to ensuring that they comply with regulations made for the purposes of subsection (3).

(5) Every local authority shall give such publicity to their arrangements for the provision of assistance under this section as they consider appropriate.

27 Co-operation between authorities

(1) Where it appears to a local authority that any authority mentioned in subsection (3) could, by taking any specified action, help in the exercise of any of their functions under this Part, they may request the help of that other authority, specifying the action in question.

(2) An authority whose help is so requested shall comply with the request if it is compatible with their own statutory or other duties and obligations and does not unduly prejudice the discharge of any of their functions.

(3) The authorities are –

    (a) any local authority;

    (b) any local education authority;

    (c) any local housing authority;

    (d) any Health Authority, Special Health Authority, Primary Care Trust or National Health Service trust; and

    (e) any person authorised by the Secretary of State for the purposes of this section.

(4) *(repealed)*

28 Consultation with local education authorities

(1) Where –

    (a) a child is being looked after by a local authority; and

    (b) the authority propose to provide accommodation for him in an establishment at which education is provided for children who are accommodated there, they shall, so far as is reasonably practicable, consult the appropriate local education authority before doing so.

(2) Where any such proposal is carried out, the local authority shall, as soon as is reasonably practicable, inform the appropriate local education authority of the arrangements that have been made for the child's accommodation.

(3) Where the child ceases to be accommodated as mentioned in subsection (1)(b), the local authority shall inform the appropriate local education authority.

(4) In this section 'the appropriate local education authority' means –

    (a) the local education authority within whose area the local authority's area falls; or

    (b) where the child has special educational needs and a statement of his needs is maintained under Part IV of the Education Act 1996, the local education authority who maintain the statement.

29 Recoupment of cost of providing services etc

(1) Where a local authority provide any service under section 17 or 18, other than advice, guidance or counselling, they may recover from a person specified in subsection (4) such charge for the service as they consider reasonable.

(2) Where the authority are satisfied that that person's means are insufficient for it to be reasonably practicable for him to pay the charge, they shall not require him to pay more than he can reasonably be expected to pay.

(3) No person shall be liable to pay any charge under subsection (1) for a service provided under section 17 or section 18(1) or (5) at any time when he is in receipt of income support under Part VII of the Social Security Contributions and Benefits Act 1992, of any element of child tax credit other than the family element, of working tax credit or of an income-based jobseeker's allowance.

(3A) No person shall be liable to pay any charge under subsection (1) for a service provided under section 18(2) or (6) at any time when he is in receipt of income support under Part VII of the Social Security and Benefits Act 1992 or of an income-based jobseeker's allowance.

(4) The persons are –

    (a) where the service is provided for a child under sixteen, each of his parents;

    (b) where it is provided for a child who has reached the age of sixteen, the child himself; and

    (c) where it is provided for a member of the child's family, that member.

(5) Any charge under subsection (1) may, without prejudice to any other method of recovery, be recovered summarily as a civil debt.

(6) Part III of Schedule 2 makes provision in connection with contributions towards the maintenance of children who are being looked after by local authorities and consists of the re-enactment with modifications of provisions in Part V of the Child Care Act 1980.

(7) Where a local authority provide any accommodation under section 20(1) for a child who was (immediately before they began to look after him) ordinarily resident within the area of another local authority, they may recover from that other authority

any reasonable expenses incurred by them in providing the accommodation and maintaining him.

(8) Where a local authority provide accommodation under section 21(1) or (2)(a) or (b) for a child who is ordinarily resident within the area of another local authority and they are not maintaining him in –

    (a)   a community home provided by them;

    (b)   a controlled community home; or

    (c)   a hospital vested in the Secretary of State or a Primary Care Trust, or any other hospital made available pursuant to arrangements made by a Strategic Health Authority, Health Authority or a Primary Care Trust,

they may recover from that other authority any reasonable expenses incurred by them in providing the accommodation and maintaining him.

(9) Except where subsection (10) applies, where a local authority comply with any request under section 27(2) in relation to a child or other person who is not ordinarily resident within their area, they may recover from the local authority in whose area the child or person is ordinarily resident any reasonable expenses incurred by them in respect of that person.

(10) Where a local authority ('authority A') comply with any request under section 27(2) from another local authority ('authority B') in relation to a child or other person –

    (a)   whose responsible authority is authority B for the purposes of section 23B or 23C; or

    (b)   whom authority B are advising or befriending or to whom they are giving assistance by virtue of section 24(5)(a),

authority A may recover from authority B any reasonable expenses incurred by them in respect of that person.

Section 29

Prospective amendment—Section prospectively amended by State Pension Credit Act 2002, s 14, Sch 2, para 30.

30 Miscellaneous

(1) Nothing in this Part shall affect any duty imposed on a local authority by or under any other enactment.

(2) Any question arising under section 20(2), 21(3) or 29(7) to (9) as to the ordinary residence of a child shall be determined by agreement between the local authorities concerned or, in default of agreement, by the Secretary of State.

(3) Where the functions conferred on a local authority by this Part and the functions of a local education authority are concurrent, the Secretary of State may by regulations provide by which authority the functions are to be exercised.

(4) The Secretary of State may make regulations for determining, as respects any local education authority functions specified in the regulations, whether a child who is being looked after by a local authority is to be treated, for purposes so specified, as a child of parents of sufficient resources or as a child of parents without resources.

PART IV

CARE AND SUPERVISION

General

31 Care and supervision orders

(1) On the application of any local authority or authorised person, the court may make an order –

    (a) placing the child with respect to whom the application is made in the care of a designated local authority; or

    (b) putting him under the supervision of a designated local authority.

(2) A court may only make a care order or supervision order if it is satisfied –

    (a) that the child concerned is suffering, or is likely to suffer, significant harm; and

    (b) that the harm, or likelihood of harm, is attributable to –

        (i) the care given to the child, or likely to be given to him if the order were not made, not being what it would be reasonable to expect a parent to give to him; or

        (ii) the child's being beyond parental control.

(3) No care order or supervision order may be made with respect to a child who has reached the age of seventeen (or sixteen, in the case of a child who is married).

(4) An application under this section may be made on its own or in any other family proceedings.

(5) The court may –

    (a) on an application for a care order, make a supervision order;

    (b) on an application for a supervision order, make a care order.

(6) Where an authorised person proposes to make an application under this section he shall –

    (a) if it is reasonably practicable to do so; and

    (b) before making the application,

consult the local authority appearing to him to be the authority in whose area the child concerned is ordinarily resident.

(7) An application made by an authorised person shall not be entertained by the court if, at the time when it is made, the child concerned is –

    (a) the subject of an earlier application for a care order, or supervision order, which has not been disposed of; or

    (b) subject to –

        (i) a care order or supervision order;

        (ii) an order under section 63(1) of the Powers of Criminal Courts (Sentencing) Act 2000; or

        (iii) *(applies to Scotland only}*.

(8) The local authority designated in a care order must be –

(a) the authority within whose area the child is ordinarily resident; or

(b) where the child does not reside in the area of a local authority, the authority within whose area any circumstances arose in consequence of which the order is being made.

(9) In this section –

'authorised person' means –

(a) the National Society for the Prevention of Cruelty to Children and any of its officers; and

(b) any person authorised by order of the Secretary of State to bring proceedings under this section and any officer of a body which is so authorised;

'harm' means ill-treatment or the impairment of health or development including, for example, impairment suffered from seeing or hearing the ill-treatment of another;

'development' means physical, intellectual, emotional, social or behavioural development;

'health' means physical or mental health; and

'ill-treatment' includes sexual abuse and forms of ill-treatment which are not physical.

(10) Where the question of whether harm suffered by a child is significant turns on the child's health or development, his health or development shall be compared with that which could reasonably be expected of a similar child.

(11) In this Act –

'a care order' means (subject to section 105(1)) an order under subsection (1)(a) and (except where express provision to the contrary is made) includes an interim care order made under section 38; and

'a supervision order' means an order under subsection (1)(b) and (except where express provision to the contrary is made) includes an interim supervision order made under section 38.

Section 31

Prospective amendment—Section prospectively amended by Adoption and Children Act 2002, s 121 (see **3.3B**).

Statute and the Human Rights Act 1998—This section contains the 'threshold criteria' that must be fulfilled on an application for either a care order or a supervision order. If the threshold criteria are satisfied it is still necessary for the court to consider s 1 of the CA 1989 and Article 8 of the European Convention on Human Rights before making any order. In the case of *Re C and B (Care Order: Future Harm)* [2001] 1 FLR 611, Hale LJ said at [33]: 'I do note that under Article 8 of the Convention both the children and the parents have the right to respect for their family and private life. If the state is to interfere with that there are three requirements: first, that it be in accordance with the law; secondly that it be for a legitimate aim (in this case, the protection of the welfare and interests of the children); and thirdly, that it be necessary in a democratic society'. The court will deprecate any attempt to use excessive and irrelevant arguments under that Convention: see *Re F (Care: Termination of Contact)* [2000] 2 FCR 481. The court will also take into account that there is a strong supposition that, all other things being equal, it is in the interests of a child that it shall remain with its natural parents, but that has to give way to particular needs in particular situations (*Re W (A Minor) (Residence Order)* [1993] 2 FLR 625, and *Re H (A Minor) (Custody Interim Care and Control)* [1991] 2 FLR 109, CA).

Twin track/split hearing—Early consideration should always be given to twin track planning in order to avoid delay (*Re D and K (Care Plan: Guidelines)* [1999] 4 All ER 893, [1999] 2 FLR 872). Further, early consideration should be given to whether there should be a separate hearing on the threshold issues prior to a subsequent hearing on welfare issues (see *Re CB and JB (Care Proceedings: Case Conduct)* [1998] 2 FLR 211, FD, which also gives guidance on the use of expert evidence as to propensity). Where separate hearings are issued, the second hearing should be heard by the same judge wherever possible (*Re G (Care Proceedings: Split Trials)* [2001] 1 FLR 872). A finding made at a threshold hearing may be reviewed at the second stage hearing, where a good reason for this is shown (*Re M and MC (Care: Issues of Fact: Drawing of Orders)* [2002] EWCA Civ 499, [2003] 1 FLR 461, CA; *Re D (Child: Threshold Criteria)* [2001] 1 FLR 274, CA). Findings made at split hearings may be appealed (*Re B (A Minor) (Split Hearings: Jurisdiction)* [2000] 1 WLR 790, [2000] 1 FLR 334, CA).

Parents' involvement—Where both parents have parental responsibility for a child, they will both be automatic respondents to the proceedings (see FPR 1991, Appendix 3 and FPC(CA 1989)R 1991, Sch 2). A father without parental responsibility should be given notice of the proceedings and of the dates and times of any hearings (ibid). The rules will only be relaxed in exceptional circumstances (*Re AB (Care Proceedings: Service on Husband Ignorant of Child's Existence)* [2004] 1 FLR 541, FD). In most circumstances a father without parental responsibility who applies to be joined into the proceedings will be permitted to do so (see, eg *Re B (Care Proceedings: Notification of Father without Parental Responsibility)* [1999] 2 FLR 408); however, where a father delays until the last minute to make an application to be joined, the application may be refused (*Re P (Care Proceedings: Father's Application to be Joined as a Party)* [2001] 1 FLR 781). Parents should be involved by the local authority in the decision-making process concerning their children (*Venema v Netherlands* [2003] 1 FLR 552, ECtHR; *Re L (Care Assessment: Fair Trial)* [2002] 2 FLR 703; and *Re G (Care: Challenge to Local Authority Decision)* [2003] 2 FLR 42 (and see cases herein under the HRA 1998, in particular, *Re L (Care Proceedings: Human Rights Claims)* [2003] 2 FLR 160, FD)).

Withdrawal—An application for a care or supervision order may only be withdrawn with the court's permission (*Re N (Leave to Withdraw Care Proceedings)* [2000] 1 FLR 134). There is no automatic assumption that care proceedings will be adjourned to take place after any criminal proceedings concerning parties to the care proceedings (see *Re TB (Care Proceedings: Criminal Trial)* [1995] 2 FLR 801, CA). Where an application is made for disclosure of papers to the police, the court will balance a number of factors, including the need to encourage frankness within the care proceedings on the one hand, and on the other hand, the public interest in the proper investigation of alleged criminal activity (see *Re M (Care Proceedings: Disclosure: Human Rights)* [2001] 2 FLR 1316, and *Re Y and K (Split Hearing: Evidence)* [2003] EWCA Civ 669, [2003] 2 FLR 273, CA). Where an application to free a child for adoption is being heard together with care proceedings, the care proceedings should be considered first (*Re D (Simultaneous Applications for Care Order and Freeing Order)* [1999] 2 FLR 49, CA; *Re D (Grant of Care Order: Refusal of Freeing Order)* [2001] 1 FLR 862, CA; and *Re M (Care Order: Freeing Application)* [2003] EWCA Civ 1874, [2004] 1 FLR 826, CA).

When—The court will decide whether the threshold criteria are satisfied by having regard to the position as it stood at the time that the protective measures were taken by the local authority in relation to the child (*Re M (A Minor) (Care Order Threshold Conditions)* [1994] 2 AC 424, [1994] 3 All ER 298, [1994] 3 WLR 558, [1994] 2 FLR 577, HL, and see also *Southwark London Borough Council v B* [1998] 2 FLR 1095, FD). This means that the court will consider the position immediately before an emergency protection order, if there is one; or an interim care order, if that is the initiation of the protection; or when a child went into voluntary care (*Northamptonshire County Council v S* [1993] 1 FLR 554). Events that occurred after the protective measures were taken may be relevant only to the extent that they show the state of affairs as at the time that the measures were taken (*Re G (Care Proceedings: Threshold Conditions)* [2001] 2 FLR 1111, CA).

Facts first – standard of proof—In deciding whether the threshold criteria are fulfilled the court should first establish the facts of the case in accordance with the balance of probability standard of proof and should then apply the facts as found to the statutory criteria in s 31 (*Re H (Minors) (Sexual Abuse: Standard of Proof)* [1996] AC 563, [1996] 1 FLR 80). The burden of proving allegations made within the care proceedings rests upon the party raising the allegation; thus a local authority will bear the burden of proving the facts that are said to justify the care or supervision orders sought (see *Re H* (above) and *Re M and R (Minors) (Sexual Abuse: Expert Evidence)* [1996] 4 All ER 239, [1996] 2 FLR 195, CA). The standard of proof in care proceedings is considered in detail in the speech of Lord Nicholls in the case of *Re H*, in which he said:

'Where the matters in issue are facts the standard of proof required in non-criminal proceedings is the preponderance of probability, usually referred to as the balance of probability. This is the established general principle. There are exceptions such as contempt of court applications, but I can see no reason for thinking that family proceedings are, or should be, an exception. By family proceedings I mean proceedings so described in the 1989 Act, ss 105 and 8(3). Despite their special features, family proceedings remain essentially a form of civil proceedings. Family proceedings often raise very serious issues, but so do other forms of civil proceedings.

The balance of probability standard means that a court is satisfied an event occurred if the court considers that, on the evidence, the occurrence of the event was more likely than not. When assessing the probabilities the court will have in mind as a factor, to whatever extent is appropriate in the particular case, that the more serious the allegation the less likely it is that the event occurred and, hence, the stronger should be the evidence before the court concludes that the allegation is established on the balance of probability. Fraud is usually less likely than negligence. Deliberate physical injury is usually less likely than accidental physical injury. A stepfather is usually less likely to have repeatedly raped and had non-consensual oral sex with his under age stepdaughter than on some occasion to have lost his temper and slapped her. Built into the preponderance of probability standard is a generous degree of flexibility in respect of the seriousness of the allegation.

Although the result is much the same, this does not mean that where a serious allegation is in issue the standard of proof required is higher. It means only that the inherent probability or improbability of an event is itself a matter to be taken into account when weighing the probabilities and deciding whether, on balance, the event occurred. The more improbable the event, the stronger must be the evidence that it did occur before, on the balance of probability, its occurrence will be established. Ungoed-Thomas J expressed this neatly in *Re Dellow's Will Trusts, Lloyds Bank Ltd v Institute of Cancer Research* [1964] 1 All ER 771 at 773, [1964] 1 WLR 451 at 455:

"The more serious the allegation, the more cogent is the evidence required to overcome the unlikelihood of what is alleged and thus to prove it."

This substantially accords with the approach adopted in authorities such as the well-known judgment of Morris LJ in *Hornal v Neuberger Products Ltd* [1956] 3 All ER 970 at 978, [1957] 1 QB 247 at 266. This approach also provides a means by which the balance of probability standard can accommodate one's instinctive feeling that even in civil proceedings a court should be more sure before finding serious allegations proved than when deciding less serious or trivial matters.

No doubt it is this feeling which prompts judicial comment from time to time that grave issues call for proof to a standard higher than the preponderance of probability. Similar suggestions have been made recently regarding proof of allegations of sexual abuse of children: see *Re G (A Minor) (Child Abuse: Standard of Proof)* [1987] 1 WLR 1461 at 1466 and *Re W (Minors) (Sexual Abuse: Standard of Proof)* [1994] 1 FLR 419 at 429. So I must pursue this a little further. The law looks for probability, not certainty. Certainty is seldom attainable. But probability is an unsatisfactorily vague criterion because there are degrees of probability. In establishing principles regarding the standard of proof, therefore, the law seeks to define the degree of probability appropriate for different types of proceedings. Proof beyond reasonable doubt, in whatever form of words expressed, is one standard. Proof on a preponderance of probability is another, a lower standard having the inbuilt flexibility already mentioned. If the balance of probability standard were departed from, and a third standard were substituted in some civil cases, it would be necessary to identify what the standard is and when it would apply. Herein lies a difficulty. If the standard were to be higher than the balance of probability but lower than the criminal standard of proof beyond reasonable doubt, what would it be? The only alternative which suggests itself is that the standard should be commensurate with the gravity of the allegation and the seriousness of the consequences. A formula to this effect has its attraction. But I doubt whether in practice it would add much to the present test in civil cases, and it would risk causing confusion and uncertainty. As at present advised I think it is better to stick to the existing, established law on this subject. I can see no compelling need for a change.

　　　I therefore agree with the recent decisions of the Court of Appeal in several cases involving the care of children, to the effect that the standard of proof is the ordinary civil standard of balance of probability (see *H v H and C (Kent County Council intervening) (child abuse: evidence)*, *K v K (Haringey London Borough Council Intervening) (Child Abuse: Evidence)* [1989] 3 All ER 740 at 745, 750, [1990] Fam 86 at 94, 100, *Re M (A Minor) (Appeal) (No 2)* [1994] 1 FLR 59 at 67, and *Re W* [1994] 1 FLR 419 at 424 per Balcombe LJ). The Court of Appeal were of the same view in the present case. It follows that the contrary observations already mentioned in *Re G* [1987] 1 WLR 1461 at 1466 and *Re W* [1994] 1 FLR 419 at 429 are not an accurate statement of the law.'

The above passage has been re-affirmed as stating the correct standard of proof in care proceedings (*Re U (Serious Injury: Standard of Proof); Re B* [2004] EWCA Civ 567, [2004] 2 FLR 263, CA, and *Re T (Abuse: Standard of Proof)* [2004] EWCA Civ 558, [2004] 2 FLR 838, CA). The decision of Bodey J in *Re ET (Serious Injuries: Standard of Proof)* [2003] 2 FLR 1205 should not be followed (*Re U; Re B* (above)). In *Re U* the court considered the impact of the decision in *R v Cannings* [2004] 1 All ER 725, CA, and said:

　　　'**[29]**　In summary the decision of the Court in *R v Cannings* [2004] EWCA Crim 1 has no doubt provided a useful warning to judges in care proceedings against ill-considered conclusions or conclusions resting on insufficient evidence. The extent of the retrospective effect remains to emerge. However practitioners should be slow to assume that past cases which have been carefully tried on a wide range of evidence will be readily reopened.

　　　[30]　In our judgment the responsibilities of local authorities have not been changed by the decision of the Court of Appeal (Criminal Division). Theirs is the task to protect the child; to assess the issues within their competence and expertise; and to rely upon the legal team for the local authority to advise on the strength and credibility of the medical evidence. They will, with their legal advisers, continue to prepare applications for care orders in suitable cases based upon the civil standard of proof as explained by Lord Nicholls in *Re H*. In our view the decision in *R v Cannings* does not affect their responsibilities under the Children Act.'

In *Re A (Non-accidental Injury: Medical Evidence)* [2001] 2 FLR 657 it was held to be wrong to apply a test of 'is there a reasonable body of medical opinion that would suggest that the injury could be accidental' (ie the *Bolam v Friern* test). A judge should state his findings clearly on any crucial expert opinion or diagnosis (*Re W and Another (A Child: Non-accidental Injury)* [2002] EWCA Civ 710, [2003] 2 FCR 346, and see *A Local Authority v S, W and T (by his guardian)* [2004] EWHC 1270 (Fam), [2004] 2 FLR 129, FD, and *Re B (Threshold Criteria: Fabricated Illness)* [2002] EWHC 20 (Fam), [2004] 2 FLR 200, FD). A judge should distinguish between medical diagnosis and judicial finding, the latter being based on the totality of the evidence and the application of the appropriate standard of proof (*Re B (Non-accidental Injury)* [2002] EWCA Civ 752, [2002] 1 FLR 1133, CA). There is a potential danger of relying too heavily on photographs to demonstrate abuse (*Re Y (Evidence of Abuse: Unreliability of Photographs)* [2003] EWHC 3090 (Fam), [2004] 1 FLR 855, FD).

'Likely'—In considering whether a child is 'likely' to suffer significant harm, the court should consider whether there is 'a real possibility, a possibility that cannot sensibly be ignored having regard to the nature and gravity of the fear of harm in the particular case' (see *Re H (Minors) (Sexual Abuse: Standard of Proof)* [1996] AC 563, [1996] 1 FLR 80). This may require both a short-term and a long-term examination of the likelihood of harm (*Re H (A Minor) (Section 37 Direction)* [1993] 2 FLR 541).

Harm—The definition of harm will be amended by the Adoption and Children Act 2002, s 120 to include 'for example, impairment suffered from seeing or hearing the ill-treatment of another'.

Perpetrator—Difficult issues arise where the court is unable to identify the perpetrator of harm in relation to a child; the phrase in the section 'care given to the child' refers primarily to the care given to the child by a parent or parents or other primary carers. However, the matter stands differently in a case where care is shared and the court is unable to distinguish in a crucial respect between the care given by the parent or the primary carers, and the care given by other carers. In such a case, the phrase 'care given to the child' is apt to embrace not merely the care given by the parents or other primary carers; it is apt to embrace the care given by any one of the carers (*Lancashire County Council v B* [2000] 2 AC 147, [2000] 2 All ER 97, [2000] 2 WLR 590, [2000] 1 FLR 593). The civil standard of proof will apply to the identification of an alleged perpetrator of abuse just as it applies to the issue of identifying the harm a child has suffered (*Re G (A Child) (Non-accidental Injury: Standard of Proof)* [2001] 1 FCR 96). If a court finds that abuse has occurred but considers that there is insufficient evidence to make a finding against any one of a number of possible perpetrators, the test is as stated in *North Yorkshire County Council v SA* [2003] 2 FLR 849 (considering *Re O and N; Re B (Children) (Non-accidental Injury)* [2003] UKHL 18, [2003] 2 All ER 305, [2003] 2 WLR 1075, [2003] 1 FLR 1169; rvsg *Re O and N (Care: Preliminary Hearing)* [2002] EWCA Civ 1271, [2002] 2 FLR 1167, affg *Re B (Non-accidental Injury: Compelling Medical Evidence* [2002] EWCA Civ 902, [2002] 2 FLR 599):

> 'In relation to … the attributable condition, it seems to me that the two most likely outcomes in "uncertain perpetrator" cases are as follows. The first is that there is sufficient evidence for the court positively to identify the perpetrator or perpetrators. Second, if there is not sufficient evidence to make such a finding, the court has to apply the test set out by Lord Nicholls as to whether there is a real possibility or likelihood that one or more of a number of people with access to the child might have caused the injury to the child. For this purpose, real possibility and likelihood can be treated as the same test. As Lord Nicholls pointed out in *Re O and N; Re B* the views and indications that the judge at the first part of a split trial may be able to set out may be of great assistance at the later stage of assessment and the provision of the protection package for the injured child. I would therefore formulate the test set out by Lord Nicholls as, "Is there a likelihood or real possibility that A or B or C was the perpetrator or a perpetrator of the inflicted injuries?". There may perhaps also be the third possibility that there is no indicator to help the court decide from whom the risk to the child may come, in which eventuality it would be very difficult for the local authority and for the court to assess where the child might be at most risk.'

Concessions—The following has been said about parents offering concessions in relation to threshold findings:

Case and court	What it says
Devon County Council v S [1992] Fam 176, [1992] 3 All ER 793, Thorpe J.	'First, and foremost, whilst undoubtedly there is an overriding duty in the court to investigate the proposals advanced by the parties, even when those proposals are fully agreed, the profundity of that investigation must reflect the reality that there is consensus amongst the parties to the litigation, particularly when the parties include a public authority with statutory duties and a guardian ad litem on behalf of the child. It seems to me quite inappropriate that two and three quarter hours of

	investigation and oral evidence should have been devoted to the hearing of the interim application on 29 November. It seems to me equally if not more inappropriate that the court should have devoted six hours to the investigation of the application for the full order including oral evidence.'
Re G (A Minor) (Care Proceedings) [1994] 2 FLR 69, Wall J	The court must feel able to investigate the factual substratum of the order where to do so is in the interests of the children.
Stockport Metropolitan Borough Council v D [1995] 1 FLR 873, Thorpe J	The local authority prepared one draft of the proposed findings. The parents prepared another. The judge held that it would be contrary to public interest to prolong the hearing in order to litigate the differences in expression. The parents' version should be preferred.
Re B (Agreed Findings of Fact) [1998] 2 FLR 968, CA	A 10-day hearing would not be appropriate in a case where the mother accepted that there should be a supervision order and faced criminal proceedings over the allegation of salt poisoning (that she denied). The case could be brought back after the criminal trial if it was felt that a further investigation was necessary.
Re M (Threshold Criteria: Parental Concessions) [1999] 2 FLR 728, CA	Children made clear allegations of sexual abuse against adoptive father. Acquitted of rape. Threshold conceded on minor allegations but sexual abuse allegations denied. The adoptive parents did not want any further contact. Should the family court investigate them? Wall J: Yes. The concessions were insufficient. The potential for future contact required the issue to be dealt with. The care plan must depend on the harm that the children have suffered. The children had their credibility impugned and had been accused of lying; fairness demanded that a judge be invited to make findings on the evidence.
Re W (Children) (Threshold Criteria: Parental Concessions) [2001] 1 FCR 139, CA	Concessions by parents have to be considered to see whether they meet the reasonable requirements of the local authority and the guardian and satisfy the justice of the case. Here the parents' concessions did not.

Court's role—Once a care order has been made, the court has no continuing role in relation to the manner in which the care order is implemented (save to the extent permitted by subsequent application or contact or discharge of the care order): see *Re S (Minors) (Care Order: Implementation of Care Plan), Re W (Minors) (Care Order: Adequacy of Care Plan)* [2002] UKHL 10, [2002] 2 AC 291, [2002] 2 WLR 720, [2002] 2 All ER 192, [2002] 1 FLR 815. Therefore, the care plan will be a document of great importance (see, eg, *Re R (Care Proceedings: Adjournment)* [1998] 2 FLR 390, CA). Interim care orders may be used so as to enable the court to safeguard the welfare of the child until such time as the court is in a position to decide whether or not it is in the best interests of the child to make a care order. When that time arrives depends on the circumstances of the case and is a matter of the judgement of the trial judge (*Re S (Minors) (Care Order: Implementation of Care Plan)*, *Re W (Minors) (Care Order: Adequacy of Care Plan)* [2002] UKHL 10, [2002] 2 AC 291, [2002] 2 WLR 720, [2002] 2 All ER 192, [2002] 1 FLR 815, HL).

Care plans—Section 121 of the Adoption and Children Act 2002 provides for the introduction of s 31(3A) of the CA 1989 by which 'no care order may be made with respect to a child until the court has considered a section 31A plan'. Section 31A (as introduced by the Adoption and Children Act 2002) will contain more detailed provisions relating to the contents of care plans.

Continued use of interim care orders as a means of controlling the care plan is inappropriate (*Re L (Sexual Abuse: Standard of Proof)* [1996] 1 FLR 116, CA, and see *Re S (Minors) (Care Order: Implementation of Care Plan)*, *Re W (Minors) (Care Order: Adequacy of Care Plan)* [2002] UKHL 10 (cited above)). A care plan should set out the local authority's plans for the child in objective and unemotional terms (*Re DH (A Minor) (Child Abuse)* [1994] 1 FLR 679). The plan should be supported by evidence (*Re J (Minors) (Care: Care Plan)* [1994] 1 FLR 253). Where the court disagrees with the care plan it may be left in the position of having to chose between two perceived 'evils' (inappropriate care plan or return to parents) (*Re S and D (Children: Powers of Court)* [1995] 2 FLR 456); the care plan may represent the only realistic solution for the child (*Re R (Care Proceedings: Adjournment)* [1998] 2 FLR 390, CA). Where a local authority fails to put into effect a care plan following the making of a care order (eg by withdrawing contact) an urgent application can be made to a judge (*Re P (Adoption: Breach of Care Plan)* [2004] EWCA Civ 355, [2004] 2 FLR 1109, CA, in which Thorpe LJ said at [20]: 'When the father sensed … that the denial of contact was both a breach of the care plan and a breach of his rights, then it was to the judge that he should have gone immediately. This failure to apply for interim relief is as significant in my judgment as the failure to apply under section 7 of the Human Rights Act 1998. Indeed… it is more significant because, although there may be some professional unfamiliarity with the section 7 route, and there may be difficulties in obtaining public funding for a section 7 application, all with any experience of public law litigation know that the judge is available at short notice to restore any rights that are being arbitrarily denied or withheld by the local authorities in possession of care orders … This was the plainest case for an urgent application to the judge to intervene'). It is wrong for a local authority to make significant changes in a care plan without involving the parents in the decision-making process, even after obtaining a care order (*X Council v B (Emergency Protection Orders)* [2004] EWHC 2015 (Fam), [2005] Fam Law 13).

A care order may still be appropriate, even if it is intended that the child should remain living with the parents (*Re S (J) (A Minor) (Care or Supervision Order)* [1993] 2 FLR 919, CA).

Satellite parties—There is no automatic right for a 'satellite' party to intervene in care proceedings in order to defend an allegation that has been made against that person; however, the interests of justice may require that such a person should be permitted to intervene to the extent of defending the allegation made against him (see *Re H (Care Proceedings: Intervener)* [2000] 1 FLR 775, CA, distinguishing *Re S (Care: Residence: Intervener)* [1997] 1 FLR 497, CA).

Care/supervision—In deciding whether to make a care order or a supervision order, a judge has to exercise a discretion on the particular facts of the individual case. In *Re O (Supervision Order)* [2001] EWCA Civ 16, [2001] 1 FLR 923, CA, Hale LJ said at [24]–[28]:

'**[24]** A care order is, however, very different from a supervision order. There are three main points. First, it gives a local authority power to remove the child without recourse even to a family proceedings court for an emergency protection order. The parents' only means of challenging that removal is by an application to discharge the care order, which usually takes some time to be heard, especially if, as in this case, it would have to be transferred to a higher court. Given the judge's findings as to the nature of risk, the slowness of any deterioration, the level of protection available from other sources including the father, it is very difficult to say that the local authority need to have this power. The care plan itself, as I have already indicated, does not suggest that they do.

[25] Secondly, it gives the local authority parental responsibility for the child coupled with the power to control the parents' exercise of that responsibility. Again, the care plan does not suggest that the local authority wish to exercise parental responsibility or control the parents' exercise of it. It expressly states, for example, 'that A's social, moral and academic education will be the responsibility of his parents'. Under 'Health' it points out that he 'continues to be in good health and he will need to receive the usual check-ups and vaccinations via the local health visitor and GP service'. This is not indicative of the suggestion that the local authority need to be in a position to arrange that for him. In any event, that could be done by inserting appropriate requirements in the supervision order.

[26] The third difference is one of timing. Mr Forbes in particular has argued that it might be difficult to achieve a further order in three years' time, but of course that difficulty would only arise if by then the risk of harm had disappeared or almost disappeared, or the need for an order had disappeared or almost disappeared. If that were not the case, the local authority would have to investigate and take any action which was thought appropriate to protect the child.

[27] All of these considerations, therefore, suggest that the judge, far from being plainly wrong to make a supervision order, was absolutely right so to do. Mr Archer has not relied upon earlier case law on the choice between care and supervision orders. He was probably wise to do so. Each case is an exercise of discretion on its own particular facts and earlier case law may be of limited help in this context. But, in any event, it has to be considered in the light of the Human Rights Act 1998 and art 8 of the Convention for the Protection of Human Rights and Fundamental Freedoms (the European Convention on Human Rights) (Rome, 4 November 1950; TS 71 (1953); Cmd 8969). As I said in the case of *Re C and B (Children) (Care Order: Future Harm)* [2000] 1 FLR 611 at 620–621 (paras 33–34):

"I do note that under art 8 of the Convention both the children and the parents have the right to respect for their family and private life. If the state is to interfere with that there are three requirements: firstly, that it be in accordance with the law; secondly, that it be for a legitimate aim (in this case the protection of the welfare and interests of the children); and thirdly, that it be 'necessary in a democratic society.' There is a long line of European Court of Human Rights jurisprudence on that third requirement, which emphasises that the intervention has to be proportionate to the legitimate aim."

[28] Proportionality, therefore, is the key. It will be the duty of everyone to ensure that, in those cases where a supervision order is proportionate as a response to the risk presented, a supervision order can be made to work, as indeed the framers of the Children Act 1989 always hoped that it would be made to work. The local authorities must deliver the services that are needed and must secure that other agencies, including the health service, also play their part, and the parents must co-operate fully.'

Conditions—These may not be attached to a care order (*Re T (A Minor) (Care Order: Conditions)* [1994] 2 FLR 423, CA). Nor may they be attached to a supervision order – the court is confined to the requirements set out in CA 1989, Sch 3 (*Re V (Care or Supervision Order)* [1996] 1 FLR 776).

Injunctions—It has been held that a county court does not have an inherent jurisdiction to grant an injunction in care proceedings (*Devon County Council v B* [1997] 1 FLR 591), although there is a debate about whether it may do so under s 38 of the County Courts Act 1984 (see **3.9**). However, the High Court may grant such injunctions under Supreme Court Act 1981, s 37 or under its inherent jurisdiction (*Re P (Care Orders: Injunctive Relief)* [2000] 2 FLR 385, FD). The county court also has no inherent jurisdiction to accept undertakings in care proceedings (*Re B (Supervision Order: Parental Undertaking)* [1996] 1 FLR 676).

Parents' evidence—Parents may be compelled to give evidence in care proceedings and proceedings for supervision orders (*Re Y and K (Split Hearing: Evidence)* [2003] EWCA Civ 669, [2003] 2 FLR 273, CA). General practice will be not to hear oral evidence from children in care proceedings (*Re O (Care Proceedings: Evidence)* [2003] EWHC 2011 (Fam), [2004] 1 FLR 161, FD). Where parents refuse to give oral evidence (and the court does not compel them to give evidence) the court may draw inferences against them that the allegations concerning them are true (*Re O*, above).

Breaches of the European Convention on Human Rights—Where there is a complaint of a breach of a Convention right during the currency of care proceedings, that complaint should be dealt with by the court (eg the family proceedings court) hearing the proceedings and as part of those proceedings. Transfer to the High Court is not necessary and is normally inappropriate (*Re L (Care Proceedings: Human Rights Claims)* [2003] 2 FLR 160, FD; *Re V (Care Proceedings: Human Rights Claims)* [2004] EWCA Civ 54, [2004] 1 FLR 944, CA). The issue of habeas corpus proceedings where care proceedings are in existence is to be deprecated (*Re S (Habeas Corpus); S v Haringey London Borough Council* [2003] EWHC 2734 (Admin), [2004] 1 FLR 590).

[31A *(Section prospectively inserted by Adoption and Children Act 2002, s 121(2) – see* **3.3B** *for text)*]

32 Period within which application for order under this Part must be disposed of

(1) A court hearing an application for an order under this Part shall (in the light of any rules made by virtue of subsection (2)) –

  (a) draw up a timetable with a view to disposing of the application without delay; and
  (b) give such directions as it considers appropriate for the purpose of ensuring, so far as is reasonably practicable, that that timetable is adhered to.

(2) Rules of court may –

  (a) specify periods within which specified steps must be taken in relation to such proceedings; and
  (b) make other provision with respect to such proceedings for the purpose of ensuring, so far as is reasonably practicable, that they are disposed of without delay.

Section 32

Protocol—*Practice Direction (Care Cases: Judicial Continuity and Judicial Case Management)* [2003] 2 FLR 798, [2003] 1 WLR 2209 (included within the Protocol for Judicial Case Management, set out at **6.2**) now contains principles for the proper determination of care cases. The terms and purpose of that protocol should be kept clearly in mind by the courts and, if that purpose requires a departure from the protocol, reasons should be given for that departure (although the protocol should not become a source for satellite or appellate litigation: *Re G (Protocol for Judicial Case Management in Public Law Cases: Application to Become Party in Family Proceedings)* [2004] EWHC 116 (Fam), [2004] 1 FLR 1119, FD).

Practice Direction (Family Proceedings: Court Bundles) [2000] 1 WLR 737, [2000] 1 FLR 536, remains in force and is to be complied with in all cases to which it applies, subject only to the protocol and to any directions which may be given in any particular care case by the case management judge (the 2000 Practice Direction is annexed to the protocol).

Paragraph 2 of the *President's Direction (Judicial Continuity)* [2002] 2 FLR 367 (which paragraph deals with case management in care/supervision proceedings) no longer has effect in any case to which the 2003 Practice Direction and protocol apply.

Paragraph 7 of the pre-hearing review (PHR) checklist in Appendix 5 of the protocol requires the court to consider whether a witness template has been completed and agreed template. Such templates had received the court's approval in *Re EC (Disclosure of Material)* [1996] 2 FLR 123, FD, and *Re T and E (Proceedings: Conflicting Interests)* [1995] 1 FLR 581, FD.

In *Re G, S and M (Wasted Costs)* [2000] 1 FLR 52, Wall J held that it was the collective responsibility of all legal representatives to ensure that, when they attend a pre-hearing review:

(1) the issues in the case to be addressed at the final hearing are clearly identified;
(2) the evidence to address those issues is either already available or that directions are sought from the court to ensure that it is available in good time for the hearing;
(3) all the expert witnesses in the case have been sent – or will prior to giving evidence be sent – all relevant material which has emerged since their reports were written; or where, as here, the material required by an expert witness had not been seen by that witness, that the material would be sent and a further report, if necessary, commissioned;
(4) the witnesses required to give evidence at the hearing have been identified;
(5) the length of time required for the evidence of each witness has been appropriately estimated;
(6) the witnesses have been timetabled;
(7) expert witnesses, in particular, have been allotted specific dates and times for their evidence; and that the length of time allotted for their evidence has been carefully assessed to ensure that it can be given without the witnesses being inconvenienced by having to return to court on a second occasion to complete their evidence;
(8) the documents required for the case are in good order and bundled appropriately; that there is a chronology and, where required, a short statement of case from each party;
(9) the guardian's report will be available in proper time for the hearing;
(10) appropriate reading time and time for an ex tempore judgment has been allowed to the judge.

As to wasted costs, see Supreme Court Act 1981, s 51; CPR 1998, r 48.7, and the Practice Direction supplementing Parts 43 to 48, paras 53.1–53.9; *B v B (Wasted Costs: Abuse of Process)* [2001] 1 FLR 843, FD; and *Medcalf v Mardell* [2002] 3 All ER 721, [2002] 3 WLR 172, HL.

Legal representation—In *P, C and S v UK* (2002) 35 EHRR, [2002] 2 FLR 631 (in which a baby was removed at birth and the mother was refused an adjournment to obtain legal representation) it was held that it was an indispensable requirement that the parents should have legal representation and that the refusal of an adjournment was in breach of Article 6 of the European Convention on Human Rights (see further at **5.6**) – see also *Re G (Children) (Adoption Proceedings: Representation of Parents)* [2001] 1 FCR 353 (mother's counsel retired on third day of care proceedings, judge should have adjourned) but cf *Re B and T (Care Proceedings: Legal Representation)* [2001] 1 FLR 485, CA (parents had changed solicitors four times and had not co-operated with assessments; fifth solicitors and counsel retired; refusal of adjournment justified).

Guardian and protocol—Under the protocol attached to the Practice Direction the children's guardian is to be appointed on day one of the proceedings (unless the court is satisfied that it is not necessary to do so to safeguard the child's interests). On the same day the court must inform CAFCASS of the decision to appoint and the request to allocate a guardian. Within two days of the issue of proceedings (ie by day three), CAFCASS must inform the court of the name of the allocated guardian or the likely date upon which an allocation will be made (see paras 1.2 and 1.3 of the protocol). When a guardian is allocated the guardian must on that day: (a) appoint a solicitor for the child; (b) inform the court of the name of the solicitor appointed; (c) in the event that the guardian's allocation is delayed and the court has already appointed a solicitor, ensure that effective legal representation is maintained (para 1.4 of the protocol, although the guardian clearly cannot do anything if he/she has not been allocated). Where a guardian is not allocated within two days of the issue of proceedings, the court must on day three: (a) consider when a guardian will be allocated; and (b) decide whether to appoint a solicitor for the child (para 1.4 of the protocol). In any event, on the day the appointment is made, the court must notify all parties on form C46 of the names of the guardian and/or the solicitor for the child who have been appointed (para 1.4).

Experts—In *Re G (Minors) (Expert Witnesses)* [1994] 2 FLR 291, Wall J gave this guidance:

'1   Generalised orders giving leave for the papers to be shown to "an expert" or "experts" should never be made. In each case the expert or area of expertise should be identified.

2   As part of the process of granting or refusing leave either for the child to be examined or for papers in the case to be shown to an expert the advocates have a positive duty to place all relevant information before the court and the court has a positive duty to inquire into that information and in particular into the following matters:

(a)   the category of expert evidence which the party in question seeks to adduce;

(b)   the relevance of the expert evidence sought to be adduced to the issues arising for decision in the case;

(c)   whether or not the expert evidence can properly be obtained by the joint instruction of one expert by two or more of the parties;

(d)   whether or not expert evidence in any given category may properly be adduced by only one party (for example by the guardian ad litem) or whether it is necessary for experts in the same discipline to be instructed by more than one party.

3   Where the court exercises its discretion to grant leave for the papers to be shown to a particular expert (whether identified by name or by category of expertise) the court should invariably go on to give directions as to:

(a)   the timescale in which the evidence in question should be produced;

(b)   the disclosure of any report written by an expert both to the parties and to the other experts in the case;

(c)   discussions between experts following future disclosure of reports;

(d)   the filing of further evidence by the experts of the parties stating the areas of agreement and disagreement between the experts.

4   Where it is impractical to give directions under para 3 above at the time leave to disclose the papers is granted, the court should set a date for a further directions appointment at which the directions set out in para 3 can be given.

5   Whether it is necessary to consider the estimated length of hearing at a directions appointment the number of expert witnesses and the likely length of their evidence should be carefully considered and the exercise which I have set out in *Re MD and TD (Minors)* [1994] 2 FLR 336, [1994] 2 FCR 94, FD, undertaken.

6   It is a commonplace of care cases for the local authority to wish at the outset to carry out an assessment. Where this occurs, the court should in my judgment adopt the following approach:

(1)   It should specify the time in which the assessment is to be carried out and direct that evidence of the outcome of the assessment be filed by a given date.

(2)   It should fix a directions appointment for a date immediately after the date fixed for the completion of the assessments and to reassess the case and give further directions for a speedy trial.

(3)   Once the local authority assessment is available, immediate thought should be given at the directions appointment following its disclosure to the evidence (expert and otherwise) required to bring the case speedily and fairly to trial. Any directions for expert evidence should identify the areas of expertise for which leave is given and lay down a time-table as per para 3 above.

(4)   Where a date for the final trial can be fixed before the assessment is complete that should be done. More commonly, however, it will only be possible to assess the likely length of a case once the initial assessment is complete and the issues in the case emerge.'

Care orders

33 Effect of care order

(1) Where a care order is made with respect to a child it shall be the duty of the local authority designated by the order to receive the child into their care and to keep him in their care while the order remains in force.

(2) Where –

    (a) a care order has been made with respect to a child on the application of an authorised person; but

    (b) the local authority designated by the order was not informed that that person proposed to make the application,

the child may be kept in the care of that person until received into the care of the authority.

(3) While a care order is in force with respect to a child, the local authority designated by the order shall –

    (a) have parental responsibility for the child; and

    (b) have the power (subject to the following provisions of this section) to determine the extent to which a parent or guardian of the child may meet his parental responsibility for him.

(4) The authority may not exercise the power in subsection (3)(b) unless they are satisfied that it is necessary to do so in order to safeguard or promote the child's welfare.

(5) Nothing in subsection (3)(b) shall prevent a parent or guardian of the child who has care of him from doing what is reasonable in all the circumstances of the case for the purpose of safeguarding or promoting his welfare.

(6) While a care order is in force with respect to a child, the local authority designated by the order shall not –

    (a) cause the child to be brought up in any religious persuasion other than that in which he would have been brought up if the order had not been made; or

    (b) have the right –

        (i)   to consent or refuse to consent to the making of an application with respect to the child under section 18 of the Adoption Act 1976;

        (ii) to agree or refuse to agree to the making of an adoption order, or an order under section 55 of the Act of 1976, with respect to the child; or

        (iii) to appoint a guardian for the child.

(7) While a care order is in force with respect to a child, no person may –

    (a) cause the child to be known by a new surname; or

    (b) remove him from the United Kingdom,

without either the written consent of every person who has parental responsibility for the child or the leave of the court.

(8) Subsection (7)(b) does not –

    (a) prevent the removal of such a child, for a period of less than one month, by the authority in whose care he is; or

    (b) apply to arrangements for such a child to live outside England and Wales (which are governed by paragraph 19 of Schedule 2).

(9) The power in subsection (3)(b) is subject (in addition to being subject to the provisions of this section) to any right, duty, power, responsibility or authority which a parent or guardian of the child has in relation to the child and his property by virtue of any other enactment.

Section 33

Prospective amendment—Section prospectively amended by Adoption and Children Act 2002, s 139(1), Sch 3, paras 54, 63 (see **3.3B**).

Generally—In deciding which local authority should be designated in an order, the court will take into account the factors identified in the cases of *Re H (Care Order: Appropriate Local Authority)* [2003] EWCA Civ 1629, [2004] 1 FLR 534, CA, *Northamptonshire County Council v Islington London Borough Council and Others* [2001] Fam 364, [1999] 2 FLR 881, CA, and *Kirklees Metropolitan Borough Council v London Borough of Brent* [2004] 2 FLR 800, FD (the provisions of s 105 of the CA 1989 do not apply to a period when the child is placed at home with a parent under an interim care order). In the case of *London Borough of Redbridge v Newport City Council* [2003] EWHC 2967 (Fam), [2004] 2 FLR 226, it was held by David Hershman QC, sitting as a deputy High Court judge, as follows:

(i) under s 105, any period that the child spent in local authority accommodation (including in a residential unit) should be disregarded, although periods at home with a parent should not;

(ii) the time for deciding on a child's 'ordinary residence' is when the case was determined by the court, and not when the proceedings were commenced.

34 Parental contact etc with children in care

(1) Where a child is in the care of a local authority, the authority shall (subject to the provisions of this section) allow the child reasonable contact with –

(a) his parents;

(b) any guardian of his;

(c) where there was a residence order in force with respect to the child immediately before the care order was made, the person in whose favour the order was made; and

(d) where, immediately before the care order was made, a person had care of the child by virtue of an order made in the exercise of the High Court's inherent jurisdiction with respect to children, that person.

(2) On an application made by the authority or the child, the court may make such order as it considers appropriate with respect to the contact which is to be allowed between the child and any named person.

(3) On an application made by –

(a) any person mentioned in paragraph (a) to (d) of subsection (1); or

(b) any person who has obtained the leave of the court to make the application,

the court may make such order as it considers appropriate with respect to the contact which is to be allowed between the child and that person.

(4) On an application made by the authority or the child, the court may make an order authorising the authority to refuse to allow contact between the child and any person who is mentioned in paragraphs (a) to (d) of subsection (1) and named in the order.

(5) When making a care order with respect to a child, or in any family proceedings in connection with a child who is in the care of a local authority, the court may make an order under this section, even though no application for such an order has been made with respect to the child, if it considers that the order should be made.

(6) An authority may refuse to allow the contact that would otherwise be required by virtue of subsection (1) or an order under this section if –

(a) they are satisfied that it is necessary to do so in order to safeguard or promote the child's welfare; and

(b) the refusal –

    (i) is decided upon as a matter of urgency; and

    (ii) does not last for more than seven days.

(7) An order under this section may impose such conditions as the court considers appropriate.

(8) The Secretary of State may by regulations make provision as to –

(a) the steps to be taken by a local authority who have exercised their power under subsection (6);

(b) the circumstances in which, and conditions subject to which, the terms of any order under this section may be departed from by agreement between the local authority and the person in relation to whom the order is made;

(c) notification by a local authority of any variation or suspension of arrangements made (otherwise than under an order under this section) with a view to affording any person contact with a child to whom this section applies.

(9) The court may vary or discharge any order made under this section on the application of the authority, the child concerned or the person named in the order.

(10) An order under this section may be made either at the same time as the care order itself or later.

(11) Before making a care order with respect to any child the court shall –

(a) consider the arrangements which the authority have made, or propose to make, for affording any person contact with a child to whom this section applies; and

(b) invite the parties to the proceedings to comment on those arrangements.

Section 34

Prospective amendment—Section prospectively amended by Adoption and Children Act 2002, s 139(1), Sch 3, paras 54, 64 (see **3.3B**).

Before making a care order—As is plain from s 34(11) the court must consider the arrangements for contact before making a care order. The provisions of s 34 should be read in association with those of CA 1989, Sch 2, para 15 (which define a local authority's duties to promote and maintain contact between a child and its family). Reference should also be made to the Contact with Children Regulations 1991, SI 1991/891, under which, for instance, an order for contact under s 34 may be varied by agreement between the local authority and the person in whose favour the order is made. *The Children Act 1989 Guidance and Regulations* (HMSO, 1991), vol 3: *Family Placements* gives guidance in relation to these provisions.

Reasonable contact—In the absence of specific order, s 34(1) states that the local authority must allow the child *reasonable contact* with the individuals listed in that subsection (see, eg, *Re S (A Minor) (Care: Contact Order)* [1994] 2 FLR 222, CA). This may not be the same as contact at the local authority's discretion (see *Re P (Minors) (Contact with Children in Care)* [1993] 2 FLR 156, CA, but cf *L v London Borough of Bromley* [1998] 1 FLR 709, FD). 'Reasonable contact' connotes an agreement between the local authority and those involved. Contact may be of benefit to a child in care even where rehabilitation is not being contemplated (*Re E (A Minor) (Care Order: Contact)* [1994] 1 FLR 146, CA). In *Re B (Minors) (Termination of Contact: Paramount Consideration)* [1993] Fam 301, [1993] 3 All ER 524, [1994] 3

WLR 63; sub nom *Re B (Minors) (Care: Contact: Local Authority's Plans)* [1993] 1 FLR 543, CA, Butler-Sloss LJ said:

'Contact applications generally fall into two main categories, those which ask for contact as such, and those which are attempts to set aside the care order itself. In the first category, there is no suggestion that the applicant wishes to take over the care of the child and the issue of contact often depends upon whether contact would frustrate long-term plans for the child in a substitute home, such as adoption where continuing contact may not be for the long-term welfare of the child. The presumption of contact, which has to be for the benefit of the child, has always to be balanced against the long-term welfare of the child and particularly where he will live in the future. Contact must not be allowed to destabilize or endanger the arrangements for the child and in many cases the plans for the child will be decisive of the contact application. There may also be cases where the parent is having satisfactory contact with the child and there are no long-term plans or those plans do not appear to the court to preclude some future contact. The proposals of the local authority, based on their appreciation of the best interests of the child, must command the greatest respect and consideration from the court, but Parliament has given to the court, and not to the local authority, the duty to decide on contact between the child and those named in s 34(1). Consequently, the court may have the task of requiring the local authority to justify their long-term plans to the extent only that those plans exclude contact between parent and child.

In the second category contact applications may be made by parents by way of another attempt to obtain the return of the children. In such a case the court is obviously entitled to take into account the failure to apply to discharge the care order and in the majority of cases the court will have little difficulty in coming to the conclusion that the applicant cannot demonstrate that contact with a view to rehabilitation with the parent is a viable proposition at that stage, particularly if it had already been rejected at the earlier hearing when the child was placed in care. The task for the parents will be too great and the court would be entitled to assume that the plans of the local authority to terminate contact are for the welfare of the child and are not to be frustrated by inappropriate contact with a view to the remote possibility, at some future date, of rehabilitation. But in all cases the welfare section has to be considered, and the local authority has the task of justifying the cessation of contact. There may also be unusual cases where either the local authority has not made effective plans or there has been considerable delay in implementing them and a parent, who had previously been found by the court unable or unwilling to care for the child so that a care order had been made, comes back upon the scene as a possible future primary caretaker. If the local authority with a care order decides not to consider that parent on the new facts, Mr Munby argued that it is for the court, with the enhanced jurisdiction of the Children Act, to consider whether even at this late stage there should be some investigation of the proposals of the parent, with the possibility of reconsidering the local authority plans. Mr Horrocks argued that the court cannot go behind the long-term plans of the local authority unless they were acting capriciously or were otherwise open to scrutiny by way of judicial review. I unhesitatingly reject the local authority argument. As I have already said, their plan has to be given the greatest possible consideration by the court and it is only in the unusual case that a parent will be able to convince the court, the onus being firmly on the parent, that there has been such a change of circumstances as to require further investigation and reconsideration of the local authority plan. If, however, a court was unable to intervene, it would make a nonsense of the paramountcy of the welfare of the child, which is the bedrock of the Act, and would subordinate it to the administrative decision of the local authority in a situation where the court is seised of the contact issue. That cannot be right.'

Prohibition of contact—Section 34(4) does not create a prohibitory jurisdiction. Therefore the court cannot order a local authority not to provide contact between a parent and a child (*Re W (Section 34(2) Orders)* [2000] 1 FLR 502).

Human rights—Section 34 is human rights compliant (*Re F (Care: Termination of Contact)* [2000] 2 FCR 481). Where the court considers issues relating to contact, the child's welfare is paramount (*Re B (Minors) (Termination of Contact: Paramount Consideration)* [1993] Fam 301, [1993] 3 All ER 524, [1994] 3 WLR 63, [1993] 1 FLR 543, CA, and *Re E (A Minor) (Care Order: Contact)* [1994] 1 FLR 146, CA). The contact provisions within a care plan will be considered by the court and will form an important part of the manner in which a local authority honours its responsibilities under Article 8 of the European Convention on Human Rights (*Re F; F v Lambeth London Borough Council* [2001] 2 FLR 1217).

Child applicant—Where the application for contact is by a person who is herself a child (eg a 17-year-old mother seeking contact with her baby) it is the welfare of the child who is the subject of the proceedings which is paramount (ie the baby) and not that of the applicant (*Birmingham City Council v H (A Minor)* [1994] 2 AC 212, [1994] 1 All ER 12, [1994] 2 WLR 31, [1994] 1 FLR 224, HL).

Review—The court may order a review of contact following the making of a contact order but should not do so as a means of controlling the care plan for the child (*Re B (A Minor) (Care Order: Review)* [1993] 1 FLR 421, FD, and *Re S (A Minor) (Care: Contact Order)* [1994] 2 FLR 222, CA).

Permissive—Under s 34(4) the court may authorise a local authority to refuse contact to those who would otherwise be entitled to reasonable contact. The CA 1989 also permits a short-term suspension of contact within the provisions of s 34(6). An order under s 34(6) is permissive (ie it permits the local authority to refuse contact) rather than mandatory (ie it does not order the local authority to refuse that contact). There must be compelling reasons for an order refusing contact (*A v M and Walsall Metropolitan Borough Council* [1993] 2 FLR 244, FD, and *Re J-S (Contact: Parental Responsibility)* [2002] EWCA Civ 1028, [2003] 1 FLR 399, CA). Where the care plan is for adoption, the termination of contact will usually be better decided at the adoption hearing (*Re P (Adoption: Freeing Order)* [1994] 2 FLR 1000, and *Re G (Adoption: Contact)* [2002] EWCA Civ 761, [2003] 1 FLR 270, CA).

Interim orders—Interim orders may be made. Unless there is a severe risk, contact should be maintained pending the final hearing (*A v M and Walsall Metropolitan Borough Council* [1993] 2 FLR 244).

Leave—On an application for leave to make an application for contact, the court will consider the provisions of CA 1989, s 10(9). It has been said that the court should consider the factors identified in *Re M (Care: Contact: Grandmother's Application for Leave)* [1995] 2 FLR 86, CA, *Re A (Section 8 Order: Grandparent Application)* [1995] 2 FLR 153, CA, and *Re W (A Child) (Contact: Leave to Apply)* [2000] 1 FCR 185, FD. However, in the case of *Re J (Leave to Issue Application for Residence Order)* [2003] 1 FLR 114, it was said that, although the test in *Re M* had served a valuable purpose in its day, the test expounded in that case should not be used as a substitute for s 10(9) on applications for permission to apply under s 8.

There has been a growing appreciation of 'what grandparents have to offer' and judges should be careful not to dismiss applications for grandparents without a full enquiry (*Re J (Leave to Issue Application for Residence Order)* [2003] 1 FLR 114).

Evidence—The court has a discretion as to the amount of evidence it should hear on an application under the CA 1989 (including contact) (*Re B (Minors) (Contact)* [1994] 2 FLR 1, CA). It will rarely be right to refuse to permit a party to give evidence (*Re I and H (Contact: Right to Give Evidence)* [1998] 1 FLR 876, CA, and *Re V (Children) (Residence: Interim Care Order)* [2002] EWCA Civ 1225, [2002] 3 FCR 562, CA). However, in exceptional circumstances the court may refuse to hear oral evidence from the party concerned (*Re B (Contact: Stepfather's Opposition)* [1997] 2 FLR 579, CA). The duty under Article 6 of the European Convention on Human Rights to ensure a fair trial subsists throughout the proceedings and is not limited to the judge's functions (*Re L (Care Assessment: Fair Trial)* [2002] EWHC 1379, [2002] 2 FLR 730, FD). In private law proceedings it has been said that a contact application should only be struck out in most exceptional circumstances and an order to that effect should only be made where the contact application has no prospect whatsoever of success (*Re T (A Minor) (Parental Responsibility: Contact)* [1993] 2 FLR 450, CA; *Re B (Minors) (Contact)* [1994] 2 FLR 1, CA; and *Re U (Children) (Contact)* [2004] 1 FCR 768, CA).

Supervision orders

35 Supervision orders

(1) While a supervision order is in force it shall be the duty of the supervisor –

    (a) to advise, assist and befriend the supervised child;

    (b) to take such steps as are reasonably necessary to give effect to the order; and

    (c) where –

        (i) the order is not wholly complied with; or

        (ii) the supervisor considers that the order may no longer be necessary,

to consider whether or not to apply to the court for its variation or discharge.

(2) Parts I and II of Schedule 3 make further provision with respect to supervision orders.

Section 35

The main provisions relating to supervision orders are to be found in CA 1989, Sch 3. Although it was held that where a supervision order was made, the proceedings did not come to an end until the supervision order expired (by reason of the original wording of the Criminal Justice and Court Services Act 2000, s 12(5) – *Re MH, Re SB and Re MB* [2001] 2 FLR 1334), the relevant words of s 12(5) were repealed as from 28 November 2003 (by Adoption and Children Act 2002, s 139(1), (3), Sch 3, Sch 5, para 118(5) (see SI 2003/3079, art 2(1)(c)).

It is not possible to attach conditions to a supervision order beyond those set out in CA 1989, Sch 3 (*Re V (Care or Supervision Order)* [1996] 1 FLR 776, CA).

An application to extend a supervision order under Sch 3, para 6(4) should be decided by applying the welfare considerations of s 1; it is not necessary to prove the s 31 threshold criteria again (*Re A (A Minor) (Supervision Order: Extension)* [1995] 3 All ER 401, [1995] 1 WLR 482). Where there are such difficulties over contact that CA 1989, s 31 is fulfilled, the court may make a supervision order to assist with those difficulties (*Re Z and A (Contact: Supervision Order)* [2000] 2 FLR 406; *Re M (Intractable Contact Dispute: Interim Care Order)* [2003] 2 FLR 636, FD).

The notes to s 31 above set out the cases dealing with when a court should make a supervision order rather than a care order (see, in particular, *Re O (Supervision Order)* [2001] EWCA Civ 16, [2001] 1 FLR 923, CA, and *Re C (Care Order or Supervision Order)* [2001] 2 FLR 466, FD).

A supervision order may be made for less than one year (*M v Warwickshire County Council* [1994] 2 FLR 593).

36 Education supervision orders

(1) On the application of any local education authority, the court may make an order putting the child with respect to whom the application is made under the supervision of a designated local education authority.

(2) In this Act 'an education supervision order' means an order under subsection (1).

(3) A court may only make an education supervision order if it is satisfied that the child concerned is of compulsory school age and is not being properly educated.

(4) For the purposes of this section, a child is being properly educated only if he is receiving efficient full-time education suitable to his age, ability and aptitude and any special educational needs he may have.

(5) Where a child is –

(a) the subject of a school attendance order which is in force under section 437 of the Education Act 1996 and which has not been complied with; or

(b) a registered pupil at a school which he is not attending regularly within the meaning of section 444 of that Act,

then, unless it is proved that he is being properly educated, it shall be assumed that he is not.

(6) An education supervision order may not be made with respect to a child who is in the care of a local authority.

(7) The local education authority designated in an education supervision order must be –

(a) the authority within whose area the child concerned is living or will live; or

(b) where –

(i) the child is a registered pupil at a school; and

(ii) the authority mentioned in paragraph (a) and the authority within whose area the school is situated agree,

the latter authority.

(8) Where a local education authority propose to make an application for an education supervision order they shall, before making the application, consult the appropriate local authority.

(9) The appropriate local authority is –

(a) in the case of a child who is being provided with accommodation by, or on behalf of, a local authority, that authority; and

(b) in any other case, the local authority within whose area the child concerned lives, or will live.

(10) Part III of Schedule 3 makes further provision with respect to education supervision orders.

Section 36

Other provision is made in relation to education or supervision orders in CA 1989, Sch 3. The application can only be made by the local education authority (s 36(1)). The proceedings are not specified within CA 1989, s 41(6), and therefore a guardian will not be appointed in relation to the child (*Essex County Council v B* [1993] 1 FLR 866). Although such orders may be the usual method of enforcing school attendance, it may be necessary to consider the making of care orders in a case where the threshold criteria under s 31 are fulfilled (*Re O (A Minor) (Care Proceedings: Education)* [1992] 4 All ER 905, [1992] 1 WLR 912).

In *A v Head Teacher and Governors of Lord Grey School* [2003] EWHC 1533, [2003] 4 All ER 1317, QBD, a claim for damages under the Human Rights Act 1998 by a child who had been excluded from the school was rejected.

Powers of court

37 Powers of court in certain family proceedings

(1) Where, in any family proceedings in which a question arises with respect to the welfare of any child, it appears to the court that it may be appropriate for a care or supervision order to be made with respect to him, the court may direct the appropriate authority to undertake an investigation of the child's circumstances.

(2) Where the court gives a direction under this section the local authority concerned shall, when undertaking the investigation, consider whether they should –

    (a) apply for a care order or for a supervision order with respect to the child;

    (b) provide services or assistance for the child or his family; or

    (c) take any other action with respect to the child.

(3) Where a local authority undertake an investigation under this section, and decide not to apply for a care order or supervision order with respect to the child concerned, they shall inform the court of –

    (a) their reasons for so deciding;

    (b) any service or assistance which they have provided, or to intend to provide, for the child and his family; and

    (c) any other action which they have taken, or propose to take, with respect to the child.

(4) The information shall be given to the court before the end of the period of eight weeks beginning with the date of the direction, unless the court otherwise directs.

(5) The local authority named in a direction under subsection (1) must be –

    (a) the authority in whose area the child is ordinarily resident; or

    (b) where the child is not ordinarily resident in the area of a local authority, the authority within whose area any circumstances arose in consequence of which the direction is being given.

(6) If, on the conclusion of any investigation or review under this section, the authority decide not to apply for a care order or supervision order with respect to the child –

    (a) they shall consider whether it would be appropriate to review the case at a later date; and

    (b) if they decide that it would be, they shall determine the date on which that review is to begin.

Section 37

It is wrong for a court to use the provisions of s 37 in private law proceedings if care or supervision orders are not in contemplation (*Re L (Section 37 Direction)* [1999] 1 FLR 984; *Re CE (Section 37 Direction)* [1995] 1 FLR 26). However, the provisions of s 37 should be widely construed and may 'include any situation which may have a bearing on the child being likely to suffer significant harm in the future' (*Re H (A Minor) (Section 37 Direction)* [1993] 2 FLR 541, FD). The procedure to be followed is specified in FPR 1991, r 4.26 and FPC(CA 1989)R 1991, r 27. The procedure to be followed is also considered in the case of *Re CE (Section 37 Direction)* [1995] 1 FLR 26, FD. Where a local authority decides that it will not apply for care or supervision orders, it should not be joined as a party to the relevant family proceedings (*F v Cambridgeshire County Council* [1995] 1 FLR 516, FD).

38 Interim orders

(1) Where –

    (a) in any proceedings on an application for a care order or supervision order, the proceedings are adjourned; or

    (b) the court gives a direction under section 37(1).

the court may make an interim care order or an interim supervision order with respect to the child concerned.

(2) A court shall not make an interim care order or interim supervision order under this section unless it is satisfied that there are reasonable grounds for believing that circumstances with respect to the child are as mentioned in section 31(2).

(3) Where, in any proceedings on an application for a care order or supervision order, a court makes a residence order with respect to the child concerned, it shall also make an interim supervision order with respect to him unless satisfied that his welfare will be satisfactorily safeguarded without an interim order being made.

(4) An interim order made under or by virtue of this section shall have effect for such period as may be specified in the order, but shall in any event cease to have effect on whichever of the following events first occurs –

    (a) the expiry of the period of eight weeks beginning with the date on which the order is made;

    (b) if the order is the second or subsequent such order made with respect to the same child in the same proceedings, the expiry of the relevant period;

    (c) in a case which falls within subsection (1)(a), the disposal of the application;

    (d) in a case which falls within subsection (1)(b), the disposal of an application for a care order or a supervision order made by the authority with respect to the child;

    (e) in a case which falls within subsection (1)(b) and in which –

        (i) the court has given a direction under section 37(4), but

        (ii) no application for a care order or supervision order has been made with respect to the child,

    the expiry of the period fixed by that direction.

(5) In subsection (4)(b) 'the relevant period' means –

    (a) the period of four weeks beginning with the date on which the order in question is made; or

    (b) the period of eight weeks beginning with the date on which the first order was made if that period ends later than the period mentioned in paragraph (a).

(6) Where the court makes an interim care order, or interim supervision order, it may give such directions (if any) as it considers appropriate with regard to the medical or psychiatric examination or other assessment of the child; but if the child is of sufficient understanding to make an informed decision he may refuse to submit to the examination or other assessment.

(7) A direction under subsection (6) may be to the effect that there is to be –

    (a) no such examination or assessment; or

    (b) no such examination or assessment unless the court directs otherwise.

(8) A direction under subsection (6) may be –

    (a) given when the interim order is made or at any time while it is in force; and

    (b) varied at any time on the application of any person falling within any class of person prescribed by rules of court for the purposes of this subsection.

(9) Paragraphs 4 and 5 of Schedule 3 shall not apply in relation to an interim supervision order.

(10) Where a court makes an order under or by virtue of this section it shall, in determining the period for which the order is to be in force, consider whether any

party who was, or might have been, opposed to the making of the order was in a position to argue his case against the order in full.

Section 38

In order for the court to make an interim care order or interim supervision order it need only have *reasonable grounds* for believing that the threshold criteria in s 31(2) are satisfied (see s 38(2)); justices' reasons should make it plain that they have applied the correct test (and not the test under s 31) (*Oxfordshire County Council v S* [2003] EWHC 2174 (Fam)).

The rights of parents under Articles 6 and 8 of the European Convention on Human Rights will require a judge to abstain from a premature determination of the case unless the welfare of the child demands it. Thus immediate separation will only be contemplated if the child's safety so demands (*Re H (A Child) (Interim Care Order)* [2002] EWCA Civ 1942, [2003] 1 FCR 350). The intention of the section is to safeguard the welfare of the child until the court is in a position to decide upon the substantive application (*Re S (Minors) (Care Order: Implementation of Care Plan), Re W (Minors) (Care Order: Adequacy of Care Plan)* [2002] 2 AC 291, [2002] 1 FLR 815, HL).

Where there are significant gaps in the care plan the court will refuse to make a final care order (*Re CH (Care or Interim Care Order)* [1998] 1 FLR 402, CA). A planned and purposeful delay may justify the making of an interim order, rather than a final order (*C v Solihull Metropolitan Borough Council* [1993] 1 FLR 290). However the court should not seek to control the exercise by the local authority of the care plan (*Re R (Care Proceedings: Adjournment)* [1998] 2 FLR 390, CA). In the case of *Hampshire County Council v S* [1993] Fam 158, [1993] 2 WLR 216, [1993] 1 FLR 559, Cazalet J gave guidance as to how magistrates should approach interim care applications. The guidance of Cazalet J has been held to apply to the High Court and county court (*Re W (A Minor) (Interim Care Order)* [1994] 2 FLR 892, CA). Guidance was as follows:

'(1) Justices should bear in mind that they are not, at an interim hearing, required to make a final conclusion; indeed it is because they are unable to reach a final conclusion that they are empowered to make an interim order. An interim order or decision will usually be required so as to establish a holding position, after weighing all the relevant risks, pending the final hearing. Nevertheless justices must always ensure that the substantive issue is tried and determined at the earliest appropriate date. Any delay in determining the question before the court is likely to prejudice the welfare of the child: see section 1(2) of the Act;

(2) If justices find they are unable to provide the appropriate hearing time, be it through pressure of work or some other reason, they must, when an urgent interim order may have to be made, consider taking steps pursuant to rule 14(2)(h) to transfer the proceedings laterally to an adjacent family proceedings court;

(3) At the end of a hearing which is concerned with interim relief, justices will usually be called upon to exercise their discretion under rule 21(2) as to the order of speeches and evidence. The circumstances prevailing will almost certainly not permit full evidence to be heard. Accordingly, in such proceedings, justices should rarely make findings as to dispute of facts. These will have to be left over to the final hearing;

(4) Justices must bear in mind that the greater the extent to which an interim order deviates from a previous order or the status quo, the more acute the need is likely to be for an early final hearing. Any disruption in a child's life almost invariably requires early resolution. Justices should be cautious about changing a child's residence under an interim order. The preferred course should be to leave the child where it is with a direction for safeguards and the earliest possible hearing;

(5) When an interim order may be made which will lead to a substantial change in a child's position, justices should consider permitting limited oral evidence to be led and challenged by way of cross-examination. However it will necessarily follow that, in cross-examination, the evidence will have to be restricted to the issues which are essential at the interim stage. To this end the court may well have to intervene to ensure that this course is followed and there is not a dress rehearsal of the full hearing;

(6) Justices should, if possible, ensure that they have before them written advice from the guardian ad litem. When there are substantial issues between the parties the guardian should, if possible, be at court to give oral evidence. A party who is opposed to a recommendation made by the guardian should normally be given an opportunity to put questions to him/her in regard to advice given to the court;

(7) Justices must always comply with the mandatory requirements of the Rules. These include compliance with (a) rule 21(1), which requires the justices to read, before the hearing, any documents which have been filed under rule 17; (b) rule 21(5), which requires the justices' clerk to make the appropriate written record of the hearing and in consultation with the justices to record the reasons for the court's decision and any findings of fact; and (c) rule 21(6) which requires the court, when making its order or giving its decision to state any findings of fact and the reasons for the court's decision;

(8) If shortage of time or some other circumstance delays the court in the preparation of its written findings of fact and reasons, justices should adjourn the making of their order or the giving of their decision until the following court day or the earliest possible date. At that further hearing it is permissible for one or other of their number to return to court and state the decision, findings of fact and reasons (see rule 21(6)). When the length of a hearing lasts beyond normal hours it will often be sensible for the court to take this court so that it is not formulating its reasons and making perhaps a difficult decision under the sort of pressure which can arise when a sitting runs late into the date.'

On an application to renew an interim order, the court may limit its enquiry to whether anything significant has changed (*Re B (Interim Care Orders: Renewal)* [2001] 2 FLR 1217, FD).

Section 38(6)—On an application for an assessment under s 38(6) the essential question should always be: 'can what is sought be broadly classified as an assessment to enable the court to obtain the information necessary for its own decision?'. The court should not distil the essential question to: 'is what is proposed assessment or therapy?'. The court should take into account the aim identified by Hale LJ in *Re C and B (Care Order: Future Harm)* [2001] 1 FLR 611, namely to reunite the family when the circumstances enable that, and thus serious and sustained efforts should be made by the relevant public authorities towards achieving that end (*Re G (Interim Care Order: Residential Assessment)* [2004] EWCA Civ 24, [2004] 1 FLR 317, and see also the cases under Article 8 of the European Convention on Human Rights). Such assessments may fall within the ambit of s 38(6) (*Re C (A Minor) (Interim Care Order: Residential Assessment)* [1997] AC 489, [1997] 1 FLR 1, HL). Where a local authority opposes an application on the grounds of expense, it must provide full evidence of the basis of that opposition and must demonstrate that it has sought contribution towards funding from other public authorities, such as the health and educational authorities (*Re C (Children) (Residential Assessment)* [2001] EWCA Civ 1305, [2001] 3 FCR 164 and *B County Council v L* [2002] EWHC 2327 (Fam)). The decision of Holman J in *Re M (Residential Assessment Directions)* [1998] 2 FLR 371 should not be regarded as a guideline case (*Re G*, above). A court may order a named social worker to carry out an assessment under s 38(6), although such orders are not to be encouraged (*Re W (Assessment of Child)* [1998] 2 FLR 130, CA).

38A Power to include exclusion requirement in interim care order

(1) Where –

    (a) on being satisfied that there are reasonable grounds for believing that the circumstances with respect to a child are as mentioned in section 31(2)(a) and (b)(i), the court makes an interim care order with respect to a child, and

    (b) the conditions mentioned in subsection (2) are satisfied,

the court may include an exclusion requirement in the interim care order.

(2) The conditions are –

(a) that there is reasonable cause to believe that, if a person ('the relevant person') is excluded from a dwelling-house in which the child lives, the child will cease to suffer, or cease to be likely to suffer, significant harm, and

(b) that another person living in the dwelling-house (whether a parent of the child or some other person) –

   (i) is able and willing to give to the child the care which it would be reasonable to expect a parent to give him, and

   (ii) consents to the inclusion of the exclusion requirement.

(3) For the purposes of this section an exclusion requirement is any one or more of the following –

(a) a provision requiring the relevant person to leave a dwelling-house in which he is living with the child,

(b) a provision prohibiting the relevant person from entering a dwelling-house in which the child lives, and

(c) a provision excluding the relevant person from a defined area in which a dwelling-house in which the child lives is situated.

(4) The court may provide that the exclusion requirement is to have effect for a shorter period than the other provisions of the interim care order.

(5) Where the court makes an interim care order containing an exclusion requirement, the court may attach a power of arrest to the exclusion requirement.

(6) Where the court attaches a power of arrest to an exclusion requirement of an interim care order, it may provide that the power of arrest is to have effect for a shorter period than the exclusion requirement.

(7) Any period specified for the purposes of subsection (4) or (6) may be extended by the court (on one or more occasions) on an application to vary or discharge the interim care order.

(8) Where a power of arrest is attached to an exclusion requirement of an interim care order by virtue of subsection (5), a constable may arrest without warrant any person whom he has reasonable cause to believe to be in breach of the requirement.

(9) Sections 47(7), (11) and (12) and 48 of, and Schedule 5 to, the Family Law Act 1996 shall have effect in relation to a person arrested under subsection (8) of this section as they have effect in relation to a person arrested under section 47(6) of that Act.

(10) If, while an interim care order containing an exclusion requirement is in force, the local authority have removed the child from the dwelling-house from which the relevant person is excluded to other accommodation for a continuous period of more than 24 hours, the interim care order shall cease to have effect in so far as it imposes the exclusion requirement.

Section 38A

Where an exclusion requirement is made, the applicant will have to serve a separate statement upon the person who is to be excluded together with a copy of the order excluding him. The procedure in relation to this is set out in FPC(CA 1989)R 1991, r 25A and FPR 1991, r 4.24A. This procedure was considered in the case of *Re W (Exclusion: Statement of Evidence)* [2000] 2 FLR 666, FD.

38B Undertakings relating to interim care orders

(1) In any case where the court has power to include an exclusion requirement in an interim care order, the court may accept an undertaking from the relevant person.

(2) No power of arrest may be attached to any undertaking given under subsection (1).

(3) An undertaking given to a court under subsection (1) –

- (a) shall be enforceable as if it were an order of the court, and
- (b) shall cease to have effect if, while it is in force, the local authority have removed the child from the dwelling-house from which the relevant person is excluded to other accommodation for a continuous period of more than 24 hours.

(4) This section has effect without prejudice to the powers of the High Court and county court apart from this section.

(5) In this section 'exclusion requirement' and 'relevant person' have the same meaning as in section 38A.

39 Discharge and variation etc of care orders and supervision orders

(1) A care order may be discharged by the court on the application of –

- (a) any person who has parental responsibility for the child;
- (b) the child himself; or
- (c) the local authority designated by the order.

(2) A supervision order may be varied or discharged by the court on the application of –

- (a) any person who has parental responsibility for the child;
- (b) the child himself; or
- (c) the supervisor.

(3) On the application of a person who is not entitled to apply for the order to be discharged, but who is a person with whom the child is living, a supervision order may be varied by the court in so far as it imposes a requirement which affects that person.

(3A) On the application of a person who is not entitled to apply for the order to be discharged, but who is a person to whom an exclusion requirement contained in the order applies, an interim care order may be varied or discharged by the court in so far as it imposes the exclusion requirement.

(3B) Where a power of arrest has been attached to an exclusion requirement of an interim care order, the court may, on the application of any person entitled to apply for the discharge of the order so far as it imposes the exclusion requirement, vary or discharge the order in so far as it confers a power of arrest (whether or not any application has been made to vary or discharge any other provision of the order).

(4) Where a care order is in force with respect to a child the court may, on the application of any person entitled to apply for the order to be discharged, substitute a supervision order for the care order.

(5) When a court is considering whether to substitute one order for another under subsection (4) any provision of this Act which would otherwise require section 31(2)

to be satisfied at the time when the proposed order is substituted or made shall be disregarded.

Section 39

An application to discharge or vary care or supervision orders will be determined through the application of the provisions of s 1 of the CA 1989 (ie the child's welfare is paramount). The burden of proof rests upon the person seeking the order (*Re MD and TD (Minors) (Time Estimates)* [1994] 2 FLR 336, FD). Public care should be discontinued as soon as circumstances permit (*KA v Finland* (App No 27751/95) [2003] 1 FLR 696).

40 Orders pending appeals in cases about care or supervision orders

(1) Where –

    (a) a court dismisses an application for a care order; and

    (b) at the time when the court dismisses the application, the child concerned is the subject of an interim care order,

the court may make a care order with respect to the child to have effect subject to such directions (if any) as the court may see fit to include in the order.

(2) Where –

    (a) a court dismisses an application for a care order, or an application for a supervision order; and

    (b) at the time when the court dismisses the application, the child concerned is the subject of an interim supervision order,

the court may make a supervision order with respect to the child to have effect subject to such directions (if any) as the court sees fit to include in the order.

(3) Where a court grants an application to discharge a care order or supervision order, it may order that –

    (a) its decision is not to have effect; or

    (b) the care order, or supervision order, is to continue to have effect but subject to such directions as the court sees fit to include in the order.

(4) An order made under this section shall only have effect for such a period, not exceeding the appeal period, as may be specified in the order.

(5) Where –

    (a) an appeal is made against any decision of a court under this section; or

    (b) any application is made to the appellate court in connection with a proposed appeal against that decision,

the appellate court may extend the period for which the order in question is to have effect, but not so as to extend it beyond the end of the appeal period.

(6) In this section 'the appeal period' means –

    (a) where an appeal is made against the decision in question, the period between the making of that decision and the determination of the appeal; and

    (b) otherwise, the period during which an appeal may be made against the decision.

Representation of child

41 Representation of child and of his interests in certain proceedings

(1) For the purpose of any specified proceedings, the court shall appoint an officer of the Service for the child concerned unless satisfied that it is not necessary to do so in order to safeguard his interests.

(2) The officer of the Service shall –

    (a) be appointed in accordance with rules of court; and

    (b) be under a duty to safeguard the interests of the child in the manner prescribed by such rules.

(3) Where –

    (a) the child concerned is not represented by a solicitor; and

    (b) any of the conditions mentioned in subsection (4) is satisfied,

the court may appoint a solicitor to represent him.

(4) The conditions are that –

    (a) no officer of the Service has been appointed for the child;

    (b) the child has sufficient understanding to instruct a solicitor and wishes to do so;

    (c) it appears to the court that it would be in the child's best interests for him to be represented by a solicitor.

(5) Any solicitor appointed under or by virtue of this section shall be appointed, and shall represent the child, in accordance with rules of court.

(6) In this section 'specified proceedings' means any proceedings –

    (a) on an application for a care order or supervision order;

    (b) in which the court has given a direction under section 37(1) and has made, or is considering whether to make, an interim care order;

    (c) on an application for the discharge of a care order or the variation or discharge of a supervision order;

    (d) on an application under section 39(4);

    (e) in which the court is considering whether to make a residence order with respect to a child who is the subject of a care order;

    (f) with respect to contact between a child who is the subject of a care order and any other person;

    (g) under Part V;

    (h) on an appeal against –

        (i) the making of, or refusal to make, a care order, supervision order or any order under section 34;

        (ii) the making of, or refusal to make, a residence order with respect to a child who is the subject of a care order; or

        (iii) the variation or discharge of, or refusal of an application to vary or discharge, an order of a kind mentioned in sub-paragraph (i) or (ii);

        (iv) the refusal of an application under section 39(4);

        (v) the making of, or refusal to make, an order under Part V; or

    (i) which are specified for the time being, for the purposes of this section, by rules of court.

(6A) The proceedings which may be specified under subsection (6)(i) include (for example) proceedings for the making, varying or discharging of a section 8 order.

(7)–(9) (*repealed*)

(10) Rules of court may make this provision as to –

    (a) the assistance which any officer of the Service may be required by the court to give to it;

    (b) the consideration to be given by any officer of the Service, where an order of a specified kind has been made in the proceedings in question, as to whether to apply for the variation or discharge of the order;

    (c) the participation of officers of the Service in reviews, of a kind specified in the rules, which are conducted by the court.

(11) Regardless of any enactment or rule of law which would otherwise prevent it from doing so, the court may take account of –

    (a) any statement contained in a report made by an officer of the Service who is appointed under this section for the purpose of the proceedings in question; and

    (b) any evidence given in respect of the matters referred to in the report,

in so far as the statement or evidence is, in the opinion of the court, relevant to the question which the court is considering.

(12) (*repealed*)

Section 41

Prospective amendment—Section prospectively amended by Adoption and Children Act 2002, s 122(1) (see **3.3B**).

Specified proceedings—This section appears as amended by the Criminal Justice and Court Services Act 2000, under which CAFCASS was established as from 1 April 2001. This section sets out the proceedings which are 'specified' and therefore effectively require the involvement of a children's guardian. Education supervision orders under CA 1989, s 36 are not included within that definition (*Essex County Council v B* [1993] 1 FLR 866). Where a court has directed an investigation under CA 1989, s 37, the proceedings will be specified for the purposes of s 41(6); however, if the local authority decides not to apply for care or supervision orders the proceedings will cease to be specified (and any future involvement of the children's guardian could only be as a result of an appointment as guardian ad litem in non-specified proceedings under FPR 1991, r 9.5) – see *Re CE (Section 37 Direction)* [1995] 1 FLR 26. Section 122(1)(a) of the Adoption and Children Act 2002 (ACA 2002) will add placement orders under s 21 of that Act to the list of proceedings that are specified for the purposes of s 41(6).

Rules and protocol for guardian—FPR 1991, rr 4.11 and 4.11A (and FPC(CA 1989)R 1991, rr 11 and 11A) govern the work of the children's guardian. See the notes to s 32 for more details.

Guardian in previous case—When appointing a children's guardian, the court must consider the appointment of anyone who has previously acted as a children's guardian of the same child (FPR 1991, r 4.10(8)). It is likely to be beneficial to appoint a guardian who has had a previous involvement with the family (*Re J (Adoption: Appointment of Guardian Ad Litem)* [1999] 2 FLR 86).

Separate representation of child—As part of the case management checklist for the first hearing in the family proceedings court and the allocation hearing/allocation directions in the other courts at first instance, the parties are required to give consideration to whether the child should be separately represented. Where it appears to the children's guardian that the child is instructing his solicitor direct or intends to conduct and is capable of conducting the proceedings on his own behalf, he must inform the court (FPR 1991, r 4.11A). Thereafter the guardian's duties are set out in that rule. Thorpe LJ in *Re H (A Minor) (Care Proceedings: Child's Wishes)* [1993] 1 FLR 440 gives guidance on this:

> 'In cases involving intelligent articulate but disturbed children, it is necessary for the court to apply rule 11 and rule 12 realistically to ensure that not only is the professional voice of the guardian ad litem heard through an advocate's presentation but that also the wishes and feelings of the child, however limited the horizon, should be similarly presented. If there is any real question as to whether the child's emotional disturbance is so intense as to destroy the capacity to give coherent and consistent instructions, then I think that question should be the subject of specific expert opinion from the expert or experts who are already involved in the case.'

See also *Re M (Minors) (Care Proceedings: Child's Wishes)* [1994] 1 FLR 749.

CAFCASS Legal and joinder of the child in non-specified proceedings—FPR 1991, r 9.5 provides for the mechanism for joining the child as a party to non-specified proceedings.

The role of CAFCASS Legal in representing children is dealt with in the CAFCASS Practice Note dated 5 April 2004 [2004] 1 FLR 1190 (see **6.19**), which replaces the Practice Note that was reported at [2001] 2 FLR 151 (and see also *Re W (Contact: Joining Child as Party)* [2001] EWCA Civ 1830, [2003] 1 FLR 681, CA). The CAFCASS Practice Note should be read in conjunction with *President's Direction (Representation of Children in Family Proceedings Pursuant to Rule 9.5 of the FPR 1991)* [2004] 1 FLR 1188 (see **6.18**). It will be rare for a child to be joined as a party ('a step that will be taken only in cases which involve an issue of significant difficulty'); however, this is a developing area of law – see the article by Munby J at [2004] Fam Law 427, and *CF v Secretary of State for Home Department* [2004] 2 FLR 517. In the case of *Re D (Intractable Contact Dispute: Publicity)* [2004] EWHC 727 (Fam), [2004] 1 FLR 1226, FD, Munby J said:

> '**[51]** As Wall J pointed out in *Re M (Intractable Contact Dispute: Interim Care Order)* [2003] EWHC 1024 (Fam), [2003] 2 FLR 636 at para [15], intractable contact disputes are one of the "prime categories" for separate representation of the children. I agree. I also agree that in this situation the court can with great advantage make use of organisations such as the National Youth Advisory Service (NYAS), an organisation whose assistance in *A v A (Shared Residence)* [2004] EWHC 142 (Fam), [2004] 1 FLR 1195 was justifiably lauded by Wall J (see at paras [24], [131]–[133]).
>
> **[52]** But children caught up in intractable contact disputes may need more than the forensic assistance of a guardian. Guardian's reports, though immensely valuable, may not be enough. The children may need a social worker who can remain with them long enough to form a long-term relationship (see *Re M* at para [127]). The children and their warring parents will often need and can often benefit from skilled social work intervention. That was the thinking that lay behind the appointment of the independent social worker in the present case by the Circuit Judge on 31 August 2001: her most vital function was to facilitate the implementation of overnight contact. Sometimes this will work, at least in part. *A v A* provides a striking example. Sometimes it will not work. In the present case it did not, largely I think because the independent social worker first came on to the scene far too late, and at a time which can be seen, albeit perhaps only with the priceless advantage of hindsight, to have been well after the point at which the situation was in all probability wholly irretrievable.'

Confidentiality of documents—The confidentiality of documents is governed by FPR 1991, r 4.23 and FPC(CA 1989)R 1991, r 23. Under the terms of that rule, confidential information should not be disclosed without the prior leave of the judge or district judge. It has been said that the confidentiality extends to information provided to a children's guardian in the preparation of a report (*Oxfordshire County Council v P* [1995] Fam 161, [1995] 1 FLR 552 – mother confessed to guardian that she had injured child). In *Re G (Social Worker: Disclosure)* [1996] 1 FLR 276 it was said that a social worker did not need the permission of the court to inform the police that oral admissions had been made, since r 4.23 only required that leave should be sought in respect of documents filed with and held by the court (see also *Re W (Minors) (Social Worker: Disclosure)* [1998] 2 FLR 135, CA). Where proceedings have been concluded, the confidentiality of the guardian's report must still be maintained and controlled by the court (*Re C (Guardian Ad Litem: Disclosure of Report)* [1996] 1 FLR 61). This issue needs to be considered with reference to Administration of Justice Act 1960, s 12; CA 1989, s 97(2); and *Re M (Disclosure: Children and Family Reporter)* [2002] 2 FLR 893.

Guardian's expertise—A children's guardian should not hold himself/herself out to be an expert in an area that requires specialist knowledge (*Re N (Child Abuse: Evidence)* [1996] 4 All ER 225, [1996] 2 FLR 214, CA). Further, a guardian cannot start proceedings in his/her own name in relation to the child without the prior permission of the court (*Re M (Prohibited Steps Order: Application for Leave)* [1993] 1 FLR 275, FD).

Judge departing from guardian's recommendation—The court must specify reasons for departing from the guardian's recommendations (*Re D (Grant of Care Order: Refusal of Freeing Order)* [2001] 1 FLR 862, CA).

Termination of role—The court may terminate the appointment of a guardian in appropriate circumstances (*Re T and A (Children) (Risk of Disclosure)* [2000] 1 FLR 859; *Re M (Terminating Appointment of Guardian ad Litem)* [1999] 2 FLR 717).

Guardian and supervision order—Although it was held that where a supervision order was made, the proceedings did not come to an end until the supervision order expired (*Re MH, Re SB and MB* [2001] 2 FLR 1334) the effect of that decision has been repealed as from 28 November 2003 by Adoption and Children Act 2002, s 139(1), (3), Sch 3, para 118(5) and Sch 5: see SI 2003/3079, Article 2(1)(c)).

42 Right of officer of the Service to have access to local authority records

(1) Where an officer of the Service has been appointed under section 41 he shall have the right at all reasonable times to examine and take copies of –

(a) any records of, or held by, a local authority or an authorised person which were compiled in connection with the making, or proposed making, by any person of any application under this Act with respect to the child concerned;

(b) any records of, or held by, a local authority which were compiled in connection with any functions which are social services functions within the meaning of the Local Authority Social Services Act 1970, so far as those records relate to that child; or

(c) any records of, or held by, an authorised person which were compiled in connection with the activities of that person, so far as those records relate to that child.

(2) Where an officer of the Service takes a copy of any record which he is entitled to examine under this section, that copy or any part of it shall be admissible as evidence of any matter referred to in any –

(a) report which he makes to the court in the proceedings in question; or

(b) evidence which he gives in those proceedings.

(3) Subsection (2) has effect regardless of any enactment or rule of law which would otherwise prevent the record in question being admissible in evidence.

(4) In this section 'authorised person' has the same meaning as in section 31.

Section 42

A children's guardian will be entitled to see a full report compiled by an Area Child Protection Committee ('a Part 8 review') (*Re R (Care Proceedings: Disclosure)* [2000] 2 FLR 751, CA). Documents produced by a local authority when acting as an adoption agency should also be made available to the guardian for inspection (*Re T (A Minor) (Guardian Ad Litem: Case Record)* [1994] 1 FLR 632, CA). No issue of public interest immunity arises in relation to the guardian's inspection of records held by the local authority (*Re J (Care Proceedings: Disclosure)* [2003] EWHC 976, [2003] 2 FLR 522). In the case of *Oxfordshire County Council v P* [1995] 1 FLR 552 it was said to be wrong for the guardian to have made a witness statement in criminal proceedings without the prior permission of the family court; guardians should make sure that records taken are stored securely.

PART V

PROTECTION OF CHILDREN

43 Child assessment orders

(1) On the application of a local authority or authorised person for an order to be made under this section with respect to a child, the court may make the order if, but only if, it is satisfied that –

  (a) the applicant has reasonable cause to suspect that the child is suffering, or is likely to suffer, significant harm;
  (b) an assessment of the state of the child's health or development, or of the way in which he has been treated, is required to enable the applicant to determine whether or not the child is suffering, or is likely to suffer, significant harm; and
  (c) it is unlikely that such an assessment will be made, or be satisfactory, in the absence of an order under this section.

(2) In this Act 'a child assessment order' means an order under this section.

(3) A court may treat an application under this section as an application for an emergency protection order.

(4) No court shall make a child assessment order if it is satisfied –

  (a) that there are grounds for making an emergency protection order with respect to the child; and
  (b) that it ought to make such an order rather than a child assessment order.

(5) A child assessment order shall –

  (a) specify a date by which the assessment is to begin; and
  (b) have effect for such period, not exceeding 7 days beginning with that date, as may be specified in the order.

(6) Where a child assessment order is in force with respect to a child it shall be the duty of any person who is in a position to produce the child –

  (a) to produce him to such person as may be named in the order; and
  (b) to comply with such directions relating to the assessment of the child as the court thinks fit to specify in the order.

(7) A child assessment order authorises any person carrying out the assessment, or any part of the assessment, to do so in accordance with the terms of the order.

(8) Regardless of subsection (7), if the child is of sufficient understanding to make an informed decision he may refuse to submit to a medical or psychiatric examination or other assessment.

(9) The child may only be kept away from home –

    (a) in accordance with directions specified in the order;
    (b) if it is necessary for the purposes of the assessment; and
    (c) for such period or periods as may be specified in the order.

(10) Where the child is to be kept away from home, the order shall contain such directions as the court thinks fit with regard to the contact that he must be allowed to have with other persons while away from home.

(11) Any person making an application for a child assessment order shall take such steps as are reasonably practicable to ensure that notice of the application is given to –

    (a) the child's parents;
    (b) any person who is not a parent of his but who has parental responsibility for him;
    (c) any other person caring for the child;
    (d) any person in whose favour a contact order is in force with respect to the child;
    (e) any person who is allowed to have contact with the child by virtue of an order under section 34; and
    (f) the child,

before the hearing of the application.

(12) Rules of court may make provision as to the circumstances in which –

    (a) any of the persons mentioned in subsection (11); or
    (b) such other person as may be specified in the rules,

may apply to the court for a child assessment order to be varied or discharged.

(13) In this section 'authorised person' means a person who is an authorised person for the purposes of section 31.

44 Orders for emergency protection of children

(1) Where any person ('the applicant') applies to the court for an order to be made under this section with respect to a child, the court may make the order if, but only if, it is satisfied that –

    (a) there is reasonable cause to believe that the child is likely to suffer significant harm if –
        (i) he is not removed to accommodation provided by or on behalf of the applicant; or
        (ii) he does not remain in the place in which he is then being accommodated;
    (b) in the case of an application made by the local authority –
        (i) enquiries are being made with respect to the child under section 47(1)(b); and

      (ii) those enquiries are being frustrated by access to the child being unreasonably refused to a person authorised to seek access and that the applicant has reasonable cause to believe that access to the child is required as a matter of urgency; or

  (c) in the case of an application made by an authorised person –

      (i) the applicant has reasonable cause to suspect that a child is suffering, or is likely to suffer, significant harm;

      (ii) the applicant is making enquiries with respect to the child's welfare; and

      (iii) those enquiries are being frustrated by access to the child being unreasonably refused to a person authorised to seek access and the applicant has reasonable cause to believe that access to the child is required as a matter of urgency.

(2) In this section –

  (a) 'authorised person' means a person who is an authorised person for the purposes of section 31; and

  (b) 'a person authorised to seek access' means –

      (i) in the case of an application by a local authority, an officer of the local authority or a person authorised by the local authority to act on their behalf in connection with the enquiries; or

      (ii) in the case of an application by an authorised person, that person.

(3) Any person –

  (a) seeking access to a child in connection with enquiries of a kind mentioned in subsection (1); and

  (b) purporting to be a person authorised to do so,

shall, on being asked to do so, produce some duly authenticated document as evidence that he is such a person.

(4) While an order under this section ('an emergency protection order') is in force it –

  (a) operates as a direction to any person who is in a position to do so to comply with any request to produce the child to the applicant;

  (b) authorises –

      (i) the removal of the child at any time to accommodation provided by or on behalf of the applicant and his being kept there; or

      (ii) the prevention of the child's removal from any hospital, or other place, in which he was being accommodated immediately before the making of the order; and

  (c) gives the applicant parental responsibility for the child.

(5) Where an emergency protection order is in force with respect to a child, the applicant –

  (a) shall only exercise the power given by virtue of subsection (4)(b) in order to safeguard the welfare of the child;

  (b) shall take, and shall only take, such action in meeting his parental responsibility for the child as is reasonably required to safeguard or promote the welfare of the child (having regard in particular to the duration of the order); and

  (c) shall comply with the requirements of any regulations made by the Secretary of State for the purposes of this subsection.

(6) Where the court makes an emergency protection order, it may give such directions (if any) as it considers appropriate with respect to –

(a) the contact which is, or is not, to be allowed between the child and any named person;

(b) the medical or psychiatric examination or other assessment of the child.

(7) Where any direction is given under subsection (6)(b), the child may, if he is of sufficient understanding to make an informed decision, refuse to submit to the examination or other assessment.

(8) A direction under subsection (6)(a) may impose conditions and one under subsection (6)(b) may be to the effect that there is to be –

(a) no such examination or assessment; or

(b) no such examination or assessment unless the court directs otherwise.

(9) A direction under subsection (6) may be –

(a) given when the emergency protection order is made or at any time while it is in force; and

(b) varied at any time on the application of any person falling within any class of person prescribed by rules of court for the purposes of this subsection.

(10) Where an emergency protection order is in force with respect to a child and –

(a) the applicant has exercised the power given by subsection (4)(b)(i) but it appears to him that it is safe for the child to be returned; or

(b) the applicant has exercised the power given by subsection (4)(b)(ii) but it appears to him that it is safe for the child to be allowed to be removed from the place in question,

he shall return the child or (as the case may be) allow him to be removed.

(11) Where he is required by subsection (10) to return the child the applicant shall –

(a) return him to the care of the person from whose care he was removed; or

(b) if that is not reasonably practicable, return him to the care of –

(i) a parent of his;

(ii) any person who is not a parent of his but who has parental responsibility for him; or

(iii) such other person as the applicant (with the agreement of the court) considers appropriate.

(12) Where the applicant has been required by subsection (10) to return the child, or to allow him to be removed, he may again exercise his powers with respect to the child (at any time while the emergency protection order remains in force) if it appears to him that a change in the circumstances of the case makes it necessary for him to do so.

(13) Where an emergency protection order has been made with respect to a child, the applicant shall, subject to any direction given under subsection (6), allow the child reasonable contact with –

(a) his parents;

(b) any person who is not a parent of his but who has parental responsibility for him;

(c) any person with whom he was living immediately before the making of the order;

(d) any person in whose favour a contact order is in force with respect to him;

(e) any person who is allowed to have contact with the child by virtue of an order under section 34; and

(f) any person acting on behalf of any of those persons.

(14) Wherever it is reasonably practicable to do so, an emergency protection order shall name the child; and where it does not name him it shall describe him as clearly as possible.

(15) A person shall be guilty of an offence if he intentionally obstructs any person exercising the power under subsection (4)(b) to remove, or prevent the removal of, a child.

(16) A person guilty of an offence under subsection (15) shall be liable on summary conviction to a fine not exceeding level 3 on the standard scale.

Section 44

This section has to be read in conjunction with s 45 (which deals with the duration of emergency protection orders and other supplemental provisions). Emergency protection orders are intended to be made when there is an emergency and it can be shown that, unless emergency action is taken, the child will be at risk of significant harm during the period of the order (*Re C and B (Care Order: Future Harm)* [2001] 1 FLR 611, CA). There need to be extraordinarily compelling reasons to justify the removal of a baby from the care of its mother immediately after birth (see *K and T v Finland* [2001] 2 FLR 707). Every application for an emergency protection order should be approached with an anxious awareness of the extreme gravity of the order that is being sought and a scrupulous regard for the Convention rights of both the child and the parents (*X Council v B (Emergency Protection Orders)* [2004] EWHC 2015 (Fam), [2005] Fam Law 13).

Only in exceptional circumstances might it be right for judicial review to be used to prevent a local authority seeking an emergency protection order (*Re M (Care Proceedings: Judicial Review)* [2003] 2 FLR 171, FD).

44A Power to include exclusion requirement in emergency protection order

(1) Where –

(a) on being satisfied as mentioned in section 44(1)(a), (b) or (c), the court makes an emergency protection order with respect to a child, and

(b) the conditions mentioned in subsection (2) are satisfied,

the court may include an exclusion requirement in the emergency protection order.

(2) The conditions are –

(a) that there is reasonable cause to believe that, if a person ('the relevant person') is excluded from a dwelling-house in which the child lives, then –

(i) in the case of an order made on the ground mentioned in section 44(1)(a), the child will not be likely to suffer significant harm, even though the child is not removed as mentioned in section 44(1)(a)(i) or does not remain as mentioned in section 44(1)(a)(ii), or

(ii) in the case of an order made on the ground mentioned in paragraph (b) or (c) of section 44(1), the enquiries referred to in that paragraph will cease to be frustrated, and

    (b)   that another person living in the dwelling-house (whether a parent of the child or some other person) –

        (i)   is able and willing to give to the child the care which it would be reasonable to expect a parent to give him, and

        (ii)   consents to the inclusion of the exclusion requirement.

(3) For the purposes of this section an exclusion requirement is any one or more of the following –

    (a)   a provision requiring the relevant person to leave a dwelling-house in which he is living with the child,

    (b)   a provision prohibiting the relevant person from entering a dwelling-house in which the child lives, and

    (c)   a provision excluding the relevant person from a defined area in which a dwelling-house in which the child lives is situated.

(4) The court may provide that the exclusion requirement is to have effect for a shorter period than the other provisions of the order.

(5) Where the court makes an emergency protection order containing an exclusion requirement, the court may attach a power of arrest to the exclusion requirement.

(6) Where the court attaches a power of arrest to an exclusion requirement of an emergency protection order, it may provide that the power of arrest is to have effect for a shorter period than the exclusion requirement.

(7) Any period specified for the purposes of subsection (4) or (6) may be extended by the court (on one or more occasions) on an application to vary or discharge the emergency protection order.

(8) Where a power of arrest is attached to an exclusion requirement of an emergency protection order by virtue of subsection (5), a constable may arrest without warrant any person whom he has reasonable cause to believe to be in breach of the requirement.

(9) Sections 47(7), (11) and (12) and 48 of, and Schedule 5 to, the Family Law Act 1996 shall have effect in relation to a person arrested under subsection (8) of this section as they have effect in relation to a person arrested under section 47(6) of that Act.

(10) If, while an emergency protection order containing an exclusion requirement is in force, the applicant has removed the child from the dwelling-house from which the relevant person is excluded to other accommodation for a continuous period of more than 24 hours, the order shall cease to have effect in so far as it imposes the exclusion requirement.

44B Undertakings relating to emergency protection orders

(1) In any case where the court has power to include an exclusion requirement in an emergency protection order, the court may accept an undertaking from the relevant person.

(2) No power of arrest may be attached to any undertaking given under subsection (1).

(3) An undertaking given to a court under subsection (1) –

    (a)   shall be enforceable as if it were an order of the court, and

    (b) shall cease to have effect if, while it is in force, the applicant has removed the child from the dwelling-house from which the relevant person is excluded to other accommodation for a continuous period of more than 24 hours.

(4) This section has effect without prejudice to the powers of the High Court and county court apart from this section.

(5) In this section 'exclusion requirement' and 'relevant person' have the same meaning as in section 44A.

45 Duration of emergency protection orders and other supplemental provisions

(1) An emergency protection order shall have effect for such period, not exceeding eight days, as may be specified in the order.

(2) Where –

    (a) the court making an emergency protection order would, but for this subsection, specify a period of eight days as the period for which the order is to have effect; but

    (b) the last of those eight days is a public holiday (that is to say, Christmas Day, Good Friday, a bank holiday or a Sunday),

the court may specify a period which ends at noon on the first later day which is not such a holiday.

(3) Where an emergency protection order is made on an application under section 46(7), the period of eight days mentioned in subsection (1) shall begin with the first day on which the child was taken into police protection under section 46.

(4) Any person who –

    (a) has parental responsibility for a child as the result of an emergency protection order; and

    (b) is entitled to apply for a care order with respect to the child,

may apply to the court for the period during which the emergency protection order is to have effect to be extended.

(5) On an application under subsection (4) the court may extend the period during which the order is to have effect by such period, not exceeding seven days, as it thinks fit, but may do so only if it has reasonable cause to believe that the child concerned is likely to suffer significant harm if the order is not extended.

(6) An emergency protection order may only be extended once.

(7) Regardless of any enactment or rule of law which would otherwise prevent it from doing so, a court hearing an application for, or with respect to, an emergency protection order may take account of –

    (a) any statement contained in any report made to the court in the course of, or in connection with, the hearing; or

    (b) any evidence given during the hearing,

which is, in the opinion of the court, relevant to the application.

(8) Any of the following may apply to the court for an emergency protection order to be discharged –

(a) the child;

(b) a parent of his;

(c) any person who is not a parent of his but who has parental responsibility for him; or

(d) any person with whom he was living immediately before the making of the order.

(8A) On the application of a person who is not entitled to apply for the order to be discharged, but who is a person to whom an exclusion requirement contained in the order applies, an emergency protection order may be varied or discharged by the court in so far as it imposes the exclusion requirement.

(8B) Where a power of arrest has been attached to an exclusion requirement of an emergency protection order, the court may, on the application of any person entitled to apply for the discharge of the order so far as it imposes the exclusion requirement, vary or discharge the order in so far as it confers a power of arrest (whether or not any application has been made to vary or discharge any other provision of the order).

(9) No application for the discharge of an emergency protection order shall be heard by the court before the expiry of the period of 72 hours beginning with the making of the order.

(10) No appeal may be made against –

(a) the making of, or refusal to make, an emergency protection order;

(b) the extension of, or refusal to extend, the period during which such an order is to have effect;

(c) the discharge of, or refusal to discharge, such an order; or

(d) the giving of, or refusal to give, any direction in connection with such an order.

(11) Subsection (8) does not apply –

(a) where the person who would otherwise be entitled to apply for the emergency protection order to be discharged –

(i) was given notice (in accordance with rules of court) of the hearing at which the order was made; and

(ii) was present at that hearing; or

(b) to any emergency protection order the effective period of which has been extended under subsection (5).

(12) A court making an emergency protection order may direct that the applicant may, in exercising any powers which he has by virtue of the order, be accompanied by a registered medical practitioner, registered nurse or registered midwife, if he so chooses.

(13) The reference in subsection (12) to a registered midwife is to such a midwife who is also registered in the Specialist Community Public Health Nurses' Part of the register maintained under article 5 of the Nursing and Midwifery Order 2001.

46 Removal and accommodation of children by police in cases of emergency

(1) Where a constable has reasonable cause to believe that a child would otherwise be likely to suffer significant harm, he may –

(a) remove the child to suitable accommodation and keep him there; or

(b) take such steps as are reasonable to ensure that the child's removal from any hospital, or other place, in which he is then being accommodated is prevented.

(2) For the purposes of this Act, a child with respect to whom a constable has exercised his powers under this section is referred to as having been taken into police protection.

(3) As soon as is reasonably practicable after taking a child into police protection, the constable concerned shall –

   (a) inform the local authority within whose area the child was found of the steps that have been, and are proposed to be, taken with respect to the child under this section and the reasons for taking them;

   (b) give details to the authority within whose area the child is ordinarily resident ('the appropriate authority') of the place at which the child is being accommodated;

   (c) inform the child (if he appears capable of understanding) –

      (i) of the steps that have been taken with respect to him under this section and of the reasons for taking them; and;

      (ii) of the further steps that may be taken with respect to him under this section;

   (d) take such steps as are reasonably practicable to discover the wishes and feelings of the child;

   (e) secure that the case is inquired into by an officer designated for the purposes of this section by the chief officer of the police area concerned; and

   (f) where the child was taken into police protection by being removed to accommodation which is not provided –

      (i) by or on behalf of a local authority; or

      (ii) as a refuge, in compliance with the requirements of section 51,

   secure that he is moved to accommodation which is so provided.

(4) As soon as is reasonably practicable after taking a child into police protection, the constable concerned shall take such steps as are reasonably practicable to inform –

   (a) the child's parents;

   (b) every person who is not a parent of his but who has parental responsibility for him; and

   (c) any other person with whom the child was living immediately before being taken into police protection,

of the steps that he has taken under this section with respect to the child, the reasons for taking them and the further steps that may be taken with respect to him under this section.

(5) On completing any inquiry under subsection (3)(e), the officer conducting it shall release the child from police protection unless he considers that there is still reasonable cause for believing that the child would be likely to suffer significant harm if released.

(6) No child may be kept in police protection for more than 72 hours.

(7) While a child is being kept in police protection, the designated officer may apply on behalf of the appropriate authority for an emergency protection order to be made under section 44 with respect to the child.

(8) An application may be made under subsection (7) whether or not the authority know of it or agree to its being made.

(9) While a child is being kept in police protection –

(a) neither the constable concerned nor the designated officer shall have parental responsibility for him; but

(b) the designated officer shall do what is reasonable in all the circumstances of the case for the purpose of safeguarding or promoting the child's welfare (having regard in particular to the length of the period during which the child will be so protected).

(10) Where a child has been taken into police protection, the designated officer shall allow –

(a) the child's parents;

(b) any person who is not a parent of the child but who has parental responsibility for him;

(c) any person with whom the child was living immediately before he was taken into police protection;

(d) any person in whose favour a contact order is in force with respect to the child;

(e) any person who is allowed to have contact with the child by virtue of an order under section 34; and

(f) any person acting on behalf of any of those persons,

to have such contact (if any) with the child as, in the opinion of the designated officer, is both reasonable and in the child's best interests.

(11) Where a child who has been taken into police protection is in accommodation provided by, or on behalf of, the appropriate authority, subsection (10) shall have effect as if it referred to the authority rather than to the designated officer.

47 Local authority's duty to investigate

(1) Where a local authority –

(a) are informed that a child who lives, or is found, in their area –
   (i) is the subject of an emergency protection order; or
   (ii) is in police protection; or
   (iii) has contravened a ban imposed by a curfew notice within the meaning of Chapter I of Part I of the Crime And Disorder Act 1998; or

(b) have reasonable cause to suspect that a child who lives, or is found, in their area is suffering, or is likely to suffer, significant harm,

the authority shall make, or cause to be made, such enquiries as they consider necessary to enable them to decide whether they should take any action to safeguard or promote the child's welfare.

In the case of a child falling within paragraph (a)(iii) above, the enquiries shall be commenced as soon as practicable and, in any event, within 48 hours of the authority receiving the information.

(2) Where a local authority have obtained an emergency protection order with respect to a child, they shall make, or cause to be made, such enquiries as they consider necessary to enable them to decide what action they should take to safeguard or promote the child's welfare.

(3) The enquiries shall, in particular, be directed towards establishing –

    (a) whether the authority should make any application to the court, or exercise any of their other powers under this Act or section 11 of the Crime and Disorder Act 1998 (child safety orders), with respect to the child;

    (b) whether, in the case of a child –

        (i) with respect to whom an emergency protection order has been made; and

        (ii) who is not in accommodation provided by or on behalf of the authority,

    it would be in the child's best interests (while an emergency protection order remains in force) for him to be in such accommodation; and

    (c) whether, in the case of a child who has been taken into police protection, it would be in the child's best interests for the authority to ask for an application to be made under section 46(7).

(4) Where enquiries are being made under subsection (1) with respect to a child, the local authority concerned shall (with a view to enabling them to determine what action, if any, to take with respect to him) take such steps as are reasonably practicable –

    (a) to obtain access to him; or

    (b) to ensure that access to him is obtained, on their behalf, by a person authorised by them for the purpose,

unless they are satisfied that they already have sufficient information with respect to him.

(5) Where, as a result of any such enquiries, it appears to the authority that there are matters connected with the child's education which should be investigated, they shall consult the relevant local education authority.

(6) Where, in the course of enquiries made under this section –

    (a) any officer of the local authority concerned; or

    (b) any person authorised by the authority to act on their behalf in connection with those enquiries –

        (i) is refused access to the child concerned; or

        (ii) is denied information as to his whereabouts,

the authority shall apply for an emergency protection order, a child assessment order, a care order or a supervision order with respect to the child unless they are satisfied that his welfare can be satisfactorily safeguarded without their doing so.

(7) If, on the conclusion of any enquiries or review made under this section, the authority decide not to apply for an emergency protection order, a care order, a child assessment order or a supervision order they shall –

    (a) consider whether it would be appropriate to review the case at a later date; and

    (b) if they decide that it would be, determine the date on which that review is to begin.

(8) Where, as a result of complying with this section, a local authority conclude that they should take action to safeguard or promote the child's welfare they shall take that action (so far as it is both within their power and reasonably practicable for them to do so).

(9) Where a local authority are conducting enquiries under this section, it shall be the duty of any person mentioned in subsection (11) to assist them with those enquiries (in particular by providing relevant information and advice) if called upon by the authority to do so.

(10) Subsection (9) does not oblige any person to assist a local authority where doing so would be unreasonable in all the circumstances of the case.

(11) The persons are –

(a) any local authority;
(b) any local education authority;
(c) any local housing authority;
(d) any Health Authority, Special Health Authority, Primary Care Trust or National Health Service trust; and
(e) any person authorised by the Secretary of State for the purposes of this section.

(12) Where a local authority are making enquiries under this section with respect to a child who appears to them to be ordinarily resident within the area of another authority, they shall consult that other authority, who may undertake the necessary enquiries in their place.

Section 47

In the case of *Re O and N; Re B* [2003] UKHL 18, [2003] 2 WLR 1075, [2003] 2 All ER 305, [2003] 1 FLR 1169, Lord Nicholls said at [18]: 'In the case of each statutory provision it is necessary to consider the language and purpose of the provision to see whether, for reasons of legal policy, any limitation should be placed on the matters the decision-maker may take into account when assessing the risk in question. An example of this concerns the duties of investigation placed upon local authorities by section 47. As Scott Baker J held in *Re S (Sexual Abuse Allegations: Local Authority Response)* [2001] EWHC Admin 334, [2001] 2 FLR 776, local authorities would be prevented from carrying out effective and timely risk assessments if they could act only on the basis of proven fact'. Under s 47(1)(b) the local authority's duty to make enquiries arises where it has reasonable cause to suspect that a child is suffering or is likely to suffer significant harm; it is not necessary for the fact of that harm to be proven before the duty to investigate arises.

48 Powers to assist in discovery of children who may be in need of emergency protection

(1) Where it appears to a court making an emergency protection order that adequate information as to the child's whereabouts –

(a) is not available to the applicant for the order; but
(b) is available to another person,

it may include in the order a provision requiring that other person to disclose, if asked to do so by the applicant, any information that he may have as to the child's whereabouts.

(2) No person shall be excused from complying with such a requirement on the ground that complying might incriminate him or his spouse of an offence; but a statement of admission made in complying shall not be admissible in evidence against either of them in proceedings for any offence other than perjury.

(3) An emergency protection order may authorise the applicant to enter premises specified by the order and search for the child with respect to whom the order is made.

(4) Where the court is satisfied that there is reasonable cause to believe that there may be another child on those premises with respect to whom an emergency protection order ought to be made, it may make an order authorising the applicant to search for that other child on those premises.

(5) Where –

    (a)   an order has been made under subsection (4);

    (b)   the child concerned has been found on the premises; and

    (c)   the applicant is satisfied that the grounds for making an emergency protection order exist with respect to him,

the order shall have effect as if it were an emergency protection order.

(6) Where an order has been made under subsection (4), the applicant shall notify the court of its effect.

(7) A person shall be guilty of an offence if he intentionally obstructs any person exercising the power of entry and search under subsection (3) or (4).

(8) A person guilty of an offence under subsection (7) shall be liable on summary conviction to a fine not exceeding level 3 on the standard scale.

(9) Where, on an application made by any person for a warrant under this section, it appears to the court –

    (a)   that a person attempting to exercise powers under an emergency protection order has been prevented from doing so by being refused entry to the premises concerned or access to the child concerned; or

    (b)   that any such person is likely to be so prevented from exercising any such powers,

it may issue a warrant authorising any constable to assist the person mentioned in paragraph (a) or (b) in the exercise of those powers, using reasonable force if necessary.

(10) Every warrant issued under this section shall be addressed to, and executed by, a constable who shall be accompanied by the person applying for the warrant if –

    (a)   that person so desires; and

    (b)   the court by whom the warrant is issued does not direct otherwise.

(11) A court granting an application for a warrant under this section may direct that the constable concerned may, in executing the warrant, be accompanied by a registered medical practitioner, registered nurse or registered midwife if he so chooses.

(11A) The reference in subsection (11) to a registered midwife is to such a midwife who is also registered in the Specialist Community Public Health Nurses' Part of the register maintained under article 5 of the Nursing and Midwifery Order 2001.

(12) An application for a warrant under this section shall be made in the manner and form prescribed by rules of court.

(13) Wherever it is reasonably practicable to do so, an order under subsection (4), an application for a warrant under this section and any such warrant shall name the child; and where it does not name him it shall describe him as clearly as possible.

49 Abduction of children in care etc

(1) A person shall be guilty of an offence if, knowingly and without lawful authority or reasonable excuse, he –

    (a) takes a child to whom this section applies away from the responsible person;

    (b) keeps such a child away from the responsible person; or

    (c) induces, assists or incites such a child to run away or stay away from the responsible person.

(2) This section applies in relation to a child who is –

    (a) in care;

    (b) the subject of an emergency protection order; or

    (c) in police protection,

and in this section 'the responsible person' means any person who for the time being has care of him by virtue of the care order, the emergency protection order, or section 46, as the case may be.

(3) A person guilty of an offence under this section shall be liable on summary conviction to imprisonment for a term not exceeding six months, or to a fine not exceeding level 5 on the standard scale, or to both.

50 Recovery of abducted children etc

(1) Where it appears to the court that there is reason to believe that a child to whom this section applies –

    (a) has been unlawfully taken away or is being unlawfully kept away from the responsible person;

    (b) has run away or is staying away from the responsible person; or

    (c) is missing,

the court may make an order under this section ('a recovery order').

(2) This section applies to the same children to whom section 49 applies and in this section 'the responsible person' has the same meaning as in section 49.

(3) A recovery order –

    (a) operates as a direction to any person who is in a position to do so to produce the child on request to any authorised person;

    (b) authorises the removal of the child by any authorised person;

    (c) requires any person who has information as to the child's whereabouts to disclose that information, if asked to do so, to a constable or an officer of the court;

    (d) authorises a constable to enter any premises specified in the order and search for the child, using reasonable force if necessary.

(4) The court may make a recovery order on the application of –

    (a) any person who has parental responsibility for the child by virtue of a care order or emergency protection order; or

(b) where the child is in police protection, the designated officer.

(5) A recovery order shall name the child and –

(a) any person who has parental responsibility for the child by virtue of a care order or emergency protection order; or

(b) where the child is in police protection, the designated officer.

(6) Premises may only be specified under subsection (3)(d) if it appears to the court that there are reasonable grounds for believing the child to be on them.

(7) In this section –

'an authorised person' means –

(a) any person specified by the court;

(b) any constable;

(c) any person who is authorised –

(i) after the recovery order is made; and

(ii) by a person who has parental responsibility for the child by virtue of a care order or an emergency protection order,

to exercise any power under a recovery order; and

'the designated officer' means the officer designated for the purposes of section 46.

(8) Where a person is authorised as mentioned in subsection (7)(c) –

(a) the authorisation shall identify the recovery order; and

(b) any person claiming to be so authorised shall, if asked to do so, produce some duly authenticated document showing that he is so authorised.

(9) A person shall be guilty of an offence if he intentionally obstructs an authorised person exercising the power under subsection (3)(b) to remove a child.

(10) A person guilty of an offence under this section shall be liable on summary conviction to a fine not exceeding level 3 on the standard scale.

(11) No person shall be excused from complying with any request made under subsection (3)(c) on the ground that complying with it might incriminate him or his spouse of an offence; but a statement or admission made in complying shall not be admissible in evidence against either of them in proceedings for an offence other than perjury.

(12) Where a child is made the subject of a recovery order whilst being looked after by a local authority, any reasonable expenses incurred by an authorised person in giving effect to the order shall be recoverable from the authority.

(13) *(applies to Scotland only)*

(14) *(applies to Northern Ireland only)*.

51 Refuges for children at risk

(1) Where it is proposed to use a voluntary home or private children's home to provide a refuge for children who appear to be at risk of harm, the Secretary of State may issue a certificate under this section with respect to that home.

(2) Where a local authority or voluntary organisation arrange for a foster parent to provide such a refuge, the Secretary of State may issue a certificate under this section

with respect to that foster parent.

(3) In subsection (2) 'foster parent' means a person who is, or who from time to time is, a local authority foster parent or a foster parent with whom children are placed by a voluntary organisation.

(4) The Secretary of State may by regulations –

(a) make provision as to the manner in which certificates may be issued;
(b) impose requirements which must be complied with while any certificate is in force; and
(c) provide for the withdrawal of certificates in prescribed circumstances.

(5) Where a certificate is in force with respect to a home, none of the provisions mentioned in subsection (7) shall apply in relation to any person providing a refuge for any child in that home.

(6) Where a certificate is in force with respect to a foster parent, none of those provisions shall apply in relation to the provision by him of a refuge for any child in accordance with arrangements made by the local authority or voluntary organisation.

(7) The provisions are –

(a) section 49;
(b) sections 82 (recovery of certain fugitive children) and 83 (harbouring) of the Children (Scotland) Act 1995, so far as they apply in relation to anything done in England and Wales;
(c) section 32(3) of the Children and Young Persons Act 1969 (compelling, persuading, inciting or assisting any person to be absent from detention etc), so far as it applies in relation to anything done in England and Wales;
(d) section 2 of the Child Abduction Act 1984.

52 Rules and regulations

(1) Without prejudice to section 93 or any other power to make such rules, rules of court may be made with respect to the procedure to be followed in connection with proceedings under this Part.

(2) The rules may in particular make provision –

(a) as to the form in which any application is to be made or direction is to be given;
(b) prescribing the persons who are to be notified of –
    (i) the making, or extension, of an emergency protection order; or
    (ii) the making of an application under section 45(4) or (8) or 46(7); and
(c) as to the content of any such notification and the manner in which, and person by whom, it is to be given.

(3) The Secretary of State may by regulations provide that, where –

(a) an emergency protection order has been made with respect to a child;
(b) the applicant for the order was not the local authority within whose area the child is ordinarily resident; and
(c) that local authority are of the opinion that it would be in the child's best interests for the applicant's responsibilities under the order to be transferred to them,

that authority shall (subject to their having complied with any requirements imposed by the regulations) be treated, for the purposes of this Act, as though they and not the original applicant had applied for, and been granted, the order.

(4) Regulations made under subsection (3) may, in particular, make provision as to –

(a) the considerations to which the local authority shall have regard in forming an opinion as mentioned in subsection (3)(c); and

(b) the time at which responsibility under any emergency protection order is to be treated as having been transferred to a local authority.

****

PART XII

MISCELLANEOUS AND GENERAL

****

91 Effect and duration of orders etc

(1) The making of a residence order with respect to a child who is the subject of a care order discharges the care order.

(2) The making of a care order with respect to a child who is the subject of any section 8 order discharges that order.

(3) The making of a care order with respect to a child who is the subject of a supervision order discharges that other order.

(4) The making of a care order with respect to a child who is a ward of court brings that wardship to an end.

(5) The making of a care order with respect to a child who is the subject of a school attendance order made under section 437 of the Education Act 1996 discharges the school attendance order.

(6) Where an emergency protection order is made with respect to a child who is in care, the care order shall have effect subject to the emergency protection order.

(7) Any order made under section 4(1) or 5(1) shall continue in force until the child reaches the age of eighteen, unless it is brought to an end earlier.

(8) Any –

(a) agreement under section 4; or
(b) appointment under section 5(3) or (4),

shall continue in force until the child reaches the age of eighteen, unless it is brought to an end earlier.

(9) An order under Schedule 1 has effect as specified in that Schedule.

(10) A section 8 order shall, if it would otherwise still be in force, cease to have effect when the child reaches the age of sixteen, unless it is to have effect beyond that age by virtue of section 9(6).

(11) Where a section 8 order has effect with respect to a child who has reached the age of sixteen, it shall, if it would otherwise still be in force, cease to have effect when he reaches the age of eighteen.

(12) Any care order, other than an interim care order, shall continue in force until the child reaches the age of eighteen, unless it is brought to an end earlier.

(13) Any order made under any other provision of this Act in relation to a child shall, if it would otherwise still be in force, cease to have effect when he reaches the age of eighteen.

(14) On disposing of any application for an order under this Act, the court may (whether or not it makes any other order in response to the application) order that no application for an order under this Act of any specified kind may be made with respect to the child concerned by any person named in the order without leave of the court.

(15) Where an application ('the previous application') has been made for –

    (a) the discharge of a care order;
    (b) the discharge of a supervision order;
    (c) the discharge of an education supervision order;
    (d) the substitution of a supervision order for a care order; or
    (e) a child assessment order,

no further application of a kind mentioned in paragraphs (a) to (e) may be made with respect to the child concerned, without leave of the court, unless the period between the disposal of the previous application and the making of the further application exceeds six months.

(16) Subsection (15) does not apply to applications made in relation to interim orders.

(17) Where –

    (a) a person has made an application for an order under section 34;
    (b) the application has been refused; and
    (c) a period of less than six months has elapsed since the refusal,

that person may not make a further application for such an order with respect to the same child, unless he has obtained the leave of the court.

Section 91

Prospective amendment—Section prospectively amended by Adoption and Children Act 2002, ss 114(3), 139(1), Sch 3, paras 54, 68 (see **3.3B**).

Generally—The power of the court to make an order under CA 1989, s 91(14) is discretionary and should be used in the best interests of the child concerned. It is a draconian order which should be used with great care and sparingly. Its use must be proportionate to the harm it is intended to avoid (*Re G (Contempt: Committal)* [2003] EWCA Civ 489, [2003] 2 FLR 58, CA). The Court of Appeal set out guidelines that should be considered on an application for an order under s 91(14) in *Re P (A Minor) (Residence Order: Child's Welfare)* [2000] Fam 15, [1999] 3 All ER 734, [1999] 3 WLR 1164, [1999] 2 FLR 573, CA, as follows:

    (1) CA 1989, s 91(14) should be read in conjunction with s 1(1) which makes the welfare of the child the paramount consideration;
    (2) the power to restrict applications to the court is discretionary and in the exercise of its discretion the court must weigh in the balance all the relevant circumstances;

(3) an important consideration is that to impose a restriction is a statutory intrusion into the right of a party to bring proceedings before the court and to be heard in matters affecting his or her child;

(4) the power is therefore to be used with great care and sparingly, the exception and not the rule;

(5) it is generally to be seen as a useful weapon of last resort in cases of repeated and unreasonable applications;

(6) in suitable circumstances (and on clear evidence) a court may impose the leave restriction in cases where the welfare of the child requires it, although there is no past history of making unreasonable applications;

(7) in cases under point (6) above, the court will need to be satisfied, first, that the facts go beyond the commonly encountered need for a time to settle to a regime ordered by the court and the all too common situation where there is animosity between the adults in dispute or between the local authority and the family, and secondly, that there is a serious risk that, without the imposition of the restriction, the child or the primary carers will be subject to unacceptable strain;

(8) a court may impose the restriction on making applications in the absence of a request from any of the parties, subject of course, to the rules of natural justice such as an opportunity for the parties to be heard on the point;

(9) a restriction may be imposed with or without limitation of time;

(10) the degree of restriction should be proportionate to the harm that it is intended to avoid. Therefore the court imposing the restriction should carefully consider the extent of the restriction to be imposed and specify, where appropriate, the type of application to be restrained and the duration of the order;

(11) it would be undesirable in other than the most exceptional cases to make the order ex parte.

In the above case of *Re P* it was also held that an absolute prohibition on making any application to the court would not be an order under s 91(14), which pre-supposes an ex parte application to the court. An order imposing an absolute prohibition would have to be made under the inherent jurisdiction of the court (see *Re R (Residence: Contact: Restricting Applications)* [1998] 1 FLR 749). Further, it was held in *Re P* that s 91(14) does not infringe Article 6 of the European Convention on Human Rights.

Where an order under s 91(14) has been made, a subsequent application to issue proceedings in relation to the child will be a distinct application which will not be subjected either to the statutory criteria contained in s 10(9) or to the elaboration of those criteria which have been introduced in subsequent decisions of the court. The test should be: does this application demonstrate that there is any need for renewed judicial intervention? (*Re A (Application for Leave)* [1998] 1 FLR 1, CA).

****

Jurisdiction and procedure etc

94 Appeals

(1) Subject to any express provisions to the contrary made by or under this Act, an appeal shall lie to the High Court against –

    (a) the making by a magistrates' court of any order under this Act; or

    (b) any refusal by a magistrates' court to make such an order.

(2) Where a magistrates' court has power, in relation to any proceedings under this Act, to decline jurisdiction because it considers that the case can more conveniently be dealt with by another court, no appeal shall lie against any exercise by that magistrates' court of that power.

(3) Subsection (1) does not apply in relation to an interim order for periodical payments made under Schedule 1.

(4) On an appeal under this section, the High Court may make such orders as may be necessary to give effect to its determination of the appeal.

(5) Where an order is made under subsection (4) the High Court may also make such incidental or consequential orders as appears to it to be just.

(6) Where an appeal from a magistrates' court relates to an order for the making of periodical payments, the High Court may order that its determination of the appeal shall have effect from such date as it thinks fit to specify in the order.

(7) The date so specified must not be earlier than the earliest date allowed in accordance with rules of court made for the purposes of this section.

(8) Where, on an appeal under this section in respect of an order requiring a person to make periodical payments, the High Court reduces the amount of those payments or discharges the order –

   (a) it may order the person entitled to the payments to pay to the person making them such sum in respect of payments already made as the High Court thinks fit; and

   (b) if any arrears are due under the order for periodical payments, it may remit payment of the whole, or part, of those arrears.

(9) Any order of the High Court made on an appeal under this section (other than one directing that an application be re-heard by a magistrates' court) shall, for the purposes –

   (a) of the enforcement of the order; and

   (b) of any power to vary, revive or discharge orders,

be treated as if it were an order of the magistrates' court from which the appeal was brought and not an order of the High Court.

(10) The Lord Chancellor may by order make provision as to the circumstances in which appeals may be made against decisions taken by courts on questions arising in connection with the transfer, or proposed transfer, of proceedings by virtue of any order under paragraph 2 of Schedule 11.

(11) Except to the extent provided for in any order made under subsection (10), no appeal may be made against any decision of a kind mentioned in that subsection.

Section 94

Prospective amendment—Section prospectively amended by Adoption and Children Act 2002, s 100 (see **3.3B**).

95 Attendance of child at hearing under Part IV or V

(1) In any proceedings in which a court is hearing an application for an order under Part IV or V, or is considering whether to make any such order, the court may order the child concerned to attend such stage or stages of the proceedings as may be specified in the order.

(2) The power conferred by subsection (1) shall be exercised in accordance with rules of court.

(3) Subsections (4) to (6) apply where –

    (a)   an order under subsection (1) has not been complied with; or

    (b)   the court has reasonable cause to believe that it will not be complied with.

(4) The court may make an order authorising a constable, or such person as may be specified in the order –

    (a)   to take charge of the child and to bring him to the court; and

    (b)   to enter and search any premises specified in the order if he has reasonable cause to believe that the child may be found on the premises.

(5) The court may order any person who is in a position to do so to bring the child to the court.

(6) Where the court has reason to believe that a person has information about the whereabouts of the child it may order him to disclose it to the court.

96 Evidence given by, or with respect to, children

(1) Subsection (2) applies in any civil proceedings where a child who is called as a witness in any civil proceedings does not, in the opinion of the court, understand the nature of an oath.

(2) The child's evidence may be heard by the court if, in its opinion –

    (a)   he understands that it is his duty to speak the truth; and

    (b)   he has sufficient understanding to justify his evidence being heard.

(3) The Lord Chancellor may by order make provision for the admissibility of evidence which would otherwise be inadmissible under any rule of law relating to hearsay.

(4) An order under subsection (3) may only be made with respect to –

    (a)   civil proceedings in general or such civil proceedings, or class of civil proceedings, as may be prescribed; and

    (b)   evidence in connection with the upbringing, maintenance or welfare of a child.

(5) An order under subsection (3) –

    (a)   may, in particular, provide for the admissibility of statements which are made orally or in a prescribed form or which are recorded by any prescribed method of recording;

    (b)   may make different provision for different purposes and in relation to different descriptions of court; and

    (c)   may make such amendments and repeals in any enactment relating to evidence (other than in this Act) as the Lord Chancellor considers necessary or expedient in consequence of the provision made by the order.

(6) Subsection (5)(b) is without prejudice to section 104(4).

(7) In this section –

    'civil proceedings' means civil proceedings, before any tribunal, in relation to which the strict rules of evidence apply, whether as a matter of law or by agreement of the parties, and references to 'the court' shall be construed accordingly;

'prescribed' means prescribed by an order under subsection (3).

Section 96

Hearsay evidence is admissible in proceedings as a result of the Children (Admissibility of Hearsay) Order 1993. Although hearsay evidence is admissible, the court must treat it cautiously and consider carefully the extent to which it can properly be relied upon (*R v B County Council ex parte P* [1991] 2 All ER 65, [1991] 1 WLR 221, CA; *Re W (Minors) (Wardship: Evidence)* [1990] 1 FLR 203, CA).

The child's welfare will be relevant but will not be the court's paramount concern in applications for orders that a child attend court pursuant to a witness summons (*Re P (Witness Summons)* [1997] 2 FLR 447, CA – see also *R v B County Council. ex parte P* (above); and *Re O (Care Proceedings: Evidence)* [2003] EWHC 2011 (Fam), [2004] 1 FLR 161 in which it was said that the general practice is not to hear evidence from children in care proceedings).

97 Privacy for children involved in certain proceedings

(1) Rules made under section 144 of the Magistrates' Courts Act 1980 may make provision for a magistrates' court to sit in private in proceedings in which any powers under this Act may be exercised by the court with respect to any child.

(2) No person shall publish any material which is intended, or likely, to identify –

    (a) any child as being involved in any proceedings before the High Court, a county court or a magistrates' court in which any power under this Act may be exercised by the court with respect to that or any other child; or

    (b) an address or school as being that of a child involved in any such proceedings.

(3) In any proceedings for an offence under this section it shall be a defence for the accused to prove that he did not know, and had no reason to suspect, that the published material was intended, or likely, to identify the child.

(4) The court or the Lord Chancellor may, if satisfied that the welfare of the child requires it, by order dispense with the requirements of subsection (2) to such extent as may be specified in the order.

(5) For the purposes of this section –

'publish' includes –

    (a) include in a programme service (within the meaning of the Broadcasting Act 1990); or

    (b) cause to be published; and

'material' includes any picture or representation.

(6) Any person who contravenes this section shall be guilty of an offence and liable, on summary conviction, to a fine not exceeding level 4 on the standard scale.

(7) Subsection (1) is without prejudice to –

    (a) the generality of the rule making power in section 144 of the Act of 1980; or

    (b) any other power of a magistrates' court to sit in private.

(8) Sections 69 (sittings of magistrates' courts for family proceedings) and 71 (newspaper reports of certain proceedings) of the Act of 1980 shall apply in relation to any proceedings (before a magistrates' court) to which this section applies subject to the provisions of this section.

Section 97

Prospective amendment—Section prospectively amended by Adoption and Children Act 2002, s 101(3) (see **3.3B**); Children Act 2004, s 62(1) (see **3.7**); and Courts Act 2003, s 109(1), Sch 8, para 337(1), (2).

Generally—This section is not incompatible with the European Convention on Human Rights; it is not an absolute prohibition, and the court can be specifically asked to exercise its discretion to permit the identity of the child to be published (*P v BW (Children Cases: Hearings in Public)* [2003] EWHC 1541 (Fam), [2004] 1 FLR 171, FD; the appeal from Bennett J was dismissed [2004] EWCA Civ 845, the Court of Appeal stating in para [38] of the judgment: 'in reality although the Family Proceedings Rules confer on the judge in any case the discretion to lift the veil of privacy, there is such a strong inherited convention of privacy that the judicial mind is almost never directed to the discretion and in rare cases where an application is made a fair exercise may be prejudiced by the tradition or an unconscious preference for the atmosphere created by a hearing in chambers. Judges need to be aware of this and to be prepared to consider another course where appropriate').

See also *B v United Kingdom* (2002) 34 EHRR 19, [2001] 2 FLR 261, ECtHR. *Re M (Disclosure: Children and Family Reporter)* [2002] EWCA Civ 1199, [2002] 2 FLR 893 provides useful guidance on the definition of 'publish' relevant to this provision and to s 12 of the Administration of Justice Act 1960.

98 Self-incrimination

(1) In any proceedings in which a court is hearing an application for an order under Part IV or V, no person shall be excused from –

    (a) giving evidence on any matter; or

    (b) answering any question put to him in the course of his giving evidence,

on the ground that doing so might incriminate him or his spouse of an offence.

(2) A statement or admission made in such proceedings shall not be admissible in evidence against the person making it or his spouse in proceedings for an offence other than perjury.

Section 98

This section should be read together with FPR 1991, r 4.23 and FPC(CA 1989)R 1991, r 23, and Administration of Justice Act 1960, s 12.

There is a continuing duty of full and frank disclosure in proceedings under the CA 1989 (see, eg, *Vernon v Bosley (No 2)* [1997] 1 All ER 614, CA, and para 4 of the *Practice Direction (Family Proceedings: Case Management)* [1995] 1 WLR 262, [1995] 1 All ER 586, [1995] 1 FLR 456). The existence of that duty does not infringe the European Convention on Human Rights (*L v UK* [2000] 2 FLR 322, ECtHR). In *S County Council v B* [2000] 2 FLR 161, FD, it was held that a father was not obliged to disclose reports obtained in criminal proceedings.

In the case of *Re EC (Disclosure of Material)* [1997] Fam 76, [1997] 2 WLR 322, [1996] 2 FLR 725, CA, the Court of Appeal gave guidelines upon when it would be appropriate for a court to permit disclosure to the police of information received in care proceedings. The court should take into account the following factors:

(1) the welfare and interests of the child or children concerned in the care proceedings. If the child is likely to be adversely affected by the order in any serious way, this will be a very important factor;

(2) the welfare and interests of other children generally;

(3) the maintenance of confidentiality in children's cases;

(4) the importance of encouraging frankness in children's cases;

(5) the public interest in the administration of justice. Barriers should not be erected between one branch of the judicature and another;

(6) the public interest in the prosecution of serious crime and the punishment of offenders;

(7) the gravity of the alleged offence and the relevance of the evidence to it;

(8) the desirability of cooperation between various agencies concerned with the welfare of children, including the social services departments, the police service, medical practitioners, health visitors, schools, etc;

(9) in a case to which s 98(2) applies, the terms of the section itself, namely that the witness was not excused from answering incriminating questions, and that any statement or admission would not be admissible against him in criminal proceedings;

(10) any other material disclosure which has already taken place.

There is no presumption in favour of disclosure (*A Chief Constable v A County Council and Others* [2002] EWHC 2198 (Fam), [2003] 2 FCR 384, FD). The court may limit the disclosure to defined classes of people (*Re C (Disclosure: Sexual Abuse Findings)* [2002] EWHC 234 (Fam), [2002] 2 FLR 375, FD). Where the disclosure of criminal papers into proceedings concerning children might compromise the criminal proceedings, disclosure may be refused (*Re P (Disclosure: Criminal Proceedings)* [2003] EWHC 1713 (Fam), [2004] 1 FLR 407).

On an application for permission to disclose information for the purposes of bringing civil proceedings the court will take into account, amongst other things:

(1) the interests of the children concerned;

(2) the interests of the good conduct of children cases generally, in preserving the confidence of those who gave evidence or information to or for the purposes of those proceedings;

(3) the interests of the administration of justice; and

(4) the interests of children generally (*Re R (Children: Disclosure)* [2003] EWCA Civ 19, [2003] 1 FCR 192, CA).

****

100 Restrictions on use of wardship jurisdiction

(1) Section 7 of the Family Law Reform Act 1969 (which gives the High Court power to place a ward of court in the care, or under the supervision, of a local authority) shall cease to have effect.

(2) No court shall exercise the High Court's inherent jurisdiction with respect to children –

(a) so as to require a child to be placed in the care, or put under the supervision, of a local authority;

(b) so as to require a child to be accommodated by or on behalf of a local authority;

(c) so as to make a child who is the subject of a care order a ward of court; or

(d) for the purpose of conferring on any local authority power to determine any question which has arisen, or which may arise, in connection with any aspect of parental responsibility for a child.

(3) No application for any exercise of the court's inherent jurisdiction with respect to children may be made by a local authority unless the authority have obtained the leave of the court.

(4) The court may only grant leave if it is satisfied that –

(a) the result which the authority wish to achieve could not be achieved through the making of any order of a kind to which subsection (5) applies; and

(b) there is reasonable cause to believe that if the court's inherent jurisdiction is not exercised with respect to the child he is likely to suffer significant harm.

(5) This subsection applies to any order –

    (a) made otherwise than in the exercise of the court's inherent jurisdiction; and

    (b) which the local authority is entitled to apply for (assuming, in the case of any application which may only be made with leave, that leave is granted).

Section 100

In the case of *C v K (Inherent Powers: Exclusion Order)* [1996] 2 FLR 506, FD, Wall J gave an extensive analysis of the inherent jurisdiction of the High Court. That inherent jurisdiction is not confined to the wardship jurisdiction. The local authority does not need leave under s 100 before applying for an injunction in care proceedings (*Re P (Care Orders: Injunctive Relief)* [2000] 2 FLR 385). In *Re S (A Child: Identity: Restriction on Publication)* [2004] Fam 43, it was held by a majority of the Court of Appeal that the High Court could prohibit identification of a child whose mother was being tried for murder.

****

105 Interpretation

(1) In this Act –

    'adoption agency' means a body which may be referred to as an adoption agency by virtue of section 1 of the Adoption Act 1976;

    'appropriate children's home' has the meaning given by section 23;

    'bank holiday' means a day which is a bank holiday under the Banking and Financial Dealings Act 1971;

    'care home' has the same meaning as in the Care Standards Act 2000;

    'care order' has the meaning given by section 31(11) and also includes any order which by or under any enactment has the effect of, or is deemed to be, a care order for the purposes of this Act; and any reference to a child who is in the care of an authority is a reference to a child who is in their care by virtue of a care order;

    'child' means, subject to paragraph 16 of Schedule 1, a person under the age of eighteen;

    'child assessment order' has the meaning given by section 43(2);

    'child minder' has the meaning given by section 71;

    'child of the family', in relation to the parties to a marriage, means –

        (a) a child of both of those parties;

        (b) any other child, not being a child who is placed with those parties as foster parents by a local authority or voluntary organisation, who has been treated by both of those parties as a child of their family;

    'children's home' has the meaning given by section 23;

    'community home' has the meaning given by section 53;

    'contact order' has the meaning given by section 8(1);

    'day care' (except in Part XA) has the same meaning as in section 18;

    'disabled', in relation to a child, has the same meaning as in section 17(11);

    'domestic premises' has the meaning given by section 71(12);

    'dwelling-house' includes –

        (a) any building or part of a building which is occupied as a dwelling;

        (b) any caravan, house-boat or structure which is occupied as a dwelling;

        and any yard, garden, garage or outhouse belonging to it and occupied with it;

    'education supervision order' has the meaning given in section 36;

'emergency protection order' means an order under section 44;

'family assistance order' has the meaning given in section 16(2);

'family proceedings' has the meaning given by section 8(3);

'functions' includes powers and duties;

'guardian of a child' means a guardian (other than a guardian of the estate of a child) appointed in accordance with the provisions of section 5;

'harm' has the same meaning as in section 31(9) and the question of whether harm is significant shall be determined in accordance with section 31(10);

'Health Authority' means a Health Authority established under section 8 of the National Health Service Act 1977;

'health service hospital' has the same meaning as in the National Health Service Act 1977;

'hospital' (except in Schedule 9A) has the same meaning as in the Mental Health Act 1983, except that it does not include a hospital at which high security psychiatric services within the meaning of that Act are provided;

'ill-treatment' has the same meaning as in section 31(9);

'income-based jobseeker's allowance' has the same meaning as in the Jobseekers Act 1995;

'independent hospital' has the same meaning as in the Care Standards Act 2000;

'independent school' has the same meaning as in the Education Act 1996;

'local authority' means, in relation to England, the council of a county, a metropolitan district, a London Borough or the Common Council of the City of London, in relation to Wales, the council of a county or a county borough and, in relation to Scotland, a local authority within the meaning of section 1(2) of the Social Work (Scotland) Act 1968;

'local authority foster parent' has the same meaning as in section 23(3);

'local education authority' has the same meaning as in the Education Act 1996;

'local housing authority' has the same meaning as in the Housing Act 1985;

'officer of the Service' has the same meaning as in the Criminal Justice and Court Services Act 2000;

'parental responsibility' has the meaning given in section 3;

'parental responsibility agreement' has the meaning given in section 4(1);

'prescribed' means prescribed by regulations made under this Act;

'Primary Care Trust' means a Primary Care Trust established under section 16A of the National Health Service Act 1977;

'private children's home' means a children's home in respect of which a person is registered under Part II of the Care Standards Act 2000 which is not a community home or a voluntary home;

'privately fostered child' and 'to foster a child privately' have the same meaning as in section 66;

'prohibited steps order' has the meaning given by section 8(1);

'protected child' has the same meaning as in Part III of the Adoption Act 1976;

'registered pupil' has the same meaning as in the Education Act 1996;

'relative', in relation to a child, means a grandparent, brother, sister, uncle or aunt (whether of the full blood or half blood or by affinity) or step-parent;

'residence order' has the meaning given by section 8(1);

'responsible person', in relation to a child who is the subject of a supervision order, has the meaning given in paragraph 1 of Schedule 3;

'school' has the same meaning as in the Education Act 1996 or, in relation to Scotland, in the Education (Scotland) Act 1980;

'service', in relation to any provision made under Part III, includes any facility;

'signed', in relation to any person, includes the making by that person of his mark;

'special educational needs' has the same meaning as in the Education Act 1996;

'Special Health Authority' means a Special Health Authority established under section 11 of the National Health Service Act 1977;

'specific issue order' has the meaning given by section 8(1);

'Strategic Health Authority' means a Strategic Health Authority established under section 8 of the National Health Service Act 1977;

'supervision order' has the meaning given by section 31(11);

'supervised child' and 'supervisor', in relation to a supervision order or an education supervision order, mean respectively the child who is (or is to be) under supervision and the person under whose supervision he is (or is to be) by virtue of the order;

'upbringing', in relation to any child, includes the care of the child but not his maintenance;

'voluntary home' has the meaning given by section 60;

'voluntary organisation' means a body (other than a public or local authority) whose activities are not carried on for profit.

(2) References in this Act to a child whose father and mother were, or (as the case may be) were not, married to each other at the time of his birth must be read with section 1 of the Family Law Reform Act 1987 (which extends the meaning of such references).

(3) References in this Act to –

(a) a person with whom a child lives, or is to live, as the result of a residence order; or

(b) a person in whose favour a residence order is in force,

shall be construed as references to the person named in the order as the person with whom the child is to live.

(4) References in this Act to a child who is looked after by a local authority have the same meaning as they have (by virtue of section 22) in Part III.

(5) References in this Act to accommodation provided by or on behalf of a local authority are references to accommodation so provided in the exercise of functions of that or any other local authority which are social services functions within the meaning of the Local Authority Social Services Act 1970.

(5A) References in this Act to a child minder shall be construed –

(a) in relation to Scotland, in accordance with section 71;

(b) in relation to England and Wales, in accordance with section 79A.

(6) In determining the 'ordinary residence' of a child for any purpose of this Act, there shall be disregarded any period in which he lives in any place –

(a) which is a school or other institution;

(b) in accordance with the requirements of a supervision order under this Act or an order under section 63(1) of the Powers of Criminal Courts (Sentencing) Act 2000; or

(c) while he is being provided with accommodation by or on behalf of a local authority.

(7) References in this Act to children who are in need shall be construed in accordance with section 17.

(8) Any notice or other document required under this Act to be served on any person may be served on him by being delivered personally to him, or being sent by post to him in a registered letter or by the recorded delivery service at his proper address.

(9) Any such notice or other document required to be served on a body corporate or a firm shall be duly served if it is served on the secretary or clerk of that body or a partner of that firm.

(10) For the purposes of this section, and of section 7 of the Interpretation Act 1978 in its application to this section, the proper address of a person –

(a) in the case of a secretary or clerk of a body corporate, shall be that of the registered or principal office of that body;

(b) in the case of a partner of a firm, shall be that of the principal office of the firm; and

(c) in any other case, shall be the last known address of the person to be served.

Section 105

Prospective amendment—Section prospectively amended by Adoption and Children Act 2002, s 139(1), Sch 3, paras 54, 70 (see **3.3B**); Care Standards Act 2002, s 117(2), Sch 6; Civil Partnership Act 2004, s 75.

****

SCHEDULE 2
LOCAL AUTHORITY SUPPORT FOR CHILDREN AND FAMILIES

PART I

PROVISION OF SERVICES FOR FAMILIES

1 Identification of children in need and provision of information

(1) Every local authority shall take reasonable steps to identify the extent to which there are children in need within their area.

(2) Every local authority shall –

(a) publish information

(i) about services provided by them under sections 17, 18, 20, 23B to 23D, 24A and 24B; and

(ii) where they consider it appropriate, about the provision by others (including, in particular, voluntary organisations) of services which the authority have power to provide under those sections; and

(b) take such steps as are reasonably practicable to ensure that those who might benefit from the services receive the information relevant to them.

1A Children's services plans

(1) Every local authority shall, on or before 31 March 1997 –

    (a) review their provision of services under sections 17, 20, 21, 23 and 24; and

    (b) having regard to that review and to their most recent review under section 19, prepare and publish a plan for the provision of services under Part III.

(2) Every local authority –

    (a) shall, from time to time review the plan prepared by them under sub-paragraph (1)(b) (as modified or last substituted under this sub-paragraph), and

    (b) may, having regard to that review and to their most recent review under section 19, prepare and publish –

        (i) modifications (or, as the case may be, further modifications) to the plan reviewed; or

        (ii) a plan in substitution for that plan.

(3) In carrying out any review under this paragraph and in preparing any plan or modifications to a plan, a local authority shall consult –

    (a) every Health Authority and Primary Care Trust the whole or part of whose area lies within the area of the local authority;

    (b) every National Health Service trust which manages a hospital, establishment or facility (within the meaning of the National Health Service and Community Care Act 1990) in the authority's area;

    (c) if the local authority is not itself a local education authority, every local education authority the whole or any part of whose area lies within the area of the local authority;

    (d) any organisation which represents schools in the authority's area which are grant-maintained schools or grant-maintained special schools (within the meaning of the Education Act 1993);

    (e) the governing body of every such school in the authority's area which is not so represented;

    (f) such voluntary organisations as appear to the local authority –

        (i) to represent the interests of persons who use or are likely to use services provided by the local authority under Part III; or

        (ii) to provide services in the area of the local authority which, were they to be provided by the local authority, might be categorised as services provided under that Part;

    (g) the chief constable of the police force for the area;

    (h) the probation committee for the area;

    (i) such other persons as appear to the local authority to be appropriate; and

    (j) such other persons as the Secretary of State may direct.

(4) Every local authority shall, within 28 days of receiving a written request from the Secretary of State, submit to him a copy of –

    (a) the plan prepared by them under sub-paragraph (1); or

    (b) where that plan has been modified or substituted, the plan as modified or last substituted.

Schedule 2, para 1A

Prospective amendment—Paragraph prospectively repealed by Children Act 2004, s 64, Sch 5.

2 Maintenance of a register of disabled children

(1) Every local authority shall open and maintain a register of disabled children within their area.

(2) The register may be kept by means of a computer.

3 Assessment of children's needs

Where it appears to a local authority that a child within their area is in need, the authority may assess his needs for the purposes of this Act at the same time as any assessment of his needs is made under –

- (a) the Chronically Sick and Disabled Persons Act 1970;
- (b) Part IV of the Education Act 1996;
- (c) the Disabled Persons (Services, Consultation and Representation) Act 1986; or
- (d) any other enactment.

4 Prevention of neglect and abuse

(1) Every local authority shall take reasonable steps, through the provision of services under Part III of this Act, to prevent children within their area suffering ill-treatment or neglect.

(2) Where a local authority believe that a child who is at any time within their area –

- (a) is likely to suffer harm; but
- (b) lives or proposes to live in the area of another local authority they shall inform that other local authority.

(3) When informing that other local authority they shall specify –

- (a) the harm that they believe he is likely to suffer; and
- (b) (if they can) where the child lives or proposes to live.

5 Provision of accommodation in order to protect child

(1) Where –

- (a) it appears to a local authority that a child who is living on particular premises is suffering, or is likely to suffer, ill treatment at the hands of another person who is living on those premises; and
- (b) that other person proposes to move from the premises,

the authority may assist that other person to obtain alternative accommodation.

(2) Assistance given under this paragraph may be in cash.

(3) Subsections (7) to (9) of section 17 shall apply in relation to assistance given under this paragraph as they apply in relation to assistance given under that section.

6 Provision for disabled children

Every local authority shall provide services designed –

- (a) to minimise the effect on disabled children within their area of their disabilities; and

(b) to give such children the opportunity to lead lives which are as normal as possible.

7 Provision to reduce need for care proceedings etc

Every local authority shall take reasonable steps designed –

(a) to reduce the need to bring –
   (i) proceedings for care or supervision orders with respect to children within their area;
   (ii) criminal proceedings against such children;
   (iii) any family or other proceedings with respect to such children which might lead to them being placed in the authority's care; or
   (iv) proceedings under the inherent jurisdiction of the High Court with respect to children;
(b) to encourage children within their area not to commit criminal offences; and
(c) to avoid the need for children within their area to be placed in secure accommodation.

8 Provision for children living with their families

Every local authority shall make such provision as they consider appropriate for the following services to be available with respect to children in need within their area while they are living with their families –

(a) advice, guidance and counselling;
(b) occupational, social, cultural or recreational activities;
(c) home help (which may include laundry facilities);
(d) facilities for, or assistance with, travelling to and from home for the purpose of taking advantage of any other service provided under this Act or of any similar service;
(e) assistance to enable the child concerned and his family to have a holiday.

9 Family centres

(1) Every local authority shall provide such family centres as they consider appropriate in relation to children within their area.

(2) 'Family centre' means a centre at which any of the persons mentioned in sub-paragraph (3) may –

(a) attend for occupational, social, cultural or recreational activities;
(b) attend for advice, guidance or counselling; or
(c) be provided with accommodation while he is receiving advice, guidance or counselling.

(3) The persons are –

(a) a child;
(b) his parents;
(c) any person who is not a parent of his but who has parental responsibility for him;
(d) any other person who is looking after him.

10 Maintenance of the family home

Every local authority shall take such steps as are reasonably practicable, where any child within their area who is in need and whom they are not looking after is living apart from his family –

(a) to enable him to live with his family; or

(b) to promote contact between him and his family,

if, in their opinion, it is necessary to do so in order to safeguard or promote his welfare.

11 Duty to consider racial groups to which children in need belong

Every local authority shall, in making any arrangements –

(a) for the provision of day care within their area; or

(b) designed to encourage persons to act as local authority foster parents,

have regard to the different racial groups to which children within their area who are in need belong.

PART II

CHILDREN LOOKED AFTER BY LOCAL AUTHORITIES

12 Regulations as to placing of children with local authority foster parents

Regulations under section 23(2)(a) may, in particular, make provision –

(a) with regard to the welfare of children placed with local authority foster parents;

(b) as to the arrangements to be made by local authorities in connection with the health and education of such children;

(c) as to the records to be kept by local authorities;

(d) for securing that a child is not placed with a local authority foster parent unless that person is for the time being approved as a local authority foster parent by such local authority as may be prescribed;

(e) for securing that where possible the local authority foster parent with whom a child is to be placed is –

(i) of the same religious persuasion as the child; or

(ii) gives an undertaking that the child will be brought up in that religious persuasion;

(f) for securing that children placed with local authority foster parents, and the premises in which they are accommodated, will be supervised and inspected by a local authority and that the children will be removed from those premises if their welfare appears to require it;

(g) as to the circumstances in which local authorities may make arrangements for duties imposed on them by the regulations to be discharged, on their behalf.

13 Regulations as to arrangements under section 23(2)(f)

Regulations under section 23(2)(f) may, in particular, make provision as to –

- (a) the persons to be notified of any proposed arrangements;
- (b) the opportunities such persons are to have to make representations in relation to the arrangements proposed;
- (c) the persons to be notified of any proposed changes in arrangements;
- (d) the records to be kept by local authorities;
- (e) the supervision by local authorities of any arrangements made.

14 Regulations as to conditions under which child in care is allowed to live with parent etc

Regulations under section 23(5) may, in particular, impose requirements on a local authority as to –

- (a) the making of any decision by a local authority to allow a child to live with any person falling within section 23(4) (including requirements as to those who must be consulted before the decision is made, and those who must be notified when it has been made);
- (b) the supervision or medical examination of the child concerned;
- (c) the removal of the child, in such circumstances as may be prescribed, from the care of the person with whom he has been allowed to live;
- (d) the records to be kept by local authorities.

15 Promotion and maintenance of contact between child and family

(1) Where a child is being looked after by a local authority, the authority shall, unless it is not reasonably practicable or consistent with his welfare, endeavour to promote contact between the child and –

- (a) his parents;
- (b) any person who is not a parent of his but who has parental responsibility for him; and
- (c) any relative, friend or other person connected with him.

(2) Where a child is being looked after by a local authority –

- (a) the authority shall take such steps as are reasonably practicable to secure that
  - (i) his parents; and
  - (ii) any person who is not a parent of his but who has parental responsibility for him,

  are kept informed of where he is being accommodated; and
- (b) every such person shall secure that the authority are kept informed of his or her address.

(3) Where a local authority ('the receiving authority') take over the provision of accommodation for a child from another local authority ('the transferring authority') under section 20(2) –

- (a) the receiving authority shall (where reasonably practicable) inform
  - (i) the child's parents; and
  - (ii) any person who is not a parent of his but who has parental responsibility for him;
- (b) sub-paragraph (2)(a) shall apply to the transferring authority, as well as the

receiving authority, until at least one such person has been informed of the change; and

(c) sub-paragraph (2)(b) shall not require any person to inform the receiving authority of his address until he has been so informed.

(4) Nothing in this paragraph requires a local authority to inform any person of the whereabouts of a child if –

(a) the child is in the care of the authority; and

(b) the authority has reasonable cause to believe that informing the person would prejudice the child's welfare.

(5) Any person who fails (without reasonable excuse) to comply with sub-paragraph (2)(b) shall be guilty of an offence and liable on summary conviction to a fine not exceeding level 2 on the standard scale.

(6) It shall be a defence in any proceedings under sub-paragraph (5) to prove that the defendant was residing at the same address as another person who was the child's parent or had parental responsibility for the child and had reasonable cause to believe that the other person had informed the appropriate authority that both of them were residing at that address.

16 Visits to or by children: expenses

(1) This paragraph applies where –

(a) a child is being looked after by a local authority; and

(b) the conditions mentioned in sub-paragraph (3) are satisfied.

(2) The authority may –

(a) make payments to –
   (i) a parent of the child;
   (ii) any person who is not a parent of his but who has parental responsibility for him; or
   (iii) any relative, friend or other person connected with him,
   in respect of travelling, subsistence or other expenses incurred by that person in visiting the child; or

(b) make payments to the child, or to any person on his behalf, in respect of travelling, subsistence or other expenses incurred by or on behalf of the child in his visiting –
   (i) a parent of his;
   (ii) any person who has parental responsibility for him; or
   (iii) any relative, friend or other person connected with him.

(3) The conditions are that –

(a) it appears to the authority that the visit in question could not otherwise be made without undue financial hardship; and

(b) the circumstances warrant the making of the payments.

17 Appointment of visitor for child who is not being visited

(1) Where it appears to a local authority in relation to any child that they are looking after that –

(a) communication between the child and –

       (i) a parent of his, or

      (ii) any person who is not a parent of his but who has parental responsibility for him,

     has been infrequent; or

  (b) he has not visited or been visited by (or lived with) any such person during the preceding twelve months,

and that it would be in the child's best interests for an independent person to be appointed to be his visitor for the purposes of this paragraph, they shall appoint such a visitor.

(2) A person so appointed shall –

  (a) have the duty of visiting, advising and befriending the child; and

  (b) be entitled to recover from the authority who appointed him any reasonable expenses incurred by him for the purposes of his functions under this paragraph.

(3) A person's appointment as a visitor in pursuance of this paragraph shall be determined if –

  (a) he gives notice in writing to the authority who appointed him that he resigns the appointment; or

  (b) the authority give him notice in writing that they have terminated it.

(4) The determination of such an appointment shall not prejudice any duty under this paragraph to make a further appointment.

(5) Where a local authority propose to appoint a visitor for a child under this paragraph, the appointment shall not be made if –

  (a) the child objects to it; and

  (b) the authority are satisfied that he has sufficient understanding to make an informed decision.

(6) Where a visitor has been appointed for a child under this paragraph, the local authority shall determine the appointment if –

  (a) the child objects to its continuing; and

  (b) the authority are satisfied that he has sufficient understanding to make an informed decision.

(7) The Secretary of State may make regulations as to the circumstances in which a person appointed as a visitor under this paragraph is to be regarded as independent of the local authority appointing him.

18 Power to guarantee apprenticeship deeds etc

(1) While a child is being looked after by a local authority, or is a person qualifying for advice and assistance, the authority may undertake any obligation by way of guarantee under any deed of apprenticeship or articles of clerkship which he enters into.

(2) Where a local authority have undertaken any such obligation under any deed or articles they may at any time (whether or not they are still looking after the person concerned) undertake the like obligation under any supplemental deed or articles.

19 Arrangements to assist children to live abroad

(1) A local authority may only arrange for, or assist in arranging for, any child in their care to live outside England and Wales with the approval of the court.

(2) A local authority may, with the approval of every person who has parental responsibility for the child arrange for, or assist in arranging for, any other child looked after by them to live outside England and Wales.

(3) The court shall not give its approval under sub-paragraph (1) unless it is satisfied that –

    (a) living outside England and Wales would be in the child's best interests;

    (b) suitable arrangements have been, or will be, made for his reception and welfare in the country in which he will live;

    (c) the child has consented to living in that country; and

    (d) every person who has parental responsibility for the child has consented to his living in that country.

(4) Where the court is satisfied that the child does not have sufficient understanding to give or withhold his consent, it may disregard sub-paragraph (3)(c) and give its approval if the child is to live in the country concerned with a parent, guardian, or other suitable person.

(5) Where a person whose consent is required by sub-paragraph (3)(d) fails to give his consent, the court may disregard that provision and give its approval if it is satisfied that that person –

    (a) cannot be found;

    (b) is incapable of consenting; or

    (c) is withholding his consent unreasonably.

(6) Section 56 of the Adoption Act 1976 (which requires authority for the taking or sending abroad for adoption of a child who is a British subject) shall not apply in the case of any child who is to live outside England and Wales with the approval of the court given under this paragraph.

(7) Where a court decides to give its approval under this paragraph it may order that its decision is not to have effect during the appeal period.

(8) In sub-paragraph (7) 'the appeal period' means –

    (a) where an appeal is made against the decision, the period between the making of the decision and the determination of the appeal; and

    (b) otherwise, the period during which an appeal may be made against the decision.

Schedule 2, para 19

Prospective amendment—Paragraph prospectively amended by Adoption and Children Act 2002, s 139(1), Sch 3, paras 54, 72 (see **3.3B**).

Preparation for ceasing to be looked after

19A It is the duty of the local authority looking after a child to advise, assist and befriend him with a view to promoting his welfare when they have ceased to look after him.

19B (1) A local authority shall have the following additional functions in relation to an eligible child whom they are looking after.

(2) In sub-paragraph (1) 'eligible child' means, subject to sub-paragraph (3), a child who –

(a) is aged sixteen or seventeen; and

(b) has been looked after by a local authority for a prescribed period, or periods amounting in all to a prescribed period, which began after he reached a prescribed age and ended after he reached the age of sixteen.

(3) The Secretary of State may prescribe –

(a) additional categories of eligible children; and

(b) categories of children who are not to be eligible children despite falling within sub-paragraph (2).

(4) For each eligible child, the local authority shall carry out an assessment of his needs with a view to determining what advice, assistance and support it would be appropriate for them to provide him under this Act –

(a) while they are still looking after him; and

(b) after they cease to look after him,

and shall then prepare a pathway plan for him.

(5) The local authority shall keep the pathway plan under regular review.

(6) Any such review may be carried out at the same time as a review of the child's case carried out by virtue of section 26.

(7) The Secretary of State may by regulations make provision as to assessments for the purposes of sub-paragraph (4).

(8) The regulations may in particular provide for the matters set out in section 23B(6).

19C Personal advisers

A local authority shall arrange for each child whom they are looking after who is an eligible child for the purposes of paragraph 19B to have a personal adviser.

20 Death of children being looked after by local authorities

(1) If a child who is being looked after by a local authority dies, the authority –

(a) shall notify the Secretary of State;

(b) shall, so far as is reasonably practicable, notify the child's parents and every person who is not a parent of his but who has parental responsibility for him;

(c) may, with the consent (so far as it is reasonably practicable to obtain it) of every person who has parental responsibility for the child, arrange for the child's body to be buried or cremated; and

(d) may, if the conditions mentioned in sub-paragraph (2) are satisfied, make payments to any person who has parental responsibility for the child, or any relative, friend or other person connected with the child, in respect of travelling, subsistence or other expenses incurred by that person in attending the child's funeral.

(2) The conditions are that –

    (a) it appears to the authority that the person concerned could not otherwise attend the child's funeral without undue financial hardship; and

    (b) that the circumstances warrant the making of the payments.

(3) Sub-paragraph (1) does not authorise cremation where it does not accord with the practice of the child's religious persuasion.

(4) Where a local authority have exercised their power under sub-paragraph (1)(c) with respect to a child who was under sixteen when he died, they may recover from any parent of the child any expenses incurred by them.

(5) Any sums so recoverable shall, without prejudice to any other method of recovery, be recoverable summarily as a civil debt.

(6) Nothing in this paragraph affects any enactment regulating or authorising the burial, cremation or anatomical examination of the body of a deceased person.

PART III

CONTRIBUTIONS TOWARDS MAINTENANCE OF CHILDREN LOOKED AFTER BY LOCAL AUTHORITIES

21 Liability to contribute

(1) Where a local authority are looking after a child (other than in the cases mentioned in sub-paragraph (7)) they shall consider whether they should recover contributions towards the child's maintenance from any person liable to contribute ('a contributor').

(2) An authority may only recover contributions from a contributor if they consider it reasonable to do so.

(3) The persons liable to contribute are –

    (a) where the child is under sixteen, each of his parents;

    (b) where he has reached the age of sixteen, the child himself.

(4) A parent is not liable to contribute during any period when he is in receipt of income support under Part VII of the Social Security Contributions and Benefits Act 1992, of any element of child tax credit other than the family element, of working tax credit or of an income-based jobseeker's allowance.

(5) A person is not liable to contribute towards the maintenance of a child in the care of a local authority in respect of any period during which the child is allowed by the authority (under section 23(5)) to live with a parent of his.

(6) A contributor is not obliged to make any contribution towards a child's maintenance except as agreed or determined in accordance with this Part of this Schedule.

(7) The cases are where the child is looked after by a local authority under –

    (a) section 21;

    (b) an interim care order;

(c)   section 92 of the Powers of Criminal Courts (Sentencing) Act 2000.

22 Agreed contributions

(1) Contributions towards a child's maintenance may only be recovered if the local authority have served a notice ('a contribution notice') on the contributor specifying –

  (a)   the weekly sum which they consider that he should contribute; and
  (b)   arrangements for payment.

(2) The contribution notice must be in writing and dated.

(3) Arrangements for payment shall, in particular, include –

  (a)   the date on which liability to contribute begins (which must not be earlier than the date of the notice);
  (b)   the date on which liability under the notice will end (if the child has not before that date ceased to be looked after by the authority); and
  (c)   the date on which the first payment is to be made.

(4) The authority may specify in a contribution notice a weekly sum which is a standard contribution determined by them for all children looked after by them.

(5) The authority may not specify in a contribution notice a weekly sum greater than that which they consider –

  (a)   they would normally be prepared to pay if they had placed a similar child with local authority foster parents; and
  (b)   it is reasonably practicable for the contributor to pay (having regard to his means).

(6) An authority may at any time withdraw a contribution notice (without prejudice to their power to serve another).

(7) Where the authority and the contributor agree –

  (a)   the sum which the contributor is to contribute; and
  (b)   arrangements for payment,

(whether as specified in the contribution notice or otherwise) and the contributor notifies the authority in writing that he so agrees, the authority may recover summarily as a civil debt any contribution which is overdue and unpaid.

(8) A contributor may, by serving a notice in writing on the authority, withdraw his agreement in relation to any period of liability falling after the date of service of the notice.

(9) Sub-paragraph (7) is without prejudice to any other method of recovery.

23 Contribution orders

(1) Where a contributor has been served with a contribution notice and has –

  (a)   failed to reach any agreement with the local authority as mentioned in paragraph 22(7) within the period of one month beginning with the day on which the contribution notice was served; or
  (b)   served a notice under paragraph 22(8) withdrawing his agreement,

the authority may apply to the court for an order under this paragraph.

(2) On such an application the court may make an order ('a contribution order') requiring the contributor to contribute a weekly sum towards the child's maintenance in accordance with arrangements for payment specified by the court.

(3) A contribution order –

    (a) shall not specify a weekly sum greater than that specified in the contribution notice; and

    (b) shall be made with due regard to the contributor's means.

(4) A contribution order shall not –

    (a) take effect before the date specified in the contribution notice; or

    (b) have effect while the contributor is not liable to contribute (by virtue of paragraph 21); or

    (c) remain in force after the child has ceased to be looked after by the authority who obtained the order.

(5) An authority may not apply to the court under sub-paragraph (1) in relation to a contribution notice which they have withdrawn.

(6) Where –

    (a) a contribution order is in force;

    (b) the authority serve another contribution notice; and

    (c) the contributor and the authority reach an agreement under paragraph 22(7) in respect of that other contribution notice,

the effect of the agreement shall be to discharge the order from the date on which it is agreed that the agreement shall take effect.

(7) Where an agreement is reached under sub-paragraph (6) the authority shall notify the court –

    (a) of the agreement; and

    (b) of the date on which it took effect.

(8) A contribution order may be varied or revoked on the application of the contributor or the authority.

(9) In proceedings for the variation of a contribution order, the authority shall specify –

    (a) the weekly sum which, having regard to paragraph 22, they propose that the contributor should contribute under the order as varied; and

    (b) the proposed arrangements for payment.

(10) Where a contribution order is varied, the order –

    (a) shall not specify a weekly sum greater than that specified by the authority in the proceedings for variation; and

    (b) shall be made with due regard to the contributor's means.

(11) An appeal shall lie in accordance with rules of court from any order made under this paragraph.

24 Enforcement of contribution orders etc

(1) A contribution order made by a magistrates' court shall be enforceable as a magistrates' court maintenance order (within the meaning of section 150(1) of the Magistrates' Courts Act 1980).

(2) Where a contributor has agreed, or has been ordered, to make contributions to a local authority, any other local authority within whose area the contributor is for the time being living may –

- (a) at the request of the local authority who served the contribution notice; and
- (b) subject to agreement as to any sum to be deducted in respect of services rendered,

collect from the contributor any contributions due on behalf of the authority who served the notice.

(3) In sub-paragraph (2) the reference to any other local authority includes a reference to –

- (a) a local authority within the meaning of section 1(2) of the Social Work (Scotland) Act 1968; and
- (b) a Health and Social Services Board established under Article 16 of the Health and Personal Social Services (Northern Ireland) Order 1972.

(4) The power to collect sums under sub-paragraph (2) includes the power to –

- (a) receive and give a discharge for any contributions due; and
- (b) (if necessary) enforce payment of any contributions,

even though those contributions may have fallen due at a time when the contributor was living elsewhere.

(5) Any contributions collected under sub-paragraph (2) shall be paid (subject to any agreed deduction) to the local authority who served the contribution notice.

(6) In any proceedings under this paragraph, a document which purports to be –

- (a) a copy of an order made by a court under or by virtue of paragraph 23; and
- (b) certified as a true copy by the justices' chief executive for the court,

shall be evidence of the order.

(7) In any proceedings under this paragraph, a certificate which –

- (a) purports to be signed by the clerk or some other duly authorised officer of the local authority who obtained the contribution order; and
- (b) states that any sum due to the authority under the order is overdue and unpaid,

shall be evidence that the sum is overdue and unpaid.

25 Regulations

The Secretary of State may make regulations –

- (a) as to the considerations which a local authority must take into account in deciding –
  - (i) whether it is reasonable to recover contributions; and
  - (ii) what the arrangements for payment should be;

(b) as to the procedures they must follow in reaching agreements with –
  (i) contributors (under paragraphs 22 and 23); and
  (ii) any other local authority (under paragraph 23).

SCHEDULE 3

SUPERVISION ORDERS

PART I
GENERAL

1 Meaning of 'responsible person'

In this Schedule, 'the responsible person', in relation to a supervised child, means –

(a) any person who has parental responsibility for the child; and
(b) any other person with whom the child is living.

2 Power of supervisor to give directions to supervised child

(1) A supervision order may require the supervised child to comply with any directions given from time to time by the supervisor which require him to do all or any of the following things –

(a) to live at a place or places specified in the directions for a period or periods so specified;
(b) to present himself to a person or persons specified in the directions at a place or places and on a day or days so specified;
(c) to participate in activities specified in the directions on a day or days so specified.

(2) It shall be for the supervisor to decide whether, and to what extent, he exercises his power to give directions and to decide the form of any directions which he gives.

(3) Sub-paragraph (1) does not confer on a supervisor power to give directions in respect of any medical or psychiatric examination or treatment (which are matters dealt with in paragraphs 4 and 5).

3 Imposition of obligations on responsible person

(1) With the consent of any responsible person, a supervision order may include a requirement –

(a) that he take all reasonable steps to ensure that the supervised child complies with any direction given by the supervisor under paragraph 2;
(b) that he take all reasonable steps to ensure that the supervised child complies with any requirement included in the order under paragraph 4 or 5;
(c) that he comply with any directions given by the supervisor requiring him to attend at a place specified in the directions for the purpose of taking part in activities so specified.

(2) A direction given under sub-paragraph (1)(c) may specify the time at which the responsible person is to attend and whether or not the supervised child is required to attend with him.

(3) A supervision order may require any person who is a responsible person in relation to the supervised child to keep the supervisor informed of his address, if it differs from the child's.

4 Psychiatric and medical examinations

(1) A supervision order may require the supervised child –

 (a) to submit to a medical or psychiatric examination; or
 (b) to submit to any such examination from time to time as directed by the supervisor.

(2) Any such examination shall be required to be conducted –

 (a) by, or under the direction of, such registered medical practitioner as may be specified in the order;
 (b) at a place specified in the order and at which the supervised child is to attend as a non-resident patient; or
 (c) at –
  (i) a health service hospital; or
  (ii) in the case of a psychiatric examination, a hospital, independent hospital or care home,
 at which the supervised child is, or is to attend as, a resident patient.

(3) A requirement of a kind mentioned in sub-paragraph (2)(c) shall not be included unless the court is satisfied, on the evidence of a registered medical practitioner, that –

 (a) the child may be suffering from a physical or mental condition that requires, and may be susceptible to, treatment; and
 (b) a period as a resident patient is necessary if the examination is to be carried out properly.

(4) No court shall include a requirement under this paragraph in a supervision order unless it is satisfied that –

 (a) where the child has sufficient understanding to make an informed decision, he consents to its inclusion; and
 (b) satisfactory arrangements have been, or can be, made for the examination.

5 Psychiatric and medical treatment

(1) Where a court which proposes to make or vary a supervision order is satisfied, on the evidence of a registered medical practitioner approved for the purposes of section 12 of the Mental Health Act 1983, that the mental condition of the supervised child –

 (a) is such as requires, and may be susceptible to, treatment; but
 (b) is not such as to warrant his detention in pursuance of a hospital order under Part III of that Act,

the court may include in the order a requirement that the supervised child shall, for a period specified in the order, submit to such treatment as is so specified.

(2) The treatment specified in accordance with sub-paragraph (1) must be –

    (a) by, or under the direction of, such registered medical practitioner as may be specified in the order;

    (b) as a non-resident patient at such a place as may be so specified; or

    (c) as a resident patient in a hospital, independent hospital or care home.

(3) Where a court which proposes to make or vary a supervision order is satisfied, on the evidence of a registered medical practitioner, that the physical condition of the supervised child is such as requires, and may be susceptible to, treatment, the court may include in the order a requirement that the supervised child shall, for a period specified in the order, submit to such treatment as is so specified.

(4) The treatment specified in accordance with sub-paragraph (3) must be –

    (a) by, or under the direction of, such registered medical practitioner as may be specified in the order;

    (b) as a non-resident patient at such place as may be so specified; or

    (c) as a resident patient in a health service hospital.

(5) No court shall include a requirement under this paragraph in a supervision order unless it is satisfied –

    (a) where the child has sufficient understanding to make an informed decision, that he consents to its inclusion; and

    (b) that satisfactory arrangements have been, or can be, made for the treatment.

(6) If a medical practitioner by whom or under whose direction a supervised person is being treated in pursuance of a requirement included in a supervision order by virtue of this paragraph is unwilling to continue to treat or direct the treatment of the supervised child or is of the opinion that –

    (a) the treatment should be continued beyond the period specified in the order;

    (b) the supervised child needs different treatment;

    (c) he is not susceptible to treatment; or

    (d) he does not require further treatment,

the practitioner shall make a report in writing to that effect to the supervisor.

(7) On receiving a report under this paragraph the supervisor shall refer it to the court, and on such a reference the court may make an order cancelling or varying the requirement.

PART II

MISCELLANEOUS

6 Life of supervision order

(1) Subject to sub-paragraph (2) and section 91, a supervision order shall cease to have effect at the end of the period of one year beginning with the date on which it was made.

(2) A supervision order shall also cease to have effect if an event mentioned in section 25(1)(a) or (b) of the Child Abduction and Custody Act 1985 (termination of existing orders) occurs with respect to the child.

(3) Where the supervisor applies to the court to extend, or further extend, a supervision order the court may extend the order for such period as it may specify.

(4) A supervision order may not be extended so as to run beyond the end of the period of three years beginning with the date on which it was made.

7 *(repealed)*

8 Information to be given to supervisor etc

(1) A supervision order may require the supervised child –

    (a)   to keep the supervisor informed of any change in his address; and

    (b)   to allow the supervisor to visit him at the place where he is living.

(2) The responsible person in relation to any child with respect to whom a supervision order is made shall –

    (a)   if asked by the supervisor, inform him of the child's address (if it is known to him); and

    (b)   if he is living with the child, allow the supervisor reasonable contact with the child.

9 Selection of supervisor

(1) A supervision order shall not designate a local authority as the supervisor unless –

    (a)   the authority agree; or

    (b)   the supervised child lives or will live within their area.

(2)–(5) *(repealed)*

10 Effect of supervision order on earlier orders

The making of a supervision order with respect to any child brings to an end any earlier care or supervision order which –

    (a)   was made with respect to that child; and

    (b)   would otherwise continue in force.

11 Local authority functions and expenditure

(1) The Secretary of State may make regulations with respect to the exercise by a local authority of their functions where a child has been placed under their supervision by a supervision order.

(2) Where a supervision order requires compliance with directions given by virtue of this section, any expenditure incurred by the supervisor for the purposes of the directions shall be defrayed by the local authority designated in the order.

PART III

EDUCATION SUPERVISION ORDERS

Effect of orders

12 (1) Where an education supervision order is in force with respect to a child, it shall be the duty of the supervisor –

    (a) to advise, assist and befriend, and give directions to –
        (i) the supervised child; and
        (ii) his parents;
        in such a way as will, in the opinion of the supervisor, secure that he is properly educated;
    (b) where any such directions given to
        (i) the supervised child; or
        (ii) a parent of his,
        have not been complied with, to consider what further steps to take in the exercise of the supervisor's powers under this Act.

(2) Before giving any directions under sub-paragraph (1) the supervisor shall, so far as is reasonably practicable, ascertain the wishes and feelings of –

    (a) the child; and
    (b) his parents;

including, in particular, their wishes as to the place at which the child should be educated.

(3) When settling the terms of any such directions, the supervisor shall give due consideration –

    (a) having regard to the child's age and understanding, to such wishes and feelings of his as the supervisor has been able to ascertain; and
    (b) to such wishes and feelings of the child's parents as he has been able to ascertain.

(4) Directions may be given under this paragraph at any time while the education supervision order is in force.

13 (1) Where an education supervision order is in force with respect to a child, the duties of the child's parents under sections 7 and 444 of the Education Act 1996 (duties to secure education of children and to secure regular attendance of registered pupils) shall be superseded by their duty to comply with any directions in force under the education supervision order.

(2) Where an education supervision order is made with respect to a child –

    (a) any school attendance order –
        (i) made under section 437 of the Education Act 1996 with respect to the child; and
        (ii) in force immediately before the making of the education supervision order,
        shall cease to have effect; and
    (b) while the education supervision order remains in force, the following provisions shall not apply with respect to the child –

     (i)   section 437 of that Act (school attendance orders);

     (ii) section 9 of that Act (pupils to be educated in accordance with wishes of their parents);

     (iii) sections 411 and 423 of that Act (parental preference and appeals against admission decisions);

  (c) a supervision order made with respect to the child in criminal proceedings, while the education supervision order is in force, may not include an education requirement of the kind which could otherwise be included under paragraph 7 of Schedule 6 to the Powers of Criminal Courts (Sentencing) Act 2000;

  (d) any education requirement of a kind mentioned in paragraph (c), which was in force with respect to the child immediately before the making of the education supervision order, shall cease to have effect.

14 Effect where child also subject to supervision order

(1) This paragraph applies where an education supervision order and a supervision order, or order under section 63(1) of the Powers of Criminal Courts (Sentencing) Act 2000, are in force at the same time with respect to the same child.

(2) Any failure to comply with a direction given by the supervisor under the education supervision order shall be disregarded if it would not have been reasonably practicable to comply with it without failing to comply with a direction given under the other order.

15 Duration of orders

(1) An education supervision order shall have effect for a period of one year, beginning with the date on which it is made.

(2) An education supervision order shall not expire if, before it would otherwise have expired, the court has (on the application of the authority in whose favour the order was made) extended the period during which it is in force.

(3) Such an application may not be made earlier than three months before the date on which the order would otherwise expire.

(4) The period during which an education supervision order is in force may be extended under sub-paragraph (2) on more than one occasion.

(5) No one extension may be for a period of more than three years.

(6) An education supervision order shall cease to have effect on –

  (a) the child's ceasing to be of compulsory school age; or

  (b) the making of a care order with respect to the child;

and sub-paragraphs (1) to (4) are subject to this sub-paragraph.

16 Information to be given to supervisor etc

(1) An education supervision order may require the child –

  (a) to keep the supervisor informed of any change in his address; and

  (b) to allow the supervisor to visit him at the place where he is living.

(2) A person who is the parent of a child with respect to whom an education supervision order has been made shall –

    (a) if asked by the supervisor, inform him of the child's address (if it is known to him); and

    (b) if he is living with the child, allow the supervisor reasonable contact with the child.

17 Discharge of orders

(1) The court may discharge any education supervision order on the application of –

    (a) the child concerned;

    (b) a parent of his; or

    (c) the local education authority concerned.

(2) On discharging an education supervision order, the court may direct the local authority within whose area the child lives, or will live, to investigate the circumstances of the child.

18 Offences

(1) If a parent of a child with respect to whom an education supervision order is in force persistently fails to comply with a direction given under the order he shall be guilty of an offence.

(2) It shall be a defence for any person charged with such an offence to prove that –

    (a) he took all reasonable steps to ensure that the direction was complied with;

    (b) the direction was unreasonable; or

    (c) he had complied with –

        (i) a requirement included in a supervision order made with respect to the child; or

        (ii) directions given under such a requirement,

and that it was not reasonably practicable to comply both with the direction and with the requirement or directions mentioned in this paragraph.

(3) A person guilty of an offence under this paragraph shall be liable on summary conviction to a fine not exceeding level 3 on the standard scale.

19 Persistent failure of child to comply with directions

(1) Where a child with respect to whom an education supervision order is in force persistently fails to comply with any direction given under the order, the local education authority concerned shall notify the appropriate local authority.

(2) Where a local authority have been notified under sub-paragraph (1) they shall investigate the circumstances of the child.

(3) In this paragraph 'the appropriate local authority' has the same meaning as in section 36.

20 Miscellaneous

The Secretary of State may by regulations make provision modifying, or displacing, the provisions of any enactment about education in relation to any child with respect to whom an education supervision order is in force to such extent as appears to the Secretary of State to be necessary or expedient in consequence of the provision made by this Act with respect to such orders.

21 Interpretation

In this part of this Schedule 'parent' has the same meaning as in the Education Act 1996.

****

3.7 CHILDREN ACT 2004
(ss 2, 3, 4(1), 10–14, 17, 62)

Note on commencement—The provisions reproduced here are in force except where otherwise stated in the annotations.

PART 1

CHILDREN'S COMMISSIONER

****

2 General function

(1) The Children's Commissioner has the function of promoting awareness of the views and interests of children in England.

(2) The Children's Commissioner may in particular under this section –

(a) encourage persons exercising functions or engaged in activities affecting children to take account of their views and interests;

(b) advise the Secretary of State on the views and interests of children;

(c) consider or research the operation of complaints procedures so far as relating to children;

(d) consider or research any other matter relating to the interests of children;

(e) publish a report on any matter considered or researched by him under this section.

(3) The Children's Commissioner is to be concerned in particular under this section with the views and interests of children so far as relating to the following aspects of their well-being –

(a) physical and mental health and emotional well-being;

(b) protection from harm and neglect;

(c) education, training and recreation;

(d) the contribution made by them to society;

(e) social and economic well-being.

(4) The Children's Commissioner must take reasonable steps to involve children in the discharge of his function under this section, and in particular to –

(a) ensure that children are made aware of his function and how they may communicate with him; and

(b) consult children, and organisations working with children, on the matters he proposes to consider or research under subsection (2)(c) or (d).

(5) Where the Children's Commissioner publishes a report under this section he must, if and to the extent that he considers it appropriate, also publish the report in a

version which is suitable for children (or, if the report relates to a particular group of children, for those children).

(6) The Children's Commissioner must for the purposes of subsection (4) have particular regard to groups of children who do not have other adequate means by which they can make their views known.

(7) The Children's Commissioner is not under this section to conduct an investigation of the case of an individual child.

(8) The Children's Commissioner or a person authorised by him may for the purposes of his function under this section at any reasonable time –

    (a) enter any premises, other than a private dwelling, for the purposes of interviewing any child accommodated or cared for there; and

    (b) if the child consents, interview the child in private.

(9) Any person exercising functions under any enactment must supply the Children's Commissioner with such information in that person's possession relating to those functions as the Children's Commissioner may reasonably request for the purposes of his function under this section (provided that the information is information which that person may, apart from this subsection, lawfully disclose to him).

(10) Where the Children's Commissioner has published a report under this section containing recommendations in respect of any person exercising functions under any enactment, he may require that person to state in writing, within such period as the Children's Commissioner may reasonably require, what action the person has taken or proposes to take in response to the recommendations.

(11) In considering for the purpose of his function under this section what constitutes the interests of children (generally or so far as relating to a particular matter) the Children's Commissioner must have regard to the United Nations Convention on the Rights of the Child.

(12) In subsection (11) the reference to the United Nations Convention on the Rights of the Child is to the Convention on the Rights of the Child adopted by the General Assembly of the United Nations on 20th November 1989, subject to any reservations, objections or interpretative declarations by the United Kingdom for the time being in force.

3 Inquiries initiated by Commissioner

(1) Where the Children's Commissioner considers that the case of an individual child in England raises issues of public policy of relevance to other children, he may hold an inquiry into that case for the purpose of investigating and making recommendations about those issues.

(2) The Children's Commissioner may only conduct an inquiry under this section if he is satisfied that the inquiry would not duplicate work that is the function of another person (having consulted such persons as he considers appropriate).

(3) Before holding an inquiry under this section the Children's Commissioner must consult the Secretary of State.

4 Other inquiries held by Commissioner

(1) Where the Secretary of State considers that the case of an individual child in England raises issues of relevance to other children, he may direct the Children's Commissioner to hold an inquiry into that case

(2)–(7) *(not reproduced here)*

****

PART 2

CHILDREN'S SERVICES IN ENGLAND

General

10 Co-operation to improve well-being

(1) Each children's services authority in England must make arrangements to promote co-operation between –

(a) the authority;

(b) each of the authority's relevant partners; and

(c) such other persons or bodies as the authority consider appropriate, being persons or bodies of any nature who exercise functions or are engaged in activities in relation to children in the authority's area.

(2) The arrangements are to be made with a view to improving the well-being of children in the authority's area so far as relating to –

(a) physical and mental health and emotional well-being;

(b) protection from harm and neglect;

(c) education, training and recreation;

(d) the contribution made by them to society;

(e) social and economic well-being.

(3) In making arrangements under this section a children's services authority in England must have regard to the importance of parents and other persons caring for children in improving the well-being of children.

(4) For the purposes of this section each of the following is a relevant partner of a children's services authority in England –

(a) where the authority is a county council for an area for which there is also a district council, the district council;

(b) the police authority and the chief officer of police for a police area any part of which falls within the area of the children's services authority;

(c) a local probation board for an area any part of which falls within the area of the authority;

(d) a youth offending team for an area any part of which falls within the area of the authority;

(e) a Strategic Health Authority and Primary Care Trust for an area any part of which falls within the area of the authority;

(f) a person providing services under section 114 of the Learning and Skills

Act 2000 in any part of the area of the authority;
(g) the Learning and Skills Council for England.

(5) The relevant partners of a children's services authority in England must co-operate with the authority in the making of arrangements under this section.

(6) A children's services authority in England and any of their relevant partners may for the purposes of arrangements under this section –

(a) provide staff, goods, services, accommodation or other resources;
(b) establish and maintain a pooled fund.

(7) For the purposes of subsection (6) a pooled fund is a fund –

(a) which is made up of contributions by the authority and the relevant partner or partners concerned; and
(b) out of which payments may be made towards expenditure incurred in the discharge of functions of the authority and functions of the relevant partner or partners.

(8) A children's services authority in England and each of their relevant partners must in exercising their functions under this section have regard to any guidance given to them for the purpose by the Secretary of State.

(9) Arrangements under this section may include arrangements relating to –

(a) persons aged 18 and 19;
(b) persons over the age of 19 who are receiving services under sections 23C to 24D of the Children Act 1989;
(c) persons over the age of 19 but under the age of 25 who have a learning difficulty, within the meaning of section 13 of the Learning and Skills Act 2000, and are receiving services under that Act.

Section 10

Commencement—Section due to come into force 1 April 2005.

11 Arrangements to safeguard and promote welfare

(1) This section applies to each of the following –

(a) a children's services authority in England;
(b) a district council which is not such an authority;
(c) a Strategic Health Authority;
(d) a Special Health Authority, so far as exercising functions in relation to England, designated by order made by the Secretary of State for the purposes of this section;
(e) a Primary Care Trust;
(f) an NHS trust all or most of whose hospitals, establishments and facilities are situated in England;
(g) an NHS foundation trust;
(h) the police authority and chief officer of police for a police area in England;
(i) the British Transport Police Authority, so far as exercising functions in relation to England;
(j) a local probation board for an area in England;
(k) a youth offending team for an area in England;
(l) the governor of a prison or secure training centre in England (or, in the case of a contracted out prison or secure training centre, its director);

(m)   any person to the extent that he is providing services under section 114 of the Learning and Skills Act 2000.

(2) Each person and body to whom this section applies must make arrangements for ensuring that –

(a)   their functions are discharged having regard to the need to safeguard and promote the welfare of children; and

(b)   any services provided by another person pursuant to arrangements made by the person or body in the discharge of their functions are provided having regard to that need.

(3) In the case of a children's services authority in England, the reference in subsection (2) to functions of the authority does not include functions to which section 175 of the Education Act 2002 applies.

(4) Each person and body to whom this section applies must in discharging their duty under this section have regard to any guidance given to them for the purpose by the Secretary of State.

Section 11

Commencement—Section not yet in force.

12 Information databases

(1) The Secretary of State may for the purpose of arrangements under section 10 or 11 above or under section 175 of the Education Act 2002 –

(a)   by regulations require children's services authorities in England to establish and operate databases containing information in respect of persons to whom such arrangements relate;

(b)   himself establish and operate, or make arrangements for the operation and establishment of, one or more databases containing such information.

(2) The Secretary of State may for the purposes of arrangements under subsection (1)(b) by regulations establish a body corporate to establish and operate one or more databases.

(3) A database under this section may only include information falling within subsection (4) in relation to a person to whom arrangements specified in subsection (1) relate.

(4) The information referred to in subsection (3) is information of the following descriptions in relation to a person –

(a)   his name, address, gender and date of birth;

(b)   a number identifying him;

(c)   the name and contact details of any person with parental responsibility for him (within the meaning of section 3 of the Children Act 1989) or who has care of him at any time;

(d)   details of any education being received by him (including the name and contact details of any educational institution attended by him);

(e)   the name and contact details of any person providing primary medical services in relation to him under Part 1 of the National Health Service Act 1977;

(f)   the name and contact details of any person providing to him services of such description as the Secretary of State may by regulations specify;

(g) information as to the existence of any cause for concern in relation to him;

(h) information of such other description, not including medical records or other personal records, as the Secretary of State may by regulations specify.

(5) The Secretary of State may by regulations make provision in relation to the establishment and operation of any database or databases under this section.

Section 12

Commencement—Section not yet in force.

Local Safeguarding Children Boards

13 Establishment of LSCBs

(1) Each children's services authority in England must establish a Local Safeguarding Children Board for their area.

(2) A Board established under this section must include such representative or representatives of –

(a) the authority by which it is established, and
(b) each Board partner of that authority,

as the Secretary of State may by regulations prescribe.

(3) For the purposes of this section each of the following is a Board partner of a children's services authority in England –

(a) where the authority is a county council for an area for which there is also a district council, the district council;

(b) the chief officer of police for a police area any part of which falls within the area of the authority;

(c) a local probation board for an area any part of which falls within the area of the authority;

(d) a youth offending team for an area any part of which falls within the area of the authority;

(e) a Strategic Health Authority and a Primary Care Trust for an area any part of which falls within the area of the authority;

(f) an NHS trust and an NHS foundation trust all or most of whose hospitals, establishments and facilities are situated in the area of the authority;

(g) a person providing services under section 114 of the Learning and Skills Act 2000 (c 21) in any part of the area of the authority;

(h) the Children and Family Court Advisory and Support Service;

(i) the governor of any secure training centre in the area of the authority (or, in the case of a contracted out secure training centre, its director);

(j) the governor of any prison in the area of the authority which ordinarily detains children (or, in the case of a contracted out prison, its director).

(4) A children's services authority in England must take reasonable steps to ensure that the Local Safeguarding Children Board established by them includes representatives of relevant persons and bodies of such descriptions as may be prescribed by the Secretary of State in regulations.

(5) A Local Safeguarding Children Board established under this section may also include representatives of such other relevant persons or bodies as the authority by

which it is established consider, after consulting their Board partners, should be represented on it.

(6) For the purposes of subsections (4) and (5), relevant persons and bodies are persons and bodies of any nature exercising functions or engaged in activities relating to children in the area of the authority in question.

(7) In the establishment and operation of a Local Safeguarding Children Board under this section –

(a) the authority establishing it must co-operate with each of their Board partners; and

(b) each Board partner must co-operate with the authority.

(8) Two or more children's services authorities in England may discharge their respective duties under subsection (1) by establishing a Local Safeguarding Children Board for their combined area (and where they do so, any reference in this section or sections 14 to 16 to the authority establishing the Board shall be read as a reference to the authorities establishing it).

Section 13

Commencement—Section not yet in force.

14 Functions and procedure of LSCBs

(1) The objective of a Local Safeguarding Children Board established under section 13 is –

(a) to co-ordinate what is done by each person or body represented on the Board for the purposes of safeguarding and promoting the welfare of children in the area of the authority by which it is established; and

(b) to ensure the effectiveness of what is done by each such person or body for those purposes.

(2) A Local Safeguarding Children Board established under section 13 is to have such functions in relation to its objective as the Secretary of State may by regulations prescribe (which may in particular include functions of review or investigation).

(3) The Secretary of State may by regulations make provision as to the procedures to be followed by a Local Safeguarding Children Board established under section 13.

Section 14

Commencement—Section not yet in force.

****

Local authority administration

17 Children and young people's plans

(1) The Secretary of State may by regulations require a children's services authority in England from time to time to prepare and publish a plan setting out the authority's strategy for discharging their functions in relation to children and relevant young persons.

(2) Regulations under this section may in particular make provision as to –

    (a) the matters to be dealt with in a plan under this section;
    (b) the period to which a plan under this section is to relate;
    (c) when and how a plan under this section must be published;
    (d) keeping a plan under this section under review;
    (e) consultation to be carried out during preparation of a plan under this section.

(3) The matters for which provision may be made under subsection (2)(a) include in particular –

    (a) the arrangements made or to be made under section 10 by a children's services authority in England;
    (b) the strategy or proposals in relation to children and relevant young persons of any person or body with whom a children's services authority in England makes or proposes to make such arrangements.

(4) The power to make regulations conferred by this section shall, for the purposes of subsection (1) of section 100 of the Local Government Act 2003 (c 26), be regarded as included among the powers mentioned in subsection (2) of that section.

(5) In this section 'relevant young persons' means persons, other than children, in relation to whom arrangements under section 10 may be made.

Section 17

Commencement—Section due to come into force 15 March 2005.

****

62 Publication of material relating to legal proceedings

(1) In section 97(2) of the Children Act 1989 (privacy for children involved in certain proceedings), after 'publish' insert 'to the public at large or any section of the public'.

(2) In section 12(4) of the Administration of Justice Act 1960 (publication of information relating to proceedings in private), at the end insert '(and in particular where the publication is not so punishable by reason of being authorised by rules of court)'.

(3) In section 66 of the Adoption Act 1976 (rules of procedure), after subsection (5) insert –

    '(5A) Rules may, for the purposes of the law relating to contempt of court, authorise the publication in such circumstances as may be specified of information relating to proceedings held in private involving children.'

(4) In section 145(1) of the Magistrates' Courts Act 1980 (rules: supplementary), after paragraph (g) insert –

    '(ga) authorising, for the purposes of the law relating to contempt of court, the publication in such circumstances as may be specified of information relating to proceedings referred to in section 12(1)(a) of the Administration of Justice Act 1960 which are held in private;'.

(5) In section 40(4) of the Matrimonial and Family Proceedings Act 1984 (family proceedings rules), in paragraph (a) after 'County Courts Act 1984;' insert –

'(aa)   authorise, for the purposes of the law relating to contempt of court, the publication in such circumstances as may be specified of information relating to family proceedings held in private;'.

(6) In section 141 of the Adoption and Children Act 2002 (rules of procedure) at the end insert –

'(6) Rules may, for the purposes of the law relating to contempt of court, authorise the publication in such circumstances as may be specified of information relating to proceedings held in private involving children.'

(7) In section 76 of the Courts Act 2003 (Family Procedure Rules: further provision) after subsection (2) insert –

'(2A) Family Procedure Rules may, for the purposes of the law relating to contempt of court, authorise the publication in such circumstances as may be specified of information relating to family proceedings held in private.'

Section 62

Commencement—Section not yet in force.

3.8 CHILDREN AND YOUNG PERSONS ACT 1933
(s 39, Sch 1)

39 Power to prohibit publication of certain matter in newspapers

(1) In relation to any proceedings in any court the court may direct that –

   (a) no newspaper report of the proceedings shall reveal the name, address, or school, or include any particulars calculated to lead to the identification, of any child or young person concerned in the proceedings, either as being the person by or against or in respect of whom the proceedings are taken, or as being a witness therein;

   (b) no picture shall be published in any newspaper as being or including a picture of any child or young person so concerned in the proceedings as aforesaid;

except in so far (if at all) as may be permitted by the direction of the court.

(2) Any person who publishes any matter in contravention of any such direction shall on summary conviction be liable in respect of each offence to a fine not exceeding level 5 on the standard scale.

(3) In this section 'proceedings' means proceedings other than criminal proceedings.

Section 39

The effect of this section is thoroughly examined in the case of *Re S (A Child) (Identification: Restriction on Publication)* [2003] EWCA Civ 963, [2004] Fam 43, CA. In the case of *Re G (Contempt: Committal)* [2003] EWCA Civ 489, [2003] 2 FLR 58, CA, the President said:

> 'In the absence of an order, as under s 39(1) of the Children and Young Persons Act 1933, it is not a breach of s 12 of the Administration of Justice Act 1960 to publish the name and address of, or to indicate the identity of, the child nor to publish the fact that proceedings are taking place (*Re W (Wards) (Publication of Information)* [1989] 1 FLR 246). It is a breach to publish details of the actual proceedings. These include the evidence given before the court, the proofs of witnesses, the contents of experts' reports and the Official Solicitor's report and the submissions of the advocates (*Re F (otherwise) (A Minor) (Publication of Information)* [1977] 1 All ER 114 at 135, [1977] Fam 58 at 105).'

FIRST SCHEDULE

OFFENCES AGAINST CHILDREN AND YOUNG PERSONS, WITH RESPECT TO WHICH SPECIAL PROVISIONS OF THIS ACT APPLY

Sections 13, 14, 15, 40, 41, 42, 43, 63, 67, 99 and 108

The murder or manslaughter of a child or young person.

Infanticide.

Any offence under sections twenty-seven, … or fifty-six of the Offences against the Person Act 1861, and any offence against a child or young person under sections five, of that Act

Common assault, or battery.

Any offence under sections one, three, four, eleven or twenty-three of this Act.

Any offence against a child or young person under any of the following sections of the Sexual Offences Act 1956, that is to say sections two to seven, ten to sixteen, nineteen, twenty, twenty-two to twenty-six and twenty-eight, and any attempt to commit against a child or young person an offence under section two, five, six, seven, ten, eleven, twelve, twenty-two or twenty-three of that Act:

Provided that for the purposes of subsection (2) of section ninety-nine of this Act this entry shall apply so far only as it relates to offences under sections ten, eleven, twelve, fourteen, fifteen, sixteen, twenty and twenty-eight of the Sexual Offences Act 1956, and attempts to commit offences under sections ten, eleven and twelve of that Act.

Any other offences involving bodily injury to a child or young person.

Schedule 1

This Schedule lists the offences that are frequently referred to collectively in proceedings under the Children Act 1989 as 'Schedule 1 offences'.

Convictions will not be regarded as spent for the purposes of the Rehabilitation of Offenders Act 1974 (ROA 1974) in proceedings 'relating to adoption, the marriage of any minor, the exercise of the inherent jurisdiction of the High Court with respect to minors or the provision by any person of accommodation, care or schooling for minors or in any proceedings brought under the Children Act 1989 or in any proceedings relating to the variation or discharge of a supervision order under section 1 of the Children and Young Persons Act 1969 or on appeal from any such proceedings': ROA 1974, s 7(2).

In *Re CB Access: Attendance of Court Welfare Officer* (1992) [1995] 1 FLR 622, CA, the judge wrongly questioned whether an unappealed Schedule 1 conviction was correct and then went on to ignore it.

3.9 COUNTY COURTS ACT 1984
(s 38)

38 Remedies available in county courts

(1) Subject to what follows, in any proceedings in a county court the court may make any order which could be made by the High Court if the proceedings were in the High Court.

(2) Any order made by a county court may be –

    (a) absolute or conditional;
    (b) final or interlocutory.

(3) A county court shall not have power –

    (a) to order mandamus, certiorari or prohibition; or
    (b) to make any order of a prescribed kind.

(4) Regulations under subsection (3) –

    (a) may provide for any of their provisions not to apply in such circumstances or descriptions of case as may be specified in the regulations;
    (b) may provide for the transfer of the proceedings to the High Court for the purpose of enabling an order of a kind prescribed under subsection (3) to be made;
    (c) may make such provision with respect to matters of procedure as the Lord Chancellor considers expedient; and
    (d) may make provision amending or repealing any provision made by or under any enactment, so far as may be necessary or expedient in consequence of the regulations.

(5) In this section 'prescribed' means prescribed by regulations made by the Lord Chancellor under this section.

(6) The power to make regulations under this section shall be exercised by statutory instrument.

(7) No such statutory instrument shall be made unless a draft of the instrument has been approved by both Houses of Parliament.

Section 38

The county court does not have an inherent jurisdiction to grant injunctions (unlike the High Court). It therefore does not have an inherent jurisdiction to make injunctions in support of care orders (*Devon County Council v B* [1997] 1 FLR 591; *D v D (County Court Jurisdiction: Injunctions)* [1993] 2 FLR 802), although an injunction may be granted in care proceedings to protect a social worker (*Tameside Metropolitan Borough Council v M (Injunctive Relief: County Courts: Jurisdiction)* [2001] Fam Law 873). Whether a county court might make an injunction ancillary to a care order by reliance upon CCA 1984, s 38 remains a matter of debate. The county court also has no inherent jurisdiction to accept undertakings in care proceedings (*Re B (Supervision Order: Parental Undertaking)* [1996] 1 FLR 676).

3.10 CRIMINAL JUSTICE AND COURT SERVICES ACT 2000
(ss 11, 12, 15, 16)

Chapter II
Children and Family Court Advisory and Support Service

11 Establishment of the Service

(1) There shall be a body corporate to be known as the Children and Family Court Advisory and Support Service (referred to in this Part as the Service) which is to exercise the functions conferred on it by virtue of this Act and any other enactment.

(2) Schedule 2 (which makes provision about the constitution of the Service, its powers and other matters relating to it) is to have effect.

(3) References in this Act or any other enactment to an officer of the Service are references to –

    (a) any member of the staff of the Service appointed under paragraph 5(1)(a) of that Schedule, and

    (b) any other individual exercising functions of an officer of the Service by virtue of section 13(2) or (4).

12 Principal functions of the Service

(1) In respect of family proceedings in which the welfare of children is or may be in question, it is a function of the Service to –

    (a) safeguard and promote the welfare of the children,

    (b) give advice to any court about any application made to it in such proceedings,

    (c) make provision for the children to be represented in such proceedings,

    (d) provide information, advice and other support for the children and their families.

(2) The Service must also make provision for the performance of any functions conferred on officers of the Service by virtue of this Act or any other enactment (whether or not they are exercisable for the purposes of the functions conferred on the Service by subsection (1)).

(3) Regulations may provide for grants to be paid by the Service to any person for the purpose of furthering the performance of any of the Service's functions.

(4) The regulations may provide for the grants to be paid on conditions, including conditions –

    (a) regulating the purposes for which the grant or any part of it may be used,

    (b) requiring repayment to the Service in specified circumstances.

(5) In this section, 'family proceedings' has the same meaning as in the Matrimonial and Family Proceedings Act 1984 and also includes any other proceedings which are family proceedings for the purposes of the Children Act 1989, but –

    (a) references to family proceedings include (where the context allows) family proceedings which are proposed or have been concluded,

    (b) *(repealed)*

Section 12

Regulations have been made under s 12(3) and (4) – see the Children and Family Court Advisory and Support Service (Provision of Grants) Regulations 2001, SI 2001/697. The Transfer of Functions (Children, Young People and Families) Order 2003, SI 2003/3191, art 3(d) transferred to the Secretary of State the former functions of the Lord Chancellor's Department under this section.

In *Re M (Disclosure: Children and Family Reporter* [2002] EWCA Civ 1199, [2002] 2 FLR 893, CA, the Court of Appeal examined the interaction between the court and the child and family reporter (see also the notes on CA 1989, s 7). Wall J said at [96]:

'(i) CFRs are not "officers of the court". They are officers of the Service (CAFCASS) with the duties and responsibilities laid upon them by s 12 of the CJCSA 2000, s 7 of the 1989 Act and r 4.11 of the FPR 1991.

(ii) CFRs are not under the control of the judiciary. Within the scope of their employment by CAFCASS, they are independent professionals who, at the request of the court, investigate issues identified by the court as relating to the welfare of the child in question and give the court any advice and assistance it requires. During the course of those investigations, they are free to exercise their professional judgment on those issues, and in particular do not need the court's permission to disclose information to local authority child protection workers.

(iii) The relationship between CFRs and the judiciary should be collaborative and co-operative. In particular, CFRs should not hesitate to seek directions from the judge in relation to issues which arise during the course of the investigation.

(iv) CFRs should advise the court immediately if a child protection issue of sufficient gravity arises such as has required the CFR to notify the local authority. The CFR in such circumstances should seek the court's directions and any decision to terminate or continue the CFR's inquiries is for the court, not the CFR.'

Although it was held that, where a supervision order was made, the proceedings did not come to an end until the supervision order expired (by reason of the original wording of the Criminal Justice and Court Services Act 2000, s 12(5): *Re MH, Re SB and Re MB* [2001] 2 FLR 1334), the relevant words of s 12(5) were repealed as from 28 November 2003 (by Adoption and Children Act 2002, s 139(1), (3), Sch 3, para 118(5) and Sch 5 (see SI 2003/3079, art 2(1)(c)).

****

15 Right to conduct litigation and right of audience

(1) The Service may authorise an officer of the Service of a prescribed description –

    (a) to conduct litigation in relation to any proceedings in any court,

    (b) to exercise a right of audience in any proceedings before any court,

in the exercise of his functions.

(2) An officer of the Service exercising a right to conduct litigation by virtue of subsection (1)(a) who would otherwise have such a right by virtue of section 28(2)(a)

of the Courts and Legal Services Act 1990 is to be treated as having acquired that right solely by virtue of this section.

(3) An officer of the Service exercising a right of audience by virtue of subsection (1)(b) who would otherwise have such a right by virtue of section 27(2)(a) of the Courts and Legal Services Act 1990 is to be treated as having acquired that right solely by virtue of this section.

(4) In this section and section 16, 'right to conduct litigation' and 'right of audience' have the same meanings as in section 119 of the Courts and Legal Services Act 1990.

Section 15

The Children and Family Court Advisory and Support Service (Conduct of Litigation and Exercise of Rights of Audience) Regulations 2001, SI 2001/698, came into force on 1 April 2001 and provided that an officer of the Service who is either: (a) a barrister or a solicitor of the Supreme Court; or (b) employed (whether wholly or in part), or is otherwise engaged, to conduct litigation and is doing so in conjunction with an officer of the Service described in sub-paragraph (a), may be authorised by the Service in accordance with s 15(1) of the Criminal Justice and Court Services Act 2000.

As to the roles of CAFCASS Legal, see the CAFCASS Practice Note [2004] 1 FLR 1190 (set out at **6.19**). The Official Solicitor will no longer represent children who are the subject of family proceedings other than in exceptional circumstances: see *Practice Note (Official Solicitor: Appointment in Family Proceedings)* [2001] 2 FLR 155.

16 Cross-examination of officers of the Service

(1) An officer of the Service may, subject to rules of court, be cross-examined in any proceedings to the same extent as any witness.

(2) But an officer of the Service may not be cross-examined merely because he is exercising a right to conduct litigation or a right of audience granted in accordance with section 15.

Section 16

In *Re M (Disclosure: Children and Family Reporter)* [2002] EWCA Civ 1199, [2002] 3 FLR 893, CA (set out at **5.8**), Wall J said at para [78]: 'By s 16 of the 2000 Act, and in a significant departure from previous practice (see *Cadman v Cadman* (1982) 3 FLR 275 at 277 referred to at [24] of Thorpe LJ's judgment) CFRs may be cross-examined in any proceedings to the same extent as any witness, although they may not be cross-examined merely because they are exercising a right to conduct litigation or a right of audience granted in accordance with s 15. This change derives from the incorporation into English law of Art 6 of the European Convention on Human Rights and Fundamental Freedoms 1950'.

****

3.11 FAMILY LAW ACT 1986
(ss 1–2A, 5, 6, 33, 34, 37, 55A–58)

PART I

CHILD CUSTODY

Chapter I
Preliminary

1 Orders to which Part I applies

(1) Subject to the following provisions of this section, in this Part 'Part I order' means –

    (a) a section 8 order made by a court in England and Wales under the Children Act 1989, other than an order varying or discharging such an order;

    (b) an order made by a court of civil jurisdiction in Scotland under any enactment or rule of law with respect to the residence, custody, care or control of a child, contact with or access to a child or the education or upbringing of a child, excluding –

        (i) an order committing the care of a child to a local authority or placing a child under the supervision of a local authority;

        (ii) an adoption order as defined in section 12(1) of the Adoption (Scotland) Act 1978;

        (iii) an order freeing a child for adoption made under section 18 of the said Act of 1978;

        (iv) an order giving parental responsibilities and parental rights in relation to a child made in the course of proceedings for the adoption of the child (other than an order made following the making of a direction under section 53(1) of the Children Act 1975);

        (v) an order made under the Education (Scotland) Act 1980;

        (vi) an order made under Part II and III of the Social Work (Scotland) Act 1968;

        (vii) an order made under the Child Abduction and Custody Act 1985;

        (viii) an order for the delivery of a child or other order for the enforcement of a Part I order;

        (ix) an order relating to the guardianship of a child;

    (c) an Article 8 order made by a court in Northern Ireland under the Children (Northern Ireland) Order 1995, other than an order varying or discharging such an order;

    (d) an order made by a court in England and Wales in the exercise of the inherent jurisdiction of the High Court with respect to children –

        (i) so far as it gives care of a child to any person or provides for contact with, or the education of, a child; but

      (ii) excluding an order varying or revoking such an order;

(e) an order made by the High Court in Northern Ireland in the exercise of its inherent jurisdiction with respect to children –

      (i) so far as it gives care of a child to any person or provides for contact with, or the education of, a child; but

      (ii) excluding an order varying or discharging such an order;

(f) an order made by a court in a specified dependent territory corresponding to an order within paragraphs (a) to (e) above.

(2) In this Part 'Part I order' does not include –

(a)–(c) (*repealed*)

(3) In this Part, 'Part I order' –

(a) includes any order which would have been a custody order by virtue of this section in any form in which it was in force at any time before its amendment by the Children Act 1989 or the Children (Northern Ireland) Order 1995, as the case may be; and

(b) (subject to sections 32 and 40 of this Act) excludes any order which would have been excluded from being a custody order by virtue of this section in any such form, and

(c) excludes any order falling within subsection (1)(f) above made before the date specified opposite the name of the territory concerned in Column 2 of Schedule 1 to the Family Law Act 1986 (Dependent Territories) Order 1991, as from time to time in force.

(6) Provision may be made by act of sederunt prescribing, in relation to orders within subsection (1)(b) above, what constitutes an application for the purposes of this Part.

Section 1

Prospective amendment—Section prospectively amended by Adoption and Children Act 2002, s 139(1), Sch 3, paras 46, 47 (see **3.3B**).

Chapter II
Jurisdiction of Courts in England and Wales

2 Jurisdiction: general

(1) A court in England and Wales shall not have jurisdiction to make a section 1(1)(a) order with respect to a child in or in connection with matrimonial proceedings in England and Wales unless –

(a) the child concerned is a child of both parties to the matrimonial proceedings and the court has jurisdiction to entertain those proceedings by virtue of the Council Regulation, or

(b) the condition in section 2A of this Act is satisfied.

(2) A court in England and Wales shall not have jurisdiction to make a section 1(1)(a) order in a non-matrimonial case (that is to say, where the condition in section 2A of this Act is not satisfied) unless the condition in section 3 of this Act is satisfied.

(3) A court in England and Wales shall not have jurisdiction to make a section 1(1)(d) order unless –

(a) the condition in section 3 of this Act is satisfied, or

(b) the child concerned is present in England and Wales on the relevant date and the court considers that the immediate exercise of its powers is necessary for his protection.

Section 2

Prospective amendment—Section prospectively amended by Adoption and Children Act 2002, s 139(1), Sch 3, paras 46, 48 (see **3.3B**).

2A Jurisdiction in or in connection with matrimonial proceedings

(1) The condition referred to in section 2(1) of this Act is that the matrimonial proceedings are proceedings in respect of the marriage of the parents of the child concerned and –

    (a) the proceedings –
        (i) are proceedings for divorce or nullity of marriage, and
        (ii) are continuing;
    (b) the proceedings –
        (i) are proceedings for judicial separation,
        (ii) are continuing,
    and the jurisdiction of the court is not excluded by subsection (2) below; or
    (c) the proceedings have been dismissed after the beginning of the trial but –
        (i) the section 1(1)(a) order is being made forthwith, or
        (ii) the application for the order was made on or before the dismissal.

(2) For the purposes of subsection (1)(b) above, the jurisdiction of the court is excluded if, after the grant of a decree of judicial separation, on the relevant date, proceedings for divorce or nullity in respect of the marriage are continuing in Scotland, Northern Ireland or a specified dependent territory.

(3) Subsection (2) above shall not apply if the court in which the other proceedings there referred to are continuing has made –

    (a) an order under section 13(6) or 19A(4) of this Act (not being an order made by virtue of section 13(6)(a)(i)), or a corresponding dependent territory order, or
    (b) an order under section 14(2) or 22(2) of this Act, or a corresponding dependent territory order, which is recorded as being made for the purpose of enabling Part I proceedings to be taken in England and Wales with respect to the child concerned.

(4) Where a court –

    (a) has jurisdiction to make a section 1(1)(a) order in or in connection with matrimonial proceedings, but
    (b) considers that it would be more appropriate for Part I matters relating to the child to be determined outside England and Wales,

the court may by order direct that, while the order under this subsection is in force, no section 1(1)(a) order shall be made by any court in or in connection with those proceedings.

****

5 Power of court to refuse application or stay proceedings

(1) A court in England and Wales which has jurisdiction to make a Part I order may refuse an application for the order in any case where the matter in question has already been determined in proceedings outside England and Wales.

(2) Where, at any stage of the proceedings on an application made to a court in England and Wales for a Part I order, or for the variation of a Part I order, other than proceedings governed by the Council Regulation, it appears to the court –

  (a) that proceedings with respect to the matters to which the application relates are continuing outside England and Wales, or

  (b) that it would be more appropriate for those matters to be determined in proceedings to be taken outside England and Wales,

the court may stay the proceedings on the application.

(3) The court may remove a stay granted in accordance with subsection (2) above if it appears to the court that there has been unreasonable delay in the taking or prosecution of the other proceedings referred to in that subsection, or that those proceedings are stayed, sisted or concluded.

(4) Nothing in this section shall affect any power exercisable apart from this section to refuse an application or to grant or remove a stay.

6 Duration and variation of custody orders

(1) If a Part I order made by a court in Scotland, Northern Ireland or a specified dependent territory (or a variation of such an order) comes into force with respect to child at a time when a Part I order made by a court in England and Wales has effect with respect to him, the latter order shall cease to have effect so far as it makes provision for any matter for which the same or different provision is made by (or by the variation of) the order made by the court in Scotland, Northern Ireland or the territory.

(2) Where by virtue of subsection (1) above a Part I order has ceased to have effect so far as it makes provision for any matter, a court in England or Wales shall not have jurisdiction to vary that order so as to make provision for that matter.

(3) A court in England and Wales shall not have jurisdiction to vary a Part I order if, on the relevant date, matrimonial proceedings are continuing in Scotland, Northern Ireland or a specified dependent territory in respect of the marriage of the parents of the child concerned.

(3A) Subsection (3) above shall not apply if –

  (a) the Part I order was made in or in connection with proceedings for divorce or nullity in England and Wales in respect of the marriage of the parents of the child concerned; and

  (b) those proceedings are continuing.

(3B) Subsection (3) above shall not apply if –

  (a) the Part I order was made in or in connection with proceedings for judicial separation in England and Wales;

  (b) those proceedings are continuing; and

  (c) the decree of judicial separation has not yet been granted.

(4) Subsection (3) above shall not apply if the court in which the proceedings there referred to are continuing has made –

(a) an order under section 13(6) or 19A(4) of this Act (not being an order made by virtue of section 13(6)(a)(i)), or a corresponding dependent territory order, or

(b) an order under section 14(2) or 22(2) of this Act, or a corresponding dependent territory order, which is recorded as made for the purpose of enabling Part I proceedings with respect to the child concerned to be taken in England and Wales,

and that order is in force.

(5) Subsection (3) above shall not apply in the case of a variation of section 1(1)(d) order if the child concerned is present in England and Wales on the relevant date and the court considers that the immediate exercise of its powers is necessary for his protection.

(6) Subsection (7) below applies where a Part I order which is –

(a) a residence order (within the meaning of the Children Act 1989) in favour of a person with respect to a child,

(b) an order made in the exercise of the High Court's inherent jurisdiction with respect to children by virtue of which a person has care of a child, or

(c) an order –

    (i) of a kind mentioned in section 1(3)(a) of this Act,

    (ii) under which a person is entitled to the actual possession of a child,

ceases to have effect in relation to that person by virtue of subsection (1) above.

(7) Where this subsection applies, any family assistance order made under section 16 of the Children Act 1989 with respect to the child shall also cease to have effect.

(8) For the purposes of subsection (7) above the references to a family assistance order under section 16 of the Children Act 1989 shall be deemed to include a reference to an order for the supervision of a child made under –

(a) section 7(4) of the Family Law Reform Act 1969,

(b) section 44 of the Matrimonial Causes Act 1973,

(c) section 2(2)(a) of the Guardianship Act 1973,

(d) section 34(5) or 36(3)(b) of the Children Act 1975, or

(e) section 9 of the Domestic Proceedings and Magistrates' Courts Act 1978;

but this subsection shall cease to have effect once all such orders for the supervision of children have ceased to have effect in accordance with Schedule 14 to the Children Act 1989.

****

33 Power to order disclosure of child's whereabouts

(1) Where in proceedings for or relating to a Part I order in respect of a child there is not available to the court adequate information as to where the child is, the court may order any person who it has reason to believe may have relevant information to disclose it to the court.

(2) A person shall not be excused from complying with an order under subsection (1) above by reason that to do so may incriminate him or his spouse of an offence; but a statement or admission made in compliance with such an order shall not be admissible in evidence against either of them in proceedings for any offence other than perjury.

(3) A court in Scotland before which proceedings are pending for the enforcement of an order relating to parental responsibilities or parental rights in relation to a child made outside the United Kingdom and any specified dependent territory which is recognised in Scotland shall have the same powers as it would have under subsection (1) above if the order were its own.

Section 33

Other relevant statutory provisions—This section should be considered together with Children Act 1989, ss 48–50 (discovery of children in need of emergency protection, abduction of children in care and recovery of abducted children). The procedure under this section is set out in FPR 1991, r 6.17 and FPC(CA 1989)R 1991, r 31A.

Police—In *S v S (Chief Constable of West Yorkshire Police Intervening)* [1999] 1 All ER 281, [1998] 2 FLR 973, CA, Butler-Sloss LJ said:

'The primary duty of the police is to find a child who is reported missing and where possible ensure the safety and well-being of that child. It would be most unsuitable, bearing in mind their scarce resources and more important duties to the public, to place on them any unnecessary burdens for which they ought not to be primarily responsible. Section 33 is capable of applying to the police, but I have no doubt that routine applications to the police under s 33, even inter partes, ought not to be made and, if made, ought to be strongly discouraged by the courts. Subject to the question of giving binding assurances as to confidentiality, with which I deal below, in my view, the police should also be helped as far as it is possible by the courts to maintain their channels of communication without the requirement to divulge the information pursuant to a s 33 application.'

Order against legal representative—Where an order is to be sought against the legal representative of the person who is thought to have the child with him (eg the abductor) reference should be made to the cases of *Re B (Abduction: Disclosure)* [1995] 1 FLR 774, and *Re H (Abduction: Whereabouts Order to Solicitors)* [2000] 1 FLR 766, FD. Where a person has been brought before the court under a bench warrant, the judge may not order his further detention where there is no continuing contempt of court (*Re B (Child Abduction: Wardship: Power to Detain)* [1994] 2 FLR 479, CA).

34 Power to order recovery of child

(1) Where –

    (a) a person is required by a Part I order, or an order for the enforcement of a Part I order, to give up a child to another person ('the person concerned'), and

    (b) the court which made the order imposing the requirement is satisfied that the child has not been given up in accordance with the order,

the court may make an order authorising an officer of the court or a constable to take charge of the child and deliver him to the person concerned.

(2) The authority conferred by subsection (1) above includes authority –

    (a) to enter and search any premises where the person acting in pursuance of the order has reason to believe the child may be found, and

(b) to use such force as may be necessary to give effect to the purpose of the order.

(3) Where by virtue of –

(a) section 14 of the Children Act 1989, or

(b) Article 14 (enforcement of residence orders) of the Children (Northern Ireland) Order 1995,

a Part I order (or a provision of a Part I order) may be enforced as if it were an order requiring a person to give up a child to another person, subsection (1) above shall apply as if the Part I order had included such a requirement.

(4) This section is without prejudice to any power conferred on a court by or under any other enactment or rule of law.

Section 34

This section should be considered along with CA 1989, ss 48–50 (discovery of children in need of emergency protection, abduction of children in care and recovery of abducted children). The procedure under this section is set out in FPR 1991, r 6.17 and FPC(CA 1989)R 1991, r 31A.

****

37 Surrender of passports

(1) Where there is in force an order prohibiting or otherwise restricting the removal of a child from the United Kingdom or from any specified part of it or from a specified dependent territory, the court by which the order was in fact made, or by which it is treated under section 36 of this Act as having been made, may require any person to surrender any United Kingdom passport which has been issued to, or contains particulars of, the child.

(2) In this section 'United Kingdom passport' means a current passport issued by the Government of the United Kingdom.

Section 37

This section relates to the surrender of a *United Kingdom* passport. The High Court may, under its inherent jurisdiction, order the surrender of a foreign passport (*Re A-K (Foreign Passport: Jurisdiction)* [1997] 2 FLR 569, CA). In the case of *Al-Kandari v JR Brown & Co* [1988] 1 QB 665, [1988] 1 All ER 833, CA, a solicitor was held to be negligent in returning a passport contrary to an undertaking that he had given to the effect that he would not do so (and see also *Hamilton Jones v David and Snape (A Firm)* [2003] EWHC 3146, [2004] 1 FLR 774, ChD – failure to re-register children with Passport Agency). In *Re A (Return of Passport)* [1997] 2 FLR 137, a judge was held to have been plainly wrong in returning a passport to a Bangladeshi father who had taken the child to Bangladesh and said that he wanted the passport returned in order that he might secure the child's return.

Communication with the Home Office or with the Passport Office should be in accordance with the *Protocol from the President's Office (Communicating with the Home Office)* [2004] 1 FLR 638 and the *Protocol from the President's Office (Communicating with the Passport Service)* [2004] 1 FLR 640 (see **6.15** and **6.16**).

****

PART III

DECLARATIONS OF STATUS

55A Declarations of parentage

(1) Subject to the following provisions of this section, any person may apply to the High Court, a county court or a magistrates' court for a declaration as to whether or not a person named in the application is or was the parent of another person so named.

(2) A court shall have jurisdiction to entertain an application under subsection (1) above if, and only if, either of the persons named in it for the purposes of that subsection –

(a) is domiciled in England and Wales on the date of the application, or
(b) has been habitually resident in England and Wales throughout the period of one year ending with that date, or
(c) died before that date and either –
  (i) was at death domiciled in England and Wales, or
  (ii) had been habitually resident in England and Wales throughout the period of one year ending with the date of death.

(3) Except in a case falling within subsection (4) below, the court shall refuse to hear an application under subsection (1) above unless it considers that the applicant has a sufficient personal interest in the determination of the application (but this is subject to section 27 of the Child Support Act 1991).

(4) The excepted cases are where the declaration sought is as to whether or not –

(a) the applicant is the parent of a named person;
(b) a named person is the parent of the applicant; or
(c) a named person is the other parent of a named child of the applicant.

(5) Where an application under subsection (1) above is made and one of the persons named in it for the purposes of that subsection is a child, the court may refuse to hear the application if it considers that the determination of the application would not be in the best interests of the child.

(6) Where a court refuses to hear an application under subsection (1) above it may order that the applicant may not apply again for the same declaration without leave of the court.

(7) Where a declaration is made by a court on an application under subsection (1) above, the prescribed officer of the court shall notify the Registrar General, in such a manner and within such period as may be prescribed, of the making of that declaration.

Section 55A

An application must be made by petition in accordance with FPR 1991, r 3.1(3) to which must be annexed a copy of the birth certificate of the person whose parentage is in issue. An affidavit must be filed in support of the petition, and the respondents to the application are to be the persons whose parentage is in issue and any person other than the petitioner who is or is alleged to be the mother or father of that person (*Re B (A Child) (Parentage: Knowledge of Proceedings)* [2004] 1 FCR 473 (in which the mother's attempt to prevent the father learning about the birth of the child failed)).

In *Re R (IVF: Paternity of Child)* [2003] EWCA Civ 182, [2003] 1 FLR 1183, CA, the following was said by Hale LJ giving the judgment of the court:

'**[32]** There are some advantages to the procedure under s 55A. If it relates to a child, the court may refuse to hear the application if it considers that the determination of the application would not be in the child's best interests: s 56A(6). Declarations made are binding upon Her Majesty and all other persons: s 58(2). The court has power to direct that the papers be sent to the Attorney-General should he wish to intervene: s 59. If a declaration is granted, the birth may be re-registered accordingly: Births and Deaths Registration Act 1953, s 14A.

[33] Of course, findings of parentage can be made in the course of other proceedings, for example under s 4 of the 1989 Act. The child's birth can be re-registered if certain orders are made but not if they are not: see the 1953 Act, s 10A. That distinction was deliberately drawn by the Law Commission in recommending the re-registration provisions: see the Law Commission Working Paper *Illegitimacy* (Law Com No 74 (1979)) para 9.28. Re-registration may not necessarily be in the child's best interests if it is not in his best interests to make a substantive order relating to his maintenance or upbringing. Generally speaking it will usually be more convenient to continue to seek findings of fact in the course of proceedings for a substantive order about the child. But if, for example, the case raises a difficult issue of law or public policy, as here, or re-registration would be desirable even without a substantive order, or of course if the child is grown up, then the s 55A procedure should be used.'

56 Declarations as to legitimacy or legitimation

(1) Any person may apply to the High Court or a county court for a declaration –

  (a) *(repealed)*
  (b) that he is the legitimate child of his parents.

(2) Any person may apply to the court for one (or for one or, in the alternative, the other) of the following declarations, that is to say –

  (a) a declaration that he has become a legitimated person;
  (b) a declaration that he has not become a legitimated person.

(3) A court shall have jurisdiction to entertain an application under this section if, and only if, the applicant –

  (a) is domiciled in England and Wales on the date of the application, or
  (b) has been habitually resident in England and Wales throughout the period of one year ending with that date.

(4) Where a declaration is made by a court on an application under subsection (1) above, the prescribed officer of the court shall notify the Registrar General, in such a manner and within such period as may be prescribed, of the making of that declaration.

(5) In this section 'legitimated person' means a person legitimated or recognised as legitimated –

  (a) under section 2 or 3 of the Legitimacy Act 1976; or
  (b) under section 1 or 8 of the Legitimacy Act 1926; or
  (c) by a legitimation (whether or not by virtue of the subsequent marriage of his parents) recognised by the law of England and Wales and effected under the law of another country.

Section 56

The procedure for such an application is set out in FPR 1991, r 3.13.

57 Declarations as to adoptions effected overseas

(1) Any person whose status as an adopted child of any person depends on whether he has been adopted by that person by either –

    (a) a Convention adoption as defined by subsection (1) of section 72 of the Adoption Act 1976 or an overseas adoption as defined by subsection (2) of that section, or

    (b) an adoption recognised by the law of England and Wales and effected under the law of any country outside the British Islands,

may apply to the High Court or a county court for one (or for one or, in the alternative, the other) of the declarations mentioned in subsection (2) below.

(2) The said declarations are –

    (a) a declaration that the applicant is for the purposes of section 39 of the Adoption Act 1976 the adopted child of that person;

    (b) a declaration that the applicant is not for the purposes of that section the adopted child of that person.

(3) A court shall have jurisdiction to entertain an application under subsection (1) above if, and only if, the applicant –

    (a) is domiciled in England and Wales on the date of the application, or

    (b) has been habitually resident in England and Wales throughout the period of one year ending with that date.

(4) ...

Section 57

Prospective amendment—Section prospectively amended by Adoption and Children Act 2002, s 139(1), Sch 3, para 49 (see **3.3B**).

Generally—The procedure for such an application is set out in FPR 1991, rr 3.15 and 3.16.

58 General provisions as to the making and effect of declarations

(1) Where on an application to a court for a declaration under this Part the truth of the proposition to be declared is proved to the satisfaction of the court, the court shall make that declaration unless to do so would manifestly be contrary to public policy.

(2) Any declarations made under this Part shall be binding on Her Majesty and all other persons.

(3) A court, on the dismissal of an application for a declaration under this Part, shall not have power to make any declaration for which an application has not been made.

(4) No declaration which may be applied for under this Part may be made otherwise than under this Part by any court.

(5) No declaration may be made by any court, whether under this Part or otherwise –

    (a) that a marriage was at its inception void;

    (b) *(repealed)*

(6) Nothing in this section shall affect the powers of any court to grant a decree of nullity of marriage.

3.12 FAMILY LAW ACT 1996
(ss 30–51, 57–59, 61–63, Sch 5)

PART IV

FAMILY HOMES AND DOMESTIC VIOLENCE

Rights to occupy matrimonial home

30 Rights concerning matrimonial home where one spouse has no estate etc

(1) This section applies if –

    (a) one spouse is entitled to occupy a dwelling-house by virtue of –
        (i) a beneficial estate or interest or contract; or
        (ii) any enactment giving that spouse the right to remain in occupation; and
    (b) the other spouse is not so entitled.

(2) Subject to the provisions of this Part, the spouse not so entitled has the following rights ('matrimonial home rights') –

    (a) if in occupation, a right not to be evicted or excluded from the dwelling-house or any part of it by the other spouse except with the leave of the court given by an order under section 33;
    (b) if not in occupation, a right with the leave of the court so given to enter into and occupy the dwelling-house.

(3) If a spouse is entitled under this section to occupy a dwelling-house or any part of a dwelling-house, any payment or tender made or other thing done by that spouse in or towards satisfaction of any liability of the other spouse in respect of rent, mortgage payments or other outgoings affecting the dwelling-house shall, whether or not it is made or done in pursuance of an order under section 40, be as good as if made or done by the other spouse.

(4) A spouse's occupation by virtue of this section –

    (a) is to be treated, for the purposes of the Rent (Agriculture) Act 1976 and the Rent Act 1977 (other than Part V and sections 103 to 106 of that Act), as occupation by the other spouse as the other spouse's residence, and
    (b) if the spouse occupies the dwelling-house as that spouse's only or principal home, is to be treated, for the purposes of the Housing Act 1985, Part I of the Housing Act 1988 and Chapter I of Part V of the Housing Act 1996, as occupation by the other spouse as the other spouse's only or principal home.

(5) If a spouse ('the first spouse') –

    (a) is entitled under this section to occupy a dwelling-house or any part of a dwelling-house, and

(b) makes any payment in or towards satisfaction of any liability of the other spouse ('the second spouse') in respect of mortgage payments affecting the dwelling-house,

the person to whom the payment is made may treat it as having been made by that other spouse, but the fact that that person has treated any such payment as having been so made does not affect any claim of the first spouse against the second spouse to an interest in the dwelling-house by virtue of the payment.

(6) If a spouse is entitled under this section to occupy a dwelling-house or part of a dwelling-house by reason of an interest of the other spouse under a trust, all the provisions of subsections (3) to (5) apply in relation to the trustees as they apply in relation to the other spouse.

(7) This section does not apply to a dwelling-house which has at no time been, and which was at no time intended by the spouses to be, a matrimonial home of theirs.

(8) A spouse's matrimonial home rights continue –

(a) only so long as the marriage subsists, except to the extent that an order under section 33(5) otherwise provides; and

(b) only so long as the other spouse is entitled as mentioned in subsection (1) to occupy the dwelling-house, except where provision is made by section 31 for those rights to be a charge on an estate or interest in the dwelling-house.

(9) It is hereby declared that a spouse –

(a) who has an equitable interest in a dwelling-house or in its proceeds of sale, but

(b) is not a spouse in whom there is vested (whether solely or as joint tenant) a legal estate in fee simple or a legal term of years absolute in the dwelling-house,

is to be treated, only for the purpose of determining whether he has matrimonial home rights, as not being entitled to occupy the dwelling-house by virtue of that interest.

31 Effect of matrimonial home rights as charge on dwelling-house

(1) Subsections (2) and (3) apply if, at any time during a marriage, one spouse is entitled to occupy a dwelling-house by virtue of a beneficial estate or interest.

(2) The other spouse's matrimonial home rights are a charge on the estate or interest.

(3) The charge created by subsection (2) has the same priority as if it were an equitable interest created at whichever is the latest of the following dates –

(a) the date on which the spouse so entitled acquires the estate or interest;

(b) the date of the marriage; and

(c) 1st January 1968 (the commencement date of the Matrimonial Homes Act 1967).

(4) Subsections (5) and (6) apply if, at any time when a spouse's matrimonial home rights are a charge on an interest of the other spouse under a trust, there are, apart from either of the spouses, no persons, living or unborn, who are or could become beneficiaries under the trust.

(5) The rights are a charge also on the estate or interest of the trustees for the other spouse.

(6) The charge created by subsection (5) has the same priority as if it were an equitable interest created (under powers overriding the trusts) on the date when it arises.

(7) In determining for the purposes of subsection (4) whether there are any persons who are not, but could become, beneficiaries under the trust, there is to be disregarded any potential exercise of a general power of appointment exercisable by either or both of the spouses alone (whether or not the exercise of it requires the consent of another person).

(8) Even though a spouse's matrimonial home rights are a charge on an estate or interest in the dwelling-house, those rights are brought to an end by –

    (a) the death of the other spouse, or
    (b) the termination (otherwise than by death) of the marriage,

unless the court directs otherwise by an order made under section 33(5).

(9) If –

    (a) a spouse's matrimonial home rights are a charge on an estate or interest in the dwelling-house, and
    (b) that estate or interest is surrendered to merge in some other estate or interest expectant on it in such circumstances that, but for the merger, the person taking the estate or interest would be bound by the charge,

the surrender has effect subject to the charge and the persons thereafter entitled to the other estate or interest are, for so long as the estate or interest surrendered would have endured if not so surrendered, to be treated for all purposes of this Part as deriving title to the other estate or interest under the other spouse or, as the case may be, under the trustees for the other spouse, by virtue of the surrender.

(10) If the title to the legal estate by virtue of which a spouse is entitled to occupy a dwelling-house (including any legal estate held by trustees for that spouse) is registered under the Land Registration Act 1925 or any enactment replaced by that Act –

    (a) registration of a land charge affecting the dwelling-house by virtue of this Part is to be effected by registering a notice under that Act; and
    (b) a spouse's matrimonial home rights are not an overriding interest within the meaning of that Act affecting the dwelling-house even though the spouse is in actual occupation of the dwelling-house.

(11) A spouse's matrimonial home rights (whether or not constituting a charge) do not entitle that spouse to lodge a caution under section 54 of the Land Registration Act 1925.

(12) If –

    (a) a spouse's matrimonial home rights are a charge on the estate of the other spouse or of trustees of the other spouse, and
    (b) that estate is the subject of a mortgage,

then if, after the date of the creation of the mortgage ('the first mortgage'), the charge is registered under section 2 of the Land Charges Act 1972, the charge is, for the purposes of section 94 of the Law of Property Act 1925 (which regulates the rights of mortgagees to make further advances ranking in priority to subsequent mortgages), to be deemed to be a mortgage subsequent in date to the first mortgage.

(13) It is hereby declared that a charge under subsection (2) or (5) is not registrable under subsection 10 or under section 2 of the Land Charges Act 1972 unless it is a charge on a legal estate.

32 Further provisions relating to matrimonial home rights

Schedule 4 re-enacts with consequential amendments and minor modifications provisions of the Matrimonial Homes Act 1983.

Occupation orders

33 Occupation orders where applicant has estate or interest etc or has matrimonial home rights

(1) If –

    (a) a person ('the person entitled') –

        (i) is entitled to occupy a dwelling-house by virtue of a beneficial estate or interest or contract or by virtue of any enactment giving him the right to remain in occupation, or

        (ii) has matrimonial home rights in relation to a dwelling-house, and

    (b) the dwelling-house –

        (i) is or at any time has been the home of the person entitled and of another person with whom he is associated, or

        (ii) was at any time intended by the person entitled and any such other person to be their home,

the person entitled may apply to the court for an order containing any of the provisions specified in subsections (3), (4) and (5).

(2) If an agreement to marry is terminated, no application under this section may be made by virtue of section 62(3)(e) by reference to that agreement after the end of the period of three years beginning with the date on which it is terminated.

(3) An order under this section may –

    (a) enforce the applicant's entitlement to remain in occupation as against the other person ('the respondent');

    (b) require the respondent to permit the applicant to enter and remain in the dwelling-house or part of the dwelling-house;

    (c) regulate the occupation of the dwelling-house by either or both parties;

    (d) if the respondent is entitled as mentioned in subsection (1)(a)(i), prohibit, suspend or restrict the exercise by him of his right to occupy the dwelling-house;

    (e) if the respondent has matrimonial home rights in relation to the dwelling-house and the applicant is the other spouse, restrict or terminate those rights;

    (f) require the respondent to leave the dwelling-house or part of the dwelling-house; or

    (g) exclude the respondent from a defined area in which the dwelling-house is included.

(4) An order under this section may declare that the applicant is entitled as mentioned in subsection (1)(a)(i) or has matrimonial home rights.

(5) If the applicant has matrimonial home rights and the respondent is the other spouse, an order under this section made during the marriage may provide that those rights are not brought to an end by –

(a) the death of the other spouse; or

(b) the termination (otherwise than by death) of the marriage.

(6) In deciding whether to exercise its powers under subsection (3) and (if so) in what manner, the court shall have regard to all the circumstances including –

(a) the housing needs and housing resources of each of the parties and of any relevant child;

(b) the financial resources of each of the parties;

(c) the likely effect of any order, or of any decision by the court not to exercise its powers under subsection (3), on the health, safety or well-being of the parties and of any relevant child; and

(d) the conduct of the parties in relation to each other and otherwise.

(7) If it appears to the court that the applicant or any relevant child is likely to suffer significant harm attributable to conduct of the respondent if an order under this section containing one or more of the provisions mentioned in subsection (3) is not made, the court shall make the order unless it appears to the court that –

(a) the respondent or any relevant child is likely to suffer significant harm if the order is made; and

(b) the harm likely to be suffered by the respondent or child in that event is as great as, or greater than, the harm attributable to conduct of the respondent which is likely to be suffered by the applicant or child if the order is not made.

(8) The court may exercise its powers under subsection (5) in any case where it considers that in all the circumstances it is just and reasonable to do so.

(9) An order under this section –

(a) may not be made after the death of either of the parties mentioned in subsection (1); and

(b) except in the case of an order made by virtue of subsection (5)(a), ceases to have effect on the death of either party.

(10) An order under this section may, in so far as it has continuing effect, be made for a specified period, until the occurrence of a specified event or until further order.

34 Effect of order under s 33 where rights are charge on dwelling-house

(1) If a spouse's matrimonial home rights are a charge on the estate or interest of the other spouse or of trustees for the other spouse –

(a) any order under section 33 against the other spouse has, except so far as a contrary intention appears, the same effect against persons deriving title under the other spouse or under the trustees and affected by the charge, and

(b) subsections 33(1), (3), (4) and (10) and 30(3) to (6) apply in relation to any person deriving title under the other spouse or under the trustees and affected by the charge as they apply in relation to the other spouse.

(2) The court may make an order under section 33 by virtue of subsection (1)(b) if it considers that in all the circumstances it is just and reasonable to do so.

35 One former spouse with no existing right to occupy

(1) This section applies if –

    (a) one former spouse is entitled to occupy a dwelling-house by virtue of a beneficial estate or interest or contract, or by virtue of any enactment giving him the right to remain in occupation;

    (b) the other former spouse is not so entitled; and

    (c) the dwelling-house was at any time their matrimonial home or was at any time intended by them to be their matrimonial home.

(2) The former spouse not so entitled may apply to the court for an order under this section against the other former spouse ('the respondent').

(3) If the applicant is in occupation, an order under this section must contain provision –

    (a) giving the applicant the right not to be evicted or excluded from the dwelling-house or any part of it by the respondent for the period specified in the order; and

    (b) prohibiting the respondent from evicting or excluding the applicant during that period.

(4) If the applicant is not in occupation, an order under this section must contain provision –

    (a) giving the applicant the right to enter into and occupy the dwelling-house for the period specified in the order; and

    (b) requiring the respondent to permit the exercise of that right.

(5) An order under this section may also –

    (a) regulate the occupation of the dwelling-house by either or both of the parties;

    (b) prohibit, suspend or restrict the exercise by the respondent of his right to occupy the dwelling-house;

    (c) require the respondent to leave the dwelling-house or part of the dwelling-house; or

    (d) exclude the respondent from a defined area in which the dwelling-house is included.

(6) In deciding whether to make an order under this section containing provision of the kind mentioned in subsection (3) or (4) and (if so) in what manner, the court shall have regard to all the circumstances including –

    (a) the housing needs and housing resources of each of the parties and of any relevant child;

    (b) the financial resources of each of the parties;

    (c) the likely effect of any order, or of any decision by the court not to exercise its powers under subsection (3) or (4), on the health, safety or well-being of the parties and of any relevant child;

    (d) the conduct of the parties in relation to each other and otherwise;

    (e) the length of time that has elapsed since the parties ceased to live together;

(f) the length of time that has elapsed since the marriage was dissolved or annulled; and

(g) the existence of any pending proceedings between the parties –

   (i) for an order under section 23A or 24 of the Matrimonial Causes Act 1973 (property adjustment orders in connection with divorce proceedings etc);

   (ii) for an order under paragraph 1(2)(d) or (e) of Schedule 1 to the Children Act 1989 (orders for financial relief against parents); or

   (iii) relating to the legal or beneficial ownership of the dwelling-house.

(7) In deciding whether to exercise its power to include one or more of the provisions referred to in subsection (5) ('a subsection (5) provision') and (if so) in what manner, the court shall have regard to all the circumstances including the matters mentioned in subsection (6)(a) to (e).

(8) If the court decides to make an order under this section and it appears to it that, if the order does not include a subsection (5) provision, the applicant or any relevant child is likely to suffer significant harm attributable to conduct of the respondent, the court shall include the subsection (5) provision in the order unless it appears to the court that –

(a) the respondent or any relevant child is likely to suffer significant harm if the provision is included in the order; and

(b) the harm likely to be suffered by the respondent or child in that event is as great as or greater than the harm attributable to conduct of the respondent which is likely to be suffered by the applicant or child if the provision is not included.

(9) An order under this section –

(a) may not be made after the death of either of the former spouses; and

(b) ceases to have effect on the death of either of them.

(10) An order under this section must be limited so as to have effect for a specified period not exceeding six months, but may be extended on one or more occasions for a further specified period not exceeding six months.

(11) A former spouse who has an equitable interest in the dwelling-house or in the proceeds of sale of the dwelling-house but in whom there is not vested (whether solely or as joint tenant) a legal estate in fee simple or a legal term of years absolute in the dwelling-house is to be treated (but only for the purpose of determining whether he is eligible to apply under this section) as not being entitled to occupy the dwelling-house by virtue of that interest.

(12) Subsection (11) does not prejudice any right of such a former spouse to apply for an order under section 33.

(13) So long as an order under this section remains in force, subsections (3) to (6) of section 30 apply in relation to the applicant –

(a) as if he were the spouse entitled to occupy the dwelling-house by virtue of that section; and

(b) as if the respondent were the other spouse.

36 One cohabitant or former cohabitant with no existing right to occupy

(1) This section applies if –

    (a) one cohabitant or former cohabitant is entitled to occupy a dwelling-house by virtue of a beneficial estate or interest or contract or by virtue of any enactment giving him the right to remain in occupation;

    (b) the other cohabitant or former cohabitant is not so entitled; and

    (c) that dwelling-house is the home in which they live together as husband and wife or a home in which they at any time so lived together or intended so to live together.

(2) The cohabitant or former cohabitant not so entitled may apply to the court for an order under this section against the other cohabitant or former cohabitant ('the respondent').

(3) If the applicant is in occupation, an order under this section must contain provision –

    (a) giving the applicant the right not to be evicted or excluded from the dwelling-house or any part of it by the respondent for the period specified in the order, and

    (b) prohibiting the respondent from evicting or excluding the applicant during that period.

(4) If the applicant is not in occupation, an order under this section must contain provision –

    (a) giving the applicant the right to enter into and occupy the dwelling-house for the period specified in the order; and

    (b) requiring the respondent to permit the exercise of that right.

(5) An order under this section may also –

    (a) regulate the occupation of the dwelling-house by either or both of the parties;

    (b) prohibit, suspend or restrict the exercise by the respondent of his right to occupy the dwelling-house;

    (c) require the respondent to leave the dwelling-house or part of the dwelling-house; or

    (d) exclude the respondent from a defined area in which the dwelling-house is included.

(6) In deciding whether to make an order under this section containing provision of the kind mentioned in subsection (3) or (4) and (if so) in what manner, the court shall have regard to all the circumstances including –

    (a) the housing needs and housing resources of each of the parties and of any relevant child;

    (b) the financial resources of each of the parties;

    (c) the likely effect of any order, or of any decision by the court not to exercise its powers under subsection (3) or (4), on the health, safety or well-being of the parties and of any relevant child;

    (d) the conduct of the parties in relation to each other and otherwise;

    (e) the nature of the parties' relationship;

- (f) the length of time during which they have lived together as husband and wife;
- (g) whether there are or have been any children who are children of both parties or for whom both parties have or have had parental responsibility;
- (h) the length of time that has elapsed since the parties ceased to live together; and
- (i) the existence of any pending proceedings between the parties –
    - (i) for an order under paragraph 1(2)(d) or (e) of Schedule 1 to the Children Act 1989 (orders for financial relief against parents), or
    - (ii) relating to the legal or beneficial ownership of the dwelling-house.

(7) In deciding whether to exercise its powers to include one or more of the provisions referred to in subsection (5) ('a subsection (5) provision') and (if so) in what manner, the court shall have regard to all the circumstances including –

- (a) the matters mentioned in subsection (6)(a) to (d); and
- (b) the questions mentioned in subsection (8).

(8) The questions are –

- (a) whether the applicant or any relevant child is likely to suffer significant harm attributable to conduct of the respondent if the subsection (5) provision is not included in the order; and
- (b) whether the harm likely to be suffered by the respondent or child if the provision is included is as great as or greater than the harm attributable to conduct of the respondent which is likely to be suffered by the applicant or child if the provision is not included.

(9) An order under this section –

- (a) may not be made after the death of either of the parties; and
- (b) ceases to have effect on the death of either of them.

(10) An order under this section must be limited so as to have effect for a specified period not exceeding six months, but may be extended on one occasion for a further specified period not exceeding six months.

(11) A person who has an equitable interest in the dwelling-house or in the proceeds of sale of the dwelling-house but in whom there is not vested (whether solely or as joint tenant) a legal estate in fee simple or a legal term of years absolute in the dwelling-house is to be treated (but only for the purpose of determining whether he is eligible to apply under this section) as not being entitled to occupy the dwelling-house by virtue of that interest.

(12) Subsection (11) does not prejudice any right of such a person to apply for an order under section 33.

(13) So long as the order remains in force, subsections (3) to (6) of section 30 apply in relation to the applicant –

- (a) as if he were a spouse entitled to occupy the dwelling-house by virtue of that section; and
- (b) as if the respondent were the other spouse.

37 Neither spouse entitled to occupy

(1) This section applies if –

    (a) one spouse or former spouse and the other spouse or former spouse occupy a dwelling-house which is or was the matrimonial home; but

    (b) neither of them is entitled to remain in occupation –

        (i) by virtue of a beneficial estate or interest or contract; or

       (ii) by virtue of any enactment giving him the right to remain in occupation.

(2) Either of the parties may apply to the court for an order against the other under this section.

(3) An order under this section may –

    (a) require the respondent to permit the applicant to enter and remain in the dwelling-house or part of the dwelling-house;

    (b) regulate the occupation of the dwelling-house by either or both of the spouses;

    (c) require the respondent to leave the dwelling-house or part of the dwelling-house; or

    (d) exclude the respondent from a defined area in which the dwelling-house is included.

(4) Subsections (6) and (7) of section 33 apply to the exercise by the court of its powers under this section as they apply to the exercise by the court of its powers under subsection (3) of that section.

(5) An order under this section must be limited so as to have effect for a specified period not exceeding six months, but may be extended on one or more occasions for a further specified period not exceeding six months.

38 Neither cohabitant or former cohabitant entitled to occupy

(1) This section applies if –

    (a) one cohabitant or former cohabitant and the other cohabitant or former cohabitant occupy a dwelling-house which is the home in which they live or lived together as husband and wife; but

    (b) neither of them is entitled to remain in occupation –

        (i) by virtue of a beneficial estate or interest or contract; or

       (ii) by virtue of any enactment giving him the right to remain in occupation.

(2) Either of the parties may apply to the court for an order against the other under this section.

(3) An order under this section may –

    (a) require the respondent to permit the applicant to enter and remain in the dwelling-house or part of the dwelling-house;

    (b) regulate the occupation of the dwelling-house by either or both of the parties;

    (c) require the respondent to leave the dwelling-house or part of the dwelling-house; or

    (d) exclude the respondent from a defined area in which the dwelling-house is included.

(4) In deciding whether to exercise its powers to include one or more of the provisions referred to in subsection (3) ('a subsection (3) provision') and (if so) in what manner, the court shall have regard to all the circumstances including –

    (a) the housing needs and housing resources of each of the parties and of any relevant child;

    (b) the financial resources of each of the parties;

    (c) the likely effect of any order, or of any decision by the court not to exercise its powers under subsection (3), on the health, safety or well-being of the parties and of any relevant child;

    (d) the conduct of the parties in relation to each other and otherwise; and

    (e) the questions mentioned in subsection (5).

(5) The questions are –

    (a) whether the applicant or any relevant child is likely to suffer significant harm attributable to conduct of the respondent if the subsection (3) provision is not included in the order; and

    (b) whether the harm likely to be suffered by the respondent or child if the provision is included is as great as or greater than the harm attributable to conduct of the respondent which is likely to be suffered by the applicant or child if the provision is not included.

(6) An order under this section shall be limited so as to have effect for a specified period not exceeding six months, but may be extended on one occasion for a further specified period not exceeding six months.

39 Supplementary provisions

(1) In this Part an 'occupation order' means an order under section 33, 35, 36, 37 or 38.

(2) An application for an occupation order may be made in other family proceedings or without any other family proceedings being instituted.

(3) If –

    (a) an application for an occupation order is made under section 33, 35, 36, 37 or 38, and

    (b) the court considers that it has no power to make the order under the section concerned, but that it has power to make an order under one of the other sections,

the court may make an order under that other section.

(4) The fact that a person has applied for an occupation order under sections 35 to 38, or that an occupation order has been made, does not affect the right of any person to claim a legal or equitable interest in any property in any subsequent proceedings (including subsequent proceedings under this Part).

40 Additional provisions that may be included in certain occupation orders

(1) The court may on, or at any time after, making an occupation order under section 33, 35 or 36 –

    (a) impose on either party obligations as to –

(i) the repair and maintenance of the dwelling-house; or

(ii) the discharge of rent, mortgage payments or other outgoings affecting the dwelling-house;

(b) order a party occupying the dwelling-house or any part of it (including a party who is entitled to do so by virtue of a beneficial estate or interest or contract or by virtue of any enactment giving him the right to remain in occupation) to make periodical payments to the other party in respect of the accommodation, if the other party would (but for the order) be entitled to occupy the dwelling-house by virtue of a beneficial estate or interest or contract or by virtue of any such enactment;

(c) grant either party possession or use of furniture or other contents of the dwelling-house;

(d) order either party to take reasonable care of any furniture or other contents of the dwelling-house;

(e) order either party to take reasonable steps to keep the dwelling-house and any furniture or other contents secure.

(2) In deciding whether and, if so, how to exercise its powers under this section, the court shall have regard to all the circumstances of the case including –

(a) the financial needs and financial resources of the parties; and

(b) the financial obligations which they have, or are likely to have in the foreseeable future, including financial obligations to each other and to any relevant child.

(3) An order under this section ceases to have effect when the occupation order to which it relates ceases to have effect.

41 Additional considerations if parties are cohabitants or former cohabitants

(1) This section applies if the parties are cohabitants or former cohabitants.

(2) Where the court is required to consider the nature of the parties' relationship, it is to have regard to the fact that they have not given each other the commitment involved in marriage.

Non-molestation orders

42 Non-molestation orders

(1) In this Part a 'non-molestation order' means an order containing either or both of the following provisions –

(a) provision prohibiting a person ('the respondent') from molesting another person who is associated with the respondent;

(b) provision prohibiting the respondent from molesting a relevant child.

(2) The court may make a non-molestation order –

(a) if an application for the order has been made (whether in other family proceedings or without any other family proceedings being instituted) by a person who is associated with the respondent; or

(b) if in any family proceedings to which the respondent is a party the court considers that the order should be made for the benefit of any other party to the proceedings or any relevant child even though no such application has been made.

(3) In subsection (2) 'family proceedings' includes proceedings in which the court has made an emergency protection order under section 44 of the Children Act 1989 which includes an exclusion requirement (as defined in section 44A(3) of that Act).

(4) Where an agreement to marry is terminated, no application under subsection (2)(a) may be made by virtue of section 62(3)(e) by reference to that agreement after the end of the period of three years beginning with the day on which it is terminated.

(5) In deciding whether to exercise its powers under this section and, if so, in what manner, the court shall have regard to all the circumstances including the need to secure the health, safety and well-being –

    (a) of the applicant or, in a case falling within subsection (2)(b), the person for whose benefit the order would be made; and

    (b) of any relevant child.

(6) A non-molestation order may be expressed so as to refer to molestation in general, to particular acts of molestation, or to both.

(7) A non-molestation order may be made for a specified period or until further order.

(8) A non-molestation order which is made in other family proceedings ceases to have effect if those proceedings are withdrawn or dismissed.

Further provisions relating to occupation and non-molestation orders

43 Leave of court required for applications by children under sixteen

(1) A child under the age of sixteen may not apply for an occupation order or a non-molestation order except with the leave of the court.

(2) The court may grant leave for the purposes of subsection (1) only if it is satisfied that the child has sufficient understanding to make the proposed application for the occupation order or non-molestation order.

44 Evidence of agreement to marry

(1) Subject to subsection (2) the court shall not make an order under section 33 or 42 by virtue of section 62(3)(e) unless there is produced to it evidence in writing of the existence of the agreement to marry.

(2) Subsection (1) does not apply if the court is satisfied that the agreement to marry was evidenced by –

    (a) the gift of an engagement ring by one party to the agreement to the other in contemplation of their marriage, or

    (b) a ceremony entered into by the parties in the presence of one or more other persons assembled for the purpose of witnessing the ceremony.

45 Ex parte orders

(1) The court may, in any case where it considers that it is just and convenient to do so, make an occupation order or a non-molestation order even though the respondent

has not been given such notice of the proceedings as would otherwise be required by rules of court.

(2) In determining whether to exercise its powers under subsection (1), the court shall have regard to all the circumstances including –

    (a) any risk of significant harm to the applicant or a relevant child, attributable to conduct of the respondent, if the order is not made immediately;

    (b) whether it is likely that the applicant will be deterred or prevented from pursuing the application if an order is not made immediately; and

    (c) whether there is reason to believe that the respondent is aware of the proceedings but is deliberately evading service and that the applicant or a relevant child will be seriously prejudiced by the delay involved –

        (i) where the court is a magistrates' court, in effecting service of proceedings; or

        (ii) in any other case, in effecting substituted service.

(3) If the court makes an order by virtue of subsection (1) it must afford the respondent an opportunity to make representations relating to the order as soon as just and convenient at a full hearing.

(4) If, at a full hearing, the court makes an occupation order ('the full order'), then –

    (a) for the purposes of calculating the maximum period for which the full order may be made to have effect, the relevant section is to apply as if the period for which the full order will have effect began on the date on which the initial order first had effect; and

    (b) the provisions of section 36(10) or 38(6) as to the extension of orders are to apply as if the full order and the initial order were a single order.

(5) In this section –

    'full hearing' means a hearing of which notice has been given to all the parties in accordance with rules of court;

    'initial order' means an occupation order made by virtue of subsection (1); and

    'relevant section' means section 33(10), 35(10), 36(10), 37(5) or 38(6).

46 Undertakings

(1) In any case where the court has power to make an occupation order or non-molestation order, the court may accept an undertaking from any party to the proceedings.

(2) No power of arrest may be attached to any undertaking given under subsection (1).

(3) The court shall not accept an undertaking under subsection (1) in any case where apart from this section a power of arrest would be attached to the order.

(4) An undertaking given to a court under subsection (1) is enforceable as if it were an order of the court.

(5) This section has effect without prejudice to the powers of the High Court and the county court apart from this section.

47 Arrest for breach of order

(1) In this section 'a relevant order' means an occupation order or a non-molestation order.

(2) If –

    (a) the court makes a relevant order; and

    (b) it appears to the court that the respondent has used or threatened violence against the applicant or a relevant child,

it shall attach a power of arrest to one or more provisions of the order unless the court is satisfied that in all the circumstances of the case the applicant or child will be adequately protected without such a power of arrest.

(3) Subsection (2) does not apply in any case where the relevant order is made by virtue of section 45(1), but in such a case the court may attach a power of arrest to one or more provisions of the order if it appears to it –

    (a) that the respondent has used or threatened violence against the applicant or a relevant child; and

    (b) that there is a risk of significant harm to the applicant or child, attributable to conduct of the respondent, if the power of arrest is not attached to those provisions immediately.

(4) If, by virtue of subsection (3), the court attaches a power of arrest to any provisions of a relevant order, it may provide that the power of arrest is to have effect for a shorter period than the other provisions of the order.

(5) Any period specified for the purposes of subsection (4) may be extended by the court (on one or more occasions) on an application to vary or discharge the relevant order.

(6) If, by virtue of subsection (2) or (3), a power of arrest is attached to certain provisions of an order, a constable may arrest without warrant a person whom he has reasonable cause for suspecting to be in breach of any such provision.

(7) If a power of arrest is attached under subsection (2) or (3) to certain provisions of the order and the respondent is arrested under subsection (6) –

    (a) he must be brought before the relevant judicial authority within the period of 24 hours beginning at the time of his arrest; and

    (b) if the matter is not then disposed of forthwith, the relevant judicial authority before whom he is brought may remand him.

In reckoning for the purposes of this subsection any period of 24 hours, no account is to be taken of Christmas Day, Good Friday or any Sunday.

(8) If the court has made a relevant order but –

    (a) has not attached a power of arrest under subsection (2) or (3) above to any provisions of the order, or

    (b) has attached that power only to certain provisions of the order,

then, if at any time the applicant considers that the respondent has failed to comply with the order, he may apply to the relevant judicial authority for the issue of a warrant for the arrest of the respondent.

(9) The relevant judicial authority shall not issue a warrant on an application under subsection (8) unless –

    (a)   the application is substantiated on oath; and

    (b)   the relevant judicial authority has reasonable grounds for believing that the respondent has failed to comply with the order.

(10) If a person is brought before a court by virtue of a warrant issued under subsection (9) and the court does not dispose of the matter forthwith, the court may remand him.

(11) Schedule 5 (which makes provision corresponding to that applying in magistrates' courts in civil cases under sections 128 and 129 of the Magistrates' Courts Act 1980) has effect in relation to the powers of the High Court and a county court to remand a person by virtue of this section.

(12) If a person remanded under this section is granted bail (whether in the High Court or a county court under Schedule 5 or in a magistrates' court under section 128 or 129 of the Magistrates' Courts Act 1980), he may be required by the relevant judicial authority to comply, before release on bail or later, with such requirements as appear to that authority to be necessary to secure that he does not interfere with witnesses or otherwise obstruct the course of justice.

48 Remand for medical examination and report

(1) If the relevant judicial authority has reason to consider that a medical report will be required, any power to remand a person under section 47(7)(b) or (10) may be exercised for the purpose of enabling a medical examination and report to be made.

(2) If such a power is so exercised, the adjournment must not be for more than 4 weeks at a time unless the relevant judicial authority remands the accused in custody.

(3) If the relevant judicial authority so remands the accused, the adjournment must not be for more than 3 weeks at a time.

(4) If there is reason to suspect that a person who has been arrested –

    (a)   under section 47(6), or

    (b)   under a warrant issued on an application made under section 47(8),

is suffering from mental illness or severe mental impairment, the relevant judicial authority has the same power to make an order under section 35 of the Mental Health Act 1983 (remand for report on accused's mental condition) as the Crown Court has under section 35 of the Act of 1983 in the case of an accused person within the meaning of that section.

49 Variation and discharge of orders

(1) An occupation order or non-molestation order may be varied or discharged by the court on an application by –

    (a)   the respondent, or

    (b)   the person on whose application the order was made.

(2) In the case of a non-molestation order made by virtue of section 42(2)(b), the order may be varied or discharged by the court even though no such application has been made.

(3) If a spouse's matrimonial home rights are a charge on the estate or interest of the other spouse or of trustees for the other spouse, an order under section 33 against the other spouse may also be varied or discharged by the court on an application by any person deriving title under the other spouse or under the trustees and affected by the charge.

(4) If, by virtue of section 47(3), a power of arrest has been attached to certain provisions of an occupation order or non-molestation order, the court may vary or discharge the order under subsection (1) in so far as it confers a power of arrest (whether or not any application has been made to vary or discharge any other provision of the order).

Enforcement powers of magistrates' courts

50 Power of magistrates' court to suspend execution of committal order

(1) If, under section 63(3) of the Magistrates' Courts Act 1980, a magistrates' court has power to commit a person to custody for breach of a relevant requirement, the court may by order direct that the execution of the order of committal is to be suspended for such period or on such terms and conditions as it may specify.

(2) In subsection (1) 'a relevant requirement' means –

    (a)   an occupation order or non-molestation order;

    (b)   an exclusion requirement included by virtue of section 38A of the Children Act 1989 in an interim care order made under section 38 of that Act; or

    (c)   an exclusion requirement included by virtue of section 44A of the Children Act 1989 in an emergency protection order under section 44 of that Act.

51 Power of magistrates' court to order hospital admission or guardianship

(1) A magistrates' court shall have the same power to make a hospital order or guardianship order under section 37 of the Mental Health Act 1983 or an interim hospital order under section 38 of that Act in the case of a person suffering from mental illness or severe mental impairment who could otherwise be committed to custody for breach of a relevant requirement as a magistrates' court has under those sections in the case of a person convicted of an offence punishable on summary conviction with imprisonment.

(2) In subsection (1) 'a relevant requirement' has the meaning given by section 50(2).

****

Jurisdiction and procedure etc

57 Jurisdiction of courts

(1) For the purposes of this Act 'the court' means the High Court, a county court or a magistrates' court.

(2) Subsection (1) above is subject to the provision made by or under the following provisions of this section, to section 59 and to any express provision as to the jurisdiction of any court made by any other provision of this Part.

(3) The Lord Chancellor may by order specify proceedings under this Act which may only be commenced in –

    (a)   a specified level of court;

    (b)   a court which falls within a specified class of court; or

    (c)   a particular court determined in accordance with, or specified in, the order.

(4) The Lord Chancellor may by order specify circumstances in which specified proceedings under this Part may only be commenced in –

    (a)   a specified level of court;

    (b)   a court which falls within a specified class of court; or

    (c)   a particular court determined in accordance with, or specified in, the order.

(5) The Lord Chancellor may by order provide that in specified circumstances the whole, or any specified part of any specified proceedings under this Part shall be transferred to –

    (a)   a specified level of court;

    (b)   a court which falls within a specified class of court; or

    (c)   a particular court determined in accordance with, or specified in, the order.

(6) An order under subsection (5) may provide for the transfer to be made at any stage, or specified stage, of the proceedings and whether or not the proceedings, or any part of them, have already been transferred.

(7) An order under subsection (5) may make provision as the Lord Chancellor thinks appropriate for excluding specified proceedings from the operation of section 38 or 39 of the Matrimonial and Family Proceedings Act 1984 (transfer of family proceedings) or any other enactment which would otherwise govern the transfer of those proceedings, or any part of them.

(8) For the purposes of subsections (3), (4) and (5), there are three levels of court –

    (a)   the High Court;

    (b)   any county court; and

    (c)   any magistrates' court.

(9) The Lord Chancellor may by order make provision for the principal registry of the Family Division of the High Court to be treated as if it were a county court for specified purposes of this Part, or of any provision made under this Part.

(10) Any order under subsection (9) may make such provision as the Lord Chancellor thinks expedient for the purpose of applying (with or without modifications) provisions which apply in relation to the procedure in county courts to the principal registry when it acts as if it were a county court.

(11) In this section 'specified' means specified by an order under this section.

58 Contempt proceedings

The powers of the court in relation to contempt of court arising out of a person's failure to comply with an order under this Part may be exercised by the relevant judicial authority.

59 Magistrates' courts

(1) A magistrates' court shall not be competent to entertain any application, or make any order, involving any disputed question as to a party's entitlement to occupy any property by virtue of a beneficial estate or interest or contract or by virtue of any enactment giving him the right to remain in occupation, unless it is unnecessary to determine the question in order to deal with the application or make the order.

(2) A magistrates' court may decline jurisdiction in any proceedings under this Part if it considers that the case can more conveniently be dealt with by another court.

(3) The powers of a magistrates' court under section 63(2) of the Magistrates' Courts Act 1980 to suspend or rescind orders shall not apply in relation to any order made under this Part.

****

61 Appeals

(1) An appeal shall lie to the High Court against –

    (a) the making by a magistrates' court of any order under this Part, or

    (b) any refusal by a magistrates' court to make such an order,

but no appeal shall lie against any exercise by a magistrates' court of the power conferred by section 59(2) of this Act.

(2) On an appeal under this section, the High Court may make such orders as may be necessary to give effect to its determination of the appeal.

(3) Where an order is made under subsection (2), the High Court may also make such incidental or consequential orders as appear to it to be just.

(4) Any order of the High Court made on an appeal under this section (other than one directing that an application be re-heard by a magistrates' court) shall, for the purposes –

    (a) of the enforcement of the order, and

    (b) of any power to vary, revive or discharge orders,

be treated as if it were an order of the magistrates' court from which the appeal was brought and not an order of the High Court.

(5) The Lord Chancellor may by order make provision as to the circumstances in which appeals may be made against decisions taken by courts on questions arising in connection with the transfer, or proposed transfer, of proceedings by virtue of any order under section 57(5).

(6) Except to the extent provided for in any order made under subsection (5), no appeal may be made against any decision of a kind mentioned in that subsection.

General

62 Meaning of 'cohabitants', 'relevant child' and 'associated persons'

(1) For the purposes of this Part –

(a) 'cohabitants' are a man and a woman who, although not married to each other, are living together as husband and wife; and

(b) 'former cohabitants' is to be read accordingly, but does not include cohabitants who have subsequently married each other.

(2) In this Part, 'relevant child', in relation to any proceedings under this Part, means –

(a) any child who is living with or might reasonably be expected to live with either party to the proceedings;

(b) any child in relation to whom an order under the Adoption Act 1976 or the Children Act 1989 is in question in the proceedings; and

(c) any other child whose interests the court considers relevant.

(3) For the purposes of this Part, a person is associated with another person if –

(a) they are or have been married to each other;

(b) they are cohabitants or former cohabitants;

(c) they live or have lived in the same household, otherwise than merely by reason of one of them being the other's employee, tenant, lodger or boarder;

(d) they are relatives;

(e) they have agreed to marry one another (whether or not that agreement has been terminated);

(f) in relation to any child, they are both persons falling within subsection (4); or

(g) they are parties to the same family proceedings (other than proceedings under this Part).

(4) A person falls within this subsection in relation to a child if –

(a) he is a parent of the child; or

(b) he has or has had parental responsibility for the child.

(5) If a child has been adopted or has been freed for adoption by virtue of any of the enactments mentioned in section 16(1) of the Adoption Act 1976, two persons are also associated with each other for the purpose of this Part if –

(a) one is a natural parent of the child or a parent of such a natural parent, and

(b) the other is the child or any person –

(i) who had become a parent of the child by virtue of an adoption order or has applied for an adoption order, or

(ii) with whom the child has at any time been placed for adoption.

(6) A body corporate and another person are not, by virtue of subsection (3)(f) or (g), to be regarded for the purposes of this Part as associated with each other.

Section 62

Prospective amendment—Section prospectively amended by Adoption and Children Act 2002, s 139(1), Sch 3, paras 54, 86, 87 (see **3.3B**).

63 Interpretation of Part IV

(1) In this Part –

'adoption order' has the meaning given by section 72(1) of the Adoption Act 1976;

'associated', in relation to a person, is to be read with section 62(3) to (6);

'child' means a person under the age of eighteen years;

'cohabitant' and 'former cohabitant' have the meaning given by section 62(1);

'the court' is to be read with section 57;

'development' means physical, intellectual, emotional, social or behavioural development;

'dwelling-house' includes (subject to subsection (4)) –

(a) any building or part of a building which is occupied as a dwelling,

(b) any caravan, house-boat or structure which is occupied as a dwelling,

and any yard, garden, garage or outhouse belonging to it and occupied with it;

'family proceedings' means any proceedings –

(a) under the inherent jurisdiction of the High Court in relation to children; or

(b) under the enactments mentioned in subsection (2),

'harm' –

(a) in relation to a person who has reached the age of eighteen years, means ill-treatment or the impairment of health; and

(b) in relation to a child, means ill-treatment or the impairment of health or development;

'health' includes physical or mental health;

'ill-treatment' includes forms of ill-treatment which are not physical and, in relation to a child, includes sexual abuse;

'matrimonial home rights' has the meaning given by section 30;

'mortgage', 'mortgagor' and 'mortgagee' have the same meaning as in the Law of Property Act 1925;

'mortgage payments' includes any payments which, under the terms of the mortgage, the mortgagor is required to make to any person;

'non-molestation order' has the meaning given by section 42(1);

'occupation order' has the meaning given by section 39;

'parental responsibility' has the same meaning as in the Children Act 1989;

'relative', in relation to a person, means –

(a) the father, mother, stepfather, stepmother, son, daughter, stepson, stepdaughter, grandmother, grandfather, grandson or granddaughter of that person or of that person's spouse or former spouse, or

(b) the brother, sister, uncle, aunt, niece or nephew (whether of the full blood or of the half blood or by affinity) of that person or of that person's spouse or former spouse,

and includes, in relation to a person who is living or has lived with another person as husband or wife, any person who would fall within paragraph (a) or (b) if the parties were married to each other;

'relevant child', in relation to any proceedings under this Part, has the meaning given by section 62(2);

'the relevant judicial authority', in relation to any order under this Part, means –

(a) where the order was made by the High Court, a judge of that court;

(b) where the order was made by a county court, a judge or district judge of that or any other county court; or

(c) where the order was made by a magistrates' court, any magistrates' court.

(2) The enactments referred to in the definition of 'family proceedings' are –

(a) Part II;

(b) this Part;

(c) the Matrimonial Causes Act 1973;

(d) the Adoption Act 1976;

(e) the Domestic Proceedings and Magistrates' Court Act 1978;

(f) Part III of the Matrimonial and Family Proceedings Act 1984;

(g) Parts I, II and IV of the Children Act 1989;

(h) section 30 of the Human Fertilisation and Embryology Act 1990.

(3) Where the question of whether harm suffered by a child is significant turns on the child's health or development, his health or development shall be compared with that which could reasonably be expected of a similar child.

(4) For the purposes of sections 31, 32, 53 and 54 and such other provisions of this Part (if any) as may be prescribed, this Part is to have effect as if paragraph (b) of the definition of 'dwelling-house' were omitted.

(5) It is hereby declared that this Part applies as between the parties to a marriage even though either of them is, or has at any time during the marriage been, married to more than one person.

Section 63

Prospective amendment—Section prospectively amended by Adoption and Children Act 2002, s 139(1), Sch 3, paras 54, 88 (see **3.3B**).

****

SCHEDULE 5

POWERS OF HIGH COURT AND COUNTY COURT TO REMAND

1 Interpretation

In this Schedule 'the court' means the High Court or a county court and includes –

(a) in relation to the High Court, a judge of that court, and

(b) in relation to a county court, a judge or district judge of that court.

2 Remand in custody or on bail

(1) Where a court has power to remand a person under section 47, the court may –

(a) remand him in custody, that is to say, commit him to custody to be brought before the court at the end of the period of remand or at such earlier time as the court may require, or

(b) remand him on bail –

(i) by taking from him a recognizance (with or without sureties) conditioned as provided in sub-paragraph (3), or

(ii) by fixing the amount of the recognizances with a view to their being taken subsequently in accordance with paragraph 4 and in the meantime committing the person to custody in accordance with paragraph (a).

(2) Where a person is brought before the court after remand, the court may further remand him.

(3) Where a person is remanded on bail under sub-paragraph (1), the court may direct that his recognizance be conditioned for his appearance –

(a) before that court at the end of the period of remand, or
(b) at every time and place to which during the course of the proceedings the hearing may from time to time be adjourned.

(4) Where a recognizance is conditioned for a person's appearance in accordance with sub-paragraph (1)(b), the fixing of any time for him next to appear shall be deemed to be a remand; but nothing in this sub-paragraph or sub-paragraph (3) shall deprive the court of power at any subsequent hearing to remand him afresh.

(5) Subject to paragraph 3, the court shall not remand a person under this paragraph for a period exceeding 8 clear days, except that –

(a) if the court remands him on bail, it may remand him for a longer period if he and the other party consent, and
(b) if the court adjourns a case under section 48(1), the court may remand him for the period of the adjournment.

(6) Where the court has power under this paragraph to remand a person in custody it may, if the remand for a period not exceeding 3 clear days, commit him to the custody of a constable.

3 Further remand

(1) If the court is satisfied that any person who has been remanded under paragraph 2 is unable by reason of illness or accident to appear or be brought before the court at the expiration of the period for which he was remanded, the court may, in his absence, remand him for a further time; and paragraph 2(5) shall not apply.

(2) Notwithstanding anything in paragraph 2(1), the power of the court under sub-paragraph (1) to remand a person on bail for a further time may be exercised by enlarging his recognizance and those of any sureties for him to a later time.

(3) Where a person remanded on bail under paragraph 2 is bound to appear before the court at any time and the court has no power to remand him under sub-paragraph (1), the court may in his absence enlarge his recognizance and those of any sureties for him to a later time; and the enlargement of his recognizance shall be deemed to be a further remand.

4 Postponement of taking of recognizance

Where under paragraph 2(1)(b)(ii) the court fixes the amount in which the principal and his sureties, if any, are to be bound, the recognizance may thereafter be taken by such person as may be prescribed by rules of court, and the same consequences shall follow as if it had been entered into before the court.

****

3.13   FAMILY LAW REFORM ACT 1969
(ss 8, 20–26)

PART I

REDUCTION OF AGE OF MAJORITY AND RELATED PROVISIONS

****

8 Consent by persons over 16 to surgical, medical and dental treatment

(1) The consent of a minor who has attained the age of sixteen years to any surgical, medical or dental treatment which, in the absence of consent, would constitute a trespass to his person, shall be as effective as it would be if he were of full age; and where a minor has by virtue of this section given an effective consent to any treatment it shall not be necessary to obtain any consent for it from his parent or guardian.

(2) In this section 'surgical, medical or dental treatment' includes any procedure undertaken for the purposes of diagnosis, and this section applies to any procedure (including, in particular, the administration of an anaesthetic) which is ancillary to any treatment as it applies to that treatment.

(3) Nothing in this section shall be construed as making ineffective any consent which would have been effective if this section had not been enacted.

Section 8

In Re *W (A Minor) (Medical Treatment: Court's Jurisdiction)* [1993] Fam 64, [1992] 4 All ER 627, CA, Lord Donaldson said:

'1. No question of a minor consenting to or refusing medical treatment arises unless and until a medical or dental practitioner advises such treatment and is willing to undertake it.

2. Regardless of whether the minor or anyone else with authority to do so consents to the treatment, that practitioner will be liable to the minor in negligence if he fails to advise with reasonable skill and care and to have due regard to the best interests of his patient.

3. This appeal has been concerned with the treatment of anorexia nervosa. It is a peculiarity of this disease that the disease itself creates a wish not to be cured or only to be cured if and when the patient decides to cure himself or herself, which may well be too late. Treatment has to be directed at this state of mind as much as to restoring body weight.

4. Section 8 of the Family Law Reform Act 1969 gives minors who have attained the age of 16 a right to consent to surgical, medical or dental treatment. Such a consent cannot be overridden by those with parental responsibility for the minor. It can, however, be overriden by the court. This statutory right does not extend to consent to the donation of blood or organs.

5. A minor of any age who is "Gillick competent" in the context of particular treatment has a right to consent to that treatment which again cannot be overriden by those with parental responsibility, but can be overridden by the court. Unlike the statutory right this common law right extends to the donation of blood or organs.

6. No minor of whatever age has power by refusing consent to treatment to override a consent to treatment by someone who has parental responsibility for the minor and *a fortiori* a consent by the court. Nevertheless, such a refusal is a very important consideration in making clinical judgments and for parents and the court in deciding whether themselves to give consent. Its importance increases with the age and maturity of the minor.

7. The effect of consent to treatment by the minor or someone else with authority to give it is limited to protecting the medical or dental practitioner from claims for damages for trespass to the person.'

In the case of *Re O (A Minor) (Blood Tests: Constraint)* [2000] 2 All ER 29, FD, it was stated that it was apparent: 'that the inherent jurisdiction had been exercised vigorously and creatively in other, often graver, circumstances'. These included involving the use of compulsion in respect of a heart transplant against the wishes of a teenager (see *Re M (Medical Treatment: Consent)* [1999] 2 FLR 1097); a liver transplant (see *Re T (A Minor) (Wardship: Medical Treatment)* [1997] 1 All ER 906, [1997] 1 WLR 242); blood transfusions against the wishes of teenage Jehovah's witnesses (see *Re E (A Minor) (Wardship: Medical Treatment)* [1993] 1 FLR 386 and *Re L (Medical Treatment: Gillick Competency)* [1998] 2 FLR 810); blood transfusion for babies against the wishes of Jehovah's witness parents (see *Re O (A Minor) (Medical Treatment)* [1993] 2 FLR 149 and *Re R (A Minor) (Blood Transfusion)* [1993] 2 FLR 757); blood testing of a baby for HIV against parents' wishes (see *Re C (HIV Test)* [1999] 2 FLR 1004); directions for medical/psychiatric treatment against the wishes of a teenager (including restriction of liberty) (see *Re W (A Minor) (Medical Treatment: Court's Jurisdiction)* [1992] 4 All ER 627, [1993] Fam 64; *South Glamorgan County Council v W and B* [1993] 1 FLR 574; and *Re C (Detention: Medical Treatment)* [1997] 2 FLR 180); the exclusion of a joint tenant from property (see *C v K (Inherent Powers: Exclusion Order)* [1996] 2 FLR 506); the restriction of free speech (see *Re Z (A Minor) (Identification: Restrictions on Publication)* [1997] Fam 1, [1995] 4 All ER 961, and *Nottingham City Council v October Films Ltd* [1999] 2 FLR 347); and the discharge of an order freeing a child for adoption (see *Re C (A Minor) (Adoption: Freeing Order)* [1999] Fam 240, [1999] 2 WLR 1079).

In *Glass v UK* [2004] 1 FLR 1019, ECHR it was held that a hospital trust's decision to override without prior court authority a parent's objection to the giving of diamorphine to a severely disabled child who was on a ventilator amounted to a breach of Article 8 of the European Convention on Human Rights.

****

PART III

PROVISIONS FOR USE OF SCIENTIFIC TESTS IN DETERMINING PATERNITY

20 Power of court to require use of scientific tests

(1) In any civil proceedings in which the parentage of any person falls to be determined, the court may, either of its own motion or on an application by any party to the proceedings, give a direction –

   (a) for the use of scientific tests to ascertain whether such tests show that a party to the proceedings is or is not the father or mother of that person; and

(b) for the taking, within a period specified in the direction, of bodily samples from all or any of the following, namely, that person, any party who is alleged to be the father or mother of that person and any other party to the proceedings;

and the court may at any time revoke or vary a direction previously given by it under this subsection.

(1A) Tests required by a direction under this section may only be carried out by a body which has been accredited for the purposes of this section by –

(a) the Lord Chancellor, or
(b) a body appointed by him for the purpose.

(2) The individual carrying out scientific tests in pursuance of a direction under subsection (1) above ('the tester') shall make to the court a report in which he shall state –

(a) the results of the tests;
(b) whether the party to whom the report relates is or is not excluded by the results from being the father or mother of the person whose parentage is to be determined; and
(c) in relation to any party who is not so excluded, the value, if any, of the results in determining whether that party is the father or mother of that person;

and the report shall be received by the court as evidence in the proceedings of the matters stated in it.

(2A) Where the proceedings in which the parentage of any person falls to be determined are proceedings on an application under section 55A or 56 of the Family Law Act 1986, any reference in subsection (1) or (2) of this section to any party to the proceedings shall include a reference to any person named in the application.

(3) A report under subsection (2) of this section shall be in the form prescribed by regulations made under section 22 of this Act.

(4) Where a report has been made to a court under subsection (2) of this section, any party may, with the leave of the court, or shall, if the court so directs, obtain from 'the tester' a written statement explaining or amplifying any statement made in the report, and that statement shall be deemed for the purposes of this section (except subsection (3) thereof) to form part of the report made to the court.

(5) Where a direction is given under this section in any proceedings, a party to the proceedings, unless the court otherwise directs, shall not be entitled to call as a witness the tester, or any other person by whom any thing necessary for the purpose of enabling those tests to be carried out was done, unless within fourteen days after receiving a copy of the report he serves notice on the other parties to the proceedings, or on such of them as the court may direct, of his intention to call the tester, or that other person; and where the tester or any such person is called as a witness the party who called him shall be entitled to cross-examine him.

(6) Where a direction is given under this section the party on whose application the direction is given shall pay the cost of taking and testing bodily samples for the purpose of giving effect to the direction (including any expenses reasonably incurred by any person in taking any steps required of him for the purpose), and of making a

report to the court under this section, but the amount paid shall be treated as costs incurred by him in the proceedings.

Section 20

In considering whether to order tests, the child's welfare is relevant but not paramount (*S v S; W v W* [1972] AC 24, [1970] 3 All ER 107). In deciding whether to order blood tests the court will recognise that the interests of justice in the abstract are best served by the ascertainment of the truth, and there must be few cases where the interests of children can be shown to be best served by the suppression of truth (*Re H and A (Paternity: Blood Tests)* [2002] 1 FLR 1145, CA, citing *S v S; W v W* (above)). Further, under Article 7 of the UN Convention on the Rights of the Child, every child has the right to know the truth of his identity unless this would be contrary to his interests (*Re H (A Minor) (Blood Tests: Parental Rights)* [1997] Fam 89, [1996] 4 All ER 28, [1996] 2 FLR 65, CA). The balancing rights under Article 8 of the European Convention on Human Rights are considered in *Re T (Paternity: Ordering Blood Tests)* [2001] 2 FLR 1190.

When considering the relevance of the merit of the substantive application, the Court of Appeal said in *Re H (A Minor) (Blood Tests: Parental Rights)* [1997] Fam 89, [1996] 4 All ER 28, [1996] 2 FLR 65 that the following approach should be adopted (see [1996] 4 All ER 28 at 41):

'1. The paternity issue must be judged as a free-standing application entitled to consideration on its own.

2. The outcome of the proceedings in which the paternity issue has been raised, in so far as it bears on the welfare of child, must be taken into account.

3. Any gain to the child from preventing any disturbance to his security must be balanced against the loss to him of the certainty of knowing who he is.

4. The terms of s 10(4) of the Children Act 1989 are explicit in giving a parent a right to apply for contact because they provide:
   "The following persons *are entitled to apply* to the court for any section 8 order with respect to a child – (a) any parent ... of the child ..."
   There is no statutory justification for transforming the paternity issue into a disguised application for leave to apply and judging the paternity issue by the criteria set out in s 10(9).

5. Accordingly, whilst the outcome of the section 8 proceedings and the risk of disruption to the child's life both by the continuance of the paternity issue as well as the pursuit of the section 8 order are obviously factors which impinge on the child's welfare, they are not, in my judgment, determinative of the blood testing question.'

The requisite consents that are necessary before a blood test can be ordered are stated in s 21. The current wording of s 21(3) appears as amended by Child Support, Pensions and Social Services Act 2000, s 82 as from 1 April 2001 (see SI 2001/777) and cases such as *Re O (A Minor) (Blood Tests: Constraint)* [2000] Fam 139, [2000] 2 All ER 29, [2000] 1 FLR 418 have to be read in the light of those amendments (although that decision remains effective insofar as it decides that there is no power to enforce a direction for blood tests to be taken). Where a parent refuses to consent to blood tests adverse inferences may be drawn against him (*Re H (A Minor) (Blood Tests: Parental Rights)* [1997] Fam 89, CA; *Re A (A Minor) (Paternity: Refusal of Blood Test)* [1994] 2 FLR 463, CA; *Re G (Parentage: Blood Sample)* [1997] 1 FLR 360, CA, and *Secretary of State for Works and Pensions v Jones* [2004] 1 FLR 282, FD ('virtually inescapable inference')).

The procedure is as stated in RSC Ord 112 (High Court) and CCR Ord 47, r 5 (county court) and the Magistrates Courts (Blood Tests) Rules 1971, as amended (family proceedings court). A Code of Practice has been published by the Ad Hoc Advisory Group for those offering genetic paternity testing services – see http://paternity.forensic.gov.uk/docs/geneticspaternity.

Where an issue arises in relation to HIV, reference should be made to *President's Direction: HIV Testing of Children* [2003] 1 FLR 1299.

Under the Blood Tests (Evidence of Paternity) (Amendment) Regulations 2001, SI 2001/773, it is now possible for samples of bodily tissue and bodily fluid to be taken rather than blood. Further scientific tests may be used to establish whether a person is the mother of the person whose parentage falls to be determined, as well as whether a person is the father. The regulations provide that tests are to be carried out by an accredited body rather than a named individual, and lay down the conditions which a body must meet if it is to be accredited. The regulations also reflect the courts' jurisdiction under s 21(3) to order that a sample be taken from a person under 16, where it would be in his best interests for the sample to be taken, even though the person with care and control of the person does not consent. The charges that a sampler may make are limited by the Blood Tests (Evidence of Paternity) (Amendment) Regulations 2004, SI 2004/596.

The laboratories that were approved by the Lord Chancellor for taking samples are:

– the Department of Haemotology, St Bartholomew's and the Royal London School of Medicine and Dentistry;
– the Department of Human Genetics, University of Newcastle upon Tyne;
– Cellmark Diagnostics, Abingdon;
– University Diagnostics Ltd, Teddington;
– Forensic Science Service, Wetherby Laboratory;
– Forensic Science Service, Metropolitan Laboratory;
– Department of Human Sciences, Loughborough University.

21 Consents etc required for taking of bodily samples

(1) Subject to the provisions of subsections (3) and (4) of this section, a bodily sample which is required to be taken from any person for the purpose of giving effect to a direction under section 20 of this Act shall not be taken from that person except with his consent.

(2) The consent of a minor who has attained the age of sixteen years to the taking from himself of a bodily sample shall be as effective as it would be if he were of full age; and where a minor has by virtue of this subsection given an effective consent to the taking of a bodily sample it shall not be necessary to obtain any consent for it from any other person.

(3) A bodily sample may be taken from a person under the age of sixteen years, not being such a person as is referred to in subsection (4) of this section –

(a) if the person who has the care and control of him consents; or
(b) where that person does not consent, if the court considers that it would be in his best interests for the sample to be taken.

(4) A bodily sample may be taken from a person who is suffering from mental disorder within the meaning of the Mental Health Act 1983 and is incapable of understanding the nature and purpose of scientific tests if the person who has the care and control of him consents and the medical practitioner in whose care he is has certified that the taking of a bodily sample from him will not be prejudicial to his proper care and treatment.

(5) The foregoing provisions of this section are without prejudice to the provisions of section 23 of this Act.

22 Power to provide for manner of giving effect to direction for use of scientific tests

(1) The Lord Chancellor may by regulations make provision as to the manner of giving effect to directions under section 20 of this Act and, in particular, any such regulations may –

(a) provide that bodily samples shall not be taken except by registered medical practitioners or members of such professional bodies as may be prescribed by the regulations;

(aa) prescribe the bodily samples to be taken;

(b) regulate the taking, identification and transport of bodily samples;

(c) require the production at the time when a bodily sample is to be taken of such evidence of the identity of the person from whom it is to be taken as may be prescribed by the regulations;

(d) require any person from whom a bodily sample is to be taken, or, in such cases as may be prescribed by the regulations, such other person as may be so prescribed, to state in writing whether he or the person from whom the sample is to be taken, as the case may be, has during such period as may be specified in the regulations suffered from any such illness or condition or undergone any such treatment as may be so specified or received a transfusion of blood;

(e) prescribe conditions which a body must meet in order to be eligible for accreditation for the purposes of section 20 of this Act;

(f) prescribe the scientific tests to be carried out and the manner in which they are to be carried out;

(g) regulate the charges that may be made for the taking and testing of bodily samples and for the making of a report to a court under section 20 of this Act;

(h) make provisions for securing that so far as practicable the bodily samples to be tested for the purpose of giving effect to a direction under section 20 of this Act are tested by the same person;

(i) prescribe the form of the report to be made to a court under section 20 of this Act;

(j) make different provision for different cases or for different descriptions of case.

(2) The power to make regulations under this section shall be exercisable by statutory instrument which shall be subject to annulment in pursuance of a resolution of either House of Parliament.

23 Failure to comply with direction for taking scientific tests

(1) Where a court gives a direction under section 20 of this Act and any person fails to take any step required of him for the purpose of giving effect to the direction, the court may draw such inferences, if any, from that fact as appear proper in the circumstances.

(2) Where in any proceedings in which the parentage of any person falls to be determined by the court hearing the proceedings there is a presumption of law that that person is legitimate, then if –

(a) a direction is given under section 20 of this Act in those proceedings, and

(b) any party who is claiming any relief in the proceedings and who for the purpose of obtaining that relief is entitled to rely on the presumption fails to take any step required of him for the purpose of giving effect to the direction,

the court may adjourn the hearing for such period as it thinks fit to enable that party to take that step, and if at the end of that period he has failed without reasonable cause to take it the court may, without prejudice to subsection (1) of this section, dismiss his claim for relief notwithstanding the absence of evidence to rebut the presumption.

(3) Where any person named in a direction under section 20 of this Act fails to consent to the taking of a bodily sample from himself or from any person named in the direction of whom he has the care and control, he shall be deemed for the purposes of this section to have failed to take a step required of him for the purpose of giving effect to the direction.

24 Penalty for personating another, etc, for purpose of providing bodily sample

If for the purpose of providing a bodily sample for a test required to give effect to a direction under section 20 of this Act any person personates another, or proffers a child knowing that it is not the child named in the direction, he shall be liable –

  (a) on conviction on indictment, to imprisonment for a term not exceeding two years, or
  (b) on summary conviction, to a fine not exceeding the prescribed sum.

25 Interpretation of Part III

In this Part of this Act the following expressions have the meanings hereby respectively assigned to them, that is to say –

  'bodily sample' means a sample of bodily fluid or bodily tissue taken for the purpose of scientific tests;
  'excluded' means excluded subject to the occurrence of mutation to section 27 of the Family Law Reform Act 1987 and to sections 27 to 29 of the Human Fertilisation and Embryology Act 1990;
  'scientific tests' means scientific tests carried out under this Part of this Act and made with the object of ascertaining the inheritable characteristics of bodily fluids or bodily tissue.

PART IV

MISCELLANEOUS AND GENERAL

26 Rebuttal of presumption as to legitimacy and illegitimacy

Any presumption of law as to the legitimacy or illegitimacy of any person may in any civil proceedings be rebutted by evidence which shows that it is more probable than not that that person is illegitimate or legitimate, as the case may be, and it shall not be necessary to prove that fact beyond reasonable doubt in order to rebut the presumption.

****

3.14 FAMILY LAW REFORM ACT 1987
(ss 1, 27)

1 General principle

(1) In this Act and enactments passed and instruments made after the coming into force of this section, references (however expressed) to any relationship between two persons shall, unless the contrary intention appears, be construed without regard to whether or not the father and mother of either of them, or the father and mother of any person through whom the relationship is deduced, have or had been married to each other at any time.

(2) In this Act and enactments passed after the coming into force of this section, unless the contrary intention appears –

    (a) references to a person whose father and mother were married to each other at the time of his birth include; and

    (b) references to a person whose father and mother were not married to each other at the time of his birth do not include,

references to any person to whom subsection (3) below applies, and cognate references shall be construed accordingly.

(3) This subsection applies to any person who –

    (a) is treated as legitimate by virtue of section 1 of the Legitimacy Act 1976;

    (b) is a legitimated person within the meaning of section 10 of that Act;

    (c) is an adopted child within the meaning of Part IV of the Adoption Act 1976; or

    (d) is otherwise treated in law as legitimate.

(4) For the purpose of construing references falling within subsection (2) above, the time of a person's birth shall be taken to include any time during the period beginning with –

    (a) the insemination resulting in his birth; or

    (b) where there was no such insemination, his conception,

and (in either case) ending with his birth.

Section 1

The Family Law Reform Act 1987 (FLRA 1987) was introduced following the recommendations of the Law Commission. The Law Commission published its first Working Paper on Illegitimacy in 1979. It then published its report, *Family Law: Illegitimacy*, Law Com No 118 (TSO, 1982). The Commission's second report (*Illegitimacy (second report)*) was published in 1986 (Law Com No 157). In the financial provision case of *J v C* [1999] 1 FLR 152, [1998] 3 FCR 79 at 82–83, Hale J traced the genesis of the FLRA 1987 and said:

'This implemented two Law Commission reports on illegitimacy. The object of those reports was to remove the differences in the legal positions of children. The underlying principle was that children should not suffer just because their parents had, for whatever reason, not been married to one another. Equally of course they should not get more. There is a long line of authority ... that children are entitled to provision during their dependency and for their education, but they are not entitled to a settlement beyond that, unless there are exceptional circumstances such as a disability, however rich their parents may be.'

In *D v Hereford and Worcester County Council* [1991] Fam 14, [1991] 1 FLR 205, FD, Ward J said:

'The Family Law Reform Act 1987 is, to quote the preamble "An Act to reform the law relating to the consequences or birth outside marriage: to make further provision with respect to the rights and duties of parents and the determination of parentage: and for connected purposes". That reform was the culmination of long deliberation and consultation. The Law Commission published its first Working Paper on Illegitimacy in 1979. The logic of sweeping away the legal distinction between the illegitimate child and the legitimate child was that in principle there should be no distinction between the parents and each should have equal parental rights and duties. As the Law Commission's Report, No 118 of 1982, made clear, that sweeping approach did not find favour and the report recommended instead that the law should provide machinery giving legal recognition to the familial links between a non-marital child and his father whenever it would be in the child's interests to do so. In 1986 the Scots Law was amended. Thus, the Law Commission in its second report, No 157 in 1986, stated that the policy emerging was that to the greatest extent possible the legal position of the child born to unmarried parents should be the same as that of one born to married parents, but as between the parents themselves, the mother alone should have the parental rights and duties, although the father should be able to acquire these by legal process. The Law Commission accordingly recommended in para 3.2: "... permitting the court to order that the father shall have full parental authority sharing it with the mother. Such an order would place him in essentially the same position as a married father. Once the father has acquired full parental status in this way, disputes between the parents will usually be dealt with in the same way as disputes between married parents, either by orders under the Guardianship Act 1973, relating to single issues, or by custody and access orders under the Guardianship of Minors Act 1971.'

****

27 Artificial insemination

(1)   Where after the coming into force of this section a child is born in England and Wales as the result of the artificial insemination of a woman who –

(a)   was at the time of the insemination a party to a marriage (being a marriage which had not at that time been dissolved or annulled); and

(b)   was artificially inseminated with the semen of some person other than the other party to that marriage,

then, unless it is proved to the satisfaction of any court by which the matter has to be determined that the other party to that marriage did not consent to the insemination, the child shall be treated in law as the child of the parties to that marriage and shall not be treated as the child of any person other than the parties to that marriage.

(2)   Any reference in this section to a marriage includes a reference to a void marriage if at the time of the insemination resulting in the birth of the child both or either of the parties reasonably believed that the marriage was valid; and for the purposes of this section it shall be presumed, unless the contrary is shown, that one of the parties so believed at that time that the marriage was valid.

(3)   Nothing in this section shall affect the succession to any dignity or title of honour or render any person capable of succeeding to or transmitting a right to succeed to any such dignity or title.

Section 27

This section should be read in association with the Human Fertilisation and Embryology Act 1990.

The effect of this section was explained in *U v W (Attorney General Intervening)* [1998] Fam 29, [1997] 3 WLR 739, FD: 'The identification in law of parents of a child born as a result of such treatment is addressed in ss 27–30 of the Act. Section 27 provides for maternity. By virtue of s 27(1) and (3) the woman who is carrying or has carried a child as a result of the placing in her of an embryo or of sperm and eggs, and no other woman, is to be treated as the mother of the child, whether she was in the United Kingdom or elsewhere at the time of such placement.'

3.15 HUMAN FERTILISATION AND EMBRYOLOGY ACT 1990
(ss 1, 27–30, 34, 35, Sch 3)

Principal terms used

1 Meaning of 'embryo', 'gamete' and associated expressions

(1) In this Act, except where otherwise stated –

    (a) embryo means a live human embryo where fertilisation is complete, and

    (b) references to an embryo include an egg in the process of fertilisation, and, for this purpose, fertilisation is not complete until the appearance of a two cell zygote.

(2) This Act, so far as it governs bringing about the creation of an embryo, applies only to bringing about the creation of an embryo outside the human body; and in this Act –

    (a) references to embryos the creation of which was brought about in vitro (in their application to those where fertilisation is complete) are to those where fertilisation began outside the human body whether or not it was completed there, and

    (b) references to embryos taken from a woman do not include embryos whose creation was brought about in vitro.

(3) This Act, so far as it governs the keeping or use of an embryo, applies only to keeping or using an embryo outside the human body.

(4) References in this Act to gametes, eggs or sperm, except where otherwise stated, are to live human gametes, eggs or sperm but references below in this Act to gametes or eggs do not include eggs in the process of fertilisation.

Section 1

Save for the provisions of ss 30 and 48(1), the Human Fertilisation and Embryology Act 1990 (HFEA 1990) came into force in 1990 and 1991 (see Commencement Orders (Nos 1 to 4) – SIs 1990/2165, 1991/480, 1991/1400, and 1991/1781). Sections 30(9) and (10) and 48(1) (so far as it relates to that subsection) came into force on 5 July 1994; the balance of ss 30 and 48 came into force on 1 November 1994 (SI 1994/1776).

The HFEA 1990 was introduced following the recommendations of *The Warnock Report*, Cmnd 9314 (1984). The Human Fertilisation and Embryology Authority has been set up in accordance with HFEA 1990, s 5 and Sch 1. Information concerning the HFEA 1990 and the Authority (together with the code of practice issued by the Authority) can be obtained from the Authority's website http://www.hfea.gov.uk. Note also that, since 18 September 2003, any man wishing to be recorded as the father of a child resulting from fertility treatment undertaken after his death must have given his written consent: see the Human Fertilisation and Embryology (Deceased Fathers) Act 2003. The Authority has produced a sample consent form which can be obtained from the above website. Licensing committees have been set up under ss 8–10 in accordance with the Human Fertilisation and Embryology Authority (Licence Committee and Appeals) Regulations 1991, SI 1991/1889. Section 3 of the Act contains prohibitions in connection with embryos and creates criminal offences (*R v The Human Fertilisation and Embryology Authority, ex parte Blood* [1999] Fam 151, [1997] 2 FLR 742). The two most important principles to be found in the HFEA 1990 are the welfare of any children born by treatment and the requirements of consent (*Leeds Teaching Hospital NHS Trust v A* [2003] EWHC 259 (QB), [2003] 1 FLR 1091, and *Mrs U v Centre for Reproductive Medicine* [2002] EWCA Civ 565, [2002] Lloyd's Rep Med 259).

The background to the HFEA 1990 and the manner in which the Act regulates certain forms of fertility treatment, the storage of gametes and the creation., storage and use of human embryos outside the body for treatment services or research are considered in detail in R *(Quintavalle) v Secretary of State for Health* [2003] EWHC 13, [2003] 2 WLR 692, [2003] 2 All ER 1 and in R *(Quintavalle) v The Human Fertilisation and Embryology Authority (Secretary of State for Health Intervening)* [2003] EWCA Civ 667, [2003] 3 WLR 878, [2003] 3 All ER 257, [2003] 2 FLR 335, CA. It has been held that the HFEA 1990 does not breach the European Convention on Human Rights (*Evans v Amicus Healthcare Ltd; Hadley v Midland Fertility Services Ltd* [2004] EWCA (Civ) 727, [2004] 2 FLR 766). The artificial insemination of a woman by a prisoner may be refused without there being a breach of Article 8 of the European Convention on Human Rights (R *(On the Application of Mellor) v Secretary of State for the Home Department* [2001] EWCA Civ 472, [2002] QB 13, [2001] 3 WLR 533).

****

Status

27 Meaning of 'mother'

(1) The woman who is carrying or has carried a child as a result of the placing in her of an embryo or of sperm and eggs, and no other woman, is to be treated as the mother of the child.

(2) Subsection (1) above does not apply to any child to the extent that the child is treated by virtue of adoption as not being the child of any person other than the adopter or adopters.

(3) Subsection (1) above applies whether the woman was in the United Kingdom or elsewhere at the time of placing in her of the embryo or the sperm and eggs.

Section 27

Prospective amendment—Section prospectively amended by Adoption and Children Act 2002, s 139(1), Sch 3, paras 54,77 (see **3.3B**).

28 Meaning of 'father'

(1) This section applies in the case of a child who is being or has been carried by a woman as the result of the placing in her of an embryo or of sperm and eggs or her artificial insemination.

(2) If –

  (a) at the time of the placing in her of the embryo or the sperm and eggs or of her insemination, the woman was a party to a marriage, and

  (b) the creation of the embryo carried by her was not brought about with the sperm of the other party to the marriage,

then, subject to subsection (5) below, the other party to the marriage shall be treated as the father of the child unless it is shown that he did not consent to the placing in her of the embryo or the sperm and eggs or to her insemination (as the case may be).

(3) If no man is treated, by virtue of subsection (2) above, as the father of the child but –

(a) the embryo or the sperm and eggs were placed in the woman, or she was artificially inseminated, in the course of treatment services provided for her and a man together by a person to whom a licence applies, and

(b) the creation of the embryo carried by her was not brought about with the sperm of that man,

then, subject to subsection (5) below, that man shall be treated as the father of the child.

(4) Where a person is treated as the father of the child by virtue of subsection (2) or (3) above, no other person is to be treated as the father of the child.

(5) Subsections (2) and (3) above do not apply –

(a) in relation to England and Wales and Northern Ireland, to any child who, by virtue of the rules of common law, is treated as the legitimate child of the parties to a marriage,

(b) *(applies to Scotland only)*, or

(c) to any child to the extent that the child is treated by virtue of adoption as not being the child of any person other than the adopter or adopters.

(6) Where –

(a) the sperm of a man who had given such consent as is required by paragraph 5 of Schedule 3 to this Act was used for a purpose for which such consent was required, or

(b) the sperm of a man, or any embryo the creation of which was brought about with his sperm, was used after his death,

he is not to be treated as the father of the child.

(7) The references in subsection (2) above to the parties to a marriage at the time there referred to –

(a) are to the parties to a marriage subsisting at that time, unless a judicial separation was then in force, but

(b) include the parties to a void marriage if either or both of them reasonably believed at that time that the marriage was valid; and for the purposes of this subsection it shall be presumed, unless the contrary is shown, that one of them reasonably believed at that time that the marriage was valid.

(8) This section applies whether the woman was in the United Kingdom or elsewhere at the time of the placing in her of the embryo or the sperm and eggs or her artificial insemination.

(9) In subsection (7)(a) above, 'judicial separation' includes a legal separation obtained in a country outside the British Islands and recognised in the United Kingdom.

Section 28

Prospective amendment—Section prospectively amended by Adoption and Children Act 2002, s 139(1), Sch 3, paras 54,78 (see **3.3B**).

29 Effect of sections 27 and 28

(1) Where by virtue of section 27 or 28 of this Act a person is to be treated as the mother or father of a child, that person is to be treated in law as the mother or, as the case may be, father of the child for all purposes.

(2) Where by virtue of section 27 or 28 of this Act a person is not to be treated as the mother or father of a child, that person is to be treated in law as not being the mother or, as the case may be, father of the child for any purpose.

(3) Where subsection (1) or (2) above has effect, references to any relationship between two people in any enactment, deed or other instrument or document (whenever passed or made) are to be read accordingly.

(4) In relation to England and Wales and Northern Ireland, nothing in the provisions of section 27(1) or 28(2) to (4), read with this section, affects –

- (a) the succession to any dignity or title of honour or renders any person capable of succeeding to or transmitting a right to succeed to any such dignity or title, or
- (b) the devolution of any property limited (expressly or not) to devolve (as nearly as the law permits) along with the dignity or title of honour.

(5) *(applies to Scotland only)*.

30 Parental orders in favour of gamete donors

(1) The court may make an order providing for a child to be treated in law as the child of the parties to a marriage (referred to in this section as 'the husband' and 'the wife') if –

- (a) the child has been carried by a woman other than the wife as the result of the placing in her of an embryo or sperm and eggs or her artificial insemination,
- (b) the gametes of the husband or the wife, or both, were used to bring about the creation of the embryo, and
- (c) the conditions in subsections (2) to (7) below are satisfied.

(2) The husband and the wife must apply for the order within six months of the birth of the child or, in the case of a child born before the coming into force of this Act, within six months of such coming into force.

(3) At the time of the application and of the making of the order –

- (a) the child's home must be with the husband and the wife, and
- (b) the husband or the wife, of both of them, must be domiciled in a part of the United Kingdom or in the Channel Islands or the Isle of Man.

(4) At the time of the making of the order both the husband and the wife must have attained the age of eighteen.

(5) The court must be satisfied that both the father of the child (including a person who is the father by virtue of section 28 of this Act), where he is not the husband, and the woman who carried the child have freely, and with full understanding of what is involved, agreed unconditionally to the making of the order.

(6) Subsection (5) above does not require the agreement of a person who cannot be found or is incapable of giving agreement and the agreement of the woman who

carried the child is ineffective for the purposes of that subsection if given by her less than six weeks after the child's birth.

(7) The court must be satisfied that no money or other benefit (other than for expenses reasonably incurred) has been given or received by the husband or the wife for or in consideration of –

    (a) the making of the order,

    (b) any agreement required by subsection (5) above,

    (c) the handing over of the child to the husband and the wife, or

    (d) the making of any arrangements with a view to the making of the order,

unless authorised by the court.

(8) For the purposes of an application under this section –

    (a) in relation to England and Wales, section 92(7) to (10) of, and Part I of Schedule 11 to, the Children Act 1989 (jurisdiction of courts) shall apply for the purposes of this section to determine the meaning of 'the court' as they apply for the purposes of that Act and proceedings on the application shall be 'family proceedings' for the purposes of that Act,

    (b) *(applies to Scotland only)*, and

    (c) in relation to Northern Ireland, 'the court' means the High Court or any county court within whose division the child is.

(9) Regulations may provide –

    (a) for any provision of the enactments about adoption to have effect, with such modifications (if any) as may be specified in the regulations, in relation to orders under this section, and applications for such orders, as it has effect in relation to adoption, and applications for adoption orders, and

    (b) for references in any enactment to adoption, an adopted child or an adoptive relationship to be read (respectively) as references to the effect of an order under this section, a child to whom such an order applies and a relationship arising by virtue of the enactments about adoption, as applied by the regulations, and for similar expressions in connection with adoption to be read accordingly,

and the regulations may include such incidental or supplemental provision as appears to the Secretary of State necessary or desirable in consequence of any provision made by virtue of paragraph (a) or (b) above.

(10) In this section 'the enactments about adoption' means the Adoption Act 1976, the Adoption (Scotland) Act 1978 and the Adoption (Northern Ireland) Order 1987.

(11) Subsection (1)(a) above applies whether the woman was in the United Kingdom or elsewhere at the time of the placing in her of the embryo or the sperm and eggs or her artificial insemination.

Section 30

Prospective amendment—Section prospectively amended by Adoption and Children Act 2002, s 139(1), Sch 3, paras 54,79 (see **3.3B**).

Generally—Section 30(2) of the Act came into force on 1 November 1994 – see the Human Fertilisation and Embryology Act 1990 (Commencement No 5) Order 1994, SI 1994/1776. The procedure is set out in FPR 1991, rr 4A.1–4A.10 and FPC(CA 1989)R 1991, rr 21A–21J.

In *Re Q (Parental Order)* [1996] 1 FLR 369, FD, the child was born to an unmarried woman; the applicants for the parental order were husband and wife. The wife had provided the egg but the husband had not provided the sperm. Since there was no father whose consent arose under HFEA 1990. s 28(2) and (3), it was open to the applicants to obtain a parental order; the judge gave retrospective authorisation for reasonable payments totalling £8,280. In *Re C, Application by Mr and Mrs X under s 30 of the Human Fertilisation and Embryology Act 1990* [2002] EWHC 157 (Fam), [2002] 1 FLR 909, the judge gave retrospective authorisation for a payment of £12,000 under s 30(7) and made a parental order on the facts of the case.

****

34 Disclosure in interests of justice

(1) Where in any proceedings before a court the question whether a person is or is not the parent of a child by virtue of sections 27 to 29 of this Act falls to be determined, the court may on the application of any party to the proceedings make an order requiring the Authority –

    (a) to disclose whether or not any information relevant to that question is contained in the register kept in pursuance of section 31 of this Act, and

    (b) if it is, to disclose so much of it as is specified in the order,

but such an order may not require the Authority to disclose any information falling within section 31(2)(b) of this Act.

(2) The court must not make an order under subsection (1) above unless it is satisfied that the interests of justice require it to do so, taking into account –

    (a) any representations made by any individual who may be affected by the disclosure, and

    (b) the welfare of the child, if under 18 years old, and of any other person under that age who may be affected by the disclosure.

(3) If the proceedings before the court are civil proceedings, it –

    (a) may direct that the whole or any part of the proceedings on the application for an order under subsection (2) above shall be heard in camera, and

    (b) if it makes such an order, may then or later direct that the whole or any part of any later stage of the proceedings shall be heard in camera.

(4) An application for a direction under subsection (3) above shall be heard in camera unless the court otherwise directs.

35 Disclosure in interests of justice: congenital disabilities etc

(1) Where for the purpose of instituting proceedings under section 1 of the Congenital Disabilities (Civil Liability) Act 1976 (civil liability to child born disabled) it is necessary to identify a person who would or might be the parent of a child but for sections 27 to 29 of this Act, the court may, on the application of the child, make an order requiring the Authority to disclose any information contained in the register kept in pursuance of section 31 of this Act identifying that person.

(2) ...

(3) Subsections (2) to (4) of section 34 of this Act apply for the purposes of this section as they apply for the purposes of that.

(4) ...

****

SCHEDULE 3
CONSENTS TO USE OF GAMETES OR EMBRYOS

Consent

1 A consent under this Schedule must be given in writing and, in this Schedule, 'effective consent' means a consent under this Schedule which has not been withdrawn.

2 (1) A consent to the use of any embryo must specify one or more of the following purposes –

    (a) use in providing treatment services to the person giving consent, or that person and another specified person together,

    (b) use in providing treatment services to persons not including the person giving consent, or

    (c) use for the purposes of any project of research,

and may specify conditions subject to which the embryo may be so used.

(2) A consent to the storage of any gametes or any embryo must –

    (a) specify the maximum period of storage (if less than the statutory storage period), and

    (b) state what is to be done with the gametes or embryo if the person who gave the consent dies or is unable because of incapacity to vary the terms of the consent or to revoke it,

and may specify conditions subject to which the gametes or embryo may remain in storage.

(3) A consent under this Schedule must provide for such other matters as the Authority may specify in directions.

(4) A consent under this Schedule may apply –

    (a) to the use or storage of a particular embryo, or

    (b) in the case of a person providing gametes, to the use or storage of any embryo whose creation may be brought about using those gametes,

and in the paragraph (b) case the terms of the consent may be varied, or the consent may be withdrawn, in accordance with this Schedule either generally or in relation to a particular embryo or particular embryos.

3 Procedure for giving consent

(1) Before a person gives consent under this Schedule –

    (a) he must be given a suitable opportunity to receive proper counselling about the implications of taking the proposed steps, and

    (b) he must be provided with such relevant information as is proper.

(2) Before a person gives consent under this Schedule he must be informed of the effect of paragraph 4 below.

4 Variation and withdrawal of consent

(1) The terms of any consent under this Schedule may from time to time be varied, and the consent may be withdrawn, by notice given by the person who gave the consent to the person keeping the gametes or embryo to which the consent is relevant.

(2) The terms of any consent to the use of any embryo cannot be varied, and such consent cannot be withdrawn, once the embryo has been used –

    (a) in providing treatment services, or
    (b) for the purposes of any project of research.

5 Use of gametes for treatment of others

(1) A person's gametes must not be used for the purposes of treatment services unless there is an effective consent by that person to their being so used and they are used in accordance with the terms of the consent.

(2) A person's gametes must not be received for use for those purposes unless there is an effective consent by that person to their being so used.

(3) This paragraph does not apply to the use of a person's gametes for the purpose of that person, or that person and another together, receiving treatment services.

6 In vitro fertilisation and subsequent use of embryo

(1) A person's gametes must not be used to bring about the creation of any embryo in vitro unless there is an effective consent by that person to any embryo the creation of which may be brought about with the use of those gametes being used for one or more of the purposes mentioned in paragraph 2(1) above.

(2) An embryo the creation of which was brought about in vitro must not be received by any person unless there is an effective consent by each person whose gametes were used to bring about the creation of the embryo to the use for one or more of the purposes mentioned in paragraph 2(1) above of the embryo.

(3) An embryo the creation of which was brought about in vitro must not be used for any purpose unless there is an effective consent by each person whose gametes were used to bring about the creation of the embryo to the use for that purpose of the embryo and the embryo is used in accordance with those consents.

(4) Any consent required by this paragraph is in addition to any consent that may be required by paragraph 5 above.

7 Embryos obtained by lavage, etc

(1) An embryo taken from a woman must not be used for any purpose unless there is an effective consent by her to the use of the embryo for that purpose and it is used in accordance with the consent.

(2) An embryo taken from a woman must not be received by any person for use for any purpose unless there is an effective consent by her to the use of the embryo for that purpose.

(3) This paragraph does not apply to the use, for the purpose of providing a woman with treatment services, of an embryo taken from her.

8 Storage of gametes and embryos

(1) A person's gametes must not be kept in storage unless there is an effective consent by that person to their storage and they are stored in accordance with the consent.

(2) An embryo the creation of which was brought about in vitro must not be kept in storage unless there is an effective consent, by each person whose gametes were used to bring about the creation of the embryo, to the storage of the embryo and the embryo is stored in accordance with those consents.

(3) An embryo taken from a woman must not be kept in storage unless there is an effective consent by her to its storage and it is stored in accordance with the consent.

****

Schedule 3

The provisions of this Schedule are examined thoroughly in the case of *Evans v Amicus Healthcare Ltd; Hadley v Midland Fertility Services Ltd* [2003] EWHC 2161 (Fam), [2004] 1 FLR 67, FD. The case concerned the withdrawal by men of consent that they had given to the IVF treatment of former partners. The judge held that the men had an unconditional statutory right to withdraw or vary consent, the embryos had not been 'used' in the provision of treatment services, the HFEA 1990 did not breach the ECHR, and the issue of promissory estoppel did not apply. The appeal from the judge's decision was dismissed – see [2004] EWCA Civ 727, [2004] 2 FLR 766.

3.16   HUMAN RIGHTS ACT 1998

OVERVIEW

Introduction

It is usually said that the Human Rights Act 1998 (HRA 1998), which came into force on 2 October 2000, incorporates the European Convention on Human Rights into our domestic law (although in passing, it is just worth being aware that not quite all of the Convention has been incorporated, some limitations having been defined by s 1 of the HRA 1998). Whether this is strictly correct does not matter for the purposes of this Handbook. What does matter is to know of the three great steps taken by the HRA 1998.

The relevance of the case-law of the European Court of Human Rights

First, s 2 of the HRA 1998 *requires domestic courts to take account of any relevant case-law of the European Court of Human Rights*. This is very important. It means that the thinking and decisions in all such case-law are potentially relevant to the domestic courts' approach to and determination of every case.[1] So, for example, when considering whether a child should be placed in the care of a local authority or the arrangements for contact for a child with members of his family, domestic courts must take into account the considerable body of European case-law on the issue.

Compatibility of domestic legislation

Secondly, s 3 of the HRA 1998 *requires domestic courts to read and give effect to domestic legislation in a way which is compatible with rights under the European Convention on Human Rights*.[2] The practical result is this: where a court has to choose between two or more possible interpretations of the wording of a piece of domestic legislation it must reject any interpretation that is incompatible with the European Convention on Human Rights in favour of one that is compatible. Where no interpretation is compatible with the Convention the court may make a declaration of incompatibility[3] which, although not changing the current domestic law (a matter for Parliament and

---

[1]   A note of caution, however. As Lord Justice Laws has said, the court's duty 'is to take account of the Strasbourg jurisprudence, not necessarily to apply it': *Gough v Chief Constable of the Derbyshire Constabulary* [2001] 4 All ER 289 at para 32.

[2]   Reference was made to this previously in the Overview when considering statutory interpretation: see **3.1** above.

[3]   HRA 1998, s 4. The courts which can make such a declaration are restricted to, in effect, the High Court upwards: see s 4(5).

not for judges), would clearly indicate to the government that such a change is necessary.

The issue of the compatibility of domestic legislation with the Convention does not, however, arise in most cases.[4] Ministers are now required to sign a declaration that new legislation will be compatible with the Convention. This is not a guarantee that it will be compatible (that would be to usurp the function of the courts) but it is some assurance that the issue of compatibility has been considered in the drafting process.

Public authorities

Thirdly, s 6 of the HRA 1998 specifically *extends the European Convention on Human Rights to the acts and failures to act of public authorities*, which includes local authorities, organisations such as CAFCASS, and, critically, courts and tribunals. So, at a stroke, all these public authorities must ensure that everything they do complies with, for example, the Article 6 right to a fair trial and the Article 8 right to respect for private and family life. This issue affects every case in the family courts, if only because the courts are themselves public authorities.

Section 7 of the HRA 1998 then provides two ways by which an individual can enforce her rights against a public authority. It can be done either by raising the rights within existing proceedings (HRA 1998, s 7(1)(b)) or by issuing a free-standing set of proceedings specifically for the purpose (HRA 1998, s 7(1)(a)). The former is routine – indeed, implicit – within all family proceedings. The latter is rare, but may sometimes be used, as for example in *Re M (Care: Challenging Decisions by Local Authority)*.[5] The remedies available are defined by s 8 of the HRA 1998 and, in appropriate proceedings before an appropriate court, can include damages.

The HRA 1998 therefore enables individuals to enforce their rights under the European Convention on Human Rights directly through the courts of England and Wales. They can, of course, still seek to do so through the European Court of Human Rights in Strasbourg but in the great majority of cases it will now be unnecessary to do this.

The extracts from the primary materials we recommend you read now are ss 2(1), 3(1), 6 and 7(1) of the HRA 1998.

The Overview continues at **4.1** Overview of Statutory Instruments.

---

[4]   There has so far been no declaration of incompatibility in respect of children law legislation.

[5]   [2001] 2 FLR 1300.

Human Rights Act 1998
(ss 1–8, 11, 12, 21)

1 The Convention Rights

(1) In this Act 'the Convention rights' means the rights and fundamental freedoms set out in –

    (a) Articles 2 to 12 and 14 of the Convention,
    (b) Articles 1 to 3 of the First Protocol, and
    (c) Articles 1 and 2 of the Sixth Protocol,

as read with Articles 16 to 18 of the Convention.

(2) Those Articles are to have effect for the purposes of this Act subject to any designated derogation or reservation (as to which see sections 14 and 15).

(3) The Articles are set out in Schedule 1.

(4) The Secretary of State may by order make such amendments to this Act as he considers appropriate to reflect the effect, in relation to the United Kingdom, of a protocol.

(5) In subsection (4) 'protocol' means a protocol to the Convention –

    (a) which the United Kingdom has ratified; or
    (b) which the United Kingdom has signed with a view to ratification.

(6) No amendment may be made by an order under subsection (4) so as to come into force before the protocol concerned is in force in relation to the United Kingdom.

Section 1

The HRA 1998 came into force on 2 October 2000 (see SI 2000/1851). The Articles to the Convention (which is set out in Part 2 at **2.4**) are contained in Schedule 1 to the Act. They are:

Article 2	Right to life
Article 3	Prohibition of torture, inhuman or degrading treatment or punishment.
Article 4	Freedom from slavery, servitude, forced or compulsory labour.
Article 5	Right to liberty and security of the person.
Article 6	Right to a fair trial.
Article 7	Prohibition of retrospective criminal liability and punishment.
Article 8	Right to respect for private and family life, home and correspondence.
Article 9	Freedom of thought, conscience and religion.
Article 10	Freedom of expression.

Article 11	Right to freedom of peaceful assembly and association.
Article 12	Right to marry and to found a family.
First Protocol (Articles 1 to 3)	(Article 1) Entitlement to peaceful enjoyment of possessions.
	(Article 2) Right to education.
	(Article 3) Right to free elections.
Sixth Protocol (Articles 1 and 2)	(Article 1) Abolition of death penalty.
	(Article 2) Death penalty in time of war.
Article 16	Restrictions on political activities of aliens.
Article 17	Prohibition of abuse of rights.
Article 18	Limitation on use of restrictions on rights.

In *D v East Berkshire Community NHS Trust; MAK v Dewsbury Healthcare NHS Trust: RK v Oldham NHS Trust* [2003] EWCA Civ 1151, [2003] 2 FLR 1166, Lord Phillips MR said at [79]:

'Section 1 of the Human Rights Act 1998 requires the court to have regard to the jurisprudence of the Strasbourg Court where relevant to proceedings under the Act. Thus any English court, when dealing with a claim under the Act in relation to action or inaction after October 2000 on the part of a local authority in relation to suspected child abuse, must take into account the decisions to which we have just referred.' The case decided that it is no longer legitimate to rule that, as a matter of law, no common law duty of care is owed to a child in relation to the investigation of suspected child abuse and the initiation and pursuit of care proceedings; each case will fall to be determined on its own facts. The position in relation to the parent is different; where child care decisions were being taken, no common law duty of care is owed to the parents.'

2 Interpretation of Convention rights

(1) A court or tribunal determining a question which has arisen in connection with a Convention right must take into account any –

(a) judgment, decision, declaration or advisory opinion of the European Court of Human Rights,

(b) opinion of the Commission given in a report adopted under Article 31 of the Convention,

(c) decision of the Commission in connection with Article 26 or 27(2) of the Convention, or

(d) decision of the Committee of Ministers taken under Article 46 of the Convention,

whenever made or given, so far as, in the opinion of the court or tribunal, it is relevant to the proceedings in which that question has arisen.

(2) Evidence of any judgment, decision, declaration or opinion of which account may have to be taken under this section is to be given in proceedings before any court or tribunal in such manner as may be provided by rules.

(3) In this section 'rules' means rules of court or, in the case of proceedings before a tribunal, rules made for the purposes of this section –

(a) by the Secretary of State, in relation to any proceedings outside Scotland;

(b) by the Secretary of State, in relation to proceedings in Scotland; or
(c) by a Northern Ireland department, in relation to proceedings before a tribunal in Northern Ireland –
    (i) which deals with transferred matters; and
    (ii) for which no rules made under paragraph (a) are in force.

Section 2

The Commission and the court—The Commission used to decide upon the admissibility of applications prior to their transmission to the ECtHR under Article 48. Applications by individuals were considered under the provisions of Articles 25 to 27. Applications relating to issues between States were considered under Article 24. Decisions on admissibility would be given (hence the provision of HRA 1998, s 2(1)); an admissible application would be referred to the ECtHR for final decision if the Commission had not been able to secure a mediated solution ('friendly settlement') to the point in issue. However, the ECtHR now itself determines all issues (including admissibility) in the unified procedure that has existed since November 1998.

Human rights and care proceedings—A distinction has to be made between issues relating to Convention rights that arise during the course of domestic proceedings (eg while care proceedings are still running) and those that arise after proceedings have ended or where no domestic proceedings are contemplated (*Re L (Care Proceedings: Human Rights Claims)* [2003] EWHC 665 (Fam), [2003] 2 FLR 160, FD). Complaints that are made whilst proceedings are still running should generally be dealt with in the court that is dealing with the proceedings. Thus, where there is a complaint of a breach of a Convention right during the currency of care proceedings, that complaint should be dealt with by the court (eg the family proceedings court) hearing the proceedings and as part of those proceedings. Transfer to the High Court is not necessary and is normally inappropriate (*Re L (Care Proceedings: Human Rights Claims)* (above); *Re V (A Child) (Care Proceedings: Human Rights Claims)* [2004] EWCA Civ 54, [2004] 1 FLR 944, CA).

Where proceedings have come to an end or are not in contemplation, the appropriate course may be to issue a free-standing application under HRA 1998, s 7(1)(a) (*Re L (Care Proceedings: Human Rights Claims)* (above), *Re C (Adoption: Religious Observance)* [2002] 1 FLR 1119, FD, and *Re P (A Child)* [2004] EWCA Civ 355, [2004] Fam Law 708, CA). As an alternative to free-standing proceedings under HRA 1998, s 7, the issue might be raised under, eg, an application to discharge a care order under Children Act 1989, s 39 or an application for contact under s 34. Where a free-standing application under HRA 1998, s 7 is made, it should be heard in the Family Division of the High Court and, if possible, by a judge with experience of sitting in the administrative court (*C v Bury Metropolitan Borough Council* [2002] EWHC 1438 (Fam), [2002] 2 FLR 868, CA).

Care plans in care proceedings—A party to public law proceedings cannot seek an order under the High Court's inherent jurisdiction to force a local authority to change its care plan (*Re S and D (Child Case: Power of Court)* [1995] 2 FLR 456, CA); nor does a court have any statutory jurisdiction under Part IV of the Children Act 1989 to dictate to a local authority what a care plan is to say (*Re S (Minors) (Care Order: Implementation of Care Plan); Re W (Minors) (Care Order: Adequacy of Care Plan)* [2002] UKHL 10, [2002] 2 AC 291, [2002] 2 WLR 720, [2002] 2 All ER 192, [2002] 1 FLR 815, HL). As a last resort a care plan might be challenged by way of judicial review, although in most cases relating to children this is likely to be a 'blunt and … unsatisfactory tool' (*Re L (Care Proceedings: Human Rights Claims)* (above)). Challenges to care plans should generally be made in the way set out above and outlined in the cases of *Re V (A Child) (Care Proceedings: Human Rights Claims)* [2004] EWCA Civ 54, [2004] 1 FLR 944, CA, and *Re L (Care Proceedings: Human Rights Claims)* [2003] EWHC 665 (Fam), [2003] 2 FLR 160, FD. Where a local authority fails to put into effect a care plan following the making of a care order (eg by withdrawing contact), an urgent application can be made to a judge (*Re P* [2004] EWCA Civ 355, [2004] Fam Law 708, CA (referred to below in the notes to s 7).

Excessive reference to ECHR case-law—Excessive and unnecessary reference to human rights legislation and case-law will be deprecated by the court (see *Re F (Care: Termination of Contact)* [2000] 2 FCR 481). It has been held that many aspects of the Children Act 1989 are human rights compliant (eg the welfare provisions in s 1: *Dawson v Wearmouth* [1999] 2 AC 308, [1999] 2 All ER 353, [1999] 2 WLR 960, [1999] 1 FLR 1167, HL; the secure accommodation provisions of s 25: *Re K (A Child) (Secure Accommodation Order: Right to Liberty)* [2001] Fam 377, [2001] 2 All ER 719, [2001] 2 WLR 1141, [2001] 1 FLR 526, CA; and the provisions of s 91(14), Part IV of the Act generally and the absence of power to compel a local authority to fund therapeutic treatment for parents: *Re V (Care Proceedings: Human Rights Claims)* [2004] EWCA Civ 54, [2004] 1 FLR 944, CA).

Citing human rights – Practice Direction—Where are human rights authorities are cited, regard should be paid to the *Practice Direction (Human Rights Act 1998: Citation of Authorities)* [2000] 2 FLR 429. Rule 10.26 of the FPR 1991 sets out procedural requirements for the raising of such issues.

Legislation

3 Interpretation of legislation

(1) So far as it is possible to do so, primary legislation and subordinate legislation must be read and given effect in a way which is compatible with the Convention rights.

(2) This section –

   (a) applies to primary legislation and subordinate legislation whenever enacted;
   (b) does not affect the validity, continuing operation or enforcement of any incompatible primary legislation; and
   (c) does not affect the validity, continuing operation or enforcement of any incompatible subordinate legislation if (disregarding any possibility of revocation) primary legislation prevents removal of the incompatibility.

Section 3

Not retrospective—Section 3 of the HRA 1998 is not retrospective – see *Bellinger v Bellinger* [2003] UKHL 21, [2003] 2 AC 467, [2003] 2 WLR 1174, [2003] 1 FLR 1043; *R v Lambert* [2001] UKHL 37, [2001] 3 All ER 577, [2001] 3 WLR 206; *R v Kansal (No 2)* [2001] UKHL 62, [2002] 1 All ER 257, [2002] 2 AC 69; and *R v Lyons* [2002] UKHL 44, [2002] 4 All ER 1028, [2002] 3 WLR 1562, at [45], [63].

Effect of section 3—This section was considered in *Re S (Minors) (Care Order: Implementation of Care Plan); Re W (Minors) (Care Order: Adequacy of Care Plan)* [2002] UKHL 10, [2002] 2 AC 291, [2002] 2 WLR 720, [2002] 2 All ER 192, [2002] 1 FLR 815, HL, where Lord Nicholls said at [38]–[41]:

   '**[38]** ... Section 3 ... is concerned with interpretation ... The existence of this limit on the scope of s 3(1) has already been the subject of judicial confirmation, more than once: see, for instance, Lord Woolf CJ in *Poplar Housing and Regeneration Community Association Ltd v Donoghue* [2001] EWCA Civ 595, [2001] 3 WLR 183 at [75], and Lord Hope of Craighead in *R v Lambert* [2001] UKHL 37, [2001] 3 WLR 206 at [79]–[81].

   [39] ... The 1998 Act reserves the amendment of primary legislation to Parliament ... Interpretation of statutes is a matter for the courts; the enactment of statutes, and the amendment of statutes, are matters for Parliament.

   [40] ... The area of real difficulty lies in identifying the limits of interpretation in a particular case ... For present purposes it is sufficient to say that a meaning which departs substantially from a fundamental feature of an Act of Parliament is likely to have crossed the boundary between interpretation and amendment. This is especially so where the departure has important practical repercussions which the court is not equipped to evaluate. In such a case the overall contextual setting may leave no scope for rendering the statutory provision Convention compliant by legitimate use of the process of interpretation. The boundary line may be crossed even though a limitation on Convention rights is not stated in express terms. Lord Steyn's observations in *R v A* [2001] UKHL 25, [2002] 1 AC 45 at [44] are not to be read as meaning that a clear limitation on Convention rights in terms is the only circumstance in which an interpretation incompatible with Convention rights may arise.

[41] ... When a court, called upon to construe legislation, ascribes a meaning and effect to the legislation pursuant to its obligation under s 3, it is important the court should identify clearly the particular statutory provision or provisions whose interpretation leads to that result.'

In the case of *Ghaidan v Godin-Mendoza* [2004] UKHL 30, [2004] 3 WLR 113, Lord Nicholls said as follows in relation to s s 3:

'[32] ... From this the conclusion which seems inescapable is that the mere fact the language under consideration is inconsistent with a Convention-compliant meaning does not of itself make a Convention-compliant interpretation under s 3 impossible. Section 3 enables language to be interpreted restrictively or expansively. But s 3 goes further than this. It is also apt to require a court to read in words which change the meaning of the enacted legislation, so as to make it Convention-compliant. In other words, the intention of Parliament in enacting s 3 was that, to an extent bounded only by what is "possible", a court can modify the meaning, and hence the effect, of primary and secondary legislation.

[33] ... Parliament, however, cannot have intended that in the discharge of this extended interpretative function the courts should adopt a meaning inconsistent with a fundamental feature of legislation. That would be to cross the constitutional boundary s 3 seeks to demarcate and preserve. Parliament has retained the right to enact legislation in terms which are not Convention-compliant. The meaning imported by application of s 3 must be compatible with the underlying thrust of the legislation being construed. Words implied must, in the phrase of my noble and learned friend Lord Rodger of Earlsferry, "go with the grain of the legislation". Nor can Parliament have intended that s 3 should require courts to make decisions for which they are not equipped. There may be several ways of making a provision Convention-compliant, and the choice may involve issues calling for legislative deliberation.'

4 Declaration of incompatibility

(1) Subsection (2) applies in any proceedings in which a court determines whether a provision of primary legislation is compatible with a Convention right.

(2) If the court is satisfied that the provision is incompatible with a Convention right, it may make a declaration of that incompatibility.

(3) Subsection (4) applies in any proceedings in which a court determines whether a provision of subordinate legislation, made in the exercise of a power conferred by primary legislation, is compatible with a Convention right.

(4) If the court is satisfied –

   (a) that the provision is incompatible with a Convention right, and
   (b) that (disregarding any possibility of revocation) the primary legislation concerned prevents removal of the incompatibility,

it may make a declaration of that incompatibility.

(5) In this section 'court' means –

   (a) the House of Lords;
   (b) the Judicial Committee of the Privy Council;

(c) the Courts-Martial Appeal Court;

(d) in Scotland, the High Court of Justiciary sitting otherwise than as a trial court or the Court of Session;

(e) in England and Wales or Northern Ireland, the High Court or the Court of Appeal.

(6) A declaration under this section ('a declaration of incompatibility') –

(a) does not affect the validity, continuing operation or enforcement of the provision in respect of which it is given; and

(b) is not binding on the parties to the proceedings in which it is made.

Section 4

Relates to compatibility of legislation—This section relates to proceedings where it is suggested that the *legislation* is incompatible with a Convention right and thus is entirely different to proceedings where it is alleged that Convention rights have been breached by a public authority. There are therefore three main types of action that might be considered in relation to the Convention:

(1) allegations made within existing proceedings that a public body has acted in breach of a Convention right (eg a local authority has made a care plan that offends Article 8). Such issues should usually be determined within the existing proceedings by the court that is hearing those proceedings (*Re V (Care Proceedings: Human Rights Claims)* [2004] EWCA Civ 54, [2004] 1 FLR 944, CA, and *Re L (Care Proceedings: Human Rights Claims)* [2003] EWHC 665 (Fam), [2003] 2 FLR 160, FD);

(2) proceedings where a declaration is sought that the legislation is itself incompatible with the Convention. This will be raised in the High Court (or appellate court, other than the county court) under HRA 1998, s 4;

(3) proceedings under HRA 1998, s 7 where it is alleged that a public body has acted in breach of a Convention right (and there are no existing proceedings, such as care proceedings, in which the issue is more properly litigated) – see s 7 below.

Children Act 1989 compatibility—It has been held that many aspects of the Children Act 1989 are human rights compliant (eg the welfare provisions in s 1: *Dawson v Wearmouth* [1999] 2 AC 308, [1999] 2 All ER 353, [1999] 2 WLR 960, 1999] 1 FLR 1167, HL; the secure accommodation provisions of s 25: *Re K (A Child) (Secure Accommodation Order: Right to Liberty)* [2001] Fam 377, [2001] 2 All ER 719, [2001] 2 WLR 1141, [2001] 1 FLR 526, CA; and the provisions of s 91(14), Part IV of the Act generally and the absence of power to compel a local authority to fund therapeutic treatment for parents: *Re V (Care Proceedings: Human Rights Claims)* [2004] EWCA Civ 54, [2004] 1 FLR 944, CA).

Procedure—Where a declaration of incompatibility is sought, the proceedings must be dealt with in the High Court and must follow the procedural requirements of FPR 1991, r 10.26 and of the *Practice Direction (Family Proceedings: Human Rights)* [2000] 4 All ER 288, [2000] 1 WLR 1782, [2000] 2 FLR 429.

5 Right of Crown to intervene

(1) Where a court is considering whether to make a declaration of incompatibility, the Crown is entitled to notice in accordance with rules of court.

(2) In any case to which subsection (1) applies –

(a) a Minister of the Crown (or a person nominated by him),

(b) a member of the Scottish Executive,

(c) a Northern Ireland Minister,

(d) a Northern Ireland department,

is entitled, on giving notice in accordance with rules of court, to be joined as a party to the proceedings.

(3) Notice under subsection (2) may be given at any time during the proceedings.

(4) A person who has been made a party to criminal proceedings (other than in Scotland) as the result of a notice under subsection (2) may, with leave, appeal to the House of Lords against any declaration of incompatibility made in the proceedings.

(5) In subsection (4) –

'criminal proceedings' includes all proceedings before the Courts-Martial Appeal Court; and

'leave' means leave granted by the court making the declaration of incompatibility or by the House of Lords.

Public authorities

6 Acts of public authorities

(1) It is unlawful for a public authority to act in a way which is incompatible with a Convention right.

(2) Subsection (1) does not apply to an act if –

(a) as the result of one or more provisions of primary legislation, the authority could not have acted differently; or

(b) in the case of one or more provisions of, or made under, primary legislation which cannot be read or given effect in a way which is compatible with the Convention rights, the authority was acting so as to give effect to or enforce those provisions.

(3) In this section 'public authority' includes –

(a) a court or tribunal, and

(b) any person certain of whose functions are functions of a public nature,

but does not include either House of Parliament or a person exercising functions in connection with proceedings in Parliament.

(4) In subsection (3) 'Parliament' does not include the House of Lords in its judicial capacity.

(5) In relation to a particular act, a person is not a public authority by virtue only of subsection (3)(b) if the nature of the act is private.

(6) 'An act' includes a failure to act but does not include a failure to –

(a) introduce in, or lay before, Parliament a proposal for legislation; or

(b) make any primary legislation or remedial order.

Section 6

Public authority—The definition of public authority is widely construed (*Poplar Housing and Regeneration Community Association Ltd v Donoghue* [2001] EWCA Civ 595, [2001] 4 All ER 604, [2001] 2 FLR 284, at para [66] of the judgment: 'while activities of housing associations need not involve the performance of public functions in this case, in providing accommodation for the defendant and then seeking possession, the role of Poplar is so closely assimilated to that of Tower Hamlets that it was performing public and not private functions'; and *Heather v Leonard Cheshire Homes* [2001] EWHC Admin 429, [2001] All ER (D) 156 (charity concerned not a public authority).

The following are examples of public authorities for the purposes of this provision:

(1) a court (*Local Authority Inquiry: Restraint on Publication*) [2003] EWHC 2746 (Fam), [2004] 1 FLR 541);

(2) a local authority (*Newham London Borough Council v Kibata* [2003] EWCA Civ 1785, [2003] 3 FCR 724);

(3) an appeal panel (*R (On the Application of Hounslow London Borough Council) v Schools Admissions Appeal Panel for Hounslow* [2002] EWCA Civ 900, [2002] 3 FCR 142).

ECHR applies to all stages of child protection—The substantive and procedural protection afforded to parents by Article 8 of the Convention applies to all stages of child protection (*Re L (Care Proceedings: Human Rights Claims)* [2003] EWHC 665 (Fam), [2003] 2 FLR 160, FD; *Re L (Care: Assessment: Fair Trial)* [2002] EWHC 1379 (Fam), [2002] 2 FLR 730; and *Re G (Care: Challenge to Local Authority's Decision)* [2003] EWHC 551 (Fam), [2003] 2 FLR 42).

7 Proceedings

(1) A person who claims that a public authority has acted (or proposes to act) in a way which is made unlawful by section 6(1) may –

(a) bring proceedings against the authority under this Act in the appropriate court or tribunal, or

(b) rely on the Convention right or rights concerned in any legal proceedings,

but only if he is (or would be) a victim of the unlawful act.

(2) In subsection (1)(a) 'appropriate court or tribunal' means such court or tribunal as may be determined in accordance with rules; and proceedings against an authority include a counterclaim or similar proceeding.

(3) If the proceedings are brought on an application for judicial review, the applicant is to be taken to have a sufficient interest in relation to the unlawful act only if he is, or would be, a victim of that act.

(4) If the proceedings are made by way of a petition for judicial review in Scotland, the applicant shall be taken to have title and interest to sue in relation to the unlawful act only if he is, or would be, a victim of that act.

(5) Proceedings under subsection (1)(a) must be brought before the end of –

(a) the period of one year beginning with the date on which the act complained of took place; or

(b) such longer period as the court or tribunal considers equitable having regard to all the circumstances,

but that is subject to any rule imposing a stricter time limit in relation to the procedure in question.

(6) In subsection (1)(b) 'legal proceedings' includes –

(a) proceedings brought by or at the instigation of a public authority; and

(b) an appeal against the decision of a court or tribunal.

(7) For the purposes of this section, a person is a victim of an unlawful act only if he would be a victim for the purposes of Article 34 of the Convention if proceedings were brought in the European Court of Human Rights in respect of that act.

(8) Nothing in this Act creates a criminal offence.

(9) In this section 'rules' means –

    (a) in relation to proceedings before a court or tribunal outside Scotland, rules made by the Secretary of State for the purposes of this section or rules of court,

    (b) in relation to proceedings before a court or tribunal in Scotland, rules made by the Secretary of State for those purposes,

    (c) in relation to proceedings before a tribunal in Northern Ireland –

        (i) which deals with transferred matters; and

        (ii) for which no rules made under paragraph (a) are in force,

        rules made by a Northern Ireland department for those purposes,

and includes provision made by order under section 1 of the Courts and Legal Services Act 1990.

(10) In making rules, regard must be had to section 9.

(11) The Minister who has power to make rules in relation to a particular tribunal may, to the extent he considers it necessary to ensure that the tribunal can provide an appropriate remedy in relation to an act (or proposed act) of a public authority which is (or would be) unlawful as a result of section 6(1), by order add to –

    (a) the relief or remedies which the tribunal may grant; or

    (b) the grounds on which it may grant any of them.

(12) An order made under subsection (11) may contain such incidental, supplemental, consequential or transitional provision as the Minister making it considers appropriate.

(13) 'The Minister' includes the Northern Ireland department concerned.

Section 7

'A longstop'—In *Re S (Minors) (Care Order: Implementation of Care Plan); Re W (Minors) (Care Order: Adequacy of Care Plan)* [2002] UKHL 10, [2002] 2 AC 291, [2002] 2 WLR 720, [2002] 2 All ER 192, [2002] 1 FLR 815, HL, Lord Nicholls characterised proceedings brought under s 7 'as a longstop', saying: 'I say "as a longstop", because other remedies, both of an administrative nature and by way of court proceedings, may also be available in the particular case. For instance, Bedfordshire council has an independent visitor, a children's complaint officer and a children's rights officer. Sometimes court proceedings by way of judicial review of a decision of a local authority may be the appropriate way to proceed. In a suitable case an application for discharge of the care order is available. One would not expect proceedings to be launched until any other remedial routes have first been explored.' (See [62].)

Free-standing—Proceedings under s 7 do not have to be joined with other pre-existing proceedings. Under CPR 1998, r 7.11 (inserted by SI 2000/2082 with effect from 2 October 2000) it is provided that: (1) a claim under s 7(1)(a) of the Human Rights Act 1998 in respect of a judicial act may be brought only in the High Court; (2) any other claim under s 7(1)(a) of that Act may be brought in any court. In relation to 'any other claim', Hale LJ said at para [73] of *Re W and B, Re W (Care Plan)* [2001] EWCA Civ 757, [2001] 2 FLR 582: 'There is no definition of "the appropriate court or tribunal" for the purpose of s 7(1)(a). The amended Practice Direction to Pt 16 of the Civil Procedure Rules requires any party who seeks to rely on the 1998 Act to state that and give certain particulars in his statement of case. A claim against a local authority under s 7(1)(a) might therefore be brought as an ordinary civil claim in the county court or High Court' (see also *Re M (Care: Challenging*

Decisions by a Local Authority) [2001] 2 FLR 1300 and R *(P and Q and QB) v Secretary of State for the Home Department* [2001] EWCA Civ 1151, [2001] 2 FLR 1122.

Procedure—For procedure, see FPR 1991, r 10.26 and CPR 1998, PD 16, para 16.1.

Local authority failure to put care plan into effect—Where a local authority fails to put into effect a care plan following the making of a care order (eg by withdrawing contact) an urgent application can be made to a judge *(Re P* [2004] EWCA Civ 355, [2004] Fam Law 708, CA, in which Thorpe LJ said at [20]: 'When the father sensed … that the denial of contact was both a breach of the care plan and a breach of his rights, then it was to the judge that he should have gone immediately. This failure to apply for interim relief is as significant in my judgment as the failure to apply under section 7 of the Human Rights Act 1998. Indeed … it is more significant because, although there may be some professional unfamiliarity with the section 7 route, and there may be difficulties in obtaining public funding for a section 7 application, all with any experience of public law litigation know that the judge is available at short notice to restore any rights that are being arbitrarily denied or withheld by local authorities in possession of care orders … This was the plainest case for an urgent application to the judge to intervene').

To what extent retrospective—Section 22(4) provides: 'Paragraph (b) of subsection (1) of section 7 applies to proceedings brought by or at the instigation of a public authority whenever the act in question took place; but otherwise that subsection does not apply to an act taking place before the coming into force of that section'. Therefore, where reliance is placed on s 7(1)(a), the alleged breach must have occurred after 2 October 2000; in proceedings brought by or at the instigation of a public authority (eg care proceedings), s 7(1)(b) can be relied upon whenever the breach occurred. The phrase 'instigated by' is broadly defined *(King v Walden (Inspector of Taxes)* [2001] STC 822 – taxpayer appealed tax assessment – held that proceedings were at the instigation of the Inland Revenue).

Victim—The person concerned must be someone who is or would be a victim of the unlawful act (see s 7(1), *Dudgeon v United Kingdom* (1981) 4 EHRR 149, and *McCann v United Kingdom* (1996) 21 EHRR 97). Therefore, groups cannot bring themselves collectively within this definition unless the individuals pursuing the claim are affected ('The Act confers rights on citizens against the Government and other public authorities, not on public authorities against the government. Public authorities have no Convention rights' – *Heather and Others v Leonard Cheshire Foundation* [2001] 1 All ER (D) 156). Where a son was beaten by his stepfather, the father could not bring himself within this definition, although the son could *(A and B v United Kingdom* [1998] 1 EHRR 82; *A v United Kingdom (Human Rights: Punishment of Child)* [1998] 2 FLR 959, [1998] Fam Law 733, ECtHR.).

8 Judicial remedies

(1) In relation to any act (or proposed act) of a public authority which the court finds is (or would be) unlawful, it may grant such relief or remedy, or make such order, within its powers as it considers just and appropriate.

(2) But damages may be awarded only by a court which has power to award damages, or to order the payment of compensation, in civil proceedings.

(3) No award of damages is to be made unless, taking account of all the circumstances of the case, including –

   (a) any other relief or remedy granted, or order made, in relation to the act in question (by that or any other court), and

   (b) the consequences of any decision (of that or any other court) in respect of that act,

the court is satisfied that the award is necessary to afford just satisfaction to the person in whose favour it is made.

(4) In determining –

    (a) whether to award damages, or

    (b) the amount of an award,

the court must take into account the principles applied by the European Court of Human Rights in relation to the award of compensation under Article 41 of the Convention.

(5) A public authority against which damages are awarded is to be treated –

    (a) in Scotland, for the purposes of section 3 of the Law Reform (Miscellaneous Provisions) (Scotland) Act 1940 as if the award were made in an action of damages in which the authority has been found liable in respect of loss or damage to the person to whom the award is made;

    (b) for the purposes of the Civil Liability (Contribution) Act 1978 as liable in respect of damage suffered by the person to whom the award is made.

(6) In this section –

    'court' includes a tribunal;
    'damages' means damages for an unlawful act of a public authority; and
    'unlawful' means unlawful under section 6(1).

Section 8

Remedies—It has been doubted whether the family courts may award damages, in the light of s 32 of the Matrimonial and Family Proceedings Act 1984 (however, see Hale LJ in *Re W and B; Re W (Care Plan)* [2001] EWCA Civ 757, [2001] 2 FLR 582 at [75] in which she says: 'all judges sitting in the county courts or the High Court can grant injunctions and award damages'. In the case of *Re V (Care: Pre-Birth Actions)* [2004] EWCA Civ 1575, [2005] 1 FLR 627, Thorpe LJ said that it was far from the case that a breach of the Convention ought to give an automatic right to damages. The principles to be applied to an award of damages are considered in *Anufrijeva v Southwark London Borough Council and Others* [2004] 1 FLR 8, CA. The level of damages is generally regarded to be modest – eg *Hansen v Turkey* [2004] 1 FLR 142, ECtHR (€15,000 for non-pecuniary loss in favour of mother whose contact with her (now adult) children had been prevented after they had been taken to Turkey when 8 and 9); *Kosmopoulou v Greece* [2004] 1 FLR 800, ECHR (€10,000 for failure to take effective measures to enforce contact); and *R (On the Application of KB and Others) v Mental Health Review Tribunal and Secretary of State for Health* [2003] EWHC 193 (Admin), [2002] 5 CCLR 458 (damages between £750 to £4,000 for delay in hearing Mental Health Review Tribunal application). See also the Law Commission report on this issue, *Damages under the Human Rights Act 1998* (Law Com No 266).

9 Judicial acts

(1) Proceedings under section 7(1)(a) in respect of a judicial act may be brought only—

    (a) by exercising a right of appeal;

    (b) on an application (in Scotland a petition) for judicial review; or

    (c) in such other forum as may be prescribed by rules.

(2) That does not affect any rule of law which prevents a court from being the subject of judicial review.

(3) In proceedings under this Act in respect of a judicial act done in good faith, damages may not be awarded otherwise than to compensate a person to the extent required by Article 5(5) of the Convention.

(4) An award of damages permitted by subsection (3) is to be made against the Crown; but no award may be made unless the appropriate person, if not a party to the proceedings, is joined.

(5) In this section –

'appropriate person' means the Minister responsible for the court concerned, or a person or government department nominated by him;
'court' includes a tribunal;
'judge' includes a member of a tribunal, a justice of the peace and a clerk or other officer entitled to exercise the jurisdiction of a court;
'judicial act' means a judicial act of a court and includes an act done on the instructions, or on behalf, of a judge;
'rules' has the same meaning as in section 7(9).

Section 9

Judicial acts—Under CPR 1998, r 7.11 (inserted by SI 2000/2082 with effect from 2 October 2000) it is provided that: (1) a claim under s 7(1)(a) of the Human Rights Act 1998 in respect of a judicial act may be brought only in the High Court; (2) any other claim under s 7(1)(a) of that Act may be brought in any court.

****

11 Safeguard for existing human rights

A person's reliance on a Convention right does not restrict –

(a) any other right or freedom conferred on him by or under any law having effect in any part of the United Kingdom, or
(b) his right to make any claim or bring any proceedings which he could make or bring apart from sections 7 to 9.

12 Freedom of expression

(1) This section applies if a court is considering whether to grant any relief which, if granted, might affect the exercise of the Convention right to freedom of expression.

(2) If the person against whom the application for relief is made ('the respondent') is neither present nor represented, no such relief is to be granted unless the court is satisfied –

(a) that the applicant has taken all practicable steps to notify the respondent; or
(b) that there are compelling reasons why the respondent should not be notified.

(3) No such relief is to be granted so as to restrain publication before trial unless the court is satisfied that the applicant is likely to establish that publication should not be allowed.

(4) The court must have particular regard to the importance of the Convention right to freedom of expression and, where the proceedings relate to material which the respondent claims, or which appears to the court, to be journalistic, literary or artistic material (or to conduct connected with such material), to –

(a) the extent to which –
(i) the material has, or is about to, become available to the public; or
(ii) it is, or would be, in the public interest for the material to be published;

(b)   any relevant privacy code.

(5) In this section –

'court' includes a tribunal; and

'relief' includes any remedy or order (other than in criminal proceedings).

Section 12

This has to be read together with Article 10 of the Convention. In the case of *Local Authority (Inquiry: Restraint on Publication)* [2003] EWHC 2746 (Fam), [2004] 1 FLR 541, FD, the President said at [76]: 'The court must also have particular regard, by s 12(4), to the importance of the Convention right to freedom of expression, although I doubt whether the report can be said to be journalistic, literary or artistic material so as to require consideration of s 12(4)(a)(i) or (ii). The court in deciding whether to exercise its jurisdiction to restrain publication has to consider both Arts 8 and 10 as independent elements. Sedley LJ said in *Douglas v Hello! Ltd* [2001] 2 All ER 289 at 323, [2001] QB 967 at 1005: "Neither element is a trump card. They will be articulated by the principles of legality and proportionality which, as always, constitute the mechanism by which the court reaches its conclusion on countervailing or qualifying rights. It will be remembered that in the jurisprudence of the Convention proportionality is tested by, amongst other things, the standard of what is necessary in a democratic society." Lord Woolf LCJ said in *A v B (A Company)* [2002] 2 All ER 545 at [6] "There is a tension between the two Articles which requires the court to hold the balance between the conflicting interests they are designed to protect. This is not an easy task but it can be achieved by the courts if, when holding the balance, they attach proper weight to the important rights which both articles are designed to protect. Each Article is qualified expressly in a way which allows the interests under the other Article to be taken into account."'

****

21 Interpretation, etc

(1) In this Act –

'amend' includes repeal and apply (with or without modifications);

'the appropriate Minister' means the Minister of the Crown having charge of the appropriate authorised government department (within the meaning of the Crown Proceedings Act 1947);

'the Commission' means the European Commission of Human Rights;

'the Convention' means the Convention for the Protection of Human Rights and Fundamental Freedoms, agreed by the Council of Europe at Rome on 4th November 1950 as it has effect for the time being in relation to the United Kingdom;

'declaration of incompatibility' means a declaration under section 4;

'Minister of the Crown' has the same meaning as in the Ministers of the Crown Act 1975;

'Northern Ireland Minister' includes the First Minister and the deputy First Minister in Northern Ireland;

'primary legislation' means any –

(a)   public general Act;

(b)   local and personal Act;

(c)   private Act;

(d)   Measure of the Church Assembly;

(e)   Measure of the General Synod of the Church of England;

(f)   Order in Council –
    (i)   made in exercise of Her Majesty's Royal Prerogative;
    (ii)   made under section 38(1)(a) of the Northern Ireland Constitution Act 1973 or the corresponding provision of the Northern Ireland Act 1998; or
    (iii)   amending an Act of a kind mentioned in paragraph (a), (b) or (c);
and includes an order or other instrument made under primary legislation (otherwise than by the National Assembly for Wales, a member of the Scottish Executive, a Northern Ireland Minister or a Northern Ireland department) to the extent to which it operates to bring one or more provisions of that legislation into force or amends any primary legislation;
'the First Protocol' means the protocol to the Convention agreed at Paris on 20th March 1952;
'the Sixth Protocol' means the protocol to the Convention agreed at Strasbourg on 28th April 1983;
'the Eleventh Protocol' means the protocol to the Convention (restructuring the control machinery established by the Convention) agreed at Strasbourg on 11th May 1994;
'remedial order' means an order under section 10;
'subordinate legislation' means any –
(a)   Order in Council other than one –
    (i)   made in exercise of Her Majesty's Royal Prerogative;
    (ii)   made under section 38(1)(a) of the Northern Ireland Constitution Act 1973 or the corresponding provision of the Northern Ireland Act 1998; or
    (iii)   amending an Act of a kind mentioned in the definition of primary legislation;
(b)   Act of the Scottish Parliament;
(c)   Act of the Parliament of Northern Ireland;
(d)   Measure of the Assembly established under section 1 of the Northern Ireland Assembly Act 1973;
(e)   Act of the Northern Ireland Assembly;
(f)   order, rules, regulations, scheme, warrant, byelaw or other instrument made under primary legislation (except to the extent to which it operates to bring one or more provisions of that legislation into force or amends any primary legislation);
(g)   order, rules, regulations, scheme, warrant, byelaw or other instrument made under legislation mentioned in paragraph (b), (c), (d) or (e) or made under an Order in Council applying only to Northern Ireland;
(h)   order, rules, regulations, scheme, warrant, byelaw or other instrument made by a member of the Scottish Executive, a Northern Ireland Minister or a Northern Ireland department in exercise of prerogative or other executive functions of Her Majesty which are exercisable by such a person on behalf of Her Majesty;
'transferred matters' has the same meaning as in the Northern Ireland Act 1998; and
'tribunal' means any tribunal in which legal proceedings may be brought.

(2) The references in paragraphs (b) and (c) of section 2(1) to Articles are to Articles of the Convention as they had effect immediately before the coming into force of the Eleventh Protocol.

(3) The reference in paragraph (d) of section 2(1) to Article 46 includes a reference to Articles 32 and 54 of the Convention as they had effect immediately before the coming into force of the Eleventh Protocol.

(4) The references in section 2(1) to a report or decision of the Commission or a decision of the Committee of Ministers include references to a report or decision made as provided by paragraphs 3, 4 and 6 of Article 5 of the Eleventh Protocol (transitional provisions).

(5) Any liability under the Army Act 1955, the Air Force Act 1955 or the Naval Discipline Act 1957 to suffer death for an offence is replaced by a liability to imprisonment for life or any less punishment authorised by those Acts; and those Acts shall accordingly have effect with the necessary modifications.

****

Schedule 1

The Articles

(*Not reproduced here*)

Schedule 1

The European Convention on the Protection of Human Rights and Fundamental Freedoms 1950 is set out in Part 2 as **2.4**.

3.17 LEGITIMACY ACT 1976
(ss 1–4, 9, 10)

1 Legitimacy of children of certain void marriages

(1) The child of a void marriage, whenever born, shall, subject to subsection (2) below and Schedule 1 to this Act, be treated as the legitimate child of his parents if at the time of the insemination resulting in the birth or, where there was no such insemination, the child's conception (or at the time of the celebration of the marriage if later) both or either of the parties reasonably believed that the marriage was valid.

(2) This section only applies where the father of the child was domiciled in England and Wales at the time of the birth or, if he died before the birth, was so domiciled immediately before his death.

(3) It is hereby declared for the avoidance of doubt that subsection (1) above applies notwithstanding that the belief that the marriage was valid was due to a mistake as to law.

(4) In relation to a child born after the coming into force of section 28 of the Family Law Reform Act 1987, it shall be presumed for the purposes of subsection (1) above, unless the contrary is shown, that one of the parties to the void marriage reasonably believed at the time of the insemination resulting in the birth or, where there was no such insemination, the child's conception (or at the time of the celebration of the marriage if later) that the marriage was valid.

Section 1

Section 11 of the Matrimonial Causes Act 1973 defines the circumstances in which a marriage celebrated after 31 July 1971 is void as: (a) where it is not a valid marriage under the provisions of the Marriage Acts 1949 to 1986, that is to say where— (i) the parties are within the prohibited degrees of relationship; (ii) either party is under the age of sixteen; or (iii) the parties have intermarried in disregard of certain requirements as to the formation of marriage; (b) where at the time of the marriage either party was already lawfully married; (c) where the parties are not respectively male and female; (d) in the case of a polygamous marriage entered into outside England and Wales, where either party was at the time of the marriage domiciled in England and Wales (for these purposes a marriage is not polygamous if at its inception neither party has any spouse additional to the other).

Where a marriage is voidable (as to which see s 12 of the Matrimonial Causes Act 1973) any child born or conceived during the marriage will be legitimate (see s 16 of the 1973 Act).

2 Legitimation by subsequent marriage of parents

Subject to the following provisions of this Act, where the parents of an illegitimate person marry one another, the marriage shall, if the father of the illegitimate person is at the date of marriage domiciled in England and Wales, render that person, if living, legitimate from the date of the marriage.

3 Legitimation by extraneous law

Subject to the following provisions of this Act, where the parents of an illegitimate person marry one another and the father of the illegitimate person is not at the time of the marriage domiciled in England and Wales but is domiciled in a country by the law of which the illegitimate person became legitimated by virtue of such subsequent marriage, that person, if living, shall in England and Wales be recognised as having been so legitimated from the date of the marriage notwithstanding that, at the time of his birth, his father was domiciled in a country the law of which did not permit legitimation by subsequent marriage.

4 Legitimation of adopted child

(1) Section 39 of the Adoption Act 1976 does not prevent an adopted child being legitimated under section 2 or 3 above if either natural parent is the sole adoptive parent.

(2) Where an adopted child (with a sole adoptive parent) is legitimated –

    (a) subsection (2) of the said section 39 shall not apply after the legitimation to the natural relationship with the other natural parent, and

    (b) revocation of the adoption order in consequence of the legitimation shall not affect section 39, 41 or 42 of the Adoption Act 1976 as it applies to any instrument made before the date of legitimation.

Section 4

Prospective amendment—Section prospectively amended by Adoption and Children Act 2002, Sch 5, para 17.

****

9 Re-registration of birth of legitimated person

(1) It shall be the duty of the parents of a legitimated person or, in cases where re-registration can be effected on information furnished by one parent and one of the parents is dead, of the surviving parent to furnish to the Registrar General information with a view to obtaining the re-registration of the birth of that person within 3 months after the date of the marriage by virtue of which he was legitimated.

(2) The failure of the parents or either of them to furnish information as required by subsection (1) above in respect of any legitimated person shall not affect the legitimation of that person.

(3) This section does not apply in relation to a person who was legitimated otherwise than by virtue of the subsequent marriage of his parents.

(4) Any parent who fails to give information as required by this section shall be liable on summary conviction to a fine not exceeding level 1 on the standard scale.

10 Interpretation

(1) In this Act, except where the context otherwise requires, –

    'disposition' includes the conferring of a power of appointment and any other disposition of an interest in or right over property;

'existing', in relation to an instrument, means one made before 1 January 1976;

'legitimated person' means a person legitimated or recognised as legitimated –

(a)   under section 2 or 3 above; or

(b)   under section 1 or 8 of the Legitimacy Act 1926; or

(c)   except in section 8, by a legitimation (whether or not by virtue of the subsequent marriage of his parents) recognised by the law of England and Wales and effected under the law of any other country:

and cognate expressions shall be construed accordingly;

'power of appointment' includes any discretionary power to transfer a beneficial interest in property without the furnishing of valuable consideration;

'void marriage' means a marriage, not being voidable only, in respect of which the High Court has or had jurisdiction to grant a decree of nullity, or would have or would have had such jurisdiction if the parties were domiciled in England and Wales.

(2) For the purposes of this Act 'legitimated person' includes, where the context admits, a person legitimated, or recognised as legitimated, before the passing of the Children Act 1975.

(3) For the purpose of this Act, except where the context otherwise requires, –

(a)   the death of the testator is the date at which a will or codicil is to be regarded as made;

(b)   an oral disposition of property shall be deemed to be contained in an instrument made when the disposition was made.

(4) (*repealed*)

(5) Except in so far as the context otherwise requires, any reference in this Act to an enactment shall be construed as a reference to that enactment as amended by or under any other enactment, including this Act.

****

3.18 LOCAL AUTHORITY SOCIAL SERVICES ACT 1970
(ss 7–7E)

****

7 Local authorities to exercise social services functions under guidance of Secretary of State

(1) Local authorities shall, in the exercise of their social services functions, including the exercise of any discretion conferred by any relevant enactment, act under the general guidance of the Secretary of State.

(2), (3) …

Section 7

Section 7(1) creates the gateway between the government and the work of social services. It is under that subsection that the government (in the guise of the Secretary of State) issues guidance to social services. Local authorities *shall* act under that guidance.

Children Act guidance—The Home Office has issued 9 volumes of the *Children Act 1989 Guidance and Regulations* under this section (published by HMSO). The local authority must follow that guidance; a necessary precursor of any decision by a local authority to provide services is an assessment of the needs of a particular child (*Re T (Judicial Review: Local Authority Decisions Concerning Child in Need)* [2003] EWHC 2515 (Admin), [2004] 1 FLR 601 in which it was held that, although judicial review of a local authority's decision relating to a child in care might force the local authority to reconsider its decision, the court can neither direct the local authority what to decide nor direct that specific provision be made for a child). Where children were lost in care there had been a failure to follow the Children Act guidance and therefore a breach of the Local Authority Social Services Act 1970 (LASSA 1970), s 7 (*Re F; F v Lambeth London Borough Council* [2002] 1 FLR 217, FD). Appendix F to the Protocol (as annexed to the *Practice Direction (Care Cases) Judicial Continuity and Judicial Case Management Direction* [2003] 2 FLR 798) now contains the Social Services Assessment and Care Planning Aide-Mémoire, which is a summary of existing guidance relating to assessment and care planning.

'Working together'—A successful application for judicial review was made where a local authority carried out an assessment which did not follow the 1999 guidance document entitled 'Working Together to Safeguard Children', and the guidance issued in March 2000, entitled 'Framework for the Assessment of Children in Need and their Families' (*R (on the Application of AB and SB) v Nottingham City Council* [2001] EWHC Admin 235, [2001] 3 FCR 350) (see also *R v Islington London Borough Council ex parte Rixon* (1996) 32 BMLR 136). In the case of *Re M (Disclosure: Police Investigation)* [2002] 1 FCR 655, FD, the judge said: 'In addition to these provisions the government has issued guidance in a document known as "Working Together", pursuant to s 7 of the Local Authority Social Services Act 1970. This provides a framework for inter-agency co-operation and highlights a number of important matters. But it deals primarily, and indeed almost exclusively, with inter-agency co-operation as it relates to the investigation, assessment and safeguarding of the child prior to care proceedings being concluded, and mainly with a decision whether or not they should be instituted. It does not address what, if anything, is to happen after the court has made a determination of the facts and has decided whether or not to make a care order or is in the process of doing so. At this stage, as this case highlights, there are real difficulties for the local authority in sharing information which it has only because it is a party to the care proceedings'.

Mixed purpose – adults and children—It has been held that a local authority did not act beyond its powers under LASSA 1970, s 7 when conducting an enquiry into a home where there were vulnerable adults as well as children (*Local Authority Inquiry: Restraint on Publication*) [2003] EWHC 2746 (Fam), [2004] 1 FLR 544, FD.

Part 8 report—A report into the death of a child under para 8.1 of Part 8 to Department of Health, *Working Together Under the Children Act 1989: a Guide to Arrangements for Inter-agency Co-operation for the Protection of Children from Abuse* (HMSO, 1991) ('*Working Together*') does fall within the local authority's functions under LASSA 1970, s 7 and, therefore, may be inspected by a guardian in care proceedings (*Re R (Care Proceedings: Disclosure)* [2000] 2 FLR 751, CA).

7A Directions by the Secretary of State as to exercise of social services functions

(1) Without prejudice to section 7 of this Act, every local authority shall exercise their social services functions in accordance with such directions as may be given to them under this section by the Secretary of State.

(2) Directions under this section—

    (a) shall be given in writing; and

    (b) may be given to a particular authority, or to authorities of a particular class, or to authorities generally.

7B Complaints procedure

(1) The Secretary of State may by order require local authorities to establish a procedure for considering any representations (including any complaints) which are made to them by a qualifying individual, or anyone acting on his behalf, in relation to the discharge of, or any failure to discharge, any of their social services functions in respect of that individual.

(2) In relation to a particular local authority, an individual is a qualifying individual for the purposes of subsection (1) above if –

    (a) the authority have a power or a duty to provide, or to secure the provision of, a service for him; and

    (b) his need or possible need for such a service has (by whatever means) come to the attention of the authority;

or if he is in receipt of payment from the authority under the Community Care (Direct Payments) Act 1996.

(3) A local authority shall comply with any directions given by the Secretary of State as to the procedure to be adopted in considering representations made as mentioned in subsection (1) above and as to the taking of such action as may be necessary in consequence of such representations.

(4) Local authorities shall give such publicity to any procedure established pursuant to this section as they consider appropriate.

Section 7B

Although a local authority's complaints procedure under s 26 of the Children Act 1989 may amount to an appropriate alternative remedy to judicial review, the procedure under LASSA 1970, s 7B would not ('Whilst it is intended local authorities should be able to set up common structures for handling representations and complaints, the 1989 Act requires the involvement of an independent person at each stage of the complaint. In my judgment, s 26 of the 1989 Act provides a suitable alternative remedy in this case and s 7B of LASSA 1970, which was not intended for review of decisions in relation to care orders, does not' – *R v East Sussex County Council ex parte W* [1998] 2 FLR 1082, but cf *R v Tower Hamlets London Borough Council ex parte Bradford and Others* (1997) 29 HLR 756, QBD). In the case of *R v Wokingham District Council ex parte J* [1999] 2 FLR 1136, QBD, it was held that a failure to use an alternative complaints procedure was only a discretionary bar to judicial review.

7C Inquiries

(1) The Secretary of State may cause an inquiry to be held in any case where, whether on representations made to him or otherwise, he considers it advisable to do so in connection with the exercise by any local authority of any of their social services functions (except in so far as those functions relate to persons under the age of eighteen).

(2) Subsections (2) to (5) of section 250 of the Local Government Act 1972 (powers in relation to local inquiries) shall apply in relation to an inquiry under this section as they apply in relation to an inquiry under that section.

7D Default powers of Secretary of State as respects social services functions of local authorities

(1) If the Secretary of State is satisfied that any local authority have failed, without reasonable excuse, to comply with any of their duties which are social services functions (other than a duty imposed by or under the Children Act 1989), he may make an order declaring that authority to be in default with respect to the duty in question.

(2) An order under subsection (1) may contain such directions for the purposes of ensuring that the duty is complied with within such period as may be specified in the order as appear to the Secretary of State to be necessary.

(3) Any such direction shall, on the application of the Secretary of State, be enforceable by mandamus.

Section 7D

Prospective amendment—Section prospectively amended by Adoption and Children Act 2002, s 139(1), Sch 3, para 13.

Generally—As to whether this would provide an alternative remedy preventing judicial review, see *R v London Borough of Brent ex parte S* [1994] 1 FLR 203, CA.

7E Grants to local authorities in respect of social services for the mentally ill

The Secretary of State may, with the approval of the Treasury, make grants out of money provided by Parliament towards any expenses of local authorities incurred in connection with the exercise of their social services functions in relation to persons suffering from mental illness.

3.19 MAGISTRATES' COURTS ACT 1980
(ss 65, 71, 73, 74)

****

65 Meaning of family proceedings

(1) In this Act 'family proceedings' means proceedings under any of the following enactments, that is to say –

   (a) the Maintenance Orders (Facilities for Enforcement) Act 1920;

   (b) section 43 of the National Assistance Act 1948;

   (c) section 3 of the Marriage Act 1949;

(d), (e) (*repealed*)

  (ee) section 35 of the Matrimonial Causes Act 1973;

   (f) Part I of the Maintenance Orders (Reciprocal Enforcement) Act 1972;

   (g) (*repealed*)

   (h) the Adoption Act 1976, except proceedings under section 34 of that Act;

   (i) section 18 of the Supplementary Benefits Act 1976;

   (j) Part I of the Domestic Proceedings and Magistrates' Courts Act 1978;

   (k) (*repealed*)

   (l) section 60 of this Act;

  (m) Part I of the Civil Jurisdiction and Judgments Act 1982, so far as that Part relates to the recognition or enforcement of maintenance orders;

 (mm) section 55A of the Family Law Act 1986;

  (n) the Children Act 1989;

  (n) section 106 of the Social Security Administration Act 1992;

  (o) section 20 (so far as it provides, by virtue of an order under section 45, for appeals to be made to a court) of the Child Support Act 1991;

  (p) Part IV of the Family Law Act 1996;

  (q) sections 11 and 12 of the Crime and Disorder Act 1998;

  (r) Council Regulation (EC) No 44/2001 of 22 December 2000 on jurisdiction and the recognition and enforcement of judgments in civil and commercial matters, so far as that Regulation relates to the recognition or enforcement of maintenance orders;

except that, subject to subsection (2) below, it does not include –

    (i) proceedings for the enforcement of any order made, confirmed or registered under any of those enactments;

   (ii) proceedings for the variation of any provision for the periodical payment of money contained in an order made, confirmed or registered under any of those enactments; or

  (iii) proceedings on an information in respect of the commission of an offence under any of these enactments.

(2) The court before which there fall to be heard any of the following proceedings, that is to say –

(a) proceedings (whether under this Act or any other enactment) for the enforcement of any order made, confirmed or registered under any of the enactments specified in paragraphs (a) to (k), (m), (n), (p) and (r) of subsection (1) above;

(b) proceedings (whether under this Act or any other enactment) for the variation of any provision for the making of periodical payments contained in an order made, confirmed or registered under any of those enactments;

(c) proceedings for an attachment of earnings order to secure maintenance payments within the meaning of the Attachment of Earnings Act 1971 or for the discharge or variation of such an order; or

(d) proceedings for the enforcement of a maintenance order which is registered in a magistrates' court under Part II of the Maintenance Orders Act 1950 or Part I of the Maintenance Orders Act 1958 or for the variation of the rate of payments specified by such an order,

(e) proceedings under section 20 (so far as it provides, by virtue of an order under section 45, for appeals to be made to a court) of the Child Support Act 1991,

may if it thinks fit order that those proceedings and any other proceedings being heard therewith shall, notwithstanding anything in subsection (1) above, be treated as family proceedings for the purposes of this Act.

(3) Where the same parties are parties –

(a) to proceedings which are family proceedings by virtue of subsection (1) above, and

(b) to proceedings which the court has power to treat as family proceedings by virtue of subsection (2) above,

and the proceedings are heard together by a magistrates' court, the whole of those proceedings shall be treated as family proceedings for the purposes of this Act.

(4) No appeal shall lie from the making of, or refusal to make, an order under subsection (2) above.

(5), (6) ...

Section 65

Prospective amendment—Section prospectively amended by Adoption and Children Act 2002, s 139(1), Sch 3, para 37 (see **3.3B**).

****

71 Newspaper reports of family proceedings

(1) In the case of family proceedings in a magistrates' court (other than proceedings under the Adoption Act 1976) it shall not be lawful for a person to whom this subsection applies –

(a) to print or publish, or cause or procure to be printed or published, in a newspaper or periodical, or

(b) to include, or cause or procure to be included, in a programme included in a programme service (within the meaning of the Broadcasting Act 1990) for reception in Great Britain, any particulars of the proceedings other than such particulars as are mentioned in subsection (1A) below.

(1A) The particulars referred to in subsection (1) above are –

(a) the names, addresses and occupations of the parties and witnesses;

(b) the grounds of the application, and a concise statement of the charges, defences and counter-charges in support of which evidence has been given;

(c) submissions on any point of law arising in the course of the proceedings and the decision of the court on the submissions;

(d) the decision of the court, and any observations made by the court in giving it.

(1B) Subsection (1) above applies –

(a) in relation to paragraph (a) of that subsection, to the proprietor, editor or publisher of the newspaper or periodical, and

(b) in relation to paragraph (b) of that subsection, to any body corporate which provides the service in which the programme is included and to any person having functions in relation to the programme corresponding to those of an editor of a newspaper.

(2) In the case of family proceedings in a magistrates' court under the Adoption Act 1976, subsection (1A) above shall apply with the omission of paragraphs (a) and (b) and the reference in that subsection to the particulars of the proceedings shall, in relation to any child concerned in the proceedings, include –

(a) the name, address or school of the child,

(b) any picture as being, or including, a picture of the child, and

(c) any other particulars calculated to lead to the identification of the child.

(3) Any person acting in contravention of this section shall be liable on summary conviction to a fine not exceeding level 4 on the standard scale.

(4) No prosecution for an offence under this section shall be begun without the consent of the Attorney General.

(5) Nothing in this section shall prohibit the printing or publishing of any matter in a newspaper or periodical of a technical character bona fide intended for circulation among members of the legal or medical professions.

(6) ...

Section 65

Prospective amendment—Section prospectively amended by Adoption and Children Act 2002, s 139(1), Sch 3, para 37 (see **3.3B**).

73 Examination of witnesses by court

Where in any family proceedings, or in any proceedings for the enforcement or variation of an order made in family proceedings, it appears to a magistrates' court that any party to the proceedings who is not legally represented is unable effectively to examine or cross-examine a witness, the court shall ascertain from that party what are the matters about which the witness may be able to depose or on which the witness ought to be cross-examined, as the case may be, and shall put, or cause to be put, to the witness such questions in the interests of that party as may appear to the court to be proper.

74 Reasons for decisions in family proceedings

(1) The power to make rules conferred by section 144 below shall, without prejudice to the generality of subsection (1) of that section, include power to make provision for the recording by a magistrates' court, in such manner as may be prescribed by the rules, of reasons for a decision made in such family proceedings or class of family proceedings as may be so prescribed, and for making available a copy of any record made in accordance with those rules of the reasons for a decision of a magistrates' court to any person who requests a copy thereof for the purposes of an appeal against that decision or for the purpose of deciding whether or not to appeal against that decision.

(2) A copy of any record made by virtue of this section of the reasons for a decision of a magistrates' court shall, if certified by such officer of the court as may be prescribed, be admissible as evidence of those reasons.

****

3.20 MATRIMONIAL AND FAMILY PROCEEDINGS ACT 1984
(s 32)

****

32 What is family business

In this Part of this Act –

'family business' means business of any description which in the High Court is for the time being assigned to the Family Division and to no other Division by or under section 61 of (and Schedule 1 to) the Supreme Court Act 1981;

'family proceedings' means proceedings which are family business;

'matrimonial cause' means an action for divorce, nullity of marriage or judicial separation;

and 'the 1973 Act' means the Matrimonial Causes Act 1973.

****

3.21 MATRIMONIAL CAUSES ACT 1973
(ss 41, 52)

****

41 Restrictions on decrees for dissolution, annulment or separation affecting children

(1) In any proceedings for a decree of divorce or nullity of marriage, or a decree of judicial separation, the court shall consider –

   (a) whether there are any children of the family to whom this section applies; and

   (b) where there are any such children, whether (in the light of the arrangements which have been, or are proposed to be, made for their upbringing and welfare) it should exercise any of its powers under the Children Act 1989 with respect to any of them.

(2) Where, in any case to which this section applies, it appears to the court that –

   (a) the circumstances of the case require it, or are likely to require it, to exercise any of its powers under the Act of 1989 with respect to any such child;

   (b) it is not in a position to exercise that power or (as the case may be) those powers without giving further consideration to the case; and

   (c) there are exceptional circumstances which make it desirable in the interests of the child that the court should give a direction under this section,

it may direct that the decree of divorce or nullity is not to be made absolute, or that the decree of judicial separation is not to be granted, until the court orders otherwise.

(3) This section applies to –

   (a) any child of the family who has not reached the age of sixteen at the date when the court considers the case in accordance with the requirements of this section; and

   (b) any child of the family who has reached that age at that date and in relation to whom the court directs that this section shall apply.

Section 41

'A child of the family' is defined by s 52 (see below). A child cannot be treated as a child of the family before it is born (*A v A (Family: Unborn Child)* [1974] Fam 6, [1974] 1 All ER 755 – father thought child was his but realised on the child's birth that it could not be – not treated as child of family). Lack of knowledge of the true paternity of a child will not prevent a finding that a child was treated as a child of the family (*W (RJ) v W (SJ)* [1972] Fam 152, [1971] 3 All ER 303).

For this definition to apply there must be a family at the time that the child was treated in the necessary way (see, eg, *M v M (Child of the Family)* [1981] 2 FLR 39, CA – child of another man born after the spouses separated; husband did not repudiate child and allowed wife's family to think that he was the father. Held: whether or not there was a family at the time is a question of fact; here there was no family at the time of the husband's treatment of the child – see also *Re A (A Minor)* (1980) 10 Fam Law 184, CA, and *Carron v Carron* [1984]

FLR 805, CA). The Principal Registry conciliation scheme is to be extended (*District Judge's Direction (Children – Conciliation)* [2004] 1 FLR 974).

****

52　Interpretation

(1)　In this Act –

'child', in relation to one or both of the parties to a marriage, includes an illegitimate child of that party or, as the case may be, of both parties;

'child of the family', in relation to the parties to a marriage, means –

(a)　a child of both of those parties; and

(b)　any other child, not being a child who is placed with those parties as foster parents by a local authority or voluntary organisation, who has been treated by both of those parties as a child of their family;

'the court' (except where the context otherwise requires) means the High Court or, where a county court has jurisdiction by virtue of Part V of the Matrimonial and Family Proceedings Act 1984, a county court;

'education' includes training;

'maintenance calculation' has the same meaning as it has in the Child Support Act 1991 by virtue of section 54 of that Act as read with any regulations in force under that section.

(2)　In this Act –

(a)　references to financial provision orders, periodical payments and secured periodical payments orders and orders for the payment of a lump sum, and references to property adjustment orders, shall be construed in accordance with section 21 above;

(aa)　references to pension sharing orders shall be construed in accordance with section 21A above; and

(b)　references to orders for maintenance pending suit and to interim orders for maintenance shall be construed respectively in accordance with section 22 and section 27(5) above.

(3)　For the avoidance of doubt it is hereby declared that references in this Act to remarriage include references to a marriage which is by law void or voidable.

(4)　Except where the contrary intention is indicated, references in this Act to any enactment include references to that enactment as amended, extended or applied by or under any subsequent enactment, including this Act.

****

3.22 PROTECTION FROM HARASSMENT
ACT 1987
(ss 1–5, 7)

1 Prohibition of harassment

(1) A person must not pursue a course of conduct –

    (a) which amounts to harassment of another, and
    (b) which he knows or ought to know amounts to harassment of the other.

(2) For the purposes of this section, the person whose course of conduct is in question ought to know that it amounts to harassment of another if a reasonable person in possession of the same information would think the course of conduct amounted to harassment of the other.

(3) Subsection (1) does not apply to a course of conduct if the person who pursued it shows –

    (a) that it was pursued for the purpose of preventing or detecting crime,
    (b) that it was pursued under any enactment or rule of law or to comply with any condition or requirement imposed by any person under any enactment, or
    (c) that in the particular circumstances the pursuit of the course of conduct was reasonable.

2 Offence of harassment

(1) A person who pursues a course of conduct in breach of section 1 is guilty of an offence.

(2) A person guilty of an offence under this section is liable on summary conviction to imprisonment for a term not exceeding six months, or a fine not exceeding level 5 on the standard scale, or both.

(3) *(repealed)*

3 Civil remedy

(1) An actual or apprehended breach of section 1 may be the subject of a claim in civil proceedings by the person who is or may be the victim of the course of conduct in question.

(2) On such a claim, damages may be awarded for (among other things) any anxiety caused by the harassment and any financial loss resulting from the harassment.

(3) Where –

    (a) in such proceedings the High Court or a county court grants an injunction for the purpose of restraining the defendant from pursuing any conduct which amounts to harassment, and
    (b) the plaintiff considers that the defendant has done anything which he is prohibited from doing by the injunction,

the plaintiff may apply for the issue of a warrant for the arrest of the defendant.

(4) An application under subsection (3) may be made –

    (a) where the injunction was granted by the High Court, to a judge of that court, and

    (b) where the injunction was granted by a county court, to a judge or district judge of that or any other county court.

(5) The judge or district judge to whom an application under subsection (3) is made may only issue a warrant if –

    (a) the application is substantiated on oath, and

    (b) the judge or district judge has reasonable grounds for believing that the defendant has done anything which he is prohibited from doing by the injunction.

(6) Where –

    (a) the High Court or a county court grants an injunction for the purpose mentioned in subsection (3)(a), and

    (b) without reasonable excuse the defendant does anything which he is prohibited from doing by the injunction,

he is guilty of an offence.

(7) Where a person is convicted of an offence under subsection (6) in respect of any conduct, that conduct is not punishable as a contempt of court.

(8) A person cannot be convicted of an offence under subsection (6) in respect of any conduct which has been punished as a contempt of court.

(9) A person guilty of an offence under subsection (6) is liable –

    (a) on conviction on indictment, to imprisonment for a term not exceeding five years, or a fine, or both, or

    (b) on summary conviction, to imprisonment for a term not exceeding six months, or a fine not exceeding the statutory maximum, or both.

4 Putting people in fear of violence

(1) A person whose course of conduct causes another to fear, on at least two occasions, that violence will be used against him is guilty of an offence if he knows or ought to know that his course of conduct will cause the other so to fear on each of those occasions.

(2) For the purposes of this section, the person whose course of conduct is in question ought to know that it will cause another to fear that violence will be used against him on any occasion if a reasonable person in possession of the same information would think the course of conduct would cause the other so to fear on that occasion.

(3) It is a defence for a person charged with an offence under this section to show that –

    (a) his course of conduct was pursued for the purpose of preventing or detecting crime,

(b) his course of conduct was pursued under any enactment or rule of law or to comply with any condition or requirement imposed by any person under any enactment, or

(c) the pursuit of his course of conduct was reasonable for the protection of himself or another or for the protection of his or another's property.

(4) A person guilty of an offence under this section is liable –

(a) on conviction on indictment, to imprisonment for a term not exceeding five years, or a fine, or both, or

(b) on summary conviction, to imprisonment for a term not exceeding six months, or a fine not exceeding the statutory maximum, or both.

(5) If on the trial on indictment of a person charged with an offence under this section the jury find him not guilty of the offence charged, they may find him guilty of an offence under section 2.

(6) The Crown Court has the same powers and duties in relation to a person who is by virtue of subsection (5) convicted before it of an offence under section 2 as a magistrates' court would have on convicting him of the offence.

5 Restraining orders

(1) A court sentencing or otherwise dealing with a person ('the defendant') convicted of an offence under section 2 or 4 may (as well as sentencing him or dealing with him in any other way) make an order under this section.

(2) The order may, for the purpose of protecting the victim of the offence, or any other person mentioned in the order, from further conduct which –

(a) amounts to harassment, or

(b) will cause a fear of violence,

prohibit the defendant from doing anything described in the order.

(3) The order may have effect for a specified period or until further order.

(4) The prosecutor, the defendant or any other person mentioned in the order may apply to the court which made the order for it to be varied or discharged by a further order.

(5) If without reasonable excuse the defendant does anything which he is prohibited from doing by an order under this section, he is guilty of an offence.

(6) A person guilty of an offence under this section is liable –

(a) on conviction on indictment, to imprisonment for a term not exceeding five years, or a fine, or both, or

(b) on summary conviction, to imprisonment for a term not exceeding six months, or a fine not exceeding the statutory maximum, or both.

****

7 Interpretation of this group of sections

(1) This section applies for the interpretation of sections 1 to 5.

(2) References to harassing a person include alarming the person or causing the person distress.

(3) A 'course of conduct' must involve conduct on at least two occasions.

(3A) A person's conduct on any occasion shall be taken, if aided, abetted, counselled or procured by another –

- (a) to be conduct on that occasion of the other (as well as conduct of the person whose conduct it is); and
- (b) to be conduct in relation to which the other's knowledge and purpose, and what he ought to have known, are the same as they were in relation to what was contemplated or reasonably foreseeable at the time of the aiding, abetting, counselling or procuring.

(4) 'Conduct' includes speech.

****

PART II

JURISDICTION

****

37 Powers of High Court with respect to injunctions and receivers

(1) The High Court may by order (whether interlocutory or final) grant an injunction or appoint a receiver in all cases in which it appears to the court to be just and convenient to do so.

(2) Any such order may be made either unconditionally or on such terms and conditions as the court thinks just.

(3) The power of the High Court under subsection (1) to grant an interlocutory injunction restraining a party to any proceedings from removing from the jurisdiction of the High Court, or otherwise dealing with, assets located within that jurisdiction shall be exercisable in cases where that party is, as well as in cases where he is not, domiciled, resident or present within that jurisdiction.

(4), (5) ...

Section 37

The High Court has a very broad and inherent jurisdiction to make injunctions to protect children. That jurisdiction is examined extensively in *Re S (A Child) (Identification: Restriction on Publication)* [2003] EWCA 963, [2003] 2 FLR 1253, CA (in which Hale LJ dissents in the outcome of the appeal but whose analysis of the law is adopted by the other members of the court). An ouster injunction may be made under the High Court's inherent jurisdiction where this is necessary to protect a child: *Re S (Minors) (Inherent Jurisdiction: Ouster)* [1994] 1 FLR 623 (Connell J).

The High Court may grant injunctions in care proceedings without the local authority obtaining the prior permission of the court under s 100 of the Children Act 1989 to make the application – *Re P (Care Orders: Injunctive Relief)* [2000] 2 FLR 385 (in which Charles J considered that such injunctions would be available under s 37 of the Supreme Court Act 1981). The county court does not have a similar inherent jurisdiction: *Devon County Council v B* [1997] 1 FLR 591.

****

41 Wards of court

(1) Subject to the provisions of this section, no minor shall be made a ward of court except by virtue of an order to that effect made by the High Court.

(2) Where an application is made for such an order in respect of a minor, the minor shall become a ward of court on the making of the application, but shall cease to be a ward of court at the end of such period as may be prescribed unless within that period an order has been made in accordance with the application.

(2A) Subsection (2) does not apply with respect to a child who is the subject of a care order (as defined by section 105 of the Children Act 1989).

(3) The High Court may, either upon an application in that behalf or without such an application, order that any minor who is for the time being a ward of court shall cease to be a ward of court.

Section 41

In the case of *Re T (A Minor) (Wardship: Representation)* [1994] Fam 49, [1993] 4 All ER 518, sub nom *Re CT (A Minor) (Wardship: Representation)* [1993] 2 FLR 278, CA, Waite LJ described how the Children Act 1989 circumscribed the use of wardship, saying:

'The scheme of the Children Act is to establish a statutory code for both the private and public law field. It implements proposals in the Law Commission Paper No 172, of which a major objective was stated (para 4.35) to be the reduction of the need to resort to the wardship jurisdiction of the High Court. "Family proceedings" is expressed by the Act (s 8(3)) to include proceedings under the jurisdiction of the High Court in relation to children, and wardship proceedings are also comprehended in the definition of "family proceedings" in r 1(2)(1) of the Family Proceedings Rules 1991. Though wardship survives as an independent jurisdiction (and was clearly intended to do so) it is now made subject to the provisions of r 9.2(A), with the result that minors may engage in wardship proceedings without a next friend or guardian ad litem with the same leave, and subject to the same conditions, as apply to other forms of "family proceedings". The jurisdiction is not only circumscribed procedurally. The courts' undoubted discretion to allow wardship proceedings to go forward in a suitable case is subject to their clear duty, in loyalty to the scheme and purpose of the Children Act legislation, to permit recourse to wardship only when it becomes apparent to the Judge in any particular case that the question which the court is determining in regard to the minor's upbringing or property cannot be resolved under the statutory procedures in Part II of the Act in a way which secures the best interests of the child; or where the minor's person is in a state of jeopardy from which he can only be protected by giving him the status of a ward of court; or where the court's functions need to be secured from the effects, potentially injurious to the child, of external influences (intrusive publicity for example) and it is decided that conferring on the child the status of a ward will prove a more effective deterrent than the ordinary sanctions of contempt of court which already protect all family proceedings. The open court statement made by the President, Sir Stephen Brown, in *Re AD (A Minor)* [1993] 1 FCR 573 appears to provide an illustration of wardship functioning usefully in that last context, although it is to be observed that the jurisdiction was in that instance accepted by all parties by agreement.'

The procedure in wardship proceedings is set out in rr 5.1–5.6 of the FPR 1991 (although it has been held that the court may make a child a ward of court without there being an application to this effect – see, eg, *O'Dare v South Glamorgan County Council* (1982) FLR 1). It is not necessary to make the child a ward of court in order to invoke the inherent jurisdiction of the High Court in relation to children. Proceedings may be transferred to the county court in accordance with the Practice Direction issued on 23 July 1987, which reads as follows:

'County courts do not have jurisdiction to deal with applications for an order that a minor be made, or cease to be, a ward of court. Section 38(2)(b) of the Matrimonial and Family Proceedings Act 1984 excludes such proceedings from the category of family proceedings which are able to be transferred from the High Court.

The current standard practice is that on the first appointment following the issue of the originating summons, the Court if it considers that wardship should continue, confirms wardship and directs that the child remains a ward of court during his minority or until further order. If such a direction is given, there is no need to repeat it in subsequent orders, including any order on the substantive hearing of the originating summons. Provided that such a direction has been given, and the matter is not one which under the President's Direction of [5 June 1992, [1992] 3 All ER 151, [1992] 1 WLR 586], as to the Distribution and Transfer of Family Business must be dealt with in the High Court, consideration should be given to transferring the case, in whole or in part, to the county court. In any case which is so transferred in which the court concludes that it is not appropriate to deal with the matter because it is of the opinion that the minor should not remain a ward, it should transfer the case back to the High Court.

Issued with the concurrence of the Lord Chancellor.'

The making of a care order in relation to a child who is a ward of court brings the wardship to an end (Children Act 1989, s 91(4)). For a case where wardship coupled with supervision orders and orders under s 8 of the Children Act 1989 were used so as to ensure that children remained with grandparents who had been rejected as foster parents, see *Re W and X (Wardship: Relatives Rejected as Foster Carers)* [2003] EWHC 2206 (Fam), [2004] 1 FLR 415, FD. In an exceptional case where there were profound difficulties within a family, Charles J made residence orders, supervision orders and orders that the children be wards of court (*Re M & J (Wardship: Supervision and Residence Orders)* [2003] 2 FLR 541, FD). In *Re D (Evidence: Facilitated Communication)* [2001] 1 FLR 148, FD, a child was assisted to communicate allegations through 'facilitated communication'; the President held that facilitated communication (facilitator holds child's hand in order to use keyboard) is highly controversial and should be regarded with the utmost caution. It was not possible to test the veracity or history of the allegations and therefore findings could not be made and the wardship was dismissed.

****

PART III

PRACTICE AND PROCEDURE

****

67 Proceedings in court and in chambers

Business in the High Court shall be heard and disposed of in court except in so far as it may, under this or any other Act, under rules of court or in accordance with the practice of the court, be dealt with in chambers.

****

SCHEDULE 1

DISTRIBUTION OF BUSINESS IN HIGH COURT

****

3 Family Division

To the Family Division are assigned –

- (a) all matrimonial causes and matters (whether at first instance or on appeal);
- (b) all causes and matters (whether at first instance or on appeal) relating to –
  - (i) legitimacy;
  - (ii) the exercise of the inherent jurisdiction of the High Court with respect to minors, the maintenance of minors and any proceedings under the Children Act 1989, except proceedings solely for the appointment of a guardian of a minor's estate;
  - (iii) adoption;
  - (iv) non-contentious or common form probate business;
- (c) applications for consent to the marriage of a minor or for a declaration under section 27B(5) of the Marriage Act 1949;
- (d) proceedings on appeal under section 13 of the Administration of Justice Act 1960 from an order or decision made under section 63(3) of the Magistrates' Courts Act 1980 to enforce an order of a magistrates' court made in matrimonial proceedings or proceedings under Part IV of the Family Law Act 1996 or with respect to the guardianship of a minor;
- (e) applications under Part III of the Family Law Act 1986;
- (e) proceedings under the Children Act 1989;
- (f) all proceedings under –
  - (i) Part IV of the Family Law Act 1996;
  - (ii) the Child Abduction and Custody Act 1985;
  - (iii) the Family Law Act 1986;
  - (iv) section 30 of the Human Fertilisation and Embryology Act 1990; and
- (fa) all proceedings relating to a debit or credit under section 29(1) or 49(1) of the Welfare Reform and Pensions Act 1999;
- (g) all proceedings for the purpose of enforcing an order made in any proceedings of a type described in this paragraph;
- (h) all proceedings under the Child Support Act 1991.

****

PART 4

STATUTORY INSTRUMENTS

' "All persons more than a mile high to leave the court."
Everybody looked at Alice.
"I'm not a mile high," said Alice.
"You are," said the King.
"Nearly two miles high," added the Queen.
"Well I sha'n't go, at any rate," said Alice; "Besides, that's not a regular rule: you invented it just now."
"It's the oldest rule in the book," said the King.
"Then it ought to be Number 1," said Alice.'

Lewis Carroll, *Alice's Adventures in Wonderland*, Chapter 12

'Investigations into paternity are forbidden'

Napoleonic Code, Article 340

'MY FOSTER FAMILY There's no point filling this bit in. I haven't got a foster family at the moment. I've had two. There was Aunty Peggy and Uncle Sid first of all. I didn't like them much and I didn't get on with the other kids so I didn't care when they got rid of me. I was in a children's home for a while and then I had this other couple. Julie and Ted. They were young and friendly and they bought me a bike and I thought it was all going to be great and I went to live with them and I was ever so good and did everything they said and I thought I'd be staying with them until my mum came to get me for good but then … I don't want to write about it. It ended up with me getting turfed out THROUGH NO FAULT OF MY OWN. I was so mad I smashed up the bike so I don't even have that anymore. And now I'm in a new children's home and they've advertised me in the papers but there weren't many takers and now I think they're getting a bit desperate. I don't care though. I expect my mum will come soon anyway.'

Jacqueline Wilson, *The story of Tracy Beaker* (Corgi Yearling, 1992)[1]

---

[1] Used by permission of The Random House Group Limited.

4.1 OVERVIEW OF STATUTORY INSTRUMENTS

Statutory instruments are also known as 'secondary legislation' or 'subordinate legislation'. However they are referred to, they are important source materials for children law. Statutes (or 'primary legislation') go through a full and usually lengthy process in Parliament, culminating in Royal Assent. Statutory instruments, by contrast, are simply laid before Parliament, and derive their authority from provisions in primary legislation. They can only do what a statute says they can do.

The typical process is for statutes to be enacted before the statutory instruments are drafted. Statutory instruments are the working out of the details, details that are often administrative and practical. The promulgation of statutory instruments is very much the province of the Secretary of State responsible for the primary legislation. Indeed, the primary legislation will have prepared the way by including words such as:

> 'Any power to make subordinate legislation conferred by the Act on the Lord Chancellor, the Secretary of State, the Scottish Ministers, the Assembly or the Registrar General is exercisable by statutory instrument.'[1]

Although presently of limited application to family proceedings,[2] we have included some extracts from the Civil Procedure Rules 1998, partly because they are likely to have a significant direct influence,[3] partly because they are likely to have a significant indirect influence in the foreseeable future,[4] and particularly because of the importance of r 35 to the work of those giving expert evidence and those instructing them.

The extracts from the primary materials we recommend you read now are Parts 1 and 35 of the Civil Procedure Rules 1998.

The Overview of Children Law continues at **4.20** Family Proceedings Rules 1991.

---

[1] This example is taken from s 140(1) of the Adoption and Children Act 2002. It nicely illustrates the point made in the Introduction to this Handbook that the power and responsibility to make statutory instruments will often be divided between, for England, several ministers in London and, for Wales, the National Assembly for Wales.

[2] For which the Family Proceedings Rules 1991 are of pre-eminent importance: see further at **4.20** below.

[3] Eg the overriding objective contained in *Practice Direction (Care Cases: Judicial Continuity and Judicial Case Management)* (see Protocol for Judicial Case Management in Public Law Children Act Cases at **6.2** below).

[4] See **4.20** below.

4.2 ADOPTION RULES 1984, SI 1984/265
(rr 1–25, 47, 49, 49A, Schs 2, 3)

PART I
INTRODUCTORY

1 Citation and commencement

These rules may be cited as the Adoption Rules 1984 and shall come into operation on 27 May 1984.

2 Interpretation

(1) In these rules, unless the context otherwise requires –

'the Act' means the Adoption Act 1976;

'adoption agency' means a local authority or approved adoption society; 'the child' means the person whom the applicant for an adoption order or an order authorising a proposed foreign adoption proposes to adopt, or, as the case may be, the person the adoption agency proposes should be freed for adoption;

'CA of the receiving State' means, in relation to a Convention country other than the United Kingdom, the Central Authority of the receiving State;

'CA of the State of origin' means, in relation to a Convention country other than the United Kingdom, the Central Authority of the State of origin;

'Central Authority' means, in relation to England, the Secretary of State for Health, and in relation to Wales, the National Assembly for Wales;

'children's guardian' means an officer of the service appointed to act on behalf of the child in accordance with section 65(1)(a) of the 1976 Act;

'Convention' means the Convention on Protection of Children and Co-operation in respect of Intercountry Adoption, concluded at the Hague on 29 May 1993;

'Convention proceedings' means proceedings in the High Court or a county court for a Convention adoption order or in connection with a Convention adoption order or a Convention adoption;

'the court' means the High Court and any county court falling within the class specified for the commencement of proceedings under the Act by an Order under Part I of Schedule 11 to the Children Act 1989;

'Hague Convention Regulations' means the Intercountry Adoption (Hague Convention) Regulations 2003;

'interim order' means an order under section 25 of the Act;

'order authorising a proposed foreign adoption' means an order under section 55 of the Act;

'process' means, in the High Court, a summons and, in a county court, an application;

'proper officer' means, in the High Court, a district judge of the Principal Registry of the Family Division and, in a county court, the person defined as 'proper officer' by Order 1(3) of the County Court Rules 1981;

'receiving State' means the state in which it is proposed that the child will become habitually resident;

'regular armed forces of the Crown' means the Royal Navy, the Regular Armed Forces as defined by section 225 of the Army Act 1955, the Regular Air Force as defined by section 223 of the Air Force Act 1955, the Queen Alexandra's Royal Naval Nursing Service and the Women's Royal Naval Service;

'reporting officer' means an officer of the service appointed in accordance with section 65(1)(b) of the Act; and

'State of origin' means the state in which the child is habitually resident.

(2) Except where a contrary intention appears, a word or phrase used in these rules shall have the same meaning as in the Children Act 1989 or, where the word or phrase does not appear in that Act, as in the Act.

(3) In these rules a form referred to by number means the form so numbered in Schedule 1 to these rules, or a form substantially to the like effect, with such variations, as the circumstances may require.

3 Extent and application of other rules

(1) These rules shall apply to proceedings in the High Court and in a county court under the Act, and Part IV of these rules shall apply to Convention proceedings, commenced on or after 1 June 2003.

(2) Subject to the provisions of these rules and to any enactment, the Rules of the Supreme Court 1965 and the County Court Rules 1981 in force immediately before 26th April 1999 shall continue to apply, with any necessary modifications, to proceedings in the High Court or a county court under the Act, and any reference in these rules to those rules shall be construed accordingly.

(3) For the purposes of paragraph (2) any provision of these rules authorising or requiring anything to be done shall be treated as if it were a provision of the Rules of the Supreme Court 1965 or the County Court Rules 1981 as the case may be.

(3A) In any proceedings concerning an adoption in accordance with the Convention relating to Adoption concluded at the Hague on 15 November 1965, the Adoption Rules 1984 in force immediately before 1 June 2003 shall continue to apply, with any necessary modifications, to proceedings in the High Court.

(4) Unless the contrary intention appears, any power which by these rules may be exercised by the court may be exercised by the proper officer.

PART II

FREEING FOR ADOPTION

4 Commencement of proceedings

(1) Proceedings to free a child for adoption shall be commenced –

(a) by originating summons in Form 1 issued out of the Principal Registry of the Family Division; or

(b) by filing in the office of a county court an originating application in Form 1.

(2) The applicant shall be the adoption agency and the respondents shall be –

(a) each parent or guardian of the child;

(b) any local authority or voluntary organisation which has parental responsibility for, is looking after, or is caring for, the child;

(f) any person liable by virtue of any order or agreement to contribute to the maintenance of the child; and

(g) in the High Court, the child.

(3) The court may at any time direct that any other person or body be made a respondent to the process.

(4) On filing the originating process the applicant shall pay the appropriate fee and supply three copies of –

(a) Form 1, together with any other documents required to be supplied, and

(b) a report in writing covering all the relevant matters specified in Schedule 2 to these rules.

5 Appointment and duties of reporting officer

(1) As soon as practicable after the originating process has been filed or at any stage thereafter, if it appears that a parent or guardian of the child is willing to agree to the making of an adoption order and is in England and Wales, the proper officer, shall appoint a reporting officer in respect of that parent or guardian, and shall send to him a copy of the originating process and any documents attached thereto and of the report supplied by the applicant.

(2) The same person may be appointed as reporting officer in respect of two or more parents or guardians of the child.

(3) The reporting officer shall not be a member or employee of the applicant or any respondent body nor have been involved in the making of any arrangements for the adoption of the child.

(4) The reporting officer shall –

(a) ensure so far as is reasonably practicable that any agreement to the making of an adoption order is given freely and unconditionally and with full understanding of what is involved;

(b) confirm that the parent or guardian has been given an opportunity of making a declaration under section 18(6) of the Act that he prefers not be involved in future questions concerning the adoption of the child;

(c) witness the signature by the parent or guardian of the written agreement to the making of an adoption order;

(d) investigate all the circumstances relevant to that agreement and any such declaration;

(e) where it is proposed to free for adoption a child whose parents were not married to each other at the time of his birth and whose father is not his guardian, interview any person claiming to be the father in order to be able to advise the court on the matters listed in section 18(7) of the Act; but if more than one reporting officer has been appointed, the proper officer shall nominate one of them to conduct the interview; and

(f) on completing his investigations make a report in writing to the court, drawing attention to any matters which, in his opinion, may be of assistance to the court in considering the application.

(5) With a view to obtaining the directions of the court on any matter, the reporting officer may at any time make such interim report to the court as appears to him to be necessary and, in particular, the reporting officer shall make a report if a parent or guardian of the child is unwilling to agree to the making of an adoption order, and in such a case the proper officer shall notify the applicant.

(6) The court may, at any time before the final determination of the application, require the reporting officer to perform such further duties as the court considers necessary.

(7) The reporting officer shall attend any hearing of the application if so required by the court.

(8) Any report made to the court under this rule shall be confidential.

6 Appointment and duties of children's guardian

(1) As soon as practicable after the originating process has been filed, or after receipt of the statement of facts supplied under rule 7, if it appears that a parent or guardian of the child is unwilling to agree to the making of an adoption order, the proper officer shall appoint a children's guardian of the child and shall send to him a copy of the originating process, together with any documents attached thereto, the statement of facts and the report supplied by the applicant.

(2) Where there are special circumstances and it appears to the court that the welfare of the child requires it, the court may at any time appoint a children's guardian of the child, and where such an appointment is made the court shall indicate any particular matters which it requires the children's guardian to investigate, and the proper officer shall send the children's guardian a copy of the originating process together with any documents attached thereto and the report supplied by the applicant.

(3) The same person may be appointed as reporting officer under rule 5(1) in respect of a parent or guardian who appears to be willing to agree to the making of an adoption order, and as children's guardian of the child under this rule, and, whether or not so appointed as reporting officer, the children's guardian may be appointed as reporting officer in respect of a parent or guardian of the child who originally was unwilling to agree to the making of an adoption order but who later signifies his or her agreement.

(4) *(repealed)*

(5) The children's guardian shall not be a member or employee of the applicant or any respondent body nor have been involved in the making of any arrangements for the adoption of the child.

(6) With a view to safeguarding the interests of the child before the court, the children's guardian shall, so far as is reasonably practicable –

(a) investigate –

(i) so far as he considers necessary, the matters alleged in the originating process, the report supplied by the applicant and, where appropriate, the statement of facts supplied under rule 7, and

(ii) any other matters which appear to him to be relevant to the making of an order freeing the child for adoption;

(b) advise whether, in his opinion, the child should be present at the hearing of the process; and

(c) perform such other duties as appear to him to be necessary or as the court may direct.

(7) On completing his investigations the children's guardian shall make a report in writing to the court, drawing attention to any matters which, in his opinion, may be of assistance to the court in considering the application.

(8) With a view to obtaining the directions of the court on any matter, the children's guardian may at any time make such interim report to the court as appears to him to be necessary.

(9) The court may, at any time before the final determination of the application, require the children's guardian to perform such further duties as the court considers necessary.

(10) The children's guardian shall attend any hearing of the application unless the court otherwise orders.

(11) Any report made to the court under this rule shall be confidential.

7 Statement of facts in dispensation cases

(1) Where the adoption agency applying for an order freeing a child for adoption intends to request the court to dispense with the agreement of a parent or guardian of the child on any of the grounds specified in section 16(2) of the Act, the request shall, unless otherwise directed, be made in the originating process, or, if made subsequently, by notice to the proper officer and there shall be attached to the originating process or notice three copies of the statement of facts on which the applicant intends to rely.

(2) Where the applicant has been informed by a person with whom the child has been placed for adoption that he wishes his identity to remain confidential, the statement of facts supplied under paragraph (1) shall be framed in such a way as not to disclose the identity of that person.

(3) Where a statement of facts has been supplied under paragraph (1), the proper officer shall, where and as soon as practicable, inform the parent or guardian of the request to dispense with his agreement and shall send to him a copy of the statement supplied under paragraph (1).

(4) The proper officer shall also send a copy of the statement supplied under paragraph (1) to the children's guardian and to the reporting officer if a different person.

8 Agreement

(1) Any document signifying the agreement of a person to the making of an adoption order may be in Form 2, and, if executed by a person outside England and Wales

before the commencement of the proceedings, shall be filed with the originating process.

(2) If the document is executed in Scotland it shall be witnessed by a Justice of the Peace or a Sheriff.

(3) If the document is executed in Northern Ireland it shall be witnessed by a Justice of the Peace.

(4) If the document is executed outside the United Kingdom it shall be witnessed by one of the following persons –

    (a) any person for the time being authorised by law in the place where the document is executed to administer an oath for any judicial or other legal purpose;

    (b) a British consular officer;

    (c) a notary public; or

    (d) if the person executing the document is serving in any of the regular armed forces of the Crown, an officer holding a commission in any of those forces.

9 Notice of hearing

(1) As soon as practicable after receipt of the originating process, the proper officer shall list the case for hearing by a judge, and shall serve notice of the hearing on all the parties, the reporting officer and the children's guardian (if appointed) in Form 3.

(2) The reporting officer and the children's guardian (if appointed), but no other person, shall be served with a copy of the originating process and the report supplied by the applicant, and that report shall be confidential.

(3) If, at any stage before the hearing of the process, it appears to the court that directions for the hearing are required, the court may give such directions as it considers necessary and, in any event, the court shall, not less than four weeks before the date fixed for the hearing under paragraph (1), consider the documents relating to the process with a view to giving such further directions for the hearing as appear to the court to be necessary.

10 The hearing

(1) On the hearing of the process, any person upon whom notice is required to be served under rule 9 may attend and be heard on the question whether an order freeing the child for adoption should be made.

(2) Any member or employee of a party which is a local authority, adoption agency or other body may address the court if he is duly authorised in that behalf.

(3) Where the court has been informed by the applicant that the child has been placed with a person (whether alone or jointly with another) for adoption and that person wishes his identity to remain confidential, the proceedings shall be conducted with a view to securing that any such person is not seen by or made known to any respondent who is not already aware of his identity except with his consent.

(4) Subject to paragraph (5), the judge shall not make an order freeing the child for adoption except after the personal attendance before him of a representative of the applicant duly authorised in that behalf and of the child.

(5) If there are special circumstances which, having regard to the report of the children's guardian (if any), appear to the court to make the attendance of the child unnecessary, the court may direct that the child need not attend.

(6) If there are special circumstances which appear to the court to make the attendance of any party necessary, the court may direct that that party shall attend.

11 Proof of identity of child etc

(1) Where the child who is the subject of the proceedings is identified in the originating process by reference to a birth certificate which is the same, or relates to the same entry in the Registers of Births, as a birth certificate exhibited to a form of agreement, the child so identified shall be deemed, unless the contrary appears, to be the child to whom the form of agreement refers.

(2) Where the child has previously been adopted, paragraph (1) shall have effect as if for the references to a birth certificate and to Registers of Births there were substituted respectively references to a certified copy of an entry in the Adopted Children Register and to that Register.

(3) Where the precise date of the child's birth is not proved to the satisfaction of the court, the court shall determine the probable date of his birth and the date so determined may be specified in the order freeing the child for adoption as the date of his birth.

(4) Where the place of birth of the child cannot be proved to the satisfaction of the court but it appears probable that the child was born in the United Kingdom, the Channel Islands or the Isle of Man, he may be treated as having been born in the registration district and sub-district in which the court sits, and in any other case (where the country of birth is not proved) the particulars of the country of birth may be omitted from the order freeing the child for adoption.

12 Application for revocation of order freeing a child for adoption

(1) An application by a former parent for an order revoking an order freeing the child for adoption shall be made in Form 4 in the proceedings commenced under rule 4.

(2) Notice of the proceedings shall be served on all parties and on any adoption agency which has parental responsibility for the child by virtue of section 21 of the Act, save that notice shall not be served on a party to the proceedings who was joined as a party by virtue of rule 4(2)(b).

(3) As soon as practicable after receipt of the application, the proper officer shall list the case for hearing by a judge and shall appoint a children's guardian of the child in accordance with rule 6(4) or (5) and shall send to him a copy of the application and any documents attached thereto.

(4) The children's guardian shall have the same duties as if he had been appointed under rule 6 but as if in that rule –

(a) the reference to an order freeing the child for adoption was a reference to the revocation of an order freeing the child for adoption; and

(b) each reference to the report supplied by the applicant was omitted.

13 Substitution of one adoption agency for another

(1) An application under section 21(1) of the Act shall be made in Form 5 in the proceedings commenced under rule 4.

(2) Notice of any order made under section 21 of the Act shall be sent by the court to the court which made the order under section 18 of the Act (if a different court) and to any former parent (as defined in section 19(1) of the Act) of the child.

PART III
ADOPTION ORDERS

14 Application for a serial number

If any person proposing to apply to the court for an adoption order wishes his identity to be kept confidential, he may, before commencing proceedings, apply to the proper officer for a serial number to be assigned to him for the purposes of identifying him in the proposed process and a number shall be assigned to him accordingly.

15 Commencement of proceedings

(1) Proceedings for an adoption order shall be commenced –

    (a) by originating summons in Form 6 issued out of the Principal Registry of the Family Division; or

    (b) by filing in the office of a county court an originating application in Form 6.

(2) The applicant shall be the proposed adopter and the respondents shall be –

    (a) each parent or guardian (not being an applicant) of the child, unless the child is free for adoption;

    (b) any adoption agency having parental responsibility for the child by virtue of sections 18 or 21 of the Act;

    (c) any adoption agency named in the application or in any form of agreement to the making of the adoption order as having taken part in the arrangements for the adoption of the child;

    (d) any local authority to whom the applicant has given notice under section 22 of the Act of his intention to apply for an adoption order;

    (e) any local authority or voluntary organisation which has parental responsibility for, is looking after, or is caring for, the child;

    (f), (g) *(revoked)*

    (h) any person liable by virtue of any order or agreement to contribute to the maintenance of the child;

    (i) *(revoked)*

    (j) where the applicant proposes to rely on section 15(1)(b)(ii) of the Act, the spouse of the applicant; and

    (k) in the High Court, the child.

(3) The court may at any time direct that any other person or body be made a respondent to the process.

(4) On filing the originating process the applicant shall pay the appropriate fee and supply three copies of –

(a) Form 6, together with any other documents required to be supplied, and

(b) where the child was not placed for adoption with the applicant by an adoption agency, save where the applicant or one of the applicants is a parent of the child, reports by a registered medical practitioner made not more than three months earlier on the health of the child and of each applicant, covering the matters specified in Schedule 3 to these rules.

16 Preliminary examination of application

If it appears to the proper officer on receipt of the originating process for an adoption order that the court –

(a) may be precluded, by virtue of section 24(1) of the Act, from proceeding to hear the application, or

(b) may for any other reason appearing in the process have no jurisdiction to make an adoption order,

he shall refer the process to the judge or district judge for directions.

17 Appointment and duties of reporting officer

(1) As soon as practicable after the originating process has been filed or at any stage thereafter, if the child is not free for adoption and if it appears that a parent or guardian of the child is willing to agree to the making of an adoption order and is in England and Wales, the proper officer shall appoint a reporting officer in respect of that parent or guardian, and shall send him a copy of the originating process and any documents attached thereto.

(2) The same person may be appointed as reporting officer in respect of two or more parents or guardians of the child.

(3) The reporting officer shall not be a member or employee of the applicant or any respondent body (except where a local authority is made a respondent only under rule 15(2)(d)) nor have been involved in the making of any arrangements for the adoption of the child.

(4) The reporting officer shall –

(a) ensure so far as is reasonably practicable that any agreement to the making of the adoption order is given freely and unconditionally and with full understanding of what is involved;

(b) witness the signature by the parent or guardian of the written agreement to the making of the adoption order;

(c) investigate all the circumstances relevant to that agreement; and

(d) on completing his investigations make a report in writing to the court, drawing attention to any matters which, in his opinion, may be of assistance to the court in considering the application.

(5) Paragraphs (5) to (8) of rule 5 shall apply to a reporting officer appointed under this rule as they apply to a reporting officer appointed under that rule.

18 Appointment and duties of children's guardian

(1) As soon as practicable after the originating process has been filed, or after receipt of the statement of facts supplied under rule 19, if the child is not free for adoption and if it appears that a parent or guardian of the child is unwilling to agree to the

making of the adoption order, the proper officer shall appoint a children's guardian of the child and shall send him a copy of the originating process together with any documents attached thereto.

(2) Subject to paragraph (2A), where there are special circumstances and it appears to the court that the welfare of the child requires it, the court may at any time appoint a children's guardian of the child and where such an appointment is made the court shall indicate any particular matters which it requires the children's guardian to investigate, and the proper officer shall send to the children's guardian a copy of the originating process together with any documents attached thereto.

(2A) Where an application is made for a Convention adoption order under rule 28, the proper officer shall as soon as possible appoint a children's guardian of the child and shall send him a copy of the originating process together with any documents attached thereto.

(3) The same person may be appointed as reporting officer under rule 17(1) in respect of a parent or guardian who appears to be willing to agree to the making of the adoption order, and as children's guardian of the child under this rule, and, whether or not so appointed as reporting officer, the children's guardian may be appointed as reporting officer in respect of a parent or guardian of the child who originally was unwilling to agree to the making of an adoption order but who later signifies his or her agreement.

(4) *(repealed)*

(5) The children's guardian shall not be a member or employee of the applicant or any respondent body (except where a local authority is made a respondent only under rule 15(2)(d)) nor have been involved in the making of any arrangements for the adoption of the child.

(6) With a view to safeguarding the interests of the child before the court the children's guardian shall, so far as is reasonably practicable –

    (a) investigate –
        (i) so far as he considers necessary, the matters alleged in the originating process, any report supplied under rule 22(1) or (2), any reports filed under the Convention or Hague Convention Regulations and, where appropriate, the statement of facts supplied under rule 19;
       (ii) any other matters which appear to him to be relevant to the making of an adoption order/Convention adoption order;
    (b) advise whether, in his opinion, the child should be present at the hearing of the process; and
    (c) perform such other duties as appear to him to be necessary or as the court may direct.

(7) Paragraphs (7) to (11) of rule 6 shall apply to a children's guardian appointed under this rule as they apply to a children's guardian appointed under that rule.

19 Statement of facts in dispensation cases

(1) Where the child is not free for adoption and the applicant for the adoption order intends to request the court to dispense with the agreement of a parent or guardian of the child on any of the grounds specified in section 16(2) of the Act, the request shall, unless otherwise directed, be made in the originating process or, if made subsequently,

by notice to the proper officer and there shall be attached to the originating process or notice three copies of the statement of facts on which the applicant intends to rely.

(2) Where a serial number has been assigned to the applicant under rule 14, the statement of facts supplied under paragraph (1) shall be framed in such a way as not to disclose the identity of the applicant.

(3) Where a statement of facts has been supplied under paragraph (1), the proper officer shall, where and as soon as practicable, inform the parent or guardian of the request to dispense with his agreement and shall send to him a copy of the statement supplied under paragraph (1).

(4) The proper officer shall also send a copy of the statement supplied under paragraph (1) to the children's guardian and to the reporting officer if a different person.

20 Agreement

(1) Any document signifying the agreement of a person to the making of the adoption order may be in Form 7, and, if executed by a person outside England and Wales before the commencement of the proceedings, shall be filed with the originating process.

(2) If the document is executed outside England and Wales it shall be witnessed by one of the persons specified in rule 8(2), (3) or (4), according to the country in which it is executed.

21 Notice of hearing

(1) Subject to paragraph (4), the proper officer shall list the case for hearing by a judge as soon as practicable after the originating process has been filed, and shall serve notice of the hearing on all the parties, the reporting officer and the children's guardian (if appointed) in Form 8.

(2) In a case where section 22 of the Act applies, the proper officer shall send a copy of the originating process and, where appropriate, of the report supplied under rule 15(4), to the local authority to whom notice under that section was given.

(3) No person other than the reporting officer, the children's guardian (if appointed) and, in cases where section 22 of the Act applies, the local authority to whom notice under that section was given, shall be served with a copy of the originating process.

(4) Where section 22 of the Act applies, the proper officer shall list the case for hearing on a date not less than three months from the date of the notice given to the local authority under that section.

(5) If, at any stage before the hearing of the process, it appears to the court that directions for the hearing are required, the court may give such directions as it considers necessary and, in any event, the court shall, not less than four weeks before the date fixed for the hearing under paragraph (1), consider the documents relating to the process with a view to giving such further directions for the hearing as appear to the court to be necessary.

22 Reports by adoption agency or local authority

(1) Where the child was placed for adoption with the applicant by an adoption agency, that agency shall supply, within six weeks of receipt of the notice of hearing under rule 21, three copies of a report in writing covering the matters specified in Schedule 2 to these rules.

(2) Where the child was not placed for adoption with the applicant by an adoption agency, the local authority to whom the notice under section 22 of the Act was given shall supply, within six weeks of receipt of the notice of hearing under rule 21, three copies of a report in writing covering the matters specified in Schedule 2 to these rules.

(3) The court may request a further report under paragraph (1) or (2) and may indicate any particular matters it requires such a further report to cover.

(4) The proper officer shall send a copy of any report supplied under paragraph (1) or (2) to the reporting officer and to the children's guardian (if appointed).

(5) No other person shall be supplied with a copy of any report supplied under paragraph (1) or (2) and any such report shall be confidential.

23 The hearing

(1) On the hearing of the process, any person upon whom notice is required to be served under rule 21 may attend and be heard on the question whether an adoption order should be made.

(2) Any member or employee of a party which is a local authority, adoption agency or other body may address the court if he is duly authorised in that behalf.

(3) If a serial number has been assigned to the applicant under rule 14, the proceedings shall be conducted with a view to securing that he is not seen by or made known to any respondent who is not already aware of the applicant's identity except with his consent.

(4) Subject to paragraphs (5) and (7), the judge shall not make an adoption order or an interim order except after the personal attendance before him of the applicant and the child.

(5) If there are special circumstances which, having regard to the report of the children's guardian (if any), appear to the court to make the attendance of the child unnecessary, the court may direct that the child need not attend.

(6) If there are special circumstances which appear to the court to make the attendance of any other person necessary, the court may direct that that party shall attend.

(7) In the case of an application under section 14(1A) or (1B) of the Act, the judge may in special circumstances make an adoption order or an interim order after the personal attendance of one only of the applicants, if the originating process is verified by an affidavit sworn by the other applicant or, if he is outside the United Kingdom, by a declaration made by him and witnessed by any of the persons specified in rule 8(4).

24 Proof of identity of child etc

(1) Where the child who is the subject of the proceedings is identified in the originating process by reference to a birth certificate which is the same, or relates to the same entry in the Registers of Births, as a birth certificate exhibited to a form of agreement, the child so identified shall be deemed, unless the contrary appears, to be the child to whom the form of agreement refers.

(2) Where the child has previously been adopted, paragraph (1) shall have effect as if for the references to a birth certificate and to the Registers of Births there were substituted respectively references to a certified copy of an entry in the Adopted Children Register and to that Register.

(3) Subject to paragraph (5), where the precise date of the child's birth is not proved to the satisfaction of the court, the court shall determine the probable date of birth and the date so determined may be specified in the adoption order as the date of his birth.

(4) Subject to paragraph (5), where the place of birth of the child cannot be proved to the satisfaction of the court but it appears probable that the child was born in the United Kingdom, the Channel Islands or the Isle of Man, he may be treated as having been born in the registration district and sub-district in which the court sits, and in any other case (where the country of birth is not proved) the particulars of the country of birth may be omitted from the adoption order.

(5) Where the child is free for adoption, any order made identifying the probable date and place of birth of the child in the proceedings under section 18 of the Act shall be sufficient proof of the date and place of birth of the child in proceedings to which this rule applies.

25 Further proceedings after interim order

Where the court has made an interim order, the proper officer shall list the case for further hearing by a judge on a date before the order expires and shall send notice in Form 8 of the date of the hearing to all the parties and to the children's guardian (if appointed) not less than one month before that date.

****

47 Application for removal, return etc of child

(1) An application –

    (a) for leave under section 27 or 28 of the Act to remove a child from the home of a person with whom the child lives,

    (b) under section 29(2) of the Act for an order directing a person not to remove a child from the home of a person with whom the child lives,

    (c) under section 29(1) of the Act for an order for the return of a child who has been removed from the home of a person with whom the child lives,

    (d) under section 30(2) of the Act for leave to give notice of an intention not to give a home to a child or not to allow a child to remain in a person's home, or

    (e) under section 20(2) of the Act for leave to place a child for adoption,

shall be made in accordance with paragraph (2).

(2) The application under paragraph (1) shall be made –

    (a) if an application for an adoption order or an order under sections 18 or 20 of the Act is pending, by process on notice in those proceedings; or

    (b) if no such application is pending, by filing an originating process in the court.

(3) *(revoked)*

(4) Any respondent to the originating process made under paragraph (2)(b) who wishes to claim relief shall do so by means of an answer to the process which shall be made within 7 days of the service of the copy of the process on the respondent.

(5) Subject to paragraph (6), the proper officer shall serve a copy of the process, and of any answer thereto, and a notice of the date of the hearing –

    (a) in a case where proceedings for an adoption order or an order under sections 18 or 20 of the Act are pending (or where such proceedings have subsequently been commenced), on all the parties to those proceedings and on the reporting officer and children's guardian, if any;

    (b) in any other case, on any person against whom an order is sought in the application and on the local authority to whom the prospective adopter has given notice under section 22 of the Act; and

    (c) in any case, on such other person or body, not being the child, as the court thinks fit.

(6) If in any application under this rule a serial number has been assigned to a person who has applied or who proposes to apply for an adoption order, or such a person applies to the proper officer in that behalf before filing the originating process and a serial number is assigned accordingly –

    (a) the proper officer shall ensure that the documents served under paragraph (5) do not disclose the identity of that person to any other party to the application under this rule who is not already aware of that person's identity, and

    (b) the proceedings on the application under this rule shall be conducted with a view to securing that he is not seen by or made known to any party who is not already aware of his identity except with his consent.

(7) Unless otherwise directed, any prospective adopter who is served with a copy of an application under this rule and who wishes to oppose the application shall file his process for an adoption order within 14 days or before or at the time of the hearing of the application under this rule, whichever is the sooner.

(8) The court may at any time give directions, and if giving directions under paragraph (7) shall give further directions, as to the conduct of any application under this rule and in particular as to the appointment of a children's guardian of the child.

(9) Where an application under paragraph (1)(a) or (d) is granted or an application under paragraph (1)(b) or (c) is refused, the judge may thereupon, if process for an adoption order has been filed, treat the hearing of the application as the hearing of the process for an adoption order and refuse an adoption order accordingly.

(10) Where an application under this rule is determined the proper officer shall serve notice of the effect of the determination on all the parties.

(11) Paragraphs (6) to (10) shall apply to an answer made under this rule as they apply to an originating process made under this rule as if the answer were the originating process.

****

49 Amendment and revocation of orders

(1) An application under paragraph 4 of Schedule 1 of the Act for the amendment of an adoption order or the revocation of a direction to the Registrar General, or under section 52 of the Act for the revocation of an adoption order, may be made ex parte in the first instance, but the court may require notice of the application to be served on such persons as it thinks fit.

(2) Where the application is granted, the proper officer shall send to the Registrar General a notice specifying the amendments or informing him of the revocation and shall give sufficient particulars of the order to enable the Registrar General to identify the case.

49A Power of court to limit cross examination

The court may limit the issues on which a children's guardian or a reporting officer may be cross-examined.

****

SCHEDULE 2

MATTERS TO BE COVERED IN REPORTS SUPPLIED UNDER
RULES 4(4), 22(1) OR 22(2)

So far as is practicable, the report supplied by the adoption agency or, in the case of a report supplied under rule 22(2), the local authority shall include all the following particulars –

1 The Child

(a) Name, sex, date and place of birth and address;
(b) whether the child's parents were married to each other at the time of his birth and, if not, whether he was subsequently legitimated;
(c) nationality;
(d) physical description;
(e) personality and social development;
(f) religion, including details of baptism, confirmation or equivalent ceremonies;
(g) details of any wardship proceedings and of any court orders relating to parental responsibility for the child or to maintenance and residence;
(h) details of any brothers and sisters, including dates of birth, arrangements concerning with whom they are to live and whether any brother or sister is the subject of a parallel application;

(i) extent of contact with members of the child's natural family and, if the child's parents were not married to each other at the time of his birth, his father, and in each case the nature of the relationship enjoyed;

(j) if the child has been in the care of a local authority or voluntary organisation, or is in such care, or is being, or has been, looked after by such an authority or organisation details (including dates) of any placements with foster parents, or other arrangements in respect of the care of the child, including particulars of the persons with whom the child has had his home and observations on the care provided;

(k) date and circumstances of placement with prospective adopter and where a Convention adoption is proposed, details of the arrangements which were made for the transfer of the child to the UK and that they were in accordance with regulation 12(8) of the Hague Convention Regulations;

(l) names, addresses and types of schools attended, with dates, and educational attainments;

(m) any special needs in relation to the child's health (whether physical or mental) and his emotional and behavioural development and whether he is subject to a statement under the Education Act 1981;

(n) what, if any, rights to or interest in property or any claim to damages, under the Fatal Accidents Act 1976 or otherwise, the child stands to retain or lose if adopted;

(o) wishes and feelings in relation to adoption and the application, including any wishes in respect of religious and cultural upbringing; and

(p) any other relevant information which might assist the court.

2 Each Natural Parent

(a) Name, date and place of birth and address;

(b) marital status and date and place of marriage (if any);

(c) past and present relationship (if any) with the other natural parent, including comments on its stability;

(d) physical description;

(e) personality;

(f) religion;

(g) educational attainments;

(h) past and present occupations and interests;

(i) so far as available, names and brief details of the personal circumstances of the parents and any brothers and sisters of the natural parent, with their ages or ages at death;

(j) wishes and feelings in relation to adoption and the application, including any wishes in respect of the child's religious and cultural upbringing;

(k) reasons why any of the above information is unavailable; and

(l) any other relevant information which might assist the court.

3 Guardian(s)

Give the details required under paragraph 2(a), (f), (j) and (l).

4 Prospective Adopter(s)

(a) Name, date and place of birth and address;

(b) relationship (if any) to the child;

(c) marital status, date and place of marriage (if any) and comments on stability of relationship;

(d) details of any previous marriage;

(e) if a parent and step-parent are applying, the reasons why they prefer adoption to a residence order;

(f) if a natural parent is applying alone, the reasons for the exclusion of the other parent;

(g) if a married person is applying alone, the reasons for this;

(h) physical description;

(i) personality;

(j) religion, and whether willing to follow any wishes of the child or his parents or guardian in respect of the child's religious and cultural upbringing;

(k) educational attainments;

(l) past and present occupations and interests;

(m) particulars of the home and living conditions (and particulars of any home where the prospective adopter proposes to live with the child, if different);

(n) details of income and comments on the living standards of the household;

(o) details of other members of the household (including any children of the prospective adopter even if not resident in the household);

(p) details of the parents and any brothers or sisters of the prospective adopter, with their ages or ages at death;

(q) attitudes to the proposed adoption of such other members of the prospective adopter's household and family as the adoption agency or, as the case may be, the local authority considers appropriate;

(r) previous experience of caring for children as step-parent, foster parent, child-minder or prospective adopter and assessment of ability in this respect, together where appropriate with assessment of ability in bringing up the prospective adopter's own children;

(s) reasons for wishing to adopt the child and extent of understanding of the nature and effect of adoption;

(t) any hope and expectations for the child's future;

(u) assessment of ability to bring up the child throughout his childhood;

(v) details of any adoption allowance payable;

(w) confirmation that any referees have been interviewed, with a report of their views and opinion of the weight to be placed thereon; and

(x) any other relevant information which might assist the court.

5 Actions of the adoption agency or local authority supplying the report

(a) Reports under rules 4(4) or 22(1) –

(i) brief account of the agency's actions in the case, with particulars and dates of all written information and notices given to the child, his natural parents and the prospective adopter;

(ii) details of alternatives to adoption considered;

(iii) reasons for considering that adoption would be in the child's best interests (with date of relevant decision); and

(iv) reasons for considering that the prospective adopter would be suitable to be an adoptive parent and that he would be suitable for this child (with dates of relevant decisions) or, if the child has not yet been placed for adoption, reasons for considering that he is likely to be so placed.

OR

(b) Reports under rule 22(2) –

(i) confirmation that notice was given under section 22 of the Act, with the date of that notice;

(ii) brief account of the local authority's actions in the case; and

(iii) account of investigations whether child was placed in contravention of section 11 of the Act.

6 Generally

(a) Whether any respondent appears to be under the age of majority or under a mental disability; and

(b) whether, in the opinion of the body supplying the report, any other person should be made a respondent (for example, a person claiming to be the father of a child whose parents were not married to each other at the time of his birth, a spouse or ex-spouse of a natural parent, a relative of a deceased parent, or a person with parental responsibility).

6A Further information to be provided in proceedings relating to a Convention adoption/foreign adoption

(a) where the UK is the State of origin confirmation that an order has been made under section 18(1) of the Act, section 18 of the Adoption (Scotland) Act 1978 or Article 17(1) or 18(1) of the Adoption Northern Ireland Order 1987;

(b) where the UK is the State of origin confirmation that, after possibilities for placement of the child within the UK have been given due consideration, an intercountry adoption is in the child's best interests;

(c) confirmation that, in the case of a foreign adoption, the requirements of regulations made under section 56A of the Adoption Act 1976 have been complied with and, in the case of a Convention adoption, that the requirements of the Intercountry Adoption (Hague Convention) Regulations 2003 have been complied with; and

(d) for the Convention adoption where the United Kingdom is either the State of origin or the receiving State confirmation that the Central Authorities of both States have agreed that the adoption may proceed. The documents supplied by the CA of the State of origin should be attached to the report together with a translation if necessary.

7 Conclusions

(This part of the report should contain more than a simple synopsis of the information above. As far as possible, the court should be given a fuller picture of the child, his natural parents and, where appropriate, the prospective adopter.)

(a) Except where the applicant or one of them is a parent of the child, a summary by the medical adviser to the body supplying the report, of the health history and state of health of the child, his natural parents and, if appropriate, the prospective adopter, with comments on the implications for the order sought and on how any special health needs of the child might be met;

(b) opinion on whether making the order sought would be in the child's best long-term interests, and on how any special emotional, behavioural and educational needs of the child might be met;

(c) opinion on the effect on the child's natural parents of making the order sought;

(d) if the child has been placed for adoption, opinion on the likelihood of full integration of the child into the household, family and community of the prospective adopter, and on whether the proposed adoption would be in the best long-term interests of the prospective adopter;

(e) opinion, if appropriate, on the relative merits of adoption and a residence order; and

(f) final conclusions and recommendations whether the order sought should be made (and, if not, alternative proposals).

SCHEDULE 3

REPORTS ON THE HEALTH OF THE CHILD AND OF THE APPLICANT(S)

This information is required for reports on the health of a child and of his prospective adopter(s). Its purpose is to build up a full picture of their health history and current state of health, including strengths and weaknesses. This will enable the local authority's medical adviser to base his advice to the court on the fullest possible information, when commenting on the health implications of the proposed adoption. The reports made by the examining doctor should cover, as far as practicable, the following matters.

1 The Child

Name, date of birth, sex, weight and height.

(a) A health history of each natural parent, so far as is possible, including –
   (i) name, date of birth, sex, weight and height;
   (ii) a family health history, covering the parents, the brothers and sisters and the other children of the natural parent, with details of any serious physical or mental illness and inherited and congenital disease;
   (iii) past health history, including details of any serious physical or mental illness, disability, accident, hospital admission or attendance at an out-patient department, and in each case any treatment given;
   (iv) a full obstetric history of the mother, including any problems in the ante-natal, labour and post-natal periods, with the results of any tests carried out during or immediately after pregnancy.
   (v) details of any present illness including treatment and prognosis;
   (vi) any other relevant information which might assist the medical adviser; and
   (vii) the name and address of any doctor(s) who might be able to provide further information about any of the above matters.

(b) A neo-natal report on the child, including –
   (i) details of the birth, and any complications;
   (ii) results of a physical examination and screening tests;
   (iii) details of any treatment given;
   (iv) details of any problem in management and feeding;
   (v) any other relevant information which might assist the medical adviser; and

     (vi) the name and address of any doctor(s) who might be able to provide further information about any of the above matters.

  (c) A full health history and examination of the child, including –

     (i) details of any serious illness, disability, accident, hospital admission or attendance at an out-patient department, and in each case any treatment given;

     (ii) details and dates of immunisations;

     (iii) a physical and developmental assessment according to age, including an assessment of vision and hearing and of neurological, speech and language development and any evidence of emotional disorder;

     (iv) for a child over five years of age, the school health history (if available);

     (v) any other relevant information which might assist the medical adviser; and

     (vi) the name and address of any doctor(s) who might be able to provide further information about any of the above matters.

  (d) The signature, name, address and qualifications of the registered medical practitioner who prepared the report, and the date of the report and of the examinations carried out.

2 The Applicant

(If there is more than one applicant, a report on each applicant should be supplied covering all the matters listed below).

  (a) (i) name, date of birth, sex, weight and height;

     (ii) a family health history, covering the parents, the brothers and sisters and the children of the applicant, with details of any serious physical or mental illness and inherited and congenital disease;

     (iii) marital history, including (if applicable) reasons for inability to have children;

     (iv) past health history, including details of any serious physical or mental illness, disability, accident, hospital admission or attendance at an out-patient department, and in each case any treatment given;

     (v) obstetric history (if applicable);

     (vi) details of any present illness, including treatment and prognosis;

     (vii) a full medical examination;

     (viii) details of any daily consumption of alcohol, tobacco and habit-forming drugs;

     (ix) any other relevant information which might assist the medical adviser; and

     (x) the name and address of any doctor(s) who might be able to provide further information about any of the above matters.

  (b) The signature, name, address and qualifications of the registered medical practitioner who prepared the report, and the date of the report and of the examinations carried out.

****

4.3 ADVOCACY SERVICES AND REPRESENTATIONS PROCEDURES (CHILDREN) (AMENDMENT) REGULATIONS 2004, SI 2004/719

1 Citation, commencement and application

(1) These Regulations may be cited as the Advocacy Services and Representations Procedure (Children) (Amendment) Regulations 2004 and shall come into force on 1st April 2004.

(2) These Regulations apply to England only.

2 Interpretation

In these Regulations –

'the Act' means the Children Act 1989;

'advocacy services' means assistance provided under arrangements made by a local authority under section 26A(1) of the Act;

'advocate' means a person who provides assistance under arrangements made by a local authority under section 26A(1) of the Act;

'complainant' means a person making representations under section 24D of the Act or a child making representations under section 26 of the Act;

'the Representations Regulations' means the Representations Procedure (Children) Regulations 1991.

3 Persons who may not provide assistance

A person may not provide assistance under the arrangements made by a local authority under section 26A(1) of the Act to persons who make or intend to make representations under section 24D of the Act or to a child who makes or intends to make representations under section 26 of the Act if –

(a) he is or may be the subject of the representations;

(b) he is responsible for the management of a person who is or may be the subject of the representations;

(c) he manages the service which is or may be the subject of the representations;

(d) he has control over the resources allocated to the service which is or may be the subject of the representations; or

(e) he is or may become involved in the consideration of the representations on behalf of the local authority.

4 Information to be provided to a complainant etc

(1) Where a local authority receive representations from a complainant they must –

(a) provide him with information about advocacy services; and

(b) offer him help in obtaining an advocate.

(2) Where a local authority become aware that a person or child intends to make representations under section 24D or, as the case may be, section 26(3) they must –

(a) provide the person or child with information about advocacy services; and

(b) offer him help in obtaining an advocate.

5 Monitoring of compliance with the Regulations

A local authority must monitor the steps that they have taken with a view to ensuring that they comply with these Regulations in particular by keeping a record about each advocate appointed under arrangements made by the local authority under section 26A(1) of the Act.

6 Amendment of the Representations Regulations

(1) The Representations Regulations shall be amended as follows.

(2) In regulation 2(1) (interpretation) after the definition of 'representations' insert '"section 26A advocate"' means a person who is appointed to provide assistance to the complainant under arrangements made by a local authority under section 26A(1) of the Act'.

(3) In regulation 4 (preliminaries) –

(a) in paragraph (2) after the word 'complainant' insert 'and any section 26A advocate';

(b) in paragraph (2A) after the word 'complainant' insert 'and any section 26A advocate'.

(4) In regulation 7 (withdrawal of representations) after the word 'them' insert 'or any section 26A advocate acting on his behalf'.

(5) In regulation 8 (notification to complainant and reference to panel) –

(a) in paragraph (1)(a) after the word 'complainant' insert 'and any section 26A advocate';

(b) in paragraph (2) after the word 'complainant' insert ', or any section 26A advocate on his behalf';

(c) in paragraph (5)(a) after the word 'complainant' insert '(or any section 26A advocate on his behalf)'; and

(d) in paragraph (6) after the word 'meeting' in the second place where it occurs insert 'by any section 26A advocate or' and after the word 'nominate' insert 'the section 26A advocate or'.

(6) In regulation 9(2)(b) (recommendations) after the word 'complainant' insert 'and any section 26A advocate'.

7 Transitional provisions

(1) Where at the time that these Regulations come into force a complainant has made representations to the local authority and the procedure for considering the representations has not come to an end, then, subject to the provisions of paragraph (2) the local authority must provide the complainant with the information and assistance which the local authority are required to provide under regulation 4.

(2) For the purpose of paragraph (1) the procedure for considering the representations is to be treated as being at an end once the panel have met to consider the representations in accordance with regulation 8 of the Representations

Regulations even if they have not made their recommendation in accordance with regulation 9 of the Representations Regulations.

Bainham, Sorry and Carebury Flagmanton Programmed i ditions 2004, will
regulations is if they have not made their recommendation in accordance with
regulation of the Representations Regulations.

4.4 ARRANGEMENTS FOR PLACEMENT OF CHILDREN (GENERAL) REGULATIONS 1991, SI 1991/890

1 Citation, commencement and interpretation

(1) These Regulations may be cited as the Arrangements for Placement of Children (General) Regulations 1991 and shall come into force on 14th October 1991.

(2) In these Regulations, unless the context otherwise requires –

'the Act' means the Children Act 1989;

'area authority' means, in relation to a child who is or is to be placed, the local authority in whose area the child is or is to be placed, where the child is looked after by a different authority;

'care case' means a case in which the child is in the care of a local authority;

'placement' subject to regulation 13 means –

    (a) the provision of accommodation and maintenance by a local authority for any child whom they are looking after by any of the means specified in section 23(2)(a), (aa) or (f) of the Act (accommodation and maintenance of child looked after by a local authority);

    (b) the provision of accommodation for a child by a voluntary organisation by any of the means specified in section 59(1)(a), (aa) or (f) of the Act (provision of accommodation by voluntary organisations), and

    (c) the provision of accommodation for a child in a private children's home,

and the expressions 'place' and 'placed' shall be construed accordingly;

'responsible authority' means –

    (a) in relation to a placement by a local authority (including one in which the child is accommodated and maintained in a voluntary home or a private children's home), the local authority which place the child,

    (b) in relation to a placement by a voluntary organisation of a child who is not looked after by a local authority, the voluntary organisation which place the child, and

    (c) in relation to a placement in a private children's home of a child who is neither looked after by a local authority nor accommodated in such a home by a voluntary organisation, the person carrying on the home.

(3) Any notice required under these Regulations is to be given in writing and may be sent by post.

(4) In these Regulations, unless the context otherwise requires –

    (a) any reference to a numbered regulation is to the regulation in these Regulations bearing that number and any reference in a regulation to a numbered paragraph is to the paragraph of that regulation bearing that number;

    (b) any reference to a numbered Schedule is to the Schedule to these Regulations bearing that number.

2 Application of Regulations

(1) Subject to paragraphs (2) and (3), these Regulations apply to placements –

    (a) by a local authority of any child;

    (b) by a voluntary organisation of a child who is not looked after by a local authority;

    (c) in a private children's home of a child who is neither looked after by a local authority nor accommodated in such a home by a voluntary organisation, by a person carrying on the home.

(2) These Regulations shall not apply to placements of a child, otherwise than by a local authority or voluntary organisation, in a school which is a children's home within the meaning of section 1(6) of the Care Standards Act 2000.

(3) These Regulations shall not apply to any placement of a child for adoption under the Adoption Act 1976.

3 Making of arrangements

(1) Before they place a child the responsible authority shall, so far as is reasonably practicable, make immediate and long-term arrangements for that placement, and for promoting the welfare of the child who is to be placed.

(2) Where it is not practicable to make those arrangements before the placement, the responsible authority shall make them as soon as reasonably practicable thereafter.

4 Considerations on making and contents of arrangements

(1) The considerations to which the responsible authority are to have regard so far as reasonably practicable in making the arrangements referred to in regulation 3 in each case are the general considerations specified in Schedule 1, the considerations concerning the health of a child specified in Schedule 2 and the considerations concerning the education of a child specified in Schedule 3.

(2) Except in a care case, the arrangements referred to in regulation 3 shall include, where practicable, arrangements concerning the matters specified in Schedule 4.

5 Notification of arrangements

(1) The responsible authority shall, so far as is reasonably practicable, notify the following persons in writing of the arrangements to place a child, before the placement is made –

    (a) any person an indication of whose wishes and feelings have been sought under section 22(4), section 61(2) or section 64(2) of the Act (consultation prior to decision making in respect of children looked after by a local authority, provided with accommodation by a voluntary organisation or in a private children's home);

    (b) the Primary Care Trust, or the Health Authority, for the area in which the child is living and, if it is different, for the area in which the child is to be placed;

    (c) the local education authority for the area in which the child is living and, if it is different, for the area in which the child is to be placed;

(d) the child's registered medical practitioner and, where applicable, any registered medical practitioner with whom the child is to be registered following the placement;

(e) ...

(f) the area authority;

(g) any person, who is caring for the child immediately before the arrangements are made;

(h) except in a care case, any person in whose favour a contact order is in force with respect to the child, and

(i) in a care case, any person who has contact with the child pursuant to section 34 of the Act (contact with a child in care by parents etc) or to an order under that section.

(2) Where it is not practicable to give the notification before the placement, it shall be given as soon as reasonably practicable thereafter.

(3) The responsible authority shall send a copy of the arrangements referred to in regulation 3 or such part of the arrangements as they consider will not prejudice the welfare of the child with the notification referred to in paragraph (1) but in the case of notification to those specified in paragraph (1)(b) to (i) they shall send details of only such part of the arrangements as they consider those persons need to know.

6 Arrangements for contact

In operating the arrangements referred to in paragraph 6 of Schedule 4, a voluntary organisation or a person carrying on a private children's home shall, unless it is not reasonably practicable or consistent with the child's welfare, endeavour to promote contact between the child and the persons mentioned in that paragraph.

7 Health requirements

(1) Subject to paragraphs (3) and (4), a responsible authority shall –

(a) before making a placement, or if that is not reasonably practicable, as soon as reasonably practicable after a placement is made, make arrangements for a registered medical practitioner to conduct an assessment, which may include a physical examination, of the child's state of health;

(b) require the registered medical practitioner who conducts the assessment to prepare a written report of the assessment which addresses the matters listed in Schedule 2; and

(c) having regard to the matters listed in Schedule 2 and, unless paragraph (4) applies, to the assessment report, prepare a plan for the future health care of the child if one is not already in existence.

unless the child has been so examined and such assessment has been made within a period of three months immediately preceding the placement or the child is of sufficient understanding and he refuses to submit to the examination.

(2) A responsible authority shall ensure that each child is provided during the placement with –

(a) health care services, including medical and dental care and treatment; and

(b) advice and guidance on health, personal care and health promotion issues appropriate to his needs.

(3) Paragraph (1) does not apply if within a period of three months immediately preceding the placement the child's health has been assessed, and a report of the assessment prepared in accordance with that paragraph.

(4) Sub-paragraphs (a) and (b) of paragraph (1) do not apply if the child, being of sufficient understanding to do so, refuses to consent to the assessment.

8 Establishment of records

(1) A responsible authority shall establish, if one is not already in existence, a written case record in respect of each child whom it places.

(2) The record shall include –

    (a) a copy of the arrangements referred to in regulation 3;

    (b) a copy of any written report in its possession concerning the welfare of the child;

    (c) a copy of any document considered or record established in the course of or as a result of a review of the child's case;

    (d) details of arrangements for contact, of contact orders and of other court orders relating to the child; and

    (e) details of any arrangements whereby another person acts on behalf of the local authority or organisation which placed the child.

9 Retention and confidentiality of records

(1) A case record relating to a child who is placed shall be retained by the responsible authority until the seventy-fifth anniversary of the date of birth of the child to whom it relates or, if the child dies before attaining the age of 18, for a period of 15 years beginning with the date of his death.

(2) The requirements of paragraph (1) may be complied with either by retaining the original written record, or a copy of it, or by keeping all of the information from such record in some other accessible form (such as by means of a computer).

(3) A responsible authority shall secure the safe keeping of case records and shall take all necessary steps to ensure that information contained in them is treated as confidential, subject only to –

    (a) any provision of or made under or by virtue of, a statute under which access to such records or information may be obtained or given;

    (b) any court order under which access to such records or information may be obtained or given.

10 Register

(1) A local authority shall, in respect of every child placed in their area (by them and any other responsible authority) and every child placed by them outside their area enter into a register to be kept for the purpose –

    (a) the particulars specified in paragraph (3), and

    (b) such of the particulars specified in paragraph (4) as may be appropriate.

(2) A voluntary organisation and a person carrying on a private children's home shall, in respect of every child placed by them, enter into a register to be kept for the purpose –

(a) the particulars specified in paragraph (3), and

(b) such of the particulars specified in paragraph (4) as may be appropriate.

(3) The particulars to be entered into the register in accordance with paragraphs (1) or (2) are –

(a) the name, sex and date of birth of the child;

(b) the name and address of the person with whom the child is placed and, if different, of those of the child's parent or other person not being a parent of his who has parental responsibility for him;

(c) in the case of a child placed on behalf of a local authority by a voluntary organisation or in a private children's home, the name of the authority;

(d) whether the child's name is entered on any local authority register indicating that the child is at risk of being abused;

(e) whether the child's name is entered on the register maintained under paragraph 2 of Schedule 2 to the Act (register of disabled children);

(f) the date on which each placement of the child began and terminated and the reason for each termination;

(g) in a care case the name of the local authority in whose care the child is;

(h) the legal provisions under which the child is being looked after or cared for.

(4) The additional particulars to be entered in the register, where appropriate in accordance with paragraphs (1) or (2) are –

(a) in the case of a child placed by a local authority in respect of whom arrangements have been made for the area authority to carry out functions pursuant to regulation 12 a note that the arrangements were made and the name of the other local authority with whom they were made; and

(b) in the case of a child who has been placed, in respect of whom arrangements have been made for supervision of the placement to be carried out on behalf of a responsible authority (otherwise than pursuant to Regulation 12), a note that the arrangements were made and the name of person with whom the arrangements were made.

(5) Entries in registers kept in accordance with this regulation shall be retained until the child to whom the entry relates attains the age of 23 or, if the child has died before attaining 23, the period of 5 years beginning with the date of his death.

(6) The requirements of paragraph (1) may be complied with either by retaining the original register, or a copy of it, or by keeping all of the information from such a register in some other accessible form (such as by means of a computer).

(7) A responsible authority shall secure the safe keeping of registers kept in accordance with this regulation and shall take all necessary steps to ensure that information contained in them is treated as confidential, subject only to –

(a) any provision of or made under or by virtue of a statute under which access to such registers or information may be obtained or given;

(b) any court order under which access to such registers or information may be obtained or given.

11 Access by officers of the service to records and register

Each voluntary organisation, where they are not acting as an authorised person, and every person carrying on a private children's home shall provide an officer of the service of a child –

    (a) such access as may be required to –
        (i) case records and registers maintained in accordance with these Regulations; and
       (ii) the information from such records or registers held in whatever form (such as by means of a computer);
    (b) such copies of the records or entries in the registers as he may require.

12 Arrangements between local authorities and area authorities

Where arrangements are made by a local authority which is looking after a child with an area authority for the area authority to carry out functions in relation to a placement on behalf of the local authority –

    (a) the local authority shall supply the area authority with all such information as is necessary to enable the area authority to carry out those functions on behalf of the local authority;
    (b) the area authority shall keep the local authority informed of the progress of the child and, in particular, shall furnish reports to the local authority following each visit to the home in which the child is placed and following each review of the case of the child carried out by the area authority on behalf of the local authority;
    (c) the local authority and the area authority shall consult each other from time to time as necessary, and as soon as reasonably practicable after each such review of the case of the child, with regard to what action is required in relation to him.

13 Application of Regulations to short-term placements

(1) This regulation applies where a responsible authority has arranged to place a child in a series of short-term placements at the same place and the arrangement is such that no single placement is to last for more than four weeks and the total duration of the placements is not to exceed 120 days in any period of 12 months.

(2) Any series of short-term placements to which this regulation applies may be treated as a single placement for the purposes of these Regulations.

SCHEDULE 1
CONSIDERATIONS TO WHICH RESPONSIBLE AUTHORITIES ARE TO HAVE REGARD

1 In the case of a child who is in care, whether an application should be made to discharge the care order.

2 Where the responsible authority is a local authority whether the authority should seek a change in the child's legal status.

3 Arrangements for contact, and whether there is any need for changes in the arrangements in order to promote contact with the child's family and others so far as is consistent with his welfare.

4 The responsible authority's immediate and long term arrangements for the child, previous arrangements in respect of the child, and whether a change in those arrangements is needed and consideration of alternative courses of action.

5 Where the responsible authority is a local authority, whether an independent visitor should be appointed if one has not already been appointed.

6 Whether arrangements need to be made for the time when the child will no longer be looked after by the responsible authority.

7 Whether plans need to be made to find a permanent substitute family for the child.

SCHEDULE 2

HEALTH CONSIDERATIONS TO WHICH RESPONSIBLE AUTHORITIES ARE TO HAVE REGARD

1 The child's state of health including his physical, emotional and mental health.

2 The child's health history including, as far as practicable, his family health history.

3 The effect of the child's health and health history on his development.

4 Existing arrangements for the child's medical and dental care and treatment and health and dental surveillance.

5 The possible need for an appropriate course of action which should be identified to assist necessary change of such care, treatment or surveillance.

6 The possible need for preventive measures, such as vaccination and immunisation, and screening for vision and hearing and for advice and guidance on health, personal care and health promotion issues appropriate to the child's needs.

SCHEDULE 3

EDUCATIONAL CONSIDERATIONS TO WHICH RESPONSIBLE AUTHORITIES ARE TO HAVE REGARD

1 The child's educational history.

2 The need to achieve continuity in the child's education.

3 The need to identify any educational need which the child may have and to take action to meet that need.

4 The need to carry out any assessment in respect of any special educational need under the Education Act 1996 and meet any such needs identified in a statement of special educational needs made under section 324 of that Act.

SCHEDULE 4

MATTERS TO BE INCLUDED IN ARRANGEMENTS TO ACCOMMODATE CHILDREN WHO ARE NOT IN CARE

1 The type of accommodation to be provided and its address together with the name of any person who will be responsible for the child at that accommodation on behalf of the responsible authority.

2 The details of any services to be provided for the child.

3 The respective responsibilities of the responsible authority and –

(a) the child;

(b) any parent of his; and

(c) any person who is not a parent of his but who has parental responsibility for him.

4 What delegation there has been by the persons referred to in paragraph 3(b) and (c) of this Schedule to the responsible authority of parental responsibility for the child's day to day care.

5 The arrangements for involving those persons and the child in decision making with respect to the child having regard –

(a) to the local authority's duty under sections 20(6) (involvement of children before provision of accommodation) and 22(3) to (5) of the Act (general duties of the local authority in relation to children looked after by them);

(b) the duty of the voluntary organisation under section 61(1) and (2) of the Act (duties of voluntary organisations); and

(c) the duty of the person carrying on a private children's home under section 64(1) and (2) of the Act (welfare of children in private children's homes).

6 The arrangements for contact between the child and –

(a) his parents;

(b) any person who is not a parent of his but who has parental responsibility for him; and

(c) any relative, friend or other person connected with him,

and if appropriate, the reasons why contact with any such person would not be reasonably practicable or would be inconsistent with the child's welfare.

7 The arrangements for notifying changes in arrangements for contact to any of the persons referred to in paragraph 6.

8 In the case of a child aged 16 or over whether section 20(11) (accommodation of a child of 16 or over despite parental opposition) applies.

9 The expected duration of arrangements and the steps which should apply to bring the arrangements to an end, including arrangements for rehabilitation of the child with the person with whom he was living before the voluntary arrangements were made or some other suitable person, having regard in particular, in the case of a local authority looking after a child, to section 23(6) of the Act (duty to place children where practicable with parents etc) and paragraph 15 of Schedule 2 to the Act (maintenance of contact between child and family).

4.5 BLOOD TESTS (EVIDENCE OF PATERNITY) REGULATIONS 1971, SI 1971/1861[1]

1 Citation and commencement

These Regulations may be cited as the Blood Tests (Evidence of Paternity) Regulations 1971 and shall come into operation on 1st March 1972.

2 Interpretation

(1) In these Regulations, unless the context otherwise requires, –

'the Act' means the Family Law Reform Act 1969;

'court' means a court which gives a direction for the use of scientific tests in pursuance of section 20(1) of the Act;

'direction' means a direction given as aforesaid;

'direction form' means Form 1 in Schedule 1 to these Regulations;

'photograph' means a recent photograph, taken full face without a hat, of the size required for insertion in a passport;

'sample' means bodily fluid or bodily tissue taken for the purpose of scientific tests;

'sampler' means a registered medical practitioner, or a person who is under the supervision of such a practitioner and is either a registered nurse or a registered medical laboratory technician, or a tester,

'subject' means a person from whom a court directs the bodily samples shall be taken;

'tester' means an individual employed to carry out tests by a body which has been accredited for the purposes of section 20 of the Act either by the Lord Chancellor or by a body appointed by him for those purposes and which has been nominated in a direction to carry out tests;

'tests' means scientific tests carried out under Part III of the Act and includes any test made with the object of ascertaining the inheritable characteristics of bodily fluids or bodily tissue.

(2) A reference in these Regulations to a person who is under a disability is a reference to a person who has not attained the age of 16 years or who is suffering from a mental disorder within the meaning of the Mental Health Act 1959 and is incapable of understanding the nature and purpose of scientific tests.

(3) The Interpretation Act 1889 shall apply to the interpretation of these Regulations as it applies to the interpretation of an Act of Parliament.

---

[1] For cases proceeding in the family proceedings court, see the Magistrates' Courts (Blood Tests) Rules 1971, SI 1971/1991.

3 Direction form

A sampler shall not take a sample from a subject unless Parts I and II of the direction form have been completed and the direction form purports to be signed by the proper officer of the court or some person on his behalf.

4 Subjects under disability to be accompanied to sampler

A subject who is under a disability who attends a sampler for the taking of a sample shall be accompanied by a person of full age who shall identify him to the sampler.

5 Taking of samples

(1) Without prejudice to the provisions of rules of court, a sampler may make arrangements for the taking of samples from the subjects or may change any arrangements already made and make other arrangements.

(2) Subject to the provisions of these Regulations, where a subject attends a sampler in accordance with arrangements made under a direction, the sampler shall take a sample from him on that occasion.

(3) A sampler shall not take a sample from a subject if –

    (i)   in the case of a blood sample he has reason to believe that the subject has been transfused with blood within the three months immediately preceding the day on which the sample is to be taken; or

   (ii)   in his opinion, tests on a sample taken at that time from that subject could not effectively be carried out for the purposes of and in accordance with the direction; or

  (iii)   in his opinion, the taking of a sample might have an adverse effect on the health of the subject.

(4) A sampler may take a sample from a subject who has been injected with a blood product or blood plasma if, in his opinion, the value of any tests done on that sample would not be thereby affected, but shall inform the tester that the subject was so injected.

(5) Where a sampler does not take a sample from a subject in accordance with arrangements made for the taking of that sample and no other arrangements are made, he shall return the direction form relating to that subject to the court, having stated on the form his reason for not taking the sample and any reason given by the subject (or the person having the care and control of the subject) for any failure to attend in accordance with those arrangements.

(6) A subject who attends a sampler for the taking of a sample may be accompanied by his legal representative.

6 Sampling procedure

(1) A sampler shall comply with the provisions of this Regulation, all of which shall be complied with in respect of one subject before any are complied with in respect of any other subject; so however that a report made in accordance with the provisions of section 20(2) of the Act or any other evidence relating to the samples or the tests made on the samples shall not be challenged solely on the grounds that a sampler has not acted in accordance with the provisions of this Regulation.

(2) Before a sample is taken from any subject who has attained the age of 12 months by the date of the direction, the sampler shall ensure that a photograph of that subject is affixed to the direction form relating to that subject.

(3) Before a sample is taken from a subject, he, or where he is under a disability the person of full age accompanying him, shall complete the declaration in Part V of the direction form (that that subject is the subject to whom the direction form relates and, where a photograph is affixed to the direction form, that the photograph is a photograph of that subject) which shall be signed in the presence of and witnessed by the sampler.

(4) (*deleted*)

(5) A sample shall not be taken from any subject unless –

    (a) he or, where he is under a disability, the person having the care and control of him, has signed a statement on the direction form that he consents to the sample being taken; or

    (b) where he is under a disability and is not accompanied by the person having the care and control of him, the sampler is in possession of a statement in writing, purporting to be signed by that person that he consents to the sample being taken; or

    (c) where he is under the age of sixteen years, and the person with care and control of him does not consent, the court has nevertheless ordered that a sample be taken.

(6) The sampler shall affix to the direction form any statement referred to in sub-paragraph (b) of the preceding paragraph.

(7) If a subject or, where he is under a disability, the person having the care and control of him, does not consent to the taking of a sample, he may record on the direction form his reasons for withholding his consent.

(8) When the sampler has taken a sample he shall place it in a suitable container and shall affix to the container a label giving the full name, age and sex of the subject from whom it was taken and the label shall be signed by the sampler.

(9) The sampler shall state in Part VII of the direction form that he has taken the sample and the date on which he did so.

7 Despatch of samples to tester

(1) When a sampler has taken samples, he shall, where he is not himself the tester, pack the containers together with the relevant direction forms and shall despatch them forthwith to the tester by post by recorded delivery or shall deliver them or cause them to be delivered to the tester by some person other than a subject or a person who has accompanied a subject to the sampler.

(2) If at any time a sampler despatches to a tester samples from some only of the subjects and has not previously despatched samples taken from the other subjects, he shall inform the tester whether he is expecting to take any samples from those other subjects and, if so, from whom and on what date.

8 Procedure where sampler nominated is unable to take the samples

(1) Where a sampler is unable himself to take samples from all or any of the subjects, he may nominate another sampler to take the samples which he is unable to take.

(2) The sampler shall record the nomination of the other sampler on the relevant direction forms and shall forward them to the sampler nominated by him.

8A Accreditation

(1) Subject to paragraph (2), a body shall not be eligible for accreditation for the purposes of section 20 of the Act unless it is accredited to ISO/IEC/17025 by an accreditation body which complies with the requirements of ISO Guide 58.

(2) A body which employs a person who at the date of the coming into force of the Blood Tests (Evidence of Paternity) (Amendment) Regulations 2001 was a tester appointed by the Lord Chancellor shall, until three years after that date, be eligible for accreditation for the purposes of section 20 of the Act notwithstanding that it does not comply with paragraph (1).

9 Testing of samples

(1) Samples taken for the purpose of giving effect to a direction shall (so far as practicable) all be tested by the same tester.

(2) A tester shall not make tests on any samples for the purpose of a direction unless he will, in his opinion, be able to show from the results of those tests (whether alone or together with the results of tests on any samples which he has received and tested or expects to receive subsequently) that a subject is or is not excluded from being the father or mother of the person whose parentage falls to be determined.

10 Report by tester

On completion of the tests in compliance with the direction, the tester shall forward to the court a report in Form 2 in Schedule 1 to these Regulations, together with the appropriate direction forms.

11 Procedure where tests not made

If at any time it appears to a tester that he will be unable to make tests in accordance with the direction, he shall inform the court, giving his reasons, and shall return the direction forms in his possession to the court.

12 Fees

(1) A sampler may charge £27.50 for making the arrangements to take a sample

(2) The charge in paragraph (1) is payable whether or not a sample is taken.

SCHEDULE 1

Forms 1–2
(Not reproduced here)

SCHEDULE 2

(repealed)

4.6 CHILD ABDUCTION AND CUSTODY (PARTIES TO CONVENTIONS) ORDER 1986, SI 1986/1159[1]

1

This Order may be cited as the Child Abduction and Custody (Parties to Conventions) Order 1986, and shall come into operation on 1st August 1986.

2

(1) In this Article of, and in Schedule 1 to, this Order, 'the Convention' means the Convention on the Civil Aspects of International Child Abduction which was signed at The Hague on 25th October 1980.

(2)

    (a) The Contracting States to the Convention shall be as specified in the first column of Schedule 1 to this Order.

    (b) Where the Convention applies, or applies only, to a particular territory or particular territories specified in a declaration made by a Contracting State under Article 39 or 40 of the Convention, the territory or territories in question shall be as specified in the second column of Schedule 1 to this Order.

    (c) The date of the coming into force of the Convention as between the United Kingdom and any State or territory so specified shall be as specified in the third column of Schedule 1 to this Order.

3

(1) In this Article of, and in Schedule 2 to, this Order, 'the Convention' means the European Convention on Recognition and Enforcement of Decisions concerning Custody of Children and on the Restoration of Custody of Children which was signed in Luxembourg on 20th May 1980.

(2)

    (a) The Contracting States to the Convention shall be as specified in the first column of Schedule 2 to this Order.

    (b) Where the Convention applies, or applies only, to a particular territory or particular territories specified by a Contracting State under Article 24 or 25 of the Convention, the territory or territories in question shall be as specified in the second column of Schedule 2 to this Order.

    (c) The date of the coming into force of the Convention as between the United Kingdom and any State or territory so specified shall be as specified in the third column of Schedule 2 to this Order.

---

[1] As most recently amended by SI 2004/3040.

SCHEDULE 1

CONVENTION ON THE CIVIL ASPECTS OF INTERNATIONAL CHILD ABDUCTION, THE HAGUE, 25TH OCTOBER 1980

State	Date in force	State	Date in force
Argentina	1 June 1991	Greece	1 June 1993
Australia. Australian States and mainland Territories	1 January 1987	Honduras	1 March 1994
Austria	1 October 1988	Hungary	1 September 1986
The Bahamas	1 January 1994	Iceland	1 November 1996
Belarus	1 September 2003	Ireland	1 October 1991
Belgium	1 May 1999	Israel	1 December 1991
Belize	1 October 1989	Italy	1 May 1995
Bosnia and Herzegovina	7 April 1992	Latvia	1 September 2003
Brazil	1 March 2005	Lithuania	1 March 2005
Burkina Faso	1 August 1992	Luxembourg	1 January 1987
Canada :		Macedonia	1 December 1991
Canada – Ontario	1 August 1986	Malta	1 March 2002
Canada – New Brunswick	1 August 1986	Mauritius	1 June 1993
Canada – British Columbia	1 August 1986	Mexico	1 September 1991
Canada – Manitoba	1 August 1986	Monaco	1 February 1993
Canada – Nova Scotia	1 August 1986	Netherlands	1 September 1990
Canada – Newfoundland	1 August 1986	New Zealand	1 August 1991
Canada – Prince Edward Island	1 August 1986	Norway	1 April 1989
Canada – Quebec	1 August 1986	Panama	1 May 1994

State	Date in force		State	Date in force
Canada – Yukon Territory	1 August 1986		Peru	1 September 2003
Canada – Saskatchewan	1 November 1986		Poland	1 November 1992
Canada – Alberta	1 February 1987		Portugal	1 August 1986
Canada – Northwest Territories	1 April 1988		Romania	1 February 1993
Chile	1 May 1994		St Kitts and Nevis	1 August 1994
China – Hong Kong Special Administrative Region	1 September 1997		Serbia and Montenegro	27 April 1992
China – Macau Special Administrative Region	1 March 1999		Slovakia	1 February 2001
Colombia	1 March 1996		Slovenia	1 June 1994
Croatia	1 December 1991		South Africa	1 October 1997
Cyprus	1 February 1995		Spain	1 September 1987
Czech Republic	1 March 1998		Sweden	1 June 1989
Denmark	1 July 1991		Switzerland	1 August 1986
Ecuador	1 April 1992		Turkey	1 August 2001
Estonia	1 September 2003		Turkmenistan	1 March 1998
Fiji	1 September 2003		United States of America	1 July 1988
Finland	1 August 1994		Uruguay	1 September 2003
France	1 August 1986		Uzbekistan	1 September 2003
Georgia	1 October 1997		Venezuela	1 January 1997
Germany	1 December 1990		Zimbabwe	1 July 1995

SCHEDULE 2

EUROPEAN CONVENTION ON RECOGNITION AND ENFORCEMENT OF DECISIONS CONCERNING CUSTODY OF CHILDREN AND ON THE RESTORATION OF CUSTODY OF CHILDREN, LUXEMBOURG, 20TH MAY 1980

State	Date in force	State	Date in force
Austria	1 August 1986	Lithuania	1 March 2005
Belgium	1 August 1986	Liechtenstein	1 August 1997
Cyprus	1 October 1986	Luxembourg	1 August 1986
Czech Republic	1 July 2000	Malta	1 February 2000
Denmark	1 August 1991	Netherlands	1 September 1990
Finland	1 August 1994	Norway	1 May 1989
France	1 August 1986	Poland	1 March 1996
Germany	1 February 1991	Portugal	1 August 1986
Greece	1 July 1993	Spain	1 August 1986
Iceland	1 November 1996	Sweden	1 July 1989
Ireland	1 October 1991	Switzerland	1 August 1986
Italy	1 June 1995	Turkey	1 June 2000
Latvia	1 August 2002		

4.7 CHILDREN (ADMISSIBILITY OF HEARSAY EVIDENCE) ORDER 1993, SI 1993/621[1] (rr 1–2)

1 Citation and commencement

This order may be cited as the Children (Admissibility of Hearsay Evidence) Order 1993 and shall come into force on 5th April 1993.

2 Admissibility of hearsay evidence

In –

(a) civil proceedings before the High Court or a county court; and

(b)

    (i) family proceedings, and

    (ii) civil proceedings under the Child Support Act 1991 in a magistrates' court,

evidence given in connection with the upbringing, maintenance or welfare of a child shall be admissible notwithstanding any rule of law relating to hearsay.

****

---

[1] Lawyers should also be aware of the general abrogation of the rule against hearsay effected by the Civil Evidence Act 1995.

4.8 CHILDREN (ALLOCATION OF PROCEEDINGS) ORDER 1991, SI 1991/1677

1 Citation, commencement and interpretation

(1) This Order may be cited as the Children (Allocation of Proceedings) Order 1991 and shall come into force on 14th October 1991.

(2) In this Order, unless the context otherwise requires –

'child' –
    (a) means, subject to sub-paragraph (b), a person under the age of 18 with respect to whom proceedings are brought, and
    (b) where the proceedings are under Schedule 1, also includes a person who has reached the age of 18;

'London commission area' has the meaning assigned to it by section 2(1) of the Justices of the Peace Act 1979;

'petty sessions area' has the meaning assigned to it by section 4 of the Justices of the Peace Act 1979; and

'the Act' means the Children Act 1989, and a section, Part or Schedule referred to by number alone means the section, Part or Schedule so numbered in that Act.

2 Classes of county court

For the purposes of this Order there shall be the following classes of county court –

    (a) divorce county courts, being those courts designated for the time being as divorce county courts by an order under section 33 of the Matrimonial and Family Proceedings Act 1984;
    (b) family hearing centres, being those courts set out in Schedule 1 to this Order;
    (c) care centres, being those courts set out in column (ii) of Schedule 2 to this Order.

Commencement of proceedings

3 Proceedings to be commenced in magistrates' court

(1) Subject to paragraphs (2) and (3) and to article 4, proceedings under any of the following provisions shall be commenced in a magistrates' court –

    (a) section 25 (use of accommodation for restricting liberty);
    (b) section 31 (care and supervision orders);
    (c) section 33(7) (leave to change name of or remove from United Kingdom child in care);
    (d) section 34 (parental contact);
    (e) section 36 (education supervision orders);
    (f) section 43 (child assessment orders);
    (g) section 44 (emergency protection orders);
    (h) section 45 (duration of emergency protection orders etc);
    (i) section 46(7) (application for emergency protection order by police officer);

(j) section 48 (powers to assist discovery of children etc);

(k) section 50 (recovery orders);

(l) section 75 (protection of children in an emergency);

(m) section 77(6) (appeal against steps taken under section 77(1));

(n) section 102 (powers of constable to assist etc);

(o) paragraph 19 of Schedule 2 (approval of arrangements to assist child to live abroad);

(p) paragraph 23 of Schedule 2 (contribution orders);

(q) paragraph 8 of Schedule 8 (certain appeals);

(r) section 21 of the Adoption Act 1976;

(s) *(deleted)*

(t) section 20 of the Child Support Act 1991 (appeals) where the proceedings are to be dealt with in accordance with the Child Support Appeals (Jurisdiction of Courts) Order 1993.

(u) section 30 of the Human Fertilisation and Embryology Act 1990 (parental orders in favour of gamete donors).

(2) Notwithstanding paragraph (1) and subject to paragraph (3), proceedings of a kind set out in sub-paragraphs (b), (e), (f), (g), (i) or (j) of paragraph (1), and which arise out of an investigation directed, by the High Court or a county court, under section 37(1), shall be commenced –

(a) in the court which directs the investigation, where that court is the High Court or a care centre, or

(b) in such care centre as the court which directs the investigation may order.

(3) Notwithstanding paragraphs (1) and (2), proceedings of a kind set out in sub-paragraph (a) to (k), (n) or (o) of paragraph (1) shall be commenced in a court in which are pending other proceedings, in respect of the same child, which are also of a kind set out in those sub-paragraphs.

4 Application to extend, vary or discharge order

(1) Subject to paragraphs (2) and (3), proceedings under the Act, or under the Adoption Act 1976 –

(a) to extend, vary or discharge an order, or

(b) the determination of which may have the effect of varying or discharging an order,

shall be commenced in the court which made the order.

(2) Notwithstanding paragraph (1), an application for an order under section 8 which would have the effect of varying or discharging an order made, by a county court, in accordance with section 10(1)(b) shall be made to a divorce county court.

(3) Notwithstanding paragraph (1), an application to extend, vary or discharge an order made, by a county court, under section 38, or for an order which would have the effect of extending, varying or discharging such an order, shall be made to a care centre.

(4) A court may transfer proceedings commenced in accordance with paragraph (1) to any other court in accordance with the provisions of articles 5 to 13.

Transfer of proceedings

5 Disapplication of enactments about transfer

Sections 38 and 39 of the Matrimonial and Family Proceedings Act 1984 shall not apply to proceedings under the Act or under the Adoption Act 1976.

6 Transfer from one magistrates' court to another

(1) A magistrates' court (the 'transferring court') shall transfer proceedings to which this article applies to another magistrates' court (the 'receiving court') where –

    (a) having regard to the principle set out in section 1(2), the transferring court considers that the transfer is in the interests of the child –

        (i) because it is likely significantly to accelerate the determination of the proceedings,

        (ii) because it would be appropriate for those proceedings to be heard together with other family proceedings which are pending in the receiving court, or

        (iii) for some other reason, and

    (b) the receiving court, by its justices' clerk (as defined by rule 1(2) of the Family Proceedings Courts (Children Act 1989) Rules 1991), consents to the transfer.

(2) This article applies to proceedings –

    (a) under the Act;

    (b) under the Adoption Act 1976;

    (c) of the kind mentioned in sub-paragraphs (t) or (u) of article 3(1) and under section 55A of the Family Law Act 1986.

    (d) under section 11 of the Crime and Disorder Act 1998 (child safety orders).

7 Transfer from magistrates' court to county court by magistrates' court

(1) Subject to paragraphs (2), (3) and (4) and to articles 15 to 18, a magistrates' court may, upon application by a party or of its own motion, transfer to a county court proceedings of any of the kinds mentioned in article 3(1) or proceedings under section 55A of the Family Law Act 1986 where it considers it in the interests of the child to do so having regard, first, to the principle set out in section 1(2) and, secondly, to the following questions –

    (a) whether the proceedings are exceptionally grave, important or complex, in particular –

        (i) because of complicated or conflicting evidence about the risks involved to the child's physical or moral well-being or about other matters relating to the welfare of the child;

        (ii) because of the number of parties;

        (iii) because of a conflict with the law of another jurisdiction;

        (iv) because of some novel and difficult point of law; or

        (v) because of some question of general public interest;

    (b) whether it would be appropriate for those proceedings to be heard together with other family proceedings which are pending in another court; and

    (c) whether transfer is likely significantly to accelerate the determination of the proceedings, where –

  (i) no other method of doing so, including transfer to another magistrates' court, is appropriate, and

  (ii) delay would seriously prejudice the interests of the child who is the subject of the proceedings.

(2) Notwithstanding paragraph (1), proceedings of the kind mentioned in sub-paragraphs (g) to (j), (l), (m), (p) or (q) of article 3(1) shall not be transferred from a magistrates' court.

(3) Notwithstanding paragraph (1), proceedings of the kind mentioned in sub-paragraph (a) or (n) of article 3(1) shall only be transferred from a magistrates' court to a county court in order to be heard together with other family proceedings which arise out of the same circumstances as gave rise to the proceedings to be transferred and which are pending in another court.

(4) Notwithstanding paragraphs (1) and (3), proceedings of the kind mentioned in article 3(1)(a) shall not be transferred from a magistrates' court which is not a family proceedings court within the meaning of section 92(1).

8 Subject to articles 15 to 18, a magistrates' court may transfer to a county court proceedings under the Act or under the Adoption Act 1976, being proceedings to which article 7 does not apply, where, having regard to the principle set out in section 1(2), it considers that in the interests of the child the proceedings can be dealt with more appropriately in that county court.

9 Transfer from magistrates' court following refusal of magistrates' court to transfer

(1) Where a magistrates' court refuses to transfer proceedings under article 7, a party to those proceedings may apply to the care centre listed in column (ii) of Schedule 2 to this Order against the entry in column (i) for the petty sessions area or London commission area in which the magistrates' court is situated for an order under paragraph (2).

(2) Upon hearing an application under paragraph (1) the court may transfer the proceedings to itself where, having regard to the principle set out in section 1(2) and the questions set out in article 7(1)(a) to (c), it considers it in the interests of the child to do so.

(3) Upon hearing an application under paragraph (1) the court may transfer the proceedings to the High Court where, having regard to the principle set out in section 1(2), it considers –

  (a) that the proceedings are appropriate for determination in the High Court, and

  (b) that such determination would be in the interests of the child.

(4) This article shall apply (with the necessary modifications) to proceedings brought under Parts I and II as it applies where a magistrates' court refuses to transfer proceedings under article 7.

10 Transfer from one county court to another

(1) Subject to articles 15 to 17, a county court (the 'transferring court') shall transfer proceedings to which this article applies to another county court (the 'receiving court') where –

    (a) the transferring court, having regard to the principle set out in section 1(2), considers the transfer to be in the interests of the child, and

    (b) the receiving court is –

        (i) of the same class or classes, within the meaning of article 2, as the transferring court, or

        (ii) to be presided over by a judge or district judge who is specified by directions under section 9 of the Courts and Legal Services Act 1990 for the same purposes as the judge or district judge presiding over the transferring court.

(2) This article applies to proceedings –

    (a) under the Act;

    (b) under the Adoption Act 1976;

    (c) of the kind mentioned in sub-paragraphs (t) or (u) of article 3(1) and under section 55A of the Family Law Act 1986.

11 Transfer from county court to magistrates' court by county court

(1) A county court may transfer to a magistrates' court before trial proceedings which were transferred under article 7(1) where the county court, having regard to the principle set out in section 1(2) and the interests of the child, considers that the criterion cited by the magistrates' court as the reason for transfer –

    (a) in the case of the criterion in article 7(1)(a), does not apply,

    (b) in the case of the criterion in article 7(1)(b), no longer applies, because the proceedings with which the transferred proceedings were to be heard have been determined,

    (c) in the case of the criterion in article 7(1)(c), no longer applies.

(2) Paragraph (1) shall apply (with the necessary modifications) to proceedings under Parts I and II brought in, or transferred to, a county court as it applies to proceedings transferred to a county court under article 7(1).

12 Transfer from county court to High Court by county court

(1) A county court may transfer proceedings to which this article applies to the High Court where, having regard to the principle set out in section 1(2), it considers –

    (a) that the proceedings are appropriate for determination in the High Court, and

    (b) that such determination would be in the interests of the child.

(2) This article applies to proceedings –

    (a) under the Act;

    (b) under the Adoption Act 1976;

    (c) of the kind mentioned in sub-paragraphs (t) or (u) of article 3(1) and under section 55A of the Family Law Act 1986.

13 Transfer from High Court to county court

(1) Subject to articles 15, 16 and 18, the High Court may transfer to a county court proceedings to which this article applies where, having regard to the principle set out in section 1(2), it considers that the proceedings are appropriate for determination in such a court and that such determination would be in the interests of the child.

(2) This article applies to proceedings –

   (a) under the Act;

   (b) under the Adoption Act 1976;

   (c) of the kind mentioned in sub-paragraphs (t) or (u) of article 3(1) and under section 55A of the Family Law Act 1986.

Allocation of proceedings to particular county courts

14 Commencement

Subject to articles 18, 19 and 20 and to rule 2.40 of the Family Proceedings Rules 1991 (Application under Part I or II of the Children Act 1989 where matrimonial cause is pending), an application under the Act or under the Adoption Act 1976 which is to be made to a county court shall be made to a divorce county court.

15 Proceedings under Part I or II or Schedule 1

(1) Subject to paragraph (3), where an application under Part I or II or Schedule 1 is to be transferred from a magistrates' court to a county court, it shall be transferred to a divorce county court.

(2) Subject to paragraph (3), where an application under Part I or II or Schedule 1, other than an application for an order under section 8, is to be transferred from the High Court to a county court, it shall be transferred to a divorce county court.

(3) Where an application under Part I or II or Schedule 1, other than an application for an order under section 8, is to be transferred to a county court for the purpose of consolidation with other proceedings, it shall be transferred to the court in which those other proceedings are pending.

16 Orders under section 8 of the Children Act 1989

(1) An application for an order under section 8 in a divorce county court, which is not also a family hearing centre, shall, if the court is notified that the application will be opposed, be transferred for trial to a family hearing centre.

(2) Subject to paragraph (3), where an application for an order under section 8 is to be transferred from the High Court to a county court it shall be transferred to a family hearing centre.

(3) Where an application for an order under section 8 is to be transferred to a county court for the purpose of consolidation with other proceedings, it may be transferred to the court in which those other proceedings are pending whether or not it is a family hearing centre; but paragraph (1) shall apply to the application following the transfer.

17 Application for adoption or freeing for adoption

(1) Subject to article 22, proceedings in a divorce county court, which is not also a family hearing centre, under section 12 or 18 of the Adoption Act 1976 shall, if the court is notified that the proceedings will be opposed, be transferred for trial to a family hearing centre.

(2) Where proceedings under the Adoption Act 1976 are to be transferred from a magistrates' court to a county court, they shall be transferred to a divorce county court.

18 Applications under Part III, IV or V

(1) An application under Part III, IV or V, if it is to be made to a county court, shall be made to a care centre.

(2) An application under Part III, IV or V which is to be transferred from the High Court to a county court shall be transferred to a care centre.

(3) An application under Part III, IV or V which is to be transferred from a magistrates' court to a county court shall be transferred to the care centre listed against the entry in column (i) of Schedule 2 to this Order for the petty sessions area or London commission area in which the relevant magistrates' court is situated.

19 Principal Registry of the Family Division

The principal registry of the Family Division of the High Court shall be treated, for the purposes of this Order, as if it were a divorce county court, a family hearing centre and a care centre listed against every entry in column (i) of Schedule 2 to this Order (in addition to the entries against which it is actually listed).

20 Lambeth, Shoreditch and Woolwich County Courts

Notwithstanding articles 14, 16 and 17, an application for an order under section 4 or 8 or under the Adoption Act 1976 may be made to and tried in Lambeth, Shoreditch or Woolwich County Court.

Miscellaneous

21 Contravention of provision of this Order

Where proceedings are commenced or transferred in contravention of a provision of this Order, the contravention shall not have the effect of making the proceedings invalid; and no appeal shall lie against the determination of proceedings on the basis of such contravention alone.

22 Transitional provision – proceedings under Adoption Act 1976

Proceedings under the Adoption Act 1976 which are commenced in a county court prior to the coming into force of this Order may, notwithstanding article 17(1), remain in that court for trial.

SCHEDULE 1
FAMILY HEARING CENTRES

Article 2

Midland Circuit

Birmingham County Court	Coventry County Court
Derby County Court	Dudley County Court
Leicester County Court	Lincoln County Court

Mansfield County Court
Nottingham County Court
Stoke-on-Trent County Court
Walsall County Court
Worcester County Court

Northampton County Court
Stafford County Court
Telford County Court
Wolverhampton County Court

Northern Circuit

Blackburn County Court
Carlisle County Court
Liverpool County Court
Oldham County Court

Bolton County Court
Lancaster County Court
Manchester County Court
Stockport County Court

North Eastern Circuit

Barnsley County Court
Darlington County Court
Doncaster County Court
Grimsby County Court
Harrogate County Court
Keighley County Court
Leeds County Court
Pontefract County Court
Scarborough County Court
Skipton County Court
Teesside County Court
York County Court

Bradford County Court
Dewsbury County Court
Durham County Court
Halifax County Court
Huddersfield County Court
Kingston-upon-Hull County Court
Newcastle-upon-Tyne County Court
Rotherham County Court
Sheffield County Court
Sunderland County Court
Wakefield County Court

South Eastern Circuit

Barnet County Court
Brighton County Court
Brentford County Court
Cambridge County Court
Chelmsford County Court
Colchester and Clacton County Court

Bedford County Court
Bow County Court
Bromley County Court
Canterbury County Court
Chichester County Court
Croydon County Court

Dartford County Court

Guildford County Court

Ilford County Court

King's Lynn County Court

Luton County Court

Medway County Court

Norwich County Court

Peterborough County Court

Romford County Court

Southend County Court

Watford County Court

Edmonton County Court

Hitchin County Court

Ipswich County Court

Kingston-upon-Thames County Court

Maidstone County Court

Milton Keynes County Court

Oxford County Court

Reading County Court

Slough County Court

Wandsworth County Court

Willesden County Court

Wales and Chester Circuit

Aberystwyth County Court

Cardiff County Court

Chester County Court

Haverfordwest County Court

Macclesfield County Court

Newport (Gwent) County Court

Rhyl County Court

Warrington County Court

Wrexham County Court

Caernarfon County Court

Carmarthen County Court

Crewe County Court

Llangefni County Court

Merthyr Tydfil County Court

Pontypridd County Court

Swansea County Court

Welshpool and Newtown County Court

Western Circuit

Barnstaple County Court

Bath County Court

Bristol County Court

Gloucester County Court

Portsmouth County Court

Southampton County Court

Taunton County Court

Weymouth County Court

Basingstoke County Court

Bournemouth County Court

Exeter County Court

Plymouth County Court

Salisbury County Court

Swindon County Court

Truro County Court

Yeovil County Court

SCHEDULE 2
CARE CENTRES

(i)	*(ii)*
Petty Sessions Areas	*Care Centres*
	Midland Circuit
Aldridge and Brownhills	Wolverhampton County Court
Alfreton and Belper	Derby County Court
Ashby-De-La-Zouch	Leicester County Court
Atherstone and Coleshill	Coventry County Court
Bewdley and Stourport	Worcester County Court
Birmingham	Birmingham County Court
Boston	Lincoln County Court
Bourne and Stamford	Lincoln County Court
Bridgnorth	Telford County Court
Bromsgrove	Worcester County Court
Burton-upon-Trent	Derby County Court
Caistor	Lincoln County Court
Cannock	Wolverhampton County Court
Cheadle	Stoke-on-Trent County Court
Chesterfield	Derby County Court
City of Hereford	Worcester County Court
Congleton	Stoke-on-Trent County Court
Corby	Northampton County Court
Coventry	Coventry County Court
Crewe and Nantwich	Stoke-on-Trent County Court
Daventry	Northampton County Court
Derby and South Derbyshire	Derby County Court
Drayton	Telford County Court
Dudley	Wolverhampton County Court
East Retford	Nottingham County Court
Eccleshall	Stoke-on-Trent County Court
Elloes	Lincoln County Court
Gainsborough	Lincoln County Court

Glossop	Derby County Court
Grantham	Lincoln County Court
Halesowen	Wolverhampton County Court
High Peak	Derby County Court
Ilkeston	Derby County Court
Kettering	Northampton County Court
Kidderminster	Worcester County Court
Leek	Stoke-on-Trent County Court
Leicester (City)	Leicester County Court
Leicester (County)	Leicester County Court
Lichfield	Stoke-on-Trent County Court
Lincoln District	Lincoln County Court
Loughborough	Leicester County Court
Louth	Lincoln County Court
Ludlow	Telford County Court
Lutterworth	Leicester County Court
Malvern Hills	Worcester County Court
Mansfield	Nottingham County Court
Market Bosworth	Leicester County Court
Market Harborough	Leicester County Court
Market Rasen	Lincoln County Court
Melton and Belvoir	Leicester County Court
Mid-Warwickshire	Coventry County Court
Mid-Worcestershire	Worcester County Court
Newark and Southwell	Nottingham County Court
Newcastle-under-Lyme	Stoke-on-Trent County Court
Northampton	Northampton County Court
North Herefordshire	Worcester County Court
Nottingham	Nottingham County Court
Nuneaton	Coventry County Court
Oswestry	Telford County Court
Pirehill North	Stoke-on-Trent County Court
Redditch	Worcester County Court
Rugby	Coventry County Court

Rugeley	Wolverhampton County Court
Rutland	Leicester County Court
Seisdon	Wolverhampton County Court
Sleaford	Lincoln County Court
Shrewsbury	Telford County Court
Solihull	Birmingham County Court
South Herefordshire	Worcester County Court
South Warwickshire	Coventry County Court
Spilsby and Skegness	Lincoln County Court
Stoke-on-Trent	Stoke-on-Trent County Court
Stone	Stoke-on-Trent County Court
Stourbridge	Wolverhampton County Court
Sutton Coldfield	Birmingham County Court
Tamworth	Stoke-on-Trent County Court
Telford	Telford County Court
Towcester	Northampton County Court
Uttoxeter	Stoke-on-Trent County Court
Vale of Evesham	Worcester County Court
Warley	Wolverhampton County Court
Walsall	Wolverhampton County Court
Wellingborough	Northampton County Court
West Bromwich	Wolverhampton County Court
West Derbyshire	Derby County Court
Wolds	Lincoln County Court
Wolverhampton	Wolverhampton County Court
Worcester City	Worcester County Court
Worksop	Nottingham County Court

Northern Circuit

Appleby	Carlisle County Court
Ashton-under-Lyne	Manchester County Court
Barrow with Bootle	Lancaster County Court
Blackburn	Blackburn County Court

Blackpool	Lancaster County Court
Bolton	Manchester County Court
Burnley	Blackburn County Court
Bury	Manchester County Court
Carlisle	Carlisle County Court
Chorley	Blackburn County Court
Darwen	Blackburn County Court
Eccles	Manchester County Court
Fylde	Lancaster County Court
Hyndburn	Blackburn County Court
Kendal and Lonsdale	Lancaster County Court
Keswick	Carlisle County Court
Knowsley	Liverpool County Court
Lancaster	Lancaster County Court
Leigh	Manchester County Court
Liverpool	Liverpool County Court
Manchester	Manchester County Court
Middleton and Heywood	Manchester County Court
North Lonsdale	Lancaster County Court
North Sefton	Liverpool County Court
Oldham	Manchester County Court
Ormskirk	Liverpool County Court
Pendle	Blackburn County Court
Penrith and Alston	Carlisle County Court
Preston	Blackburn County Court
Ribble Valley	Blackburn County Court
Rochdale	Manchester County Court
Rossendale	Blackburn County Court
St Helens	Liverpool County Court
Salford	Manchester County Court
South Lakes	Lancaster County Court
South Ribble	Blackburn County Court
South Sefton	Liverpool County Court
South Tameside	Manchester County Court

Stockport	Manchester County Court
Trafford	Manchester County Court
West Allerdale	Carlisle County Court
Whitehaven	Carlisle County Court
Wigan	Liverpool County Court
Wigton	Carlisle County Court
Wirral	Liverpool County Court
Wyre	Lancaster County Court

North Eastern Circuit

Bainton Beacon	Kingston-upon-Hull County Court
Barnsley	Sheffield County Court
Batley and Dewsbury	Leeds County Court
Berwick-upon-Tweed	Newcastle-upon-Tyne County Court
Beverley	Kingston-upon-Hull County Court
Blyth Valley	Newcastle-upon-Tyne County Court
Bradford	Leeds County Court
Brighouse	Leeds County Court
Calder	Leeds County Court
Chester-le-Street	Newcastle-upon-Tyne County Court
Claro	York County Court
Coquetdale	Newcastle-upon-Tyne County Court
Darlington	Teesside County Court
Derwentside	Newcastle-upon-Tyne County Court
Dickering	Kingston-upon-Hull County Court
Doncaster	Sheffield County Court
Durham	Newcastle-upon-Tyne County Court
Easington	Sunderland County Court
Easingwold	York County Court
Gateshead	Newcastle-upon-Tyne County Court
Grimsby and Cleethorpes	Kingston-upon-Hull County Court
Goole and Howdenshire	Kingston-upon-Hull County Court
Hartlepool	Teesside County Court

Holme Beacon	Kingston-upon-Hull County Court
Houghton-le-Spring	Sunderland County Court
Huddersfield	Leeds County Court
Keighley	Leeds County Court
Kingston-upon-Hull	Kingston-upon-Hull County Court
Langbaurgh East	Teesside County Court
Leeds	Leeds County Court
Middle Holderness	Kingston-upon-Hull County Court
Morley	Leeds County Court
Morpeth Ward	Newcastle-upon-Tyne County Court
Newcastle-upon-Tyne	Newcastle-upon-Tyne County Court
Northallerton	Teesside County Court
North Holderness	Kingston-upon-Hull County Court
North Lincolnshire	Kingston-upon-Hull County Court
North Tyneside	Newcastle-upon-Tyne County Court
Pontefract	Leeds County Court
Pudsey and Otley	Leeds County Court
Richmond	Teesside County Court
Ripon Liberty	York County Court
Rotherham	Sheffield County Court
Ryedale	York County Court
Scarborough	York County Court
Sedgefield	Newcastle-upon-Tyne County Court
Selby	York County Court
Sheffield	Sheffield County Court
Skyrack and Wetherby	Leeds County Court
South Holderness	Kingston-upon-Hull County Court
South Hunsley Beacon	Kingston-upon-Hull County Court
South Tyneside	Sunderland County Court
Staincliffe	Leeds County Court
Sunderland	Sunderland County Court
Teesdale and Wear Valley	Newcastle-upon-Tyne County Court
Teesside	Teesside County Court
Todmorden	Leeds County Court

Tynedale	Newcastle-upon-Tyne County Court
Wakefield	Leeds County Court
Wansbeck	Newcastle-upon-Tyne County Court
Whitby Strand	Teesside County Court
Wilton Beacon	Kingston-upon-Hull County Court
York	York County Court

South Eastern Circuit

Abingdon	Oxford County Court
Ampthill	Luton County Court
Arundel	Brighton County Court
Ashford and Tenterden	Canterbury County Court
Aylesbury	Milton Keynes County Court
Barnet	Principal Registry of the Family Division
Barking and Dagenham	Principal Registry of the Family Division
Basildon	Chelmsford County Court
Battle and Rye	Brighton County Court
...	
Bedford	Luton County Court
Bexhill	Brighton County Court
Bexley	Principal Registry of the Family Division
Bicester	Oxford County Court
Biggleswade	Luton County Court
Bishop's Stortford	Watford County Court
Brent	Principal Registry of the Family Division
Brentwood	Chelmsford County Court
Brighton	Brighton County Court
Bromley	Principal Registry of the Family Division
Buckingham	Milton Keynes County Court
Burnham	Milton Keynes County Court

Cambridge	Cambridge County Court
Canterbury and St Augustine	Canterbury County Court
Chelmsford	Chelmsford County Court
Chertsey	Guildford County Court
Cheshunt	Watford County Court
Chichester and District	Brighton County Court
Chiltern	Milton Keynes County Court
Colchester	Chelmsford County Court
Crawley	Brighton County Court
Cromer	Norwich County Court
Crowborough	Brighton County Court
Croydon	Principal Registry of the Family Division
Dacorum	Watford County Court
Dartford	Medway County Court
Didcot and Wantage	Oxford County Court
Diss	Norwich County Court
Dorking	Guildford County Court
Dover and East Kent	Canterbury County Court
Downham Market	Norwich County Court
Dunmow	Chelmsford County Court
Dunstable	Luton County Court
Ealing	Principal Registry of the Family Division
Eastbourne	Brighton County Court
East Cambridgeshire	Cambridge County Court
East Dereham	Norwich County Court
East Oxfordshire	Oxford County Court
Enfield	Principal Registry of the Family Division
Epping and Ongar	Chelmsford County Court
Epsom	Guildford County Court
Esher and Walton	Guildford County Court
Fakenham	Norwich County Court
Farnham	Guildford County Court

Faversham and Sittingbourne	Medway County Court
Fenland	Peterborough County Court
Folkestone and Hythe	Canterbury County Court
The Forest	Reading County Court
Freshwell and South Hinckford	Chelmsford County Court
Godstone	Guildford County Court
Guildford	Guildford County Court
Gravesham	Medway County Court
Great Yarmouth	Norwich County Court
Hailsham	Brighton County Court
Halstead and Hedingham	Chelmsford County Court
Harlow	Chelmsford County Court
Harrow Gore	Principal Registry of the Family Division
Haringey	Principal Registry of the Family Division
Harwich	Chelmsford County Court
Hastings	Brighton County Court
Haverhill and Sudbury	Ipswich County Court
Havering	Principal Registry of the Family Division
Henley	Oxford County Court
Hertford and Ware	Watford County Court
Hillingdon	Principal Registry of the Family Division
Horsham	Brighton County Court
Hounslow	Principal Registry of the Family Division
Hove	Brighton County Court
Hunstanton	Norwich County Court
Huntingdonshire	Peterborough County Court
King's Lynn	Norwich County Court
Kingston-upon-Thames	Principal Registry of the Family Division
Leighton Buzzard	Luton County Court
Lewes	Brighton County Court

Luton	Luton County Court
Maidenhead	Reading County Court
Maidstone	Medway County Court
Maldon and Witham	Chelmsford County Court
Medway	Medway County Court
Merton	Principal Registry of the Family Division
Mid-Hertfordshire	Watford County Court
Mid-Sussex	Brighton County Court
Milton Keynes	Milton Keynes County Court
Newham	Principal Registry of the Family Division
North East Suffolk	Ipswich County Court
North Hertfordshire	Watford County Court
North Oxfordshire and Chipping Norton	Oxford County Court
North Walsham	Norwich County Court
North West Suffolk	Ipswich County Court
Norwich	Norwich County Court
Oxford	Oxford County Court
Peterborough	Peterborough County Court
Reading and Sonning	Reading County Court
Redbridge	Principal Registry of the Family Division
Reigate	Guildford County Court
Richmond-upon-Thames	Principal Registry of the Family Division
Rochford and Southend-on-Sea	Chelmsford County Court
Saffron Walden	Chelmsford County Court
St Albans	Watford County Court
St Edmundsbury and Stowmarket	Ipswich County Court
Sevenoaks	Medway County Court
Slough	Reading County Court
South East Suffolk	Ipswich County Court
South Mimms	Watford County Court

Staines and Sunbury	Guildford County Court
Stevenage	Watford County Court
Steyning	Brighton County Court
Sutton	Principal Registry of the Family Division
Swaffham	Norwich County Court
Tendring	Chelmsford County Court
Thanet	Canterbury County Court
Thetford	Norwich County Court
Thurrock	Chelmsford County Court
Tonbridge and Malling	Medway County Court
Tunbridge Wells and Cranbrook	Medway County Court
Waltham Forest	Principal Registry of the Family Division
Watford	Watford County Court
West Berkshire	Reading County Court
Windsor	Reading County Court
Witney	Oxford County Court
Woking	Guildford County Court
Woodstock	Oxford County Court
Worthing	Brighton County Court
Wycombe	Milton Keynes County Court
Wymondham	Norwich County Court

Wales and Chester Circuit

Ardudwy-is-Artro	Caernarfon County Court
Ardudwy-uwch-Artro	Caernarfon County Court
Bangor	Caernarfon County Court
Bedwellty	Newport (Gwent) County Court
Berwyn	Rhyl County Court
Brecon	Pontypridd County Court
Caernarfon and Gwyrfai	Caernarfon County Court
Cardiff	Cardiff County Court
Carmarthen North	Swansea County Court

Carmarthen South	Swansea County Court
Ceredigion Ganol	Swansea County Court
Chester	Chester County Court
Cleddau	Swansea County Court
Colwyn	Rhyl County Court
Congleton	Stoke-on-Trent County Court
Conwy and Llandudno	Caernarfon County Court
Crewe and Nantwich	Stoke-on-Trent County Court
Cynon Valley	Pontypridd County Court
De Ceredigion	Swansea County Court
Dinefwr	Swansea County Court
Dyffryn Clywd	Rhyl County Court
East Gwent	Newport (Gwent) County Court
Eifionydd	Caernarfon County Court
Ellesmere Port and Neston	Chester County Court
Estimaner	Caernarfon County Court
Flint	Rhyl County Court
Gogledd Ceredigion	Swansea County Court
Gogledd Preseli	Swansea County Court
Halton	Warrington County Court
Hawarden	Rhyl County Court
Llandrindod Wells	Pontypridd County Court
Llanelli	Swansea County Court
Lliw Valley	Swansea County Court
Lower Rhymney Valley	Cardiff County Court
Macclesfield	Warrington County Court
Machynlleth	Chester County Court
Merthyr Tydfil	Pontypridd County Court
Miskin	Pontypridd County Court
Mold	Rhyl County Court
Nant Conwy	Caernarfon County Court
Neath	Swansea County Court
Newcastle and Ogmore	Cardiff County Court
Newport	Newport (Gwent) County Court

Newtown	Chester County Court
North Anglesey	Caernarfon County Court
Penllyn	Caernarfon County Court
Port Talbot	Swansea County Court
Pwllheli	Caernarfon County Court
Rhuddlan	Rhyl County Court
South Anglesey	Caernarfon County Court
South Pembrokeshire	Swansea County Court
Swansea	Swansea County Court
Talybont	Caernarfon County Court
Upper Rhymney Valley	Pontypridd County Court
Vale of Glamorgan	Cardiff County Court
Vale Royal	Chester County Court
Warrington	Warrington County Court
Welshpool	Chester County Court
Wrexham Maelor	Rhyl County Court
Ystradgynlais	Swansea County Court

Western Circuit

Alton	Portsmouth County Court
Andover	Portsmouth County Court
Axminster	Taunton County Court
Barnstaple	Taunton County Court
Basingstoke	Portsmouth County Court
Bath and Wansdyke	Bristol County Court
Bideford and Great Torrington	Taunton County Court
Blandford and Sturminster	Bournemouth County Court
Bodmin	Truro County Court
Bournemouth	Bournemouth County Court
Bristol	Bristol County Court
Bridport	Bournemouth County Court
Cheltenham	Bristol County Court
Christchurch	Bournemouth County Court

Cirencester, Fairford and Tetbury	Swindon County Court
Cullompton	Taunton County Court
Dorchester	Bournemouth County Court
Droxford	Portsmouth County Court
Dunheved and Stratton	Truro County Court
Eastleigh	Portsmouth County Court
East Penwith	Truro County Court
East Powder	Truro County Court
Exeter	Plymouth County Court
Exmouth	Plymouth County Court
Falmouth and Kerrier	Truro County Court
Fareham	Portsmouth County Court
Forest of Dean	Bristol County Court
Gloucester	Bristol County Court
Gosport	Portsmouth County Court
Havant	Portsmouth County Court
Honiton	Taunton County Court
Hythe	Bournemouth County Court
Isle of Wight	Portsmouth County Court
Isles of Scilly	Truro County Court
Kennet	Swindon County Court
Kingsbridge	Plymouth County Court
Long Ashton	Bristol County Court
Lymington	Bournemouth County Court
Mendip	Taunton County Court
North Avon	Bristol County Court
North Cotswold	Bristol County Court
North Wiltshire	Swindon County Court
Odiham	Portsmouth County Court
Okehampton	Plymouth County Court
Penwith	Truro County Court
Petersfield	Portsmouth County Court
Plymouth	Plymouth County Court
Plympton	Plymouth County Court

Portsmouth	Portsmouth County Court
Poole	Bournemouth County Court
Pydar	Truro County Court
Ringwood	Bournemouth County Court
Romsey	Bournemouth County Court
Salisbury	Swindon County Court
Sedgemoor	Taunton County Court
Shaftesbury	Bournemouth County Court
Sherborne	Bournemouth County Court
Southampton	Portsmouth County Court
South East Cornwall	Plymouth County Court
South Gloucestershire	Bristol County Court
South Molton	Taunton County Court
South Somerset	Taunton County Court
Swindon	Swindon County Court
Taunton Deane	Taunton County Court
Tavistock	Plymouth County Court
Teignbridge	Plymouth County Court
Tewkesbury	Bristol County Court
Tiverton	Taunton County Court
Torbay	Plymouth County Court
Totnes	Plymouth County Court
Totton and New Forest	Bournemouth County Court
Truro and South Powder	Truro County Court
Wareham and Swanage	Bournemouth County Court
West Somerset	Taunton County Court
Weston-Super-Mare	Bristol County Court
West Wiltshire	Swindon County Court
Weymouth and Portland	Bournemouth County Court
Wimborne	Bournemouth County Court
Winchester	Portsmouth County Court
Wonford	Plymouth County Court

(i)	*(ii)*
London Commission Area	*Care Centre*
Inner London Area and City of London	Principal Registry of the Family Division

4.9 CHILDREN (ALLOCATION OF PROCEEDINGS) (APPEALS) ORDER 1991, SI 1991/1801

1 Citation, commencement and interpretation

(1) This Order may be cited as the Children (Allocation of Proceedings) (Appeals) Order 1991 and shall come into force on 14 October 1991.

(2) In this Order –

'district judge' includes an assistant district judge and a deputy district judge; and
'circuit judge' means any person who is capable of sitting as a judge for a county court district and who is allocated to hear appeals permitted by this Order in accordance with directions given under section 9 of the Courts and Legal Services Act 1990.

2 Appeals

Where a district judge orders the transfer of proceedings to a magistrates' court in accordance with article 11 of the Children (Allocation of Proceedings) Order 1991 an appeal may be made against that decision –

(a) to a judge of the Family Division of the High Court, or
(b) except where the order was made by a district judge or deputy district judge of the principal registry of the Family Division, to a circuit judge.

4.10 CHILDREN LEAVING CARE (ENGLAND) REGULATIONS 2001, SI 2001/2874[1] (ss 1–12, Sch)

1 Citation, commencement and extent

(1) These Regulations may be cited as the Children (Leaving Care) (England) Regulations 2001 and shall come into force on 1st October 2001.

(2) These Regulations extend to England only.

2 Interpretation

(1) In these Regulations, unless the context otherwise requires –

'the Act' means the Children Act 1989;

'placement' means the provision of accommodation and maintenance by a local authority for a child they are looking after by any of the means specified in section 23(2)(a) to (d) or (f) of the Act;

'responsible authority' –

    (a) in relation to an eligible child, means the local authority looking after him; and

    (b) in relation to a relevant child or a former relevant child, has the meaning given to it by section 23A(4) of the Act.

(2) In these Regulations, a reference –

    (a) to a numbered regulation or Schedule is to the regulation in, or Schedule to, these Regulations bearing that number;

    (b) in a regulation or Schedule to a numbered paragraph, is to the paragraph in that regulation or Schedule bearing that number.

3 Eligible children

(1) For the purposes of paragraph 19B(2)(b) of Schedule 2 to the Act, the prescribed period is 13 weeks and the prescribed age is 14.

(2) A child falling within paragraph (3) is not an eligible child despite falling within paragraph 19B(2) of Schedule 2 to the Act.

(3) A child falls within this paragraph if he has been looked after by a local authority in circumstances where –

    (a) the local authority has arranged to place him in a pre-planned series of short-term placements, none of which individually exceeds four weeks (even though they may amount in all to the prescribed period); and

    (b) at the end of each such placement the child returns to the care of his parent, or a person who is not a parent but who has parental responsibility for him.

---

[1] The equivalent regulations in Wales are the Children Leaving Care (Wales) Regulations 2001, SI 2001/2189.

4 Relevant children

(1) For the purposes of section 23A(3), children falling within paragraph (2) are an additional category of relevant children.

(2) Subject to paragraph (3) a child falls within this paragraph if –

    (a) he is aged 16 or 17;

    (b) he is not subject to a care order; and

    (c) at the time when he attained the age of 16 he was detained or in hospital and immediately before he was detained or admitted to hospital he had been looked after by a local authority for a period or periods amounting in all to at least 13 weeks, which began after he reached the age of 14.

(3) In calculating the period of 13 weeks referred to in paragraph (2)(c), no account is to be taken of any period in which the child was looked after by a local authority in any of a pre-planned series of short-term placements, none of which individually exceeded four weeks, where at the end of each such placement the child returned to the care of his parent, or a person who is not a parent but who has parental responsibility for him.

(4) For the purposes of this regulation –

    (a) 'detained' means detained in a remand centre, a young offenders institution or a secure training centre, or any other institution pursuant to an order of a court; and

    (b) 'hospital' means –

        (i) any health service hospital within the meaning of the National Health Service Act 1977; or

        (ii) any mental nursing home being a home in respect of which the particulars of registration are for the time being entered in the separate part of the register kept for the purposes of section 23(5)(b) of the Registered Homes Act 1984.

(5) Subject to paragraph (7), any child who has lived with a person falling within section 23(4) of the Act ('a family placement') for a continuous period of six months or more is not to be a relevant child despite falling within section 23A(2) of the Act.

(6) Paragraph (5) applies whether the period of six months commences before or after a child ceases to be looked after by a local authority.

(7) Where a family placement within the meaning of paragraph (5) breaks down and the child ceases to live with the person concerned, the child is to be treated as a relevant child.

5 Assessments and pathway plans – general

(1) The responsible authority must prepare a written statement describing the manner in which the needs of each eligible and relevant child will be assessed.

(2) The written statement must include, in relation to each child whose needs are to be assessed, information about, in particular –

    (a) the person responsible for the conduct and co-ordination of the assessment;

    (b) the timetable for the assessment;

    (c) who is to be consulted for the purposes of the assessment;

(d) the arrangements for recording the outcome of the assessment;

(e) the procedure for making representations in the event of a disagreement.

(3) The responsible authority must make a copy of the statement available to the child and the persons specified in regulation 7(5).

(4) Nothing in these Regulations shall prevent the carrying out of any assessment or review under these Regulations at the same time as any assessment, review or consideration under any other enactment.

6 Involvement of the child or young person

(1) The responsible authority in carrying out an assessment and in preparing or reviewing a pathway plan shall, unless it is not reasonably practicable –

(a) seek and have regard to the views of the child or young person to whom it relates; and

(b) take all reasonable steps to enable him to attend and participate in any meetings at which his case is to be considered.

(2) The responsible authority shall without delay provide the child or young person with copies of –

(a) the results of his assessment,

(b) his pathway plan, and

(c) each review of his pathway plan,

and shall ensure that the contents of each document are explained to him in accordance with his level of understanding unless it is not reasonably practicable to do so.

7 Assessment of needs

(1) The responsible authority shall assess the needs of each eligible child, and each relevant child who does not already have a pathway plan, in accordance with these Regulations.

(2) The assessment is to be completed –

(a) in the case of an eligible child, not more than three months after the date on which he reaches the age of 16 or becomes an eligible child after that age; and

(b) in the case of a relevant child who does not already have a pathway plan, not more than three months after the date on which he becomes a relevant child.

(3) Each responsible authority shall ensure that a written record is kept of –

(a) the information obtained in the course of an assessment;

(b) the deliberations at any meeting held in connection with any aspect of an assessment; and

(c) the results of the assessment.

(4) In carrying out an assessment the responsible authority shall take account of the following considerations –

(a) the child's health and development;

(b) the child's need for education, training or employment;

(c) the support available to the child from members of his family and other persons;

(d) the child's financial needs;

(e) the extent to which the child possesses the practical and other skills necessary for independent living; and

(f) the child's needs for care, support and accommodation.

(5) The responsible authority shall, unless it is not reasonably practicable to do so, seek and take into account the views of –

(a) the child's parents;

(b) any person who is not a parent but has parental responsibility for the child;

(c) any person who on a day to day basis cares for, or provides accommodation for the child;

(d) any school or college attended by the child, or the local education authority for the area in which he lives;

(e) any independent visitor appointed for the child;

(f) any person providing health care or treatment to the child;

(g) the personal adviser appointed for the child; and

(h) any other person whose views the responsible authority, or the child consider may be relevant.

8 Pathway plans

(1) A pathway plan prepared under paragraph 19B of Schedule 2 to, or section 23B of, the Act, must be prepared as soon as possible after the assessment and must include, in particular, the matters referred to in the Schedule.

(2) The pathway plan must, in relation to each of the matters referred to in the Schedule, set out –

(a) the manner in which the responsible authority proposes to meet the needs of the child; and

(b) the date by which, and by whom, any action required to implement any aspect of the plan will be carried out.

(3) The pathway plan must be recorded in writing.

9 Review of pathway plans

(1) The responsible authority shall review the pathway plan of each eligible, relevant and former relevant child in accordance with this regulation.

(2) The responsible authority shall arrange a review –

(a) if requested to do so by the child or young person;

(b) if it, or the personal adviser considers a review necessary; and

(c) in any other case, at intervals of not more than six months.

(3) In carrying out a review, the responsible authority shall, to the extent it considers it appropriate to do so, seek and take account of the views of the persons mentioned in regulation 7(5).

(4) The responsible authority conducting a review must consider –

(a) in the case of an eligible or relevant child, whether, in relation to each of the matters set out in the Schedule, any change to the pathway plan is necessary; and

(b) in the case of a former relevant child, whether in relation to the matters set out in paragraphs 1, 3 and 4 of the Schedule, any change to the pathway plan is necessary.

(5) The results of the review must be recorded in writing.

10 Retention and confidentiality of records

(1) Records relating to assessments, pathway plans and their review shall be retained by the responsible authority until the seventy-fifth anniversary of the date of birth of the child or young person to whom they relate, or if the child dies before attaining the age of 18, for a period of fifteen years beginning with the date of his death.

(2) The requirement in paragraph (1) may be complied with by retaining the original written records or copies of them, or by keeping all or part of the information contained in them in some other accessible form such as a computer record.

(3) The records mentioned in paragraph (1) must be kept securely and may not be disclosed to any person except in accordance with –

(a) any provision of, or made under, or by virtue of, a statute under which access to such records is authorised; or

(b) any court order authorising access to such records.

11 Support and accommodation

(1) For the purposes of section 23B(8)(c) (support for relevant children), the responsible local authority must provide assistance in order to meet the child's needs in relation to education, training or employment as provided for in his pathway plan.

(2) For the purposes of section 23B(10), 'suitable accommodation' means accommodation –

(a) which so far as reasonably practicable is suitable for the child in the light of his needs, including his health needs and any needs arising from any disability;

(b) in respect of which the responsible authority has satisfied itself as to the character and suitability of the landlord or other provider; and

(c) in respect of which the responsible authority has so far as reasonably practicable taken into account the child's –
(i) wishes and feelings; and
(ii) education, training or employment needs.

(3) For the purposes of section 24B(5) (provision of vacation accommodation) –

(a) 'higher education' means education provided by means of a course of a description referred to in regulations made under section 22 of the Teaching and Higher Education Act 1998;

(b) 'further education' has the same meaning as in the Education Act 1996 save that for the purposes of this regulation it only includes further education which is provided on a full-time residential basis.

12 Functions of personal advisers

A personal adviser shall have the following functions in relation to an eligible or a relevant child or a young person who is a former relevant child –

(a) to provide advice (including practical advice) and support;

(b) where applicable, to participate in his assessment and the preparation of his pathway plan;

(c) to participate in reviews of the pathway plan;

(d) to liaise with the responsible authority in the implementation of the pathway plan;

(e) to co-ordinate the provision of services, and to take reasonable steps to ensure that he makes use of such services;

(f) to keep informed about his progress and wellbeing; and

(g) to keep a written record of contacts with him.

****

SCHEDULE

MATTERS TO BE DEALT WITH IN THE PATHWAY PLAN AND REVIEW

1. The nature and level of contact and personal support to be provided, and by whom, to the child or young person.

2. Details of the accommodation the child or young person is to occupy.

3. A detailed plan for the education or training of the child or young person.

4. How the responsible authority will assist the child or young person in relation to employment or other purposeful activity or occupation.

5. The support to be provided to enable the child or young person to develop and sustain appropriate family and social relationships.

6. A programme to develop the practical and other skills necessary for the child or young person to live independently.

7. The financial support to be provided to the child or young person, in particular where it is to be provided to meet his accommodation and maintenance needs.

8. The health needs, including any mental health needs, of the child or young person, and how they are to be met.

9. Contingency plans for action to be taken by the responsible authority should the pathway plan for any reason cease to be effective.

4.11 CHILDREN (PRIVATE ARRANGEMENTS FOR FOSTERING) REGULATIONS 1991, SI 1991/2050

1 Citation, commencement and interpretation

(1) These Regulations may be cited as the Children (Private Arrangements for Fostering) Regulations 1991 and shall come into force on 14th October 1991.

(2) In these Regulations, unless the context otherwise requires –

    (a) 'the Act' means the Children Act 1989;

    (b) 'address' includes a temporary address;

    (c) any reference to a numbered regulation is to the regulation in these Regulations bearing that number and any reference in a regulation to a numbered paragraph is to the paragraph of that regulation bearing that number.

2 General welfare of children

(1) In carrying out functions under section 67 of the Act, as to the welfare of children who are privately fostered within their area, a local authority (including any officer of the authority making a visit under regulation 3) shall satisfy themselves as to such of the matters specified in paragraph (2) as are relevant in the particular circumstances.

(2) The matters referred to in paragraph (1) are –

    (a) the purpose and intended duration of the fostering arrangement;

    (b) the child's physical, intellectual, emotional, social and behavioural development;

    (c) whether the child's needs arising from his religious persuasion, racial origin and cultural and linguistic background are being met;

    (d) the financial arrangements for the care and maintenance of the child;

    (e) the suitability of the accommodation;

    (f) the arrangements for the child's medical and dental care and treatment and, in particular, that the child is included on the list of a general medical practitioner who provides general medical services under Part II of the National Health Service Act 1977, or the list of a doctor performing personal medical services in connection with a pilot scheme under the National Health Service (Primary Care) Act 1997 (or a list held jointly by two or more such doctors in connection with a pilot scheme under that Act);

    (g) the arrangements for the child's education and, in particular, that the local education authority have been informed of the fostering arrangement;

    (h) the standard of care which the child is being given;

    (i) the suitability of the foster parent to look after the child and the suitability of the foster parent's household;

    (j) whether the foster parent is being given any necessary advice;

    (k) whether the contact between the child and his parents, or any other person with whom contact has been arranged, is satisfactory;

(l) whether the child's parents, or any other person, are exercising parental responsibility for the child; and

(m) the ascertainable wishes and feelings of the child regarding the fostering arrangements.

3 Visits to children

(1) A local authority shall make arrangements for each child who is privately fostered within their area to be visited by an officer of the authority from time to time as the authority consider necessary in order to safeguard and promote the welfare of the child and when reasonably requested by the child or foster parent and in particular –

(a) in the first year of the fostering arrangement, within one week from its beginning and then at intervals of not more than six weeks;

(b) in any second or subsequent year, at intervals of not more than three months.

(2) For the purpose of making visits under this regulation the officer shall, if he considers it appropriate, arrange to see the child alone.

(3) The officer shall make a written report to the local authority after each visit.

4 Notifications by prospective and actual foster parents

(1) Any person who proposes to foster privately a child for whom he is not already caring and providing accommodation shall notify the appropriate local authority not less than six, nor more than thirteen, weeks before he receives the child, unless he receives him in an emergency.

(2) A person who is privately fostering a child –

(a) whom he received in an emergency; or

(b) for whom he was already caring and providing accommodation when he became a foster child,

shall notify the appropriate local authority not more than 48 hours after the fostering arrangements began.

(3) A notice under paragraph (1) or (2) shall specify –

(a) the name, sex, date and place of birth, religious persuasion, racial origin and cultural and linguistic background of the child;

(b) the name and address of the person giving the notice and any previous address within the last 5 years;

(c) the purpose and intended duration of the fostering arrangement;

(d) the name and address of any parent of the child and of any other person who has parental responsibility for the child and (if different) of any person from whom the child was, or is to be, received;

(e) the name and address of any person, other than a person specified in sub-paragraph (d) above, who is involved directly or indirectly in making the fostering arrangement; and

(f) the intended date of the beginning of the fostering arrangement or, as the case may be, the date on which the arrangement actually began.

(4) A person giving notice under paragraph (1) or (2) shall include in the notice particulars of –

    (a) any offence of which he has been convicted;

    (b) any disqualification or prohibition imposed on him under (as the case may be) section 68 or 69 of the Act or under any previous enactment of either of those sections; and

    (c) any such conviction, disqualification or prohibition imposed on any other person living in, or employed at, the same household.

(5) Any person who is fostering a child privately shall notify the appropriate local authority of –

    (a) any change in his address;

    (b) any person who begins, or ceases, to be part of his household; and

    (c) any further conviction, disqualification or prohibition as mentioned in sub-paragraphs (a) to (c) of paragraph (4).

(6) A notice under paragraph (5) shall be given –

    (a) in advance if practicable; and

    (b) in any other case, not more than 48 hours after the change of circumstances,

and if the new address is in the area of another local authority, or of a local authority in Scotland, the authority to whom the notice is given shall inform the other authority of the new address and of the particulars given to them under sub-paragraphs (a) and (d) of paragraph (3).

(7) Paragraphs (4)(a) and (c) and (5)(c) are subject to the Rehabilitation of Offenders Act 1974.

5 Notifications by former foster parents

(1) Subject to paragraphs (2) and (3), any person who has been fostering a child privately, but has ceased to do so, shall notify the appropriate local authority within 48 hours and shall include in the notice the name and address of the person into whose care the child was received.

(2) Where the reason for the ending of the fostering arrangement is the death of the child the foster parent shall notify forthwith the local authority and also the person from whom the foster parent received the child.

(3) Paragraph (1) shall not apply where the foster parent intends to resume the fostering arrangement after an interval of not more than 27 days but if –

    (a) he subsequently abandons his intention; or

    (b) the interval expires without his having given effect to his intention,

he shall thereupon give notice to the local authority within 48 hours of abandoning his intention or as the case may be the expiry of the interval.

6 Other notifications

(1) Any person who is, or proposes to be, involved (whether or not directly) in arranging for a child to be fostered privately shall notify the appropriate local authority not less than six, nor more than thirteen, weeks before the fostering arrangement begins unless the fostering arrangement is made in an emergency in which case the notification shall be not more than 48 hours after the fostering arrangement begins.

(2) A parent of a child, and any other person who has parental responsibility for the child, who knows that it is proposed that the child should be fostered privately shall notify the appropriate local authority not less than six, nor more than thirteen, weeks before the fostering arrangement begins unless the fostering arrangement is made in an emergency in which case the notification shall be not more than 48 hours thereafter.

(3) Any notice under paragraph (1) or (2) shall specify –

    (a)   the information mentioned in sub-paragraphs (a) to (c) of regulation 4(3);

    (b)   the arrangements for the care of any brother or sister of the child who is not included in the fostering arrangement;

    (c)   the name and address of any other person involved (whether or not directly) in the fostering arrangement;

    (d)   where the notice is given under paragraph (1), the relationship to the child of the person giving the notice and also the information specified in sub-paragraph (d) of regulation 4(3).

(4) Any parent of a privately fostered child, and any other person who has parental responsibility for the child, shall notify the appropriate local authority of –

    (a)   the ending of the fostering arrangement; and

    (b)   any change in his own address.

7 Form of notifications

Any notice required under regulations 4 to 6 shall be given in writing and may be sent by post.

4.12 CHILDREN (SECURE ACCOMMODATION) REGULATIONS 1991, SI 1991/1505

1 Citation and commencement

These Regulations may be cited as the Children (Secure Accommodation) Regulations 1991 and shall come into force on 14th October 1991.

2 Interpretation

(1) In these Regulations, unless the context otherwise requires –

'the Act' means the Children Act 1989;

'children's home' means a private children's home, a community home or a voluntary home;

'independent visitor' means a person appointed under paragraph 17 of Schedule 2 to the Act;

'secure accommodation' means accommodation which is provided for the purpose of restricting the liberty of children to whom section 25 of the Act (use of accommodation for restricting liberty) applies.

(2) Any reference in these regulations to a numbered regulation shall be construed as a reference to the regulation bearing that number in these Regulations, and any reference in a regulation to a numbered paragraph is a reference to the paragraph bearing that number in that regulation.

3 Approval by Secretary of State of secure accommodation in a children's home

Accommodation in a children's home shall not be used as secure accommodation unless it has been approved by the Secretary of State for such use and approval shall be subject to such terms and conditions as he sees fit.

4 Placement of a child aged under 13 in secure accommodation in a children's home

A child under the age of 13 years shall not be placed in secure accommodation in a children's home without the prior approval of the Secretary of State to the placement of that child and such approval shall be subject to such terms and conditions as he sees fit.

5 Children to whom section 25 of the Act shall not apply

(1) Section 25 of the Act shall not apply to a child who is detained under any provision of the Mental Health Act 1983 or in respect of whom an order has been made under section 90 or 91 of the Powers of the Criminal Courts (Sentencing) Act 2000 (detention at Her Majesty's pleasure or for specified period).

(2) Section 25 of the Act shall not apply to a child –

   (a) to whom section 20(5) of the Act (accommodation of persons over 16 but under 21) applies and who is being accommodated under that section,

   (b) in respect of whom an order has been made under section 43 of the Act (child assessment order) and who is kept away from home pursuant to that order.

6 Detained and remanded children to whom section 25 of the Act shall have effect subject to modifications

(1) Subject to regulation 5, section 25 of the Act shall have effect subject to the modification specified in paragraph (2) in relation to children who are being looked after by a local authority and are of the following descriptions –

   (a) children detained under section 38(6) of the Police and Criminal Evidence Act 1984 (detained children), and

   (b) children remanded to local authority accommodation under section 23 of the Children and Young Persons Act 1969 (remand to local authority accommodation) but only if –

      (i) the child is charged with or has been convicted of a violent or sexual offence, or of an offence punishable in the case of an adult with imprisonment for a term of 14 years or more, or

     (ii) the child has a recent history of absconding while remanded to local authority accommodation, and is charged with or has been convicted of an imprisonable offence alleged or found to have been committed while he was so remanded.

(2) The modification referred to in paragraph (1) is that, for the words 'unless it appears' to the end of subsection (1), there shall be substituted the following words –

   'unless it appears that any accommodation other than that provided for the purpose of restricting liberty is inappropriate because –

   (a)   the child is likely to abscond from such other accommodation, or
   (b)   the child is likely to injure himself or other people if he is kept in any such other accommodation'.

7 Children to whom section 25 of the Act shall apply and have effect subject to modifications

(1) Subject to regulation 5 and paragraphs (2) and (3) of this regulation section 25 of the Act shall apply (in addition to children looked after by a local authority) –

   (a) to children, other than those looked after by a local authority, who are accommodated by health authorities, Primary Care Trusts, National Health Service trusts established under section 5 of the National Health Service and Community Care Act 1990 or local education authorities, and

   (b) to children, other than those looked after by a local authority, who are accommodated in care homes or independent hospitals.

(2) In relation to the children of a description specified in paragraph (1)(a) section 25 of the Act shall have effect subject to the following modifications –

   (a) for the words 'who is being looked after by a local authority' in subsection (1) there shall be substituted the words 'who is being provided with accommodation by a health authority, a Primary Care Trust, a National

Health Service trust established under section 5 of the National Health Service and Community Care Act 1990 or a local education authority'.

(b) for the words 'local authorities' in subsection (2)(c) there shall be substituted the words 'health authorities, Primary Care Trusts, National Health Service trusts or local education authorities'.

(3) In relation to the children of a description specified in paragraph (1)(b), section 25 of the Act shall have effect subject to the following modifications –

(a) for the words 'who is being looked after by a local authority' in subsection (1) there shall be substituted the words 'who is being provided with accommodation in a residential care home, a nursing home or a mental nursing home'; and

(b) for the words 'local authorities' in subsection (2)(c) there shall be substituted the words 'persons carrying on care homes or independent hospitals'.

8 Applications to court

Subject to section 101 of the Local Government Act 1972 or to provisions in or under sections 14 to 20 of the Local Government Act 2000, applications to a court under section 25 of the Act in respect of a child shall be made only by the local authority which are looking after that child.

9 Duty to give information of placement in children's homes

Where a child is placed in secure accommodation in a children's home which is managed by a person, organisation or authority other than the local authority which is looking after him, the person who, or the organisation or the authority which manages that accommodation shall inform the authority which are looking after him that he has been placed there, within 12 hours of his being placed there, with a view to obtaining their authority to continue to keep him there if necessary.

10 Maximum period in secure accommodation without court authority

(1) Subject to paragraphs (2) and (3), the maximum period beyond which a child to whom section 25 of the Act applies may not be kept in secure accommodation without the authority of a court is an aggregate of 72 hours (whether or not consecutive) in any period of 28 consecutive days.

(2) Where authority of a court to keep a child in secure accommodation has been given, any period during which the child has been kept in such accommodation before the giving of that authority shall be disregarded for the purposes of calculating the maximum period in relation to any subsequent occasion on which the child is placed in such accommodation after the period authorised by the court has expired.

(3) Where a child is in secure accommodation at any time between 12 midday on the day before and 12 midday on the day after a public holiday or a Sunday, and

(a) during that period the maximum period specified in paragraph (1) expires, and

(b) the child had, in the 27 days before the day on which he was placed in secure accommodation, been placed and kept in such accommodation for an aggregate of more than 48 hours, the maximum period does not expire until 12 midday on the first day, which is not itself a public holiday or a Sunday, after the public holiday or Sunday.

11 Maximum initial period of authorisation by a court

Subject to regulations 12 and 13 the maximum period for which a court may authorise a child to whom section 25 of the Act applies to be kept in secure accommodation is three months.

12 Further periods of authorisation by a court

Subject to regulation 13 a court may from time to time authorise a child to whom section 25 of the Act applies to be kept in secure accommodation for a further period not exceeding 6 months at any one time.

13 Maximum periods of authorisation by court for remanded children

(1) The maximum period for which a court may from time to time authorise a child who has been remanded to local authority accommodation under section 23 of the Children and Young Persons Act 1969 to be kept in secure accommodation (whether the period is an initial period or a further period) is the period of the remand.

(2) Any period of authorisation in respect of such a child shall not exceed 28 days on any one occasion without further court authorisation.

14 Duty to inform parents and others in relation to children in secure accommodation in a children's home

Where a child to whom section 25 of the Act applies is kept in secure accommodation in a children's home and it is intended that an application will be made to a court to keep the child in that accommodation, the local authority which are looking after the child shall if practicable inform of that intention as soon as possible –

  (a) his parents,
  (b) any person who is not a parent of his but who has parental responsibility for him,
  (c) the child's independent visitor, if one has been appointed, and
  (d) any other person who that local authority consider should be informed.

15 Appointment of persons to review placement in secure accommodation in a children's home

Each local authority looking after a child in secure accommodation in a children's home shall appoint at least three persons, at least one of whom is neither a member nor an officer of the local authority by or on behalf of which the child is being looked after, who shall review the keeping of the child in such accommodation for the purposes of securing his welfare within one month of the inception of the placement and then at intervals not exceeding three months where the child continues to be kept in such accommodation.

16 Review of placement in secure accommodation in a children's home

(1) The persons appointed under regulation 15 to review the keeping of a child in secure accommodation shall satisfy themselves as to whether or not –

(a)   the criteria for keeping the child in secure accommodation continue to apply;
(b)   the placement in such accommodation in a children's home continues to be necessary; and
(c)   any other description of accommodation would be appropriate for him,

and in doing so shall have regard to the welfare of the child whose case is being reviewed.

(2) In undertaking the review referred to in regulation 15 the persons appointed shall, if practicable, ascertain and take into account the wishes and feelings of –

(a)   the child,
(b)   any parent of his,
(c)   any person not being a parent of his but who has parental responsibility for him,
(d)   any other person who has had the care of the child, whose views the persons appointed consider should be taken into account,
(e)   the child's independent visitor if one has been appointed, and
(f)   the person, organisation or local authority managing the secure accommodation in which the child is placed if that accommodation is not managed by the authority which is looking after that child.

(3) The local authority shall, if practicable, inform all those whose views are required to be taken into account under paragraph (2) of the outcome of the review what action, if any, the local authority propose to take in relation to the child in the light of the review, and their reasons for taking or not taking such action.

17 Records to be kept in respect of a child in secure accommodation in a children's home

Whenever a child is placed in secure accommodation in a children's home the person, organisation or local authority which manages that accommodation shall ensure that a record is kept of –

(a)   the name, date of birth and sex of that child,
(b)   the care order or other statutory provision by virtue of which the child is in the children's home and in either case particulars of the local authority involved with the placement of the child in that home,
(c)   the date and time of his placement in secure accommodation, the reason for his placement, the name of the officer authorising the placement and where the child was living before the placement,
(d)   all those informed by virtue of regulation 9, regulation 14 or regulation 16(3) in their application to the child,
(e)   court orders made in respect of the child by virtue of section 25 of the Act,
(f)   reviews undertaken in respect of the child by virtue of regulation 15,
(g)   the date and time of any occasion on which the child is locked on his own in any room in the secure accommodation other than his bedroom during usual bedtime hours, the name of the person authorising this action, the reason for it and the date on which and time at which the child ceases to be locked in that room, and
(h)   the date and time of his discharge and his address following discharge from secure accommodation,

and the Secretary of State may require copies of these records to be sent to him at any time.

4.13 CHILDREN (SECURE ACCOMMODATION) (NO 2) REGULATIONS 1991, SI 1991/2034

1 Citation and commencement

(1) These Regulations may be cited as the Children (Secure Accommodation) (No 2) Regulations 1991 and shall come into force on 14th October 1991 immediately after the Children (Secure Accommodation) Regulations 1991.

2 Applications to court – special cases

(1) Applications to a court under section 25 of the Children Act 1989 in respect of a child provided with accommodation by a health authority , a Primary Care Trust, a National Health Service trust established under section 5 of the National Health Service and Community Care Act 1990 or a local education authority shall, unless the child is looked after by a local authority, be made only by the health authority Primary Care Trust, National Health Service trust or local education authority providing accommodation for the child.

(2) Applications to a court under section 25 of the Children Act 1989 in respect of a child provided with accommodation in a care home or an independent hospital shall, unless the child is looked after by a local authority, be made only by the person carrying on the home in which accommodation is provided for the child.

4.14 CHILDREN'S HOMES REGULATIONS 2001, SI 2001/3967
(regs 1–5, 11–24, 28–30, Schs 1, 3–5)

PART I

GENERAL

1 Citation, commencement and extent

(1) These Regulations may be cited as the Children's Homes Regulations 2001 and shall come into force on 1st April 2002.

(2) These Regulations extend to England only.

2 Interpretation

(1) In these Regulations –

'the Act' means the Care Standards Act 2000;
'the 1989 Act' means the Children Act 1989;
'child protection enquiry' has the meaning given to it by regulation 16(3);
'children's guide' means the guide produced in accordance with regulation 4(3);
'general practitioner' means a registered medical practitioner who –
    (a) provides general medical services under Part II of the National Health Service Act 1977;
    (b) performs personal medical services in connection with a pilot scheme under the National Health Service (Primary Care) Act 1997; or
    (c) provides services which correspond to services provided under Part II of the National Health Service Act 1977, otherwise than in pursuance of that Act;
'organisation', other than in regulation 17, means a body corporate or any unincorporated association other than a partnership;
'placement plan' means the written plan prepared in accordance with regulation 12(1);
'placing authority' in relation to a child accommodated in a children's home means –
    (a) in the case of a child who is looked after by a local authority, that local authority;
    (b) in the case of a child who is not looked after by a local authority -
        (i) if he is being provided with accommodation by a voluntary organisation, that voluntary organisation;
        (ii) if he is accommodated in a qualifying school under arrangements made by a local education authority or a local authority, that local education authority or local authority as the case may be;
        (iii) in any other case, the child's parent;

'qualifying school' means a school which is a children's home within the meaning of section 1(6) of the Act;

'registered dental practitioner' means a person registered in the dentists register under the Dentists Act 1984;

'registered manager', in relation to a children's home, means a person who is registered under Part II of the Act as the manager of that home;

'registered person', in relation to a children's home, means any person who is the registered provider or the registered manager of the home;

'registered provider', in relation to a children's home, means a person who is registered under Part II of the Act as the person carrying on that home[9];

'responsible individual' shall be construed in accordance with regulation 6(2)(c); and

'statement of purpose' means the written statement compiled in accordance with regulation 4(1).

(2) In these Regulations, a reference –

(a) to a numbered regulation or Schedule is to the regulation in, or Schedule to, these Regulations bearing that number;

(b) in a regulation or Schedule to a numbered paragraph, is to the paragraph in that regulation or Schedule bearing that number;

(c) in a paragraph to a lettered or numbered sub-paragraph, is to the sub-paragraph in that paragraph bearing that letter or number.

(3) In these Regulations, references to employing a person include employing a person whether or not for payment, and whether under a contract of service or a contract for services, and allowing a person to work as a volunteer, and references to an employee or to a person being employed shall be construed accordingly.

3 Excepted establishments

(1) For the purposes of the Act, establishments of the following descriptions are excepted from being a children's home –

(a) any institution within the further education sector as defined by section 91(3) of the Further and Higher Education Act 1992;

(b) subject to paragraph (2), any establishment providing accommodation for children for less than 28 days in any twelve month period in relation to any one child, for the purposes of –
  (i) a holiday; or
  (ii) recreational, sporting, cultural or educational activities;

(c) subject to paragraph (2), any premises at which a person provides day care within the meaning of Part XA of the 1989 Act for less than 28 days in any twelve month period in relation to any one child;

(d) subject to paragraph (2), any establishment providing accommodation for children aged 16 and over –
  (i) to enable them to undergo training or apprenticeship;
  (ii) for the purposes of a holiday; or
  (iii) for recreational, sporting, cultural or educational purposes;

(e) any approved bail hostel or approved probation hostel; and

(f) any institution provided for young offenders under or by virtue of section 43(1) of the Prison Act 1952.

(2) The exceptions in paragraphs (1)(b), (c) and (d) do not apply to any establishment or premises in which the children who are accommodated are wholly or mainly of a description falling within section 3(2) of the Act.

(3) For the purposes of calculating the period of 28 days mentioned in paragraph (1)(c), no account is to be taken of any period of 24 hours during which at least 9 hours are spent by a child in the care of his parent or relative, and day care is not provided for him during that time.

4 Statement of purpose and children's guide

(1) The registered person shall compile in relation to the children's home a written statement (in these Regulations referred to as 'the statement of purpose') which shall consist of a statement as to the matters listed in Schedule 1.

(2) The registered person shall provide a copy of the statement of purpose to the Commission and shall make a copy of it available upon request for inspection by –

    (a) any person who works at the children's home;
    (b) any child accommodated in the children's home;
    (c) the parent of any child accommodated in the children's home;
    (d) the placing authority of any child accommodated in the home; and
    (e) in the case of a qualifying school, the Secretary of State, and Her Majesty's Inspector of Schools in England,

and in this paragraph references to a child who is accommodated in the children's home include a child in respect of whom accommodation in the children's home is being considered.

(3) The registered person shall produce a guide to the children's home (in these Regulations referred to as 'the children's guide') which shall include –

    (a) a summary of the home's statement of purpose;
    (b) a summary of the complaints procedure established under regulation 24; and
    (c) the address and telephone number of the Commission.

(4) The children's guide shall be produced in a form appropriate to the age, understanding and communication needs of the children to be accommodated in the home.

(5) The registered person shall supply a copy of the children's guide to the Commission and, on admission, to each child accommodated in the home.

(6) Subject to paragraph (7), the registered person shall ensure that the children's home is at all times conducted in a manner which is consistent with its statement of purpose.

(7) Nothing in paragraph (6) or in regulation 31 shall require or authorise the registered person to contravene or not comply with –

    (a) any other provision of these Regulations; or
    (b) the conditions for the time being in force in relation to the registration of the registered person under Part II of the Act.

5 Review of the statement of purpose and children's guide

The registered person shall –

(a) keep under review and, where appropriate, revise the statement of purpose and the children's guide;

(b) notify the Commission of any such revision within 28 days; and

(c) if the children's guide is revised, supply a copy to each child accommodated in the home.

****

PART III

CONDUCT OF CHILDREN'S HOMES

Chapter 1
Welfare of children

11 Promotion of welfare

(1) The registered person shall ensure that the children's home is conducted so as to –

(a) promote and make proper provision for the welfare of children accommodated there; and

(b) make proper provision for the care, education, supervision and, where appropriate, treatment, of children accommodated there.

(2) The registered person shall make suitable arrangements to ensure that the home is conducted –

(a) in a manner which respects the privacy and dignity of children accommodated there; and

(b) with due regard to the sex, religious persuasion, racial origin, and cultural and linguistic background and any disability of children accommodated there.

12 Child's placement plan

(1) The registered person shall, before providing accommodation for a child in a children's home, or if that is not reasonably practicable, as soon as possible thereafter, prepare in consultation with the child's placing authority a written plan (in these Regulations referred to as the 'placement plan') for the child setting out, in particular –

(a) how, on a day to day basis, he will be cared for, and his welfare safeguarded and promoted by the home;

(b) the arrangements made for his health care and education; and

(c) any arrangements made for contact with his parents, relatives and friends.

(2) The registered person shall keep under review and revise the placement plan as necessary.

(3) In preparing or reviewing the placement plan the registered person shall, so far as practicable having regard to the child's age and understanding, seek and take account of his views.

(4) The registered person shall so far as is reasonably practicable –

  (a) ensure that the placement plan is consistent with any plan for the care of the child prepared by his placing authority; and
  (b) comply with requests made by the child's placing authority to –

    (i) provide it with information relating to the child; and
    (ii) provide a suitable representative to attend any meetings it may hold concerning the child.

13 Food provided for children

(1) The registered person shall ensure that children accommodated in a children's home are provided with –

  (a) food which –
    (i) is served in adequate quantities and at appropriate intervals;
    (ii) is properly prepared, wholesome and nutritious;
    (iii) is suitable for their needs and meets their reasonable preferences; and
    (iv) is sufficiently varied; and
  (b) access to fresh drinking water at all times.

(2) The registered person shall ensure that any special dietary need of a child accommodated in the home, which is due to his health, religious persuasion, racial origin or cultural background, is met.

14 Provision of clothing, pocket money and personal necessities

(1) The registered person shall ensure that the needs and reasonable preferences of each child accommodated in the home for clothing including footwear, and personal necessities are met.

(2) The registered person shall provide children accommodated in the home with such sums of money in respect of their occasional personal expenses as is appropriate to their age and understanding.

15 Contact and access to communications

(1) The registered person shall –

  (a) subject to paragraphs (6) and (8), promote the contact of each child with his parents, relatives and friends in accordance with the arrangements set out in his placement plan; and
  (b) subject to paragraph (3), ensure that suitable facilities are provided within the children's home for any child accommodated there to meet privately at any reasonable time with his parents, relatives and friends, and the persons listed in paragraph (2).

(2) The persons are –

  (a) any solicitor or other adviser or advocate acting for the child;
  (b) any officer of the Children and Family Court Advisory and Support Service appointed for him;
  (c) any social worker for the time being assigned to the child by his placing authority;
  (d) any person appointed in respect of any requirement of the procedure specified in the Representations Procedure (Children) Regulations 1991;

(e) any person appointed as a visitor for him in accordance with paragraph 17 of Schedule 2 to the 1989 Act;

(f) any person authorised by the Commission;

(g) any person authorised by the local authority in whose area the children's home is situated;

(h) any person authorised in accordance with section 80(2) of the 1989 Act by the Secretary of State to conduct an inspection of the children's home and the children there.

(3) In the case of a home in respect of which a certificate under section 51 of the 1989 Act is in force, the facilities may be at a different address.

(4) Subject to paragraphs (6) and (8), the registered person shall ensure that children accommodated in the home are provided at all reasonable times with access to the following facilities which they may use without reference to persons working in the home –

(a) a telephone on which to make and receive telephone calls in private; and

(b) facilities to send and receive post and, if the necessary facilities are provided for the use of children accommodated in the home, electronic mail, in private.

(5) The registered person shall ensure that any disabled child accommodated in the home is provided with access to such aids and equipment which he may require as a result of his disability in order to facilitate his communication with others.

(6) The registered person may (subject to paragraphs (7) and (8)) impose such restriction, prohibition or condition upon a child's contact with any person under paragraph (1) or access to communications under paragraph (4) which he is satisfied is necessary for the purpose of safeguarding or promoting the welfare of the child in question.

(7) No measure may be imposed by the registered person in accordance with paragraph (6) unless –

(a) the child's placing authority consents to the imposition of the measure; or

(b) the measure is imposed in an emergency, and full details are given to the placing authority within 24 hours of its imposition.

(8) This regulation is subject to the provisions of any relevant order of the court relating to contact between the child and any person.

16 Arrangements for the protection of children

(1) The registered person shall prepare and implement a written policy which –

(a) is intended to safeguard children accommodated in the children's home from abuse or neglect; and

(b) sets out the procedure to be followed in the event of any allegation of abuse or neglect.

(2) The procedure under paragraph (1)(b) shall in particular provide for –

(a) liaison and co-operation with any local authority which is, or may be, making child protection enquiries in relation to any child accommodated in the children's home;

(b) the prompt referral to the local authority in whose area the children's home is situated, of any allegation of abuse or neglect affecting any child accommodated in the children's home;

(c) notification (in accordance with regulation 30) of the instigation and outcome of any child protection enquiries involving any child accommodated in the children's home, to the Commission and the child's placing authority;

(d) written records to be kept of any allegation of abuse or neglect, and of the action taken in response;

(e) consideration to be given to the measures which may be necessary to protect children in the children's home following an allegation of abuse or neglect;

(f) a requirement for persons working at the home to report any concerns about the welfare or safety of a child accommodated there to one of the following –
  (i) the registered person;
  (ii) a police officer;
  (iii) an officer of the Commission;
  (iv) an officer of the local authority in whose area the home is situated, or
  (v) an officer of the National Society for the Prevention of Cruelty to Children;

(g) arrangements to be made for persons working at the home and children accommodated there, to have access at all times and in an appropriate form, to information which would enable them to contact the local authority in whose area the children's home is situated, or the Commission, concerning the welfare or safety of children accommodated in the home.

(3) In this regulation 'child protection enquiries' means any enquiries carried out by a local authority in the exercise of any of its functions conferred by or under the 1989 Act relating to the protection of children.

(4) The registered person shall prepare and implement as required –

(a) a written policy for the prevention of bullying in the children's home, which shall in particular set out the procedure for dealing with an allegation of bullying; and

(b) a procedure to be followed when any child accommodated in a children's home is absent without permission.

17 Behaviour management, discipline and restraint

(1) No measure of control, restraint or discipline which is excessive, unreasonable or contrary to paragraph (5) shall be used at any time on children accommodated in a children's home.

(2) The registered person shall prepare and implement a written policy (in this regulation referred to as 'the behaviour management policy') which sets out –

(a) the measures of control, restraint and discipline which may be used in the children's home; and

(b) the means whereby appropriate behaviour is to be promoted in the home.

(3) The registered person shall –

(a) keep under review and where appropriate revise the behaviour management policy; and

(b)   notify the Commission of any such revision within 28 days.

(4) The registered person shall ensure that within 24 hours of the use of any measure of control, restraint or discipline in a children's home, a written record is made in a volume kept for the purpose which shall include –

(a)   the name of the child concerned;
(b)   details of the child's behaviour leading to the use of the measure;
(c)   a description of the measure used;
(d)   the date, time and location of, the use of the measure, and in the case of any form of restraint, the duration of the restraint;
(e)   the name of the person using the measure, and of any other person present;
(f)   the effectiveness and any consequences of the use of the measure; and
(g)   the signature of a person authorised by the registered provider to make the record.

(5) Subject to paragraphs (6) and (7) of this regulation, the following shall not be used as disciplinary measures on children accommodated in a children's home -

(a)   any form of corporal punishment;
(b)   any punishment relating to the consumption or deprivation of food or drink;
(c)   any restriction, other than one imposed by a court or in accordance with regulation 15, on –
    (i)   a child's contact with his parents, relatives or friends;
    (ii)   visits to him by his parents, relatives or friends;
    (iii)   a child's communications with any of the persons listed in regulation 15(2); or
    (iv)   his access to any telephone helpline providing counselling for children;
(d)   any requirement that a child wear distinctive or inappropriate clothes;
(e)   the use or withholding of medication or medical or dental treatment;
(f)   the intentional deprivation of sleep;
(g)   the imposition of any financial penalty, other than a requirement for the payment of a reasonable sum (which may be by instalments) by way of reparation;
(h)   any intimate physical examination of the child;
(i)   the withholding of any aids or equipment needed by a disabled child;
(j)   any measure which involves -
    (i)   any child in the imposition of any measure against any other child; or
    (ii)   the punishment of a group of children for the behaviour of an individual child.

(6) Nothing in this regulation shall prohibit –

(a)   the taking of any action by, or in accordance with the instructions of, a registered medical practitioner or a registered dental practitioner which is necessary to protect the health of a child;
(b)   the taking of any action immediately necessary to prevent injury to any person or serious damage to property; or
(c)   the imposition of a requirement that a child wear distinctive clothing for sporting purposes, or for purposes connected with his education or with any organisation whose members customarily wear uniform in connection with its activities.

18 Education, employment and leisure activity

(1) The registered person shall promote the educational attainment of children accommodated in a children's home, in particular by ensuring that –

    (a) the children make use of educational facilities appropriate to their age, aptitude, needs, interests and potential;

    (b) the routine of the home is organised so as to further children's participation in education, including private study; and

    (c) effective links are maintained with any schools attended by children accommodated in the home.

(2) The registered person shall ensure that children accommodated in the home are –

    (a) encouraged to develop and pursue appropriate leisure interests; and

    (b) provided with appropriate leisure facilities and activities.

(3) Where any child in a children's home has attained the age where he is no longer required to receive compulsory full-time education, the registered person shall assist with the making of, and give effect to, the arrangements made for his education, training and employment.

19 Religious observance

The registered person shall ensure that each child accommodated in a children's home is enabled, so far as practicable –

    (a) to attend the services of;

    (b) to receive instruction in; and

    (c) to observe any requirement (whether as to dress, diet or otherwise) of,

the religious persuasion to which he belongs.

20 Health needs of children

(1) The registered person shall promote and protect the health of the children accommodated in a children's home.

(2) In particular the registered person shall ensure that –

    (a) each child is registered with a general practitioner;

    (b) each child has access to such medical, dental, nursing, psychological and psychiatric advice, treatment and other services, as he may require;

    (c) each child is provided with such individual support, aids and equipment as he may require as a result of any particular health needs or disability he may have;

    (d) each child is provided with guidance, support and advice on health and personal care issues appropriate to his needs and wishes;

    (e) at all times, at least one person on duty at the children's home has a suitable first aid qualification;

    (f) any person appointed to the position of nurse at the children's home is a registered nurse.

21 Medicines

(1) The registered person shall make suitable arrangements for the recording, handling, safekeeping, safe administration and disposal of any medicines received into the children's home.

(2) In particular the registered person shall ensure, subject to paragraph (3), that –

    (a) any medicine which is kept in a children's home is stored in a secure place so as to prevent any child accommodated there having unsupervised access to it;

    (b) any medicine which is prescribed for a child is administered as prescribed, to the child for whom it is prescribed, and to no other child; and

    (c) a written record is kept of the administration of any medicine to any child.

(3) Paragraph (2) does not apply to a medicine which –

    (a) is stored by the child for whom it is provided in such a way that others are prevented from using it; and

    (b) may be safely self-administered by that child.

(4) In this regulation, 'prescribed' means –

    (a) ordered for a patient for provision to them –

        (i) under or by virtue of the National Health Service Act 1977; or

        (ii) as part of the performance of personal medical services in connection with a pilot scheme under the National Health Service (Primary Care) Act 1997; or

    (b) in a case not falling within sub-paragraph (a), prescribed for a patient under section 58 of the Medicines Act 1968.

22 Use of surveillance

Subject to any requirements for electronic monitoring imposed by a court under any enactment, the registered person shall ensure that electronic or mechanical monitoring devices for the surveillance of children are not used in a children's home, except for the purpose of safeguarding and promoting the welfare of the child concerned, or other children accommodated in the children's home, and where the following conditions are met –

    (a) the child's placing authority consents to the use of the measure in question;

    (b) it is provided for in the child's placement plan;

    (c) so far as practicable in the light of his age and understanding, the child in question is informed in advance of the intention to use the measure; and

    (d) the measure is no more restrictive than necessary, having regard to the child's need for privacy.

23 Hazards and safety

The registered person shall ensure that –

    (a) all parts of the home to which children have access are so far as reasonably practicable free from hazards to their safety;

    (b) any activities in which children participate are so far as reasonably practicable free from avoidable risks;

(c) unnecessary risks to the health or safety of children accommodated in the home are identified and so far as possible eliminated,

and shall make suitable arrangements for persons working at the children's home to be trained in first aid.

24 Complaints and representations

(1) Subject to paragraph (8), the registered person shall establish a written procedure for considering complaints made by or on behalf of children accommodated in the home.

(2) The procedure shall, in particular, provide –

   (a) for an opportunity for informal resolution of the complaint at an early stage;

   (b) that no person who is the subject of a complaint takes any part in its consideration other than, if the registered person considers it appropriate, at the informal resolution stage only;

   (c) for dealing with complaints about the registered person;

   (d) for complaints to be made by a person acting on behalf of a child;

   (e) for arrangements for the procedure to be made known to –
      (i) children accommodated in the home;
      (ii) their parents;
      (iii) placing authorities; and
      (iv) persons working in the home.

(3) A copy of the procedure shall be supplied on request to any of the persons mentioned in paragraph (2)(e).

(4) The copy of the procedure supplied under paragraph (3) shall include –

   (a) the name, address and telephone number of the Commission; and

   (b) details of the procedure (if any) which has been notified to the registered person by the Commission for the making of complaints to it relating to children's homes.

(5) The registered person shall ensure that a written record is made of any complaint, the action taken in response, and the outcome of the investigation.

(6) The registered person shall ensure that –

   (a) children accommodated in the home are enabled to make a complaint or representation; and

   (b) no child is subject to any reprisal for making a complaint or representation.

(7) The registered person shall supply to the Commission at its request a statement containing a summary of any complaints made during the preceding twelve months and the action that was taken.

(8) This regulation (apart from paragraph (6)) does not apply to any matter to which the Representations Procedure (Children) Regulations 1991 applies.

****

Chapter 3
Records

28 Children's case records

(1) The registered person shall maintain in respect of each child who is accommodated in a children's home a record in permanent form which –

    (a) includes the information, documents and records specified in Schedule 3 relating to that child;

    (b) is kept up to date; and

    (c) is signed and dated by the author of each written entry.

(2) The record mentioned in paragraph (1) may not be disclosed to any person except in accordance with –

    (a) any provision of, or made under, or by virtue of, a statute under which access to such records is authorised; or

    (b) any court order authorising access to such records.

(3) The record mentioned in paragraph (1) shall be –

    (a) kept securely in the children's home so long as the child to whom it relates is accommodated there; and

    (b) thereafter retained in a place of security,

for at least seventy-five years from the date of birth of the child to whom it relates or, if the child dies before attaining the age of 18, for a period of fifteen years from the date of his death.

29 Other records

(1) The registered person shall maintain in the children's home the records specified in Schedule 4 and ensure that they are kept up to date.

(2) The records referred to in paragraph (1) shall be retained for at least fifteen years from the date of the last entry, except for records of menus, which need be kept only for one year.

30 Notifiable events

(1) If, in relation to a children's home, any of the events listed in column 1 of the table in Schedule 5 takes place, the registered person shall without delay notify the persons indicated in respect of the event in column 2 of the table.

(2) The registered person shall without delay notify the parent of any child accommodated in the home of any significant incident affecting the child's welfare unless to do so is not reasonably practicable or would place the child's welfare at risk.

(3) Any notification made in accordance with this regulation which is given orally shall be confirmed in writing.

****

SCHEDULE 1

MATTERS TO BE INCLUDED IN THE STATEMENT OF PURPOSE

(1) A statement of the overall aims of the children's home, and the objectives to be attained with regard to children accommodated in the home.

(2) A statement of the facilities and services to be provided for the children accommodated in the children's home.

(3) The name and address of the registered provider, and of the registered manager if applicable.

(4) The relevant qualifications and experience of the registered provider and, if applicable, the registered manager.

(5) The number, relevant qualifications and experience of persons working at the children's home, and if the workers are all of one sex, a description of the means whereby the home will promote appropriate role models of both sexes.

(6) The arrangements for the supervision, training and development of employees.

(7) The organisational structure of the children's home.

(8) The following particulars –

    (a) the age-range, sex and numbers of children for whom it is intended that accommodation should be provided;

    (b) whether it is intended to accommodate children who are disabled, have special needs or any other special characteristics; and

    (c) the range of needs (other than those mentioned in sub-paragraph (b)) that the home is intended to meet.

(9) Any criteria used for admission to the home, including the home's policy and procedures for emergency admissions, if the home provides for emergency admissions.

(10) If the children's home provides or is intended to provide accommodation for more than six children, a description of the positive outcomes intended for children in a home of such a size, and of the home's strategy for counteracting any adverse effects arising from its size, on the children accommodated there.

(11) A description of the children's home's underlying ethos and philosophy, and where this is based on any theoretical or therapeutic model, a description of that model.

(12) The arrangements made to protect and promote the health of the children accommodated at the home.

(13) The arrangements for the promotion of the education of the children accommodated there, including the facilities for private study.

(14) The arrangements to promote children's participation in recreational, sporting and cultural activities.

(15) The arrangements made for consultation with the children accommodated about the operation of the children's home.

(16) The arrangements made for the control, restraint and discipline of children.

(17) The arrangements made for child protection and to counter bullying.

(18) The procedure for dealing with any unauthorised absence of a child from the children's home.

(19) A description of any electronic or mechanical means of surveillance of children which may be used in the children's home.

(20) The fire precautions and associated emergency procedures in the children's home.

(21) The arrangements for the children's religious instruction and observance.

(22) The arrangements for contact between a child and his parents, relatives and friends.

(23) The arrangements for dealing with complaints.

(24) The arrangements for dealing with reviews of placement plans.

(25) The type of accommodation, including the sleeping accommodation, provided, and, where applicable, how children are to be grouped, and in what circumstances they are to share bedrooms.

(26) Details of any specific therapeutic techniques used in the home, and arrangements for their supervision.

(27) A description of the children's home's policy in relation to anti-discriminatory practice as respects children and children's rights.

****

SCHEDULE 3

INFORMATION TO BE INCLUDED IN THE CASE RECORDS OF CHILDREN ACCOMMODATED IN CHILDREN'S HOMES

(1) The child's name and any name by which the child has previously been known, other than a name used by the child prior to adoption.

(2) The child's date of birth and sex.

(3) The child's religious persuasion, if any.

(4) A description of the child's racial origin, cultural and linguistic background.

(5) The child's address immediately prior to entering the home.

(6) The name, address and telephone number of the child's placing authority.

(7) The statutory provision (if any) under which he is provided with accommodation.

(8) The name, address, telephone number and the religious persuasion, if any, of the child's parents.

(9) The name, address and telephone number of any social worker for the time being assigned to the child by the placing authority.

(10) The date and circumstances of all absences of the child from the home, including whether the absence was authorised and any information relating to the child's whereabouts during the period of absence.

(11) The date of, and reason for, any visit to the child whilst in the home.

(12) A copy of any statement of special educational needs maintained in relation to the child under section 324 of the Education Act 1996], with details of any such needs.

(13) The date and circumstances of any measures of control, restraint or discipline used on the child.

(14) Any special dietary or health needs of the child.

(15) The name, address and telephone number of any school or college attended by the child, and of any employer of the child.

(16) Every school report received in respect of the child while accommodated in the home.

(17) Arrangements for, including any restrictions on, contact between the child, his parents, and any other person.

(18) A copy of any plan for the care of the child prepared by his placing authority, and of the placement plan.

(19) The date and result of any review of the placing authority's plan for the care of the child, or of his placement plan.

(20) The name and address of the general practitioner with whom the child is registered, and of the child's registered dental practitioner.

(21) Details of any accident or serious illness involving the child while accommodated in the home.

(22) Details of any immunisation, allergy, or medical examination of the child and of any medical or dental need or treatment of the child.

(23) Details of any health examination or developmental test conducted with respect to the child at or in connection with his school.

(24) Details of any medicines kept for the child in the home, including any medicines which the child is permitted to administer to himself, and details of the administration of any medicine to the child.

(25) The dates on which any money or valuables are deposited by or on behalf of a child for safekeeping, and the dates on which any money is withdrawn, and any valuables are returned.

(26) The address, and type of establishment or accommodation, to which the child goes when he ceases to be accommodated in the home.

SCHEDULE 4

OTHER RECORDS WITH RESPECT TO CHILDREN'S HOMES

(1) A record in the form of a register showing in respect of each child accommodated in a children's home –

    (a) the date of his admission to the home;

    (b) the date on which he ceased to be accommodated there;

    (c) his address prior to being accommodated in the home;

    (d) his address on leaving the home;

    (e) his placing authority;

    (f) the statutory provision (if any) under which he is accommodated.

(2) A record showing in respect of each person working at the home –

    (a) his full name;

    (b) his sex;

    (c) his date of birth;

    (d) his home address;

    (e) his qualifications relevant to, and experience of, work involving children;

    (f) whether he works at the home full-time or part-time (whether paid or not), and if part-time, the average number of hours worked per week; and

    (g) whether he resides at the home.

(3) A record of any persons who reside or work at any time at the children's home, who are not mentioned in the records kept in accordance with paragraphs 1 or 2.

(4) A record of all accidents occurring in the children's home, or to children whilst accommodated by the home.

(5) A record of the receipt, disposal and administration of any medicine to any child.

(6) A record of every fire drill or fire alarm test conducted, with details of any deficiency in either the procedure or the equipment concerned, together with details of the steps taken to remedy that deficiency.

(7) A record of all money deposited by a child for safekeeping, together with the date on which that money was withdrawn, or the date of its return.

(8) A record of all valuables deposited by a child and the date of their return.

(9) Records of all accounts kept in the children's home.

(10) A record of menus served.

(11) A copy of the staff duty roster of persons working at the children's home, and a record of the actual rosters worked.

(12) A daily log of events occurring in the home.

(13) A record of all visitors to the home and to children accommodated in the home, including the names of visitors and the reasons for the visit.

SCHEDULE 5

EVENTS AND NOTIFICATIONS

Column 1	Column 2					
Event:	To be notified to:					
	Commission	Placing authority	Secretary of State	Local authority	Police	Primary care trust
Death of a child accommodated in the home	yes	yes	yes	yes		yes
Referral to the Secretary of State pursuant to section 2(1)(a) of the Protection of Children Act 1999 of an individual working at the home	yes	yes				
Serious illness or serious accident sustained by a child accommodated in the home	yes	yes				
Outbreak of any infectious disease which in the opinion of a registered medical practitioner attending children at the home is sufficiently serious to be so notified	yes	yes				yes

	Commission	Placing authority	Secretary of State	Local authority	Police	Primary care trust
Allegation that a child accommodated at the home has committed a serious offence		yes			yes	
Involvement or suspected involvement of a child accommodated at the home in prostitution	yes	yes		yes	yes	
Serious incident necessitating calling the police to the home	yes	yes				
Absconding by a child accommodated at the home		yes				
Any serious complaint about the home or persons working there	yes	yes				
Instigation and outcome of any child protection enquiry involving a child accommodated at the home	yes	yes				

4.15 CIVIL PROCEDURE RULES 1998, SI 1998/3132 (Part 1, r 2.1, Parts 35, 52)

1.1 The overriding objective

(1) These Rules are a new procedural code with the overriding objective of enabling the court to deal with cases justly.

(2) Dealing with a case justly includes, so far as is practicable –

    (a) ensuring that the parties are on an equal footing;

    (b) saving expense;

    (c) dealing with the case in ways which are proportionate –

        (i) to the amount of money involved;

        (ii) to the importance of the case;

        (iii) to the complexity of the issues; and

        (iv) to the financial position of each party;

    (d) ensuring that it is dealt with expeditiously and fairly; and

    (e) allotting to it an appropriate share of the court's resources, while taking into account the need to allot resources to other cases.

1.2 Application by the court of the overriding objective

The court must seek to give effect to the overriding objective when it –

    (a) exercises any power given to it by the Rules; or

    (b) interprets any rule.

1.3 Duty of the parties

The parties are required to help the court to further the overriding objective.

1.4 Court's duty to manage cases

(1) The court must further the overriding objective by actively managing cases.

(2) Active case management includes –

    (a) encouraging the parties to co-operate with each other in the conduct of the proceedings;

    (b) identifying the issues at an early stage;

    (c) deciding promptly which issues need full investigation and trial and accordingly disposing summarily of the others;

    (d) deciding the order in which issues are to be resolved;

    (e) encouraging the parties to use an alternative dispute resolution procedure if the court considers that appropriate and facilitating the use of such procedure;

    (f) helping the parties to settle the whole or part of the case;

    (g) fixing timetables or otherwise controlling the progress of the case;

    (h) considering whether the likely benefits of taking a particular step justify the cost of taking it;

(i) dealing with as many aspects of the case as it can on the same occasion;

(j) dealing with the case without the parties needing to attend at court;

(k) making use of technology; and

(l) giving directions to ensure that the trial of a case proceeds quickly and efficiently.

2.1 Application of the Rules

(1) Subject to paragraph (2), these Rules apply to all proceedings in –

(a) county courts;

(b) the High Court; and

(c) the Civil Division of the Court of Appeal.

(2) These Rules do not apply to proceedings of the kinds specified in the first column of the following Table (proceedings for which rules may be made under the enactments specified in the second column) except to the extent that they are applied to those proceedings by another enactment –

Proceedings	*Enactments*
1. Insolvency proceedings	Insolvency Act 1986, ss 411 and 412
2. Non-contentious or common form probate proceedings	Supreme Court Act 1981, s 127
3. Proceedings in the High Court when acting as a Prize Court	Prize Courts Act 1894, s 3
4. Proceedings before the judge within the meaning of Part VII of the Mental Health Act 1983	Mental Health Act 1983, s 106
5. Family proceedings	Matrimonial and Family Proceedings Act 1984, s 40
6. Adoption proceedings	Adoption Act 1976, s 66
7. Election petitions in the High Court	Representation of the People Act 1983, s 182

****

PART 35

EXPERTS AND ASSESSORS

35.1 Duty to restrict expert evidence

Expert evidence shall be restricted to that which is reasonably required to resolve the proceedings.

35.2 Interpretation

A reference to an 'expert' in this Part is a reference to an expert who has been instructed to give or prepare evidence for the purpose of court proceedings.

35.3 Experts – overriding duty to the court

(1) It is the duty of an expert to help the court on the matters within his expertise.

(2) This duty overrides any obligation to the person from whom he has received instructions or by whom he is paid.

35.4 Court's power to restrict expert evidence

(1) No party may call an expert or put in evidence an expert's report without the court's permission.

(2) When a party applies for permission under this rule he must identify –

    (a) the field in which he wishes to rely on expert evidence; and
    (b) where practicable the expert in that field on whose evidence he wishes to rely.

(3) If permission is granted under this rule it shall be in relation only to the expert named or the field identified under paragraph (2).

(4) The court may limit the amount of the expert's fees and expenses that the party who wishes to rely on the expert may recover from any other party.

35.5 General requirement for expert evidence to be given in a written report

(1) Expert evidence is to be given in a written report unless the court directs otherwise.

(2) (*not reproduced here*)

35.6 Written questions to experts

(1) A party may put to –

    (a) an expert instructed by another party; or
    (b) a single joint expert appointed under rule 35.7,

written questions about his report.

(2) Written questions under paragraph (1) –

    (a) may be put once only;

(b) must be put within 28 days of service of the expert's report; and

(c) must be for the purpose only of clarification of the report;

unless in any case,

     (i) the court gives permission; or

     (ii) the other party agrees.

(3) An expert's answers to questions put in accordance with paragraph (1) shall be treated as part of the expert's report.

(4) Where –

(a) a party has put a written question to an expert instructed by another party in accordance with this rule; and

(b) the expert does not answer that question,

the court may make one or both of the following orders in relation to the party who instructed the expert –

     (i) that the party may not rely on the evidence of that expert; or

     (ii) that the party may not recover the fees and expenses of that expert from any other party.

35.7 Court's power to direct that evidence is to be given by a single joint expert

(1) Where two or more parties wish to submit expert evidence on a particular issue, the court may direct that the evidence on that issue is to given by one expert only.

(2) The parties wishing to submit the expert evidence are called 'the instructing parties'.

(3) Where the instructing parties cannot agree who should be the expert, the court may –

(a) select the expert from a list prepared or identified by the instructing parties; or

(b) direct that the expert be selected in such other manner as the court may direct.

35.8 Instructions to a single joint expert

(1) Where the court gives a direction under rule 35.7 for a single joint expert to be used, each instructing party may give instructions to the expert.

(2) When an instructing party gives instructions to the expert he must, at the same time, send a copy of the instructions to the other instructing parties.

(3) The court may give directions about –

(a) the payment of the expert's fees and expenses; and

(b) any inspection, examination or experiments which the expert wishes to carry out.

(4) The court may, before an expert is instructed –

(a) limit the amount that can be paid by way of fees and expenses to the expert; and

(b)   direct that the instructing parties pay that amount into court.

(5) Unless the court otherwise directs, the instructing parties are jointly and severally liable for the payment of the expert's fees and expenses.

35.9 Power of court to direct a party to provide information

Where a party has access to information which is not reasonably available to the other party, the court may direct the party who has access to the information to –

(a)   prepare and file a document recording the information; and
(b)   serve a copy of that document on the other party.

35.10 Contents of report

(1) An expert's report must comply with the requirements set out in the relevant practice direction.

(2) At the end of an expert's report there must be a statement that –

(a)   the expert understands his duty to the court; and
(b)   he has complied with that duty.

(3) The expert's report must state the substance of all material instructions, whether written or oral, on the basis of which the report was written.

(4) The instructions referred to in paragraph (3) shall not be privileged against disclosure but the court will not, in relation to those instructions –

(a)   order disclosure of any specific document; or
(b)   permit any questioning in court, other than by the party who instructed the expert,

unless it is satisfied that there are reasonable grounds to consider the statement of instructions given under paragraph (3) to be inaccurate or incomplete.

35.11 Use by one party of expert's report disclosed by another

Where a party has disclosed an expert's report, any party may use that expert's report as evidence at the trial.

35.12 Discussions between experts

(1) The court may, at any stage, direct a discussion between experts for the purpose of requiring the experts to –

(a)   identify and discuss the expert issues in the proceedings; and
(b)   where possible, reach an agreed opinion on those issues.

(2) The court may specify the issues which the experts must discuss.

(3) The court may direct that following a discussion between the experts they must prepare a statement for the court showing –

(a)   those issues on which they agree; and
(b)   those issues on which they disagree and a summary of their reasons for disagreeing.

(4) The content of the discussion between the experts shall not be referred to at the trial unless the parties agree.

(5) Where experts reach agreement on an issue during their discussions, the agreement shall not bind the parties unless the parties expressly agree to be bound by the agreement.

35.13 Consequence of failure to disclose expert's report

A party who fails to disclose an expert's report may not use the report at the trial or call the expert to give evidence orally unless the court gives permission.

35.14 Expert's right to ask court for directions

(1) An expert may file a written request for directions to assist him in carrying out his function as an expert.

(2) An expert must, unless the court orders otherwise, provide a copy of any proposed request for directions under paragraph (1) –

    (a) to the party instructing him, at least 7 days before he files the request; and
    (b) to all other parties, at least 4 days before he files it.

(3) The court, when it gives directions, may also direct that a party be served with a copy of the directions.

****

PART 52

APPEALS

Section I – General Rules about Appeals

52.1 Scope and interpretation

(1) The rules in this Part apply to appeals to –

    (a) the civil division of the Court of Appeal;
    (b) the High Court; and
    (c) a county court.

(2) This Part does not apply to an appeal in detailed assessment proceedings against a decision of an authorised court officer.

(Rules 47.21 to 47.26 deal with appeals against a decision of an authorised court officer in detailed assessment proceedings)

(3) In this Part –

    (a) 'appeal' includes an appeal by way of case stated;
    (b) 'appeal court' means the court to which an appeal is made;
    (c) 'lower court' means the court, tribunal or other person or body from whose decision an appeal is brought;
    (d) 'appellant' means a person who brings or seeks to bring an appeal;

 (e) 'respondent' means –

   (i) a person other than the appellant who was a party to the proceedings in the lower court and who is affected by the appeal; and

   (ii) a person who is permitted by the appeal court to be a party to the appeal; and

 (f) 'appeal notice' means an appellant's or respondent's notice.

(4) This Part is subject to any rule, enactment or practice direction which sets out special provisions with regard to any particular category of appeal.

52.2 Parties to comply with the practice direction

All parties to an appeal must comply with the relevant practice direction.

52.3 Permission

(1) An appellant or respondent requires permission to appeal –

 (a) where the appeal is from a decision of a judge in a county court or the High Court, except where the appeal is against –

   (i) a committal order;

   (ii) a refusal to grant habeas corpus; or

   (iii) a secure accommodation order made under section 25 of the Children Act 1989; or

 (b) as provided by the relevant practice direction.

(Other enactments may provide that permission is required for particular appeals)

(2) An application for permission to appeal may be made –

 (a) to the lower court at the hearing at which the decision to be appealed was made; or

 (b) to the appeal court in an appeal notice.

(Rule 52.4 sets out the time limits for filing an appellant's notice at the appeal court. Rule 52.5 sets out the time limits for filing a respondent's notice at the appeal court. Any application for permission to appeal to the appeal court must be made in the appeal notice (see rules 52.4(1) and 52.5(3)))

(Rule 52.13(1) provides that permission is required from the Court of Appeal for all appeals to that court from a decision of a county court or the High Court which was itself made on appeal)

(3) Where the lower court refuses an application for permission to appeal, a further application for permission to appeal may be made to the appeal court.

(4) Where the appeal court, without a hearing, refuses permission to appeal, the person seeking permission may request the decision to be reconsidered at a hearing.

(5) A request under paragraph (4) must be filed within seven days after service of the notice that permission has been refused.

(6) Permission to appeal will only be given where –

 (a) the court considers that the appeal would have a real prospect of success; or

 (b) there is some other compelling reason why the appeal should be heard.

(7) An order giving permission may –

(a) limit the issues to be heard; and

(b) be made subject to conditions.

(Rule 3.1(3) also provides that the court may make an order subject to conditions)

(Rule 25.15 provides for the court to order security for costs of an appeal)

52.4 Appellant's notice

(1) Where the appellant seeks permission from the appeal court it must be requested in the appellant's notice.

(2) The appellant must file the appellant's notice at the appeal court within –

(a) such period as may be directed by the lower court; or

(b) where the court makes no such direction, 14 days after the date of the decision of the lower court that the appellant wishes to appeal.

(3) Unless the appeal court orders otherwise, an appeal notice must be served on each respondent –

(a) as soon as practicable; and

(b) in any event not later than 7 days,

after it is filed.

52.5 Respondent's notice

(1) A respondent may file and serve a respondent's notice.

(2) A respondent who –

(a) is seeking permission to appeal from the appeal court; or

(b) wishes to ask the appeal court to uphold the order of the lower court for reasons different from or additional to those given by the lower court,

must file a respondent's notice.

(3) Where the respondent seeks permission from the appeal court it must be requested in the respondent's notice.

(4) A respondent's notice must be filed within –

(a) such period as may be directed by the lower court; or

(b) where the court makes no such direction, 14 days, after the date in paragraph (5).

(5) The date referred to in paragraph (4) is –

(a) the date the respondent is served with the appellant's notice where –

(i) permission to appeal was given by the lower court; or

(ii) permission to appeal is not required;

(b) the date the respondent is served with notification that the appeal court has given the appellant permission to appeal; or

(c) the date the respondent is served with notification that the application for permission to appeal and the appeal itself are to be heard together.

(6) Unless the appeal court orders otherwise a respondent's notice must be served on the appellant and any other respondent –

    (a) as soon as practicable; and

    (b) in any event not later than 7 days,

after it is filed.

52.6 Variation of time

(1) An application to vary the time limit for filing an appeal notice must be made to the appeal court.

(2) The parties may not agree to extend any date or time limit set by –

    (a) these Rules;

    (b) the relevant practice direction; or

    (c) an order of the appeal court or the lower court.

(Rule 3.1(2)(a) provides that the court may extend or shorten the time for compliance with any rule, practice direction or court order (even if an application for extension is made after the time for compliance has expired))

(Rule 3.1(2)(b) provides that the court may adjourn or bring forward a hearing)

52.7 Stay

Unless –

    (a) the appeal court or the lower court orders otherwise; or

    (b) the appeal is from the Immigration Appeal Tribunal,

an appeal shall not operate as a stay of any order or decision of the lower court.

52.8 Amendment of appeal notice

An appeal notice may not be amended without the permission of the appeal court.

52.9 Striking out appeal notices and setting aside or imposing conditions on permission to appeal

(1) The appeal court may –

    (a) strike out the whole or part of an appeal notice;

    (b) set aside permission to appeal in whole or in part;

    (c) impose or vary conditions upon which an appeal may be brought.

(2) The court will only exercise its powers under paragraph (1) where there is a compelling reason for doing so.

(3) Where a party was present at the hearing at which permission was given he may not subsequently apply for an order that the court exercise its powers under sub-paragraphs (1)(b) or (1)(c).

52.10 Appeal court's powers

(1) In relation to an appeal the appeal court has all the powers of the lower court.

(Rule 52.1(4) provides that this Part is subject to any enactment that sets out special provisions with regard to any particular category of appeal – where such an enactment gives a statutory power to a tribunal, person or other body it may be the case that the appeal court may not exercise that power on an appeal)

(2) The appeal court has power to –

    (a) affirm, set aside or vary any order or judgment made or given by the lower court;

    (b) refer any claim or issue for determination by the lower court;

    (c) order a new trial or hearing;

    (d) make orders for the payment of interest;

    (e) make a costs order.

(3) In an appeal from a claim tried with a jury the Court of Appeal may, instead of ordering a new trial –

    (a) make an order for damages; or

    (b) vary an award of damages made by the jury.

(4) The appeal court may exercise its powers in relation to the whole or part of an order of the lower court.

(Part 3 contains general rules about the court's case management powers)

52.11 Hearing of appeals

(1) Every appeal will be limited to a review of the decision of the lower court unless –

    (a) a practice direction makes different provision for a particular category of appeal; or

    (b) the court considers that in the circumstances of an individual appeal it would be in the interests of justice to hold a re-hearing.

(2) Unless it orders otherwise, the appeal court will not receive –

    (a) oral evidence; or

    (b) evidence which was not before the lower court.

(3) The appeal court will allow an appeal where the decision of the lower court was –

    (a) wrong; or

    (b) unjust because of a serious procedural or other irregularity in the proceedings in the lower court.

(4) The appeal court may draw any inference of fact which it considers justified on the evidence.

(5) At the hearing of the appeal a party may not rely on a matter not contained in his appeal notice unless the appeal court gives permission.

52.12 Non-disclosure of Part 36 offers and payments

(1) The fact that a Part 36 offer or Part 36 payment has been made must not be disclosed to any judge of the appeal court who is to hear or determine –

    (a) an application for permission to appeal; or

    (b) an appeal,

until all questions (other than costs) have been determined.

(2) Paragraph (1) does not apply if the Part 36 offer or Part 36 payment is relevant to the substance of the appeal.

(3) Paragraph (1) does not prevent disclosure in any application in the appeal proceedings if disclosure of the fact that a Part 36 offer or Part 36 payment has been made is properly relevant to the matter to be decided.

Section II – Special Provisions applying to the Court of Appeal

52.13 Second appeals to the court

(1) Permission is required from the Court of Appeal for any appeal to that court from a decision of a county court or the High Court which was itself made on appeal.

(2) The Court of Appeal will not give permission unless it considers that –

    (a) the appeal would raise an important point of principle or practice; or

    (b) there is some other compelling reason for the Court of Appeal to hear it.

52.14 Assignment of appeals to the Court of Appeal

(1) Where the court from or to which an appeal is made or from which permission to appeal is sought ('the relevant court') considers that –

    (a) an appeal which is to be heard by a county court or the High Court would raise an important point of principle or practice; or

    (b) there is some other compelling reason for the Court of Appeal to hear it,

the relevant court may order the appeal to be transferred to the Court of Appeal.

(The Master of the Rolls has the power to direct that an appeal which would be heard by a county court or the High Court should be heard instead by the Court of Appeal – see section 57 of the Access to Justice Act 1999)

(2) The Master of the Rolls or the Court of Appeal may remit an appeal to the court in which the original appeal was or would have been brought.

52.15 Judicial review appeals

(1) Where permission to apply for judicial review has been refused at a hearing in the High Court, the person seeking that permission may apply to the Court of Appeal for permission to appeal.

(2) An application in accordance with paragraph (1) must be made within 7 days of the decision of the High Court to refuse to give permission to apply for judicial review.

(3) On an application under paragraph (1), the Court of Appeal may, instead of giving permission to appeal, give permission to apply for judicial review.

(4) Where the Court of Appeal gives permission to apply for judicial review in accordance with paragraph (3), the case will proceed in the High Court unless the Court of Appeal orders otherwise.

52.16 Who may exercise the powers of the Court of Appeal

(1) A court officer assigned to the Civil Appeals Office who is –

(a)   a barrister; or

(b)   a solicitor

may exercise the jurisdiction of the Court of Appeal with regard to the matters set out in paragraph (2) with the consent of the Master of the Rolls.

(2)   The matters referred to in paragraph (1) are –

(a)   any matter incidental to any proceedings in the Court of Appeal;

(b)   any other matter where there is no substantial dispute between the parties; and

(c)   the dismissal of an appeal or application where a party has failed to comply with any order, rule or practice direction.

(3)   A court officer may not decide an application for –

(a)   permission to appeal;

(b)   bail pending an appeal;

(c)   an injunction ;

(d)   a stay of any proceedings, other than a temporary stay of any order or decision of the lower court over a period when the Court of Appeal is not sitting or cannot conveniently be convened.

(4)   Decisions of a court officer may be made without a hearing.

(5)   A party may request any decision of a court officer to be reviewed by the Court of Appeal.

(6)   At the request of a party, a hearing will be held to reconsider a decision of –

(a)   a single judge; or

(b)   a court officer,

made without a hearing.

(6A)   A request under paragraph (5) or (6) must be filed within 7 days after the party is served with notice of the decision.

(7)   A single judge may refer any matter for a decision by a court consisting of two or more judges.

(Section 54(6) of the Supreme Court Act 1981 provides that there is no appeal from the decision of a single judge on an application for permission to appeal)

(Section 58(2) of the Supreme Court Act 1981 provides that there is no appeal to the House of Lords from decisions of the Court of Appeal that –

(a)   are taken by a single judge or any officer or member of staff of that court in proceedings incidental to any cause or matter pending before the civil division of that court; and

(b)   do not involve the determination of an appeal or of an application for permission to appeal,

and which may be called into question by rules of court. Rules 52.16(5) and (6) provide the procedure for the calling into question of such decisions)

Section III – Provisions about Reopening Appeals

52.17 Reopening of final appeals

(1) The Court of Appeal or the High Court will not reopen a final determination of any appeal unless –

    (a) it is necessary to do so in order to avoid real injustice;

    (b) the circumstances are exceptional and make it appropriate to reopen the appeal; and

    (c) there is no alternative effective remedy.

(2) In paragraphs (1), (3), (4) and (6), 'appeal' includes an application for permission to appeal.

(3) This rule does not apply to appeals to a county court.

(4) Permission is needed to make an application under this rule to reopen a final determination of an appeal even in cases where under rule 52.3(1) permission was not needed for the original appeal.

(5) There is no right to an oral hearing of an application for permission unless, exceptionally, the judge so directs.

(6) The judge will not grant permission without directing the application to be served on the other party to the original appeal and giving him an opportunity to make representations.

(7) There is no right of appeal or review from the decision of the judge on the application for permission, which is final.

(8) The procedure for making an application for permission is set out in the practice direction.

4.16 CONTACT WITH CHILDREN REGULATIONS 1991, SI 1991/891

1 Citation, commencement and interpretation

(1) These Regulations may be cited as the Contact with Children Regulations 1991, and shall come into force on 14th October 1991.

(2) Any notice required under these Regulations is to be given in writing and may be sent by post.

(3) In these Regulations unless the context requires otherwise –

(a) any reference to a numbered section is to the section in the Children Act 1989 bearing that number;

(b) any reference to a numbered regulation is to the regulation in these Regulations bearing that number; and

(c) any reference to a Schedule is to the Schedule to these Regulations.

2 Local authority refusal of contact with child

Where a local authority has decided under section 34(6) to refuse contact with a child that would otherwise be required by virtue of section 34(1) or a court order, the authority shall, as soon as the decision has been made, notify the following persons in writing of those parts of the information specified in the Schedule as the authority considers those persons need to know –

(a) the child, if he is of sufficient understanding;

(b) the child's parents;

(c) any guardian of his;

(d) where there was a residence order in force with respect to the child immediately before the care order was made, the person in whose favour the order was made;

(e) where immediately before the care order was made, a person had care of the child by virtue of an order made in the exercise of the High Court's inherent jurisdiction with respect to children, that person; and

(f) any other person whose wishes and feelings the authority consider to be relevant.

3 Departure from terms of court order on contact under section 34

The local authority may depart from the terms of any order under section 34 (parental contact etc with children in care) by agreement between the local authority and the person in relation to whom the order is made and in the following circumstance and subject to the following condition –

(a) where the child is of sufficient understanding, subject to agreement also with him; and

(b) a written notification shall be sent to the persons specified in regulation 2 containing those parts of the information specified in the Schedule as the authority considers those persons need to know, within seven days of the agreement to depart from the terms of the order.

4 Notification of variation or suspension of contact arrangements

Where a local authority varies or suspends any arrangements made (otherwise than under an order made under section 34) with a view to affording any person contact with a child in the care of that local authority, written notification shall be sent to those persons specified in regulation 2 containing those parts of the information specified in the Schedule as the authority considers those persons need to know, as soon as the decision is made to vary or suspend the arrangements.

SCHEDULE

INFORMATION TO BE CONTAINED IN WRITTEN NOTIFICATION

1 Local authority's decision.

2 Date of the decision.

3 Reasons for the decision.

4 Duration (if applicable).

5 Remedies available in case of dissatisfaction.

4.17 EMERGENCY PROTECTION ORDER (TRANSFER OF RESPONSIBILITIES) REGULATIONS 1991, SI 1991/1414

1 Citation and commencement

These Regulations may be cited as the Emergency Protection Order (Transfer of Responsibilities) Regulations 1991 and shall come into force on 14th October 1991.

2 Transfer of responsibilities under emergency protection orders

Subject to regulation 5 of these Regulations, where –

    (a) an emergency protection order has been made with respect to a child;

    (b) the applicant for the order was not the local authority within whose area the child is ordinarily resident; and

    (c) that local authority are of the opinion that it would be in the child's best interests for the applicant's responsibilities under the order to be transferred to them,

that authority shall (subject to their having complied with the requirements imposed by regulation 3(1) of these Regulations) be treated, for the purposes of the Children Act 1989, as though they and not the original applicant had applied for, and been granted, the order.

3 Requirements to be complied with by local authorities

(1) In forming their opinion under regulation 2(c) of these Regulations the local authority shall consult the applicant for the emergency protection order and have regard to the following considerations –

    (a) the ascertainable wishes and feelings of the child having regard to his age and understanding;

    (b) the child's physical, emotional and educational needs for the duration of the emergency protection order;

    (c) the likely effect on him of any change in his circumstances which may be caused by a transfer of responsibilities under the order;

    (d) his age, sex, family background;

    (e) the circumstances which gave rise to the application for the emergency protection order;

    (f) any directions of a court and other orders made in respect of the child;

    (g) the relationship (if any) of the applicant for the emergency protection order to the child, and

    (h) any plans which the applicant may have in respect of the child.

(2) The local authority shall give notice, as soon as possible after they form the opinion referred to in regulation 2(c), of the date and time of the transfer to –

    (a) the court which made the emergency protection order,

    (b) the applicant for the order, and

(c)   those (other than the local authority) to whom the applicant for the order
gave notice of it.

(3) A notice required under this regulation shall be given in writing and may be sent
by post.

4 When responsibility under emergency protection order transfers

The time at which responsibility under any emergency protection order is to be
treated as having been transferred to a local authority shall be the time stated as the
time of transfer in the notice given in accordance with regulation 3 of these
Regulations by the local authority to the applicant for the emergency protection order
or the time at which notice is given to him under that regulation, whichever is the
later.

5 Exception for children in refuges

These Regulations shall not apply where the child to whom the emergency protection
order applies is in a refuge in respect of which there is in force a Secretary of State's
certificate issued under section 51 of the Children Act 1989 (refuges for children at
risk) and the person carrying on the home or, the foster parent providing the refuge,
having taken account of the wishes and feelings of the child, has decided that the child
should continue to be provided with the refuge for the duration of the order.

4.18 FAMILY PROCEEDINGS (ALLOCATION TO JUDICIARY) DIRECTIONS 1999

****

2

In these Directions, in the absence of a contrary implication –

> 'family proceedings' and 'judge' bear the meanings assigned to them in section 9 of the Courts and Legal Services Act 1990;
>
> 'nominated' in relation to a judge means a judge who has been approved as one to whom family proceedings may be allocated by the President of the Family Division;
>
> 'opposed hearing' includes an application made ex parte; and
>
> 'Schedule' means the Schedule to these Directions.

3

These Directions shall apply where proceedings of a class specified in column (i) of the Schedule are pending in a county court or, by virtue of section 42 of the Matrimonial and Family Proceedings Act 1984, a provision of the Children (Allocation of Proceedings) Order 1991 or of the Family Law Act 1996 (Part IV) (Allocation of Proceedings) Order 1997, treated as pending in a county court in the Principal Registry of the Family Division of the High Court.

4

Subject to the following paragraphs of these Directions, the proceedings in column (i) of the Schedule may be allocated to a judge of the description specified in the corresponding entry in column (ii), in the circumstances specified in the corresponding entry in column (iii).

5

Without prejudice to the provisions of the Schedule, any of the proceedings in column (i) of the Schedule may be allocated to –

(a) a judge of the Family Division of the High Court;

(b) a person acting as a judge of the Family Division of the High Court in pursuance of a request made under section 9(1) of the Supreme Court Act 1981 other than a former judge of the Court of Appeal or a former puisne judge of the High Court; but public family law proceedings shall be allocated only to a judge who has been nominated for them;

(c) a person sitting as a recorder who has been authorised to act as a judge of the Family Division of the High Court under section 9(4) of the Supreme Court Act 1981.

(d) a person sitting as a recorder who is a district judge (Magistrates' Courts) and who is nominated for public family law proceedings in the county court.

(e) a person sitting as a recorder who is a district judge of the Principal Registry of the Family Division.

5A

When a person sitting as a recorder is also a district judge nominated for public family law proceedings, any proceedings may be allocated to him which, under these Directions, may be allocated to a district judge nominated for public family law proceedings.

6

Where any family proceedings include proceedings of more than one class specified in column (i) of the Schedule, the Schedule shall apply to those classes as if they did not form part of the same proceedings.

7

For the purposes of paragraphs (f), (g), (h) and (i) of the Schedule, where –

(a) unopposed proceedings become opposed during the course of the hearing; and

(b) the judge before whom the hearing takes place does not fall within a description of judge to whom the proceedings would have been allocated if the proceedings had been opposed at the commencement of the trial,

he shall adjourn the hearing to a judge to whom such a hearing would be allocated by these Directions.

SCHEDULE

ALLOCATION OF PROCEEDINGS

(i) DESCRIPTION OF PROCEEDINGS	*(ii)* DESCRIPTION OF JUDGE	*(iii)* CIRCUMSTANCES IN WHICH ALLOCATION APPLIES
(a) Family proceedings for which no express provision is made in this Schedule.	A circuit judge, deputy circuit judge or recorder nominated for private or public family law proceedings; a district judge of the Principal Registry of the Family Division of the High Court; or a district judge or deputy district judge.	All circumstances.

(b)		
Non-contentious or common form probate business within the meaning of section 128 of the Supreme Court Act 1981 (c 54).	A judge.	All circumstances.
(c)		
Proceedings under any of the provisions in Part IV of the Family Law Act 1996 (c.27).	A circuit judge or deputy circuit judge nominated for private or public family law proceedings;	All circumstances.
	a recorder nominated for public family law proceedings; or	All circumstances.
	a district judge of the Principal Registry of the Family Division of the High Court; or	All circumstances.
	a district judge,	All circumstances.
	a recorder nominated for private family law proceedings, a recorder or a deputy district judge.	All circumstances except proceedings to enforce an order made under Part IV.
(d)		
Hearing of contested petition for a decree of divorce, nullity or judicial separation.	A circuit judge, deputy circuit judge or a recorder nominated for private or public family law proceedings.	All circumstances.
(e)		
Proceedings under any of the following provisions of the Adoption Act 1976 (c 36):	A circuit judge nominated for adoption proceedings; or	All circumstances.

section 14 (adoption by married couple); section 15 (adoption by one person);	a deputy circuit judge or recorder nominated for adoption proceedings; or	All circumstances.
section 18 (freeing child for adoption); section 20 (revocation of order under section 18); section 27, 28 or 29 (restrictions on removal of child); section 55 (adoption of children abroad).	a circuit judge nominated for public family law proceedings; or	All circumstances where proceedings under section 18 (freeing child for adoption) are heard in conjunction with care proceedings under s 31 of the Children Act 1989 (c 41) and relate to the same child.
	a district judge of the Principal Registry of the Family Division of the High Court; or	Interlocutory matters.
	a district judge nominated for adoption proceedings; or	Interlocutory matters.
	a deputy district judge nominated for adoption proceedings; or	Interlocutory matters.
	a district judge nominated for public family law proceedings.	Interlocutory matters where proceedings under section 18 (freeing child for adoption) are heard in conjunction with care proceedings under s 31 of the Children Act 1989 (c 41) and relate to the same child.

(f)

Proceedings under any of the following provisions of the Children Act 1989 (c 41):	A circuit judge nominated for private or public family law proceedings; or	All circumstances.
section 4(1)(a) (applications for parental responsibility by father);	a deputy circuit judge or recorder nominated for private or public family law proceedings; or	All circumstances.
section 4(3) (termination of parental responsibility);	a district judge of the Principal Registry of the Family Division of the High Court; or	All circumstances.
section 5(1) (appointment of guardian);	a district judge nominated for private or public family law proceedings;	All circumstances.
section 6(7) (termination of guardianship); paragraph 11(3) of Schedule 14 (discharge of existing custody etc orders).	a district judge or deputy district judge.	(1) Interlocutory matters; or (2) unopposed hearings.

(g)

Proceedings under any of the following provisions of the Children Act 1989 (c 41):	A circuit judge nominated for private or public family law proceedings; or	All circumstances.
section 13(1) (change of child's name or removal from jurisdiction);	a deputy circuit judge or recorder nominated for private or public family law proceedings; or	All circumstances.
section 16(6) (reference of question of variation or discharge of section 8 order);	a district judge of the Principal Registry of the Family Division of the High Court; or	All circumstances.
applications under section 10 of the Children Act 1989 (c 41) for an order under section 8.	a district judge nominated for private or public family law proceedings;	All circumstances.
	a district judge;	(1) Interlocutory matters; (2) unopposed hearings; or (3) opposed hearings where

		(a) the application is for a contact order and the principle of contact with the applicant is unopposed; or (b) the order (i) is (or is one of a series of orders which is) to be limited in time until the next hearing or order, and (ii) the substantive application is returnable before a judge within column (ii) of this paragraph who has full jurisdiction in all circumstances.
	a deputy district judge.	(1) Interlocutory matters; or (2) unopposed hearings.

(h)

Proceedings under any of the following provisions of the Children Act 1989 (c 41):	A circuit judge nominated for public family law proceedings; or	All circumstances.
section 25 (secure accommodation);	a district judge of the Principal Registry of the Family Division of the High Court;	All circumstances.
section 31 (care and supervision orders);		
section 33(7) (change of child's name or removal from jurisdiction);	a district judge nominated for public family law proceedings.	(1) Interlocutory matters; or (2) unopposed hearings; or (3) opposed hearings where the application is for an order under section 34 (a contact order) and the principle of contact is unopposed.
section 39(1), (2) or (4) (discharge and variation of care and supervision orders);		
paragraph 6 of Schedule 3 (supervision order);		
section 34 (parental contact etc with child in care);		
paragraph 19(1) of Schedule 2 (arrangements to assist children to live abroad).		

(i)		
Proceedings under section 38 of the Children Act 1989 (c 41) (interim care or supervision orders).	A circuit judge nominated for public family law proceedings;	All circumstances.
	a district judge of the Principal Registry of the Family Division of the High Court; or	All circumstances.
	a district judge nominated for public family law proceedings.	All circumstances.
(j)		
Proceedings under any of the following provisions of the Children Act 1989 (c 41):	A circuit judge nominated for public family law proceedings;	All circumstances.
section 39(3) (variation of supervision order);	a district judge of the Principal Registry of the Family Division of the High Court; or	All circumstances.
section 36(1) (education supervision order);	a district judge nominated for public family law proceedings.	All circumstances.
paragraph 15(2), or 17(1) of Schedule 3 (extension and discharge of education supervision order);		
section 43 (child assessment order);		
sections 44, 45(4), 45(8), 46(7), 48(9) (order for emergency protection of child);		
section 50 (recovery order);		
applications for leave under section 91(14), (15) or (17) (further applications);		
applications under section 21 of the Adoption Act 1976 (c 36) (substitution of adoption agencies).		

(k)		
Proceedings under any of the following provisions of the Child Support Act 1991 (c 48):	A circuit judge nominated for private family law proceedings; or	All circumstances.
section 20 (appeals)	a district judge of the Principal Registry of the Family Division of the High Court.	All circumstances.

(l)		
The hearing of an appeal under:	A person capable of sitting as a judge of a county court district and nominated for private or public family law proceedings.	Where, under these directions, such person would have been able to hear the matter at first instance but subject to the exception contained in article 2(b) of the 1991 Order.
(i) rule 8.1 of the Family Proceedings Rules 1991;		
(ii) Order 37, rule 6 of the County Court Rules 1981 as applied by the said rule 8.1; or		
(iii) the Children (Allocation of Proceedings) (Appeals) Order 1991 ('the 1991 Order').		

(m)		
Proceedings under s 30 of the Human Fertilisation and Embryology Act 1990 (c 37).	A circuit judge nominated for private or public family law proceedings; or	All circumstances.
	a district judge of the Principal Registry of the Family Division of the High Court; or	Interlocutory matters.
	a district judge	Interlocutory matters.

(n)		
Proceedings under any of the following provisions of the Family Law Act 1986 (c 55) in respect of proceedings or orders made under section 8 of the Children Act 1989 (c 41):	A circuit judge nominated for private or public family proceedings; or	All circumstances.
	a district judge of the Principal Registry of the Family Division of the High Court; or	All circumstances.
section 33 (power to order child's whereabouts);	a district judge nominated for private orpublic family law proceedings.	All circumstances.
section 34 (power to order recovery of child);		
section 37 (surrender of passports).		
(o)		
Proceedings under any of the following provisions of the Family Law Act 1986 (c 55):	A circuit judge nominated for private or public family law proceedings; or	All circumstances.
section 55 (declaration as to marital status);	a district judge of the Principal Registry of the Family Division of the High Court; or	Interlocutory matters.
section 55A (declarations of parentage);		
section 56 (declarations of legitimacy or legitimation);	a district judge.	Interlocutory matters.
section 57 (declarations as to adoptions effected overseas).		

4.19 FAMILY PROCEEDINGS COURTS (CHILDREN ACT 1989) RULES 1991, SI 1991/1395

The Family Proceedings Courts (Children Act 1989) Rules 1991 (FPC(CA)R 1991) apply to family proceedings in the family proceedings court.[1] They are not set out in this Handbook, since, for most purposes it is sufficient to work on the basis that:

- rr 1–21 of the FPC(CA)R 1991 correspond to rr 4.1–4.21 in Part IV of the Family Proceedings Rules 1991 (FPR 1991);
- rr 21A–21J of the FPC(CA)R 1991 correspond to the rules in Part IVA of the FPR 1991; and
- rr 23, 25 to 27, and 31 of the FPC(CA)R 1991 correspond to rr 4.23, 4.24–4.26, and 4.27, respectively in Part IV of the FPR 1991,

with minor modifications essentially to reflect the differences in structure between, on the one hand, the family proceedings court and, on the other hand, the High Court and county court.

Much more important than any minor differences between these two sets of court rules is the fact that the FPC(CA)R 1991 mirror only Parts IV and IVA of the FPR 1991. There are no equivalents to the other Parts of the FPR 1991. This reflects important limitations on the sorts of case that can be heard by the family proceedings court. In particular, such courts cannot hear applications for orders under the Child Abduction and Custody Act 1985 or applications in wardship, nor do they have the discretionary power to make a child party to proceedings in the way that the High Court and county court can do pursuant to FPR 1991, r 9.5.

---

[1] Ie the magistrates' court.

4.20 FAMILY PROCEEDINGS RULES 1991

OVERVIEW

General

The Family Proceedings Rules 1991 (FPR 1991) came into effect on 14 October 1991 to coincide with the coming into effect of the Children Act 1989. They apply to family proceedings in the county court and High Court.[1] They have been amended from time to time (for example, from 1 April 2001 with the establishment of CAFCASS), and now require further revision. It is intended that a new set of rules – the Family Procedure Rules – will be issued in stages, starting with an overriding objective and adoption rules in time for the commencement of the main provisions of the Adoption and Children Act 2002 in September 2005. The new set of rules will mark two vital developments: they will apply across all courts dealing with family cases (ie there will no longer be separate rules for the family proceedings court) and they will be harmonised with the Civil Procedure Rules 1998 (indeed the CPR 1998 will act as default provision).[2] In the meantime there will be some further amendments to the FPR 1991 in connection with the amended definition of 'harm' in s 31(9) of the Children Act 1989 and in connection with Brussels II.

The FPR 1991 are themselves divided into a number of Parts: Part I is headed 'Preliminary', Part II 'Matrimonial Causes', Part III 'Other Matrimonial etc Proceedings', Part IV 'Proceedings under the Children Act 1989', Part IVA 'Proceedings under section 30 of the Human Fertilisation and Embryology Act 1990', Part V 'Wardship', Part VI 'Child Abduction and Custody', Part VII 'Enforcement of Orders', Part VIII 'Appeals', Part IX 'Disability' and Part X 'Procedure (General)'. Appendix 1 prescribes the use of certain forms, and Appendix 3[3] defines who is to be a respondent to various applications concerning children, and those persons who, though not respondents, must be sent notice of the application.

Part IV

It should be clear from this list that it is Part IV of the FPR 1991 which provides the rules of court for the great majority of cases concerning children that proceed in the High Court and county court (the main exception to this

---

[1] But not to such proceedings in the family proceedings court, to which the Family Proceedings Court (Children Act 1989) Rules 1991 apply.

[2] To this end the Family Procedure Rules Committee has been established pursuant to s 77 of the Courts Act 2003.

[3] Which is not always easy to follow.

being cases brought under the Adoption Act 1976, which proceed under their own rules). Very broadly, Part IV can be broken down into three groups:

- some important preliminaries of general application, including the meaning of particular words and phrases within Part IV (r 4.1(1)), the cases to which Part IV applies (r 4.1(2)), and the definitions of certain matters prescribed by the Children Act 1989, including additional categories of 'specified proceedings' in which the court shall appoint a CAFCASS officer as children's guardian unless satisfied that it is not necessary to do so in order to safeguard the child's interests (r 4.2(2));

- rules concerning each of the steps that are typically taken in proceedings relating to children, from applications for leave to commence proceedings (r 4.3), to parties and service (rr 4.7 and 4.8), the appointment and various roles of CAFCASS officers, a solicitor for the child and a local authority social worker writing a report in accordance with s 7(1)(b) of the Children Act 1989 (rr 4.10–4.13), directions (r 4.14), evidence (rr 4.17–4.20 including, at r 4.18(1) that 'No person may, without the leave of the court, cause a child to be medically or psychiatrically examined, or otherwise assessed, for the purpose of the preparation of expert evidence for use in the proceedings'), and hearings, appeals and confidentiality of documents (rr 4.21–4.23 respectively);

- finally, an assortment of provisions relating to particular issues, including secure accommodation, investigation under s 37 of the Children Act 1989 and directions to local education authorities to apply for an education supervision order (rr 4.24–4.27).

Part IX

After Part IV, it is Part IX that is probably of greatest importance in proceedings affecting children. This Part is titled 'Disability', the use of which in this context should surely now be regarded as outmoded. The term refers to the deeply rooted concept in the law of England and Wales that neither the mentally ill nor children have the capacity to conduct their own litigation and that, therefore, where they are parties to litigation, a competent adult must stand in to do so, usually by instructing solicitors on their behalf.

This restriction, so far as it relates to children, has been substantially modified by:

- section 41(4)(b) of the Children Act 1989, FPR 1991, r 4.12 and r 9.2A, which establish that mature children are legally capable of directly instructing a solicitor; and

- section 41 of the Children Act 1989, FPR 1991, r 4.7 and Appendix 3, and r 9.5, which establish that a child will be a party to 'specified proceedings'[4] and may be a party to other family proceedings. The

---

[4] Section 122 of the Adoption and Children Act 2002 holds out the prospect of extending this further by extending the definition of 'specified proceedings'.

President's *Practice Direction: Representation of Children in Family Proceedings pursuant to FPR 1991, Rule 9.5*[5] gives essential guidance about cases in which it may be appropriate for a court to make a child party to proceedings.

CAFCASS officers reading this Overview should read and be familiar with rr 4.10, 4.11, 4.11A, 4.11B, 4.12, 9.2A and 9.5.

The **Overview of Children Law** continues at **5.1** Overview of Case-law..

---

[5] [2004] 1 FLR 1188. This, and the CAFCASS Practice Note accompanying it at [2004] 1 FLR 1190, are set out below at **6.18** and **6.19** respectively.

Family Proceedings Rules 1991, SI 1991/1247
(rr 1.1–1.5, 4.1–4.28, 4A.1–4A.10, 5.1–5.6, 6.1–6.17,
9.1–9.5, 10.14A, 10.26, App 3)

PART I
PRELIMINARY

1.1 Citation and commencement

These rules may be cited as the Family Proceedings Rules 1991 and shall come into force on 14 October 1991.

1.2 Interpretation

(1) In these rules, unless the context otherwise requires –

'the Act of 1973' means the Matrimonial Causes Act 1973;
'the Act of 1984' means the Matrimonial and Family Proceedings Act 1984;
'the Act of 1986' means the Family Law Act 1986;
'the Act of 1989' means the Children Act 1989;
'the Act of 1991' means the Child Support Act 1991;
'ancillary relief' means –
>   (a) an avoidance of disposition order,
>   (b) a financial provision order,
>   (c) an order for maintenance pending suit,
>   (d) a property adjustment order,
>   (e) a variation order, or
>   (f) a pension sharing order;

'avoidance of disposition order' means an order under section 37(2)(b) or (c) of the Act of 1973;
'business day' has the meaning assigned to it by rule 1.5(6);
'cause' means a matrimonial cause as defined by section 32 of the Act of 1984 or proceedings under section 19 of the Act of 1973 (presumption of death and dissolution of marriage);
'child' and 'child of the family' have, except in Part IV, the meanings respectively assigned to them by section 52(1) of the Act of 1973;
'consent order' means an order under section 33A of the Act of 1973;
'Contracting State' means –
>   (a) one of the original parties to the Council Regulation, that is to say Belgium, Germany, Greece, Spain, France, Ireland, Italy, Luxembourg, the Netherlands, Austria, Portugal, Finland, Sweden and the United Kingdom, and
>   (b) a party which has subsequently adopted the Council Regulation;

'the Council Regulation' means Council Regulation (EC) No 1347/2000 of 29 May 2000 on jurisdiction and the recognition and enforcement of judgments in matrimonial matters and in matters of parental responsibility for children of both spouses;

'court' means a judge or the district judge;

'court of trial' means a divorce county court designated by the Lord Chancellor as a court of trial pursuant to section 33(1) of the Act of 1984 and, in relation to matrimonial proceedings pending in a divorce county court, the principal registry shall be treated as a court of trial having its place of sitting at the Royal Courts of Justice;

'defended cause' means a cause not being an undefended cause;

'district judge', in relation to proceedings in the principal registry, a district registry or a county court, means the district judge or one of the district judges of that registry or county court, as the case may be;

'district registry', except in rule 4.22(2A), means any district registry having a divorce county court within its district;

'divorce county court' means a county court so designated by the Lord Chancellor pursuant to section 33(1) of the Act of 1984;

'divorce town', in relation to any matrimonial proceedings, means a place at which sittings of the High Court are authorised to be held outside the Royal Courts of Justice for the hearing of such proceedings or proceedings of the class to which they belong;

'document exchange' means any document exchange for the time being approved by the Lord Chancellor;

'family proceedings' has the meaning assigned to it by section 32 of the Act of 1984;

'financial provision order' means any of the orders mentioned in section 21(1) of the Act of 1973 except an order under section 27(6) of that Act;

'financial relief' has the same meaning as in section 37 of the Act of 1973;

'judge' does not include a district judge;

'notice of intention to defend' has the meaning assigned to it by rule 10.8;

'officer of the service' has the same meaning as in the Criminal Justice and Court Services Act 2000;

'order for maintenance pending suit' means an order under section 22 of the Act of 1973;

'person named' includes a person described as 'passing under the name of A.B.';

'the President' means the President of the Family Division or, in the case of his absence or incapacity through illness or otherwise or of a vacancy in the office of President, the senior puisne judge of that Division;

'principal registry' means the Principal Registry of the Family Division;

'proper officer' means –

   (a) in relation to the principal registry, the family proceedings department manager, and

   (b) in relation to any other court or registry, the court manager,

or other officer of the court or registry acting on his behalf in accordance with directions given by the Lord Chancellor;

'property adjustment order' means any of the orders mentioned in section 21(2) of the Act of 1973;

'registry for the divorce town' shall be construed in accordance with rule 2.32(6);

'Royal Courts of Justice', in relation to matrimonial proceedings pending in a divorce county court, means such place, being the Royal Courts of Justice or elsewhere, as may be specified in directions given by the Lord Chancellor pursuant to section 42(2)(a) of the Act of 1984;

'senior district judge' means the senior district judge of the Family Division or, in his absence from the principal registry, the senior of the district judges in attendance at the registry;

'special procedure list' has the meaning assigned to it by rule 2.24(3);

'undefended cause' means –

    (i) a cause in which no answer has been filed or any answer filed has been struck out, or

    (ii) a cause which is proceeding only on the respondent's answer and in which no reply or answer to the respondent's answer has been filed or any such reply or answer has been struck out, or

    (iii) a cause to which rule 2.12(4) applies and in which no notice has been given under that rule or any notice so given has been withdrawn, or

    (iv) a cause in which an answer has been filed claiming relief but in which no pleading has been filed opposing the grant of a decree on the petition or answer or any pleading or part of a pleading opposing the grant of such relief has been struck out, or

    (v) any cause not within (i) to (iv) above in which a decree has been pronounced;

'variation order' means an order under section 31 of the Act of 1973.

(2) Unless the context otherwise requires, a cause begun by petition shall be treated as pending for the purposes of these rules notwithstanding that a final decree or order has been made on the petition.

(3) Unless the context otherwise requires, a rule or Part referred to by number means the rule or Part so numbered in these rules.

(4) In these rules a form referred to by number means the form so numbered in Appendix 1 or 1A to these rules with such variation as the circumstances of the particular case may require.

(5) In these rules any reference to an Order and rule is –

    (a) if prefixed by the letters 'CCR', a reference to that Order and rule in the County Court Rules 1981, and

    (b) if prefixed by the letters 'RSC', a reference to that Order and rule in the Rules of the Supreme Court 1965.

(5A) In these rules a reference to a Part or rule, if prefixed by the letters 'CPR', is a reference to that Part or rule in the Civil Procedure Rules 1998.

(6) References in these rules to a county court shall, in relation to matrimonial proceedings, be construed as references to a divorce county court.

(7) In this rule and in rule 1.4, 'matrimonial proceedings' means proceedings of a kind with respect to which divorce county courts have jurisdiction by or under section 33, 34 or 35 of the Act of 1984.

1.3 Application of other rules

(1) Subject to the provisions of these rules and of any enactment the County Court Rules 1981 and the Rules of the Supreme Court 1965 shall continue to apply, with the necessary modifications, to family proceedings in a county court and the High Court respectively.

(2) For the purposes of paragraph (1) any provision of these rules authorising or requiring anything to be done in family proceedings shall be treated as if it were, in the

case of proceedings pending in a county court, a provision of the County Court Rules 1981 and, in the case of proceedings pending in the High Court, a provision of the Rules of the Supreme Court 1965.

1.4 County court proceedings in principal registry

(1) Subject to the provisions of these rules, matrimonial proceedings pending at any time in the principal registry which, if they had been begun in a divorce county court, would be pending at that time in such a court, shall be treated, for the purposes of these rules and of any provision of the County Court Rules 1981 and the County Courts Act 1984, as pending in a divorce county court and not in the High Court.

(2) Unless the context otherwise requires, any reference to a divorce county court in any provision of these rules which relates to the commencement or prosecution of proceedings in a divorce county court, or the transfer of proceedings to or from such a court, includes a reference to the principal registry.

1.5 Computation of time

(1) Any period of time fixed by these rules, or by any rules applied by these rules, or by any decree, judgment, order or direction for doing any act shall be reckoned in accordance with the following provisions of this rule.

(2) Where the act is required to be done not less than a specified period before a specified date, the period starts immediately after the date on which the act is done and ends immediately before the specified date.

(3) Where the act is required to be done within a specified period after or from a specified date, the period starts immediately after that date.

(4) Where, apart from this paragraph, the period in question, being a period of seven days or less, would include a day which is not a business day, that day shall be excluded.

(5) Where the time so fixed for doing an act in the court office expires on a day on which the office is closed, and for that reason the act cannot be done on that day, the act shall be in time if done on the next day on which the office is open.

(6) In these rules 'business day' means any day other than –

    (a) a Saturday, Sunday, Christmas Day or Good Friday; or

    (b) a bank holiday under the Banking and Financial Dealings Act 1971, in England and Wales.

****

PART IV

PROCEEDINGS UNDER THE CHILDREN ACT 1989

4.1 Interpretation and application

(1) In this Part of these rules, unless a contrary intention appears –

a section or schedule referred to means the section or schedule so numbered in the Act of 1989;

'a section 8 order' has the meaning assigned to it by section 8(2);

'application' means an application made under or by virtue of the Act of 1989 or under these rules, and 'applicant' shall be construed accordingly;

'child', in relation to proceedings to which this Part applies –

(a) means, subject to sub-paragraph (b), a person under the age of 18 with respect to whom the proceedings are brought, and

(b) where the proceedings are under Schedule 1, also includes a person who has reached the age of 18;

'children and family reporter' means an officer of the service who has been asked to prepare a welfare report under section 7(1)(a);

'children's guardian' –

(a) means an officer of the service appointed under section 41 for the child with respect to whom the proceedings are brought; but

(b) does not include such an officer appointed in relation to proceedings specified by Part IVA;

'directions appointment' means a hearing for directions under rule 4.14(2);

'emergency protection order' means an order under section 44;

'leave' includes permission and approval;

'note' includes a record made by mechanical means;

'parental responsibility' has the meaning assigned to it by section 3;

'recovery order' means an order under section 50;

'specified proceedings' has the meaning assigned to it by section 41(6) and rule 4.2(2); and

'welfare officer' means a person who has been asked to prepare a welfare report under section 7(1)(b).

(2) Except where the contrary intention appears, the provisions of this Part apply to proceedings in the High Court and the county courts –

(a) on an application for a section 8 order;

(b) on an application for a care order or a supervision order;

(c) on an application under section 4(1)(c), 4(3), 5(1), 6(7), 13(1), 16(6), 33(7), 34(2), 34(3), 34(4), 34(9), 36(1), 38(8)(b), 39(1), 39(2), 39(3), 39(4), 43(1), 43(12), 44, 45, 46(7), 48(9), 50(1) or 102(1);

(d) under Schedule 1, except where financial relief is also sought by or on behalf of an adult;

(e) on an application under paragraph 19(1) of Schedule 2;

(f) on an application under paragraph 6(3), 15(2) or 17(1) of Schedule 3;

(g) on an application under paragraph 11(3) or 16(5) of Schedule 14; or

(h) under section 25.

4.2 Matters prescribed for the purposes of the Act of 1989

(1) The parties to proceedings in which directions are given under section 38(6), and any person named in such a direction, form the prescribed class for the purposes of section 38(8) (application to vary directions made with interim care or interim supervision order).

(2) The following proceedings are specified for the purposes of section 41 in accordance with subsection (6)(i) thereof –

(a) proceedings under section 25;

(b) applications under section 33(7);
(c) proceedings under paragraph 19(1) of Schedule 2;
(d) applications under paragraph 6(3) of Schedule 3;
(e) appeals against the determination of proceedings of a kind set out in sub-paragraphs (a) to (d).

(3) The applicant for an order that has been made under section 43(1) and the persons referred to in section 43(11) may, in any circumstances, apply under section 43(12) for a child assessment order to be varied or discharged.

(4) The following persons form the prescribed class for the purposes of section 44(9) (application to vary directions) –

(a) the parties to the application for the order in respect of which it is sought to vary the directions;
(b) the children's guardian;
(c) the local authority in whose area the child concerned is ordinarily resident;
(d) any person who is named in the directions.

4.3 Application for leave to commence proceedings

(1) Where the leave of the court is required to bring any proceedings to which this Part applies, the person seeking leave shall file –

(a) a written request for leave in Form C2 setting out the reasons for the application; and
(b) a draft of the application (being the documents referred to in rule 4.4(1A)) for the making of which leave is sought together with sufficient copies for one to be served on each respondent.

(2) On considering a request for leave filed under paragraph (1), the court shall –

(a) grant the request, whereupon the proper officer shall inform the person making the request of the decision, or
(b) direct that a date be fixed for the hearing of the request, whereupon the proper officer shall fix such a date and give such notice as the court directs to the person making the request and such other persons as the court requires to be notified, of the date so fixed.

(3) Where leave is granted to bring proceedings to which this Part applies the application shall proceed in accordance with rule 4.4; but paragraph (1)(a) of that rule shall not apply.

(4) In the case of a request for leave to bring proceedings under Schedule 1, the draft application under paragraph (1) shall be accompanied by a statement setting out the financial details which the person seeking leave believes to be relevant to the request and containing a declaration that it is true to the maker's best knowledge and belief, together with sufficient copies for one to be served on each respondent.

4.4 Application

(1) Subject to paragraph (4), an applicant shall –

(a) file the documents referred to in paragraph (1A) below (which documents shall together be called the 'application') together with sufficient copies for one to be served on each respondent, and

(b) serve a copy of the application together with Form C6 and such (if any) of Forms C7 and C10A as are given to him by the proper officer under paragraph (2)(b) on each respondent such number of days prior to the date fixed under paragraph (2)(a) as is specified for that application in column (ii) of Appendix 3 to these rules.

(1A) The documents to be filed under paragraph (1)(a) above are –

    (a) (i) whichever is appropriate of Forms C1 to C4 or C51, and

        (ii) such of the supplemental Forms C10 or C11 to C20 as may be appropriate, or

    (b) where there is no appropriate form a statement in writing of the order sought,

and where the application is made in respect of more than one child, all the children shall be included in one application.

(2) On receipt of the documents filed under paragraph (1)(a) the proper officer shall –

    (a) fix the date for a hearing or a directions appointment, allowing sufficient time for the applicant to comply with paragraph (1)(b),

    (b) endorse the date so fixed upon Form C6 and, where appropriate, Form C6A, and

    (c) return forthwith to the applicant the copies of the application and Form C10A if filed with it, together with Form C6 and such of Forms C6A and C7 as are appropriate.

(3) The applicant shall, at the same time as complying with paragraph (1)(b), serve Form C6A on the persons set out for the relevant class of proceedings in column (iv) of Appendix 3 to these rules.

(4) An application for –

    (a) a section 8 order,

    (b) an emergency protection order,

    (c) a warrant under section 48(9),

    (d) a recovery order, or

    (e) a warrant under section 102(1)

may be made ex parte in which case the applicant shall –

        (i) file the application in the appropriate form in Appendix 1 to these rules –

            (a) where the application is made by telephone, within 24 hours after the making of the application, or

            (b) in any other case, at the time when the application is made, and

        (ii) in the case of an application for a section 8 order or an emergency protection order, serve a copy of the application on each respondent within 48 hours after the making of the order.

(5) Where the court refuses to make an order on an ex parte application it may direct that the application be made inter partes.

(6) In the case of proceedings under Schedule 1, the application under paragraph (1) shall be accompanied by a statement in Form C10A setting out the financial details

which the applicant believes to be relevant to the application, together with sufficient copies for one to be served on each respondent.

4.5 Withdrawal of application

(1) An application may be withdrawn only with leave of the court.

(2) Subject to paragraph (3), a person seeking leave to withdraw an application shall file and serve on the parties a written request for leave setting out the reasons for the request.

(3) The request under paragraph (2) may be made orally to the court if the parties and either the children's guardian or the welfare officer or children and family reporter are present.

(4) Upon receipt of a written request under paragraph (2) the court shall –

- (a) if –
  - (i) the parties consent in writing,
  - (ii) the children's guardian has had an opportunity to make representations, and
  - (iii) the court thinks fit,

  grant the request, in which case the proper officer shall notify the parties, the children's guardian and the welfare officer or children and family reporter of the granting of the request, or
- (b) direct that a date be fixed for the hearing of the request in which case the proper officer shall give at least 7 days' notice to the parties, the children's guardian and the welfare officer or children and family reporter, of the date fixed.

4.6 Transfer

(1) Where an application is made, in accordance with the provisions of the Allocation Order, to a county court for an order transferring proceedings from a magistrates' court following the refusal of the magistrates' court to order such a transfer, the applicant shall –

- (a) file the application in Form C2, together with a copy of the certificate issued by the magistrates' court, and
- (b) serve a copy of the documents mentioned in sub-paragraph (a) personally on all parties to the proceedings which it is sought to have transferred,

within 2 days after receipt by the applicant of the certificate.

(2) Within 2 days after receipt of the documents served under paragraph (1)(b), any party other than the applicant may file written representations.

(3) The court shall, not before the fourth day after the filing of the application under paragraph (1), unless the parties consent to earlier consideration, consider the application and either –

- (a) grant the application, whereupon the proper officer shall inform the parties of that decision, or
- (b) direct that a date be fixed for the hearing of the application, whereupon the proper officer shall fix such a date and give not less than 1 day's notice to the parties of the date so fixed.

(4) Where proceedings are transferred from a magistrates' court to a county court in accordance with the provisions of the Allocation Order, the county court shall consider whether to transfer those proceedings to the High Court in accordance with that Order and either –

(a) determine that such an order need not be made,

(b) make such an order,

(c) order that a date be fixed for the hearing of the question whether such an order should be made, whereupon the proper officer shall give such notice to the parties as the court directs of the date so fixed, or

(d) invite the parties to make written representations, within a specified period, as to whether such an order should be made; and upon receipt of the representations the court shall act in accordance with sub-paragraph (a), (b) or (c).

(5) The proper officer shall notify the parties of an order transferring the proceedings from a county court or from the High Court made in accordance with the provisions of the Allocation Order.

(6) Before ordering the transfer of proceedings from a county court to a magistrates' court in accordance with the Allocation Order, the county court shall notify the magistrates' court of its intention to make such an order and invite the views of the clerk to the justices on whether such an order should be made.

(7) An order transferring proceedings from a county court to a magistrates' court in accordance with the Allocation Order shall –

(a) be in Form C49, and

(b) be served by the court on the parties.

(8) In this rule 'the Allocation Order' means the Children (Allocation of Proceedings) Order 1991 or any Order replacing that Order.

4.7 Parties

(1) The respondents to proceedings to which this Part applies shall be those persons set out in the relevant entry in column (iii) of Appendix 3 to these rules.

(2) In proceedings to which this Part applies, a person may file a request in Form C2 that he or another person –

(a) be joined as a party, or

(b) cease to be a party.

(3) On considering a request under paragraph (2) the court shall, subject to paragraph (4) –

(a) grant it without a hearing or representations, save that this shall be done only in the case of a request under paragraph (2)(a), whereupon the proper officer shall inform the parties and the person making the request of that decision, or

(b) order that a date be fixed for the consideration of the request, whereupon the proper officer shall give notice of the date so fixed, together with a copy of the request –

    (i) in the case of a request under paragraph (2)(a), to the applicant, and

    (ii) in the case of a request under paragraph (2)(b), to the parties, or

(c) invite the parties or any of them to make written representations, within a specified period, as to whether the request should be granted; and upon the expiry of the period the court shall act in accordance with sub-paragraph (a) or (b).

(4) Where a person with parental responsibility requests that he be joined under paragraph (2)(a), the court shall grant his request.

(5) In proceedings to which this Part applies the court may direct –

    (a)   that a person who would not otherwise be a respondent under these rules be joined as a party to the proceedings, or

    (b)   that a party to the proceedings cease to be a party.

4.8 Service

(1) Subject to the requirement in rule 4.6(1)(b) of personal service, where service of a document is required under this Part (and not by a provision to which section 105(8) (Service of notice or other document under the Act) applies) it may be effected –

    (a)   if the person to be served is not known by the person serving to be acting by solicitor –

        (i)   by delivering it to him personally, or

        (ii)   by delivering it at, or by sending it by first-class post to, his residence or his last known residence, or

    (b)   if the person to be served is known by the person serving to be acting by solicitor –

        (i)   by delivering the document at, or sending it by first-class post to, the solicitor's address for service,

        (ii)   where the solicitor's address for service includes a numbered box at a document exchange, by leaving the document at that document exchange or at a document exchange which transmits documents on every business day to that document exchange, or

        (iii)   by sending a legible copy of the document by facsimile transmission to the solicitor's office.

(2) In this rule 'first-class post' means first-class post which has been pre-paid or in respect of which pre-payment is not required.

(3) Where a child who is a party to proceedings to which this Part applies is not prosecuting or defending them without a next friend or guardian ad litem under rule 9.2A and is required by these rules or other rules of court to serve a document, service shall be effected by –

    (a)   the solicitor acting for the child, or

    (b)   where there is no such solicitor, the children's guardian or the guardian ad litem, or

    (c)   where there is neither such a solicitor nor a children's guardian nor a guardian ad litem, the court.

(4) Service of any document on a child who is not prosecuting or defending the proceedings concerned without a next friend or guardian ad litem under rule 9.2A shall, subject to any direction of the court, be effected by service on –

    (a)   the solicitor acting for the child, or

    (b)   where there is no such solicitor, the children's guardian or the guardian ad litem, or

    (c) where there is neither such a solicitor nor a children's guardian nor a guardian ad litem, with leave of the court, the child.

(5) Where the court refuses leave under paragraph (4)(c) it shall give a direction under paragraph (8).

(6) A document shall, unless the contrary is proved, be deemed to have been served –

    (a) in the case of service by first-class post, on the second business day after posting, and

    (b) in the case of service in accordance with paragraph (1)(b)(ii), on the second business day after the day on which it is left at the document exchange.

(7) At or before the first directions appointment in, or hearing of, proceedings to which this Part applies the applicant shall file a statement in Form C9 that service of –

    (a) a copy of the application and other documents referred to in rule 4.4(1)(b) has been effected on each respondent, and

    (b) notice of the proceedings has been effected under rule 4.4(3);

and the statement shall indicate –

        (i) the manner, date, time and place of service, or
        (ii) where service was effected by post, the date, time and place of posting.

(8) In proceedings to which this Part applies, where these rules or other rules of court require a document to be served, the court may, without prejudice to any power under rule 4.14, direct that –

    (a) the requirement shall not apply;

    (b) the time specified by the rules for complying with the requirement shall be abridged to such extent as may be specified in the direction;

    (c) service shall be effected in such manner as may be specified in the direction.

4.9 Answer to application

(1) Within 14 days of service of an application for a section 8 order or an application under Schedule 1, each respondent shall file, and serve on the parties, an acknowledgement of the application in Form C7.

(2) (*deleted*)

(3) Following service of an application to which this Part applies, other than an application under rule 4.3 or for a section 8 order, a respondent may, subject to paragraph (4), file a written answer, which shall be served on the other parties.

(4) An answer under paragraph (3) shall, except in the case of an application under section 25, 31, 34, 38, 43, 44, 45, 46, 48 or 50, be filed, and served, not less than 2 days before the date fixed for the hearing of the application.

4.10 Appointment of children's guardian

(1) As soon as practicable after the commencement of specified proceedings, or the transfer of such proceedings to the court, the court shall appoint a children's guardian, unless –

    (a) such an appointment has already been made by the court which made the transfer and is subsisting, or

(b) the court considers that such an appointment is not necessary to safeguard the interests of the child.

(2) At any stage in specified proceedings a party may apply, without notice to the other parties unless the court directs otherwise, for the appointment of a children's guardian.

(3) The court shall grant an application under paragraph (2) unless it considers such an appointment not to be necessary to safeguard the interests of the child, in which case it shall give its reasons; and a note of such reasons shall be taken by the proper officer.

(4) At any stage in specified proceedings the court may, of its own motion, appoint a children's guardian.

(4A) The court may, in specified proceedings, appoint more than one children's guardian in respect of the same child.

(5) The proper officer shall, as soon as practicable, notify the parties and any welfare officer or children and family reporter of an appointment under this rule or, as the case may be, of a decision not to make such an appointment.

(6) Upon the appointment of a children's guardian the proper officer shall, as soon as practicable, notify him of the appointment and serve on him copies of the application and of documents filed under rule 4.17(1).

(7) A children's guardian appointed by the court under this rule shall not –

(a) be a member, officer or servant of a local authority which, or an authorised person (within the meaning of section 31(9)) who, is a party to the proceedings;
(b) be, or have been, a member, officer or servant of a local authority or voluntary organisation (within the meaning of section 105(1)) who has been directly concerned in that capacity in arrangements relating to the care, accommodation or welfare of the child during the five years prior to the commencement of the proceedings; or
(c) be a serving probation officer who has, in that capacity, been previously concerned with the child or his family.

(8) When appointing a children's guardian the court shall consider the appointment of anyone who has previously acted as children's guardian of the same child.

(9) The appointment of a children's guardian under this rule shall continue for such time as is specified in the appointment or until terminated by the court.

(10) When terminating an appointment in accordance with paragraph (9), the court shall give its reasons in writing for so doing.

(11) Where the court appoints a children's guardian in accordance with this rule or refuses to make such an appointment, the court or the proper officer shall record the appointment or refusal in Form C47.

4.11 Powers and duties of officers of the service

(1) In carrying out his duty under section 7(1)(a) or section 41(2), the officer of the service shall have regard to the principle set out in section 1(2) and the matters set out in section 1(3)(a) to (f) as if for the word 'court' in that section there were substituted the words 'officer of the service'.

(2) The officer of the service shall make such investigations as may be necessary for him to carry out his duties and shall, in particular –

(a) contact or seek to interview such persons as he thinks appropriate or as the court directs;
(b) obtain such professional assistance as is available to him which he thinks appropriate or which the court directs him to obtain.

(3) In addition to his duties, under other paragraphs of this rule, or rules 4.11A and 4.11B, the officer of the service shall provide to the court such other assistance as it may require.

(4) A party may question the officer of the service about oral or written advice tendered by him to the court.

4.11A Additional powers and duties of children's guardian

(1) The children's guardian shall –

(a) appoint a solicitor to represent the child unless such a solicitor has already been appointed; and
(b) give such advice to the child as is appropriate having regard to his understanding and, subject to rule 4.12(1)(a), instruct the solicitor representing the child on all matters relevant to the interests of the child including possibilities for appeal, arising in the course of the proceedings.

(2) Where the children's guardian is an officer of the service authorised by the Service in the terms mentioned by and in accordance with section 15(1) of the Criminal Justice and Court Services Act 2000, paragraph 1(a) shall not require him to appoint a solicitor for the child if he intends to have conduct of the proceedings on behalf of the child unless –

(a) the child wishes to instruct a solicitor direct; and
(b) the children's guardian or the court considers that he is of sufficient understanding to do so.

(3) Where it appears to the children's guardian that the child –

(a) is instructing his solicitor direct, or
(b) intends to conduct and is capable of conducting the proceedings on his own behalf,

he shall inform the court and from then he –

(i) shall perform all of his duties set out in rule 4.11 and this rule, other than duties under paragraph (1)(a) of this rule, and such other duties as the court may direct;
(ii) shall take such part in the proceedings as the court may direct; and
(iii) may, with leave of the court, have legal representation in the conduct of those duties.

(4) Unless excused by the court, the children's guardian shall attend all directions appointments in and hearings of the proceedings and shall advise the court on the following matters –

(a) whether the child is of sufficient understanding for any purpose including the child's refusal to submit to a medical or psychiatric examination or other assessment that the court has power to require, direct or order;

(b)   the wishes of the child in respect of any matter relevant to the proceedings, including his attendance at court;

(c)   the appropriate forum for the proceedings;

(d)   the appropriate timing of the proceedings or any part of them;

(e)   the options available to it in respect of the child and the suitability of each such option including what order should be made in determining the application; and

(f)   any other matter concerning which the court seeks his advice or concerning which he considers that the court should be informed.

(5) The advice given under paragraph (4) may, subject to any order of the court, be given orally or in writing; and if the advice be given orally, a note of it shall be taken by the court or the proper officer.

(6) The children's guardian shall, where practicable, notify any person whose joinder as a party to those proceedings would be likely, in the opinion of the children's guardian, to safeguard the interests of the child of that person's right to apply to be joined under rule 4.7(2) and shall inform the court –

(a)   of any such notification given;

(b)   of anyone whom he attempted to notify under this paragraph but was unable to contact; and

(c)   of anyone whom he believes may wish to be joined to the proceedings.

(7) The children's guardian shall, unless the court otherwise directs, not less than 14 days before the date fixed for the final hearing of the proceedings –

(a)   file a written report advising on the interests of the child; and

(b)   serve a copy of the filed report on the other parties.

(8) The children's guardian shall serve and accept service of documents on behalf of the child in accordance with rule 4.8(3)(b) and (4)(b) and, where the child has not himself been served, and has sufficient understanding, advise the child of the contents of any document so served.

(9) If the children's guardian inspects records of the kinds referred to in section 42, he shall bring to the attention of –

(a)   the court; and

(b)   unless the court otherwise directs, the other parties to the proceedings,

all records and documents which may, in his opinion, assist in the proper determination of the proceedings.

(10) The children's guardian shall ensure that, in relation to a decision made by the court in the proceedings –

(a)   if he considers it appropriate to the age and understanding of the child, the child is notified of that decision; and

(b)   if the child is notified of the decision, it is explained to the child in a manner appropriate to his age and understanding.

4.11B Additional powers and duties of a children and family reporter

(1) The children and family reporter shall –

   (a) notify the child of such contents of his report (if any) as he considers appropriate to the age and understanding of the child, including any reference to the child's own views on the application and the recommendation of the children and family reporter; and

   (b) if he does notify the child of any contents of his report, explain them to the child in a manner appropriate to his age and understanding.

(2) Where the court has –

   (a) directed that a written report be made by a children and family reporter; and

   (b) notified the children and family reporter that his report is to be considered at a hearing,

the children and family reporter shall –

      (i) file the report; and

     (ii) serve a copy on the other parties and on the children's guardian (if any),

by such time as the court may direct and if no direction is given, not less than 14 days before that hearing.

(3) The court may direct that the children and family reporter attend any hearing at which his report is to be considered.

(4) The children and family reporter shall advise the court if he considers that the joinder of a person as a party to the proceedings would be likely to safeguard the interests of the child.

(5) The children and family reporter shall consider whether it is in the best interests of the child for the child to be made a party to the proceedings.

(6) If the children and family reporter considers the child should be made a party to the proceedings he shall notify the court of his opinion together with the reasons for that opinion.

4.12 Solicitor for child

(1) A solicitor appointed under section 41(3) or in accordance with rule 4.11A(1)(a) shall represent the child –

   (a) in accordance with instructions received from the children's guardian (unless the solicitor considers, having taken into account the views of the children's guardian and any direction of the court under rule 4.11A(3), that the child wishes to give instructions which conflict with those of the children's guardian and that he is able, having regard to his understanding, to give such instructions on his own behalf in which case he shall conduct the proceedings in accordance with instructions received from the child), or

   (b) where no children's guardian has been appointed for the child and the condition in section 41(4)(b) is satisfied, in accordance with instructions received from the child, or

   (c) in default of instructions under (a) or (b), in furtherance of the best interests of the child.

(2) A solicitor appointed under section 41(3) or in accordance with rule 4.11A(1)(a) shall serve and accept service of documents on behalf of the child in accordance with rule 4.8(3)(a) and (4)(a) and, where the child has not himself been served and has sufficient understanding, advise the child of the contents of any document so served.

(3) Where the child wishes an appointment of a solicitor under section 41(3) or in accordance with rule 4.11A(1)(a) to be terminated, he may apply to the court for an order terminating the appointment; and the solicitor and the children's guardian shall be given an opportunity to make representations.

(4) Where the children's guardian wishes an appointment of a solicitor under section 41(3) to be terminated, he may apply to the court for an order terminating the appointment; and the solicitor and, if he is of sufficient understanding, the child, shall be given an opportunity to make representations.

(5) When terminating an appointment in accordance with paragraph (3) or (4), the court shall give its reasons for so doing, a note of which shall be taken by the court or the proper officer.

(6) Where the court appoints a solicitor under section 41(3) or refuses to make such an appointment, the court or the proper officer shall record the appointment or refusal in Form C48.

4.13 Welfare officer

(1) Where the court has directed that a written report be made by a welfare officer in accordance with section 7(1)(b), the report shall be filed at or by such time as the court directs or, in the absence of such a direction, at least 14 days before a relevant hearing; and the proper officer shall, as soon as practicable, serve a copy of the report on the parties and any children's guardian.

(2) In paragraph (1), a hearing is relevant if the proper officer has given the welfare officer notice that his report is to be considered at it.

(3) After the filing of a report by a welfare officer, the court may direct that the welfare officer attend any hearing at which the report is to be considered; and

(a) except where such a direction is given at a hearing attended by the welfare officer the proper officer shall inform the welfare officer of the direction; and

(b) at the hearing at which the report is considered any party may question the welfare officer about his report.

(3A) The welfare officer shall consider whether it is in the best interests of the child for the child to be made a party to the proceedings.

(3B) If the welfare officer considers the child should be made a party to the proceedings he shall notify the court of his opinion together with the reasons for that opinion.

(4) This rule is without prejudice to any power to give directions under rule 4.14.

4.14 Directions

(1) In this rule, 'party' includes the children's guardian and, where a request or a direction concerns a report under section 7, the welfare officer or children and family reporter.

(2) In proceedings to which this Part applies the court may, subject to paragraph (3), give, vary or revoke directions for the conduct of the proceedings, including –

(a) the timetable for the proceedings;

    (b) varying the time within which or by which an act is required, by these rules or by other rules of court, to be done;

    (c) the attendance of the child;

    (d) the appointment of a children's guardian, a guardian ad litem, or of a solicitor under section 41(3);

    (e) the service of documents;

    (f) the submission of evidence including experts' reports;

    (g) the preparation of welfare reports under section 7;

    (h) the transfer of the proceedings to another court;

    (i) consolidation with other proceedings.

(3) Directions under paragraph (2) may be given, varied or revoked either –

    (a) of the court's own motion having given the parties notice of its intention to do so, and an opportunity to attend and be heard or to make written representations,

    (b) on the written request in Form C2 of a party specifying the direction which is sought, filed and served on the other parties, or

    (c) on the written request in Form C2 of a party specifying the direction which is sought, to which the other parties consent and which they or their representatives have signed.

(4) In an urgent case the request under paragraph (3)(b) may, with the leave of the court, be made –

    (a) orally, or

    (b) without notice to the parties, or

    (c) both as in sub-paragraph (a) and as in sub-paragraph (b).

(5) On receipt of a written request under paragraph (3)(b) the proper officer shall fix a date for the hearing of the request and give not less than 2 days' notice in Form C6 to the parties of the date so fixed.

(6) On considering a request under paragraph (3)(c) the court shall either –

    (a) grant the request, whereupon the proper officer shall inform the parties of the decision, or

    (b) direct that a date be fixed for the hearing of the request, whereupon the proper officer shall fix such a date and give not less than 2 days' notice to the parties of the date so fixed.

(7) A party may apply for an order to be made under section 11(3) or, if he is entitled to apply for such an order, under section 38(1) in accordance with paragraph (3)(b) or (c).

(8) Where a court is considering making, of its own motion, a section 8 order, or an order under section 31, 34 or 38, the power to give directions under paragraph (2) shall apply.

(9) Directions of a court which are still in force immediately prior to the transfer of proceedings to which this Part applies to another court shall continue to apply following the transfer, subject to any changes of terminology which are required to apply those directions to the court to which the proceedings are transferred, unless varied or discharged by directions under paragraph (2).

(10) The court or the proper officer shall take a note of the giving, variation or revocation of a direction under this rule and serve, as soon as practicable, a copy of the note on any party who was not present at the giving, variation or revocation.

4.15 Timing of proceedings

(1) Where these rules or other rules of court provide a period of time within which or by which a certain act is to be performed in the course of proceedings to which this Part applies, that period may not be extended otherwise than by direction of the court under rule 4.14.

(2) At the –

  (a) transfer to a court of proceedings to which this Part applies,
  (b) postponement or adjournment of any hearing or directions appointment in the course of proceedings to which this Part applies, or
  (c) conclusion of any such hearing or directions appointment other than one at which the proceedings are determined, or so soon thereafter as is practicable,

the court or the proper officer shall –

  (i) fix a date upon which the proceedings shall come before the court again for such purposes as the court directs, which date shall, where paragraph (a) applies, be as soon as possible after the transfer, and
  (ii) give notice to the parties, the children's guardian or the welfare officer or children and family reporter of the date so fixed.

4.16 Attendance at directions appointment and hearing

(1) Subject to paragraph (2), a party shall attend a directions appointment of which he has been given notice in accordance with rule 4.14(5) unless the court otherwise directs.

(2) Proceedings or any part of them shall take place in the absence of any party, including the child, if –

  (a) the court considers it in the interests of the child, having regard to the matters to be discussed or the evidence likely to be given, and
  (b) the party is represented by a children's guardian or solicitor;

and when considering the interests of the child under sub-paragraph (a) the court shall give the children's guardian, the solicitor for the child and, if he is of sufficient understanding, the child an opportunity to make representations.

(3) Subject to paragraph (4), where at the time and place appointed for a hearing or directions appointment the applicant appears but one or more of the respondents do not, the court may proceed with the hearing or appointment.

(4) The court shall not begin to hear an application in the absence of a respondent unless –

  (a) it is proved to the satisfaction of the court that he received reasonable notice of the date of the hearing; or
  (b) the court is satisfied that the circumstances of the case justify proceeding with the hearing.

(5) Where, at the time and place appointed for a hearing or directions appointment one or more of the respondents appear but the applicant does not, the court may

refuse the application or, if sufficient evidence has previously been received, proceed in the absence of the applicant.

(6) Where at the time and place appointed for a hearing or directions appointment neither the applicant nor any respondent appears, the court may refuse the application.

(7) Unless the court otherwise directs, a hearing of, or directions appointment in, proceedings to which this Part applies shall be in chambers.

4.17 Documentary evidence

(1) Subject to paragraphs (4) and (5), in proceedings to which this Part applies a party shall file and serve on the parties, any welfare officer or children and family reporter and any children's guardian of whose appointment he has been given notice under rule 4.10(5) –

  (a) written statements of the substance of the oral evidence which the party
      intends to adduce at a hearing of, or a directions appointment in, those
      proceedings, which shall –
      (i)   be dated,
      (ii) be signed by the person making the statement,
      (iii) contain a declaration that the maker of the statement believes it to be
            true and understands that it may be placed before the court; and
      (iv) show in the top right hand corner of the first page –
            (a) the initials and surname of the person making the statement,
            (b) the number of the statement in relation to the maker,
            (c) the date on which the statement was made, and
            (d) the party on whose behalf it is filed; and
  (b) copies of any documents, including experts' reports, upon which the party
      intends to rely at a hearing of, or a directions appointment in, those
      proceedings,

at or by such time as the court directs or, in the absence of a direction, before the hearing or appointment.

(2) A party may, subject to any direction of the court about the timing of statements under this rule, file and serve on the parties a statement which is supplementary to a statement served under paragraph (1).

(3) At a hearing or a directions appointment a party may not, without the leave of the court –

  (a) adduce evidence, or
  (b) seek to rely on a document,

in respect of which he has failed to comply with the requirements of paragraph (1).

(4) In proceedings for a section 8 order a party shall –

  (a) neither file nor serve any document other than as required or authorised by
      these rules, and
  (b) in completing a form prescribed by these rules, neither give information, nor
      make a statement, which is not required or authorised by that form,

without the leave of the court.

(5) In proceedings for a section 8 order no statement or copy may be filed under paragraph (1) until such time as the court directs.

4.18 Expert evidence – examination of child

(1) No person may, without the leave of the court, cause the child to be medically or psychiatrically examined, or otherwise assessed, for the purpose of the preparation of expert evidence for use in the proceedings.

(2) An application for leave under paragraph (1) shall, unless the court otherwise directs, be served on all parties to the proceedings and on the children's guardian.

(3) Where the leave of the court has not been given under paragraph (1), no evidence arising out of an examination or assessment to which that paragraph applies may be adduced without the leave of the court.

4.19 Amendment

(1) Subject to rule 4.17(2), a document which has been filed or served in proceedings to which this Part applies, may not be amended without the leave of the court which shall, unless the court otherwise directs, be requested in writing.

(2) On considering a request for leave to amend a document the court shall either –

    (a) grant the request, whereupon the proper officer shall inform the person making the request of that decision, or

    (b) invite the parties or any of them to make representations, within a specified period, as to whether such an order should be made.

(3) A person amending a document shall file it and serve it on those persons on whom it was served prior to amendment; and the amendments shall be identified.

4.20 Oral evidence

The court or the proper officer shall keep a note of the substance of the oral evidence given at a hearing of, or directions appointment in, proceedings to which this Part applies.

4.21 Hearing

(1) The court may give directions as to the order of speeches and evidence at a hearing or directions appointment, in the course of proceedings to which this Part applies.

(2) Subject to directions under paragraph (1), at a hearing of, or directions appointment in, proceedings to which this Part applies, the parties and the children's guardian shall adduce their evidence in the following order –

    (a) the applicant,
    (b) any party with parental responsibility for the child,
    (c) other respondents,
    (d) the children's guardian,
    (e) the child, if he is a party to the proceedings and there is no children's guardian.

(3) After the final hearing of proceedings to which this Part applies, the court shall deliver its judgment as soon as is practicable.

(4) When making an order or when refusing an application, the court shall –

    (a) where it makes a finding of fact state such finding and complete Form C22; and

    (b) state the reasons for the court's decision.

(5) An order made in proceedings to which this Part applies shall be recorded, by the court or the proper officer, either in the appropriate form in Appendix 1 to these rules or, where there is no such form, in writing.

(6) Subject to paragraph (7), a copy of an order made in accordance with paragraph (5) shall, as soon as practicable after it has been made, be served by the proper officer on the parties to the proceedings in which it was made and on any person with whom the child is living.

(7) Within 48 hours after the making ex parte of –

    (a) a section 8 order, or

    (b) an order under section 44, 48(4), 48(9) or 50,

the applicant shall serve a copy of the order in the appropriate form in Appendix 1 to these Rules on –

    (i) each party,

    (ii) any person who has actual care of the child or who had such care immediately prior to the making of the order, and

    (iii) in the case of an order referred to in sub-paragraph (b), the local authority in whose area the child lives or is found.

(8) At a hearing of, or directions appointment in, an application which takes place outside the hours during which the court office is normally open, the court or the proper officer shall take a note of the substance of the proceedings.

4.21A Attachment of penal notice to section 8 order

CCR Order 29, rule 1 (committal for breach of order or undertaking) shall apply to section 8 orders as if for paragraph (3) of that rule there were substituted the following –

    '(3) In the case of a section 8 order (within the meaning of section 8(2) of the Children Act 1989) enforceable by committal order under paragraph (1), the judge or the district judge may, on the application of the person entitled to enforce the order, direct that the proper officer issue a copy of the order, indorsed with or incorporating a notice as to the consequences of disobedience, for service in accordance with paragraph (2), and no copy of the order shall be issued with any such notice indorsed or incorporated save in accordance with such a direction'.

4.22 Appeals

(1) Where an appeal lies –

    (a) to the High Court under section 94, or

    (b) from any decision of a district judge to the judge of the court in which the decision was made, it shall be made in accordance with the following provisions; and references to 'the court below' are references to the court from which, or person from whom, the appeal lies.

(2) The appellant shall file and serve on the parties to the proceedings in the court below, and on any children's guardian –

    (a) notice of the appeal in writing, setting out the grounds upon which he relies;

    (b) a certified copy of the summons or application and of the order appealed against, and of any order staying its execution;

    (c) a copy of any notes of the evidence;

    (d) a copy of any reasons given for the decision.

(2A) In relation to an appeal to the High Court under section 94, the documents required to be filed by paragraph (2) shall, –

    (a) where the care centre listed in column (ii) of Schedule 2 to the Children (Allocation of Proceedings) Order 1991 against the entry in column (i) relating to the petty sessions area or London commission area in which the court below is situated –

        (i) is the principal registry, or

        (ii) has a district registry in the same place,

      be filed in that registry, and

    (b) in any other case, be filed in the district registry, being in the same place as a care centre within the meaning of article 2(c) of the said Order, which is nearest to the court below.

(3) The notice of appeal shall be filed and served in accordance with paragraph (2)(a)

    (a) within 14 days after the determination against which the appeal is brought, or

    (b) in the case of an appeal against an order under section 38(1), within 7 days after the making of the order, or

    (c) with the leave of the court to which, or judge to whom, the appeal is to be brought, within such other time as that court or judge may direct.

(4) The documents mentioned in paragraph (2)(b) to (d) shall, subject to any direction of the court to which, or judge to whom, the appeal is to be brought, be filed and served as soon as practicable after the filing and service of the notice of appeal under paragraph (2)(a).

(5) Subject to paragraph (6), a respondent who wishes –

    (a) to contend on the appeal that the decision of the court below should be varied, either in any event or in the event of the appeal being allowed in whole or in part, or

    (b) to contend that the decision of the court below should be affirmed on grounds other than those relied upon by that court, or

    (c) to contend by way of cross-appeal that the decision of the court below was wrong in whole or in part,

shall, within 14 days of receipt of notice of the appeal, file and serve on all other parties to the appeal a notice in writing, setting out the grounds upon which he relies.

(6) No notice under paragraph (5) may be filed or served in an appeal against an order under section 38.

(7) In the case of an appeal mentioned in paragraph (1)(a) an application to –

    (a) withdraw the appeal,
    (b) have the appeal dismissed with the consent of all the parties, or
    (c) amend the grounds of appeal,

may be heard by a district judge.

(8) An appeal of the kind mentioned in paragraph (1)(a) shall, unless the President otherwise directs, be heard and determined by a single judge.

4.23 Confidentiality of documents

(1) Notwithstanding any rule of court to the contrary, no document, other than a record of an order, held by the court and relating to proceedings to which this Part applies shall be disclosed, other than to –

    (a) a party,
    (b) the legal representative of a party,
    (c) the children's guardian,
    (d) the Legal Aid Board, or
    (e) a welfare officer or children and family reporter,
    (f) an expert whose instruction by a party has been authorised by the court,

without leave of the judge or district judge.

(2) Nothing in this rule shall prevent the notification by the court or the proper officer of a direction under section 37(1) to the authority concerned.

(3) Nothing in this rule shall prevent the disclosure of a document prepared by an officer of the service for the purpose of –

    (a) enabling a person to perform functions required by regulations under section 62(3A) of the Justices of the Peace Act 1997;
    (b) assisting an officer of the service who is appointed by the court under any enactment to perform his functions.

(4) Nothing in this rule shall prevent the disclosure of any document relating to proceedings by an officer of the service to any other officer of the service unless that other officer is involved in the same proceedings but on behalf of a different party.

4.24 Notification of consent

(1) Consent for the purposes of –

    (a) section 16(3), or
    (b) section 38A(2)(b)(ii) or 44A(2)(b)(ii), or
    (c) paragraph 19(3)(c) or (d) of Schedule 2,

shall be given either –

        (i) orally in court, or
        (ii) in writing to the court signed by the person giving his consent.

(2) Any written consent given for the purposes of subsection (2) of section 38A or section 44A, shall include a statement that the person giving consent –

    (a) is able and willing to give to the child the care which it would be reasonable to expect a parent to give him; and

(b) understands that the giving of consent could lead to the exclusion of the relevant person from the dwelling-house in which the child lives.

4.24A Exclusion requirements: interim care orders and emergency protection orders

(1) This rule applies where the court includes an exclusion requirement in an interim care order or an emergency protection order.

(2) The applicant for an interim care order or emergency protection order shall –

(a) prepare a separate statement of the evidence in support of the application for an exclusion requirement;

(b) serve the statement personally on the relevant person with a copy of the order containing the exclusion requirement (and of any power of arrest which is attached to it);

(c) inform the relevant person of his right to apply to vary or discharge the exclusion requirement.

(3) Where a power of arrest is attached to an exclusion requirement in an interim care order or an emergency protection order, a copy of the order shall be delivered to the officer for the time being in charge of the police station for the area in which the dwelling-house in which the child lives is situated (or of such other station as the court may specify) together with a statement showing that the relevant person has been served with the order or informed of its terms (whether by being present when the order was made or by telephone or otherwise).

(4) Rules 3.9(5), 3.9A (except paragraphs (1) and (3)) and 3.10 shall apply, with the necessary modifications, for the service, variation, discharge and enforcement of any exclusion requirement to which a power of arrest is attached as they apply to an order made on an application under Part IV of the Family Law Act 1996.

(5) The relevant person shall serve the parties to the proceedings with any application which he makes for the variation or discharge of the exclusion requirement.

(6) Where an exclusion requirement ceases to have effect whether –

(a) as a result of the removal of a child under section 38A(10) or 44A(10),

(b) because of the discharge of the interim care order or emergency protection order, or

(c) otherwise,

the applicant shall inform –

(i) the relevant person,

(ii) the parties to the proceedings

(iii) any officer to whom a copy of the order was delivered under paragraph (3), and

(iv) (where necessary) the court.

(7) Where the court includes an exclusion requirement in an interim care order or an emergency protection order of its own motion, paragraph (2) shall apply with the omission of any reference to the statement of the evidence.

4.25 Secure accommodation – evidence

In proceedings under section 25, the court shall, if practicable, arrange for copies of all written reports before it to be made available before the hearing to –

    (a) the applicant;
    (b) the parent or guardian of the child;
    (c) any legal representative of the child;
    (d) the children's guardian; and
    (e) the child, unless the court otherwise directs;

and copies of such reports may, if the court considers it desirable, be shown to any person who is entitled to notice of the proceedings in accordance with these rules.

4.26 Investigation under section 37

(1) This rule applies where a direction is given to an appropriate authority by the High Court or a county court under section 37(1).

(2) On giving a direction the court shall adjourn the proceedings and the court or the proper officer shall record the direction in Form C40.

(3) A copy of the direction recorded under paragraph (2) shall, as soon as practicable after the direction is given, be served by the proper officer on the parties to the proceedings in which the direction is given and, where the appropriate authority is not a party, on that authority.

(4) When serving the copy of the direction on the appropriate authority the proper officer shall also serve copies of such of the documentary evidence which has been, or is to be, adduced in the proceedings as the court may direct.

(5) Where a local authority informs the court of any of the matters set out in section 37(3)(a) to (c) it shall do so in writing.

4.27 Direction to local education authority to apply for education supervision order

(1) For the purposes of section 40(3) and (4) of the Education Act 1944 a direction by the High Court or a county court to a local education authority to apply for an education supervision order shall be given in writing.

(2) Where, following such a direction, a local education authority informs the court that they have decided not to apply for an education supervision order, they shall do so in writing.

4.28 Transitional provision

Nothing in any provision of this Part of these rules shall affect any proceedings which are pending (within the meaning of paragraph 1 of Schedule 14 to the Act of 1989) immediately before these rules come into force.

PART IVA

PROCEEDINGS UNDER SECTION 30 OF THE HUMAN FERTILISATION AND EMBRYOLOGY ACT 1990

4A.1 Interpretation

(1) In this Part of these Rules –

'the 1990 Act' means the Human Fertilisation and Embryology Act 1990;

'the birth father' means the father of the child, including a person who is treated as being the father of the child by section 28 of the 1990 Act where he is not the husband within the meaning of section 30 of the 1990 Act;

'the birth mother' means the woman who carried the child;

'the birth parents' means the birth mother and the birth father;

'the husband and wife' means the persons who may apply for a parental order where the conditions set out in section 30(1) of the 1990 Act are met;

'parental order' means an order under section 30 of the 1990 Act (parental orders in favour of gamete donors) providing for a child to be treated in law as a child of the parties to a marriage.

'parental order reporter' means an officer of the service appointed under section 41 of the Children Act 1989 in relation to proceedings specified by paragraph (2).

(2) Applications under section 30 of the 1990 Act are specified proceedings for the purposes of section 41 of the Children Act 1989 in accordance with section 41(6)(i) of that Act.

4A.2 Application of Part IV

Subject to the provisions of this Part, the provisions of Part IV of these Rules shall apply as appropriate with any necessary modifications to proceedings under this Part except that rules 4.7(1), 4.9, 4.10(1)(b), 4.10(11), 4.11A(1), 4.11A(3) and 4.12 shall not apply.

4A.3 Parties

The applicants shall be the husband and wife and the respondents shall be the persons set out in the relevant entry in column (iii) of Appendix 3.

4A.4 Acknowledgement

Within 14 days of the service of an application for a parental order, each respondent shall file and serve on all the other parties an acknowledgement in Form C52.

4A.5 Appointment and duties of the parental order reporter

(1) As soon as practicable after the application has been filed the court shall consider the appointment of a parental order reporter in accordance with section 41(1) of the Children Act 1989.

(2), (3) (*revoked*)

(4) In addition to such of the matters set out in rules 4.11 and 4.11A as are appropriate to the proceedings, the parental order reporter shall –

(i) investigate the matters set out in section 30(1) to (7) of the 1990 Act;

(ii) so far as he considers necessary, investigate any matter contained in the application form or other matter which appears relevant to the making of a parental order;

(iii) advise the court on whether there is any reason under section 6 of the Adoption Act 1976, as applied with modifications by the Parental Orders (Human Fertilisation and Embryology) Regulations 1994, to refuse the parental order.

4A.6 Personal attendance of applicants

The court shall not make a parental order except upon the personal attendance before it of the applicants.

4A.7 Copies of orders

(1) Where a parental order is made by a court sitting in Wales in respect of a child who was born in Wales and the applicants so request before the order is drawn up, the proper officer shall obtain a translation into Welsh of the particulars set out in the order.

(2) Within 7 days after the making of a parental order, the proper officer shall send a copy of the order to the Registrar General.

(3) A copy of any parental order may be supplied to the Registrar General at his request.

4A.8 Amendment and revocation of orders

(1) An application under paragraph 4 of Schedule 1 to the Adoption Act 1976 as modified by the Parental Orders (Human Fertilisation and Embryology) Regulations 1994 for the amendment of a parental order or the revocation of a direction to the Registrar General may be made ex parte in the first instance but the court may require notice of the application to be served on such persons as it thinks fit.

(2) Where the application is granted, the proper officer shall send to the Registrar General a notice specifying the amendments or informing him of the revocation and shall give sufficient particulars of the order to enable the Registrar General to identify the case.

4A.9 Custody, inspection and disclosure of documents and information

(1) All documents relating to proceedings for a parental order shall, while they are in the custody of the court, be kept in a place of special security.

(2) Any person who obtains any information in the course of, or relating to proceedings for a parental order shall treat that information as confidential and shall only disclose it if –

  (a) the disclosure is necessary for the proper exercise of his duties, or
  (b) the information is requested –
    (i) by a court or public authority (whether in Great Britain or not) having power to determine proceedings for a parental order and related matters, for the purpose of discharge of its duties in that behalf, or

        (ii) by a person who is authorised in writing by the Secretary of State to obtain the information for the purposes of research.

4A.10 Application for removal, return etc of child

(1) An application under sections 27(1), 29(1) or 29(2) of the Adoption Act 1976 as applied with modifications by the Parental Orders (Human Fertilisation and Embryology) Regulations 1994 shall be made on notice in proceedings under section 30 of the 1990 Act.

(2) The proper officer shall serve a copy of the application and a notice of the date of the hearing on all the parties to the proceedings under section 30, on the guardian ad litem and on any other person or body, not being the child, as the court thinks fit.

(3) The court may at any time give directions as to the conduct of the application under this rule.

PART V

WARDSHIP

5.1 Application to make a minor a ward of court

(1) An application to make a minor a ward of court shall be made by originating summons and, unless the court otherwise directs, the plaintiff shall file an affidavit in support of the application when the originating summons is issued.

(2) Rule 4.3 shall, so far as applicable, apply to an application by a local authority for the leave of the court under section 100(3) of the Act of 1989.

(3) Where there is no person other than the minor who is a suitable defendant, an application may be made ex parte to a district judge for leave to issue either an ex parte originating summons or an originating summons with the minor as defendant thereto; and, except where such leave is granted, the minor shall not be made a defendant to an originating summons under this rule in the first instance.

(4) Particulars of any summons issued under this rule in a district registry shall be sent by the proper officer to the principal registry for recording in the register of wards.

(5) The date of the minor's birth shall, unless otherwise directed, be stated in the summons, and the plaintiff shall –

      (a) on issuing the summons or before or at the first hearing thereof lodge in the registry out of which the summons issued a certified copy of the entry in the Register of Births or, as the case may be, in the Adopted Children Register relating to the minor, or

      (b) at the first hearing of the summons apply for directions as to proof of birth of the minor in some other manner.

(6) The name of each party to the proceedings shall be qualified by a brief description, in the body of the summons, of his interest in, or relation to, the minor.

(7) Unless the court otherwise directs, the summons shall state the whereabouts of the minor or, as the case may be, that the plaintiff is unaware of his whereabouts.

(8) Upon being served with the summons, every defendant other than the minor shall forthwith lodge in the registry out of which the summons issued a notice stating the address of the defendant and the whereabouts of the minor or, as the case may be, that the defendant is unaware of his whereabouts and, unless the court otherwise directs, serve a copy of the same upon the plaintiff.

(9) Where any party other than the minor changes his address or becomes aware of any change in the whereabouts of the minor after the issue, or, as the case may be, service of the summons, he shall, unless the court otherwise directs, forthwith lodge notice of the change in the registry out of which the summons issued and serve a copy of the notice on every other party.

(10) The summons shall contain a notice to the defendant informing him of the requirements of paragraphs (8) and (9).

(11) In this rule any reference to the whereabouts of a minor is a reference to the address at which and the person with whom he is living and any other information relevant to the question where he may be found.

5.2 Enforcement of order by tipstaff

The power of the High Court to secure, through an officer attending upon the court, compliance with any direction relating to a ward of court may be exercised by an order addressed to the tipstaff.

5.3 Where minor ceases to be a ward of court

(1) A minor who, by virtue of section 41(2) of the Supreme Court Act 1981, becomes a ward of court on the issue of a summons under rule 5.1 shall cease to be a ward of court –

    (a) if an application for an appointment for the hearing of the summons is not made within the period of 21 days after the issue of the summons, at the expiration of that period;

    (b) if an application for such an appointment is made within that period, on the determination of the application made by the summons unless the court hearing it orders that the minor be made a ward of court.

(2) Nothing in paragraph (1) shall be taken as affecting the power of the court under section 41(3) of the said Act to order that any minor who is for the time being a ward of court shall cease to be a ward of court.

(3) If no application for an appointment for the hearing of a summons under rule 5.1 is made within the period of 21 days after the issue of the summons, a notice stating whether the applicant intends to proceed with the application made by the summons must be left at the registry in which the matter is proceeding immediately after the expiration of that period.

5.4 Adoption of minor who is a ward of court

(1) An application for leave –

    (a) to commence proceedings to adopt a minor who is a ward, or

    (b) to commence proceedings to free such a minor for adoption,

may be ex parte to a district judge.

(2) Where a local authority has been granted leave to place a minor who is a ward with foster parents with a view to adoption it shall not be necessary for an application to be made for leave under paragraph (1)(a) or (b) unless the court otherwise directs.

(3) If the applicant for leave under paragraph (1)(a) or (b), or a local authority which has applied for leave as referred to in paragraph (2), or a foster parent so requests, the district judge may direct that any subsequent proceedings shall be conducted with a view to securing that the proposed adopter is not seen by or made known to any respondent or prospective respondent who is not already aware of his identity except with his consent.

(4) In paragraphs (1) and (3) 'proceedings' means proceedings in the High Court or in a county court.

5.5 Orders for use of secure accommodation

No order shall be made with the effect of placing or keeping a minor in secure accommodation, within the meaning of section 25(1) of the Act of 1989 unless the minor has been made a party to the summons.

5.6 Notice to provider of refuge

Where a child is staying in a refuge which is certified under section 51(1) or 51(2) of the Act of 1989, the person who is providing that refuge shall be given notice of any application under this Part of these rules in respect of that child.

PART VI
CHILD ABDUCTION AND CUSTODY

6.1 Interpretation

In this Part, unless the context otherwise requires –

(a) 'the Act' means the Child Abduction and Custody Act 1985 and words or expressions bear the same meaning as in that Act;

(b) 'the Hague Convention' means the convention defined in section 1(1) of the Act and 'the European Convention' means the convention defined in section 12(1) of the Act.

6.2 Mode of application

(1) Except as otherwise provided by this Part, every application under the Hague Convention and the European Convention shall be made by originating summons, which shall be in Form No 10 in Appendix A to the Rules of the Supreme Court 1965 and issued out of the principal registry.

(2) An application in custody proceedings for a declaration under section 23(2) of the Act shall be made by summons in those proceedings.

6.3 Contents of originating summons: general provisions

(1) The originating summons by which any application is made under the Hague Convention or the European Convention shall state –

    (a) the name and date of birth of the child in respect of whom the application is made;

    (b) the names of the child's parents or guardians;

    (c) the whereabouts or suspected whereabouts of the child;

    (d) the interest of the plaintiff in the matter and the grounds of the application; and

    (e) particulars of any proceedings (including proceedings out of the jurisdiction and concluded proceedings) relating to the child,

and shall be accompanied by all relevant documents including but not limited to the documents specified in Article 8 of the Hague Convention or, as the case may be, Article 13 of the European Convention.

6.4 Contents of originating summons: particular provisions

(1) In applications under the Hague Convention, in addition to the matters specified in rule 6.3 –

    (a) the originating summons under which an application is made for the purposes of Article 8 for the return of a child shall state the identity of the person alleged to have removed or retained the child and, if different, the identity of the person with whom the child is presumed to be;

    (b) the originating summons under which an application is made for the purposes of Article 15 for a declaration shall identify the proceedings in which the request that such a declaration be obtained was made.

(2) In applications under the European Convention, in addition to the matters specified in rule 6.3, the originating summons shall identify the decision relating to custody or rights of access which is sought to be registered or enforced or in relation to which a declaration that it is not to be recognised is sought.

6.5 Defendants

The defendants to an application under the Act shall be –

    (a) the person alleged to have brought into the United Kingdom the child in respect of whom an application under the Hague Convention is made;

    (b) the person with whom the child is alleged to be;

    (c) any parent or guardian of the child who is within the United Kingdom and is not otherwise a party;

    (d) the person in whose favour a decision relating to custody has been made if he is not otherwise a party; and

    (e) any other person who appears to the court to have a sufficient interest in the welfare of the child.

6.6 Acknowledgement of service

The time limit for acknowledging service of an originating summons by which an application is made under the Hague Convention or the European Convention shall be seven days after service of the originating summons (including the day of service) or, in the case of a defendant referred to in rule 6.5(d) or (e), such further time as the Court may direct.

6.7 Evidence

(1) The plaintiff, on issuing an originating summons under the Hague Convention or the European Convention, may lodge affidavit evidence in the principal registry in support of his application and serve a copy of the same on the defendant with the originating summons.

(2) A defendant to an application under the Hague Convention or the European Convention may lodge affidavit evidence in the principal registry and serve a copy of the same on the plaintiff within seven days after service of the originating summons on him.

(3) The plaintiff in an application under the Hague Convention or the European Convention may within seven days thereafter lodge in the principal registry a statement in reply and serve a copy thereof on the defendant.

6.8 Hearing

Any application under the Act (other than an application (a) to join a defendant, (b) to dispense with service or extend the time for acknowledging service, or (c) for the transfer of proceedings) shall be heard and determined by a judge and shall be dealt with in chambers unless the court otherwise directs.

6.9 Dispensing with service

The court may dispense with service of any summons (whether originating or ordinary) in any proceedings under the Act.

6.10 Adjournment of summons

The hearing of the originating summons under which an application under the Hague Convention or the European Convention is made may be adjourned for a period not exceeding 21 days at any one time.

6.11 Stay of proceedings

(1) A party to proceedings under the Hague Convention shall, where he knows that an application relating to the merits of rights of custody is pending in or before a relevant authority, file in the principal registry a concise statement of the nature of the application which is pending, including the authority before which it is pending.

(2) A party –

(a) to pending proceedings under section 16 of the Act, or
(b) to proceedings as a result of which a decision relating to custody has been registered under section 16 of the Act,

shall, where he knows that such an application as is specified in section 20(2) of the Act or section 42(2) of the Child Custody Act 1987 (an Act of Tynwald) is pending in or before a relevant authority, file a concise statement of the nature of the application which is pending.

(3) The proper officer shall on receipt of such a statement as is mentioned in paragraph (1) or (2) notify the relevant authority in which or before whom the application is pending and shall subsequently notify it or him of the result of the proceedings.

(4) On the court receiving notification under paragraph (3) above or equivalent notification from the Court of Session, the High Court in Northern Ireland or the High Court of Justice of the Isle of Man –

    (a) where the application relates to the merits of rights of custody, all further proceedings in the action shall be stayed unless and until the proceedings under the Hague Convention in the High Court, Court of Session, the High Court in Northern Ireland or the High Court of Justice of the Isle of Man, as the case may be, are dismissed, and the parties to the action shall be notified by the proper officer of the stay and of any such dismissal accordingly, and

    (b) where the application is such a one as is specified in section 20(2) of the Act, the proper officer shall notify the parties to the action.

(5) In this rule 'relevant authority' includes the High Court, a county court, a magistrates' court, the Court of Session, a sheriff court, a children's hearing within the meaning of Part III of the Social Work (Scotland) Act 1968, the High Court in Northern Ireland, a county court in Northern Ireland, a court of summary jurisdiction in Northern Ireland, the High Court of Justice of the Isle of Man, a court of summary jurisdiction in the Isle of Man or the Secretary of State.

6.12 Transfer of proceedings

(1) At any stage in the proceedings under the Act the court may, of its own motion or on the application by summons of any party to the proceedings issued on two days' notice, order that the proceedings be transferred to the Court of Session, the High Court in Northern Ireland or the High Court of Justice of the Isle of Man.

(2) Where an order is made under paragraph (1) the proper officer shall send a copy of the order, which shall state the grounds therefor, together with the originating summons, the documents accompanying it and any evidence, to the Court of Session, the High Court in Northern Ireland or the High Court of Justice of the Isle of Man, as the case may be.

(3) Where proceedings are transferred to the Court of Session, the High Court in Northern Ireland or the High Court of Justice of the Isle of Man the costs of the whole proceedings both before and after the transfer shall be at the discretion of the Court to which the proceedings are transferred.

(4) Where proceedings are transferred to the High Court from the Court of Session, the High Court in Northern Ireland or the High Court of Justice of the Isle of Man the proper officer shall notify the parties of the transfer and the proceedings shall continue as if they had begun by originating summons under rule 6.2.

6.13 Interim directions

An application for interim directions under section 5 or section 19 of the Act may where the case is one of urgency be made ex parte on affidavit but shall otherwise be made by summons.

6.14 *(revoked)*

6.15 Revocation and variation of registered decisions

(1) This rule applies to decisions which have been registered under section 16 of the Act and are subsequently varied or revoked by an authority in the Contracting State in which they were made.

(2) The court shall, on cancelling the registration of a decision which has been revoked, notify –

(a) the person appearing to the court to have care of the child,

(b) the person on whose behalf the application for registration of the decision was made, and

(c) any other party to that application,

of the cancellation.

(3) The court shall, on being notified of the variation of a decision, notify –

(a) the person appearing to the court to have care of the child, and

(b) any party to the application for registration of the decision

of the variation and any such person may apply by summons in the proceedings for the registration of the decision, for the purpose of making representations to the court before the registration is varied.

(4) Any person appearing to the court to have an interest in the matter may apply by summons in the proceedings for the registration of a decision for the cancellation or variation of the registration.

6.16 Orders for disclosure of information

At any stage in proceedings under the European Convention the court may, if it has reason to believe that any person may have relevant information about the child who is the subject of those proceedings, order that person to disclose such information and may for that purpose order that the person attend before it or file affidavit evidence.

6.17 Applications and orders under sections 33 and 34 of the Family Law Act 1986

(1) In this rule 'the 1986 Act' means the Family Law Act 1986.

(2) An application under section 33 of the 1986 Act shall be in Form C4 and an order made under that section shall be in Form C30.

(3) An application under section 34 of the 1986 Act shall be in Form C3 and an order made under that section shall be in Form C31.

(4) An application under section 33 or section 34 of the 1986 Act may be made ex parte in which case the applicant shall file the application –

(a) where the application is made by telephone, within 24 hours after the making of the application, or

(b) in any other case at the time when the application is made, and shall serve a copy of the application on each respondent 48 hours after the making of the order.

(5) Where the court refuses to make an order on an ex parte application it may direct that the application be made inter partes.

****

PART IX
DISABILITY

9.1 Interpretation and application of Part IX

(1) In this Part –

'patient' means a person who, by reason of mental disorder within the meaning of the Mental Health Act 1983, is incapable of managing and administering his property and affairs;
'person under disability' means a person who is a minor or a patient;
'Part VII' means Part VII of the Mental Health Act 1983.

(2) So far as they relate to minors who are the subject of applications, the provisions of this Part of these rules shall not apply to proceedings which are specified proceedings within the meaning of section 41(6) of the Children Act 1989 and, with respect to proceedings which are dealt with together with specified proceedings, this Part shall have effect subject to the said section 41 and Part IV of these rules.

(3) Rule 9.2A shall apply only to proceedings under the Act of 1989 or the inherent jurisdiction of the High Court with respect to minors.

9.2 Person under disability must sue by next friend etc

(1) Except where rule 9.2A or any other rule otherwise provides, a person under disability may begin and prosecute any family proceedings only by his next friend and may defend any such proceedings only by his guardian ad litem and, except as otherwise provided by this rule, it shall not be necessary for a guardian ad litem to be appointed by the court.

(2) No person's name shall be used in any proceedings as next friend of a person under disability unless he is the Official Solicitor or the documents mentioned in paragraph (7) have been filed.

(3) Where a person is authorised under Part VII to conduct legal proceedings in the name of a patient or on his behalf, that person shall, subject to paragraph (2) be entitled to be next friend or guardian ad litem of the patient in any family proceedings to which his authority extends.

(4) Where a person entitled to defend any family proceedings is a patient and there is no person authorised under Part VII to defend the proceedings in his name or on his behalf, then –

(a) the Official Solicitor shall, if he consents, be the patient's guardian ad litem, but at any stage of the proceedings an application may be made on not less than four days' notice to the Official Solicitor, for the appointment of some other person as guardian;

(b) in any other case, an application may be made on behalf of the patient for the appointment of a guardian ad litem;

and there shall be filed in support of any application under this paragraph the documents mentioned in paragraph (7).

(5) Where a petition, answer, originating application or originating summons has been served on a person whom there is reasonable ground for believing to be a person under disability and no notice of intention to defend has been given, or answer or affidavit in answer filed, on his behalf, the party at whose instance the document was served shall, before taking any further steps in the proceedings, apply to a district judge for directions as to whether a guardian ad litem should be appointed to act for that person in the cause, and on any such application the district judge may, if he considers it necessary in order to protect the interests of the person served, order that some proper person be appointed his guardian ad litem.

(6) Except where a minor is prosecuting or defending proceedings under rule 9.2A, no notice of intention to defend shall be given, or answer or affidavit in answer filed, by or on behalf of a person under disability unless the person giving the notice or filing the answer or affidavit –

(a) is the Official Solicitor or, in a case to which paragraph (4) applies, is the Official Solicitor or has been appointed by the court to be guardian ad litem; or

(b) in any other case, has filed the documents mentioned in paragraph (7).

(7) The documents referred to in paragraphs (2), (4) and (6) are –

(a) a written consent to act by the proposed next friend or guardian ad litem;

(b) where the person under disability is a patient and the proposed next friend or guardian ad litem is authorised under Part VII to conduct the proceedings in his name or on his behalf, an office copy, sealed with the seal of the Court of Protection, of the order or other authorisation made or given under Part VII; and

(c) except where the proposed next friend or guardian ad litem is authorised as mentioned in sub-paragraph (b), a certificate by the solicitor acting for the person under disability –

(i) that he knows or believes that the person to whom the certificate relates is a minor or patient, stating (in the case of a patient) the grounds of his knowledge or belief and, where the person under disability is a patient, that there is no person authorised as aforesaid, and

(ii) that the person named in the certificate as next friend or guardian ad litem has no interest in the cause or matter in question adverse to that of the person under disability and that he is a proper person to be next friend or guardian.

9.2A Certain minors may sue without next friend etc

(1) Where a person entitled to begin, prosecute or defend any proceedings to which this rule applies, is a minor to whom this Part applies, he may subject to paragraph (4),

begin, prosecute or defend, as the case may be, such proceedings without a next friend or guardian ad litem –

   (a) where he has obtained the leave of the court for that purpose; or
   (b) where a solicitor –
        (i) considers that the minor is able, having regard to his understanding, to give instructions in relation to the proceedings; and
        (ii) has accepted instructions from the minor to act for him in the proceedings and, where the proceedings have begun, is so acting.

(2) A minor shall be entitled to apply for the leave of the court under paragraph (1)(a) without a next friend or guardian ad litem either –

   (a) by filing a written request for leave setting out the reasons for the application, or
   (b) by making an oral request for leave at any hearing in the proceedings.

(3) On considering a request for leave filed under paragraph (2)(a), the court shall either –

   (a) grant the request, whereupon the proper officer shall communicate the decision to the minor and, where the leave relates to the prosecution or defence of existing proceedings, to the other parties to those proceedings, or
   (b) direct that the request be heard ex parte, whereupon the proper officer shall fix a date for such a hearing and give to the minor making the request such notice of the date so fixed as the court may direct.

(4) Where a minor has a next friend or guardian ad litem in proceedings and the minor wishes to prosecute or defend the remaining stages of the proceedings without a next friend or guardian ad litem, the minor may apply to the court for leave for that purpose and for the removal of the next friend or guardian ad litem; and paragraph (2) shall apply to the application as if it were an application under paragraph (1)(a).

(5) On considering a request filed under paragraph (2) by virtue of paragraph (4), the court shall either –

   (a) grant the request, whereupon the proper officer shall communicate the decision to the minor and next friend or guardian ad litem concerned and to all other parties to the proceedings, or
   (b) direct that the request be heard, whereupon the proper officer shall fix a date for such a hearing and give to the minor and next friend or guardian ad litem concerned such notice of the date so fixed as the court may direct;

provided that the court may act under sub-paragraph (a) only if it is satisfied that the next friend or guardian ad litem does not oppose the request.

(6) Where the court is considering whether to –

   (a) grant leave under paragraph (1)(a), or
   (b) grant leave under paragraph (4) and remove a next friend or guardian ad litem,

it shall grant the leave sought and, as the case may be, remove the next friend or guardian ad litem if it considers that the minor concerned has sufficient understanding to participate as a party in the proceedings concerned or proposed without a next friend or guardian ad litem.

(6A) In exercising its powers under paragraph (6) the court may order the next friend or guardian ad litem to take such part in the proceedings as the court may direct.

(7) Where a request for leave is granted at a hearing fixed under paragraph (3)(b) (in relation to the prosecution or defence of proceedings already begun) or (5)(b), the proper officer shall forthwith communicate the decision to the other parties to the proceedings.

(8) The court may revoke any leave granted under paragraph (1)(a) where it considers that the child does not have sufficient understanding to participate as a party in the proceedings concerned without a next friend or guardian ad litem.

(9) Without prejudice to any requirement of CCR Order 50, rule 5 or RSC Order 67, where a solicitor is acting for a minor in proceedings which the minor is prosecuting or defending without a next friend or guardian ad litem by virtue of paragraph (1)(b) and either of the conditions specified in the paragraph (1)(b)(i) and (ii) cease to be fulfilled, he shall forthwith so inform the court.

(10) Where –

    (a) the court revokes any leave under paragraph (8), or

    (b) either of the conditions specified in paragraph (1)(b)(i) and (ii) is no longer fulfilled,

the court may, if it considers it necessary in order to protect the interests of the minor concerned, order that some proper person be appointed his next friend or guardian ad litem.

(11) Where a minor is of sufficient understanding to begin, prosecute or defend proceedings without a next friend or guardian ad litem –

    (a) he may nevertheless begin, prosecute or defend them by his next friend or guardian ad litem; and

    (b) where he is prosecuting or defending proceedings by his next friend or guardian ad litem, the respective powers and duties of the minor and next friend or guardian ad litem, except those conferred or imposed by this rule shall not be affected by the minor's ability to dispense with a next friend or guardian ad litem under the provisions of this rule.

9.3 Service on person under disability

(1) Where a document to which rule 2.9 applies is required to be served on a person under disability, it shall be served –

    (a) in the case of a minor who is not also a patient, on his father or guardian or, if he has no father or guardian, on the person with whom he resides or in whose care he is;

    (b) in the case of a patient –

        (i) on the person (if any) who is authorised under Part VII to conduct in the name of the patient or on his behalf the proceedings in connection with which the document is to be served, or

        (ii) if there is no person so authorised, on the Official Solicitor if he has consented under rule 9.2(4) to be the guardian ad litem of the patient, or

        (iii) in any other case, on the person with whom the patient resides or in whose care he is:

Provided that the court may order that a document which has been, or is to be served on the person under disability or on a person other than one mentioned in sub-paragraph (a) or (b) shall be deemed to be duly served on the person under disability.

(2) Where a document is served in accordance with paragraph (1) it shall be indorsed with a notice in Form M24; and after service has been effected the person at whose instance the document was served shall, unless the Official Solicitor is the guardian ad litem of the person under disability or the court otherwise directs, file an affidavit by the person on whom the document was served stating whether the contents of the document were, or its purport was, communicated to the person under disability and, if not, the reasons for not doing so.

9.4 Petition for nullity on ground of mental disorder

(1) Where a petition for nullity has been presented on the ground that at the time of the marriage the respondent was suffering from mental disorder within the meaning of the Mental Health Act 1983 of such a kind or to such an extent as to be unfitted for marriage, then, whether or not the respondent gives notice of intention to defend, the petitioner shall not proceed with the cause without the leave of the district judge.

(2) The district judge by whom an application for leave is heard may make it a condition of granting leave that some proper person be appointed to act as guardian ad litem of the respondent.

9.5 Separate representation of children[6]

(1) Without prejudice to rules 2.57 and 9.2A, if in any family proceedings it appears to the court that it is in the best interests of any child to be made a party to the proceedings, the court may appoint –

    (a) an officer of the service;

    (b) (if he consents) the Official Solicitor; or

    (c) (if he consents) some other proper person,

to be the guardian ad litem of the child with authority to take part in the proceedings on the child's behalf.

(2) An order under paragraph (1) may be made by the court of its own motion or on the application of a party to the proceedings or of the proposed guardian ad litem.

(3) The court may at any time direct that an application be made by a party for an order under paragraph (1) and may stay the proceedings until the application has been made.

(4) *(revoked)*

(5) Unless otherwise directed, a person appointed under this rule or rule 2.57 to be the guardian ad litem of a child in any family proceedings shall be treated as a party for the purpose of any provision of these rules requiring a document to be served on or notice to be given to a party to the proceedings.

---

[6] See further the *President's Direction (Representation of Children in Family Proceedings Pursuant to Rule 9.5 of the Family Proceedings Rules 1991)* [2004] 1 FLR 1188, and the CAFCASS Practice Note accompanying it [2004] 1 FLR 1190, set out at **6.18** and **6.19**, respectively.

(6) Where the guardian ad litem appointed under this rule is an officer of the service, rules 4.11 and 4.11A shall apply to him as they apply to a children's guardian appointed under section 41 of the Children Act 1989.

****

10.14A Power of court to limit cross-examination

The court may limit the issues on which an officer of the service may be cross-examined.

****

10.26 Human Rights Act 1998

(1) In this rule –

'originating document' means a petition, application, originating application, originating summons or other originating process;
'answer' means an answer or other document filed or served by a party in reply to an originating document (but not an acknowledgement of service);
'Convention right' has the same meaning as in the Human Rights Act 1998;
'declaration of incompatibility' means a declaration of incompatibility under section 4 of the Human Rights Act 1998.

(2) A party who seeks to rely on any provision of or right arising under the Human Rights Act 1998 or seeks a remedy available under that Act –

(a) shall state that fact in his originating document or (as the case may be) answer; and
(b) shall in his originating document or (as the case may be) answer:
(i) give precise details of the Convention right which it is alleged has been infringed and details of the alleged infringement;
(ii) specify the relief sought;
(iii) state if the relief sought includes a declaration of incompatibility.

(3) A party who seeks to amend his originating document or (as the case may be) answer to include the matters referred to in paragraph (2) shall, unless the court orders otherwise, do so as soon as possible and in any event not less than 28 days before the hearing.

(4) The court shall not make a declaration of incompatibility unless 21 days' notice, or such other period of notice as the court directs, has been given to the Crown.

(5) Where notice has been given to the Crown a Minister, or other person permitted by the Human Rights Act 1998, shall be joined as a party on giving notice to the court.

(6) Where a party has included in his originating document or (as the case may be) answer:

(a) a claim for a declaration of incompatibility, or
(b) an issue for the court to decide which may lead to the court considering making a declaration of incompatibility,

then the court may at any time consider whether notice should be given to the Crown as required by the Human Rights Act 1998 and give directions for the content and service of the notice.

(7) In the case of an appeal for which permission to appeal is required, the court shall, unless it decides that it is appropriate to do so at another stage in the proceedings, consider the issues and give the directions referred to in paragraph (6) when deciding whether to give such permission.

(8) If paragraph (7) does not apply, and a hearing for directions would, but for this rule, be held, the court shall, unless it decides that it is appropriate to do so at another stage in the proceedings, consider the issues and give the directions referred to in paragraph (6) at the hearing for directions.

(9) If neither paragraph (7) nor paragraph (8) applies, the court shall consider the issues and give the directions referred to in paragraph (6) when it considers it appropriate to do so, and may fix a hearing for this purpose.

(10) Where a party amends his originating document or (as the case may be) answer to include any matter referred to in paragraph (6)(a), then the court will consider whether notice should be given to the Crown and give directions for the content and service of the notice.

(11) In paragraphs (12) to (16), 'notice' means the notice given under paragraph (4).

(12) The notice shall be served on the person named in the list published under section 17 of the Crown Proceedings Act 1947.

(13) The notice shall be in the form directed by the court.

(14) Unless the court orders otherwise, the notice shall be accompanied by the directions given by the court and the originating document and any answers in the proceedings.

(15) Copies of the notice shall be served on all the parties.

(16) The court may require the parties to assist in the preparation of the notice.

(17) Unless the court orders otherwise, the Minister or other person permitted by the Human Rights Act 1998 to be joined as a party shall, if he wishes to be joined, give notice of his intention to be joined as a party to the court and every other party, and where the Minister has nominated a person to be joined as a party the notice must be accompanied by the written nomination.

(18) Where a claim is made under section 7(1) of the Human Rights Act 1998 in respect of a judicial act the procedure in paragraphs (6) to (17) shall also apply, but the notice to be given to the Crown:

    (a) shall be given to the Lord Chancellor and shall be served on the Treasury Solicitor on his behalf; and

    (b) shall also give details of the judicial act which is the subject of the claim and of the court that made it.

(19) Where in any appeal a claim is made under section 7(1) of that Act and section 9(3) and 9(4) applies –

    (a) that claim must be set out in the notice of appeal; and

    (b) notice must be given to the Crown in accordance with paragraph (18).

(20) The appellant must in a notice of appeal to which paragraph (19)(a) applies –

(a) state that a claim is being made under section 7(1) of the Human Rights Act 1998 in respect of a judicial act and section 9(3) of that Act applies; and

(b) give details of –
    (i) the Convention right which it is alleged has been infringed;
    (ii) the infringement;
    (iii) the judicial act complained of; and
    (iv) the court which made it.

(21) Where paragraph (19) applies and the appropriate person (as defined in section 9(5) of the Human Rights Act 1998) has not applied within 21 days, or such other period as the court directs, after the notice is served to be joined as a party, the court may join the appropriate person as a party.

(22) On any application or appeal concerning –

(a) a committal order;
(b) a refusal to grant habeas corpus; or
(c) a secure accommodation order made under section 25 of the Act of 1989,

if the court ordering the release of the person concludes that his Convention rights have been infringed by the making of the order to which the application or appeal relates, the judgment or order should so state, but if the court does not do so, that failure will not prevent another court from deciding the matter.

****

APPENDIX 3

NOTICES AND RESPONDENTS

(i) *Provision under which proceedings brought*	(ii) *Minimum number of days prior to hearing or directions appointment for service under rule 4.4(1)(b)*	(iii) *Respondents*	(iv) *Persons to whom notice is to be given*
All applications.	See separate entries below	Subject to separate entries below: every person whom the applicant believes to have parental responsibility for the child;	Subject to separate entries below: local authority providing accommodation for the child;

		where the child is the subject of a care order, every person whom the applicant believes to have had parental responsibility immediately prior to the making of the care order;	persons who are caring for the child at the time when the proceedings are commenced;
			in the case of proceedings brought in respect of a child who is alleged to be staying in a refuge which is certificated under section 51(1) or (2), the person who is providing the refuge.
		in the case of an application to extend, vary or discharge an order, the parties to the proceedings leading to the order which it is sought to have extended, varied or discharged;	
		in the case of specified proceedings, the child.	
Section 4(1)(c), 4(3), 5(1), 6(7), 8, 13(1), 16(6), 33(7), Schedule 1, paragraph 19(1) of Schedule 2, or paragraph 11(3) or 16(5) of Schedule 14.	14 days.	As for 'all applications' above, and:	As for 'all applications' above, and:
		in the case of proceedings under Schedule 1, those persons whom the applicant believes to be interested in or affected by the proceedings;	in the case of an application for a section 8 order, every person whom the applicant believes —
		in the case of an application under paragraph 11(3)(b) or 16(5) of Schedule 14, any person, other than the child, named in the order or directions which it is sought to discharge or vary.	(i) to be named in a court order with respect to the same child, which has not ceased to have effect,

(ii) to be a party to pending proceedings in respect of the same child, or

(iii) to be a person with whom the child has lived for at least 3 years prior to the application, unless, in a case to which (i) or (ii) applies, the applicant believes that the court order or pending proceedings are not relevant to the application;

in the case of an application under paragraph 19(1) of Schedule 2, the parties to the proceedings leading to the care order;

in the case of an application under section 5(1), the father of the child if he does not have parental responsibility.

Section 36(1), 39(1), 39(2), 39(3), 39(4), 43(1), or paragraph 6(3), 15(2) or 17(1) of Schedule 3.	7 days.	As for 'all applications' above, and: in the case of an application under section 39(2) or (3), the supervisor; in the case of proceedings under paragraph 17(1) of Schedule 3, the local education authority concerned; in the case of proceedings under section 36 or paragraph 15(2) or 17(1) of Schedule 3, the child.	As for 'all applications' above, and: in the case of an application for an order under section 43(1) – (i) every person whom the applicant believes to be a parent of the child, (ii) every person whom the applicant believes to be caring for the child, (iii) every person in whose favour a contact order is in force with respect to the child, and (iv) every person who is allowed to have contact with the child by virtue of an order under section 34.
Section 31, 34(2), 34(3), 34(4), 34(9) or 38(8)(b).	3 days.	As for 'all applications' above, and:	As for 'all applications' above, and:

		in the case of an application under section 34, the person whose contact with the child is the subject of the application.	in the case of an application under section 31 – (i) every person whom the applicant believes to be a party to pending relevant proceedings in respect of the same child, and (ii) every person whom the applicant believes to be a parent without parental responsibility for the child.
Section 43(12).	2 days.	As for 'all applications' above.	Those of the persons referred to in section 43(11)(a) to (e) who were not party to the application for the order which it is sought to have varied or discharged.
Section 25, 44(1), 44(9)(b), 45(4), 45(8), 46(7), 48(9), 50(1), or 102(1).	1 day.	As for 'all applications' above, and: in the case of an application under section 44(9)(b) – (i) the parties to the application for the order in respect of which it is sought to vary the directions;	Except for applications under section 102(1), as for 'all applications' above, and: in the case of an application under section 44(1), every person whom the applicant believes to be a parent of the child;

(ii) any person who was caring for the child prior to the making of the order, and

(iii) any person whose contact with the child is affected by the direction which it is sought to have varied;

in the case of an application under section 50, the person whom the applicant alleges to have effected or to have been or to be responsible for the taking or keeping of the child.

in the case of an application under section 44(9)(b) –

(i) the local authority in whose area the child is living, and

(ii) any person whom the applicant believes to be affected by the direction which it is sought to have varied;

in the case of an application under section 102(1), the person referred to in section 102(1) and any person preventing or likely to prevent such a person from exercising powers under enactments mentioned in subsection (6) of that section.

Section 30 of the Human Fertilisation and Embryology Act 1990	14 days.	The birth parents (except where the applicants seek to dispense with their agreement under section 30(6) of the Human Fertilisation and Embryology Act 1990) and any other persons or body with parental responsibility for the child at the date of the application.	Any local authority or voluntary organisation that has at any time provided accommodation for the child.

4.21 FOSTERING SERVICES REGULATIONS 2002, SI 2002/57[1] (regs 1–4, 11–19, 24–43, 49–50, Schs 2, 3, 6–8)

PART I

GENERAL

1 Citation, commencement and extent

(1) These Regulations may be cited as the Fostering Services Regulations 2002 and shall come into force on 1st April 2002.

(2) These Regulations extend to England only.

2 Interpretation

(1) In these Regulations, unless the context otherwise requires –

'the 1989 Act' means the Children Act 1989;

'the 2000 Act' means the Care Standards Act 2000;

'approval' means approval as a foster parent in accordance with regulation 28 and references to a person being approved shall be construed accordingly;

'area authority' means the local authority in whose area a child is placed, in any case where that local authority is not the child's responsible authority;

'assessment' shall be construed in accordance with regulation 27(1);

'child protection enquiries' has the meaning given to it by regulation 12(4);

'children's guide' means the written guide produced in accordance with regulation 3(3);

'foster care agreement' has the meaning given to it by regulation 28(5)(b);

'foster placement agreement' has the meaning given to it by regulation 34(3);

'foster parent' means a person with whom a child is placed, or may be placed under these Regulations, except that, in Parts IV and V of these Regulations it does not include a person with whom a child is placed under regulation 38(2);

'fostering panel' means a panel established in accordance with regulation 24;

'fostering service' means –

(a) a fostering agency within the meaning of section 4(4) of the 2000 Act; or

(b) a local authority fostering service;

'fostering service provider' means –

(a) in relation to a fostering agency, a registered person; or

(b) in relation to a local authority fostering service, a local authority;

'general practitioner' means a registered medical practitioner who –

---

[1]   The equivalent regulations in Wales are the Fostering Services (Wales) Regulations 2003.

(a) provides general medical services under Part II of the National Health Service Act 1977;

(b) performs personal medical services in connection with a pilot scheme under the National Health Service (Primary Care) Act 1997; or

(c) provides services which correspond to services provided under Part II of the National Health Service Act 1977 otherwise than in pursuance of that Act;

'independent fostering agency' means a fostering agency falling within section 4(4)(a) of the 2000 Act (discharging functions of local authorities in connection with the placing of children with foster parents);

'local authority fostering service' means the discharge by a local authority of relevant fostering functions within the meaning of section 43(3)(b) of the 2000 Act;

'organisation' means a body corporate or any unincorporated association other than a partnership;

'parent' in relation to a child, includes any person who has parental responsibility for him;

'placement' means any placement of a child made by –

(a) a local authority under section 23(2)(a) of the 1989 Act or a voluntary organisation under section 59(1)(a) of the 1989 Act which is not –

(i) a placement with a person who falls within section 23(4) of that Act; or

(ii) a placement for adoption; and

(b) except in Part V of these Regulations includes a placement arranged by an independent fostering agency acting on behalf of a local authority,

and references to a child who is placed shall be construed accordingly;

'registered manager' in relation to a fostering agency means a person who is registered under Part II of the 2000 Act as the manager of the fostering agency;

'registered person' in relation to a fostering agency means any person who is the registered provider or the registered manager of the fostering agency;

'registered provider' in relation to a fostering agency means a person who is registered under Part II of the 2000 Act as the person carrying on the fostering agency;

'responsible authority' means, in relation to a child, the local authority or voluntary organisation as the case may be, responsible for the child's placement;

'responsible individual' shall be construed in accordance with regulation 5(2)(c)(i);

'statement of purpose' means the written statement compiled in accordance with regulation 3(1).

(2) In these Regulations, a reference –

(a) to a numbered regulation or Schedule is to the regulation in, or Schedule to, these Regulations bearing that number;

(b) in a regulation or Schedule to a numbered paragraph, is to the paragraph in that regulation or Schedule bearing that number;

(c) in a paragraph to a lettered or numbered sub-paragraph is to the sub-paragraph in that paragraph bearing that letter or number.

(3) In these Regulations, references to employing a person include employing a person whether or not for payment, and whether under a contract of service or

a contract for services, and allowing a person to work as a volunteer, but do not include allowing a person to act as a foster parent, and references to an employee or to a person being employed shall be construed accordingly.

3 Statement of purpose and children's guide

(1) The fostering service provider shall compile, in relation to the fostering service, a written statement (in these Regulations referred to as 'the statement of purpose') which shall consist of –

> (a) a statement of the aims and objectives of the fostering service; and
> (b) a statement as to the services and facilities to be provided by the fostering service.

(2) The fostering service provider shall provide a copy of the statement of purpose to the Commission and shall make it available, upon request, for inspection by –

> (a) any person working for the purposes of the fostering service;
> (b) any foster parent or prospective foster parent of the fostering service;
> (c) any child placed with a foster parent by the fostering service; and
> (d) the parent of any such child.

(3) The fostering service provider shall produce a written guide to the fostering service (in these Regulations referred to as 'the children's guide') which shall include –

> (a) a summary of the statement of purpose;
> (b) a summary of the procedure established –
> > (i) in the case of an independent fostering agency, under regulation 18(1);
> > (ii) in the case of a local authority fostering service, under section 26(3) of the 1989 Act; and
> > (iii) in the case of a fostering agency falling within section 4(4)(b) of the 2000 Act, under section 59(4)(b) of the 1989 Act; and
> (c) the address and telephone number of the Commission.

(4) The fostering service provider shall provide a copy of the children's guide to the Commission, to each foster parent approved by the fostering service provider and (subject to his age and understanding), to each child placed by it.

(5) Subject to paragraph (6) of this regulation the fostering service provider shall ensure that the fostering service is at all times conducted in a manner which is consistent with its statement of purpose.

(6) Nothing in paragraph (5) shall require or authorise the fostering service provider to contravene or not comply with –

> (a) any other provision of these Regulations; or
> (b) in the case of a fostering agency, any conditions for the time being in force in relation to the registration of the registered person under Part II of the 2000 Act.

4 Review of statement of purpose and children's guide

The fostering service provider shall –

> (a) keep under review and where appropriate revise the statement of purpose and children's guide;
> (b) notify the Commission of any such revision within 28 days; and

    (c) if the children's guide is revised, supply a copy to each foster parent approved by the fostering service provider and (subject to his age and understanding), to each child placed by it.

****

PART III

CONDUCT OF FOSTERING SERVICES

11 Independent fostering agencies – duty to secure welfare

The registered person in respect of an independent fostering agency shall ensure that –

    (a) the welfare of children placed or to be placed with foster parents is safeguarded and promoted at all times; and

    (b) before making any decision affecting a child placed or to be placed with foster parents due consideration is given to –

        (i) the child's wishes and feelings in the light of his age and understanding; and

        (ii) his religious persuasion, racial origin and cultural and linguistic background.

12 Arrangements for the protection of children

(1) The fostering service provider shall prepare and implement a written policy which –

    (a) is intended to safeguard children placed with foster parents from abuse or neglect; and

    (b) sets out the procedure to be followed in the event of any allegation of abuse or neglect.

(2) The procedure under paragraph (1)(b) shall, subject to paragraph (3), provide in particular for –

    (a) liaison and co-operation with any local authority which is, or may be, making child protection enquiries in relation to any child placed by the fostering service provider;

    (b) the prompt referral to the area authority of any allegation of abuse or neglect affecting any child placed by the fostering service provider;

    (c) notification of the instigation and outcome of any child protection enquiries involving a child placed by the fostering service provider, to the Commission;

    (d) written records to be kept of any allegation of abuse or neglect, and of the action taken in response;

    (e) consideration to be given to the measures which may be necessary to protect children placed with foster parents following an allegation of abuse or neglect; and

    (f) arrangements to be made for persons working for the purposes of a fostering service, foster parents and children placed by the fostering service,

to have access to information which would enable them to contact –
  (i)   the area authority; and
  (ii) the Commission,

regarding any concern about child welfare or safety.

(3) Sub-paragraphs (a), (c) and (f)(i) of paragraph (2) do not apply to a local authority fostering service.

(4) In this regulation 'child protection enquiries' means any enquiries carried out by a local authority in the exercise of any of its functions conferred by or under the 1989 Act relating to the protection of children.

13 Behaviour management and absence from foster parent's home

(1) The fostering service provider shall prepare and implement a written policy on acceptable measures of control, restraint and discipline of children placed with foster parents.

(2) The fostering service provider shall take all reasonable steps to ensure that –
  (a)   no form of corporal punishment is used on any child placed with a foster parent;
  (b)   no child placed with foster parents is subject to any measure of control, restraint or discipline which is excessive or unreasonable; and
  (c)   physical restraint is used on a child only where it is necessary to prevent likely injury to the child or other persons or likely serious damage to property.

(3) The fostering service provider shall prepare and implement a written procedure to be followed if a child is absent from a foster parent's home without permission.

14 Duty to promote contact

The fostering service provider shall, subject to the provisions of the foster placement agreement and any court order relating to contact, promote contact between a child placed with a foster parent and his parents, relatives and friends unless such contact is not reasonably practicable or consistent with the child's welfare.

15 Health of children placed with foster parents

(1) The fostering service provider shall promote the health and development of children placed with foster parents.

(2) In particular the fostering service provider shall ensure that –
  (a)   each child is registered with a general practitioner;
  (b)   each child has access to such medical, dental, nursing, psychological and psychiatric advice, treatment and other services as he may require;
  (c)   each child is provided with such individual support, aids and equipment which he may require as a result of any particular health needs or disability he may have; and
  (d)   each child is provided with guidance, support and advice on health, personal care and health promotion issues appropriate to his needs and wishes.

16 Education, employment and leisure activities

(1) The fostering service provider shall promote the educational attainment of children placed with foster parents.

(2) In particular the fostering service provider shall –

    (a) establish a procedure for monitoring the educational attainment, progress and school attendance of children placed with foster parents;

    (b) promote the regular school attendance and participation in school activities of school aged children placed with foster parents; and

    (c) provide foster parents with such information and assistance, including equipment, as may be necessary to meet the educational needs of children placed with them.

(3) The fostering service provider shall ensure that any education it provides for any child placed with foster parents who is of compulsory school age but not attending school is efficient and suitable to the child's age, ability, aptitude, and any special educational needs he may have.

(4) The fostering service provider shall ensure that foster parents promote the leisure interests of children placed with them.

(5) Where any child placed with foster parents has attained the age where he is no longer required to receive compulsory full-time education, the fostering service provider shall assist with the making of, and give effect to, the arrangements made for his education, training and employment.

17 Support, training and information for foster parents

(1) The fostering service provider shall provide foster parents with such training, advice, information and support, including support outside office hours, as appears necessary in the interests of children placed with them.

(2) The fostering service provider shall take all reasonable steps to ensure that foster parents are familiar with, and act in accordance with the policies established in accordance with regulations 12(1) and 13(1) and (3).

(3) The fostering service provider shall ensure that, in relation to any child placed or to be placed with him, a foster parent is given such information, which is kept up to date, as to enable him to provide appropriate care for the child, and in particular that each foster parent is provided with appropriate information regarding –

    (a) the state of health and health needs of any child placed or to be placed with him; and

    (b) the arrangements for giving consent to the child's medical or dental examination or treatment.

18 Independent fostering agencies – complaints and representations

(1) Subject to paragraph (7), the registered person in respect of an independent fostering agency shall establish a written procedure for considering complaints made by or on behalf of children placed by the agency and foster parents approved by it.

(2) The procedure shall, in particular, provide –

    (a) for an opportunity for informal resolution of the complaint at an early stage;

(b) that no person who is the subject of a compliant takes part in its consideration other than, if the registered person considers it appropriate, at the informal resolution stage only;

(c) for dealing with complaints about the registered person;

(d) for complaints to be made by a person acting on behalf of a child;

(e) for arrangements for the procedure to be made known to –
  (i) children placed by the agency;
  (ii) their parents;
  (iii) persons working for the purposes of the independent fostering agency.

(3) A copy of the procedure shall be supplied on request to any of the persons mentioned in paragraph (2)(e).

(4) The copy of the procedure supplied under paragraph (3) shall include –

(a) the name, address and telephone number of the Commission; and

(b) details of the procedure (if any) which has been notified to the registered person by the Commission for the making of complaints to it relating to independent fostering agencies.

(5) The registered person shall ensure that a written record is made of any complaint or representation, the action taken in response to it, and the outcome of the investigation.

(6) The registered person shall ensure that –

(a) children are enabled to make a complaint or representation; and

(b) no child is subject to any reprisal for making a complaint or representation.

(7) The registered person shall supply to the Commission at its request a statement containing a summary of any complaints made during the preceding twelve months and the action taken in response.

(8) This regulation (apart from paragraph (5)) does not apply in relation to any matter to which the Representations Procedure (Children) Regulations 1991 applies.

19 Staffing of fostering service

The fostering service provider shall ensure that there is, having regard to –

(a) the size of the fostering service, its statement of purpose, and the numbers and needs of the children placed by it; and

(b) the need to safeguard and promote the health and welfare of children placed with foster parents,

a sufficient number of suitably qualified, competent and experienced persons working for purposes of the fostering service.

****

22 Records with respect to fostering services

(1) The fostering service provider shall maintain and keep up to date the records specified in Schedule 2.

(2) The records referred to in paragraph (1) shall be retained for at least 15 years from the date of the last entry.

****

PART V

PLACEMENTS

33 General duty of responsible authority

A responsible authority shall not place a child with a foster parent unless it is satisfied that –

(a) it is the most suitable way of performing its duty under (as the case may be) section 22(3) or 61(1)(a) and (b) of the 1989 Act; and

(b) a placement with the particular foster parent is the most suitable placement having regard to all the circumstances.

34 Making of placements

(1) Except in the case of an emergency or immediate placement under regulation 38, a responsible authority may only place a child with a foster parent if –

(a) the foster parent is approved –
  (i) by the responsible authority proposing to make the placement; or
  (ii) provided the conditions specified in paragraph (2) are satisfied, by another fostering service provider;

(b) the terms of his approval are consistent with the proposed placement; and

(c) he has entered into a foster care agreement.

(2) The conditions referred to in paragraph (1)(a)(ii) are –

(a) that the fostering service provider by whom the foster parent is approved, consents to the placement;

(b) that any other responsible authority which already has a child placed with the foster parent, consents to the placement;

(c) where applicable, that the area authority is consulted, its views are taken into account, and it is given notice if the placement is made; and

(d) where the foster parent is approved by an independent fostering agency, the requirements of regulation 40 are complied with.

(3) Before making a placement, the responsible authority shall enter into a written agreement (in these regulations referred to as the 'foster placement agreement') with the foster parent relating to the child, which covers the matters specified in Schedule 6.

35 Supervision of placements

(1) A responsible authority shall satisfy itself that the welfare of each child placed by it continues to be suitably provided for by the placement, and for that purpose the authority shall make arrangements for a person authorised by the authority to visit the child, in the home in which he is placed –

(a) from time to time as circumstances may require;

(b) when reasonably requested by the child or the foster parent; and

(c) in any event (subject to regulation 37) –

    (i) in the first year of the placement, within one week from its beginning and then at intervals of not more than six weeks;

    (ii) subsequently, at intervals of not more than 3 months.

(2) In the case of an immediate placement under regulation 38, the local authority shall arrange for the child to be visited at least once in each week during the placement.

(3) On each occasion on which the child is visited under this regulation the responsible authority shall ensure that the person it has authorised to carry out the visit –

    (a) sees the child alone unless the child, being of sufficient age and understanding to do so, refuses; and

    (b) prepares a written report of the visit.

36 Termination of placements

(1) A responsible authority shall not allow the placement of a child with a particular person to continue if it appears to them that the placement is no longer the most suitable way of performing their duty under (as the case may be) section 22(3) or 61(1)(a) and (b) of the Act.

(2) Where it appears to an area authority that the continuation of a placement would be detrimental to the welfare of the child concerned, the area authority shall remove the child forthwith.

(3) An area authority which removes a child under paragraph (2) shall forthwith notify the responsible authority.

37 Short-term placements

(1) This regulation applies where a responsible authority has arranged to place a child in a series of short-term placements with the same foster parent and the arrangement is such that –

    (a) no single placement is to last for more than four weeks; and

    (b) the total duration of the placements is not to exceed 120 days in any period of 12 months.

(2) A series of short-term placements to which this regulation applies may be treated as a single placement for the purposes of these Regulations, but with the modifications set out in paragraphs (3) and (4).

(3) Regulation 35(1)(c)(i) and (ii) shall apply as if they required arrangements to be made for visits to the child on a day when he is in fact placed ('a placement day') –

    (a) within the first seven placement days of a series of short-term placements; and

    (b) thereafter, if the series of placements continues, at intervals of not more than six months or, if the interval between placements exceeds six months, during the next placement.

(4) Regulation 41 shall apply as if it required arrangements to be made for visits to the child on a placement day within the first seven placement days of a series of short-term placements.

38 Emergency and immediate placements by local authorities

(1) Where a child is to be placed in an emergency, a local authority may for a period not exceeding 24 hours place the child with any foster parent approved by the local authority or any other fostering service provider provided that –

    (a) the foster parent has made a written agreement with the local authority to carry out the duties specified in paragraph (3); and

    (b) the local authority are satisfied as to the provisions of regulation 33(a).

(2) Where a local authority are satisfied that the immediate placement of a child is necessary, they may place the child with a person who is not a foster parent after interviewing him, inspecting the accommodation and obtaining information about other persons living in his household, for a period not exceeding six weeks, provided that –

    (a) the person is a relative or friend of the child;

    (b) the person has made a written agreement with the local authority to carry out the duties specified in paragraph (3); and

    (c) the local authority are satisfied as to the provisions of regulation 33(a).

(3) The duties referred to in paragraphs (1)(a) and (2)(b) are –

    (a) to care for the child as if he were a member of that person's family;

    (b) to permit any person authorised by the local authority or (if applicable) the area authority, to visit the child at any time;

    (c) where regulation 36 applies, to allow the child to be removed at any time by the local authority or (if applicable) the area authority;

    (d) to ensure that any information which that person may acquire relating to the child, his family or any other person, which has been given to him in confidence in connection with the placement is kept confidential and is not disclosed except to, or with the agreement of, the local authority; and

    (e) to allow contact with the child in accordance with the terms of any court order relating to contact or any arrangements made or agreed by the local authority.

(4) Where a local authority make a placement under this regulation outside their area they shall notify the area authority.

39 Placements outside England

(1) A voluntary organisation shall not place a child outside the British Islands.

(2) Where a responsible authority makes arrangements to place a child outside England it shall ensure, so far as reasonably practicable, that the requirements which would have applied under these Regulations had the child been placed in England, are complied with.

(3) *(revoked)*

40 Independent fostering agencies – discharge of local authority functions

(1) A local authority may make arrangements in accordance with this regulation for the duties imposed on it as a responsible authority by regulations 34, 35, 36(1) and 37

and where paragraph (3) applies, 33(b) to be discharged on its behalf by a registered person.

(2) Subject to paragraph (3), no arrangements may be made under this regulation in respect of a particular child, unless a local authority has performed its duties under regulation 33 in relation to that child.

(3) Where a local authority makes arrangements with a registered person for the registered person to provide foster parents for the purposes of a short-term placement within the meaning of regulation 37(1), the local authority may also make arrangements for the registered person to perform the local authority's duty under regulation 33(b) in relation to that placement on its behalf.

(4) No arrangements may be made under this regulation unless a local authority has entered into a written agreement with the registered person which sets out –

(a) which of its duties the local authority proposes to delegate in accordance with this regulation;
(b) the services to be provided to the local authority by the registered person;
(c) the arrangements for the selection by the local authority of particular foster parents from those approved by the registered person;
(d) a requirement for the registered person to submit reports to the local authority on any placement as may be required by the authority, and in particular following any visit carried out under regulation 35; and
(e) the arrangements for the termination of the agreement.

(5) Where a local authority proposes to make an arrangement under this regulation in respect of a particular child the local authority shall enter into an agreement with the registered person in respect of that child which sets out –

(a) details of the particular foster parent with whom the child is to be placed;
(b) details of any services the child is to receive;
(c) the terms (including as to payment) of the proposed foster placement agreement;
(d) the arrangements for record keeping about the child, and for the return of records at the end of the placement;
(e) a requirement for the registered person to notify the local authority immediately in the event of any concerns about the placement; and
(f) whether and on what basis other children may be placed with the foster parent.

(6) A foster parent with whom a child is placed in accordance with arrangements made under this regulation is, in relation to that placement, to be treated for the purposes of paragraph 12(d) of Schedule 2 to the 1989 Act as a local authority foster parent.

(7) A local authority shall report to the Commission any concerns it may have about the services provided by a registered person.

(8) In this regulation 'registered person' means a person who is the registered person in respect of an independent fostering agency.

PART VI

LOCAL AUTHORITY VISITS

41 Local authority visits to children placed by voluntary organisations

(1) Every local authority shall arrange for a person authorised by the local authority to visit every child who is placed with a foster parent within their area by a voluntary organisation as follows –

    (a) subject to regulation 37(4), within 28 days of the placement;

    (b) within 14 days of receipt of a request from the voluntary organisation which made the placement to visit a child;

    (c) as soon as reasonably practicable if it is informed that the welfare of the child may not be being safeguarded or promoted; and

    (d) at intervals of not more than six months where the local authority are satisfied, following a visit to a child under this regulation that the child's welfare is being safeguarded and promoted.

(2) Every local authority shall ensure that a person carrying out a visit in accordance with paragraph (1) –

    (a) sees the child during the course of the visit, or if the child is not there, makes arrangements to see the child as soon as reasonably practicable; and

    (b) takes steps to discover whether the voluntary organisation which placed the child have made suitable arrangements to perform their duties under these Regulations, and those under section 61 of the 1989 Act.

(3) A local authority shall report to the Commission any concerns it may have about the voluntary organisation.

PART VII

FOSTERING AGENCIES – MISCELLANEOUS

42 Review of quality of care

(1) The registered person shall establish and maintain a system for –

    (a) monitoring the matters set out in Schedule 7 at appropriate intervals; and

    (b) improving the quality of foster care provided by the fostering agency.

(2) The registered person shall supply to the Commission a report in respect of any review conducted by him for the purposes of paragraph (1) and make a copy of the report available upon request to the persons mentioned in regulation 3(2).

(3) The system referred to in paragraph (1) shall provide for consultation with foster parents, children placed with foster parents, and their responsible authority (unless, in the case of a fostering agency which is a voluntary organisation, it is also the responsible authority).

43 Notifiable events

(1) If, in relation to a fostering agency, any of the events listed in column 1 of the table in Schedule 8 takes place, the registered person shall without delay notify the persons indicated in respect of the event in column 2 of the table.

(2) Any notification made in accordance with this regulation which is given orally shall be confirmed in writing.

****

48 Offences

(1) A contravention or failure to comply with any of the provisions of regulations 3 to 23 and 42 to 46 shall be an offence.

(2) The Commission shall not bring proceedings against a person in respect of any contravention or failure to comply with those regulations unless –

(a) subject to paragraph 4, he is a registered person;

(b) notice has been given to him in accordance with paragraph (3);

(c) the period specified in the notice, within which the registered person may make representations to the Commission, has expired; and

(d) in a case where, in accordance with paragraph (3)(b), the notice specifies any action that is to be taken within a specified period, the period has expired and the action has not been taken within that period.

(3) Where the Commission considers that the registered person has contravened or failed to comply with any of the provisions of the regulations mentioned in paragraph (1), it may serve a notice on the registered person specifying –

(a) in what respect in its opinion the registered person has contravened or is contravening any of the regulations, or has failed or is failing to comply with the requirements of any of the regulations;

(b) where it is practicable for the registered person to take action for the purpose of complying with any of those regulations, the action which, in the opinion of the Commission, the registered person should take for that purpose;

(c) the period, not exceeding three months, within which the registered person should take any action specified in accordance with sub-paragraph (b);

(d) the period, not exceeding one month, within which the registered person may make representations to the Commission about the notice.

(4) The Commission may bring proceedings against a person who was once, but no longer is, a registered person, in respect of a failure to comply with regulation 22, and for this purpose, references in paragraphs (2) and (3) to a registered person shall be taken to include such a person.

49 Compliance with regulations

Where there is more than one registered person in respect of a fostering agency, anything which is required under these Regulations to be done by the registered person shall, if done by one of the registered persons, not be required to be done by any of the other registered persons.

****

SCHEDULE 2

RECORDS TO BE KEPT BY FOSTERING SERVICE PROVIDERS

1 A record in the form of a register showing in respect of each child placed with foster parents –

    (a) the date of his placement;

    (b) the name and address of the foster parent;

    (c) the date on which he ceased to be placed there;

    (d) his address prior to the placement;

    (e) his address on leaving the placement;

    (f) his responsible authority (if it is not the fostering service provider);

    (g) the statutory provision under which he is placed with foster parents.

2 A record showing in respect of each person working for the fostering service provider –

    (a) his full name;

    (b) his sex;

    (c) his date of birth;

    (d) his home address;

    (e) his qualifications relevant to, and experience of, work involving children;

    (f) whether he is employed by the fostering service provider under a contract of service or a contract for services, or is employed by someone other than the fostering service provider;

    (g) whether he works full-time or part-time and, if part-time, the average number of hours worked per week.

3 A record of all accidents occurring to children whilst placed with foster parents.

SCHEDULE 3

INFORMATION AS TO PROSPECTIVE FOSTER PARENT AND OTHER MEMBERS OF HIS HOUSEHOLD AND FAMILY

1 His full name, address and date of birth.

2 Details of his health (supported by a medical report), personality, marital status and details of his current and any previous marriage or similar relationship.

3 Particulars of any other adult members of his household.

4 Particulars of the children in his family, whether or not members of his household, and any other children in his household.

5 Particulars of his accommodation.

6 His religious persuasion, and his capacity to care for a child from any particular religious persuasion.

7 His racial origin, his cultural and linguistic background and his capacity to care for a child from any particular origin or cultural or linguistic background.

8 His past and present employment or occupation, his standard of living and leisure activities and interests.

9 His previous experience (if any) of caring for his own and other children.

10 His skills, competence and potential relevant to his capacity to care effectively for a child placed with him.

11 The outcome of any request or application made by him or any other member of his household to foster or adopt children, or for registration for child minding or day care, including particulars of any previous approval or refusal of approval relating to him or to any other member of his household.

12 The names and addresses of two persons who will provide personal references for the prospective foster parent.

13 In relation to the prospective foster parent, either –

- (a) an enhanced criminal record certificate issued under section 115 of the Police Act 1997 including the matters specified in section 115(6A) of that Act; or
- (b) where any certificate of information on any matters referred to in sub-paragraph (a) is not available to an individual because any provision of the Police Act 1997 has not been brought into force, details of any criminal offences –
  - (i) of which the person has been convicted, including details of any convictions which are spent within the meaning of section 1 of the Rehabilitation of Offenders Act 1974 and which may be disclosed by virtue of the Rehabilitation of Offenders Act 1974 (Exceptions) Order 1975; or
  - (ii) in respect of which he has been cautioned by a constable and which, at the time the caution was given, he admitted; and

  in relation to each member of the household aged 18 or over, details of any criminal offences such as are mentioned in sub-paragraphs (i) and (ii) of paragraph 13(b).

****

SCHEDULE 6

MATTERS AND OBLIGATIONS IN FOSTER PLACEMENT AGREEMENTS

1 A statement by the responsible authority containing all the information which the authority considers necessary to enable the foster parent to care for the child and, in particular, information as to –

- (a) the authority's arrangements for the child and the objectives of the placement in the context of its plan for the care of the child;
- (b) the child's personal history, religious persuasion and cultural and linguistic background and racial origin;
- (c) the child's state of health and identified health needs;
- (d) the safety needs of the child, including any need for any special equipment or adaptation;
- (e) the child's educational needs; and

(f) any needs arising from any disability the child may have.

2 The responsible authority's arrangements for the financial support of the child during the placement.

3 The arrangements for giving consent to the medical or dental examination or treatment of the child.

4 The circumstances in which it is necessary to obtain in advance the approval of the responsible authority for the child to take part in school trips, or to stay overnight away from the foster parent's home.

5 The arrangements for visits to the child by the person authorised by or on behalf of the responsible authority, and the frequency of visits and reviews under the Review of Children's Cases Regulations 1991.

6 The arrangements for the child to have contact with his parents and any other specified persons, and details of any court order relating to contact.

7 Compliance by the foster parent with the terms of the foster care agreement.

8 Co-operation by the foster parent with the responsible authority regarding any arrangements it makes for the child.

SCHEDULE 7

MATTERS TO BE MONITORED BY THE REGISTERED PERSON

1 Compliance in relation to each child placed with foster parents, with the foster placement agreement and the responsible authority's plan for the care of the child.

2 All accidents, injuries and illnesses of children placed with foster parents.

3 Complaints in relation to children placed with foster parents and their outcomes.

4 Any allegations or suspicions of abuse in respect of children placed with foster parents and the outcome of any investigation.

5 Recruitment records and conduct of required checks of new workers.

6 Notifications of events listed in Schedule 8.

7 Any unauthorised absence from the foster home of a child accommodated there.

8 Use of any measures of control, restraint or discipline in respect of children accommodated in a foster home.

9 Medication, medical treatment and first aid administered to any child placed with foster parents.

10 Where applicable, the standard of any education provided by the fostering service.

11 Records of assessments.

12 Records of fostering panel meetings.

13 Duty rosters of persons working for the fostering agency, as arranged and as actually worked.

14 Records of appraisals of employees.

15 Minutes of staff meetings.

SCHEDULE 8
EVENTS AND NOTIFICATIONS

Column 1	*Column 2*					
Event:	*To be notified to:*					
	Commission	*Responsible authority*	*Secretary of State*	*Area authority*	*Police*	*Primary Care Trust*
Death of a child placed with foster parents	yes	yes	yes	yes		yes
Referral to the Secretary of State pursuant to section 2(1)(a) of the Protection of Children Act 1999 of an individual working for a fostering service	yes	yes				
Serious illness or serious accident of a child placed with foster parents	yes	yes				
Outbreak at the home of a foster parent of any infectious disease which in the opinion of a registered medical practitioner attending the home is sufficiently serious to be so notified	yes	yes				yes

	Commission	Responsible authority	Secretary of State	Area authority	Police	Primary Care Trust
Allegation that a child placed with foster parents has committed a serious offence		yes			yes	
Involvement or suspected involvement of a child placed with foster parents in prostitution	yes	yes		yes	yes	
Serious incident relating to a child placed with foster parents necessitating calling the police to the foster parent's home	yes	yes				
Absconding by a child placed with foster parents		yes				
Any serious complaint about any foster parent approved by the fostering agency	yes	yes				
Instigation and outcome of any child protection enquiry involving a child placed with foster parents	yes	yes				

4.22 MAGISTRATES' COURTS (ADOPTION) RULES 1984, SI 1984/661

The Magistrates' Courts (Adoption) Rules 1984 (MC(A)R 1984) apply to adoption proceedings in the family proceedings court.[1] They are not set out in this Handbook since, for most purposes, it is sufficient to work on the basis that:

- rr 1–25 of the MC(A)R 1984 correspond to rr 1–25 of the Adoption Rules 1984 (AR 1984);
- rr 27–29 of the MC(A)R 1984 correspond to rr 47, 49 and 49A of the AR 1984; and
- Schedules 2 and 3 are identical in the MC(A)R 1984 and the AR 1984,

with minor modifications essentially to reflect the differences in structure between, on the one hand, the family proceedings court and, on the other, the High Court and county court.

Much more important than any minor differences between these two sets of court rules are that:

- the AR 1984 contains special provisions for proceedings in relation to the Hague Convention on Protection of Children and Co-operation in respect of Intercountry Adoption (such proceedings cannot be brought in the family proceedings court); and
- under the AR 1984 the child must be a party if the proceedings are in the High Court and may be a party if the proceedings are in the county court,[2] but under the MC(A)R 1984 the child cannot be a party to adoption proceedings in the family proceedings court.[3]

---

[1] Ie the magistrates' court.

[2] Rule 4(2)(g) and (3) of the AR 1984.

[3] Rule 4(3) of the MC(A)R 1984.

4.23 PARENTAL ORDERS (HUMAN FERTILISATION AND EMBRYOLOGY) REGULATIONS 1994, SI 1994/2767
(regs 1, 2, 4, Schs 1, 3)

1 Citation, commencement, interpretation and extent

(1) These Regulations may be cited as the Parental Orders (Human Fertilisation and Embryology) Regulations 1994 and shall come into force on 1st November 1994.

(2) In these Regulations unless the context otherwise requires –

'the 1990 Act' means the Human Fertilisation and Embryology Act 1990;
'the 1976 Act' means the Adoption Act 1976 and references to sections are to sections of the 1976 Act;
'the Order' means the Adoption (Northern Ireland) Order 1987 and references to articles are to articles of the Order;
'parental order' means an order under section 30 of the 1990 Act (parental orders in favour of gamete donors) providing for a child to be treated in law as a child of the parties to a marriage.

(3) These Regulations extend to England and Wales and Northern Ireland.

2 Application of Adoption Act 1976 provisions with modifications to parental orders and applications for such orders

The provisions of the 1976 Act set out in column 1 of Schedule 1 to these Regulations shall have effect with the modifications (if any) set out in column 2 of that Schedule in relation to parental orders made in England and Wales and applications for such orders, as they have effect in relation to adoption and applications for adoption orders.

****

4 References in enactments to be read as references to parental orders etc

Schedule 3 shall have effect so that the references mentioned in column 2, where they appear in the enactments mentioned in relation to them in column 1, shall be read in relation to parental orders and applications for such orders as provided for in column 2.

SCHEDULE 1

APPLICATION OF ADOPTION ACT 1976 PROVISIONS WITH MODIFICATIONS TO PARENTAL ORDERS AND APPLICATIONS FOR SUCH ORDERS

Column 1	*Column 2*
provisions of the 1976 Act	*modifications*

Applications by Gamete Donors for a parental order

1 (a) Section 6 (duty to promote the welfare of the child)	(i) As if for the words 'the adoption of a child' there were substituted the words 'an application for a parental order'; and
	(ii) as if the words 'or adoption agency' were omitted.
(b) Section 12(1) to (3) (adoption orders)	(i) As if for the words 'an adoption order' on each occasion they appear there were substituted the words 'a parental order';
	(ii) as if in subsection (1) for the word 'adopters' there were substituted the words 'husband and wife' and as if for the words 'an authorised' there were substituted the word 'the'.
(c) Section 24(1) (restrictions on making adoption orders)	(i) As if for the words 'an adoption order' there were substituted the words 'a parental order'; and
	(ii) as if for the words 'a British adoption order' there were substituted the words 'such an order'.
(d) Section 27(1) (restrictions on removal while application is pending)	As if for the words 'an adoption order is pending in a case where a parent or guardian of the child has agreed to the making of the adoption order (whether or not he knows the identity of the applicant)' there were substituted the words 'a parental order is pending'.
(e) Section 29 (return of a child taken away in breach of section 27 or 28 of the 1976 Act)	(i) As if for paragraphs (a) to (c) of subsections (1) and (2) there were substituted the words

'(a) section 27 as applied with modifications by regulation 2 of and paragraph 1(d) of Schedule 1 to the Parental Orders (Human Fertilisation and Embryology) Regulations 1994,

(b) section 27 of the Adoption (Scotland) Act 1978 as applied with modifications by regulation 2 of and Schedule 1 to the Parental Orders (Human Fertilisation and Embryology) (Scotland) Regulations 1994,

(c) Article 28 of the Adoption (Northern Ireland) Order 1987 as applied with modifications by regulation 3 of and paragraph 2(d) of Schedule 2 to the Parental Orders (Human Fertilisation and Embryology) Regulations 1994.'; and

(ii) as if for the words 'an authorised' there were substituted on each occasion they appear the word 'the'.

Effect of a parental order

2 Section 39(1)(a), (2), (4) and (6) (status conferred by adoption)

(i) As if for the words 'an adopted child' there were substituted, on each occasion they appear, the words 'a child who is the subject of a parental order';

(ii) as if in section 39(1)(a) the words 'where the adopters are a married couple,' were omitted and for the words 'child of the marriage' there were substituted the words 'child of the marriage of the husband and wife';

(iii) as if in section 39(2) for the word 'adopters' there were substituted the words 'persons who obtain the parental order' and the words 'or adopter' and the words 'subject to subsection (3),' were omitted;

(iv) as if in section 39(6) for the word 'adoption' there were substituted the words 'the making of the parental order' and the words 'Subject to the provisions of this Part,' and ', or after 31st December 1975, whichever is the later' were omitted.

Interpretation of certain events consequent upon the making of a parental order

3 (a) Section 42 (rules of construction for instruments concerning property)

(i) As if in section 42(2) for the words 'section 39(1)' there were substituted the words 'section 39(1)(a) as applied with modifications by regulation 2 of and paragraph 2 of Schedule 1 to the Parental Orders (Human Fertilisation and Embryology) Regulations 1994';

(ii) as if in section 42(2), for the words 'of the adoptive parent or parents' there were substituted the words 'in respect of whom the husband and wife have obtained a parental order';

(iii) as if in section 42(2)(a) for the words 'adopted child' there were substituted the words 'child the subject of the parental order' and for the word 'adoption' there were substituted the words 'the parental order';

(iv) as if in section 42(2)(b) for the words 'adopted' there were substituted the words 'in respect of whom parental orders were made';

(v) as if in section 42(4) for the word 'adoption' there were substituted the words 'making of the parental order' and for the words 'adopted child' there were substituted the words 'child the subject of the parental order';

(vi) as if in section 42(5) for the word 'adopt' there were substituted the words 'obtain a parental order in respect of' and as if after the words in section 42(4) 'section 39(2)' and, in section 42(5) 'section 39', there were inserted the words 'as applied with modifications by regulation 2 of and paragraph 2 of Schedule 1 to the Parental Orders (Human Fertilisation and Embryology) Regulations 1994'.

(b) Section 44 (property devolving with peerages etc)	As if for the words 'an adoption' on each occasion they appear there were substituted the words 'the making of a parental order'.
(c) Section 45 (protection of trustees and personal representatives)	As if in section 45(1) for the words 'adoption has been effected' there were substituted the words 'parental order has been made'.
(d) Section 46 (meaning of 'disposition')	(i) As if for the words 'this Part' on each occasion they appear and in section 46(5) the words 'the Part', there were substituted the words 'sections 39, 42, 44, 45 and 47 as applied with modifications by regulation 2 of and paragraphs 2 and 3(a), (b), (c) and (e) respectively of Schedule 1 to the Parental Orders (Human Fertilisation and Embryology) Regulations 1994'; and
	(ii) as if in section 46(2) for the word 'applies' there were substituted the word 'apply'.
(e) Section 47 (miscellaneous enactments)	(i) As if for subsection (1) there were substituted the words
	'(1) Section 39(2) as applied with modifications by regulation 2 of and paragraph 2 of Schedule 1 to the Parental Orders (Human Fertilisation and Embryology) Regulations 1994 does not apply so as to prevent a child who is the subject of a parental order from continuing to be treated as the child of a person who was in law the child's mother or father before the order was made, for the purposes of the table of kindred and affinity in Schedule 1 to the Marriage Act 1949 and of Sections 10 and 11 (incest) of the Sexual Offences Act 1956' and

(ii) as if in subsection (2) for the words 'Section 39' there were substituted the words 'Section 39 as applied with modifications by regulation 2 of and paragraph 2 of Schedule 1 to the Parental Orders (Human Fertilisation and Embryology) Regulations 1994'.

Registration

4 (a) Section 50 (Adopted Children Register)

(i) As if for the words 'Adopted Children Register' on each occasion they appear, except on the second occasion in section 50(3), there were substituted the words 'Parental Order Register';

(ii) as if in section 50(1) for the words 'adoption orders' there were substituted the words 'parental orders';

(iii) as if in section 50(2) for the word 'adoption' there were substituted the words 'parental order';

(iv) as if in section 50(2) for the words 'adopted person' there were substituted the words 'person who is the subject of the parental order';

(v) as if in section 50(3) for the words 'every person shall be entitled to search that index and to have a certified copy of any entry in the Adopted Children Register in all respects upon and subject to the same terms' there were substituted the following words:

'the Registrar General shall—

(a) cause a search to be made of that index on behalf of any person or permit that person to search that index himself, and

(b) issue to any person a certified copy of any entry in the Parental Order Register,

in all respects, except as to the entitlement of any person to search that index, upon and subject to the same terms';

(vi) as if in section 50(4) for the words 'marked 'Adopted'' there were substituted the words 'marked 'Re-registered by the Registrar General' pursuant to paragraph 1(3) of Schedule 1 as applied with modifications by regulation 2 of and paragraph 8(a) of Schedule 1 to the Parental Orders (Human Fertilisation and Embryology) Regulations 1994';

(vii) as if in section 50(5) after the words 'section 51' there were inserted the words 'as applied with modifications by regulation 2 of and paragraph 4(b) of Schedule 1 to the Parental Orders (Human Fertilisation and Embryology) Regulations 1994';

(viii) as if in section 50(5)(c) and (6) for the words 'an adoption order' on each occasion they appear there were substituted the words 'a parental order'; and

(ix) as if in section 50(7) for the words 'adoptions and the amendment of adoption orders' there were substituted the words 'parental orders and the amendment of such orders'.

(b) Section 51(1) to (6) and (9) (disclosure of birth records of adopted children)

(i) As if in section 51(1) for the words 'an adopted person' there were substituted the words 'a person who is the subject of a parental order';

(ii) as if in section 51(2) for the words 'an adopted person under the age of 18 years' there were substituted the words 'a person who is the subject of a parental order and who is under the age of 18 years';

(iii) as if section 51 (3)(a)(i) and (d) were omitted;

(iv) as if in section 51(3)(a)(iii), (b)(ii) and (c)(ii) for the words 'adoption order' there were substituted the words 'parental order';

(v) as if in section 51(4) for the words from 'Where' to '1978' there were substituted the words 'Where a person who is the subject of a parental order and who is in England and Wales applies for information under subsection (1),'; and

(vi) as if section 51(5)(a) and (c) were omitted.

Procedure

5 (a) Section 61(1) (evidence of agreement and consent)

(i) As if for the words 'this Act' there were substituted the words 'section 30 of the Human Fertilisation and Embryology Act 1990';

(ii) as if the words '(other than an order to which section 17(6) applies)' were omitted; and

(iii) as if for the words 'and, if the document signifying the agreement or consent is witnessed in accordance with rules, it' there were substituted 'and any such written consent'.

(b) Section 63(2) (appeals etc)

(i) As if the words 'Subject to subsection (3)' were omitted; and

(ii) as if for the words 'this Act' there were substituted the words 'section 30 of the Human Fertilisation and Embryology Act 1990'.

(c) Section 64 (proceedings to be in private)

As if for the words 'under this Act' there were substituted the words 'pursuant to section 30 of the Human Fertilisation and Embryology Act 1990'.

Orders, rules and regulations

6 Section 67(1), (2), (5) and (6) (orders, rules and regulations)

(i) As if after the words 'this Act' on each occasion they appear, there were inserted the words 'as applied with modifications by regulation 2 of and Schedule 1 to the Parental Orders (Human Fertilisation and Embryology) Regulations 1994';

(ii) as if in section 67(2) the words ', except section 3(1),' were omitted; and

(iii) as if in section 67(6) after the words 'paragraph 1(1)' there were inserted the words 'as applied with modifications by regulation 2 of and paragraphs 4(b) and 8(a) respectively of Schedule 1 to the Parental Orders (Human Fertilisation and Embryology) Regulations 1994'.

Interpretation

7 Section 72(1) (interpretation)

(i) As if after the definition of 'guardian' there were inserted the words '"husband and wife" means, in relation to the provisions of this Act as they have effect in relation to parental orders and applications for such orders, the husband and wife as defined in section 30 of the Human Fertilisation and Embryology Act 1990;'; and

(ii) as if after the definition of 'parent' there were inserted the words '"parental order" means an order under section 30 of the Human Fertilisation and Embryology Act 1990;'.

Schedule 1 to the 1976 Act (registration of adoptions)

8 (a) Schedule 1, paragraph 1

(i) As if in paragraph 1(1) for the words 'adoption order' there were substituted the words 'parental order';

(ii) as if in paragraph 1(1) for the words 'Adopted Children Register' there were substituted the words 'Parental Order Register';

(iii) as if paragraph 1(2) were omitted;

(iv) as if in paragraph 1(3) for the words from 'application to a court' to 'time in force)' there were substituted the words 'application to a court for a parental order';

(v) as if in paragraph 1(3) for the words 'any adoption order' there were substituted the words 'any parental order';

(vi) as if in paragraph 1(3) for the words 'marked with the word "Adopted"' there were substituted the words 'marked with the words "Re-registered by the Registrar General"';

(vii) as if paragraph 1(4) were omitted; and

(viii) as if in paragraph 1(5) for the words 'an adoption order' there were substituted the words 'a parental order'.

(b) Schedule 1, paragraph 2

(i) As if in paragraph 2(1) for the words 'an adoption order' there were substituted the words 'a parental order';

(ii) as if in paragraph 2(1) the words 'or the Adopted Children Register' were omitted;

(iii) as if in paragraph 2(1) for the words '"Adopted (Scotland)" or, as the case may be, "Re-adopted (Scotland)"' there were substituted the words '"Re-registered (Scotland)"';

(iv) as if in paragraph 2(1) the words from 'and where, after an entry has been so marked' to the end of the sub-paragraph were omitted;

(v) as if in paragraph 2(2) for the words 'register of adoptions' there were substituted the words 'register of parental orders';

(vi) as if in paragraph 2(2) for the words 'an order has been made in that country authorising the adoption of a child' there were substituted the words 'a parental order has been made in that country in respect of a child';

(vii) as if in paragraph 2(2) the words 'or the Adopted Children Register' were omitted;

(viii) as if in paragraph 2(2) for the words 'marked with the word "Adopted" or "Re-adopted", as the case may require' there were substituted the words 'marked with the word "Re-registered"'; and

(ix) as if in paragraph 2(3) for the words 'so marked' there were substituted the words 'marked in accordance with the provisions of sub-paragraph (1) or (2)'; and

(x) as if paragraph 2(4) and (5) were omitted.

(c) Schedule 1, paragraph 4

(i) As if for the words 'an adoption order' on each occasion they appear there were substituted the words 'a parental order';

(ii) as if for the words 'Adopted Children Register' on each occasion they appear there were substituted the words 'Parental Order Register';

(iii) as if in paragraph 4(1) for the words 'adopter or of the adopted person' there were substituted the words 'husband or wife or of the person who is the subject of the parental order';

(iv) as if in paragraph 4(1)(a) for the words 'adopter or the adopted person' there were substituted the words 'husband or wife or the child who is the subject of the parental order';

(v) as if in paragraph 4(1)(a) for the words 'given to the adopted person' there were substituted the words 'given to that child' and the words ', or taken by him,' were omitted;

(vi) as if in paragraph 4(1)(b) the words 'or (4)' were omitted;

(vii) as if in paragraph 4(4) after the words 'section 50' there were inserted the words 'as applied with modifications by regulation 2 of and paragraph 4(a) of Schedule 1 to the Parental Orders (Human Fertilisation and Embryology) Regulations 1994'; and

(viii) as if paragraph 4(5) were omitted.

****

SCHEDULE 3

REFERENCES IN ENACTMENTS TO BE READ AS REFERENCES TO PARENTAL ORDERS ETC

Column 1	*Column 2*
1 Article 37 of the Birth and Deaths Registration (Northern Ireland) Order 1976	In article 37(1) the words 'article 52(1)(a)' and 'article 50' shall be read as though they were followed by the words 'as applied with modifications by regulation 3 of and

paragraph 5(c) of Schedule 2 to the Parental Orders (Human Fertilisation and Embryology) Regulations 1994.' and the reference to 'Adopted Children Register' shall be read as a reference to 'Parental Order Register'.

2 Paragraph 5(a) of Schedule 8 to the Children Act 1989

The reference in sub-paragraph (a) to a person who proposes to adopt a child under arrangements made by an adoption agency within the meaning of the Acts or Order mentioned in that sub-paragraph shall be read as including a reference to a person who proposes to be treated as the parent of a child by virtue of a parental order and the enactments about adoption as applied by these Regulations.

3 Sections 27(2) and 28(5)(c) of the 1990 Act

The references to a child who is treated by virtue of adoption as not being the child of any person other than the adopter or adopters shall be read as references to a child who is treated by virtue of the making of a parental order as not being the child of any person other than the husband and wife as defined by section 30 of the 1990 Act.

4.24 PARENTAL RESPONSIBILITY AGREEMENT REGULATIONS 1991, SI 1991/1478
(regs 1–3)

1 Citation, commencement and interpretation

(1) These Regulations may be cited as the Parental Responsibility Agreement Regulations 1991 and shall come into force on 14th October 1991.

(2) In these Regulations, 'the Principal Registry' means the principal registry of the Family Division of the High Court.

2 Form of parental responsibility agreement

A parental responsibility agreement shall be made in the form set out in the Schedule to these Regulations.

3 Recording of parental responsibility agreement

(1) A parental responsibility agreement shall be recorded by the filing of the agreement, together with two copies, in the Principal Registry.

(2) Upon the filing of documents under paragraph (1), an officer of the Principal Registry shall seal the copies and send one to the child's mother and one to the child's father.

(3) The record of an agreement under paragraph (1) shall be made available, during office hours, for inspection by any person upon –

   (a) written request to an officer of the Principal Registry, and
   (b) payment of such fee as may be prescribed in an Order under section 41 of the Matrimonial and Family Proceedings Act 1984 (fees in family proceedings).

SCHEDULE

Parental responsibility agreement form
(*not reproduced here*)

4.25 PLACEMENT OF CHILDREN WITH PARENTS REGULATIONS 1991, SI 1991/893

1 Citation, commencement and interpretation

(1) These Regulations may be cited as the Placement of Children with Parents etc Regulations 1991 and shall come into force on 14th October 1991.

(2) In these Regulations, unless the context otherwise requires –

'the Act' means the Children Act 1989;

'area authority' means, in relation to a child who is or is to be placed, the local authority in whose area the child is or is to be placed where the child is in the care of a different authority;

'placement' means allowing a child who is in the care of a local authority to live pursuant to section 23(5) of the Act (placement of a child in care with parents etc) with

    (a) a parent of the child,

    (b) a person who is not a parent of the child but who has parental responsibility for him, or

    (c) where there was a residence order in force with respect to him immediately before the care order was made a person in whose favour the residence order was made,

and the expressions 'place' and 'placed' shall be construed accordingly and 'placed with' a person means being allowed to live with that person pursuant to that section;

'placement decision' means a decision to place a child which is made in accordance with regulation 5(2) (placement decisions by director of social services or nominated person);

'supervisory duties' means the duties imposed by regulation 9 (support and supervision of placements).

(3) Any notice required under these Regulations is to be in writing and any such notice may be sent by post.

(4) In these Regulations, unless the context otherwise requires –

    (a) any reference to a numbered regulation is to the regulation in these Regulations bearing that number and any reference in a regulation to a numbered paragraph is to the paragraph of that regulation bearing that number;

    (b) any reference to a numbered Schedule is to the Schedule to these Regulations bearing that number.

2 Scope of Regulations

(1) These Regulations shall apply to every child who is in the care of a local authority and who is or is proposed to be placed.

(2) Where a child who is to be placed is aged 16 or over regulations 3, 6, 7, 8, 9 and 12 shall not apply.

(3) These Regulations shall not apply to the placement of a child for adoption pursuant to the Adoption Act 1976.

(4) Nothing in these Regulations shall require the temporary removal of a child from the person with whom he is already living and with whom he may be placed, before a placement decision is made concerning him.

(5) These Regulations shall not apply in a case to the extent that they are incompatible with any order made by a court under section 34 of the Act (parental contact with children in care etc), or any direction of a court which has effect under paragraph 16(5) of Schedule 14 to the Act (transitional provision as to directions) in that case.

3 Enquiries and assessment

(1) Before a placement decision is made, a local authority shall make all necessary enquiries in respect of –

    (a) the health of the child;
    (b) the suitability of the person with whom it is proposed that the child should be placed;
    (c) the suitability of the proposed accommodation, including the proposed sleeping arrangements;
    (d) the educational and social needs of the child; and
    (e) the suitability of all other members of the household, aged 16 and over, in which it is proposed a child will live.

(2) In considering the suitability of a person as required by paragraph (1)(b) or (e), the local authority shall, so far as practicable, take into account the particulars specified in paragraphs 1 and 2 respectively of Schedule 1.

4 Duties of local authorities in relation to placements

A local authority shall satisfy themselves that the placement of a child is the most suitable way of performing their duty under section 22(3) of the Act (general duty of local authority in respect of children looked after by them) and that the placement is the most suitable having regard to all the circumstances.

5 Placement decisions by director of social services or nominated person

(1) A placement shall be made only after a placement decision has been made.

(2) The decision to place a child shall be made on behalf of the local authority by the director of social services appointed by the authority under section 6 of the Local Authority Social Services Act 1970 (director of social services) or by an officer of the local authority nominated in writing for that purpose by the director.

6 Immediate placements

(1) Subject to paragraph (2), nothing in regulation 3 shall prevent the immediate placement of a child pursuant to a placement decision in circumstances in which the local authority consider that to be necessary and in accordance with their duty under

section 22(3) of the Act and in such a case the authority shall take steps to ensure that the provisions of these Regulations that would otherwise have to be complied with before the placement decision is made are complied with as soon as practicable thereafter.

(2) Before an immediate placement is made pursuant to this regulation a local authority shall –

    (a) arrange for the person with whom the child is to be placed to be interviewed in order to obtain as much of the information specified in paragraph 1 of Schedule 1 as can be readily ascertained at the interview, and

    (b) arrange to obtain as much of the information specified in paragraph 2 of Schedule 1 in relation to other members of the household aged 16 and over, in which it is proposed the child will live, as can be readily ascertained at the time of that interview.

7 Provisions of agreements

Following a placement decision the local authority shall seek to reach agreement with the person with whom the child is to be placed on all the particulars, so far as is practicable, specified in Schedule 2 and the placement shall not be put into effect unless and until such an agreement on all such particulars has been reached and recorded in writing and a copy of it has been given or sent to that person.

8 Notification of placements

(1) Subject to paragraph (3) the local authority shall, so far as practicable, give notice to all the persons whose wishes and feelings have been sought in relation to the decision to place the child pursuant to section 22(4) of the Act (persons to be consulted concerning local authority decisions) and to those persons specified in paragraph (4) of –

    (a) the placement decision, and

    (b) details of where the child is to be placed.

(2) Where the child is placed with a person other than a parent the local authority's notice under paragraph (1) to the persons referred to in the paragraph shall contain –

    (a) the name and address of the person with whom the child is placed;

    (b) particulars of arrangements for contact with the child;

    (c) any other particulars relating to the care and welfare of the child which it appears to the local authority ought to be supplied.

(3) A local authority shall not be required to give notice under paragraph (1) in the case of a person whose whereabouts are unknown to the authority, or cannot be readily ascertained, or in any case where the authority determine that to give such notice would not be in accordance with their duty under section 22(3) of the Act.

(4) For the purposes of paragraph (1) the persons specified are –

    (a) the Primary Care Trust, the Health Authority, for the area in which the child is living and, if it is different, for the area in which the child is to be placed;

    (b) the local education authority for the area in which the child is living and, if it is different, for the area in which the child is to be placed;

    (c) the child's registered medical practitioner and, where applicable, any registered medical practitioner with whom the child is to be registered following the placement;

    (d)   the area authority;

    (e)   any person, not being an officer of a local authority, who has been caring for the child immediately before the placement; and

    (f)   where there was a residence order in force with respect to the child immediately before the care order was made, the person in whose favour the residence order was made.

9 Support and supervision of placements

(1) A local authority shall satisfy themselves that the welfare of each child who has been placed by them continues to be appropriately provided for by his placement and for that purpose the authority shall –

    (a)   give such advice and assistance to the person with whom the child is placed as appears to the local authority to be necessary;

    (b)   make arrangements for a person authorised by the local authority to visit the child from time to time as necessary but in any event –

        (i)   within one week of the beginning of the placement,

        (ii)   at intervals of not more than 6 weeks during the first year of the placement,

        (iii)   thereafter at intervals of not more than three months and also whenever reasonably requested by the child or the person with whom the child is placed

    and for the person so authorised to make arrangements, so far as practicable, on each visit to see the child alone.

(2) On each occasion on which a child is visited in pursuance of this regulation by any person authorised by the local authority which placed the child the local authority shall cause a written report on the child to be prepared by that person.

10 Placements outside England and Wales

A local authority which make arrangements to place a child outside England and Wales in accordance with the provisions of paragraph 19 of Schedule 2 to the Act (placement of child in care outside England and Wales) shall take steps to ensure that, so far as is reasonably practicable, requirements corresponding with the requirements of these Regulations are complied with in relation to that child as would be required to be complied with under these Regulations if the child were placed in England and Wales.

11 Termination of placements

(1) If it appears to a local authority that the placement is no longer in accordance with their duty in respect of the child under section 22(3) of the Act or would prejudice the safety of the child, they shall terminate the placement and shall remove the child forthwith from the person with whom he is placed.

(2) Where, in the case of a child who has been placed in the area of an area authority by another local authority, it appears to the area authority that it would be detrimental to the welfare of the child if he continued to be so placed, the area authority may remove the child forthwith from the person with whom he is placed.

(3) Where a child is removed under paragraph (2) the area authority shall forthwith notify the other authority of that fact and that authority shall make other arrangements for the care of the child as soon as is practicable.

12 Notification of termination of placements

In relation to a decision to terminate a placement a local authority shall, so far as is reasonably practicable –

- (a) give notice in writing of any decision to terminate the placement before it is terminated to –
  - (i) the child, having regard to his age and understanding,
  - (ii) the other persons whose wishes and feelings have been sought in relation to the decision to terminate the placement pursuant to section 22(4) of the Act,
  - (iii) the person with whom the child is placed,
  - (iv) the other persons to whom regulation 8(1) refers; and
- (b) give notice in writing of the termination of the placement to all those persons, other than the child and the person with whom the child was placed.

13 Application of Regulations to short-term placements

(1) This regulation applies where a local authority has arranged to place a child in a series of short-term placements with the same person and the arrangement is such that no single placement is to last for more than four weeks and the total duration of the placements is not to exceed 120 days in any period of 12 months.

(2) Any series of short-term placements to which this regulation applies may be treated as a single placement for the purpose of these Regulations.

(3) Regulation 9(1)(b) shall apply in relation to short-term placements to which this regulation applies as if for paragraphs (1)(b)(i) to (iii) of that regulation there were substituted –

- '(i) on a day when the child is in fact placed ("a placement day") within the first seven placement days of a series of short-term placements, and
- (ii) thereafter, if the series of short-term placements continues, on placement days falling at intervals of not more than six months or, if the interval between placements exceeds six months, during the next placement.'

SCHEDULE 1

PARTICULARS TO BE TAKEN INTO ACCOUNT IN CONSIDERING SUITABILITY OF PERSONS AND HOUSEHOLDS

1 In respect of a person with whom it is proposed the child should be placed –

- (a) age;
- (b) health;
- (c) personality;
- (d) marital status and particulars of any previous marriage;

   (e)   previous experience of looking after and capacity to look after children and capacity to care for the child;

   (f)   the result of any application to have a child placed with him or to adopt a child or of any application for registration for child minding or day care and details of any prohibition on his acting as a child-minder, providing day care, or caring for foster children privately or children in a voluntary or registered children's home;

   (g)   details of children in his household, whether living there or not;

   (h)   religious persuasion and degree of observance, racial origin and cultural and linguistic background;

   (i)   past and present employment and leisure activities and interests;

   (j)   details of the living standards and particulars of accommodation of his household;

   (k)   details of any criminal offences of which he has been convicted, or in respect of which he has been cautioned by a constable and which, at the time the caution was given, he admitted.

2 In respect of members of the household aged 16 and over of a person with whom a child is to be placed, so far as is practicable, all the particulars specified in paragraph 1(a), (b), (c), (d), (f), (i), and (k) of this Schedule.

SCHEDULE 2

PARTICULARS ON WHICH THERE SHOULD BE AGREEMENT WITH THE PERSON WITH WHOM A CHILD IS TO BE PLACED

1 The authority's plans for the child and the objectives of the placement.

2 The arrangements for support of the placement.

3 Arrangements for visiting the child in connection with the supervision of the placement by the person authorised by or on behalf of the local authority or area authority, and frequency of visits and reviews of the child's case under regulations made under section 26 of the Act (review of cases).

4 Arrangements for contact, if any, (including prohibition of contact) in pursuance of section 34 of the Act (parental contact etc for children in care).

5 Removal of the child from the placement in the circumstances specified in regulation 11.

6 The need to notify the local authority of relevant changes in circumstances of the person with whom the child is placed, including any intention to change his address, changes in the household in which the child will live and any serious occurrence involving the child such as injury or death.

7 The provision of a statement concerning the health of the child, the child's need for health care and surveillance, and the child's educational needs and the local authority's arrangements to provide for all such needs.

8 Any arrangements for any delegation and exercise of responsibility for consent to medical examination or treatment.

9 The need to ensure that any information relating to any child or his family or any other person given in confidence to the person with whom the child is placed in

connection with the placement is kept confidential and that such information is not disclosed to any person without the consent of the local authority.

10 The circumstances in which it is necessary to obtain in advance the approval of the local authority for the child living, even temporarily, in a household other than the household of the person with whom the child has been placed.

11 The arrangements for requesting a change in the agreement.

4.26 REPRESENTATIONS PROCEDURE (CHILDREN) REGULATIONS 1991, SI 1991/894

PART I

INTRODUCTORY

1 Citation and commencement

These Regulations may be cited as the Representations Procedure (Children) Regulations 1991, and shall come into force on 14th October 1991.

2 Interpretation

(1) In these Regulations, unless the context otherwise requires –

'the Act' means the Children Act 1989;

'complainant' means a person falling within section 23A, 23C, 24, or 24B(3) of the Act making any representations about the discharge of their functions by a local authority under Part III of the Act in relation to him, or a person specified in section 26(3)(a) to (e) of the Act making any representations;

'independent person' means in relation to representations made to, or treated as being made to, a local authority, a person who is neither a member nor an officer of that authority;

'panel' means a panel of 3 persons;

'representations' means representations referred to in sections 24D(1) or 26(3) of the Act.

(2) Any notice required under these Regulations is to be given in writing and may be sent by post.

(3) In these Regulations unless the context requires otherwise –

(a) any reference to a numbered section is to the section in the Act bearing that number;

(b) any reference to a numbered regulation is to the regulation in these Regulations bearing that number, and any reference in a regulation to a numbered paragraph is to the paragraph of that regulation bearing that number.

PART II

REPRESENTATIONS AND THEIR CONSIDERATION

3 Local authority action

(1) The local authority shall appoint one of their officers to assist the authority in the co-ordination of all aspects of their consideration of the representations.

(2) The local authority shall take all reasonable steps to ensure that everyone involved in the handling of the representations, including independent persons, is familiar with the procedure set out in these Regulations.

3A Local resolution

(1) Where a local authority receive any representation from a person specified in section 24D(1) they shall –

    (a) provide the person appointed under regulation 3(1) with a written summary of the representation;

    (b) endeavour by informal means to reach a settlement to the satisfaction of the complainant within 14 days; and

    (c) if at the end of 14 days no resolution has been achieved, notify the person appointed under regulation 3(1).

4 Preliminaries

(1) Where

    (a) a person to whom it applies is dissatisfied with the outcome of the procedure set out in regulation 3A; or

    (b) a local authority receive representations from any other complainant, except from a person to whom section 26(3)(e) may apply,

the local authority shall send to the complainant an explanation of the procedure set out in these Regulations, and offer assistance and guidance on the use of the procedure, or give advice on where he may obtain it.

(2) Where oral representations are made, the authority shall forthwith cause them to be recorded in writing, and sent to the complainant, who shall be given the opportunity to comment on the accuracy of the record.

(2A) The authority shall consider any comments made by the complainant under paragraph (2) and shall make any amendments to the record which they consider to be necessary.

(3) For the purposes of the following provisions of these Regulations, the written record referred to in paragraph (2), as amended where appropriate in accordance with paragraph (2A), shall be deemed to be the representations.

(4) Where a local authority receive representations from a person to whom they consider section 26(3)(e) may apply they shall –

    (a) forthwith consider whether the person has a sufficient interest in the child's welfare to warrant his representations being considered by them;

    (b) if they consider that he has a sufficient interest, cause the representations to be dealt with in accordance with the provisions of these Regulations, and send to the complainant an explanation of the procedure set out in the Regulations, and offer assistance and guidance on the use of the procedure, or give advice on where he may obtain it;

(c) if they consider that he has not got a sufficient interest they shall notify him accordingly in writing, and inform him that no further action will be taken;

(d) if they consider it appropriate to do so having regard to his understanding, they shall notify the child of the result of their consideration.

(5) Where paragraph (4)(b) applies, the date at which the authority conclude that the person has a sufficient interest shall be treated for the purpose of these Regulations as the date of receipt of the representations.

5 Appointment of independent person

Where the local authority receive representations under regulation 4 they shall appoint an independent person to take part in the consideration of them, unless regulation 4(4)(c) applies.

6 Consideration by local authority with independent person

(1) The local authority shall consider the representations with the independent person and formulate a response within 28 days of their receipt.

(2) The independent person shall take part in any discussions which are held by the local authority about the action (if any) to be taken in relation to the child in the light of the consideration of the representations.

7 Withdrawal of representations

The representations may be withdrawn at any stage by the person making them.

8 Notification to complainant and reference to panel

(1) The local authority shall give notice within the period specified in regulation 6 to –

(a) the complainant;

(b) if different, the person on whose behalf the representations were made, unless the local authority consider that he is not of sufficient understanding or it would be likely to cause serious harm to his health or emotional condition;

(c) the independent person;

(d) any other person whom the local authority consider has sufficient interest in the case

of the proposed result of their consideration of the representations and the complainant's right to have the matter referred to a panel under paragraph (2).

(2) If the complainant informs the authority in writing within 28 days of the date on which notice is given under paragraph (1) that he is dissatisfied with the proposed result and wishes the matter to be referred to a panel for consideration of the representations, a panel shall be appointed by the local authority for that purpose.

(3) The panel shall include at least one independent person.

(4) The panel shall meet within 28 days of the receipt by the local authority of the complainant's request that the matter be referred to a panel.

(5) At that meeting the panel shall consider –

(a) any oral or written submissions that the complainant or the local authority wish to make; and

(b) if the independent person appointed under regulation 5 is different from the independent person on the panel, any oral or written submissions which the independent person appointed under regulation 5 wishes to make.

(6) If the complainant wishes to attend the meeting of the panel he may be accompanied throughout the meeting by another person of his choice, and may nominate that other person to speak on his behalf.

9 Recommendations

(1) When a panel meets under regulation 8, they shall decide on their recommendations and record them with their reasons in writing within 24 hours of the end of the meeting referred to in regulation 8.

(2) The panel shall give notice of their recommendations to –

(a) the local authority;
(b) the complainant;
(c) the independent person appointed under regulation 5 if different from the independent person on the panel;
(d) any other person whom the local authority considers has sufficient interest in the case.

(3) The local authority shall, together with the independent person appointed to the panel under regulation 8(3) consider what action if any should be taken in relation to the child in the light of the representation, and that independent person shall take part in any discussions about any such action.

PART III
REVIEW

10 Monitoring of operation of procedure

(1) Each local authority shall monitor the arrangements that they have made with a view to ensuring that they comply with the Regulations by keeping a record of each representation received, the outcome of each representation, and whether there was compliance with the time limits specified in regulations 6(1), 8(4) and 9(1).

(2) For the purposes of such monitoring, each local authority shall, at least once in every period of twelve months, compile a report on the operation in that period of the procedure set out in these Regulations.

(3) The first report referred to in paragraph (2) shall be compiled within twelve months of the date of coming into force of these Regulations.

PART IV

APPLICATION OF REGULATIONS TO VOLUNTARY ORGANISATIONS AND PRIVATE CHILDREN'S HOMES AND IN SPECIAL CASES

11 Application to voluntary organisations and private children's homes

(1) The provisions of Parts I to III of these Regulations shall apply where accommodation is provided for a child by a voluntary organisation, and he is not looked after by a local authority, as if –

(a) for references to 'local authority' there were substituted references to 'voluntary organisation';

(b) for the definition in regulation 2(1) of 'complainant' there were substituted –

"'complainant" means
(a) any child who is being provided with accommodation by a voluntary organisation;
(b) any parent of his;
(c) any person who is not a parent of his but who has parental responsibility for him;
(d) such other person as the voluntary organisation consider has a sufficient interest in the child's welfare to warrant his representations being considered by them.';

(c) for the definition in regulation 2(1) of 'independent person' there were substituted –

"'independent person" means in relation to representations made to, or treated as being made to a voluntary organisation, a person who is not an officer of that voluntary organisation nor a person engaged in any way in furthering its objects, nor the spouse of any such person;' and

(d) for the definition in regulation 2(1) of 'representations' there were substituted –

"'representations" means representations referred to in section 59(4) about the discharge by the voluntary organisation of any of their functions relating to section 61 and any regulations made under it in relation to the child.';

(e) for the reference in regulation 4(1) and (4) to a person to whom section 26(3)(e) may apply or to whom the local authority consider section 26(3)(e) may apply there was substituted a reference to a person who may fall within sub-paragraph (d) in the definition of 'complainant' in these Regulations.

(2) The provisions of Parts I to III of these Regulations shall apply where accommodation is provided for a child in a private children's home, but where a child is neither looked after by a local authority nor accommodated on behalf of a voluntary organisation, as if –

(a) for references to 'local authority' there were substituted references to 'the person carrying on the home';

(b) for the definition in regulation 2(1) of 'complainant' there were substituted –

"'complainant" means
  (i) any child who is being provided with accommodation in a private children's home;
  (ii) a parent of his;
  (iii) any person who is not a parent of his but who has parental responsibility for him;
  (iv) such other person as the person carrying on the home considers has a sufficient interest in the child's welfare to warrant his representations being considered by them;'

(c) for the definition in regulation 2(1) of 'independent person' there were substituted –

"'independent person" means in relation to representations made to a person carrying on a private children's home, a person who is neither involved in the management or operation of that home nor financially interested in its operation, nor the spouse of any such person;'

(d) for the definition in regulation 2(1) of 'representations' there were substituted –

"'representations" means any representations (including any complaint) made in relation to the person carrying on the private children's home by a complainant about the discharge of his functions relating to section 64.';

(e) for the reference in regulation 4(1) and (4) to a person to whom section 26(3)(e) may apply or to whom the local authority consider section 26(3)(e) may apply there was substituted a reference to a person who may fall within sub-paragraph (d) in the definition of 'complainant' in these Regulations.

11A Exceptions to application of Regulations

These Regulations shall not apply to representations made by a child or a person in respect of a child who is being provided with accommodation, otherwise than by a local authority or voluntary organisation, in a school which is a children's home within the meaning of section 1(6) of the Care Standards Act 2000.

12 Special cases including application to representations by foster parents

(1) Where representations would fall to be considered by more than one local authority, they shall be considered by the authority which is looking after the child or by the authority within whose area the child is ordinarily resident where no authority has that responsibility.

(2) The provisions of Parts I to III of, and of regulation 12(1) of, these Regulations, shall apply to the consideration by a local authority of any representations (including any complaint) made to them by any person exempted or seeking to be exempted under paragraph 4 of Schedule 7 to the Act (foster parents: limits on numbers of foster children) about the discharge of their functions under that paragraph as if –

(a) for the definition in regulation 2(1) of 'complainant' there were substituted: 'a person exempted or seeking to be exempted under paragraph 4 of Schedule 7 to the Act making any representations;'

(b) for the definition in regulation 2(1) of 'representations' there were substituted: 'representations referred to in paragraph 6 of Schedule 7 to the Act.';

(c) in regulation 4(1) the words 'except from a person to whom section 26(3)(e) may apply' were omitted;

(d) regulation 4(4) and (5) were omitted.

4.27 REVIEW OF CHILDREN'S CASES REGULATIONS 1991, SI 1991/895

1 Citation, commencement and interpretation

(1) These Regulations may be cited as the Review of Children's Cases Regulations 1991 and shall come into force on 14th October 1991.

(2) In these Regulations, unless the context otherwise requires –

'the Act' means the Children Act 1989;
'independent visitor' means an independent visitor appointed under paragraph 17 of Schedule 2 to the Act;
'responsible authority' means in relation to –
  (a) a child who is being looked after by a local authority, that authority,
  (b) a child who is being provided with accommodation by a voluntary organisation otherwise than on behalf of a local authority, that voluntary organisation,
  (c) a child who is being provided with accommodation in a private children's home otherwise than on behalf of a local authority or voluntary organisation, the person carrying on that home;

(3) Any notice required under these Regulations is to be given in writing and may be sent by post.

(4) In these Regulations, unless the context otherwise requires –

  (a) any reference to a numbered regulation is to the regulation in these Regulations bearing that number and any reference in any regulation to a numbered paragraph is to the paragraph of that regulation bearing that number;
  (b) any reference to a numbered Schedule is to the Schedule to these Regulations bearing that number.

2 Review of children's cases

Each responsible authority shall review in accordance with these Regulations the case of each child while he is being looked after or provided with accommodation by them.

3 Time when case is to be reviewed

(1) Each case is first to be reviewed within four weeks of the date upon which the child begins to be looked after or provided with accommodation by a responsible authority.

(2) The second review shall be carried out not more than three months after the first and thereafter subsequent reviews shall be carried out not more than six months after the date of the previous review.

4 Manner in which cases are to be reviewed

(1) Each responsible authority shall set out in writing their arrangements governing the manner in which the case of each child shall be reviewed and shall draw the written arrangements to the attention of those specified in regulation 7(1).

(2) The responsible authority which are looking after or providing accommodation for a child shall make arrangements to coordinate the carrying out of all aspects of the review of that child's case.

(3) The responsible authority shall appoint one of their officers to assist the authority in the coordination of all the aspects of the review.

(4) The manner in which each case is reviewed shall, so far as practicable, include the elements specified in Schedule 1.

(5) Nothing in these Regulations shall prevent the carrying out of any review under these Regulations and any other review, assessment or consideration under any other provision at the same time.

5 Considerations to which responsible authorities are to have regard

The considerations to which the responsible authority are to have regard so far as is reasonably practicable in reviewing each case are the general considerations specified in Schedule 2 and the considerations concerning the health of the child specified in Schedule 3.

6 Health reviews

(1) Subject to paragraph (2), the responsible authority shall, in respect of each child who continues to be looked after or provided with accommodation by them –

- (a) arrange for an assessment, which may include a physical examination, of the child's state of health, to be conducted by a registered medical practitioner, or a registered nurse or registered midwife acting under the supervision of a registered medical practitioner –
  - (i) at least once in every period of six months before the child's fifth birthday; and
  - (ii) at least once in every period of twelve months after the child's fifth birthday;
- (b) require the person who carried out the assessment to prepare a written report which addresses the matters listed in Schedule 2; and
- (c) review the plan for the future health of the child prepared under regulation 7(1)(c) of the Arrangements for Placement of Children (General) Regulations 1991 at the intervals set out in sub-paragraphs (i) and (ii) of paragraph (a).

(2) Sub-paragraphs (a) and (b) of paragraph (1) do not apply if the child, being of sufficient understanding to do so, refuses to consent to the assessment.

7 Consultation, participation and notification

(1) Before conducting any review the responsible authority shall, unless it is not reasonably practicable to do so, seek and take into account the views of –

- (a) the child;
- (b) his parents;

    (c) any person who is not a parent of his but who has parental responsibility for him; and

    (d) any other person whose views the authority consider to be relevant;

including, in particular, the views of those persons in relation to any particular matter which is to be considered in the course of the review.

(2) The responsible authority shall so far as is reasonably practicable involve the persons whose views are sought under paragraph (1) in the review including, where the authority consider appropriate, the attendance of those persons at part or all of any meeting which is to consider the child's case in connection with any aspect of the review of that case.

(3) The responsible authority shall, so far as is reasonably practicable, notify details of the result of the review and of any decision taken by them in consequence of the review to –

    (a) the child;

    (b) his parents;

    (c) any person who is not a parent of his but who has parental responsibility for him; and

    (d) any other person whom they consider ought to be notified.

8 Arrangements for implementation of decisions arising out of reviews

The responsible authority shall make arrangements themselves or with other persons to implement any decision which the authority propose to make in the course, or as a result, of the review of a child's case.

9 Monitoring arrangements for reviews

Each responsible authority shall monitor the arrangements which they have made with a view to ensuring that they comply with these Regulations.

10 Recording review information

Each responsible authority shall ensure that –

    (a) information obtained in respect of the review of a child's case,

    (b) details of the proceedings at any meeting arranged by the authority at which the child's case is considered in connection with any aspect of the review of that case, and

    (c) details of any decisions made in the course of or as a result of the review

are recorded in writing.

11 Application of Regulations to short periods

(1) This regulation applies to cases in which a responsible authority has arranged that a child should be looked after or provided with accommodation for a series of short periods at the same place and the arrangement is such that no single period is to last for more than four weeks and the total duration of the periods is not to exceed 120 days in any period of 12 months.

(2) Regulation 3 shall not apply to a case to which this regulation applies, but instead –

(a) each such case is first to be reviewed within three months of the beginning of the first of the short periods;

(b) if the case continues, the second review shall be carried out not more than six months after the first; and

(c) thereafter, if the case continues, subsequent reviews shall be carried out not more than six months after the date of the previous review.

(3) For the purposes of regulation 6, a child shall be treated as continuing to be looked after or provided with accommodation throughout the period that this regulation applies to his case.

12 Transitional provisions

(1) Where immediately before 14th October 1991 a child is being accommodated by a local authority, a voluntary organisation or in a private children's home, regulation 3 (time when each case is to be reviewed) shall have effect subject to the following provisions of this regulation.

(2) Where a child has been accommodated by a local authority, voluntary organisation or in a private children's home for less than four weeks before 14th October 1991 and –

(a) there has not been a review of the case, that child's case shall be reviewed within four weeks of 14th October 1991 and thereafter in accordance with regulation 3(2);

(b) there has been a review of the case before 14th October 1991 that child's case shall be reviewed thereafter in accordance with regulation 3(2).

(3) Where a child has been accommodated by a local authority, voluntary organisation or in a private children's home for four weeks or more, but for less than three months, before 14th October 1991 and –

(a) there has not been a review of the case, that child's case shall be reviewed within three months of 14th October 1991 and thereafter not more than six months after the date of the previous review;

(b) there has been a review of the case before 14th October 1991, that child's case shall be reviewed thereafter not more than six months after the date of the previous review.

(4) Where a child has been accommodated by a local authority, voluntary organisation or in a private children's home for three months or more, but for less than six months, before 14th October 1991 and

(a) there has not been a review of the case, that child's case shall be reviewed within six months of the day on which the child was first so accommodated and thereafter not more than six months after the date of the previous review;

(b) there has been a review of the case by 14th October 1991 that child's case shall be reviewed thereafter not more than six months after the date of the previous review.

(5) Where a child has been accommodated in a private children's home otherwise than by a local authority or voluntary organisation for more than 6 months before 14th October 1991 that child's case shall be reviewed within 6 months of 14th October 1991 and thereafter not more than 6 months after the date of the previous review.

13 Exceptions to application of Regulations

These Regulations shall not apply in the case of a child who is being provided with accommodation, otherwise than by a local authority or a voluntary organisation, in a school which is a children's home within the meaning of section 1(6) of the Care Standards Act 2000.

13A

These Regulations shall not apply in the case of a child who is placed for adoption under the Adoption Act 1976.

SCHEDULE 1

ELEMENTS TO BE INCLUDED IN REVIEW

1 Keeping informed of the arrangements for looking after the child and of any relevant change in the child's circumstances.

2 Keeping informed of the name and address of any person whose views should be taken into account in the course of the review.

3 Making necessary preparations and providing any relevant information to the participants in any meeting of the responsible authority which considers the child's case in connection with any aspect of the review.

4 Initiating meetings of relevant personnel of the responsible authority and other relevant persons to consider the review of the child's case.

5 Explaining to the child any steps which he may take under the Act including, where appropriate –

   (a) his right to apply, with leave, for a section 8 order (residence, contact and other orders with respect to children),
   (b) where he is in care, his right to apply for the discharge of the care order, and
   (c) the availability of the procedure established under the Act for considering representations.

6 Making decisions or taking steps following review decisions arising out of or resulting from the review.

SCHEDULE 2

CONSIDERATIONS TO WHICH RESPONSIBLE AUTHORITIES ARE TO HAVE REGARD

1 In the case of a child who is in care, whether an application should be made to discharge the care order.

2 Where the responsible authority are a local authority whether they should seek a change in the child's legal status.

3 Arrangements for contact, and whether there is any need for changes in the arrangements in order to promote contact with the child's family and others so far as is consistent with his welfare.

4 Any special arrangements that have been made or need to be made for the child, including the carrying out of assessments either by a local authority or other persons, such as those in respect of special educational need under the Education Act 1996.

5 The responsible authority's immediate and long term arrangements for looking after the child or providing the child with accommodation (made pursuant to the provisions of the Arrangements for Placement of Children (General) Regulations 1991), whether a change in those arrangements is needed and consideration of alternative courses of action.

6 Where the responsible authority are a local authority, whether an independent visitor should be appointed if one has not already been appointed.

7 The child's educational needs, progress and development.

8 Whether arrangements need to be made for the time when the child will no longer be looked after or provided with accommodation by the responsible authority.

9 Whether plans need to be made to find a permanent substitute family for the child.

SCHEDULE 3

HEALTH CONSIDERATIONS TO WHICH RESPONSIBLE AUTHORITIES ARE TO HAVE REGARD

1 The child's state of health including his physical, emotional and mental health.

2 The child's health history including, as far as practicable, his family health history.

3 The effect of the child's health and health history on his development.

4 Existing arrangements for the child's medical and dental care and treatment and health and dental surveillance.

5 The possible need for an appropriate course of action which should be identified to assist necessary change of such care, treatment or surveillance.

6 The possible need for preventive measures, such as vaccination and immunisation, and screening for vision and hearing, and for advice and guidance on health, personal care and health promotion issues appropriate to the child's needs.

PART 5

CASE-LAW

'The single most important feature in the diagnosis of abuse is a clear statement by the child'

Physical signs of sexual abuse in children (Royal College of Physicians, 2nd edn), Summary and Conclusions, para 1, where the words are printed in bold typeface[1]

'I would really Like to be a TV journaliste on ITN. I would love to be rich and donate £2,000,000 to social services to help other children in care. I think that it is important for every young person to get what they deserve. I would love to get in contact with my Dad and find out about my history and my Mum. There are a lot of secrets in my family and no one is willing to share them with me. I want to know why my Mum is manic-depressive, I want to know why Nan and Grandad split up. I want to know why none of my uncles apart from two came to see me when I was younger. I want to prove to everyone who had stereotypical views about me to be put to shame and shown that foster children can get really far if they just believe in themselves. I want to live a wonderful life where all my dreams come true. I'm sick of the constant nightmares in my life and it's about time that I woke up smiling instead of crying.'

An extract (p 37) from *Your Shout!*, a survey of the views of 706 children and young people in public care, by Judith Timms and June Thoburn (NSPCC, 2003)[2]

'Mrs Boyle: I can hardly be held responsible. We had reports from welfare worker … One tries to do a public duty and all one gets is abuse …
Mollie: They say that what happened when you're a child matters more than anything else.
Miss Casewell: They say – they say. Who says?
Mollie: Psychologists
Miss Casewell: All humbug. Just a damned lot of nonsense. I've no use for psychologists and psychiatrists.'

Agatha Christie, *The Mousetrap*, Act 1 Scene 2 (HarperCollins Publishers Ltd, 1995)[3]

---

[1] By permission of the Royal College of Physicians.

[2] By permission of the NSPCC.

[3] By permission of HarperCollins Publishers Ltd. (c) 1952 Agatha Christie. Copyright in the customised version vests in Jordans.

5.1 OVERVIEW OF CASE-LAW

How case-law works as a source of law

Law books are, by definition, full of statements about what the law is. For every such statement the reader is entitled to ask 'on what basis are you saying this is the law?' to which, in England and Wales, the author's answer will normally either be 'because Parliament has said so' or 'because the courts have said so'.[1] We have already considered the former in the Overviews of statutes and statutory instruments. It is now time to consider the latter.

The so-called 'common law' system,[2] the origins of which go back before the concept and emergence of Parliament (early though they are in England and Wales),[3] is a system in which judges do, effectively, make law. A judge's basic task is to determine facts and apply the law to those facts in the cases that are brought before him, and to do so impartially and fairly. Parliament remains sovereign, but in applying the law laid down by Parliament questions of interpretation inevitably arise. It is a necessary part of a judge's job to do this, and once a judge (or group of judges) has done so his decision may be used as an authority on the point. This is known as *the doctrine of precedent*.[4]

Just how authoritative a judge's decision is depends on several factors, of which two are particularly important:

- whether the particular statement was an essential part of the judge's reasoning on the point in question, or whether it was, to a greater or lesser degree, peripheral observation.[5] Only the 'essential reasoning' can be binding. The rest may be persuasive; and

- the level of court in which the judge was sitting.[6] Decisions of the House of Lords are binding on all courts except the House of Lords itself.[7] Decisions of the Court of Appeal are binding on all lower courts, and upon the Court of Appeal itself save in very limited circumstances.[8]

---

[1] Which is why many of the footnotes in this text are references to sections in statutes, rules in statutory instruments and to cases: they are authorities for the propositions being made.

[2] A phrase often used in contradistinction to continental codified and Roman-based law.

[3] Both are attested by Chaucer in his description of the sergeant of the law in the General Prologue to the *Canterbury Tales*. It was only shortly before that, in 1362, that English itself was used in law courts and Parliament (source: *The Norton Anthology of English Literature*, 7th edn (WW Norton & Co, 2000), Vol 1).

[4] Historically known as 'stare decisis'.

[5] The 'essential reasoning' is still usually known as 'ratio decidendi' and the 'peripheral observations' as 'obiter dicta' despite the strong general tendency to do away with latinisms.

[6] The structure of the court system in England and Wales is illustrated at **7.10** below.

[7] Ie the House of Lords has the right to change its mind: see *Practice Statement* [1966] 3 All ER 77.

[8] *Young v Bristol Aeroplane Co Ltd* [1944] 2 All ER 293, affirmed at [1946] AC 163, [1946] 1 All ER 98.

Decisions of the High Court sitting at first instance are binding on lower courts[9] but not on other High Court judges. Decisions of circuit judges and district judges are not binding.

Typically this leaves two main potential areas for argument: whether a particular statement was or was not 'essential reasoning'; and whether the circumstances of a subsequent case are the same as or to be distinguished from those of the earlier one.

Burden and standard of proof

The '*burden of proof*' is about who has to prove something. The basic rule is straightforward. The burden of proof is on whoever asserts it. In practice it means that the burden of proof is on whoever brings the application. A local authority that applies for a care order must prove the grounds on which a care order is made; a woman who seeks a non-molestation order must prove the grounds on which a non-molestation order is made; a father seeking a contact order must prove the grounds on which a contact order is made;[10] and so on. It will also mean proving the facts on which the applicant relies to make out the relevant legal grounds.

The '*standard of proof*' is about how conclusively that something must be proved. The basic rule is straightforward, but it becomes more difficult after that. The basic rule in civil proceedings is that the standard of proof is 'the balance of probabilities' or 'more likely than not'. However a series of recent decisions, not just in the field of children law,[11] have meant that this simple proposition does not have a simple interpretation or application. In the field of children law, the leading decision is that of the House of Lords in *Re H (Minors) (Sexual Abuse: Standard of Proof)*.[12] At its heart is the statement:

> 'The more serious the allegation the more cogent is the evidence required to overcome the unlikelihood of what is alleged and thus to prove it.'[13]

---

[9]   See, eg *Re V (Care Proceedings: Human Rights Claims)* [2004] EWCA Civ 54, [2004] 1 FLR 944 at [6].

[10]   Albeit this will readily be achieved: see *Re O (Contact: Imposition of Conditions)* [1995] 2 FLR 124 and at **5.3** below.

[11]   *B v Chief Constable of the Avon and Somerset Constabulary* [2001] 1 All ER 562; *R (McCann and Others) v Crown Court at Manchester; Clingham v Kensington and Chelsea Royal London Borough Council* [2002] UKHL 39, [2002] 4 All ER 593.

[12]   [1996] 1 All ER 1, [1996] 1 FLR 80, and set out at **5.4** below. Note that, under the doctrine of precedent, the decision is binding on all courts in England and Wales except the House of Lords itself. The principles have recently been reasserted by the Court of Appeal in two children law cases in the aftermath of the quashing of the conviction of Angela Cannings: *Re U, Re B (Serious Injury: Standard of Proof)* [2004] EWCA (Civ) 567, [2004] 2 FLR 263. The House of Lords refused leave to appeal against this decision.

[13]   Lord Nicholls (at p 96 in the FLR), quoting Ungoed-Thomas J in *Re Dellow's Will Trusts* [1964] 1 WLR 451 – an example of using a decision that was not binding as nevertheless of some persuasive value.

Evidence

Evidence, like statutory interpretation, is one of the great oceans in our earlier likening of the law to a map or globe of the world, and as with statutory interpretation it is a subject on which we can only point the way in this Handbook:[14]

- the starting point is that the general law of evidence applies to children law cases in the same way as it does to others, subject to certain exceptions;

- in particular, this means that evidence must be relevant for it to be admitted,[15] and that opinion can only be given by an expert;[16]

- it is the court that determines issues, not the expert witness. Although the court will normally accept the evidence of an expert witness it can and should reject it where the evidence is not capable of withstanding logical analysis, in which case the court must give its reasons for doing so;[17]

- the old general rule against hearsay evidence being admitted has been abrogated by the Civil Evidence Act 1995 in general and by the Children (Admissibility of Hearsay) Order 1993 in particular. The court will, however, have to determine what weight it should attach to such evidence;

- there are further exceptions to the general law of evidence made by the Children Act 1989, particularly in relation to the reports of CAFCASS officers.[18] It also makes specific provision in relation to the evidence of children[19] and creates an exception to the rule against self-incrimination (ie the rule that no one shall be required to give evidence that may incriminate himself);[20]

- there is a general duty of disclosure of information to the court and to the other parties.[21] There are exceptions, such as under the doctrine of public interest immunity (essentially that there is a greater public interest

---

[14] For detailed consideration of the laws of evidence see, eg, *Cross and Tapper on Evidence* (LexisNexis Butterworths, 10th edn, 2004).

[15] 'Evidence is relevant if it is logically probative or disprobative of some matter which requires proof': Lord Simon of Glaisdale in *DPP v Kilbourne* [1973] AC 729 at 756.

[16] An expert may give opinion evidence on any relevant matter on which he is qualified to do so: see Civil Evidence Act 1972, s 3. In relation to expert evidence generally, see r 35 of the CPR 1998. It is for the court to determine whether someone is suitably qualified. Social workers, including CAFCASS officers, are experts who are entitled to, and should, give opinion evidence within their own area of expertise.

[17] Eg *Re B (Split Hearings: Jurisdiction)* [2000] 1 FLR 334; *Re L (Contact: Domestic Violence), Re V, Re M and Re H* [2000] 2 FLR 334 at 349.

[18] See Children Act 1989, ss 7(4), 41(11) and 42(2).

[19] Children Act 1989, s 96.

[20] Children Act 1989, s 98.

[21] 'It is a duty owed to the court both by the parties and by their legal representatives to give full and frank disclosure ... in all matters in respect of children': *Practice Direction (Family Proceedings: Cse Management)* [1995] 1 FLR 456, and see also, eg, *Re D (Adoption Reports: Confidentiality)* [1995] 2 FLR 687 and *Re L (Care: Assessment: Fair Trial)* [2002] 2 FLR 730.

in the non-disclosure of particular information than there is in its disclosure[22]) but these will not readily be made out;

- there is a difficult area in relation to legal professional privilege[23] which can be subdivided into legal advice privilege (communications between solicitor and client) which is absolute,[24] and litigation privilege (communications with third parties for the purposes of litigation) which is not absolute;[25]

- there is another difficult area in relation to disclosure of information to third parties. The starting point is to be aware that there are multiple legal obstacles to such disclosure, each of which must be considered: the Data Protection Act 1998; Administration of Justice Act 1960, s 12; Children Act 1989, s 97(2); Family Proceedings Rules 1991, r 4.23; and the provisions of Article 8 of the European Convention on Human Rights 1950 and its application under the Human Rights Act 1998.[26] This is an issue which is currently under review and is prospectively amended by s 62 of the Children Act 2004.

Our selection of cases

The references to case decisions throughout this Handbook are testimony to the importance of case-law to children law in England and Wales, but those references only go so far. We have had to decide whether, and if so, how, to illustrate this. It is clearly impossible to set out the full judgments of all the cases we have referred to in such a Handbook, but at the same time we want to give a feel for what lies behind these single line references. We have therefore decided to include the headnotes[27] of, and brief extracts from, eight case reports taken from the law reports.

The cases we have chosen are not held out by us to be the eight most important children law cases (although, if such a thing could be determined, some of them surely would be) nor are they necessarily the eight cases most frequently referred to in court. We have chosen them instead for the way in

---

[22]　Eg *D v NSPCC* [1978] AC 171.

[23]　See generally *S County Council v B* [2000] 2 FLR 161.

[24]　*R v Derby Magistrates' Court ex parte B* [1996] 1 FLR 513.

[25]　*Re L (A Minor) (Police Investigation: Privilege)* [1997] AC 16. The European Court of Human Rights ruled the mother's challenge to this decision to be inadmissible: *L v United Kingdom* [2000] 2 FLR 322.

[26]　See, for example, *Re B (A Child) (Disclosure)*, *Re* [2004] EWHC 411 (Fam), [2004] 2 FLR 142. 'It is much more questionable whether it is right to prohibit the publication of general non-identified information with a view to seeking such guidance and assistance as the fellow members of Families Need Fathers may wish to supply to him. Again, I have to say, having read many of the communications in question, a great deal of very helpful advice and sound wisdom was provided to the father as a result of his communications in that discussion' per Hale LJ, endorsed by Butler-Sloss P in *Re G (Contempt: Committal)* [2003] 2 FLR 58 at 69. Note also the rather different approach of the European Court of Human Rights to the question of confidentiality. It routinely gives the full names of the parties in its published judgments.

[27]　It is the judgments that are authoritative, or rather from which the essential (and perhaps binding) reasoning and persuasive observations must be extracted, not the headnotes, although these remain a useful summary.

which, individually and collectively, they illuminate legal reasoning and the subject of children law. Each is preceded by a brief introduction.

The Overview continues at **6.1** Overview of Practice Directions.

5.2 G v G (MINORS: CUSTODY APPEAL)
[1985] FLR 70

Court of Appeal

Sir John Arnold P and Sheldon J

14 June 1984

Introductory comments

The subject of appeals is complex, and one that we have decided largely goes beyond this Handbook.[1] However, we have included this case, which is key to an understanding of appeals, to dispel the popular belief that there is only one 'right' answer in any particular case. This is only partly true. It is true in the sense that there is only one right answer to the law that is to be applied, and if a judge errs in this then it must be corrected on appeal. However, it is not true in the sense that the law often leaves matters to the discretion of the judge, and an appeal court will not intervene in matters of discretion merely because another judge might have reached a different conclusion. Putting it starkly, different judges could reach different conclusions, and make different orders, having heard the same case, yet both may be 'right' in the sense that the decision of neither would necessarily be overturned on appeal.

The most important illustration of this in children law is the application of s 1 of the Children Act 1989. A judge has no alternative but to apply its principles in the circumstances defined by the section itself, and failure to do so will result in a successful appeal. But the judge has a great deal of discretion in determining the weight to be attached to the various elements set out in the welfare checklist of s 1(3)[2] and thus in determining the court's paramount consideration – the child's welfare – as required by s 1(1).

---

[1] Apart from this case, lawyers should be aware of the line of authority emerging in *Re T (Contact: Alienation: Permission to Appeal)* [2003] 1 FLR 531 and *Re B (Appeal: Lack of Reasons)* [2003] 2 FLR 1035: (1) in the vast majority of cases, practitioners should follow the guidance contained in the notes to r 52.3(2) of the CPR 1998 and apply for leave to the trial judge at the point of judgment; (2) on receipt of an application for permission to appeal on the ground of lack of reasons, a judge should consider whether the judgment was defective for lack of reasons and, if necessary, remedy the defect by the provision of additional reasons refusing permission to appeal; (3) advocates should draw to the judge's attention any material omission in a judgment of which they are aware to allow the judge at first instance to remedy that possible defect in the judgment, rather than the matter being taken on appeal; (4) adequacy of reasons depends on the nature of the case: there is no duty on a judge to deal with every argument presented by the parties' advocates – 'the bottom line is that the essential reasoning must be clear' (per Arden LJ in *Re T*).

[2] As well as to the weight to be attached to the evidence of particular witnesses.

Headnote

Appeal – Function of appellate court – Appeal from discretionary jurisdiction – Deciding issue of custody of children – Circumstances in which appellate court will interfere

Children – Custody – Appeal – Grounds for interfering with discretion of court below – Examination of balancing exercise

The parties were married in 1976. Michelle aged 18 and Christopher aged 16 were the children of the father by his first marriage and following their mother's death in 1975 had always lived with him. There was no issue as to their custody. E, a girl aged 15, and J and B, boys aged 13 and 12, were the children of the mother by her first marriage which ended in 1972 when their father died. They had always lived with the mother and there was no issue as to their custody. D, a boy aged 7, and M, a girl aged 5, were the natural children of the mother and father. The marriage had been unhappy and there had been a number of separations. The mother finally left the matrimonial home about the third week in September 1983 leaving D and M with the father. She sought custody of D and M.

On 20 March 1984 the judge heard evidence that J and B had been involved in breaking into cars, a minor sexual aberration, an instance of factory breaking, an attempt to steal a car and an attempt to steal a car radio. He was concerned about the alleged criminal activities. There was no record of J and B being either prosecuted or cautioned and he accepted that in no case did the police take action. Evidence was also given that E engaged in truancy. This was explained away by the mother but the welfare officer thought it would be of a delinquent nature to some extent. The judge was very favourably impressed by Michelle and expressed himself satisfied that due to her D and M were being better looked after than by the father and mother or either of them. It was contended on behalf of the mother that the time during which Michelle continued to fulfil this role in so satisfactory a manner might well be limited. The judge accepted the possibility but also recognized that Michelle might be available for a protracted period. He accepted that the mother had a great love for the children and recognized that when she left the children with the father it was not her fault. The welfare report indicated that D and M had formed an attachment for the father and that it would be very distressing for them to be removed from his care but, considering the position overall, recommended that the children should go to their mother. The judge ordered custody to the father.

On appeal by the mother it was contended (i) on the evidence, the alleged criminal activities and truancy were either irrelevant or had been given too much weight by the judge; (ii) he erred in method because he was in substance awarding the custody to Michelle whereas the issue before him was whether the custody should go to the mother or father; (iii) he erred in method in that he regarded the welfare of D and M as being relevantly coincident with the availability of Michelle which was likely to be for a short-term duration thereby neglecting to take into account the long-term welfare of the children; (iv) he gave no weight or too little weight to the fact that the mother was able to give full-time care to the children – the children were small and one of them was a young girl; (v) his conclusion was wrong so that he must have gone wrong in the performance of the balancing exercise.

Held – dismissing appeal –

(1) Before a discretionary decision can be overturned there had to be something more than the possibility that the appellate court might itself have exercised the discretion in a different way.

(2) The court would do so where (i) a matter irrelevant to the decision had been taken into account in any decisive fashion by the court below; (ii) a matter which was germane in any decisive manner to the making of the discretionary decision had been left out of account; (iii) there was so blatant an error in the conclusion that it could only have been reached if the judge had erred in his method of decision – sometimes called the balancing exercise.

(3) There was nothing to suggest a later move to the mother would be more distressing than an earlier move. The judge envisaged a prospect of improved access from which it was reasonable to infer the opposite would be the case. For that reason the circumstance that Michelle might not cease to be available was very important and one the judge was fully entitled to take into account.

(4) Counsel for the mother had addressed the judge only a few minutes before he gave his judgment during which counsel had prominently argued that the mother was available for the care of the children full-time, that the children were small and included a small girl. It was inconceivable that the judge should have forgotten those matters.

(5) Acting as a reasonable balancer, the judge was entitled to reach the conclusion he did. The height of what could be said about the judge's conclusion was that it was a decision which other judges might have taken in the opposite direction.

Extracts from the judgment of Sir John Arnold, President

[Having referred to three previous authorities, he continued...] It is again a discernible unanimity that if the court observes that a matter irrelevant to the decision has been taken into account in any decisive fashion by the court below in making its discretionary order, that will be set aside; similarly, if it emerges, from an observation of the reasons of the judge, that there has been left out of account a matter which is germane and proper to be taken into account in any decisive manner in making the discretionary decision, that too will be a cause of upset. It is when one gets beyond that that the difficulty appears to occur. It is the duty of the appellate court, as the cases say, to do justice – one does not doubt that – and if the court comes to the clear conclusion that the judge below was wrong, or if the court comes to the conclusion that the judge below was clearly wrong, or if the court comes to the conclusion that the judge below was plainly wrong, then, even though the exposition of the judge's thought processes has not thrown up either the omission of a relevant circumstance of a decisive nature, or the inclusion of an irrelevant circumstance in a decisive way, the appellate court can nevertheless come to the conclusion that because of this clear conclusion that the judge was wrong, or conclusion that the judge was plainly, or clearly, wrong, then the court is at liberty to overset the decision and either order a new trial or substitute its own conclusion as the case may seem to require.

But running all through this consideration of the different circumstances with which the appellate court has to deal is the word 'wrong'. What is it that 'wrong' means, which is not and cannot be, as is on all hands conceded, identical with 'in a way different from that which the members of the appellate court would themselves have resolved the issue'? It is the answer to that question which provides the difficulty.

I believe that there is a way of reconciling these cases. I believe that if the court comes to the conclusion, when examining the decision at first instance, that there is so blatant an error in the conclusion that it could only have been reached if the judge below had erred in his method of decision – sometimes called the balancing exercise – then the court is at liberty to interfere; but that, if the observation of the appellate court extends no further than that the decision in terms of the result of the balancing exercise was one with which they might, or do, disagree as a matter of result, then that by itself is not enough, and that falls short of the conclusion, which is essential, that the judge has erred in his method. I cannot think of any case in which this particular issue has had to be faced, in which that method of determination is not intellectually satisfactory, logically supportable or consistent with the result of any of the cases in the appellate courts; and I shall approach this case on the footing that what this court should seek to do is to answer the question whether the court discerns a wrongness in the result of so striking a character as to make it a legitimate conclusion that there must have been an error of method – apart, of course, from a disclosed inclusion of irrelevant or exclusion of relevant matters. With that, I hope, comprehensible introduction, I come now to the particular matters of complaint.

[...]

In my judgment, the judge was entitled, acting as a reasonable balancer, to reach the conclusion which he did. I do not find the conclusion which he reached so wrong that one ought to draw any conclusion from it other than that it was a decision which other judges might have taken in the opposite direction. That, it seems to me, is the height of what can be said about this judge's conclusion in the matter and I would dismiss the appeal.

5.3 RE O (CONTACT: IMPOSITION OF CONDITIONS) [1995] 2 FLR 124

Court of Appeal

Sir Thomas Bingham MR, Simon Brown and Swinton Thomas LJJ

14 March 1995

Introductory comments

This case needs little introduction. It is commonly treated as the general starting point for any discussion of the application of the welfare principle to private law contact cases, the most basic and most numerous, though often by no means the most straightforward, children law cases that the courts have to determine.

Headnote

Contact – Indirect contact order – Conditions attached to order – Whether court having power to order intransigent mother to send father photographs of child, school report, and medical reports or to order mother to read and show child letters written by father

The parents never married, and separated prior to the child's birth. The mother was opposed to the father having contact to the child. In 1993 and 1994 direct contact orders were made but there were immediate difficulties. The mother was not prepared to participate in the contact. The court made a further contact order attaching conditions. The mother subsequently issued an application to discharge one of the conditions as she did not want to come into contact with the father herself. The judge refused to amend his order in the terms that the mother sought. The mother appealed.

Held – dismissing the appeal – section 11(7) of the Children Act 1989 conferred wide and comprehensive powers on the court to ensure contact between the child and the non-custodial parent, where it promoted the welfare of the child. The parents' interests were only relevant where they affected the welfare of the child. Where parents were separated it was almost always in the child's interests to have contact with the other parent. In infrequent cases the court may consider that direct contact should not be ordered. Indirect contact was then desirable provided that it was not abused. The caring parent had reciprocal obligations. An intransigent mother had no right of veto over contact. The court had ample power to compel a mother to send information to the father to promote meaningful contact.

Extract from the judgment of Sir Thomas Bingham, Master of the Rolls

It may perhaps be worth stating in a reasonably compendious way some very familiar but none the less fundamental principles. First of all, and overriding all else as provided in s 1(1) of the 1989 Act, the welfare of the child is the paramount consideration of any court concerned to make an order relating to the upbringing of a child. It cannot be emphasised too strongly that the court is concerned with the interests of the mother and the father only insofar as they bear on the welfare of the child.

Secondly, where parents of a child are separated and the child is in the day-to-day care of one of them, it is almost always in the interests of the child that he or she should have contact with the other parent. The reason for this scarcely needs spelling out. It is, of course, that the separation of parents involves a loss to the child, and it is desirable that that loss should so far as possible be made good by contact with the non-custodial parent, that is the parent in whose day-to-day care the child is not. This has been said on a very great number of occasions and I cite only two of them. In *Re H (Minors) (Access)* [1992] 1 FLR 148 at p 151A, Balcombe LJ quoted, endorsing as fully as he could, an earlier passage in a judgment of Latey J in which that judge had said:

> '... where the parents have separated and one has the care of the child, access by the other often results in some upset in the child. Those upsets are usually minor and superficial. They are heavily outweighed by the long-term advantages to the child of keeping in touch with the parent concerned so that they do not become strangers, so that the child later in life does not resent the deprivation and turn against the parent who the child thinks, rightly or wrongly, has deprived him, and so that the deprived parent loses interest in the child and therefore does not make the material and emotional contribution to the child's development which that parent by its companionship and otherwise would make.'

My second citation is from *Re J (A Minor) (Contact)* [1994] 1 FLR 729 at p 736B–C, where Balcombe LJ said:

> 'But before concluding this judgment I would like to make three general points. The first is that judges should be very reluctant to allow the implacable hostility of one parent (usually the parent who has a residence order in his or her favour), to deter them from making a contact order where they believe the child's welfare requires it. The danger of allowing the implacable hostility of the residential parent (usually the mother) to frustrate the court's decision is too obvious to require repetition on my part.'

Thirdly, the court has power to enforce orders for contact, which it should not hesitate to exercise where it judges that it will overall promote the welfare of the child to do so. I refer in this context to the judgment of the President of the Family Division in *Re W (A Minor) (Contact)* [1994] 2 FLR 441 at p 447H, where the President said:

> 'However, I am quite clear that a court cannot allow a mother, in such circumstances, simply to defy the order of the court which was, and is, in force, that is to say that there should be reasonable contact with the father. That was indeed made by consent as I have already observed. Some constructive step must be taken to permit and encourage the boy to resume contact with his father.'

At p 449A the President added:

'I wish to make it very clear to the mother that this is an order of the court. The court cannot be put in a position where it is told, "I shall not obey an order of the court".'

Fourthly, cases do, unhappily and infrequently but occasionally, arise in which a court is compelled to conclude that in existing circumstances an order for immediate direct contact should not be ordered, because so to order would injure the welfare of the child. In *Re D (A Minor) (Contact: Mother's Hostility)* [1993] 2 FLR 1 at p 7G, Waite LJ said:

'It is now well settled that the implacable hostility of a mother towards access or contact is a factor which is capable, according to the circumstances of each particular case, of supplying a cogent reason for departing from the general principle that a child should grow up in the knowledge of both his parents. I see no reason to think that the judge fell into any error of principle in deciding, as he clearly did on the plain interpretation of his judgment, that the mother's present attitude towards contact puts D at serious risk of major emotional harm if she were to be compelled to accept a degree of contact to the natural father against her will.'

I simply draw attention to the judge's reference to a serious risk of major emotional harm. The courts should not at all readily accept that the child's welfare will be injured by direct contact. Judging that question the court should take a medium-term and long-term view of the child's development and not accord excessive weight to what appear likely to be short-term or transient problems. Neither parent should be encouraged or permitted to think that the more intransigent, the more unreasonable, the more obdurate and the more unco-operative they are, the more likely they are to get their own way. Courts should remember that in these cases they are dealing with parents who are adults, who must be treated as rational adults, who must be assumed to have the welfare of the child at heart, and who have once been close enough to each other to have produced the child. It would be as well if parents also were to bear these points in mind.

Fifthly, in cases in which, for whatever reason, direct contact cannot for the time being be ordered, it is ordinarily highly desirable that there should be indirect contact so that the child grows up knowing of the love and interest of the absent parent with whom, in due course, direct contact should be established. This calls for a measure of restraint, common sense and unselfishness on the part of both parents. If the absent parent deluges the child with presents or writes long and obsessive screeds to the child, or if he or she uses his or her right to correspond to criticise or insult the other parent, then inevitably those rights will be curtailed. The object of indirect contact is to build up a relationship between the absent parent and the child, not to enable the absent parent to pursue a feud with the caring parent in a manner not conducive to the welfare of the child.

The caring parent also has reciprocal obligations. If the caring parent puts difficulties in the way of indirect contact by withholding presents or letters or failing to read letters to a child who cannot read, then such parent must understand that the court can compel compliance with its orders; it has sanctions available and no residence order is to be regarded as irrevocable. It is entirely reasonable that the parent with the care of the child should be obliged to report on the progress of the child to the absent parent, for the obvious reason that an absent parent cannot correspond in a meaningful way if unaware of the child's concerns, or of where the child goes to school, or what it does when it gets there, or what games it plays, and so on. Of course judges must not impose duties which parents cannot realistically be expected to perform, and it would accordingly be absurd to expect, in a case where this was the case, a semi-literate parent to write monthly reports. But some means of communication, directly or indirectly, is essential if indirect contact is to be meaningful, and if the welfare of the child is not to suffer.

5.4 RE H AND R (CHILD SEXUAL ABUSE: STANDARD OF PROOF)[1] [1996] 1 FLR 80

House of Lords

Lord Goff of Chieveley, Lord Browne-Wilkinson, Lord Mustill,
Lord Lloyd of Berwick, Lord Nicholls of Birkenhead

14 December 1995

Introductory comments

In the introductory comments to *G v G (Minors: Custody Appeal)* (at **5.2**) we made the point that there is only one right answer to the law that is to be applied. The first thing to notice about this case is that although there is only one right answer to the law that is to be applied, even the best legal minds can disagree about what it is. Here the judges in the House of Lords were divided three to two on the main point at issue – the standard of proof to be applied in determining whether or not a material fact alleged (sexual abuse of a child within the family) had occurred.

Although we have already referred to this issue in the Overview we have included the case in this section of the Handbook as: (1) the issue is of fundamental importance to the operation of the family justice system and hence to the work of all professionals involved in matters of child protection and welfare; (2) the decision is controversial, at least in some quarters, in some of the reasoning and in its consequences for child protection and welfare; (3) the case is also authority on other important issues, namely the meaning of 'likely' in s 31 of the Children Act 1989 and that unproved allegations (lingering suspicions) cannot form the basis for a finding that the threshold criteria in s 31 have been crossed. This last point also links it with *Re O and N; Re B* [2003] 1 FLR 1169, a case included later in this selection (at **5.9**).

Headnote

Care – Evidence – Local authority applying for care orders for three children based on allegations of sexual abuse of older sister by mother's cohabitant – Judge finding allegations not established – Whether standard of proof on balance of probabilities – Whether judge should proceed to consider future risk to children when primary allegation not proved – Children Act 1989, s 31

---

[1] The case is also known as *Re H (Minors) (Sexual Abuse: Standard of Proof)* [1996] AC 563 and *Re H and Others (Minors) (Sexual Abuse: Standard of Proof)* [1996] 1 All ER 1.

The mother had four children, all girls. D1 and D2 were children of her marriage to Mr H. They separated and the mother lived with Mr R. They had two children, D3 and D4. When she was 15, D1 said she had been sexually abused by Mr R and he was charged with rape. Interim care, followed by interim supervision, orders were made in respect of the three other girls. Mr R was acquitted. The local authority proceeded with applications for care orders for D2, D3 and D4, then aged 13, 8 and 2 years, the case based solely on the alleged abuse of D1 by Mr R. Relying on the different standard of proof applicable in civil and criminal matters, the judge was asked to find that Mr R had sexually abused D1 or at least that there was a substantial risk he had done so, thereby, so it was said, satisfying the conditions of s 31(2) of the Children Act 1989 for the making of a care order. The applications were dismissed by the judge who could not be sure 'to the requisite high standard of proof' that D1's allegations were true. An appeal to the Court of Appeal was dismissed by a majority, which stated that having fairly weighed up the matters relating to the allegations of sexual abuse and having concluded that those allegations had not been established to the requisite standard of proof, ie the balance of probabilities, the judge had rightly dismissed the applications. It was not open to him, on the evidence, since he had rejected the only allegation which gave rise to the applications, to go on to a second stage and consider the likelihood of future harm to the children. The local authority appealed.

Held – dismissing the appeal (Lord Browne-Wilkinson and Lord Lloyd of Berwick dissenting) –

(1) Sexual abuse not having been proved, there were no facts upon which the judge could properly conclude there was a likelihood of harm to the three younger girls. 'Likely' in the context of s 31(2)(a) was being used in the sense of a real possibility, a possibility that could not sensibly be ignored, having regard to the nature and gravity of the feared harm in the particular case.

(2) The standard of proof in cases involving the care of children was the ordinary civil standard of balance of probability. The more improbable the event, the stronger must be the evidence that it did occur before, on the balance of probability, its occurrence would be established.

(3) The rejection of a disputed allegation as not proved on the balance of probability left scope for the possibility that the non-proven allegation might be true after all. Those unresolved doubts and suspicions could no more form the basis of a conclusion that the second limb of the threshold condition in s 31(2)(a) of the 1989 Act ('likely to suffer') had been established than they could form the basis of a conclusion that the first ('is suffering') had been established.

(4) Unproved allegations of maltreatment could not form the basis for a finding by the court that either limb of s 31(2)(a) was established. It was, however, open to a court to conclude that there was a real possibility that the child would suffer harm in the future although harm in the past had not been established. There would be cases where, although the alleged maltreatment was not proved, the evidence did establish a combination of profoundly worrying features affecting the care of the child within the family. In such cases it would be open to a court in appropriate circumstances to find that, although not satisfied the child was yet suffering significant harm, on the basis of such facts as were proved there was a likelihood that he would do so in the future.

Decision in *Re H and R (Child Sexual Abuse: Standard of Proof)* [1995] 1 FLR 643 upheld.

Extracts from the judgment of Lord Nicholls of Birkenhead

'Likely' to suffer harm

I shall consider first the meaning of 'likely' in the expression 'likely to suffer significant harm' in s 31. In your Lordships' House Mr Levy QC advanced an argument not open in the courts below. He submitted that likely means probable, and that the decision of the Court of Appeal to the contrary in *Newham London Borough Council v AG* [1993] 1 FLR 281 was wrong. I cannot accept this contention.

In everyday usage one meaning of the word likely, perhaps its primary meaning, is probable, in the sense of more likely than not. This is not its only meaning. If I am going walking on Kinder Scout and ask whether it is likely to rain, I am using likely in a different sense. I am inquiring whether there is a real risk of rain, a risk that ought not to be ignored. In which sense is likely being used in this subsection?

In s 31(2) Parliament has stated the prerequisites which must exist before the court has power to make a care order. These prerequisites mark the boundary line drawn by Parliament between the differing interests. On one side are the interests of parents in caring for their own child, a course which prima facie is also in the interests of the child. On the other side there will be circumstances in which the interests of the child may dictate a need for his care to be entrusted to others. In s 31(2) Parliament has stated the minimum conditions which must be present before the court can look more widely at all the circumstances and decide whether the child's welfare requires that a local authority shall receive the child into their care and have parental responsibility for him. The court must be satisfied that the child is already suffering significant harm. Or the court must be satisfied that, looking ahead, although the child may not yet be suffering such harm, he or she is likely to do so in the future. The court may make a care order if, but only if, it is satisfied in one or other of these respects.

In this context Parliament cannot have been using likely in the sense of more likely than not. If the word likely were given this meaning, it would have the effect of leaving outside the scope of care and supervision orders cases where the court is satisfied there is a real possibility of significant harm to the child in the future but that possibility falls short of being more likely than not. Strictly, if this were the correct reading of the Act, a care or supervision order would not be available even in a case where the risk of significant harm is as likely as not. Nothing would suffice short of proof that the child will probably suffer significant harm.

The difficulty with this interpretation of s 31(2)(a) is that it would draw the boundary line at an altogether inapposite point. What is in issue is the prospect, or risk, of the child suffering *significant* harm. When exposed to this risk a child may need protection just as much when the risk is considered to be less than fifty-fifty as when the risk is of a higher order. Conversely, so far as the parents are concerned, there is no particular magic in a threshold test based on a probability of significant harm as distinct from a real possibility. It is otherwise if there is no real possibility. It is eminently understandable that Parliament should provide that where there is no real possibility of significant harm, parental responsibility should remain solely with the parents. That makes sense as a threshold in the interests of the parents and the child in a way that a higher threshold, based on probability, would not.

In my view, therefore, the context shows that in s 31(2)(a) likely is being used in the sense of a real possibility, a possibility that cannot sensibly be ignored having regard to the nature and gravity of the feared harm in the particular case. By parity of reasoning, the expression likely to suffer significant harm bears the same meaning elsewhere in the Act; for instance, in ss 43, 44 and 46. Likely also bears a similar meaning, for a similar reason, in the requirement in s 31(2)(b) that the harm or likelihood of harm must be attributable to the care given to the child or 'likely' to be given to him if the order were not made.

The burden of proof

The power of the court to make a care or supervision order only arises if the court is 'satisfied' that the criteria stated in s 31(2) exist. The expression 'if the court is satisfied', here and elsewhere in the Act, envisages that the court must be judicially satisfied on proper material. There is also inherent in the expression an indication of the need for the subject matter to be affirmatively proved. If the court is left in a state of indecision the matter has not been established to the level, or standard, needed for the court to be 'satisfied'. Thus in s 31(2), in order for the threshold to be crossed, the conditions set out in paras (a) and (b) must be affirmatively established to the satisfaction of the court.

The legal burden of establishing the existence of these conditions rests on the applicant for a care order. The general principle is that he who asserts must prove. Generally, although there are exceptions, a plaintiff or applicant must establish the existence of all the preconditions and other facts entitling him to the order he seeks. There is nothing in the language or context of s 31(2) to suggest that the normal principle should not apply to the threshold conditions.

The standard of proof

Where the matters in issue are facts the standard of proof required in non-criminal proceedings is the preponderance of probability, usually referred to as the balance of probability. This is the established general principle. There are exceptions such as contempt of court applications, but I can see no reason for thinking that family proceedings are, or should be, an exception. By family proceedings I mean proceedings so described in the 1989 Act, ss 105 and 8(3). Despite their special features, family proceedings remain essentially a form of civil proceedings. Family proceedings often raise very serious issues, but so do other forms of civil proceedings.

The balance of probability standard means that a court is satisfied an event occurred if the court considers that, on the evidence, the occurrence of the event was more likely than not. When assessing the probabilities the court will have in mind as a factor, to whatever extent is appropriate in the particular case, that the more serious the allegation the less likely it is that the event occurred and, hence, the stronger should be the evidence before the court concludes that the allegation is established on the balance of probability. Fraud is usually less likely than negligence. Deliberate physical injury is usually less likely than accidental physical injury. A stepfather is usually less likely to have repeatedly raped and had non-consensual oral sex with his under-age stepdaughter than on some occasion to have lost his temper and slapped her. Built into the preponderance of probability standard is a serious degree of flexibility in respect of the seriousness of the allegation.

Although the result is much the same, this does not mean that where a serious allegation is in issue the standard of proof required is higher. It means only that the inherent probability or improbability of an event is itself a matter to be taken into account when weighing the probabilities and deciding whether, on balance, the event occurred. The more improbable the event, the stronger must be the evidence that it did occur before, on the balance of probability, its occurrence will be established. Ungoed-Thomas J expressed this neatly in *Re Dellow's Will Trusts, Lloyd's Bank v Institute of Cancer Research* [1964] 1 WLR 451 at p 455:

> 'The more serious the allegation the more cogent is the evidence required to overcome the unlikelihood of what is alleged and thus to prove it.'

This substantially accords with the approach adopted in authorities such as the well-known judgment of Morris LJ in *Hornal v Neuberger Products Ltd* [1957] 1 QB 247 at p 266. This approach also provides a means by which the balance of probability standard can accommodate one's instinctive feeling that even in civil proceedings a court should be more sure before finding serious allegations proved than when deciding less serious or trivial matters.

[...]

A conclusion based on facts

The starting-point here is that courts act on evidence. They reach their decisions on the basis of the evidence before them. When considering whether an applicant for a care order has shown that the child is suffering harm or is likely to do so, a court will have regard to the undisputed evidence. The judge will attach to that evidence such weight, or importance, as he considers appropriate. Likewise with regard to disputed evidence which the judge accepts as reliable. None of that is controversial. But the rejection of a disputed allegation as not proved on the balance of probability leaves scope for the possibility that the non-proven allegation may be true after all. There remains room for the judge to have doubts and suspicions on this score. This is the area of controversy.

In my view these unresolved judicial doubts and suspicions can no more form the basis of a conclusion that the second threshold condition in s 31(2)(a) has been established than they can form the basis of a conclusion that the first has been established.

[...]

I must now put this into perspective by noting, and emphasising, the width of the range of facts which may be relevant when the court is considering the threshold conditions. The range of facts which may properly be taken into account is infinite. Facts include the history of members of the family, the state of relationships within a family, proposed changes within the membership of a family, parental attitudes, and omissions which might not reasonably have been expected, just as much as actual physical assaults. They include threats, and abnormal behaviour by a child, and unsatisfactory parental responses to complaints or allegations. And facts, which are minor or even trivial if considered in isolation, when taken together may suffice to satisfy the court of the likelihood of future harm. The court will attach to all the relevant facts the appropriate weight when coming to an overall conclusion on the crucial issue.

I must emphasise a further point. I have indicated that unproved allegations of maltreatment cannot form the basis for a finding by the court that either limb of s 31(2)(a) is established. It is, of course, open to a court to conclude there is a real possibility that the child will suffer harm in the future although harm in the past has not been established. There will be cases where, although the alleged maltreatment itself is not proved, the evidence does establish a combination of profoundly worrying features affecting the care of the child within the family. In such cases it would be open to a court in appropriate circumstances to find that, although not satisfied the child is yet suffering significant harm, *on the basis of such facts as are proved* there is a likelihood that he will do so in the future.

That is not the present case. The three younger girls are not at risk unless D1 was abused by Mr R in the past. If she was not abused, there is no reason for thinking the others may be. This is not a case where Mr R has a history of abuse. Thus the one and only relevant fact is whether D1 was abused by Mr R as she says. The other surrounding facts, such as the fact that D1 made a complaint and the fact that her mother responded unsatisfactorily, lead nowhere relevant in this case if they do not lead to the conclusion that D1 was abused. To decide that the others are at risk because there is a possibility that D1 was abused would be to base the decision, not on fact, but on suspicion: the suspicion that D1 *may* have been abused. That would be to lower the threshold prescribed by Parliament.

Conclusion

I am very conscious of the difficulties confronting social workers and others in obtaining hard evidence, which will stand up when challenged in court, of the maltreatment meted out to children behind closed doors. Cruelty and physical abuse are notoriously difficult to prove. The task of social workers is usually anxious and often thankless. They are criticised for not having taken action in response to warning signs which are obvious enough when seen in the clear light of hindsight. Or they are criticised for making applications based on serious allegations which, in the event, are not established in court. Sometimes, whatever they do, they cannot do right.

I am also conscious of the difficulties facing judges when there is conflicting testimony on serious allegations. On some occasions judges are left deeply anxious at the end of a case. There may be an understandable inclination to 'play safe' in the interests of the child. Sometimes judges wish to safeguard a child whom they fear may be at risk without at the same time having to fasten a label of very serious misconduct onto one of the parents.

These are among the difficulties and considerations Parliament addressed in the Children Act when deciding how, to use the fashionable terminology, the balance should be struck between the various interests. As I read the Act, Parliament decided that the threshold for a care order should be that the child is suffering significant harm, or there is a real possibility that he will do so. In the latter regard the threshold is comparatively low. Therein lies the protection for children. But, as I read the Act, Parliament also decided that proof of the relevant facts is needed if this threshold is to be surmounted. Before the s 1 welfare test and the welfare 'checklist' can be applied, the threshold has to be crossed. Therein lies the protection for parents. They are not to be at risk of having their child taken from them and removed into the care of the local authority on the basis only of suspicions, whether of the judge or of the local authority or anyone else. A conclusion that the child is suffering or is likely to suffer harm must be based on facts, not just suspicion.

5.5 RE L (CONTACT: DOMESTIC VIOLENCE); RE V (CONTACT: DOMESTIC VIOLENCE); RE M (CONTACT: DOMESTIC VIOLENCE); RE H (CONTACT: DOMESTIC VIOLENCE)

[2000] 2 FLR 334

Court of Appeal

Dame Elizabeth Butler-Sloss P, Thorpe and Waller LJJ

19 June 2000

Introductory comments

If *Re O (Contact: Imposition of Conditions)* (at **5.3**) provides the general starting point for any discussion of the application of the welfare principle to private law contact cases then *Re L, Re V, Re M and Re H* is the particular starting point for those cases in which there is an allegation of domestic violence.

Apart from the importance of the issue and the decision, the practical application of which continues to need to be worked through, the case was notable for the way in which the Court of Appeal drew heavily upon the work of the Children Act Sub-Committee of the Lord Chancellor's Advisory Board on Family Law and a specially commissioned report by Drs Sturge and Glaser, 'Contact and Domestic Violence – The Experts' Report',[1] that set out principles about contact applicable to all cases and then applied those principles to the situation in which there had been domestic violence.[2]

Headnote

Contact – Domestic violence – Welfare of child – Refusal of direct contact

In each case a father's application for direct contact had been refused by the judge, against a background of domestic violence between the parents, and the father had appealed. The court considered the report of the Children Act Sub-Committee of the Advisory Board on Family Law on parental contact in domestic violence cases, and a joint expert report prepared by two child psychiatrists for the Official Solicitor.

---

[1]   [2000] Fam Law 615.

[2]   Reading the documents reveals an important difference between the experts, who tended towards a presumption against contact where there had been domestic violence, and the judges, who held that as a matter of law this was not the case.

Held – dismissing all four appeals –

(1) A court hearing a contact application in which allegations of domestic violence were raised should consider the conduct of both parties towards each other and towards the children, the effect of the violence on the children and on the residential parent, and the motivation of the parent seeking contact. On an application for interim contact, when the allegations of domestic violence had not yet been adjudicated on, the court should give particular consideration to the likely risk of harm to the child, whether physical or emotional, if contact were granted or refused. The court should ensure, as far as possible, that any risk of harm to the child was minimised and that the safety of the child and the residential parent was secured before, during and after any such contact. Family judges and magistrates needed to have a heightened awareness of the existence and consequences for children of exposure to domestic violence between their parents or other partners. Where allegations of domestic violence were made which might have an effect on the outcome, those allegations must be adjudicated upon, and found proved or not proved. There was not, and should not be a presumption that on proof of domestic violence the offending parent had to surmount a prima facie barrier of no contact, but such violence was a factor in the delicate balancing exercise of discretion carried out by the judge applying the welfare principle and the welfare checklist in s 1(1) and (3) of the Children Act 1989. In cases of proved domestic violence, the court had to weigh the seriousness of the domestic violence, the risks involved and the impact on the child against the positive factors, if any, of contact. The ability of the offending parent to recognise his past conduct, to be aware of the need to change and to make genuine efforts to do so would be likely to be an important consideration when performing that balancing exercise.

(2) Where there was a conflict between the rights and interests of a child and those of a parent, the interests of the child had to prevail under Art 8(2) of the European Convention for the Protection of Human Rights and Fundamental Freedoms 1950.

Extracts from the judgment of Dame Elizabeth Butler-Sloss, President

There are however a number of general comments I wish to make on the advice given to us. The family judges and magistrates need to have a heightened awareness of the existence of and consequences (some long term), on children of exposure to domestic violence between their parents or other partners. There has, perhaps, been a tendency in the past for courts not to tackle allegations of violence and to leave them in the background on the premise that they were matters affecting the adults and not relevant to issues regarding the children. The general principle that contact with the non-resident parent is in the interests of the child may sometimes have discouraged sufficient attention being paid to the adverse effects on children living in the household where violence has occurred. It may not necessarily be widely appreciated that violence to a partner involves a significant failure in parenting – failure to protect the child's carer and failure to protect the child emotionally.

In a contact or other s 8 application, where allegations of domestic violence are made which might have an effect on the outcome, those allegations must be adjudicated upon and found proved or not proved. It will be necessary to scrutinise such allegations which may not always be true or may be grossly exaggerated. If however there is a firm basis for finding that violence has occurred, the psychiatric advice becomes very important. There is not, however, nor should there be, any presumption that, on proof of domestic violence, the offending parent has to surmount a prima facie barrier of no contact. As a matter of principle, domestic violence of itself cannot constitute a bar to contact. It is one factor in the difficult and delicate balancing exercise of discretion. The court deals with the facts of a specific case in which the degree of violence and the seriousness of the impact on the child and on the resident parent have to be taken into account. In cases of proved domestic violence, as in cases of other proved harm or risk of harm to the child, the court has the task of weighing in the balance the seriousness of the domestic violence, the risks involved and the impact on the child against the positive factors (if any), of contact between the parent found to have been violent and the child. In this context, the ability of the offending parent to recognise his past conduct, be aware of the need to change and make genuine efforts to do so, will be likely to be an important consideration. Wall J in *Re M (Contact: Violent Parent)* [1999] 2 FLR 321 suggested at 333 that often in cases where domestic violence had been found, too little weight had been given to the need for the father to change. He suggested that the father should demonstrate that he was a fit person to exercise contact and should show a track record of proper behaviour. Assertions, without evidence to back it up, may well not be sufficient.

In expressing these views I recognise the danger of the pendulum swinging too far against contact where domestic violence has been proved. It is trite but true to say that no two child cases are exactly the same. The court always has the duty to apply s 1 of the Children Act 1989 that the welfare of the child is paramount and, in considering that welfare, to take into account all the relevant circumstances, including the advice of the medical experts as far as it is relevant and proportionate to the decision in that case. It will also be relevant in due course to take into account the impact of Art 8 of the European Convention for the Protection of Human Rights and Fundamental Freedoms 1950 on a decision to refuse direct contact.

The propositions set out above are not, in my view, in any way inconsistent with earlier decisions on contact. The fostering of a relationship between the child and the non-resident parent has always been and remains of great importance. It has equally been intended to be for the benefit of the child rather than of the parent. Over the last 40 years there has been a movement away from rights towards responsibilities of the parents and best interests of the child.

[…]

In conclusion, on the general issues, a court hearing a contact application in which allegations of domestic violence are raised should consider the conduct of both parties towards each other and towards the children, the effect on the children and on the residential parent and the motivation of the parent seeking contact. Is it a desire to promote the best interests of the child or a means to continue violence and/or intimidation or harassment of the other parent? In cases of serious domestic violence, the ability of the offending parent to recognise his or her past conduct, to be aware of the need for change and to make genuine efforts to do so, will be likely to be an important consideration.

On an application for interim contact, when the allegations of domestic violence have not yet been adjudicated upon, the court should give particular consideration to the likely risk of harm to the child, whether physical or emotional, if contact is granted or refused. The court should ensure, as far as it can, that any risk of harm to the child is minimised and that the safety of the child and the residential parent is secured before, during and after any such contact.

5.6 P, C AND S v UNITED KINGDOM
[2002] 2 FLR 631

European Court of Human Rights

Mr J-P Costa, President, Mr AB Baka, Sir Nicolas Bratza, Mr Gaukur Jörundsson,
Mr L Loucaides, Mr C Birsan, Mr M Ugrekhelidze, Judges, and Mr TL Early,
Deputy Section Registrar

16 July 2002

Introductory comments

This is a decision of the European Court of Human Rights which concerns what we would call public law, although it is important to realise that the principles of the European Convention on Human Rights apply across all areas of children law – public, private and adoption – essentially without distinction.

We have chosen this particular case as: (1) it involved findings against the United Kingdom in relation to three of the main areas for children law identified in the Overview of the European Convention on Human Rights – Article 6, procedural rights under Article 8, and substantive rights under Article 8 – and as such illustrates them; (2) the issue of the removal of children shortly after their birth from their parents is an acute one for many professionals involved in child protection ('there must be extraordinarily compelling reasons …' before doing so); and (3) despite the European Court of Human Rights' decision, one is still left with the question: what else could the judge at first instance (with whom the Court of Appeal agreed) have done?[1]

Headnote

Care proceedings – Freeing for adoption – Legal representation – Arts 6 and 8 of European Convention for the Protection of Human Rights and Fundamental Freedoms 1950

During the 1990s an American mother lost custody of her son and was convicted of an offence after it was found that she had deliberately caused the child's numerous illnesses by the administration of laxatives. She was required to undergo therapy for Munchausen Syndrome by Proxy (MSBP) and thereby met her second husband, a social worker who was carrying out research into that condition. They subsequently

---

[1] The underlying problem was essentially one of what was practicable under the family justice system (if the case had been adjourned to allow the parents to be represented, when would it have been heard?), but it would take quite something to design and operate a system that could have dealt with the circumstances of this case without compromising other vital interests, particularly those of the child.

married in the UK and the mother became pregnant. The local authority learned of the pregnancy and received information about the mother's past from the American authorities. The local authority expressed concern about the risk of harm to the unborn child, a case conference was held and the mother and husband reluctantly agreed to assessment by an expert. The day the child was born she was removed to foster care under an emergency protection order and the parents and both sets of grandparents later had successful contact. Meanwhile the local authority's application for a care order was transferred to the High Court and both the guardian ad litem and psychiatrist reported that the parents posed a risk to the child. The care plan proposed that she be placed with an adoptive family as soon as possible. At the hearing of the care application the father withdrew from the proceedings, and the mother's legal team also withdrew on the basis that she was requiring them to conduct her case unreasonably. A second adjournment was refused and the mother, albeit distressed on occasion, proceeded to conduct her own case with the assistance of a McKenzie friend. A care order and a freeing order were subsequently made. The judge refused the mother leave to appeal and her renewed application in person before the Court of Appeal was refused. The court concluded that no error of law or any failure of procedural unfairness had been demonstrated. The child was adopted in March 2000 and no provision for future direct contact was made. The parents alleged that the removal of the child at birth and the care and freeing orders breached Art 8 of the European Convention for the Protection of Human Rights and Fundamental Freedoms 1950 and that the procedures which followed were in breach of Art 6.

Held – unanimously finding violations of Arts 6 and 8 with respect to the removal of the child at birth, and Art 8 by six votes to one with respect to procedures concerning the care and freeing applications; unanimously holding that no separate issue arose under Art 12 and that damages were payable under Art 44 –

(1) The complexity of the case, importance of what was at stake and highly emotive subject matter led to the conclusion that the principles of effective access to the court and fairness required that the mother receive the assistance of a lawyer. The procedures adopted prevented the parents from putting forward their case in a proper and effective manner and although it was desirable for the child's future to be settled as soon as possible, the draconian action of proceeding to a full and complex care hearing, followed within one week by the freeing application, both without legal assistance, was not necessary. The parents did not have a fair and effective access to court as required by Art 6 as the possibility of some delay was not so prejudicial to the child's interests as to justify the procedure adopted and the assistance of a lawyer was indispensable.

(2) The local authority had to be able to take appropriate steps to prevent harm to the child and the decision to obtain an emergency protection order after her birth was necessary in a democratic society to safeguard her health and rights. However, there was no suspicion of life-threatening conduct from the mother immediately after the birth and it was not apparent why the child could not have spent some time with her in hospital under supervision. Removing the child from her mother after birth was not supported by relevant and sufficient reasons and could not be regarded as having been necessary in a democratic society for the purpose of safe-guarding the child. There was therefore a breach of the parent's rights under Art 8. The circumstances leading to a breach of Art 6, having regard to the seriousness of what was at stake, also prevented them from being involved in the decision-making process to a degree sufficient to provide them with the requisite protection of the interests under Art 8.

Extracts from the judgment

[...]

D. The hearing of the application for a care order in the High Court February–March 1999

[57] At a hearing, beginning on 2 February 1999 and ending on 1 March 1999, the High Court heard the local authority's application for a care order in respect of S. The local authority informed the judge that there were nine families available and wanting to adopt S. P and C were parties as were S's paternal grandparents, while S was represented by a professional guardian ad litem, solicitors and both senior and junior counsel.

[58] On 4 February 1999, C applied for leave to withdraw from the proceedings, on the ground that he saw no prospect of success in obtaining custody of S and that the stress of the proceedings was likely to lead to a breakdown in his health. On 5 February 1999, the judge granted him leave to withdraw. C's parents also withdrew from the proceedings.

[59] On the same date, P's legal representatives (leading counsel and solicitors) withdrew from the case, informing the judge that her legal aid had been withdrawn. It was later stated by the judge that they had withdrawn as P was requiring them to conduct the case unreasonably. Her legal aid had not in fact been withdrawn as the judge made clear in his judgment. The legal aid certificate could not be formally discharged until P had been given the opportunity to show cause why that should not happen.

[60] P asked for an adjournment until 9 February 1999, which was granted. On 9 February 1999, P asked for a further adjournment in order to apply for the reinstatement of her legal aid certificate.

[61] The judge refused the adjournment. As a result of this decision, P conducted her own case, assisted by a 'McKenzie friend', Mrs H. The applicant stated that she found conducting her own case immensely difficult. At one stage, she told the judge that she simply could not continue because she was so distressed. That was after cross-examining her own husband C, which she found very painful. However, the judge said that she should carry on. The solicitor for the guardian ad litem and a social worker visited P that evening to persuade her to carry on.

[62] In his judgment, the judge explained his refusal of an adjournment:

> 'In the first place I was satisfied that the mother had a very clear grasp of the voluminous documentation, at least as good and if not better a grasp than the lawyers in the case. Secondly, it was clear to me from the documents that the mother, who is an intelligent woman, was fully able to put her case in a clear and coherent way, an assessment that has been amply borne out by the hearing itself.
>
> Thirdly, I was confident that the Bar, in the form of leading and junior counsel for the local authority and the guardian ad litem, would not only treat the mother fairly but in the tradition of the Bar would assist her in the presentation

of any points she wished to advance, insofar as it would be professionally proper for them to do so. Once again that assessment has been fully justified by the conduct of counsel during the hearing. As examples, the local authority both facilitated and paid for the attendance of Dr Toseland, consultant toxicologist, to attend as part of the mother's case. Junior counsel for the local authority ... struggled manfully to ensure that the mother had a complete set of the ever growing documentation. There were other examples.

Fourthly, the outcome of the case seemed to me to hinge or be likely to hinge substantially on the mother's cross-examination, an area of the case in which the ability of lawyers to protect her was limited.

Finally, and most importantly, I was concerned about the prejudice to [S] of what would have had to have been a very lengthy adjournment. Section 1(2) of the Children Act 1989 expresses the general principle that delay in resolving a child's future is prejudicial to that child's welfare. In this particular case intensive preparation for the hearing had been going on effectively since [S's] birth in May 1998 and up until the outset of the hearing before me the mother had had the benefit of advice from her lawyers, latterly of course from leading counsel. An adjournment would have involved a very substantial delay in resolving [S's] future.

The hearing was estimated to last, and did indeed, last something in the order of 20 working days. A fresh legal team, assuming legal aid was restored, would have needed a substantial amount of time to master the voluminous documentation and to take instructions. 20 days of court time simply cannot be conjured out of thin air.

Furthermore the evidence of Dr Bentovim, the consultant child psychiatrist jointly instructed to advise me, amongst other things, on [S's] placement, was that a decision on her long-term future needed to be both made and if possible implemented before her first birthday.

The consequence of the events I have described was that the mother has been obliged to conduct her case in person with the assistance of a McKenzie friend, Mrs [H]. In their closing submissions Mr David Harris QC and Miss Roddy for the guardian ad litem paid tribute to the manner in which the mother had conducted her case. They described her as fighting bravely, resourcefully and skilfully for the return of her daughter. I would like to echo that tribute. I would also like to express my gratitude to the mother's McKenzie friend ... who was clearly a considerable support to the mother throughout the case.

If the mother had been represented by counsel her case would, I think, have been conducted differently, but I am entirely satisfied that the result would have been the same. As so often happens the mother was given a latitude which would not be given to a litigant who was legally represented. For example, I allowed her to call a witness, Professor Robinson, who had not provided a statement prior to the hearing. I was also prepared for her to call a consultant psychologist who had given evidence in the American proceedings, Dr [P] who in the event was unable to attend. I also allowed the mother to cross-examine witnesses twice ... I have throughout the hearing endeavoured to ensure that the mother was treated fairly.

I am the first to acknowledge that the court room is not a friendly environment and ... that those who are not used to it find it difficult. However much

experience the mother may have had of the legal system in the USA, I accept …
that she is not a lawyer. Further the hearing has had in [S's] interests to delve
into matters which were highly distressing to the parents and which are normally
intensely private and would have remained private.

It is my judgment that the mother's case has been fully heard and that the
hearing has been fair … I reject any suggestion that had the mother been legally
represented the result would have been different.'

[…]

E.   The hearing in the High Court of the application to free S for adoption and subsequent appeals

[66] On 15 March 1999, the same High Court judge heard the application to
free S for adoption. The transcript of his previous judgment was not yet
available. The final order of 15 March 1999 listed P, C and S as respondents.
According to the applicants, C was present throughout and was specifically
asked in court if he consented to a freeing order being made, and C indicated
that he did not.

[67] At the commencement of the hearing, P informed the court that without
legal representation she was significantly disadvantaged and was being
deprived of a proper opportunity to advance her case. Both P and C had valid
legal aid certificates in force. The judge declined to defer the proceedings,
finding that P was capable of representing her interests and that she would
have been put on notice by her lawyers at an earlier stage that the freeing
application would follow the care order. Though he noted that there might
appear to be 'an element of railroading', on balancing the parents' interests
against the need of S to have her future decided at the earliest possible
opportunity, he considered S's interests prevailed. On the issue of the freeing
application, the judge concluded that the parents were withholding their
consent to adoption unreasonably as they should have accepted, in the light of
the previous proceedings, that there was no realistic prospect of the
rehabilitation of S to their care. He therefore issued an order freeing S for
adoption. That permanently severed legal ties between S and her parents. As
regards contact, he stated:

'I'm assured by [the local authority] that there will be conventional letterbox
contact. But it will in due course (if an adoption order is made) be essentially a
matter for the adoptive parents as to precisely what contact [S] has with her
natural family.'

[68] The judge refused P leave to appeal against the order. Her renewed
application before the Court of Appeal was refused after a hearing on
5 July 1999, where she and C appeared in person. Though the Court of
Appeal noted that C was not a party to the appeal, it referred to the fact that C
had addressed the court at some length on the issues. It noted that the trial
was of exceptional complexity, with enormous documentation, much expert
evidence and lasting 20 days. It found however that the judge had carefully
and thoroughly weighed all the issues of fact and that he had been meticulous

throughout in ensuring fairness. No error of law or any failure of procedural fairness had been demonstrated.

[...]

B. The court's assessment

1. General principles

[88] There is no automatic right under the Convention for legal aid or legal representation to be available for an applicant who is involved in proceedings which determine his or her civil rights. Nonetheless Art 6 may be engaged under two inter-related aspects.

[89] First, Art 6(1) of the Convention embodies the right of access to a court for the determination of civil rights and obligations (see *Golder v UK* (1979–80) 1 EHRR 524, at para 36). Failure to provide an applicant with the assistance of a lawyer may breach this provision, where such assistance is indispensable for effective access to court, either because legal representation is rendered compulsory as is the case in certain Contracting States for various types of litigation, or by reason of the complexity of the procedure or the type of case (see *Airey v Ireland* (1979–80) 1 EHRR 305, at paras 26–28, where the applicant was unable to obtain the assistance of a lawyer in judicial separation proceedings). Factors identified as relevant in the *Airey* case in determining whether the applicant would be able to present her case properly and satisfactorily without the assistance of a lawyer included the complexity of the procedure, the necessity to address complicated points of law or to establish facts, involving expert evidence and the examination of witnesses, and the fact that the subject-matter of the marital dispute entailed an emotional involvement that was scarcely compatible with the degree of objectivity required by advocacy in court. In such circumstances, the court found it unrealistic to suppose that the applicant could effectively conduct her own case, despite the assistance afforded by the judge to parties acting in person.

[90] It may be noted that the right of access to court is not absolute and may be subject to legitimate restrictions. Where an individual's access is limited either by operation of law or in fact, the restriction will not be incompatible with Art 6 where the limitation did not impair the very essence of the right and where it pursued a legitimate aim, and there was a reasonable relationship of proportionality between the means employed and the aim sought to be achieved (*Ashingdane v UK* (1985) 7 EHRR 528, at para 57). Thus, though the pursuit of proceedings as a litigant in person may on occasion not be an easy matter, the limited public funds available for civil actions renders a procedure of selection a necessary feature of the system of administration of justice, and the manner in which it functions in particular cases may be shown not to have been arbitrary or disproportionate, or to have impinged on the essence of the right of access to court (see the judgment *Del Sol v France* (unreported), of 26 February 2002, *Ivison v UK* (unreported) 16 April 2002). It may be the case that other factors concerning the administration of justice (eg the necessity for expedition or the rights of other individuals) could also play a limiting role as

regards the provision of assistance in a particular case, though such restriction would also have to satisfy the tests set out above.

[91] Secondly, the key principle governing the application of Art 6 is fairness. In cases where an applicant appears in court notwithstanding lack of assistance of a lawyer and manages to conduct his or her case in the teeth of all the difficulties, the question may nonetheless arise as to whether this procedure was fair (see, for example, *McVicar v UK* (unreported) 7 May 2002, paras 50–51 (to be published in EHRR)). There is the importance of ensuring the appearance of the fair administration of justice and a party in civil proceedings must be able to participate effectively, inter alia, by being able to put forward the matters in support of his or her claims. Here, as in other aspects of Art 6, the seriousness of what is at stake for the applicant will be of relevance to assessing the adequacy and fairness of the procedures.

[...]

[94] The court has paid careful attention to the reasons given by the trial judge in this case, whose long judgment received merited praise in the Court of Appeal for the thoroughness of his analysis and who had first-hand experience of the events and participants. It also notes that the Court of Appeal considered that the proceedings had been fair, an opinion shared by counsel for the guardian ad litem, who represented S.

[95] Nonetheless, P was required as a parent to represent herself in proceedings which as, the Court of Appeal observed, were of exceptional complexity, extending over the course of 20 days in which the documentation was voluminous and which required a review of highly complex expert evidence relating to the applicant's fitness to parent their daughter. Her alleged disposition to harm her own children, along with her personality traits, were at the heart of the case, as well as her relationship with her husband. The complexity of the case, along with the importance of what was at stake and the highly emotive nature of the subject matter, lead this court to conclude that the principles of effective access to court and fairness required that P receive the assistance of a lawyer. Even if P was acquainted with the vast documentation in the case, the court is not persuaded that she should have been expected to take up the burden of conducting her own case. It notes that at one point in the proceedings, which were conducted at the same time as she was coping with the distress of the removal of S at birth, P broke down in the court room and the judge, counsel for the guardian ad litem and a social worker, had to encourage her to continue (see para [61] above).

[96] The court notes that the judge himself commented that if P had been represented by a lawyer her case would have been conducted differently. Though he went on in his judgment to give the opinion that this would not have affected the outcome of the proceedings, this element is not decisive as regards the fairness of the proceedings. Otherwise, a requirement to show actual prejudice from a lack of legal representation would deprive the guarantees of Art 6 of their substance (*Artico v Italy* (1981) 3 EHRR 1, at

para 35). Similarly, while the judge considered that the case would turn on the cross-examination of P, where a lawyer would only have been able to give limited assistance, that assistance would nonetheless have furnished P with some safeguards and support.

[97] While it is also true that P and C were aware that the freeing application was likely to follow the care application within a short time, this does not mean however that they were in an adequate position to cope with the hearing when it occurred. This hearing also raised difficult points of law and emotive issues, in particular since the issuing of the care order, and the rejection of the applicants' claims to have S returned home, must have had a significant and distressing impact on the parents.

[98] Nor is the court convinced that the importance of proceeding with expedition, which attaches generally to childcare cases, necessitated the draconian action of proceeding to a full and complex hearing, followed within one week by the freeing for adoption application, both without legal assistance being provided to the applicants. Though it was doubtless desirable for S's future to be settled as soon as possible, the court considers that the imposition of one year from birth as the deadline appears a somewhat inflexible and blanket approach, applied without particular consideration of the facts of this individual case. S was, according to the care plan, to be placed for adoption and it was not envisaged that there would be any difficulty in finding a suitable adoptive family (eight couples were already identified by 2 February 1999). Yet though S was freed for adoption by the court on 15 March 1999, she was not in fact placed with a family until 2 September 1999, a gap of over 5 months for which no explanation has been given, while the adoption order which finalised matters on a legal basis was not issued until 27 March 2000, more than one year later. Her placement was therefore not achieved by her first birthday in May in any event. It is not possible to speculate at this time as to how long the adjournment would have lasted had it been granted in order to allow the applicant P to have representation at the care proceedings, or for both parent applicants to be represented at the freeing for adoption proceedings. It would have been entirely possible for the judge to place strict time limits on any lawyers instructed, and for instructions to be given for re-listing the matter with due regard to priorities. As the applicants have pointed out, S was herself in a successful foster placement and unaffected by the ongoing proceedings. The court does not find that the possibility of some months' delay in reaching a final conclusion in those proceedings was so prejudicial to her interests as to justify what the trial judge himself regarded as a procedure which gave an appearance of 'railroading' her parents.

[99] Recognising that the courts in this matter were endeavouring in good faith to strike a balance between the interests of the parents and the welfare of S, the court is nevertheless of the opinion that the procedures adopted not only gave the appearance of unfairness but prevented the applicants from putting forward their case in a proper and effective manner on the issues which were important to them. For example, the court notes that the judge's

decision to free S for adoption gave no explanation of why direct contact was not to be continued or why an open adoption with continued direct contact was not possible, matters which the applicants apparently did not realise could, or should, have been raised at that stage. The assistance afforded to P by the counsel for other parties' and the latitude granted by the judge to P in presenting her case was no substitute, in a case such as the present, for competent representation by a lawyer instructed to protect the applicants' rights.

[100] The court concludes that the assistance of a lawyer during the hearing of these two applications which had such crucial consequences for the applicants' relationship with their daughter was an indispensable requirement. Consequently, the parents did not have fair and effective access to court as required by Art 6(1) of the Convention. There has, therefore, been a breach of this provision as regards the applicant parents, P and C.

[...]

B.   The court's assessment

1.   General principles

[113] The mutual enjoyment by parent and child of each other's company constitutes a fundamental element of family life, and domestic measures hindering such enjoyment amount to an interference with the right protected by Art 8 of the Convention (see, amongst others, *Johansen v Norway* (1996) 23 EHRR 33, at para 52). Any such interference constitutes a violation of this Article unless it is 'in accordance with the law', pursues an aim or aims that are legitimate under para 2 of Art 8 and can be regarded as 'necessary in a democratic society'.

[114] In determining whether the impugned measures were 'necessary in a democratic society', the court will consider whether, in the light of the case as a whole, the reasons adduced to justify these measures were relevant and sufficient for the purpose of para 2 of Art 8 of the Convention (see, inter alia, *Olsson v Sweden* (1988) 10 EHRR 259, at para 68).

[115] It must be borne in mind that the national authorities have the benefit of direct contact with all the persons concerned (see *Olsson v Sweden (No 2)* (1992) 17 EHRR 134, at para 90). It follows from these considerations that the court's task is not to substitute itself for the domestic authorities in the exercise of their responsibilities for the regulation of the public care of children and the rights of parents whose children have been taken into care, but rather to review under the Convention the decisions taken by those authorities in the exercise of their power of appreciation (see, for instance, *Hokkanen v Finland* (1995) 19 EHRR 139, [1996] 1 FLR 289, at para 55 and the above-mentioned *Johansen* judgment, at para 64).

[116] The margin of appreciation so to be accorded to the competent national authorities will vary in the light of the nature of the issues and the seriousness of the interests at stake. While the authorities enjoy a wide margin

of appreciation in assessing the necessity of taking a child into care, in particular where an emergency situation arises, the court must still be satisfied in the circumstances of the case that there existed circumstances justifying the removal of the child, and it is for the respondent State to establish that a careful assessment of the impact of the proposed care measure on the parents and the child, as well as of the possible alternatives to taking the child into public care, was carried out prior to implementation of a care measure (see *K and T v Finland* (2000) 31 EHRR 484, [2000] 2 FLR 79, at para 166 and *Kutzner v Germany* (unreported) 26 February 2002, at para 67). Furthermore, the taking of a new-born baby into public care at the moment of its birth is an extremely harsh measure. There must be extraordinarily compelling reasons before a baby can be physically removed from its mother, against her will, immediately after birth as a consequence of a procedure in which neither she nor her partner has been involved (*K and T* judgment cited above, at para 168).

[117] Following any removal into care, a stricter scrutiny is called for in respect of any further limitations by the authorities, for example on parental rights of access, as such further restrictions entail the danger that the family relations between the parents and a young child are effectively curtailed (the above-mentioned judgments, *Johansen*, at para 64, and *Kutzner*, at para 67). The taking into care of a child should normally be regarded as a temporary measure to be discontinued as soon as the circumstances permit, and any measures of implementation of temporary care should be consistent with the ultimate aim of reuniting the natural parent and child (*Olsson v Sweden* (1988) 10 EHRR 259, at para 81; *Johansen v Norway* (1996) 23 EHRR 33, at para 78 and *EP v Italy* (unreported) 16 September 1999, at para 69). In this regard a fair balance has to be struck between the interests of the child remaining in care and those of the parent in being reunited with the child (see *Olsson v Sweden (No 2)* (1992) 17 EHRR 134, at para 90 and *Hokkanen v Finland* (1995) 19 EHRR 139, [1996] 1 FLR 289, at para 55). In carrying out this balancing exercise, the court will attach particular importance to the best interests of the child which, depending on their nature and seriousness, may override those of the parent (*Johansen*, at para 78).

[118] As regards the extreme step of severing all parental links with a child, the court has taken the view that such a measure would cut a child from its roots and could only be justified in exceptional circumstances or by the overriding requirement of the child's best interests (*Johansen*, at para 84 and *Gnahoré v France* (2002) 34 EHRR 38, at para 59). That approach however may not apply in all contexts, depending on the nature of the parent–child relationship (see the *Soderback v Germany* judgment of 28 October 1998, *Reports of Judgments and Decisions* 1998–IV, at paras 31–34, where the severance of links between a child and father, who had never had care and custody of the child, was found to fall within the margin of the appreciation of the courts which had made the assessment of the child's best interests).

[119] The court further recalls that whilst Art 8 contains no explicit procedural requirements, the decision-making process involved in measures of

interference must be fair and such as to afford due respect to the interests safeguarded by Art 8:

> '[W]hat has to be determined is whether, having regard to the particular circumstances of the case and notably the serious nature of the decisions to be taken, the parents have been involved in the decision-making process, seen as a whole, to a degree sufficient to provide them with the requisite protection of their interests. If they have not, there will have been a failure to respect their family life and the interference resulting from the decision will not be capable of being regarded as "necessary" within the meaning of Art 8.' (see *W v United Kingdom* (1988) 10 EHRR 29, at paras 62 and 64)

[120] It is essential that a parent be placed in a position where he or she may obtain access to information which is relied on by the authorities in taking measures of protective care or in taking decisions relevant to the care and custody of a child. Otherwise the parent will be unable to participate effectively in the decision-making process or put forward in a fair or adequate manner those matters militating in favour of his or her ability to provide the child with proper care and protection (see *McMichael v United Kingdom* (1995) 20 EHRR 205, at para 92, where the authorities did not disclose to the applicant parents reports relating to their child, and *TP and KM v United Kingdom* [2001] 2 FLR 549, where the applicant mother was not afforded an early opportunity to view a video of an interview of her daughter, crucial to the assessment of abuse in the case; also *Buchberger v Austria* (unreported) 20 December 2001).

2. The state of domestic law

[121] The applicants have complained that the law governing adoption in the UK is in breach of the Convention, in that it permits, if not facilitates, the removal of very young babies from their parents with subsequent adoption and severance of all legal links.

[122] It is not however the court's role to examine domestic law in the abstract. In any event, since there are circumstances which may be envisaged where a young baby might be adopted in conformity with Art 8 of the Convention, it cannot be considered that the law per se is in breach of this provision. The court will examine rather whether the measures taken in this particular case were in compliance with the guarantees of Art 8 of the Convention.

3. The removal of S at birth

[123] The court recalls that S was born on 7 May 1998, at 4.42 am, after P was brought into hospital for an emergency caesarean. The local authority obtained an emergency protection order at about 10.30 am which placed S under their care. At about 4 pm, the social workers took S from the hospital and placed her with foster parents. It is uncontested that these matters constituted interferences with the applicants' rights under the first paragraph of Art 8 and that it falls to be determined whether they complied with the requirements of the second paragraph. As it is also not in dispute that the measures taken were in accordance with the law and pursued the legitimate aim of the protection of health and the rights of others, namely of S, the court's examination concentrates on the necessity of the measures as that term has been interpreted in its case-law (see paras [114]–[119] above).

[...]

[128] Questions of emergency care measures are, by their nature, decided on a highly provisional basis and on an assessment of risk to the child reached on the basis of the information, inevitably incomplete, available at the time. The court considers that it was within the proper role of the local authority in its child protection function to take steps to obtain an emergency protection order. It finds that there were relevant and sufficient reasons for this measure, in particular the fact that P had been convicted for harming her son B and had been found by an expert in those proceedings to suffer from a syndrome which manifested itself in exaggerating and fabricating illness in a child, with consequent significant physical and psychological damage to the child.

[...]

[130] In the circumstances, the court considers that the decision to obtain the emergency protection order after S's birth may be regarded as having been necessary in a democratic society to safeguard the health and rights of the child. The local authority had to be able to take appropriate steps to ensure that no harm came to the baby and, at the very least, to take the legal power to prevent C or any other relative removing the baby with a view to foiling the local authority's actions, and thereby placing the baby at risk.

[131] It has nonetheless given consideration as to the manner of implementation of the order, namely, the steps taken under the authority of the order. As stated above (para [116]), the removal of a baby from its mother at birth requires exceptional justification. It is a step which is traumatic for the mother and places her own physical and mental health under a strain, and it deprives the new-born baby of close contact with its birth mother and, as pointed out by the applicants, of the advantages of breast-feeding. The removal also deprived the father, C, of being close to his daughter after the birth.

[132] The reasons put forward by the Government for removing the baby from the hospital, rather than leaving her with her mother or father under supervision, are that the hospital staff stated that they could not assure the child's safety and alleged tensions with the family. No details or documentary substantiation of this assertion are provided. P, who had undergone a caesarean section and was suffering the after-effects of blood loss and high blood pressure, was, at least in the first days after the birth, confined to bed. Once she had left the hospital, she was permitted to have supervised contact visits with S. It is not apparent to the court why it was not at all possible for S to remain in the hospital and to spend at least some time with her mother under supervision. Even on the assumption that P might be a risk to the baby, her capacity and opportunity for causing harm immediately after the birth must be regarded as limited, considerably more limited than once she was discharged. Furthermore, on the information available to the authorities at that stage, P's manifestation of the syndrome, sometimes known as MSBP, indicated a prevalence for exaggerating symptoms of ill-health in her children and that she had gone so far as to use laxatives to induce diarrhoea. Though the harm which such conduct poses to a child, particularly if continued over a long period of time cannot be underestimated, there was in the present case no suspicion of life-threatening conduct. This made the risk to be guarded against more manageable and it has not been shown that supervision could not have provided adequate protection against this risk, as was the case in the many contact visits over the months leading up to the care proceedings when both parents were allowed to feed the baby (see Dr Bentovim's report, para 54(vii)).

[133] The court concludes that the draconian step of removing S from her mother shortly after birth was not supported by relevant and sufficient reasons and that it cannot be regarded as having been necessary in a democratic society for the purpose of safeguarding S. There has therefore been, in that respect, a breach of the applicant parents' rights under Art 8 of the Convention.

[...]

[137] The lack of legal representation of P during the care proceedings and of P and C during the freeing for adoption proceedings, together with the lack of any real lapse of time between the two procedures, has been found above to have deprived the applicants of a fair and effective hearing in court. Having regard to the seriousness of what was at stake, the court finds that it also prevented them from being involved in the decision-making process, seen as a whole, to a degree sufficient to provide them with the requisite protection of their interests under Art 8 of the Convention. Emotionally involved in the case as they were, the applicant parents were placed at a serious disadvantage by these elements, and it cannot be excluded that this might have had an effect on the decisions reached and eventual outcome for the family as a whole.

[138] In the circumstances of this case, the court concludes that there has been in this regard a breach of P, C and S's rights under Art 8 of the Convention.

[...]

[149] Turning to the claims for non-pecuniary damage, the court does not consider that it can be asserted that S would not have been adopted if the flaws identified in the procedures had not occurred, though it cannot be excluded that the situation of the family might have been different in some respects. They thereby suffered a loss of opportunity. In addition, the applicants P and C certainly suffered non-pecuniary damage through distress and anxiety.

[150] The court thus concludes that the applicants P and C sustained some non-pecuniary damage which is not sufficiently compensated by the finding of

a violation of the Convention (see, for example, *Elsholz v Germany* (2002) 34 EHRR 58, [2000] 2 FLR 486, at paras 70–71). While S might also be regarded as having lost an opportunity of contact with her birth parents, she was, to the knowledge of the court, protected from the trauma of the court proceedings. Having regard to the fact that P and C have no legal ties with S or any direct contact, it considers it inappropriate to make any award to them to hold on trust for S or to make any award to S who is settled in her adoptive family and unaware of these proceedings.

[151] Making an assessment on an equitable basis, it awards the sum of 12,000 euros each to the applicants P and C.

5.7 RE L (CARE: ASSESSMENT: FAIR TRIAL) [2002] EWHC 1379 (Fam), [2002] 2 FLR 730

Family Division

Munby J

1 July 2002

Introductory comments

From a decision of the European Court of Human Rights we now come to a decision of a domestic court that is very much founded upon the European Convention on Human Rights and the jurisprudence of the Strasbourg court.

The full judgment is long and involved but we hope that the headnote will give a flavour of it and be sufficient for lawyers for their everyday purposes, while the short extract we have included summarises vitally important expectations of other professionals involved in child protection.[1]

Headnote

Care – Human rights – Disclosure – Fair trial – Need for transparent and transparently fair procedure at all stages

Human rights – Right to fair trial – Care – Disclosure – Need for transparent and transparently fair procedure at all stages

The mother had a child who died aged 4 months, probably of suffocation, with a variety of non-accidental injuries including rib fractures and facial bruising. A baby born to the mother in April 2001 went onto the Child Protection Register, and the local authority began care proceedings, placing the baby with foster carers. The threshold conditions having been made out, a consultant child and family psychiatrist was jointly instructed to determine whether it was appropriate to assess the mother with a view to possible rehabilitation of the baby with her. The psychiatrist's initial assessment was not very positive, but he recommended a 3-day in-patient assessment of the mother alone, on the basis that a 2-week residential assessment of the mother and child together would only be worthwhile if the mother moved significantly towards a greater degree of acknowledgement of her responsibility for having harmed the dead child. Reporting on the 3-day assessment the psychiatrist initially advised that the longer residential assessment would be worthwhile. After various communications

---

[1] For a similarly trenchant analysis by the same judge of what the European Convention on Human Rights requires of the family justice system in private law, see *Re D (Intractable Contact Dispute: Publicity)* [2004] EWHC 727 (Fam), [2004] 1 FLR 1226.

between the local authority and the psychiatrist, some of which were not shared with the mother, the psychiatrist sought a meeting with the local authority and the guardian. At that meeting, which the mother was aware of but not permitted to attend, the psychiatrist revealed that he wished to reconsider the decision to admit the mother for assessment. A number of concerns over and criticisms of the mother's care were raised at that meeting, although they had not been discussed with the mother. The mother was not informed of the outcome of the meeting, and no minutes were taken, but the psychiatrist prepared a new report, which was made available to the parties, in which he recommended that a residential assessment was not appropriate because there was no reasonable possibility that the baby could be placed in the mother's care. The local authority's care plan was thereafter for adoption. The judge asked the psychiatrist to explain his change of position in a new report, and the mother's solicitors asked the psychiatrist to identify what oral information he had received, from what source, and to produce minutes of any meetings. At a subsequent directions hearing the local authority was ordered to produce all contact notes and a number of internal documents evaluating the mother's relationship with the child. The guardian asked the psychiatrist to produce his clinical notes. A number of important documents, including the clinical notes and the psychiatrist's notes of the decisive meeting did not become available until the disposal hearing was already underway. At the hearing the mother opposed the local authority care plan for adoption, arguing that various breaches of good practice had denied her any, or any adequate involvement in the decision-making process, and any proper or fair opportunity to present her case in court.

Held – dismissing the mother's application for further assessment by the psychiatrist, making the care order, approving the amended care plan for adoption and adjourning the local authority application for an order terminating direct contact –

(1) The fair trial guaranteed by Art 6 of the European Convention for the Protection of Human Rights and Fundamental Freedoms 1950 was not confined to the purely judicial part of the proceedings. Unfairness at any stage of the litigation process might involve breaches not merely of the Art 8 right to respect for family and personal life, but also of Art 6. This was potentially very important because whereas rights under Art 8 were inherently qualified, a parent's right to a fair trial under Art 6 was absolute, and could not be qualified by reference to, or balanced against any rights under Art 8 (see para [113]).

(2) Where a jointly instructed or other sole expert's report, though not binding on the court, was 'likely to have a preponderant influence on the assessment of the facts' by the court, there might be a breach of Art 6 if a litigant were denied the opportunity, before the expert produced his report, (a) to examine and comment on the documents being considered by the expert and (b) to cross-examine witnesses interviewed by the expert and on whose evidence the report was based, in short to participate effectively in the process by which the report was produced (see para [113]).

(3) The state, in the form of the local authority, assumed a heavy burden when it sought to take a child into care, and part of that burden was the need, in the interests not merely of the parent but also of the child, for a transparent and transparently fair procedure at all stages of the process, both in and out of the court. Documents must be made openly available and crucial meetings at which a family's future was being decided must be conducted openly and with the parents, if they wished, either present or represented (see para [151]).

(4) It was not necessary for the local authority to make disclosure by way of a list of all relevant documents. Automatic or routine general discovery by list was neither necessary nor desirable (see para [160]).

(5) In this case the decision-making process seen as a whole had not involved the mother sufficiently to provide her with the requisite protection of her interests. She had been wrongly excluded from meetings, crucially the decisive meeting which she had specifically asked to attend, had had no opportunity to answer criticisms of her which had been put to the psychiatrist at the decisive meeting, had been kept in the dark by the local authority's failure to disclose a whole series of documents and communications, and had been marginalised by the lack of direct contact with the local authority key worker (see paras [201], [209], [212]).

(6) The earlier unfairness in the decision-making process had been overcome, as the psychiatrist's decisive change of position had come about because of the mother's lack of acknowledgement of responsibility, which had been investigated and confirmed during the hearing, not because of any information provided to him by the local authority (see paras [230], [236], [240]).

Per curiam: detailed precepts were set out which all those involved in such cases were advised to bear in mind if they were to avoid the criticism that the decision-making process had been unfair to a parent (see para [154]).

Extract from judgment

[153] I do not propose even to attempt to summarise all this learning, let alone to formulate a comprehensive statement of good practice in cases such as this. That is a task for others. But there are certain principles of practice in public law cases, particularly pertinent perhaps in the circumstances of this case, to which attention can usefully be drawn. What follows is based in large measure on the closing submissions carefully crafted by Mr Keehan and Ms Henke, for whose assistance in this respect, as in others, I am grateful.

[154] If those involved in cases such as this are in future to avoid the criticisms which, understandably and, as it seems to me with no little justification, have been levelled against some of those involved in the present case they would be well advised to bear the following precepts in mind:

(i)   Social workers should, as soon as ever practicable:
  (a)   notify parents of material criticisms of and deficits in their parenting or behaviour and of the expectations of them; and
  (b)   advise them how they may remedy or improve their parenting or behaviour.
(ii) All the professionals involved (social workers, social work assistants, children's guardians, expert witnesses and others) should at all times keep clear, accurate, full and balanced notes of all relevant conversations and meetings between themselves and/or with parents, other family members and others involved with the family.
(iii) The local authority should at an early stage of the proceedings make full and frank disclosure to the other parties of all key documents in its possession or available to it, including in particular contact recordings, attendance notes of meetings and conversations and minutes of case

conferences, core group meetings and similar meetings. Early provision should then be afforded for inspection of any of these documents. Any objection to the disclosure or inspection of any document should be notified to the parties at the earliest possible stage in the proceedings and raised with the court by the local authority without delay.

(iv) Social workers and guardians should routinely exhibit to their reports and statements notes of relevant meetings, conversations and incidents.

(v) Where it is proposed that the social workers and/or guardian should meet with a jointly appointed or other sole expert witness instructed in the case (what I will refer to as a 'professionals' meeting', as opposed to a meeting of experts chaired by one of the legal representatives in the case – usually the children's guardian's solicitor):

(a) there should be a written agenda circulated in advance to all concerned;

(b) clear written notice of the meeting should be given in advance to the parents and/or their legal representative, accompanied by copies of the agenda and of all documents to be given or shown to the expert and notice of all issues relating to or criticisms of a parent, or a non-attending party, which it is intended to raise with the expert;

(c) the parent, or non-attending party, should have a clear opportunity to make representations to the expert prior to and/or at the meeting on the documents, issues and/or criticisms of which he or she has been given notice;

(d) a parent or other party who wishes to should have the right to attend and/or be represented at the professionals' meeting;

(e) clear, accurate, full and balanced minutes of the professionals' meeting (identifying in particular what information has been given to the expert and by whom) should be taken by someone nominated for that task before the meeting begins;

(f) as soon as possible after the professionals' meeting the minutes should be agreed by those present as being an accurate record of the meeting and then be immediately disclosed to all parties.

[155] I emphasise that these are not intended to be comprehensive guidelines. Nor are they intended in any way to water down, let alone replace, anything said by Wall J, Cazalet J and Charles J in the cases to which I have referred.[2] I build on those earlier analyses. I intend, simply by way of supplement, to draw attention to some particular aspects of proper procedure which need to be observed if in future other parents are to be spared the unfairness to which D was, as it seems to me, subjected in this case and if in future proper regard is to be paid not merely to what domestic law and practice have long recognised as appropriate but to what Arts 6 and 8 now require if there is to be proper compliance with what the Convention demands.

---

[2] Cazalet J in *Re C (Expert Evidence: Disclosure: Practice)* [1995] 1 FLR 204; Wall J in *Re CB and JB (Care Proceedings: Guidelines)* [1998] 2 FLR 211; and Charles J in *Re R (Care: Disclosure: Nature of Proceedings)* [2002] 1 FLR 755. See also the further decision of Munby J in *Re G (Care: Challenge to Local Authority's Decision)* [2003] EWHC 551 (Fam), [2003] 2 FLR 42 at [45].

5.8 RE M (DISCLOSURE: CHILDREN AND FAMILY REPORTER)

[2002] EWCA Civ 1199, [2002] 2 FLR 893

Court of Appeal

Thorpe LJ and Wall J

31 July 2002

Introductory comments

In this case the Court of Appeal had to consider the relatively narrow issue of whether or not it was lawful for a CAFCASS officer, acting in the role of a Children and Family Reporter (CFR), to disclose information discovered in the course of her enquiries to social services or the police without first obtaining permission to do so from the court. That issue would be much too narrow to warrant anything more than a brief reference in this Handbook, but we have included it as a separate item as: (1) the general issue about the rules on disclosure in connection with children law cases is of considerable importance; (2) Thorpe LJ's single paragraph summary of what a CFR should do if faced with such a situation is such a model of interdisciplinary awareness it is worth including for that reason alone;[1] and (3) both judges, and Wall J in particular, took the opportunity to comment on the relationship between CAFCASS, its officers and the courts, a relationship that is at the heart of the interdisciplinary operation of the family justice system.

Headnote

Disclosure – Whether children and family reporter needs court leave to disclose to relevant social services department concerns about possible child abuse – Relevance of FPR 1991, r 4.23, Administration of Justice Act 1960, s 12, and Children Act 1989, s 97

The parents of a girl born on 11 February 1997 were involved in a private law dispute over the child's residence. The parents had separated in April 1999 and the child had moved to live with her father in September 2001. On 10 February 2002 the mother attempted to remove the child from the father's care by retaining her at the end of a period of staying contact. On 25 February the mother applied for a residence order. On 28 February the district judge ordered the return of the child to the father's care by 1 March. A direction was given for a report to be prepared by a CAFCASS officer

---

[1] Compare with the similarly helpful summary by Munby J in *Re L*, the preceding case in this selection. Note also the practice employed by Wall J in *Evans v Amicus Healthcare Ltd; Hadley v Midland Fertility Services Ltd* [2003] EWHC 2161 (Fam), [2004] 1 FLR 67, and *Re O (Contact: Withdrawal of Application)* [2003] EWHC 3031 (Fam), [2004] 1 FLR 1258 of issuing a press release to accompany the judgment.

by 23 May. On 26 March the county court judge heard the mother's application for an interim residence order. Following a firm indication given during the course of the mother's evidence, a consent order was made confirming the status quo, ie that the child should live with the father. On 30 April the CAFCASS officer appointed to report for the court interviewed the mother and her sister. They alleged that the father had behaved inappropriately in front of the child. The CAFCASS officer contacted the judge and suggested there might need to be an investigation under s 47 of the Children Act 1989 by the local authority. At a subsequent hearing the judge heard from the CAFCASS officer and counsel for both parties. The judge refused leave for the CAFCASS officer to disclose the material to the local authority. The judge granted the mother and CAFCASS permission to appeal his decision.

Held –

(1) Leave of the court is not required for the CAFCASS officer to disclose material to the local authority as a matter of law. Rule 4.23 of the Family Proceedings Rules 1991 expressly protects the confidentiality of documents and it cannot be argued that the CAFCASS officer is prevented from reporting to the local authority concerns resulting from investigation simply because at a later date they will be recorded in the report to the judge (see para [19]).

(2) Communication between two professionals exchanging information in the course of their respective functions, each acting in furtherance of the protection of children, does not constitute publication breaching the privacy of the contemporaneous Children Act proceedings (see paras [21], [66], [67]).

(3) The children and family reporter (CFR) is a member of a new statutory service, the success of which depends in part on the support of other disciplines including the judiciary. The CFR acts independently and exercises an independent discretion as to the nature and extent of his investigations and inquiries. In the absence of any statutory prohibition on the discretionary communication from the CFR to the social worker the court was not prepared to find one in the common law or in the inherent nature of the functions of the CFR or in the inherent relationship between the CFR and the court (see paras [26], [96]).

(4) The relationship between the judge and the CFR is a collaborative one. Both share the ultimate objective, namely, the protection of children and advancement of their welfare. The CFR executes that part of the judge's function which is inquisitorial. The judge should give due weight to the outcome of the CFR's investigations (see paras [26], [85]).

(5) There is a need for communication between the family justice system in private law proceedings and the local authority in discharging its statutory functions for the protection and care of children at risk of significant harm. In exercising an independent discretion the CFR should be mindful of the judge's power within private law proceedings to order a s 37 investigation and in an emergency situation the power to intervene under s 44 of the Children Act 1989. The CFR should always consider taking his concerns to the judge in the case rather than to the local authority. Much may depend on the state of the proceedings – the later in the proceedings the more likely it is that the judge will have knowledge of the parties and insight built up over the course of previous hearings (see para [27]).

(6) Allegations from a party to the dispute of neglect or misconduct by the other party should be distinguished especially where they were made by an applicant for a residence order or an order for extended or defined contact. It is the function of the

judge to determine such allegations as a prelude to his conclusion and a CFR would be wiser to avoid direct involvement with the social services. The party raising allegations has the opportunity to raise them in the proceedings before the judge but also has the right to approach the local authority director at any time (see paras [33], [35], [43]).

(7) Where the CFR's suspicions are raised by interview with the child alone or by a home visit he must exercise an independent professional judgment. There may be circumstances in which the decision will be to go immediately to the judge. Alternatively, his instinct may be to go to the social services without delay. As a matter of practice the exercise of that discretion cannot be fettered by any rule of practice requiring prior referral to the court. Any such referral to the local authority should be reported to the judge at the earliest convenient opportunity to enable the judge, who controls the proceedings, to consider the impact of the development and the need for consequential directions. Any decision to suspend an inquiry must be that of the judge and not the CFR (see paras [38], [43]).

Per Wall J: CFRs are not 'officers of the court'. They are officers of the service (CAFCASS) (see para [96]).

Extracts from the judgment of Thorpe LJ

[19] On this fundamental issue I accept the rival submissions of Mr Spon-Smith and Mr McFarlane. Rule 4.23 expressly protects the confidentiality of documents. I do not think it is justifiably extended by the submission that the gist of the interview on 30 April would subsequently be included in the report to be filed with the court. This issue was considered by this court in the case of *Re G (Social Worker: Disclosure)* [1996] 1 WLR 1407, [1996] 1 FLR 276. Butler-Sloss LJ, at 1414 and 282 respectively, set out the possibility of a narrow construction of r 4.23 confined to documents and a wider construction extended to material that would or might end up on the court file. She said at 1415 and 283G respectively:

> 'I would on balance and in the absence of argument give the more restrictive interpretation to r 4.23 and limit it to documents held by the court in the court file. I doubt that it extends to documents created for the purposes of the proceedings even if intended to be filed with the court, since they may not in fact become part of the court file. It is important that the rule should not be widely and loosely interpreted so as to bring within its ambit information at a stage when I am sure it was not intended to be covered and which would be contrary to wider considerations of the best interests of the child.'

[20] Following that approach it can, in my opinion, hardly be argued that the CFR is prevented from reporting to social services concerns resulting from investigations simply because at a later date they will be recorded in the report to the judge.

[21] Both ss 12 and 97 raise the same question: what is meant by publication? Mr Spon-Smith offers us the definition in the *Shorter Oxford Dictionary*. Mr Everall counters with *Arlidge, Eady and Smith on Contempt* (Sweet and Maxwell, 2nd edn, 2000) at paras 8–79. The authors there submit that the statutory language should be given the wide interpretation of the law of defamation: it should not be confined to information communicated through the media but should extend to private communications to individuals. I do not read a narrower sense in the dictionary definition and would accept that a conversation between the CFR and another individual might amount to publication, but I cannot accept that a CFR publishes, and thereby exposes himself to a risk of contempt, when he reports concerns to the relevant statutory authority charged with the collection and investigation of material suggestive of child abuse. Such a communication between two professionals exchanging information in the course of their respective functions, each acting in furtherance of the protection of children, does not constitute a publication breaching the privacy of contemporaneous Children Act proceedings.

[…]

[43] Since in this judgment I offer guidance to those who do not of choice read the law reports I will endeavour a brief summary:

(i)   The relationship between the CFR and the judge is collaborative. Each has distinct functions and responsibilities in the discharge of which each exercises independently both judgment and discretion.

(ii)   If in the course of inquiries in private law proceedings the CFR is alerted to the possible abuse of a child he should consider the following analysis:

    (a)   Is this either:

        (i)   a discovery or direct report; alternatively

        (ii)   is the CFR listening to an account of someone else's discovery or to a second-hand report?

    (b)   If the latter:

        (i)   Has the information been relayed to social services or the police already?

        (ii)   Is there a history or pattern of past complaints?

        (iii) How plausible is the report?

        (iv) Was the informant a party to the proceedings?

        (v)   If yes, has he put this statement in evidence?

    (c)   Would the abuse, if established, amount to significant harm or the risk of significant harm within the meaning of s 31?

    (d)   Is there a need for urgent action? What are the risks of delay?

(iii) The answers that this analysis elicits should help to decide the appropriate course of action. It will seldom be necessary for the CFR to relay second-hand reports to social services. Furthermore such reports are unlikely to be urgent. Accordingly there will ordinarily be no obstacle to consultation with the judge before taking any action.

(iv) The CFR should always be alert to the danger of being enmeshed in the strategy of the manipulative litigant. The independence and impartiality of the CFR are crucial and if one party perceives that the CFR has taken sides with the other the judge's ultimate task, both to promote the welfare of the child and to impress the parties with the fairness of the proceedings, is rendered more difficult.

(v)   Where the CFR makes a discovery or receives a direct report an
immediate report to social services or to the police may be indicated. In
such a situation the CFR must exercise an unfettered independent
discretion. The only rule is that he must inform the judge of the steps he
has taken at the earliest convenient opportunity to enable the judge, who
controls the proceedings, to consider the impact of the development and
the need for consequential directions.

Extracts from the judgment of Wall J

[78] By s 16 of CJCSA 2000, and in a significant departure from previous
practice (see *Cadman v Cadman* (1982) 3 FLR 275 at 277 referred to at para [24]
of Thorpe LJ's judgment) CFRs may be cross-examined in any proceedings to
the same extent as any witness, although they may not be cross-examined
merely because they are exercising a right to conduct litigation or a right of
audience granted in accordance with s 15. This change derives from the
incorporation into English law of Art 6 of the European Convention for
the Protection of Human Rights and Fundamental Freedoms 1950.

[80] I have set out the provisions of CJCSA 2000 in such detail because, in
my judgment, it is important to recognise that CAFCASS is a new body with a
multiplicity of functions. It has been given a pivotal role to play in the family
justice system, and it needs to establish its identity and its status as swiftly and
authoritatively as possible. Its structure and the functions which it has been
given by Parliament clearly provide the opportunity, for the first time in the
family justice system, to create a coherent and integrated service for families
and children involved in relationship breakdown.

[81] We are in this case, of course, only concerned with one aspect of
CAFCASS's functions, albeit one of considerable importance. We need to
remember, however, that the flexible structure of CAFCASS enables the
person appointed as CFR in a private law case to be appointed the children's
guardian in a public law case.

[82] CAFCASS is going to have to identify and define the principles and
national standards under which it will carry out its functions under the
1989 Act and FPR 1991. It also follows from this very substantial change that
the relationship between CAFCASS and the judiciary – and in particular the
status and functions of CFRs – is an issue which needs to be addressed. It is,
accordingly, to this topic which I now turn.

The relationship between the court and the CFR

[83] Whilst we must, of course, learn from and build upon past experience,
we cannot, in my judgment import previous concepts into CAFCASS unless
they fit comfortably with the new service and are in the interests of the
children involved in the proceedings. Thus, in my judgment, the phrase
'officer of the court', whilst mellifluous and reassuringly resonant, is no longer
apt to describe the functions of the CFR. They are officers of the service

(CAFCASS), with professional duties and responsibilities defined by CJCSA 2000 and FPR 1991 as amended.

[84] This is particularly important, in my judgment, when it comes to considering the relationship between the CFR and the judiciary. Under s 7 of the 1989 Act the judge 'asks' an officer of CAFCASS to report to the court. No doubt the request is contained in an order of the court, and the CFR has a duty under s 12(1)(b) of CJCSA 2000 and FPR 1991, r 4.11 to investigate, to advise and to 'provide the court with such other assistance as it may require'. Other powers and duties are set out in FPR 1991, r 4.11B. But in my judgment, the language used is significant. The court 'asks'. The CFR investigates, advises and assists. The language is to be contrasted with s 37 of the 1989 Act, where the court directs.

[85] The relationship between the judiciary and the CFR should be, accordingly, one of collaboration and mutual co-operation. It is no more for the judge to tell CFRs how to go about their inquiries than it is for the CFR to intrude on the judicial function by making findings of fact.

[86] In my judgment, the relationship between the CFR and the judge requires the latter to identify the issues in the case on which he or she seeks the assistance of the CFR, and to ask the CFR to report on them. The brief is contained in the court order, which should identify those issues. The CFR has professional duties and responsibilities which the judge must respect. Thus, as is illustrated by this case, if CFRs feel professionally obliged to communicate information about the child to local authority duty social workers, they must not be inhibited from doing so by the feeling that they are, in some way, under the court's control as an 'officer of the court'.

[87] That is not, of course, to say that there should not be ongoing communication between the CFR and the court. To the contrary, important child protection information of the type envisaged in the previous paragraph should be immediately communicated to the judge. Equally, the relationship between the CFR and the judge should be such that CFRs should not feel it any derogation from their professional status to go back to the judge to ask for advice on unforeseen developments in the course of their inquiries.

[…]

[93] … Judges do not have a monopoly of wisdom on the manner in which other professional organisations regard it as appropriate to perform their functions, and judges in my view should be aware of the limitations of the judicial function.

[94] On the other side of the equation, of course, CFRs need to be acutely aware of the risk that a parent may be behaving manipulatively by making allegations of child abuse against the other parent. Allegations of sexual abuse in particular are very easy to make, and very difficult to refute. In the instant case, the child is living with her father and the allegations (if untrue) are likely to have an ulterior, tactical purpose. In the instant case, an exchange of information between the CFR and the local authority would have revealed a previous complaint by the mother which had been investigated and found to be baseless. In these circumstances, the CFR and the social worker might well have concluded that the information given to the former was a matter she should report to the judge so that the judge could decide how it should be addressed in the private law proceedings.

[95] Like Thorpe LJ, I disagree with the final 13 words of para 4.19 of the old *National Standards for Probation Service Family Court Welfare Work*, which he has set out at para [39] of his judgment. These seem to me to impinge inappropriately on the judicial function. If CFRs feel professionally obliged to relay child protection information to a local authority, they should immediately inform the judge and seek the judge's directions as to the future of their inquiries. The decision to suspend or terminate inquiries is for the judge who has the conduct of the private law proceedings. This point has a particular relevance to the question of the interface between private law proceedings and an inquiry by the local authority under s 47, to which I will turn in a moment.

[96] In summary, therefore, my conclusions on this important part of the case are:

(i)   CFRs are not 'officers of the court'. They are officers of the Service (CAFCASS) with the duties and responsibilities laid upon them by s 12 of CJCSA 2000, s 7 of the 1989 Act and r 4.11 of the FPR 1991.

(ii)   CFRs are not under the control of the judiciary. Within the scope of their employment by CAFCASS, they are independent professionals who, at the request of the court, investigate issues identified by the court as relating to the welfare of the child in question and give the court any advice and assistance it requires. During the course of those investigations, they are free to exercise their professional judgment on those issues, and in particular do not need the court's permission to disclose information to local authority child protection workers.

(iii)   The relationship between CFRs and the judiciary should be collaborative and co-operative. In particular, CFRs should not hesitate to seek directions from the judge in relation to issues which arise during the course of the investigation.

(iv)   CFRs should advise the court immediately if a child protection issue of sufficient gravity arises such as has required the CFR to notify the local authority. The CFR in such circumstances should seek the court's directions and any decision to terminate or continue the CFR's inquiries is for the court, not the CFR.

5.9 RE O AND N; RE B
[2003] UKHL 18, [2003] 1 FLR 1169

House of Lords

Lord Nicholls of Birkenhead, Lord Hoffmann, Lord Millett, Lord Scott of
Foscote, Lord Walker of Gestingthorpe

3 April 2003

Introductory comments

This case, which in some ways picks up from where the decision in
Re H and R (at **5.4**) left off, concerns the approach the court must take
in child protection cases in which it is not clear which of a number of
people has injured a child. It is included because: (1) the issue is of
immense practical importance in a small but significant number of child
protection cases; and (2) it is one over which there has been much
dispute over the last few years (being the second case on this general
issue to reach the House of Lords in a couple of years[1]).

Although we have not set them out in full we have also flagged up for
lawyers the important obiter remarks ('peripheral observations') about
the place of unproven allegations: (1) when applying the second
(welfare) test to a care application; and (2) when applying the welfare
test in private law proceedings. The next steps for lawyers wanting to
pursue these issues are to read the whole of paras [37] to [45] of the
judgment in this case and then to read the decision of the Court of
Appeal in *Re M and R (Child Abuse: Evidence)* [1996] 2 FLR 195.

Headnote

*Care proceedings – Risk – 'Uncertain perpetrator' – Threshold criteria met – Physical harm to child
but not clear which parent caused harm or whether both caused harm – Correct approach*

In the first case, the younger child had been pronounced dead on arrival at hospital
with serious external and internal non-accidental injuries. At the preliminary care
hearing in respect of an elder child, the judge found that the mother's male partner
was the perpetrator of the injuries inflicted on the younger child, and that the mother
who could be exonerated, had not failed to protect him. The Court of Appeal allowed
the local authority's appeal, on the basis that there was insufficient evidence that the
mother's male partner was the sole perpetrator, that the judge could not disregard the
risk posed to the child by the mother and that there was no doubt that the mother had

---

[1]   The other being *Lancashire County Council v B* [2000] 1 FLR 583.

failed to protect him. The mother appealed to the House of Lords. In the second case, the child was found to be suffering from a fractured skull and several other fractures. The father accepted responsibility for the skull injury, but not the other injuries. The judge found that the injuries were non-accidental, that the father was responsible for the skull fracture, that neither parent had given any explanation to account for the other injuries which had been caused by either or both parents while the child was in their care, that neither parent could be exculpated as a possible perpetrator, and that the parents individually or jointly had failed to protect the child. The Court of Appeal allowed the mother's appeal in part, on the basis that it had not been established on a balance of probabilities that any of the injuries had been caused by her, and that she must therefore be treated as if she had not caused the child significant harm, although she had failed to protect her from injury by the father. The local authority appealed to the House of Lords.

Held – dismissing the mother's appeal in the first case and allowing the local authority's appeal in the second case –

(1) Where a child suffered significant harm, but the court was unable to identify which parent had been the perpetrator, or, indeed, whether both had been, the court should proceed at the welfare stage on the footing that each of the parents was a possible perpetrator. It would be grotesque if, because neither parent had been proved to be the perpetrator, the court had to proceed at the welfare stage as though the child were not at risk from either parent, even though one or other of them was the perpetrator of significant harm. When the facts found at the preliminary 'threshold' hearing left open the possibility that a parent or other carer was a perpetrator of proved harm, it would not be right for that conclusion to be excluded from consideration at the disposal hearing as one of the matters to be taken into account, as that would risk distorting the court's assessment of where, having regard to all the circumstances, the best interests of the child lay (see paras [27], [28], [31]).

(2) A finding of failure to protect could not be relied upon to protect the child, as such a finding was not always made when the court was unable to identify which of the parents had inflicted the harm. In any event, a finding of failure to protect was not a reason for leaving out of account at the welfare stage the undoubted fact that one or other of the parents inflicted the physical harm on the child (see para [30]).

(3) In cases of split hearings, judges must be astute to express at the preliminary hearing such views as they are able to, in order to assist social workers and psychiatrists in making their assessments and drafting the care plan. To that end transcripts of judgments given at the preliminary hearing should always be made readily available when required so that reliance did not have to be placed on summaries or even bare statements of conclusions (see para [35]).

Per curiam: to have regard at the welfare stage to allegations of harm rejected as not proven at the threshold stage would have the effect of depriving the child and the family of the protection intended to be afforded by the threshold criteria and accordingly at the welfare stage the court should proceed on the footing that the unproven allegations were no more than that (see para [38]).

Per curiam: although full argument had not been heard, the court was attracted by the Court of Appeal's reasoning in *Re M and R (Child Abuse: Evidence)* and *Re P (Sexual Abuse: Standard of Proof)* which suggested that the court might not infer in private proceedings that a child was at risk of suffering harm in the future where the only evidence that the child was at risk was an unproved allegation that he had suffered harm in the past (see paras [44], [45]).

Extracts from the judgment of Lord Nicholls of Birkenhead

The threshold criteria: the 'attributable' condition

[19] In *Lancashire County Council v B* [2000] 2 AC 147, [2000] 1 FLR 583 the House of Lords considered how threshold condition (b), the 'attributable' condition, should be applied in cases such as the present two appeals, where the significant harm condition is satisfied but the court is unable to decide which of two or more carers was the perpetrator of the physical harm in question. The House decided that in such 'uncertain perpetrator' cases the phrase 'the care given to the child' in s 31(2)(b)(i) includes the care given by any of the carers, so that this condition is fulfilled even though the identity of the particular carer who was the perpetrator is not known.

[20] Section 31 and its associated emergency and interim provisions comprise the only court mechanism available to a local authority to protect a child from risk. The interpretation of the 'attributable' condition adopted by the House is necessary to avoid the unacceptable consequence that, otherwise, if the court cannot identify which of the child's carers was responsible for inflicting the injuries the child will remain wholly unprotected. As Wall J observed in *Re B (Minors) (Care Proceedings: Practice)* [1999] 1 WLR 238, at 248, that would render the statutory provisions ineffective to deal with a commonplace aspect of child protection. The interpretation adopted by the House avoids this result while, at the same time, encroaching to the minimum extent necessary on the general principle underpinning s 31(2).

[21] In reaching this conclusion on the interpretation of the legislation your Lordships' House had very much in mind that, in consequence, judges will find themselves faced with the particularly difficult problem of proceeding with the care application but not knowing which individual was responsible for inflicting the injuries. And parents who may be wholly innocent, and whose care may not have fallen below that of a reasonable parent, will face the possibility of losing their child: see *Lancashire County Council v B* [2000] 2 AC 147, [2000] 1 FLR 583 at 166–167 and 589 respectively.

[22] The House now has to consider some of the practical implications of this decision at the welfare stage.

[...]

[25] The Children Act 1989 directs the court, when making a decision regarding a child's welfare, to have particular regard to the factors set out in the welfare checklist in s 1(3). One of these factors is any harm the child 'has suffered or is at risk of suffering': s 1(3)(e). Questions have arisen on the interaction of this paragraph and s 31(2) as interpreted in *Re H (Minors) (Sexual Abuse: Standard of Proof)* [1996] AC 563, sub nom *Re H and R (Child Sexual Abuse: Standard of Proof)* [1996] 1 FLR 80 and *Lancashire County Council v B* [2000] 2 AC 147, [2000] 1 FLR 583. The questions have arisen in three areas.

The welfare stage: 'uncertain perpetrator' cases

[26] The first area concerns cases of the type involved in the present appeals, where the judge finds a child has suffered significant physical harm at the hands of his parents but is unable to say which. I stress one feature of this type of case. These are cases where it has been proved, to the requisite standard of proof, that the child is suffering significant harm or is likely to do so.

[27] Here, as a matter of legal policy, the position seems to me straightforward. Quite simply, it would be grotesque if such a case had to proceed at the welfare stage on the footing that, because neither parent, considered individually, has been proved to be the perpetrator, therefore the child is not at risk from either of them. This would be grotesque because it would mean the court would proceed on the footing that neither parent represents a risk even though one or other of them was the perpetrator of the harm in question.

[28] That would be a self-defeating interpretation of the legislation. It would mean that, in 'uncertain perpetrator' cases, the court decides that the threshold criteria are satisfied but then lacks the ability to proceed in a sensible way in the best interests of the child. The preferable interpretation of the legislation is that in such cases the court is able to proceed at the welfare stage on the footing that each of the possible perpetrators is, indeed, just that: a possible perpetrator. As Hale LJ said in *Re G (Care Proceedings: Split Trials)* [2001] 1 FLR 872, at 882:

> 'the fact that a judge cannot always decide means that when one gets to the later hearing, the later hearing has to proceed on the basis that each is a possible perpetrator.'

This approach accords with the basic principle that in considering the requirements of the child's welfare the court will have regard to all the circumstances of the case.

[29] In such cases the judge at the preliminary hearing, while unable to identify the perpetrator, may decide that one or other of the parents, perhaps both, was guilty of failure to protect. It was submitted that herein lies a better solution to the problem. The court should assess future risk on the basis of this proved shortcoming. This would be a better way to proceed because it would avoid attaching to each parent the stigma of possible perpetrator.

[30] I do not believe this would be a satisfactory alternative. Inability to identify the perpetrator is not always accompanied by a finding of failure to protect. The judge may find that the child was injured in only one incident, by one or other of the parents, in a momentary loss of self-control. Further, when assessing future risk, failure to protect is one matter, perpetration is another. A finding of failure to protect is not a reason for leaving out of account at the welfare stage the undoubted fact that one or other of the parents inflicted the physical harm on the child. This may be important in cases where circumstances have changed since the injuries were inflicted and the parents are no longer living together.

[31] In 'uncertain perpetrator' cases the correct approach must be that the judge conducting the disposal hearing will have regard, to whatever extent is appropriate, to the facts found by the judge at the preliminary hearing. Nowadays the same judge usually conducts both hearings, but this is not always so. When the facts found at the preliminary hearing leave open the possibility that a parent or other carer was a perpetrator of proved harm, it would not be right for that conclusion to be excluded from consideration at the disposal hearing as one of the matters to be taken into account. The importance to be attached to that possibility, as to every feature of the case, necessarily depends on the circumstances. But to exclude that possibility altogether from the matters the judge may consider would risk distorting the court's assessment of where, having regard to all the circumstances, the best interests of the child lie.

[32] Similarly, and for the same reason, the judge at the disposal hearing will take into account any views expressed by the judge at the preliminary hearing on the likelihood that one carer was or was not the perpetrator, or a perpetrator, of the inflicted injuries. Depending on the circumstances, these views may be of considerable value in deciding the outcome of the application: for instance, whether the child should be rehabilitated with his mother.

[...]

[35] ... in cases of split hearings judges must be astute to express such views as they can at the preliminary hearing to assist social workers and psychiatrists in making their assessments and preparing the draft care plan. For their part social workers, I do not doubt, will have well in mind the need to consider all the circumstances when assessing the risk posed by a carer who is, but who is no more than, a possible perpetrator. To this end transcripts of judgments given at the preliminary hearing should always be made readily available when required, so that reliance does not have to be placed on summaries or even bare statements of conclusions: see Dame Elizabeth Butler-Sloss P in *Re G (Care Proceedings: Split Trials)* [2001] 1 FLR 872, at 876.

[36] I must mention a further point. The burden of proof on care order applications rests on the local authority. But, it was submitted, to proceed as mentioned above would improperly reverse the burden of proof. The parent would have the onus of exculpating himself when the local authority failed to prove he was a perpetrator but the possibility that he was a perpetrator was left open. I am unable to accept this submission. It cannot stand with the decision in *Lancashire County Council v B* [2000] 2 AC 147, [2000] 1 FLR 583. As already noted, the effect of this decision was that a care order may be made in this type of case even though the local authority failed to prove, to the requisite standard of proof, which parent was the perpetrator of the physical harm. The approach described above does no more than give effect to this

decision at the welfare stage in the only sensible way which is possible. On the present appeals, I add, no submission was made that the House should reconsider the decision in *Lancashire County Council v B*, nor have I heard anything to suggest the House should do so.

The welfare stage: unproved allegations of harm

[37] The second area where a question has arisen about the interaction of s 1(3)(e) and s 31(2) does not directly concern the present appeals. Nevertheless I should comment briefly so that the observations made above are seen in context. This second area relates to the type of case where the threshold criteria are satisfied on one ground, such as neglect or failure to protect, but not on another ground, such as physical harm. At the welfare stage, to what extent may the court take into account the possibility that the non-proven allegation might, after all, be true?

[...]

Private law cases and s 1(3)(e)

[42] The reasoning of the decision in *Re M and R (Child Abuse: Evidence)* [1996] 2 FLR 195 raises a further question on the interaction of s 1(3)(e) and s 31(2). The question is whether the interpretation of s 31(2)(a) adopted in *Re H (Minors) (Sexual Abuse: Standard of Proof)* [1996] AC 563, sub nom *Re H and R (Child Sexual Abuse: Standard of Proof)* [1996] 1 FLR 80 is applicable to s 1(3)(e) in private law proceedings. Butler-Sloss LJ considered that it is: see *Re M and R (Child Abuse: Evidence)*, at 203.

PART 6

PRACTICE DIRECTIONS, PRACTICE
NOTES, CIRCULARS AND GUIDANCE

'For who would bear … the law's delay … when he himself might his quietus make with a bare bodkin'

William Shakespeare, *Hamlet*, Act 3: Scene 1

'Defend the children of the poor and punish the wrongdoer'

Psalm 72:4, Authorised Version, inscribed above the entrance to the Central Criminal Court (the Old Bailey), London

'"Poor little monkey!" she at last exclaimed: and the words were an epitaph for the tomb of Maisie's childhood. She was abandoned to her fate. What was clear to any spectator was that the only link binding her to either parent was this lamentable fact of her being a vessel for bitterness, a deep little porcelain cup in which biting acids could be mixed. They had wanted her not for any good they could do her, but for the harm they could, with her unconscious aid, do each other. She should serve their anger and seal their revenge, for husband and wife had been alike crippled by the heavy hand of justice, which in the last resort met on neither side their indignant claim to get, as they called it, everything.'

Henry James, *What Maisie Knew*, Chapter 1

6.1 OVERVIEW OF PRACTICE DIRECTIONS

There are all sorts of things which are not 'law' in a strict sense of the term but which direct or guide the way in which legal practice takes place. These include:

- Practice Directions, issued by the President of the Family Division and therefore carrying the authority of that judicial office;
- Practice Notes, which are essentially administrative;
- an increasing number of Statements of Good Practice, generally produced by a committee led by a senior judge or by professional bodies such as the Law Society;
- government circulars issued by the relevant government department to those within the public sector for which they are responsible. In children law the most important of these are the local authority circulars issued under s 7(1) of the Local Authority Social Services Act 1970, which states:

    'Local authorities shall, in the exercise of their social services functions, including the exercise of any discretion conferred by any relevant enactment, act under the general guidance of the Secretary of State.'[1]

We have included a selection of these, of which the most important must be the Protocol for Judicial Case Management in Public Law Children Act Cases.[2] This Protocol carries the authority of a Practice Direction by the President[3] which makes it clear that the Protocol applies to all courts[4] hearing applications issued by local authorities under Part IV of the Children Act 1989 (defined as 'care cases' but in fact wider than that) issued or transferred up after 1 November 2003.

There are two particularly important things to know about the Protocol. First, that the overriding objective, set out in the Practice Direction,[5] is:

    '... to enable the Court to deal with every care case

---

[1] See also ss 7A–7E of the same Act.

[2] See **6.2**.

[3] As well as a Foreword by not only the President but also the Lord Chancellor and the Secretary of State for Education and Skills.

[4] Including family proceedings courts.

[5] This was confirmed by Hedley J in *Re G (Protocol for Judicial Case Management in Public Law Children Act Cases: Application to become Party in Family Proceedings)* [2004] EWHC 116 (Fam), [2004] 1 FLR 1119: '(1) the Protocol must be understood and applied in the light of the purposes set out in the Practice Direction; (2) if the pursuit of that purpose requires departure from terms of the Protocol then that must be done with proper reasons being given for such departure; (3) the Protocol is a tool to improve family justice, not to impair it; (4) the Protocol is not to be allowed to become the source of satellite litigation.'

(a)   justly, expeditiously, fairly and with the minimum of delay;

(b)   in ways which ensure, so far as is practicable, that

    (i)   the parties are on an equal footing;

    (ii)   the welfare of the children involved is safeguarded; and

    (iii) distress to all parties is minimised;

(c)   so far as is practicable, in ways which are proportionate

    (i)   to the gravity and complexity of the issues; and

    (ii)   to the nature and extent of the intervention proposed in the private and family life of the children and adults involved.'

And secondly, that the paramount objective is:

'that save in exceptional or unforeseen circumstances every care case is finally determined within 40 weeks of the application being issued.'

Appendix C sets out information of the foremost importance about the instruction and role of experts in such proceedings, guidance that is not limited to public law proceedings. It is also worth noting that the Protocol also incorporates an earlier Practice Direction about court bundles.

The other documents to which we wish to draw specific attention in this Overview are:

- the President's Practice Direction concerning the representation of children in private law proceedings pursuant to Family Proceedings Rules 1991, r 9.5.[6] This gives important guidance about the sort of situations in which it may be appropriate to make a child party to and represented in such cases;

- the President's Private Law Programme.[7] This is not a full-blown protocol but it does indicate important features of a reshaped system for dealing with private law cases.

The extract from the primary materials we recommend you read now is Appendix C (Code of Guidance for Expert Witnesses) in the Protocol for Judicial Case Management in Public Law Children Act Cases set out at **6.2**.

The Overview of Children Law ends here.

---

[6]   See **6.18**.

[7]   See **6.20**.

6.2 PROTOCOL FOR JUDICIAL CASE MANAGEMENT IN PUBLIC LAW CHILDREN ACT CASES
[2003] 2 FLR 719

June 2003

Foreword

by the President of the Family Division, the Lord Chancellor and the Secretary of State for Education and Skills

After over a decade of otherwise successful implementation of the Children Act there remains a large cloud in the sky in the form of delay. Delay in care cases has persisted for too long. The average care case lasts for almost a year. This is a year in which the child is left uncertain as to his or her future, is often moved between several temporary care arrangements, and the family and public agencies are left engaged in protracted and complex legal wranglings. Though a fair and effective process must intervene before a child is taken from its parents, we believe it is essential that unnecessary delay is eliminated and that better outcomes for children and families are thereby achieved. This protocol sets a guideline of 40 weeks for the conclusion of care cases. Some cases will need to take longer than this, but many more cases should take less.

The causes of delay have become clear from the Scoping Study published by the Department in March 2002, and through the work of the Advisory Committee that finalised this protocol. There is now a real enthusiasm among all the agencies involved for tackling these causes. Other work has begun and the momentum is building. Overt efforts have been made locally, both by Care Centres and by Family Proceedings Courts. Additional judicial sitting days for care work are being found. Measures are being taken to help improve the performance of CAFCASS. This protocol will form the backbone of these other efforts.

The Advisory Committee has involved all of the agencies and organisations that have a significant role to play in the care process and has striven to produce a consensus as to the content of this protocol. We are grateful to all the members of the Committee and to everyone else who engaged with the consultation process.

This protocol has been prepared on the basis that a change in the whole approach to case management and a clarification of focus, among all those involved in care cases, is the best way forward. This protocol is not a fresh start – it is a collation and distillation of best practice – we do ask you to engage it wholeheartedly with all your usual enthusiasm and dedication.

Dame Elizabeth Butler-Sloss
President
Lord Falconer of Thoroton
The Secretary of State for Constitutional Affairs and Lord Chancellor
Rt Hon Charles Clarke MP
Secretary of State for Education and Skills

THE PROTOCOL – ROUTE MAP – THE 6 STEPS

1		2		3
The Application		**The First Hearing in the FPC**		**Allocation Hearing and Directions**
Day 1 to Day 3		**On (or before) Day 6**		**By Day 11 (CC) 15 (HC)**
Objective: LA to provide sufficient information to identify issues/make early welfare and case management decisions		**Objective:** To decide what immediate steps are necessary/contested ICO/preventing delay/appropriate court		**Objective:** To make provision for continuous/consistent judicial case management
Action: • LA file application in Form C1/C3 **on Day 1 [1.1]** • Directions on Issue by court - fixing First Hearing - Appointment of guardian **on Day 1 [1.2]** • Allocation of guardian by CAFCASS **by Day 3 [1.2–3]** • Appointment of solicitor for the child - no appointment of guardian - Notification to parties of name of guardian/solicitor **on Day 3 [1.4]** • LA file and serve documents **by Day 3 [1.5]**	►	**Action:** • Parties [2.2] • Contested interim care orders [2.3] • Transfer [2.4] and transfer arrangements [2.5] • Initial case management and checklist [2.6] including: - Case Management Conference - Final Hearing - Pre-Hearing Review - Evidence - Disclosure - Core Assessment - Standard Directions Form **by Day 6**	► **5 days** ►	**Action:** **Care centre court officer shall:** • Allocate 1–2 judges (including Final Hearing judge) [3.2] • Attach SDF with proposed date for CMC, Final Hearing and PHR **by Day 8 [3.2]:** **Judge (at Allocation Hearing) considers:** • Transfer, ICO, CM Checklist, dates for CMC, Final Hearing, PHR, Disclosure, Core Assessment, SDF **by Day 11 [3.4]** • Case management documents [3.4] ▼ **1 day** ▼ **In High Court:** • Court officer **by Day 12 [3.6]** • Case management judge **by Day 15 [3.7]** **Within 54 days**

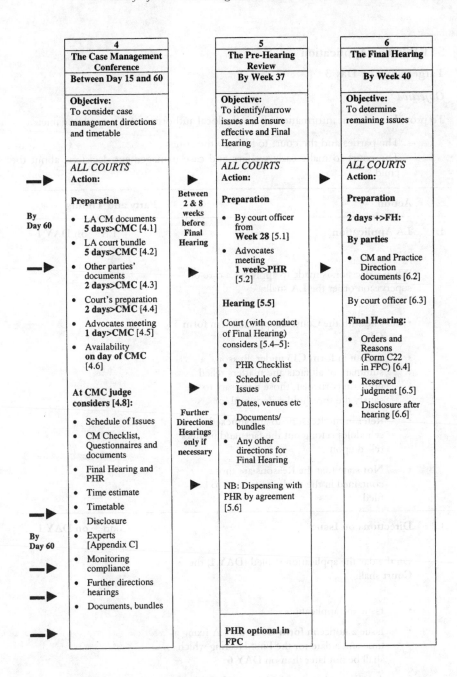

4		5		6
The Case Management Conference		**The Pre-Hearing Review**		**The Final Hearing**
Between Day 15 and 60		**By Week 37**		**By Week 40**

Objective: To consider case management directions and timetable		**Objective:** To identify/narrow issues and ensure effective and Final Hearing		**Objective:** To determine remaining issues	

ALL COURTS
Action:

Preparation

By Day 60

- LA CM documents **5 days>CMC** [4.1]
- LA court bundle **5 days>CMC** [4.2]
- Other parties' documents **2 days>CMC** [4.3]
- Court's preparation **2 days>CMC** [4.4]
- Advocates meeting **1 day>CMC** [4.5]
- Availability **on day of CMC** [4.6]

At CMC judge considers [4.8]:

- Schedule of Issues
- CM Checklist, Questionnaires and documents
- Final Hearing and PHR
- Time estimate
- Timetable
- Disclosure

By Day 60

- Experts [Appendix C]
- Monitoring compliance
- Further directions hearings
- Documents, bundles

Between 2 & 8 weeks before Final Hearing

Further Directions Hearings only if necessary

ALL COURTS
Action:

Preparation

- By court officer from **Week 28** [5.1]
- Advocates meeting **1 week>PHR** [5.2]

Hearing [5.5]

Court (with conduct of Final Hearing) considers [5.4–5]:

- PHR Checklist
- Schedule of Issues
- Dates, venues etc
- Documents/bundles
- Any other directions for Final Hearing

NB: Dispensing with PHR by agreement [5.6]

PHR optional in FPC

ALL COURTS
Action:

Preparation

2 days +>FH:

By parties

- CM and Practice Direction documents [6.2]

By court officer [6.3]

Final Hearing:

- Orders and Reasons (Form C22 in FPC) [6.4]
- Reserved judgment [6.5]
- Disclosure after hearing [6.6]

Days

Where target times are expressed in days, the days are "court business days" in accordance with the Rules (principles of application para 10)

STEP 1: The Application

Target time: by Day 3

Objective

To provide sufficient information about the local authority's (LA) case to enable:

- The parties and the court to identify the issues
- The court to make early welfare and case management decisions about the child.

	Action	Party and Timing
1.1	**LA Application**	LA **on DAY 1**
	When a decision is made to apply for a care or supervision order the **LA** shall:	
	• File with the Court an application in **form C1**	
	• Set out in **form C13** under 'Reasons' a summary of all facts and matters relied upon, in particular, those necessary to satisfy the threshold criteria and/or	
	• Refer in the Reasons to any annexed schedules setting out the facts and matters relied upon	
	• **Not** state that the Reasons are those contained in the evidence filed or to be filed.	
1.2	**Directions on Issue**	Court **on DAY 1**
	On the day the application is filed (**DAY 1**) the **Court** shall:	
	• Issue the application	
	• Issue a notice in **form C6** to the LA fixing a time and a date for the First Hearing which shall be not later than on **DAY 6**	
	• Appoint a Guardian (unless satisfied that it is not necessary to do so to safeguard the child's interests)	
	• Inform CAFCASS of the decision to appoint and the request to allocate a Guardian	

Action	Party and Timing
1.3 **Allocation of the Guardian by CAFCASS**	CAFCASS **by DAY 3**

Within **2 days** of issue (by **DAY 3**) **CAFCASS** shall inform the Court of:

- The name of the allocated Guardian or
- The likely date upon which an application will be made.

Action	Party and Timing
1.4 **Appointment of the Solicitor for the Child**	Guardian **on DAY 3**

When a Guardian is allocated the **Guardian** shall on that day:

- Appoint a solicitor for the child
- Inform the Court of the name of the solicitor appointed
- In the event that the Guardian's allocation is delayed and the Court has already appointed a solicitor, ensure that effective legal representation is maintained

Where a Guardian is not allocated within **2 days** of issue, the **Court** shall on **DAY 3**:   FPC **on DAY 3**

- Consider when a Guardian will be allocated
- Decide whether to appoint a solicitor for the child

In any event on the day the appointment is made the **Court** shall: FPC **on DAY 3**

- Notify all parties on **form C47** of the names of the Guardian and/or the solicitor for the child who have been appointed.

Action	Party and Timing
1.5 **LA Documents**	LA **by DAY 3**

Within **2 days** of issue (by **DAY 3**) the **LA** shall file and serve on all parties, the solicitor for the child and CAFCASS the following documents:

- The **forms C1 and C13** and any supplementary forms and notices issued by the Court

Action	Party and Timing
• Any relevant **court orders** relating to the child (together with the relevant Justices Facts and Reasons in **form C22** and any relevant **judgments** that exist)	
• The **initial social work statement** (appendix B/3)	
• The **social work chronology** (appendix B/2)	
• The **core or initial assessment** reports (appendix F)	
• Any other **additional evidence** including specialist assessments or reports which then exist and which are relied upon by the LA.	

STEP 2: The First Hearing in the FPC

Target time: by Day 6

Objective

To decide what immediate steps are necessary to safeguard the welfare of the child by:

- Determining contested interim care order applications/with whom the child will live
- Identifying how to prevent delay
- Identifying the appropriate court
- Transferring to the appropriate court.

	Action	Party and Timing
2.1	**The First Hearing**	FPC **on DAY 6**

The First Hearing shall take place in the Family Proceedings Court (FPC) on or before **DAY 6**. At every First Hearing the **FPC** shall:

- Consider who should be a **party** to the proceedings (step 2.2)

- Make arrangements for contested **interim care applications** to be determined (step 2.3)

- Consider whether the proceedings should be **transferred** to the Care Centre or another FPC (step 2.4)

- Where the proceedings are not transferred, make **initial case management** decisions (step 2.6).

Action	Party and Timing
2.2 Parties and Service	FPC **on DAY 6**

At the First Hearing the **FPC** shall:

- Obtain confirmation that all those who are entitled to be parties have been served

- Consider whether any other person should be joined as a party

- Give directions relating to party status and the service of documents upon parties.

2.3 Contested Interim Care Orders	FPC **on DAY 6**

In any proceedings where the application for an interim care order (ICO) is not agreed at the First Hearing, the **FPC** shall:

- Decide whether to grant an order and if so what order; or

- List the application for an urgent contested interim hearing in an FPC prior to the Case Management Conference (CMC); and

- Give such case management directions as are necessary to ensure that the interim hearing will be effective; or

- Transfer the proceedings to be heard at the Care Centre.

2.4 Urgency and Transfer	FPC **on DAY 6**

At the First Hearing the **FPC** shall:

- Hear submissions as to complexity, gravity and urgency

- Consider whether transfer to another Court is appropriate and in any event determine any application made by a party for transfer

- Give reasons for any transfer decision made and record the information provided by the parties relating to transfer on **form C22** (including any intention to apply for transfer to the High Court)

- Send the court file and the Order of transfer in **form C49** to the receiving court within **1 day** of the First Hearing (by **DAY 7**)

Action	Party and Timing
2.5 **Proceedings Transferred to the Care Centre**	FPC **on DAY 6**

Where a decision is made to transfer to the Care Centre, the **FPC** shall:

- In accordance with the arrangements set out in the **Care Centre Plan** (CCP) and the **FPC Plan** (FPCP) (**appendix E**), immediately inform the court officer at the Care Centre of the transfer and of the reasons set out on **form C22**

- Obtain a date and time from the court officer for an **Allocation Hearing**/contested interim hearing in the Care Centre which shall be between **3** and **5** days of the decision to transfer (by **DAY 11**)

- Notify the parties of the Care Centre to which the proceedings are transferred and of the date and time of the Allocation Hearing/contested interim hearing

- Direct the LA or the child's solicitor to prepare a **case synopsis** (**appendix B/1**) which shall be filed with the Care Centre and served within **2 days** of the First Hearing in the FPC (by **DAY 8**)

- Except as to disclosure of documents, make only those **case management directions upon transfer** as are agreed with the Care Centre as set out in the CCP and the FPCP.

2.6 **Case Management in the FPC**	FPC **on DAY 6**

In any case where the proceedings are **NOT** transferred to the care centre the **FPC** shall at the First Hearing:

- Consider the **case management checklist** (**appendix A/3**)

- Fix a date and time for a **Case Management Conference** (CMC) in the FPC within **54 days** of the First Hearing (between **DAYS 15 and 60**) unless all of the case management decisions set out at step 4.8 of this protocol can be taken at the First Hearing and the application can be listed for Final Hearing

Action	Party and Timing
• Fix a date for the **Final Hearing** or if it is not possible to do so fix a hearing window (either of which shall be not later than in the **3 week** period commencing the **37th WEEK** after the application was issued)	
• Consider whether a **Pre Hearing Review** (PHR) is necessary and if so fix a PHR not later than **2 weeks** and no earlier than **8 weeks** before the Final Hearing date/window	
• Give such **case management directions** as are necessary to ensure that all steps will have been taken prior to the CMC to enable it to be effective, in particular:	
• that a **statement of evidence** from each party (including the child where of sufficient age and understanding, but excluding the child's Guardian) is filed and served replying to the facts alleged and the proposals made by the LA in the initial social work statement	
• whether directions as to full and frank **disclosure** of all relevant documents need to be given and in any event give directions where necessary to ensure that the disclosure of relevant documents by the LA occurs within **20 days** of the First Hearing (by **DAY 26**)	
• whether a **core assessment** (**appendix F**) exists or should be directed to be undertaken by the LA before the CMC	
• Record on the **Standard Directions Form** (**SDF**) (**appendix A/1**) the Court's case management decisions and reasons and serve the directions given on the parties	
2.7 The **FPC** shall give a direction at the First Hearing that **no further documents** shall be filed without the Court's permission unless in support of a new application or in accordance with case management directions given at that hearing (the Court will consider directions relating to the filing of comprehensive evidence and documents at the CMC)	

STEP 3: Allocation Hearing & Directions

Target time: by Day 11

Objective

To make provision for continuous and consistent judicial case management.

	Action	Party and Timing
3.1	**Following Transfer**	Care **from DAY 6** Centre

Following transfer to the **Care Centre** or to the **High Court** all further hearings in the proceedings shall be conducted:

- So as to ensure **judicial continuity of case management** in accordance with the protocol;

- By one or not more than 2 judges who are identified as **case management judges** in the CCP (**appendix E/1**), one of whom may be and where possible should be the judge who will conduct the Final Hearing

3.2	**Allocation in the Care Centre**	Court **by DAY 8** Officer

Within **2 days** of the order transferring proceedings to the Care Centre (normally by **DAY 8**) the **court officer** shall:

- Allocate one and not more than two **case management judges** (one of whom may be and where possible should be the Judge who will conduct the Final Hearing) to case manage the proceedings in accordance with the protocol and the CCP

- Where possible, identify the judge who is to be the **Final Hearing judge**

- Upon receipt of the court file from the FPC, attach to the file the **form C22** issued by the FPC, the **case synopsis (appendix B/1)** and a **Standard Directions Form (SDF) (appendix A/1)** and complete the SDF to the extent only of:
  - the names of the **allocated and identified judges**

Action	Party and Timing

- the proposed date of the **CMC** (which shall be within **54 days** of the date of the First Hearing in the FPC ie between **DAYS 15 and 60**)
- the proposed **Final Hearing** date or hearing window (which shall be not later than in the **3 week** period commencing the **37th WEEK** after the application was issued)
- the proposed date of the **PHR** (which shall be not later than **2 weeks** and no earlier than **8 weeks** before the Final Hearing/trial window)

- Inform the case management judge in writing:
  - of any other circumstances of **urgency**
  - of any contested interim hearing for an **ICO**
  - of any application to **transfer to the High Court**
  - of the date and time of the **Allocation Hearing** (which shall be between **3 and 5 days** of the First Hearing in the FPC ie by **DAY 11**)

- Notify the parties of the date, time and venue fixed for the Allocation Hearing, together with the identity of the allocated/nominated judges

	Action	Party and Timing
3.3	**Section 37 Request for a Report and Transfer to a Care Centre**	Court Officer **within 2 days of the order of transfer**

Where in any family proceedings a Court decides to direct an appropriate LA to investigate a child's circumstances, the Court shall follow the guidance set out at **appendix G**.

Where, following a section 37 request for a report, proceedings are transferred to the Care Centre:

- The **transferring court** shall make a record of the Court's reasons for the transfer on **form C22** and the **court officer** of the transferring court shall send the court file, the order of transfer in **form C49** and the record of reasons to the Care Centre within **1 day** of the order

Action	Party and Timing

• The **court officer** in the care centre shall within **2 days** of the order transferring the proceedings take the steps set out at paragraph 3.2 and shall also:
  • inform the case management judge in writing of the transfer (and such circumstances as are known)
  • request the case management judge to consider giving directions as to the **appointment of a Guardian and/or a solicitor for the child** at or before the Allocation Hearing
  • notify all parties on **form C47** of the names of the Guardian and/or the solicitor for the child when they are appointed
  • inform the LA solicitor or the child's solicitor of the requirement that a **case synopsis (appendix B/1)** be prepared which shall be filed with the care centre and served not later than **2 days** before the date fixed for the Allocation Hearing.	

3.4 **Allocation Hearing**	Case Manage-ment Judge	**by DAY 11**

The Allocation Hearing in the Care Centre shall take place between **3 and 5 days** of the First Hearing in the FPC (by **DAY 11**). At the Allocation Hearing the **case management judge** shall:

• Consider whether the proceedings should be **transferred to the High Court or re-transferred to the FPC**

• Determine any **contested interim application** for a care or supervision order

• Where **the proceedings have been transferred from a court following a section 37 request** consider:
  • whether directions should be given to appoint a Guardian and/or a solicitor for the child in accordance with steps 1.2 to 1.4 of the protocol
  • whether any directions need to be given for the filing and service of LA documents in accordance with step 1.5 of the protocol

Action	Party and Timing
• Consider the **case management checklist (appendix A/3)**	
• Fix a date and time for a **CMC** which shall be within **54 days** of the First Hearing in the FPC (between **DAYS 15 and 60**)	
• Fix a date for the **Final Hearing** and confirm the identity of the Final Hearing judge or if it is not possible to do so fix a hearing window (either of which shall be not later than in the **3 week** period commencing the **37th WEEK** after the application was issued)	
• Fix a date and time for a **PHR** which shall be not later than **2 weeks** and no earlier than **8 weeks** before the Final Hearing date or window	
• Give such **case management directions** as are necessary to ensure that all steps will have been taken prior to the CMC to enable it to be effective, in particular:	
• that a **statement of evidence from each party** (including the child where of sufficient age and understanding, but excluding the child's Guardian) is filed and served replying to the facts alleged and the proposals made by the LA in the initial social work statement	
• whether directions as to full and frank **disclosure** of all relevant documents need to be given and in any event give directions where necessary to ensure that the disclosure of relevant documents by the LA occurs within **20 days** of the First Hearing (by **DAY 26**)	
• whether a **core assessment (appendix F)** exists or should be directed to be undertaken by the LA before the CMC	
• Having regard to the *Practice Direction (Family Proceedings: Court Bundles)* [2000] 1 FLR 536 (**appendix D**), if applicable, give directions to the LA setting out which of the following **case management documents** in addition to the **case management questionnaire (appendix A/2)** are to be filed and served for use at the CMC:	
• a **schedule of findings of fact** which the Court is invited to make (in particular so as to satisfy the threshold criteria)	

Action	Party and Timing
• any update to the **social work chronology (appendix B/2)** that may be required • the **initial care plan (appendix F)** • if there is a question of law; a **skeleton argument with authorities** • a **summary of the background** (only if necessary to supplement the case synopsis) • an **advocate's chronology** (only if necessary to supplement the social work chronology or the case synopsis) • Having regard to **appendix D**, give directions to the LA setting out the form of **bundle or documents index** that the Court requires • Complete the **SDF (appendix A/1)** to record the Court's case management decisions and reasons.	

3.5	**Case Management Questionnaire**	Court Officer · **on DAY 12**

Within **1 day** of the Allocation Hearing (on **DAY 12**) the **court officer** shall serve on each party:

• the completed **SDF** together with a

• **case management questionnaire (appendix A/2)**.

3.6	**Allocation in the High Court**	Court Officer · **on DAY 12**

Where an application is transferred to the High Court, the **court officer** shall within **1 day** of the Allocation Hearing (on **DAY 12**):

• In consultation with the Family Division Liaison Judge (or if the proceedings are transferred to the RCJ, the Clerk of the Rules) allocate a judge of the High Court who shall be the **case management judge** (and who may be the judge who will conduct the final hearing) to case manage the proceedings in accordance with the protocol and the CCP

Action	Party and Timing
• If necessary to accord with the CCP, allocate a **second case management judge** in the Care Centre who shall be responsible to the allocated High Court judge for case management of the proceedings	
• Where possible, identify a judge of the High Court to be the **Final Hearing judge**	

• Attach to the court file the **form C22** issued by the FPC, the **case synopsis (appendix B/1)** and a **SDF (appendix A/1)** and complete the SDF to the extent only of:
  • the names of the **allocated judges**
  • the date of the **CMC** (which shall be within **54 days** of the date of the First Hearing in the FPC ie between **DAYS 15 and 60**)
  • the proposed **Final Hearing** date or window (which shall be not later than in the **3 week** period commencing the **37th WEEK** after the application was issued) Action
  • the proposed date of the **PHR** (which shall be not later than **2 weeks** and no earlier than **8 weeks** before the Final Hearing or window)	

• Inform the case management judge in writing of:
  • any other circumstance of **urgency**
  • any contested hearing for an **ICO**	

• Within **1 day** of receipt of the court file and **completed SDF** from the allocated High Court judge (by **DAY 16**), send to each party a copy of the completed SDF together with a **case management questionnaire (appendix A/2)**	Court Officer **on DAY 16**

3.7	**Allocation Directions in the High Court**	Case Manage-ment Judge **by DAY 15**

Within **3 days** of receipt of the court file (by **DAY 15**) the allocated **case management judge** shall:

• Consider the **case management checklist (appendix A/3)**

• Complete the **SDF (appendix A/1)** having regard to those matters set out at step 3.4

Action	Party and Timing
• Return the court file and the completed SDF to the court officer.	

STEP 4: The Case Management Conference

Target time: between Days 15 and 60

Objective

To consider what case management directions are necessary

— To ensure that a fair hearing of the proceedings takes place
— To timetable the proceedings so that the Final Hearing is completed within or before the recommended hearing window.

	Action	Party and Timing	
4.1	**LA Case Management Documents** In every case the **LA** shall not later than **5 days** before the CMC prepare, paginate, index, file and serve: • The **case management documents** for the CMC that have been directed at the Allocation Hearing/Directions (step 3.4) and • A **case management questionnaire** (**appendix A/2**)	LA	**not later than 5 days before the CMC**
4.2	**The Court Bundle** Not later than **5 days** before the date fixed for the CMC, the **LA** shall: • For hearings to which the *Practice Direction (Family Proceedings: Court Bundles)* [2000] 1 FLR 536 (**appendix D**) applies or in accordance with any direction given at a First Hearing or Allocation Hearing, file with the Court a **bundle** • Serve on each of the represented parties an **index** to the bundle • Serve on any un-represented party a copy indexed bundle • For hearings to which **appendix D does not apply**, serve on all parties an **index** of the documents that have been filed	LA	**not later than 5 days before the CMC**

Action	Party and Timing	

4.3 **Other Party's Case Management Documents**

All Parties except the LA — **not later than 2 days before the CMC**

Not later than **2 days** before the date of the CMC **each party other than the LA** shall:

- File with the court and serve on the parties the following **case management documents**
    - a **position statement** which sets out that party's response to the case management documents filed by the LA indicating the issues that are agreed and those that are not agreed. (A Guardian's position statement on behalf of the child should comment on the LA's arrangements and plans for the child)
    - a completed **case management questionnaire (appendix A/2)**
- **Not** file any **other case management documents** without the prior direction of the Court

4.4 **The Court's Preparation**

Court Officer — **not later than 2 days before the CMC**

Not later than 2 days before the CMC the court officer shall:

- Place the **case management documents of all parties** at the front of the court file and at the front of any bundle that is filed by the LA

- Deliver the court file and bundle to the case management judge who is to conduct the CMC

- Ensure that any arrangements for video and telephone conferencing and with criminal and civil listing officers have been made

4.5 **Advocates Meeting**

Advocates — **on or before the day of the CMC**

Before **the day** fixed for the **CMC** or (where it has not been practicable to have an earlier meeting) not later than **1 hour** before the time fixed for the CMC, the **parties and/or their lawyers** shall:

- Meet to **identify and narrow the issues** in the case

Action	Party and Timing
• Consider the **case management checklist** (appendix A/3)	
• Consider the **case management questionnaires (appendix A/2)**	
• Consider in accordance with the **experts code of guidance (appendix C)** whether and if so why any application is to be made to instruct an **expert**	
• Consider whether full and frank **disclosure** of all relevant documents has taken place	All Parties **on DAY 34**
• Draft a composite **schedule of issues (appendix B/4)** which identifies: • a summary of the issues in the case • a summary of issues for determination at the CMC by reference to the case management questionnaires/case management checklist • the timetable of legal and social work steps proposed • the estimated length of hearing of the PHR and of the Final Hearing • the order which the Court will be invited to make at the CMC	

4.6 Availability

On **the day** of the CMC **the parties** shall complete and file with the Court:

- **witness non-availability form (appendix A/4)**

- A schedule (so far as it is known) of the names and contact details (professional address, telephone, fax, DX and e-mail) of:
  - the lead social worker and team manager
  - the Guardian
  - solicitors and counsel/advocates for each party
  - un-represented litigants
  - any experts upon whose evidence it is proposed to rely

Action	Party and Timing

4.7   Conduct of the CMC

The CMC shall be conducted by one of the allocated case management judges or as directed by the FPC case management legal adviser in accordance with the protocol. It is the essence of the protocol that case management through to Final Hearing must be consistently provided by the same case management judges/legal advisers/FPCs.

All advocates who are retained to have conduct of the final hearing shall:

- Use their best endeavours to attend the CMC and must do so if directed by the Court

- Bring to the CMC details of their own availability for the 12 month period following the CMC

- Attend the advocates meeting before the CMC

4.8   The Hearing   Case Manage-
                                                                    ment Judge

At the CMC the **case management judge/court** shall:

- Consider the parties' composite **schedule of issues (appendix B/4)**

- Consider the **case management checklist (appendix A/3)**

- Consider the parties' **case management questionnaires (appendix A/2)** and **case management documents** (steps 3.4 and 4.3)

- If not already fixed at the First or Allocation Hearing, fix the date of the **Final Hearing** which shall be not later than in the **3 week** period commencing the **37th WEEK** after the application was issued

- If not already fixed, fix the date and time of the **PHR** which shall be not later than **2 weeks** before and no earlier than **8 weeks** before the Final Hearing

Action	Party and Timing
• Give a **time estimate** for each hearing that has been fixed	
Consider whether any hearing can take place using video, telephone or other **electronic means**	
• Consider any outstanding application of which notice has been given to the Court and to the parties in accordance with the rules	
• Give all necessary **case management directions** to:	
• **timetable** all remaining legal and social work steps	
• ensure that full and frank **disclosure** of all relevant documents is complete	
• ensure that a **core assessment** (**appendix F**) or other appropriate assessments materials will be available to the Court	
• ensure that if any **expert** is to be instructed the expert and the parties will complete their work for the Court within the Court's timetable and in accordance with the **experts code of guidance** (**appendix C**)	
• provide for **regular monitoring** of the Court's case management directions to include certification of compliance at each ICO renewal and the notification to the Court by the Guardian and by each responsible party of any material non compliance	
• permit a **further directions hearing** before the allocated case management judge in the event of a change of circumstances or significant non compliance with the directions of the Court	
• update, file and serve such of the **existing case management documents** as are necessary	
• update, file and serve a **court bundle/index** for the PHR and for the final Hearing	
• ensure that the PHR and Final Hearing will be effective	

STEP 5: The Pre-Hearing Review

Target time: by Week 37

Objective

To identify and narrow the remaining issues between the parties and ensure that the Final Hearing is effective.

Action	Party and Timing
5.1 The Court's Preparation The **court officer** shall: • In circumstances where **no PHR direction** has been given, send the court file/bundle to the case management judge during **WEEK 28** with a request for confirmation that no PHR is necessary or for a direction that a PHR be listed • **Notify** the parties of any **PHR direction** given by the case management judge • **List a PHR** where directions have been given by the case management judge (not earlier than **8 weeks** and not later than **2 weeks** before the Final Hearing ie between **WEEKS 29 and 37**) • Not later than **2 days** before the PHR: 　• place the **updated case management documents** directed at the CMC (if any) at the front of the court file and at the front of any bundle that is filed by the LA 　• deliver the court file/bundle to the judge/FPC nominated to conduct the PHR 　• ensure that any arrangements for video and telephone conferencing and with criminal and civil listing officers have been made	Court Officer **from WEEK 28**
5.2 Advocates Meeting In the **week** before the PHR **the advocates** who have conduct of the **Final Hearing** shall:	Advocates **in the week before the PHR**

Action	Party and Timing

• Communicate with each other and if necessary meet to **identify and narrow the issues** to be considered by the Court at the PHR and the Final Hearing
 	
 • Consider the **pre-hearing review checklist (appendix A/5)**
 	
 • **2 days** before the PHR file a composite **schedule of issues (appendix B/4)** which shall set out:
   • a summary of issues in the case
   • a summary of issues for determination at the PHR
   • a draft witness template
   • the revised estimated length of hearing of the Final Hearing
   • whether the proceedings are ready to be heard and if not, what steps need to be taken at the PHR to ensure that the proceedings can be heard on the date fixed for the Final Hearing
   • the order which the Court will be invited to make at the PHR	

5.3	**Case Management Documents** **No case management documents** are to be filed for use at a PHR except: • Any **updated case management documents** directed by the case management judge at the CMC (step 4.8) • The composite **schedule of issues (appendix B/4)** • Documents in support of a **new application**.	Advocates **between WEEKS 29 and 30**

5.4 Conduct of the PHR

The **PHR** (or any directions hearing in the FPC which immediately precedes a Final Hearing) shall be listed before the judge/FPC nominated to conduct the Final Hearing. In exceptional circumstances the Court may in advance approve the release of the PHR but only to one of the allocated case management judges.

The **advocates** who are retained to have conduct of the Final Hearing shall:

Action	Party and Timing

- Use their best endeavours to secure their release from any other professional obligation to enable them to attend the PHR

- Update the case management documents as directed at the CMC

- Attend the advocates meeting.

5.5 The Hearing   Court   **at the PHR**

At the PHR the **Court** shall:

- Consider the **pre-hearing review checklist (appendix A/5)**

- Consider the parties' composite **schedule of issues (appendix B/4)**

- Confirm or give a **revised time estimate** for the Final Hearing

- Confirm the **fixed dates, venues and the nominated judge** for the Final Hearing

- Give such directions as are necessary to **update the existing case management documents** and the Court **bundle/index** having regard to the application of the *Practice Direction (Family Proceedings: Court Bundles)* [2000] 1 FLR 536 (**appendix D**)

- Give such directions as are necessary to ensure that the Final Hearing will be effective

5.6 Dispensing with the PHR   All Parties   **before the PHR**

Where the requirements of an advocates meeting have been complied with and all parties certify (in the composite **schedule of issues**) that:

- The proceedings are ready to be heard

- There has been compliance with the directions of the Court and

- There is agreement by all parties to all of the directions proposed having regard to the **pre-hearing review checklist (appendix A/5)**

Action	Party and Timing
The Court may decide to **dispense with the PHR** or deal with it on paper or by electronic means, including computer, video or telephone conferencing	

STEP 6: The Final Hearing

Target time: by Week 40

Objective

To determine the remaining issues between the parties.

	Action	Party and Timing
6.1	**The Hearing**	Judge/FPC nominated for the Final Hearing
	• The judge or FPC identified in the allocation directions as confirmed at the PHR	
	Where one of the allocated case management judges or an FPC has heard a substantial factual issue or there has been a 'preliminary hearing' to determine findings of fact it is necessary for the same judge/magistrates who conducted the preliminary hearing to conduct the Final Hearing.	
6.2	**Case Management and Practice Direction Documents** Not later than **2 days** before the Final Hearing **the parties** shall: • Prepare, file and serve the **case management documents** for the Final Hearing as directed by the Court at the PHR • Prepare, file and serve the **court bundle or index of court documents** as directed by the Court at the PHR	All Parties **not later than 2 days before the Final Hearing**
6.3	**The Court's Preparation** Not later than 2 days before the Final Hearing the Court officer shall: • Place any **case management documents** at the front of the court file and at the front of any bundle that is filed by the LA	Court Officer **not later than 2 days before the Final Hearing**

Action	Party and Timing

- Deliver the **court file/bundle** to the judge/FPC nominated to conduct the Final Hearing

- Ensure that any arrangements for the reception of evidence by video link and telephone conferencing, interpreters, facilities for disabled persons and special measures for vulnerable or intimidated witnesses have been made

6.4 Orders and Reasons	Court **at the Final Hearing**

At the conclusion of the Final Hearing the **Court** shall:

- Set out the basis/reasons for the orders made or applications refused in a **judgment** and where appropriate in the form of **recitals** to the order or in the case of an FPC in **form C22**

- Annexe to the order the **agreed or approved documents** setting out the threshold criteria and the care plan for the child

- Where the judgment is not in writing give consideration to whether there should be a **transcript** and if so who will obtain and pay for it

6.5 Reserved judgment	Judge **at the end of submissions**

In a complex case a judge (but not an FPC) may decide to reserve judgment and take time for consideration. Where judgment is reserved the Court will endeavour to fix a date for judgment to be given or handed down within **20 days** (4 weeks) of the conclusion of submissions. Advocates may be invited to make oral or written submissions as to consequential orders and directions at the conclusion of submissions or when the draft judgment is released.

6.6 Disclosure	Court **at the end of the Final Hearing**

At the end of every Final Hearing the **Court** shall consider whether to give directions for **disclosure of documents**, for example:

Action	Party and Timing
• In any case where it is proposed that the child should be placed for adoption and so that subsequent adoption proceedings are not delayed, to the LA adoption panel, specialist adoption agency and/or proposed adopters and their legal advisers for use in subsequent adoption proceedings • For any medical or therapeutic purpose • For a claim to be made to the CICA	

APPENDIX A/1:   Standard Directions Form

IN THE HIGH COURT OF JUSTICE
FAMILY DIVISION

COUNTY COURT/FPC

	Case Number

Application of | Local Authority |

Re | Child(ren) |

Standard directions by Case Management Judge/Magistrates/Legal Adviser

Date of this order | |

Upon reading the papers filed by the applicant:

IT IS ORDERED by   **The Honourable**
                            His/Her Honour
                            District Judge
                            Magistrates/Justices Clerk

Allocation Directions

This case is allocated for case management to:

The Honourable
His/Her Honour   and
District Judge
Magistrates/Justices Clerk

Contact Telephone No
(Judge's Clerk/Court Officer/Legal Adviser)

The allocated judge(s) will be responsible for the continuous case management of this case

All future hearings in this case will be conducted by one of the allocated judges and *not* by the urgent applications judge or by any other judge unless on application to one of the allocated judges (if necessary in case of urgency by telephone) the allocated judge releases the case to another judge.
(*Where it is possible to identify the Final Hearing Judge/Magistrates*).

The judge who will be responsible for the PHR and the conduct of the Final Hearing is:

Case Management Conference

There will be a   **The Honourable**
Case Management   **His/Her Honour**
Conference before   **District Judge**
                         Magistrates/Justices Clerk

                         at   venue

                         on the   date

                         at   time

The parties and their lawyers shall consider each of the matters set out at Steps 1 to 4 of the Protocol and in the CMC Checklist.

The parties shall prepare, file and serve **the Evidence and Case Management Documents** listed below. No documents other than those identified shall thereafter be filed with the Court without the Court's permission, unless in support of a new application.

Local Authority Preparation for the CMC

The LOCAL AUTHORITY shall not later than **2pm 5 days before** the date of the Case Management Conference prepare and file with the Court the following:
(Delete as appropriate)

(a) a Bundle prepared in accordance with the [*Practice Direction (Family Proceedings: Court Bundles)* [2000] 1 FLR 536] *[....or   specify the form]*.
The Local Authority shall at the same time serve on each of the Respondents an Index to the Bundle and on any unrepresented party a copy of the bundle;

(b) an Index of the Documents filed with the Court. The Local Authority shall at the same time serve on each of the Respondents a copy of the Index;

(c) the following case management documents *(delete if not required)*:

* A **case management questionnaire**
* A schedule of the **findings of fact** which the Court is to be invited to make (in particular so as to satisfy the threshold criteria)
* Any update to the **social work chronology**
* The **interim care plan**(s)
* A **skeleton argument** limited to legal questions with accompanying authorities.
* A clear and concise **summary of the background** on one page of A4 paper (only where necessary to supplement the Case Synopsis)
* An **advocates** chronology (only where necessary to supplement the Case Synopsis or the social work chronology)

Respondent's Preparation for the CMC

The RESPONDENTS shall not later than **2pm 2 working days before** the date of the Case Management Conference prepare and file with the Court and serve on the Local Authority copies of:

- A statement of evidence in **reply to** the local authorities **initial social work statement** (unless already filed).
- A **case management questionnaire**.
- A **position statement** (setting out what is agreed and what is not agreed).

The Advocates Meeting

The parties lawyers and any un-represented party shall attend an **Advocates Meeting**:

at		venue
on the		date
at		time

to discuss those matters set out at Step 4.5 of the Protocol and shall prepare a composite **schedule of issues** which shall be filed with the Court:

not later than		time
on the		date

in default of the advocates meeting taking place and in any event, the lawyers for all parties and any un-represented party shall attend at Court on the day of the Case Management Conference NOT LATER THAN **1 hour before** the time fixed for the hearing so that they can all meet together to discuss the issues and draft the composite **schedule of issues**.

Experts

Any party that proposes to ask the Court's permission to instruct an **expert witness** shall comply with the **experts code of guidance** and shall set out the required particulars in their case management questionnaire

Availability and Contact Details

The parties' legal representatives shall bring to the advocates meeting and to the CMC:

- Their professional diaries for the next 12 months.
- Details (so far as can be known) of the names and the availability of anybody who it is proposed should conduct any assessment or provide any expert evidence so that a **witness availability form** can be prepared and filed at the CMC.

- Details (so far as can be known) of the names and contact details (professional addresses and telephone / fax / DX / e-mail numbers for) so that a **schedule** can be prepared and filed at the CMC with particulars of:
  - the lead social worker
  - the Children's Guardian
  - the solicitors and counsel/advocates for each party
  - any experts and assessors who have been or may be instructed

Disclosure of Documents

Any outstanding disclosure of relevant documents between the parties shall take place:

by	date

Pre-Hearing Review

There will be a PHR before the Final Hearing Judge:

at	venue
on the	date
at	time
with a time estimate of	time estimate

Final Hearing

The Final Hearing will take place before the Final Hearing Judge

at	venue
on the	date
at	time
with a time estimate of	time estimate

ADDITIONAL DIRECTIONS (if any)

OBSERVATIONS

Signed

Case Management Judge/Magistrates/Justices Clerk

APPENDIX A/2: Case Management Questionnaire

This questionnaire is completed [by][on behalf of],

Note:
Please state your party status.

who is the [ ] [Applicant] [Respondent]
[   ] [other]
in these proceedings.

In the
[Family Proceedings Court]
[District Registry] [County Court]
[Principal Registry of the Family Division]
[The High Court of Justice]

Case Number

Please read the following notes before completing the Case Management Questionnaire.

- **The Local Authority** must file and serve this questionnaire (together with the other case management documents directed at steps 3.4 and 4.1 of the protocol) **not later than 5 days** before the date fixed for the Case Management Conference.

- **All other parties** must file and serve this questionnaire (together with the other case management documents listed at step 4.3 of the protocol) **not later than 2 days** before the date fixed for the Case Management Conference.

- Your answers to the following questions should be given **in summary form only**. However, if you need more space for your answers use a separate sheet of paper. Please put your full name and case number at the top of any additional sheet and mark clearly which question the information refers to. Please ensure that any additional sheets are firmly attached to the questionnaire.

Have you served a copy of the completed questionnaire [and the other documents required by the protocol] on the other [party][parties]?

Yes ☐   No ☐

A. Complexity/Urgency

Are the proceedings complex?   Yes ☐   No ☐

Are there are any urgent features that the Court should know about?   Yes ☐   No ☐

If **'Yes'**, to either question please explain briefly why the proceedings are complex and or what urgent features the Court should be aware of:

```
┌─────────────────────────────────────────────────────────────┐
│                                                             │
│                                                             │
│                                                             │
│                                                             │
│                                                             │
│                                                             │
│                                                             │
│                                                             │
└─────────────────────────────────────────────────────────────┘
```

B. Urgent/Preliminary Hearings

Do you wish there to be an urgent hearing?   Yes ☐   No ☐

Do you wish there to be a preliminary hearing?   Yes ☐   No ☐

If **'Yes'**, to either question please explain briefly why such a hearing is required and what question(s) the Court will be asked to answer at that hearing.

```
┌─────────────────────────────────────────────────────────────┐
│                                                             │
│                                                             │
│                                                             │
│                                                             │
│                                                             │
│                                                             │
│                                                             │
│                                                             │
│                                                             │
│                                                             │
│                                                             │
│                                                             │
└─────────────────────────────────────────────────────────────┘
```

C. Evidence

Part 1 – Witnesses/Reports

Are there any **witness statements** or **clinical reports** upon which you intend to rely?

Yes ☐   No ☐

If 'Yes', please provide the information requested in the box below:

Author	Date of Report:	Nature of Evidence:

Part 2 – Further Assessments/Expert Evidence

Do you propose to ask for a further assessment?   Yes ☐   No ☐

Do you propose to seek permission to use expert evidence?   Yes ☐   No ☐

If you answer 'Yes' to either of the above questions, for each further assessment or expert you propose please give those details required by the Experts Code of Guidance (step 2.3) on a separate sheet and attach it to this questionnaire.

D. Other Evidence including Evidence of Ethnicity, Language, Religion, Culture, Gender and Vulnerability

Is any other evidence needed for example, relating to the ethnicity, language, religion, culture, gender and vulnerability of the child or other significant person?   Yes ☐   No ☐

If 'Yes', please give brief details of the evidence that you propose:

E. Legal and Social Work Timetable

Please give details of the Legal and Social Work timetable that is proposed:

Date Proposed:	Step Proposed:	Party Responsible:

F. Hearing and Reading Time

How long do you think the Case Management Conference will take? ☐ hour(s) ☐ minutes

How long do you think the Pre-Hearing Review will take? ☐ hour(s) ☐ minutes

How long do you think the Final Hearing will take? ☐ day(s) ☐ hour(s)

Give details of the recommended reading list for the Case Management Conference:

G. Proposed Directions

(Parties should agree directions at the Advocates Meeting. A list of proposed directions or orders should be attached to this questionnaire using the standard variable directions forms wherever possible.)

Have you attached a list of the directions (or orders)
you wish the Court to consider at the CMC:

(a) to ensure that the matters set out in the protocol   Yes ☐   No ☐
are complied with; and

(b) that are required for any other purpose, in particular,   Yes ☐   No ☐
compliance with the Experts Code of Guidance (Step 2.4)
and to ensure that disclosure of relevant documents takes place.

H. Other Information

In the space below, set out any other information you consider will help the judge or court to manage this case.

Signed [   ]   date [   ]

[Counsel] [Solicitor] for the
[   ][Applicant] [Respondent] [   ][other]

Please enter your contact name, reference number and full postal address including
(if appropriate) details of DX, fax or e-mail.

Name:	Reference:
Address:	Telephone number:
	Fax number:
	DX number:
	e-mail:

APPENDIX A/3   Case Management Checklist

Objective

The following checklist is to be used for the First Hearing in the FPC, the Allocation Hearing in the care centre, Allocation Directions in the High Court and for the CMC.

Representation of the Child

1   Has CAFCASS been notified of any decision to appoint a ☐
Guardian? If so, has a Guardian been allocated or is the likely
date of allocation known?

2   Are there any other relevant proceedings? If so, was a ☐
Guardian appointed and has CAFCASS been informed of the
nature/number of the other/previous proceedings and the
identity of the Guardian?

3   If a decision has been made to appoint a Guardian but no ☐
allocation has yet taken place by CAFCASS: are any directions
necessary for the representation of the child including the
appointment of a solicitor?

4   Have the parties been notified of the names of the Guardian ☐
and of the solicitor appointed in form C47?

5   Should consideration be given to the separate representation of ☐
the child?

Parties

☐

6   Have all significant persons involved in the child's care been
identified, in particular those persons who are automatically
Respondents to the application? Are any directions required to
ensure service upon a party?

7   Has consideration been given to notifying a father without ☐
parental responsibility and informing other significant adults in
the extended family of the proceedings?

8   Should any other person be joined as a party to the ☐
proceedings (whether upon application or otherwise)? Are any
directions necessary for the service of documents. If so, which
documents?

ICO

9   Are the grounds for making an ICO agreed? Have they been   ☐
recorded on form C22 or in a document approved by the
Court?

10   If the grounds for making an ICO are not agreed has a date   ☐
been fixed for an urgent hearing of the contested interim
application or are the proceedings to be transferred to the Care
Centre?

11   Have all case management directions been given to ensure that   ☐
the contested interim hearing will be effective?

Urgency, Transfer and Re-Transfer

12   Are there any features of particular urgency and if so what   ☐
directions are necessary to provide for that urgency or to
minimise delay eg lateral or upwards transfer?

13   Have any circumstances of complexity, gravity and urgency   ☐
been considered and has any decision to transfer the
proceedings to the Care Centre/High Court been made and
notified to the parties?

14   Have the directions that are set out in the CCP and the FPCP   ☐
been made upon transfer?

15   After transfer, have the circumstances of complexity, gravity   ☐
and urgency that remain been re-considered and is it
appropriate to transfer back to the Care Centre or FPC?

16   In relation to any question of re-transfer, has the availability of   ☐
the Court been ascertained and have the parties been notified?

Protocol Documents

17   **LA Documents on Issue of Application.** Are any directions   ☐
necessary relating to the preparation, filing and service of those
LA documents that are required by the protocol within 2 days
of the proceedings being issued?

18   **Case Synopsis.** Are any directions necessary to ensure that   ☐
the LA or the Child's solicitor prepares, files and serves a case
synopsis?

19   **The Court Bundle/Index.** Are any directions necessary to   ☐
ensure that a court bundle is prepared and filed or that an
index to the Court documents is prepared, filed and served?

20	Have directions been given to update the court bundle/index, in particular the responsibility for, the format of and arrangements for updating (or the compilation of an application bundle) and whether updates can be provided to the Court/judge by e-mail?	☐
21	**Local Authority Case Management Documents.** Are any directions necessary to ensure that the LA case management documents are prepared, filed and served?	☐
22	**Other Party's Case Management Documents.** Are any directions necessary to ensure that the case management documents of other parties are prepared, filed and served?	☐
23	**Case Management Questionnaires.** Are any directions necessary to ensure that the parties prepare, file and serve case management questionnaires?	☐
24	**Recommended Reading List.** For any hearing where no case management questionnaire or schedule of issues will be available, are any directions necessary for the parties to provide the Court with a joint reading list?	☐
25	**Witness Non-Availability Form.** Are any directions necessary to ensure that a witness availability form and schedule of contact details are completed/updated?	☐

Preliminary Directions

26	**Statements of Evidence from Each Party.** Have directions been given for the parties other than the LA to prepare, file and serve evidence in reply to the LA's initial social work statement?	☐
27	**Disclosure.** Have directions been given to ensure that all relevant documents are disclosed by the LA within 20 days of the First Hearing?	☐
28	**Allocation.** Have all allocation directions been given?	☐
29	**Standard Directions Form.** Has the SDF been completed and served?	☐

Listing

| 30 | **CMC.** Has a date and time been fixed for the CMC (between days 15 and 60)? Is the date, time and time estimate recorded on the draft SDF? | ☐ |
| 31 | If a CMC is not to be listed have all case management directions been given for the Final Hearing and are they recorded on the draft SDF? | ☐ |

32   **PHR.** Is a PHR necessary? Is the date, time and time estimate   ☐
        recorded on the draft SDF (not later than 2 weeks and no
        earlier than 8 weeks before the Final Hearing)?

33   If a PHR is not necessary have all case management directions   ☐
        set out in the PHR checklist been considered in giving
        directions for the Final Hearing?

34   **Final Hearing.** Has a date or hearing window been fixed for   ☐
        the Final Hearing (not later than in the 3 weeks commencing
        the 37th week after issue) and are the dates recorded on the
        draft SDF together with the time estimate?

35   **Venue/Technology.** Have directions been given for the   ☐
        venue of each hearing and whether video link, telephone
        conferencing or electronic communication with the Court can
        be used? If so, have arrangements been made for the same?

Evidence

36   **Other Proceedings.** Has consideration been given to the   ☐
        relevance of any other/previous proceedings and as to whether
        the Judgment/Reasons given or evidence filed should be
        admitted into evidence?

37   **Disclosure.** Has the Guardian read the social work files? If   ☐
        not when will that task be complete? Having read the files has
        the Guardian confirmed that either they contain no other
        relevant documents or that an application for specific
        disclosure is necessary?

38   Are there any applications relating to the disclosure of   ☐
        documents?

39   **The Child's Evidence.** Should evidence be prepared, filed   ☐
        and served concerning the child's wishes and feelings?

40   **The Issues.** What are the issues in the case?   ☐

41   Are any directions necessary for the filing of further factual   ☐
        evidence (including clinical evidence of treatment) by any party
        and if so to which issue(s) is such evidence to be directed?

42   Are any directions necessary for any party to respond to the   ☐
        LA's factual evidence and/or to the LA's proposed threshold
        criteria and schedule of findings of fact sought?

43   **LA Core Assessment.** Has a core assessment been   ☐
        completed? If not, are any directions necessary for the
        preparation, service and filing of an assessment?

44	**Additional Assessments and Expert Evidence.** In respect of every question relating to a request for expert evidence, is the request in accordance with the Experts Code of Guidance?	☐
45	What are the issues to which it is proposed expert evidence or further assessment should be directed?	☐
46	Who is to conduct the assessment or undertake the report, what is the expert's discipline, has the expert confirmed availability, what is the timetable for the report, the responsibility for instruction and the likely costs on both an hourly and global basis, what is the proposed responsibility for or apportionment of costs of jointly instructed experts as between the LA and the publicly funded parties (including whether there should be a section 38(6) direction?	☐
47	Are any consequential directions necessary (eg to give permission for examination or interview)?	☐
48	Are any directions necessary to provide the expert with the documents/further documents?	☐
49	Are any directions necessary for the conduct of experts meetings/discussions and the preparation, filing and service of statements of agreement and disagreement?	☐
50	**Ethnicity, Language, Religion and Culture.** Has consideration been given to the ethnicity, language, religion and culture of the child and other significant persons and are any directions necessary to ensure that evidence about the same is available to the Court?	☐

Care Plans and Final Evidence

51	**LA.** Have directions been given for the preparation, filing and service of the final proposals of the LA and in particular its final statements of evidence and care plan?	☐
52	**Other Parties.** Have directions been given for the preparation, filing and service of the parents' and other parties responses to the LA's proposals?	☐
53	**Guardian.** Are any directions necessary for the preparation, filing and service of the Guardian's report?	☐

Other Case Management Steps

54	**Advocates Meetings and Schedules of Issue.** Are any directions necessary to ensure that an advocates meeting takes place and that a composite Schedule of Issues is drafted?	☐
55	**Preliminary/Split Hearing.** Is a finding of fact hearing necessary and if so, what is the discrete issue of fact that is to be determined, by whom and when?	☐
56	**Family Group Conference/ADR.** Has consideration been given to whether a family group conference or alternative dispute resolution can be held and would any directions assist to facilitate the conference resolution?	☐
57	**Twin Track Planning.** Are any directions necessary to ensure that in the appropriate case twin track planning has been considered and where appropriate, directions given in relation to any concurrent freeing for adoption proceedings and for the filing and service of evidence relating to placement options and their feasibility? In particular have dates been fixed for the filing of the parallel plan and in respect of the Adoption/Fostering/Permanent Placement Panel timetable?	☐
58	**Adoption Directions.** Are any directions necessary to ensure that the Adoption Practice Direction is complied with and in particular that any proposed (concurrent) freeing proceedings have been commenced?	☐
59	**Placement.** Are any directions necessary for the filing and service of evidence relating to placement options including extended family placements and their feasibility, information about the timetable for the assessment and planning processes and any proposed referrals to Adoption/Fostering and/or Permanence Panels?	☐
60	**Court's Timetable.** Has a timetable of all legal and social work steps been agreed and is the timetable set out in the Court order or as an approved document annexed to the order?	☐
61	**Monitoring and Compliance.** What directions are necessary to ensure that the Court's timetable and directions are monitored and complied with, in particular have directions been given for the certification of compliance upon ICO renewals and for any further directions or a return to Court in the event of a significant non-compliance?	☐
62	**Change of Circumstance.** What directions are necessary to make provision for the parties to return to court in the event of a significant change of circumstance?	☐

63 **Preparation for Final Hearing.** Is any consideration □
necessary of the case management directions set out in the
PHR checklist in particular:

- Use of interpreters?
- Special Measures for Vulnerable or intimidated
  witnesses?
- Children's evidence or attendance at court?
- Facilities for persons with a disability?
- Evidence or submissions by video or telephone
  conference or on paper or by e-mail?
- Video and audio recordings and transcripts?

APPENDIX A/4:   Witness Non-availability

This questionnaire is completed [by][on behalf of],

<table>
<tr><td></td><td></td></tr>
</table>

Note:
Please state
your party
status.

who is the [ ] [Applicant] [Respondent]
[   ] [other]
in these proceedings. ·

In the
[Family Proceedings Court]
[District Registry] [County Court]
[Principal Registry of the Family Division]
[The High Court of Justice]

Case Number

Sheet No.   of

**Note: This form may be used for a maximum of six witnesses. If you intend to ask for
more than six witnesses to give evidence on your behalf, please continue on a second
sheet. You should indicate how many sheets you have used by completing the box above.**

Date of Final Hearing (where known)

Location of Final Hearing (where known)

Witness Details:

Witness Number: Witness Name: Description:

1.
2
3.
4.
5.
6.

Completion of the Non-Availability Grid:

NOTE:
Mark dates when Experts and other witnesses are <u>NOT</u> available. Codes for use in the grid are as follows: H = Holiday, C = Course, S = Sickness or medical appointment, T = Attendance at another trial/hearing, O = Other

The person signing this form must be fully familiar with all the details of non-availability given on the Grid overleaf. If there are other issues the Court should be aware of concerning witness availability please state these below:

Signed: [   ]   Date: [   ]

    [Counsel] [Solicitor] for the
    [   ] [Applicant] [Respondent] [   ]

Date	MONTH				
	Witness Number				
1					
2					
3					
4					
5					
6					
7					
8					
9					
10					
11					
12					
13					
14					
15					
16					
17					
18					
19					
20					
21					
22					
23					
24					
25					
26					
27					
28					
28					
29					
30					
31					

Date	MONTH				
	Witness Number				
1					
2					
3					
4					
5					
6					
7					
8					
9					
10					
11					
12					
13					
14					
15					
16					
17					
18					
19					
20					
21					
22					
23					
24					
25					
26					
27					
28					
28					
29					
30					
31					

Date	MONTH				
	Witness Number				
1					
2					
3					
4					
5					
6					
7					
8					
9					
10					
11					
12					
13					
14					
15					
16					
17					
18					
19					
20					
21					
22					
23					
24					
25					
26					
27					
28					
28					
29					
30					
31					

Date	MONTH				
	Witness Number				
1					
2					
3					
4					
5					
6					
7					
8					
9					
10					
11					
12					
13					
14					
15					
16					
17					
18					
19					
20					
21					
22					
23					
24					
25					
26					
27					
28					
28					
29					
30					
31					

Date	MONTH				
	Witness Number				
1					
2					
3					
4					
5					
6					
7					
8					
9					
10					
11					
12					
13					
14					
15					
16					
17					
18					
19					
20					
21					
22					
23					
24					
25					
26					
27					
28					
28					
29					
30					
31					

Date	MONTH				
	Witness Number				
1					
2					
3					
4					
5					
6					
7					
8					
9					
10					
11					
12					
13					
14					
15					
16					
17					
18					
19					
20					
21					
22					
23					
24					
25					
26					
27					
28					
28					
29					
30					
31					

APPENDIX A/5   PHR Checklist

Objective

The following checklist is to be used for the Pre-Hearing Review.

1	Have the protocol and other practice direction steps been complied with?	☐
2	Have each of the directions given at the CMC and any subsequent hearing been complied with?	☐
3	Have the issues to be determined at the Final Hearing been identified and recorded in the draft PHR order?	☐
4	Which witnesses are to be called, by whom and in relation to what issue(s)?	☐
5	Are any experts required to give oral evidence, if so why and in relation to what issue(s)?	☐
6	What is the extent of the examination in chief and cross-examination of each witness that is proposed?	☐
7	Has a witness template been completed and agreed?	☐
8	What, if any, of the written evidence is agreed or not in issue (and accordingly is to be read by the Court on that basis)?	☐
9	Are interpretation facilities necessary and if so have they been directed and/or arranged (Note the special arrangements to be made for deaf signing)?	☐
10	Are any facilities needed for a party or witness with a disability? If so have arrangements been made?	☐
11	Are any special measures or security measures applied for in relation to vulnerable or intimidated witnesses including, for example, live video link, screens or witness support? If so what are the arrangements, if any, that are directed to be made?	☐
12	Is it intended that the child will attend to see the judge and/or give evidence at the Final Hearing and have the arrangements been agreed and made?	☐
13	Is any evidence is to be taken indirectly by live video link eg for an expert or witness who is overseas or otherwise unable to attend Court. If so have the arrangements been made?	☐

14 Are any video or audio recordings to be used and if so: ☐

    (a)   have the relevant excerpts of the recordings been agreed?
    (b)   have agreed transcripts been obtained and?
    (c)   have the arrangements been made to view/listen to the
        recordings?

---

15 Are there questions of law to be determined, and if so when ☐
should the submissions be heard and what provision should be
made for the consideration of the authorities and skeleton
arguments that will be required?

---

16 Is there a recommended reading list for the Court? ☐

---

17 What is the timetable for the final hearing including opening ☐
and closing submissions and judgment/reasons?

---

18 What is the estimated length of the Final Hearing? ☐

---

19 Who is/are the judge/magistrates nominated to conduct the ☐
Final Hearing?

---

20 Where is the venue for the Final Hearing? ☐

---

21 Does the *Practice Direction (Family Proceedings: Court Bundles)* ☐
[2000] 1 FLR 536 apply to the Final Hearing and/or are any
other case management documents to be updated, prepared,
filed and served by the parties and if so: by whom and when?

---

22 Are the proceedings ready for Final Hearing and have all steps ☐
and directions been complied with so that the PHR can be
dispensed with or considered by the Court in the absence of
the parties?

APPENDIX B   Standard Documents

Objective

The following documents are identified in the Protocol and their contents are prescribed below.

1   **Case Synopsis** shall contain such of the following information as is known in summary form for use at the Allocation Hearing and shall normally be limited to 2 sides of A4:

- The identities of the parties and other significant persons
- The applications that are before the Court
- A very brief summary of the precipitating incident(s) and background circumstances
- Any particular issue that requires a direction to be given at the Allocation Hearing (eg relating to a social services core assessment)
- Any intention to apply to transfer the proceedings to the High Court
- The parties interim proposals in relation to placement and contact
- The estimated length of the Allocation Hearing (to include a separate estimate relating to a contested ICO where relevant)
- A recommended reading list and a suggested reading time for the Allocation Hearing
- Advance notice of any other decisions or proceedings that may be relevant, to include: criminal prosecutions, family law proceedings, disciplinary, immigration and mental health adjudications

---

2   **Social Work Chronology** is a schedule containing a succinct summary of the significant dates and events in the child's life in chronological order. It is a running record ie it is to be updated during the proceedings. The schedule headings are:

- serial number
- date
- event-detail
- witness or document reference (where applicable)

---

3   **Initial Social Work Statement**. The initial social work statement filed
     by the LA within 2 days of the issue of an application is strictly limited
     to the following evidence:

-    The precipitating incident(s) and background circumstances
     relevant to the grounds and reasons for making the application
     including a brief description of any referral and assessment
     processes that have already occurred
-    Any facts and matters that are within the social worker's
     personal knowledge
-    Any emergency steps and previous court orders that are relevant
     to the application
-    Any decisions made by the LA that are relevant to the
     application
-    Information relevant to the ethnicity, language, religion, culture,
     gender and vulnerability of the child and other significant
     persons in the form of a 'family profile' together with a narrative
     description and details of the social care services that are relevant
     to the same
-    Where the LA is applying for an ICO and/or is proposing to
     remove or seeking to continue the removal of a child under
     emergency protection: the LA's initial proposals for the child
     including placement, contact with parents and other significant
     persons and the social care services that are proposed
-    The LA's initial proposals for the further assessment of the
     parties during the proceedings including twin track planning
-    The social work timetable, tasks and responsibilities so far as
     they are known.

4   **Schedule of Issues**. The composite schedule of issues produced by
     the advocates at the end of the advocates' meetings prior to the CMC
     and the PHR should be agreed so far as is possible and where not
     agreed should set out the differing positions as to the following:

-    A summary of the issues in the case (including any diverse
     cultural or religious contexts)
-    A summary of issues for determination of the CMC/PHR by
     reference to the questionnaires/checklists
-    For the CMC: the timetable of legal and social work steps
     proposed
-    The estimated length of hearing of the PHR and the Final
     Hearing
-    For the PHR: whether the Final Hearing is ready to be heard and
     if not, what steps need to be taken
-    The order which the Court will be invited to make at the
     CMC/PHR

APPENDIX C   Code of Guidance for Expert Witnesses in Family Proceedings

Objective

The objective of this Code of Guidance is to provide the court with early information to enable it to determine whether it is necessary and/or practicable to ask an expert to assist the court:

- To identify, narrow and where possible agree the issues between the parties
- To provide an opinion about a question that is not within the skill and experience of the court
- To encourage the early identification of questions that need to be answered by an expert
- To encourage disclosure of full and frank information between the parties, the court and any expert instructed.

Action	Party and Timing
1 The Duties of Experts	
1.1 Overriding Duty: An **expert in family proceedings has an overriding duty to** the Court that takes precedence over any obligation to the person from whom he has received instructions or by whom he is paid.	
1.2 Particular Duties: Among any other duties an expert may have, **an expert shall** have regard to the following duties: • To assist the Court in accordance with the overriding duty • To provide an opinion that is independent of the party or parties instructing the expert • To confine an opinion to matters material to the issues between the parties and in relation only to questions that are within the expert's expertise (skill and experience). If a question is put which falls outside that expertise the expert must say so	

Action	Party and Timing	
• In expressing an opinion take into consideration all of the material facts including any relevant factors arising from diverse cultural or religious contexts at the time the opinion is expressed, indicating the facts, literature and any other material that the expert has relied upon in forming an opinion • To indicate whether the opinion is provisional (or qualified, as the case may be) and the reason for the qualification, identifying what further information is required to give an opinion without qualification • Inform those instructing the expert without delay of any change in the opinion and the reason for the change		

Action	Party and Timing	
2 Preparation for the CMC **2.1 Preliminary Enquiries of the Expert**: Not later than 10 days before the CMC the solicitor for the party proposing to instruct the expert (or lead solicitor/solicitor for the child if the instruction proposed is joint) shall approach the expert with the following information: • The nature of the proceedings and the issues likely to require determination by the Court; • The questions about which the expert is to be asked to give an opinion (including any diverse cultural or religious contexts) • When the Court is to be asked to give permission for the instruction (if unusually permission has already been given the date and details of that permission) • Whether permission is asked of the Court for the instruction of another expert in the same or any related field (ie to give an opinion on the same or related questions) • The volume of reading which the expert will need to undertake • Whether or not (in an appropriate case) permission has been applied for or given for the expert to examine the child • Whether or not (in an appropriate case) it will be necessary for the expert to conduct interviews (and if so with whom) • The likely timetable of legal and social work steps • When the expert's opinion is likely to be required	Solicitor instructing the expert	**10 days before the CMC**

Action	Party and Timing
• Whether and if so what date has been fixed by the Court for any hearing at which the expert may be required to give evidence (in particular the Final Hearing).	

Action	Party and Timing
2.2 **Expert's Response:** Not later than 5 days before the CMC the solicitors intending to instruct the expert shall obtain the following information from the expert: • That the work required is within the expert's expertise • That the expert is available to do the relevant work within the suggested time scale • When the expert is available to give evidence, the dates and/or times to avoid, and, where a hearing date has not been fixed, the amount of notice the expert will require to make arrangements to come to Court without undue disruption to their normal clinical routines. • The cost, including hourly and global rates, and likely hours to be spent, of attending at experts/professionals meetings, attending court and writing the report (to include any examinations and interviews).	Solicitor instructing the expert **5 days before the CMC**

Action	Party and Timing
2.3 **Case Management Questionnaire:** **Any party** who proposes to ask the Court for permission to instruct an expert shall not later than 2 days before the CMC (or any hearing at which the application is to be made) file and serve a case management questionnaire setting out the proposal to instruct the expert in the following detail: • The name, discipline, qualifications and expertise of the expert (by way of CV where possible) • The expert's availability to undertake the work • The relevance of the expert evidence sought to be adduced to the issues in the proceedings and the specific questions upon which it is proposed the expert should give an opinion (including the relevance of any diverse cultural or religious contexts) • The timetable for the report • The responsibility for instruction	The Party proposing to instruct the expert **not later than 2 days before the CMC**

Action		Party and Timing
	• Whether or not the expert evidence can properly be obtained by the joint instruction of the expert by two or more of the parties.	
	• Whether the expert evidence can properly be obtained by only one party (eg on behalf of the child)	
	• Whether it is necessary for more than one expert in the same discipline to be instructed by more than one party	
	• Why the expert evidence proposed cannot be given by social services undertaking a core assessment or by the Guardian in accordance with their different statutory duties	
	• The likely cost of the report on both an hourly and global basis.	
	• The proposed apportionment of costs of jointly instructed experts as between the Local Authority and the publicly funded parties.	
2.4	**Draft Order for the CMC:** **Any party** proposing to instruct an **expert** shall in the draft order submitted at the CMC request the Court to give directions (among any others) as to the following:	Any Party **not later than 2 days before the CMC**
	• The party who is to be responsible for drafting the letter of instruction and providing the documents to the expert	
	• The issues identified by the Court and the questions about which the expert is to give an opinion	
	• The timetable within which the report is to be prepared, filed and served	
	• The disclosure of the report to the parties and to any other expert	
	• The conduct of an experts' discussion	
	• The preparation of a statement of agreement and disagreement by the experts following an experts discussion	
	• The attendance of the expert at the Final Hearing unless agreement is reached at or before the PHR about the opinions given by the expert.	

Action		Party and Timing	
3	**Letter of Instruction**	Solicitor instructing the expert	**within 5 days of the CMC**
3.1	**The solicitor instructing the expert** shall within 5 days of the CMC prepare (agree with the other parties where appropriate) file and serve a letter of instruction to the expert which shall:		

- Set out the context in which the expert's opinion is sought (including any diverse ethnic, cultural, religious or linguistic contexts)
- Define carefully the specific questions the expert is required to answer ensuring
  - **that they are within the ambit of the expert's area of expertise and**
  - **that they do not contain unnecessary or irrelevant detail**
  - **that the questions addressed to the expert are kept to a manageable number and are clear, focused and direct**
  - **that the questions reflect what the expert has been requested to do by the Court**
- List the documentation provided or provide for the expert an indexed and paginated bundle which shall include:
  - **a copy of the order (or those parts of the order) which gives permission for the instruction of the expert immediately the order becomes available**
  - **an agreed list of essential reading**
  - **all new documentation when it is filed and regular updates to the list of documents provided or to the index to the paginated bundle**
  - **a copy of this code of guidance and of the protocol**
- Identify the relevant lay and professional people concerned with the proceedings (eg the treating clinicians) and inform the expert of his/her right to talk to the other professionals provided an accurate record is made of the discussion
- Identify any other expert instructed in the proceedings and advise the expert of his/her right to talk to the other experts provided an accurate record is made of the discussion

Action	Party and Timing
• Define the contractual basis upon which the expert is retained and in particular the funding mechanism including how much the expert will be paid (an hourly rate and overall estimate should already have been obtained) when the expert will be paid, and what limitation there might be on the amount the expert can charge for the work which he/she will have to do. There should also be a brief explanation of the 'detailed assessment process' in cases proceeding in the Care Centre or the High Court which are not subject to a high cost case contract • In default of agreement the format of the letter of instruction shall be determined by the Court, which may determine the issue upon written application with representations from each party.	

4 **The Expert's Report**	The Expert **in accordance with the Court's timetable**
4.1 **Content of the Report:**	

The expert's report shall be addressed to the Court and shall:

- Give details of the expert's qualifications and experience
- Contain a statement setting out the substance of all material instructions (whether written or oral) summarising the facts stated and instructions given to the expert which are material to the conclusions and opinions expressed in the report
- Give details of any literature or other research material upon which the expert has relied in giving an opinion
- State who carried out any test, examination or interview which the expert has used for the report and whether or not the test, examination or interview has been carried out under the expert's supervision.
- Give details of the qualifications of any person who carried out the test, examination or interview
- Where there is a range of opinion on the question to be answered by the expert:
  - summarise the range of opinion and
  - give reasons for the opinion expressed

	Action	Party and Timing
	• Contain a summary of the expert's conclusions and opinions • Contain a statement that the expert understands his duty to the Court and has complied with that duty • Where appropriate be verified by a statement of truth.	

4.2	**Supplementary Questions:** Any party wishing to ask supplementary questions of an expert for the purpose of clarifying the expert's report must put those questions in writing to the parties not later than 5 days after receipt of the report. Only those questions that are agreed by the parties or in default of agreement approved by the Court may be put to the expert The Court may determine the issue upon written application with representations from each party.	Any party	**within 5 days of the receipt of the report**

5	**Experts Discussion (Meeting)**	The Court	**at the CMC**
5.1	**Purpose:** The Court will give directions for the experts to meet or communicate: • To identify and narrow the issues in the case. • To reach agreement on the expert questions • To identify the reasons for disagreement on any expert question and to identify what if any action needs to be taken to resolve any outstanding disagreement/question • To obtain elucidation or amplification of relevant evidence in order to assist the Court to determine the issues • To limit, wherever possible, the need for experts to attend Court to give oral evidence.		
5.2	**The Arrangements for a Discussion/Meeting: In accordance with the directions given by** the Court **at the CMC**, the solicitor for the child or such other professional who is given the responsibility by the Court shall make arrangements for there to be a discussion between the experts within 10 days of the filing of the experts reports. The following matters should be considered:	Child's Solicitor	**within 10 days of the filing of the experts' reports**

Action	Party and Timing
• Where permission has been given for the instruction of experts from different disciplines a global discussion may be held relating to those questions that concern all or most of them.	
• Separate discussions may have to be held among experts from the same or related disciplines but care should be taken to ensure that the discussions complement each other so that related questions are discussed by all relevant experts	
• 7 days prior to a discussion or meeting the solicitor for the child or other nominated professional should formulate an agenda to include a list of the questions for consideration. This may usefully take the form of a list of questions to be circulated among the other parties in advance. The agenda should comprise all questions that each party wishes the experts to consider. The agenda and list of questions should be sent to each of the experts not later than 2 days before the discussion	
• The discussion should usually be chaired by the child's solicitor or in exceptional cases where the parties have applied to the Court at the CMC, by an independent professional identified by the parties or the Court. In complex medical cases it may be necessary for the discussion to be jointly chaired by an expert. A minute must be taken of the questions answered by the experts, and a Statement of Agreement and Disagreement must be prepared which should be agreed and signed by each of the experts who participated in the discussion. The statement should be served and filed not later than 5 days after the discussion has taken place	
• Consideration should be given in each case to whether some or all of the experts participate by telephone conference or video link to ensure that minimum disruption is caused to clinical schedules.	

5.3	**Positions of the Parties:** Where any party refuses to be bound by an agreement that has been reached at an experts' discussion that party must inform the Court at or before the PHR of the reasons for refusing to accept the agreement.	Any Party **at the PHR**

Action	Party and Timing
5.4 **Professionals Meetings:** In proceedings where the Court gives a direction that a professionals meeting shall take place between the Local Authority and any relevant named professionals for the purpose of providing assistance to the Local Authority in the formulation of plans and proposals for the child, the meeting shall be arranged, chaired and minuted in accordance with directions given by the Court.	
6 **Arranging for the Expert to attend Court**	Every Party **by the** responsible **PHR**
6.1 **Preparation:** The party who is responsible for the instruction of an expert witness shall ensure: • That a date and time is fixed for the Court to hear the expert's evidence that is if possible convenient to the expert and that the fixture is made substantially in advance of the Final Hearing and no later than at the PHR (ie no later than 2 weeks before the Final Hearing) • That if the expert's oral evidence is not required the expert is notified as soon as possible • That the witness template accurately indicates how long the expert is likely to be giving evidence, in order to avoid the inconvenience of the expert being delayed at Court.	for the instruction of an expert
6.2 **All parties shall ensure:** • That where expert witnesses are to be called the advocates attending the PHR have identified at the advocates meeting the issues which the experts are to address • That wherever possible a logical sequence to the evidence is arranged with experts of the same discipline giving evidence on the same day(s) • That at the PHR the Court is informed of any circumstance where all experts agree but a party nevertheless does not accept the agreed opinion so that directions can be given for the proper consideration of the experts' evidence and the parties reasons for not accepting the same • That in the exceptional case the Court is informed of the need for a witness summons.	All Parties **at the PHR**

	Action	Party and Timing
7	**Post Hearing Action**	Solicitor **within 10**
		instructing **days of the**
7.1	Within 10 days of the Final Hearing the solicitor	the expert **Final**
	instructing the expert should provide feedback	**Hearing**
	to the expert by way of a letter informing the	
	expert of the outcome of the case, and the use	
	made by the Court of the expert's opinion.	
	Where the Court directs that a copy of the	
	transcript can be sent to the expert, the solicitor	
	instructing the expert should obtain the	
	transcript within 10 days of the Final Hearing.	

APPENDIX D   Practice Direction (Family Proceedings: Court Bundles)

[Editorial note: This Practice Direction is reproduced as *President's Direction (Family Proceedings: Court Bundles) (10 March 2000)* at **6.10** below.]

APPENDIX E/1   The Care Centre Plan

Objective

To implement the Protocol (without modification) on a local basis and to ensure that in each care centre judicial and administrative resources are deployed in order to achieve the highest practical level of continuity of judicial case management and the earliest possible resolution of cases.

---

1   **Responsibility for the Preparation and Operation of the CCP:**
The Designated Family Judge (DFJ) in each Care Centre shall be responsible for the preparation and operation of the CCP

---

2   **Consultees:** When preparing the CCP the DFJ shall consult fully with each of the Circuit and District Judges nominated to do Public Law work at the Care Centre as well as with:

- The Court Service
- All relevant Family Proceedings Courts (FPCs)
- CAFCASS
- All relevant Local Authorities
- Other local professional bodies

---

3   **Contents of the CCP:** The CCP shall provide for the following:

(a)   The arrangements for transfer and retransfer of cases between the FPCs and the Care Centre and the job title and contact particulars of the person responsible for administering transfers at each court

(b) How and when cases will be allocated to one and not more than two case management judges (one of whom may be and where possible should be the judge who will conduct the Final Hearing) to case manage the proceedings in accordance with the protocol and the CCP

(c) Where two judges are allocated, for the division of work between them

(d) Where the case management judge or judges are not able to be the Final Hearing judge, how and when the Final Hearing judge for the case is to be identified

(e) Wherever possible, for the release of the allocated judges from other business to hear applications and the arrangements for the case to follow the allocated judge or to be heard by telephone conferencing or video link.

(f) Where, exceptionally, no allocated judge is available to hear an application, for the referral of the proceedings to one of the allocated judges or the DFJ before it is listed before another judge

(g) The identity of the DFJ, the judges to whom cases may be allocated for case management and the other Nominated Circuit Judges and Nominated District Judges at the Care Centre (All judges of the Family Division of the High Court are available to act as case management judges)

(h) The local agreement with each MCC as to the directions to be given by FPCs on the transfer of cases to the Care Centre

(i) The local arrangements for joint directions in cases where there are concurrent relevant criminal proceedings

(j) The arrangements in the Care Centre for the allocation of the judiciary to conduct Public Law Children Act cases

(k) The arrangements for the monitoring by the local Family Court Business Committee of the implementation of the protocol and the CCP

(l) The arrangements for active liaison between the Care Centre and the FPCs

4 **Authorisation of the Care Centre Plan:** Each CCP shall be subject to the final approval of the Family Division Liaison Judge (FDLJ) of the relevant Circuit before implementation.

5 **Timetable for Preparation and Lodging of the CCP:** The first CCP for each Care Centre shall be submitted to the FDLJ by the DFJ by the 1st October 2003. The CCP as approved by the FDLJ shall be lodged at the office of the President of the Family Division by the 31st October 2003.

6 **Review and Amendment of the CCP:** Not later than 1st October 2004 the first CCP shall be reviewed in the same way as it was prepared. Thereafter the CCP shall be reviewed in the same way every 2 years unless the DFJ determines that it is necessary to do so earlier or the President or the FDLJ so direct. Revised or updated plans shall be lodged at the President's office within 10 days of their approval by the FDLJ.

APPENDIX E/2   The Family Proceedings Court Plan

Objective

To implement the protocol (without modification) on a local basis and to ensure that in each FPC and administrative centre resources are deployed in order to achieve the highest practical level of continuity of case management and the earliest possible resolution of cases.

1   **Responsibility for the Preparation and Operation of the FPCP:** The Justices' Chief Executive (JCE) for each Magistrates Courts Committee (MCC) area shall be responsible for arranging for the preparation and administrative operation of the Family Proceedings Court Plan (FPCP).

2   **Consultees:** When preparing the FPCP the JCE should consult fully with each of the Chairs of the Family Panels, the District Judges (Magistrates Courts) nominated to do Public Law cases in the MCC area and the Justices Clerk(s) as well as with:

- The Court Service
- CAFCASS
- All relevant Local Authorities
- Other local professional bodies.

3   **Contents of the FPCP:** The FPCP shall provide for the following:

(a)   The arrangements for transfer and retransfer of cases between the FPCs and between FPCs and the Care Centre and the job title and contact particulars of the court officers responsible for administering transfers at each court

(b)   The local arrangements with the Care Centre as to the directions to be given by FPCs on the transfer of cases to the Care Centre

(c)   The best practical arrangements to maximise effective and continuous case management. Where practicable within existing resources, this could include allocation to no more than 2 legal advisers and to no more than 6 identified magistrates (or 2 DJs(MC)); or to a team of specialist family legal advisers. If possible, however, the objective of continuous case management by allocation of each case to a single legal adviser and to a single bench for case management and Final Hearing should be pursued.

(d)   Arrangements for active liaison between the FPCs and the Care Centre.

4   **Authorisation of the FPC Plan:** The FPCP for each MCC shall be subject to the final approval of the JCE after consultation with the relevant Designated Family Judge(s) (DFJ) and the Family Division Liaison Judge (FDLJ) of the relevant Circuit before implementation.

5   **Timetable for Preparation and Lodging of the FPCP:** The first FPCP for each MCC area should be returned to the FDLJ by the JCE by the 1st October 2003. The FPCP should be lodged at the office of the President of the Family Division by the 31st October 2003.

6   **Review and Amendment of the FPCP:** Not later than the 1st April 2004 the first FPCP shall be reviewed in the same way as it was prepared. Thereafter the FPCP shall be reviewed in the same way every year unless the JCE determines that it is necessary to do so earlier (in consultation with the FDLJ). Revised or updated plans shall be lodged at the President's office within 28 days of their submission to the FDLJ.

APPENDIX F   Social Services Assessment and Care Planning Aide-Memoire

Days

The reference in this appendix to 'Days' is independent of the 'Days' referred to in The 6 Steps.

	Recommended Guidance	Recommended timetable
1	**Referral** A referral to a Council with Social Services Responsibilities (CSSR) in England and a Local Authority in Wales (ie a request for services including child protection) triggers the following Government guidance:	**On DAY 1**
2	**Initial Decision** Within 1 working day of a referral social services should make a decision about what response is required including a decision to take no action or to undertake an initial assessment. The parents or carers (the family), where appropriate, the child and (unless inappropriate) the referrer should be informed of the initial decision and its reasons by social services	**On DAY 2**
3	**Initial Assessment** An initial assessment (if undertaken) should be completed by social services within a maximum of 7 working days of the date of the referral (ie 6 working days from the date of the decision about how to respond to a referral)	**By DAY 7**
4	As part of an initial assessment social services should: • Obtain and collate information and reports from other agencies • Interview family members and the child • In any event, see the child	
5	At the conclusion of an initial assessment social services will make a decision about whether the child is a child in need and about further action including whether to undertake a core assessment. It will inform the family, the child and other relevant agencies of the decision and its reasons. Social services will record the response of each person and agency consulted	

	Recommended Guidance	**Recommended timetable**
6	**Initial Assessment Record** Social services will make and keep a record of the initial assessment and decision making process. The Department of Health (DH) and Welsh Assembly Government (WAG) publish an 'Initial Assessment Record' for this purpose.	
7	**Child in Need Plan** Where social services decide that the child is a child in need they will make a plan which sets out the services to be provided to meet the child's needs.	
8	**Strategy Discussion/Record** Where social services has evidence that the child is suspected to be suffering or is likely to suffer significant harm it should ensure that an inter agency strategy discussion takes place to decide whether to initiate an enquiry under section 47 of the Children Act. This should also result in the child in need plan being updated. A record of the strategy discussion will be made.	
9	**Achieving Best Evidence in Criminal Proceedings** Where a child is the victim of or witness to a suspected crime the strategy discussion shall include a discussion about how any interviews are to be conducted with the child. These may be as part of a police investigation and /or a section 47 enquiry initiated by social services, These interviews should be undertaken in accordance with Government guidance 'Achieving Best Evidence in Criminal Proceedings'.	
10	**Complex Child Abuse Investigations** Where a complex child abuse investigation has been initiated by social services or the police there will be inter agency strategy discussions to make recommendations relating to the planning, co-ordination and management of the investigation and assessment processes in accordance with the guidance given in 'Working Together', 'Complex Child Abuse Investigations: Inter Agency Issues' (England only - to be published in Wales, Summer 2003)	

	Recommended Guidance	**Recommended timetable**
11	**Section 47 Enquiries** If during a strategy discussion it is decided that there is reasonable cause to suspect that the child is suffering or is likely to suffer significant harm, section 47 enquiries will be initiated by social services. This means that a core assessment will be commenced under section 47 of the Children Act 1989. It should be completed within 35 working days of the completion of the initial assessment or the strategy discussion at which it was decided to initiate section 47 enquiries.	**By DAY 42 or within 35 days of the last strategy discussion**
12	**Core Assessment** Where social services decides to undertake a core assessment it should be completed within 35 working days of the initial assessment or the date of the subsequent strategy discussion A timetable for completion of specialist assessments should be agreed with social services	**By DAY 42 or within 35 days of the last strategy discussion**
13	At the conclusion of a core assessment social services should consult with the family, the child and all relevant agencies before making decisions about the plan for the child. Social Services will record the response of each person and agency consulted.	
14	**Core Assessment Record** Social services will make and keep a record of the core assessment and decision making process. The DH and WAG publish a 'Core Assessment Record' for this purpose.	
15	**Child Protection Conferences** Where social services undertakes section 47 enquiries and it is concluded that a child is at continuing risk of suffering or is likely to suffer significant harm, social services will consider whether to convene a child protection conference. A child protection conference determines whether the child is at continuing risk of significant harm and therefore requires a child protection plan to be put in place when determining whether to place the child's name on the child protection register. It agrees an outline child protection plan. An initial child protection working days of the last strategy discussion	**By DAY 22 or within 15 days of the end of the last strategy discussion**

Recommended Guidance	Recommended timetable
(ie by day 22) in accordance with the Government guidance given in 'Working Together to Safeguard Children: a guide to inter-agency working to safeguard and promote the welfare of children'	

16 **Decision to Apply for a Care Order** At the conclusion of the core assessment which may have been undertaken under section 47 of the Children Act and where no earlier decision has been made social services should decide whether to apply for a statutory order and should be able to identify by reference to the conclusions in the core assessment

- The needs of the child (including for protection),
- The services that will be provided,
- The role of other professionals and agencies,
- Whether additional specialist assessments are to be undertaken,
- The timetable and
- The responsibilities of those involved.

17 **Plans** At the conclusion of a core assessment social services will prepare one or more of the following plans:

- A children in need plan
- A child protection plan for a child whose name is on the child protection register
- A care plan (where the child is a looked after child)

The DH and WAG publish formats and/or guidance for each of these plans.

18 **Interim Care Plans** Where social services decide to make an application to the Court it will be necessary to satisfy the Court that an order would be better for the child than making no order at all. An interim care plan should be prepared, filed and served so as to be available to the Court for the CMC in accordance with steps 3.4 and 4.1 of the protocol.

Recommended Guidance	Recommended timetable
19 In cases where no core assessment has been undertaken (eg because the interim care order had to be taken quickly before one could be begun/completed) it should be begun/completed as soon as possible. The interim care plan should be developed from the initial assessment information	

20 **Care Plans** Care Plans should be written so as to comply with the Government guidance given in **LAC(99) 29** in England and *Care Plans and Care Proceedings under the CA 1989* **NAFWC 1/2000** in Wales. While interim care plans will necessarily be in outline and contain less comprehensive information, the plan should include details of the following:
 	
 • The aim of the plan and a summary of the social work timetable
 • A summary of the child's needs and how these are to be met including
  • placement
  • contact with family and other significant persons
  • education, healthcare and social care services
  • the role of parents and other significant persons
  • the views of others
 • Implementation and management of the plan	

21 **Emergency Protection** Where at any time there is reasonable cause to believe that a child is suffering or is likely to suffer significant harm, an application for a child assessment order or an emergency protection order may be made (among others) by social services. The child may be removed or remain in a safe place under police powers of protection. In each case agency and/or court records of the application and reasons will exist.	

	Recommended Guidance	Recommended timetable
22	**Adoption** Government guidance is given on the assessment and decision making process relating to adoption in England in **LAC (2001) 33** which from the 1st April 2003 incorporates the 'National Adoption Standards for England'. The processes and timescales of assessment and decision making for a child for whom adoption is identified as an option are set out in detail in the Standards.	

APPENDIX G: Section 37 Request

Target time: by Day 40

Objective

To provide a recommended procedure within the existing rules for the timely determination of s 37 requests by the court.

	Action	Party and Timing
1	**The Test** Where, in any family proceedings in which a question arises with respect to the welfare of any child, it appears to the Court that it may be appropriate for a care or supervision order to be made with respect to the child, the **Court** may direct the appropriate local authority (LA) to undertake an investigation of the child's circumstances.	Court **on DAY 1**
2	**The Court's Request** On the same day the **Court** shall: • Identify the LA that is to prepare the s 37 report • Fix the date for the next hearing • Specify the date for the s 37 report to be filed by the LA • Direct the court officer to give notice of the order and the form C40 to the LA court liaison manager/lawyer (as set out in the CCP) by fax on the day the order is made • Direct each party to serve upon the LA all further documents filed with the Court.	Court **on DAY 1**
3	Where a s 37 report is required in less than 8 weeks, the **Court** should make direct enquiries of the Court liaison manager/lawyer of the LA to agree the period within which a report can be written.	Court **on DAY 1**
4	Within 24 hours of the order being made (on **DAY 2**) the **court officer** shall serve on the LA a sealed copy of the order and such other documents as the Court has directed.	Court Officer **on DAY 1**

Action	Party and Timing
5 **LA Responsibility** Within 24 hours of the receipt of the sealed order (on **DAY 3**) the Court liaison manager/lawyer of the **LA** shall ensure that the request is allocated to a social services team manager who shall: • Be responsible for the preparation of the report and the allocation of a social worker/team to carry out any appropriate assessment • Ensure that the request is treated and recorded as a formal referral by social services in respect of each child named in the order • Notify the Court and the lawyers acting for all parties of his/her identity and contact details and the identity of the team that has been allocated • Follow Government guidance in relation to referral and assessment processes (see appendix F).	LA **on DAY 3**
6 Any **assessment** including a core assessment that is undertaken by social services should be completed within 35 days of the allocation above ie within 36 days of the service of the sealed court order.	Social Services **by DAY 38**
7 At the conclusion of the social services enquiries **social services** shall: • Consult with the family, the child and all relevant agencies before making decisions about a plan for the child. The LA will record the response of each person and agency consulted • Decide whether to apply to the Court for a statutory order • File the section 37 report with the Court and serve it upon the parties on or before the date specified in the Court's order.	Social Services **between DAYS 38 and 40**
8 Where social services decide not to apply for a care or supervision order they should as part of their report set out the decisions they have made and the reasons for those decisions and any plan they have made for the child (including the services to be provided) in accordance with Government guidance (see appendix F).	

PRACTICE DIRECTION

Practice Direction (Care Cases: Judicial Continuity and Judicial Case Management)

29 July 2003

1.1 This Practice Direction, which includes the annexed Principles and the annexed Protocol, is issued by the President of the Family Division with the concurrence of the Lord Chancellor. It is intended to implement the recommendations of the Final Report, published in May 2003, of the Lord Chancellor's Advisory Committee on Judicial Case Management in Public Law Children Act Cases chaired by Munby and Coleridge JJ.

1.2 The Practice Direction, Principles and Protocol apply to all Courts, including Family Proceedings Courts, hearing applications issued by local authorities under Part IV (Care and Supervision) of the Children Act 1989 ("care cases") where

(a) the application is issued on or after 1 November 2003; or
(b) the proceedings are transferred on or after 1 November 2003 from the Family Proceedings Court to a Care Centre, or from a County Court to a Care Centre or from a Care Centre to the High Court.

1.3 *Practice Direction (Family Proceedings: Court Bundles)* [2000] 1 WLR 737, [2000] 1 FLR 536, remains in force and is to be complied with in all cases to which it applies, subject only to the Protocol and to any directions which may be given, in any particular care case by the case management judge.

1.4 Paragraph 2 of the *President's Direction (Judicial Continuity)* [2002] 2 FLR 367 shall cease to have effect in any case to which this Practice Direction applies.

2 **Purpose of the Practice Direction, Principles and Protocol**

2.1 The purpose of the Practice Direction, Principles and Protocol is to ensure consistency in the application of best practice by all Courts dealing with care cases and, in particular, to ensure:

(a) that care cases are dealt with in accordance with the overriding objective;
(b) that there are no unacceptable delays in the hearing and determination of care cases; and
(c) that save in exceptional or unforeseen circumstances every care case is finally determined within 40 weeks of the application being issued.

2.2 The Principles are the principles which govern the application of the Practice Direction and Protocol by the Courts and the parties.

3 **The Overriding Objective**

3.1 The overriding objective is to enable the Court to deal with every care case

(a)   justly, expeditiously, fairly and with the minimum of delay;

(b)   in ways which ensure, so far as is practicable, that

  (i)   the parties are on an equal footing;

  (ii) the welfare of the children involved is safeguarded; and

  (iii) distress to all parties is minimised;

(c)   so far as is practicable, in ways which are proportionate

  (i)   to the gravity and complexity of the issues; and

  (ii) to the nature and extent of the intervention proposed in the private family life of the children and adults involved.

3.2   The Court should seek to give effect to the overriding objective when it exercises any power given to it by the Family Proceedings Courts (Children Act 1989) Rules 1991 or the Family Proceedings Rules 1991 (as the case may be) or interprets any rule.

3.3   The parties are required to help the Court to further the overriding objective.

3.4   The Court will further the overriding objective by actively managing cases as required by sections 11 and 32 of the Children Act 1989 and in accordance with the Practice Direction, Principles and Protocol.

---

4   **Avoiding Delay**

4.1   Section 1(2) of the Children Act 1989 requires the Court to "have regard to the general principle that any delay in determining any question is likely to prejudice the welfare of the child".

4.2   Decisions of the European Court of Human Rights emphasise the need under article 6 of the European Convention for the Protection of Human Rights and Fundamental Freedoms for "exceptional diligence" in this context: *Johansen v Norway* (1996) 23 EHRR 33, para [88].

4.3   One of the most effective means by which unnecessary delay can be avoided in care cases is by active case management by a specialist judiciary.

---

5   **Judicial Case Management**

5.1   The key principles underlying the Practice Direction, Principles and Protocol are

(a)   **judicial continuity**: each care case will be allocated to one or not more than two case management judges, who will be responsible for every stage in the proceedings down to the final hearing and one of whom may be, and where possible should be, the judge who will conduct the final hearing;

(b)   **active case management**: each care case will be actively case managed by the case management judge(s) with a view at all times to furthering the overriding objective;

(c)   **consistency by standardisation** of steps: each care case will so far as possible be managed in a consistent way

  (i)   in accordance with the standardised procedures laid down in the Protocol; and

  (ii) using, wherever possible, standardised forms of order and other standardised documents;

(d)   **the case management conference**: in each care case there will be a
case management conference to enable the case management judge to
actively case manage the case and, at the earliest practicable
opportunity, to
(i)   identify the relevant issues; and
(ii)   fix the timetable for all further directions and other hearings
(including the date of the final hearing).

| 6 | **Implementing the Protocol** |

6.1   The Protocol is based on, and is intended to promote the adoption in all
Courts and in all care cases of, the best practice currently adopted by Courts
dealing with care cases.

6.2   The Protocol will be implemented:

(a)   in each Care Centre by reference to the Care Centre Plan which will be
drafted locally (see appendix E/1 to the Protocol); and
(b)   in each Family Proceedings Court by reference to the FPC Plan which
will be drafted locally (see appendix E/2 to the Protocol).

6.3   The target times specified in the Protocol for the taking of each step should
be adhered to wherever possible and treated as the maximum permissible
time for the taking of that step. Save in exceptional or unforeseen
circumstances every care case should be finally determined within 40 weeks
of the application being issued. Simpler cases can often be finally determined
within a shorter time.

6.4   Unless the case management judge is satisfied that some other direction is
necessary in order to give effect to the overriding objective, the case
management judge should, and, unless the case management judge has
otherwise ordered, the parties and any expert who may be instructed in the
case must (as the case may be):

(a)   use or require the parties to use the forms and standard documents
referred to in Appendix A to the Protocol;
(b)   prepare or require the parties to prepare the documents referred to in
Appendix B to the Protocol in accordance with that Appendix;
(c)   comply or require the parties and every expert to comply with the Code
of Guidance for Expert Witnesses in Family Proceedings contained in
Appendix C to the Protocol; and
(d)   make every order and direction in the form of any relevant form which
may from time to time be approved by the President of the Family
Division for this purpose.

6.5   Appendix D to the Protocol contains the text of the President's *Practice
Direction (Family Proceedings: Court Bundles)* [2000] 1 WLR 737, [2000] 1 FLR
536.

6.6   Appendix F to the Protocol contains the Social Services Assessment and
Care Planning Aide-Memoire, which is a summary of existing guidance
relating to assessment and care planning.

6.7   Appendix G to the Protocol is a summary of best practice guidance relating
to requests made under section 37 of the Children Act 1989.

6.8	Cases in which there are concurrent care proceedings and criminal proceedings are to be dealt with in accordance with the Care Centre Plan.

7   Monitoring and Compliance

7.1   It is the responsibility of the Designated Family Judge in conjunction with the Court Service and in consultation with the Family Division Liaison Judge

(a)   to monitor the extent to which care cases in the Courts for which he is responsible are being conducted in compliance with the protocol and with directions previously given by the Court;

(b)   to arrange for the collection and collation of such statistical and other information and in such form as the Family Division Liaison Judge and the President of the Family Division may from time to time direct.

ANNEX TO THE PRACTICE DIRECTION

Principles of Application

The principles which govern the application of the Practice Direction and Protocol by the courts and the parties:

1   The **Aim** of the Practice Direction and Protocol is to reduce delay and improve the quality of justice for children and families by the following means:

- Proper Court control of proceedings
- Identifying and promoting best practice
- The consistent application of best practice by all Courts
- Providing predictable standards which the Courts will treat as the normal and reasonable approach to the conduct of proceedings by parties

2   In order to achieve the **Aim** the Practice Direction gives effect to:

- A **protocol** which sets out predictable standards as specific steps to be taken in all care proceedings by reference to identified best practice
- An **overriding objective** to provide consistency of case management decisions
- **Court plans** to maximise the use of judicial and administrative resources
- Best practice **guidance**

3   **Court Control:** Proper Court control of care proceedings requires forward planning so that:

- A specialist judiciary is identified and trained
- Arrangements are made for continuous case management in the High Court, and in each Care Centre and Family Proceedings Court
- The arrangements for continuous case management are supervised by the specialist judiciary in conjunction with dedicated court officers, in particular
  - the matching and allocation of judicial and administrative resources to cases; and
  - the allocation and listing of cases,
- There is continuous and active case management of each case by allocated case management judges/benches

- There is continuous monitoring of the progress of all proceedings against target times to help minimise delay

4   **Continuity of Case Management:** The continuity of case management is to be achieved:

- In the Care Centre and the High Court by a **care centre plan** (CCP); and
- In the Family Proceedings Courts, by a **family proceedings courts plan** (FPCP)
- By the **identification of the specialist judiciary** and the **dedicated court officers** in the plans

Guidelines for the preparation and implementation of the plans are set out at appendix E to the protocol.

5   **Active Case Management:** Active case management is to be achieved by giving directions to ensure that the determination of proceedings occurs quickly, efficiently and with the minimum of delay and risk to the child (and where appropriate other persons) by:

- Identifying the appropriate Court to conduct the proceedings and transferring the proceedings as early as possible to that Court
- Identifying all facts and matters that are in issue at the earliest stage and then at each case management step in the proceedings
- Deciding which issues need full investigation and hearing and which do not
- Considering whether the likely benefits of taking a particular social work or legal step justify the delay which will result and the cost of taking it
- Encouraging the parties to use an alternative dispute resolution procedure such as a family group conference and facilitating the use of such a procedure
- Helping the parties to reach agreement in relation to the whole or part of a case, quickly, fairly and with the minimum of hostility
- Encouraging the parties to co-operate with each other in the conduct of the proceedings
- Identifying the timetable for all legal and social work steps
- Fixing the dates for all appointments and hearings
- Standardising, simplifying and regulating:
  - the use of case management documentation and forms
  - the court's orders and directions
- Controlling:
  - the use and cost of experts
  - the nature and extent of the documents which are to be disclosed to the parties and presented to the Court
  - whether and if so in what manner the documents disclosed are to be presented to the Court
- Monitoring the Court's timetable and directions against target times for the completion of each protocol step to prevent delay and non-compliance

6   **Standard Directions, Forms and Documents:** In order to simplify and provide consistency in the exchange of information: such standard variable directions, forms (appendix A) and standard documents (appendix B) as may be approved from time to time by the President are to be used unless otherwise directed by the Court.

7   **Controlling the Use and Cost of Experts:** Expert evidence should be proportionate to the issues in question and should relate to questions that are outside the skill and experience of the Court. To assist the Court in its control of

the use and cost of experts a Code of Guidance is incorporated as appendix C to the protocol. The Code of Guidance is to be followed by the parties when a party proposes that the court gives permission for the use of an expert. The Code of Guidance should form part of every letter of instruction so that experts can adopt best practice guidance in the formulation of their reports and advices to the Court.

8   **Disclosure:** Disclosure of relevant documents should be encouraged at the earliest opportunity. Where disclosure is in issue the Court's control of the extent of disclosure will have regard to whether the disclosure proposed is proportionate to the issues in question and the continuing duty of each party to give *full* and frank disclosure of information to each other and the Court.

9   **Inter-Disciplinary Good Practice:** The Court's process and its reliance upon best practice should acknowledge and encourage inter-disciplinary best practice and in particular pre-application investigation, assessment, consultation and planning by statutory agencies (including local authorities) and other potential parties (an aide-memoire of local authority guidance is annexed to the protocol at appendix F).

10 **Target Time:** The target times specified in the protocol for the taking of each step should be adhered to wherever possible and treated as the maximum permissible time for the taking of that step. Where target times are expressed in days, the days are 'court business days' in accordance with the Rules. Save in exceptional or unforeseen circumstances every care case should be finally determined within 40 weeks of the application being issued. Simpler cases can often be finally determined within a shorter time. Target times should only be departed from at the direction of the Court and for good reason in accordance with the overriding objective.

11 **Monitoring and Compliance:** To facilitate directions being given to deal with a change of circumstances or to remedy a material non-compliance at the earliest opportunity the Court should consider requiring regular certification of compliance with the Court's timetable and directions by the parties, for example on interim care order renewal certificates. In addition the Court might consider other mechanisms to monitor the progress of a case without the need for the parties or their representatives to attend Court.

12 **Technology:** Where the facilities are available to the Court and the parties, the Court should consider making *full* use of technology including electronic information exchange and video or telephone conferencing.

6.3 PRACTICE DIRECTION: CHILDREN ACT 1989: APPLICATIONS BY CHILDREN

[1993] 1 FLR 668

Applications for leave to be transferred to High Court – Children Act 1989, ss 8, 10 – Family Proceedings Rules 1991, r 4.3 – Family Proceedings Courts (Children Act 1989) Rules 1991, r 3

Under s 10 of the Children Act 1989, the prior leave of the court is required in respect of applications by the child concerned for s 8 orders (contact) prohibited steps, residence and specific issue orders). Rule 4.3 of the Family Proceedings Rules 1991 and r 3 of the Family Proceedings Courts (Children Act 1989) Rules 1991 set out the procedure to be followed when applying for leave.

Such applications raise issues which are more appropriate for determination in the High Court and should be transferred there for hearing.

Issued with the concurrence of the Lord Chancellor.

SIR STEPHEN BROWN
President

22 February 1993

6.4 PRACTICE NOTE: CHILD ABDUCTION UNIT: LORD CHANCELLOR'S DEPARTMENT

[1993] 1 FLR 804

CHILD ABDUCTION AND CUSTODY ACT 1985

Duties of the Central Authority for England and Wales under Article 21 of the Hague Convention on the Civil Aspects of International Child Abduction

In the case of *Re G (A Minor) (Hague Convention: Access)* [1993] 1 FLR 669 the Court of Appeal considered the duties of the Central Authority for England and Wales on receiving an application in respect of rights of access under Art 21 of the Hague Convention.

The Court of Appeal took the view that Art 21 conferred no jurisdiction to determine matters relating to access, or to recognise or enforce foreign access orders. It provides, however, for executive co-operation in the enforcement of such recognition as national law allows.

Accordingly, the duty of this Central Authority is to make appropriate arrangements for the applicant by providing solicitors to act on his behalf in applying for legal aid and instituting proceedings in the High Court under s 8 of the Children Act 1989.

If, during the course of proceedings under Art 12 of the Convention, the applicant decides to seek access instead of the return of the child, but no agreement can be reached and the provisions of the European Convention on the Recognition and Enforcement of Decisions Concerning Custody of children and on Restoration of custody of children are not available, a separate application under s 8 of the children Act 1989 will have to be made.

Central Authority for England and Wales

5 March 1993

6.5 B v B (COURT BUNDLES: VIDEO EVIDENCE) (PRACTICE NOTE)

[1994] 1 FLR 323

After consultation with the President and with his approval Wall J made the following statement about the efficient preparation of court bundles.

1 Careful thought should always be given by the solicitors carrying the burden of the litigation to the preparation of the bundles to be used in court. This should preferably be done in consultation with counsel who is to have the conduct of the case in court and should certainly be done in consultation with the solicitors for the other parties. There should always be liaison and co-operation between the parties' legal advisers in the preparation of documents for use in court. This should be done in good time before the trial: documents which arrive late or at the last minute can then be added to existing bundles or bundled separately.

2 Where the mechanical task of putting bundles together is delegated to a clerk or junior member of staff it remains the responsibility of the solicitor or managing clerk who has the conduct of the case to check the bundles before they leave the solicitors' offices to ensure that they are in order.

3 In particular, a check should be made to ensure that all the documents copied are legible and that the photocopying process has not truncated any document so that part of it is missing. Elementary as this may sound, illegible or truncated documents are frequently found in court bundles. Where a document is found to be illegible or will not copy properly (for example because it is itself a copy or because it is an original which has been highlighted over the text) a typed version of the document should be made and inserted in the bundle next to the illegible copy.

4 Documents should be presented in a logical (usually chronological) order. The preparer of the bundles should attempt to put himself or herself in the position of the judge who is coming to the papers for the first time. Nothing is more frustrating than to open a bundle of documents and to read 'I make this statement further to my previous statement of such and such a date and in answer to the respondent's statement'. The judge then has the choice either of reading something which answers an allegation he has yet to read or searching the bundle for the document to which it is a reply. For these reasons it is not appropriate to bundle each party's evidence separately in different bundles or in different sections of a bundle. A chronological presentation enables the judge to read a bundle through from beginning to end without the distraction of having to search for documents which are out of sequence.

5 All bundles should be properly indexed with a description of each document and the page number at which it begins and ends.

6 Bundles should be individually paginated, and the pagination should be continuous throughout each bundle. A master bundle should be prepared and copy bundles should only be made after the master bundle has been paginated, not before. By these means only can it be ensured that everyone in court has the same document with identical pagination. Equally documents should not be presented with generalised

numbering – for example, document 1 is the applicant's statement, document 2 is the respondent's statement, and so on. The aim in court is to be able to refer to bundle A page x, not bundle A, document 2, and page x of that document. The latter process is very time-wasting.

7 It is common practice for solicitors to prepare bundles for their own use and for the use of the court and to provide indices only to the solicitors for the other parties. In my judgement it is preferable for the solicitors having the conduct of the litigation to prepare all the bundles and distribute them after making a charge for photocopying. Where, however, indices only are supplied, it is the duty of the recipient solicitors to ensure that the bundles which they make up from the indices have identical pagination to the master bundles. A simple telephone call should obviate any difficulty in this regard.

8 Whilst each case varies in relation to the issues which arise from it, thought should always be given to the categorisation of documents and their distribution into individual bundles. Usually it is sensible to have a bundle of statements or affidavits (chronologically arranged) another for formal court documents and interlocutory court orders (also in chronological order) another for bundles of expert or medical reports (likewise arranged in chronological sequence) and so on.

9 Where medical records are relevant and reproduced every effort should be made to ensure that the copies are legible and photocopied in the correct order and are presented the right way up. In rare cases where a bundle of solicitors' correspondence is relevant, that correspondence should likewise be presented in chronological order. Where there are documents in manuscript (such as letters between the parties) typed copies should be provided unless the manuscript is clearly legible.

10 Rigorous pruning of unnecessary material should take place and duplication should be avoided. If a document is exhibited to an affidavit or statement and should more logically appear elsewhere (for example as a medical report in a medical bundle) a page can be inserted in the bundle from which it has been removed stating where it is to be found.

11 Wherever possible the chronology prepared by the applicant should be cross-referenced to the relevant page in the relevant bundle. Such a process can only be achieved if the person preparing the chronology has access to the bundles in their final state, but the process is of enormous assistance to the judge. Equally a dramatis personae which identifies the parties and the principal witnesses and where their evidence is to be found is extremely useful to the judge.

12 There should always be a 'witness bundle' that is to say a spare bundle for use by witnesses in the witness box. When a document needs to be put to a witness it is at the very least a discourtesy to the witness if the document has to be retrieved from a solicitor's file or counsel's papers. It is also time wasting. Moreover, the witness bundles must be kept up to date during the trial. It is the duty of the advocate having the conduct of the proceedings to ensure that this is done.

13 Bundles should be presented in a way which enables them to lie flat when opened. It is very irritating when cross-referencing documentation or making a note if the bundle snaps shut as soon as the hand is taken off it. Furthermore, staples, treasury tags or other means of holding papers together should be removed once the papers are in a file or ring binder.

14 Documents frequently arrive or emerge during the course of a trial. Provided there is agreement for their inclusion in the court bundles they should be paginated, photocopied, hole punched and inserted in the relevant bundle at the relevant place and, if possible, the index to the particular bundle amended to cover their inclusion.

15 Where videos of interviews with children form part of the evidence in the case there should either be a directions appointment at which their use is discussed and directions about their use given, alternatively the parties' respective solicitors should attempt to agree about the manner in which they are to be used. Thus:

(a) where there is to be a challenge to the technique used or debate as to the interpretation of what the child or interviewer has said, transcripts should be obtained and placed in a separate bundle;

(b) if the judge is to be asked to view the videos in private before the trial begins:

   (i)   the agreement of all the parties to this course should be obtained,

   (ii) the parties should endeavour to agree those parts of the interviews which the judge should look at,

   (iii) a transcript should be provided to the judge;

(c) where it is intended that the video should be played in court in addition or as an alternative to a private viewing made by the judge, early arrangements should be made for the provision of the relevant equipment, agreement reached on the parts of the interviews which are to be played and transcripts provided.

6.6 PRACTICE DIRECTION: CASE MANAGEMENT

[1995] 1 FLR 456

1 The importance of reducing the cost and delay of civil litigation makes it necessary for the court to assert greater control over the preparation for and conduct of hearings than has hitherto been customary. Failure by practitioners to conduct cases economically will be visited by appropriate orders for costs, including wasted costs orders.

2 The court will accordingly exercise its discretion to limit –

    (a) discovery;
    (b) the length of opening and closing oral submissions;
    (c) the time allowed for the examination and cross-examination of witnesses;
    (d) the issues on which it wishes to be addressed;
    (e) reading aloud from documents and authorities.

3 Unless otherwise ordered, every witness statement or affidavit shall stand as the evidence in chief of the witness concerned. The substance of the evidence which a party intends to adduce at the hearing must be sufficiently detailed, but without prolixity; it must be confined to material matters of fact, not (except in the case of the evidence of professional witnesses) of opinion; and if hearsay evidence is to be adduced, the source of the information must be declared or good reason given for not doing so.

4 It is a duty owed to the court both by the parties and by their legal representatives to give full and frank disclosure in ancillary relief applications and also in all matters in respect of children. The parties and their advisers must also use their best endeavours:

    (a) to confine the issues and the evidence called to what is reasonably considered to be essential for the proper presentation of their case;
    (b) to reduce or eliminate issues for expert evidence;
    (c) in advance of the hearing to agree which are the issues or the main issues.

5 *(ceased to have effect – see President's Direction of 10 March 2000)*

6 In cases estimated to last for five days or more and in which no pre-trial review has been ordered, application should be made for a pre-trial review. It should when practicable be listed at least three weeks before the hearing and be conducted by the judge or district judge before whom the case is to be heard and should be attended by the advocates who are to represent the parties at the hearing. Whenever possible, all statements of evidence and all reports should be filed before the date of the review and in good time for them to have been considered by all parties.

7 Whenever practicable and in any matter estimated to last five days or more, each party should, not less than two clear days before the hearing, lodge with the court, or the Clerk of the Rules in matters in the Royal Courts of Justice in London, and deliver to other parties, a chronology and a skeleton argument concisely summarising that

party's submissions in relation to each of the issues, and citing the main authorities relied upon. It is important that skeleton arguments should be brief.

8   *(ceased to have effect – see President's Direction of 10 March 2000)*

9 The opening speech should be succinct. At its conclusion other parties may be invited briefly to amplify their skeleton arguments. In a heavy case the court may in conjunction with final speeches require written submissions, including the findings of fact for which each party contends.

10 This practice direction which follows *Practice Direction (Civil Litigation: Case Management)* [1995] 1 WLR 262 handed down by Lord Taylor of Gosforth CJ and Sir Richard Scott V-C to apply in the Queen's Bench and Chancery Divisions, shall apply to all family proceedings in the High Court and in all care centres, family hearing centres and divorce county courts.

11 Issued with the concurrence of the Lord Chancellor.

SIR STEPHEN BROWN
President

31 January 1995

6.7 PRESIDENT'S DIRECTION: (CHILDREN ACT 1989: EXCLUSION REQUIREMENT)

[1998] 1 FLR 495

Exclusion requirement – Power of court in ex parte order – person arrested under power of arrest – Committal orders

Under s 38A(5) and s 44A(5) of the Children Act 1989 the court may attach a power of arrest to an exclusion requirement included in an interim care order or an emergency protection order. In cases where an order is made which includes an exclusion requirement, the following shall apply:

(1) If a power of arrest is attached to the order then unless the person to whom the exclusion requirement refers was given notice of the hearing and attended the hearing, the name of that person and that an order has been made including an exclusion requirement to which a power of arrest has been attached shall be announced in open court at the earliest opportunity. This may be either on the same day when the court proceeds to hear cases in open court or where there is no further business in open court on that day at the next listed sitting of the court.

(2) When a person arrested under a power of arrest cannot conveniently be brought before the relevant judicial authority sitting in a place normally used as a court room within 24 hours after the arrest, he may be brought before the relevant judicial authority at any convenient place but, as the liberty of the subject is involved, the press and the public should be permitted to be present, unless security needs make this impracticable.

(3) Any order of committal made otherwise than in public or in a courtroom open to the public, shall be announced in open court at the earliest opportunity. This may be either on the same day when the court proceeds to hear cases in open court or where there is no further business in open court on that day at the next listed sitting of the court. The announcement shall state (a) the name of the person committed, (b) in general terms the nature of the contempt of the court in respect of which the order of committal has been made and (c) the length of the period of committal.

Issued with the concurrence of the Lord Chancellor.

SIR STEPHEN BROWN
President
17 December 1997

6.8 LOCAL AUTHORITY CIRCULAR LAC(1999)29: CARE PLANS AND CARE PROCEEDINGS UNDER THE CHILDREN ACT 1989

12 August 1999

Introduction

1. This circular is issued under section 7 of the Local Authority Social Services Act 1970 which requires local authorities to act under the guidance of the Secretary of State. It contains guidance to local authorities on the preparation of care plans in care proceedings applications under section 31 of the Children Act 1989. It supplements guidance originally issued in The Children Act 1989: Guidance and Regulations, Volumes 3 and 4. Following consultation issued in March 1999, the guidance in this circular has been approved by the President of the Family Division.

2. Local authorities are asked to bring this circular to the attention of senior managers with responsibilities for care applications at court; to local authority legal staff dealing with such cases and to Guardians ad Litem and Reporting Officers panel managers.

Aim and Scope of the Circular

3. The guidance in this circular seeks to address concerns that care planning, although considered to have steadily improved during the 1990s, lacks consistency between and within authorities across the country. These differences may be in the style, format and level of detail set out in the care plan but also who contributes to its completion, including family members. There are also believed to be continuing uncertainties about the status of the contents of care plans, particularly regarding key decisions and timetable. This in turn gives rise to differing expectations from those involved in the court proceedings, including the judiciary, about the strictness with which the care plan should be implemented. There is general acceptance that family circumstances do change and that plans may well need to be adjusted to reflect the changing needs of the child who is the subject of the care order. Typically, this will be one of the main tasks of the statutory reviews which are required to be undertaken for all looked after children.

4. The circular covers practice and policy matters, including:

    i. background issues on care planning;
    ii. advice in the circular in relation to the current law;
    iii. structure and contents of the care plan;
    iv. reasons and time-scales;
    v. format of care plans;
    vi. applications involving siblings;
    vii. endorsement of the plan within the local authority;
    vii. care plans and assessment;
    viii. care plans and Looked After Children System;

    ix. care plans and children who are disabled;
    x. race, culture, religion and language;
    xi. care proceedings prior to an adoption care plan;
    xii. care plans and care leavers;
    xiii. reviewing the implementation of the care plan;
    xiv. commencement;
    xv. transitional arrangements.

5. Implementation of the guidance, alongside other important initiatives such as the Quality Protects programme, will help achieve high standards of care planning within care applications at court and consistent practice regarding their preparation and use during and after the proceedings.

Background issues on care planning

6. Care planning is a crucial ingredient in the preparation of a local authority's application to court for a care order because it explains how the proposed care order will be implemented in order to achieve specific outcomes for the child. Before making a care order, courts have to be satisfied that the 'threshold criteria' at section 3l(2) ('significant harm') are satisfied. They will have regard to the 'welfare checklist' at section l(3). But they then have to address whether, under section l(5), making any order will be better for the child than making no order. This judgement will often rely to a considerable extent on the details presented by the local authority to the court in the papers commonly known as the care plan. This is one of the most important documents considered by courts in care proceedings.

7. Guidance about planning for children looked after by local authorities was issued by the Department of Heath in 1991 as part of the Children Act 1989 Regulations and Guidance (Volumes 3 Family Placements and Volume 4 Residential Care, both at paragraphs 2.43–2.62). The guidance does not use the exact phrase 'care plans' but instead addresses the need for planning in the context of the Arrangements for Placement Regulations 1991 (SI 1991 No 890). **These requirements are not affected by the guidance in this circular**.

8. The 1991 guidance was written mainly to address the needs of children and local authorities in the context of looked after children rather than for direct use by courts dealing with care applications for a care or supervision order. The guidance was adopted by the Family Division as applicable to care applications and since 1994 has been considered a requirement for any such application (*Re J (Minors) (Care Plan)* [1994] FLR 253).

9. Inter-professional debate, publications and research during the 1990s have reinforced a number of good practice messages. These include:

    – Local authority circular 'Adoption – Achieving The Right Balance' LAC (89)20 issued in August 1998, included guidance about care proceedings and adoption which, in the light of representations to the Department of Health was superseded by CI (99)6 (*see below paragraphs 28–33*);
    – Department of Health funded research undertaken by Hunt et al 'The Last Resort – Child Protection, the Courts and the 1989 Children Act' (Stationery

Office 1999); Harwin et al research on care plan implementation (publication planned early 2000);

- The SSI study ('Care Planning and Court Orders' April 1998);
- President's Inter-disciplinary Conference (1997) and publication of the conference papers on care planning ('Divided Duties – care planning within the family justice system,' edited by the Rt Hon Lord Justice Thorpe and Elizabeth Clarke – Family Law 1998);
- 'Reporting to Court under the Children Act – a Handbook for Social Services' (Joyce Plotnikoff and Richard Woolfson HMSO 1996);
- 'Avoiding Delay in Children Act Cases' (Dame Margaret Booth DBE Lord Chancellor's Department 1996).

10. Alongside all these developments has been the steady progress in the introduction of the Looking After Children Assessment and Action Record System (LAC) across the country, one element of which is the care plan. These materials are now in widespread use and one of the purposes has been to ensure a consistent approach and format for care plans across the local authority.

Advice in the circular in relation to the current law

11. Seventeen of the 18 areas which were set out in the 1991 guidance are included below in this circular. A few are separated out, repeated or expanded to give greater emphasis and to reflect practice experience since 1991. One of the 18 areas is not included 'arrangements for ending the placement (if made under voluntary arrangements)' as this is not applicable in the context of a care plan to implement a care order. The guidance in this circular concerning the structure and contents of the care plan, as set out below at paragraphs 12–13, is considered to be entirely consistent with legal precedents to date and should not therefore pose legal questions for local authorities following it.

- Authorities will also wish to bear in mind the principles underpinning Article 8 of the European Convention on Human Rights ('Right to respect for private and family life'). In this context, for example, careful attention should be given to the issues about consulting with parents, as set out in paragraphs 13 (Section 3) and 14.

Structure and contents of the care plan

12. The advised contents of the care plan items are set out within a structure of five sections:

- Overall aim
- Child's needs including contact
- Views of others
- Placement details and timetable
- Management and support by local authority

13. The complete list of matters that the guidance advises should be included within each of the care plan's five sections is as follows:

Section 1: Overall aim

1.1 Aim of the plan and summary of timetable.

Section 2: Child's needs including contact

2.1 The child's identified needs, including needs arising from race, culture, religion or language, special education, health or disability.

2.2 The extent to which the wishes and views of the child have been obtained and acted upon; and

2.3 The reasons for supporting this or explanations of why wishes/views have not been given absolute precedence;

2.4 Summary of how those needs might be met;

2.5 Arrangements for, and purpose of, contact in meeting the child's needs (specifying contact relationship eg parent, step-parent, other family member, former carer, friend, siblings, including those looked after who may have a separate placement); any proposals to restrict or terminate contact.

Section 3: Views of others

3.1 The extent to which the wishes and views of the child's parents and anyone else with a sufficient interest in the child (including representatives of other agencies, current and former carers) have been obtained and acted upon, and

3.2 The reasons for supporting them or explanations of why wishes/views have been given absolute precedence.

Section 4: Placement details and timetable

4.1 Proposed placement – type and details (or details of alternative placements);

4.2 Time that is likely to elapse before proposed placement is made;

4.3 Likely duration of placement (or other placement);

4.4 Arrangements for health care (including consent to examination and treatment);

4.5 Arrangements for education (including any pre-school day care/activity);

4.6 Arrangements for reunification (often known as 'rehabilitation') (see also 4.8);

4.7 Other services to be provided to the child;

4.8 Other services to be provided to parents and other family members;

4.9 Details of proposed support services in placement for the carers;

4.10 Specific details of the parents' role in day to day arrangements.

Section 5: Management and support by local authority

5.1 Who is to be responsible for implementing the overall plan;

5.2 Who is to be responsible for implementing specific tasks within the plan;

5.3 Dates of review;

5.4 Contingency plan, if placement breaks down or if preferred placement is not available;

5.5 Arrangements for input by parents, the child and others into the ongoing decision-making process;

5.6 Arrangements for notifying the responsible authority of disagreements about the implementation of the care plan or making representations or complaints.

Reasons and time-scales

14. Care plans need to be understood by a range of professionals, the child and the child's family. The following should be reflected in the wording of the care plan:

- Confusion and mistrust can inadvertently be generated where care plans explain **what** is proposed but give insufficient detail as to **why** a particular placement or course of action has been chosen.
- Attention to this aspect of the care plan may reduce time spent later, often in court itself, explaining the basis on which the local authority has made certain key decisions, including those around contact.
- Similarly, it is important that everyone concerned with the finalisation of the care plan considers **achievable time-scales** leading up to **specific outcomes** for overall implementation, as well as for each of the key steps within it. This should be made clear within the plan.
- These will also help at a later stage if a care order is made. Reviewing officers monitoring the implementation of care plans will be able to identify any delays and, as necessary, ensure that these are addressed.

Format of care plan

15. The care plan in the proceedings is a distinct and separate formal court document. It is not required to be presented as a sworn statement or affidavit. It should not be incorporated into a local authority statement of evidence. It should not inappropriately duplicate information in such statements, such as the child's history and evidential aspects of the proceedings.

16. Each page of the care plan should be typed/word processed on A4, single-sided paper. The first and separate page should be headed 'Care Plan – Front Sheet' and include the following information:

- full name of child
- date of birth
- court case number
- name of court hearing application
- date of the court hearing
- type of hearing (ie directions, interim or final hearing)
- name of local authority
- number of plan
- date of plan

Where during proceedings several plans have been produced, each should be numbered to avoid confusion. This will help ensure that after the care order is made, the particular numbered care plan is that understood by all parties and the court as being the operative one and may be referred to as such in any formal judicial communication.

The subsequent pages (also single-sided) should set out the main elements of the care plan under clearly marked headings. These should correspond with sections 1 to 5 as shown above in this circular. Paragraph numbers will aid communication in court.

17. Care plans, although incomplete, may sometimes be needed at an interim stage in the care proceedings. These will not necessarily represent the local authority's confirmed views that will brought to the final hearing. It is therefore important that the first page of the care plan under 'type of hearing' should clearly distinguish between interim care plans for interim court hearings and the complete care plan for the final hearing.

18. The last and separate page of the care plan should include the following information:

- full name and professional position of the person who has prepared the care plan
  This should normally be the social worker allocated to the case, although a range of other people within the authority and from other agencies may have contributed to aspects of the plan, as also may have the child, the child's family and the guardian ad litem.
- signature
- date
- work address and telephone number

followed by

- full name(s) and professional position(s) of the person(s) endorsing the plan for the final hearing on behalf of the local authority making the application
  Such an endorsement is only needed for the complete plan prepared for the final hearing (see paragraphs 17 above and 20–22 below)
- signature(s)
- date(s)
- work address and telephone number(s)

Applications involving siblings

19. A separate care plan is needed for each child who is the subject of care proceedings. Some of the information within the care plans for siblings may be similar or identical. Other material may be different because of the need to address the distinct characteristics of each child and the way the plan proposes to meet each child's needs. The court will wish to scrutinise the care plans for each sibling child. It is important that the court's attention is drawn to any important differences between the respective plans reflecting the individual needs of siblings. These can be made prominent by use of **highlighting,** *italics* or underlining, as illustrated in this sentence.

Endorsement of plan within local authority

20. The care plan presented by the local authority is intended to be an authoritative statement made in good faith about the child's needs, the best way of responding to those needs, and the detailed arrangements setting out how the local authority will provide services to promote and protect the child's welfare whilst he or she is the subject of the care order.

- The local authority commitment to the plan given as part of the final hearing in the care proceedings goes far beyond the professional responsibility of the child's front line key-worker.

- That commitment may require input from a range of services and may have far-reaching resource implications. These will always include the social services but in many cases may also involve an input from health and education. If this is the case, an agreement should have been reached with these agencies in respect of services included in the care plan.
- Where the child's proposed placement is outside the local authority's own area, it will also be necessary to discuss and agree the provision of appropriate services to meet the child's needs with local agencies and for these to be included in the care plan.

21. One or more relevant senior officers within the local authority should endorse the care plan for the final hearing, as an authority wide statement of its commitment to the plan. The choice of one or more senior officers designated to endorse care plans on behalf of the local authority is for the authority to determine. Considerations which it may be helpful to take into account in selecting designated persons include:

- the size and structure of the Social Services Department
- the average number of care plans for court prepared annually
- arrangements for the provision of services for children looked after
- arrangements for reviewing the cases of children looked after
- delegated funding and authorisation arrangements within the authority
- arrangements for monitoring the implementation of all care plans within the authority
- and, in the shorter term, arrangements for implementing the Quality Protects programme.

22. In exceptional cases and where the court considers it necessary, a designated officer or other senior manager may be required to attend court and give evidence on behalf of the local authority. This might cover wider considerations which may have influenced the authority's choice within the care plan, such as the overall aim of the plan or the selection of a particular placement or other resource.

Care plans and assessment

23. The new framework for assessing children and families will be launched later in 1999. It applies to all children in need, not just those where child abuse has been identified or is suspected. Using the framework children's needs will be assessed, according to the same seven child developmental dimensions in the Looking After Children System, as will the capacities of their parents, carers and significant others in the child's life to respond to the child's identified needs. The findings from the assessment will inform the plan which sets out the help required by the child and their family in order to achieve optimal outcomes for the child. This could include applying for a statutory order. The completed assessment should provide a clear evidential base for the judgments made by social workers and subsequent decisions. The social work assessment may also indicate where other professionals might be required to undertake assessments within their own specialities, for example, paediatricians, speech therapists, educational psychologists, child and family psychiatrists.

24. The assessment framework will provide a structure within which the child's developmental needs, and need to be safe, can be clearly set out as can their parents'

capacities to respond appropriately to these needs, within time-scales appropriate to the child.

Care plans and the Looked After Children System

25. The Looking After Children Care Plan is not suitable as it stands for use as a court care plan. It has to be suitable for the needs of children in accommodation as well as those involved in care proceedings and therefore needs to encompass a broader range of issues. Only in a minority of cases will an accommodated child become the subject of court proceedings. However, in order to facilitate the making of a care plan for court the relevant questions are highlighted with a shaded margin box.

Care plans and disabled children

26. A substantial minority of looked after children are disabled, about one quarter according to the best available if rather outdated figures – Department of Health 1998, Disabled Children: Directions for their Future Care. There is also evidence that disabled children are placed in residential care more often than non-disabled children, and that disabled children tend to remain away from home for longer periods. The care plans for disabled children will have to show that what is proposed is the best way to meet the assessed needs of the particular child in question. The plans should pay particular attention to any physical or other characteristics in the environment, which exacerbate the impact of any impairment the child may have. The educational component of the plan should be informed by the DfEE's policy of promoting more widely the inclusion of disabled children in mainstream education. From October 1999 further provisions of the Disability Discrimination Act 1995 will be implemented which will require service providers to take reasonable steps to change practice, policies or procedures which make it impossible or unreasonably difficult for disabled people to use a service; provide auxiliary aids or services which would enable disabled people to use a service; and overcome physical barriers by providing a service by a reasonable alternative method.

Race, culture, religion and language

27. It is important that care plans should fully reflect the dimensions of race, culture, religion and language in respect of the child and child's family. Relevant guidance was included in 'Adoption – Achieving the Right Balance' (LAC (98)20 paragraphs 11 to 18). There is also research to draw on including, for example, 'Social Care and Black Communities' (Dutt and Mizra – Race Equality Unit 1995).

Care proceedings prior to an adoption care plan

28. In a minority of applications for a care order, it becomes apparent during the proceedings that adoption will be the preferred option set out in the care plan, should a care order be made at the final hearing. Some courts are presented at the final care application hearing with evidence about the preliminary steps that the local authority has taken to effect an adoption placement should a care order be made. Elsewhere, courts are informed that no or only minimal preparatory work has been undertaken. This poses the

likelihood of serious delay before placement and, as such, may well be detrimental to the child's welfare. Because each child and family situation is different, guidance setting out the preferred approach has to be flexible. Where adoption is the probable option, the courts will need to be advised of the likely steps and time-scales to implement the plan. The following paragraphs offer a framework where adoption is envisaged which is intended to achieve greater consistency within both the care proceedings and the preparation of the care plan.

29. Where the facts of the case remain in dispute up to the final hearing, the choice of placement may significantly depend on findings of fact and, indeed, in some cases no care order is made at all. It is these cases where it is likely to be most difficult to effect much, if any, detailed preparatory work prior to the final hearing concerning possible adoptive placement. But even here, it should normally be possible to explain within the care plan, the principal steps which would need to be taken before an adoptive placement could be made and give estimated time-scales for each of the key steps. This would include those cases where it is necessary to time-table therapeutic work with the child before preparing the child for placement.

30. Even where the facts in certain cases of the care application are not disputed and the preferred option in the care plan is adoption, it is important that local authorities have satisfied themselves that sufficient assessment has taken place to rule out rehabilitation or placement with relatives, for example, under a section 8 residence order. In these cases, local authority procedures should facilitate the process of finding an adoptive placement. How much progress can be made before the final hearing will depend on a range of factors, including the overall time-scale of the care proceedings. In addition, sensitivity is needed to ensure that the child's parent(s) understands that the care hearing under the Children Act is not the same as any later hearing under adoption legislation which would need to address questions of parental consent, unless a freeing application is being considered at the same time (see paragraph 32 below).

31. In respect of the cases described in paragraph 30 where the local authority has ruled out rehabilitation or placement with relatives and has confirmed adoption as the preferred option, the following should always be addressed:

    a. the local authority should take appropriate steps to co-ordinate information between the team responsible for the care proceedings application and those responsible for family finding and to allocate responsibilities for carrying out the necessary work;

    b. the BAAF Form E (details about the child) should be completed as far as possible, including obtaining from the parent(s) relevant medical and other details, although there may be difficulty in obtaining the necessary medical and other information from the parents;

    c. the adoption panel should consider the case, with a view to making a recommendation on whether adoption is in the child's best interests;

    d. the local authority should have identified the key steps and timetable, including family finding and any necessary therapy, and issues of contact (for inclusion in the care plan) which would lead to an adoptive placement, if the court made a care order;

    e. the care plan should include a contingency plan for use in specified circumstances if the preferred option for adoption cannot be achieved;

    f. consideration should be given as to whether a freeing application is appropriate (see paragraph 32 below).

32. There are also some (but not many) care cases with a view to adoption which may also require the child to be freed for adoption as soon as possible. It is important that there is full discussion with the local authority's legal advisors to ensure that such cases are identified as early as possible so that evidence and time-tabling of the court hearings can be co-ordinated. It is expensive for the local authority, stressful for the parent and possible unnecessary further delay for the child to have a care application followed months later by a freeing application, both of which may be contested.

33. However, it is not appropriate before the final care hearing for there to have been introductions between the child and the prospective adopters or for the agency to have confirmed the panel's recommendations.

Care plans and care leavers

34. In respect of a teenage child, the care plan may well need to consider the arrangements for leaving care. The Government is committed to develop new arrangements for young people living in and leaving care aimed at developing life skills and clarifying responsibility for financial support. In July 1999, a consultation paper was issued 'Me, Survive, Out There? New Arrangements for Young People Living in and Leaving Care' (LASSL (99)15).

Reviewing the implementation of the care plan

35. Reviews of the implementation of care plans take place within the statutory framework of the Review of Children's Cases Regulations 1991 (SI 1991 No. 895). This circular reiterates the importance of providing oversight of the implementation of care plans within the framework of reviews, as set out in 1991 in the Children Act Regulations and Guidance (Volumes 3 and 4). Local authorities will be aware of how these issues are being addressed with the Quality Protects programme launched by the Department of Health in September 1998. Therefore this circular does not extend current guidance in respect of reviews.

36. Monitoring individual children's care plans through the reviewing system will also generate management information about any difficulties, such as a lack of key services or other inputs, which may have contributed to delay in implementing a plan. This information may then usefully inform the children's services planning process.

Commencement

37. This circular comes into force on the date shown on the top right hand side of page 1.

Transitional arrangements

38. The intention of this guidance is not to delay care proceedings by the courts. Where the final hearing of a care application is scheduled to take place within 3 months of the date this circular comes into force, the care plan should, as far as it is practical, comply with this guidance. However, where a final care plan is not structured or endorsed in the

way advised by the circular, this should not alone be construed as sufficient grounds for delaying the final hearing. This approach is also commended after the 3 months transitional period.

6.9 PRESIDENT'S DIRECTION: FAMILY PROCEEDINGS: COURT BUNDLES

[2000] 1 FLR 536

1 The following practice applies to all hearings in family proceedings in the High Court, to all hearings of family proceedings in the Royal Courts of Justice and to hearings with a time estimate of half a day or more in all care centres, family hearing centres and divorce county courts (including the Principal Registry of the Family Division when so treated), except as specified in paragraph 2.3 below, and subject to specific directions given in any particular case. 'Hearing' extends to all hearings before judges and district judges and includes the hearing of any application.

2.1 A bundle for the use of the court at the hearing shall be provided by the party in the position of applicant at the hearing or by any other party who agrees to do so. It shall contain copies of all documents relevant to the hearing in chronological order, paginated and indexed and divided into separate sections, as follows:

(a) applications and orders;
(b) statements and affidavits;
(c) experts' reports and other reports including those of a guardian ad litem; and
(d) other documents, divided into further sections as may be appropriate.

2.2 Where the nature of the hearing is such that a complete bundle of all documents is unnecessary, the bundle may comprise only those documents necessary for the hearing but the summary (paragraph 3.1(a) below) must commence with a statement that the bundle is limited or incomplete. The summary should be limited to those matters which the court needs to know for the purpose of the hearing and for management of the case.

2.3 The requirement to provide a bundle shall not apply to the hearing of any urgent application where the circumstances are such that it is not reasonably practicable for a bundle to be provided.

3.1 At the commencement of the bundle there shall be:

(a) a summary of the background to the hearing limited, if practicable, to one A4 page;
(b) a statement of the issue or issues to be determined;
(c) a summary of the order or directions sought by each party;
(d) a chronology if it is a final hearing or if the summary under (a) is insufficient;
(e) skeleton arguments as may be appropriate, with copies of all authorities relied on.

3.2 If possible the bundle shall be agreed. In all cases, the party preparing the bundle shall paginate it and provide an index to all other parties prior to the hearing.

3.3 The bundle should normally be contained in a ring binder or lever arch file (limited to 350 pages in each file). Where there is more than one bundle, each should be clearly distinguishable. Bundles shall be lodged, if practicable, 2 clear days prior to the hearing. For hearings in the Royal Courts of Justice bundles shall be lodged with the Clerk of the Rules. All bundles shall have clearly marked on the outside, the title and number of the case, the hearing date and time and, if known, the name of the judge hearing the case.

4 After each hearing which is not a final hearing, the party responsible for the bundle shall retrieve it from the court. The bundle with any additional documents shall be re-lodged for further hearings in accordance with the above provisions.

5 This direction replaces paragraphs 5 and 8 of *Practice Direction (Case Management)* [1995] 1 FLR 456 dated 31 January 1995 and shall have effect from 2 May 2000.

6 Issued with the approval and concurrence of the Lord Chancellor.

DAME ELIZABETH BUTLER-SLOSS
President
10 March 2000

6.10 PRESIDENT'S DIRECTION: HUMAN RIGHTS ACT 1998

[2000] 2 FLR 429

1 It is directed that the following practice shall apply as from 2 October 2000 in all family proceedings:

Citation of authorities

2 When an authority referred to in s 2 of the Human Rights Act 1998 ('the Act') is to be cited at a hearing:

> (a) the authority to be cited shall be an authoritative and complete report;
> (b) the court must be provided with a list of authorities it is intended to cite and copies of the reports:
>> (i) in cases to which *Practice Direction (Family Proceedings: Court Bundles)* (10 March 2000) [2000] 1 FLR 536 applies, as part of the bundle;
>> (ii) otherwise, not less than 2 clear days before the hearing; and
> (c) copies of the complete original texts issued by the European Court and Commission, either paper based or from the Court's judgment database (HUDOC) which is available on the internet, may be used.

Allocation to judges

3(1) The hearing and determination of the following will be confined to a High Court judge:

> (a) a claim for a declaration of incompatibility under s 4 of the Act; or
> (b) an issue which may lead to the court considering making such a declaration.

(2) The hearing and determination of a claim made under the Act in respect of a judicial act shall be confined in the High Court to a High Court judge and in county courts to a circuit judge.

Issued with the concurrence and approval of the Lord Chancellor.

DAME ELIZABETH BUTLER-SLOSS
President
24 July 2000

6.11 PRACTICE DIRECTION (CITATION OF AUTHORITIES)

[2001] 1 WLR 1001

Introduction

(1)   In recent years, there has been a substantial growth in the number of readily available reports of judgments in this and other jurisdictions, such reports being available either in published reports or in transcript form. Widespread knowledge of the work and decisions of the courts is to be welcomed. At the same time, however, the current weight of available material causes problems both for advocates and for courts in properly limiting the nature and amount of material that is used in the preparation and argument of subsequent cases.

(2)   The latter issue is a matter of rapidly increasing importance. Recent and continuing efforts to increase the efficiency, and thus reduce the cost, of litigation, whilst maintaining the interests of justice, will be threatened if courts are burdened with a weight of inappropriate and unnecessary authority, and if advocates are uncertain as to the extent to which it is necessary to deploy authorities in the argument of any given case.

(3)   With a view to limiting the citation of previous authority to cases that are relevant and useful to the court, this Practice Direction lays down a number of rules as to what material may be cited, and the manner in which that cited material should be handled by advocates. These rules are in large part such as many courts already follow in pursuit of their general discretion in the management of litigation. However, it is now desirable to promote uniformity of practice by the same rules being followed by all courts.

(4)   It will remain the duty of advocates to draw the attention of the court to any authority not cited by an opponent which is adverse to the case being advanced.

(5)   This Direction applies to all courts apart from criminal courts, including within the latter category the Court of Appeal (Criminal Division).

Categories of judgments that may only be cited if they fulfil specified requirements

(6.1)   A judgment falling into one of the categories referred to in para 6.2 below may not in future be cited before any court unless it clearly indicates that it purports to establish a new principle or to extend the present law. In respect of judgments delivered after the date of this Direction, that indication must take the form of an express statement to that effect. In respect of judgments delivered before the date of this Direction that indication must be present in or clearly deducible from the language used in the judgment.

(6.2)   Paragraph 6.1 applies to the following categories of judgment:

- applications attended by one party only;
- applications for permission to appeal;

— decisions on applications that only decide that the application is arguable;
— county court cases, unless:

(a) cited in order to illustrate the conventional measure of damages in a personal injury case; or

(b) cited in a county court in order to demonstrate current authority at that level on an issue in respect of which no decision at a higher level of authority is available.

(6.3) These categories will be kept under review, such review to include consideration of adding to the categories.

Citation of other categories of judgment

(7.1) Courts will in future pay particular attention, when it is sought to cite other categories of judgment, to any indication given by the court delivering the judgment that it was seen by that court as only applying decided law to the facts of the particular case; or otherwise as not extending or adding to the existing law.

(7.2) Advocates who seek to cite a judgment that contains indications of the type referred to in para 7.1 will be required to justify their decision to cite the case.

Methods of citation

(8.1) Advocates will in future be required to state, in respect of each authority that they wish to cite, the proposition of law that the authority demonstrates, and the parts of the judgment that support that proposition. If it is sought to cite more than one authority in support of a given proposition, advocates must state the reason for taking that course.

(8.2) The demonstration referred to in para 8.1 will be required to be contained in any skeleton argument and in any appellant's or respondent's notice in respect of each authority referred to in that skeleton or notice.

(8.3) Any bundle or list of authorities prepared for the use of any court must in future bear a certification by the advocate responsible for arguing the case that the requirements of this paragraph have been complied with in respect of each authority included.

(8.4) The statements referred to in para 8.1 should not materially add to the length of submissions or of skeleton arguments, but should be sufficient to demonstrate, in the context of the advocate's argument, the relevance of the authority or authorities to that argument and that the citation is necessary for a proper presentation of that argument.

Authorities decided in other jurisdictions

(9.1) Cases decided in other jurisdictions can, if properly used, be a valuable source of law in this jurisdiction. At the same time, however, such authority should not be cited without proper consideration of whether it does indeed add to the existing body of law.

(9.2) In future therefore, any advocate who seeks to cite an authority from another jurisdiction must:

(i) comply, in respect of that authority, with the rules set out in para 8 above;

(ii) indicate in respect of each authority what that authority adds that is not to be found in authority in this jurisdiction; or, if there is said to be justification for adding to domestic authority, what that justification is;

(iii) certify that there is no authority in this jurisdiction that precludes the acceptance by the court of the proposition that the foreign authority is said to establish.

(9.3) For the avoidance of doubt, paras 9.1 and 9.2 do not apply to cases decided in either the European Court of Justice or the organs of the European Convention of Human Rights. Because of the status in English law of such authority, as provided by, respectively, s 3 of the European Communities Act 1972 and s 2(1) of the Human Rights Act 1998, such cases are covered by the earlier paragraphs of this Direction.

THE LORD CHIEF JUSTICE OF ENGLAND AND WALES
9 April 2001

6.12 PRESIDENT'S DIRECTION: COMMITTAL APPLICATIONS AND PROCEEDINGS IN WHICH A COMMITTAL ORDER MAY BE MADE

[2001] 1 FLR 949

President's Direction – Committal applications – Proceedings in which committal order may be made

(1) As from the date of this direction, the Civil Procedure *Practice Direction* supplemental to the Rules of the Supreme Court 1965 (SI 1965/1766), Ord 52 (Sch 1 to the Civil Procedure Rules 1998 (SI 1998/3132)) and the County Court Rules 1981 (SI 1981/1687), Ord 29 (Sch 2 to the Civil Procedure Rules 1998) ('the CPR Direction'), shall apply to all applications in family proceedings for an order of committal in the same manner and to the same extent as it applies to proceedings governed by the Civil Procedure Rules 1998 ('the CPR') but subject to:

(a)   the provisions of the Family Proceedings Rules 1991 (SI 1991/1247) ('the FPR') and the Rules applied by those Rules namely, the Rules of the Supreme Court 1965 ('RSC') and the County Court Rules 1981 ('CCR') in force immediately before 26 April 1999; and

(b)   the appropriate modifications consequent upon the limited application of the CPR to family proceedings.

(1.1) In particular, the following modification should apply:

(a)   Where the alleged contempt is in connection with existing proceedings (other than contempt in the face of the court) or with an order made or an undertaking given in existing proceedings, the committal application shall be made in those proceedings;

(b)   As required by the FPR, r 7.2, committal applications in the High Court are to be made by summons. In county court proceedings applications are to be made in the manner prescribed by CCR, Ord 29. References in the CPR Direction to 'claim form' and 'application notice' are to be read accordingly;

(c)   In instances where the CPR Direction requires more information to be provided than is required to be provided under the RSC and the CCR, the court will expect the former to be observed;

(d)   Having regard to the periods specified in RSC, Ord 52, r 3, Ord 32, r 3(2)(a) and CCR, Ord 3, r 1(2), the time specified in para 4.2 of the CPR Direction shall not apply. Nevertheless, the court will ensure that adequate time is afforded to the respondent for the preparation of his defence;

(e)   Paragraph 9 of the CPR Direction is to be read with para 3 of each of the Directions issued on 17 December 1997, entitled 'Children Act 1989 – Exclusion requirement' and 'Family Law Act 1996 – Part IV'.

(2) In any family proceedings (not falling within (1) above), in which a committal order may be made, including proceedings for the enforcement of an existing order by way

of judgment summons or other process, full effect will be given to the Human Rights Act 1998 and to the rights afforded under that Act. In particular, Art 6 of the European Convention for the Protection of Human Rights and Fundamental Freedoms 1950 (as set out in Sch 1 to the Human Rights Act 1998) is fully applicable to such proceedings. Those involved must ensure that in the conduct of the proceedings there is due observance of the Human Rights Act 1998 in the same manner as if the proceedings fell within the CPR *Direction*.

(3) As with all family proceedings, the CPR costs provisions apply to all committal proceedings.

(4) Issued with the approval and concurrence of the Lord Chancellor.

DAME ELIZABETH BUTLER-SLOSS
President
16 March 2001

6.13 LORD CHANCELLOR'S PRACTICE NOTE (OFFICIAL SOLICITOR: APPOINTMENT IN FAMILY PROCEEDINGS)

[2001] 2 FLR 155

Practice Note – Official Solicitor – Appointment as guardian ad litem – Appointment as next friend – Terms of appointment

[1] This *Practice Note* supersedes *Practice Note (Official Solicitor: Appointment in Family Proceedings)* (4 December 1998) [1999] 1 FLR 310 issued by the Official Solicitor in relation to his appointment in family proceedings. It is issued in conjunction with a *Practice Note* dealing with the appointment of officers of CAFCASS Legal Services and Special Casework in family proceedings. This *Practice Note* is intended to be helpful guidance, but always subject to *Practice Directions*, decisions of the court and other legal guidance.

[2] The Children and Family Court Advisory and Support Service (CAFCASS) has responsibilities in relation to children in family proceedings in which their welfare is or may be in question (Criminal Justice and Court Services Act 2000, s 12). From 1 April 2001, the Official Solicitor will no longer represent children who are the subject of family proceedings (other than in very exceptional circumstances and after liaison with CAFCASS).

[3] This *Practice Note* summarises the continuing role of the Official Solicitor in family proceedings. Since there are no provisions for parties under disability in the Family Proceedings Courts (Children Act 1989) Rules 1991 (SI 1991/1395), the Official Solicitor can only act in the High Court or in a county court, pursuant to Part IX of the Family Proceedings Rules 1991 (SI 1991/1247). The Official Solicitor will shortly issue an updated *Practice Note* about his role for adults under disability who are the subject of declaratory proceedings in relation to their medical treatment or welfare.

Adults under disability

[4] The Official Solicitor will, in the absence of any other willing and suitable person, act as next friend or guardian ad litem of an adult party under disability, a 'patient'. 'Patient' means someone who is incapable by reason of mental disorder of managing and administering his property and affairs (Family Proceedings Rules 1991, r 9.1). Medical evidence will usually be required before the Official Solicitor can consent to act and his staff can provide a standard form of medical certificate. Where there are practical difficulties in obtaining such medical evidence, the Official Solicitor should be consulted.

Non-subject children

[5] Again in the absence of any other willing and suitable person, the Official Solicitor will act as next friend or guardian ad litem of a child party whose own welfare is not the subject of family proceedings (Family Proceedings Rules 1991, r 2.57, r 9.2 and r 9.5). The most common examples will be:

(a) a child who is also the parent of a child, and who is a respondent to a Children Act 1989 or Adoption Act 1976 application. If a child respondent is already represented by a CAFCASS officer in pending proceedings of which he or she is the subject, then the Official Solicitor will liaise with CAFCASS to agree the most appropriate arrangements;

(b) a child who wishes to make an application for a Children Act 1989 order naming another child (typically a contact order naming a sibling). The Official Solicitor will need to satisfy himself that the proposed proceedings would benefit the child applicant before proceeding;

(c) a child witness to some disputed factual issue in a children case and who may require intervener status. In such circumstances the need for party status and legal representation should be weighed in the light of *Re H (Care Proceedings: Intervener)* [2000] 1 FLR 775;

(d) a child party to a petition for a declaration of status under Part III of the Family Law Act 1986;

(e) a child intervener in divorce or ancillary relief proceedings (r 2.57 or r 9.5);

(f) a child applicant for, or respondent to, an application for an order under Part IV of the Family Law Act 1996. In the case of a child applicant, the Official Solicitor will need to satisfy himself that the proposed proceedings would benefit the child before pursuing them, with leave under Family Law Act 1996, s 43 if required.

[6] Any children who are parties to Children Act 1989 or inherent jurisdiction proceedings may rely on the provisions of Family Proceedings Rules 1991, r 9.2A if they wish to instruct a solicitor without the intervention of a next friend or guardian ad litem. Rule 9.2A does not apply to Adoption Act 1976, Family Law Act 1986/1996 or Matrimonial Causes Act 1973 proceedings.

Older children who are also patients

[7] Officers of CAFCASS will not be able to represent anyone who is over the age of 18. The Official Solicitor may therefore be the more appropriate next friend or guardian ad litem of a child who is also a patient and whose disability will persist beyond his or her eighteenth birthday, especially in non-emergency cases where the substantive hearing is unlikely to take place before the child's eighteenth birthday. The Official Solicitor may also be the more appropriate next friend or guardian ad litem in medical treatment cases such as sterilisation or vegetative state cases, in which his staff have particular expertise deriving from their continuing role for adult patients.

Advising the court

[8] The Official Solicitor may be invited to act or instruct counsel as a friend of the court (amicus) if it appears to the court that such an invitation is more appropriately addressed to him rather than (or in addition to) CAFCASS Legal Services and Special Casework.

Liaison with CAFCASS

[9] In cases of doubt or difficulty, staff of the Official Solicitor's office will liaise with staff of CAFCASS Legal Services and Special Casework to avoid duplication and ensure the most suitable arrangements are made.

Invitations to act in new cases

[10] Solicitors who have been consulted by a child or an adult under disability (or by someone acting on their behalf, or concerned about their interests) should write to the Official Solicitor setting out the background to the proposed case and explaining why there is no other willing and suitable person to act as next friend or guardian ad litem. Where the person concerned is an adult, medical evidence in the standard form of the Official Solicitor's medical certificate should be provided.

Invitations to act in pending proceedings

[11] Where a case is already before the court, an order appointing the Official Solicitor should be expressed as being made subject to his consent. The Official Solicitor aims to provide a response to any invitation within 10 working days. He will be unable to consent to act for an adult until satisfied that the party is a 'patient'. A further directions appointment after 28 days may therefore be helpful. If he accepts appointment the Official Solicitor will need time to prepare the case on behalf of the child or patient and may wish to make submissions about any substantive hearing date. The following documents should be forwarded to the Official Solicitor without delay:

(a) a copy of the order inviting him to act (with a note of the reasons approved by the judge if appropriate);

(b) the court file;

(c) if available, a bundle with summary, statement of issues and chronology (as required by the President's *Practice Direction (Family Proceedings: Court Bundles)* (10 March 2000) [2000] 1 FLR 536).

Contacting the Official Solicitor

[12] It is often helpful to discuss the question of appointment with the Official Solicitor or one of his staff by telephoning 020 7911 7127. Enquiries about family proceedings should be addressed to the Team Manager, Family Litigation.

The Official Solicitor's address is:
81 Chancery Lane
London WC2A 1DD

DX 0012 London Chancery Lane
Fax: 020 7911 7105
Email: officialsolicitor@offsol.gsi.gov.uk

LAURENCE OATES
Official Solicitor
2 April 2001

6.14 PRESIDENT'S DIRECTION: HIV TESTING OF CHILDREN

[2003] 1 FLR 1299

President's Direction – Medical treatment – HIV testing of child – Appropriate court for applications – Where application necessary and where unnecessary – Notice of application to CAFCASS

[1] The procedure, initiated by the decision in *Re HIV Tests (Note)* [1994] 2 FLR 116, whereby applications are made to a High Court judge to permit the testing of a child for the presence of Human Immunodeficiency Virus (HIV) is to be revised in the light of judicial experience and having regard to developments in medical science.

[2] The need to make application to the court is likely to arise only rarely. In cases where application to permit HIV testing is a necessary step, the application to permit testing should be made to the appropriate county court and only to the High Court if proceedings concerning the child are pending there or the application is made for an order under the inherent jurisdiction of the High Court.

[2.1] If there are proceedings concerning the child pending in a family proceedings court, the application to permit HIV testing should be transferred to county court level for determination; the proceedings may then be remitted to the family proceedings court following the hearing of the application in the county court.

[2.2] Applications made to, or transferred to, the county court should be determined by a judge or district judge nominated (at least) for private law children cases. In the High Court, the application may be determined by a High Court district judge unless the application is made for an order under the inherent jurisdiction, in which case the application should be made directly to a High Court judge.

[3] In cases where a child of sufficient understanding to make an informed decision opposes the testing, reference to the court is necessary. If there are no pending proceedings, the application should be made under the inherent jurisdiction of the High Court. Notice of the application should be given to the Legal Services and Special Casework department of the Children and Family Court Advisory and Support Service (CAFCASS Legal Services). Another category of case in which CAFCASS Legal Services should be given notice is where a decision about testing is urgently required and the parents may not be legally represented.

[3.1] It should be noted that where all those with parental responsibility agree to the testing (and it is not opposed by the child) no reference to court is necessary, unless the testing is for the preparation of expert evidence.

[4] Issued with the approval and concurrence of the Lord Chancellor.

DAME ELIZABETH BUTLER-SLOSS
President
15 May 2003

6.15 PROTOCOL FROM THE PRESIDENT'S OFFICE (COMMUNICATING WITH THE HOME OFFICE)

[2004] 1 FLR 638

Practice – Communication with Home Office – Request or order for information

[1] Where a request is made of or an order is made against the Home Office, the judge should ask the court to draw up and immediately to provide a copy of the relevant request or order in a separate document to:

Ms Ananda Hall
Family Division Lawyer
President's Chambers
Royal Courts of Justice
Strand, London WC2A 2LL
T: 020 7947 7197
F: 020 7947 7274
Ananda.Hall@courtservice.gsi.gov.uk

[2] The request or order should either state or be accompanied by a letter to the Family Division Lawyer stating the following details in respect of all parties about whom they are seeking information:

– full name including all middle names;
– nationality;
– full date of birth; and
– any known Home Office reference number.

[3] The request or order should state the time by which the information is required, where possible allowing a reasonable period for the Home Office to investigate and prepare its statement to the court.

[4] The request or order should identify the questions it wishes to be answered by the Home Office.

[5] The request or order should be forwarded to the Family Division Lawyer together with such information as is sufficient to enable the President's Office and the Home Office to understand the nature of the case, to identify whether the case involves an adoption, and to identify whether the immigration issues raised might relate to an asylum or non-asylum application.

[6] The Family Division Lawyer will then send to an appropriate enquiries officer in the Home Office the enquiry, together with a copy of any request or order made. The Home Office official will be personally responsible for either:

(a) answering the query herself, by retrieving the file and preparing a statement for the court; or

(b) if the request is for more than mere information (eg requiring speculation as to the possible effect of an order or the likelihood of a party being granted special leave to remain), by either obtaining information from, or passing the court's order to, the relevant official with carriage of that particular file.

[7] The Family Division Lawyer will follow up as required in order to ensure that the information is received by the court in time, and will receive the statement before forwarding it on as instructed by the judge or court making the request.

1 December 2003

6.16 PROTOCOL FROM THE PRESIDENT'S OFFICE (COMMUNICATING WITH THE PASSPORT SERVICE)

[2004] 1 FLR 640

Practice – Communication with Passport Service – Request or order for information

[1] Where a request is made of or an order is made against the UK Passport Service, the judge should ask the court to draw up and immediately to provide a copy of the relevant request or order in a separate document to:

Ms Ananda Hall
Family Division Lawyer
President's Chambers
Royal Courts of Justice
Strand, London WC2A 2LL
T: 020 7947 7197
F: 020 7947 7274
Ananda.Hall@courtservice.gsi.gov.uk

[2] The request or order should either state or be accompanied by a letter to the Family Division Lawyer stating the following details in respect of all parties about whom they are seeking information:

– full name including all middle names;
– full date of birth; and
– any known passport numbers.

[3] The request or order should state the time by which the information is required, where possible allowing a reasonable period for the Passport Service to search their records.

[4] The request or order should identify the information required from the Passport Service.

[5] The Family Division Lawyer will then send to disclosure of information officers the enquiry, together with a copy of any request or order made. The disclosure of information officer will be responsible for retrieving the information and forwarding this to the Family Division Lawyer.

[6] The Family Division Lawyer will follow up as required in order to ensure that the information is received by the court in time, and will receive the statement before forwarding it on as instructed by the judge or court making the request.

21 November 2003

6.17 GUIDANCE FROM THE PRESIDENT'S OFFICE (UK PASSPORT APPLICATIONS ON BEHALF OF CHILDREN IN THE ABSENCE OF THE SIGNATURE OF A PERSON WITH PARENTAL RESPONSIBILITY)

[2004] 1 FLR 746

Children – Issue of passport in best interests – Adult with parental responsibility refusing to sign – Application form

[1] This guidance deals with situations in which the court has decided that it is in a child's best interests that s/he be issued with a passport, but the adult/s with parental responsibility have refused to sign the passport application form.

[2] This kind of situation might arise where a child is voluntarily accommodated by a local authority and, for example, wishes to go on holiday independently or with his/her carers.

[3] The UK Passport Application form is in a standard form which will not be entirely suitable in these kinds of circumstances.

[4] The UK Passport Service has therefore agreed that it will be acceptable to complete the form in the following manner:

SECTIONS 1–6

[5] These sections must be completed.

SECTION 7 (RELEVANT ONLY RE: CHILDREN AGED 16 OR 17)

[6] If no person with parental responsibility is prepared to sign section 7, and the court has decided that it is in the best interests of the child that a passport be issued to the child, then the section may be left blank provided that the application is accompanied by an order of the court that:

  (a) the parent/s (as appropriate) should not use their parental responsibility to veto the application; and
  (b) that the court considers it to be in the best interests of the child that a passport be issued.

SECTION 8

[7] This question should be completed if relevant to the application.

SECTION 9

[8] *Where a child is aged 16 or 17*: the child may personally sign this section.

[9] *Where a child is aged under 16*: it is imperative that an adult sign this section. In the absence of a person holding parental responsibility, there will presumably be another adult in a position to sign the form (eg the adult with whom the child is going on holiday). It would not be necessary or proper for the judge to sign the form personally.

[10] If the adult signing the form is not a parent or guardian with parental responsibility for the child, the section can be manually altered as follows:

    (a) Clauses 2, 3, 4 and 6 may be deleted, if any of them causes any concern or difficulty for the adult signing the form.

    (b) Clauses 1, 5, 7 and 8 must not be deleted: they are mandatory declarations without which the application will not be processed.

[11] If any clauses are deleted in accordance with para [10] above, then the application form must be accompanied by:

    (a) An order of the court that:

        (i)   the parent/s (as appropriate) should not use their parental responsibility to veto the application; and

        (ii)   that the court considers it to be in the best interests of the child that a passport be issued; plus

    (b) A statement from the adult signing s 9 setting out a written explanation as to why they are making the application on the child's behalf, what their relationship is to the child, and in the case of a child being accommodated by a local authority an explanation from that authority.

[12] Additionally, if cl 3 is deleted, then the adult signing the form must instead enter at s 8 a statement in the following terms: 'The person named at s 2 is, to the best of my knowledge and belief, a British national and has not lost or renounced his/her national status'.

ANANDA HALL
Family Division Lawyer
21 January 2004

6.18 PRESIDENT'S DIRECTION: REPRESENTATION OF CHILDREN IN FAMILY PROCEEDINGS PURSUANT TO FAMILY PROCEEDINGS RULES 1991, RULE 9.5

[2004] 1 FLR 1188

Children Act proceedings – Representation of children in non-specified proceedings – Practice

[1] The proper conduct and disposal of proceedings concerning a child which are not specified proceedings within the meaning of s 41 of the Children Act 1989 may require the child to be made a party. Rule 9.5 of the Family Proceedings Rules 1991 (FPR) provides for the appointment of a guardian ad litem (a guardian) for a child party unless the child is of sufficient understanding and can participate as a party in the proceedings without a guardian, as permitted by FPR r 9.2A.

[2] Making the child a party to the proceedings is a step that will be taken only in cases which involve an issue of significant difficulty and consequently will occur in only a minority of cases. Before taking the decision to make the child a party, consideration should be given to whether an alternative route might be preferable, such as asking an officer of the Children and Family Court Advisory and Support Service (CAFCASS) to carry out further work or by making a referral to social services or possibly, by obtaining expert evidence.

[3] The decision to make the child a party will always be exclusively that of the judge, made in the light of the facts and circumstances of the particular case. The following are offered, solely by way of guidance, as circumstances which may justify the making of an order:

[3.1] Where a CAFCASS officer has notified the court that in his opinion the child should be made a party (see FPR r 4.11B(6)).

[3.2] Where the child has a standpoint or interests which are inconsistent with or incapable of being represented by any of the adult parties.

[3.3] Where there is an intractable dispute over residence or contact, including where all contact has ceased, or where there is irrational but implacable hostility to contact or where the child may be suffering harm associated with the contact dispute.

[3.4] Where the views and wishes of the child cannot be adequately met by a report to the court.

[3.5] Where an older child is opposing a proposed course of action.

[3.6] Where there are complex medical or mental health issues to be determined or there are other unusually complex issues that necessitate separate representation of the child.

[3.7] Where there are international complications outside child abduction, in particular where it may be necessary for there to be discussions with overseas authorities or a foreign court.

[3.8] Where there are serious allegations of physical, sexual or other abuse in relation to the child or there are allegations of domestic violence not capable of being resolved with the help of a CAFCASS officer.

[3.9] Where the proceedings concern more than one child and the welfare of the children is in conflict or one child is in a particularly disadvantaged position.

[3.10] Where there is a contested issue about blood testing.

[4] It must be recognised that separate representation of the child may result in a delay in the resolution of the proceedings. When deciding whether to direct that a child be made a party, the court will take into account the risk of delay or other facts adverse to the welfare of the child. The court's primary consideration will be the best interests of the child.

[5] When a child is made a party and a guardian is to be appointed:

[5.1] Consideration should first be given to appointing an officer of CAFCASS as guardian. Before appointing an officer, the court will cause preliminary enquires to be made of CAFCASS. For the procedure, reference should be made to *CAFCASS Practice Note (Representation of Children in Family Proceedings Pursuant to Family Proceedings Rules 1991, Rule 9.5)* (6 April 2004) [2004] 1 FLR 1190.

[5.2] If CAFCASS is unable to provide a guardian without delay, or if for some other reason the appointment of a CAFCASS officer is not appropriate, FPR r 9.5(1) makes further provision for the appointment of a guardian.

[6] In cases proceeding in a county court, the court may, at the same time as deciding whether to join a child as a party, consider whether the nature of the case or the complexity or importance of the issues require transfer of the case to the High Court.

[7] Issued with the concurrence and approval of the Lord Chancellor.

ELIZABETH BUTLER-SLOSS
President
5 April 2004

6.19 CAFCASS PRACTICE NOTE: REPRESENTATION OF CHILDREN IN FAMILY PROCEEDINGS PURSUANT TO FAMILY PROCEEDINGS RULES 1991, RULE 9.5

[2004] 1 FLR 1190

Children Act proceedings – Representation of children in non-specified proceedings – Practice

Introduction

[1] This practice note is issued in conjunction with the *President's Direction (Representation of Children in Family Proceedings Pursuant to Family Proceedings Rules 1991, Rule 9.5)* (5 April 2004) [2004] 1 FLR 1188 with the President's approval. It supersedes *CAFCASS Practice Note (Officers of CAFCASS Legal Services and Special Casework: Appointment in Family Proceedings)* (March 2001) [2001] 2 FLR 151.

Appointment of CAFCASS officers in private law proceedings pursuant to Family Proceedings Rules 1991 (FPR) r 9.5

[2] Where the court has decided to appoint an officer of the Children and Family Court Advisory and Support Service (CAFCASS) as guardian the preferred order should simply state that '[name of child] is made party to the proceedings and pursuant to Family Proceedings Rules 1991 r 9.5 an officer of CAFCASS be appointed as his/her guardian'. It is also helpful for CAFCASS to know whether the court considers there is any reason why any CAFCASS officer who has dealt with the matter so far should not continue to deal with it in the role of guardian.

[3] The decision about which particular officer of CAFCASS to allocate as guardian is a matter for CAFCASS.

[4] In cases proceeding in the High Court, a copy of the court file, including the order making the r 9.5 appointment and any information about the court's reasons, should be sent for the attention of The Manager, CAFCASS Legal, 1st Floor, Newspaper House, 8–16 Great New Street, London, EC4A 3BN or by document exchange to DX 144 London Chancery Lane. If the appointment of a CAFCASS officer as guardian is urgent then the judge or a member of the Court Service is encouraged, if possible, to telephone on 020 7904 0867 to discuss the matter before an order is made; alternatively, the order and any information about the court's reasons can be faxed to CAFCASS Legal on 020 7904 0868.

[5] In cases proceeding in the county court, the order making the r 9.5 appointment should be faxed to the local CAFCASS office responsible for private law cases unless the case falls within any of the categories identified in para [10] below when it should be referred to CAFCASS Legal following the procedure in para [4] above.

[6] In either case CAFCASS will make a decision within 5 working days of receipt of the papers from the court about whether it will provide an officer of the service locally (as will be the case in most county court cases) or from CAFCASS Legal (as will be the case in most High Court cases) to act as guardian. It is the responsibility of the local CAFCASS service manager and CAFCASS Legal to liaise whenever necessary to ensure that the most appropriate CAFCASS officer is appointed as guardian.

[7] The CAFCASS office that is to be responsible for the matter will notify the court of the name and professional address and telephone number of the particular officer who will act as guardian. If for whatever reason there is likely to be any significant delay in an officer of the service being made available CAFCASS will notify the court accordingly to enable the court to consider whether some other proper person should instead be appointed as guardian.

[8] If the CAFCASS officer to be appointed as guardian is based at CAFCASS Legal there will normally be no need for a solicitor for the child also to be appointed as the litigation will usually be conducted in-house pursuant to s 15 of the Criminal Justice and Court Services Act 2000.

[9] If the CAFCASS officer to be appointed as guardian is based at a local CAFCASS office then legal representation will be provided either through CAFCASS Legal or by the appointment of a local solicitor to act for the child. It is normally the guardian's responsibility to appoint a solicitor pursuant to the combined effect of FPR rr 9.5(6) and 4.11A(1). A local solicitor can apply for legal aid for the child in the ordinary way enabling the guardian (funded by CAFCASS) and the child's solicitor (funded by the Legal Services Commission) to work together in the same way as they routinely do in specified proceedings.

Cases that should be referred to CAFCASS Legal whether or not involving an appointment pursuant to FPR r 9.5 and whether proceeding in the High Court or the county court

[10] Whilst the great majority of cases are likely to continue to be referred by courts to local CAFCASS offices the following categories of case should be referred to CAFCASS Legal:

[10.1] Cases in which the children's divisions of the Official Solicitor or CAFCASS Legal previously acted for the child;

[10.2] Exceptionally complex international cases where legal or other substantial enquiries abroad will be necessary or where there is a dispute as to which country's courts should have jurisdiction over the child's affairs (for example, a case in which two children previously the subject of adoption and then care proceedings in two other countries were brought to England illegally and made the subject of further care proceedings here);

[10.3] Exceptionally complex adoption cases (for example, where there is a need to investigate a suspected illegal payment or placement; adoption proceedings following a mistake during fertility treatment involving the use of unauthorised sperm; and the circumstances arising in *Flintshire County Council v K* [2001] 2 FLR 476);

[10.4] All medical treatment cases where the child is old enough to have views which need to be taken into account, or where there are particularly difficult ethical issues such as the withdrawal of treatment, unless the issue arises in existing proceedings already being handled locally when the preferred arrangement will usually be for the matter to continue to be dealt with locally but with additional advice provided by CAFCASS Legal;

[10.5] Any freestanding human rights applications pursuant to s 7(1)(a) of the Human Rights Act 1998 in which it is thought that it may be possible and appropriate for any part to be played by CAFCASS or its officers;

[10.6] Any additional categories of case for referral to CAFCASS Legal that may from time to time be added to this list.

[11] In such cases the referral to CAFCASS Legal should follow a similar procedure to that set out in para [4] above.

Other cases that may be referred to CAFCASS Legal

[12] Other family proceedings in which the welfare of children is or may be in question may be referred to CAFCASS Legal where they are exceptionally difficult, unusual or sensitive (for example, a care case in which death threats were made against the child and other professionals necessitating special security measures including false identities for some of those under threat; and an adoption case in which there had been serious misconduct by the local CAFCASS officer originally appointed).

CAFCASS Legal acting as Advocate to the Court

[13] CAFCASS Legal may be invited to act or instruct counsel to appear as Advocate to the Court in family proceedings in which the welfare of children is or may be in question (for example, in a recent case an issue arose about the extent of the court's powers in Hague Convention1 proceedings to give directions designed to prevent further abduction pending trial, which led to CAFCASS Legal briefing counsel as Advocate to the Court).

[14] Sometimes it will be more appropriate for the Attorney-General or the Official Solicitor to fulfil this role. Reference should be made to the memorandum on requests for the appointment of an Advocate to the Court issued by the Attorney-General and the Lord Chief Justice on 19 December 2001.

Liaison between CAFCASS Legal and the Official Solicitor

[15] In cases in which there is any doubt as to whether CAFCASS or the Official Solicitor should provide representation, staff of CAFCASS Legal will liaise with staff of the Official Solicitor's office to ensure that the most suitable arrangements are made.

Provision of general assistance by CAFCASS Legal

[16] CAFCASS Legal is available to provide legal advice to officers of CAFCASS, whether employed or self-employed, in connection with their professional responsibilities.

[17] CAFCASS Legal is also available to offer informal advice to judges and other professionals engaged in family proceedings in which the welfare of children is or may be in question without necessarily being appointed as a guardian or Advocate to the Court (for instance in relation to passport applications for accommodated children).

---

1   Editor's note: Hague Convention on the Civil Aspects of International Child Abduction 1980.

[18] Lawyers at CAFCASS Legal take it in turn to carry a mobile telephone through which they can be contacted any day of the year by the High Court out-of-hours duty judge if their help is needed, for instance in relation to a medical treatment emergency.

CHARLES PREST
Director of Legal Services, CAFCASS
6 April 2004

6.20 THE PRIVATE LAW PROGRAMME: GUIDANCE ISSUED BY THE PRESIDENT OF THE FAMILY DIVISION

Introduction
From: the Rt Hon Dame Elizabeth Butler-Sloss, GBE

On 21 July 2004 I announced the implementation of a new **Framework for Private Law** cases. This gave advanced warning to the Designated Family Judges of the principles and key elements of the **Private Law Programme** to enable the judiciary, managers from the Her Majesty's Courts Service[1] (HMCS), and the Children and Family Court Advisory and Support Service (CAFCASS) to begin their discussions about local schemes.

The full text of the guidance, which was published on 9 November 2004, follows this Introduction. It is intended that the Programme will be a gradual process involving a National roll out of best practice together with the development of local schemes, having in mind good local initiatives already in place, based upon these principles and key elements. The detail has been discussed and agreed by a judicial working party in consultation with representatives of HMCS and CAFCASS.

The guidance provides assistance to the judiciary, HMCS and CAFCASS managers to help develop local schemes and includes examples of information sheets and other documents for court users and certain basic minimum considerations that will be necessary to make the Programme effective.

It is expected that careful consideration will be given to schemes that already exist at Family Proceedings Court level so that they can be incorporated into or enlarged upon in the development of family dispute resolution mechanisms. It is hoped that in due course the Programme will be formally extended to all Family Proceedings Courts.

It is my intention that in each of the Care Centres there will now be a process of consultation between the judiciary, HMCS, CAFCASS and interest groups represented on local Family Court Business Committees and Forums. Having regard to that consultation, local schemes will be implemented by Designated Family Judges as soon as it is practicable to do so in each region.

ELIZABETH BUTLER-SLOSS
President

---

[1] On 1 April 2005 Her Majesty's Courts Service will become the new executive agency, which will incorporate the Court Service, and be responsible for running all courts below the House of Lords – comprising of the Court of Appeal, High Court, Crown Court, County Courts and Magistrates' Family Proceedings Courts.

Guidance: The Private Law Programme

The court process exists in the wider context of parental separation and relationship breakdown. The court's aim is to assist parents to safeguard their children's welfare. It is hoped that many families will have received out of court assistance and early intervention from professionals before or upon making an application to the court eg by referral to a Family Resolutions Pilot Project and/or information, advice and assistance from specialist legal advisors and others (eg through the Family Advice and Information Service: FAInS). The court to which an application is made will always investigate whether the family has had the benefit of these or similar services and whether any available form of alternative dispute resolution can be utilised.

Principles:

Where an application is made to the court under Part II of the Children Act 1989, the welfare of the child will be safeguarded by the application of the overriding objective of the family justice system in 3 respects:

1. Dispute resolution at a First Hearing
2. Effective court control including monitoring outcomes against aims
3. Flexible facilitation and referrals (matching resources to families)

The overriding objective is as follows:

'... *to enable the court to deal with every (children) case*

(a) *justly, expeditiously, fairly and with the minimum of delay;*
(b) *in ways which ensure, so far as is practicable, that*
    a. *the parties are on an equal footing;*
    b. *the welfare of the children involved is safeguarded; and*
    c. *distress to all parties is minimised;*
(c) *so far as is practicable, in ways which are proportionate*
    a. *to the gravity and complexity of the issues; and*
    b. *to the nature and extent of the intervention proposed in the private and family life of the children and adults involved*'

1. FIRST HEARING DISPUTE RESOLUTION

*   In every case there shall be an early **First Hearing** dispute resolution appointment:

    *   That identifies **immediate safety issues**
    *   That exercises **effective court control** so as to **identify the aim** of the proceedings, the timescale within which the aim can be achieved, the issues between the parties, the opportunities for the resolution of those issues by appropriate referrals for support and assistance and any subsequent steps that may be permitted or required

- That, wherever possible, a **CAFCASS** practitioner shall be available to the court and to the family whose purpose and priority is to **facilitate early dispute resolution** rather than the provision of a formal report
- That, save in exceptional circumstances (eg safety) or where immediate agreement is possible so that the principle of **early dispute resolution** can be **facilitated**: directs that **the family** shall be **referred for support and assistance** to:
    - ♦ A Family Resolutions Pilot Project (where available)
    - ♦ Locally available resolution services (eg ADR, including mediation and conciliation, and/or other service, support, facilitation, treatment and therapy options) that are to be listed and publicised by the Family Justice Council / Family Court Business Committee for each Care Centre (eg provided by CAFCASS, service partnerships – Councils with Social Services Responsibilities and the NHS and/or by voluntary service providers – NACCC (National Association of Child Contact Centres) resources and outreach voluntary workers)

2. EFFECTIVE COURT CONTROL

- The overriding objective shall be furthered by **continuous** and **active case management** of every case which shall include:
    - **Judicial Availability**: the identification of gatekeeper district judges to undertake early First Hearing dispute resolution appointments
    - **Judicial Continuity**: the allocation to the case of private law family judiciary and the identification of dedicated court and CAFCASS practitioners
    - **Continuous case management** by the allocated judiciary and identified court officers which shall include a listing scheme in each hearing centre that describes local listing arrangements to ensure judicial availability, continuity and access to the court for review and/or enforcement
    - The **avoidance of unnecessary delay** by the early identification of issues and timetabling of the case from the outset
    - Maximising Family Court Resources: guidance for the flexible **transfer of cases** between every level of family court so as to make best use of court facilities, judges and FPCs, having regard to availability, urgency and in some cases, complexity
    - Identifying **and** achieving **the aim** of each hearing
    - **Monitoring** and **reviewing** the **outcome** (if needs be at short notice)
    - **Enforcing** the court's orders (if needs be at short notice)
    - **Controlling** the use and **cost** of resources

3. FLEXIBLE FACILITATION AND REFERRAL

- Best interests decisions and agreements shall be **facilitated** by:
    - The use of **Parenting Plans** to assist parents to agree routine childcare questions

- The use of a **CAFCASS practitioner** who where possible shall be continuously involved **to facilitate** and/or supervise the orders made by the court and the arrangements that are necessary to make orders and agreements work
- The flexible use of **rehabilitative, training, therapy, treatment** and **enforcement** powers
- Directions that require parties, referral agencies and, where appropriate, the CAFCASS practitioner to report the **progress** or **outcome** of any step so that the court might respond by **urgent review** to safeguard the welfare of the child

4. PROCESS

- **Information**: The DFJ responsible for each family hearing centre shall liaise with HMCS and CAFCASS and local service providers and shall set out in judicial, listing, parent and child information sheets the procedures, arrangements and facilities that are available to the court and families in the local area.

- The **First Hearing** dispute resolution appointment:
  - Shall be listed within a **target window** from the issue of the application of **4 to 6 working weeks**;
  - Shall be attended by the **parents** and in court centres where the local scheme provides for it and where resources exist may be attended by any **child** aged 9 or over
  - In court centres where resources exist to provide 'in-court conciliation':
    - the First Hearing dispute resolution appointment shall be listed so that a **duty CAFCASS practitioner is available** to the parties and to the court **to facilitate** agreements, the identification of issues and any appropriate referrals for assistance;
    - where the local scheme provides for it, the detailed content of the conciliation discussions may remain confidential;
    - the court may adjourn a First Hearing dispute resolution appointment for further in-court conciliation or a report upon the availability or success of any proposal.
  - In court centres where a duty CAFCASS practitioner is not available:
    - the court will identify the issues between the parties and use its best endeavours to facilitate agreements and referrals for assistance;
    - in appropriate cases where advice is necessary, the court may adjourn the First Hearing dispute resolution appointment for a CAFCASS practitioner to provide oral or short written advice to the parties and the court limited to the facilitation of matters that are agreed and referrals for further assistance.
  - In all cases at the conclusion of the First Hearing dispute resolution appointment and generally at the end of any subsequent hearing that may be required the court shall identify on the face of the order:
    - the issues that are determined, agreed or disagreed;
    - the aim of the order, agreement, referral or hearing that is set out in the order;

♦ any other basis for the order or directions that are made or the agreement that is recorded;

♦ in respect of issues that are not agreed and that need to be determined so as to safeguard the welfare of the child:

  o the level of court (and where appropriate the allocated judge(s)) before whom all future non-conciliation hearings and applications are to be heard;

  o the timetable and the sequence of the steps that are required to lead to an early hearing;

  o the filing and service of evidence limited to such of the issues as the court may identify;

  o whether a CAFCASS practitioner's report is necessary and if so, the issues to which the report is to be directed;

  o in respect of all orders, agreements and referrals directions for

    * the facilitation of the same (in particular by a CAFCASS practitioner);

    * the monitoring of the outcome, including by urgent reserved re-listing before the same court **within 10 working days** of a request by CAFCASS;

    * Enforcement

PART 7

A JACKDAW'S COLLECTION

'My heart leaps up when I behold
A rainbow in the sky:
So was it when my life began;
So is it now I am a man;
So be it when I shall grow old,
Or let me die!
The Child is father of the Man;
And I could wish my days to be
Bound each to each by natural piety.

William Wordsworth, 'My heart leaps up when I behold'

'It also ... demonstrates not only that in this particular field which we summarise as "cot deaths", even the most distinguished expert can be wrong, but also provides a salutary warning against the possible dangers of an over-dogmatic expert approach. ... We cannot avoid the thought that some of the honest views expressed with reasonable confidence in the present case (on both sides of the argument) will have to be revised in years to come, when the fruits of continuing medical research, both here and internationally, become available. What may be unexplained today may be perfectly well understood tomorrow. Until then, any tendency to dogmatise should be met with an answering challenge.'

Judge LJ in *R v Angela Cannings* [2004] EWCA Crim 01
at paras [17] and [22]

'Though the children did not know Levin well and did not remember when they had seen him, they did not show towards him any of that strange shyness and hostility so often felt by children toward grown-up people who "pretend", which causes them to suffer so painfully. Pretence about anything sometimes deceives the wisest and shrewdest man, but, however cunningly it is hidden, a child of the meanest capacity feels it and is repelled by it.'

Leo Tolstoy, *Anna Karenina*, Part 3, Chapter 9[1]

---

[1]   By permission of Oxford University Press. Part 3, p 267 (75 words) from *Anna Karenina* (OWC), edited by Maude, Louise and Aylmer (1979). Free permission.

7.1 A SUMMARY OF BASICS ABOUT ARTICLE 8 OF THE EUROPEAN CONVENTION ON HUMAN RIGHTS

Article 8 of the European Convention on Human Rights 1950 provides:

'(1) Everyone has the right to respect for his private and family life, his home and his correspondence.

(2) There shall be no interference by a public authority with the exercise of this right except such as is in accordance with the law and is necessary in a democratic society in the interests of national security, public safety or the economic well-being of the country, for the prevention of disorder or crime, for the protection of health or morals, or for the protection of the rights and freedoms of others.'

The main elements in a dispute about a breach of Article 8 are therefore as follows.

- Was there family life?[1]
- Was the right to respect for that private/family life interfered with by the State, bearing in mind the positive obligations a State has in this respect?
- Was any such interference in accordance with law?
- Was such interference in pursuit of an aim or aims that are legitimate under Article 8(2)?
- Was the interference necessary in a democratic society? This often proves to be the main issue of contention and is where many of the great principles of ECHR jurisprudence (eg the margin of appreciation, proportionality, etc) are brought to bear.

Pursuant to the Human Rights Act 1998:

- domestic courts must take account of any relevant case-law of the ECtHR (s 2);
- domestic courts must read and give effect to domestic legislation in a way which is compatible with rights under the ECHR (s 3); and
- the ECHR is specifically extended to the acts and failures to act of public authorities (s 6), and two ways are provided by which an individual can enforce such rights – within existing proceedings (s 7(1)(b)) or by issuing a free-standing set of proceedings (s 7(1)(a)).

---

[1] If the issue is a breach of the right to respect for family life. If it is the right to respect for private life this is irrelevant.

7.2 AN OUTLINE OF THE EUROPEAN CONVENTION ON HUMAN RIGHTS, ARTICLE 8 RIGHTS THAT MIGHT BE RELEVANT TO AN 'ORDINARY' APPLICATION BY A FATHER FOR CONTACT WITH HIS CHILD

Father

- A right to 'sufficient involvement' in the proceedings.
- That delay should not be determinative of the issue.
- The positive obligation on the State to achieve a re-unification between him and the child …
  - … including a positive obligation on the State to enforce such contact …,
  - … itself including the taking of 'preparatory measures'/'coercive measures',
- but these rights/positive obligations are not absolute as the rights and freedoms of all concerned must be taken into account, particularly the best interests of the child and her rights.

Mother

- A right to 'sufficient involvement' in the proceedings.
- That delay should not be determinative of the issue.
- Within her right to respect for private life, a right to her physical integrity (safety).
- A right to have her rights and freedoms taken into account in determining the nature and extent of the State's positive obligation to achieve a re-unification between the father and the child.

Child

- A right to 'sufficient involvement' in the proceedings.
- That delay should not be determinative of the issue.
- The positive obligation on the State to achieve a re-unification between her and her father…
  - … including a positive obligation on the State to enforce such contact …,
  - … itself including the taking of 'preparatory measures'/'coercive measures',
- a right to have her rights and freedoms (which may indeed be paramount) taken into account in determining the nature and extent of

the State's positive obligation to achieve a re-unification between father and child.

- Within her right to respect for private life, a right to her physical integrity (safety).
- Within the right to respect for her private life, an emerging right to self-determination in accordance with her increasing age and maturity.

The general interest

- In ensuring respect for the rule of law (enforcement).

7.3 THE WELFARE CHECKLIST – AN EXPLANATION FOR CHILDREN AND YOUNG PEOPLE

Reproduced here with the kind permission of the author, Gill Timmis.[1]

JUDGES HAVE RULES TOO! When a judge is thinking about plans for you he or she has to think about all these things before he is allowed to make a decision about what should happen to you. These are the things that the judge has to think about when he or she is deciding about plans for you:

What are your wishes and feelings?

What do you think and feel about what's happening and the plans that are being made, balanced with how old you are and how much you understand.

What do you need?

What you need to help you grow up OK. Things like: being looked after, loved and cared for and going to school.

What if something changed?

What would happen if anything changed for you, would things get better or worse or stay the same?

What are the special things that make you who you are?

The judge must be told about all the special things about you, how old you are, where you come from, who your family is, and anything else about you that's important.

Have you been hurt or harmed?

If you've been hurt or harmed by what has happened to you.

Can your parents manage?

Whether your parents can manage to look after you properly.

What can the court do?

What orders the court is allowed to make.

---

[1] Previously published in 'Seen and Heard', vol 11, issue 1 at p 45 and also included in 'Powerpack', an information pack for children and young people involved in care proceedings, published in 2001 by the NSPCC, CAFCASS and Warwick Law School.

7.4 WHEN THE WELFARE OF THE CHILD IS NOT PARAMOUNT

It is generally sufficient for most interdisciplinary workers to work on the basis that 'the child's welfare is the paramount consideration' is the golden rule of children law in England and Wales. It is, but it is also important to be aware of some exceptions and limitations to the application of that golden rule. The starting point to understanding this is that there is no general statutory or common law principle that says that 'the child's welfare is the paramount consideration'. It only applies if and to the extent that a statute says it does.

- There are all sorts of statutes affecting the welfare of children that do not contain the paramountcy principle. The most important of these at the moment is the Adoption Act 1976, although this will be put right by the implementation of s 1 of the Adoption and Children Act 2002. But there are other examples, such as when courts are considering making occupation and non-molestation orders under the Family Law Act 1996, or when determining financial relief under the Matrimonial Causes Act 1973, or when dealing with an application under the Child Abduction and Custody Act 1985.

- Even where a statute contains the paramountcy principle, the exact way in which it is expressed must be carefully considered and applied. Section 1(1) of the Children Act 1989 limits its application to 'when a court determines any question with respect to (a) the upbringing of a child; or (b) the administration of a child's property or the application of any income from it'. The paramountcy principle does not apply to applications for leave to apply for a section 8 order (pursuant to s 10),[1] for financial relief (pursuant to s 15), or for a secure accommodation order (pursuant to s 25).[2]

- The paramountcy principle under the Children Act 1989 only applies to decisions of the court. It does not apply to parents in the exercise of their parental responsibility or to local authorities in the exercise of their functions.

- There are some other important exceptions to the paramountcy principle including judicial decisions about whether someone should be joined as, or discharged from being, a party to Children Act 1989 proceedings

---

[1] See *G v F (Contact and Shared Residence: Applications for Leave)* [1998] 2 FLR 799.

[2] See s 25(4), and *Re M (Secure Accommodation Order)* [1995] 1 FLR 418.

(pursuant to r 4.7 of the Family Proceedings Rules 1991)[3] and about whether to grant an injunction to restrict publicity.[4]

---

[3] See *North Yorkshire County Council v G* [1993] 2 FLR 732 and *Re W (Discharge of Party to Proceedings)* [1997] 1 FLR 128.

[4] See *Re S (Identification: Restrictions on Publication)* [2003] EWCA Civ 963, [2003] 2 FLR 1253.

7.5 WHO HAS PARENTAL RESPONSIBILITY?

As at 1 January 2005 the following have parental responsibility:

- a child's mother (Children Act 1989 (CA 1989), s 2) unless it has been extinguished by an order freeing the child for adoption or by an adoption order;
- a child's father if married to the mother at the time of the child's birth or if they have subsequently married (CA 1989, s 2) again unless it has been extinguished by an order freeing the child for adoption or by an adoption order;
- a child's father if formally registered as such on or after 1 December 2003[1] (CA 1989, s 4, as amended by Adoption and Children Act 2002, s 111) unless it has been extinguished by an order freeing the child for adoption or by an adoption order;
- a child's father if he has acquired it by entering into a parental responsibility agreement with the mother (CA 1989, s 4) unless it has been extinguished by an order freeing the child for adoption or by an adoption order or if the court has made an order bringing the parental responsibility agreement to an end;
- a child's father if he has acquired it by a court order (CA 1989, s 4) unless it has been extinguished by an order freeing the child for adoption or by an adoption order or if the court has made an order bringing the earlier court order to an end;
- a child's father if he obtains a residence order in respect of the child, in which case the court must also make a parental responsibility order in his favour (CA 1989, s 12). Parental responsibility obtained in these circumstances does not automatically come to an end if the residence order is revoked although the court has the power to revoke the parental responsibility order at the same time. It also comes to an end if it has been extinguished by an order freeing the child for adoption or by an adoption order;
- a child's guardian has parental responsibility for a child when the appointment takes effect (CA 1989, s 5). Such an appointment can be brought to an end by disclaimer by the guardian or by an order of the court, and is extinguished by an order freeing the child for adoption or by an adoption order;
- any other person in whose favour a residence order is made (CA 1989, s 12). Parental responsibility acquired in this way comes to an end if and when the residence order ends;

---

[1] Ie 'on the birth certificate'.

- any person (typically a local authority, although the law does not prevent a private individual from making the application) who applies for and obtains an emergency protection order (CA 1989, s 44). Parental responsibility acquired in those circumstances ends when the emergency protection order ends;

- a local authority to which a care order (including an interim care order, which itself includes where an interim care order is made pursuant to the CA 1989, s 37) has been made (CA 1989, s 33). Parental responsibility acquired in this way comes to an end when the care order ends, for example, the making of a residence order, an order freeing the child for adoption or an adoption order;

- an adoption agency that has obtained an order freeing a child for adoption (Adoption Act 1976 (AA 1976), s 18). This continues unless the order is revoked (in which case some but not all categories of person who previously had parental responsibility for the child will have it restored to them: AA 1976, s 20) or until some other order is made such as a residence or an adoption order;

- an adoptive parent in whose favour an adoption order is made (AA 1976, s 12) unless it has been extinguished by a further order freeing the child for adoption or by an adoption order.

Once the Adoption and Children Act 2002 (ACA 2002) is fully implemented the following will have parental responsibility:

- a child's mother (CA 1989, s 2) unless it has been extinguished by an adoption order;

- a child's father if married to the mother at the time of the child's birth or if they have subsequently married (CA 1989, s 2) again unless it has been extinguished by an adoption order;

- a child's father if formally registered as such on or after 1 December 2003[2] (CA 1989, s 4, as amended by ACA 2002, s 111) unless it has been extinguished by an adoption order;

- a child's father if he has acquired it by entering into a parental responsibility agreement with the mother (CA 1989, s 4) unless it has been extinguished by an adoption order or if the court has made an order bringing the parental responsibility agreement to an end;

- a child's father if he has acquired it by a court order (CA 1989, s 4) unless it has been extinguished by an adoption order or if the court has made an order bringing the earlier court order to an end;

- a child's father if he obtains a residence order in respect of the child, in which case the court must also make a parental responsibility order in his favour (CA 1989, s 12). Parental responsibility obtained in these circumstances does not automatically come to an end if the residence order is revoked although the court has the power to revoke the parental

---

[2] Ie 'on the birth certificate'.

responsibility order at the same time. It also comes to an end if it has been extinguished by an adoption order;

- a step-parent who has obtained a parental responsibility agreement from the other parent or parents who hold parental responsibility (CA 1989, s 4A, as amended by ACA 2002, s 112). It comes to an end if a court so orders or if the child is subsequently adopted;

- a child's guardian has parental responsibility for a child when the appointment takes effect (CA 1989, s 5). Such an appointment can be brought to an end by disclaimer by the guardian or by an order of the court, and is extinguished by an adoption order;

- any other person in whose favour a residence order is made (CA 1989, s 12). Parental responsibility acquired in this way comes to an end if and when the residence order ends;

- others in whose favour a special guardianship order has been made (CA 1989, s 14C as amended by the ACA 2002, s 115). Parental responsibility acquired in this way comes to an end if and when the special guardianship order ends;

- any person (typically a local authority, although the law does not prevent a private individual from making the application) who applies for and obtains an emergency protection order (CA 1989, s 44). Parental responsibility acquired in those circumstances ends when the emergency protection order ends;

- a local authority to which a care order (including an interim care order, which itself includes where an interim care order is made pursuant to the CA 1989, s 37) has been made (CA 1989, s 33). Parental responsibility acquired in this way comes to an end when the care order ends, for example, the making of a residence order or an adoption order;

- an adoption agency while a child is placed for adoption with parental consent, or which is authorised to place a child for adoption with parental consent, or when a placement order is in force in respect of the child (ACA 2002, s 25). The adoption agency's parental responsibility comes to an end when these circumstances end;

- prospective adopters, while the child is placed with them (ACA 2002, s 25(3));

- an adoptive parent in whose favour an adoption order is made (ACA 2002, s 46) unless it has been extinguished by a further adoption order.

7.6 PARENTAL RESPONSIBILITY: HELPING PARENTS AGREE WHAT EACH CAN AND CANNOT DO

The following is taken from an annex to the judgment of Wall J in *A v A (Shared Residence)*.[1] It was prepared at the instigation of the NYAS[2] caseworker acting as guardian ad litem on behalf of the children pursuant to r 9.5 of the Family Proceedings Rules 1991. It provides a very helpful and practical example of the sort of issues that may need to be agreed between parents who share parental responsibility and points the way in which professionals involved with them can help them address these issues.[3]

'1   Decisions that could be taken independently and without any consultation or notification to the other parent:
- how the children are to spend their time during contact;
- personal care for the children;
- activities undertaken;
- religious and spiritual pursuits;
- continuance of medicine treatment prescribed by a GP.

2   Decisions where one parent would always need to inform the other parent of the decision, but did not need to consult or take the other parent's views into account:
- medical treatment in an emergency;
- booking holidays or to take the children abroad in contact time;
- planned visits to the GP and the reasons for this.

3   Decisions that you would need to both inform and consult the other parent prior to making the decision:
- schools the children are to attend, including admissions applications. With reference to which senior school C should attend this is to be decided taking into account C's own views and in consultation and with advice from her teachers;
- contact rotas in school holidays;
- planned medical and dental treatment;
- stopping medication prescribed for the children;

[1]   [2004] EWHC 142 (Fam), [2004] 1 FLR 1195.

[2]   National Youth Advocacy Service: contact details are included in **7.21** below.

[3]   See also 'Parenting Plan' produced by the Lord Chancellor's Department in 2002. It is available on the Department for Constitutional Affairs' website: www.dca.gov.uk. Printed copies can be obtained from FREEPOST, PO Box 2001, Burgess Hill, West Sussex RH15 8BR. Work is being done to produce a new version of this useful document.

- attendance at school functions so they can be planned to avoid meetings wherever possible;
- age that children should be able to watch videos, ie videos recommended for children over 12 and 18.'

7.7 THE INCREASING THRESHOLD IN PUBLIC LAW PROCEEDINGS

Step	local authority duty to investigate, and child assessment order	police protection, and emergency protection order	interim care and interim supervision order	care and supervision order
Key words preceding 'is suffering, or is likely to suffer, significant harm'	'reasonable cause to suspect'	'reasonable cause to believe'	'reasonable grounds for believing'	–
Full statutory reference	CA 1989, ss 47 and 43	CA 1989, ss 46 and 44	CA 1989, s 38	CA 1989, s 31

7.8 AN INTERDISCIPLINARY CURRICULUM

The Education and Training Sub-Committee of the President's Interdisciplinary Committee[1] has worked on an inclusive curriculum for continuing education for those who work with vulnerable children and families within the court system. It is intended that this will be published by on the website of the Family Justice Council (www.family-justice-council.org.uk).

---

[1] Now a sub-committee of the Family Justice Council.

7.9 SOCIO-LEGAL RESEARCH

Even excluding research within other relevant fields (notably medical) we are acutely conscious that such a considerable amount of valuable socio-legal research has been conducted, is currently taking place or is already planned, both in the United Kingdom and overseas, that we could not begin mention it all here even if we were aware of it or qualified to comment on it.

However, many lawyers and others within the family justice system are eager to have better information bearing on what they do, while many researchers seem understandably frustrated that the work they do is not more widely known and used to inform policy and practice.

So, with considerable hesitation, we have decided we should make some attempt, albeit very limited and highly selective, to identify some such research. The items have been selected because they are stimulating and readable. Many of them argue powerfully for changes in the way in which children should be involved following family break-up. We are particularly grateful to Harriet Bretherton[1] for her help to us in making this selection, but the responsibility for this, as with everything else in this Handbook, is ours.

Private law

- Claire Sturge and Danya Glaser 'Contact and Domestic Violence — The Experts' Report'. This seminal report, much relied upon by the Court of Appeal in *Re L, Re V, Re M and Re H (Contact: Domestic Violence)*, sets out principles about contact applicable to all cases and then applies them to cases in which there has been domestic violence.[2]
- Bren Neale and Amanda Wade *Parent Problems: Children's Views on Life When Parents Split Up* (Young Voice, 2000).[3] A gathering of the direct comments of children, as readable as it is powerful.
- Ian Butler, Lesley Scanlon, Margaret Robinson, Gillian Douglas and Mervyn Murch *Divorcing Children: Children's Experience of their Parents' Divorce* (Jessica Kingsley Publishers, 2003). The same topic considered at greater length by adult professionals but still giving a clear voice to the children themselves.
- Bren Neale and Carol Smart *Good to Talk: Conversations with Children after Divorce* (Young Voice, 2001). Argues for children to be seen as agents and competent in relation to their own lives (the citizenship model) rather than as victims and in need of protection (the welfare model).

---

[1] Research Co-ordinator, CAFCASS.

[2] See [2000] 2 FLR 334, and at **5.5** above. The report is available at [2000] Fam Law 615 (and to CAFCASS officers on their intranet).

[3] A follow-up publication is due to be published shortly.

- Andrew Bainham, Bridget Lindley, Margaret Richards and Liz Trinder (eds) *Children and their Families: Contact Rights and Welfare* (Hart, 2003). A stimulating set of essays on contact post-separation, including what makes for effective contact and the role of law.

- Liz Trinder, Mary Beek and Jo Connolly *Making Contact: How Parents and Children Negotiate and Experience Contact After Divorce* (Joseph Rowntree Foundation, 2002). Helpfully identifies: (a) three main groups of family behaviour, the consensually committed, the faltering and the conflicted, and a total of nine subtypes; and (b) factors affecting why contact varies.

- Joan Hunt *Researching Contact* (One Parent Families, 2003). An admirable summary of the research that exists and identifying areas where further research is needed.

Public law

- Judith Timms and June Thoburn *Your Shout* (NSPCC, 2003). A survey of the views of 706 children and young people in public care. Full of the direct comments of the children and young people themselves. Particularly striking is their desire for more contact with family and friends.

- Julia Brophy, Jagbir Jhutti-Johal and Charlie Owen *Significant Harm: Child Protection Litigation in a Multi-Cultural Setting* (Lord Chancellor's Department, 2003). Addresses the extent to which the family justice system understands and meets the needs of diverse communities.

- Judith Masson et al 'Working in the Dark' (2001) and 'Emergency Protection Orders: court orders for child protection crises' (2004). Research into practice relating to police protection and emergency protection orders.[4]

- Jane Aldgate and June Statham *The Children Act Now: Messages from Research* (Department of Health, 2001). This report summarises 24 studies funded by the DOH to monitor the effect of the Children Act 1989 and synthesises the key findings.

- John Triselotis 'Long-term foster care or adoption? The evidence examined' in *Child and Family Social Work 2002* vol 7, at pp 23–33. A paper examining the relative merits of adoption and long-term foster care in terms of outcomes including breakdown of placement and emotional security.

Adoption

- Alan Rushton *The Adoption of Looked After Children: A Scoping Review* (Social Care Institute for Excellence, 2003). This review identifies key findings from published research on the adoption of children from care.

---

[4]   Available at www2.warwick.ac.uk/fac/soc/law/about/staff/masson.

It covers recruitment, preparation, outcomes, contact and support services.[5] It contains a useful list of references.

- Roy Parker *Adoption Now: Messages from Research* (Wiley, 1999). This report gives an overview of the findings from 10 studies funded by the Department of Health.

- Hedi Argent (ed) *Staying Connected: Managing Contact Arrangement in Adoption* (British Association for Adoption and Fostering, 2002). A series of articles covering a wide range of issues relating to contact after adoption.

7.10 STRUCTURE OF THE COURT SYSTEM OF ENGLAND AND WALES

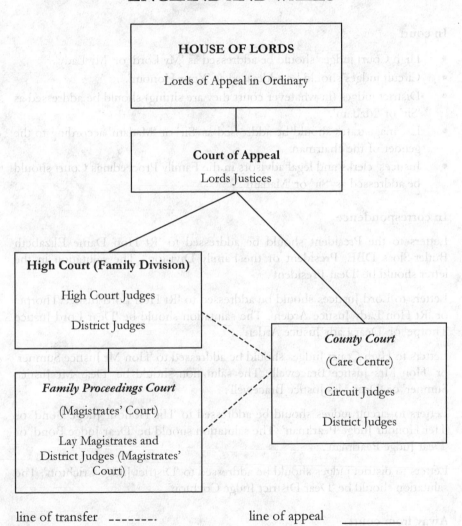

HOUSE OF LORDS

Lords of Appeal in Ordinary

Court of Appeal

Lords Justices

High Court (Family Division)

High Court Judges

District Judges

County Court

(Care Centre)

Circuit Judges

District Judges

Family Proceedings Court

(Magistrates' Court)

Lay Magistrates and
District Judges (Magistrates'
Court)

line of transfer - - - - - - -

line of appeal ＿＿＿＿＿

Notes:

- Appeals from decisions made by district judges are to a circuit judge if the case is proceeding in the county court, and to a High Court judge if it is proceeding in the High Court.
- District judges in the Principal Registry have an increased jurisdiction and can, for example, hear a full and contested application for a care order.
- As part of a significant programme of constitutional change, the final appeal court may cease to be the House of Lords and instead be a separately constituted Supreme Court.

7.11 ADDRESSING JUDGES AND MAGISTRATES

In court

- High Court judges should be addressed as 'My Lord' or 'My Lady'.
- Circuit judges should be addressed as 'Your Honour'.
- District judges (in whatever court they are sitting) should be addressed as 'Sir' or 'Madam'.
- Lay magistrates should be addressed as 'Sir' or 'Madam' according to the gender of the chairman.
- Justices' clerks and legal advisors in the Family Proceedings Court should be addressed as 'Sir' or 'Madam'.

In correspondence

Letters to the President should be addressed to 'Rt Hon Dame Elizabeth Butler-Sloss DBE, President of the Family Division'. The salutation in the letter should be 'Dear President'.

Letters to Lord Justices should be addressed to 'Rt Hon Lord Justice Thorpe' or 'Rt Hon Lady Justice Arden'. The salutation should be 'Dear Lord Justice Thorpe' or 'Dear Lady Justice Arden'.

Letters to High Court Judges should be addressed to 'Hon Mr Justice Sumner' or 'Hon Mrs Justice Bracewell'. The salutation should be 'Dear Mr Justice Sumner' or 'Dear Mrs Justice Bracewell'.

Letters to circuit judges should be addressed to 'His Honour Judge Bond' or 'Her Honour Judge Pearlman'. The salutation should be 'Dear Judge Bond' or 'Dear Judge Pearlman'.

Letters to district judges should be addressed to 'District Judge Crichton'. The salutation should be 'Dear District Judge Crichton'.

Away from court

Away from court (for example, at Family Court Business Committee meetings, lectures, or if a judge telephones you) all judges can be addressed as 'Judge' except for the President of the Family Division who should be addressed as 'President'.

7.12 ADVICE ABOUT GIVING EVIDENCE[1]

'Give your evidence,' said the King: 'and don't be nervous, or I'll have you executed on the spot.'

Lewis Carroll, *Alice's Adventures in Wonderland*, Chapter 11

It will not be like this, but this is probably what you will feel it is going to be like just before you give your evidence, at any rate until you have become experienced at it. For what it is worth, we do know what it is like. We have both had to give evidence in a variety of circumstances and it is a salutary experience that perhaps all advocates should have to undergo.

A good professional witness

All professional witnesses should be fully aware of the guidance that has been given about their role that is contained in Part 35 of the Civil Procedure Rules 1998 and in Appendix C of the Protocol for the Judicial Case Management in Public Law Children Act cases.[2] This clearly sets out the duties of experts.

The hallmarks of a good professional witness are that she:

- has the requisite professional qualifications and experience (clearly the degree of experience and specialism, and therefore of expertise, will vary);
- has carefully considered all the available information, and in particular what is said by anyone on behalf of the family;
- states if there is further information it is necessary to obtain, or if there are relevant matters outside her own area of expertise;
- clearly sets out her opinions, and the basis on which they are held, in her report and oral evidence; and
- acts independently and objectively throughout.[3]

Desperately trying to remember a long list of do's and don't's is probably just about the least helpful thing you can be doing immediately before you give oral evidence. We suggest it is much more helpful:

- to be clear about your role (we have just been looking at this);

---

[1] For fuller advice, look no further than Mr Justice Wall (as he then was) *A Handbook for Expert Witnesses in Children Act Cases* (Family Law, 2000).

[2] See **4.15** and **6.2**, respectively. It is also helpful to be aware of guidance given within case-law as, for example, by Munby J in *Re L (Care: Assessment: Fair Trial)* [2002] 2 FLR 730, set out at **5.6** above.

[3] This particularly includes drawing attention to matters that point against the expert's conclusion and giving whatever credit can be given to members of the family.

- to have produced a well-considered and well-written report (this is evidence too and it is the foundation for all your oral evidence);
- to be clear about what you believe and why you believe it;
- to have a general understanding of what to expect in court (the rest of our advice is about this).

When it comes to giving oral evidence it is important to remember the promise you will make. Whether you choose to take an oath or to make the affirmation,[4] you will promise that the evidence you give 'will be the truth, the whole truth and nothing but the truth'. Knowing that is what you are trying to do, to the best of your knowledge and understanding, and that it is all you can be asked to do, is probably the best way of getting a good night's sleep on the night before, and the night after, you give oral evidence.

The sequence of events

Unless you are asked to sit in court and hear the evidence of any other witness the first thing you will be asked to do is to take the oath or make the affirmation. Exactly what happens after this is a matter for the judge but the normal sequence is for questions to be put to you in the following order:

- first, by the advocate for the party that is calling you to give evidence. This is called *examination-in-chief*. This will often be brief – perhaps little more than confirming who you are, that you are the author of your report and that nothing has happened since you wrote your report to change the opinions you expressed in it. Examination-in-chief is only likely to be extensive if important events have taken place since you wrote your report in which case you should be asked about the implications (if any) of those events. Have they strengthened your opinions? Have they weakened them? Have they changed them altogether? It is also an important opportunity to correct any errors in your written report;
- secondly, by the advocates for each of the other parties. This is called *cross-examination*. This is likely to be longer and more difficult than examination-in-chief since the client of at least one of the advocates must, to a greater or lesser extent, disagree with some or all of your report (if everyone agrees with everything you have said, no one will have asked you to attend court to give oral evidence). However it does not follow that the clients of all those who cross-examine you disagree with what you have said. There may well be a range of views among the clients of the advocates who cross-examine you. One may want you to change your opinion entirely, another only to draw out or emphasise aspects of your report. There is no reason why you should not be told the basic position of each party before you give your evidence and in our view it is both courteous and helpful for witnesses to be told by each advocate which party they represent before questions are asked on behalf

---

[4]   Ie a solemn promise to tell the truth but without invoking God.

of that party (although this practice is by no means universally applied and might not be agreed by some);

- thirdly, you may be asked some follow-up questions by the advocate who originally called you to give evidence. This is called *re-examination*. This should be limited to matters arising out of cross-examination (if anything new is introduced you will find yourself going round the loop of cross-examination once again).

The judge may intervene at any stage. Usually this will be to clarify or confirm an answer you have been giving, but it may be to explore a wholly new area the judge thinks may be important. The judge may also intervene to make clear to an advocate that she has had enough of a particular line of questioning. You will probably have felt that several minutes earlier, but the judge has to allow some margin to an advocate – it does not help anyone, particularly the child who is the subject of the proceedings, if after the hearing a party can make any reasonable complaint that his advocate was prevented from putting his case. Finally, it may be some consolation to know that judges are much more likely to be cross with one or more of the advocates than with any professional witness who is doing her honest best to help the court, even if, for the reason just given, the judge may choose to bite her lip about it.

Traps

This is an area where the imagination of the professional witness seems to know no bounds. Most advocates have long since stopped even dreaming about such skills. There really is nothing that can properly be called a trap. Instead, the realities are these:

- *honest questions* – there is the possibility that you may be mistaken in parts of your evidence. This may be as to matters of fact (you may have relied on information given to you by others that turns out to have been inaccurate, or you may be mistaken in your own direct observations) or as to your opinions (for example, there may be new research or theories with which you are not familiar, or with which you are very familiar but about which there is as yet no settled consensus within your profession). It is always legitimate, as well as surely always being in the best interests of the child, for such matters to be explored and exposed. Indeed so far as possible this should be done in your report and/or in the course of examination-in-chief;
- *legitimate techniques* – there are techniques an advocate may properly use in an effort to limit damage or maximise advantage to his client. This *may* be as simple as the way in which a question is put: the same issue underlies the questions 'You accept that it is possible the bruises you saw could have been caused accidentally don't you?' and 'Do you have any real doubt that the bruises you saw were caused non-accidentally?' but they have very different emphases. It may be the way in which the words are spoken: the meaning of the Charles Lamb quotation at the start of this book depends very much on how much stress is put on the word

'suppose'. In many cases advocates know they are unlikely to be able significantly to discredit your opinions and are therefore much more likely to be concentrating upon minimising their impact or opening up a new alternative for you and the court to consider: 'What if Dad underwent anger management?', 'You didn't have the advantage of seeing them 24 hours a day – what about a residential assessment that we have just established could be done?', 'If the children can't live with their parents and ought to be adopted, wouldn't it be in their interests to continue to have direct contact with their natural family?' and so on;

- *errors, dishonest questions and illegitimate techniques* – these include misquoting what you or another witness have said or, more commonly, quoting something out of its full and proper context or giving the gist of what someone has said in a way that is in fact incomplete or inaccurate; interrupting you or not allowing you to complete the answer you are giving; or bullying you.[5] It will help if you are alert to these possibilities but it is also something that the advocate who called you should be alert to and, in the final analysis, is the responsibility of the judge.

A few suggestions

- Before giving evidence, ask what the position is of the different parties, check whether there are any further reports or statements that you should have read (it is not your responsibility to do this but all too often it is forgotten) and reread your own report and those of any other professional from your field;

- remember to take with you to court your contemporaneous notes and other records on which you have relied. You should also take with you copies of any research or other professional literature you rely on if this was not attached to your report;

- try to arrange to meet the advocate who is going to call you before you give evidence – it is usually sufficient to do so in the morning or at lunchtime immediately before you are going to give evidence;

- listen carefully to the questions that are put to you. If you need them to be explained or repeated do say so;

- if you need it, allow yourself time to think before answering a question or to refer to what is written in your report or another document in the court bundle;

- try to answer the questions that are put to you as clearly and straightforwardly as you can;

- try to speak a little more slowly than you might normally do. It is easy to gabble when you are nervous. If that happens, you will not express yourself as clearly as you want to, and others, who will be trying to make

---

5   Just how common this is no doubt depends to some extent upon one's definition of bullying and perhaps needs to be the subject of further discussion between judges, lawyers and representatives of experts and other groups of witnesses.

a note of what you are saying, are less likely to understand it or give due weight to it;

- try to address your answers to the judge. This may feel strange at first because the questions are coming from the advocates, but after a while it will become natural;

- any hostility in the questioning is best met with calm and charm;

- do not be afraid of letting your personal qualities (thoughtfulness, humanity, concern, good humour, humility) come across;

- do not be afraid to concede the obvious, nor to stick to what you believe unless and until you really are persuaded otherwise.

7.13 CAFCASS OFFICER ROLES[1]

Private law

There are two main roles CAFCASS officers can fulfil in private law proceedings: the more common is that of the children and family reporter, the less common that of the guardian ad litem.[2]

The role of *children and family reporter* is defined by s 7 of the Children Act 1989 and by rr 4.11 and 4.11B of the Family Proceedings Rules 1991 (rr 11 and 11B of the Family Proceedings Courts (Children Act 1989) Rules 1991 if the case is proceeding in the family proceedings court).

The role of *guardian ad litem* is defined by r 9.5 of the Family Proceedings Rules 1991.[3] However, r 9.5(6) also applies rr 4.11 and 4.11A to a CAFCASS officer fulfilling this role (but not to anyone else fulfilling this role) but the rights of a CAFCASS officer to have access to local authority records pursuant to s 42 of the Children Act 1989 do not apply to this role. A reminder: this role does not exist in the family proceedings court.

Public law

The role of a CAFCASS officer in public law proceedings is that of the *children's guardian*. The role is defined by ss 41–42 of the Children Act 1989 and by rr 4.10, 4.11 and 4.11A of the Family Proceedings Rules 1991 (rr 10, 11 and 11A of the Family Proceedings Courts (Children Act 1989) Rules 1991 if the case is proceeding in the family proceedings court).

Adoption, and cases brought under the Human Fertilisation and Embryology Act 1990

There are currently two roles CAFCASS officers can fulfil in adoption proceedings: that of the reporting officer and that of the children's guardian.

Where there is parental agreement to the adoption, the role is that of a *reporting officer* which is defined by s 65 of the Adoption Act 1976 and (in freeing for adoption) by r 5 and (in adoption) by r 17 of the Adoption Rules 1984

---

[1]   The functions of CAFCASS are defined by s 12 of the Criminal Justice and Court Services Act 2000.

[2]   There is also a role without a title pursuant to s 26 of the Domestic Proceedings and Magistrates' Courts Act 1978 whereby proceedings can be adjourned if there is a reasonable possibility of a reconciliation between the parties. A CAFCASS officer can be requested to attempt to effect a reconciliation and shall report in writing to the court whether the attempt has been successful or not. We are not aware of it ever having been used since CAFCASS was created on 1 April 2001.

[3]   As to when this may be appropriate and how it should be arranged see, respectively, the President's *Practice Direction (Representation of Children in Family Proceedings)* [2004] 1 FLR 1188 and the *CAFCASS Practice Note* [2004] 1 FLR 1190, reproduced at **6.18** and **6.19** below.

(rr 5 and 17 respectively of the Magistrates' Courts (Adoption) Rules 1984 if the matter is proceeding in the family proceedings court).

Where there is no parental agreement to the adoption, the role is that of a children's guardian which is defined by s 65 of the Adoption Act 1976 and (in freeing for adoption) by r 6 and (in adoption) by r 18 of the Adoption Rules 1984 (rr 6 and 18 respectively of the Magistrates' Courts (Adoption) Rules 1984 if the matter is proceeding in the family proceedings court).

Under the Adoption and Children Act 2002, the roles of a CAFCASS officer will be defined by ss 102–103 and by new adoption rules. These have yet to be finalised, but current drafts set out three different roles: that of reporting officer, that of children and family reporter, and that of children's guardian. [4]

On an application for an order pursuant to s 30 of the Human Fertilisation and Embryology Act 1990, the role of a CAFCASS officer is that of the *parental order reporter*. The role is defined by s 41 of the Children Act 1989 and r 4A.5 of the Family Proceedings Rules 1991 (r 21E of the Family Proceedings Courts (Children Act 1989) Rules 1991 if the matter is proceeding in the Family Proceedings Court).[5]

Other

In circumstances that will presumably be rare, it may be possible for a CAFCASS officer to fulfil the role of *litigation friend* if none of the other roles is appropriate but the proceedings are nevertheless 'family proceedings in which the welfare of children is or may be in question' (Criminal Justice and Court Services Act 2000, s 12(1)).[6]

---

[4] There may also be the possibility of a CAFCASS officer acting as a litigation friend to a mother in adoption proceedings who is herself a child, although this is likely normally to be a role for the Official Solicitor.

[5] Helpful guidance about such cases was issued by the Department of Health in its Local Authority Circular LAC(94) 25.

[6] An important example of where this is relevant arises in relation to s 118 of the Adoption and Children Act 2002. On the implementation of that section in September 2004, independent reviewing officers became able to refer the cases of looked after children to CAFCASS Legal, for CAFCASS – in the absence of anyone else able to do so – to consider bringing proceedings on behalf of the child. Such proceedings might include a free-standing application under s 7(1)(a) of the Human Rights Act 1998 or an application for judicial review.

7.14   JUDICIAL REVIEW

Judicial review is its own specialist area of legal practice and any detailed handling of the subject is beyond the scope of this Handbook. However it is an important tool in the protection of children and enforcement of their rights. Some interdisciplinary professionals may need to be aware of the possibility of its use, so here is a brief outline of its compass:

- the law defining judicial review and its process is contained in s 31 of the Supreme Court Act 1981 and Part 54 of the Civil Procedure Rules 1998;
- judicial review is a means by which courts scrutinise executive and administrative decisions;
- it is a review of what falls within public law, not what falls within private law, although the boundary between them is by no means always clear;
- it is a mechanism of review, not of appeal;
- generally, the greater the element of policy in a decision, the greater the judicial reticence in reviewing it is likely to be;
- if the court upholds an application for judicial review it can make a mandatory order, a quashing order, a prohibiting order, a declaration, an injunction and, in certain circumstances, may award damages;
- it is important to note that these remedies are discretionary: the court is not obliged to make any of them even though it has upheld the application;
- the applicant must have a sufficient interest in the matter in order to be allowed to bring it;
- the application must be made promptly, and in any event within three months, unless the court grants an extension of time;
- the applicant must normally exhaust other available forms of relief before bringing judicial review proceedings;
- the classic summary lists the grounds on which judicial review can be brought as illegality, irrationality and procedural impropriety[1] although these should not be treated as rigid categories;
- putting this more illustratively:

> '... there are many cases where, although the tribunal had jurisdiction to enter on the enquiry, it has done or failed to do something in the course of the enquiry which is of such a nature that its decision is a nullity. It may have given the decision in bad faith. It may have made a decision which it had no power to make. It may have failed in the course of the enquiry to comply with the requirements of natural justice. It may in perfect good faith have misconstrued the provisions giving it power to act so that it failed to deal with the question remitted to it and decided some question

---

[1] Lord Diplock in *Council of Civil Service Union v Minister for the Civil Service* [1985] AC 374 at 410.

which was not remitted to it. It may have refused to take into account something which it was required to take into account. Or it may have based its decision on some matter which, under the provisions setting it up, it had no right to take into account. I do not intend this list to be exhaustive.' [2]

- 'legality' means that the decision-maker must have correctly interpreted the law under which the decision is made;

- 'rationality' means that no reasonable authority, acting reasonably, could have come to it.[3] Rationality also includes the concept of proportionality,[4] failing to take into account relevant considerations and taking into account irrelevant considerations; [5]

- 'procedural propriety' means that the decision-maker must follow procedures that have been set down by legislation and, more generally, must act fairly ('in accordance with the principles of natural justice'). Fairness means the absence of bias and allowing representations to be made before a decision is reached.[6] It also embraces the doctrine of legitimate expectation;[7]

- 'the scope and extent of the principles of natural justice depend on the subject matter to which they are sought to be applied';[8]

- in determining the principles of fairness, note that:

  '(1) Where an Act Parliament confers an administrative power there is a presumption that it will be exercised in a manner which is fair in all the circumstances. (2) The standards of fairness are not immutable. (3) The principles of fairness are not to be applied by rote identically in every situation. What fairness demands is dependent on the context of the decision, and this is to be taken into account in all its aspects. (4) An essential feature of the context is the statute which creates the discretion as regards both its language and the shape of the legal and administrative system within which the decision is taken ...'[9]

- for all that judicial review is an important tool in the protection of children and the enforcement of their rights, it should not be misused.

---

[2] Lord Reid in *Anisminic Ltd v Foreign Compensation Commission* [1969] 2 AC 147 at 171.

[3] So-called 'Wednesbury unreasonableness' after the decision in *Associated Provisional Picture Houses Ltd v Wednesbury Corporation* [1948] 1 KB 223.

[4] Compare with the same concept in the jurisprudence of the European Court of Human Rights referred to at **2.4** above.

[5] These last two aspects of rationality were expressly referred to in the *Wednesbury* case cited above, although this is often forgotten.

[6] For a brief and entertaining review of the origins of this principle see the decision of Munby J in *Re G (Care: Challenge to Local Authority's Decision)* [2003] 2 FLR 42 at [28]–[29].

[7] See, for example, *R (NAGALRO) v CAFCASS* [2002] 1 FLR 255.

[8] Brightman LJ in *Payne v Lord Harris of Greenwich* [1981] 1 WLR 754 at 766.

[9] Lord Mustill in *R v Secretary of State for the Home Department ex parte Doody* [1994] 1 AC 531 at 560.

The law reports are full of examples in which either judicial review was not an appropriate remedy or the application was obviously weak.[10]

---

10   The law on the use and, more particularly, misuse of judicial review (and other remedies such as habeas corpus and free-standing applications under s 7(1)(a) of the Human Rights Act 1998) is helpfully summarised by Munby J in *Re S (Habeas Corpus); S v Haringey London Borough Council* [2003] EWHC 2734 (Admin), [2004] 1 FLR 590. For an example of the proper use of judicial review, see *Re T (Judicial Review: Local Authority Decisions Concerning Child in Need)* [2003] EWHC 2515 (Admin), [2004] 1 FLR 601 – the next report in the *Family Law Reports*.

7.15 MAJOR CHILD ABUSE INQUIRIES

1974   **Report of the Committee of Inquiry into the Care and Supervision Provided in Relation to Maria Colwell**: Maria Colwell returned to live with her mother and stepfather, initially under a care order. The care order was revoked on the application of Maria's mother, supported by the local authority, and a supervision order was substituted. Her well-being was not sufficiently monitored and she was killed by her stepfather. She was less than eight years old.

1985   **A Child in Trust: Jasmine Beckford**: Like Maria Colwell, Jasmine Beckford was killed by her stepfather while living with him and her mother, but unlike Maria Colwell, Jasmine Beckford was not under the supervision of the local authority but in its care when this happened. She was four and a half years old.

1987   **Whose Child?** Tyra Henry was less than two years old when she was murdered by her father. Like Jasmine Beckford, Tyra was in the care of the local authority when this happened.

1987   **A Child in Mind; Protection of Children in a Responsible Society**: Kimberley Carlile was in voluntary care on several occasions before being returned to the care of her mother and stepfather. She was murdered by her stepfather when she was four and a half years old.

1991   **Report of the Inquiry into Child Abuse in Cleveland 1987**: Unlike the enquiries referred to above, this concerned not the certain physical abuse of a single child leading to her death but the possibility of the sexual abuse of at least of 121 children, both boys and girls.

'The child is a person and not an object of concern'

> Dame Elizabeth Butler-Sloss:
> extract from recommendation 2 of
> the Report of the Inquiry into
> Child Abuse in Cleveland 1987.

1991   **The Pindown Experience and the Protection of Children: The Report of the Staffordshire Child Care Inquiry**: This concerned a regime of isolation and humiliation in the name of behaviour modification resulting in the abuse of 132 children in four children's homes.

1992 **Report of the Inquiry into the Removal of Children from Orkney in February 1991**: Allegations of ritual abuse led to nine children being removed from their parents' care. In a glare of publicity, the case was dismissed several weeks later and the children returned.

1993 **The Leicestershire Inquiry 1992 ('The Kirkwood Report')** and **The Inquiry into Police Investigation of Complaints of Child and Sexual Abuse in Leicestershire Children's Homes**: As with the Pindown Report, these two reports concern the abuse of children in residential care. This time up to 200 children suffered abuse, including sexual abuse.

2000 **Lost in care: Report of the Tribunal of Enquiry into the Abuse of Children in Care in the Former County Council Areas of Gwynedd and Clwyd since 1974**: Like the Staffordshire and Leicestershire inquiries this identified the extensive abuse of children in residential care and the failures that had allowed it to happen.

2003 **The Victoria Climbié Inquiry Report**: Victoria's great-aunt and her partner murdered Victoria when she was eight years old. This happened despite Victoria having been abused over a prolonged period, her being known to a series of agencies whose responsibility it was to protect her, and when nothing more than basic good practice was needed to save her.

> 'What is needed are managers with a clear set of values about the role of public services, particularly in addressing the needs of vulnerable people, combined with the ability to "lead from the front" ... robust leadership must replace bureaucratic administration. The adherence to inward-looking processes must give way to more flexible deployment of staff and resources in the search for better results for children and families ... little I heard in this Inquiry convinced me that local authorities[1] accept that in public service, the needs of the public must come first. This must change.'

> Lord Laming, paras 1.27, 1.48 and 1.54 of the
> Victoria Climbié Inquiry Report

---

[1] The principle, of course, is not confined to local authorities but extends to all public bodies that exist to provide services for children and families.

7.16 COMPENSATION FOR CHILDREN

Child abuse raises a variety of legal issues including the protection and future welfare of the child, whether any criminal proceedings should be brought, and whether the child is or may be entitled to compensation.

There are several ways in which the issue of compensation can be addressed. It can be awarded in criminal proceedings, under the Human Rights Act 1998 or by the European Court of Human Rights. In practice, two ways predominate. First, the child, or rather someone on his or her behalf, may issue civil proceedings for damages, either against the abuser or against an individual or organisation who, one way or another, should have prevented it from happening. The second is for an application to be made to the Criminal Injuries Compensation Authority for compensation.

Most children law specialists would not hold themselves out as being the right person to help with either of these. Many will be able to refer to another lawyer within their own firm or in their area, but in the event of any doubt contact can be made with the Association of Child Abuse Lawyers.[1]

---

[1] Details are included at **7.21** below.

7.17 NUMBER AND OUTCOME OF CHILDREN LAW CASES IN ENGLAND AND WALES

Source: Judicial Statistics, issued annually by the Department of Constitutional Affairs (formerly the Lord Chancellor's Department).[1]

	Private law	Public law	Adoption
1993	108,201	16,754	6,751
1994	102,801	18,660	6,326
1995	102,000	17,136	5,317
1996	106,292	16,066	4,936
1997	103,335	17,942	4,266
1998	114,518	17,284	4,675
1999	90,381	19,770	3,962
2000	95,407	22,000	4,438
2001	112,012	24,134	4,452
2002	111,562	23,637	4,120
2003	115,944	22,725	4,870

Outcome of contact applications in private law cases

	Withdrawn	Order refused	No Order	Order made
1998	8,385	1,911	3,298	49,313
1999	7,210	1,752	2,600	41,862
2000	5,419	1,276	2,067	46,070
2001	3,226	713	1,168	55,030
2002	2,373	518	945	61,356
2003	2,753	601	1,522	67,184

---

[1]   Information available at www.dca.gov.uk/judicial/.

7.18 LEGAL AID EXPENDITURE IN FAMILY PROCEEDINGS

Legal Aid expenditure on children cases in England and Wales

Source: the Legal Services Commission

Private Law £m	Total	Solicitors	Disbursements	Counsel
99/00	132.2	98.8	9.7	23.6
00/01	129.9	95.4	9.7	24.7
01/02	115.4	84.2	8.5	22.7
02/03	117.9	87.3	9.3	21.3
03/04	120.0	91.9	10.3	17.7

Public Law £m	Total	Solicitors	Disbursements	Counsel
99/00	107.9	76.2	11.0	20.6
00/01	137.4	94.6	14.4	28.4
01/02	141.6	94.5	15.2	31.9
02/03	164.6	109.4	17.9	37.3
03/04	181.9	125.1	22.3	34.5

Total £m	Total	Solicitors	Disbursements	Counsel
99/00	240.0	175.1	20.7	44.3
00/01	267.3	190.0	24.2	53.1
01/02	257.0	178.7	23.7	54.5
02/03	282.5	196.6	27.2	58.6
03/04	301.9	217.0	32.6	52.2

Legal aid budgets in Europe

Source: Annex F of the Law Society Consultation Paper, 'The Future of Publicly Funded Legal Services' (February 2003).

'The amount spent on legal aid per year varies greatly between the individual countries. England and Wales, for example, spend about €2.6 billion per year, whereas Latvia only spends €258,000. In the list of countries with the highest legal aid budgets, England and Wales is followed at a considerable distance by Germany (€358m), France (€235m) and Scotland (€207m).'

'... the ranking changes if the relative amounts based on expenditure per capita are taken into account. Here, England and Wales come first, too, with €49, followed by Scotland with €40 and Liechtenstein with €36. With a per capita expenditure of €16.8, Norway ranks before Ireland (€10) Finland (€8), Denmark (€6.6) and Germany (€6). These countries are followed closely by France (€3.99), Austria (€3), Italy (€2.6), Belgium (€2.5) and Sweden (€2.1). Per capita expenditure is lowest in Luxembourg (€1.1), Estonia (€1) Lithuania (€0.24) and Latvia (€0.1).'

7.19 KEY PUBLICATIONS

Professionals who are not lawyers

There are two obvious next steps for professionals who are not lawyers who want to develop their understanding about children law and practice in England and Wales.

One possibility is to buy a legal textbook. There are several to choose from. For a general textbook covering the whole field, we suggest Andrew Bainham *Children: The Modern Law* (Family Law, 3rd edn, 2005). However if your main interest is child protection then we suggest Christina Lyon *Child Abuse* (Family Law, 3rd edn, 2003); if it is children's rights then Jane Fortin *Children's Rights and the Developing Law* (Lexis Nexis Butterworths, 2nd edn, 2003); and if the Children Act 1989 then White, Carr and Lowe *The Children Act in Practice* (Lexis Nexis Butterworths, 3rd edn, 2003).

The other is to start reading one of the relevant journals. There is no shortage to choose from. The following, which have different emphases and styles, are all excellent and highly recommended:[1]

- *Family Law*: although its remit includes financial matters, this is the first journal for most lawyers practising children law. With an emphasis on what is current, its case reports are often several months ahead of the law reports. There is a socio-legal spread among its articles which are written by practitioners from the different professional disciplines. Published monthly by Family Law;
- *International Family Law*: probably not for most practitioners but the ever-increasing: (a) influence of international law; (b) number of cases in which international co-operation is needed; and (c) realisation that there is much to learn from the way in which other jurisdictions and cultures address similar problems, make this an important journal for some. Published quarterly, also by Family Law;
- *Child and Family Law Quarterly*: with its emphasis specifically on children, this complements *Family Law*, providing a place for longer articles, many of which are written by academics and help to give a perspective that practitioners might otherwise miss. Published quarterly, again by Family Law;
- *Representing Children*: this has a strongly child-centred focus and a rights-based philosophy. It consistently challenges current attitudes and

---

[1] More specialist publications include: *Adoption and Fostering*; the *British Journal of Social Work*; *Child Abuse Review*; the *International Journal of Law, Policy and the Family*; the AIRE Centre newsletter (particularly about the latest from the European Court of Human Rights), the *Medico-Legal Journal*; the *Medical Law Review*, the *Bulletin of Medical Ethics*, and *Children and Society*.

processes concerning the participation and representation of children in legal and administrative decisions that affect them, although it is by no means confined to this. Published quarterly by the National Youth Advocacy Service;

- *childRIGHT*: also with a rights-based philosophy, this is highly informative, topical and 'newsy' about a broader range of matters affecting children. Published monthly by the Children's Legal Centre in association with the University of Essex.

Suggestions about a basic library for lawyers

It is hard to imagine the following not being found in the library of every children lawyer:

- a specialist lawyers' textbook such as Hershman and McFarlane *Children Law and Practice* (Family Law, looseleaf);
- *Family Law*, and
- the *Family Law Reports*.

As you build your library we suggest you think about the following categories:

- another journal or textbook (see above);
- statements of good practice produced by professional bodies. For example, all solicitors practising children law should be familiar with two Law Society publications, the *Family Law Protocol* and *Good Practice in Child Care Cases*;[2]
- good practice guidance and newsletters from professional associations such as the Solicitors Family Law Association,[3] the Association of Lawyers for Children, the Family Law Bar Association and NAGALRO;
- reports from major child abuse inquiries;[4]
- key publications from central government, including *Working Together to Safeguard Children, Framework for the Assessment of Children in Need and their Families, Achieving Best Evidence in Criminal Proceedings, Provision of Therapy for Child Witnesses Prior to a Criminal Trial, Guidance for Vulnerable or Intimidated Witnesses including Children*, and *Safeguarding Children in whom Illness is Fabricated or Induced*;[5]
- a selection of publications by professionals from other disciplines, such as *Communicating with Vulnerable Children* by David Jones; the Royal College of Physicians' *Physical Signs of Sexual Abuse in Children*; and one of

---

[2]   Solicitors, in particular, should look out for a forthcoming book by Liz Goldthorpe and Pat Monro also to be published by the Law Society. Its provisional title is 'Child Law – A Good Practice Guide' and it is likely to be published in early 2005.

[3]   As well as its general Code of Practice, the SFLA has published a 'Guide to Good Practice for Solicitors Acting for Children'.

[4]   See **7.15**.

[5]   As well as formal consultation papers and responses published from time to time.

the following: Roy Meadow (ed), *ABC of Child Abuse*,[6] Chris Hobbs and Jane Wynne, *Physical Signs of Child Abuse*, or Chris Hobbs, Helga Hanks and Jane Wynne, *Child Abuse and Neglect: A Clinician's Handbook*;

- a collection of contemporary research;[7]
- legal textbooks and law reports in related fields (eg human rights, education law, housing law, immigration law, criminal law);
- a selection of specialist children's books and other publications, such as those produced by organisations such as the British Association for Adoption and Fostering.[8]

---

6   The concerns arising out of the recent acquittals of Sally Clark, Trupti Patel and Angela Cannings should not be allowed to invalidate a lifetime's professional work.

7   See **7.9** above.

8   A knowledge of the works of JK Rowling is surely essential, and those of Jacqueline Wilson perhaps even more desirable.

7.20 WEBSITES FOR CHILDREN AND YOUNG PEOPLE

Here is a selection of websites that have been specifically designed for children and young people.

www.cafcass.gov.uk

This website contains separate sections for 'children', 'teenagers' and 'parents and families'. Within each section are subsections addressing issues like 'My mum and dad are splitting up. They can't agree about where I'll live'; 'My mum and dad can't agree about how much time I spend with each of them or with other people in my family'; 'I might be adopted by a new family'; 'My step-mum or step-dad wants to adopt me'; and 'Social services are worried about me and are going to ask a court to decide about how best to help me and my family'. The site won the 2003 Crystalmark award for best new website. Also in Welsh.

www.carelaw.org.uk

Describes itself as '… an information site for children and young people in care in England & Wales. It covers many topics from your rights in care to what happens when you leave care. It also explains how the law is different if you are "accommodated", as opposed to being under a care order. The information is given in a question and answer format. The information is updated every 6 months. The site has now been updated to include the Human Rights Act'. The site has been created by the NCH with the Solicitors Family Law Association in consultation with many other parties.

www.cf.ac.uk/claws/kids

Website designed by researchers from Cardiff University, about children's perspectives and experience of the divorce process. Includes direct quotations from children.

www.funkydragon.org

Website for young people in Wales. 'Have your say on issues that affect you. Click on the "your say" link on the left and tell it like it is. You can put your views, on any issue you like, to the Welsh Assembly. You can comment on the topics on our discussion boards or start your own strand. Your views will be fed through to the people with the power to make things happen. They look at this site regularly because they want to know what you think. That's the truth.'

www.itsnotyourfault.org

'It's not your fault. Are you worried that your parents are splitting up? If so, you might be feeling sad and confused. This website is for children like you, to help you understand and feel a bit better. Remember it's not your fault.' Produced by the NCH, with separate sections for children, teenagers and parents. Full of reassurance.

www.there4me.org

An NSPCC website: 'If you've got worries or need some advice, There4me.com can help. The site is for 12–16-year-olds living in England, Wales, Northern Ireland and the Channel Islands. It's to help you find solutions to your problems. There's on screen advice about all sorts of things … bullying, relationships, exams, drugs, difficulties at home, to name just a few. Or you can send an e-letter to Sam, our agony aunt. If you'd prefer a confidential private session, you can talk 1-2-1 in "real time" with an NSPCC adviser, or email for a reply within 24 hours. You don't have to say who you are – you stay in control.'

www.worriedneed2talk.org.uk

Another NSPCC website for young people. Also in Welsh.

7.21 ADDRESSES AND WEBSITES FOR PROFESSIONALS

The organisations referred to here have been placed in one of three groups: (1) professional associations; (2) government bodies and courts; and (3) non-governmental organisations.

Part 1: Professional associations

Association of Child Abuse Lawyers
PO Box 466
Chorleywood
Rickmansworth
Hertfordshire
WD3 5LG
01923 286 888
www.childabuselawyers.com

Association of Lawyers for Children
PO Box 283
East Molesey
Surrey
KT8 0WH
020 8224 7071
www.alc.org.uk

Bar Council
289–293 High Holborn
London
WC1V 7HZ
020 7242 0082
www.barcouncil.org.uk

British Association for the Study and Prevention of Child Abuse and Neglect
BASPCAN National Office
10 Priory Street
York
YO1 6EZ
01904 613605
www.baspcan.org.uk

British Association of Social Workers
16 Kent Street
Birmingham
B5 6RD
0121 622 3911
www.basw.co.uk

British Medical Association
BMA House
Tavistock Square
London
WC1H 9JP
020 7387 4499
www.bma.org.uk

British Paediatric Association
5 St Andrew's Place
Regents Park
London
NW1 4LB
020 7486 6151

British Psychological Society
St Andrews House
48 Princess Road East
Leicester
LE1 7DR
0116 254 9568
www.bps.org.uk

Family Law Bar Association
289–293 High Holborn
London
WC1V 7HZ
020 7242 1289
www.FLBA.co.uk

Justices' Clerks Society
2nd Floor
Port of Liverpool Building
Pier Head
Liverpool
L3 1BY
0151 255 0790
www.jc-society.co.uk

Law Society
113 Chancery Lane
London
WC2A 1PL
020 7242 1222
www.lawsociety.org.uk

Magistrates Association
28 Fitzroy Square
London
W1T 6DD
020 7387 2353
www.magistrates-
association.org.uk

NAGALRO
PO Box 264
Esher
Surrey
KT10 0W
01372 818504
www.nagalro.com

National Family Mediation
Alexander House
Bristol
BS1 4BS
0117 904 2825
www.nfm.u-net.com

Nursing and Midwifery Council
23 Portland Place
London
W1B 1P
020 7637 7181
www.nmc-uk.org

Resolution[1]
PO Box 302
Orpington
Kent
BR6 8QX
01689 850227
www.sfla.co.uk

Royal College of Physicians
11 St Andrews Place
Regents Park
London
NW1 4LE
020 7935 1174
www.rcplondon.ac.uk

Royal College of Psychiatrists
17 Belgrave Square
London
SW1X 8PG
020 7235 2351
www.rcpsych.ac.uk

Social Care Institute for Excellence
1st Floor
Goldings House
2 Hays Lane
London
SE1 2HB
020 7089 6840
www.scie.org.uk

---

[1] Formerly known as the Solicitors Family
Law Association.

UK College of Family Mediators
24-32 Stephenson Way
London
NW1 2HX
020 7391 9162
www.ukcfm.co.uk

Part 2: Government bodies and courts

CAFCASS
8th Floor
Wyndham House
189 Marsh Wall
London
E14 9SX
020 7510 7000
www.cafcass.gov.uk

Central Office of Information
6 Hercules Road
London
SE1 7DU
020 7928 2345
www.coi.gov.uk

Child Abduction Unit
81 Chancery Lane
London
WC2A 1DD
020 7911 7047
www.offsol.demon.co.uk

Child Support Agency Headquarters
Office of the Chief Executive
CSA Room 158A
Benton Park Road
Newcastle
NE98 1YX
08457 133133
www.dss.gov.uk/csa

Criminal Injuries Compensation Authority
Morley House
26–30 Holborn Viaduct
London
EC1A 2JQ
020 7842 6800
www.cica.gov.uk

Crown Prosecution Service
50 Ludgate Hill
London
EC4M 7EX
020 7796 8000
www.cps.gov.uk

Department for Constitutional Affairs
Selborne House
54–60 Victoria Street
London
SW1E 6QW
020 7210 8500
www.dca.gov.uk

Department for Education and Skills
Sanctuary Buildings
Great Smith Street
London
SW1P 3BT
0870 000 2288
www.dfes.gov.uk

Department of Health
Richmond House
79 Whitehall
London
SW1A 2NL
020 7210 4850
www.doh.gov.uk

Family Justice Council
WG 23
West Green
Royal Courts of Justice
Strand
London
WC2A 2LL
020 7947 7333
www.family-justice-council.org.uk

Foreign and Commonwealth Office
King Charles Street
London
SW1A 2AH
020 7008 1500
www.fco.gov.uk

Home Office
7th Floor
50 Queen Anne's Gate
London
SW1H 9AT
020 7273 4000
www.homeoffice.gov.uk

Legal Services Commission
85 Gray's Inn Road
London
WC1X 8TX
020 7759 0000
www.legalservices.gov.uk

Local Government Ombudsman
21 Queen Anne's Gate
London
SW1H 9BU
020 7915 3210
www.lgo.org.uk

National Assembly for Wales
Cardiff Bay
Cardiff
CF99 1NA
0292 082 5111
www.wales.gov.uk

Office for National Statistics
1 Drummond Gate
London
SW1V 2QQ
0845 601 3034
www.statistics.gov.uk

Office of the Official Solicitor
81 Chancery Lane
London
WC2A 1DD
020 7911 7127
www.off.sol.demon.co.uk

Principal Registry
First Avenue House
42–49 High Holborn
London
WC1V 6NP
020 7947 6000

Royal Courts of Justice
Strand
London
WC2A 2LL
020 7947 6000

Part 3: Non-governmental organisations

AIRE Centre[1]
Third Floor
17 Red Lion Square
London
WC1R 4QH
020 7831 4276
www.airecentre.org

ChildLine
45 Folgate Street
London
E1 6GL
020 7650 3200
www.childline.org.uk

Children's Legal Centre
University of Essex
Wivenhoe Park
Colchester
Essex
CO4 3SQ
01206 872466
www.childrenslegalcentre.com

Families Need Fathers
134 Curtain Road
London
EC2A 3AR
020 7613 5060
www.fnf.org.uk

Family Rights Group
The Print House
18 Ashwin Street
London
E8 3DL
020 7923 2628
www.frg.org.uk

Fathers Direct
Herald House
Lambs Passage
Barnhill Row
London
EC1Y 8TQ
0845 634 1328
www.fathersdirect.com

Gingerbread[2]
7 Sovereign Close
Sovereign Court
London
E1 3HW
020 7488 9300
www.gingerbread.org.uk

Grandparents Association
Moot House
The Stow
Harlow
Essex
CM20 3AG
01279 428040
www.grandparents-
federation.org.uk

---

[1] AIRE stands for 'Advice on Individual Rights in Europe'. The Centre frequently assists in bringing cases before the European Court of Human Rights.

[2] An organisation for lone parents and their children.

Joseph Rowntree Foundation
The Homestead
40 Water End
York
North Yorkshire
YO30 6WP
01904 629241
www.jrf.org.uk

National Association of Child Contact Centres
Minerva House
Spaniel Row
Nottingham
NG1 6EP
0870 770 3269
www.naccc.org.uk

NCB
8 Wakley Street
London
EC1V 7QE
020 7843 6000
www.ncb.org.uk

NCH
85 Highbury Park
London
N5 1UD
020 7704 7000
www.nch.org.uk

National Council for One Parent Families
255 Kentish Town Road
London
NW5 2LX
020 7428 5400

National Family and Parenting Institute
430 Highgate Studios
53-70 Highgate Road
London
NW5 1TL
020 7424 3460

NSPCC
Weston House
42 Curtain Road
London
EC2A 3NH
020 7815 2500
www.nspcc.org.uk

National Youth Advocacy Service
(NYAS)
99–105 Argyle Street
Birkenhead
Wirral
CH41 6AD
0151 649 8700
www.nyas.net

Nuffield Foundation
28 Bedford Square
London
WC1B 3JS
020 7631 0566
www.nuffieldorganisation.org

Relate
Herbert Gray College
Little Church Street
Rugby
Warwickshire
CV21 3AP
01788 573 241
www.relate.org.uk

Reunite[3]
PO Box 7124
Leicester
LE1 7XX
0116 2555 345
www.reunite.org

Rights of Women
52–54 Featherstone Street
London
EC1Y 8RT
020 7251 6577
www.rightsofwomen.org.uk

Who Cares? Trust[4]
Kemp House
152-160 City Road
London
EC1V 2NP
020 7251 3117
www.thewhocarestrust.org.uk

Women's Aid Federation of England
PO Box 391
Bristol
BS99 7WS
0117 944 4411
www.womensaid.org.uk

---

[3] Reunite provides advice and support to families in child abduction cases.

[4] The Who Cares? Trust promotes the interests of children and young people in public care.